HEALTH CARE LAW:

Text, Cases and Materials

AUSTRALIA
LBC Information Services

CANADA AND USA
Carswell, Toronto

NEW ZEALAND
Brooker's, Auckland

SINGAPORE AND MALAYSIA
Thomson Information (S.E. Asia), Singapore

HEALTH CARE LAW:

Text, Cases and Materials

Jean McHale
LL.B., M.Phil.,
Lecturer in Law, University of Manchester

Marie Fox
LL.B., M.Jur.,
Lecturer in Law, University of Manchester

John Murphy
LL.B., LL.M.,
Lecturer in Law, University of Manchester

London
Sweet & Maxwell
1997

Published by
Sweet & Maxwell Limited of
100 Avenue Road,
London NW3 3PF
http://www.smlawpub.co.uk

Computerset by LBJ Enterprises Ltd,
Aldermaston and Chilcompton
Printed in England by Clays Ltd,
St Ives plc

Reprinted 1999

A CIP catalogue record
for this book is available
from The British Library.

ISBN 0 421 51180 X

No natural forests were destroyed to make this product, only farmed timber was used and re-planted.

Preface

Legal issues relating to health care practice are rarely out of the headlines today. Academic and professional lawyers alike have become increasingly aware of the practical importance and complexity of health care issues. This book focuses upon and reflects the legal, professional and technological developments which have taken place in this area in recent years. It is designed to provide an accessible and stimulating collection of materials with accompanying text.

Health Care Law: Text, Cases and Materials is designed to be suitable as a core text for the wide range of undergraduate and postgraduate health care/medical law courses available. It is also intended that this book may be used by health care professionals undertaking degree and diploma courses. The volume considers various changes in health practice, notably the developing structure of the NHS, the increasing concern with rights to health care and the expansion of the role undertaken by nurses. Whilst this text covers many familiar issues arising out of the doctor-patient relationship, its scope is broader. This reflects both the burgeoning legal scholarship in the area with its focus on health rather than illness; regulation as opposed to simply litigation. We must also emphasise that this discipline is itself the subject of constant change, one which is moreover subject not only to the vaguries of judicial interpretation but also clinical and scientific developments. Nevertheless, we offer what we hope is a useful framework for study and further reading.

The focus of this book is the legal regulation of health care practice in England. We do not attempt to provide detailed decriptions of the approaches adopted in other jurisdictions. Comprehension of comparative approaches may be difficult unless jurisprudential developments are set in the broader context of the structures of health care provision. To attempt such a task alongside our account of English health care law would also have negated one of our aims which is to produce a book manageable in size for students. Where appropriate the reader's attention is drawn to particularly pertinent overseas authority; for example, where this jurisprudence has been considered in the English courts. Some reference is also made to overseas literature as further reading. This area has spawned a vast amount of literature, particularly over the last half decade. In general, reference to articles on the specific issue under discussion are incorporated within the body of the text, while at the end each chapter provides a select bibliography indicating useful, although clearly not exhaustive, further reading.

All the authors have read and commented on the several chapters and take responsibility for the whole book. Chapter 1 was written by Jonathan Montgomery and Chapter 8 by Michael Gunn. For the remainder of the text primary responsibility for Chapter 9, 10, 13, 14, 15 was taken by Jean McHale, Chapters 2, 5, 6, 11 by Marie Fox. Chapters 7 and 12 were written by Marie Fox and John Murphy; Chapters 3 and 4 were written by Jean McHale and John Murphy. (The initial draft of Chapter 6 was prepared by Jonathan Montgomery).

A number of people read through drafts of this manuscript at various stages. Special thanks to Margaret Brazier, Caroline Bridge, Therese Murphy, Sally Sheldon, Bernadette Walsh and Noel Whitty.

Our thanks also to Andrew Bainham, David Casement, Ray Geary, Joanne Goddard, Bob Lee, Melanie Latham, Simon Lee, Brian Liberman, Maureen Mulholland, Katherine O'Donovan, Aurora Plomer, Mike Redmayne, Tricia Suzuki, Jenny Urwin and Martin Wasik.

We all owe a considerable debt to our students on undergraduate and postgraduate health care law courses who acted as sounding boards for some of our ideas and some of whom "road tested" draft chapters.

We would also like to thank the "team" at Sweet & Maxwell for their support and encouragement through the long writing process.

On terminology, for the purposes of this text health care professionals are referred to as "she" and patients as "he". The case extracts are, where available, taken from the All England Law Reports.

The law is stated at January 1, 1997.

Acknowledgments

Grateful acknowledgment is made for permission to reproduce from the undermentioned works:

British Medical Association. Extracts from *Surrogacy: Ethical Considerations.*

Butterworths Ltd. Extracts from the following reports: *A.G. v. Able* [1984] 1 All E.R. 277; *A.-G. v. Guardian Newspapers (No. 2)* [1988] 3 All E.R. 545 at 658; *Airedale NHS Trust v. Bland* [1993] 1 All E.R. 521; *Attorney-General's Reference (No. 3)* [1996] 2 All E.R. 10; *B. v. Croydon Health Authority* [1995] 1 All E.R. 683; *Bolam v. Friern Hospital Management Committee* [1957] 2 All E.R. 118; *Bravery v. Bravery* [1954] 3 All E.R. 59; *C v. S* [1987] 1 All E.R. 1230; *Cassidy v. Ministry of Health* [1951] 1 All E.R. 574; *Chatterton v. Gerson* [1981] 1 All E.R. 257; *Clark v. Maclennan* [1983] 1 All E.R. 416; *Doughty v. General Dental Council* [1987] 3 All E.R. 843; *Emeh v. Chelsea and Kensington Area Health Authority* [1984] 1 All E.R. 1044; *Eyre v. Measday* [1986] 1 All E.R. 488; *F. v. West Berkshire Health Authority* [1989] 2 All E.R. 545; *Freeman v. Home Office* [1984] 1 All E.R. 1036; *Frenchay Healthcare National Health Service Trust v. S* [1994] 2 All E.R. 403; *Gold v. Haringey Health Authority* [1987] 2 All E.R. 888; *Health Authority and Another* [1985] 3 All E.R. 402; *Hotson v. East Berkshire Area Health Authority* [1987] 2 All E.R. 909; *Hunter v. Mann* [1974] 2 All E.R. 414; *Janaway v. Salford Area Health Authority* [1988] 3 All E.R. 1079; *Mahon v. Osborne* [1939] 1 All E.R. 535; *Maynard v. West Midlands Regional Health Authority* [1985] 1 All E.R. 635; *McKay v. Essex Area Health Authority* [1982] 2 All E.R. 771; *R. v. Adomako* [1994] 3 All E.R. 79; *R. v. Bourne* [1938] 3 All E.R. 615; *R. v. Cambridge DHA, ex p. B* [1995] 2 All E.R. 129; *R. v. Cannons Park MHRT, ex p. A* [1994] 2 All E.R. 659; *R. v. Mid Glamorgan Family Health Services Authority, ex p. Martin* [1995] 1 All E.R. 356; *Re B (A Minor) (Wardship: Sterilisation)* [1987] 2 All E.R. 206; *Re B* [1987] 2 All E.R. 206; *Re B* [1990] 3 All E.R. 927; *Re C (Adult: Refusal of Treatment)* [1994] 1 All E.R. 819; *Re C* [1989] 2 All E.R. 782; *Re D* [1976] 1 All E.R. 326; *Re F (In Utero)* [1988] 2 All E.R. 193; *Re J* [1990] 3 All E.R. 930; *Re J* [1992] 4 All E.R. 614; *Re A (A Minor) (Medical Treatment: Court's Jurisdiction)* [1992] 4 All E.R. 627; *Re S (Adult Refusal of Treatment)* [1992] 4 All E.R. 671; *Re S (Hospital Patient: Court's Jurisdiction)* [1995] 3 All E.R. 290; *Re T (Adult: Refusal of Treatment)* [1992] 4 All E.R. 649; *Re T* [1992] 4 All E.R. 649; *Re T* [1992] 4 All E.R. 649; *Re W (A Minor) (Medical Treatment: Court's Jurisdiction)* [1992] 4 All E.R. 627; *Royal College of Nursing v. Department of Health and Social Security* [1981] 1 All E.R. 545; *Sidaway v. Bethlem RHG* [1985] 1 All E.R. 643; *Thake v. Maurice* [1986] 1 All E.R. 497; *W. v. Egdell* [1990] 1 All E.R. 835; *Whitehouse v. Jordan* [1981] 1 All E.R. 267; *Wilsher v. Essex Area Health Authority* [1986] 3 All E.R. 801; *Wilsher v. Essex Area Health Authority* [1988] 1 All E.R. 871; *X v. Y* [1988] 2 All E.R. 648; *X v. Bedfordshire C.C.; M v. Newham L.B.C.; E v. Dorset C.C.* [1995] 3 All E.R. 353.

Fourth Estate Ltd. Extracts reprinted by permission from *Fertility and the Family: The Glover Report on Reproductive Technologies to the European Commission.*

Institute of Public Policy Research. Extracts from P. Alderson and J. Montgomery, *Health Care Choices — Making Decisions with Children.*

Jordans Publishing Ltd. Extracts from the following reports: *A v. C* [1985] F.L.R. 445; *A v. C* [1984] Fam.Law 241; *C v. S* [1987] 2 F.L.R. 5; *F v. West Berkshire Health Authority* [1989] 2 F.L.R. 476; *Frenchay Healthcare National Health Service Trust v. S* [1994] 1 F.L.R. 485; *Gillick v. West Norfolk and Wisbech Area Health Authority and Another* [1986] 1 F.L.R. 224; *Gold v. Haringey Health Authority* [1988] 1 F.L.R. 55; *Janaway v. Salford Area Health Authority* [1989] 1 F.L.R. 1; *R. v. Ethical Committee of St. Mary's Hospital (Manchester), ex p. Harriott* [1988] F.L.R. 165; *R. v. Ethical Committee of St. Mary's Hospital (Manchester), ex p. Harriott* [1988] 1 F.L.R. 512; *Re B (A Minor) (Wardship: Sterilisation)* [1987] F.L.R. 314; [1985] F.L.R. 846; *Re C (Adult: Refusal of Treatment)* [1994] 1 F.L.R. 31; *Re E (A Minor) (Medical Treatment)* [1991] 2 F.L.R. 585; *Re E (A Minor) (Wardship: Medical Treatment)* [1993] 1 F.L.R. 386; *Re K, W and H (Minors) (Medical Treatment)* [1993] 1 F.L.R. 854; *Re P (A Minor) (Wardship: Sterilisation)* [1989] 1 F.L.R. 182; *Re P (A Minor) (Wardship: Sterilisation)* [1989] 1 Fam.Law 102; *Re P (Minors) (Wardship: Surrogacy)* [1987] 2 F.L.R. 421; *Re R (A Minor) (Blood Transfusion)* [1993] 2 F.L.R. 757; *Re R (A Minor) (Blood Transfusion)* [1993] Fam.Law 577; *Re R (A Minor) (Wardship: Medical Treatment)* [1992] 1 F.L.R. 190; *Re R* [1996] 2 F.L.R. 99; *Re S (A Minor) (Medical Treatment)* [1994] 2 F.L.R. 1065; *Re T (Adult: Refusal of Treatment)* [1992] 2 F.L.R. 458; *Re T* [1992] 2 F.L.R. 458; *Re W (A Minor) (Medical Treatment: Court's Jurisdiction)* [1993] 1 F.L.R. 1, [1992] 2 F.L.R. 785; *Re W (A Minor) (Medical Treatment: Court's Jurisdiction)* Fam.Law 541; *South Glamorgan County Council v. W and B* [1993] 1 F.L.R. 574.

Royal College of Psychiatrists. Extracts from *Guidelines for Psychiatric Research Involving Human Subjects.*

Weidenfield and Nicolson. Extracts from S. Trombley, *The Right to Reproduce: A History of Coercive Sterilisation.*

While every care has been taken to establish and acknowledge copyright, and contact the copyright owners, the publishers tender their apologies for any accidental infringement. They would be pleased to come to a suitable arrangement with the rightful owners in each case.

Contents

PART THREE

PART FOUR

PART FIVE

TABLE OF CASES

TABLE OF STATUTES

TABLE OF STATUTORY INSTRUMENTS

PART I

INTRODUCTION

The first part of this book introduces the context, institutional and ethical, in which health care law operates. Many of the problems explored in the pages that follow raise profound ethical problems and grappling with them requires an awareness of the discipline of ethics. Chapter 2 introduces the main schools of moral thought and explores some of the key concepts and distinctions used by moral philosophers. These include the ideas of justice, paternalism and autonomy, and also the role of rights. These are discussed in a separate Chapter because they are relevant to most of the substantive areas explored later in the book. To deal with them as if they were only relevant to particular areas would obscure the importance of taking a reflective approach to the problems. Thus, Chapter 2 provides some tools to assess how satisfactory the current law is, and considers what reforms might be necessary.

In addition to introducing the main themes of ethical thinking in relation to health care ethics, a number of specific debates are considered. Many dilemmas would be quickly resolved if we adopted the principle that life is so sacred that it is never acceptable to cease striving to maintain it, whatever the cost. The meaning and strength of this principle of the "sanctity of life" is a key question in the ethics of caring for the dying or severely disabled. Its scope may determine the proper approach to abortion and embryo research. The issues that it raises are explored in extracts from the work of ethicists.

Some thinkers suggest that the distinction between acts and omissions can resolve many of the problems that are presented by life and death decisions. They suggest that it is permissible to allow patients to die by letting 'nature take its course' but not to take active steps to kill them. This approach may enable decisions to offer only palliative care to patients to be reconciled with a commitment to the sanctity of life. However, the moral significance of this distinction has been rejected by some philosophers. It cannot be accepted without critical consideration, even though the courts have made some use of it.

The possibility that ethics and law may make different use of the same distinctions raises a more general problem in jurisprudence (the philosophy of law). That is the proper relation between law and morality. Although most people would agree that health care gives rise to ethical problems, it is not necessarily right simply to use the law to impose good ethics on those involved. Society may not be entitled to force individuals to adopt the morality of others. Thus, we have to ask whether we are entitled to prevent someone who believes that it is acceptable to terminate a pregnancy doing so merely because we believe that they are misguided. We may also believe that there are ethical issues that are specific to the role of the health care professions, including the possibility that they should be given rights of conscientious objection.

One persistent problem that can easily be overlooked is the role of gender in debate about health care law. Many of the most contentious areas of health care law raise issues that cannot be seen as gender neutral. Abortion is clearly a more personal issue for the pregnant women than for anyone else. Many of the developments in reproductive technology impact more directly on women than men. However, gender issues are not confined to questions about the patients involved. Feminist ethics has highlighted the extent to which the dominant traditions of health care ethics have often stressed independence and autonomy at the expense of recognising the social world in which we live. We need to consider how far our approaches to moral thinking have blinkered our understanding of the problems as well as illuminating them.

The ethical dimension of health care is not the only context that we need to consider. Health care is not important so much in itself as for what it can achieve. This is not always to make people better, sometimes it may be to prevent people becoming sick, or to help them accept illness or disability and live their lives in spite of them. Sometimes, health care may aim to be palliative, caring for patients' needs without trying to cure them. Often, however, health care is aimed at protecting or improving people's health. This wider interest in health is reflected in international law, which sees rights to heath care as part of broader rights to health.

The place of law in promoting these broader rights to health is explored in Chapter 1. Although this book is mainly about health care law, we must not forget that often factors outside the health care system will have a major impact on the health of citizens. Sometimes these factors are environmental; water and air quality, housing and poverty play important roles. Such issues are regulated by law, but are not dealt with in this book. However, some legal interventions are closely related to the international health rights of citizens to health. Chapter 1 selects examples to illustrate the role of law and the issues raised. It makes no attempt to be comprehensive in this section, but to provide material to enable the potential for the use of the law to be considered.

Health care law itself is more narrowly focused. In the United Kingdom most health care is delivered within the National Health Service. Chapter 1 also sets out the legal entitlements of citizens to access health services. It can be seen that the Secretary of State for Health is obliged to secure a comprehensive range of such services. This provides United Kingdom citizens with health care services which go beyond the strict requirements of international law. However, the Chapter also shows how difficult it is to enforce those rights. The reluctance of the courts to intervene is probably related to a more general reticence on the part of the law to dictate to health professionals. This will be seen elsewhere in the book. The NHS is probably better characterised as an organisation directed by officials on behalf of patients, rather than a service that treats them as if they were paying customers. This raises questions about the accountability, openness and responsiveness of the NHS, which are also touched upon in the first Chapter.

The first part of this book thus provides an understanding of the issues that underpin the range of specific issues that are considered in later chapters. The general position of patients needs to be seen in the context of a national health service providing care for the whole population, not an individualised service for those who can afford to call the tune. While a substantial private industry exists in health care, the law has been shaped by the overwhelming dominance of the NHS. Without understanding the NHS context, the judicial attitude to patients is hard to understand. Many of the problems that will be considered can only be resolved with a consideration of the ethical issues that arise, and Chapter 2 introduces the main tools that are needed to grapple with them. Equipped with an appreciation of these areas, it is much easier to make sense of the body of detailed law that follows.

1

RIGHTS TO HEALTH AND HEALTH CARE

1. INTRODUCTION: THE SCOPE OF HEALTH RIGHTS

Good health is a fundamental precondition of much human activity. It follows that the value of health is rarely challenged. What the importance of health means for governments is more controversial. There is room for considerable disagreement about the definition and level of health that should be used to define what citizens can legitimately expect governments and the law to seek to ensure. Some argue that the role of the State is to ensure that people are as healthy as possible, others that the only concern of the law is with preventing people being, or remaining ill (see J. Montgomery "Recognising a Right to Health" in R. Beddard and D. Hill (eds) *Economic, Social and Cultural Rights, Progress and Achievements*, Basingstoke; Macmillan (1992). There is also a continuing debate about the relative responsibilities of governments and individuals for taking steps to improve health and health services, and about the relationship between health services, health professionals and market forces. The international law of human rights includes recognition of health and health care issues, and the relevant provisions can be used to consider the scope of health rights and their place in the law of this country.

There is no single source of health rights in International Law, but many of the Conventions include them. Article 25 of the Universal Declaration of Human Rights, establishes the over-arching principle:

"Everyone has the right to a standard of living adequate for the health and well-being of himself and his family, including food, clothing, housing and medical care and necessary social services . . . "

This aims to guarantee the preconditions of good health, including the availability of health services.

The International Covenant on Economic, Social & Cultural Rights, Article 12, is concerned with the level of health to which human rights law is committed:

"the right to enjoyment of the highest attainable standard of physical and mental health."

These two statements provide a general orientation for human rights law. More detail is provided by the European Social Charter of 1961, to which the British government is a signatory. Articles 11 and 13 of Part I establish the following principles:

"everyone has the right to benefit from any measures enabling him to enjoy the highest standard of health attainable", and

"anyone without adequate resources has the right to social and medical assistance"

The meaning of these rights is expanded in Part II of the Convention. Under Article 11 of that Charter, the Government has undertaken:

1. to remove so far as possible the causes of ill-health;
2. to provide advisory and educational facilities for the promotion of health and the encouragement of individual responsibility in matters of health;
3. to prevent as far as possible epidemic, endemic and other diseases.

Under Article 13, the United Kingdom has undertaken to ensure, so that the right to social and medical assistance can be effectively exercised,

"that any person who is without adequate resources and who is unable to secure such resources either by his own efforts or from other sources . . . be granted adequate assistance, and, in the case of sickness, the care necessitated by his condition."

Human rights law has also recognised that the implications of health rights for specific groups often need to be spelt out to ensure that appropriate concrete steps are taken. Thus, the United Nations Convention on the Rights of the Child contains both a general statement of children's health rights, and a series of specific commitments. For full discussion see G. Van Bueren, *The International Law on the Rights of the Child*, London: Martinus Nijhoff, 1995, Chapter 11.

Article 24:

(1) States Parties recognise the right of the child to the enjoyment of the highest attainable standard of health and to facilities for the treatment of illness and rehabilitation of health. States Parties shall strive to ensure that no child is deprived of his or her right of access to health services.
(2) States Parties shall pursue full implementation of this right and, in particular, shall take appropriate measures:

    (a) to diminish infant and child mortality;
    (b) to ensure the provision of necessary medical assistance and health care to all children with emphasis on the development of primary health care;
    (c) to combat disease and malnutrition, including within the framework of primary care, through *inter alia*, the application of readily available technology and through the provision of adequate nutritious foods and clean drinking water, taking into consideration the dangers and risks of environmental pollution;

    (d) to ensure appropriate pre-natal and post-natal care for mothers;

    (e) to ensure that all segments of society, in particular parents and children, are informed, have access to education and are supported in the use of basic knowledge of child health and nutrition, the advantages of breast-feeding, hygiene and environmental sanitation and the prevention of accidents;

    (f) to develop preventive health care, guidance for parents and family planning education and services.

(3) States Parties shall take all effective and appropriate measures with a view to abolishing traditional practices prejudicial to the health of children.

NOTES:

1. Paragraph 4, concerning international co-operation, has been omitted here.
2. Article 4 of the Convention limits the obligations of contracting states by reference to their available resources.

The United Nations Convention on the Elimination of All Forms of Discrimination against Women similarly reaffirms the entitlement of women to benefit from the general right of access to health care (Articles 11(f) and 14(b)) but also recognises the specific problems confronting women (see R. J. Cook, *Woman's Health and Human Rights*, Philadelphia: Philadelphia and Pennsylvania Press, 1994).

Article 12

(1) States Parties shall take all appropriate measures to eliminate discrimination against women in the field of health care in order to ensure, on a basis of equality of men and women, access to health care services, including those related to family planning.

(2) Notwithstanding the provisions of paragraph 1 of this article, States Parties shall ensure to women appropriate services in connection with pregnancy, confinement and the post-natal period, granting free services where necessary, as well as adequate nutrition during pregnancy and lactation.

QUESTION:

1. Do you think that this provision serves to protect the interests of women or their children?

It is clear from these provisions that the health rights of citizens are concerned with more than merely access to services under a health service. Preventive measures are also required, and citizens should be given the opportunity to improve their own health. The role of the law in removing the causes of ill-health, and the issues that are raised are explored in the next section of this Chapter. It may be that health rights are actually more valuable than rights to health care. The latter are merely one component of the broader bundle of rights (J. Montgomery, "Recognising a right to health" in R. Beddard and D. Hill (eds) *Economic, Social and Cultural Rights: Progress and Achievements*, Basingstoke: Macmillan (1992)). Often, health care will be sought to restore good health, or to reduce the impact of ill-health. It would be preferable to prevent health being impaired in the first place. We need, therefore, to consider what the law can do in this respect. We also need to consider the dangers that may arise in using the law to promote good health. While it is difficult to argue that good health is not valuable, it is quite another matter to suggest that its value outweighs all other concerns. Promoting health may raise questions of civil liberties. We must balance the freedom of people with infectious diseases to live normally against the interests of those who are put at risk. We must consider how far it is permissible to persuade people to take responsibility for their own health. Should we merely inform them of their options, seek to persuade them, or possibly even coerce them, to become healthier. It would be impossible to consider all the areas of law that relate to health. Good health is inextricably linked with broader environmental, housing and economic issues. For this Chapter, five areas have been selected to illustrate the issues. These concern provisions that are specifically related to health rights.

Section two considers health promotion and disease control. The first examples considered concern contagious disease control and the provisions governing the fluoridation of water. These demonstrate the interaction between health rights and more general principles of civil liberties. The former is an example of control of specific threats to individual health. The latter raises the question of taking proactive steps to protect the dental health of the population through improving resistance to the causes of decay that do not themselves come from water. The fluoridation debate also requires consideration of how far people are entitled to choose to take risks with their own health. The scope of this 'right to be ill' is amongst the issues arising from the provisions of the National Assistance Acts permitting compulsory admission to hospital. Similar problems arise in the context of mental health, see Chapter 8 below. The role of the law in relation to education and advice is illustrated by the requirements for general medical practitioners to counsel patients about their lifestyles. The problems of tobacco and alcohol advertising are also considered as examples of some of the problems thrown up in connection with the exercise of choice.

The third section of this Chapter looks at access to health care. It sets out the obligations of the National Health Service to provide services, considers the institutional framework for delivery of those services, and looks at the scope for patients enforcing the duties to provide care through the courts. Taken together, these areas of law constitute the rights of citizens to health services. It will be seen that this goes beyond the requirements of human rights law, in that the NHS is a comprehensive public service available to all, not merely to those unable to pay for their own care (as envisaged by the right to health care defined in Article 13 of the European Social Charter).

2.   HEALTH PROMOTION & DISEASE PREVENTION

(a) Contagious Disease Control

We begin by considering the law's contribution to protecting citizens from ill health. The threat to health may sometimes come from other people rather than impersonal substances or environmental situations. The most obvious example of this is contagious diseases, where one individual may infect another. Clearly, the right to health, and sometimes the right to life, of the 'victim' can be called upon to provide a justification for legal measures to prevent such contagion. Equally clearly, limiting the behaviour of people who are already infected raises questions about their own civil rights.

English law uses two main techniques to deal with this area. The first can be described as 'control powers.' These permit public health officials to take steps to reduce the risk of infection. They operate to identify and segregate those who may infect others. These powers seek to prevent infection by restraining risky behaviour. The second approach operates after infection has occurred, or been irresponsibly risked. Here those who have jeopardised the health of others are made liable to criminal penalties or to compensate those who have been made ill. This approach is principally remedial, compensating for or punishing wrongdoing. However, it is hoped that it would also provide a deterrent effect, which would reduce the incidence of infection.

There is a wide range of control powers provided by English law (see J. Montgomery, *Health Care Law*, Oxford: OUP (1997), Chapter 2). The main statute is the Public Health (Control of Disease) Act 1984. Some of the provisions of that Act are used here to illustrate the issues. The first step in their use is the identification of individuals who are infected by, or carry infectious diseases. Sometimes this information is already known, and merely needs to be communicated to the proper authorities. Thus, doctors are obliged to inform public health officials when they know someone has a 'notifiable' disease.

The Act specifies five diseases, cholera, plague, relapsing fever, smallpox, and typhus as notifiable. Others have been specified by regulations, and there is provision for diseases to be specified for specific geographical areas where necessary (section 16). While AIDS and tuberculosis come within the Act they are not strictly notifiable diseases because section 11 does not apply. The Public Health (Infectious Diseases) Regulations 1988 extend the Act to the following diseases:

ADAPTED FROM SCHEDULE 1 TO THE PUBLIC HEALTH (INFECTIOUS DISEASES)
REGULATIONS 1988 (S.I. 1988 NO. 1546)

Diseases	Enactments applied
Acquired immune deficiency syndrome	ss.35, 37, 38 (as modified by reg. 5), 43, 44
Acute encephalitis Acute poliomyelitis Meningitis Meningococcal septicaemia (without meningitis)	ss.11, 17, 19, 35 (as modified by reg. 4), 37, 38, 44, 45
Anthrax	ss.11, 17, 19, 35 (as modified by reg. 4), 37, 38, 43–45
Diphtheria Dysentery (amoebic or bacillary) Paratyphoid fever Typhoid fever Viral hepatitis	ss.11, 17, 19, 3–538, 44, 45.
Leprosy	ss.11, 17, 19, 35 (as modified by reg. 4), 37, 38, 44.
Leptospirosis Mumps Rubella Whooping cough	ss.11, 17, 19, 35 (as modified by reg. 4), 38, 44 and 45.
Malaria Tetanus Yellow fever	ss.11, and 35 (as modified by reg. 4).
Ophthalmia neonatorum	ss.11, 17.
Rabies	ss.11, 17, 19, 38.
Scarlet fever	ss.11, 17, 19, 35–38, 44, 45.
Tuberculosis	ss.17, 19, 35 (as modified by reg. 4), 44, 45; in addition— (a) s.11 shall apply where the opinion of the registered medical practitioner that a person is suffering from tuberculosis is formed from evidence not derived solely from tuberculin tests, and (b) ss.37 and 38 shall apply to tuberculosis of the respiratory tract in an infectious state.
Viral haemorrhagic fever	ss.11, 17, 19, 35–38, 43–45.

NOTES

1. Not all the sections of the Act are applicable in relation to these diseases. This table has been edited to deal only with a selection of these provisions, primarily those which are considered in more detail below. The sections mentioned concern notifiability (s.11) criminal

offences of endangerment (ss.17, 19), compulsory examination (ss.35, 36), removal to hospital (s.37), detention in hospital (s.38), dealings with corpses of those dying while suffering from the disease (ss.43–45).

2. The modification of s.35 made by reg. 4 is to omit s.35(1)(a)(ii) (see below).

QUESTION:

1. The Regulations do not define AIDS. Do you think that someone who tested positive for HIV, but had no symptoms of AIDS has "AIDS" within the meaning of the regulations? Compare C. d'Ecca, "Medico-legal Aspects of AIDS" in D. Harris and R. Hough, *AIDS: A Guide to the Law*, London: Routledge, 1990, J. Montgomery, "Victims or Threats? The Framing of HIV" (1992) XII *Liverpool Law Review* 25.
2. Do you agree with the way in which these various disease are categorised?

It may also be necessary to examine people to see whether they carry a disease within the Act. The main power for this purpose is to be found in section 35. That provides as follows.

Public Health (Control of Disease Act) 1984, s.35(1)(3)

35.—(1) If a justice of the peace (acting, if he deems it necessary, ex parte) is satisfied, on a written certificate issued by a registered medical practitioner nominated by the local authority for a district:
　(a) that there is reason to believe that some person in the district:
　　　(i)　is or has been suffering from a notifiable disease, or
　　　(ii)　though not suffering from such a disease, is carrying an organism that is capable of causing it, and
　(b) that in his own interest, or in the interest of his family, or in the public interest, it is expedient that he should be medically examined, and
　(c) that he is not under the treatment of a registered medical practitioner or that the registered medical practitioner who is treating him consents to the making of an order under this section,
the justice may order him to be medically examined by a registered medical practitioner so nominated . . .
　(3) In this section, references to a person's being medically examined shall be construed as including references to his being submitted to bacteriological and radiological tests and similar investigations.

NOTES:

1. For some diseases, s.35(1)(a)(ii) is omitted by reg. 4. See above for the diseases to which this applies.
2. There is a power under s.38 to order the examination of a group of people, where one of them is believed to suffer from a relevant disease.

QUESTION:

1. This provision contains a number of safeguards: the involvement of a magistrate; the need to satisfy the magistrate that there is reason to believe that the person is infected; the need to satisfy the magistrate that a medical examination is required in someone's interests; and the consent of the person's doctor (if they have one). However, there is no guarantee that the person to be examined will be a party to the application. An order may nevertheless be made in their 'own interest.' Do you think those safeguards are sufficient?

Once a person has been identified as having a relevant infectious disease, public health officials may have the power to remove them to hospital under s.37.

Public Health (Control of Disease) Act 1984, s.37(1)(2)

37.—(1) Where a justice of the peace (acting, if he deems it necessary, *ex parte*) is satisfied, on the application of the local authority, that a person is suffering from a notifiable disease and —

(a) that his circumstances are such that proper precautions to prevent the spread of infection cannot be taken, or that such precautions are not being taken, and
(b) that serious risk of infection is thereby caused to other persons, and
(c) that accommodation for him is available in a suitable hospital vested in the Secretary of State or, pursuant to arrangements made by a Health Authority (whether under an NHS contract or otherwise), in a suitable hospital vested in an NHS trust or other person,

the justice may, with the consent of the Health Authority in whose area lies the area, or the greater part of the area, of the local authority, order him to be removed to it.

(2) An order under this section may be addressed to such officer of the local authority as the justice may think expedient, and that officer and any officer of the hospital may do all acts necessary for giving effect to the order.

QUESTIONS:

1. Are the criteria for making such orders sufficiently precise?
2. Do they give the right weight to the interests of the infected person ?
3. Is it right that this power does not apply to those who are carriers of a disease, but not suffering from it?

Once a person is in hospital, a magistrate may authorise their detention there under section 38:

Public Health (Control of Disease Act) 1984, s.38(1)–(4)

38.—(1) Where a justice of the peace (acting, if he deems it necessary, ex parte) in and for the place in which a hospital for infectious diseases is situated is satisfied, on the application of any local authority, that an inmate of the hospital who is suffering from a notifiable disease would not on leaving the hospital be provided with lodging or accommodation in which proper precautions could be taken to prevent the spread of the disease by him, the justice may order him to be detained in the hospital.

(2) An order made under subsection (1) above may direct detention for a period specified in the order, but any justice of the peace acting in and for the same place may extend a period so specified as often as it appears to him to be necessary to do so.

(3) Any person who leaves a hospital contrary to an order made under this section for his detention there shall be liable on summary conviction to a fine not exceeding level 1 on the standard scale, and the court may order him to be taken back to the hospital.

(4) An order under this section may be addressed —

(a) in the case of an order for a person's detention, to such officer of the hospital, and
(b) in the case of an order made under subsection (3) above, to such officer of the local authority on whose application the order for detention was made,

as the justice may think expedient, and that officer and any officer of the hospital may do all acts necessary for giving effect to the order.

In relation to AIDS, the wording of section 38 has been amended by regulation 5 of the 1988 Regulations.

Regulation 5. In its application to acquired immune deficiency syndrome section 38(1) of the Act shall apply so that a justice of the peace (acting if he deems it necessary ex parte) may on the application of any local authority make an order for the detention in hospital of an inmate of that hospital suffering from acquired immune deficiency syndrome, in addition to the circumstances specified in that section, if the justice is satisfied that on his leaving the hospital proper precautions to prevent the spread of that disease would not be taken by him:

(a) in his lodging or accommodation, or
(b) in other places to which he may be expected to go if not detained in the hospital.

QUESTIONS:

1. Why was this amendment made?
2. Does it expose a weakness in the drafting of section 38 that is applicable more widely than just to AIDS?
3. A person suffering from a notifiable disease can be compulsorily tested, removed to hospital against their will, and detained there involuntarily. However, there is no provision for compulsory treatment under the Act. Should there be?

The only example of a power to treat someone without consent seems to be found in section 85 of the Public Health Act 1936.

Public Health Act 1936, s.85(1)–(4)

85.—(1) Upon the application of any person, a county council or a local authority may take such measures as are, in their opinion, necessary to free him and his clothing from vermin.

(2) Where it appears to a county council or a local authority, upon a report from their medical officer of health or, in the case of a local authority, from their sanitary inspector, that any person, or the clothing of any person, is verminous, then, if that person consents to be removed to a cleansing station, they may cause him to be removed to such a station, and, if he does not so consent, they may apply to a court of summary jurisdiction, and the court, if satisfied that it is necessary that he or his clothing should be cleansed, may make an order for his removal to such a station and for his detention therein for such period and subject to such conditions as may be specified in the order.

(3) Where a person has been removed to a cleansing station in pursuance of the last preceding subsection, the county council or local authority shall take such measures as may, in their opinion, be necessary to free him and his clothing from vermin.

(4) The cleansing of females under this section shall be carried out only by a registered medical practitioner, or by a woman duly authorised by the medical officer of health.

QUESTION:

1. Do you think this power is an aberration?

The European Convention on Human Rights and Fundamental Freedoms recognises that it may be legitimate for someone carrying an infections disease to be detained against their will.

European Convention on Human Rights and Fundamental Freedoms 1950

Article 5:

(1) Everyone has the right to liberty and security of the person. No one shall be deprived of this liberty save in the following cases and in accordance with a procedure prescribed by law . . .

(e) the lawful detention for the prevention of the spreading of infectious diseases, of persons of unsound mind, alcoholics or drug addicts or vagrants;
    . . .

This is the most precise example of the fact that public health issues may limit the application of fundamental human rights. However, many of the rights guaranteed by the Convention are limited when they come into conflict with actions that are 'necessary in a democratic society in the interests of . . . public safety . . . for the protection of health or morals, or for the protection of the rights and freedoms of others.' The rights to privacy, freedom of assembly, expression, thought, conscience and religion are all limited in this way (Arts. 8 to 11 of the Convention).

The extent to which interventions can be justified in the interests of the public health was explored in *Acmanne v. Belgium* (1985) 40 DR 251. This case concerned a compulsory screening programme for tuberculosis. The applicants had been convicted for refusing to undergo, or permit their children to undergo, tests. They argued that the infringement of their right to privacy under Article 8 of the Convention was not justified as being necessary to protect health. The Commission accepted that compulsory testing was an interference with the right of respect for private life. However, it ruled the complaint inadmissible as being manifestly ill-founded. They did so because they considered that the screening programme pursued a legitimate aim, protecting both the public health and the health of the individual applicants. The interference with the applicants' rights that was involved was proportionate to that aim. Finally, the interference was necessary to protect health within a democratic society under Article 8(2) of the Convention.

The Commission explained its finding on the legitimacy of the screening programme in the following terms.

> "According to the Court's case-law a restriction on a Convention right cannot be regarded as necessary in a democratic society — two hallmarks of which are tolerance and broadmindedness — unless, amongst other things, it is proportionate to the legitimate aim pursued . . . In assessing the necessity of the interference with the applicants' private life, the Commission takes into account the reasoning in the Liege Court of Appeal . . . In particular, it notes that, finding that the applicants had not produced evidence of disadvantages comparable to the former ravages of tuberculosis, particularly among the deprived, the Court held that the individual had a social duty to defer to the general interest and not endanger the health of others where his life was not in danger."

QUESTIONS:

1. Do you think that the provisions of the 1984 Act are consistent with human rights law?
2. Do you think that this reasoning would enable compulsory treatment for infectious diseases to be reconciled with human rights law?

The Public Health (Control of Disease) Act 1984 also provides examples of the use of the law to deter people from taking risks with the health of others. There are criminal offences of knowingly exposing others to the risk of infections from a notifiable disease under sections 17 and 19 of the 1984 Act.

Public Health (Control of Disease) Act 1984, ss.17(1)(2), 19

17.—(1) A person who:

(a) knowing that he is suffering from a notifiable disease, exposes other persons to the risk of infection by his presence or conduct in any street, public place, place of entertainment or assembly, club, hotel, inn or shop,

(b) having the care of a person whom he knows to be suffering from a notifiable disease, causes or permits that person to expose other persons to the risk of infection by his presence or conduct in any such place as aforesaid, or

(c) gives, lends, sells, transmits or exposes, without previous disinfection, any clothing, bedding or rags which he knows to have been exposed to infection from any such disease, or any other article which he knows to have been so exposed and which is liable to carry such infection, shall be liable on summary conviction to a fine not exceeding level 1 on the standard scale.

(2) A person shall not incur any liability under this section by transmitting with proper precautions any article for the purpose of having it disinfected.

19.—A person who, knowing that he is suffering from a notifiable disease, engages in or carries on any trade, business or occupation which he cannot engage in or carry on without risk of spreading the disease shall be liable on summary conviction to a fine not exceeding level 1 on the standard scale.

QUESTIONS:

1. These offences have not been extended to AIDS. If they were, would it be an offence to be a prostitute if you were HIV positive?
2. Would you support the creation of a general offence of endangerment in relation to infectious diseases, as proposed by K. J. M. Smith, 'Risking death by dangerous sexual behaviour and the criminal law' in D. Morgan and R. Lee (eds) *Death Rites: law and ethics and the end of life* London: Routledge, 1994?
3. Should there be specific offences of deliberately transmitting a serious disease (see S. Bronitt, "Spreading disease and the Criminal Law" [1994] *Crim.L.R.* 21 and M. Brazier and J. Harris "Public Health and Private Lives" (1996) *Medical Law Review* 171 and Chapter 6?

It is possible that even without these specific offences, a prosecution could be brought where one person knowingly infected another. Public nuisance may also provide a duty to take steps to protect those at risk from infection (see M. Mulholland "Public Nuisance—A New Use for an Old Tool (1995) 11 *Professional Negligence* 70). In *R. v. Vantandillo* (1815) 4 M. & S. 73, 105 E.R. 762 an infected child was carried through the streets. Le Blanc J. found that an offence had been committed, and defined it in these terms:
"if a person unlawfully, injuriously and with full knowledge of the fact, exposes in a public highway a person infected with a contagious disorder, it is a common nuisance to all the subjects, and indictable as such."
He also found that there was no need to show that there was any intention to infect. It is also possible in principle that a civil action might lie for compensation against a person who negligently infected another, or failed to take steps to protect them.

QUESTION:

1. What are the advantages and disadvantages of using criminal and civil liability to deter people from infecting others? (See P. Old and J. Montgomery "Law Coercion and Public Health" (1992) 304 *BMJ* 891.)

(b) Water & Fluoridation

The legal regulation of drinking water provides an interesting case study of the issues involved in protecting and promoting good health. Unsafe water is a major cause of ill-health, and ensuring that water is safe for human consumption is an example of the practical requirement of the duty to prevent disease and remove the causes of ill-health imposed under the European Social Charter. The issues raised by the fluoridation of drinking water test the limit of the right, and duty, of Government to use the power to regulate the supply of water. Water would be safe to drink without the presence of fluoride, but appropriate levels of the chemical in drinking water can contribute to the reduction of tooth decay. This does not operate by removing the causes of that decay, but by increasing the protection that teeth have against it. Thus, fluoridation can be seen as a measure taken to prevent disease (under Article 11(3) of the Social Charter) although not as removing a cause of disease (under Article 11(1)).

Even though fluoridation may be brought within the scope of the right to health, it also raises significant issues of practice and principle arising out of the possibility that other civil rights may conflict. The issues were put succinctly by Edward Leigh M.P. in the debates on the Water (Fluoridation) Act 1985:

H.C. Vol. 71, Col. 124, January 14, 1985

"First, given that every human being is largely made up of water, has not every individual a right to drink water the treatment of which has been limited to cleaning? Secondly, is the fact that fluoride occurs naturally somewhere, an argument that it should be imposed on everyone somewhere everywhere?

Thirdly, accepting that water itself does not cause decay and that people cause decay to their teeth by their eating habits, what is the logic in saying that their eating habits should be exercised according to choice, and their drinking habits according to compulsion? Fourthly, are there not ample opportunities for individuals to apply fluoride to their own teeth?

Fifthly, if it is said that the decision to administer fluoride should be made locally, is it not right that water and health authorities are appointed and not elected? Sixthly, if fluoride is considered desirable, why should not other drugs, substances or chemicals be applied? Why should the line be drawn after fluoride? Where is the logic in that?

Seventhly, is it not a fact that far from fluoride benefiting everyone, it benefits only some, that is children? Eighthly, is it not true that some doctors and researchers still have doubts about the safety of fluoride? Is it right, therefore, to make it compulsory?

Ninthly, is it not true that whether or not fluoride is dangerous, some people still consider it to be dangerous? Some of my constituents said to me that it affects their health. Why should they be forced to take it, even if their fears are groundless? Tenthly, do not people have the right to choose?"

The relevant legal provisions are now to be found in the Water Industry Act 1991. The basic obligation of water undertakers is to provide 'wholesome' water (section 68). This permits them to put substances into

the water in order to purify it. However, legal action on the Scottish
provisions (using the same term) has established that this does not imply
that all treatment can be administered. In *McColl v. Strathclyde* [1983] S.C.
225 a woman brought a legal action objecting to the fluoridation of her
drinking water. One of her arguments was that the addition of fluoride
could not be justified under the claim that it made the water 'wholesome.'
The particular issue of fluoridation is now the subject of specific provisions
(see below) but the case remains authoritative on the meaning of
'wholesome.'

McColl v. Strathclyde Regional Council [1983] S.C. 225

LORD JAUNCEY:
"... It is not disputed that the regional council as a statutory body have power
only to do those things which are expressly authorised by statute or which are
fairly and reasonably to be considered as incidental to or consequential upon
those things which are expressly authorised. The issue therefore in this part of
the case depends upon the proper construction of the words "wholesome water"
in section 6 and section 8 of the 1980 Act. The Oxford English Dictionary
defines wholesome water inter alia as: "promoting or conducive to health;
favourable to or good for health; health-giving or health-preserving; salubrious".
It also defines it as: "free from disease or taint; healthy". Is wholesome in
relation to health to be restricted to health consequent upon contamination of
water, that is to say, is wholesome water no more than that which is neither
contaminated nor in any other way dangerous to health nor obnoxious to sight
or smell? Alternatively is wholesome to be construed as embracing also a positive
benefit to health so that not only the health of the consumer consequent upon
drinking the water in its natural state can be looked at but also any possible
benefit to his general health? The petitioner contends for the former construction
and the respondents for the latter. The practical effect of these alternative
constructions is that the petitioner maintained that the respondents have power
only to treat the water in such a way that it will be free from contamination and
safe and pleasant to drink whereas the respondents maintained that they have
power to go further and in certain circumstances to treat the water in such a way
as to confer a positive health benefit on the consumers or some of them.
   At the moment the water supply for the respondents, and particularly that
from Loch Katrine, is wholesome in the sense that it is neither contaminated nor
in any other way dangerous to health. If it were fluoridated in accordance with
the respondent's proposals it would still be wholesome in this sense. There are
some 18 different chemicals which are added to different supplies in Strathclyde
and whose purpose is to achieve purity. The decision to increase the fluoride
content of the water supplies to one ppm was taken at the instigation of various
health boards who approached the respondents. In the event of the respondents
proceeding to fluoridate water supplies the decision as to the appropriate fluoride
compound and as to which supplies to fluoridate would be made by the
appropriate health board which would pay for the cost thereof. The decisions as
to the addition of the other 18 chemicals were taken by the respondents and not
by the health boards. Fluoride would thus be in a unique position in that it would
be the only chemical added to the water by the water authority in respect of
which they had not taken the decision to add. It would also be unique, argued the
petitioner, in that the purpose of its addition would be to treat a limited number
of consumers of the water rather than the water itself. The respondents however
replied that what they were proposing was to adjust the concentration of a

naturally occurring ingredient for the purpose of making good a deficiency which causes caries. I prefer the petitioner's approach to the matter to that of the respondents since I have already concluded that the present concentration in the water of Strathclyde does not cause caries. The various chemicals used by the respondents have four main objects, namely, disinfection which is effected by chlorine, removal of colour and turbidity which is effected by aluminium sulphate, the raising of the pH or the concentration of hydrogen ions to reduce the amount of lead dissolved from the pipes by the water as it passes through (plumbosolvency) which is effected by lime in the case of Loch Katrine and by sulphuric or hydrochloric acid where aluminium sulphate is also used, and the control of algae which is effected by copper sulphate. Each of these chemicals is intended to produce the desired reaction or prevent the undesirable reaction (plumbosolvency) before the water leaves the tap of the consumer and enters his body. Fluoride is intended to produce a positive effect on the body of the consumer after ingestion. Thus the water instead of being the object of treatment becomes the means whereby fluoride is carried into the consumer's body to effect a result which could also be achieved by the consumption of fluoride pills or of food and drink containing high levels of fluoride.

The petitioner advanced a number of reasons why "wholesome" should be construed not as giving the respondents a discretion to decide how to benefit the health of a community but as meaning the promoting of the consumer's health by achieving lack of contamination in the water supply. Some of these appeared to me to be little more than different ways of putting the same point. In determining whether the proposed actings of the respondents would be ultra vires they should be looked at objectively to see whether they could fairly be regarded as conducive or incidental to the purposes authorised by the statute and subjectively to see whether they were in fact directed to an ulterior purpose not authorised by the statute. I do not consider that this argument assists the petitioner. If the statute authorises the respondents to supply water which has been treated in such a way as to confer a positive health benefit on the consumer then the addition of fluoride would be in implement of the respondents' primary purpose and not merely an action conducive or incidental thereto. If on the other hand the statute merely empowers the respondents to supply water which has been treated so that it is neither contaminated, discoloured nor liable to dissolve lead from pipes then the addition of fluoride will achieve none of these objects and could not be conducive or incidental thereto. Equally the subjective test would not arise because the supply of water treated with fluoride would either be for a purpose authorised by the statute or one which was not. Standing the role which fluoride plays I do not see how there could be an authorised use thereof for an unauthorised purpose.

A more formidable reason for construing "wholesome" as the petitioner contends is that it is *prima facie* unlikely that Parliament in 1946 would, in a Water Act, have conferred upon a local water authority a power to supply water which had been treated in such a way as not only to render it safe and pleasant to drink but also to serve as a convenient means of achieving a beneficial effect on the health of consumers generally. When the relevant provisions of the 1946 Act were re-enacted in 1980 Parliament must have been aware of the passing of the National Health Service (Scotland) Act 1947 and subsequent National Health Service Acts which set up health boards charged with the duty of advancing general health. Furthermore since fluoride would involve an encroachment on individual rights to the extent that persons would be forced to drink water containing a substance, fluoride, which they did not wish to drink, a liberal construction which permitted such a result should not be adopted.

. . . fluoridation of water would inevitably involve the ingestion of the added fluoride by many persons to whom such ingestion would be of no benefit, either because they were edentulous or being dentate had reached an age when the fluoride would no longer perform its preventive role in relation to caries, and also by persons upon whom fluoride might confer a benefit but who were unwilling for personal reasons to ingest it in the quantities proposed. Such a situation would necessarily involve a restriction on the freedom of choice of the individual who would have little alternative but to consume the fluoridated water whether he liked it or not . . . I consider that there is some force in the petitioner's argument that if two possible constructions of the statute are available that construction should be preferred which encroaches to the minimum on the personal rights of the individual. To put the matter in another way the individual's right to choose how to care for his own body should only be encroached upon by statutory provisions in clear and unambiguous language . . .

In my view the word "wholesome" falls properly to be construed in the more restricted sense advocated by the petitioner as relating to water which was free from contamination and pleasant to drink. It follows that fluoridation which in no way facilitates nor is incidental to the supply of such water is outwith the powers of the respondents. The petitioner therefore succeeds on this branch of her case."

QUESTIONS:

1. Is the meaning of "wholesomeness" in this case influenced by the judge's attitude to the legitimacy of fluoridation?
2. The judge considered the rights of choice of the population, but not their health rights, would it have made any difference if he had looked at the latter rights?
3. Why is the difference between the "positive" and "negative" aspects of wholesomeness significant?

Following this decision, Parliament enacted the Water (Fluoridation) Act 1985 to make it clear that fluoridation was lawful. The provisions of that Act have now been consolidated into the Water Industry Act 1991. Section 87 makes it clear that a water authority may fluoridate water if requested to do so by the relevant health authority. The cost of fluoridation, and any liabilities incurred, can, and in practice will, be borne by the National Health Service (section 90).

Water Industry Act 1991, s.87(1)–(6)(8)

87.—(1) Where a Health Authority have applied in writing to a water undertaker for the water supplied within an area specified in the application to be fluoridated, that undertaker may, while the application remains in force, increase the fluoride content of the water supplied by the undertaker within that area.

(2) For the purposes of subsection (1) above an application under this section shall remain in force until the Health Authority, after giving reasonable notice to the water undertaker, withdraw it.

(3) The area specified in an application under this section may be the whole, or any part of, the area of the Health Authority making the application.

(4) Where in exercise of the power conferred by this section, the fluoride content of any water is increased, the increase may be effected only by the addition of one or more of the following compounds of fluorine, that is to say —

hexafluorosilicic acid (H2SiF6)
disodium hexafluorosilicate (Na2SiF6).

(5) Any Health Authority making arrangements with a water undertaker in pursuance of an application under this section shall ensure that those arrangements include provisions designed to secure that the concentration of fluoride in the water supplied to consumers in the area in question is, so far as reasonably practicable, maintained at one milligram per litre.

(6) Water to which fluoride has been added by a water undertaker in exercise of the power conferred by this section (with a view to its supply in any area) may be supplied by that or any other undertaker to consumers in any other area if the undertaker or undertakers concerned consider that it is necessary to do so —
(a) for the purpose of dealing with any serious deficiency in supply; or
(b) in connection with the carrying out of any works (including cleaning and maintenance) by the undertaker concerned or, as the case may be, by any of the undertakers concerned . . .

(8) In this section "serious deficiency in supply" means any existing or threatened serious deficiency in the supply of water (whether in quantity or quality) caused by an exceptional lack of rain or by any accident or unforeseen circumstances.

NOTE:

1. Subsections (7) and (9) have been omitted.
2. The opponents of fluoridation have argued that it is unsafe. However, their claims were rejected by Lord Jauncey in *McColl v. Strathclyde*, and by a committee of experts convened by the Government at the same time (E. G. Knox, *Fluoridation of water and cancer: a review of the epidemiological evidence*, London: HMSO, 1981). The scientific consensus (although there are a few vociferous critics) is that fluoridation at the levels permitted by the statute does not present any health risks. The Act therefore introduces safeguards by specifying which compounds of fluoridation may be used and limiting the concentration to be used (subss. (4), (5)). It is still suggested by some that if there is any doubt, then fluoridation should not be permitted.

The main argument of principle against fluoridation is based on liberty. Nicholas Fairbairn M.P. expressed this objection particularly trenchantly in the debates on the 1985 Act:

H.C. Vol. 71, Col. 93, January 14, 1985

"We have a Conservative Government trying to legislate compulsory force-feeding, in other words to legalise assault. I doubt that that action would stand up in the European Court of Human Rights. Never has any remedial or preventive measure been made legitimate, far less compulsory, except in the interest of the person concerned. Force-feeding of the insane is exceptional, but all medical treatment of the sane requires the consent of the patient or, if he is comatose, of those who are able to give that consent. This measure suggests that every citizen should be compelled to be medicated — not for his own benefit but for the possible benefit of some other citizens who form a minute proportion of the population.

Vaccination is in the interests of the person who is vaccinated. Seat belts are in the interests of the person who drives. No measure of compulsion forces a person to undergo any measure that benefits someone else, and certainly no medicinal measure does so. The legislation proposes that we should all be compelled to ingest a substance — whether it is harmless does not matter — so that some people may obtain a benefit for a complaint which is never fatal and which is, at most, irritating."

NOTES:

1. For the law relating to force-feeding of the "insane" see Chapter 9. For questions of consent for the incapacitated, see Chapter 5.
2. Although it may be true that tooth decay itself is not fatal, the removal of decayed teeth under general anaesthetic carries a risk of death.

QUESTIONS:

1. Do you think Nicholas Fairbairn M.P. was correct to say that fluoridation would be a breach of the European Convention on Human Rights? Consider the case of *Acmanne v. Belgium*, above at page 165.
2. Is vaccination purely in the interests of the person to be vaccinated, or does it also benefit the whole population by reducing the risk that they will be infected?

A further elaboration of this argument was put by Ivan Lawrence M.P.:

H.C. Vol. 71, Col. 127–128, January 14, 1985

"Others have argued that only a tiny bit of freedom is involved, so it does not really matter. That is exactly the argument we had in relation to seat belts. There is no such thing as a tiny bit of freedom. There is the principle of freedom or no freedom. It is a seamless web, and the degree is irrelevant. What matters is whether we are prepared to stand up for the liberty of the individual, which can be so easily eroded. If governments are allowed to say, through the medical authorities, not 'this is a medicine that we advise you to take' but 'this is good for you and you must take it', who can say where that will lead? We should be saying, 'This is good for children's teeth and, even though you are not a child, you will take it', and 'Even though you have no teeth, you will take it, but that is only a little infringement of liberty because people without teeth cannot possibly be harmed by it.'

John Stuart Mill said that the individual is sovereign over his own body and mind, and I believe that the right hon. member for South Down has made similar references to the importance of safeguarding small freedoms. If we infringe freedom in this way, where will the process end? Will doctors tell us that because in their view it is good for us to take vitamins — tranquillisers, stimulants, contraceptives or whatever — we shall have to take them? Once we give that kind of licence to administrators, very little of our freedom will be left in a very short time."

QUESTIONS:

1. In *On Liberty* (1859), to which Ivan Lawrence M.P. refers, John Stuart Mill wrote that the 'only purpose for which power may be

rightfully exercised over any member of a civilised community, against his will, is to prevent harm to others.' Do you think fluoridation can be justified under Mill's 'liberty principle'? (For further discussion of this principle see Chapter 2.)

2. Do you think that the arguments put forward in the name of liberty take proper account of the rights to health of those whose dental health would be improved by fluoridation?

One way of meeting the libertarian objections to fluoridation is to ensure that there is a degree of democracy in decisions to introduce it. Thus, the law requires health authorities to consult the local population before they request that a scheme be implemented. The relevant provisions are as follows.

Water Industry Act 1991, s.89(1)–(7)

89.—(1) This section applies where a Health Authority propose to make or withdraw an application under section 87 above.

(2) At least three months before implementing their proposal the Health Authority shall

(a) publish details of the proposal in one or more newspapers circulating within the area affected by the proposal; and

(b) give notice of the proposal to every local authority whose area falls wholly or partly within that area.

(3) Before implementing the proposal the Health Authority shall consult each of the local authorities to which they are required, by virtue of subsection (2)(b) above, to give notice of the proposal.

(4) The Health Authority shall, not earlier than seven days after publishing details of the proposal in the manner required by subsection (2)(a) above, republish them in that manner.

(5) Where a Health Authority have complied with this section in relation to the proposal they shall, in determining whether or not to proceed, have such regard as they consider appropriate —

(a) to any representations which have been made to them with respect to it; and

(b) to any consultations under subsection (3) above.

(6) The Secretary of State may direct that this section shall not apply in relation to any proposal of a Health Authority to withdraw an application under section 87 above.

(7) Where, at any meeting of a Health Authority, consideration is given to the question whether the Health Authority should make or withdraw an application under section 87 above, section 1(2) of the Public Bodies (Admission to Meetings) Act 1960 (which allows the exclusion of the public in certain circumstances) shall not apply to any proceedings on that question.

QUESTIONS:

1. Does the consultation required by this section satisfy the need for democratic decisions?

2. Would a local referendum be more satisfactory?
3. What account does a health authority have to take of local views?

The legal framework for fluoridation was intended to facilitate the introduction of new schemes. However, it does not in fact seem to have done so. Water companies have proved resistant to suggestions that they should fluoridate the water they supply, and have relied on the discretion given to them under the Act (Castle, "The future of the water industry and its implications for water fluoridation" (1992) 9 *Community Dental Health* 323).

QUESTIONS:

1. Do you think that privatised water companies would be more reluctant to fluoridate than those which are publicly owned. Why might that be?
2. Would you support the amendment of the Act so that water undertakers were obliged to fluoridate if asked to do so?

(c) Compulsory Care and the Right to be Ill

One of the features of a mass preventive measure such as fluoridation, and indeed the treatment of water to make it safe to drink, is that it reduces the scope for choice. Clearly, this is a paternalistic approach. However, the paternalism is put forward in the general public good. Freedom of choice is limited in order to promote the rights and interests of a large body of the population, possibly, but not necessarily including the individual whose choice is curtailed. In so far as the limitation of freedom is made in order to protect others, it is compatible with John Stuart Mill's principle of liberty. The problems presented where compulsion is used purely in the interests of the person compelled are more stark. We have already seen how the Public Health (Control of Disease) Act 1984 permits the interests of the person to be tested to be taken into account. Under the Mental Health Act 1983 (see Chapter 9 below) patients may be detained in their own interests as well as to protect others from harm. Under the National Assistance Acts the patient's interest is the principal justification for intervention.

National Assistance Act 1948, s.47(1)–(4) (6)–(9), (11)

47.—(1) The following provisions of this section shall have effect for the purposes of securing the necessary care and attention for persons who —
　(a) are suffering from grave chronic disease or, being aged, infirm or physically incapacitated, are living in insanitary conditions, and
　(b) are unable to devote to themselves, and are not receiving from other persons, proper care and attention.

(2) If the medical officer of health certifies in writing to the appropriate authority that he is satisfied after thorough inquiry and consideration that in the interests of

any such person as aforesaid residing in the area of the authority, or for preventing injury to the health of, or serious nuisance to, other persons, it is necessary to remove any such person as aforesaid from the premises in which he is residing, the appropriate authority may apply to a court of summary jurisdiction having jurisdiction in the place where the premises are situated for an order under the next following subsection.

(3) On any such application the court may, if satisfied on oral evidence of the allegations in the certificate, and that it is expedient so to do, order the removal of the person to whom the application relates, by such officer of the appropriate authority as may be specified in the order, to a suitable hospital or other place in, or within convenient distance of, the area of the appropriate authority, and his detention and maintenance therein:

Provided that the court shall not order the removal of a person to any premises, unless either the person managing the premises has been heard in the proceedings or seven clear days' notice has been given to him of the intended application and of the time and place at which it is proposed to be made.

(4) An order under the last foregoing subsection may be made so as to authorise a person's detention for any period not exceeding three months, and the court may from time to time by order extend that period for such further period, not exceeding three months, as the court may determine . . .

(6) At any time after the expiration of six clear weeks from the making of an order under subsection (3) or (4) of this section an application may be made to the court by or on behalf of the person in respect of whom the order was made, and on any such application the court may, if in the circumstances it appears expedient so to do, revoke the order.

(7) No application under this section shall be entertained by the court unless, seven clear days before the making of the application, notice has been given of the intended application and of the time and place at which it is proposed to be made:

  (a) where the application is for an order under subsection (3) or (4) of this section, to the person in respect of whom the application is made or to some person in charge of him;
  (b) where the application is for the revocation of such an order, to the medical officer of health.

(8) Where in pursuance of an order under this section a person is maintained neither in hospital accommodation provided by the Minister of Health under the National Health Service Act 1977 . . . nor in premises where accommodation is provided by, or by arrangement with, a local authority under Part III of this Act, the cost of his maintenance shall be borne by the appropriate authority.

(9) Any expenditure incurred under the last foregoing subsection shall be recoverable from the person maintained or from any person who for the purposes of this Act is liable to maintain that person; and any expenditure incurred by virtue of this section in connection with the maintenance of a person in premises where accommodation is provided under Part III of this Act shall be recoverable in like manner as expenditure incurred in providing accommodation under the said Part III.

(11) Any person who wilfully disobeys, or obstructs the execution of, an order under this section shall be guilty of an offence and liable on summary conviction to a fine not exceeding level 1 on the standard scale.

NOTE:

  1. Subs. 10 has been repealed, subss. 5, 12–14 have been omitted.

QUESTIONS:

  1. Who determines whether care and attention is "necessary"? The person concerned, the doctor, or the court?

2. Are the provisions for applications to have the order revoked sufficient? Is it right that an application may not be brought for six weeks?
3. Is it right that a person's vulnerability to being forcibly removed depends on the availability of others to care for them (section 47(1)(b))?
4. Can people effectively force their relatives to go to hospital by refusing to care for them?

Under section 47, the person to be removed must be given notice of the application. In 1951, the National Assistance (Amendment) Act 1951 introduced an *ex parte* procedure where the medical officer of health and another doctor certify that 'in their opinion it is necessary in the interest of that person to remove him without delay' (section 1(1)). Orders made under this statute last only three weeks, and must be extended under the provisions of section 47 if this is necessary.

A study published in 1981 indicated that about 200 people were compulsorily removed under these provisions each year (J. Muir Gray 'Section 47' (1981) 7 *Journal of Medical Ethics* 146). Almost all (94 per cent) of these were removed under the emergency powers in the 1951 Act. The provisions of the National Assistance Act 1948 were considered by the Law Commission in their report *Mental Incapacity* (London: HMSO, 1995). They noted the responses to their earlier consultation paper to the effect that there was need for reform of the 1948 Act stating that "The existing law was said to be ineffective in protecting elderly, disabled and other vulnerable people from abuse and neglect and inadquate in its approach to autonomy and individual rights. It appeared to be counter-productive being so draconian that it was rarely used." (para. 9.1). Other powers do exist enabling the removal of vulnerable persons. Section 135 of the Mental Health Act 1983 enables an approved social worker to obtain a warrant from a magistrate to remove a person suffering from a mental disorder to a place of safety. Muir Gray pointed out that these powers of compulsion under the 1948 Act differed from those under the Mental Health Act 1983 in that the person to be removed was recognised to be competent to decide whether they wished to leave. In contrast mental health patients are declared unable to recognise what was good for them, and treated in their interests. The Law Commission have now recommended a series of new powers in relation to vulnerable persons "at risk" which would streamline the existing system (*Mental Incapacity* (London: HMSO, 1995)).

QUESTIONS:

1. Muir Gray suggested that the National Assistance Acts needed amending, but not repealing. Do you agree?
2. What amendments might be made? (See further Law Commission, *Mental Incapacity* (London: HMSO, 1995), para. 9.12 onwards.)

(d) Health Promotion

The measures considered in the preceding two sections are essentially paternalistic. They adopt professional views as to what promotes health and well-being. However, Article 11(2) of the European Social Charter implies that the proper way to deal with many health issues is to enable people to take decisions for themselves. It obliges governments to provide advice and information on health matters and to encourage people to take responsibility for themselves, rather than require them to be healthy. A number of examples of the law facilitating this process can be found. Thus, general medical practitioners are obliged to ensure that patients are offered advice on their diet and lifestyle. They are encouraged to persuade their patients to accept immunisation programmes by financial incentive payments (under regulation 34 of the NHS (General Medical Services) Regulations 1992 (S.I. 1992 No. 635)). Enabling people to make informed choices also involves some regulation. Health pressures have led to constraints, currently voluntary, on the advertising of certain products. Foods must be properly labelled so that consumers can take decisions on the basis of their true constituents. Sometimes, however, the government pursues policies which are designed to influence choice without removing it. Examples of these, which are underpinned by legislation, are the licensing of outlets, and restriction on their opening, and taxation.

Within the duties of a general medical practitioner, there is a specific obligation to 'give advice, where appropriate, to a patient in connection with the patient's general health and in particular about the significance of diet, exercise, the use of tobacco, the consumption of alcohol and the misuse of drugs and solvents' (NHS (General Medical Services) Regulations 1992 (S.I. 1992 No 635) Schedule 1 paragraph 12(2)(a)). The G.P. contract also seeks to ensure that patients are examined and given advice in relation to the state of their health. Thus, doctors should invite new patients to undergo an examination within a month of joining the practice which covers the following areas:

NHS (General Medical Services) Regulations 1992 (S.I. 1992 No. 635) Schedule 2

14.—(2) Where a patient (or, in the case of a patient who is a child, his parent) agrees to participate in a consultation mentioned in sub-paragraph (1), the doctor shall, in the course of that consultation:

(a) seek details from the patient as to his medical history and, so far as may be relevant to the patient's medical history, as to that of his consanguineous family, in respect of:

   (i) illnesses, immunisations, allergies, hereditary conditions, medication and tests carried out for breast or cervical cancer,

   (ii) social factors (including employment, housing and family circumstances) which may affect his health,

    (iii) factors of his lifestyle (including diet, exercise, use of tobacco, consumption of alcohol, and misuse of drugs or solvents) which may affect his health, and

    (iv) the current state of his health;

  (b) offer to undertake a physical examination of the patient, comprising —

    (i) the measurement of his height, weight and blood pressure, and

    (ii) the taking of a urine sample and its analysis to identify the presence of albumen and glucose;

  (c) record, in the patient's medical records, his findings arising out of the details supplied by, and any examination of, the patient under this sub-paragraph;

  (d) assess whether and, if so, in what manner and to what extent he should render personal medical services to the patient;

  (e) in so far as it would not, in the opinion of the doctor, be likely to cause serious damage to the physical or mental health of the patient to do so, offer to discuss with the patient (or, where the patient is a child, the parent) the conclusions the doctor has drawn as a result of the consultation as to the state of the patient's health.

Doctors are also obliged to offer similar examinations to patients who have not been seen within three years (paragraph 15).

NOTE:

  1. There is considerable controversy over the effectiveness of some of these measures. Some argue that doctors are being required to give advice on the basis of poor scientific data. If the 'lifestyle' information imparted in consultations is unreliable then the respect for patients' rights to health information is of little value.

QUESTION:

  1. If the value of lifestyle consultations is uncertain, has the Government been misled by the expectations of health information rights into introducing a legal obligation that is unhelpful?

Encouraging freedom of choice may also involve taking steps to ensure that the information on which decisions are taken is as balanced as possible. Although the Government has resisted legislation to control advertising, this has largely been because the industry has voluntarily introduced restrictions on the way in which certain products are advertised. Thus, advertisements for smoking should follow the following rules.

British Code of Advertising Practice: Cigarette Code; British Codes of Advertising and Sales Promotion

  66.13 No advertisement should incite people to stop smoking.

  66.14 Advertisements should not encourage smokers to increase their consumption or smoke to excess. Smokers should not be encouraged to buy or stock large quantities of cigarettes.

66.15 Advertisements for coupon brands should not feature products unless these can be obtained through the redemption of coupons over a reasonable period of average consumption.

66.16 Advertisements should never suggest that smoking is safe, healthy, natural, necessary for relaxation and concentration, popular or appropriate in the circumstances. Cigarettes should not be shown in the mouth and advertisements should not associate with healthy eating and drinking.

66.17 No more than half those shown in groups should be smoking; smoking should not be shown in public places where it is usually not permitted.

66.18 People can be shown smoking while engaged in work or leisure activities provided that the advertisement does not illustrate inappropriate smoking situations.

66.19 Smoking should not be associated with social, sexual, romantic or business success and advertisements should not be sexually titillating, though the choice of a particular brand may be linked to taste and discernment. In particular, advertisements should not link smoking with people who are evidently wealthy, fashionable, sophisticated or successful or who possess other attributes or qualities that may reasonably be expected to command admiration or encourage emulation.

66.20 Advertisements should not contain actual or implied testimonials or endorsements from well-known people, famous fictitious characters or people doing jobs or occupying positions which are generally regarded as admirable.

66.21 No heroic figure, personality cult or partime or fashion trend should be featured in advertisements in a way that would appeal to those who are adventurous or rebellious, particularly the young.

66.22 No advertisement should play on the susceptibilities of those who are physically or emotionally vulnerable, particularly the young or immature. Advertisements should therefore avoid employing any approach which is more likely to attract the attention or sympathy of those under the age of eighteen.

66.23 Anyone shown smoking should always be, and clearly be seen to be, over twenty-five.

66.24 No advertisement should exaggerate the pleasure of smoking or claim that it is daring or glamorous to smoke or that smoking enhances people's masculinity, feminity, appearance or independence.

66.25 Advertisements that employ outdoor locations or those that depict people or animals should avoid any suggestion of a healthy or wholesome style of life. Any locations, people and objects depicted should not have undue aspirational, historical or cultural associations.

66.26 Advertisements should not associate smoking with sport or with outdoor games. Advertisements for sports sponsorship are governed by a separate voluntary agreement with the Department of National Heritage, on behalf of HM Government and the tobacco industry.

QUESTIONS:

1. Do these restrictions represent the desire to prevent inaccurate advertising, or are they based on the policy objective to reduce the consumption of tobacco without actually banning it?
2. Should advertising be banned completely?
3. Do you think that these guidelines, or something like them, should be enforced by the law?
4. What sanctions should be applied for breach of these principles?

A further way of influencing people's decisions to engage in practices that may affect their health is to increase their cost. This provides a disincentive for indulging in such behaviour, and as such may promote better health.

QUESTIONS:

1. Is taxation primarily a method for reducing consumption or increasing revenue?
2. Should the fact that those who consume alcohol and tobacco and pay high taxes on those items have the consequence that their right to treatment for smoking/alcohol related diseases is not affected?
3. Would your answer differ if the revenue from taxing tobacco and alcohol was earmarked for expenditure on health services as some have proposed?

3. ACCESS TO HEALTH SERVICES

The most specific entitlement set out in the international law of health rights concerns access to health services. It should be noted that Governments are not obliged to provide comprehensive services to all citizens, but to support those unable to make provision for themselves. However, the United Kingdom has committed itself to providing a more extensive service than the internationally recognised rights of citizens would require. To adopt the position taken by the House of Commons Select Committee on Social Services, the National Health Service is said to be committed to providing a comprehensive service that is equally available to all according to need and free of charge at the point of delivery (Social Services Select Committee, *The Future of the National Health Service*, H.C. Pap. 1987–1988 No. 613, para. ix). This section considers the legal framework that seeks to guarantee that those aims are properly met. The first element of the framework is the duties to provide services that are imposed under the NHS Act 1977 and related legislation. The second is the ability of patients to enforce their rights to health care services.

(a) Duties to Provide Services

(i) General Obligations

The general obligation that defines the scope of the National Health Service is set out in the NHS Act 1977.

National Health Service Act 1977, s.1(1–2)

1.—(1) It is the Secretary of State's duty to continue the promotion in England and Wales of a comprehensive health service designed to secure improvement:

(a) in the physical and mental health of the people of these counties, and
(b) in the prevention, diagnosis and treatment of illness,

and for the purpose to provide or secure the effective provision of services in accordance with this Act.

(2) The services so provided shall be free of charge except in so far as the making and recovery of charges is expressly provided for by or under any enactment, whenever passed.

NOTES:

1. Section 128 provides that "'illness' includes mental disorder within the meaning of the Mental Health Act 1983 and any injury or disability requiring medical or dental treatment or nursing."
2. For a survey of the provisions which permit charging for services, see J. Finch, *Spellers Law Relating to Hospitals* (7th edn., London: Chapman and Hall, 1994) Chap. 22.

Section 3 of the Act further specifies the general duty as follows.

National Health Service Act 1977, s.3(1)

3.—(1) It is the Secretary of State's duty to provide throughout England and Wales, to such extent as he considers necessary to meet all reasonable requirements:

(a) hospital accommodation;
(b) other accommodation for the purpose of any service provided under this Act;
(c) medical, dental, nursing and ambulance services;
(d) such other facilities for the care of expectant and nursing mothers and young children as he considers are appropriate as part of the health service;
(e) such facilities for the prevention of illness, the care of persons suffering from illness and the after-care of persons who have suffered from illness as he considers are appropriate as part of the health service;
(f) such other services as are required for the diagnosis and treatment of illness.

Section 5 contains a number of more detailed duties and powers to provide services. These largely consolidate provisions which were previously scattered amongst different pieces of NHS legislation. This accounts for the fact that some of the services would already fall within the general duties. The relevant parts of section 5 read as follows.

National Health Service Act 1977, s.5(1)(1A)(2)

5.—(1) It is the Secretary of State's duty:

(a) to provide for the medical inspection at appropriate intervals of pupils in attendance at schools maintained by local education authorities or at grant-maintained schools and for the medical . . . treatment of such pupils;
(b) to arrange, to such extent as he considers necessary to meet all reasonable requirements in England and Wales, for the giving of advice on contraception, the medical examination of persons seeking advice on contraception, the treatment of such persons and the supply of contraceptive substances and appliances.

(1A) It is also the Secretary of State's duty to provide, to such extent as he considers necessary to meet all reasonable requirements.

(a) for the dental inspection of pupils in attendance at schools maintained by local education authorities or at grant-maintained schools;
(b) for the dental treatment of such pupils; and
(c) for the education of such pupils in dental health . . .

(2) The Secretary of State may:

(a) provide invalid carriages for persons appearing to him to be suffering from severe physical defect or disability and, at the request of such a person, may provide for him a vehicle other than an invalid carriage . . .
(b) arrange to provide accommodation and treatment outside Great Britain for persons suffering from respiratory tuberculosis;
(c) provide a microbiologies service, which may include the provision of laboratories, for the control of the spread of infectious diseases and carry on such other activities as in his opinion can conveniently be carried on in conjunction with that service;
(d) conduct, or assist by grants or otherwise (without prejudice to the general powers and duties conferred on him under the Ministry of Health Act 1919) any person to conduct, research into any matters relating to the causation, prevention, diagnosis or treatment of illness, and into any such other matters connected with any service provided under this Act as he considers appropriate.

QUESTIONS:

1. How far are these general duties subject to the political will of the Secretary of State of the day?
2. Do you think any one will be easier to enforce than any other? Compare the requirements of school medical examinations and family planning.

Added to these NHS duties is the area of community care. This refers to a range of services provided by local authorities. They are the provision of accommodation for adults who cannot look after themselves; services for adults who are blind, deaf, dumb, or substantially and permanently handicapped by illness, injury or congenital disability, including the adaptation of homes and provision of meals and special equipment; services promoting the welfare of elderly people. Community care also includes non-residential services for pregnant women and mothers, home help and laundry facilities for households caring for a person who is ill, handicapped, or pregnant. With the Secretary of State's approval, local authorities may also provide services for those who are ill, including after-care and preventive care. Finally, community care services cover after-care for those discharged from mental health services.

The primary obligation in relation to these services is to assess the need of individual patients for them.

National Health Service & Community Care Act 1990, s.47(1–3)(7)

47.—(1) Subject to subsections (5) and (6) below, where it appears to a local authority that any person for whom they may provide or arrange for the provision of community care services may be in need of any such services, the authority:

(a) shall carry out an assessment of his needs for those services; and
(b) having regard to the results of that assessment, shall then decide whether his needs call for the provision by them of any such services.

(2) If at any time during the assessment of the needs of any person under subsection (1)(a) above it appears to a local authority that he is a disabled person, the authority:

(a) shall proceed to make such a decision as to the services he requires as is mentioned in section 4 of the Disabled Persons (Services, Consultation and Representation) Act 1986 without his requesting them to do so under that section; and
(b) shall inform him that they will be doing so and of his rights under that Act.

(3) If at any time during the assessment of the needs of any person under subsection (1)(a) above, it appears to a local authority-

(a) that there may be a need for the provision to that person by such Health Authority as may be determined in accordance with regulations of any services under the National Health Service Act 1977, or
(b) that there may be a need for the provision to him of any services which fall within the functions of a local housing authority (within the meaning of the Housing Act 1985) which is not the local authority carrying out the assessment,

the local authority shall notify that Health Authority or local housing authority and invite them to assist, to such extent as is reasonable in the circumstances, in the making of the assessment; and, in making their decision as to the provision of the services needed for the person in question, the local authority shall take into account any services which are likely to be made available for him by that Health Authority or local housing authority . . .

(7) This section is without prejudice to section 3 of the Disabled Persons (Services, Consultation and Representation) Act 1986.

In general, there is no specific obligation actually to provide services. However, it may become easier to show that authorities have acted unlawfully if they refuse to offer services that patients have been identified as needing (see below).

In certain circumstances the law does go further. Thus the Chronically Sick and Disabled Persons Act 1970, s.2, imposes a duty to actually provide services.

Chronically Sick and Disabled Persons Act 1970, s.2(1)

Section 2(1) Where a local authority having functions under section 29 of the National Assistance Act 1948 are satisfied in the case of any person to whom that section applies who is ordinarily resident in their area that it is necessary in order to meet the needs of that person for that authority to make arrangements for all or any of the following matters, namely —

(a) the provision of practical assistance for that person in his home;
(b) the provision for that person of, or assistance to that person in obtaining, wireless, television, library or similar recreational facilities;
(c) the provision for that person of lectures, games, outings or other recreational facilities outside his home or assistance to that person in taking advantage of educational facilities available to him;

(d) the provision for that person of facilities for, or assistance in, travelling to and from his home for the purpose of participating in any services provided under arrangements made by the authority under the said section 29 or, with the approval of the authority, in any services provided otherwise than as aforesaid which are similar to services which could be provided under such arrangements;

(e) the provision of assistance for that person in arranging for the carrying out of any works of adaptation in his home or the provision of any additional facilities designed to secure his greater safety, comfort or convenience;

(f) facilitating the taking of holidays by that person, whether at holiday homes or otherwise and whether provided under arrangements made by the authority or otherwise;

(g) the provision of meals for that person whether in his home or elsewhere;

(h) the provision for that person of, or assistance to that person in obtaining, a telephone and any special equipment necessary to enable him to use a telephone . . . then, . . . subject . . . to the provisions of section 7(1) of the Local Authority Social Services Act 1970 (which requires local authorities in the exercise of certain functions, including functions under the said section 29, to act under the general guidance of the Secretary of State) and to the provisions of section 7A of that Act (which requires local authorities to exercise their social services functions in accordance with directions given by the Secretary of State), it shall be the duty of that authority to make those arrangements in exercise of their functions under the said section 29.

The Secretary of State carries out these general duties in two main ways. The first is by contracting, under a statutory contract, with general medical practitioners for the provision of primary care services. These are defined relatively loosely, and in a circular manner as 'personal medical services' being 'all necessary and appropriate personal medical services of the type usually provided by general medical practitioners.' (NHS (General Medical Services) Regulations 1992 (S.I. 1992 No. 635), Schedule 2, paragraph 12(1)). This general definition is supplemented by a list of examples. These are included within the range of personal medical services, but do not constitute an exhaustive list.

National Health Service (General Medical Services) Regulations 1992 (S.I. 1992 No. 635), Schedule 2

12.—(2) The services which a doctor is required by sub-paragraph (1) to render shall include the following:

(a) giving advice, where appropriate, to a patient in connection with the patient's general health, and in particular about the significance of diet, exercise, the use of tobacco, the consumption of alcohol and the misuse of drugs or solvents;

(b) offering to patients consultations and, where appropriate, physical examinations for the purpose of identifying, or reducing the risk of, disease or injury;

(c) offering to patients, where appropriate, vaccination or immunisation against measles, mumps, rubella, pertussis, poliomyelitis, diphtheria and tetanus;

(d) arranging for the referral of patients, as appropriate, for the provision of any other services under the Act; and

(e) giving advice, as appropriate, to enable patients to avail themselves of services provided by a local social services authority.

General medical services are additionally defined by the exclusion of certain areas. These services will not automatically be available at all practices. G.P.s may specifically decide to offer them, but need not do so. Separate lists are kept by Health Authorities of G.P.s who provide these services. These areas are set out in paragraph 12(3)(l). It is also possible for a G.P. to offer only a restricted sub-set of services:

National Health Service (General Medical Services) Regulations 1992 (S.I. 1992 No. 635), Schedule 2, para. 12(3)

12.—(3) A doctor is not required by sub-paragraph (1) or (2):

(a) to provide to any person child health surveillance services, contraceptive services, minor surgery services nor, except in an emergency, maternity medical services, unless he has previously undertaken to the H.A. to provide such services to that person; or
(b) where he is a restricted services principal, to provide any category of general medical services which he has not undertaken to provide.

General medical practitioners are obliged to provide these services to their "patients". These are identified by paragraph 4 of Schedule 2 to the National Health Service (General Medical Services) Regulations 1992. They are the following.

National Health Service (General Medical Services) Regulations 1992 (S.I. 1992 No. 635), Schedule 2, 4(1)

4.—(1)(a) persons who are recorded by the H.A. as being on his list;
(b) persons whom he has accepted or agreed to accept on his list, whether or not notification of that acceptance has been received by the HA, and who have not been notified to him by the H.A. as having ceased to be on his list;
(c) for the limited period specified in sub-paragraph (4), persons whom he has refused to accept;
(d) persons who have been assigned to him under regulation 21;
(e) for the limited period specified in sub-paragraph (5), persons in respect of whom he has been notified that an application has been made for assignment to him in a case to which regulation 21(3)(b) applies;
(f) persons whom he has accepted as temporary residents;
(g) in respect of services under paragraph 8, persons to whom he has agreed to provide those services;
(h) persons to whom he may be requested to give treatment which is immediately required owing to an accident or other emergency at any place in his practice area, provided that:
    (i) he is not, at time of the request, relieved of liability to give treatment under paragraph 5, and
    (ii) he is not, at the time of the request, relieved, under paragraph 19(2), of his obligation to give treatment personally, and
    (iii) he is available to provide such treatment, and any persons by whom he is requested, and agrees, to give treatment which is immediately

required owing to an accident or other emergency at any place in the locality of any H.A. in whose medical list he is included, provided there is no doctor who, at the time of the request, is under an obligation otherwise than under this head to give treatment to that person, or there is such a doctor but, after being requested to attend, he is unable to attend and give treatment immediately required;

(k) in respect of child health surveillance services, contraceptive services, maternity medical services, or minor surgery services persons for whom he has undertaken to provide such services;

NOTES:

1. Subparagraphs (i), (j), and (l) relate to patients who are primarily the responsibility of another general medical practitioner, and have been omitted here.

2. Sub-paragraph (4) requires general medical practitioners to treat for 14 days people they refuse to accept as patients. This gives the opportunity for them to find another G.P. who is wiling to accept them, or for the Health Authority to exercise its power to oblige G.P.s to accept patients against their wishes for a limited period under reg. 21.

3. Paragraph 8 concerns the provision of cervical smears for a patient whom a doctor has accepted for maternity or contraceptive services, and the provision of such smears, vaccinations, or immunisations for temporary residents. These may be provided to people without them being on the doctor's "list".

4. Paragraph 5 relieves doctors who are elderly or infirm, who whom the Health Authority has exempted, from the obligation to provide emergency services.

5. Paragraph 19 usually requires doctors to provide services personally, but paragraph 19(2) permits the use of deputising services.

QUESTION:

1. Do you think that paragraph 4(1)(h) requires doctors who are driving past a road accident in their practice area to stop and provide assistance?

Under paragraph 9 of the Terms of Service, a G.P. is entitled to have a patient removed from his list without giving a reason. While the Health Authority has the power to require GPs to accept patients that they do not want, this can only be done for a temporary period (reg 21). Thus, it is possible for Health Authorities to ensure that a person receives primary care, but not that they receive continuity of care from the same doctor.

QUESTIONS:

1. Do you think that Health Authorities should be able to require doctors to take on patients that they do not want?

2. Would you support the lesser requirement that doctors should at least be required to explain why they are rejecting a patient? Can you identify some reasons that would be acceptable for doing this? And some that should be proscribed?

The second way in which the Secretary of State ensures that other NHS services are available is through the commissioning of services through a mechanism of contracts for services. The NHS is divided into purchasers and providers. Each geographical area has a Health Authority, to whom the obligations of securing services are delegated. Some G.P.s, known as G.P. Fundholders, also play a purchasing role (in addition to their functions as providers of primary care). On the other side of the equation, obligations to provide services are delegated to NHS Trusts. The picture is complicated somewhat by the fact that certain "special Health Authorities" exist, which are in fact providers of services (not always clinical services). Further, some bodies independent of direct NHS control may be delivering NHS services under contracts with Health Authorities. Some of these will be private businesses, others operating on a non-profit-making basis. However, the main elements of the system can be considered by considering the position of Health Authorities and NHS Trusts, which constitute the main contracting agencies.

The functions of Health Authorities are delegated to them by the Secretary of State under the NHS Functions (of Health Authorities and Administration Arrangements) Regulations 1996 (S.I. 1996 No. 708, as amended). They include all the functions extracted under above sections 2, 3 and 5 of the NHS Act 1977 except those under section 5(2)(a)–(c). The provision of community care services falls upon local authority social services departments, who either provide or arrange for the provision of those services through contracts. These contracts may be with health service bodies.

Health Authorities are usually made up of five executive officers, up to seven non-executives and a chairman. The latter two categories are appointed by the Secretary of State. If circumstances warrant it, up to four more members may be appointed, provided that the balance of executives and non-executives is maintained. The core tasks of health authorities are to oversee the work of general practitioners and to purchase hospital and community health services. This latter function includes assessing the health and health care needs of the local population and developing strategies to meet those needs within national guidelines and priorities (Department of Health *Statement of Responsibilities and Accountabilities: public health, the NHS and social care*, London: DOH, 1995). Mostly, the method used to secure services will be to enter into a "NHS contract" with a "NHS Trust". Each of these are legal entities created by the NHS and Community Care Act 1990.

(ii) National Health Service Trusts

The functions of NHS Trusts are partly determined by the NHS and Community Care Act 1990, and partly by each Trust's individual establishment order. Under section 5(1) of the 1990 Act, NHS Trusts are established:

(a) to assume responsibility, in accordance with this Act for the ownership and management of hospitals or other establishments or facilities which were previously managed or provided by Regional, District or Special Health Authorities; or

(b) to provide and manage hospitals or other establishments or facilities.

As an example of the way in which this is further specified for individual NHS Trusts, Southampton Community Health Services NHS Trust is established for the purpose set out in section 5(1), and its functions are as follows:

(a) to own and manage hospital accommodation and services provided at Lymington Hospital . . . and associated hospitals (including the management of its teaching and research facilities);

(b) to manage community health services provided from Central Health Clinic . . . Southampton . . . and to own the associated premises. (The Southampton Community Health Services NHS Trust (Establishment) Order 1992, S.I. 1992 No. 2584, art. 3(2))

'Community health services' are defined as 'any services which the Secretary of State may provide under section 3(1)(d) or (e) of, or Schedule 1 to the National Health Service Act 1977 and any service which she has a duty to provide under section 5(1) or (1A) of that Act' (The Southampton Community Health Services NHS Trust (Establishment) Order 1992 (S.I. 1992 No. 2584), art. 1(2)).

All Trusts are required to meet certain statutory financial obligations:

National Health Service & Community Care Act 1990, s.10(1–2)

10.—(1) Every NHS Trust shall ensure that its revenue is not less than sufficient, taking one financial year with another, to meet outgoings properly charged to revenue account.

(2) It shall be the duty of every NHS Trust to achieve such financial objectives as may from time to time be set by the Secretary of State with the consent of the Treasury and as are applicable to it; and any such objectives may be made applicable to NHS Trusts generally, or to a particular NHS Trust or to NHS Trusts of a particular description.

NOTES:

1. Subsection (1) imposes an obligation to break even each year.
2. There are two financial objectives currently set for NHS Trusts. The first is to obtain a 6 per cent return on their assets. This is designed to ensure that those assets are not regarded as a 'free good.' By forcing NHS Trusts to pay for all the assets they own, this provision encourages them to make sure that those assets are either productive or are sold off. The second financial objective for NHS Trusts is to stay within their 'external financing limit.' This refers to the amount of money that they are permitted to borrow.

These statutory obligations are elaborated in Schedule II to the Act. This includes the following provisions:

National Health Service & Community Care Act 1990, Schedule II, 6(1)(2), 7(1)–(3), 8

6.—(1) An NHS trust shall carry out effectively, efficiently and economically the functions for the time being conferred on it by an order under section 5(1) of this Act and by the provisions of this Schedule and, with respect to the exercise of the powers conferred by section 5(10) of this Act and paragraphs 10 to 15 below, shall comply with any directions given to it by the Secretary of State whether of a general or a particular nature.

(2) An NHS trust shall comply with any directions given to it by the Secretary of State with respect to all or any of the following matters:

(a) the qualifications of persons who may be employed as officers of the trust;
(b) the employment, for the purpose of performing functions specified in the direction, of officers having qualifications or experience of a description so specified;
(c) the manner in which officers of the trust are to be appointed;
(d) prohibiting or restricting the disposal of, or of any interest in, any asset which, at the time the direction is given, the Secretary of State reasonably considers to have a value in excess of such sum as may be specified in an order under section 5(1) of this Act and in respect of which the Secretary of State considers that the interests of the National Health Service require that the asset should not be disposed of;
(e) compliance with guidance or directions given (by circular or otherwise) to Health Authorities or Special Health Authorities particular descriptions of Health Authorities or Special Health Authorities; and
(f) the implementation of awards relating to the distinction or merit of medical practitioners or dental practitioners or any class or classes of such practitioners;

and with any directions given to it under section 1(1A) of the Hospital Complaints Procedure Act 1985.

7.—(1) For each accounting year an NHS trust shall prepare and send to the Secretary of State an annual report in such form as may be determined by the Secretary of State.

(2) At such time or times as may be prescribed, an NHS trust shall hold a public meeting at which its audited accounts and annual report and any report on the

accounts made pursuant to subsection (3) of section 15 of the Local Government Finance Act 1982 shall be presented.

(3) In such circumstances and at such time or times as may be prescribed, an NHS trust shall hold a public meeting at which such document as may be prescribed shall be presented.

8. An NHS trust shall furnish to the Secretary of State such reports, returns and other information, including information as to its forward planning, as, and in such form as, he may require.

QUESTIONS:

1. These paragraphs are designed to ensure that NHS Trusts are accountable to the Secretary of State, do you think that they are sufficient?
2. Do you think that the law indicates a greater concern with financial affairs of NHS Trusts than with clinical effectiveness or accountability to the public?

(iii) NHS Contracts

The arrangements made between health authorities and health service bodies such as NHS trusts are known as 'NHS Contracts.' While in many respects taking the form of contracts as operate at common law it was not intended that they would be judicially enforceable.

National Health Service & Community Care Act 1990, s.4(1)(3)–(8)

4.—(1) In this Act the expression "NHS contract" means an arrangement under which one health service body ("the acquirer") arranges for the provision to it by another health service body ("the provider") of goods or services which it reasonably requires for the purposes of its functions . . .

(3) Whether or not an arrangement which constitutes an NHS contract would, apart from this subsection, be a contract in law, it shall not be regarded for any purpose as giving rise to contractual rights or liabilities, but if any dispute arises with respect to such an arrangement, either party may refer the matter to the Secretary of State for determination under the following provisions of this section.

(4) If, in the course of negotiations intending to lead to an arrangement which will be an NHS contract, it appears to a health service body:

(a) that the terms proposed by another health service body are unfair by reason that the other is seeking to take advantage of its position as the only, or the only practicable, provider of the goods or services concerned or by reason of any other unequal bargaining position as between the prospective parties to the proposed arrangement, or
(b) that for any other reason arising out of the relative bargaining position of the prospective parties any of the terms of the proposed arrangement cannot be agreed, that health service body may refer the terms of the proposed arrangement to the Secretary of State for determination under the following provisions of this section.

(5) Where a reference is made to the Secretary of State under subsection (3) or subsection (4) above, the Secretary of State may determine the matter himself or, if

he considers it appropriate, appoint a person to consider and determine it in accordance with regulations.

(6) By his determination of a reference under subsection (4) above, the Secretary of State or, as the case may be, the person appointed under subsection (5) above may specify terms to be included in the proposed arrangement and may direct that it be proceeded with; and it shall be the duty of the prospective parties to the proposed arrangement to comply with any such directions.

(7) A determination of a reference under subsection (3) above may contain such directions (including directions as to payment) as the Secretary of State or, as the case may be, the person appointed under subsection (5) above considers appropriate to resolve the matter in dispute; and it shall be the duty of the parties to the NHS contract in question to comply with any such directions.

(8) Without prejudice to the generality of his powers on a reference under subsection (3) above, the Secretary of State or, as the case may be, the person appointed under subsection (5) above may by his determination in relation to an arrangement constituting an NHS contract vary the terms of the arrangement or bring it to an end; and where an arrangement is so varied or brought to an end:

(a) subject to paragraph (b) below, the variation or termination shall be treated as being effected by agreement between the parties; and

(b) the directions included in the determination by virtue of subsection (7) above may contain such provisions as the Secretary of State or, as the case maybe, the person appointed under subsection (5) above considers appropriate in order satisfactorily to give effect to the variation or to bring the arrangement to an end.

NOTES:

1. It appears that s.4(3) will exclude an action from being brought in contract. There has been some debate as to the possibility of actions being brought in restitution. (See J. Jacob, "Lawyers go to Hospital" [1991] *Public Law* 255 and K. Barker "NHS Contracts, Restitution and the Internal Market" (1993) *56 Modern Law Review* 832.)

2. Where disputes arise in relation to contracts in the internal market a number of mechanisms exist for their resolution. In contrast with private sector contracting, disputes about the formation of contracts (and not just their performance) can be subject to those processes for dispute resolution. Parties are encouraged by central NHS management to resolve the matter at local level. Where agreement cannot be reached parties are expected to involve a conciliator who will, almost invariably, be an NHS manager. If the dispute cannot be resolved in this manner then ultimately it may be referred to a special statutory dispute resolution mechanism (NHS Contracts (Dispute Resolution) Regulations 1996 (S.I. 1996 No. 623)). Disputes are to be referred to an adjudicator. He has the power to find for one party or the other—what is known as "pendulum arbitration". It is not intended that these proceedings will be judicial in nature and there is no right to an oral hearing. To date this statutory procedure has only been used on one occasion, in Wales. It has been suggested that this may be due to a combination of factors, not least strong encouragement from central NHS management for the contracting parties to settle their

disputes on a local basis. (See further J. McHale, D. Hughes and L. Griffiths, "Disputes, Regulation and Relationships" (1996) 2 *Medical Law International* 273, and I. Harden and D. Longley, "NHS Contracts" in J. Birds, J. Bradgate and C. Villiers (eds) *Termination of Contracts*, Law Chancery: Chichester, 1995.)

3. The Secretary of State also has 'default powers' under s.85 of the NHS Act 1977 which enable him to take over the running of NHS bodies. Powers to direct NHS bodies on how they should operate are provided by ss.13–17 of that Act.

QUESTIONS:

1. Do these provisions ensure that ultimate control over the NHS rests with the Secretary of State? Are they sufficient?

(iv) Corporate Governance in the NHS

Concern has been expressed about the introduction of competition and other market forces in the NHS leading to the erosion of accountability and ethical principles in the Service (see J. Jacob "Lawyers go to Hospital" [1991] *Public Law* 255, D. Longley, *Public Law and Health Service Accountability*, Buckingham: Open UP, 1993 and D. Longley, *Healthcare Constitutions*, London: Cavendish Publishing, 1996). Amongst other pressures, this has led to the production of three Codes to influence behaviour. The Code of Conduct for NHS Boards (1994) includes a statement of Public Sector Values which are to govern the NHS:

Code of Conduct for NHS Boards (1994)

There are three crucial public service values which must underpin the work of the health service.

Accountability — everything done by those who work in the NHS must be able to stand the test of parliamentary scrutiny, public judgements on propriety and professional codes of conduct.

Probity — there should be an absolute standard of honesty in dealing with the assets of the NHS: integrity should be the hallmark of all personal conduct in decisions affecting patients, staff and suppliers, and in the use of information acquired in the course of NHS duties.

Openness — there should be sufficient transparency about NHS activities to promote confidence between the NHS authority or trust and its staff, patients and the public.

All Board members are required to subscribe to these Codes on appointment. It is these Board members who are expected to provide the necessary direction for the NHS. The Code of Accountability for NHS Boards (1994) sets out their responsibilities as follows:

Code of Accountability for NHS Boards (1994)

NHS boards have six key functions for which they are held accountable by the NHS Executive on behalf of the Secretary of State:

- to set the strategic direction of the organisation within the overall policies and priorities of the Government and the NHS, define its annual and longer term objectives and agree plans to achieve them,
- to oversee the delivery of planned results by monitoring performance against objectives and ensuring corrective action is taken when necessary,
- to ensure effective financial stewardship through value for money, financial control and financial planning and strategy,
- to ensure that high standards of corporate governance and personal behaviour are maintained in the conduct of the business of the whole organisation,
- to appoint, appraise and remunerate senior executives, and
- to ensure that there is effective dialogue between the organisation and the local community on its plans and performance and that these are responsive to the community's needs.

The following, from the same source, is a summary of the reporting requirements on NHS Trusts and their Directors:

Code of Accountability for NHS Boards (1994)

Reporting and Controls

It is the board's duty to present through the timely publication of an annual report, annual accounts and other means, a balanced and readily understood assessment of the authority's or trust's performance to:

- The NHS Executive on behalf of the Secretary of State,
- The Audit Commission and its appointed auditors, and
- the local community.

The detailed guidance issued by the NHS Executive, including the role of internal and external auditors, must be scrupulously observed.

Declarations of Interests

It is a requirement that chairmen and all board members should declare any conflict of interest, that arises in the course of conducting NHS business. That requirement continues in force. Chairmen and board members should declare on appointment any business interests, position of authority, in a charity or voluntary body in the field of health and social care and any connection with a voluntary or other body contracting for NHS services. These should be formally recorded in the minutes of the Board, and entered into a register which is available to the public. Directorships and other significant interests held by NHS board members should be declared on appointment, kept up to date and set out in the annual report.

Accountability to the local community is probably the weakest element of this network. In order to improve the position, a Code of Practice on Openness in the NHS was issued in 1995.

Code of Practice on Openness in the NHS

5. Information Which Must be Provided

Apart from the exemptions set out in paragraph 9. below, NHS Trusts and Authorities must publish or otherwise make available the following information (further details are given in Annexes A, B, C and D [not reproduced here]):

- information about what services are provided, the targets and standards set and results achieved, and the costs and effectiveness of the service;
- details about important proposals on health policies or proposed changes in the way services are delivered, including the reasons for those proposals. This information will normally be made available when proposals are announced and before decisions are made;
- details about important decisions on health policies and decisions on changes to the delivery of services. This information, and the reasons for the decisions, will normally be made available when the decisions are announced;
- information about the way in which health services are managed and provided and who is responsible;
- information about how the NHS communicates with the public, such as details of public meetings, consultation procedures, suggestion and complaints systems;
- information about how to contact Community Health councils and the Health Service Commissioner (Ombudsman);
- information about how people can have access to their own personal health records.

9. Information Which May be Withheld

NHS Trusts and Authorities must provide the information requested unless it falls within one of the following exempt categories:

(i) Personal information. People have a right of access to their own health records but not normally to information about other people.

(ii) Requests for information which are manifestly unreasonable, far too general, or would require unreasonable resources to answer.

(iii) Information about internal discussion and advice, where disclosure would harm frank internal debate, except where this disclosure would be outweighed by the public interest.

(iv) Management information, where disclosure would harm the proper and effective operation of the NHS organisation.

(v) Information about legal matters and proceedings, where disclosure would prejudice the administration of justice and the law.

(vi) Information which could prejudice negotiations or the effective conduct of personnel management or commercial or contractual activities. This does not cover information about internal NHS contracts.

(vii) Information given in confidence. The NHS has a common law duty to respect confidences except when it is clearly outweighed by the public interest.

(viii) Information which will soon be published or where disclosure would be premature in relation to a planned announcement or publication.

(ix) Information relating to incomplete analysis, research or statistics where disclosure could be misleading or prevent the holder from publishing it first.

QUESTIONS

1. Do you think that the three Codes go far enough? (See A. Belcher "Codes of Conduct and Accountability for NHS Boards" [1995] *Public Law* 288.)

2. NHS directors are protected from personal liability for their actions (NHS Act 1977, s.125.) Should they be liable to surcharge in the same way as local councillors?

(b) Enforcement of Duties to Provide Services

This section considers the role of the courts in enforcing the duties to provide health care examined in the preceding section. It can be argued that the Government is meeting its international obligations to provide health services without giving aggrieved patients the possibility of bringing legal actions to enforce their rights. However, to many patients, unless they can personally bring redress in the courts, their so-called rights are worth little. Two main options are available. The first is the public law action for judicial review. This enables the decisions of public bodies to be challenged on the basis that they have been taken irrationally, illegally or were undermined by serious procedural irregularities (*Council of Civil Service Unions v. Minister for the Civil Service* [1985] 1 A.C. 374, 410 per Lord Diplock). This type of action can be used when services are refused to try to force the relevant health service body to provide them.

The second type of legal action available for patients claiming that their rights to receive health care have been breached is a claim for compensation. This will be available to those who have suffered damage because of a failure to provide the services to which they claim they were entitled. Clearly it relates to past failures, and will not usually lead to the desired services actually being provided. Rather the existence of this type of claim provides health care providers with an incentive to provide appropriate services in order to avoid being sued.

The cases reviewed in the following pages show how reluctant the courts have proved to scrutinise the decisions of health service bodies who deny patients access to services they want. In practice, they may prefer to use the NHS complaints procedures to put pressure on the health service to deliver the care they need. Those procedures are considered in Chapter 4. In relation to service failures by a general medical practitioner, the health authority may bring proceedings before a disciplinary committee because there will have been a breach of the G.P.'s contract (see J. Montgomery, *Health Care Law*, Oxford: OUP, 1997, Chapter 4).

(i) Judicial Review

R. v. Secretary of State for Social Services, ex p. Hincks (1980) 1 BMLR 93

In 1971, plans were made to expand a hospital in Staffordshire. The expansion would have improved facilities for orthopaedic surgery. In 1978, the expansion was postponed for ten years, and virtually abandoned, because it was found to be too expensive. It was acknowledged that there was a need to improve services, but the scheme was not regarded as having sufficient priority for funding. Four patients who were awaiting orthopaedic surgery brought proceedings for judicial review, alleging that the Secretary of State was in breach of his duties under section 3 of the 1977 Act (see above). They argued (as summarised by Lord Denning) that there was no limitation on those duties in respect of available resources:

> "that duty must be fulfilled. If the Secretary of State needs money to do it, then he must see that Parliament gives it to him. Alternatively if Parliament does not give it to him, then a provision should be put in the statute to excuse him from his duty. Mr Blom-Cooper [for the patients] says that that duty is plain and imperative, and it ought to be fulfilled by the Secretary of State."

All three judges in the Court of Appeal rejected the patients' case. Their reasons are explained by Lord Denning:

LORD DENNING M.R.:
" . . . That is an attractive argument, because there is no express limitation on the duty of the Secretary of State in the statute. But, in the course of the argument, many illustrations have been taken showing how necessary it is for a Secretary of State to have regard to forward planning (as it is called), to estimated changes in the population, for instance — or maybe the ageing population. He has to estimate for the future. For instance, when in 1971 the Good Hope Hospital scheme was approved, it was necessarily contemplated that it would be possible within the resources available. Indeed, as the discussion proceeded, it seemed to me inevitable that this provision had to be implied into section 3, 'to such extent as he considers necessary to meet all reasonable requirements such as can be provided within the resources available'. That seems to me to be a very necessary implication to put on that section, in accordance with the general legislative purpose. It cannot be supposed that the Secretary of State has to provide all the latest equipment. As Oliver L.J. said in the course of argument, it cannot be supposed that the Secretary of State has to provide all the kidney machines which are asked for, or for all the new developments such as heart transplants in every case where people would benefit from them. It cannot be that the Secretary of State has a duty to benefit from them. It cannot be that the Secretary of State has a duty to provide everything that is asked for in the changed circumstances which have come about. That includes the numerous pills that people take nowadays: it cannot be said that he has to provide all these free for everybody.
I would like to read a few words from the judgment of Wien J., who gave a very comprehensive and good judgment in this matter. He said:
'The question remains: has there been a breach of duty? Counsel for the [Secretary of State] submits that section 3 does not impose an absolute duty. I agree. He further submits it does, by virtue of the discretion given, include an evaluation of financial resources or the lack of them is at the root of the whole problem in this case. If funds were unlimited, then of course regions and areas could go ahead and provide all sorts of services. But funds are not unlimited. The funds are voted by Parliament, and the health service has to do the best it can with the total allocation of financial resources.'
I agree with that approach of the judge in this case. But there is a further aspect which he dealt with. He said, instead of looking at the health service as a whole, could you pinpoint a particular hospital or a particular area like the Good Hope Hospital in Birmingham, and say, 'That does require an extension, and it is a breach

of duty for the Secretary of State not to provide for that hospital and that area'? It seems to me — as, indeed, Mr Richard Moyle said in the course of his letter — that you cannot pinpoint any particular hospital or any particular area. The Secretary of State has to do his best having regard to his wide responsibilities. For instance, there are 12 hospitals in this particular area. The service has to be provided over the whole country. Upon that point, the judge said:

'I have come to the conclusion that it is impossible to pinpoint any breach of statutory duty on the part of the Secretary of State. If he is entitled to take into account financial resources, as in my judgment he is, then it follows that every thing that can be done within the limit of the financial resources available has been done in the region and in the area. I doubt very much whether under section 3(1) it is permissible to put the spotlight, as it were, upon one particular department of one particular hospital and to say that conditions there are unsatisfactory.'

It seems to me that those two paragraphs in the judge's judgment express the position very accurately. It is an interesting point, and it is important from the public point of view because of the grievances which many people feel nowadays about the long waiting list to get into hospital. So be it. The Secretary of State says that he is doing the best he can with the financial resources available to him: and I do not think that he can be faulted in the matter."

QUESTION:

1. Do you think that it would be lawful under this decision for the Secretary of State to decide that there should be no provision of kidney dialysis at all under the NHS?

If it is very difficult to challenge the global allocation of NHS resources, it might nevertheless be open to patients to use judicial review to complain that local managerial decisions, within services that have been funded, are in breach of the statutory duties.

R. v. Central Birmingham H.A., ex p. Walker (1987) 3 BMLR 32

In 1987 the parents of a baby were told that he would not receive heart surgery because there were insufficient nurses available to look after him. They sought leave to bring judicial review against the health authority. The authority accepted that they were subject to judicial review, but argued that this was not a case that should be examined by the courts. The Court of Appeal agreed and refused to grant leave.

SIR JOHN DONALDSON M.R.:

" . . . It is not for this court, or indeed any court, to substitute its own judgment for the judgment of those who are responsible for the allocation of resources. This court could only intervene where it was satisfied that there was a *prima facie* case, not only of failing to allocate resources in the way in which others would think that resources should be allocated, but of a failure to allocate resources to an extent which was Wednesbury unreasonable, if one likes to use the lawyers' jargon, or, in simpler words, which involves a breach of a public law duty (see *Associated Provincial Picture Houses v. Wednesbury Corp* [1947] 2 All E.R. 680). Even then, of course, the court has to exercise a judicial discretion. It has to take account of all the circumstances of the particular case with which it is concerned.

Taking account of the evidence which has been put before us and all the circumstances, it seems to me that this would be an inappropriate case in which to give leave. If other circumstances arose in this case or another case it might be different, because the jurisdiction does exist. But we have to remember, as I think I have already indicated, that if the court is prepared to grant leave in all or even most cases where patients are, from their points of view, very reasonably disturbed at what is going on, we should ourselves be using up National Health Service resources by requiring the authority to stop doing the work for which they were appointed and to meet the complaints of their patients. It is a very delicate balance. As I have made clear and as Mr Bailey has made clear, the jurisdiction does exist. But it has to be used extremely sparingly.

NOTE:

1. In the *Wednesbury* case, to which Lord Donaldson refers, the court identified a type of 'unreasonableness' which would permit them to quash decisions. This would be present when the decision was one that no reasonable public body of the type in question could have reached. There can be a variety of decisions in any particular case, a number of which may be reasonable, but that does not prevent the court criticising those which are not within that range. However, it is not enough to persuade the judge that a better decision could have been made.

An indication of when the courts might be prepared to strike down decisions about resource allocation can be found in a case concerning community care where the court suggested that he could envisage circumstances in which it would be so unreasonable not to provide services that a court could intervene. A number of cases were heard together in which the Social Services Departments had decided to withdraw services from clients currently receiving them in order to reduce their overall expenditure. The extract here concerns the action against Gloucestershire County Council, who lost the case because it had been guilty of a procedural impropriety in not giving individual attention to the specific needs of each clients. Instead, a decision to remove services from a whole class of people had been made because of a general lack of resources. The duties to provide services in issue in this case arose under the Chronically Sick and Disabled Persons Act 1970, section 2 (see above).

R. v. Gloucestershire CC, ex p. Mahfood; R. v. Islington, ex p. McMillan, The Times, June 21, 1995

McCOWAN L.J.:
" . . . Mr. Gordon Q.C. has appeared for all the applicants. His position is a simple one. He says that individual need is the only criterion. Sufficiency of resources in the provider or the number of disabled persons in the area who are also in need are irrelevant. His argument was illuminated by homely examples. First there were the six tired advocates who only had five chairs. There was clearly a need of a sixth chair and that need existed none the less because there was no money available to

buy it. Again, there was the chairless museum attendant. He either needs a chair, or he does not. The cost of the chair to the administrator of the museum does not come into it. Moreover, once it has been determined that the attendant does need a chair, his need does not become. less because the museum has decided to employ more attendants who will also need chairs.

The word used in the relevant sections, says Mr Gordon, is 'need', and once that is assessed arrangements have to be made to meet it. It is not qualified by any expression such as 'to the best of their ability' or 'provided it is reasonably practicable for the local authority to meet the need'. The duty, in his submission, is an absolute and specific one aimed at the satisfaction of individual need and not a target duty, as explained by Woolf L.J. as he then was in *R. v. Inner London Education Authority* [1990] ALR 822.

What then if the County Council simply do not have the resources to meet all the 'needs' in their area, not only those of the five applicants but, according to Mr Eccles Q.C. appearing for the County Council, perhaps as many as 1500 persons in a similar position? In answer to that, Mr Gordon reminded us that he no longer presses claim for mandamus. He asks only for declaratory relief, which he says would signal the illegality on the part of the Council.

For the council, Mr Eccles says that its Social Services Department has a strong professional commitment. The problem has arisen from an unexpected decision of the Government in December 1993 which had the immediate effect of withdrawing £3m of the grant upon which the Council's plans had been based, a change whose, consequences the Government has not been prepared to assist the Council to cope with. In the result the Council had insufficient funds to keep up their commitments to the applicants and others like them and decided to give greater priority to the more seriously disabled.

It is not for us to decide whether Gloucestershire's explanation of why they acted as they did is accurate or acceptable. The question is whether they have acted unlawfully. Mr Eccles says they have not, because at each stage at which they have made a decision in these matters, resources have been, and properly have been within the statutes, the dominant factor. Any duty cast upon them was no more than a target duty. If resources diminish, as they have done in Gloucestershire's case, then the services have to be withdrawn or reduced.

Mr Eccles further submitted that if he is wrong in his prime argument on interpretation, he would further argue (boldly, as he admitted) that in every statute which appears to place an absolute duty there should be a term implied that unless the contrary is stated, a local authority is obliged to comply with a statutory duty only if it has the revenue to do so.

Mr Eccles accepted that the Council had not done a re-assessment of the applicants' needs in the light of the cut in the Council's resources. The reason was that the decisions made were not related to the applicants' individual situations. There was no need to do more than send out a standard form of letter telling — them of the removal or reduction of the benefits; and indeed nothing that the applicants could have said would have made any difference.

Finally Mr Eccles submitted that even if there has been any breach by the Council it has come about as a result of circumstances over which they have no control and they have done all they could honestly and honourably to meet their obligations. Hence, he contended, the Court should not grant even declaratory relief, since such a declaration would be considered by the Council a serious matter to which they must respond.

The case advanced by Mr Fleming Q.C. for the Secretary of State for Health differed materially from that of both Mr Gordon and Mr Eccles. Mr Fleming submitted that when assessing need the local authority must take into account all relevant factors, one of them being resources. Then, when considering whether it is 'necessary in order to meet the needs of that person for that authority to make arrangements', the local authority will have to take into account whether other persons or organisations could more appropriately meet the needs identified, but it will have to take into account the resources available to the authority. If, however, the authority has satisfied itself that it is necessary for it to make the arrangements for any of the matters listed in section 2(1) of the 1970 Act, it is not permissible for it to decline or cease to make those arrangements because of shortage of funds. There is no reason, however, why a local authority should not from time to time re-assess the needs of an individual, taking account of the current needs of the individual and all other relevant factors, including resources. In fact, he submitted, it is good practice so to do, recommended to local authorities in a Practitioners' Guide to 'Care Management and Assessment' issued by the Department of Health . . .

At first sight, there appears much force in Mr Gordon's basic contention. A person's need is none the less a need because there is a shortage of resources to meet it and competing needs of other persons; and once a need has been established it cannot be reduced or eliminated by virtue of a reduction in the resources available to meet it. On further reflection, however, I have been driven to the view that such an interpretation would be impractical and unrealistic and hence one to be avoided if at possible. In assessing need, those doing so will inevitably compare the extent of the disabilities of the persons concerned in order to arrive at a view as to who needs help more. That comparative exercise is obviously related to resources. Indeed, it seems to me that a local authority faces an impossible task unless they can have regard to the size of the cake so that in turn they know how fairest and best to cut it.

I am strengthened in that view by the following factors:

(1) The broad nature of the factors under (a) to (h) seems to demonstrate the very broad spectrum covered by the word 'needs'.
(2) The expression 'necessary in order to meet the needs' again suggests to my mind that resources are a relevant factor.
(3) The demand for resources and the resources themselves are bound to fluctuate. Hence inevitably resources will be a relevant factor.
(4) Under section 2(1) the local authority is to make the arrangements in exercise of their functions under section 29 of the 1948 Act. Those functions are to make welfare arrangements for persons who are substantially and perma-nently handicapped by among other things disabilities. This points, in my view, in the direction of having to take account of other needs of other disabled persons when looking at the needs of a particular disabled person.

For these reasons I for my part have concluded that a local authority is right to take account of resources both when assessing needs and when deciding whether it is necessary to make arrangements to meet those needs. I should stress, however, that there will, in my judgment, be situations where a reasonable authority could only conclude that some arrangements were necessary to meet the needs of a particular disabled person and in which it could not reasonably conclude that a lack of resources provided an answer. Certain persons would be at severe physical risk if they were unable to have some practical assistance in their homes. In those situations, I cannot conceive that an authority would be held to have acted reasonably if it used shortage of resources as a reason for not being satisfied that some arrangement should be made to meet those persons' needs.

On any view section 2(1) is needs-led by reference to the particular needs of a particular disabled person. A balancing exercise must be carried out assessing the particular needs of that person in the context of the needs of others and the resources available, but if no reasonable authority could conclude other than that some practical help was necessary, that would have to be its decision.

Furthermore, once they have decided that it is necessary to make the arrange-ments, they are under an absolute duty to make them. It is a duty owed to a specific individual and not a target duty. No term is to be implied that the local authority is obliged to comply with the duty only if it has the revenue to do so. In fact, once under that duty, resources do not come into it.

It would certainly have been open to the Gloucestershire County Council to re-assess the individual applicants as individuals, judging their current needs and taking into account all relevant factors including the resources now available and the competing needs of other disabled persons. What they were not entitled to do, but what in my judgment they in fact did, was not to re-assess at all but simply to cut the services they were providing because their resources in turn had been cut.

This amounted to treating the cut in resources as the sole factor to be taken into account, and that was, in my judgment, unlawful. Moreover, I see no reason to deny the applicants a declaration to that effect." [AUTHOR'S COMMENT: On the approach taken by the High Court, Gloucestershire C.C. would almost certainly have won the case if they had considered each case individually and then reached the same decisions to withdraw funding. The court accepted that it had been legal for other councils in the case who had reached such decision to withdraw services because of lack of resources. However, the case was taken to the Court of Appeal, where the majority went further still. It found that not only was it improper to treat resources as the sole relevant factor, it was (in the context of the 1970 Act) unlawful to take resources into account at all.]

R. v. Gloucester C.C., ex p. Barry; R. v. Lancashire C.C., ex p. RADAR, The Times, July 12, 1996.

SWINTON THOMAS L.J.:
"[Where] the person who is being assessed is disabled then he or she falls into a distinct category. That in turn triggers the duty laid down in section 4 of the 1986 Act to make a decision which, in turn, triggers the duty to decide whether the needs of the disabled person call for the provision of any services in accordance with section 2(1) of the 1970 Act. Accordingly, section 47(2) of the 1990 Act takes one back to the provisions of section 2 of the 1970 Act.

I can find nothing in the provisions of the legislation enacted by Parliament either before or after the passing of the 1970 Act which in any way indicates that it was the intention of Parliament when passing the 1970 Act that resources should be a relevant consideration when a local authority is required to carry out is statutory duty to a disabled person under section 2(1). If Parliament had intended to incorporate the duties laid down by section 2 of the 1970 Act into the Community Care regime of the 1990 Act it could readily have passed amending or repealing legislation within the provisions of the 1990 Act. That Parliament chose not to do so supports the contentions argued for by the appellants in these appeals.

It is conceded by Mr Eccles for Gloucestershire that once the duty under section 2 had arisen it is an absolute duty owed to a specific individual. The duty in the section is aimed at 'any person to whom that section applies' and to meet the needs of 'that person'. *i.e.* the disabled person. Accordingly, the duty is plainly individu-ally orientated. It was said on behalf of the Respondents and the Secretary of State that the word 'need' is not defined in section 2 or in any of the other sections in the legislations to which we were referred. That is true but hardly surprising. Need is an ordinary English word and in my judgment, in this context, it means a basic or essential requirement. The *Oxford English Dictionary* equates need with require-ment. It was the central plank of the Respondents' submissions that an assessment of need involves a discretion. In my view, that is the fundamental flaw in the argument. A need is a question of assessment and judgment, not discretion. Whether or not a disabled person has a need must be assessed in precisely the same way as an assessment as to whether he is disabled.

A clear distinction must be drawn in the case of a disabled person between a need and what may be desirable for the disabled person to have. There is a duty to meet the need under section 2 of the 1970 Act. There is a power to provide that which is desirable under section 29 of the 1948 Act and section 47(1) of the 1990 Act. Thus, for example, in the case of Mr Barry his need is for laundry and cleaning services. The need for cleaning services may be met by a person cleaning his house once a week, even though it may be desirable that his house be cleaned every day. In the case of some disabled persons the assessment might be that it is desirable that they are provided with assistance in the house but they do not have that need. In such a case, no duty under section 2 arises . . .

In my judgment an individual's need is something which can be assessed or in respect of which a judgment can be formed. It is difficult indeed to see how a third party's resources or the needs of others can be relevant to making such an assessment or making such a judgment in relation to a disabled person. Once the need is identified, then, following the language of section 2, it becomes a duty to make the provision that is necessary to meet that need.

Resources cannot in my judgment be relevant to a judgment that provision is necessary to meet the needs of the disabled person. If it were otherwise, then it seems to me to be inescapable that if a local authority has no money in the relevant budget then it would be open to the local authority to make an assessment or judgment that a disabled person has a need which it is necessary to meet applying objective criteria but they are not required to meet it because of shortage of funds, resulting in an unmet need. The concept of an unmet need seems to me to fly in the face of the plain language of section 2 of the 1970 Act. Indeed, Mr Fleming on behalf of the Secretary of States concedes that if a local authority have satisfied themselves that in order to meet the needs of a person to whom the section applies it is necessary to make particular arrangements for any of the matters listed in section 2(1) it would not be permissible for a local authority to decline to make those arrangements because of an absence of funds."

NOTE:

1. All the members of the Court of Appeal regarded the duties set out in the 1970 Act as different from the general obligations and powers to provide health and community care services. They explicitly accepted that resources remained a relevant consideration in relation to these other statutory provisions.

QUESTIONS:

1. Do you think that resource considerations should be excluded from decisions about the provision of services even in relation to the more general duties to provide services? What problems would be thrown up if health authorities were not entitled to take resources into account?
2. What examples can you think of which would be cases where it would be so unreasonable to refuse to provide services that a court would step in?

Where decisions have to be taken about the provisions of services to individuals, resource issues are likely to be closely linked to questions of clinical judgment. This can be seen in a highly controversial case from 1995.

R. v. Cambridge DHA, ex p. B [1995] 2 All E.R. 129, [1995] 1 W.L.R. 898

The father of a 10-year-old girl brought a judicial review of the decision of Cambridge DHA not to fund further treatment for her. She had leukemia, and had previously had a bone marrow transplant and chemotherapy. Her doctors in Cambridge, reinforced by a second opinion from the Royal Marsden Hospital in London, believed that it would be inappropriate to offer a further course of chemotherapy and, if this was successful, a second bone marrow transplant. The father found other doctors in London who believed that further treatment should be given. When the health authority declined to pay for it, he sought to use the courts to force them to do so. He was successful in the High Court, but lost in the Court of Appeal. The arguments used by each court are instructive.

JOHN LAWS J.:
" . . . I entertained the greatest doubt whether the decisive touchstone for the legality of the responents' decision was the crude Wednesbury bludgeon. It seemed to me that the fundamental right, the right to life, was engaged in the case . . .
 . . . the law requires that where a public body enjoys a discretion whose exercise may infringe such a right, it is not to be permitted to perpetrate any such infringement unless it can show a substantial objective justification on public interest grounds. The public body itself is the first judge of the question whether such a justification exists. The court's role is secondary as Lord Bridge said. Such a distribution of authority is required by the nature of the judicial review jurisdiction, and the respect which the courts are certainly obliged to pay to the powers conferred by Parliament upon bodies other than themselves. But the decision-maker has to recognise that he can only infringe such a fundamental right by virtue of an objection of substance put forward in the public interest . . .
 In the light of these materials the first two questions I must decide, it seems to me, are whether the respondents in the present case have: (a) taken a decision which interferes with the applicant's right to life; and (b) if they have, whether they have offered a substantial public interest justification for doing so. Mr Pitt much pressed the submission that his clients had done no positive act to threaten anyone's life; they had done nothing whatever to violate the applicant's right to life; all they had done was to arrive at a decision about the use of public funds. But the fact is that without funding for Dr Gravett's treatment, the applicant will soon certainly die. If the funding is made available, she might not. As things stand at present, the respondents are the only apparent source of the necessary funds. I do not consider that, in the relation to the putative infringement of a fundamental right, there is as regards the obligation of a public body a difference of principle between act and omission. In other areas of law, notably the criminal law, such a distinction may possess a high importance. But in a public law case like the present the question is whether a distinct administrative decision is lawful. The decision-maker is answerable to the court whether the decision is in negative or affirmative form. The decision in this case has, to the knowledge of the decision-maker, materially affected for the worse the applicant's chances of life. I hold that the applicant's right to life is assaulted by it, and accordingly the decision can only be justified on substantial public interest grounds.
 It follows that the next question for my determination is whether the reasons for the decision put forward by the respondents, which I have described, may reasonably constitute such justification.
 The first reason, namely that the proposed treatment would not be in B's best interests, requires some little analysis. I entirely accept these submissions put forward by Mr Pitt:

(a) there are no perceptible circumstances in which a doctor might properly be ordered to administer treatment contrary to his own clinical judgment or his professional conscience: see *Re J (A Minor) (Child in Care: Medical Treatment)* [1992] 2 FLR 165. But there is no question of such an order being made in this case. The doctor who would treat B, Dr Gravatt, is entirely willing to do so;

(b) it is reasonable and proper for the respondents, in making a decision whether to fund a particular course of treatment, to give determinative weight to the views of the specialist doctors whom they consult (here, essentially, Dr Broadbent and Dr Pinkerton) upon the medical issues arising in the case; and there is no whisper of a suggestion that the high competence of the doctors on whose opinions Dr Zimmern relied should be called in question. The difficulty, however, is as to the nature of the issue upon which their opinion was given and in due course acted upon.

The expertise of Dr Broadbent and Dr Pinkerton was rightly deployed by the respondents, as it seems to me, in relation to two questions: (1) What chances of success, in terms first of a remission after chemotherapy, and secondly as to the results of a further transplant, might be expected from Dr Gravett's proposed treatment? As to that, there is no significant difference between them and Dr Gravatt. (2) What are the objective disadvantages of the treatment, in terms of the suffering the patient would be likely to endure, and the risks to life which the treatment itself would involve, when set against the quality of life which the applicant might enjoy in the short time left to her if she were treated palliatively? Those are the objective questions which in essence only the medical experts can answer. But there is a third question: given authoritative advice as to these first two issues, is it in the best interests of the patient to undergo the treatment or decline it? In the present case, Dr Broadbent and Dr Pinkerton have put forward their own views in answer to this third question. Their advice has not been limited to the first two. But in my judgment the third question is not one upon which the doctors possess an authoritative voice. At least in a case like the present it is not, in the end, a medical question at all. Test it by supposing that the patient was not a little girl, but a grown adult of sound understanding. The options would surely be put to him. The pros and cons would be explained. Upon the question what course of action was in his best interests, his views would be respected. I apprehend they would be treated as determinative. If he decided not to undergo the treatment, that would be the end of the matter. If he decided that he wished to take his chance with it, neither the doctors nor the health authority would turn round and say, it is against his best interests, and of those interests they are the sole judges. The treatment might perhaps still be refused as an unjustifiable use of scarce resources; but that engages the respondents' second reason for their decision, with which I am not presently dealing.

Mr Pitt was at pains to submit that I an not here concerned with a case of an adult, so that such an analogy is of no assistance. I disagree. Of course it may readily be assumed that a 10-year-old child, in circumstances like those of this case, cannot make for herself an informed decision upon the question which course of action is in her best interests. That being so, someone else must take the decision for her. But it should not be the doctors; it should be her family, here — her father. He has duties and responsibilities to her shared by no one else. The doctors' obligation is to ascertain and explain all the medical facts, and in the light of them articulate the choice that must be faced. Their expert views on the medical issues, however, do not constitute the premises of a syllogism from which an inevitable conclusion as to what is in the best interests of the patient may be deduced. It is not at all a matter of deduction from the medical facts. It is a personal question which the patient, if he is of full age and capacity, will decide in the light of medical advice. In the case of a little child, others must decide it — not the experts, but those having, legally and morally, overall care of the patient. I do not consider that *Re J* (to which I have already referred) is inconsistent with this result. There, the patient was in a permanent vegetative state. The views of the medical experts as to how his condition should be administered occupied quite a different, and larger, place than is necessarily possessed by the doctors upon the wholly different facts of the present case.

The difficulty in this case does not merely consist in the fact the doctors, on whose opinion Dr Zimmern relied, purported to decide what was in B.'s best interests. It is also clear (though Mr Pitt vehemently submitted to the contrary) that Zimmern did not regard the father's wish that the treatment be carried out as a relevant circumstance for the purpose of his decision whether to authorise funding. First, Dr Zimmern told the father (by his letter of February 21, 1995) that he had 'a policy of not speaking or corresponding directly with patients or their relatives about extra-contractual referrals'. I am at a loss to understand what rational justification might exist for such a policy, but the point was exposed only in Mr McIntyre's reply and I heard no distinct argument about it from Mr Pitt. I shall therefore assume nothing against the respondents arising solely from this policy. And it is right to say that on February 22, 1995 Dr Zimmern sent a reasoned letter to B's father. However, the policy provides the backdrop for the next, and much more important, point which is this: it is plain in particular from paragraph 5 of Dr Zimmern's affidavit that his careful consideration of the case took into account only the medical opinions put before him. That paragraph deals with what in his view was 'clinically appropriate' for B. In deciding that question he had no regard to the father's views as a material factor concerning the question what was in B's best interests. He supposed, wrongly, that the child's best interests engaged only a medical question.

In these circumstances the first reason put forward for the respondents' decision cannot amount to a substantial justification for their depriving B of such chance of life as Dr Gravett's proposed treatment would offer. But in my judgment this conclusion does not depend only on the jurisprudence which I have sought to outline concerning fundamental rights. The ordinary Wednesbury principle produces the result, on the facts here, that the respondents have at the least failed to have regard to a relevant consideration, namely B's family's views — which are the legitimate surrogate for her own — as to whether the proposed treatment would be in her best interests . . .

But the real argument as to the respondents' second justification for their decision depends, I think, in considerable measure upon Dr Zimmern's evidence about the deployment of resources. As I have recorded, he says 'the extra-contractual referral budget is finite'. The proposed treatment 'would not be an effective use of resources. The amount of funds available for health care are not limitless'. He had to bear in mind 'the present and future needs of other patients'.

On February 21, 1995, in a letter to which I have referred earlier, Dr Zimmern said to B's father:

'Should there be any misunderstanding I should state quite clearly that any decision taken by the Commission will be made taking all clinical and other relevant matters into consideration and not on financial grounds.'

His affidavit was sworn precisely a fortnight later. The father might, I think, be forgiven for reflecting that it amounted to something of a volte-face; however, it is no doubt self-evident that funds available for health care are indeed not limitless. And of course it is the respondents, not I, who must decide how they are to be distributed. But merely to point to the fact that resources are finite tells one nothing about the wisdom or, what is relevant for my purposes, the legality of a decision to withhold funding in a particular case, if any, might be prejudiced if the respondents were to fund B's treatment. I have no idea where in the order of things the respondents place a modest chance of saving the life of a 10-year-old girl. I have no evidence about the respondents' budget either generally or in relation to the 'extra-contractual referrals'. Dr Zimmern's evidence about money consists only in grave and well-rounded generalities. I quite accept, as *Re J* enjoins me, that the court should not make orders with consequences for the use of health service funds in ignorance of the knock-on effect on other patients. But where the question is whether the life of a 10-year-old child might be saved, by however slim a chance, the responsible authority must in my judgment do more than toll the bell of tight resources. They must explain the priorities that have led them to decline to fund the treatment. They have not adequately done so here."

John Laws J. quashed the health authority's decision, and required it to re-examine the question, although he did not order the treatment to be funded. The authority appealed to the Court of Appeal.

Sir Thomas Bingham M.R.:
" . . . [T]his is a case involving the life of a young patient and that that is a fact which must dominate all consideration of all aspects of the case. Our society is one in which a very high value is put on human life. No decision affecting human life is one that can be regarded with other than the greatest seriousness.

The second general comment which should be made is that the courts are not, contrary to what is sometimes believed, arbiters as to the merits of cases of this kind. Were we to express opinions as to the likelihood of the effectiveness of medical treatment, or as to the merits of medical judgment, then we should be straying far from the sphere which under our constitution is accorded to us. We have one function only, which is to rule upon the lawfulness of decisions. That is a function to which we should strictly confine ourselves.

The four criticisms made by the learned judge of the authority's decision were these. First, he took the view that Dr Zimmern as the decision-maker had wrongly failed to have regard to the wishes of the patient, as expressed on behalf of the patient by her family, and in particular by her father. Our attention was directed to the affidavits that I have mentioned. The point was made that nowhere does one see an express statement that among the factors that led Dr Zimmern to his decision was a consideration of the wishes of the family. In that situation, the learned judge held that the authority had failed to take a vitally important factor into consideration and that the decision was accordingly flawed.

I feel bound for my part to differ from the judge. It seems to me that the learned judge's criticism entirely fails to recognise the realities of this situation. When the case was first presented to the authority, it was presented on behalf of the patient, B, as a case calling for the co-operation and funding of the authority. At all times Dr Zimmern was as vividly aware as he could have been of the fact that the family, represented by B's father, were urgently wishing the authority to undertake this treatment; by 'undertake' I of course mean provide the funding for it. He was placed under considerable pressure by the family and, in the first instance, perhaps unfortunately, made reference to his policy of not corresponding directly with patients or their relatives about what he called 'extra-contractual referrals', meaning requests for the purchase of medical services outside the health authority.

The inescapable fact is, however, that he was put under perfectly legitimate, but very obvious, pressure by the family to procure this treatment and he was responding to that pressure. It was because he was conscious of that pressure that he obviously found the decision which he had to make such an agonizing one and one calling for such careful consideration. To complain that he did not in terms say that he had regard to the wishes of the patient as expressed by the family is to shut one's eyes to the reality of the situation with which he was confronted. It is also worthy of note, and there is no hint of criticism in this, that the accusation that he did not take the patient's wishes into account was not made in the grounds annexed to Form 86A. It was not, therefore, recognised as an accusation calling for a specific rebuttal.

The second criticism that is made is of the use of the expression 'experimental' to describe this treatment. The learned judge took the view, and Mr McIntyre on behalf of B urges, that that is not a fair or accurate description given the estimates of success which have been put by reputable practitioners, and given the willingness of Dr Gravett to accept that there was a worthwhile chance of success. The fact, however, is that even the first course of treatment had a chance of success of something between 10 and 20%. It was only if, contrary to the probabilities, that was totally successful, that it would be possible to embark on the second phase of the treatment which itself had a similar chance of success.

The plain fact is that, unlike many courses of medical treatment, this was not one that had a well-tried track record of success. It was, on any showing, at the frontier of medical science. That being so, it does not, in my judgment, carry weight to describe this decision as flawed because of the use of this expression.

The third criticism that is made by the judge is of the reference to resources. The learned judge held that Dr Zimmern's evidence about money consisted only of grave and well-rounded generalities. The judge acknowledged that the court should not make orders with consequences for the use of health service funds in ignorance of the knock-on effect on other patients. He went on to say that 'where the question is whether the life of a 10-year-old child might be saved by however slim a chance, the responsible authority . . . must do more than toll the bell of tight resources'. The learned judge said: 'They must explain the priorities that have led them to decline to fund the treatment', and he found they had not adequately done so here.

I have no doubt that in a perfect world any treatment which a patient, or a patient's family, sought would be provided if doctors were willing to give it, no matter how much it cost, particularly when a life was potentially at stake. It would however, in my view, be shutting one's eyes to the real world if the court were to proceed on the basis that we do live in such a world. It is common knowledge that health authorities of all kinds are constantly pressed to make ends meet. They cannot pay their nurses as much as they would like; they cannot provide all the treatments they would like; they cannot purchase all the extremely expensive medical equipment they would like; they cannot carry out all the research they would like; they cannot build all the hospitals and specialist units they would like. Difficult and agonizing judgments have to be made as to how a limited budget is best allocated to the maximum advantage of the maximum number of patients. That is not a judgment which the court can make. In my judgment, it is not something that a health authority such as this authority can be fairly criticised for not advancing before the court.

Mr McIntyre went so far as to say that if the authority has money in the bank which it has not spent, then they would be acting in plain breach of their statutory duty if they did not procure this treatment. I am bound to say that I regard that submission as manifestly incorrect. Unless the health authority had sufficient money to purchase everything which in the interests of patients it would wish to do, then that situation would never ever be reached. I venture to say that no real evidence is needed to satisfy the court that no health authority is in that position.

I furthermore think, differing I regret from the judge, that it would be totally unrealistic to require the authority to come to the court with its accounts and seek to demonstrate that if this treatment were provided for B then there would be a patient, C, who would have to go without treatment. No major authority could run its financial affairs in a way which would permit such a demonstration.

NOTES:

1. It is unclear how far the Court of Appeal was prepared to disentangle issues related to funding from those concerning the conflict of medical opinion. It may be that medical judgment is almost impossible to override. In *Re J.* (a minor) [1992] 4 All E.R. 614 the court went so far as to say that it would be an abuse of the powers of the court to order a doctor to treat a patient in a manner contrary to her clinical judgment. Possibly, if all the doctors available to treat a patient refuse to do so on clinical grounds, the courts would hold themselves powerless to intervene. In the Cambridge case, however, there was a doctor prepared to treat the patient.
2. With hindsight, it has become clear that the doctors' original assessment of the child's likely survival was inaccurate. The medical advice to the health authority had suggested that she would live beyond March of 1995. In fact she lived until May 1996.

QUESTIONS:

1. Do you prefer the approach of John Laws J. or Sir Thomas Bingham M.R.?
2. Which factors were more important, those relating to clinical judgment or those concerning resource allocation?
3. Will a challenge of a health authority decision be possible in the future in cases where it has not acted wholly unreasonably? (See P. Wilson casenote (1995) *Journal of Social Welfare and Family Law*, 359.)

It may also be possible to challenge decisions on the basis of procedural defects. In one case, the failure to probe the reluctance of doctors to provide services to see whether another source of care could be identified was such a defect (see *R. v. Ealing DHA, ex p Fox* [1993] 3 All E.R. 170, considered in Chapter 8). It is usually necessary for decision makers to give those adversely affected an opportunity to put their case. The issue was raised in the Cambridge case, but the Court of Appeal rejected the suggestion that the views of the girl's father had not been considered. This problem was also discussed in the case of *R. v. Ethical Committee of St Mary's Hospital (Manchester), ex p Harriott* [1988] 1 FLR 512, which concerned access to infertility treatment and is extracted in Chapter 11.

More importantly, for this Chapter, the Harriott case also suggested that decisions could be attacked for being based on improper reasons. The judge gave race, as an example, referring to the illegality of denying treatment to Jews or those with different coloured skin. These are areas where discrimination is prohibited by law. Presumably unjustifiable sex discrimination would also constitute an unlawful basis for determining access to health care.

It is possible that the Disability Discrimination Act 1995 will introduce important considerations here. That Act prohibits discrimination on the basis of disability, which is defined in terms that would include some groups with health problems. However it may be that the type of discrimination prohibited by the Act would be deemed irrelevant to treatment decisions because it would cover almost all patients and not give rise to any useable distinctions between them. If so, the distinctions made when deciding who to treat would have to be made on other grounds which would fall outside the Act.

Disability Discrimination Act 1995, s.1(1)

1.—(1) Subject to the provisions of Schedule 1, a person has a disability for the purposes of this Act if he has a physical or mental impairment which has a substantial and long-term adverse effect on his ability to carry out normal day-to-day activities.'
Schedule 1 paragraph 4(1). An impairment is to be taken to affect the ability of the person concerned to carry out normal day-to-day activities only if it affects one of the following:

(a) mobility;
(b) manual dexterity;
(c) physical co-ordination;
(d) continence;
(e) ability to lift, carry or otherwise move everyday objects;
(f) speech, hearing or eyesight;
(g) memory or ability to concentrate, learn or understand; or
(h) perception of the risk of physical danger.

NOTE:

1. Schedule 1 also states that mental impairment includes an impairment resulting from mental illness only if the illness is clinically well recognised. It defines long-term as being at least a year (with special provisions for some circumstances). It also provides for regulations to further define the meaning of disability.

QUESTION:

1. Could a patient with a learning difficulty who was denied an operation because his quality of life was too poor claim that the decision was based on factors that are prohibited by the Disability Discrimination Act 1995?
2. In the light of the case law that has now been considered, do you think that it would be possible to persuade a court to strike down a decision by a health authority not to fund either of the following procedures?
   (i) heart operations for those who refuse to give up smoking (some doctors argue for such a policy on the basis that the chances of

the operation being successful are much smaller than they would be in the case of non-smokers)

(ii) kidney transplants for those over seventy years of age (on the basis that their life expectancy is too short, and their quality of life is likely to be poor, in comparison to younger patients).

(ii) Actions for Compensation

A second way in which patients may seek to enforce their rights to services is to sue for compensation when they have been injured by the failure to provide proper care. The leading case in this area is a House of Lords decision in relation to the responsibilities of local authorities in relation to child protection and education. The facts of the cases are not relevant here, but Lord Browne-Wilkinson explained the principles of law, which would also be applied in the health context, in the extracts set out below.

X. v. Bedfordshire C.C.; M. v. Newham L.B.C.; E. v. Dorset C.C. [1995] 3 All E.R. 353

LORD BROWNE-WILKINSON:
". . . I am seeking to set out a logical approach to the wide ranging arguments advanced . . .

(A) Breach of statutory duty simpliciter:

This category comprises those cases where the statement of claim alleges simply (i) the statutory duty, (ii) a breach of that duty, causing (iii) damage to the plaintiff. The cause of action depends neither on proof of any breach of the plaintiffs' common law rights nor on any allegation of carelessness by the defendant.

The principles applicable in determining whether such statutory cause of action exists are now well established, although the application of those principles in any particular case remains difficult. The basic proposition is that in the ordinary case a breach of statutory duty does not, by itself, give rise to any private law cause of action. However, a private law cause of action will arise if it can be shown, as a matter of construction of the statute, that the statutory duty was imposed for the protection of a limited class of the public and that Parliament intended to confer on members of that class a private right of action for breach of the duty. There is no general rule by reference to which it can be decided whether a statute does create such a right of action but there are a number of indicators. If the statute provides no other remedy for its breach and the Parliamentary intention to protect a limited class is shown, that indicates that there may be a private right of action since otherwise there is no method of securing the protection the statute was intended to confer. If the statute does provide some other means of enforcing the duty that will normally indicate that the statutory right was intended to be enforceable by those means and not by private right of action: see *Cutler v. Wandsworth Stadium Ltd* [1949] 1 All E.R. 544 and *Lonrho Ltd v. Shell Petroleum Co. Ltd* [1981] 2 All E.R. 456. However, the mere existence of some other statutory remedy is not necessarily decisive. It is still possible to show that on the true construction of the statute the protected class was intended by Parliament to have a private remedy . . .

Although the question is one of statutory construction and therefore each case turns on the provisions in the relevant statute, it is significant that your Lordships were not referred to any case where it had been held that statutory provisions establishing a regulatory system or a scheme of social welfare for the benefit of the public at large had been held to give rise to a private right of action for damages for breach of statutory duty. Although regulatory or welfare legislation affecting a particular area of activity does in fact provide protection to those individuals particularly affected by that activity, the legislation is not to be treated as being passed for the benefit of those individuals but for the benefit of society in general. Thus legislation regulating the conduct of betting or prisons did not give rise to a statutory right of action vested in those adversely affected by the breach of the statutory provisions, *i.e.* bookmakers and prisoners: see *Cutler v. Wandsworth Stadium Ltd* and *Hague v. Deputy Governor of Parkhurst Prison* [1991] 3 All E.R. 733. The cases where a private right of action for breach of statutory duty have been held to arise are all cases in which the statutory duty has been very limited and specific as opposed to general administrative functions imposed on public bodies and involving the exercise of administrative discretions . . .

(c) The common law duty of care

In this category, the claim alleges either that a statutory duty gives rise to a common law duty of care owed to the plaintiff by the defendant to do or refrain from doing a particular act, or (more often) that in the course of carrying out a statutory duty the defendant has brought about such a relationship between himself and the plaintiff as to give rise to a duty of care at common law . . .

(1) Co-existence of statutory duty and common law duty of care

It is clear that a common law duty of care may arise in the performance of statutory functions. But a broad distinction has to be drawn between: (a) cases in which it is alleged that the authority owes a duty of care in the manner in which it exercises a statutory discretion; and (b) cases in which a duty of care is alleged to arise from the manner in which the statutory duty has been implemented in practice.

An example of (a) in the educational field would be a decision whether or not to exercise a statutory discretion to close a school, being a decision which necessarily involves the exercise of a discretion. An example of (b) would be the actual running of a school pursuant to the statutory duties. In such latter case a common law duty to take reasonable care for the physical safety of the pupils will arise. The fact that the school is being run pursuant to a statutory duty is not necessarily incompatible with a common law duty of care arising from the proximate relationship between a school and the pupils it has agreed to accept. The distinction is between (a) taking care in exercising a statutory discretion whether or not to do an act and (b) having decided to do that act, taking care in the manner in which you do it.

(2) Discretion, justiciability and the policy/operational test

(a) Discretion

Most statutes which impose a statutory duty on local authorities confer on the authority a discretion as to the extent to which, and the methods by which, such statutory duty is to be performed. It is clear both in principle and from the decided cases that the local authority cannot be liable in damages for doing that which Parliament has authorised. Therefore if the decisions complained of fall within the ambit of such statutory discretion they cannot be actionable in common law. However, if the decision complained of is so unreasonable that it falls outside the ambit of the discretion conferred upon the local authority, there is no priori reason for excluding all common law liability . . . "

Lord Browne-Wilkinson reviewed the authorities and concluded.

" . . . From these authorities I understand the applicable principles to be as follows. Where Parliament has conferred a statutory discretion on a public authority, it is for that authority, not for the courts, to exercise the discretion: nothing which the authority does within the ambit of the discretion can be actionable at common law. If the decision complained of falls outside the statutory discretion, it can (but not necessarily will) give rise to common law liability. However, if the factors relevant to the exercise of the discretion include matters of policy, the court cannot adjudicate on such policy matters and therefore cannot reach the conclusion that the decision was outside the ambit of the statutory discretion. Therefore a common law duty of care in relation to the taking of decisions involving policy matters cannot exist.

(3) If justiciable, the ordinary principles of negligence apply.

If the plaintiff's complaint alleges carelessness, not in the taking of a discretionary decision to do some act, but in the practical manner in which that act has been performed (*e.g.* the running of a school) the question whether or not there is a common law duty of care falls to be decided by applying the usual principles, *i.e.* those laid down in *Caparo Industries plc v. Dickman* [1990] 1 All E.R. 568 at 573–574. Was the damage to the plaintiff reasonably foreseeable? Was the relationship between the plaintiff and the defendant sufficiently proximate? Is it just and reasonable to impose a duty of care? See *Rowling v. Takaro Properties Ltd* and *Hill v. Chief Constable of West Yorkshire* [1988] 2 All E.R. 238.

However, the question whether there is such a common law duty and if so its ambit, must be profoundly influenced by the statutory framework within which the acts complained of were done. The position is directly analogous to that in which a tortious duty of care owed by A to C can arise out of the performance by A of a contract between A and B. In *Henderson v. Merrett Syndicates Ltd* [1994] 3 All E.R. 506 your Lordships held that A (the managing agent) who had contracted with B (the members' agent) to render certain services for C (the names) came under a duty of care to C in the performance of those services. It is clear that any tortious duty of care owed to C in those circumstances could not be inconsistent with the duty owed in contract by A to B. Similarly, in my judgment, a common law duty of care cannot be imposed on a statutory duty if the observance of such common law duty of care would be inconsistent with, or have a tendency to discourage, the due performance by the local authority of its statutory duties."

These principles of law provide severe restrictions upon the scope of actions for breach of statutory duty in the context of welfare agencies. The House of Lords noted that there was no case in which it had been held that the general duties of such agencies gave rise to rights of individual enforcement. The fullest discussion of the scope for bringing an action for breach of statutory duty in respect of the NHS Act 1977 is to be found in the following case.

Re HIV Haemophiliac Litigation, The Independent, October 2, 1990

The issue arose in the course of a preliminary action for discovery of documents in relation to a case in which haemophiliacs who had contracted HIV from contaminated blood transfusions were suing the Department of Health. The plaintiffs based their claim on two alternative arguments. The first was that the Department was in breach of its statutory duties, and that this gave them a right to compensation. The second was that the general law of negligence permitted them to sue. One of the grounds on which the Department resisted disclosure was that the actions were doomed to failure because the law did not permit such actions to be brought.

In relation to the suggestion that an action might be brought on the basis of breach of statutory duty, Gibson L.J. found that:

"the duties imposed by the 1977 Act [the plaintiffs relied upon subsections 1, 3(1), and 5(2), see above] . . . do not clearly demonstrate the intention of Parliament to impose a duty which is to be enforced by civil action."

Both the other judges in the Court of Appeal expressed their agreement with this assessment. However, in part the Court of Appeal's view was based on their belief that the law of negligence already provided a remedy. If that were not the case they would have found the argument from breach of statutory duty more plausible. This implies that where a negligence action would not be permitted, then an action for breach of statutory duty might have more chance of success. Although Gibson LJ doubted whether an action would be brought for breach of statutory duty, he did not regard the matter as so far beyond argument that the claim should be struck out. His comment does not, therefore preclude such a claim in the future.

In relation to possibility of liability in negligence, the Department of Health argued against the imposition of a duty of care on the Secretary of State for decisions about the way in which blood products were provided and screened to avoid contamination in the following terms:

"The nature of the relationship between the plaintiffs [*i.e.* patients] and the Central Defendants [*i.e.* the Department of Health, the Welsh Office, the Committee of Safety of Medicines and the licensing authority under the Medicines Act 1968] is such that it is not just and reasonable to impose a duty of care directly enforceable by any member of the public. His protection should be by an action for negligence, if there is a breach of duty, against those who directly provide care and treatment to him; and the remedy for imperfections in the performance of duties imposed by the 1977 Act should be within Parliament or through the ballot box. All the alleged duties upon which the plaintiffs rely contain elements of discretion."

Gibson L.J. accepted that the court hearing the full case might reach the conclusion that a duty of care existed, and concentrated on the problems of proving that there has been a *breach* of that duty:

"It is obvious that it would be rare for a case on negligence to be proved having regard to the nature of the duties under the 1977 Act, and to the fact that, in the law of negligence, it is difficult to prove a negligent breach of duty when the party charged with negligence is required to exercise discretion and to form judgments upon the allocation of public resources. That, however, is not sufficient, in my judgment, to make it clear, for the purposes of these proceedings, that there can in law be no claim in negligence."

QUESTIONS:

1. Since this case was decided, the NHS and Community Care Act 1990 has created a system in which resource allocation has been delegated down to Health Authorities. Those Authorities are not elected, they are appointed by the Secretary of State. However, the Secretary of State would almost certainly not regard himself as answerable in Parliament for the purchasing decisions of individual Authorities. If the ballot box and Parliament can no longer provide a method to challenge decisions, how does this affect the arguments put forward by the Department of Health?
2. Do you think it would be easier to bring an action against a Health Authority alleging that they negligently purchased services than against the Department in this case?

Even if it is possible to show that a negligence action may be brought, because there is a duty of care, many NHS cases will come up against the argument that they concern non-justiciable policy decisions. In the Befordshire case, the House of Lords pointed out that there was no rigid distinction between policy and operational decisions, but held that the policy aspects of decisions would only be justiciable in the most extreme case. Resource allocation decisions will almost always involve policy considerations, and will therefore be unlikely to give rise to compensation unless they are wholly unreasonable, in the public law sense discussed above. Clinical decisions are also regarded by the courts as largely non-justiciable, to be judged against reasonable professional practice rather than the views of the judge (see the test established in *Bolam v. Friern HMC* [1957] 2 All E.R. 118, discussed in Chapter 3). The prospects for success of compensations claims for failures to provide services will therefore depend on how the courts define what constitutes a policy consideration in the context of health care. This issue was examined in a case concerning the mass vaccination of young children.

D.H.S.S. v. Kinnear (1984) 134 NLJ 886

The plaintiffs alleged that they had suffered injuries as a result of receiving whooping cough vaccine. They sued the Department of Health and Social Security, alleging that they had been negligent in promoting, on expert advice, a widespread policy of vaccination. The Department of Health applied to have the writ against them struck out as disclosing no cause of action. They accepted that there was sufficient proximity between the plaintiff and the Department to raise a duty of care in negligence (note that this concession was not made in the later HIV Haemophiliac case, above). They also accepted that the damage caused was of a kind that was foreseeable. However, they argued that the action could not succeed because it challenged a decision that was within the limits of a bona fide exercise of discretion under their statutory powers. Stuart Smith J. considered that he should strike out the application so far as it related to policy decisions, but that he should not prevent the challenges to operational matters going ahead. Thus in relation to one plaintiff he said:

STUART SMITH J.:
" . . . Her case is that, between the first and second vaccination, she suffered from a respiratory disease; that, although the plaintiff's mother told the doctor administering the vaccination this, he nevertheless administered the dose. The gravamen of the case against the D.H.S.S. is that, by the circulars which they issued to Health Authorities and general practitioners, they advised how and in what circumstances the treatment should be administered, but that this advice was misleading and negligent because it did not indicate that a respiratory disease was a contra indication for vaccination. Mr. Prynne submits that, in giving advice on these matters, the D.H.S.S. were acting in the operational sphere and were no longer protected by the limits of discretion. His particular complaint was that, while in the earlier editions (*i.e.* those of 1963 and 1968) of the D.H.S.S. document entitled "Active Immunisation against Infectious Disease" it was stated that "no prophylactic should be given routinely to the individual in poor health or one suffering from intercurrent illness", this warning was omitted from the editions current at the time of Naomi Finn's vaccination . . .
In my view, [the circulars] clearly give advice on procedure of vaccination, dealing amongst other things with the time when it should take place, how the vaccine should be stored, what to do in the event of adverse reactions, and what matters contra indicate its use. To my mind, it is at least arguable, in giving such advice, that the D.H.S.S. had entered the operational area."

The judge's understanding of the distinction between policy and operational issues can perhaps best be seen by looking at those allegations which he struck out. These were that the D.H.S.S.:

- failed to heed early enough or in time the numerous published articles indicating that neurological damage was a side effect of the pertussis vaccine;
- failed to take any or sufficient heed of the investigation and report of the Medical Research Council carried out between 1952 and 1957;
- failed to carry out, or initiate the carrying out of, any adequate investigation following the report of the Medical Research Council;
- failed to give any or adequate warnings to the parents and/or guardians of infants being vaccinated with pertussis vaccine of the risks to which they were exposing the child under their care;
- failed to have any or any sufficient regard to the opinion of the parents of children to be vaccinated which expressed itself by the refusal of parents to permit their child to be immunised with pertussis vaccine from 1972 onwards;
- failed to give any or any proper regard to the risk to which the individual child was being exposed;
- failed to give any or any proper regard to the possibility that either the pertussis vaccine should be discontinued in general use; alternatively, that it should be used on a selective basis, to be administered to children at special risk;
- failed to require the manufacturers of the vaccine, the second defendants, to make proper investigations as to the extent of the risk of side effects;
- failed to require the manufacturers to investigate the risk of side effects and to investigate what contra indications there were in its use;

- if the vaccine was supplied in multi-dose use, failed to require the manufacturers to supply it in single dose units.

Stuart Smith J regarded the following two allegations as more difficult to
classify. These were that the D.H.S.S. had:
"failed to publish guidelines as a consequence of the failure to carry out research
as aforesaid, in any sufficient detail before 1974 (it not being thereby admitted
that these were either adequate or exhaustive)";
and that the Department had:
"failed to give any proper supervision and/or instructions to the servants or
agents of the third defendants, who were the local Health Authority, in the
respects as set forth hereinafter under the particulars of negligence of the third
defendants."

Considering them Stuart Smith J. said:

"If and insofar as those sub-paragraphs allege that the D.H.S.S. gave misleading
and negligent advice to the second defendants and their employees [*i.e.* the health
authority and medical staff] as to the contra indications to the administration of
the vaccine, they are relevant and should not be struck out. Otherwise, they are
not relevant and do not disclose a cause of action."

NOTES:

1. The European Commission of Human Rights has rejected the suggestion that there was insufficient respect for the right to life of
   recipients of the vaccine in the decision to promote mass vaccination.
2. The Vaccine Damage Payments Act 1979 was passed to provide
   compensation for the victims of the whooping cough vaccine, on a
   no-fault basis, see Chapter 3 below.
3. In subsequent litigation for negligence against the health authority
   and doctors who were responsible for vaccinating Kinnear, the case
   was dismissed, see *Kinnear v. D.H.S.S.* [1989] Fam. Law 146. A
   plaintiff in a similar position failed to prove a causal link between the
   vaccine and the injuries suffered in *Loveday v. Renton* [1990] 1 Med.
   L.R. 117.

QUESTION:

1. In 1995 the Department of Health promoted mass vaccination of
   school children for measles and rubella. They did so on advice that
   there was expected to be a measles epidemic. A number of cases of
   serious reactions to the vaccine have been reported. Do you think
   that it would be possible to sue the Department of Health for injuries
   that could be traced to the rubella vaccine (for which no epidemic has
   been suggested)?

SELECT BIBLIOGRAPHY

Department of Health, Review of Law on Infectious Disease Control: Consultation Document, London: DoH, 1989.

M. Brazier "Rights and Health Care" in R. Blackburn (ed.) *Rights of Citizenship*, London: Mansell, 1993.

M. Brazier and J. Harris "Public Health and Private Lives" (1996) 4 Medical Law Review 165.

J. Jacob, 'Lawyers Go To Hospital' [1991] *Public Law* 255.

D. Longley, *Public Law and Health Service Accountability*, Buckingham: Open University Press, 1993.

D. Longley, *Health Care Constitutions*, London: Cavendish Publishing, 1996.

J. Montgomery "Recognising a Right to Health" in R. Beddard & D. Hill (eds.), *Economic, Social and Cultural Rights: Progress and Achievement*, Basingstoke: Macmillan, 1992.

J Montgomery, "Rights to Health and Health Care" in A. Coote (ed.), *The Welfare of Citizens: Developing New Social Rights*, London: Institute for Public Policy Research, 1992.

J. A. Muir Gray, "The Ethics of Compulsory Removal" in M. Lockwood (ed.), *Moral Dilemmas in Modern Medicine*, Oxford: Oxford University Press, 1985.

C. Newdick, *Who Shall we Treat?*, Oxford: Oxford University Press, 1995.

P. Old & J. Montgomery, "Law, Coercion and the Public Health" (1992) 304 *BMJ* 891.

R. Porter & D. Porter "AIDS: Law, Liberty and Public Health" in P. Byrne (ed.) *Health, Rights and Resources*, London: King's Fund, 1988.

A. Smith & B. Jacobson (eds.), *The Nation's Health: A Strategy for the 1990s*, London: King's Fund, 1988.

A. Yarrow, *Politics, Society and Preventive Medicine: a Review*, London: Nuffield Provincial Hospitals Trust, 1986.

2

HEALTH CARE ETHICS

1. INTRODUCTION

This Chapter provides an overview of competing ethical approaches to various substantive legal issues which will be addressed throughout the book. We have three main reasons for considering ethical approaches separately from and prior to examining the law in depth. First, many of the legal principles we will consider purport to be based on ethical foundations — for example, it is claimed that our law on consent to treatment is based on respect for autonomy. Secondly, on many of the topics we will consider, law is insufficiently developed to provide guidance for health care professionals — this is true, for instance, of the equitable remedy of breach of confidentiality. Thirdly, there may be ethical reasons for not attempting to extend law into certain areas — for example, some would argue that this is the case with attempts to regulate the behaviour of pregnant women, which may be better influenced by education and provision of information rather than law. (See further A. Buchanan and D. Brock, *Deciding for Others: the Ethics of Surrogate Decision Making*, Cambridge and New York: Cambridge University Press, 1989, at pages 4–5.) Rather than to endorse any particular ethical theory, the aim of this Chapter is to introduce you to some of the main theories that are of relevance to decision-making in a health-care context. However, you should give some thought to which of the approaches discussed best reflects your instinctive response to some of the dilemmas encountered by health care professionals, judges and others who have to make difficult ethical decisions concerning the delivery of health care. You should also reflect upon whether your intuitive response can be rationally defended. The focus of orthodox medical ethics has been on the ethics of decision-making by doctors. Indeed much of the tradition has been derived from the professional codes which govern the practice of medicine. In essence this tradition might more properly be regarded as a body of rules of etiquette governing the behaviour of professionals. However, recent years have marked a growing literature on what may be termed 'critical medical ethics' which has been developed by 'outsiders' such as philosophers, ethicists, theologians, economists and lawyers as well as health care

71

practitioners. This body of medical ethics has been based upon the professional duties of nonmaleficence, beneficence, autonomy and justice. (See R. Gillon, *Philosophical Medical Ethics*, Chichester: John Wiley & Sons, 1985.) However, in this book we would suggest that a broader perspective needs to be adopted. First, there has been increased recognition of the need for participation in medical decision-making by the whole multi-disciplinary team involved in the care of the patient. Secondly, decisions taken at other levels, such as those by NHS managers may impact upon and constrain the decisions that health professionals can make (see Chapter 1). Furthermore, the health professional's power to make decisions will also be affected by the broader political context in which health care is delivered — in particular whether health care is funded by the state or delivered privately. Where relevant throughout the book we will refer you back to ethical theories considered in this Chapter.

We begin in section 2 with perhaps the most fundamental of the ethical debates, which pertains to whether one adopts a deontological or utilitarian approach to ethical controversies. In sections 3 and 4 we explore another pivotal issue — that of the competing values of autonomy and paternalism in the delivery of health care. Section 5 offers an introduction to rights-based theories; section 6 examines competing conceptions of justice and section 7 explores the relationship between law and morality. In section 8 we consider the challenge posed to traditional health care ethics by feminist ethics and in section 9 whether a new forum is needed to debate these issues, rather than leaving the formulation of ethical guidance to the professions themselves — a practice which is considered in section 10. Leaving such issues to the professions themselves may be particularly problematic in view of the tremendous deference which has traditionally been accorded to health care professionals, or at least to doctors. In the past their status has been such that they have largely been entrusted with defining the concept of illness. This role and how it may be changing is explored in section 11. Finally, in section 12 we examine the extent of the rights of the health professional to conscientiously object to participation in the provision of health care.

2.   DEONTOLOGICAL AND UTILITARIAN THEORIES

We begin with a distinction which has been fundamentantal to most debates in ethical theory — between theories which judge the rightfulness of actions in terms of their consequences [utilitarian] and theories which decree actions to be intrinsically right or wrong [deontological].

T. Beauchamp and J. Childress, *Principles of Biomedical Ethics*, (3rd edn.) Oxford and New York: Oxford University Press, 1989, pages 25–41

Consequentialism is the moral theory that actions are right or wrong according to their consequences rather than any intrinsic features they may have, such as truthfulness or fidelity. The most prominent consequentialist theory is utilitarianism . . . Utilitarians maintain that the moral rightness of actions is determined by their consequences, in particular by the maximisation of the nonmoral value produced by the action. The value produced — such as pleasure, friendship, knowledge or health, is said to be *nonmoral* because it is the general goal of many human activities, such as art, athletics, and academics, and thus is not a distinctly moral value like fulfilling a moral obligation. A common feature of these theories is that standards of obligation and right conduct depend on and are subordinated to standards of the good.

Deontological theories deny much that consequentialist theories affirm. Their classical origins are more diverse and include, for example, some religious traditions that concentrate on divine commands. However, the ethical theory of Immanuel Kant (1734–1804) is generally regarded as the first unambiguous formulation of a deontological ethical theory. Deontologists maintain that the concepts of obligation and right are independent of the concept of good and that right actions are not determined exclusively by the production of good consequences. Whereas the consequentialist . . . holds that acts are determined to be right or wrong by only one of their features, namely their consequences, the deontologist contends that even if this feature sometimes determines the rightness and wrongness of acts, it does not always do so. Other features of an action may also be relevant, such as the fact that it involves telling a lie or compromising one's integrity . . .

Utilitarian theories

All utilitarians share the conviction that human actions are to be morally assessed in terms of their production of maximum nonmoral value. But how are we to determine what value should be produced in any given circumstance? Here we encounter disputes among utilitarians concerning how the theory is best characterised, as well as disputes over which values are most important. Some grasp of these internal disputes is required in order to understand utilitarian ethics.

Many utilitarians agree that ultimately we ought to look to the production of agent-neutral or intrinsic values, those that do not vary from person to person. That is, what is good in itself, not merely what is good as a means to something else, ought to be produced. For example, neither undergoing nor performing an abortion is intrinsically good. However, many people would consider an abortion as extrinsically good in some circumstances — for instance, as a means to the end of protecting a pregnant woman's life and health, which are intrinsic goods. Many utilitarians believe that we ought to produce those conditions in life that are good in themselves without reference to their future consequences and that all actions are ultimately to be gauged in terms of these intrinsic values. Health and freedom from pain are often included among such values. From this perspective, the whole point of the institution of morality is to promote these values by maximizing benefits and minimizing harms.

Within utilitarian theories of intrinsic value a major distinction is drawn between hedonistic and pluralistic utilitarians. Bentham and Mill are said to be hedonistic because they conceive utility entirely in terms of happiness or pleasure, two broad terms they treat as synonymous . . .

Later utilitarian philosophers have not always looked favorably on this monistic conception of intrinsic value. They have argued that other values besides happiness possess intrinsic worth; among these values are friendship, knowledge, health and beauty. According to G.E. Moore, even some states of consciousness can be valuable apart from their pleasantness. The idea that there are several basic kinds of intrinsic value eventually received widespread acceptance among utilitarians. Its proponents held that the greatest aggregate good, as well as moral rightness or wrongness, is to be assessed in terms of the total range of intrinsic values ultimately produced by an action.

However, both hedonists and pluralists have been challenged on grounds that individual preferences rather than agent-neutral values should determine utility. For this approach, the concept of utility refers not to experiences or states of affairs but rather to individuals' actual preferences. Utility is thus translated into the satisfaction of those desires that individuals prefer to have satisfied . . .

The preference approach is not trouble-free . . . A major problem of utilitarianism arises when individuals have what are judged by the common morality to be morally unacceptable preferences. For example, if a skilled researcher derived supreme satisfaction from inflicting pain on animals or on human subjects in experiments, we would condemn and discount this person's preference and would seek to prevent it from being actualized. Utilitarianism based on subjective preferences is a defensible theory only if a range of acceptable preferences can be formulated, where 'acceptability' is agent-neutral and thus not a matter of preferences. But this task seems inconsistent with a pure preference approach, because that approach logically ties human values to preferences, which are by their nature not agent-neutral . . .

Another significant distinction is between act and rule utilitarianism. For all utilitarians the principle of utility is the ultimate source of appeal for the determination of morally right and wrong actions. Controversy has arisen, however, over whether this principle is to be applied to *particular acts* in particular circumstances in order to determine which act is right, or whether it is to be applied instead to *general rules* that determine which acts are right and wrong . . .

One of the major nineteenth-century figures in academic medicine and medical ethics, Dr. Worthington Hooker, was a rule utilitarian who paid particularly close attention to the importance of rules of truth telling in medicine. In a trenchant analysis of deception by physicians, Hooker argues as follows:

'The good, which may by done by deception in a *few* cases, is almost as nothing, compared with the evil which it does in *many*, when the prospect of its doing good was just as promising as it was in those in which it succeeded. And when we add to this the evil which would result from a *general* adoption of a system of deception, the importance of a strict adherence to the truth in our intercourse with the sick, even on the ground of expediency, becomes incalculably great.'

Hooker was aware that a patient's health may sometimes maximally be advanced through deception, but he did not believe that a physician can successfully predict the beneficent outcomes in particular cases, and he held that the use of deception will have an incremental effect over time and cause more harm than good. He therefore defended the rule that deception not be practised in medicine . . .

A contemporary act utilitarian, J.J.C. Smart, has argued that . . . there is a third possibility between never obeying a rule and always obeying it, namely that it should *sometimes* be obeyed. From this perspective, physicians do not and should not always tell the truth to their patient. They sometimes withhold information and even lie in order to give hope to a patient. They do so because they think it is better for the patient and all concerned, and they do not think their acts undermine general observance of moral rules. Smart's position seems in the end to rely on the empirical prediction that we will be better off in the moral life if we sometimes obey and sometimes disobey rules, because this selective obedience will not erode either moral rules or our general respect for morality. Rules, then are stabilizing but nonbinding guides in the moral life; that is they are useful rules of thumb that are dispensable in some circumstances.

Deontological theories

By contrast to consequentialist theories, deontological theories hold that some features of acts other than, or in addition to, their consequences make them right or wrong and that the grounds of right or obligation are not wholly dependent on the production of good consequences. The essence of the deontological perspective is that some actions are right (or wrong) for reasons other than their consequences.

If a therapist deceives a patient by substituting a placebo, a deontologist might point to both the feature of the deception itself . . . and the therapist's motives. For many deontologists deception is a wrong-making characteristic for reasons independent of its consequences. A deontologist need not hold that deception or any other type of action is absolutely wrong and never justifiable, but to qualify as a deontologist, one must hold that at least some acts are right and others wrong, not because of their consequences but because of right-making characteristics such as fidelity to promises, truthfulness, and justice . . .

[D]eontologists try in different ways to vindicate their judgments that certain acts are right or wrong. Some writers in religious traditions appeal to divine revelation (e.g., to God's promulgation of the Ten Commandments), whereas others appeal to natural law and natural right,which they contend can be known by human reason. Some philosophers, including W.D. Ross, find intuition and common sense sufficient. Still others, such as John Rawls, develop a contractarian theory by deriving their principles from a hypothetical social contract; they ask which principles rational contractors would adopt if they were blind to their particular talents, abilities, and conceptions of the good life . . . [for a fuller discussion of Rawls's theory see pp. 95–98 below].

Like utilitarian theories, deontological theories may be monistic or pluralistic. A monistic theory holds that there is a single principle or rule from which all other rules or judgments about right and wrong can be derived . . . Alan Donagan and many contemporary deontologists are indebted to Immanuel Kant's classic proposal of a single 'categorical imperative' for testing all rules of action. Kant held that the moral worth of an agent's action depends exclusively on the moral acceptability of the rule on which the person is acting; or, as Kant prefers to say, (moral acceptability depends on the rule that determines an agent's will.) An action has moral worth only if performed by an agent who possesses what Kant calls a good will; and a person has a good will only if moral duty based on a valid rule is the sole motive of action. As an example of Kant's thesis, consider a man who desperately needs money and knows that he will not be able to borrow it unless he promises repayment in a definite time, even though he knows that he will not be able to repay it within this period. He decides to make a promise that he knows he will break. According to Kant, when we examine the maxim of this man's action — "When I think myself in want of money, I will borrow money and promise to pay it back, although I know that I cannot do so" — we discover that it cannot pass the basic test of what he calls the categorical imperative, which requires that maxims be universalisable. (The categorical imperative is *categorical* because it admits of no exceptions and is absolutely binding. It is *imperative* because it gives instruction about how one morally must act.) . . .

Pluralist deontologists, by contrast, affirm more than one basic rule or principle. For example, Ross holds that there are several basic and irreducible moral principles, such as fidelity, beneficence, and justice. This pluralistic approach at first seems more plausible than monistic approaches because it is more closely attuned to our commonsense judgments, but it encounters the difficulty . . . of what to do when these principles or rules come into conflict.

[For instance] a physician has to determine whether to tell the truth or break a confidence. He cannot do both, yet each of two moral rules commands his allegiance. The pluralistic deontologist may give little guidance about which rules or principles take priority in such cases of conflict. For example, Ross holds that the principle of nonmaleficence (noninfliction of harm) takes precedence over the principle of beneficence (production of benefit) when they come into conflict, but he gives no account of the priorities among the other principles except to say that certain duties (such as keeping promises) have "a great deal of stringency". Ultimately, as he quotes Aristotle, "The decision rests with perception". While we intuit moral principles, according to Ross, we do not intuit what is right in the situation; rather, we have to find "the greatest balance" of right over wrong . . .

Finally, like utilitarians, deontologists may focus on acts or on rules that cover classes of cases. However, few philosophers or theologians have tried to defend act deontology, despite traces of it here and there ... For rule deontologists, by contrast, the heart of morality is a set of binding principles and rules that classify acts as right, wrong, obligatory, or prohibited ...

Rule deontology is widely represented in contemporary biomedical ethics. Major controversies among rule deontologists often stem from their different judgments regarding which principles or rules are primary or more stringent. For example, Paul Ramsey's rule deontology affirms that various principles and rules can be derived from love or covenant fidelity and his derivative principles include the sanctity of life. Because of this derivative principle, it is permissible in his system to override even a competent patient's refusal of lifesaving medical treatment when there is a medically indicated reason. Ramsey thus recognises the legitimacy of strong paternalism ... By contrast, both Robert Veatch and H. Tristram Engelhardt, Jr., defend the priority of the principle of respect for autonomy: A competent patient has the right to refuse even life-saving medical treatment, and strong paternalism is never justified. However, when Veatch and Engelhardt consider the allocation of health-care resources, a further division is evident among these two deontologists. Veatch argues for the priority of the principle of equality, while Engelhardt again opts for the priority of the principle of respect for autonomy.

NOTES:

1. For reasons of succinctness, the above extract is taken from the third edition of *Principles of Biomedical Ethics*. For a fuller evaluation of various utilitarian and deontological theories see the 4th edition of the text at pages 47–62.
2. One of the attractions of utilitarianism as a moral theory is its egalitarianism — the idea that everyone's pleasures are taken into account and count equally. However, attempts to formulate what are acceptable pleasures or preferences would appear to undercut this egalitarianism and pose a serious problem for preference utilitarians.
3. For a practical application of both types of reasoning see case note on *R. v. Cambridgeshire Health Authority, ex p. B* in (1996) 112 L.Q.R. 182.

QUESTION:

1. Do you think it makes sense to argue, as deontologists do, that actions are intrinsically good or bad, as opposed to producing good or bad consequences?

3. AUTONOMY

The last extract ended by introducing another fundamental debate in medical ethics – that of autonomy (or patient self-determination) versus paternalism (or the view that the health professional is best placed to decide for the patient). Even if one accepts, that the training of a doctor means that she is well placed to diagnose and treat our illnesses, injuries and diseases — a view which is increasingly contested especially in relation to the diagnosis of incapacity, mental illness and reproductive health (see Chapters 5, 8, and 11–13), it may not follow that such knowledge places her in the best position to assess the optimium course of action for the patient to adopt in the light of her diagnosis. Many of the issues pertaining to health care are not purely clinical matters, but need to take account of the values held by the patient (see Chapter 6 at pages 354–355). This has led some ethicists to stress the importance of respecting the patient's right to make his own choices — *i.e.* his autonomy or self-determination. Since the 1950s this has become recognised as perhaps the dominant principle of medical ethics.

R. Gillon, "Autonomy and Consent" in M. Lockwood (ed.) *Moral Dilemmas in Modern Medicine*, Oxford, Oxford University Press, 1985, pages 114–117

The concept of autonomy must be distinguished from what is often known as the principle of autonomy, which is essentially the moral requirement to respect others people's autonomy. In practice, everyone accepts this principle to some extent: we all want our own autonomy respected (who would accept arbitrary imprisonment without even a *feeling* of moral outrage?) and we are all prepared to accept that we ought to respect the autonomy of at least some others in at least some circumstances. In the case of autonomy of action, however, the need for some restriction on respect for the autonomy of others is obvious; otherwise we should be morally required to respect any deliberated course of action no matter how horrible the consequences might be for others. Two great philosophers, one a founding father of utilitarianism, the other an exemplar of deontological (duty based) ethical theorists, both argued vigorously for the moral importance of respecting people's autonomy; and both offered restrictions which, although expressed very differently, have, perhaps, some similarities. John Stuart Mill argued that respect for another's autonomy was required in so far as such respect did not result in harm to others and in so far as the people thus respected possessed a fairly basic level of maturity (a capability 'of being improved by free and equal discussion'). Immanuel Kant argued that both autonomy and respect for the autonomy of others were necessary features of any rational agent in so far as their exercise conformed to the 'categorical imperative'. Let me offer very brief, very rough, and oversimplified accounts of their respective claims.

Kant's metaphysics divides what exist into two great realms, the intelligible or 'noumenal' world — the world of reason — and the phenomenal world, the world of sense perception. What exists in both these realms works in accordance with universal laws. A rational being has 'the power to act in accordance with his idea of laws'. Non-rational beings, however, are acted upon, and their behaviour is causally necessitated or determined by causes outside themselves. Human beings are an amalgam of the rational and the non-rational; it is the will that links these aspects of man, enabling him to use his reason to produce effects on the non-rational world, including the non-rational aspects of himself. 'Will is a kind of causality belonging to living beings so far as they are rational. Freedom would then be the property this causality has of being able to work independently of determination by alien causes.' In so far as human beings are ruled by forces other than their own will, including the 'impulsions of animal nature', they act heteronomously. In so far as they are rational agents they are ruled by their own will and are thus autonomous. Now, as we have seen, whatever exists in either sphere works according to universal laws and Kant argues that there is only one objective moral law for the autonomous will, though it may be presented in several ways. This is his famous 'categorical imperative' that requires us to 'act only on that maxim through which you can at the same time will that it should become a universal law'. His argument for this is that all objective moral laws necessarily apply to all rational agents and therefore no maxim (principle on which we in fact act) *could* be consistent with such objective moral laws unless the maxim could consistently be willed by the agent to be a universal law applying to all rational agents. The inherent dignity of any person (by which Kant means any rational being) lies in his ability not merely to conform to the moral law, but to choose to do so, to accept the law for himself (as distinct, for instance, from being forced by someone else to obey it which is just as heteronomous as allowing one's 'animal impulsions' to make one behave contrary to the moral law).

It is in this way that people can be both subject to universal moral laws and yet at the same time be authors of those laws, in that they have subjected themselves willingly to them. Rational beings necessarily have wills, according to Kant, and thus are by their nature ends in themselves as distinct from mere means; and this is true both objectively and subjectively, in that this is how men necessarily conceive of their own existence. Any application of the categorical imperative must recognize that fact. From this Kant derives (or some would say purports to derive) his other formulations of the categorical imperative: 'Act in such a way that you always treat humanity, whether in your own person or in the person of any other, never simply as a means but always at the same time as an end' and 'a rational being must always regard himself as making laws in a kingdom of ends', where a kingdom of ends is a 'systematic union of different rational beings under common laws'.

For Kant, then, self-rule — autonomy — is a fundamental and logically necessary feature of being a rational agent: 'Autonomy is therefore the ground of the dignity of human nature and of every rational nature.'

J. S. Mill also argued for the moral requirement to respect the autonomy of others, supporting this claim (as does Oxford's Professor R.M. Hare) on the utilitarian grounds that such respect (which should, according to Mill, 'govern absolutely the dealings of society with the individual in the way of compulsion and control') would maximize human welfare. Mill has traditionally been pilloried for attempting to square the circle in endorsing both an absolute principle of respect for liberty (by which he clearly means autonomy) and utilitarianism; but in a recent book, the Oxford philosopher John Gray puts up a good case for Mill's consistency here. Gray points out that Mill, while insisting that the principle of utility is 'the ultimate appeal on all ethical questions', also stresses that it must be utility understood 'in the largest sense grounded on the permanent interests of a man as a progressive being'. Thus understood, the principle of utility maybe seen as having the principle of respect for autonomy as a corollary. This is because human happiness is constituted, in part, by the exercise of individual autonomy.

Moreover, each person exercises his autonomy differently, and thus his happiness (in the broad Aristotelian sense of *eudaemonia* or flourishing), which partially depends upon his fulfilment of the demands of his own nature, will also be different. Maximal respect for the exercise of individual autonomy (so far as this does not harm others) is thus a precondition for the utilitarian objective of maximizing human welfare. It is in this context that I now quote Mill's introductory assertion in *On Liberty:*

'The object of this Essay is to assert one very simple principle, as entitled to govern absolutely the dealings of society with the individual in the way of compulsion and control . . . . That principle is, that the sole end for which mankind are warranted, individually or collectively, in interfering with the liberty of action of any of their number, is self-protection. That the only purpose for which power can rightfully be exercised over any member of a civilized community, against his will, is to prevent harm to others. His own good, either physical or moral, is not a sufficient warrant.'

To summarize the argument thus far: autonomy is the capacity to think, to decide, and to act on the basis of such thought and decision. Respect for autonomy is the moral principle that people should have their autonomy respected to the extent that such respect is consistent with respect for the autonomy of others (and I have not gone into the problems surrounding this condition). Part of what such respect for autonomy implies, in practical terms, is not interfering with people without their consent — not imposing interference on people. Mill defends this moral principle on the utilitarian grounds that such respect for autonomy furthers human welfare. Kant defends it on the grounds that rational agents — and therefore men in so far as they are, and are acting as, rational agents — necessarily recognize the requirement to treat people as ends in themselves — as self-ruling or autonomous — and not merely as means.

I am not sure that I accept the Kantian argument that all rational agents *necessarily* recognize the moral obligation to respect others as autonomous, as ends in themselves. Perhaps it depends on the sense of necessity involved. But there can be little doubt that whenever one does not recognize and respect another's autonomy, then one is necessarily not treating him as (allowing him to be) a rational agent; for rational agency by definition requires autonomy. (It is action grounded in one's deliberation and decision.) Thus whenever, for example, one imposes decisions upon people without consulting them, let alone against their will, whether or not these decisions are designed to be beneficial, one is treating them as things or as animals or as children, but not as rational agents, not as ends in themselves.

QUESTION:

1. Do you agree with Mill's view that a person's autonomy should be respected unless it causes harm to others? How are 'harm' and 'others' to be defined? For instance, if a gynaecologist considers that a pregnant woman should undergo a Caesarian section delivery in the interests of the foetus she is carrying, and she refuses to submit to the operation, should her autonomy be respected? (See the case of *Re S (Adult: Refusal of Medical Treatment)* [1992] 4 All E.R. 649 in Chapter 13.) (For difficulties with this formulation see pages 104–107 below.) Would you impose any other limitations on a patient's right to self-determination?

In the following extract, Glover discusses the necessary preconditions which must exist before someone may be said to act autonomously.

J. Glover, *Causing Death and Saving Lives*, Harmondsworth: Penguin, 1977, pages 76–77

Respect for a person's autonomy and the associated restriction on paternalism can arise only in the context of a person who has a preference at the time when the decision affecting him is to be taken. Whatever outcome you may in future come to prefer, there can be no question of anyone now overriding your autonomy if you now have no views about the decision to be taken. (Though respect for your autonomy at least requires that this is found out by asking you.) There are three presuppositions that must be made by anyone who thinks that your autonomy should be respected in a present situation:

(a) **The existence condition:** You must already exist. There is no such thing as overriding the autonomy of a potential person. It is true that we can do things that restrict the freedom of action of future generations, perhaps by allowing the erosion of civil liberties or by using up scarce resources, but such acts are objectional because of the weight we ought to give to the interest or liberty of future people, not because we can now be said to be flouting their autonomy.

(b) **The developmental condition:** You must be at a level of development where you can have the relevant desires. Perhaps my three-year-old son will one day have the ambition to produce a unified field theory. If I do not take steps to see he has an adequate scientific education, this may prevent him even having a chance to satisfy the ambition. But this would again be a matter of restricting his future opportunities. I cannot, if I take a decision about his education now, be overriding his autonomy. This is because, although he is in existence, he is not at the stage of development where he even *could* have the desire whose satisfaction I may be ruling out.

(c) **The possession condition:** You must have the desire whose satisfaction is in question. I override your autonomy only where I take a decision on your behalf which goes against what you actually do want, not where the decision goes against what you would want if you were more knowledgeable or more intelligent. (To say this is to talk of desires in a dispositional sense: you do not have to be conscious of your desire at the moment it is overridden. Such a condition as that would license any decision I take on your behalf the moment you are asleep. And to think of desires in this dispositional sense should also allow us to respect desires that have a stable role in a person's outlook even when they are temporarily eclipsed by conditions such as hypnosis or being drugged.)

NOTES:

1. The existence of conditions for the exercise of autonomy, as outlined by Glover in the above extract, means that the autonomy of incompetent and mentally handicapped adults, and many children may have to be circumscribed. (See Chapters 5, 7 and 8.)
2. The idea of autonomy is closely related to the notion of choice (See J. Harris, *The Value of Life*, London: Routledge and Kegan Paul, 1985, pages 195–200). Doyal argues that there may be a tendency on the part of those theorists who value autonomy to presuppose that patients' choices about what they want are informed. (See L. Doyal, Medical Ethics and Moral Indeterminacy" (1990) 17 *Journal of Law and Society* 1 at page 12.) The issue of choice is explored in more detail in Chapters 11–13 on reproductive choices. When you read Chapters 5, 6 and 11–13 you should consider the extent to which law does in fact respect the patient's right to autonomy.
3. On the application of the principle of autonomy in a health care context, see M. Brazier, "Patient Autonomy and Consent to Treatment" (1987) 7 *Legal Studies* 169; H. Teff, "Consent to Medical Procedures: Paternalism, Self-Determination or Therapeutic Alliance" (1985) 101 *Law Quarterly Review* 432.
4. In the context of the doctor-patient relationship, where most power resides with the doctor, it is common to focus on the limitations of

patient autonomy. However the issue of the autonomy of the doctor is becoming increasingly significant given radical changes in the structure of the NHS. In addition to considering how the decisions and actions of the health professional may limit the patient's autonomy, it is increasingly becoming necessary to consider how decisions taken by NHS managers or NHS Trusts may limit the health professional's autonomy to make decisions which she considers appropriate to patient care. (See D. Longley, *Public Law and Health Service Accountability*, Buckingham: Open University Press, 1993; C. Newdick, *Who Should We Treat? — Law, Patients and Resources in the N.H.S.* Oxford: Oxford University Press, 1995; A. Wall and R. Rowden "Managerial Accountability" in G. Hunt (ed.), *Whistleblowing in the Health Service*, London: Edward Arnold 1995). The health professional's ability to make autonomous decisions may also vary according to whether she is employed by the NHS or under a private contract. For example, the resources which an NHS Trust is prepared to make available may affect the service which the doctor is able to provide. By contrast, in the private sector such decisions may be limited only by the patient's ability to pay.

5. It is also relevant to consider the extent to which health professionals other than doctors have autonomy within the health care team. As their role is changing, nurses and other health professionals may be gaining more autonomy, as nurses come to act more as nurse practitioners and as advocates on behalf of their patients and increasingly to carry out tasks previously entrusted only to doctors. (See Chapter 6 at pages 337 and N. Fletcher, J. Holt, M. Brazier and J. Harris, *Ethics, Law and Nursing*, Manchester: Manchester University Press, 1995, Chap. 7; L. L. Curtin, "The nurse as advocate: A philosophical foundation for nursing" (1979) 3 *Advances in Nursing Science* 1; E. Bernal "The Nurse as Patient Advocate" (1992) 22 *Hastings Center Report* 18.)

QUESTIONS:

1. What if respecting someone's autonomy leads him into actions which are fool-hardy or pose a danger to his life or health? Should we nevertheless respect his right to make such fool-hardy decisions? For example, if one of your friends is feeling depressed and confides in you that he is planning to commit suicide does respect for his autonomy mean that you should take no steps to prevent him from killing himself? At what point, if any, would intervention by you cease to be justified? (See G. Fairbairn, "Suicide and Paternalism" in M. Brazier and M. Lorbjoit (eds) *Protecting the Vulnerable: Autonomy and Consent in Health Care* London: Routledge 1992.)

2. Following on from the last question, how do we judge whether or not an action is fool-hardy? Given that such a judgement is inherently value-laden, can we ever justifiably label an action 'fool-hardy'?

3. The difficulty of judging actions may be complicated by the religious
   or cultural beliefs held by the patient. For example, a female patient
   may need to control her fertility for health reasons, but find this
   difficult to accept or discuss for cultural reasons. Is it more respectful
   of her autonomy to accept her decision to reject contraception
   without comment or to seek to counsel her so that she may change
   her mind? (See L. Doyal, "Needs and Rights of Patients in Different
   Cultures" in K. W. M. Fulford *et al*, *Essential Practice in Patient-
   Centred Care*, Oxford: Blackwells, 1996)
4. Are there any factors which will always impose constraints on patient
   autonomy and rights to choose? (See J. Harris, *The Value of Life*,
   London: Routledge and Kegan Paul, 1985, Chapter 10.)

4.   PATERNALISM

As noted above, the notion of autonomy began to assume immense
significance in the context of health care provision in the late 1950s and
1960s. (See R. R. Faden and T. Beauchamp, *A History and Theory of
Informed Consent*, New York: Oxford University Press 1986). It was at this
time that a new conception of the doctor's role became apparent. The
traditional model of health care provision was based on the notion of
beneficence – which may be broadly defined as all forms of action intended
to benefit others. (See T. L. Beauchamp and J. L. Childress, *Principles of
Biomedical Ethics* 4th edn, New York: Oxford University Press, 1994 at
page 260.) The notion of beneficence has played a central role in many
ethical theories. As Gillon notes, in health care terms it is reflected in the
notion that "the patient's interests come first", and that the doctor's role is
to devote herself to furthering her patient's interests. (See R. Gillon,
Philosophical Medical Ethics, Chichester: Wiley 1985 at pages 73–79.)
However, this raises the important question of who defines what the
patient's interests are. Thus the notion of beneficence with its aim of
promoting the patient's interests may easily slide into paternalism – the
notion that doctors know best. Paternalism rests largely on the presumption that the sole aim of the patient is to be cured and that he is willing to
entrust his well-being completely to the doctor's care. This model has
gradually been replaced by one based on the idea that the delivery of health
care was best served by a partnership between the patient and a team of
health professionals. Around the same time the notion of patients' rights
began to be more influential. The movement originated in the United
States, which continues to be in the fore-front of such developments. (For
further discussion of rights see pages 87–94 below.) However, vestiges of
the old medical paternalism linger on, particularly in the areas of consent
and capacity and provision of reproductive advice and treatment, where
the law in many instances has appeared to endorse the old view that
doctors do know best. (See Chaps 5, 6 and 11–13.)

R. Gillon, *Philosophical Medical Ethics*, Chichester: John Wiley & Sons, 1985, pages 67–71

Sometimes one has as a doctor to be paternalistic to one's patients — that is, do things against their immediate wishes or without consulting them, indeed perhaps with a measure of deception, to do what is in their best interest . . . Just as parents may sometimes have to make important decisions in a child's best interests against the child's will or by deception or without telling the child, so doctors sometimes have to act on behalf of their patients. As Dr Ingelfinger put it, "If you agree that the physician's primary function is to make the patient feel better, a certain amount of authoritarianism, paternalism and domination are the essence of the physician's effectiveness" . . . Here I shall consider some arguments offered in support of medical paternalism.

The first such argument is that medical ethics since Hippocratic times has required doctors to do the best for their patients. The Hippocratic oath requires that "I will follow that system or regimen which, according to my ability and judgment I consider for the benefit of my patients." It says nothing about doing what patients wish, explaining likely consequences, good or bad, or describing alternative courses of action.

Put so baldly this way of expressing the duty to do the best for one's patients may not sound attractive. Put in terms of various real life circumstances, however, with patients terrified by their diseases, perhaps suffering great pain and other highly unpleasant symptoms such as breathlessness, intractable itching, disordered sensation, misery and depression, and, often, utter bewilderment, it becomes far more plausible to think, especially if one is that patient's doctor, relative, or friend, that the last thing one should do is add to the misery and worry by passing on the results of the biopsy, the risk of treatment, the unsatisfactory options, or whatever other nasty bits of information the doctor has up his sleeve. More plausible indeed, but how justifiable?

Even if one accepts the claim that the overriding moral requirement is to do one's best to improve one's patients' health, minimise their suffering, and prolong their lives, it is by no means clear that these ends are furthered by, for example, false confidence, paternalistic decision making, evasions, deceit, and downright lies. Of course, such behaviour (the hearty slap on the back, "Well of course we're not magicians old boy but we'll do our best for you, you can rest assured of that, and we've had some excellent results . . . ") greatly reduces the anguish for the doctor: honest discussion with people who, for example, have a fatal disease concerning their condition and prospect are emotionally demanding, as is the necessary follow up; it is far less difficult to "look on the bright side". The assumption, however, that this generally makes such patients happier is highly suspect.

What is more, it is often only the patient who is deceived and treated thus, while a relative or relatives are told the truth; the deceit that this imposes on the family (and also on other medical and nursing staff) may itself provoke considerable distress, not to mention the breaking of normal medical confidentiality and the effects of doing so. Then there is the suffering of the patient who suspects that something nasty is afoot but cannot discover what. Finally, there is the suffering of a fatally ill patient on discovering that he or she has been deceived by his or her doctor and family. What a way to go.

Of course, some patients really do want their doctors to shield them from any unpleasant information and to take over decision making on all fronts concerning their illness. Doing what the patient wants, however, is not (by definition) paternalism. My point is that not all patients want doctors to behave like this, and for those who do not it is highly dubious to suppose that their suffering is reduced by it or their health improved or even their lives prolonged. Still, time, and effort are required to find out what the patient really wants, whereas in practice it is often merely assumed that the patient "doesn't want to know".

A second line of justification of paternalistic behaviour is that patients are not capable of making decisions about medical problems: they are too ignorant medically speaking, and such knowledge as they have is too partial in both senses of the word. Thus they are unlikely to understand the situation even if it is explained to them and so are likely to make worse decisions than the doctor would.

Even if one were to accept that "best decisions" are the primary moral determinant it is worth distinguishing the sorts of decisions that doctors might be expected to make better than their patients from those where little or no reason exists to expect this. In the technical area for which they have been specially and extensively trained there is little doubt that doctors are likely to make more technically or medically correct (and hence in that sense better) decisions than their medically ignorant patients. The doctor who advises his patients that to continue her pregnancy would, because of coexisting medical condition, be from her point of view appreciably more dangerous than to have a termination and that therefore a termination would be better may be giving medically sound advice based on superior medical knowledge. If he insisted or even advised that a termination would be better in some moral sense he would be stepping outside his realm of competence: he is not better trained professionally to make moral assessments than is his patient, and even if he were many would object that it is not the doctor's role even to advise on his patient's moral decisions let alone make them.

The counterargument just offered meets the paternalist on his own ground by agreeing that there are some areas, notably the technical, in which doctors may be expected to make better decisions than their patients. It points out that in other areas, including the moral sphere, there is little reason to expect them to do so. A further matter on which it is doubtful whether doctors are qualified or likely to make better decisions than their patients concerns what course of action is likely to produce most happiness or least unhappiness for everyone, all things considered (the utilitarian objective).

Some doctors believe, for example, that in perplexing cases such as those of severely handicapped newborn infants it is up to them to "shoulder the burden", assess what course of action will produce the greatest benefit all things considered, and than implement it. As one paediatrician wrote, "In the end it is usually the doctor who has to decide the issue: it is . . . cruel to ask the parents whether they want their child to live or die."

The philosopher Professor Allen Buchanan has pointed out that if a doctor undertakes to assess which of various available courses of action (including informing the parents of the options and asking them which they favour) is most likely to produce the greatest happiness all things considered he must consider an awful lot of factors.

' . . . [T]he physician must first make intrapersonal comparisons of harm and benefit of each member of the family, if the information is divulged. Then he must somehow coalesce these various intrapersonal net harm judgements into an estimate of total net harm which divulging the information will do to the family as a whole. Then he must make similar intrapersonal and interpersonal net harm judgments about the results of not telling the truth. Finally he must compare these totals and determine which course of action will minimise harm to the family as a whole.'

Buchanan makes a similar analysis for the doctor who tries seriously to assess whether it would be best, all things considered, to tell a dying patient the truth about his predicament. After showing the complexity of any such analysis and its necessarily morally evaluative components Buchanan concludes:

'Furthermore, once the complexity of these judgments is appreciated and once their evaluative character is understood it is implausible to hold that the physician is in a better position to make them the patient or his family. The failure to ask what sorts of harm/benefit judgments may properly be made by the physician in his capacity as a physician is a fundamental feature of medical paternalism.'

Of course, such assessments — moral and preference assessments — are difficult for anyone to make. The point is that there is no *prima facie* reason to suppose that doctors make them better than their patients. Even in the strongest case, that of technical medical assessment, the argument from patient ignorance is suspect for in practice many doctors can explain technical medical issues to their patients' satisfaction. Better postgraduate training in effective communication or delegation to colleagues who have these skills, or both, are alternatives to arguing that such effective communication cannot be achieved.

All the preceding counterarguments meet the defence of paternalism on its own ground by accepting its assumption that the overriding moral objective is to maximise the happiness of the patient alone, of the family, or of society as a whole. Kantians (for whom the principle of respect for autonomy is morally supreme) and pluralist deontologists (who believe that an adequate moral theory requires a variety of potentially conflicting moral principles including that of respect for autonomy) will argue that there are many circumstances in which a person's autonomy must be respected even if to do so will result in an obviously worse decision in terms of the patient's, the family's, or, even, a particular society's happiness. . . . [T]his conclusion is also supported by many utilitarians on the grounds that respect for people's autonomy is required if human welfare really is to be maximised.

Sir Richard Bayliss has movingly described the case of a Christian Scientist whose decision to turn to orthodox medicine for treatment of her thyrotoxicosis came too late to save her life. Few who do not accept Christian Scientism can believe she made a "better" decision in relation to her longevity and health when she rejected the advice of her original doctor in favour of her cults's. Those, however, for whom the principle of respect for autonomy is morally important would not deny her the respect of allowing her to refuse medical help in the first place even though this was highly likely to be fatal and thus cause her family and medical attendant great anguish and even though paternalistic intervention could have saved her life.

NOTE:

1. In the light of developments in the law relating to non-treatment or withdrawal of treatment from handicapped neonates, which indicate that courts may lawfully sanction controversial withdrawals of treatment (see Chapter 14) it may be more difficult to sustain the argument that it is the doctor who shoulders the burden of deciding whether the neonate should live or die.

QUESTION:

1. Who is best equipped to make these awesome decisions about the lives of others? Should it be the relatives, the doctors, the courts or some other body? (See P. Weir, *Selective Non Treatment of Handicapped New Borns*, Oxford and New York: Oxford University Press, 1979.)

In the following extract, Jonathan Glover also deals with how the necessary balance is to be struck between respecting autonomy whilst permitting paternalistic intervention in some circumstances.

J. Glover, *Causing Death and Saving Lives*, Harmondsworth: Penguin 1977, pages 75–76

Rejection of paternalism . . . raises a number of disputed questions. Is it always wrong to prevent, in his own interests, an adult capable of weighing alternatives from doing or having what he wants? Many people say we never have a right to interfere on paternalist grounds. They follow Mill in thinking that restrictions of liberty may sometimes be justified by appealing to the interests of other people, but that to restrict someone's freedom for his own good is not permissible.

But in some cases we may be doubtful about giving this absolute priority to autonomy. If someone wants to start taking heroin, I will think it right to stop him if I can. This results from giving less weight to his autonomy in this matter than to sparing him the appalling suffering involved in the slow death of a heroin addict. (The heroin addict also causes suffering to people who care about him, and is a drain on the community's medical resources. These are extra reasons, of a non-paternalist kind, for stopping people taking heroin. But the concession to paternalism made here is the admission that prevention would be right even in the absence of these reasons involving other people.)

Anyone who rejects paternalism entirely has no problem in explaining his view that it is directly wrong to kill someone who want to live. But those of us who are sometimes prepared to override a person's autonomy in what we take to be his own interest do have to face problems of drawing boundaries. If it is directly wrong to kill someone against his will, is it directly wrong to keep someone alive against his will? How can it be right that I should be forced to stay alive at great cost in pain to myself, but not be right for me to take heroin if I want, at the same cost to myself?

There are three main arguments for paternalistic prevention of heroin addiction:

(i) The suffering is very great: we can be very confident that the normal person is better off than the addict.

(ii) There is very little uncertainty that the suffering will occur.

(iii) The process is not readily reversible, so the person starting on heroin greatly restricts his future freedom of choice. (This might appeal as an argument to those whose anti-paternalism stems from valuing freedom much more than utilitarian considerations.)

It would be hard to make out a case that killing someone against his will but 'in his interests' had anything like this kind of justification. Reasons (i) and (ii) might in very rare cases apply: we would have to imagine that I am a doctor with a lot of experience of patients with your terminal illness, and I know that on our plague-ridden island medical supplies are so low that, unless I kill you now, there will be no means of avoiding your agony later. Even here, the decision about how bad a life must be for the person to be better off dead has to be taken before reason (i) applies.

Consideration of reason (iii) shows a central difference between paternalistic killing and either the heroin case or paternalistic prevention of suicide. There is the finality of an act of killing. Paternalistic prevention of suicide is different. I feel justified in stopping you killing yourself because I expect you will be glad later that I did. If I am mistaken, you will have opportunities for other attempts. Similarly, there will be other opportunities to start on heroin. But, if I kill you, this is final. You will not have second thoughts, and mine will come too late.

NOTES:

1. In a legal context paternalism by health professionals often manifests itself in the doctrine of 'therapeutic privilege' — the idea that the doctor may withhold certain information if she believes that it would have an adverse impact on the patient's chances of recovery. For discussion of this doctrine see the speech of Lord Scarman in *Sidaway v. Bethlem* [1985] 1 All E.R. 643 at pages 341–345 in Chapter 6.

2. Doyal points out that, aside from the argument that paternalism is an unwarranted interference with the individual's autonomy, there exists the practical objection that the effects of paternalism cannot be accurately predicted. (See L. Doyal, "Medical Ethics and Moral Indeterminacy" (1990) 17 *Journal of Law and Society* 1.)

QUESTIONS:

1. Are Gillon and Glover in complete agreement in the arguments they make in the two extracts above?
2. Do you agree with the final point made in each extract?
3. Although paternalism has generally had a bad press in recent years, do you think it is a justifiable ethical stance to adopt in some instances? Are you persuaded by the counter-arguments put forward by Gillon?
4. Can you distinguish between the concepts of paternalism and beneficence?

5. RIGHTS THEORIES V. UTILITARIANISM

Already it should be clear to you that the concept of rights is an extremely important one when discussing ethical issues. Rights-based theories have become the most pervasive and influential of the various deontological theories discussed above, with the result that rights discourse has dominated discussion of health care provision in the last couple of decades. For example, not only is the issue of a right to health care very contested (see Chapter 1), but it is common to discuss abortion in terms of the conflicting rights of the pregnant woman and the foetus, or to talk of patients' rights to information, or to assert claims on behalf of embryos or animals in terms of rights. In short, it has become a powerful rhetorical strategy to translate claims of grievance into rights-based claims. Moreover, rights discourse can be politically empowering — it may build a community of understanding and confer identity on particular groups — think, for example, of groups who campaign on behalf of foetal rights like LIFE and the Society for the Protection of the Unborn Child. A further advantage is that the language of rights claims can with relative ease be translated into law. (See M. Freeden, *Rights*, Milton Keynes: Open University Press, 1991; A. R. White, *Rights*, Oxford: Oxford University Press, 1984.) However, not all rights can be or have been encoded in law. For this reason you need to think critically about what you mean when you invoke rights language. Freedon points out (*op. cit.* at p. 2) that "all too often analyses of rights pay little regard to the concrete and variegated ways in which the concept is underpinned by a host of related terms that act crucially to establish its different meanings", and that "lawyers, philosophers and historians of political ideas all approach the subject from very different perspectives."

Legal rights are usually an expression of more abstract moral rights which
are the product of reasoned moral analysis. (See I. Kennedy, "Patients,
Doctors, and Human Rights" in I. Kennedy, *Treat Me Right*, Oxford:
Clarendon, 1988.) The advantage of being able to assert a legal right is that
it is more concrete than moral rights, which are extremely unlikely to
command universal acceptance. When rights are codified in law one can
point to a specific source of entitlement — a case or a statute. If a
particular right is recognised by law, the law will usually impose a duty on
someone else to give effect to that right and it will be enforceable by legal
sanctions. However, not all legal rights are enshrined in domestic law.
They may instead be contained in international treaties or conventions
such as the European Convention on Human Rights. Although the
Convention has not been incorporated into United Kingdom law (see
Chapter 1) and in the past has been overlooked by lawyers and judges in
relevant cases, there are signs that it is increasingly influential upon the
thinking of British lawyers. (The Convention is discussed in the Introduction to Part IV at pages 623–626 in the context of reproductive rights.)
Rights contained in such documents tend to be codified in rather vague and
general terms and they may also be difficult to enforce. Nonetheless rights
which are protected under such conventions are recognised as having a
special moral weight — they are fundamental rights which purport to
protect basic human entitlements such as those to life and privacy.
Kennedy (*op. cit.*) has persuasively contended that medical law is best
regarded as a branch of human rights law. The political appeal of rights
discourse in a context where patients have traditionally been disem-
powered *vis-à-vis* doctors is obvious. The significance of rights discourse in
health care law is reflected in the way the Patient's Charter champions
patient's rights in the NHS, although the rhetoric of such rights may be
more impressive than the reality. (See J. Montgomery, "Patients First: The
Role of Rights" in K. W. M. Fulford *et al.* (eds), *Essential Practice in
Patient-Centred Care*, Oxford: Blackwell, 1996; M. Brazier "Rights and
Health Care" in R. Blackburn (ed.) *Rights of Citizenship*, London: Mansell
Publishing Ltd, 1993).

In the following extract, Joseph Raz explains the concept of legal rights:

J. Raz, *The Morality of Freedom* Oxford: Clarendon Press, 1986, pages
165–6, 168–9, 170–1 (footnotes omitted)

> . . . Philosophical definitions of rights attempt to capture the way the term is
> used in legal, political and moral writing and discourse. They both explain the
> existing tradition of moral and political debate and declare the author's
> intention of carrying on the debate within the boundaries of that tradition. At
> the same time they further that debate by singling out certain features of rights,
> as traditionally understood, for special attention, on the grounds that they are
> the features which best explain the role of rights in moral, political, and legal
> discourse . . .
>   Some rights derive from others. Just as rights are grounds for duties and

powers so they can be for other rights. I shall call a right which is grounded in another right a derivative right. Non-derivative rights are core rights. The relation between a derivative right and the core right (or any other right) from which it derives is a justificatory one. The statement that the derivative right exists must be a conclusion of a sound argument (non-redundantly) including a statement entailing the existence of the core right. But not every right thus entailed is a derivative one. The premisses must also provide a justification for the existence of the derivative right (and not merely evidence or even proof of its existence). To do so their truth must be capable of being established without relying on the truth of the conclusion. An example may illustrate the point.

Let us assume that I own a whole street because I bought (in separate transactions) all its houses. My ownership of a house in the street does not derive from my ownership of the street as a whole, even though the statement that I own a house in the street is entailed by the statement that I own the street. For in attempting to provide a normative justification for my rights I have to refer to the individual transaction by which I acquired the houses. Therefore my right in the street derives from my rights in the houses and not the other way round. Had I inherited the whole street from my grandfather the situation would have been reversed.

Without grasping the relation between core and derivative rights one is liable to fall into confusion. My right to walk on my hands is not directly based on an interest served either by my doing so or by others having duties not to stop me. It is based on my interest in being free to do as I wish, on which my general right to personal liberty is directly based. The right to walk on my hands is one instance of the general right to personal liberty. The right to personal liberty is the core right from which the other derives. Similarly my right to make the previous statement is a derivative of the core right of free speech, and my right to spoil the cigarette I am holding at the moment derives from my ownership in it, and so on . . .

It is sometimes argued that to every duty there is a corresponding right. It is evident from the proposed definition that there are no conceptual reasons for upholding such a view. Some moral theories may yield such a correlativity thesis as a result of their moral principles, but this possibility cannot be explored here. A more popular thesis maintains that to every right there is a correlative duty. Since a right is a ground for duties there is a good deal of truth in this kind of correlativity thesis. Yet most of its common formulations are very misleading. R. Brandt's definition can serve as an example of many: 'X has an absolute right to enjoy, have or be secured in Y' means the same as 'It is someone's objective overall obligation to secure X in, or in the possession of, or in the enjoyment of Y, if X wishes it.' He proceeds to define prima facie rights in terms of prima facie obligations. First, note that Brandt misleadingly suggests that to every right there corresponds one duty, that that duty is to guarantee the enjoyment or possession of the object of the right, and that it is conditional on the desire of the right-holder. All three points are mistaken. A right to education grounds a duty to provide educational opportunities to each individual, whether he wishes it or not. Many rights ground duties which fall short of securing their object, and they may ground many duties not one. A right to personal security does not require others to protect a person from all accident or injury. The right is, however, the foundation of several duties, such as the duty not to assault, rape or imprison the right-holder.

Secondly, and more importantly, Brandt fails to notice that the right is the ground of the duty. It is wrong to translate statements of rights into statements of 'the corresponding' duties. A right of one person is not a duty on another. It is the ground of a duty, ground which, if not counteracted by conflicting considerations, justifies holding that other person to have the duty.

Thirdly, there is no closed list of duties which correspond to the right. The existence of a right often leads to holding another to have a duty because of the existence of certain facts peculiar to the parties or general to the society in which they live. A chance of circumstances may lead to the creation of new duties based on the old right. The right to political participation is not new, but only in modern states with their enormously complex bureaucracies does this right justify, as I think it does, a duty on the government to make public its plans and proposals before a decision on them is reached, as well as a duty to publish its reasons for a decision once reached (except in special categories of cases such as those involving defence secrets). This dynamic aspect of rights, their ability to create new duties, is fundamental to any understanding of their nature and function in practical thought. Unfortunately, most if not all formulations of the correlativity thesis disregard the dynamic aspect of rights . . .

NOTE:

1. Over the past couple of decades many scholars, especially those associated with the "critical legal studies" movement in legal theory, have questioned the value of legal rights, arguing that rights are never revolutionary, are always claims to a stake in the given order of things, and can easily be taken away. (See for example, M. Tushnet, "An essay on rights", (1984) 62 *Texas Law Review* 1363.) Many feminist scholars are sympathetic to this critique (see, for instance, E. Kingdom, *What's Wrong With Rights: Problems for Feminist Politics of Law* Edinburgh: Edinburgh University Press, 1991) but others have argued that the assertion of legal rights is politically empowering. (See, for example, P. Williams, *The Alchemy of Race and Rights* Cambridge, Massachusetts: Harvard University Press, 1991.)

QUESTIONS:

1. Given your reading of Chapter 1, how successfully do you think rights discourse has been translated into a health care context? Is it meaningful to talk of a right to health-care? Does such a claim have any real substance? If you make such a claim, are you claiming a moral or a legal right?
2. Adopting Raz's terminology, is a right to health care a core or a derivative right?
3. Can a duty be imposed on the state to provide health care, so as to enable citizens to claim a right to health care, given that the demand for health care is inexhaustible? Indeed, can there be any absolute rights against a backdrop of limited resources? (See Chapter 1 and M. Brazier, "Rights and Health Care" in R. Blackburn (ed) *Rights of Citizenship*, London: Mansell Publishing Ltd, 1993.)

Rights theories form one of the major strands of competing ethical theory in vogue today. The other main competing strand is utilitarianism. As we have seen, utilitarian theories depend on evaluation of the consequences of alternative courses of action. In the extract below the Glover report applies these competing perspectives to issues arising out of the proliferation of reproductive options (discussed more fully in Chapter 11).

"Fertility and The Family": *The Glover Report on Reproductive Technologies to the European Commission*, London: Fourth Estate, 1989, pages 24–31

Some of the questions [we consider] are difficult because there are conflicts of interest. We look first at ways of thinking about these conflicts. Our discussion here of these approaches applies not only to parents, donors and children. The same underlying issues arise in other conflicts, for instance between the possible interests of the embryo and the interests of those who may benefit from embryo research . . .

The utilitarian approach to conflicts of interest

One approach is the utilitarian one. Everyone's interests are taken into account, and weighed against each other. The right policy is determined by how many people stand to gain or lose by one decision or the other, and by how much the gains or losses matter to them.

Take the case of whether sperm donors should have their identity revealed to their biological children. Utilitarian thinking about this starts by trying to assess how serious a loss it is not to know your biological origins. This loss to the child is compared with the disadvantages to the donor of later contact with offspring he might rather forget about. The ideal here would be to be able to consult substantial numbers of people who had two characteristics: being products of unknown sperm donors, and also being donors who were known to (and had been approached by) those their donation had produced.

The donors and their offspring are not the only people for a utilitarian to take into account. If lack of anonymity reduces the numbers of donors, some potential parents will be denied children. Their deprivation has to be included in the assessment. And, more controversially, some versions of utilitarianism would include the interests of those who will be born only if there are more donors.

It is obvious that in real life much of the evidence ideally required is not available. So the utilitarian 'calculation' has to depend on a mixture of indirect evidence and intuitive assessment. The utilitarian may regret this limitation, but may not see it as a devastating objection to the approach. Moral decisions simply may not be susceptible to precise scientific methods; and any plausible moral view gives some weight to the effects of actions and policies on people's interests, and so shares with utilitarianism this limitation.

An objection more specifically directed at utilitarianism is that it disregards people's rights. It is often said that, for a utilitarian 'the end justifies the means', and that pursuit of the general good may mean riding roughshod over individuals. On the issue of donor anonymity, it may be held that the child has a right to know his or her biological origins. If there is such a right, the need for donors does not justify denying the child this knowledge. If the utilitarian supports anonymity as the policy with the best consequences, critics will see this as a case where utilitarianism gives what is morally the wrong answer, and does so by treating a right as merely another interest to be considered.

Utilitarians have in general been sensitive to criticisms of this sort. Refined versions of utilitarianism have been produced in response to them. One such version is 'rule utilitarianism', according to which the consequences of individual acts are not what matters. On this view, we should calculate the consequences of obeying different rules, choose the best set of rules and use them to judge individual actions. Another is the 'two level' theory of R. M. Hare, where at the 'intuitive' level we should act on rules or cultivated dispositions, while at the 'critical' level we should evaluate the rules or dispositions on the basis of their utility (R. M. Hare: *Moral Thinking, Its Levels, Method and Point*, Oxford, 1981).

Consider for a moment the utilitarian approach to some issues outside the field of reproductive ethics. Certain interests have a special importance for us: these include life, freedom from arbitrary arrest, freedom of speech, and not — except in clearly defined circumstances and with our consent — having our lives put at risk by doctors carrying out medical experiments. It has been held that people will only feel secure if there is some guarantee that these vital interests will be protected. Many utilitarians have, on these grounds, been prepared to justify the adoption of rules protecting these interests, such as the principle that research should never be carried out on patients without their informed consent, even in circumstances where other interests appear to outweigh the need for security.

A sophisticated utilitarian can recognize that limitations on the scope of utilitarian calculation can themselves be justified on utilitarian grounds. Although utilitarians do not believe in absolute rights, this approach produces a *de facto* recognition of frontiers which closely correspond to rights.

These oblique strategies are themselves controversial. One question is whether they generate a stable position which is still utilitarian. Perhaps the rule against risking patients' lives in medical experiments which will not benefit them is based on people's need for security. This consideration may often outweigh the short-term utilitarian case in support of such experimentation. But what is to be done in the extreme case where the utilitarian calculation may go the other way, even if the long-term considerations are included? (Perhaps the experiment would save huge numbers of future lives.) In such a case, to stick to the rule is to abandon utilitarianism. And to stick to utilitarianism is to violate what others take to be a right. Those who believe in such rights may feel that utilitarianism does not provide a secure enough basis for them.

Rights, dignity, respect for persons

An alternative approach centres around the idea that people have a certain dignity, or should be treated with a certain respect. An ethic based on respect for persons sometimes finds expression in Kant's phrase that people should be treated 'always as ends in themselves and never merely as means'. This gives a reason for objecting to the medical experiment, even if calculation of consequences comes out in favour of it. On this view, the doctor may not simply look through the patient to the future beneficiaries of the research. The patient has a claim to more respect than merely having his or her interests given equal weight with those of any one of the potential beneficiaries.

It would be too stringent to require that no-one's interests are ever put second to those of others. That would rule out any solution to most cases of conflict of interests. The more plausible interpretation is that certain interests are too central to be sacrificed: in other words, that they generate certain rights which should not be violated.

One problem is that this seems to give us the framework of an approach to moral problems, without its substance. Everything depends on what rights we have; and more fundamentally, on what procedure we use to determine what rights there are. Rights theorists disagree both over what rights there are and about the justification for claims about rights.

There is also a problem about whether rights should be thought of as absolutely inviolable. For instance, there are conflicts between different rights. Suppose we think that a child has a right to be born into a family of a certain kind, perhaps a family with two parents. A single woman gets pregnant. Are we to say that she has a duty to have an abortion, whatever her own wishes or convictions? Or does she too have rights to be considered? The content of the child's right is indeterminate until such questions are answered. If the woman has relevant rights too, some order of priority seems necessary.

Another aspect of the problem of whether rights are absolutely inviolable has to do with the priority that rights take over other considerations. Suppose we say that the child resulting from AID [Artificial Insemination by Donor] has a right to know his or her biological parents. Would this right have to be respected even if so many donors were deterred that the infertility programme collapsed?

In an attractive image drawn from card-playing, Ronald Dworkin has suggested that rights are trumps (*Taking Rights Seriously*, 2nd impression, London, 1977, page xi). This captures something distinctive about rights, but brings out a certain rigidity in rights theory. It may seem procrustean to suppose that all moral claims we care about can be sorted into the two categories of rights and non-rights, such that the least right trumps any claim in the other category, no matter how substantial. We may become cautious about recognizing rights until we have thought out the extent to which we may be boxed in by them, unable to avoid a disaster because the only way of doing so involves some rights violation of minor importance.

Rights theorists have in general been aware of these problems. They have developed sophisticated theories, with various rules of precedence between rights. And they have produced accounts of *prima facie* rights, which can be overridden in circumstances of great necessity. A difficulty for sophisticated forms of rights theory is whether they can keep to the fine line between the perhaps excessive flexibility of utilitarian theories and the perhaps excessive rigidity of the simpler rights theories.

Convergence

We have seen that neither the utilitarian approach nor the rights-based approach is free of problems. It is not yet clear that there is a stable utilitarian position which gives individuals the kind of protection which would generally be accepted as adequate. And it is not yet clear that believers in rights can provide a satisfactory justification for drawing the distinction between rights and other interests in one place rather than another (or that they have yet provided a satisfactory account of how conflicts of rights should be adjudicated). If utilitarianism seems alarmingly flexible, the two-tier approach of rights theory seems disturbingly rigid. This central region of ethical theory is one of problems still unsolved.

There are several possible explanations for why this might be so. Perhaps both approaches are fundamentally flawed, and some as yet undiscovered third approach is needed. Or, it may be that people have irreducibly different values, so that the search for the theory which will seem satisfactory to us all is misguided. Or, it may be that some further improved version either of utilitarianism or of a rights theory would escape the problems of current versions.

Simple versions of utilitarianism and of rights theory are clearly opposed. They each have difficulties the other avoids. Sophisticated versions of each try to incorporate some of the strengths of the other. But in doing this, they tend towards convergence. The problem for each is to incorporate the strengths of the other while retaining its own identity. While this may be a problem for theorists, those of us trying to solve practical ethical problems may be encouraged. Perhaps a plausible set of solutions is to be found in the area of convergence between the sophisticated versions of the two approaches. This area seems worth exploring regardless of which label turns out to fit better the most acceptable approach.

We do not as a committee feel able to solve these central issues of ethical theory. In the absence of such solutions of the theoretical level, perhaps the best that can be hoped for is to get as close as possible to what John Rawls has called 'reflective equilibrium' (John Rawls: *A Theory of Justice*, Harvard, 1971).

As Rawls describes this, it is approached by formulating general principles which seem plausible, and then seeing to what extent their application fits our intuitive responses to particular cases. Where there is conflict between intuition and theory, we need to reconsider both. We need to ask whether the theory should be modified to accommodate the intuitive response. And we also need to ask whether the intuition is one which, on reflection, we are prepared to abandon. The hope is that, by a process of mutual adjustment, we may reach a state of equilibrium, where we have a stable set of principles and of intuitions, which are in harmony with each other.

There are, of course, questions about how far an individual person's values are susceptible of being harmoniously systematized in this way. And there are perhaps even bigger problems about the emergence of any social consensus from this process. Even if each of us reaches our own reflective equilibrium, perhaps the resulting views will diverge radically from each other.

We take it that what degree of consensus will emerge is an open empirical question. Particularly in a new field of ethics of the kind we are dealing with, it is hard to be sure to what extent disagreements are mere surface phenomena, the product of insufficient experience and thought, or expressions of deep differences of values.

Our approach here has been to consider the interests of the different people involved with a certain flexibility. We do not have a prior commitment to the idea that simply summing utilities will give the best answers. But nor do we feel committed to the view that any of the parties has rights which may never be overridden. In this way our approach is somewhere in the middle ground shared by sophisticated versions of utilitarianism and of rights theory, from both of which we have borrowed something. Perhaps one way of mapping that middle ground is to look in detail at such particular conflicts as we are concerned with here. If intuitively acceptable resolutions of them can be found, these may in turn help us to evaluate claims made on behalf of more general theoretical views.

NOTE:

1. You should attempt to adopt a similar approach to Glover's in addressing the ethical and legal issues considered in this book. Try to assess whether a rights-based approach, or utilitarianism, or some combination of the two, as suggested by Glover, provides the most satisfactory guidance to resolving difficult ethical problems.

QUESTIONS:

1. Do you agree with the authors of the Glover Report, that sophistic-ated versions of rights theories and utilitarianism do ultimately converge or collapse into one another?
2. Is Glover's attempt to produce recommendations based on a synthesis of rights discourse and utilitarianism successful, or is it incoherent?

6. JUSTICE

In the above extract, Glover refers to Rawls' theory of justice. Many of the issues discussed Chapter 1 and throughout this book are concerned with questions of justice. As noted in the extract from Beauchamp and Childress above, justice is derived from a Kantian version of deontological theory. Questions of distributive justice are essentially concerned with allocation of scarce resources. This is a major issue in a health care context, since all societies have to ration health care. It is the choice between different methods of rationing health care which raises ethical questions. (See R. Persaud, "What future for ethical medical practice in the new National Health Service?" (1991) 17 *Journal of Medical Ethics* 10.) The issue is certain to become increasingly significant as the question of how health care should be rationed and how priorities should be set becomes more visible and contested. In the light of such developments, health care economists are assuming an increasingly prominent role in the debate about how health care should be delivered. As we have seen in Chapter 1, scarcity of resources renders it impossible to talk in absolute terms of a right to health care. Nevertheless, in setting priorities it is important to try to assess competing claims according to some criterion of justice. A major problem in debating the justice of political arrangements for the delivery of health care and other scarce resources is the difficulty of choosing between competing theories of justice. Some of the differing conceptions of justice are surveyed in the following extract.

T. Beauchamp and L. Walters (eds), *Contemporary Issues in Bioethics*, Belmont, California: Wadsworth Publishing Co., (1989) pages 25–26, 32–34

Every civilized society is a cooperative venture structured by moral, legal, and cultural principles that define the terms of social cooperation. Beneficence and respect for autonomy are principles in this fabric of social order, but *justice* has been the subject of more treatises on the terms of social cooperation than any other principle.

A person has been treated in accordance with the principle of justice if treated according to what is fair, due, or owed. For example, if equal political rights are due all citizens, then justice is done when those rights are accorded. Any denial of a good, service, or piece of information to which a person has a right or entitlement based in justice is an injustice. It is also an injustice to place an undue burden on the exercise of a right — for example, to make a piece of information owed to a person unreasonably difficult to obtain.

The more restricted expression 'distributive justice' refers to the proper distribution of social benefits and burdens. Usually it refers to the distribution of primary social goods, such as economic goods and fundamental political rights. But social burdens must also be considered. Paying taxes and being drafted into the armed services to fight a war are distributed burdens; Medicare checks and grants to do research are distributed benefits. Recent literature on distributive justice has tended to focus on considerations of fair economic distribution, especially unjust distributions in the form of inequalities of income between different classes of persons and unfair tax burdens on certain classes. But there are many problems of distributive justice besides issues about income and wealth, including the issues raised in prominent contemporary debates over health care distribution . . .

The notion of justice has been analysed in different ways in rival theories. But common to all theories of justice is this minimal principle: Like cases should be treated alike — or, to use the language of equality, equals ought to be treated equally and unequals unequally. The elementary principle is referred to as the formal principle of justice, or sometimes as the formal principle of equality — formal because it states no particular respects in which people ought to be treated. It merely asserts that whatever respects are under consideration, if persons are equal in those respects they should be treated alike. Thus the formal principle of justice does not tell us how to determine equality or proportion in those matters, and it therefore lacks substance as a specified guide to conduct. Because in any group of persons there will be many respects in which they are both similar and different, this account of equality must be understood as "equality irrelevant respect".

Because this formal principle leaves space for differences in the interpretation of how justice applies to particular situations, philosophers have developed diverse theories of justice. These theories attempt to be more specific than the formal principle by elaborating how people are to be compared and what it means to give people their due. Philosophers attempt to achieve the needed precision and specificity by developing material principles of justice — so called because they put material content into a theory of justice. Each material principle of justice identifies a relevant property on the basis of which burdens and benefits should be distributed.

The following is a sample list of major candidates for the position of valid principles of distributive justice (though other lists have been proposed): 1. To each person an equal share. 2. To each person according to individual need. 3. To each person according to acquisition in a free market. 4. To each person according to individual effort. 5. To each person according to societal contribution. 6. To each person according to merit. There is no obvious barrier to acceptance of more than one of these principles, and some theories of justice accept all six as valid. Most societies use several in the belief that different rules are appropriate to different situations.

Egalitarian theories of justice emphasise equal access to primary goods, libertarian theories emphasise rights to social and economic liberty, and utilitarian theories emphasise a mixed use of such criteria so that public and private utility are maximised. The utilitarian theory follows the main lines of the explanation of utilitarianism above, and thus economic justice is viewed as one among a number problems concerning how to maximize value. The ideal economic distribution, utilitarians argue, is any arrangement that would have this maximizing effect.

Egalitarianism is the theory that individual differences are not significant in an account of social justice. Distributions of burdens and benefits in a society are just to the extent they are equal, and deviations from equality in distribution are unjust. Most egalitarian accounts of justice are guardedly formulated, so that only *some* basic equalities among individuals take priority over their differences. In recent years an egalitarian theory . . . has enjoyed wide currency: John Rawls's *A Theory of Justice*. This book has as its central contention that we should distribute all economic goods and services equally except in those cases in which an unequal distribution would actually work to everyone's advantage, or at least would benefit the worse off in society. Rawls considers social institutions to be just if and only if they conform to his two principles of justice . . .

[Rawls] presents a deontological theory as a direct challenge to utilitarianism on grounds of social justice. Rawls' basic objection to utilitarianism is that social distributions produced by maximising utility could entail violations of basic individual liberties and rights that ought to be guaranteed. Utilitarianism, which is concerned with total satisfaction in a society, is indifferent as to the distribution of satisfactions among individuals. This indifference would, in Rawls' view, permit the infringement of some people's rights and liberties if the infringement genuinely promised to produce a proportionately greater utility for others.

Rawls therefore sets as his task the development of an alternative ethical theory capable of sustaining non-utilitarian principles of justice. Rawls turns for this purpose to a hypothetical social contract procedure that is strongly indebted to what he calls the 'Kantian conception of equality'. According to this social contract account, valid principles of justice are those to which we would all agree if we could freely and impartially consider the social situation from a standpoint (the 'original position') outside any actual society. Impartiality is guaranteed in this situation by a conceptual device Rawls calls the 'veil of ignorance'. This notion stipulates that, in the original position, each person is (at last momentarily) ignorant of all his or her particular fortuitous characteristics. For example, the person's sex, race, I.Q., family background, and special talents or handicaps are unrevealed in this hypothetical circumstance.

The veil of ignorance prevents people from promoting principles of justice biased towards their own combinations of talents and characteristics. Rawls argues that under these conditions, people would unanimously agree on two fundamental principles of justice. The first requires that each peson be permitted the maximum amount of equal basic liberty compatible with a similar liberty for others. The second stipulates that once this equal basic liberty is assured, inequalities in primary social goods (for example, income, rights and opportunities) are to be allowed only if they benefit everyone and only if everyone has fair equality of opportunity. Rawls considers social institutions to be just if and only if they are in conformity with these two basic principles.

Rawls' theory makes equality a basic characteristic of the original position from which the social contract is forged. Equality is built into that hypothetical position in the form of a free and equal bargain among all parties, where there is equal ignorance of all characteristics and advantages that persons have or will have in their daily lives. Furthermore, people behind this veil of ignorance would choose to make the equal possession of basic liberties the first commitment of their social institutions. Nevertheless, Rawls rejects radical egalitarianism, arguing that equal distribution cannot be justified as the sole moral principle. If inequalities were to be introduced that rendered everyone better off by comparison to initial equality, those inequalities would be desirable — as long as they are consistent with equal liberty and fair opportunity. More particularly, if these inequalities work to enhance the position of the most disadvantaged persons in society, then it would be self-defeating for the least advantaged or anyone else to seek to prohibit the inequalities. Rawls thus rejects radical egalitarianism in favour of his second principle of justice.

The first part of his second principle is called the 'difference principle'. This principle permits inequalities of distribution as long as they are consistent with equal liberty and fair opportunity. Rawls formulates this principle more precisely so that such inequalities are justifiable only if they most enhance the position of the 'representative least advantaged' person — that is, a hypothetical individual particularly unfortunate in the distribution of fortuitous characteristics or social advantages. Formulated in this way, the difference principle would allow, for instance, extraordinary economic rewards to the entrepreneurs if the resulting economic stimulation were to produce improved job opportunities and working conditions for the least advantaged members of society. A strong egalitarian flavour is retained, however, in that such inequalities would be permissible only if it could be demonstrated that they worked to the greatest advantage of those who were worse off.

The difference principle rests on the view that because inequalities of birth, historical circumstances, and natural endowment are undeserved, society should correct them by improving the unequal situation of naturally disadvantaged members. This is a deontologically based demand that Rawls believes fundamental to moral life in society . . .

The libertarian theory is sharply opposed to egalitarianism. What makes libertarian theories *libertarian* is the priority afforded to distinctive processes, procedures, or mechanisms for ensuring that liberty rights are recognized in economic practice — typically the rules and procedures governing social liberty and economic acquisition and exchange in free-market systems. Because free choice is the pivotal goal, libertarians place a premium on the principle of respect for autonomy. In some libertarian systems, this principle is the sole basic moral principle, and there thus are no unique principles of justice . . . Many philosophers believe that this approach is fundamentally wrong because economic value is generated through an essentially communal process that our health policies must reflect if justice is to be done.

Libertarian theorists, however, explicitly reject the conclusion that egalitarian patterns of distribution represent a normative ideal. People may be equal in a host of morally significant respects (for example, entitled to equal treatment under the law and equally valued as ends in themselves), but the libertarian contends that it would be a basic violation of *justice* to regard people as deserving of equal economic returns. In particular, people are seen as having a fundamental right to own and dispense with the products of their labour as they choose, even if exercise of this right leads to large inequalities of wealth in society. Equality and utility principles, from this libertarian perspective, sacrifice basic liberty rights to the larger public interest by coercively extracting financial resources through taxation.

These theories of justice all capture some of our intuitive convictions about justice, and each exhibits strengths as a theory of justice. Perhaps, then, there are several equally valid, or at least equally defensible, theories of justice and just taxation. This situation of completing and apparently viable theories has led some writers to note that there seem to be severe limits to philosophy's capacity to resolve public-policy issues through theories of distributive justice. They believe these theories are simply unsuited for public-policy formulation.

QUESTIONS:

1. Which of the competing conceptions of justice outlined in the above extract would you endorse, and on what grounds?

2. In practical terms what does it mean for like cases to be decided alike? For example, take the case of Mr Sage whose kidney dialysis was stopped by Oxfordshire Area Health authority in 1985 on the grounds that he did not have 'a sufficiently high quality of life'. Although there appeared to be an adequate supply of dialysis machines in this health authority area, the doctors involved had doubts about his life-style, which involved living rough, and his reaction to medical treatment. (See *Lancet* January 19, 1985 and S. Lee *Law and Morals*, Oxford: Oxford University Press, 1986, Chapter 10.) Does it follow that all homeless people or all single people should be regarded as like cases and thus a lower priority for dialysis treatment than those with families?

3. Brazier argues that doctors forced to choose between patients because of scarcity of resources have to resort to criteria other than clinical need, so that they inevitably have regard to non-medical, social criteria. (See M. Brazier, "Rights and Health Care" in R. Blackburn (ed) *Rights of Citizenship* London: Mansell Publishing Ltd, 1993.) Given this, should individual doctors be entrusted with such decisions? (See page 136 below for discussion of the role that might be played by ethical committees or clinical ethicists in assisting doctors to make these decisions.)

4. If you think that it is inevitable that doctors will continue to make these decisions, is there any way in which they could be trained to make 'better' and more informed decisions? (For the contested role of ethics-teaching in the education of doctors and other health professionals see D. Seedhouse, "Against medical ethics: a philosopher's view" (1991) 25 *Medical Education* 280; P. D. Toon, "After

bioethics and towards virtue?" (1993) 19 *Journal of Medical Ethics* 17; D. Seedhouse, "What I actually said about medical ethics: a brief response to Toon" (1995) 21 *Journal of Medical Ethics* 45; R. Grundstein-Amado, "Values education: a new direction for medical education" (1995) 21 *Journal of Medical Ethics* 174.)

The problem of applying abstract theories of justice to the question of allocation of scarce resources, has led some economists to propose more concrete measures.

C. Newdick, *Who Should we Treat? Law, Patients and Resources in the N.H.S.*, Oxford: Oxford University Press, pages 19–20

Health economists have begun to make a significant contribution to the way in which we consider these matters. Economics has been described as: 'the study of how men and society end up choosing, with or without the use of money, to employ scarce productive resources that could have alternative uses, to produce various commodities and distribute them for consumption among various people and groups in society. It analyses the costs and benefits of improving patterns of production'.

The question is entirely pertinent to the health service. Health economists start with the proposition that health service resources are scarce and that hard decisions between patients are unavoidable. Given the scarcity of those resources, economists ask, for example, should priority be given to the elderly, rather than the mentally ill and what criteria should be used in deciding? Should more surgical patients be treated as day patients? Should a new hospital be built? Is prevention 'better' than cure, always or just sometimes? Economics encourages us to consider an uncomfortable truth. It is all too easy in considering 'need' to assume that if a treatable condition exists, therefore (1) it should be treated and (2) it should be treated in the 'best' possible way . . . If this were accepted, this would mean that all needs should be treated and only the most effective treatments should be used. Both of these ignore the facts that resources are scarce and an overall better use of resources may be obtained from employing less effective but cheaper policies.

Economics analyses the cost-benefit implications of our decisions about treatment. Common sense says we should not always try to preserve all lives for as long as possible. In some cases it would simply be cruel to do so. What is misleadingly called 'heroic' treatment is often frowned upon for this reason. It may extend the quantity of a patient's life but, in doing so, leave him or her with such an impoverished quality of life that we would not wish upon ourselves. It is also criticised simply as a waste of money. It may deny treatment to others who could benefit from it. But the question is also asked of those for whom treatment could be effective. What about cases in which the patient could indeed benefit from treatment, but the expense involved in providing it would be so great as to deprive other patients from care?

One of the most influential economic approaches to determining priorities in health care is that of the 'quality adjusted life year' (QALY). This approach attempts to evaluate health care outcomes according to a generic scale by asking first, to what extent and for how long will a particular treatment improve the quality of a patient's life, and secondly, how much that treatment costs.

M. Lockwood, "Quality of Life and Resource Allocation" in J. M. Bell and
S. Mendus (eds), *Philosophy and Medical Welfare*, Cambridge: Cambridge
University Press, 1988, pages 36–38

The essence of a QALY is that is takes a year of healthy life expectancy to be worth
1, but regards a year of unhealthy life expectancy as worth less than 1. Its precise
value is lower the worse the quality of life of the unhealthy person (which is what
the 'quality adjusted' bit is all about). If being dead is worth zero, it is, in principle,
possible for a QALY to be negative, *i.e.* for the quality of someone's life to be
judged worse than being dead.

The general idea is that a beneficial health care activity is one that generates a
positive amount of QALYs, and that an efficient health care activity is one where
the cost per QALY is as low as it can be. A high priority health care activity is one
where the cost-per-QALY is low, and a low priority activity is one where cost-per-
QALY is high.

The assumption here is that there is some rational way of trading off length of
life against quality of life, so that one could say, for example, that three years of life
with some specified degree of discomfort, loss of mobility or whatever was worth
two years of normal life. Such tradeoffs are, of course, often inescapable in medical
practice. Take, for example, a patient suffering from larngial carcinoma, where the
choice of treatments is between laryngectomy, which is incompatible with normal
speech, but has a 60 per cent five-year survival rate, and radiotherapy, which
preserves normal speech but has only a 30–40 per cent five-year survival rate. Here,
presumably, the ethically appropriate thing for the doctor to do is put the choice to
the patient — both on the grounds of autonomy and on the grounds that the
patient is probably better able to judge, in terms of his own values and way of life,
what sort of impact on the quality of his own life the inability to speak normally is
likely to have. (For what it is worth, nearly all patients, faced with this particular
choice, in fact opt for surgery). But the resource of passing the decision back to the
individual patient is unavailable in microallocation cases, where different patients
are competing for the same resource, and would both choose to be treated, or in
macroallocation cases, where again we are dealing with different patients, this time
mainly future patients, and with questions of overall funding.

What economists who favour the QALY approach do, in a micro-allocation
context, is take a checklist of health factors that are likely to affect the perceived
quality of life of normal people, and assign weightings to them. There is, of course,
an inescapable element of arbitrariness here, both in the choice of factors to be
taken into account and in the relative weightings that are attached to them, which,
as already pointed out, would differ markedly from patient to patient. (Immobility,
for example, is likely to prove far more irksome to the athlete than to the
philosopher.) But the factors and their associated weightings are mostly so chosen
as to reflect the feelings and considered judgments which the average or representative patient is likely to evince in practice, when faced with various forms of
disability or discomfort, either in prospect or, better, having actually experienced
them. On this basis, a given form of treatment is assigned a QALY value,
corresponding to the number of QALYs such a patient can look forward to with the
treatment minus the number of QALYs the patient can look forward to if untreated.
One then calculates what each QALY gained by these means actually costs.

Whatever philosophical reservations one might have about such an exercise [. . .],
it has yielded some interesting, indeed surprising, results. In Britain there is (or
certainly was in the recent past) a widespread feeling that heart transplants
represent a wasteful use of medical resources, that the benefits yielded are simply
not sufficiently great to justify the cost. But on the other hand, people who say this
will usually argue that not enough funds are, in Britain, allocated to long-term renal

dialysis. It is widely regarded as a scandal that a treatment that is so effective in extending life should not be made universally available. Williams, evaluating these and other forms of treatment using the notion of a QALY, has come to a very different conclusion. Williams assigns to heart transplantation a QALY value of 4.5 (the point, neglected by most critics of heart transplant, being that their effect, when successful, on the quality of life is dramatic), whereas home and hospital dialysis receive QALY values of 6 and 5 respectively (the neglected point here being that, for most people, long-term dialysis represents a considerable ordeal). Nevertheless, dialysis, so far, comes out somewhat ahead of heart transplants. But now the cost per patient of long-term dialysis is considerably greater than that of a heart transplant. So the cost per QALY is only £5,000 in the case of heart transplants, as compared to £11,000 and £14,000 respectively, in the case of home and hospital dialysis.

Actually, all three figures turned out to be very high as compared with, say, hip replacement or heart value replacement and pacemaker implantation, whereas Williams assesses the cost per QALY gained as, respectively, £750, £900 and £700; in these latter operations one gets far more QALYs for one's money. In most parts of Britain there are waiting lists for all these operations; in the case of hip replacement operations the average waiting list under the National Health Service is three years (and in some areas is as high as five years) — it is not in the least unusual for people to die before they reach the head of the queue! Someone who believed that macroallocation in health care should be determined wholly on the basis of directing funds to where they can generate the maximum number of QALYs might well conclude from these figures that given a fixed health care budget, it would be rationally appropriate actually to transfer funds from such relatively high cost-per-QALY, albeit life-saving, forms of treatment as renal dialysis, to such things as hip-replacement operations, right up to the point at which the waiting lists had been eliminated — even if this meant providing no long-term dialysis at all!

QUESTIONS:

1. Given the surprising results which are produced by adopting the QALY approach do you think that it can be justified?

2. Would the application of this approach ever justify health care providers in refusing to treat a particular category of patient at all? For instance, as we shall see in Chapter 11, some English health authorities refuse to fund IVF treatment. Is this stance acceptable if one endorses the QALY approach? (For other forms of treatment which it is claimed could justly be ruled out, even if one declines to adopt the QALY approach, see R. Dworkin, "Justice in the Distribution of Health Care" (1993) 38 *McGill Law Journal* 883.)

3. Are the implications of the QALY scale ageist? Is it rational to allocate a large percentage of the NHS budget to the very old, especially as the proportion of old people in our society is increasing?

4. Does the QALY scale put those who are already disadvantaged by reason of a permanent disability or illness under a form of "double jeopardy", in that not only do they have to suffer the disability or illness, but because of it, a low priority is given in their case to forms of health care that can prolong their lives? (See J. Harris, "QALYfying the value of human life" (1987) 13 *Journal of Medical Ethics* 117; P. Singer *et al.*, "Double Jeopardy and the use of QALYs in health

care allocation" (1995) 21 *Journal of Medical Ethics* 144; J. Harris, "Double jeopardy and the veil of ignorance – a reply" (1995) 21 *Journal of Medical Ethics* 151).

An alternative to the QALY approach has been suggested in Oregon, USA.

C. Newdick, *Who Should we Treat? Law, Patients and Resources in the N.H.S.*, Oxford: Clarendon Press, 1995, pages 30–36

A variation of the principle of spreading scarce health services resources across the largest number of patients has been proposed in Oregon, USA. For those who are too poor to obtain health service insurance, Oregon receives funding from central government under the Medicaid system (like almost every other state in the Nation). However, the Medicaid grant is insufficient to cover the health care requirements of all those who fall below the relevant level of income (the federal poverty level). Rather than axe entire categories of treatment, such as dentistry and prescription medicines, a policy was devised which attempted to compile 'a list of health services, ranked by priority, from the most important to the least important, representing the comparative benefits of each service to the population to be served.' A Health Service Commission was established to undertake the task. The Commission listed services by reference to specific treatments and specific conditions (e.g. appendicitis and appendectomy). The list comprised 709 condition-treatments subdivided into seventeen general service categories which distinguished acute and chronic illness, illnesses from which complete, or only partial recovery would be expected, illnesses which cause death or disability, effective and ineffective treatment, preventive and comfort care.

. . . [C]ategories . . . were developed in which numbers 1–9 were considered 'essential' and 10–13 were designated very important'.

A separate ranking process took place within each category according to the 'net benefit' gained from specific treatment which produced a final list of over 700 procedures. The net benefit was assessed by reference to treatment outcomes and, in a very general way, public opinion as to the value of different attributes of health care. The Health Service Commission also felt obliged to add its own preference for priority treatments after it found that the results of the first list seemed perverse (*e.g.* obstetrical care was ranked low on the list and infertility treatment high.) The treatment conditions were given a score from one to zero, representing the difference between perfect health and death . . .

On this basis, given the Medicaid funds made available to provide for those without health insurance, only the first 587 treatment-conditions could be provided under the scheme. The remainder would not be made available under Medicaid . . .

Newdick concludes:

The Oregon scheme presents a number of major problems which have yet to be resolved. First, despite the list of 709 treatment conditions and a spectacular equation, the system is often too crude to differentiate sensibly between individuals. Many conditions are not included on the list and patients often present themselves with more than one condition. A patient with two conditions, only one of which was funded under the scheme, could not sensibly be treated for that complaint alone, particularly if the untreated disease were the more serious.

NOTES:

1. Whatever the problems with the Oregon plan, it does at least have the merit of taking the concept of rationing out of the closet, thus

openly inviting public scrutiny. (See D. Haldorn, "The Oregon Priority-Setting Exercise: Quality of Life and Public Policy", (1991) *Hasting Center Report* 11.)

2. It is becoming increasingly difficult to avoid dealing with the commercialisation of health care issues, however distasteful this may seem. As we shall see, the commercialisation of body parts, tissue, human gametes and embryos is an issue with which law has had to grapple. It has also moved to outlaw commercial surrogacy. (On the role of market systems within health care see N. Duxbury, "Do Markets Degrade?" (1996) 59 M.L.R. 33.)

QUESTIONS:

1. Do you think that the Oregon scheme might have the effect of expanding access to health care?
2. Can a scheme, like the Oregon Plan, which effectively excludes the poor from certain forms of medical treatment ever be regarded as just?
3. Is the language of property and contract appropriate to dealing with transactions involving body parts and products of human beings, and even potential human beings – i.e embryos, sperm and ova? (See further Chapters 11 and 15; and Duxbury, *op. cit.*)
4. In Chapter 6 we shall discuss the issue of information disclosure, and the extent to which law should compel doctors to reveal the risks of medical procedures to patients so that the patient can make an informed choice in relation to treatment. Should the patient also be fully advised of the cost of that treatment? (See M. Brazier, "Rights and Health Care" in R. Blackburn (ed.) *Rights of Citizenship* London: Mansell Publishing Ltd, 1993.)

7. LAW AND MORALITY

(a) A Framework for Thinking About Law and Morality

Questions concerning the allocation of resources also raise serious issues of law and morality. As noted at the outset of this Chapter, there are important limitations to law, which may mean that in some cases it is better not to resort to legal regulation. For example, it could be argued with regard to abortion that rather than leaving the decision in the hands of the medical profession (which is effectively the stance adopted by our law — see Chapter 12), the decision should be entrusted to the pregnant woman. The most famous jurisprudential debate concerning the limits of law occurred in the 1950s between Patrick Devlin, later to become a Law Lord, and H.L.A. Hart, professor of Jurisprudence at Oxford University. Devlin argued in *The Enforcement of Morals* (Oxford: Oxford University

Press, 1965) that there were few limits to the power of the state to legislate
where questions of morality were concerned. In his view, the suppression
of vice was as much the law's business as the suppression of treason. By
contrast, Hart argued, in *Law, Liberty and Morality* (Oxford: Oxford
University Press, 1963), in favour of J. S. Mill's contention that law was
only justified in interfering with an individual's liberty when his actions
caused harm to others.

Such debates are relevant in a health care context for four reasons. First,
in this context we frequently must define the limits of law with regard to
some very fundamental personal issues, such as whether law should
interfere with a parental decision to allow a disabled baby to die (see
Chapter 15) or with a pregnant woman's decision to terminate her
pregnancy (see Chapter 12). Secondly, in drawing these limits we have to
grapple with the question of whose morality counts. This issue can be
particularly troublesome where we are concerned with the shape that
families might take (see Chapter 11). Thirdly, given that we all have
intuitive responses to the type of issues addressed in this book, we need to
interrogate our moral intuitions in order to determine how valid they are.
A crucial issue is the extent to which one's moral intuitions would provide
a sound basis for legislation. For example, as we shall see in Chapter 11,
the Human Fertilisation and Embryology Act 1990 (which tackled some of
the most contentious moral issues in relation to the provision of infertility
treatment, abortion and embryo research) banned the creation of cross-
species hybrids, or cloning of embryos or the placing of human embryos in
an animal. Yet Lee poses the question of whether there is a rational basis
for our disgust at such activities. What is rationally wrong with the
creation, for example, of gorilla-women or the use of camels as surrogate
mothers? The fourth issue we need to confront is whether our arguments
have to be consistent across a range of moral issues. In an attempt to deal
with these issues, in the extract below Lee proposes a new framework for
considering moral issues.

S. Lee, *Law and Morals: Warnock, Gillick and Beyond*, Oxford: Oxford
University Press, 1986, pages 31–35

There is no need to wait for a generalised statement of principle with which to
analyze moral problems and the law's response thereto. If an agreed and helpful
standard existed, it might enable us to achieve consistency across time and subject
matter. But as there isn't an agreed and helpful standard, we would only be
concealing important disagreements over society's values by trying to use some
pithy formula. Instead, we need to rethink and reargue the old problems in their
new contexts. There is a danger in spending so much time on what Mill, Hart and
Devlin thought in general, that we never get round to deciding what *we* think on
particular topics . . .

I would like to offer a different framework which has evolved through discussing
law and morals with innumerable students. Whereas the harm-to-others principle
tends, in my experience, to obscure the real sources of disagreement in controversies, I have found that the separation of factual predictions and moral assumptions
helps to clarify thought.

Discussions on law and morals benefit from the attempt to locate precisely the points of dispute. These tend to be, firstly, different predictions of the consequences which would be likely to flow from the alternative courses of action proposed for the law; and secondly, different sets of moral values, or different conceptions of those values, or different weights attached to the values.

Recognition of these elements does not provide an answer to the question of what the law should do about a particular moral dilemma. But such recognition might help us to structure our own thoughts and society's decision-making procedures in an appropriate way to resolve the dispute.

An example might be the issue of violence on television and whether the law should impose censorship. Our first concern might be to argue about the consequences of allowing violence on television. Some of us might be prepared to restrict freedom of expression if a direct link to violence in the real world could be established, but might dispute that any such connection has been demonstrated. Whether or not we can reach agreement on the effect of violence on television, we then have to establish the significance we attach to broadcasters' freedom of expression as against the familiarity of our society with violence.

My emphasis on these two aspects of controversies is intended to direct us towards concentrating on the same points and explicitly on the precise issues of disagreement. Once we establish what is at stake, we can go away to research into the effects of violence on television or to think about the value of freedom of expression before returning to the fray.

Within the second area of competing moral outlooks, it is not my intention to suggest a way of resolving all controversies; but we can perhaps post some guidelines.

First, some values will usually feature in the equation on the side of restraint, namely Devlin's 'drastic' principles such as tolerance of individual liberty and respect for privacy. Second, it should be possible to trace the values on which we are relying back to some test of morality, such as the premise of utility or intuitions as to rights. These alternative bases of moralities are not themselves susceptible to 'proof' (otherwise they would not be bases, nor would all of them still be competing for our attention). Nevertheless, there is a virtue both in rationality and in appreciating its limits. Third, if we find ourselves regularly regarding certain values or interests as especially worthy of strong protection, we might call these interests 'rights'. A right exists when 'a person has a guaranteed expectation that some choice of his will be respected or some interest protected or advanced. 'Rights, in one vision of morality, are paramount considerations. Rights trump other moral values. In particular, rights will normally trump arguments based on utility or the collective good of society. They protect the individual from being sacrificed in the interests of society as a whole. But why not sacrifice an individual for the good of the rest of us? The assertion that there is a right to life or to freedom of expression, may be one moral conclusion. Yet another view might be that all such claims can be defeated by the requirements of society.

Time and again, then, the debates which follow could be represented as controversy between those who believe in rights and those who believe in utilitarianism. Believing in rights does not solve all one's moral problems. What are the specific rights and what do they require in particular circumstances? Moreover, rights may conflict with one another and a balance will have to be struck. Nor does believing in utilitarianism make moral dilemmas easily resolvable. Utilitarianism requires weighing up the happiness or pleasure caused by an action or a rule, and weighing that against the unhappiness or pain caused by it. But how can we measure happiness or pleasure, how can we compare your pleasure with my pain and how can we know what pain or pleasure will result? It is sometimes said that a rights-based approach may be all very well for one's private morality but that utilitarianism is the inevitable criterion for a public morality. Public morality has to involve compromise, give and take. It cannot deal in absolutes, especially where the law is concerned. I do not find this supposed distinction between 'private' and 'public' particularly helpful in relation to morality. Certainly, I see no reason to assume that the law should always plump for utilitarianism.

Nevertheless, there is here perhaps a warning which is of vital importance to our endeavours. Where we are trying to influence the actions of others, as through the law, we should always remember that there are certain 'rights' (for example, to privacy, liberty) or certain 'pains' (for example, the unhappiness caused by coercion restricting one's liberty) which militate against intervention. As I have tried to indicate by the alternative formulations of 'rights' and 'pains', this can be accommodated within a rights-based or a utilitarian moral code. It follows that one should never leap from the premise that something is immoral to the conclusion that it should therefore automatically be made illegal. Whether or not to make the leap is itself a moral problem and one which requires careful thought. Given that we have different moral perspectives, let alone different perceptions of the factual context and consequences, we should expect disagreement on the morality of the relationship between law and morals. I hope that the injunction to focus on predicted consequences and moral values will serve as useful way in which to clarify our thoughts.

There is one other theme on which the reader should ponder. What should we do, in our democracy, when there is disagreement about the proper legal response to a moral dilemma? Should we count up all those in favour of, and all those against, a proposal, and implement the wishes of the majority? Or should we do what is 'right', whatever the majority thinks, and if so of course, how do we determine what is right? As a final reminder before we tackle some practical problems of law and morals, we ought to analyse our own methods of analysis.

In my view, it is most helpful to recognise that these controversies can be reduced to differences of opinion on the practical effects of various options and on the morality of the conduct in question. But, traditionally, people have relied on Mill's harm-to others principle. If you cannot resist adopting that approach, I would at least stress that the important questions to ask, if Mill's principle is accepted are:

1. What is the harm?
2. Who or what is harmed?
3. How serious is that harm?
4. Are there any countervailing benefits?
5. Do those harmed need or deserve society's protection?
6. What level of protection is most appropriate, ranging from social pressure to life imprisonment for those causing the harm, bearing in mind the costs or disadvantages of such intervention?

Whichever structure one finds most useful can now form the frame-work for an examination of some controversies in law and morals. Moreover, as we reflect on each topic we should pause to examine the consistency of our moral stances. We shall begin by questioning the internal consistency of the Warnock Report [a report commissioned by the Government to consider the implication of new developments in embryology and infertility treatment, see further Chapter 11]. Then, in the context of the Gillick case [see Chapter 7], we should ask whether those who claim that parents have absolute rights over their 15-year old children are thereby committed to accepting that parents have the right to sanction experiments on their 15-day old embryos, or the right to abort their 15-week old foetuses.

But it is also important for readers to test their attitudes across the range of topics we discuss-and beyond. In relation to the Warnock Report, for example, it is obviously interesting to compare our attitudes to experimenting on early embryos with our views on aborting more mature foetuses. Less obviously, perhaps, those who condemn surrogate motherhood might ask themselves whether they are thereby condemning the use of nannies and child-minders. They might reject the analogy, or soften their attitude to surrogacy, or harden their attitude towards the practice of post-natal surrogate parenthood which affects so many more people than does the use of ante-natal nannies. Or they could reject the ideal of consistency, arguing that we hold many conflicting values which we balance in different ways. But nobody should pretend that it is easy to resolve all these dilemmas.

As we consider each problem, we should bear in mind the wise words of the Archbishop of York: ' . . . in practice most contentious ethical issues arise in the murky area where principles conflict, facts are ambiguous and differences are largely a question of degree'.

QUESTIONS:

1. Is it important to try to formulate a moral theory which will lead to one adopting a consistent approach across a range of moral issues, or is it more important to do what is morally 'right' in each particular context?

2. What are the implications of Lee's view that we should recognise that moral controversies can frequently be reduced to differences about the practical effects of the options available?

(b) The Sanctity of Life

One important moral argument has to do with the sanctity of human life. Some would claim that this is the supreme moral value. However, it is the type of argument which can be difficult to sustain across a range of issues. For example, those on the right of the political spectrum are frequently opposed to abortion but in favour of capital punishment. Are such moral positions reconcilable? You should reflect on the circumstances, if any, in which you would permit the taking of life (see Chapters 12 and 14) and also whether the ethical position you adopt in relation to issues like suicide, euthanasia and neonaticide is consistent with your standpoint on abortion (see Chapter 12) and experimentation which involves taking the lives of embryos and animals (see Chapter 10).

J. Glover, *Causing Death and Saving Lives*, Harmondsworth: Penguin 1977, pages 39, 45–46, 50–53

Most of us think it is wrong to kill people. Some think it is wrong in all circumstances, while others think that in special circumstances (say, in a just war or in self-defence) some killing may be justified. But even those who do not think killing is always wrong normally think that a special justification is needed. The assumption is that killing can at best only be justified to avoid a greater evil. It is not obvious to many people what the answer is to the question '*Why* is killing wrong?' It is not clear whether the wrongness of killing should be treated as a kind of moral axiom, or whether it can be explained by appealing to some more fundamental principle or set of principles. One very common view is that some principle of the sanctity of life has to be included among the ultimate principles of any acceptable moral system . . .

Someone who thinks that taking life is intrinsically wrong may explain this by saying that the state of being alive is itself intrinsically valuable. This claim barely rises to the level of an argument for the sanctity of life, for it simply asserts that there is value in what the taking of life takes away.

Against such a view, cases are sometimes cited of people who are either very miserable or in great pain, without any hope of cure. Might such people not be better off dead? But this could be admitted without giving up the view that life is intrinsically valuable. We could say that life has value but that not being desperately miserable can have even more value.

I have no way of refuting someone who holds that being alive, even though unconscious, is intrinsically valuable. But it is a view that will seem unattractive to those of us who, in our own case, see a life of permanent coma as in no way preferable to death. From the subjective point of view, there is nothing to choose between the two. Schopenhauer saw this clearly when he said of the destruction of the body:

'But actually we feel this destruction only in the evils or illness or of old age; on the other hand, for the *subject*, death itself consists merely in the moment when consciousness vanishes, since the activity of the brain ceases. The extension of the stoppage to all the other parts of the organism which follows this is really already an event after death. Therefore, in a subjective respect, death concerns only consciousness.'

Those of us who think that the direct objections to killing have to do with death considered from the standpoint of the person killed will find it natural to regard life as being of value only as a necessary condition of consciousness. For permanently comatose existence is subjectively indistinguishable from death, and unlikely often to be thought intrinsically preferable to it by people thinking of their own future . . .

It is worth mentioning that the objection to taking human life should not rest on what is sometimes called 'speciesism': human life being treated as having a special priority over animal life *simply* because it is human. The analogy is with racism, in its purest form, according to which people of a certain race ought to be treated differently *simply* because of their membership of that race, without any argument referring to special features of that race being given. This is objectionable partly because of its moral arbitrariness: unless some relevant empirical characteristics can be cited, there can be no argument for such discrimination. Those concerned to reform our treatment of animals point out that speciesism exhibits the same arbitrariness. It is not in itself sufficient argument for treating a creature less well to say simply that it is not a member of our species. An adequate justification must cite relevant differences between the species. We still have the question of what features of a life are of intrinsic value.

I have suggested that in destroying life or mere consciousness, we are not destroying anything intrinsically valuable. These states only matter because they are necessary for other things that matter in themselves. If a list could be made of all the things that are valuable for their own sake, these things would be the ingredients of a 'life worth living'.

One objection to the idea of judging that a life is worth living is that this seems to imply the possibility of comparing being alive and being dead. And, as Wittgenstein said, 'Death is not an event in life: we do not live to experience death.'

But we can have a preference for being alive over being dead, or for being conscious over being unconscious, without needing to make any 'comparisons' between these states. We prefer to be anaesthetized for a painful operation; queuing for a bus in the rain at midnight, we wish we were at home asleep; but for the most part we prefer to be awake and experience our life as it goes by. These preferences do not depend on any view about 'what it is like' being unconscious, and our preference for life does not depend on beliefs about 'what it is like' being dead. It is rather that we treat being dead or unconscious as nothing, and then decide whether a stretch of experience is better or worse than nothing. And this claim, that life of a certain sort is better than nothing, is an expression of our preference.

Any list of the ingredients of a worth-while life would obviously be disputable. Most people might agree on many items but many others could be endlessly argued over. It might be agreed that a happy life is worth living, but people do not agree on what happiness is. And some things that make life worth living may only debatably be to do with happiness. (Aristotle: 'And so they tell us that Anaxagoras answered a man who was raising problems of this sort and asking why one should choose rather to be born than not — "for the sake of viewing the heavens and the whole order of the universe".'.)

A life worth living should not be confused with a morally virtuous life. Moral virtues such as honesty or a sense of fairness can belong to someone whose life is relatively bleak and empty. Music may enrich someone's life, or the death of a friend impoverish it, without him growing more or less virtuous.

I shall not try to say what sorts of things do make life worth living. (Temporary loss of a sense of the absurd led me to try to do so. But, apart from the disputability of any such list, I found that the ideal life suggested always sounded ridiculous.) I shall assume that a life worth living has more to it that mere consciousness. It should be possible to explain the wrongness of killing partly in terms of the destruction of life worth living, without presupposing more than minimal agreement as to exactly what makes life worth-while.

I shall assume that, where someone's life is worth living, this is a good reason for holding that it would be directly wrong to kill him. This is what can be extracted from the doctrine of the sanctity of life by someone who accepts the criticisms made here of that view. If life is worth preserving only because it is the vehicle for consciousness, and consciousness is of value only because it is necessary for something else, then that 'something else' is the heart of this particular objection to killing. It is what is meant by a 'life worth living' or a 'worth while life'.

The idea of dividing people's lives into ones that are worth living and ones that are not is likely to seem both presumptuous and dangerous. As well as seeming to indicate an arrogant willingness to pass godlike judgements on other people's lives, it may remind people of the Nazi policy of killing patients in mental hospitals. But there is really nothing godlike in such a judgement. It is not moral judgement we are making, if we think that someone's life is so empty and unhappy as to be not worth living. It results from an attempt (obviously an extremely fallible one) to see his life from his own point of view and to see what he gets out of it. It must also be stressed that no suggestion is being made that it automatically becomes right to kill people whose lives we think are not worth living. It is only being argued that, if someone's life is worth living, this is *one* reason why it is directly wrong to kill him.

QUESTIONS:

1. Do you agree with all of Glover's conclusions?
2. How might his arguments be applied in the following cases:
   (a) withdrawal of treatment from those certified to be in a persistent vegetative state (see Chapter 14);
   (b) abortion (see Chapter 12);
   (c) medical research which involves the killing of non-human animals (see Chapter 10)?
3. When you have read the Chapters referred to in the last question, you should reflect on the following question: to what extent does our law endorse the sanctity of life principle? (See P. Singer, *Rethinking Life and Death: The Collapse of Our Traditional Ethics*, Oxford: OUP, 1995.)

(c) Who Matters Morally?

The last extract raises another important issue, which is, who counts morally? More specifically, should the interests of all living creatures count equally in making decisions and judgments in a health care context? As Lee points out, the fact that Mill ducked this crucial issue is one of the problems with his 'harm to others' formula. Who exactly counts as 'other'? Does it include the foetus who is aborted, the embryo or animal which is experimented upon, the mentally incapacitated who are denied rights to make decisions or to reproduce?

J. Harris, *The Value of Life: An Introduction to Medical Ethics*, London: Routledge and Kegan Paul, 1985, pages 7–18

The ultimate question for medical ethics, indeed for any ethics, is also in a sense the very first question that arises when we begin to grapple with moral problems. The question is simply: what makes human life valuable and, in particular, what makes it more valuable than other forms of life? . . . Ironically, many of the day-to-day decisions taken in medical practice presuppose particular answers to this question. Abortion, for example, could be permissible only in cases where there is no danger to the mother and where the foetus is normal on the assumption that it is somehow less valuable than adults, and so lacks the protection and rights that adults have . . . When we ask what makes human life valuable we are not .concerned with what might make for differences in value between individuals, but with what makes individuals of a particular kind more valuable than others . . . When we ask what makes human life valuable we are trying to identify those features, whatever they are, which both incline us and entitle us to value ourselves and one another and which license our belief that we are more valuable (and not just to ourselves) than animals, fish or plants . . . [We] need a way of recognising others as persons rather than animals, machines or collections of living human cells.

Each of us will have our own reasons for valuing our own lives and each of us is able to appreciate that the same is true of others, that they too value their own lives. What we have in common is our *capacity* to value our own lives and those of others, however different our *reasons* for doing so may be or may seem to be. I believe those rather simple, even formal features of what it takes to be a person — that persons are beings capable of valuing their own lives — can tell us a good deal about what it is to treat someone as a person. They can tell us how to recognise other beings as people, and they also tell us why it is wrong to kill such creatures against their will. They are people because they are capable of valuing life, and its wrong to kill them because they do value life . . . It is important to be clear that it is the *capacity* to value one's own life that is crucial, for of course those with the capacity to value their own lives may not in fact do so.

QUESTIONS:

1. For Harris, then, the crucial criterion for determining whose interests should count morally is the capacity to value one's own life. On Harris' account, could embryos, newborn babies, the severely mentally disabled, or animals count as persons? (See Chapters 5, 8 and 14.)

2. Can the moral status of a particular entity vary across different contexts? For example, if you argue that an embryo has rights which

would render embryo research impermissible (contrary to the stance taken by English law), does it logically follow that abortion is also impermissible? (See Chapters 10 and 12.)

(d) Acts and Omissions

A further issue which needs to be considered is how we conceptualise our moral duties and responsibilities. In particular, this begs the question whether there is a moral difference between acting and omitting to act. English law generally does not impose liability for a failure to act. For example, in the absence of a special relationship or obligation there is no duty to rescue in English law. In the leading case on withdrawal of treatment, the House of Lords in *Airedale NHS Trust v. Bland* [1993] 1 All E.R. 821 confirmed the existence of the acts/omissions dichotomy (although the thrust of their Lordships' opinions is that the distinction in practice may not be that important — see Chapter 14 at pages 842–850). Whether distinguishing between acts and omissions is morally defensible is considered in the following extract:

J. Glover, *Causing Death and Saving Lives*, Harmondsworth: Penguin, 1977, pages 92–94

Is it worse to kill someone than not to save his life? What we may call the 'acts and omission doctrine' says that, in certain contexts, failure to perform an act, with certain foreseen bad consequences of that failure, is morally less bad than to perform a different act which has the identical foreseen bad consequences.

It is worse to kill someone than to allow them to die. Philippa Foot has discussed a case which illustrates this view. She says, 'most of us allow people to die of starvation in India and Africa, and there is surely something wrong with us that we do'; it would be nonsense, however, to pretend that it is only in law that we make a distinction between allowing people in the underdeveloped countries to die of starvation and sending them poisoned food'.

Another case where our intuitive response to killing differs from our response to not striving to keep alive concerns old-age pensioners. Until the introduction of automatic regular increases, the Chancellor of the Exchequer in his annual budget normally either failed to increase the old-age pension or else put it up by an inadequate amount. In either case, it was predictable that a certain number of old-age pensioners would not be able to afford enough heating in winter, and so would die of cold. We think that the decision of such a Chancellor was not a good one, but we do not think it nearly as bad as if he had decided to take a machine-gun to an old people's home and to kill at once the same number of people.

Apart from this support the acts and omissions doctrine derives from our intuitive responses to such cases, it might be argued that to abandon it would place an intolerable burden on people. For, we may think that, without it, we would have morally to carry the whole world on our shoulders. It is arguable that we would have to give money to fight starvation up to the point where we needed it more than those we were helping: perhaps to the point where we would die without it. For not to do so would be allow more people to die, and this would be like murder. And, apart from this huge reduction in our standard of living, we should also have to give up our spare time, either to raising money or else to persuading the government to give more money. For, if a few pounds saves a life, not to raise that money would again be like murder.

Finally, it could be said that for us the acts and omissions doctrine is a 'natural' one: that it is presupposed by the way in which we use moral language. There is in our vocabulary a distinction between duties and those good acts that go beyond the call of duty. A doctor has no duty to risk his life by going from England to a plague-infested town in an Asian country at war in order to save lives there, and we do not blame him if he does not do so. If he does go, we think of him as a hero. But, if we abandoned the acts and omissions doctrine, we might have to abandon our present distinction between acts of moral duty and supererogation.

It will be argued here that we ought to reject the acts and omission doctrine. I have no formal argument to show that it is self-contradictory or in any way incoherent. I cannot show that it is a doctrine which any rational person must reject. The argument to be used is less conclusive than that. I shall present a diagnosis of why people hold the doctrine, a cluster of reasons which seem more impressive before they are separated out than after critical examination.

The acts and omissions doctrine draws its strength from the following sources:
(a) Confusion between different kinds of omission.
(b) The fact that the doctrine is itself confused with negative utilitarianism.
(c) Other factors only contingently associated with the act-omission distinction.
(d) Other moral priorities that are themselves questionable.
(e) A failure to separate the standpoint of the agent from the standpoint of the moral critic or judge.

QUESTIONS:

1. Do you agree with Glover that it is worse to kill someone than to allow them to die. Does this proposition hold in all cases? (See Chapter 14.)

2. Should our law continue to judge acts and omissions differently? (See Singer, *op. cit.*)

John Harris, *The Value of Life: An Introduction to Medical Ethics*, London: Routledge and Kegan Paul, 1985 pages 29–30

The distinction between positive and negative ways of influencing the world can be drawn in many ways, and in each case the apparent force of the distinction and the meaning of the terms may be slightly different. We can act or we can fail or omit or decline to act. We can do things, or we can forbear or neglect to do things, or we can refrain from doing them. We can sometimes make things happen, and sometimes we allow or permit or let them occur. We can set trains of events in motion, or we can fail to stop them or derail them. To emphasise just one example of the differences of meaning here, a simple *omission* to act may bear a different construction than an emphatic *neglect* of an action. To make things more complicated it is always possible (albeit with some labour and loss of elegance) to re-formulate any action description or any omission description so that each becomes the other. I can for example shoot you or fail to omit to shoot you.

For our purposes I think the best way of drawing the distinction is in terms of positive and negative responsibility, and I'll try to make clear exactly what is meant by these terms and the importance of drawing the distinction in this way. Quite simply, *where something happens, or a state of affairs obtains because someone did something, I will say that the agent is positively responsible for its occurrence; and where a particular state of affairs obtains or something happens because an agent did not do something I will say that the agent is negatively responsible for its occurrence.* For example, a piece of apparatus — a respirator — may be off and the patient connected to it dead because someone switched it off (positive responsibility) or because someone did not switch it on (negative responsibility). Of course for someone to be negatively responsible for the machine's being off it must have been *possible* for her to switch it on — she could not possibly be responsible for the occurrence of something the prevention of which would have been impossible.

So, someone will be responsible for an event or state of affairs when that event or state of affairs obtains and the agents could have so conducted themselves that the event or state of affairs did not obtain. When their conduct is positive the responsibility is positive, and when the conduct is negative the responsibility is negative.

I must make two further features of this account of the difference between positive and negative responsibility clear now, although these features will become more obvious when we turn in a moment to some examples. The first is that we can be negatively responsible for something even though it is not the case that we ought to have prevented its occurrence, or where we had no duty or contractual obligation to prevent it. I will be negatively responsible for the occurrence of something I could have prevented simply because I could have prevented it, not because I should have prevented it. The second, related qualification is that this will be the case, even where I did not know that I could have prevented the event. So where I am negatively responsible for something that I genuinely didn't realise I could prevent, I may well not be to *blame* for its occurrence, but I am still *responsible* for it.

The point of drawing the distinction in this way is to reveal what I take to be a truth about our ability to affect the World and it is simply this: that where we are able to intervene decisively, whether or not we ought to intervene, whether or not we have a duty to intervene, and even whether or not we know we can intervene, our conduct is crucial . . .

At this point, Harris offers a critique of the practice and arguments of Dr John Lorber, former professor of paediatrics at the University of Sheffield, who has written explicitly of his practice of selecting some severely handicapped neonates for an early death, while continuing to oppose active euthanasia. His opposition is based on the brutalising effects of euthanasia on those who carry it out, the fact that babies and children cannot consent to withdrawal of treatment, that stopping treatment rules out the possibility of correcting a wrong diagnosis, and that it brings into play slippery slope arguments. Harris rejects all of these arguments. (See Harris's discussion at pages 34–45 of *The Value of Life*, and H. Kuhse and P. Singer, *Should the Baby Live? The Problem of Handicapped Infants*, Oxford: Oxford University Press, 1985, pages 87–95; see also Chapter 14.) Harris concludes:

In his discussion of a doctor's duties to terminal patients, Ian Kennedy, in his stimulating *The Unmasking of Medicine* displays uncharacteristic nervousness in dealing with the distinction between positive and negative responsibility. He believes that the 'question which fascinates so many, that of when it is proper to turn off a respirator, can be shown to be one of the more simple questions to answer'. There are two strands to his solution. One is to show, quite rightly, that the crucial issue is the effect the respirator's being on has on the patient, and to argue that if that effect is deleterious the respirator should not be on. However, the nervousness emerges in his discussion of just how the respirator comes to be off. Kennedy seems to think that the moral dilemma is somehow solved if circumstances can be so arranged that the machine is off when the crucial decision is taken, rather that on. The trick is to take the patient off the respirator for some independent reason, like testing his breathing, and then to decide not to put him back on again.

If the patient's condition is so irreversibly hopeless, the doctor is entitled to desist from returning him to the respirator . . . . The ethical question thus becomes not one of turning off the respirator but rather of turning it back on again.

After showing us three separate sorts of circumstances in which this trick can be accomplished, Kennedy concludes:

'From this brief outline it can be seen that the ethically relevant decision is not whether to turn off the respirator. Rather, it is the decision whether to put the patient on the respirator, or to turn it back on again having turned it off in the light of the prognosis.'

I hope it is now clear that this cannot be the ethically relevant decision. Nothing of moral significance can hinge on whether the patient dies as a consequence of the respirator's not being turned on, rather than as a consequence of its being turned off. The ethically relevant decision is quite different. It is contained in the other strand of Kennedy's account, and it is simply 'in all the circumstances of the case is it better for this patient to be connected to the respirator or not? If the answer is 'yes' then the respirator should not be switched off or should be switched on, whichever is required to keep the patient on the machine. And if the answer is 'no' then the machine must not be switched on if it happens to be off and must be switched off if it happens to be on. Nothing can hang on the issue of whether the relevant decision is to switch off the machine or not to switch it on.

It is this conclusion that is of fundamental importance in medical care: that what matters is how our actions and decisions affect the world and other people, not whether our responsibility for the effect is positive or negative.

NOTES:

1. Another issue which is frequently raised in moral discussions, and which many would claim is as disingenuous as Harris suggests is the acts/omissions distinction, is the principle of double effect. As Harris states (*op. cit.* at page 43), this principle is often cited as explaining an important difference between positive and negative responsibility, although he questions whether it really operates on that distinction. What it does do is distinguish between consequences which are directly intended, and those which are foreseeable results of our act. For instance, although Catholic theology forbids abortion it will permit doctors to remove a cancerous womb from a pregnant woman. Although this will inevitably result in the death of the foetus, the doctor does not directly intend its death; her aim is to save the woman's life. (For another example of the doctrine, see the discussion of Arthur's Case at pages 821–822 in Chapter 14).

2. Harris goes on to point out that under the doctrine of double effect, once again, much depends upon how the action is described. He uses an example posited by the Linacre Centre:

> "Imagine a pot-holer stuck with people behind him and water rising up to drown them. And suppose two cases: in one he can be blown up; in the other a rock can be moved to open another escape route, but it will crush him to death . . . There might be people among them who seeing the consequence, would move the rock, though they would not blow up the man because that would be choosing his death as the means of escape."

Harris comments:

> "Anyone who thinks that . . . those who choose to save themselves by crushing the potholer rather than by blowing him up are those 'who show themselves as people who will absolutely reject any policy making the death of innocent people a means or end' [as the Linacre Centre had suggested] is simply and comprehensively deceiving himself."

3. The significance of the language in which we frame actions applies to much ethical debate, as all language is morally and politically loaded. For example, in the abortion debate it may be significant whether we frame the debate in terms of a clash between the rights of the potential 'mother' and her 'unborn child', or between a 'pregnant' woman and a 'foetus' (see Chapter 12). Similarly, in debates about the ethics of experimenting on embryos, it is significant that those in favour of embryo experimentation up to 14 days, coined the term 'pre-embryo' to describe the embryo of less than 14 days, thereby seeking to signify that it was of lesser value (see Chapter 10).

QUESTIONS:

1. Do you agree with Harris that both the acts/omissions doctrine and the principle of double effect are disingenuous?
2. Do you feel intuitively that Kennedy is right in suggesting that there is a valid distinction in switching off a respirator and omitting to switch one back on? If so, what force should be given to your intuition?
3. Can you think of other matters of ethical debate where the language in which it is framed may determine the outcome?

(e) Slippery Slope Arguments and Their Place in Ethical Reasoning

A further type of argument which commonly rears its head in the context of disputes about law and morality is the slippery slope (or 'thin end of the wedge') argument. For example, in the context of experimentation, proponents of the slippery slope argument claim that if we allow research on embryos up to 14 days we will eventually reach the stage of permitting research on the foetus and then on human beings; in relation to genetic screening their claim is that efforts to eliminate genetic diseases will ultimately lead to attempts to engineer the perfect baby; while in the context of euthanasia they allege that if we permit voluntary euthanasia in certain cases we will end up sanctioning involuntary euthanasia. This was one of Lorber's concerns in his debate with Harris (above). At issue here is whether these arguments are always invalid.

B. Williams, "Which Slopes are Slippery?" in M. Lockwood (ed.) *Moral Dilemmas in Modern Medicine*, Oxford: Oxford University Press, 1985, pages 126–127, 132–134

In many ethical connections, including those in which the discussion concerns what the law should be, there is a well-known argument against allowing some practice that it leads to, or is at the top of, or is on, a slippery slope. The argument is of course often applied to matters of medical practice. If X is allowed, the argument goes, then there will be a *natural progression* to Y; and since the argument is intended as an objection to X, Y is presumably agreed to be objectionable, while X is not (although of course it may be objectionable to the proponent of the argument — the slippery slope may be only one of his objections to it). The central question that needs to be asked about such arguments is what is meant by a 'natural progression'. Before coming to that, however, we need to make one or two preliminary points. First, it is worth distinguishing two types of slippery-slope argument. The first type — the *horrible result* argument — objects, roughly speaking, to what is at the bottom of the slope. The second type objects to the fact that it is a slope: this may be called the *arbitrary result* argument.

An example of *horrible result* argument is that sometimes used against *in vitro* fertilization of human ova, or at least against practices that are associated with that. IVF gives rise to extra fertilized ova, and experimentation is at least permitted, and perhaps required, on those ova. The period of time during which such experiments are allowed is limited, but (the argument goes) there is a natural progression to longer and longer such periods being permitted, until we arrive at the horrible result of experimentation on developed embryos.

All the arguments that I shall be considering use the idea that there is no point at which one can non-arbitrarily get off the slope once one has got on to it — that is what makes the slope slippery.

Arguments that belong to the first type that I have distinguished involve, in addition, the further idea that there is a clearly objectionable practice to which the slope leads.

The second type of argument, by contrast, relies merely on the point that after one has got on to the slope, subsequent discriminations will be arbitrary. Suppose that some tax relief or similar benefit is allowed to couples only if they are legally married. It is proposed that the benefit be extended to some couples who are not married. Someone might not object to the very idea of the relief being given to unmarried couples, but nevertheless argue that the only non-arbitrary line that could be drawn was between the married couples and the unmarried, and that as soon as any unmarried couple was allowed the benefit, there would be too many arbitrary discriminations to be made.

Not all cases in which a slippery slope comes in to the discussion are genuinely slippery-slope arguments. Sometimes the slope is invoked in order to express some other ground of objection. This is sometimes the case with Catholic objections to abortion. If it is said that early abortion is a slippery slope that ends in infanticide, this may be a way of expressing another objection, itself regarded as basic, to the effect that early abortion is an example of killing an innocent human being. The slippery-slope considerations are intended to make one see that point, but the point itself goes beyond them . . .

When may one rightly appeal to a process of this kind, and what are the correct conclusions to be drawn from it? The first requirement — to repeat a point that has already been made — is that it should be probable in actual social fact that such a process will occur. That requires that there should be some motive for people to move from one step to the next. Those who favour conservative policies sometimes simply assume this, perhaps because they have in mind a model of social addiction: once started in some given direction, society has, like the incipient alcoholic, an irresistible urge to go progressively further down the same path. In some cases, there certainly are reasons for thinking that the process is likely to occur. Besides the sort of examples suggested up to now, where interested parties have the same motive in relation to later cases as such parties had with earlier cases, there is also the competitive or many-party situation, supposedly exemplified by the arms race, in which each party has a reason to take the next step because some other party took the last step. The conditions for a slide can be fulfilled in various different ways, but one must try as best one may to find out whether in a given situation they will be fulfilled or not. Possible cases are not enough, and the situation must have some other feature which means that those cases have to be confronted. Suppose it is plausible that there will be a slide, and that there will be, at each stage, pressure to take the next step. What follows from that? The slippery-slope argument concludes that one should not start, and that the first case (whatever exactly that may be) should not be allowed, on the ground that after the first step there is nowhere to stop. In terms of the paradox, the argument wants us not to let premiss (1) above be true. But there is an obvious alternative. Granted that we are now considering cases in which a definite rule or practice is needed, which can be applied to any case and does not rely on what I called earlier 'restricted judgement', we have the alternative of sharpening the normative predicate in question, and drawing a sharp line between cases that are allowed and cases that are not. In terms of the paradox, the effect will be that premiss (2), the induction step, is falsified: for some n, we shall have decided that F applies to $0[n]$ but not to $0[n + 1]$. We lay down a maximum length of pregnancy for abortion, a number of days during which experiments on a fertilized ovum are permitted, a minimum age for admission to certain sorts of films, and so on.

Is drawing a line in this way reasonable? Can it be effective? The answer to both these questions seems to me evidently to be 'yes, sometimes', and as that unexciting reply suggests, there is not a great deal to be brought to deciding them beyond good sense and relevant information. It may be said that a line of this kind cannot possibly be reasonable since it has to be drawn between two adjacent cases in the range — that is to say, between two cases that were not different enough to distinguish. The answer is that they are indeed not different enough to distinguish, if that means that their characteristics, unsupported by anything else, would have led one to draw a line there. That follows from the conjunction of three things. First, it is reasonable to distinguish in some way unacceptable cases from acceptable cases; secondly, the only way of doing that in these circumstances is to draw a sharp line; thirdly, it cannot be an objection to drawing the line just here that it would have been no worse to draw it somewhere else — if that were an objection, one could conclude, by cumulation, that one had no reason to draw it anywhere, a path that leads to the grave of Buridan's ass (which allegedly starved through indecision, when placed between two equally attractive bales of hay). In practice, of course, the point at which the line is drawn is often chosen because it is salient in some way. Moreover, and significantly, it is rarely set directly in terms of the characteristic that the argument is about (development of a foetus, emotional maturity of a film-goer), but is based rather on something else (a date, an age) which can be clearly established and is roughly correlated with the relevant characteristics. This makes it all the clearer that it is not the precise merits of one rather than another step in the range that is in question when the line is drawn.

The proposed line may be unreasonable on some other ground, but it is not so merely because it is this kind of line. Whether it will be effective is another question. If it is less effective than the alternative of allowing no cases at all, that will be because of special circumstances, such as those in which there is a consensus for allowing no cases, if that is all that can be achieved, but no consensus for anything else. Equally familiar, on the other hand, is the situation in which there is a consensus for allowing something rather than nothing, and a further consensus gradually emerges about what is to be allowed — formed, perhaps, as a result of action taken in advance of any consensus.

QUESTION:

1. Can you think of other areas, aside from embryo experimentation, abortion, genetic engineering or euthanasia, where slippery slope arguments are commonly employed? Using William's criteria, do slippery slope arguments have any validity in that context?

A recurring theme in slippery slope arguments is the spectre of Naziism. In the 1920s and 1930s, in Germany, Hitler's regime embarked on the programme which was to lead to the Holocaust, by sterilising and experimenting upon those who were considered 'unfit'. Hence, arguments against research on human embryos (see Chapter 10) or the sterilisation of mentally handicapped women (see Chapter 13) frequently invoke the image of Nazi death camps to suggest that permitting such actions now, will inevitably lead to such an end. The Nazi programme was partially based on the theory of eugenics, which, having been discredited by the Nazi experience, is now beginning to creep back into ethical discourse.

S. Trombley, *The Right to Reproduce: A History of Coercive Sterilization*, London: Weidenfeld and Nicolson, 1988, page 2

The term [eugenics] was coined by Sir Francis Galton in 1883 to describe the use of genetics to 'improve' the human race. The assumption was made that disease and 'defect' (not only mental or physical defects, but drunkenness, criminality, immorality, etc.) were inherited. Eugenists ignored the fact that poor environmental conditions might be contributory factors or the cause of phenomena such as learning disabilities. Indeed, many eugenists went so far as to say that poor environments were actually the *result* of genetic deficiency.

Eugenics fell into two categories: positive and negative. *Positive eugenics* was concerned with identifying the carriers of the best genetic material and encouraging their mating and high rate of reproduction. *Negative eugenics* was concerned with curbing the fertility of the 'unfit' in order to reduce the incidence of defect in the population. Two solutions to this problem were offered by negative eugenics. One was the *segregation* of defective persons under controlled conditions in which they were not allowed to reproduce. This was the model which encouraged the growth of hospitals, colonies and asylums in the U.S. and Britain.

The second solution was *sterilisation*. As with segregation, the use of sterilization was based on the assumption that most socially undesirable characteristics were hereditary, and that control of the fertility of the unfit would lead to a brave new world of, if not perfect, at least 'normal' persons. Through sterilisation, not only would disease and defect be eradicated, but social problems such as alcohol and drug abuse, prostitution, crime and so on might also be solved. Sterilisation would also obviate the need for segregation of the unfit who, if deprived of the right to reproduce, could be assumed to present a limited danger to society.

NOTES:

1. Eugenics has a long history, which is not confined to Nazi Germany. It was a popular theory in Britain and the United States in the early years of this century, and many sterilisation operations on the

mentally incompetent were performed in the United States (See S. Trombley, *op. cit.*). Although it was discredited as a result of the Nazi experience, some commentators would argue that it is a factor in decisions authorising the sterilisation of mentally incompetent women and girls in Britain, despite the fact that the courts have been quick to deny this (see Chapter 13 at pages 754–772). Moreover, arguments about eugenics have surfaced as a result of amendments to the Abortion Act 1967 (see Chapter 12 at pages 713–718) and in the context of neonaticide. Indeed, it could be argued that there now exists a third solution to the problem of the unfit, which involves sanctioning neonaticide in the case of seriously handicapped infants (see Chapter 14).

2. Those who advocate eugenics must be working on the basis of an implicit idea of what the norm is. As Ian Kennedy points out (at pages 137–138 below), choosing what is the norm is a matter of social and political judgment.

QUESTIONS:

1. Could the introduction of reproductive techniques which permit fertilisation to occur outside the body and thus open the process up to medical supervision and control (see Chapter 11), revitalise the notion of positive eugenics?
2. Are late abortions performed on the grounds of foetal handicap justifiable according to any of the theories so far discussed?

8. A FEMINIST APPROACH TO ETHICS?

The extracts so far considered have relied heavily upon the discourse of justice and rights. It is worth noting that most of the commentators have been male. Yet many of the issues addressed in this book, particularly in relation to reproductive choices (see Chapters 11–13) are issues which traditionally have been feminist concerns. Women continue to be under-represented in the upper echelons of the medical profession, the judiciary and in Parliament, and on government committees such as the Warnock Committee. (Although it should be noted that in the composition of the Human Fertilisation and Embryology Authority, introduced to regulate the provision of infertility treatment services, gender is a factor to be taken into account — see Chapter 11). The involvement of women in decision-making processes is highly important, if, as some feminists contend, women and men reason in significantly different ways. This proposition has led feminist scholars to suggest that the language of rights, justice, autonomy and choice which we have discussed in this Chapter pertains to essentially 'male' concepts which have little relevance to the way in which women reason and conceptualise problems. The leading exponent of this thesis is psychologist Carol Gilligan. Her book, *In a Different Voice* (Cambridge, Mass: Harvard University Press, 1982) has had a significant impact on the development of feminist ethical theories. (See, for instance, M. J. Larrabee (ed.), *An Ethic of Care*, London: Routledge, 1993.) The implications of Gilligan's approach for the development of a feminist theory of ethics is considered in the following extract.

S. Sherwin, "Ethics, 'Feminine Ethics', and Feminist Ethics" in D. Shogan (ed.), *A Reader in Feminist Ethics*, Toronto: Canadian Scholar' Press Inc., 1993, pages 16–23

Feminist ethics is different from feminine ethics. It derives from the explicitly political perspective of feminism, wherein the oppression of women is seen to be morally and politically unacceptable. Hence, it involves more than recognition of women's actual experiences and moral practices; it incorporates a critique of the specific practices that constituted their oppression. Nevertheless, it is not altogether separate from what I have termed 'feminine ethics'.

In my view, feminist ethics must recognize the moral perspective of women; insofar as that includes the perspective described as an ethics of care, we should expand our moral agenda accordingly. Feminists have reason, however, to be cautious about the place of caring in their approach to ethics; it is necessary to be wary of the implications of gender traits within a sexist culture. Because gender differences are central to the structures that support dominance relations, it is likely that women's proficiency at caring is somehow related to women's subordinate status.

Within dominance relations, those who are assigned the subordinate positions, that is, those with less power, have special reason to be sensitive to the emotional pulse of others, to see things in relational terms, and to be pleasing and compliant. Thus the nurturing and caring at which women excel are, among other things, the survival skills of an oppressed group that live in the close contact with its oppressors.

Just as the gender associations that Gilligan identified have developed in a particular historical context, the attitudes that Ruddick described as maternal thinking reflect the usual experience of mothering in Western, middle-class life, where a socially and economically defined nuclear family is assumed to be the norm. We should be wary of assuming gender-based dichotomies of moral thought too readily, whatever their empirical origin; such dualisms perpetuate assumptions of deep difference between men and women and limit our abilities to think creatively about genuinely gender-neutral ethical and power structures.

Another danger inherent in proposals for feminine ethics is that caring about the welfare of others often leads women to direct all their energies toward meeting the needs of others; it may even lead them to protect the men who oppress them. Hence, feminists caution against valorising the traits that help perpetuate women's subordinate status.

Within the existing patterns of sexism, there is a clear danger that women will understand the prescriptions of feminine ethics to be directing them to pursue the virtues of caring, while men continue to focus on abstractions that protect their rights and autonomy. Although Gilligan sees the two perspectives of moral reasoning as complementary, not competitive, and believes that both elements must be incorporated into any adequate moral view, it is easy to read her evidence as entrenching the gender differences she uncovers. In a society where the feminine is devalued and equated with inferiority, it is not easy to perceive men embracing a moral approach described as feminine. Because the world is still filled with vulnerable, dependent persons who need care, if men do not assume the respon-sibilities of caring, then the burden for doing so remains on women.

Nonetheless, despite its politically suspect origins, caring is often a morally admirable way of relating to others. Feminists join with feminine ethicists in rejecting the picture that male stream ethicists offer of a world organized around purely self-interested agents — a world many women judge to be an emotionally and morally barren place that we would all do well to avoid. Feminists perceive that the caring that women do is morally valuable, but most feminists believe that women need to distinguish between circumstances in which care is appropriately offered and those in which it is better withheld. Therefore, an important task of feminist ethics is to establish moral criteria by which we can determine when caring should be offered and when it should be withheld.

Feminist ethics also takes from feminine ethics its recognition that personal feelings, such as empathy, loyalty, or guilt, can play an ethically significant role in moral deliberations. I think, however, that the proponents of abstraction are right to insist that there are limits to the place of caring in ethics. We should guard against allowing preferences, especially those tied to feelings of personal animosity, from being granted full range in ethical matters. For example, it would not be appropriate to decide to withdraw life support from a patient because she has been aggressive, complaining, and uncooperative, and hence her care givers do not like her. Although there is something morally abhorrent about the obligation to make moral decisions without regard for the effect on loved ones, there is also great danger in believing we are only responsible for the interests of those for whom we feel affection. Morality must include respect for sentiments, but it cannot give full authority to particular sentiments without considering both their source and their effects. Because feminism arises from moral objections to oppression, it must maintain a commitment to the pursuit of social justice; that commitment is not always compatible with preferences derived from existing relationships and atti-tudes. Hence we must recognize that feminist ethics involves a commitment to considerations of justice, as well as to those of caring. . . .

[F]eminist ethics shares with feminine ethics a rejection of the paradigm of moral subjects as autonomous, rational, independent, and virtually indistinguishable from one another; it seems clear that an ontology that considers only isolated, fully developed beings is not adequate for ethics. We must reconceive the concept of the individual, which has been taken as the central concept of ethical theory in Western thought. People have historical roots; they develop within specific human contexts, and they are persons, to a significant degree, by virtue of their relations to others like themselves. We value persons as unique individuals as the central unit of analysis, however, without considering that persons only exist in complex, social relationships. Unless we recognize that a person's desires, needs and beliefs are formed only within human society, we may mistakenly imagine ourselves and our interests to be independent from others and their interests. . . .

From a feminist perspective, one can see clearly the significance of the social situation of persons to moral deliberations. In place of the isolated, independent, rational agent of traditional moral theory, feminist ethics appeals to a more realistic and politically accurate notion of a self as socially constructed and complex, defined in the context of relationships with others. Moral analysis needs to examine persons and their behaviour in the context of political relations and experiences, but this dimension has been missing so far from most ethical debates.

In this regard, feminism seems closely allied with communitarianism, another recent response to the abstract, liberal vision of contractarian theories. . . .

Most important, feminist ethics is characterized by its commitment to the feminist agenda of eliminating the subordination of women — and of other oppressed persons — in all of its manifestations. The principal insight of feminist ethics is that oppression, however it is practised, is morally wrong. Therefore, moral considerations demand that we uncover and examine the moral injustice of actual oppression in its many guises. When pressed, other sorts of moral theorists will acknowledge that oppressive practices are wrong but such general declarations are morally inadequate in the face of insidious systematic oppression. If we want moral change and not mere moral platitudes, then the particular practices that constitute oppression of one group by another must be identified and subjected to explicit moral condemnation; feminists demand the elimination of each oppressive practice.

In practice, the constraints imposed by feminist ethics mean that for instance, we cannot discuss abortion purely in terms of the rights of foetuses, without noticing that foetuses are universally housed in women's bodies. We cannot discuss the acceptability of institutionalizing patients for mental illness without noting that women are far more likely to be diagnosed as mentally ill than are men. Any morally adequate discussion of such practices must come to terms with the fact that the resulting social policy will have profound implications on the lives of women. Feminist ethics demands that the effects of any decision on women's lives be a feature of moral discussion and decision-making.

In its appeal to contextual features, feminist ethics resists the model of traditional ethics, wherein the principal task is to define a totalizing or universal theory that prescribes rules for all possible worlds. Feminist ethics focuses instead on the need to develop a moral analysis that fits the actual world in which we live, without worrying about the implications of these considerations in some radically different set of circumstances. That is not to say that feminist ethics involves no concern with principles. It encompasses theories that are committed to concerns about social justice, because it demands criticism of the various patterns of dominance, oppression, and exploitation of one group of persons by another. Concern about justice, however, cannot be adequately defined in the abstract. To speak meaningfully about justice, it is necessary to examine the actual forces that undermine it, as well as those that support it.

Feminism is not, however, solely interested in issues of oppression. It is also concerned with the possibilities of women's agency, despite their oppression. . . .

I label this approach 'feminist ethics' and not simply 'ethics', because only feminists (male and female) have really concerned themselves with the details of oppression. The leading moral theorists in the mainstream tradition have not only failed to object to the oppression of women; they have often actively contributed to its perpetuation. They legitimized the subjection of women by insisting on women's moral, rational, and epistemological inferiority. Hence the ethical systems they proposed are not only inadequate but also morally wrong, because they promote behaviour and relationships that are morally reprehensible. In a world where women are systematically oppressed, an adequate ethics must address that oppression. Feminist ethics, in making explicit the moral offense of sexism and illuminating some of its many forms, is the only approach to ethics that lives up to this obligation.

In keeping with the insights of Annette Baier and Virginia Held and many other commentators, both male and female, I do not envision feminist ethics to be a comprehensive, universal, single-principle theory that can be expected to resolve every moral question with which it is confronted. It is a theoretical perspective that must be combined with other considerations to address the multitude of moral dilemmas that confront human beings. What feminist ethics claims is that oppression is a pervasive and insidious moral wrong and that moral evaluation of practice must be sensitive to questions of oppression, no matter what other moral considerations are also of interest. Such analysis requires an understanding not only of the nature of oppression in general but also of the nature of specific forms of oppression.

I believe that anyone with a genuine interest in ethics should be interested in the connections between specific practices and the patterns of dominance in society. I recognize that not all ethics will be persuaded to become thoroughgoing feminists, in the sense of adopting a version of feminism as a world view and a way of life; not every ethicist will wish to become involved in political activism. Nevertheless, I think all ethicists can and should include discussions of racism, anti-Semitism, heterosexualism, and so on. Although very little of the literature in ethics addresses the issue of sexism or any other form of systematic oppression, surely the responsibility to do so in one's moral evaluations is implicit. Feminist ethics has assumed leadership in pursuing such analysis.

In the following extract, Sherwin demonstrates how feminist ethics could inform and reform medical ethics.

S. Sherwin, "Feminist and Medical Ethics: Two Different Approaches to Contextual Ethics" in H. Bequaert Holmes and L. M. Purdy, *Feminist Perspectives in Medical Ethics*, Bloomington and Indianapolis: Indiana University Press, 1992

For medical ethics to be thought feminist, it must also reflect a political dimension, but this is mostly lacking in the literature to date. Although there are currently many diverse attempts to characterize feminist ethics, all share some political analysis of the unequal power of women and men, of white people and people of colour, of first world and third world people, of rich and poor, of healthy and disabled, etc. Ours is a world structured by hierarchies and a sense of supremacy on the part of the powerful; there are numerous social patterns which shape the people we are and the sorts of relationships we will have with one another. In attending to the quality of actual interactions among people in ethics, we need to account for the influence of social and political factors on the nature of those relationships. From either the caring or the justice perspective (to use Gilligan's language), we can see that empowerment of people who are currently victims of oppression is an ethical as well as a political issue, and ethical investigations of particular problem areas should reflect these dimensions. Many feminist critics have observed that current medical practice constitutes a powerful social institution which contributes to the oppression of women. They have demonstrated that the practice of medicine serves as an important instrument in the continuing disempowerment of women (and members of other oppressed groups) in society and thrives on hierarchial power structures. By medicating socially induced depression and anxiety, medicine helps to perpetuate unjust social arrangements. With its authority to define what is normal and what is pathological and to coerce compliance to its norms, medicine tends to strengthen patterns of stereotyping and reinforce existing power inequalities. It serves to legitimize practices such as woman battering or male sexual aggression that might otherwise be evaluated in moral and political terms.

Nonetheless, the discussion in medical ethics to date has been largely myopic, failing to comment on this important political role of medicine. That is, the institution of medicine is usually accepted as given in discussion of medical ethics, and debate has focused on certain practices within that structure: for example, truth-telling, obtaining consent, preserving confidentiality, the limits of paternalism, allocation of resources, dealing with incurable illness, and matters of reproduction. The effect is to provide an ethical legitimization of the institution overall, with acceptance of its general structures and patterns. With the occasional exception of certain discussions of resource allocation, it would appear from much of the medical ethics literature that all that is needed to make medical interactions ethically acceptable is a bit of fine-tuning in specific problem cases.

A good indication of the legitimizing function of medical ethics can be seen by noting its gradual acceptance among those who are influential within the medical profession. Increasingly, medical practitioners seem to be recognizing the value of incorporating discussions of medical ethics within their own work, for they can thereby demonstrate their serious interest in moral matters. Such serious professional concern in matters of medical ethics serves to encourage the public to place even greater trust in their judgment. Keeping the scope of medical ethics narrowed to specific problems of interaction helps physicians maintain their supportive stance towards it.

Feminists must be critical of the fact that medical ethics has remained largely silent about the patriarchal practice of medicine. Few authors writing on medical ethics have been critical of practices and institutions that contribute to the oppression of women. The deep questions about the structure of medical practice and its role in a patriarchal society are largely inaccessible within this framework, they are not considered part of the standard curriculum in textbooks of medical ethics. Consequently, medical ethics, as it is mostly practiced to date, does not amount to a feminist approach to ethics.

There are other important differences, as well. Feminist theory has gone beyond medical ethics in the criticism of traditional ethics by re-conceiving some of the central concepts of ethical theory. It has, for instance, provided grounds for rejecting an ontology of persons conceived as isolated, fully developed individuals. Rather, it acknowledges the social roots of a person as a being who develops within a specific social context and who is, to a significant degree, a product of that context. Although we may continue to consider the individual to be a key unit of ethical analysis to the extent that we value persons as unique individuals whose lives are of concern to us, most feminists reject the assumption of individualism underlying contractarian approaches to ethics through which individuals are encouraged to consider themselves and their interests as independent from others. Persons do not exist in abstraction (*i.e.*, not apart from their social circumstances), and moral directives to disregard the details of personal life under some imaginary "veil of ignorance" [as Rawls advocated] are actually pernicious for ethical and political analysis because of their trivialisation of these important facts. Moral analysis should examine persons and their behaviour in the context of political relations and experiences, but this dimension has so far being missing from most of the debates in medical ethics.

NOTES:

1. Gilligan suggests that caring is an ethic which is generally devalued in our society, with the result that girls who adopt an "ethics of care" are frequently seen as lacking in moral development when compared with boys of the same age, whom she claims adopt an ethics of justice. Some commentators have argued, along similar lines, that caring is insufficiently valued within a health care context, which treats nurses and midwives as mere handmaidens to doctors, and pays them accordingly.

2. One particular way in which the different voices might manifest themselves in a health care context is suggested by Stefan. She argues that women figure disproportionately highly amongst those who are deemed by doctors and the legal system to be incompetent (see Chapter 5). She suggests that although the concept of capacity, and its application, appears to be gender neutral, women who wish to refuse medical treatment are more likely than men to be deemed to lack capacity. She also suggests that in legal judgments women are more likely to be portrayed as unreflective, emotional and immature.

(You should assess whether this is true of the judgments in cases involving the competence of young girls discussed in Chapter 7, see S. Stefan, "Silencing the Different Voice: Competence, Feminist Theory and the Law" (1993) 47 *University of Miami Law Review* 763.)

3. In the second of the above extracts Sherwin refers to the view that medicine serves as an important social institution which contributes to the oppression of women. Not only is this reflected in the traditional low status accorded to nurses, but also in the fact that in the United Kingdom women have been relatively invisible in the debate about the major changes going on in the NHS. (See L. Doyal, "Changing Medicine? Gender and the politics of health care" in J. Gabe, D. Kelleher and G. Williams, *Challenging Medicine* London: Routledge 1994.)

QUESTIONS:

1. Does the development of the hospice movement and schemes for helping patients with AIDS suggest that caring is beginning to be more highly valued in the health profession? (See N. James, "From Vision to System: The Maturing of the Hospice Movement" in R. Lee and D. Morgan (eds.) *Death Rites: Law and ethics at the end of life*, London: Routledge, 1994.)

2. Do you agree with the suggestion that there are different masculine and feminine ways of thinking? Does Gilligan's analysis suggest that women might be especially well-suited to particular roles within the health care profession? For example, might it be true that women make better nurses?

3. Do you agree with Sherwin that there are limits to the place of caring in ethics and that it is therefore important for feminist ethics to establish criteria for when caring should be withheld as well as when it should be offered? Or should caring be unconditional? Should *all* ethical theories establish when caring should be offered/withdrawn? How might this apply in the context of withdrawing treatment? (See Chapter 14.)

4. Can Sherwin's vision of feminist ethics work, or is it necessary to have a 'comprehensive, universal, single-principle' theory?

The last question raises the issue of how we select a theory of ethics to govern our own judgments of whether decisions and actions in a health care context are ethical. Beauchamp and Childress offer the following tests which an ethical theory should satisfy, although they caution that no one theory fully satisfies all of the following tests.

T. L. Beauchamp and J. F. Childress, *Principles of Biomedical ethics*, (4th ed.) New York: Oxford University Press, 1994, pages 45–47

Criteria for Theory Construction

We begin with eight conditions of adequacy for an ethical theory. These proposals for theory construction set forth exemplary conditions for theories, but not so exemplary that a theory could not satisfy them. That all available theories only partially satisfy the demands in these conditions is not of concern here. The objective is to provide a basis from which to assess the defects and the strengths of theories. Satisfaction of these conditions protects a theory from criticism as a mere list of disconnected norms generated from our pretheoretic beliefs. The same general criteria of success in a moral theory can be used for any type of theory (for example, a scientific theory or a political theory). The eight conditions that follow express these criteria.

1. *Clarity.* First, a theory should be as clear as possible, as a whole and in its parts. Although we can expect only as much precision of language as is appropriate, more obscurity and vagueness exists in the literature of ethical theory and biomedical ethics than is necessary or justified by the subject matter.

2. *Coherence.* Second, an ethical theory should be internally coherent. There should be neither conceptual inconsistencies (for example, "strong medical paternalism is justified only by consent of the patient") nor contradictory statements (for example, "to be virtuous is a moral obligation, but virtuous conduct is not obligatory"). Ralph Waldo Emerson dismissed a foolish consistency as "the hobgoblin of little minds, adored by little statement and philosophers and divines." However, consistency is not a *sufficient* condition of a good theory, only a *necessary* condition. If an account has implications that are incoherent with other established parts of the account, some aspect of the theory needs to be changed in a way that does not produce further incoherence. . . .[A] major goal of a theory is to bring into coherence all its various normative elements (principles, rights, considered judgments, etc.).

3. *Completeness and Comprehensiveness.* A theory should be as complete and comprehensive as possible. A theory would be entirely comprehensive if it included all moral values. Any theory that includes fewer moral values will be somewhere on a continuum from partially complete to void of important values. Although the principles presented in this book under the headings of respect for autonomy, nonmaleficence, beneficence, and justice are far from a complete system for general normative ethics, they do, when specified, provide a sufficiently comprehensive general framework for *biomedical* ethics. We do not need additional principles such as promise keeping, avoiding killing, keeping contracts, and the like. However, we draw on our principles to help justify rules of promise keeping, truthfulness, privacy, and confidentiality, among others . . . and these norms increase the system's comprehensiveness by specifying commitments in the fundamental principles.

4. *Simplicity.* If a theory with a few basic norms generates sufficient moral content, then that theory is preferable to a theory with more norms but no additional content. A theory should have no more norms than are necessary, and no more than people can use without confusion. However, morality is complicated, and any comprehensive moral theory will be immensely complex. We can demand only as much simplicity in a moral theory as its subject matter permits.

5. *Explanatory Power.* A theory has explanatory power when it provides enough insight to help us understand the moral life; its purpose, its objective or subjective status, how rights are related to obligations, and the like.

6. *Justificatory Power.* A theory should also give us grounds for *justified* belief, not a reformulation of beliefs we already possess. For example, the distinction

between acts and omissions underlies many critical beliefs in biomedical ethics, such as the belief that killing is impermissible and allowing to die permissible. But a moral theory would be impoverished if it only expressed this distinction without determining whether the distinction justifiably grounds those beliefs. A good theory also should have the power to criticize defective beliefs, no matter how widely accepted those beliefs may be.

7. *Output power.* A theory has output power when it produces judgments that were not in the original data base of particular and general considered judgments on which the theory was constructed. If a theory did no more than repeat the list of judgments thought to be sound prior to the construction of the theory, nothing would have been accomplished. For example, if the parts of a theory pertaining to obligations of beneficence do not yield new judgments about role obligations of care in medicine beyond those assumed in constructing the theory, this failure of output suggests that the theory is purely a classification scheme. A theory, then, must generate more than a list of the axioms present in pretheoretic belief.

8. *Practicability.* A proposed moral theory is unacceptable if its requirements are so demanding that they probably cannot be satisfied or could be satisfied by only a few extraordinary persons or communities. A moral theory that presents utopian ideals, paltry expectations, or unfeasible recommendations fails the criterion of practicability. For example, if a theory proposed such high requirements for personal autonomy . . . or such lofty standards of social justice. . . that, realistically, no person could be autonomous and no society could be just, the proposed theory would be deeply defective.

Other general criteria could be formulated, but the eight sketched above are the most important for our purposes. A theory can receive a high score on the basis of one criterion and a low score on the basis of another. For example, early in this chapter utilitarianism is depicted as an internally coherent, simple, and comprehensive theory with exceptional output power, yet it is not coherent with some of our vital considered judgments, especially with certain judgments about justice, human rights, and the importance of personal projects. By contrast, Kantian theories are consistent with many of our considered judgments, but their clarity, simplicity, and output power are limited.

A contested and appropriately criticized moral theory may nonetheless be defensible in light of the criteria we have proposed. Although we currently have no perfect or even best moral theory, several good theories are available.

NOTE:

1. In this Chapter we have been moving from a consideration of different ethical theories at a rather abstract level to their application in the form of practical decisions that must be made every day by health care providers. In the last extract Beauchamp and Childress concede that no one ethical theory can satisfy all of their tests, and indeed each of the authors endorses a different theory. However, this poses the interesting issue of whether conflicting theories can be reconciled in practice if different professionals on the same health care team follow different theories.

QUESTIONS:

1. Which of the theories considered in this chapter do you think best fulfils the criteria of Beauchamp and Childress? Is it necessary to

select one theory to guide one's intuitions, decisions and actions in relation to the provision of health care? Would it be justifiable to apply different theories to help resolve different problems?

2. The Glover Commission discussed how rights-based theories might ultimately converge with utilitarianism, thus suggesting that there may be no clear demarcation between them. Could it be argued that this is true of all ethical theories?

9.   A New Forum for Ethical Decision-Making

The problems of decision-making and policy formulation in a health care context have led many commentators to propose that we should establish a special commission to oversee these issues at a national level.

S. Lee, "Re-Reading Warnock" in P. Byrne (ed.), *Rights and Wrongs in Medicine*, King Edward's Hospital Fund for London, 1986, pages 47–50

Medical law and ethics is all the rage . . . Unfortunately we have no one suitable forum for structuring debate, educating a fascinated public and providing authoritative guidance on these vital issues.

The Courts, for instance, can only provide a sporadic *ex post facto* review of problems, depending on the vagaries of litigation, nor is the traditional English court procedure appropriate to consider the vast amount of scientific, medical, moral and economic evidence which is germane to, say, the question of allocating kidney dialysis machines. The long-running *Gillick* saga illustrates another disadvantage of course: as appeal follows appeal there is often confusion and uncertainty.

The Warnock committee could have been a more encouraging model but . . . it was only an ad hoc body, set up to consider a particular set of issues and now disbanded. Over two years the committee built up some expertise in the area and received evidence from some 250 organisations and about 700 members of the public. Its report, however flawed, has stimulated great debate and interest. A record two million people have been spurred to sign a petition in favour of a private member's bill (albeit one opposing the Warnock majority view).

What we need now is a Super-Warnock: a permanent body to keep under review the whole range of issues in medical law and ethics. Given time, such a body would be able to produce suggested codes of practice covering areas such as *in vitro* fertilisation, treatment of the young, allocation of scarce resources within the NHS and the requirements of a sensible doctrine of informed consent.

Within its own narrow field, Warnock saw the need for such an authority. Indeed the committee regarded the establishment of a new statutory authority with advisory and executive functions as 'by far the most urgent' of its recommendations.

The *raison d'etre* of its executive licensing function might well disappear if Parliament eventually bans all experiments on embryos. Nevertheless we should rescue the advisory, monitoring role and expand it to cover all the questions of medical ethics which so concern us.

It may be unfashionable to suggest new quangos but very occasionally this is just what is required. A permanent advisory committee would fulfil a need which forms of surrogate quangohood (such as the courts, administrative fiats and ad hoc committees) cannot satisfactorily meet.

Who would oppose such a body? The government would no doubt balk at large expenditure on a secretariat so the new quango might have to rely initially on the existing infrastructure of research for some of its information. Nevertheless, the government seems ready to accept the principle behind Warnock's proposed authority. The medical establishment might be tempted to oppose the quango but any legitimacy in that position has been undermined by their reluctant approval of Warnock's licensing body. Doctors and researchers would have accepted that as the price for public acquiescence in their experiments. The public, however, may seize on that concession, while refusing to allow experiments, in order to create a more general review body which would be in everyone's interests, helping patients and doctors alike, by extensive and expert consideration of their ethical dilemmas.

What would the new quango do? Ignoring the specific references to *in vitro fertilisation*, Warnock's explanation is a good one: 'We believe it should issue general guidance, to those working in the field, on good practice . . . and on the types of research which . . . it finds broadly ethically acceptable. It should also offer advice to Government on specific issues as they arise, and be available to Ministers to consult for specific guidance. As part of its responsibility to protect the public interest, it should publish and present to parliament, an Annual Report'.

Who would be on the committee? Warnock again has the answer. 'The new body will need access to expert medical and scientific advice. We would therefore envisage a significant representation of scientific and medical interests among the membership. It would also need to have members experienced in the organisation and provision of services. However, this is not exclusively, or even primarily, a medical or scientific body. It is concerned essentially with broader matters and with the protection of the public interest. If the public is to have confidence that this is an independent body, which is not to be unduly influenced by sectional interests, its membership must be wide-ranging and in particular the lay interests should be well represented.' Within the term 'lay', I would include experts in medical law and ethics.

Until recently the USA had such a quango — the inelegantly titled but otherwise admirable President's Commission for the Study of Ethical Problems in Medicine and Biomedical and Behavioral Research. Building on that model we could surely construct an institution which was able to tackle the important task of establishing codes of practice on medical ethics in a systematic and informed way. Above all, we need to have guidelines *before* doctors and researchers face the moral dilemmas directly and this is an area where, as we have seen, 'both medical science and opinion within society may advance with startling rapidity'. Although much of the Warnock report is rightly being criticised, the committee did have the beginnings of a good idea in recommending an advisory body. That suggestion should be developed. It would be a tragedy if the embryo of a much-needed innovation is thrown out with the Warnock bath water.

NOTE:

1. Brazier has noted that investigation of ethical issues by such a multi-disciplinary Commission must be pro-active rather than reactive, and suggests that issues to be considered (such as the implications of our growing ability to screen for genetic disease) ultimately refer back to central issues to do with autonomy and parental rights, so that the primary role of such a commission would be to define the fundamental rights and obligations in health care. (See M. Brazier, *Medicine, Patients and the Law* (2nd ed.), Harmondsworth: Penguin, 1992 at pages 747–9.)

QUESTION:

1. Should such a Commission be centrally funded by the Government and charged with over-seeing all ethical developments in health care, as Brazier and Lee suggest, or is it better to have small and independent *ad hoc* committees which review specific areas?

Although no central Commission of the type envisaged by Brazier and Lee exists, there are a number of influential bodies which aim to shape public debate on how law should respond to health care issues. One of the most influential is the Law Commission — a statutory law reform body for England and Wales established in 1965:

"to take and keep under review all the law with which [it is] concerned with a view to its systematic development and reform, including in particular the codification of such law, the elimination of anomalies, the repeal of obsolete and unnecessary enactments, the reduction of the number of separate enactments and generally the simplification and modernisation of the Law". (Law Commissions Act 1965, section 3(1).)

The Law Commission has been involved in proposing reforms of health care law; for example on mental incapacity (see Chapter 5) and consent in the criminal law (see Chapter 6). It was also largely responsible for certain legislative enactments such as the Congenital Disabilities (Civil Liability) Act 1976 (see Chapter 13).

Parliamentary bodies may also be established to report on particular issues. A recent example is the report of the House of Lords Select Committee on Euthanasia (see Chapter 15). Additionally, a number of non governmental bodies exist to examine issues of particular ethical difficulty. For example, the Nuffield Council on Bioethics establishes committees which have recently reported on genetic screening (see Chapter 10) and human tissue (see Chapter 14), while the Kings Fund has undertaken and commissioned research in the area of health policy, notably in relation to compensation for victims of medical accidents and concerning shortages in the supply of organs for transplantation (see Chapter 15). It is noteworthy that reports issued by both Nuffield and the Kings Fund draw on expertise from a number of disciplines. This demonstrates that legal reform cannot be isolated from wider considerations of ethics, health policy, economics and sociology. The policy debates may also be informed by input from groupings of academics in these fields. Prominent amongst such recent developments is the United Kingdom Forum — a grouping of lawyers, health care practitioners and ethicists with an interest in biomedical ethics.

10.   PROFESSIONAL ETHICS

Although the existence of multi-disciplinary ethical decision-making has been widely applauded, traditionally ethical guidance has been in the hands of the professional bodies which regulate health care professionals, which have generally sought to make such guidance available in professional codes of practice. This tradition stems from the Hippocratic Oath — one version of which is extracted below:

The Hippocratic Oath

I swear by Apollo the Physician and Asclepius and Hygieia and Panaceia and all the gods and goddesses, making them my witnesses, that I will fulfil according to my ability and judgment this oath and this covenant:

To hold him who has taught me this art as equal to my parents and to live my life in partnership with him, and if he is in need of money to give him a share of mine, and to regard his offspring as equal to my brother's in male lineage and to teach them this art — if they desire to learn it — without fee and covenant; to give a share of precepts and oral instruction and all the other learning to my sons and to the sons of him who has instructed me and to pupils who have signed the covenant and have taken an oath according to medical law, but to no one else.

I will apply dietetic measures for the benefit of the sick according to my ability and judgment; I will keep them from harm and injustice.

I will neither give a deadly drug to anybody if asked for it, nor will I make a suggestion to this effect. Similarly I will not give to a woman an abortive remedy. In purity and holiness I will guard my life and my art.

I will not use the knife, not even on sufferers from stone, but will withdraw in favour of such men as are engaged in this work.

Whatever houses I may visit, I will come for the benefit of the sick, remaining free of all international injustice, of all mischief and in particular of sexual relations with both female and male persons, be they free or slaves.

What I may see or hear in the course of the treatment or even outside of the treatment in regard to the life of men, which on no account one must spread abroad, I will keep to myself holding such things shameful to be spoken about.

If I fulfil this oath and do not violate it, may it be granted to me to enjoy life and art, being honoured with fame among all men for time all to come; if I transgress it and swear falsely, may the opposite of all this be my lot.

NOTES:

1. For discussion of the broader Hippocratic tradition see J. Montgomery, "Medical Law in the Shadow of Hippocrates" (1989) 52 M.L.R. 566. As Thompson points out, although doctors like to boast of the historical tradition of medical ethics stretching back over more than 2000 years to Hippocrates (about 420 BC), examination of this tradition shows the oath was never universally subscribed to and its tradition has actually been confused and discontinuous. He argues that the oath only re-emerged as the basis of medical codes of practice in the nineteenth century, and that it represented a self-conscious attempt to invest medicine with a respectable image based in an ethical tradition going back to the Greeks. (See I. E. Thompson, "Fundamental ethical principles in health care" (1987) 295 BMJ 1461; and also R. M. Veatch, *A Theory of Medical Ethics* New York: Basic Books, 1981, Chapter 1.)

2. Although not all medical students do now swear the Hippocratic oath it has continued to exert an influence on conceptions of ethical

practice, and has been the foundation for many newer codes of ethics. The Hippocratic Oath has been superceded by modern international declarations such as the Declaration of Geneva (amended 1968) and the International Code of Medical Ethics. (See appendices to J. K. Mason and R. A. McCall Smith, *Law and Medical Ethics* (4th ed.), London: Butterworths, 1994; R. Gillon, *Philosophical Medical Ethics*, Chichester: John Wiley & Sons, 1985, Chapter 2).) Recently there has been evidence of a Hippocratic Oath comeback movement.

3. As Beauchamp and Childress point out, whilst professional codes are beneficial if they effectively incorporate defensible moral norms, some professional codes oversimplify moral requirements or claim more completeness and authority than they are entitled to. The result may be that professionals mistakenly suppose that they satisfy all moral requirements if they obediently follow the rules laid down in the code. (See T. L. Beauchamp and J. F. Childress, *Principles of Biomedical Ethics* (4th ed.), New York: Oxford University Press, 1994 at pages 6–8.)

4. There may also be a tendency on the part of the courts to rely too heavily on codes of professional conduct. Certainly, in the leading British case on confidentiality, the Court of Appeal accorded great weight to the GMC guidelines on confidentiality. (See *W. N. v. Egdell* [1990] 1 All E.R. 835, discussed in Chapter 9 below.)

QUESTION:

1. How far do you think professional codes are truly concerned with ethics rather than simply maintaining professional privileges and decorum? Do they simply specify rules of etiquette and responsibilities to other members of the profession?

The General Medical Council is the professional body of doctors and its current guidance to the medical profession was issued in October 1995.

GMC, Duties of a Doctor *(October 1995)*

Providing a good standard of practice and care

1. Patients are entitled to good standards of practice and care from their doctors. Essential elements of this are professional competence, good relationships with patients and colleagues and observance of professional ethical obligations.

Good clinical care

2. You must take suitable and prompt action when necessary.
   This must include:

- an adequate assessment of the patient's condition, based on the history and clinical signs including, where necessary, an appropriate examination;

- providing or arranging investigation or treatment where necessary;
- referring the patient to another practitioner, when indicated.

3. In providing care you must:

- recognise the limits of your professional competence;
- be willing to consult colleagues;
- be competent when making diagnoses and when giving or arranging treatment;
- keep clear, accurate and contemporaneous patient records which report the relevant clinical findings, the decisions made, information given to patients and any drugs or other treatment prescribed;
- keep colleagues well informed when sharing the care of patients;
- pay due regard to efficacy and the use of resources;
- prescribe only the treatment, drugs, or appliances that serve patient's needs.

Treatment in emergencies

4. In an emergency, you must offer anyone at risk the treatment you could reasonably be expected to provide.

Keeping up to date

5. You must maintain the standard of your performance by keeping your knowledge and skills up to date throughout your working life. In particular, you should take part regularly in educational activities which relate to your branch of medicine.
6. You must work with colleagues to monitor and improve the quality of health care. In particular, you should take part in regular and systematic clinical audit.
7. Some parts of medical practice are governed by law. You must observe and keep up to date with the laws which affect your practice.

Teaching

8. The GMC encourages you to help the public to be aware of and understand health issues and to contribute to the education and training of other doctors, medical students and colleagues.
9. All doctors should be prepared to supervise less experienced colleagues.
10. If you have special responsibilities for teaching you should develop the skills of a competent teacher. If you are responsible for training junior colleagues you must make sure they are responsibly supervised

Professional relationships with patients

11. Successful relationships between doctors and patients depend on trust. To establish and maintain that trust you must:

- listen to patients and respect their views;
- treat patients politely and considerately;
- respect patient's privacy and dignity;
- give patients the information they ask for or need about their condition, its treatment and prognosis;
- give information to patients in a way they can understand;
- respect the right of patients to be fully involved in decisions about their care;
- respect the right of patients to refuse treatment or to take part in teaching or research;
- respect the right of patients to a second opinion;

- ask patients' permission, if possible, before sharing information with their spouses, partners, or relatives;
- be accessible to patients when you are on duty;
- respond to criticisms and complaints promptly and constructively.

12. You must not allow your views about a patients' lifestyle, culture, belief, race, colour, sex, sexuality, age, social status, or perceived economic worth to prejudice the treatment you give or arrange.

13. If you feel that your beliefs might affect the treatment you provide, you must explain this to patients, and tell them of their right to see another doctor.

14. You must not refuse or delay treatment because you believe that patients' actions may have contributed to their condition, or because you may be putting yourself at risk.

15. Because the doctor-patient relationship is based on trust you have a special responsibility to make the relationship with your patients work. If the trust between you and a patient breaks down either of you may end the relationship. If this happens, you must do your best to make sure that arrangements are made promptly for the continuing care of the patient. You should hand over records or other information for use by the new doctor as soon as possible.

Working with colleagues

23. You must not discriminate against colleagues, including doctors applying for posts, because of your views of their lifestyle, culture, beliefs, race, colour, sex, sexuality or age.

24. You must not make any patient doubt a colleague's knowledge or skills by making unnecessary or unsustainable comments about them.

Working in teams

25. Health care is increasingly provided by multi-disciplinary teams. You are expected to work constructively within such teams and to respect the skills and contributions of colleagues.

26. If you are leading a team, you must do your best to make sure that the whole team understands the need to provide a polite and effective service and to treat patient information as confidential.

27. If you disagree with your team's decision, you may be able to persuade other team members to change their minds. If not, and you believe that the decision would harm the patient, tell someone who can take action. As a last resort, take action yourself to protect the patient's safety or health.

Arranging cover

30. You must be satisfied that, when you are off duty, suitable arrangements are made for your patients' medical care. These arrangements should include effective handover procedures and clear communication between doctors.

31. General practitioners must satisfy themselves that doctors who stand in for them have the qualifications, experience, knowledge and skills, to perform the duties for which they will be responsible. A deputising doctor is accountable to the GMC for the care of patients while on duty . . . .

Decisions about access to medical care

33. You should always seek to give priority to the investigation and treatment of patients solely on the basis of clinical need . . .

Conflicts of interest

39. You must act in your patients' best interests when making referrals and providing or arranging treatment or care. So you must not ask for or accept any inducement, gift or hospitality which may affect or be seen to affect your judgment. You should not offer such inducement to colleagues.

40. If you have financial or commercial interests in organisations providing health care or in pharmaceutical or other biomedical companies, these must not affect the way you prescribe for or refer patients.

Code of Professional Conduct for the Nurse, Midwife and Health Visitor, Third edition, originally published as Code of Professional Conduct for the Nurse, Midwife and Health Visitor, by the United Kingdom Central Council for Nursing, Midwifery and Health Visiting (June 1992)

- Each registered nurse, midwife and health visitor shall act, at all times, in such a manner as to:
- safeguard and promote the interest of individual patients and clients;
- serve the interest of society;
- justify public trust and confidence and
- uphold and enhance the good standing and reputation of the professions.

As a registered nurse, midwife or health visitor, you are personally accountable for your practice and, in the exercise of your professional accountability, must:

1. act always in such a manner as to promote and safeguard the interests and well being of patients and clients;
2. ensure that no action or omission on your part, or within your sphere of responsibility, is detrimental to the interests, condition or safety of patients and clients;
3. maintain and improve your professional knowledge and competence;
4. acknowledge any limitations in your knowledge and competence and decline any duties or responsibilities unless able to perform them in a safe and skilled manner;
5. work in an open co-operative manner with patients, clients and their families, foster their independence and recognise and respect their involvement in the planning and delivery of care;
6. work in a collaborative and co-operative manner with health care professionals and others involved in providing care, and recognise and respect their particular contributions within the care team;
7. recognise and respect the uniqueness and dignity of each patient and client, and respond to their need for care, irrespective of their ethnic origin, religious beliefs, personal attributes, the nature of their health problems or any other factor;
8. report to an appropriate person or authority, at the earliest possible time, any conscientious objection which may be relevant to your professional practice;
9. avoid any abuse of your privileged relationship with patients and clients and of the privileged access allowed to their person, property, residence or workplace;
10. protect all confidential information concerning patients and clients obtained in the course of professional practice and make disclosures only with consent, where required by the order of a court or where you can justify disclosure in the wider public interest;
11. report to an appropriate person or authority, having regard to the physical, psychological and social effects on patients and clients, and circumstances in the environment of care which could jeopardise standards of practice;

12. report to an appropriate person or authority any circumstances in which safe and appropriate care for patients and clients cannot be provided;
13. report to an appropriate person or authority where it appears that the health or safety of colleagues is at risk, as such circumstances may compromise standards of practice and care;
14. assist professional colleagues, in the context of your own knowledge, experience and sphere of responsibility, to develop their professional competence, and assist others in the care team, including informal carers, to contribute safely and to a degree appropriate to their roles;
15. refuse any gift, favour or hospitality from patients or clients currently in your care which might be interpreted as seeking to exert influence to obtain preferential consideration and
16. ensure that your registration status is not used in the promotion of commercial products or services, declare any financial or other interests in relevant organisations providing such goods or services and ensure that your professional judgement is not influenced by any commercial considerations.

NOTES:

1. On the legal significance of codes of conduct issued by a professional body, and the role which such codes play in ensuring accountability, see Chapter 4.
2. Thompson argues that health care professions other than medicine have recently begun to promulgate their own codes of practice, which may be seen as mimicking medicine, both in terms of seeking professional credibility and respectability by 'professing' a code of ethics and by asserting principles in the Hippocratic tradition. However he notes that nursing and social work codes endorse a much more explicit recognition of patient rights. (See I. E. Thompson, "Fundamental ethical principles in health care" (1987) 295 BMJ 1461.) (The issue of legally regulating complementary medicine is addressed in J. Stone and J. Matthews, *Complementary Medicine and the Law*, Oxford: OUP, 1996.)
3. A further possible source of guidance to health care professionals would be to follow the North American example and introduce institutional ethics committees, which have existed in hospitals in the United States for the last fifteen or so years. The role of these committees is primarily advisory. They are not intended to interfere with the clinical decisions of health professionals, and their decisions are not binding on health professionals. They may, however, issue advice on policy issues and on decision-making in individual cases. Thus, they may play a valuable role in facilitating decision-making by health professionals and ensuring that it is informed. (See A. McCall Smith, "Committee Ethics? Clinical Ethics Committees and their Introduction in the United Kingdom" (1990) 17 *Journal of Law and Society* 124.)
4. Another recent development in North America has been the introduction of a third party intermediary in the making of health care decisions, in the form of a clinical ethicist. This individual will

typically have a legal, medical, or philosophical background and have undertaken postgraduate study in bioethical theory. She may work as a sole practitioner advising in the clinical situation, or as a participant on a hospital ethics committee. (See J. V. McHale, "The clinical ethicist, a brave new decision maker?" (1991) 7 *Professional Negligence* 128.)

QUESTIONS:

1. Which of the extracts from the above codes do you consider provides the better ethical guidance to health professionals? What criteria did you use in assessing the value of these codes? (Note that the UKCC also issues extensive guidance on their code: see, for instance, pages 140–141 below.)
2. Overall, what do you think is the best method of regulating health care professionals? If you opt for legal regulation over self-regulation by the profession, what form of law should be used? Is statute law preferable, or does the incremental, pragmatic growth of the common law (judge-made law) provide certain advantages in this sphere?
3. What qualifications, if any, do judges have for making decisions in a health care context?

11. THE ROLE OF HEALTH CARE PROFESSIONALS

The power of the medical profession to promulgate codes of ethics may be seen as particularly problematic because of the deference society accords to doctors. One of the most vexed questions with which health care law has to grapple concerns the power differential which exists between health care providers and patients. Their training and experience equips health professionals, with knowledge and information pertaining to the patient and his condition, which the patient lacks. These issues will be addressed in the Chapters on consent and confidentiality which deal with the question of how much information a doctor is compelled to disclose to the patient. In the extract below, Kennedy discusses the authoritative role which we, as a society, have conferred upon doctors.

I. Kennedy, *The Unmasking of Medicine*, London: Allen & Unwin, 1981, pages 7–8, 10–11, 16

[I]llness, a central concept of medicine, is not a matter of objective scientific fact. Instead, it is a term used to describe deviation from a notional norm. So, a choice exists whether to call someone ill. The choice depends upon the norm chosen and this is a matter of social and political judgement. As the great American scholar Oliver Wendell Holmes remarked, at the end of the nineteenth century, "the truth is that medicine, professedly founded on observation, is as sensitive to outside influences, political, religious, philosophical, imaginative, as is the barometer to the changes of atmospheric density". Ordinarily there will be widespread agreement about what objective facts, what physical states are appropriately described as abnormal. But this does not belie the fact that there is an inherent vagueness in the term "illness". And this is only the beginning. Even when it has been decided that the physical conditions warrant the description "abnormal", there is still the second step. They have to be *judged* to be an illness. An evaluation has to take place.

This should cause us to pause. Who does the evaluating? What are the values involved? Does this mean that the vagueness we previously noticed is compounded? Does this mean that the concept of illness can be manipulated, that it has no clear and certain boundaries? We began with the cosy assumption that illness was a descriptive term, applied to a set of objective facts. It appears now that illness is an indeterminate concept, the product of social, political and moral values, which, as we have seen, fluctuate. The implications of this will strike you immediately. If illness is a judgement, the practice of medicine can be understood in terms of power. He who makes the judgment wields the power.

Let me explain what follows from this . . . The treatment of illness is for the doctors. A social institution has grown up defined and managed by doctors, the role of which is to persuade us that our preoccupations must be related to them, and them alone (since they alone have competence).

We appear, perforce, naked both physically and emotionally. However willing we may be, and however well intentioned the doctor, it is hard to overstate the power which this vests in the doctor. It is hard to overstate how such a social arrangement may undermine the notion of individual responsibility and of course, ultimately, individual liberty.

Michael Foucault, a contemporary French philosopher, captures the point perfectly, as Richard Sennett makes clear in his review in the *New Yorker* of Foucault's most recent book, *The History of Sexuality*. Foucault, writes Sennett, argues that "in the modern world all too often there is no clear line between concern for the welfare of others and coercive control of their lives. A new kind of power relationship has arisen in modern society," he goes on. "Authorities who understand our bodies have gained the right to make and enforce rules about morality." The nature of the power relationship is seen in terms of confession, now to medical rather than priestly "authorities". In the past the person who confessed furnished the raw data, the confessor the meaning, and so it is today, according to Foucault.

Interpretation and with it judgment and prescription become the preserve of authority, since, knowing what we do not know about ourselves, doctors acquire the right to show us how to behave. Let me take this further. So far, I have mentioned only the interplay between illness and morality. A far more significant interplay exists on a political and social plane. Just because illness is associated with objective facts, it appears that illness *is* those facts, that illness is a thing. But, as we have seen, illness is not a thing, it is a judgemental term. Being ill is not a state, it is a status, to be granted or withheld by those who have the power to do so. Status connotes a particular position in society, assumed only after satisfying others that certain conditions have been observed.

The conclusion exists that illness is a spurious scientific term and that the doctor in purporting to determine its existence as an objective fact is engaged in a series of moral, social and political choices which we permit him to make. Of course, many doctors find the position they are in most unsavoury. Frequent protests led the Department of Health to change the form of the sickness note in 1976. But the basic system remained and with it the power. The doctor is engaged in a process of socialisation, of ensuring that the prevailing social and political attitudes and values are reinforced and are adhered to by those who, by their behaviour, may be seen as potential deviants. For, as Muir Gray puts it, "deviance is not a property inherent in certain forms of behaviour: it is a property conferred upon these forms by the audience which witnesses them" . . .

In conclusion, I am not saying that we should abandon the use of the word "illness". I am merely urging that we understand what it involves. Since the diagnosis of illness always calls for a judgement, it is right for us all to consider when it is properly to be applied and who should apply it. We should consider what limits may properly be placed by us on the power of doctors to manipulate the concept. I am not suggesting that we take a vote. But we must make it our business to ensure that the judgements arrived at reflect the considered views of all of us. Each diagnosis is an ethical decision.

NOTES:

1. The power differential which Kennedy highlights is particularly crucial in certain situations. A good illustration of this process is where a health professional is attempting to assess a patient's capacity to consent to or refuse treatment (see Chapter 5). Stefan has commented of this situation:

   "Although competence is a matter of a dynamic or dialogue between doctor and patient. . . legal doctrine sets up this dialogue so that the powerful half of the conversation remains entirely invisible. In most of these situations, the. . . doctor raising the question of competence describes only the client's or patient's inability to communicate. . . his perspective is transformed into an authoritative account of the client's incapacity. . . Competence assessments are not a matter of communication between equals or even between two individuals, but rather are communication between an individual and a professional representing a system that has power over that individual. . . Often competence is raised as an issue when a less powerful person questions a more powerful person's version of reality." (See S. Stefan, "Silencing the Different Voice: Competence, Feminist Theory and Law" (1993) 47 *University of Miami Law Review* 763 at pages 783–4.)

2. The authority which our society has conferred on doctors would appear to be reflected in the way in which medical law is constructed to emphasise the primacy of the relationship between the doctor and the patient. In the cases discussed throughout this book you will note that it is rare for nurses, midwives or other health professionals to be the central players in caselaw (some of the few exceptions are examined in Chapter 12 on abortion). The doctor's authority is also reflected in the traditional hierarchial power structure within the health care team which provides treatment and care, where nurses and other health care providers are traditionally viewed as the handmaidens of doctors. (See J. Montgomery, "Doctors' handmaidens: the legal contribution" in S. McVeigh and S. Wheeler, *Law, Health and Medical Regulation*, Aldershot: Dartmouth, 1992; T. Murphy, "Bursting Binary Bubbles: Law, Literature and the Sexed Body" in J. Morison and C. Bell (eds) *Tall Stories? Reading Law and Literature*, Aldershot: Dartmouth 1996.) However, this relationship is now changing in recognition of the contribution made by all members of a multi-disciplinary health-care team to the care of the patient, and the changing role of the nurse as practitioner. (See J. Montgomery, "Medicine, Accountability and Professionalism" (1989) 16 *Journal of Law and Society* 319.)

QUESTIONS:

1. Do you think that deferential attitudes to doctors are now changing?
    If so, in what ways are such changes manifested? (See further
    Chapters 3 and 4 on professional accountability.)
2. In what ways do you think the doctor's power to manipulate the
    concept of illness could be limited? Would it be desirable to limit her
    power in these ways?

12. CONSCIENTIOUS OBJECTION

Thus far in this Chapter we have considered how ethical theories may
impact upon the health professional's decision-making and the extent to
which professional codes of practice may guide those decisions. The
remaining thirteen Chapters consider in detail how law regulates such
health care decisions. However, like her patients, the health care professional will have her own values which may influence her health care
practice. Formal legal rights of conscientious objection are limited. Currently they are only found in two statutes — the Abortion Act 1967 (see
Chapter 12) and the Human Fertilisation and Embryology Act 1990 (see
Chapter 11). If the doctor does have conscientious objection to providing
these services, her obligation is to refer the patient to another doctor. (For
the position of other health professionals see Chapter 12.) However,
notwithstanding the statutory right to conscientious objection in such cases
some health practitioners have claimed that refusal to participate in the
provision of such services may affect promotion prospects.

United Kingdom Central Council for Nursing, Midwifery and Health
Visiting, *Guidelines for professional practice* (1996)

Conscientious objection
    46. In today's developing health service, you may find yourselves in situations
which you find very uncomfortable. There may be many circumstances in which a
practitioner, due to personal morality or religious beliefs, will not wish to be
involved in a certain type of treatment or care. Clause 8 of the Code of Professional
Conduct states that:

> "As a registered nurse, midwife or health visitor, you are personally accountable
> for your practice and, in the exercise of your professional accountability, must
> . . . report to an appropriate person or authority, at the earliest possible time,
> any conscientious objection which may be relevant to your professional
> practice;"

    47. In law, you have the right conscientiously to object to take part in care in
only two areas. These are the Abortion Act (Scotland, England, and Wales), which
gives you the right to refuse to take part in an abortion, and the Human
Fertilisation and Embryology Act 1990, which gives you the right to refuse to
participate in technological procedures to achieve contraception and pregnancy.

48. However, in an emergency, you would be expected to provide care. You should carefully consider whether or not to accept employment in an area which carries out treatment or procedures to which you object. If, however, a situation arises in which you do not want to take part in a form of treatment or care, then it is important that you declare your objection in time for managers to make alternative arrangements. In certain circumstances this may mean providing counselling for the staff involved in these decisions. You do not have the right to refuse to take part in emergency treatment.

49. Refusing to be involved in the care of patients because of their condition or behaviour, in unacceptable. The UKCC expects all registered practitioners to be non-judgmental when providing care. This is one of the issues addressed by clause 7 of the code, which states that:

"As a registered nurse, midwife or health visitor, you are personally accountable for your practice and, in the exercise of your professional accountability, must . . . recognise and respect the uniqueness and dignity of each patient and client, and respect their need for care, irrespective of their ethnic origin, religious beliefs, personal attributes, the nature of their health problems or any other factor;"

NOTES:

1. In considering the position of doctors who have a conscientious objection to *withholding* treatment which the patient has refused, the Law Commission was of the view that there was no need for special provision to cater for this — the law clearly states that a valid refusal of treatment must be respected (see Chapters 5 and 6).

2. Objections to providing (or withholding) treatment are most likely to arise where the doctor and patient have different value and belief systems. In a multi-cultural society such clashes of values may be expected to occur with increasing frequency. (See D. Pearl, "Legal issues arising out of medical provision for ethnic groups" in A. Grubb and M. J. Mehlman (eds) *Justice and Health Care: Comparative Perspectives*, Chichester: John Wiley & Sons, 1995; L. Doyal, "Needs, Rights and the Duty of Care Towards Patients of Radically Different Cultures" in K. W. M. Fulford, *et al*, *Essential Practice in Patient-Centred Care*, Oxford: Blackwell Science, 1996).

QUESTIONS:

1. Should there be greater statutory provision allowing health professionals to conscientiously object to certain medical procedures? For example, should nurses be required to participate in nursing a patient in a persistent vegetative state from whom treatment has been withdrawn? (See Chapter 14.)

2. Should any form of sensitivity to being involved in distressing procedures be allowed to ground a right to conscientious objection?

3. Given that the Abortion Act 1967 does not extend to Northern Ireland, but that at common law abortion has now been declared to be lawful in certain circumstances in that jurisdiction (see Chapter

12) could there be an implied right for a doctor to conscientiously object to performing an abortion in Northern Ireland (provided that it was not an emergency)?

SELECT BIBLIOGRAPHY

T. Beauchamp and L. Walters, *Contemporary Issues in Bioethics*, Belmont, California: Wadsworth Publishing Co., 1989.

T. Beaumont and J. Childress, *Principles of Biomedical Ethics*, Oxford and New York: Oxford University Press, 1994.

L. Doyal and L. Doyal (eds), *Legal and Moral Dilemmas in Modern Medicine*, Oxford: Blackwells, 1990.

R. Dworkin, "Justice in the Distribution of Health Care" (1993) 38 *McGill Law Journal* 883.

R. Gillon, *Philosophical Medical Ethics*, Chichester: John Wiley & Sons, 1985.

J. Glover, *Causing Death and Saving Lives*, Harmondsworth: Penguin, 1977.

J. Harris, *The Value of Life: An Introduction to Medical Ethics*, London: Routledge and Kegan Paul, 1985.

H. Bequaert Holmes and L. M. Purdy (eds.), *Feminist Perspectives in Medical Ethics*, Bloomington and Indianapolis: Indiana University Press, 1992.

I. Kennedy, *The Unmasking of Medicine*, London: Allen & Unwin, 1981.

P. Komesaroff (ed.), *Troubled Bodies: Critical Perspectives on Postmodernism, Medical Ethics and the Body*, Durham and London, Duke University Press, 1995.

P. Singer, *Rethinking Life and Death: The Collapse of Our Traditional Ethics*, Oxford: OUP, 1995.

S. Lee, *Law and Morals: Warnock, Gillick and Beyond*, Oxford: Oxford University Press, 1986.

M. Lockwood (ed.) *Moral Dilemmas in Modern Medicine*, Oxford: Oxford University Press, 1985.

C. Newdick, *Who Should We Treat? — Law, Patients and Resources in the N.H.S.*, Oxford: Oxford University Press, 1995.

R. M. Veatch, *A Theory of Medical Ethics* New York: Basic Books, 1981.

PART II

PART II

INTRODUCTION

This part considers the accountability of health professionals for their actions. Over the past decade continuing concern has been evidenced by the health professions, particularly the medical profession, as to the growth of a "malpractice crisis". Individuals dissatisfied with the treatment given are, it is alleged, increasingly likely to take their claims to court. One consequence of the rise in claims has been that in certain areas where litigation is likely due to the type of clinical practice involved defensive medicine is practised. One further dimension is that the cost of litigation has led to funds being diverted from the health care budget with a consequent reduction of what are already limited resources. Concern regarding litigation has led to the growth of what is known as "risk management" practices in an attempt to reduce where possible the risk of adverse incidents.

While the courts may, at first sight, appear to provide the most effective method of ensuring the accountability of professionals, on closer inspection difficulties are apparent. Litigation is expensive, litigants are less likely today to be able to avail themselves of state assistance when bringing legal proceedings due to cuts in the legal aid budget. Moreover, it is claimed that the scales are weighted in favour of the medical profession. Where it is alleged that conduct is negligent the standard of care is to be ascertained by reference to what is known as the "professional practice standard" or the *Bolam* test, *Bolam v, Friern Hospital Management Company* [1957] 2 All E.R. 118. Health professionals will not generally be held to be negligent as long as they comply with a standard supported by a responsible body of professional practice, even though other health care practitioners may disagree with that approach. Even if the conduct of a health professional can be shown to have fallen short of the *Bolam* test the litigant may still fall at the hurdle of causation because he cannot establish that it was the negligent conduct of the defendant which caused the harm which he suffered. Chapter 3 examines these issues, considers how satisfactory this system is, and to what extent there is any scope for reform.

The judicial system provides one potential means of ensuring accountability. The primary aim of a tort action is to provide compensation, not to administer punishment. Professional misconduct which is grossly negligent may result in a criminal prosecution and indeed there has been increasing use of the criminal law over the last few years. Nevertheless, such prosecutions make up only a tiny fraction of all situations of alleged misconduct by health professionals.

There are, however, many cases in which the misconduct alleged is not grave or where the patient does not have compensation as his primary concern. This does not mean that the health professional should not be held accountable for her actions. In such situations investigating an alleged harm suffered may have a number of perceived advantages. It may provide a patient with an explanation of precisely what happened in that particular situation. It may identify problems in the structure of the provision of care and thus lead to changes in the delivery of care for patients as a whole. We noted in chapter 1 the expectations of patients raised by the Patients' Charter. The Charter states that the patient has the right to:

> "have any complaint about NHS services (whoever provides them) investigated and to get a quick, full written reply from the chief executive or general manager."

A new NHS complaints system was introduced in April 1996. This followed a wide ranging examination of the complaints process by a government appointed committee, the Williams Committee, whose report *Being Heard* was published in 1994 (DoH: 1994). We consider this system in Chapter 4 below.

The expectation of accountability in the context of health complaints may be seen as partly the result of the increasing perception of the patient as consumer. Accountability through knowledge is the result of an operational complaints system. But it may also lead to accountability in the form of disciplinary proceedings being brought by an employer if adverse findings are made against a health professional. Health professionals may also be the subject of practices of audit and accreditation.

Further systems of accountability are provided through systems of professional self-regulation. Health professionals are, almost invariably, subject to a professional ethical code. In Chapter 2 above, we considered the nature of such codes. It is worthy of note that the obligations placed upon health professionals by their ethical codes and those of their employers may diverge, raising difficult issues in relation to the interests of patients.

In Chapter 4 below we examine the scope of professional self-regulation and the role of professional discipline where, for instance, codes of conduct are broken, taking the General Medical Council as a case study.

This part provides a "snapshot" of the structures of accountability. The present system is undergoing considerable change. It may be too early to say as to what extent accountability will be truly facilitated by recent developments in professional practice and NHS structure.

3

PROFESSIONAL ACCOUNTABILITY I

1. INTRODUCTION

There has been a rise in "claims consciousness" in the population generally and that this is reflected in the provision of health care. The issue is as to whether this consciousness has spilt over into a "malpractice crisis". Certainly this has been a fear amongst health professionals and has been the subject of considerable academic debate. (See C. Ham, R. Dingwall, P. Fenn and D. Harris *Medical Negligence, Compensation and Accountability* London: Kings Fund Institute 1988.) It has been alleged that health professionals in areas in which litigation is potentially most likely due to the nature of the speciality have "been practising defensive medicine", namely altering their clinical practice to what may be perceived to be the "safest" therapy, even though this may not be the most appropriate or convenient for the patient, on the basis that this will reduce the risk of actions being brought. Another identifiable consequence of the increase in litigation has been that practitioners have deserted high risk specialities such as obstetrics (see P. Hoyte, "Unsound Practice: The Epidemiology of Medical Negligence" (1995) 3 *Medical Law Review* 53). Further signs of the growth in malpractice claims are that today more lawyers specialise in medical negligence. A feature of the last decade has been that firms of solicitors have begun to work in concert in major medical negligence claims, most notably, as we shall see later, in the context of litigation against drug firms. It is undoubtedly true that the number of claims have been rising steadily. Nevertheless, set against this is the fact that bringing a claim may be difficult for a number of reasons. These relate to both the substantive law in this area and also to the mechanics of bringing a claim, such as the difficulties in obtaining funding to bring an action. Jones has commented that "From the patient's perspective it could be argued that a 'malpractice crisis' arises from too few patients being able to litigate, rather than too many doctors becoming defendants." (See M. Jones, *Medical Negligence* (2nd ed.), London: Sweet and Maxwell 1996 at page 5.)

In this chapter we consider the basis on which health care professionals may be held accountable in law for careless acts or omissions. In section two, the general principles of the law of negligence as it applies to health professionals are examined. Particular problems in establishing liability in the context of medical negligence are considered, notably the reliance on the professional practice standard. A patient will face considerable problems in establishing that there was a breach of duty of care if the health professional can put forward evidence to show that a responsible body of professional opinion would have supported her actions. Even if breach of duty can be shown, a patient may experience difficulties in establishing causation, which may frustrate the claim. In section three, we consider the issue of statutory liability for defective drugs and appliances, an area in which English law has been strongly influenced by initiatives from the European Union. In section four we explore the use of multi-party actions as a means of facilitating proceedings, for example in relation to defective drugs. While medical malpractice may lead to a negligence action, grave instances of malpractice resulting in the death of the patient may result in a criminal prosecution being brought against the health professional. This issue is discussed in section five. Finally, we consider the effectiveness of the law of tort as a means of redress for those injured as a consequence of medical malpractice, and proposals which have been advanced for reform of the law in this area.

2. THE MALPRACTICE ACTION

(a) Introduction

Where a patient suffers harm through treatment provided by a health professional he may bring an action in negligence for damages. For his action to succeed, the patient must be able to show three things. First, that the doctor or nurse concerned owed him a duty of care; secondly, that she was in breach of that duty (*i.e.* that she failed to provide care of an adequate standard); thirdly, that he suffered harm in consequence of that breach which was not so unforeseeable as to be regarded in law as too remote.

(b) The Duty of Care

In the absence of an established duty of care, English law does not impose upon doctors (or other health care professionals or institutions) any obligation to provide treatment to those who require it. To this rule, however, there are two limited exceptions. First, where a patient presents at a hospital casualty department, there is an obligation to provide care (*Barnett v. Chelsea and Kensington Hospital Management Committee* [1968] 1 All E.R. 1068). Similarly, a duty also arises — under the National Health Service (General Medical Services) Regulations 1992, Schedule 2, paragraph 4(1)(h) — where the patient is treated by a General Practitioner (G.P.) as an emergency patient.

Where a patient cannot bring himself within either of these exceptions, he must be able positively to show that he was owed a duty of care before he can bring a medical negligence action. As to the circumstances in which such a duty arises, it is necessary to distinguish two types of case. First, where the patient seeks care from a G.P. on a non-emergency basis, and secondly, where he seeks hospital care. In the former instance, the obligation to treat the patient only crystallises once (a) he is registered with the G.P. (in accordance with the National Health Service (General Medical Services) Regulations 1992) *and* (b) he has consulted the G.P. on the occasion in question. In the latter, the duty does not arise until the hospital has formally accepted the patient. In either case, the existence of a duty of care is ultimately dependent upon the presence of an express or implied undertaking that he will be treated (*Cassidy v. Ministry of Health* [1951] 1 All E.R. 574).

Where a negligence action is brought, it is rare for an health care professional to be sued personally. It is more likely that an action will be brought against his employer on the basis that they are vicariously liable.

Where care is provided privately, *i.e.* outside the NHS, the doctor-patient relationship is governed by a contract for services. One consequence of this is that, in addition to her tortious duty of care, the doctor will owe a contemporaneous *contractual* duty which is almost identical in substance. Under section 13 of the Supply of Goods and Services Act 1982, the doctor is obliged to exercise reasonable care and skill while discharging his contractual obligations.

Where care is provided on a contractual basis, liability may arise not only in connection with the manner in which the care is provided, but also in relation to the quality and suitability of any medicines or surgical appliances that might be supplied. (See A. Bell, "The Doctor and the Supply of Goods and Services Act 1982" (1984) 4 *Legal Studies* 175.)

As far as the costs of litigation are concerned, these are rarely born by the individual practitioner. Health care practitioners have long carried health insurance. In the case of those who were employed by the NHS the cost of premiums were paid by the employers.

By the late 1980s much concern was being expressed over the rise in doctors insurance premiums. This led to the introduction by the government of a scheme known as "NHS indemnity" in 1991. (See M. Brazier, "NHS Indemnity: The Implications for Medical Litigation" (1990) 6 *Professional Negligence* 88.) This has the effect that NHS hospital doctors are directly idemnified by their employers. This scheme did not apply to G.P.'s who continue to require insurance. NHS trusts must bear the cost of claims themselves or they may join the Clinical Negligence scheme for Trusts which allows them to spread the cost of claims. Since March 1, 1996 it has been administered by a new body, the NHS Litigation Authority for Trusts. (See B. Millar, "CNST Update" (1996) *Health Care Risk Report* 7.)

In the majority of situations the NHS employer will be vicariously liable for the actions of health professionals. However, in some circumstances there may also be what is known as *direct* liability.

Cassidy v. Ministry of Health [1951] 1 All E.R. 574; [1951] 2 K.B. 343; [1951] W.L.R. 147 (for facts see page 170 below)

DENNING L.J.:

" . . . [W]hen hospital authorities undertake to treat a patient and themselves select and appoint and employ the professional men and women who are to give the treatment, they are responsible for the negligence of those persons in failing to give proper treatment, no matter whether they are doctors, surgeons, nurses, or anyone else. Once hospital authorities are held responsible for the nurses and radiographers as they have been in *Gold's* case (*Gold v. Essex County Council* [1942] 2 All E.R. 237), I can see no possible reason why they should not also be responsible for the house surgeons and resident medical officers on their permanent staff . . . "

After setting out the basis for the vicarious liability of the hospital, his Lordship considered whether there was, in fact, any negligence for which it could be held liable. He continued:

" . . . The hospital authorities accepted the plaintiff as a patient for treatment and it was their duty to treat him with reasonable care. They selected, employed, and paid all the surgeons and nurses who looked after him. He had no say in their selection at all. If those surgeons and nurses did not treat him with proper care and skill, then the hospital authorities must answer for it, for it means that they themselves did not perform their duty to him. I decline to enter into the question whether any of the surgeons were employed only under a contract for services, as distinct from a contract of service. The evidence is meagre enough in all conscience on that point, but the liability of the hospital authorities should not, and does not, depend on nice considerations of that sort. The plaintiff knew nothing of the terms on which they employed their staff. All he knew was that he was treated in the hospital by people whom the hospital authorities appointed, and the hospital authorities must be answerable for the way in which he was treated."

NOTES:

1. Lord Denning cited his statement in *Cassidy* in two subsequent decisions, *Roe v. Ministry of Health* [1954] 2 Q.B. 66 and *Jones v. Manchester Corporation* [1957] 2 All E.R. 125. (For further discussion on this see M. Brazier, *Street on Torts* (9th ed.), London: Butterworths, 1991 at pages 492–495; note criticism of the *Cassidy* approach in a Canadian case *Yepremian v. Scarborough General Hospital* (1980) 110 DLR (3d) 513 (Ont. C.A.).)
2. There may be a non-delegable duty arising from the statutory obligations imposed by s.3 of the National Health Service Act 1977 (see Chapter 1 above, at pages 32–39). (See *Razzel v. Snowball* [1954] 1 W.L.R. 1382, and M. Jones, *Medical Negligence* (2nd ed.), London: Sweet and Maxwell, 1996, para. 7–029.)

(c) The Standard of Care

The law of negligence requires only that health care professionals exercise reasonable care in the performance of their particular skills. This raises the issue of what amounts to "reasonable care". It also begs the question of who must prove the absence or observance of this standard.

Bolam v. Friern Hospital Management Committee [1957] 2 All E.R. 118, [1957] 1 W.L.R. 582

The plaintiff, John Bolam, was a psychiatric patient suffering depressive illness. He was advised by Dr de Bastarrechea, a consultant attached to Friern Hospital, to undergo electro-convulsive therapy. He signed a consent form but was not alerted to the risk of fracture that can occur because of fit-like convulsions that such treatment induces. In due course he received this treatment, but he was not given any relaxant drugs. As a consequence, he suffered several injuries. These included dislocation of the hip joints and fractures to the pelvis on both sides caused by the femur on both sides being driven through the cup of the pelvis.

Bolam claimed damages from Friern hospital, alleging that the provision of electro-convulsive therapy without the prior administration of relaxant drugs, or without restraining his convulsions manually, amounted to negligence.

McNair J.:
"... On the evidence it is clear, is it not, that the science of electro-convulsive therapy is a progressive science? Its development has been traced for you over the few years in which it has been used in this country. You may think on this evidence that, even today, there is no standard settled technique to which all competent doctors will agree. The doctors called before you have mentioned in turn different variants of the technique that they use. Some use restraining sheets, some use relaxant drugs, some use manual control; but the final question about which you must make up your minds is this — whether Dr Allfrey, following on the practice that he had learned at Friern Hospital and following on the technique which had been shown to him by Dr De Bastarrechea, was negligent in failing to use relaxant drugs or, if he decided not to use relaxant drugs, that he was negligent in failing to exercise any manual control over the patient beyond merely arranging for his shoulders to be held, the chin supported, a gag used, and a pillow put under his back. No one suggests that there was any negligence in the diagnosis, or in the decision to use electro-convulsive therapy. Furthermore, no one suggests that Dr Allfrey, or anyone at the hospital, was in any way indifferent to the care of their patients. The only question is really a question of professional skill.

Before I turn to that, I must explain what in law we mean by 'negligence'. In the ordinary case which does not involve any special skill, negligence in law means this: some failure to do some act which a reasonable man in the circumstances would do, or doing some act which a reasonable man in the circumstances would not do; and if that failure or doing of that act results in injury, then there is a cause of action. How do you test whether this act or failure is negligent? In an ordinary case it is generally said, that you judge that by the action of the man in the street. He is the ordinary man. In one case it has been said that you judge it by the conduct of the man on the top of a Clapham omnibus. He is the ordinary man. But where you get a situation which involves the use of some special skill or competence, then the test whether there has been negligence or not is not the test of the man on the top of a Clapham omnibus, because he has not got this special skill. The test is the standard of the ordinary skilled man exercising and professing to have that special skill. A man need not possess the highest skill at the risk of being found negligent. It is well established law that it is sufficient if he exercises the ordinary skill of an ordinary competent man exercising that particular art. I do not think that I quarrel much with any of the submissions in law which have been put before you by counsel. Counsel for the plaintiff put it in this way, that in the case of a medical man negligence means failure to act in accordance with the standards of reasonably competent medical men at the time. That is a perfectly accurate statement, as long as it is remembered that there may be one or more perfectly proper standards; and if a medical man conforms with one of those proper standards then he is not negligent. Counsel for the plaintiff was also right, in my judgment, in saying that a mere personal belief that a particular technique is best is no defence unless that belief is based on reasonable grounds. That again is unexceptionable. But the emphasis which is laid by counsel for the defendants is on this aspect of negligence: he submitted to you that the real question on which you have to make up your mind on each of the three major points to be considered is whether the defendants, in acting in the way in which they did, were acting in accordance with a practice of competent respected professional opinion. Counsel for the defendants submitted that if you are satisfied that they were acting in accordance with a practice of a competent body of professional opinion, then it would be wrong for you to hold that negligence was established. I referred, before I started these observations, to a statement which is contained in a recent Scottish case, *Hunter v. Hanley* ([1955] SLT 213 at 217), which dealt with medical matters, where the Lord President said:

'In the realm of diagnosis and treatment there is ample scope for genuine difference of opinion, and one man clearly is not negligent merely because his conclusion differs from that of other professional men, nor because he has displayed less skill or knowledge than others would have shown. The true test for establishing negligence in diagnosis or treatment on the part of a doctor is whether he has been proved to be guilty of such failure as no doctor of ordinary skill would be guilty of if acting with ordinary care.'

If that statement of the true test is qualified by the words 'in all the circumstances', counsel for the plaintiff would not seek to say that that expression of opinion does not accord with English law. It is just a question of expression. I myself would prefer to put it this way. A doctor is not guilty of negligence if he has acted in accordance with a practice accepted as proper by a responsible body of medical men skilled in that particular art. I do not think there is much difference in sense. It is just a different way of expressing the same thought. Putting it the other way round, a doctor is not negligent, if he is acting in accordance with such a practice, merely because there is a body of opinion that takes a contrary view. At the same time, that does not mean that a medical man can obstinately and pig-headedly carry on with some old technique if it has been proved to be contrary to what is really substantially the whole of informed medical opinion. Otherwise you might get men today saying: 'I don't believe in anaesthetics. I don't believe in antiseptics. I am going to continue to do my surgery in the way it was done in the eighteenth century.' That clearly would be wrong.

Before I deal with the details of the case, it is right to say this, that it is not essential for you to decide which of two practices is the better practice, as long as you accept that what Dr Allfrey did was in accordance with a practice accepted by responsible persons; but if the result of the evidence is that you are satisfied that his practice is better than the practice spoken of on the other side, then it is a stronger case. Finally, bear this in mind, that you are now considering whether it was negligent for certain action to be taken in August, 1954, not in February, 1957; and in one of the well-known cases on this topic it has been said you must not look through 1957 spectacles at what happened in 1954."

NOTES:

1. Although *Bolam* was a first instance decision, it has since been expressly approved by the House of Lords.
2. Today there are a number of factors which may affect the operation of the *Bolam* test. What constitutes the standard to be expected of a responsible professional practice may be influenced by elements external to that profession. Audit is routinely undertaken. This involves the systematic analysis of quality of care and includes reviews of diagnosis and treatment processes. Expectations raised by audit may effect what is seen as acceptable professional practice. In addition a term "evidence based medicine" has developed. This refers to clinical practice being based upon certain factors ascertained through research with the aim of determining clinical and cost effectiveness. An important part of evidence-based medicine is the dissemination of research findings. (See J. Applebey, K. Walsh, C. Ham, "Acting on the Evidence", National Association of Health Authorities and Trusts, 1995.) If a particular approach exists which has received the support of a powerful body of scientific evidence, then acting contrary to this may become increasingly difficult to justify. (See K. Walsh, "Evidence Based Health Care — A Brave New World?" (1996) *Health Care Risk Report* 16.) The new Clinical Negligence Scheme for Trusts may also have an impact on standards of health care. This scheme is administered by a new authority, the NHS litigation authority. This body has approved a set of standards and assessment procedures. Those bodies who comply with those standards may earn substantial discounts on their contributions to the scheme. Standards include, for example, requirements that patients should be provided with appropriate information as to the risks and benefits of proposed treatments and available alternatives (CNST *Manual of Guidance*, Bristol: CNST, 1996). It may only be a matter of time before compliance with such standards becomes mandatory and failure to comply with such standards may constitute negligence. Finally, stipulations in NHS contracts, such as inclusion of Patient Charter Targets may have an impact upon standards of patient care. (See further K. Barker, "NHS Contracting: Shadows in the Law of Tort" (1995) 3 *Medical Law Review* 161.)

3. In *Crawford v. Charing Cross Hospital* (*The Times*, December 8, 1953) the court rejected a claim that an anaesthetist was negligent because he had not read an article published in *The Lancet* six months before. Nevertheless, while the health care professional does not have to read everything on her subject she is expected to keep abreast of important developments. (See McNair J. at page 152 above.)

4. Both parties to the litigation are likely to adduce, if possible, expert medical opinion as to what constitutes a responsible body of professional practice. This may lead to difficulties in ascertaining whether the defendant has been negligent, which we explore further in the context of *Maynard v. West Midlands HA* at pages 156–159, below. Calling expert evidence increases the costs of the proceedings.

Whitehouse v. Jordan [1981] 1 All E.R. 267, [1981] 1 W.L.R. 246

The defendant was in charge of the plaintiff's delivery. The plaintiff, Stuart Whitehouse, was born with severe and irreparable brain damage, following a high risk pregnancy. After Stuart's mother had been in labour for 22 hours, the defendant decided to carry out a test to see whether forceps could be used to assist the delivery. He made six attempts to deliver the baby with the forceps before quickly and competently proceeding to a caesarian section. Acting through his mother, as next friend, the plaintiff claimed damages for negligence alleging (i) that the defendant had been negligent in pulling too long and too hard with the forceps — the six attempts with the forceps had taken some 25 minutes — and (ii) that in doing so he had caused the brain damage.

Lord Edmund-Davies:
". . . The principal questions calling for decision are: (a) in what manner did Mr Jordan use the forceps? and (b) was that manner consistent with the degree of skill which a member of his profession is required by law to exercise? Surprising though it is at this late stage in the development of the law of negligence, counsel for Mr Jordan persisted in submitting that his client should be completely exculpated were the answer to question (b), 'Well, at the worst he was guilty of an error of clinical judgment'. My Lords, it is high time that the unacceptability of such an answer be finally exposed. To say that a surgeon committed an error of clinical judgment is wholly ambiguous, for, while some such errors may be completely consistent with the due exercise of professional skill, other acts or omissions in the course of exercising 'clinical judgment' may be so glaringly below proper standards as to make a finding of negligence inevitable. Indeed, I should have regarded this as a truism were it not that, despite the exposure of the 'false antithesis' by Donaldson L.J. in his dissenting judgment in the Court of Appeal, counsel for the defendants adhered to it before your Lordships.

But doctors and surgeons fall into no special category, and, to avoid any future disputation of a similar kind, I would have it accepted that the true doctrine was enunciated, and by no means for the first time, by McNair in *Bolam v. Friern Hospital Management Committee* [1957] 2 All E.R. 118 at 121 in the following words, which were applied by the Privy Council in *Chin Keow v. Government of Malaysia* [1967] 1 W.L.R. 813:

'. . . where you get a situation which involves the use of some special skill or competence, then the test as to whether there has been negligence or not is not the test of the man on the top of a Clapham omnibus because he has not got this special skill. The test is the standard of the ordinary skilled man exercising and professing to have that special skill.'

If a surgeon fails to measure up to that standard in *any* respect ('clinical judgment' or otherwise), he has been negligent and should be so adjudged."

LORD FRASER:

"After a long trial, the learned judge held negligence established against the registrar, but the Court of Appeal by a majority (Lord Denning M.R. and Lawton L.J., Donaldson L.J. dissenting) reversed his decision. They did so not because they considered that the learned trial judge had misstated the relevant law. Clearly he did not; he said, rightly in my opinion, that negligence for the purposes of this case meant 'a failure . . . to exercise the standard of skill expected from the ordinary competent specialist having regard to the experience and expertise that specialist holds himself out as possessing'. He added the proviso that the skill and expertise to be considered were those applying in 1969 to 1970. Although that statement was not criticised in the Court of Appeal, Lord Denning M.R. did criticise a later sentence in the judgment because, in his view, it suggested that the law made no allowance for errors of judgment by a professional man. Referring to medical men, Lord Denning M.R. said: [1980] 1 All E.R. 650 at 658 'If they are to be found liable [*sic.* for negligence] whenever they do not effect a cure, or whenever anything untoward happens, it would do a great disservice to the profession itself.' That is undoubtedly correct, but he went on to say this: 'We must say, and say firmly, that, in a professional man an error of judgment is not negligent.' Having regard to the context, I think that Lord Denning M.R. must have meant to say that an error of judgment 'is not *necessarily negligent*'. But in my respectful opinion, the statement as it stands is not an accurate statement of the law. Merely to describe something as an error of judgment tells us nothing about whether it is negligent or not. The true position is that an error of judgment may, or may not, be negligent; it depends on the nature of the error. If it is one that would not have been made by a reasonably competent professional man professing to have the skill that the defendant held himself out as having, and acting with ordinary care, then it is negligent. If, on the other hand, it is an error that a man, acting with ordinary care, might have made, then it is not negligence.

The main reason why the Court of Appeal reversed the judge's decision was that they differed from him on the facts. The question therefore is whether the Court of Appeal was entitled to reverse the judge's decision on a pure question of fact. The view of the judge who saw and heard the witnesses as to the weight to be given to their evidence is always entitled to great respect. We were reminded particularly of dicta to that effect in *The Hontestroom* [1927] A.C. 37 and *Powell v. Streatham Manor Nursing Home* [1935] All E.R. 58, and there is other high authority to the same effect. But in this case, unlike cases such as *Powell* and *The Hontestroom*, no direct issue of credibility arises. It is not suggested that any witness, or body of witnesses, was giving dishonest evidence. The only witness whose reliability is seriously in question is Mrs Whitehouse, the mother of the plaintiff, and I shall refer to the critical part of her evidence in a moment. Apart from her evidence, the important facts are almost entirely inferences from the primary facts, and in determining what inferences should properly be drawn, an appellate court is just as well placed as the trial judge. Accordingly this is a case where the judge's decision on fact is more open to be reassessed by an appellate court that it often is."

QUESTIONS:

1. According to McNair J., who sets the standard of care to which doctors must conform, the courts or the doctors themselves? Who should set the standard? (See J. Montgomery, "Medicine, Accountability and Professionalism" (1989) 16 *Journal of Law and Society* 319.)

2. According to Lord Edmund-Davies: " . . . an error of judgment may, or may not, be negligent; it depends on the nature of the error. If it is one that would not have been made by a reasonably competent professional man . . . acting with ordinary care, then it is negligent". Are you convinced by this reasoning or would you prefer to see some reference to the gravity of the error? (*cf.* the opinion of Lord Bridge in *Sidaway v. Board of Governors of the Bethlem Royal Hospital and Maudsley Hospital* [1985] 1 All E.R. 643.)

3. Do you think that it was appropriate for their Lordships, in *Whitehouse v. Jordan*, to question the facts found at first instance?

Difficulties may arise where there is a divergence of professional opinion. A further difficulty relates to what happens in the event of failure to follow *any* approved practice. These questions were dealt with, respectively, in the cases of *Maynard v. West Midlands Regional Health Authority* and *Clark v. MacLennan*.

Maynard v. West Midlands Regional Health Authority [1985] 1 All E.R. 635, [1984] 1 W.L.R. 634

Two consultants, employed by the defendant health authority, were treating the plaintiff for a chest complaint. They believed her to be suffering from tuberculosis but thought there was a possibility that it might be Hodgkin's disease. Since Hodgkin's disease is fatal unless treated in its very early stages, they decided that, rather than wait for the results of a sputum test (designed to ascertain whether she had tuberculosis), it was sensible to conduct an exploratory operation, a mediastinoscopy, to determine whether she had Hodgkin's disease.

The operation, which was carried out properly, showed her to have tuberculosis and not Hodgkin's disease. The plaintiff claimed damages from the defendant health authority, alleging that the decision to carry out the mediastinoscopy rather than await the result of the sputum test had been negligent. At the trial, the judge was impressed by the evidence of an expert witness on behalf of the plaintiff who stated that the case had almost certainly been one of tuberculosis from the outset and that it had been dangerous and wrong to undertake the operation. He gave judgment for the plaintiff. The Court of Appeal reversed his decision. The plaintiff appealed to the House of Lords.

LORD SCARMAN:

" . . . The only issue for the House is whether the two medical men, Dr Ross who was the consultant physician and Mr Stephenson the surgeon, were guilty of an error of judgment amounting to a breach of their duty of care to their patient. Both accept that the refusal to make a firm diagnosis until they had available the findings of the diagnostic operation was one for which they were jointly responsible.

The issue is essentially one of fact: but there remains the possibility, which it will be necessary to examine closely, that the judge, although directing himself correctly as to the law, failed to apply it correctly when he came to draw the inferences upon which his conclusion of negligence was based. Should this possibility be established as the true interpretation to be put upon his judgment, he would, of course, be guilty of an error of law.

In English law the appeal process is a rehearing of fact and law. But the limitations upon an appellate court's ability to review findings of fact are severe, and well-established. Lord Thankerton stated the principles in *Watt (or Thomas) v. Thomas* [1947] 1 All E.R. 582; and recently the cases and the principles have been reviewed by this House in *Whitehouse v. Jordan* [1981] 1 All E.R. 267, itself a medical negligence case. It is, therefore, unnecessary now to restate them. I would, however, draw attention to some observations by Lord Bridge of Harwich in the *Whitehouse* case and by Brandon L.J. in a Court of Appeal case, *Joyce v. Yeomans* [1981] 2 All E.R. 21, since they are directly relevant to the problems facing your Lordships in this appeal. Lord Bridge of Harwich said ([1981] 1 All E.R. 267, at 270, 286):

'I recognise that this is a question of pure fact and that in the realm of fact, as the authorities repeatedly emphasise, the advantages which the judge derives from seeing and hearing the witnesses must always be respected by an appellate court. At the same time the importance of the part played by those advantages in assisting the judge to any particular conclusion of fact varies through a wide spectrum from, at one end, a straight conflict of primary fact between witnesses, where credibility is crucial and the appellate court can hardly ever interfere, to, at the other end, an inference from undisputed primary facts, where the appellate court is in just as good a position as the trial judge to make the decision.'

The primary facts in this case are undisputed. But there are gaps in our knowledge of some details of the medical picture due to a loss of hospital notes. These gaps occur in the critical period during which the two doctors made the decision which is said to be negligent. The gaps have to be bridged by inference. In this task, the trial judge, it must be recognised, had the advantage of seeing and hearing the two medical men whose professional judgment, reached during that period, is impugned. We are not, therefore at the extreme end of Lord Bridge's 'wide spectrum', though we are near it. There is room for a judgment on credibility for the reasons given by Brandon L.J. in *Joyce v. Yeomans* [1981] 2 All E.R. 21 at 26–27. Speaking of expert evidence, he made this comment:

'There are various aspects of such evidence in respect of which the trial judge can get the 'feeling' of a case in a way in which an appellate court, reading the transcript, cannot. Sometimes expert witnesses display signs of partisanship in a witness box or lack of objectivity. This may or may not be obvious from the transcript, yet it may be quite plain to the trial judge. Sometimes an expert witness may refuse to make what a more wise witness would make, namely, proper concessions to the viewpoint of the other side. Here again this may or may not be apparent from the transcript, although plain to the trial judge. I mention only two aspects of the matter, but there are others.'

These are wise words of warning, but they do not modify Lord Thankerton's statement of principle nor were they intended to do so. The relevant principle remains, namely that an appellate court, if disposed to come to a different conclusion from the trial judge on the printed evidence, should not do so unless satisfied that the advantage enjoyed by him of seeing and hearing the witnesses is not sufficient to explain or justify his conclusion. But if the appellate court is satisfied that he has not made a proper use of his advantage, 'the matter will then become at large for the appellate court' (see [1947] 1 All E.R. 582 at 587).

The only other question of law in the appeal is as to the nature of the duty owed by a doctor to his patient. The most recent authoritative formulation is that by Lord Edmund-Davies in the *Whitehouse* case. Quoting from the judgment of McNair J. in *Bolam v. Friern Hospital Management Committee* [1957] 2 All E.R. 118 he said, at [1981] 1 All E.R. 267 at 277:

'"The test is the standard of the ordinary skilled man exercising and professing to have that special skill." If a surgeon fails to measure up to that standard in *any* respect ("clinical judgment" or otherwise), he has been negligent . . . '
(Lord Edmund-Davies's emphasis.)

The present case may be classified as one of clinical judgment. Two distinguished consultants, a physician and a surgeon experienced in the treatment of chest diseases, formed a judgment as to what was, in their opinion, in the best interests of their patient. They recognised that tuberculosis was the most likely diagnosis. But, in their opinion, there was an unusual factor, *viz* swollen glands in the mediastinum unaccompanied by any evidence of lesion in the lungs. Hodgkin's disease, carcinoma and sarcoidosis were, therefore, possibilities. The danger they thought was Hodgkin's disease; though unlikely, it was, if present, a killer (as treatment was understood in 1970) unless remedial steps were taken in its early stage. They, therefore, decided on mediastinoscopy, an operative procedure which would provide them with a biopsy from the swollen glands which could be subjected to immediate microscopic examination. It is said that the evidence of tuberculosis was so strong that it was unreasonable and wrong to defer diagnosis and to put their patient to the risks of the operation. The case against them is not mistake or carelessness in performing the operation, which it is admitted was properly carried out, but an error of judgment in requiring the operation to be undertaken.

A case which is based on an allegation that a fully considered decision of two consultants in the field of their special skill was negligent clearly presents certain difficulties of proof. It is not enough to show that there is a body of competent professional opinion which considers that there was a wrong decision, if there also exists a body of professional opinion, equally competent, which supports the decision as reasonable in the circumstances. It is not enough to show that subsequent events show that the operation need never have been performed, if at the time the decision to operate was taken it was reasonable in the sense that a responsible body of medical opinion would have accepted it as proper. I do not think that the words of Lord President Clyde in *Hunter v. Hanley* 1955 SLT 213 at 217 can be bettered:

'In the realm of diagnosis and treatment there is ample scope for genuine difference of opinion and one man clearly is not negligent merely because his conclusion differs from that of other professional men . . . The true test for establishing negligence in diagnosis or treatment on the part of a doctor is whether he has been proved to be guilty of such failure as no doctor of ordinary skill would be guilty of if acting with ordinary care . . .'

I would only add that a doctor who professes to exercise a special skill must exercise the ordinary skill of his speciality. Differences of opinion and practice exist, and will always exist, in the medical as in other professions. There is seldom any one answer exclusive of all others to problems of professional judgment. A court may prefer one body of opinion to the other: but that is no basis for a conclusion of negligence.

His Lordship stated the facts and evidence in detail, and continued:

At the trial and in the Court of Appeal there were two issues — causation and negligence. The judge decided both in favour of the plaintiff appellant. The Court of Appeal had no hesitation in upholding the judge on causation but reversed him on negligence. Thus it is that the only issue now is negligence. On this the judge's conclusions were that the operation was unnecessary, wrong, and in the circumstances unreasonable and a breach of the duty of care. He found that Dr Ross instigated the operation and that Mr Stephenson in failing to object to it and in sharing the decision was also in breach of his duty of care. The learned judge accepted the evidence of Dr Hugh-Jones, the appellant's principal expert witness, that it was almost certainly a case of tuberculosis from the outset and should have been so diagnosed, and that it was wrong and dangerous to undertake the operation. His detailed findings against Dr Ross were that he should not have used the operation where the right diagnosis was almost certainly tuberculosis, and that he should at the very least have waited for the pathological reports on the sputum, which in fact turned out to be positive. Dr Ross's defence that because of the risk of Hodgkin's disease he could not delay was rejected by the judge on the grounds that a delay of four to six weeks, up to 10 at maximum, would not have mattered and that the fear of Hodgkin's disease being present was not a reasonable fear in the circumstances. The judge recognised that the defence had called a formidable number of distinguished experts, amongst whom it was legitimate to include Dr Ross and Mr Stephenson themselves, all of whom expressed a contrary view to his and approved the course of action taken in deferring diagnosis and performing the operation. The judge accepted not only the expertise of all the medical witnesses called before him but also their truthfulness and honesty. But he found Dr Hugh-Jones 'an outstanding witness; clear, definite, logical and persuasive'. The judge continued:

'I have weighed his evidence against that of the distinguished contrary experts. I do not intend or wish to take away from their distinction by holding that in the particular circumstances of this particular case I prefer his opinions and his evidence to theirs.'

My Lords, even before considering the reasons given by the majority of the Court of Appeal for reversing the findings of negligence, I have to say that a judge's 'preference' for one body of distinguished professional opinion to another also professionally distinguished is not sufficient to establish negligence in a practitioner whose actions have received the seal of approval of those whose opinions, truthfully expressed, honestly held, were not preferred. If this was the real reason for the judge's finding, he erred in law even though elsewhere in his judgment he stated the law correctly. For in the realm of diagnosis and treatment, negligence is not established by preferring one respectable body of professional opinion to another. Failure to exercise the ordinary skill of a doctor (in the appropriate speciality, if he be a specialist) is necessary.

My Lords, it would be doing an injustice to the careful and detailed reasoning elsewhere evident in the judgment of the trial judge to dismiss this appeal upon the basis of this one passage. But, to borrow a telling phrase from Cumming-Bruce L.J. in the Court of Appeal, it certainly suggests that his finding of negligence is 'vulnerable to attack'. It gives rise to doubt whether he succeeded in making proper use of his advantage of seeing and hearing the witnesses who gave oral evidence."

His Lordship considered the Court of Appeal's criticisms of certain parts of the trial judge's judgment, which he found to be justified, and stated that the Court of Appeal had, therefore, been justified in treating the issue of negligence as being at large for them to draw the appropriate inferences and to reach their own conclusion. He also stated that the final conclusion, as expressed by Cumming-Bruce L.J., that the judge's finding that the decision to operate was unreasonable, could not be supported. He then concluded:

> "The judge thought that Dr Ross might have had an '*idée fixe*' about the possibility of Hodgkin's disease. This, with respect, is not a possible view of his evidence read as a whole, especially in the light of the judge's own appraisal of him as a witness. Nor is it consistent with the existence of a strong body of evidence given by distinguished medical men supporting and approving of what he did in the circumstances of this case as they presented themselves to him at the time when he made his decision.
>
> My Lords, the House in this case has reviewed the evidence. The review has led me to the clear conclusion that the Court of Appeal was right to reverse the judge's finding of negligence. I would dismiss the appeal."

NOTES:

1. The other four Law Lords who heard the case, Lords Elwyn-Jones, Fraser, Roskill and Templeman, delivered short opinions expressing their agreement with Lord Scarman.
2. Lord Scarman stated, "in the realm of diagnosis and treatment negligence is not established by preferring one respectable body of professional opinion to another". Nonetheless, this view has since been qualified by the *obiter dicta* of two members of the Court of Appeal in *Bolitho v. City and Hackney Health Authority* (1992) 13 BMLR 111, a case on the issue of causation (see below at pages 182–187). According to Dillon L.J., the court would be entitled to:

> "reject [one body] of medical opinion on the ground that . . . the court, fully conscious of its own lack of medical knowledge and clinical experience, was none the less clearly satisfied that the views of that group of doctors were *Wednesbury* unreasonable, *i.e.* views such as no reasonable body of doctors could have held" (see *Associated Provincial Picture Houses v. Wednesbury Corporation* [1947] 2 All E.R. 680).

Similarly, Farquharson L.J. stated:

> "It is not enough for a defendant to call a number of doctors to say what he had done was in accord with clinical practice. It is necessary for the judge to consider that evidence and decide whether that clinical practice puts the patient unnecessarily at risk".

The *obiter* views expressed in *Bolitho* are reminiscent of those expressed in the earlier case *Hucks v. Cole* (1968) 112 *Sol J.* 483 where Sachs L.J. stated:

> " . . . the fact that other practitioners would have done the same thing as the defendant is a very weighty matter to be put in the scales on his behalf; but it is not . . . conclusive. The court must see whether the reasons given for putting the patient at risk are valid."

Jones has questioned the applicability of the *Wednesbury* test in *Bolitho*. (M. Jones, *Medical Negligence*, London: Sweet and Maxwell, 1995 at page 105.) It is doubtful whether the use of a *Wednesbury* test would lead to a different result from that achieved through the application of *Maynard*. It is very rare in public law cases for public bodies to be held to have acted so unreasonably that no reasonable body would have reached such a decision.

3. In *De Freitas v. O'Brien* [1993] 4 Med. L.R. 281, the court again illustrated its unwillingness to question a body of professional medical opinion. Here the plaintiff underwent an operation on her spine. The procedure was one which only a very small number of doctors would undertake (in this case four or five out of some 250 neurosurgeons countrywide) although the neurosurgeons claimed that they had a very high degree of expertise. The surgeon was held not to be negligent, even though the exploratory surgery which had been undertaken carried an unavoidable risk of infection. Nevertheless, the judge in this case did state that the view of a body of medical opinion could be scrutinised by the court following the approach of Dillon L.J. in *Bolitho*. (See I. Kennedy "Medical Negligence: Bolam and Professional Practice" [1994] Medical Law Review 210).

In *Joyce v. Wandsworth H.A.* [1996] 7 Medical Law Review 1, the Court of Appeal again used the "new *Bolam*" approach and departed from the view of a responsible body of professional opinion, although the action ultimately foundered on the question of causation. (See further A. Grubb "Medical Negligence Breach of Duty and Causation" [1996] 4 *Medical Law Review* 86–8.)

Further illustration of judicial scrutiny is provided in the following case.

Clark v. MacLennan [1983] 1 All E.R. 416

Soon after giving birth in the hospital of the second defendant, the health authority, the plaintiff began to suffer from stress incontinence causing normal bladder control to be lost when she was subjected to mild physical stress. Her disability was particularly acute and after conventional treatment had failed, the first defendant, a gynaecologist, performed an anterior colporrhaphy operation to restore the bladder to its normal position and support the bladder neck. It was not, however, normal practice among gynaecologists to perform this operation until at least three months after birth. The delay was designed to help ensure the success of the operation and avert the risk of subsequent haemorrhage. In this case, the operation was not a success, a haemorrhage occurred causing the repair to break down. Accordingly, two further anterior colporrhaphy operations were necessary but these, too, were unsuccessful, leaving the plaintiff with irremediable stress incontinence.

The plaintiff brought an action for damages claiming that the defendants had been negligent in her care and treatment.

The judge began by considering the statement of McNair J. in *Bolam* and the decision in *Whitehouse and Jordan*, before stating:

PETER PAIN J.:

" . . . It follows from these authorities that a doctor owes a duty to his patient to observe the precautions which are normal in the course of the treatment that he gives. But, where there are two schools of thought as to the right course to be followed, he may not be charged with negligence simply because he chooses one course rather than the other.

Where however there is but one orthodox course of treatment and he chooses to depart from that, his position is different. It is not enough for him to say as to his decision simply that it was based on his clinical judgment. One has to inquire whether he took all proper factors into account which he knew or should have known, and whether his departure from the orthodox course can be justified on the basis of these factors.

The burden of proof lies on the plaintiff. To succeed she must show, first, that there was a breach of duty and, second, that her damage flowed from that breach. It is against the second defendants that her attack is principally directed. They are liable for all the mistakes that were made, whether by Professor Turnbull or the staff.

In his final speech, counsel for the plaintiff very fairly did not press the case against the first defendant. The evidence made it apparent that he was acting under the direction of Professor Turnbull. I accept, as he said, that he would not have made the decision to operate on his own.

But an important question arises as to the burden of proof. It may seem that to base one's judgment on the burden of proof is the last resort of a judge who cannot make up his mind. But, when one is faced by medical evidence made more difficult by the fact that medical experts disagree on a number of matters of medical fact, it seems to me to be a legitimate resort.

Counsel for the plaintiff relied heavily on *McGhee v. National Coal Board* [1972] 3 All E.R. 1008 for this purpose . . .

On the basis of this authority, counsel for the plaintiff contended that, if the plaintiff could show (1) that there was a general practice not to perform an anterior colporrhaphy until at least three months after birth, (2) that one of the reasons for this practice was to protect the patient from the risk of haemorrhage and a breakdown of the repair, (3) that an operation was performed within four weeks and (4) that haemorrhage occurred and the repair broke down, then the burden of showing that he was not in breach of duty shifted to the defendants.

It must be correct on the basis of *McGhee* to say that the burden shifts so far as damages are concerned. But does the burden shift so far as the duty is concerned? Must the medical practitioner justify his departure from the usual practice?

It is very difficult to draw a distinction between the damage and the duty where the duty arises only because of a need to guard against the damage. In *McGhee's* case it was accepted there was a breach of duty. In the present case the question of whether there was a breach remains in issue.

It seems to me that it follows from *McGhee* that where there is a situation in which a general duty of care arises and there is a failure to take a precaution, and that very damage occurs against which the precaution is designed to be a protection, then the burden lies on the defendant to show that he was not in breach of duty as well as to show that the damage did not result from his breach of duty. I shall therefore apply this approach to the evidence in this case. I first have to ask myself whether the plaintiff has established that it is a general practice among gynaecologists that an anterior colporrhaphy should not ordinarily be performed until at least three months after birth. That this is the general practice was accepted by Professor Huntingford, Mr Smallwood, Mr

Rickford, the first defendant and Sir John Dewhurst. Professor Turnbull suggested late in the case that this will apply only where there was prolapse of the bladder or uterus without stress incontinence.

I am satisfied that this is the general practice. It is not an absolute rule: Mr Rickford made passing reference to considering the operation at six weeks in a particular case. Professor Huntingford, in one of his reports, refers to waiting 8 to 12 weeks. Exceptions can be considered, but they require justification. I am satisfied that this is not a case where there are two schools of thought. This is the general practice among gynaecologists and any departure from it requires justification.

No witness, despite the vast experience that they combined, was able to point to any instance where this operation had been performed at less than three months let alone four weeks . . .

As of today I am satisfied that there is a general practice from which Professor Turnbull departed when he asked the first defendant to undertake this operation. He was misled by a misunderstanding about the plaintiff's first discharge, he was sceptical about the reasons for the general practice and he was mistrustful of conservative measures; the only conservative measure which he really valued was to allow time to pass, but in this case only a very short period had elapsed without improvement.

I find the second defendants vicariously responsible both for him and for his staff who had misled him. They were in breach of duty."

A further question that arises in relation to the standard of care to be observed is whether inexperience has the effect of lowering it. The matter was dealt with by the Court of Appeal in the *Wilsher* case.

Wilsher v. Essex Area Health Authority [1986] 3 All E.R. 801, [1987] 1 Q.B. 730, [1987] 2 W.L.R. 425, 3 BMLR 37, C.A.

The plaintiff, Martin Wilsher, was an infant who had been born prematurely with various illnesses, one of which was oxygen deficiency. There was a low probability that Martin would survive. He was placed in the hospital's 24-hour special care baby unit. The unit was staffed by a medical team made up of two consultants, a senior registrar and several junior doctors and trained nurses. While Martin was in the unit, an inexperienced junior doctor undertook to monitor the oxygen level in his bloodstream. However, in doing so he inserted a catheter into a vein rather than an artery by mistake. He then requested that the senior registrar check what he had done. The registrar, Dr Kawa, failed to notice his mistake and several hours later, when replacing the catheter made the same mistake himself. In both instances the catheter monitor failed to give an accurate reading of the amount of oxygen in Martin's blood. The result was that he was given an excess of oxygen. He therefore brought an action in negligence against the health authority, alleging that the excess oxygen in his bloodstream had caused an incurable condition of the retina (RLF) resulting in near blindness.

At first instance, the action succeeded. The defendant health authority appealed to the Court of Appeal, contending, *inter alia*, that there had been no breach of the duty of care owed to the plaintiff because the standard of care required was only that reasonably required of doctors having the same formal qualifications and practical experience as the doctors actually in the unit.

Mustill L.J.:

" . . . I now turn to the real content of the standard of care. Three propositions were advanced, the first by junior counsel for the plaintiff. It may, I think, be fairly described as setting a 'team' standard of care, whereby each of the persons who formed the staff of the unit held themselves out as capable of undertaking the specialised procedures which that unit set out to perform.

I acknowledge the force of this submission, so far as it calls for recognition of the position which the person said to be negligent held within this specialised unit. But, in so far as the proposition differs from the last of those referred to below, I must dissent, for it is faced with a dilemma. If it seeks to attribute to each individual member of the team a duty to live up to the standards demanded of the unit as a whole, it cannot be right, for it would expose a student nurse to an action in negligence for a failure to possess the skill and experience of a consultant. If, on the other hand, it seeks to fix a standard for the performance of the unit as a whole, this is simply a reformulation of the direct theory of liability which leading counsel for the plaintiff has explicitly disclaimed.

The second proposition (advanced on behalf of the defendants) directs attention to the personal position of the individual member of the staff about whom the complaint is made. What is expected of him is as much as, but no more than, can reasonably be required of a person having his formal qualifications and practical experience. If correct, this proposition entails that the standard of care which the patient is entitled to demand will vary according to the chance of recruitment and rostering. The patient's right to complain of faulty treatment will be more limited if he has been entrusted to the care of a doctor who is a complete novice in the particular field (unless perhaps he can point to some fault of supervision in a person further up the hierarchy) than if he has been in the hands of a doctor who has already spent months on the same ward, and his prospects of holding the health authority vicariously liable for the consequences of any mistreatment will be correspondingly reduced.

To my mind, this notion of a duty tailored to the actor, rather than to the act which he elects to perform, has no place in the law of tort. Indeed, the defendants did not contend that it could be justified by any reported authority on the general law of tort. Instead, it was suggested that the medical profession is a special case. Public hospital medicine has always been organised so that young doctors and nurses learn on the job. If the hospitals abstained from using inexperienced people, they could not staff their wards and theatres, and the junior staff could never learn. The longer-term interests of patients as a whole are best served by maintaining the present system, even if this may diminish the legal rights of the individual patient, for, after all, medicine is about curing, not litigation.

I acknowledge the appeal of this argument, and recognise that a young hospital doctor who must get onto the wards in order to qualify without necessarily being able to decide what kind of patient he is going to meet is not in the same position as another professional man who has a real choice whether or not to practice in a particular field. Nevertheless, I cannot accept that there should be a special rule for doctors in public hospitals, and I emphasise *public*, since presumably those employed in private hospitals would be in a different category. Doctors are not the only people who gain their experience, not only from lectures or from watching others perform, but from tackling live clients or customers, and no case was cited to us which suggested that any such variable duty of care was imposed on others in a similar position. To my mind, it would be a false step to subordinate the legitimate expectation of the patient that he will receive from each person concerned with his care a degree of skill appropriate to the task which he undertakes to an understandable wish to minimise the psychological and financial pressures on hard-pressed young doctors.

For my part, I prefer the third of the propositions which have been canvassed. This relates the duty of care, not to the individual, but to the post which he occupies. I would differentiate 'post' from 'rank' or 'status'. In a case such as the present, the standard is not just that of the averagely competent and well-informed junior houseman (or whatever the position of the doctor) but of such a person who fills a post in a unit offering a highly specialised service. But, even so, it must be recognised that different posts make different demands. If it is borne in mind that the structure of hospital medicine envisages that the lower ranks will be occupied by those of whom it would be wrong to expect too much, the risk of abuse by litigious patients can be mitigated, if not entirely eliminated."

GLIDEWELL L.J.:

" . . . I have had the great advantage of reading in draft the judgments of Sir Nicholas Browne-Wilkinson V.-C. and Mustill L.J. I shall comment only about two subjects on which they do not agree. Firstly, what is the proper test to be applied to decide whether a doctor, engaged as were the doctors in this case in a special unit caring for premature babies, has been negligent? The test usually applied is that adopted in his judgment by Peter Pain J. from the charge to a jury by McNair J. in *Bolam v. Friern Hospital Management Committee* [1957] 2 All E.R. 118 . . . ."

His Lordship set out the *Bolam* test then continued . . .

"I agree with the judge that this is the correct test by which to weigh the conduct of all the doctors in the present case.

If I understand him correctly, Sir Nicholas Browne-Wilkinson V-C would apply a less stringent test to a newly-qualified practitioner, who has accepted an appointment in order to gain experience. The suggested test would only hold such a doctor liable 'for acts or omissions which a careful doctor with his qualifications and experience would not have done or omitted'. With great respect, I do not believe this is the correct test. In my view, the law requires the trainee or learner to be judged by the same standard as his more experienced colleagues. If it did not, inexperience would frequently be urged as a defence to an action for professional negligence.

If this test appears unduly harsh in relation to the inexperienced, I should add that, in my view, the inexperienced doctor called on to exercise a specialist skill will, as part of that skill, seek the advice and help of his superiors when he does or may need it. If he does seek such help, he will often have satisfied the test, even though he may himself have made a mistake. It is for this reason that I agree that Dr Wiles was not negligent. He made a mistake in inserting the catheter into a vein, and a second mistake in not recognising the signs that he had done so on the X-ray. But, having done what he thought right, he asked Dr Kawa, the senior registrar, to check what he had done, and Dr Kawa did so. Dr Kawa failed to recognise the indication on the X-ray that the catheter was in the vein, and some hours later himself inserted a replacement catheter, again in the vein, and again failed to recognise that it was in the vein. Whichever of the suggested tests of negligence should be applied to Dr Wiles, we are all agreed that Dr Kawa was negligent, and that the defendants must therefore be liable for any damage to the plaintiff proved to have been caused by that negligence."

SIR NICHOLAS BROWNE-WILKINSON V.-C. (DISSENTING):

" . . . The first point on which I differ from Mustill L.J. relates to the question of negligence. On this issue I disagree, not with his decision, but with the process whereby he reaches his conclusion. I enter into this field with hesitation since it is one in which I have virtually no experience. But I cannot accept that the standard of care required of an individual doctor holding a post in a hospital is an objective standard to be determined irrespective of his experience or the reason why he is occupying the post in question.

In English law, liability for personal injury requires a finding of personal fault (*e.g.* negligence) against someone. In cases of vicarious liability such as this, there must have been personal fault by the employee or agent of the defendant for whom the defendant is held vicariously liable. Therefore, even though no claim is made against the individual doctor, the liability of the defendant health authority is dependent on a finding of personal fault by one or more of the individual doctors. The general standard of care required of a doctor is that he would exercise the skill of a skilled doctor in the treatment which he has taken on himself to offer.

Such being the general standard of care required of a doctor, it is normally no answer for him to say the treatment he gave was of a specialist or technical nature in which he was inexperienced. In such a case, the fault of the doctor lies in embarking on giving treatment which he could not skilfully offer: he should not have undertaken the treatment but should have referred the patient to someone possessing the necessary skills.

But the position of the houseman in his first year after qualifying or of someone (like Dr Wiles in this case) who has just started in a specialist field in order to gain the necessary skill in that field is not capable of such analysis. The houseman has to take up his post in order to gain full professional qualification. Anyone who, like Dr Wiles, wishes to obtain specialist skills has to learn those skills by taking a post in a specialist unit. In my judgment, such doctors cannot in fairness be said to be at fault if, at the start of their time, they lack the very skills which they are seeking to acquire.

In my judgment, if the standard of care required of such a doctor is that he should have the skill required of the post he occupies, the young houseman or the doctor seeking to obtain specialist skill in a special unit would be held liable for shortcomings in the treatment without any personal fault on his part at all. Of course, such a doctor would be negligent if he undertook treatment for which he knows he lacks the necessary experience and skill. But one of the chief hazards of inexperience is that one does not always know the risks which exist. In my judgment, so long as the English law rests liability on personal fault, a doctor who has properly accepted a post in a hospital in order to gain necessary experience should only be held liable for acts or omissions which a careful doctor with his qualifications and experience would not have done or omitted. It follows that, in my view, the health authority could not be held vicariously liable (and I stress the word *vicariously*) for the acts of such a learner who has come up to those standards, notwithstanding that the post he held required greater experience than he in fact possessed.

The only argument to the contrary (and it is a formidable one) is that such a standard of care would mean that the rights of a patient entering hospital will depend on the experience of the doctor who treats him. This, I agree, would be wholly unsatisfactory. But, in my judgment, it is not the law. I agree with the comments of Mustill L.J. as to the confusion which has been caused in this case both by the pleading and by the argument below which blurred the distinction between the vicarious liability of the health authority for the negligence of its doctors and the direct liability of the health authority for negligently failing to provide skilled treatment of the kind that it was offering to the public. In my judgment, a health authority which so conducts its hospital that it fails to provide doctors of sufficient skill and experience to give the treatment offered at the hospital may be directly liable in negligence to the patient. Although we were told in argument that no case has ever been decided on this ground and that it is not the practice to formulate claims in this way, I can see no reason why, in principle, the health authority should not be so liable if its organisation is at fault: see *McDermid v. Nash Dredging and Reclamation Co. Ltd* [1986] 2 All E.R. 676 especially at 684–685 (reported since the conclusion of the argument).

Claims against a health authority that it has itself been directly negligent, as opposed to vicariously liable for the negligence of its doctors, will, of course, raise awkward questions. To what extent should the authority be held liable if (*e.g.* in the use of junior housemen) it is only adopting a practice hallowed by tradition? Should the authority be liable if it demonstrates that, due to the financial stringency under which it operates, it cannot afford to fill the posts with those possessing the necessary experience? But, in my judgment, the law should not be distorted by making findings of personal fault against individual doctors who are, in truth, not at fault in order to avoid such questions. To do so would be to cloud the real issues which arise. In the modern world with its technological refinements, is it sensible to persist in making compensation for those who suffer from shortcomings in technologically advanced treatment depend on proof of fault, a process which the present case illustrates can consume years in time and huge sums of money in costs? Given limited resources, what balance is to be struck in the allocation of such resources between compensating those whose treatment is not wholly successful and the provision of required treatment for the world at large? These are questions for Parliament, not the courts. But I do not think the courts will do society a favour by distorting the existing law so as to conceal the real social questions which arise."

NOTES:

1. In *Wilsher*, the Court of Appeal made it clear that inexperience on the part of the hospital staff provided no defence to an action in negligence. If *Wilsher* seems unduly harsh on the medical profession, it is perhaps worth noting that inexperience in other contexts is similarly regarded by the courts as providing no excuse for failure to meet the standard of care expected of a more experienced individual. In *Nettleship v. Weston* [1971] 3 All E.R. 581, for example, a learner driver, Lavinia Weston, was held liable for failure to attain the standard of care in driving a car expected of someone who had passed their driving test. In the words of Lord Denning M.R. "the law lays down, for all drivers of motor cars, a standard of care to which all must conform . . . even a learner driver, so long as he is the sole driver, must attain the same standard".

2. Browne-Wilkinson L.J. raises the issue as to liability of a health authority which is subject to financial constraints. This question was explored further by Mustill L.J. in his judgment in *Bull v. Devon Area Health Authority* [1993] 4 Med. L.R. 22. He said there that:

   " . . . It is not necessarily an answer to allegations of unsafety that there were insufficient resources to enable administrators to do everything which they would like to do. I do not for a moment suggest that public medicine is precisely analogous to other public services, but there is perhaps a danger in assuming that it is completely *sui generis*, and that it is necessarily a complete defence to say that even if the system in any hospital was unsatisfactory, it was no more unsatisfactory than those in force elsewhere."

Clearly, then, his Lordship envisages a certain minimal standard of care below which health care providers should not fall, regardless of how (in)adequately they are funded.

3. In *Wilsher*, Browne Wilkinson L.J. suggests that liability may be imposed directly upon the hospital authorities in such a situation rather than on the health professional. This echoes what was said by Denning in *Cassidy* (see pages 150–151 above).

4. A further issue which arises out of *Wilsher* is the extent to which liability may be imposed where treatment services have been curtailed due to policy decisions at governmental level. (See further Chapter 1 at pages 47–61 above.)

QUESTIONS:

1. In *Johnstone v. Bloomsbury Health Authority* [1991] 2 All E.R. 293 the Court of Appeal recognised the scope for young, overworked doctors bringing actions against health authorities in respect of injury to their health caused by such excessive working hours. Do you think it follows that patients injured by such over-tired doctors, because of their exhaustion, should also be able to sue the health authority?

2. Even if, as we saw above, limited resources do not form a complete defence to a negligence action, is it nonetheless possible that they may have the effect of lowering the standard of care required? (See *Knight v. Home Office* [1990] 3 All E.R. 237, 247 on the question of the standard of psychiatric services that can be expected in a prison, as opposed to any other, hospital.)

(d) The Burden of Proof

The burden of proof always rests with the plaintiff. It is for him to show, on the balance of probabilities, that the defendant has failed to meet the standard of care demanded by the law. In cases where there are very finely balanced views as to whether the doctor in question was negligent, discharging the burden of proof can be extremely problematic. Occasionally, however, a case might occur in which the plaintiff can plead *res ipsa loquitur*. Literally translated, it means "the thing speaks for itself". The plaintiff may invoke this rule if he can show three things. First, that he has been injured and that there is no explanation of how the injury arose. Secondly, that his injury arose in circumstances in which such an injury would not normally occur, and thirdly, that the defendant was in control of the situation in which context the injury occurred. There have been differing views expressed as to the impact of *res ipsa loquitur*. One approach is that once *res ipsa* is pleaded it is for the defendant to explain what has taken place and bring forward some evidence to rebut the allegation. The other is that *res ipsa loquitur* has the effect of reversing the burden of proof. (See M. Jones, *Medical Negligence* (2nd ed.), London:

Sweet and Maxwell, 1996, paras. 3.114–3.119.) This means that it is for the defendant to prove that he was not negligent.

Res ipsa loquitur has received discussion in only a limited number of medical negligence cases.

Mahon v. Osborne [1939] 1 All E.R. 535, [1939] 2 K.B. 14, (1939) 108 LJKB 567, (1939) L.T. 329

A difficult abdominal operation was performed by the appellant, assisted by a theatre sister and two nurses. At the end of the operation, the number of swabs used and retrieved from the patient's body was counted, and stated to the surgeon to be correct. However, one month later, when the patient underwent a second operation, it was discovered that a swab had been left inside his body. The patient did not survive the second operation.

It was common ground that the patient's death was caused, not by the second operation, but by the swab that had been left in his body. In addition, it was held that the system employed by the hospital for counting swabs — fully described in the evidence laid before the court — was satisfactory. The patient's mother, therefore, brought an action in negligence against the individual surgeon who had performed the operation contending that the doctrine of *res ipsa loquitur* was applicable.

SCOTT L.J.:
"... It is difficult to see how the principle of *res ipsa loquitur* can apply generally to actions for negligence against a surgeon for leaving a swab in a patient, even if in certain circumstances the presumption may arise. If it applied generally, plaintiff's counsel, having, by a couple of answers to interrogatories, proved that the defendant performed the operation and that a swab was left in, would be entitled to ask for judgment, unless evidence describing the operation was given by the defendant. Some positive evidence of neglect of duty is surely needed. It may be that a full description of the actual operation will disclose facts sufficiently indicative of want of skill or care to entitle a jury to find neglect of duty to the patient. It may be that expert evidence in addition will be requisite. To treat the maxim as applying in every case where the swab is left in the patient seems to me an error of law. The very essence of the rule, when applied to an action for negligence, is that, upon the mere fact of the event happening, for example, an injury to the plaintiff, there arise two presumptions of fact, (i) that the event was caused by a breach by somebody of the duty of care towards the plaintiff, and (ii) that the defendant was that somebody. The presumption of fact arises only because it is an inference which the reasonable man, knowing the facts, would naturally draw, and that is, in most cases, for two reasons, (i) that the control over the happening of such an event rested solely with the defendant, and (ii) that in the ordinary experience of mankind such an event does not happen unless the person in control has failed to exercise due care. The nature even of abdominal operations varies widely, and many considerations enter into it, the degree of urgency, the state of the patient's inside, the complication of his disorder or injury, the condition of his heart, the effects of the anaesthetic, the degree and kind of help which the surgeon has — for example, whether he is assisted by another surgeon — the efficiency of the team of theatre nurses, the extent of the surgeon's experience and the limits of wise discretion in the particular circumstances — for example, the complications arising out of the

operation itself, and the fear of the patient's collapse. In the present case, all the above considerations combine to present a state of things of which the ordinary experience of mankind knows nothing, and, therefore, to make it unsafe to beg the question of proof."

NOTES:

1. Although there is a discretion to enable a jury to be called, contained in section 69(3) of the Supreme Court Act 1981, juries are today almost never used in negligence suits in this country.
2. Scott L.J. was clearly very sceptical about the ability of lay patients to knowledgeably invoke the *res ipsa* principle. Brazier, while perhaps not as sceptical, has also commented: "As most people are not medically qualified, how could they know whether the accident to the patient was one which could or could not happen if proper care was taken" (M. Brazier, *Medicine Patients and the Law*, (2nd ed.), Harmondsworth: Penguin, 1992 at page 156).

QUESTION:

1. Do you think that a present day court would, like Scott L.J., regard "the extent of the surgeon's experience" as a relevant factor in assessing whether he had performed an operation negligently? (Bear in mind the comments of the Court of Appeal on the matter in the *Wilsher* case.)

Cassidy v. Ministry of Health [1951] 1 All E.R. 574, [1951] 2 K.B. 343, [1951] W.L.R. 147

The plaintiff in this case underwent an operation on his hand at the defendant's hospital which was performed by Dr Fahrni, a full-time assistant medical officer. After the operation, his hand and forearm were bandaged to a splint in which position they were kept firmly for the next fourteen days. Throughout that period, the plaintiff complained of pain but nothing was done by either the doctor who had operated or the house surgeon, except that he was given sedatives. Both Dr Fahrni and the house surgeon were hospital employees. When the bandages were finally removed the plaintiff's hand had become stiff and practically useless for the purposes of his work which involved using a pick and shovel.

By section 6(2) of the National Health Service Act 1946 the hospital was substituted by the Ministry of Health as the defendant, against whom the plaintiff brought an action alleging negligence in relation to the post-operational treatment that he had received.

DENNING L.J.:
"If the plaintiff had to prove that some particular doctor or nurse was negligent, he would not be able to do it, but he was not put to that impossible task. He says:

'I went into the hospital to be cured of two stiff fingers. I have come out with four stiff fingers, and my hand is useless. That should not have happened if due care had been used. Explain it, if you can.' I am quite clearly of the opinion that that raises a *prima facie* case against the hospital authorities: see *Mahon v. Osborne* [1939] 1 All E.R. 535 at p 561 *per* Goddard L.J. They have nowhere explained how it could have happened without negligence. They have busied themselves in saying that this member or that member of their staff was not negligent, but they have called not a single person to say that the injuries were consistent with due care on the part of all the members of their staff. They called some of the people who actually treated the plaintiff, namely, Dr Fahrni, Dr Ronaldson, and Sister Hall each of whom protested that he was careful in his or her part, but they did not call the senior surgeon, Mr Moroney, or any expert at all, to say that what occurred might happen despite all care. They have not, therefore, displaced the *prima facie* case against them and are liable in damages to the plaintiff."

NOTES:

1. The scope for the invocation of *res ipsa loquitur* in medical negligence cases should not be overestimated. *Cassidy* is an exceptional case. Equally, modern hospital care, which involves the diligent making of notes, means that the chances of an accident occurring without any evidence as to why, are probably very slim. This diminished scope for the *res ipsa* doctrine was recognised judicially in *Bull v. Devon Area Health Authority* [1993] 4 Med. L.R. 22, a case in which the first plaintiff, Mrs Bull, alleged that the asphyxia suffered by her son at birth was attributable to the defendant's negligence. There, Mustill L.J. stressed the fact that "[t]he plaintiff's advisers were able to put in evidence from the records as part of their case the outlines of what actually happened". He then added:

   "I do not see how the present situation calls for recourse to an evidentiary presumption applicable in cases where the defendant does, and the plaintiff does not, have within his grasp the means of knowing how the accident took place. Here, all the facts that are ever going to be known are before the court. The judge held that they pointed to liability, and I agree."

(e) Causation

It is insufficient in a malpractice action for the plaintiff to show merely that he was owed a duty of care and that a breach of that duty took place; he must also be able to show that he has suffered some form of harm or injury that was *caused by* the defendant's breach of duty. Normally, the plaintiff endeavours to prove causation, that is, to show that the harm of which he complains was caused by the defendant's breach of duty. To do this, the plaintiff must, according to *Barnett v. Chelsea and Kensington Hospital Management Committee* [1968] 1 All E.R. 1068, demonstrate that *but for* the defendant's negligence, he would not have suffered the harm in respect of which he seeks damages.

Unfortunately for victims of medical malpractice, proof of causation is not always amenable to a straightforward application of the "but for" test.

Four particular problems commonly arise. First, the plaintiff may have difficulty in proving that any exacerbation of his ill health was attributable to the negligence of the doctor or nurse rather than a simple progression of his illness. Second, medical knowledge has its limits, and the aetiology of illness cannot always be understood, even by those with medical expertise (see *e.g. Kay v. Ayrshire and Arran Health Board* [1987] 2 All E.R. 417). The plaintiff may have been treated with drugs, the full range of whose side-effects are not fully known or understood (see, for example *Loveday v. Renton* [1990] 1 Med. L.R. 117).

The third and fourth difficulties, the most problematic by far, can conveniently be taken together. They are, establishing causation where there is more than one causal agent at work, and establishing causation to the requisite standard of proof. (Note the standard of proof — *i.e.* the level of certainty with which one must show causation — must be distinguished from the burden of proof — *i.e.* upon whom the onus of proving their case lies.) Both of these issues have been considered by the House of Lords. The following two cases deal respectively with them.

Wilsher v. Essex Area Health Authority [1988] 1 All E.R. 871, [1988] 1 A.C. 1074, (1988) 3 BMLR 37 H.L.

The facts of *Wilsher* were set out at pages 163–164 above when we considered the Court of Appeal's discussion of the standard of care required in this case.

Lord Bridge:
" . . . My Lords, I understand that all your Lordships agree that this appeal has to be allowed and that the inevitable consequence of this is that the outstanding issue of causation must, unless the parties can reach agreement, be retried by another judge. In these circumstances, for obvious reasons, it is undesirable that I should go into the highly complex and technical evidence on which the issue depends any further than is strictly necessary to explain why, in common with all your Lordships, I feel ineluctably driven to the unpalatable conclusion that it is not open to the House to resolve the issue one way or the other, so that a question depending on the consequence of an event occurring in the first two days of Martin's life will now have to be investigated all over again when Martin is nearly ten years old. On the other hand, the appeal raises a question of law as to the proper approach to issues of causation which is of great importance and of particular concern in medical negligence cases. This must be fully considered . . .

The starting point for any consideration of the relevant law of causation is the decision of this House in *Bonnington Castings Ltd v. Wardlaw* [1956] 1 All E.R. 615. This was the case of a pursuer who, in the course of his employment by the defenders, contracted pneumoconiosis over a period of years by the inhalation of invisible particles of silica dust from two sources. One of these (pneumatic hammers) was an 'innocent' source, in the sense that the pursuer could not complain that his exposure to it involved any breach of duty on the part of his employers. The other source (swing grinders), however, arose from a breach of statutory duty by the employer. Delivering the leading speech in the House Lord Reid said ([1956] 1 All E.R. at 617–618):
'The Lord Ordinary and the majority of the First Division have dealt with this case on the footing that there was an onus on the defenders, the appellants, to

prove that the dust from the swing grinders did not cause the respondent's disease. This view was based on a passage in the judgment of the Court of Appeal in *Vyner v. Waldenberg Bros Ltd* [1945] 2 All E.R. 547 at 549 *per* Scott L.J.: 'If there is a definite breach of a safety provision imposed on the occupier of a factory, and a workman is injured in a way which could result from the breach, the onus of proof shifts on to the employer to show that the breach was not the cause. We think that that principle lies at the very basis of statutory rules of absolute duty' . . . Of course the onus was on the defendants to prove delegation (if that was an answer) and to prove contributory negligence, and it may be that that is what the Court of Appeal has in mind. But the passage which I have cited appears to go beyond that and, in so far as it does so, I am of opinion that it is erroneous. It would seem obvious in principle that a pursuer or plaintiff must prove not only negligence or breach of duty but also that such fault caused, or materially contributed to, his injury, and there is ample authority for that proposition both in Scotland and in England. I can find neither reason nor authority for the rule being different where there is breach of a statutory duty. The fact that Parliament imposes a duty for the protection of employees has been held to entitle an employee to sue if he is injured as a result of a breach of that duty, but it would be going a great deal further to hold that it can be inferred from the enactment of a duty that Parliament intended that any employee suffering injury can sue his employer merely because there was a breach of duty and it is shown to be possible that his injury may have been caused by it. In my judgment, the employee must, in all cases, prove his case by the ordinary standard of proof in civil actions he must make it appear at least that, on a balance of probabilities, the breach of duty caused, or materially contributed to, his injury.'

Lord Tucker said of Scott L.J.'s dictum in *Vyner v. Waldenberg Bros Ltd*:

' . . . I think it is desirable that your Lordships should take this opportunity to state in plain terms that no such onus exists unless the statute or statutory regulation expressly or impliedly so provides, as in several instances it does. No. distinction can be drawn between actions for common law negligence and actions for breach of statutory duty in this respect. In both, the plaintiff or pursuer must prove (a) breach of duty, and (b) that such breach caused the injury complained of (see *Wakelin v. London & South Western Ry Co* (1886) 12 App. Cas. 41), and *Caswell v. Powell Duffryn Associated Collieries Ltd* [1939] 3 All E.R. 722. In each case, it will depend on the particular facts proved, and the proper inferences to be drawn therefrom, whether the respondent has sufficiently discharged the onus that lies on him.' (See [1956] 1 All E.R. 615 at 621.)

Lord Keith said ([1956] 1 All E.R. at 621):

'The onus is on the respondent [the pursuer] to prove his case, and I see no reason to depart from this elementary principle by invoking certain rules of onus said to be based on a correspondence between the injury suffered and the evil guarded against by some statutory regulation. I think most, if not all, of the cases which professed to lay down or to recognise some such rule could have been decided as they were on simple rules of evidence, and I agree that *Vyner v. Waldenberg Bros Ltd* [1945] 2 All E.R. 547, in so far as it professed to enunciate a principle of law inverting the onus of proof, cannot be supported.'

Viscount Simonds and Lord Somervell agreed.

Their Lordships concluded, however, from the evidence that the inhalation of dust to which the pursuer was exposed by the defender's breach of statutory duty had made a material contribution to his pneumoconiosis which was sufficient to discharge the onus on the pursuer of proving that his damage was caused by the defenders' tort. A year later the decision in *Nicholson v. Atlas Steel Foundry and Engineering Co Ltd* [1957] 1 All E.R. 776 followed the decision in *Bonnington Castings Ltd v. Wardlaw* and held, in another case of pneumoconiosis, that the employers were liable for employee's disease arising from the inhalation of dust from two sources, one 'innocent' the other 'guilty', on facts virtually indistinguishable from those in *Bonnington Castings Ltd v. Wardlaw*.

In *McGhee v. National Coal Board* [1972] 3 All E.R. 1008 the pursuer worked in a brick kiln in hot and dusty conditions in which brick dust adhered to his sweaty skin. No breach of duty by his employers, the defenders, was established in respect of his working conditions. However, the employers were held to be at fault in failing to provide adequate washing facilities which resulted in the pursuer having to bicycle home after work with his body still caked in brick dust. The pursuer contracted dermatitis and the evidence that this was caused by the brick dust was accepted. Brick dust adhering to the skin was a recognised cause of industrial dermatitis and the provision of showers to remove it after work was a usual precaution to minimise the risk of the disease. The precise mechanism of causation of the disease however, was not known and the furthest the doctors called for the pursuer were able to go was to say that the provision of showers would have materially reduced the risk of dermatitis. They were unable to say that it would probably have prevented the disease.

The pursuer failed before the Lord Ordinary and the First Division of the Court of Session on the ground that he had not discharged the burden of proof of causation. He succeeded on appeal to the House of Lords. Much of the academic discussion to which this decision has given rise has focused on the speech of Lord Wilberforce, particularly on two paragraphs. He said ([1972] 3 All E.R. 1008 at 1012):

'But the question remains whether a pursuer must necessarily fail if, after he has shown a breach of duty, involving an increase of risk of disease, he cannot positively prove that this increase of risk caused or materially contributed to the disease while his employers cannot positively prove the contrary. In this intermediate case there is an appearance of logic in the view that the pursuer, on whom the onus lies, should fail — a logic which dictated the judgments below. The question is whether we should be satisfied in factual situations like the present, with this logical approach. In my opinion, there are further considerations of importance. First, it is a sound principle that where a person has, by breach of duty of care, created a risk, and injury occurs within the area of that risk, the loss should be borne by him *unless he shows that it had some other cause*. Secondly, from the evidential point of view, one may ask, why should a man who is able to show that his employer should have taken certain precautions, because without them there is a risk, or an added risk, of injury or disease, and who in fact sustains exactly that injury or disease, have to assume the burden of proving more: namely, that it was the addition to the risk, caused by the breach of duty, which caused or materially contributed to the injury? In many cases of which the present is typical, this is impossible to prove, just because honest medical opinion cannot segregate the causes of an illness between compound causes. And if one asks which of the parties, the workman or the employers should suffer from this inherent evidential difficulty, the answer as a matter in policy or justice should be that it is the creator of the risk who, *ex hypothesi*, must be taken to have foreseen the possibility of damage, who should bear its consequences.' (My emphasis.)

He then referred to *Bonnington Castings Ltd v. Wardlaw* and *Nicholson v. Atlas Steel Foundry and Engineering Co. Ltd* and added ([1972] 3 All E.R. 1008 at 1013):

'The present factual situation has its differences: the default here consisted not in adding a material quantity to the accumulation of injurious particles but by failure to take a step which materially increased the risk that the dust already present would cause injury. And I must say that, at least in the present case, to bridge the evidential gap by inference seems to me something of a fiction, since it was precisely this inference which the medical expert declined to make. But I find in the cases quoted an analogy which suggests the conclusion that, *in the absence of proof that the culpable condition had, in the result, no effect*, the employers should be liable for an injury, squarely within the risk which they created and that they, not the pursuer, should suffer the consequence of the impossibility, foreseeably inherent in the nature of his injury, of segregating the precise consequence of their default.' (My emphasis.)

My Lords, it seems to me that both these paragraphs, particularly in the words I have emphasised, amount to saying that, in the circumstances, the burden of proof of causation is reversed and thereby to run counter to the unanimous and emphatic opinions expressed in *Bonnington Castings Ltd v. Wardlaw* [1956] 1 All E.R. 615 to the contrary effect. I find no support in any of the other speeches for the view that the burden of proof is reversed and, in this respect, I think Lord Wilberforce's reasoning must be regarded as expressing a minority opinion.

A distinction is, of course, apparent between the facts of *Bonnington Castings Ltd v. Wardlaw* where the 'innocent' and 'guilty' silica dust particles which together caused the pursuer's lung disease were inhaled concurrently and the facts of *McGhee v. National Coal Board* where the 'innocent' and 'guilty' brick dust was present on the pursuer's body for consecutive periods. In the one case the concurrent inhalation of 'innocent' and 'guilty' dust must both have contributed to the cause of the disease. In the other case the consecutive periods when 'innocent' and 'guilty' brick dust was present on the pursuer's body may both have contributed to the cause of the disease or, theoretically at least, one or other may have been the sole cause. But where the layman is told by the doctors that the longer the brick dust remains on the body, the greater the risk of dermatitis, although the doctors cannot identify the process of causation scientifically, there seems to be nothing irrational in drawing the inference, as a matter of common sense, that the consecutive periods when brick dust remained on the body probably contributed cumulatively to the causation of the dermatitis. I believe that a process of inferential reasoning on these general lines underlies the decision of the majority in *McGhee's* case."

Lord Bridge sought then to support this view by reference to passages from the speeches of Lords Reid, Simon, Kilbrandon and Salmon in *McGhee's* case. He then continued:

" . . . *McGhee v. National Coal Board* laid down no new principle of law whatever. On the contrary, it affirmed the principle that the onus of proving causation lies on the pursuer or plaintiff. Adopting a robust and pragmatic approach to the undisputed primary facts of the case, the majority concluded that it was a legitimate inference of fact that the defenders' negligence had materially contributed to the pursuer's injury. The decision, in my opinion, is of no greater significance than that and the attempt to extract from it some esoteric principle which in some way modifies, as a matter of law, the nature of the burden of proof of causation which a plaintiff or pursuer must discharge once he has established a relevant breach of duty is a fruitless one.

In the Court of Appeal in the instant case Sir Nicholas Browne-Wilkinson V-C, being in a minority, expressed his view on causation with understandable caution. But I am quite unable to find any fault with the following passage in his dissenting judgment [1986] 3 All E.R. 801 at 834–835:

'To apply the principle in *McGhee v. National Coal Board* [1972] 3 All E.R. 1008 to the present case would constitute an extension of that principle. In *McGhee* there was no doubt that the pursuer's dermatitis was physically caused by brick dust the only question was whether the continued presence of such brick dust on the pursuer's skin after the time when he should have been provided with a shower caused or materially contributed to the dermatitis which he contracted. There was only one possible agent which could have caused the dermatitis, *viz* brick dust, and there was no doubt that the dermatitis from which he suffered was caused by that brick dust. In the present case the question is different. There are a number of different agents which could have caused the RLF. Excess oxygen was one of them. The defendants failed to take reasonable precautions to prevent one of the possible causative agents (*e.g.* excess oxygen) from causing RLF. But no one can tell in this case whether excess oxygen did or did not cause or contribute to the RLF suffered by the plaintiff. The plaintiff's RLF may have been caused by some completely different agent or agents, *e.g.* hypercarbia, intraventricular haemorrhage, apnoea or patent ductus arteriosus. In addition to oxygen, each of those conditions has been implicated as a possible cause of RLF. This baby suffered from each of those conditions at various times in the first two months of his life. There is no satisfactory evidence that excess oxygen is more likely than any of those other four candidates to have caused RLF in this baby. To my mind, the occurrence of RLF following a failure to take a necessary precaution to prevent excess oxygen causing RLF provides no evidence and raises no presumption that it was excess oxygen rather than one or more of the four other possible agents which caused or contributed to RLF in this case. The position, to my mind, is wholly different from that in *McGhee*, where there was only one candidate (brick dust) which could have caused the dermatitis, and the failure to take a precaution against brick dust causing dermatitis was followed by dermatitis caused by brick dust. In such a case, I can see the common sense, if not the logic, of holding that, in the absence of any other evidence, the failure to take the precaution caused or contributed to the dermatitis. To the extent that certain members of the House of Lords decided the question on inferences from evidence or presumptions, I do not consider that the present case falls within their reasoning. A failure to take preventive measures against one out of five possible causes is no evidence as to which of those five caused the injury.'

Since, on this view, the appeal must, in any event, be allowed, it is not strictly necessary to decide whether it was open to the Court of Appeal to resolve one of the conflicts between the experts which the judge left unresolved and to find that the oxygen administered to Martin in consequence of the misleading Po_2 levels derived from the misplaced catheter was capable of having caused or materially contributed to his RLF. I very well understand the anxiety of the majority to avoid the necessity for ordering a retrial if that was at all possible. But, having accepted, as your Lordships and counsel have had to accept, that the primary conflict of opinion between the experts whether excessive oxygen in the first two days of life probably did cause or materially contribute to Martin's RLF cannot be resolved by reading the transcript, I doubt, with all respect, if the Court of Appeal was entitled to try to resolve the secondary conflict whether it could have done so. Where expert witnesses are radically at issue about complex technical questions within their own field and are examined and cross-examined at length about their conflicting theories, I believe that the judge's advantage in seeing them and hearing them is scarcely less important than when he has to resolve some conflict of primary fact between lay witnesses in purely mundane matters. So here, in the absence of relevant findings of fact by the judge, there was really no alternative to a retrial."

Notes:

1. The remaining four Law Lords in *Wilsher* delivered short speeches expressing their agreement with Lord Bridge.
2. *Wilsher* graphically illustrates the difficulty in establishing causation. In this case there were five separate possible causes. In that respect it can be contrasted with the decision in *McGhee*, in that case the causes were cumulative.

QUESTION:

1. What constitutes a "material contribution" to the damage caused?

The House of Lords have also considered the standard of proof required in order to satisfy the court that the defendant's culpable act or omission was the factual cause of the plaintiff's injury.

Hotson v. East Berkshire Area Health Authority [1987] 2 All E.R. 909, [1987] 1 A.C. 750

In 1977, when the plaintiff was 13, he fell from a tree and injured his hip. He was taken to the defendant's hospital where his injury was incorrectly diagnosed. He was sent back home where, for the following five days, he remained in severe pain. After this time he was taken back to the defendant's hospital where X-rays revealed that he had suffered an acute traumatic fracture of the left femoral epiphysis. On the next day he underwent an operation to pin the joint but it did not prevent him suffering avascular necrosis of the epiphysis which led to a deformity of the hip joint and, by the time he was 20 years old, left him with a permanent disability.

The defendant health authority admitted negligence in respect of the delay in diagnosis but denied that the delay had caused the plaintiff's long-term condition. At first instance, the trial judge found that even if the defendant's staff had correctly diagnosed his condition when he was first seen at the hospital, there was still a 75 per cent chance that the disability would have developed in any case. He then held that the defendant's breach of duty had resulted in a loss of a 25 per cent chance of recovery and made an award of damages which reflected this. The defendant authority appealed first, and unsuccessfully, to the Court of Appeal, and then to the House of Lords.

LORD BRIDGE:
" . . . The plaintiff sued the authority, who admitted negligence in failing to diagnose the injury on April 26, 1977. Simon Brown J., in a judgment delivered on March 15, 1985, *sub nom. Hotson v. Fitzgerald* [1985] 3 All E.R. 167, awarded £150 damages for the pain suffered by the plaintiff from April 26 to May 1, 1977 which he would have been spared by prompt diagnosis and treatment. This element of the damages is not in dispute. The authority denied liability for any other element of damages. The judge expressed his findings of fact as follows [1985] 3 All E.R. 167 at 171:
'1. Even had the defendants correctly diagnosed and treated the plaintiff on 26 April there is a high probability, which I assess as a 75 per cent risk, that the plaintiff's injury would have followed the same course as it in fact has, *i.e.* he would have developed avascular necrosis of the whole femoral head with all the same adverse consequences as have already ensued and with all the same adverse future prospects. 2. That 75 per cent risk was translated by the defendants' admitted breach of duty into inevitability. Putting it the other way, the defendants' delay in diagnosis denied the plaintiff the 25 per

cent chance that, given immediate treatment, avascular necrosis would not have developed. 3. Had avascular necrosis not developed, the plaintiff would have made a very nearly full recovery. 4. The reason why the delay sealed the plaintiff's fate was because it followed the pressure caused by haemarthrosis (the bleeding of ruptured blood vessels into the joint) to compress and thus block the intact but distorted remaining vessels with the result that even had the fall left intact sufficient vessels to keep the epiphysis alive (which, as finding no 1 makes plain, I think possible but improbable) such vessels would have become occluded and ineffective for this purpose.'

On the basis of these findings he held, as a matter of law, that the plaintiff was entitled to damages for the loss of the 25 per cent chance that, if the injury had been promptly diagnosed and treated, it would not have resulted in avascular necrosis of the epiphysis and the plaintiff would have made a very nearly full recovery. He proceeded to assess the damages attributable to the consequences of the avascular necrosis at £46,000. Discounting this by 75 per cent, he awarded the plaintiff £11,500 for the lost chance of recovery. The authority's appeal against this element in the award of damages was dismissed by the Court of Appeal (Sir John Donaldson M.R., Dillon and Croom-Johnson L.JJ., [1987] 1 All E.R. 210). The authority now appeal by leave of your Lordships' House.

I would observe at the outset that the damages referable to the plaintiff's pain during the five days by which treatment was delayed in consequence of failure to diagnose the injury correctly, although sufficient to establish the authority's liability for the tort of negligence, have no relevance to their liability in respect of the avascular necrosis. There was no causal connection between the plaintiff's physical pain and the development of the necrosis. If the injury had been painless, the plaintiff would have to establish the necessary causal link between the necrosis and the authority's breach of duty in order to succeed. It makes no difference that the five days' pain gave him a cause of action in respect of an unrelated element of damage . . .

In analysing the issue of law arising from his findings the judge said [1985] 3 All E.R. 167 at 175:

'In the end the problem comes down to one of classification. Is this on true analysis a case where the plaintiff is concerned to establish causative negligence or is it rather a case where the real question is the proper quantum of damage? Clearly the case hovers near the border. Its proper solution in my judgment depends on categorising it correctly between the two. If the issue is one of causation then the defendants succeed since the plaintiff will have failed to prove his claim on the balance of probabilities. He will be lacking an essential ingredient of his cause of action. If, however, the issue is one of quantification then the plaintiff succeeds because it is trite law that the quantum of a recognised head of damage must be evaluated according to the chances of the loss occurring.'

He reached the conclusion that the question was one of quantification and thus arrived at his award to the plaintiff of one quarter of the damages appropriate to compensate him for the consequences of the avascular necrosis.

It is here, with respect, that I part company with the judge. The plaintiff's claim was for damages for physical injury and consequential loss alleged to have been caused by the authority's breach of their duty of care. In some cases, perhaps particularly medical negligence cases, causation may be so shrouded in mystery that the court can only measure statistical chances. But that was not so here. On the evidence there was a clear conflict as to what had caused the avascular necrosis. The authority's evidence was that the sole cause was the original traumatic injury to the hip. The plaintiff's evidence, as its highest, was that the delay in treatment was a material contributory cause. This was a conflict, like any other about some relevant past event, which the judge could not avoid resolving on a balance of probabilities. Unless the plaintiff proved on a balance of probabilities that the delayed treatment was at least a material contributory cause of the avascular necrosis he failed on the issue of causation and no question of quantification could arise. But the judge's findings of fact, as stated in the numbered paragraphs (1) and (4) which I have set out earlier in this opinion, are unmistakably to the effect that on a balance of probabilities the injury caused by the plaintiff's fall left insufficient blood vessels intact to keep the epiphysis alive. This amounts to a finding of fact that the fall was the sole cause of the avascular necrosis . . .

There is a superficially attractive analogy between the principle applied in such cases as *Chaplin v. Hicks* [1911–13] All E.R. 224 (award of damages for breach of contract assessed by reference to the lost chance of securing valuable employment if the contract had been performed) and *Kitchen v. Royal Air Forces Association* [1958] 2 All E.R. 241 (damages for solicitors' negligence assessed by reference to the lost chance of prosecuting a successful civil action) and the principle of awarding damages for the lost chance of avoiding personal injury or, in medical negligence cases, for the lost chance of a better medical result which might have been achieved by prompt diagnosis and correct treatment. I think there are formidable difficulties in the way of accepting the analogy. But I do not see this appeal as a suitable occasion for reaching a settled conclusion as to whether the analogy can ever be applied.

As I have said, there was in this case an inescapable issue of causation first to be resolved. But if the plaintiff had proved on a balance of probabilities that the authority's negligent failure to diagnose and treat his injury promptly had materially contributed to the development of avascular necrosis, I know of no principle of English law which would have entitled the authority to a discount from the full measure of damage to reflect the chance that, even given prompt treatment, avascular necrosis might well still have developed. The decisions of this House in *Bonnington Castings Ltd v. Wardlaw* [1956] 1 All E.R. 615 and *McGhee v. National Coal Board* give no support to such a view.

I would allow the appeal to the extent of reducing the damages awarded to the plaintiff by £11,500 and the amount of any interest on that sum which is included in the award."

LORD MACKAY:

" . . . In their printed case the health authority first took the position that they were entitled to succeed in this appeal because the plaintiff had not proved that any loss or damage (other than five days' pain and suffering) had been caused by the authority's breach of duty. They also submitted that damages for loss of a chance were not recoverable in tort and at the close of the hearing counsel for the authority invited your Lordships to decide this case not only on the ground of fact which he submitted was available but also on the more general ground that damages for loss of a chance could not be awarded. This latter submission has been discussed in the course of the hearing very fully and I wish to add some observations, particularly on that aspect of the case.

When counsel for the plaintiff was invited to say what he meant by a chance he said that in relation to the facts of this case as found by the judge what was meant by a chance was that if 100 people had suffered the same injury as the plaintiff 75 of them would have developed avascular necrosis of the whole femoral head and 25 would not. This, he said, was an asset possessed by the plaintiff when he arrived at the authority's hospital on April 26, 1977. It was this asset which counsel submits the plaintiff lost in consequence of the negligent failure of the authority to diagnose his injury properly until May 1, 1977.

The case closest on its facts to the present from the United Kingdom, cited at the hearing before your Lordships, is *Kenyon v. Bell* 1953 S.C. 125. In that case the lower lid of a child's eye was cut as a result of an accident and subsequently the eye had to be removed by operation. An action for damages was raised against the medical practitioner who had first treated the injury, alleging that he had failed to exercise reasonable care and ordinary professional skill in carrying out his examination and treatment of the injury and that as a result the child had not been given certain treatment which 'would have made the saving of the eye a certainty or alternatively . . . would have materially increased the chance of saving the eye'. The medical practitioner contended that since all that was being offered to be proved was the weaker of the two alternative statements the case should not be allowed to proceed to proof since the weaker alternative alleging that the treatment would materially have increased the chance of saving the eye did not justify a claim for damages. Lord Guthrie held that the loss of a chance of saving the eye was not of itself a matter which would entitle the claim to succeed but founding particularly on the use of the word 'material' in the pleadings to qualify the chance of saving the eye by proper treatment Lord Guthrie held that on the evidence the chance of saving the eye by proper treatment might be proved to be so material that the natural and reasonable inference to draw from the evidence would be that the loss of the eye was due to the absence of such treatment. In that event, the claim would succeed. Accordingly he allowed it to go to proof. This illustrates that where what is at issue is a patient's condition on being presented to a medical practitioner the question whether the condition was such that proper treatment could effect a particular result is to be determined on the balance of probabilities and that one way of describing that balance is to say that there was at that time a sufficient chance that the particular result could be attained to justify holding that the loss of that result was caused by the absence of proper treatment. On the other hand, Lord Guthrie made it clear that, in his opinion, while the fault could be charged against the doctor as being failure to give the child the opportunity of having an eye preserved by proper treatment, unless the eye would have been saved by such treatment no loss would have been established and no claim for damages justified in respect thereof.

After the proof, Lord Strachan in a decision (9 April, 1954, unreported) held that the defender had established that the boy's eye was irreparably injured on 15 March, 1951 and that no treatment could have made any difference because the initial injury involved a perforating wound of the sclera with consequent haemorrhaging into the interior of the eye . . .

As I have said, the fundamental question of fact to be answered in this case related to a point in time before the negligent failure to treat began. It must, therefore, be a matter of past fact. It did not raise any question of what might have been the situation in a hypothetical state of facts. To this problem the words of Lord Diplock in *Mallett v. McMonagle* [1969] 2 All E.R. 178 at 191 apply:

'In determining what did happen in the past a court decides on the balance of probabilities. Anything that is more probable than not it treats as certain.'

In this respect this case is the same, in principle, as any other in which the state of facts existing before alleged negligence came into play has to be determined. For example, if a claimant alleges that he sustained a certain fracture in a fall at work and there is evidence that he had indeed fallen at work, but that shortly before he had fallen at home and sustained the fracture, the court would have to determine where the truth lay. If the claimant denied the previous fall, there would be evidence, both for and against the allegation, that he had so fallen. The issue would be resolved on the balance of probabilities. If the court held on that balance that the fracture was sustained at home, there could be no question of saying that since all that had been established was that it was more probable than not that the injury was not work-related, there was a possibility that it was work-related and that this possibility or chance was a proper subject of compensation.

I should add in this context that where on disputed evidence a judge reaches a conclusion on the balance of probabilities it will not usually be easy to assess a specific measure of probability for the conclusion at which he has arrived. As my noble and learned friend Lord Bridge observed in the course of the hearing, a judge deciding disputed questions of fact will not ordinarily do it by use of a calculator.

On the other hand, I consider that it would be unwise in the present case to lay it down as a rule that a plaintiff could never succeed by proving loss of a chance in a medical negligence case. In *McGhee v. National Coal Board* [1972] 3 All E.R. 1008 this House held that where it was proved that the failure to provide washing facilities for the pursuer at the end of his shift had materially increased the risk that he would contract dermatitis it was proper to hold that the failure to provide such facilities was a cause to a material extent of his contracting dermatitis and thus entitled him to damages from his employers for their negligent failure measured by his loss resulting from dermatitis. Material increase of the risk of contraction of dermatitis is equivalent to material decrease in the chance of escaping dermatitis. Although no precise figures could be given in that case for the purpose of illustration and comparison with this case one might, for example, say that it was established that of 100 people working under the same conditions as the pursuer and without facilities for washing at the end of their shift 70 contracted dermatitis: of 100 people working in the same conditions as the pursuer when washing facilities were provided for them at the end of the shift 30 contracted dermatitis. Assuming nothing more were known about the matter than that, the decision of this House may be taken as holding that in the circumstances of that case it was reasonable to infer that there was a relationship between contraction of dermatitis in these conditions and the absence of washing facilities and therefore it was reasonable to hold that absence of washing facilities was likely to have made a material contribution to the causation of the dermatitis. Although neither party in the present appeal placed particular reliance on the decision in *McGhee* since it was recognised that *McGhee* is far removed on its facts from the circumstances of the present appeal your Lordships were also informed that cases are likely soon to come before the House in which the decision in *McGhee* will be subjected to close analysis. Obviously in approaching the matter on the basis adopted in *McGhee* much will depend on what is known of the reasons for the differences in the figures which I have used to illustrate the position. In these circumstances I think it unwise to do more than say that unless and until this House departs from the decision in *McGhee* your Lordships cannot affirm the proposition that in no circumstances can evidence of loss of a chance resulting from the breach of a duty of care found a successful claim of damages, although there was no suggestion that the House regarded such a chance as an asset in any sense."

NOTES:

1. Lord Brandon, Lord Goff and Lord Ackner agreed with Lords Bridge and Mackay.
2. The House of Lords in *Hotson* do not totally reject the possibility of a successful action for loss of a chance. Nevertheless the plaintiff would have to adduce weighty expert evidence to the effect that the mismanagement/delay had reduced the prospect of recovery, and attempt to identify a specific percentage. In the subsequent case of *Tahir v. Haringey HA* (1995), Otton L.J. speaking *obiter*, expressed the view that there was no action for loss of a chance in English law. (See A. Grubb, "Medical Negligence: Causation" (1996) 1 *Medical Law Review* 92.)
3. In some circumstances there may be recovery for loss if this is more than loss of a chance of recovery. In *Sutton v. Population Services Family Planning Programme Ltd*, *The Times*, November 7, 1981 the plaintiff's cancer was not diagnosed sufficiently early. She suffered a

premature on-set of the menopause as a consequence and also lost an additional four years of life because she was denied care which would have postponed the on-set of the cancer. She recovered damages.

4. On occasions the plaintiff's conduct will be held to break the chain of causation. Generally refusal of an abortion in a situation in which a plaintiff becomes pregnant due to the negligence of the defendant will not break the chain of causation, although there may be some exceptional circumstances in which this does occur. (See *Emeh v. Chelsea and Kensington AHA* [1984] 3 All E.R. 1044 and Chapter 13 below at pages 807–810.) The plaintiff generally is also under an obligation to mitigate his loss and this may include seeking appropriate further medical care.

QUESTIONS:

1. In the context of medical negligence, how satisfactory is it to treat "causation on the balance of probabilities" as the relevant threshold requirement given the scope for significant differences of expert opinion as to the precise aetiology of a particular disease or illness?

A final issue concerns the relevance of the *Bolam* standard of "responsible medical opinion" in establishing whether the defendant's breach of duty caused the plaintiff's injury or illness. This issue arose in the following case.

Bolitho v. City and Hackney Health Authority (1993) *Medical Law Reports* 381; (1992) 13 BMLR 111

In 1984 the appellant, Patrick, aged two, was being treated for breathing difficulties in the respondent health authority's hospital. On one particular day, he suffered two attacks of acute shortness of breath, and on both occasions the ward sister made an urgent summons to a doctor for assistance. However, the doctor failed to attend or send a replacement doctor. Later that day, Patrick suffered a respiratory and cardiac arrest. Although the medical staff managed to resuscitate him, he nonetheless suffered severe brain damage as a consequence of the cardiac arrest. He then brought an action against the respondent alleging that the failure to attend him whilst he was suffering the acute breathing problems amounted to actionable negligence. The respondent admitted negligence (in the narrow sense) in failing to attend Patrick when summoned, but denied liability, contending that causation had not been established. It was agreed that even if Patrick had been attended, he would still have suffered the respiratory and cardiac arrest and consequent brain damage since the doctor who had been summoned stated that she would still not have intubated Patrick. The respondent health authority succeeded at first instance, so Patrick appealed to the Court of Appeal.

FARQUHARSON L.J.:
" . . . By an amended notice of appeal the plaintiffs raise two further points. The first relates to the issue of causation. In *Maynard's* case Lord Scarman when

advancing the test of 'responsible medical opinion' was dealing with breach of duty. He was not dealing with causation. Accordingly, it is argued that causation was a matter for the judge to decide in the normal way and on ordinary common law principles as set out in such cases as *Wilsher v. Essex Area Health Authority* [1988] A.C. 1074, namely had the admitted negligence on the part of Dr Horn caused or materially contributed to the injury suffered by Patrick? Counsel submits that the test of responsible medical opinion is not relevant to this issue of causation. Applying those principles he argues that there is a formidable case for saying that the failure of Dr Horn to attend in answer to the two calls made to her was the probable cause of the cardiac arrest. The factual position was that all the staff concerned with Patrick knew that he was seriously ill. Dr Horn had been in charge of his treatment during the first stay in hospital when he was found to be suffering from acute croup. Although he had been discharged his parents had to bring him back to hospital within a matter of hours. During January 17 there had been two life threatening incidents. In all these circumstances and knowing that intubation caused no risk or at worst, only a slight risk, a judge should be bound to hold that if she had attended when required to do so Dr Horn would probably have given instructions that Patrick should be intubated. While the judge may be guided by expert evidence he is not on this issue to be directed by it.

While these are powerful arguments I cannot accede to them. In this case the judge was dealing with a breach of duty which consisted of an omission, and it was necessary for him to decide what course of events would have followed had the duty been discharged. Even though he was dealing with causation the learned judge was in these circumstances bound to rely on the evidence of the experts available to him. Whether Dr Horn's failure to appear would have made any difference in the event depended upon what she would have done had she been present. It was for the plaintiffs to prove that she would probably have intubated, and further that if she did not do so 'failure was contrary to accepted medical practice'."

DILLON L.J.:

" . . . The question for us is therefore essentially one of causation, *viz* was the admitted negligence causative of the damage which Patrick undoubtedly suffered? As to this it is not in doubt that the onus remained on Patrick to prove causation *i.e.* to prove that the fault of Dr Horn and Dr Rodgers caused, or materially contributed to, his injury. See *Bonnington Castings Ltd v. Wardlaw* [1956] A.C. 613 and *Wilsher v. Essex Area Health Authority* [1988] A.C. 1074. What that means, in a case where the fault of the defendant has been a failure to act, is explained by Devlin L.J. in *Corn v. Weir's Glass (Hanley) Ltd* [1960] 2 All E.R. 300 at page 306; after referring to *Bonnington Castings Ltd v. Wardlaw* he said:

'The rule requires the plaintiff to show that if before the accident the regulation had been complied with, his injury probably would not have occurred; and this test of probability means, I think, that the Court should consider independently of the accident how the employer would probably have complied with the regulation if he had done as he ought. If there are two or more ways in which he might have done so and one would, on the facts of the accident, have protected the plaintiff and the others would not have protected him and if no one can say that any one way is more likely to have been chosen than the others, then the plaintiff as a matter of probability fails.'

As to this, we have on the one side a most impressive body of cogent medical evidence called on behalf of Patrick to the effect that the proper course for any doctor attending on Patrick after Sister Sallabank's second urgent call to Dr Horn at 14.00 would have been to intubate Patrick. There would have been time for that to have been done before 14.35 and it is common ground that, if it had been done, he would not have suffered the disastrous collapse, respiratory arrest and consequent cardiac arrest at 14.35. As against that, Dr Horn says that if she had attended after the 14.00 call she would not have intubated Patrick. She would merely have had him kept under close observation to see what happened next. Dr Dinwiddie, a paediatrician specialising in respiratory disease and a consultant at Great Ormond Street Hospital, agreed with Dr Horn and said that in the circumstances he too would not have intubated Patrick, despite the risk, which he appreciated that course involved, of a sudden respiratory arrest. Dr Roberton, a consultant paediatrician at Addenbrookes Hospital, would also not have intubated Patrick . . .

In my judgment, the court could only adopt the approach of Sachs L.J. [in *Hucks v. Cole* (1968) 112 *Sol J.* 483] and reject medical opinion on the ground that the reasons of one group of doctors do not really stand up to analysis, if the court, fully conscious of its own lack of medical knowledge and clinical experience, was none the less clearly satisfied that the views of that group of doctors were *Wednesbury* unreasonable, *i.e.* views such as no reasonable body of doctors could have held (see *Associated Provincial Picture Houses Ltd v. Wednesbury Corp* [1947] 2 All E.R. 680). But, in my judgment, that would be an impossibly strong thing to say of the honest views of experts of the distinction of Dr Dinwiddie and Dr Roberton, in the present case.

The difficulty is that after each of the two episodes of respiratory distress which caused Sister Sallabank to telephone Dr Horn at 12.50 and 14.00 Patrick apparently recovered very speedily and presented as an active, healthy little boy with a good colour. Even over the last half-hour before 14.35 Patrick was not in a state of respiratory distress progressing inexorably to hypoxia and respiratory failure; he was in general quite well but subject to two sudden acute episodes. The defendants' experts therefore regarded the two sudden acute episodes as chance episodes, unconnected to each other, from which Patrick had recovered. They therefore considered the risk of a third chance episode as slight. As against that, Dr Dinwiddie shrank from intubating an active and apparently healthy little boy, since to intubate him would involve sedating him for quite a time, while Dr Roberton thought that intubation carried a danger of leading to a sense of false security as to the true reason for Patrick's sudden crises.

The matter is one of clinical judgment. I am unable to regard the views of Dr Dinwiddie, and for that matter Dr Roberton, as *Wednesbury* unreasonable. Therefore, I cannot disregard their views or prefer the views of the witnesses who would have intubated Patrick. Therefore it must follow, in accordance with the authorities cited above, that causation of damage has not been proved, and Patrick's claim for damages must fail."

SIMON BROWN L.J. (DISSENTING):
" . . . Turning to the argument advanced upon the appeal, I share My Lords' views that it would be quite wrong for this court to disturb the learned judge's conclusion that Dr Dinwiddie's approach to the question when a patient should be intubated was one representative of a respectable body of medical opinion. I would certainly not feel entitled to reject it, as Mr Brennan urged us to do, on the footing suggested by this court's decision in *Hucks v. Cole* . . . *i.e.* as unreasonable and unable to stand up to analysis.

I proceed, therefore, to Mr Brennan's second argument, that the judge should have applied the probability test rather than the *Maynard* test to the issue of causation.

Although this argument lies at the heart of the appeal, I do not propose to spend long on it. Frankly it seems obviously right. The *Maynard* test, following as it does the well recognised jurisprudential path marked out by such decisions as *Hunter v. Hanley* [1955] S.L.T. 213 and *Bolam v. Friern Hospital Management Committee* [1957] 2 All E.R. 118, was forged specifically in the context of liability, of negligence, not of causation. And one can readily detect and accept the underlying principle: that differences of medical opinion do exist and, where each is shown to be respectable, it would be quite wrong to brand as negligent those who choose to adhere to one rather than another such body of opinion.

But, as it seems to me, quite different considerations come into play when the issue is one of causation, arising in the particular way that the issue arises in the present case. This case does not involve a doctor adhering to one body of responsible medical opinion rather than another. No doctor in this case ever took a decision whether or not to intubate. The plain fact here is that no doctor ever arrived at Patrick's bedside. It is that want of attention that constitutes the undoubted negligence in the case.

I have no doubt that the resultant issue, the issue of causation, was correctly formulated by the judge . . . applying the test of probability. More particularly, in the light of his subsequent medical findings, it could have been formulated thus: had Dr Horn or a suitable substitute attended when called, would Patrick on the balance of probabilities have been intubated? I see no reason why the position here should be any different to that arising if a nurse's call is not responded to and no evidence exists as to which of several doctors might have attended. The question surely is: what would an attending doctor probably have done? And given that the doctor would probably do that which she or he should do, the question becomes: what should a doctor do in such circumstances? How then should that question be approached?

It is convenient to start with the burden of proof. This, there can be no doubt, rests upon the plaintiff. It is for the plaintiff to prove that the defendants' negligence caused or materially contributed to his injury. It is not discharged merely by the plaintiff pointing to the combination of the defendants' admitted breach of duty and his own subsequent catastrophe. That is to confuse exposure to the risk of injury with the causing of it — not necessarily the same thing — see the decision of the House of Lords in *Wilsher v. Essex Area Health Authority* [1988] A.C. 1074. Nor will the burden be discharged merely by the plaintiff demonstrating some prospect that whichever doctor arrived would have decided to intubate, not even by proof that 50 per cent of doctors would have intubated. That much too is plain — see the decision of the House of Lords in *Hotson v. East Berkshire Area Health Authority* [1987] 1 A.C. 750. And these are the decisions upon which the defendants now primarily rely. Given, they argue, that doctors could properly take either one of the two views espoused respectively by Dr Heaf and Dr Dinwiddie, how can it be said that whoever had attended would more probably have belonged to Dr Heaf's school of thought than to Dr Dinwiddie's? Superficially the argument is appealing; on analysis, however, it seems to me ill-founded.

Let me deal first with *Hotson*. That, clearly, was a decision on very different facts, raising a very different principle. The negligence there consisted of the defendants' failure to diagnose correctly and treat promptly the plaintiff's already sustained injury. In the light of the finding of fact that there was a 75 per cent chance that the plaintiff's injury was such that prompt treatment would not in any event have benefited him, the question of law raised was: should the patient recover 25 per cent of the claim's full value for loss of a chance, or nothing for having failed to prove on the balance of probabilities that the admitted negligence caused him loss? The House of Lords held the latter. But this plaintiff is not suing on the footing that he lost a 50 per cent chance that whichever doctor attended would have intubated him. His case is that he probably would have been intubated.

I turn next to *Wilsher*, clearly somewhat closer in point. The facts there were that the infant plaintiff suffered a serious retinal condition (RLF) which could have been caused by the defendants' negligence in exposing him to excess oxygen but could instead have resulted from any one of four other possible causes. The trial judge held that, since the hospital had failed to take proper precautions to prevent excess oxygen being administered, and since the plaintiff had suffered the injury against which the precautions were designed to protect, the burden lay on the health authority to show that the damage did not result from the breach. The Court of

Appeal supported the decision on the ground that the breach of duty and the plaintiff's injury were such that the hospital was to be taken as having caused the injury notwithstanding that the existence and extent of the contribution made by the hospital's breach of duty could not be ascertained. The House of Lords allowed the defendants' appeal, holding that, where a plaintiff's injury was attributable to a number of possible causes, the combination of the defendants' breach of duty and the plaintiff's injury did not give rise to a presumption that the defendant had caused the injury; instead the burden remained on the plaintiff to prove the causative link.

The question here, of course, is not 'which of two or more possible causes resulted in this plaintiff's catastrophe?', but rather 'would the doctor who should have attended Patrick have intubated him?'. But *Wilsher* is nevertheless in my judgment illuminating in the present context for the light it throws upon the court's proper approach to such a question.

Much of Lord Bridge's speech in *Wilsher* was devoted to explaining the earlier misunderstanding and mis-application of *McGhee v. National Coal Board* [1972] 3 W.L.R. *McGhee* had not, as had been thought, introduced a fiction into the law, the fiction that when negligence increases the risk of injury and injury then occurs, the negligence is assumed without more to have caused it. *McGhee* was rather an illustration as was *Bonnington Castings Ltd v. Wardlaw* before it, of the courts '[adopting] a robust and pragmatic approach to the undisputed primary facts of the case [and concluding] that it was a legitimate inference of fact that the defenders' negligence had materially contributed to the pursuer's injury.' (per Lord Bridge in *Wilsher* [1988] A.C. 1074 at 1090D).

Both *Bonnington Castings* and *McGhee* were, it may be noted, cases where the proved breach of duty materially contributed to, rather than solely caused, the plaintiff's injury. Both involved exposure to a mixture of 'guilty' and 'innocent' contamination. *Bonnington* was a pneumoconiosis case where the plaintiff inhaled damaging dust particles for some only of which the defendants were liable; *McGhee* was a dermatitis case where the plaintiff's condition arose from exposure to brick dust, the defendants' liability consisting of exposing him to contamination for longer than was necessary by their failure to provide proper washing facilities. As Lord Bridge said in *Wilsher* [1988] A.C. 1074 at page 1088:

'... the consecutive periods when 'innocent' and 'guilty' brick dust was present on the pursuer's body may both have contributed to the cause of the disease or, theoretically at least, one or other may have been the sole cause. But where the layman is told by the doctors that the longer the brick dust remains on the body, the greater the risk of dermatitis, although the doctors cannot identify the process of causation scientifically, there seems to be nothing irrational in drawing the inference, as a matter of common sense, that the consecutive periods when brick dust remained on the body probably contributed cumulatively to the causation of the dermatitis. I believe that a process of inferential reasoning on these general lines underlines the decision of the majority in *McGhee's* case.'

Lord Bridge then cited with apparent approval passages from a number of the speeches in *McGhee*, including this from Lord Reid):

'Nor can I accept the distinction drawn by the Lord Ordinary between materially increasing the risk that the disease will occur and making a material contribution to its occurrence. There may be some logical ground for such a distinction where our knowledge of all the material factors is complete. But it has often been said that the legal concept of causation is not based on logic or philosophy.'

In short, I understand *Wilsher* to recognise that, when the court's knowledge of all the material factors is not complete, on occasion it will be legitimate to adopt a robust and pragmatic approach and infer from those facts which are established that the defendants' proven negligence did indeed cause or contribute to the plaintiff's injury ...

When it comes to deciding what inferences here may legitimately be drawn from the established primary facts, prominent amongst the factors to be borne in mind are surely these. First, the literature in this field of medicine, and not least the generally accepted statements (as found by the judge) that 'respiratory failure . . . is a common complication in many disease processes and should always be readily suspected, especially if there are unexplained signs and symptoms', and 'any child who reaches the hospital alive should not . . . die from upper airway obstruction'. Second, that the very purpose of Sister Sallabank calling for the senior paediatric registrar was to ensure that whatever needed to be done for Patrick was done. The initial assumption must surely be that the doctor's attendance would have been of some use. Third is the indisputable fact that intubation alone would have benefited the child. Given all that, and given, fourth, the entire history of this case as it would have presented itself to an attending doctor — the background to Patrick's re-admission on January 16, his being 'specialled' that day, Sister Sallabank's view at the time of the first episode that something was so acutely wrong that she wanted Patrick seen by the senior paediatric registrar and not merely the senior houseman, her decision that a nurse should then remain permanently with him, and, when the second episode occurred, her renewed worry and decision again to call the senior paediatric registrar — I have no difficulty in inferring that whichever doctor had attended would have acted in the one way which would have been effective. In so deciding, I do not overlook Nurse Newbold's evidence nor Dr Dinwiddie's school of thought. But it is all very well for the specialists now to theorise over what would or would not have appeared to be indicated by second-hand descriptions of the child's developing condition; the reality is that no one will ever know quite how that condition would have presented itself to a competent doctor, learning the history as he would have done and examining the patient for himself. In my judgment, therefore, the case called for the 'robust and pragmatic approach' endorsed by *Wilsher*, and the assumption of causation suggested by the speeches in *Cumming (or McWilliams) v. Sir William Arrol & Co.* [1962] 1 All E.R. 623. So at least it strikes me, although not, as I recognise, my Lords.

In the final analysis the judge's conclusion that Dr Dinwiddie's views represented those of a respectable body of medical opinion, so far from being decisive in the defendants' favour, is in my judgment an irrelevance. Unless only it suffices to rebut the assumptions otherwise arising in Patrick's favour and to defeat the inferences otherwise to be drawn that a doctor's attendance was not merely required but would probably have benefited the child, it serves no purpose. And that to my mind it cannot do: it certainly fails to persuade me that attendance in response to Sister Sallabank's calls would have been useless."

[NOTE: Bolitho was also approved by the Court of Appeal in the later case of *Joyce v. Wandsworth LBC* [1996] 7 *Medical Law Review* 1 (see A. Grubb, "Medical Negligence: Breach of Duty and Causation" (1996) 4 *Medical Law Review* 86.)]

QUESTIONS:

1. Is the appropriate question whether the doctor was negligent in not intubating, or do you prefer Simon Brown L.J.'s view that the critical question is whether, on the balance of probabilities, a doctor would ordinarily intubate in such circumstances?
2. Do you detect in any of the three judgments anything to suggest a weakening of the *Bolam* principle? (See A. Grubb, "Causation and the *Bolam* Test" [1993] 1 *Medical Law Review* 241.)

3. Defective Medicinal Products and Drugs

The most common form of medical treatment is the administration of drugs. Thus if there is negligence in development, manufacture or supply the number of potential plaintiffs is considerable. There have been a number of notable instances of legal proceedings being brought in relation to defective drug products.

Concern over the use of the tort system as a means of redress for harm caused by defective drugs was illustrated by the Thalidomide case (H. Teff and C. Munro, *Thalidomide: The Legal Aftermath*, Farnborough: Saxon House, 1976). A number of women were given the drug Thalidomide during pregnancy. When born the children were discovered to be suffering from multiple handicaps. The litigation continued over a number of years with the claims being eventually settled. Despite a number of other high profile cases involving what were alleged to be defective drug products, for instance the actions brought in relation to the anti-arthritis drug, Opren (see below at page 194) such claims have not led to findings being made in court against the drug manufacturers in the court room, instead, either settlements have been reached or the claim has failed because causation could not be established (see P. R. Ferguson, *Drug Injuries and the Pursuit of Compensation*, London: Sweet and Maxwell, 1996, pages 10–15).

The difficulties in bringing actions in relation to drug products are in establishing who is responsible for the injury caused and in ascertaining whether the defect caused the harm suffered. A further problem relates to the fact that drug-related injuries may involve a large number of claimants which makes it difficult to co-ordinate such claims: we return to this issue at page 193 below.

Before drugs are allowed to be marketed they are subject to a statutory scheme requiring testing to take place (Medicines Act 1968). New drugs are required to be licensed by the Committee on the Safety of Medicines. (This body also issues clinical trial certificates for new drugs.) There is a reporting system where defects in drugs are detected although the efficacy of this system has been questioned. (See P. R. Ferguson, *Drug Injuries and the Pursuit of Compensation*, London: Sweet and Maxwell, 1996, at page 34.) Nevertheless despite this, problems may arise.

A statutory scheme is now in existence which imposes strict liability on defective products including defective drugs. Legislation was passed providing strict liability in relation to pharmaceutical products in 1987. The Consumer Protection Act 1987. This statute was enacted as a result of the E.C. Product Liability Directive (95/374).

Consumer Protection Act 1987

Section 2(1) Subject to the following provisions of this Part, where any damage is caused wholly or partly by a defect in a product, every person to whom subsection(2) below applies shall be liable for the damage.

(2) This subsection applies to:

(a) The producer of the product;
(b) any person who, by putting his name on the product or by using a trade mark or other distinguishing mark in relation to the product, has held himself out to be the producer of the product;
(c) any person who has imported the product into a member State from a place outside the Member States in order, in the course of any business of his, to supply it to another.

(3) Subject as aforesaid, where any damage is caused wholly or partly by a defect in a product, any person who supplied the product (whether to the person who suffered the damage, to the producer of any product in which the product in question is comprised or to any other person) shall be liable for the damage if —

(a) the person who suffered the damage requests the supplier to identify one or more of the persons(whether still in existence or not) to whom subsection (2) above applies in relation to the product;
(b) that request is made within a reasonable period after the damage occurs and at a time when it is not reasonably practicable for the person making the request to identify all those persons; and
(c) the supplier fails, within a reasonable period after receiving the request, either to comply with the request or to identify the person who supplied the product to him.

(4) Neither subsection (2) nor subsection (3) above shall apply to a person in respect of any defect in any game or agricultural produce if the only supply of the game or produce to that person was at a time when it had not undergone an industrial process.

(5) Where two or more persons are liable by virtue of this Part for the same damage, their liability shall be joint and several.

(6) This section shall be without prejudice to any liability arising otherwise than by virtue of this Part.

Section 3(1) Subject to the following provisions of this section, there is a defect in a product for the purposes of this Part if the safety of the product is not such as persons generally are entitled to expect; and for those purposes "safety", in relation to a product, shall include safety with respect to products comprised in that product and safety in the context of risks of damage to property, as well as in the context of risks of death or personal injury.

(2) In determining for the purpose of subsection (1) above what persons generally are entitled to expect in relation to a product all circumstances shall be taken into account including:

(a) the manner in which, and purposes for which, the product has been marketed, its get-up, the use of any mark in relation to the product and any instructions for, or warnings with respect to, doing or refraining from doing anything with or in relation to the product;
(b) what might reasonably be expected to be done with or in relation to the product; and
(c) the time when the product was supplied by its producer to another; and nothing in this section shall require a defect to be inferred from the fact alone that the safety of a product which is supplied after that time is greater than the safety of the product in question.

Section 4(1) In any civil proceedings by virtue of this Part against any person ("the person proceeded against") in respect of a defect in a product it shall be a defence for him to show —

(a) that the defect is attributable to compliance with any requirement imposed by or under any enactment or with any Community obligation; or
(b) that the person proceeded against did not at any time supply the product to another; or
(c) that the following conditions are satisfied, that is to say —
  (i) that the only supply of the product to another by the person proceeded against was otherwise than in the course of business of that person's; and
  (ii) that section 2(2) above does not apply to that person or applies to him by virtue only of things done by virtue only of things done otherwise than with a view to profit; or
(d) that the defect did not exist in the product at the relevant time; or
(e) that the state of scientific and technical knowledge at the relevant time was not such that a producer of products of the same description as the product in question might be expected to discover the defect, if it had existed in his products while they were under his control; or
(f) that the defect —
  (i) constituted a defect in a product ("the subsequent product") in which the product in question had been comprised; and
  (ii) was wholly attributable to the design of the subsequent product or to compliance by the producer of the product in question with instructions given by the producer of the product in question with instructions given by the producer of the subsequent product.

(2) In this section "the relevant time", in relation to electricity means the time at which it was generated, being a time before it was transmitted or distributed, and in relation to any other product, means —

(a) if the person proceeded against us a person to whom subsection(2) of section 2 above applies in relation to the product, the time when he supplied the product to another;
(b) if that subsection does not apply to that person in relation to the product, the time when the product was last supplied by a person to whom that subsection does apply in relation to the product.

Section 5(1) Subject to the following provisions of this section, in this Part "damage" means death or personal injury or any loss of or damage to any property (including land).

(2) A person shall not be liable under section 2 above in respect of any defect in a product for loss of or damage to the product itself or for the loss of or damage to the whole or any part of a product which has been supplied with the product in question comprised in it.

(3) A person shall not be liable under section 2 above for any loss or damage to property which at the time it is lost or damaged is not —

(a) a description of property ordinarily intended for private use, occupation or consumption; and
(b) intended by the person suffering the loss or damage mainly for his own private use, occupation or consumption.

(4) No damages shall be awarded to any person by virtue of this Part in respect of any loss of or damage to any property if the amount which would fall to be so awarded to that person, apart from this subsection and any liability for interest, does not exceed £270.

(5) In determining for the purposes of this Part who has suffered loss or damage to property and whether any such loss or damage occurred, the loss or damage shall

be regarded as having occurred at the earliest time at which a person with an interest in the property had knowledge of the material facts about loss or damage.

(6) For the purposes of subsection (5) above the material facts about any loss of or damage to property are such facts about the loss and damage as would lead a reasonable person with an interest in the property to consider the loss sufficiently serious to justify him launching proceedings for damages against a defendant who did not dispute liability and who was thus able to satisfy a judgment.

(7) For the purpose of subsection (5) above a person's knowledge includes knowledge which he might reasonably have been expected to acquire:

(a) from facts observable or ascertainable by him; or
(b) from facts ascertainable by him with the help of appropriate expert advice which it is reasonable for him to seek;
but a person shall not be taken by virtue of this subsection to have knowledge of a fact ascertainable by him only with the help of expert advice unless he has failed to take all reasonable steps to obtain and (where appropriate, to act on) that advice.

Section 46(1) Subject to the following provisions of this section, references in this Act to supplying goods shall be construed as references to doing any of the following, whether as principal or agent, that is to say —

(a) selling, hiring out or lending the goods;
(b) entering into a hire purchase agreement to furnish the goods;
(c) the performance or any contract of work and materials to furnish the goods;
(d) providing the goods in exchange for any consideration(including trading stamps) other than money;
(e) providing the goods in or in connection with the performance of any statutory function; or
(f) giving the goods as a prize or otherwise making a gift of the goods;
and in relation to gas or water, those references shall be construed as including references to providing the service by which the gas or water is made available for use.

(2) For the purposes of any reference to this Act to supplying goods, where a person ("the ostensible supplier") supplies goods to another person ("the customer") under a hire-purchase agreement, conditional sale agreement or credit-sale agreement or under an agreement for the hiring of goods (other than a hire purchase agreement) and the ostensible supplier:

(a) carries on the business of financing the provision of goods for others by means of such agreement; and
(b) in the course of that business acquired his interest in the goods supplied to the customer as a means of financing the provision of them for the customer by a further person ('the effective supplier"),

the effective supplier and not the ostensible supplier shall be treated as supplying the goods to the customer.

NOTES:

1. Actions can only be brought under the legislation in relation to drug products manufactured after March 1, 1988. Where a person is

injured by a defective product manufactured before that date they must bring their action at common law.

2. While proceedings under the Act will usually be brought against producers of defective products, suppliers may also be held liable. The supplier will be liable where the patient asks her to identify the producer of the product and she is unable to do so (section 2(3)). This may include pharmacists or doctors who dispense their own drugs.

3. There may be difficulties in establishing liability where the company who produced the drug cannot be identified. This issue arose in the United States in the 1950s when a drug, Debendox, was distributed with the aim of reducing miscarriages in pregnant women. This drug was supplied by many firms under a generic name. Certain United States courts were prepared to impose liability collectively on the manufacturers by ascertaining their liability in relation to their proportion of the market share. However this approach was not uniformly accepted in the United States and it may be questioned whether such an argument would be accepted by an English court. (See C. Newdick, "Special Problems of Compensating those Damaged by Medicinal Products." in S. McLean (ed.), *Compensation for Damage: An International Perspective*, Aldershot: Dartmouth (1993)).

4. It is unclear whether defects in bodily products such as blood or organs are included within the scope of the legislation. The Pearson Commission were in favour of such an inclusion and this approach has received the support of some commentators and the Nuffield Council on Bioethics (see *Human Tissue: Legal and Ethical Issues*, London: Nuffield Council on Bioethics, 1995 and Chapter 11 below at page 692, though *cf.* M. Brazier, *Street on Torts* (9th ed.), London: Butterworths, 1993, at page 338).

5. A defect is likely to become evident in the early years of the use of a product such as a drug if it is not uncovered in the course of a clinical trial. The Act requires the court to consider whether the product is safe (section 3(1)). Drugs and other products are not expected to be absolutely safe. Issues such as side effects require consideration and need to be assessed against the potential benefit from the drug/ product. A relevant factor may be approval given to the drug by the Committee on the Safety of Medicines. A further factor is whether the manufacturer has given warnings as to the use of the product, for instance whether an information sheet has been enclosed with the drug/product.

6. One major difficulty in establishing liability under this Act is likely to be causation. The House of Lords in *Wilsher* confirmed that the plaintiff must establish causation and it is not sufficient to establish liability that the defendant's conduct was one of a number of factors contributing to the harm suffered.

7. Section 4 provides a "developmental risk defence". The introduction of such a defence was opposed both by the Law Commission and by

the Pearson Commission. The defence itself is derived from the European Directive. Jones has noted that the definition contained in the Directive is narrower than that provided in section 4. Article 7(e) of the directive states that there is a defence "where the state of scientific and technical knowledge at the time when he put the product into circulation was not such as to enable the existence of the defect to be discovered." (See M. Jones, *Medical Negligence* (2nd ed.), London: Sweet and Maxwell, 1996, at page 452 and C. Newdick, "The Development Risk Defence of the Consumer Protection Act 1987", (1988) 47 *C.L.J.* 455.) Jones suggests that this may be the subject of challenge before the European Court of Justice on the basis that the statute has not fully implemented the Directive. Where litigation over a defective product does take place, a question may arise as to whether it is a manufacturing defect rather than a design defect. The distinction between such defects may be crucial. This is because the section 4 defence would not apply if it is shown that a defect is caused by failure to adhere to manufacturing standards as opposed to a defect in product design. In addition it appears that the developmental risk defence will not apply in a situation in which, although some loss was foreseeable, the precise extent of that loss was not.

QUESTION:

1. Where a patient is harmed through a defective drug, can an action be brought against the Committee on the Safety of Medicines? (See M. Brazier, *Medicines, Patients and the Law* (2nd ed.), Harmondsworth: Penguin, 1992 at page 184.)

4. MULTI-PARTY ACTIONS

In certain situations where medical negligence has taken place it may be considered appropriate to bring a multi-party action. A multi-party action allows a large number of similar actions to be dealt with at the same time. There are a number of advantages in such an approach. It can rationalise the costs of the action, particularly where claims are likely to be long and complex and there is need for considerable disclosure of documents. Such an action may be particularly appropriate, for example, in relation to injuries from drug products where there are likely to be many claims. However, such actions are problematic, as illustrated by the Opren litigation (*Davies v. Eli Lilly & Co.* [1987] 3 All E.R. 94). Here a class action was brought in relation to the drug, Opren, introduced with the intention of relieving symptoms of arthritis. (See K. Oliphant, "Innovations in procedure and practice in multi-party medical cases" in A. Grubb (ed.)

Choices and Decisions in Health Care, Chichester: John Wiley, 1994 and P. Ferguson, *Drug Injuries and the Pursuit of Compensation*, London: Sweet and Maxwell, 1996, p. 157 *et seq.*) Some persons who had taken the drug suffered serious side effects and actions were brought against the manufacturers. Difficulties in bringing a class action here included the fact that a wide range of differing side effects had been experienced. Hirst J. established a scheme applicable to the litigation. It was intended that some of the potential difficulties with the action could be addressed by themes common to all the claims being initially identified and then some claims being placed in subgroups. Some 15 "lead cases" were to be heard in which findings of liability could be established. While these findings would not be binding in relation to future cases they would nevertheless be influential. It has been argued that relitigation would be found to be an abuse of process (see K. Oliphant *op. cit.*). Twenty "lead" groups of solicitors were established who were in association with a wide range of other firms. While such a procedure may be desirable as a means of pursuing such litigation, there are difficulties, which the *Opren* litigation itself highlighted. Notable amongst these is the question of the apportionment of costs. In the *Opren* case the judge ruled that, while the lead 20 cases had been selected from person who qualified for legal aid, when it came to assessing the costs of such a claim then they were to be equally apportioned between all the plaintiffs should they lose the claim. The judge commented on the unfairness of all the costs being borne by the legal aid fund. The consequence of this decision meant that the claims would have had to be abandoned save for the fact that funding was provided by a private benefactor.

The judge in the *Opren* case was not of the view that this approach should prove binding upon subsequent cases. He instead proposed that there should be an enabling rule which allowed the court to establish a scheme in relation to an individual case. A guide to multi-party actions was subsequently produced by the Supreme Court Procedure Committee. This proposed that solicitors involved in such actions should co-ordinate themselves in order that a steering committee of a handful of firms could administer the actions.

Newdick points out that the cost of organising of multi-party actions may deter solicitors from being involved in them. (See C. Newdick, "Compensating those damaged by medical products" in S. McLean (ed.), *Compensation for Damage*, Aldershot: Dartmouth, 1993.) Special provisions were introduced to enable the legal aid board to contract with certain solicitors' firms to run multi-party actions and they would be the only firms who would run such actions (Legal Aid Act 1988, s.4). These provisions would have the effect that only those who brought the claim within the arrangements would be able to claim legal aid. Multi-party actions have now been the subject of recommendations made in the Woolf Report (see below at page 208).

5. GROSS NEGLIGENCE AND CRIMINAL LIABILITY

In most situations a malpractice action brought against a health professional is unlikely to also give rise to liability in criminal law. Nevertheless there is the possibility that a criminal prosecution may be brought in certain situations. We explore certain aspects of the scope of criminal liability in relation to issues consequent upon failure to obtain consent to treatment in Chapter 6 below. Prosecutions have been brought in recent times against health care professionals where a patient had died allegedly as a consequence of a gravely negligent action by the doctor. While the courts in earlier centuries were prepared to impose liability in manslaughter for mere carelessness this was later limited to conduct amounting to gross negligence. In *R. v. Bateman* (1925) 19 Cr.App.R. 8, the court laid down the basis for liability for gross negligence manslaughter. It must be shown that the defendant owed the deceased a duty to take care, he was in breach of that duty and this breach caused the deceased's death. Finally, it is necessary to show that the negligence was gross; namely that it showed such a disregard for the life and safety of other persons as to constitute a crime and be worthy of punishment. This approach has been criticised. In the later case of *R. v. Seymour* [1983] 2 A.C. 493, the court took a different approach, requiring it to be established that the conduct of the defendant amounted to an "obvious and serious" risk of death. Some commentators were of the view that the offence of gross negligence manslaughter was redundant. However, its existence was confirmed by the House of Lords in the later case of *R v. Adomako*, where the judgment in Seymour was disapproved.

R v. Adomako [1994] 3 All E.R. 79; [1995] 1 A.C. 624

An anaesthetist in the course of an eye operation failed to notice that the endotracheal tube used to assist the patient's breathing had become disconnected. After nine minutes, the patient suffered a heart attack and died. Expert evidence described his failure to identify the problem and remedy it as "abysmal" and as a "gross dereliction of care".

LORD MACKAY L.C.:
" . . . [I]n my opinion the principles of the law of negligence apply to ascertain whether or not the defendant has been in breach of a duty of care towards the victim who has died. If such breach of duty is established the next question is whether that breach of duty caused the death of the victim. If so, the jury must go on to consider whether that breach of duty should be characterised as gross negligence and therefore as a crime. This will depend on the seriousness of the breach of duty committed by the defendant in all the circumstances in which the defendant was placed when it occurred. The jury will have to consider whether the extent to which the defendant's conduct departed from the proper standard of care incumbent upon him, involving as it must have done a risk of death to the patient, was such that it should be judged criminal.
It is true that to a certain extent this involves an element of circularity, but in this branch of the law I do not believe that is fatal to its being correct as a test of how

far conduct must depart from accepted standards to be characterised as criminal. This is necessarily a question of degree and an attempt to specify that degree more closely is I think likely to achieve only a spurious precision. The essence of the matter, which is supremely a jury question, is whether, having regard to the risk of death involved, the conduct of the defendant was so bad in all the circumstances to amount in their judgment to a criminal act or omission . . .

I consider it perfectly appropriate that the word 'reckless' should be used in cases of involuntary manslaughter, but as Lord Atkin put it 'in the ordinary connotation of that word'. Examples in which this was done, to my mind, with complete accuracy are *R v. Stone, R v. Dobinson* [1977] 2 All E.R. 341 and *R v. West London Coroner, ex p. Gray* [1987] 2 All E.R. 129.

In my opinion it is quite unnecessary in the context of gross negligence to give the detailed directions with regard to the meaning of the word 'reckless' associated with *R v. Lawrence* [1981] 1 All E.R. 974. The decision of the Court of Appeal, Criminal Division, in the other cases with which they were concerned at the same time as they heard the appeal in this case indicates that the circumstances in which involuntary manslaughter has to be considered may make the somewhat elaborate and rather rigid directions inappropriate. I entirely agree with the view that the circumstances to which a charge of involuntary manslaughter may apply are so various that it is unwise to attempt to categorise or detail specimen directions. For my part I would not wish to go beyond the description of the basis in law which I have already given."

NOTES:

1. The only full judgment was that of Lord Mackay with whom the other members of the House of Lords Keith, Goff, Browne-Wilkinson and Woolf agreed.
2. The return to a *Bateman* type test has been criticised. For example, Virgo has argued that the reasoning is circular "gross negligence and consequent criminal liability will exist whenever the jury considers that the defendant has departed to such an extent from the proper standards of care that it should be judged criminal". He is of the view that without considerable judicial guidance the case could result in uncertainty and unpredictability. (See G. Virgo, "Reconstructing Manslaughter on Defective Foundation" [1995] *C.L.J.* 14.)
3. It has been suggested that in addition to an action for gross negligence manslaughter, a manslaughter prosecution may also be brought on the basis of subjective recklessness; (see J. C. Smith, "Manslaughter" [1994] *Crim L.R.* 758). That is to say that liability will arise for conduct in a situation which includes "Causing death by an act done being aware that it is highly probable that it will cause serious bodily harm". A prosecution may be appropriate if for example, a surgeon operates while under the influence of drugs or drink. Note that such conduct is likely to lead to action being taken against the health professional by her professional disciplinary body. (See Chapter 4 below at pages 246–261.)
4. The Law Commission have suggested various reforms in this area. (*Involuntary Manslaughter: Legislating the Criminal Code*, Law Com. Rep. 231, London: HMSO, 1996.) It proposed that there should be a

new offence of reckless killing (paras. 5.12–5.13). This would be committed if

"(1) a person by his or her conduct causes the death of another;
(2) he or she is aware of a risk that his or her conduct will cause death or serious injury: and
(3) it is unreasonable for him or her to take that risk, having regard to all the circumstances as he or she knows or believes them to be."

The Law Commission notes that this offence would be committed even in a situation in which the deceased consented to the risk for instance, in consenting to a highly risky surgical operation (para. 5.12). This obviously raises the issue of what precisely an individual may or may not consent to. (This issue is explored fully in Chapter 6 below at pages 322–325.)

It also recommends that there should be a new offence of "killing by gross carelessness" (para. 5.34). This would apply if

"(1) a person by his or her conduct will cause the death of another:
(2) a risk that his or her conduct will cause death or serious injury would be obvious to a reasonable person in his or her position;
(3) he or she is capable of appreciating that risk at the material time; and
(4) either
    (a) his or her conduct falls far below what can reasonably be expected of him or her in the circumstances, or
    (b) he or she intends by his or her conduct to cause some injury, or is aware of, and unreasonably takes, the risk that it may do so, *and* the conduct causing (or intended to cause) the injury constitutes an offence" (para. 5.34).

The Law Commission suggest that obvious in this context means "immediately apparent", "striking" or "glaring".

5. Whether a health care professional would be held liable in gross negligence manslaughter for an omission such as a failure to treat a patient who subsequently dies is unclear (see Law Commission, *Legislating the Criminal Code Involuntary Manslaughter*, London: HMSO, 1996, paras 3.13–3.14 and for further discussion of cases in relation to liability for omissions where death results see Chapter 14 below).

6. The decision in *R v. Adomako* focuses upon the liability of the individual health professional. But if there are situations in which the standard of care provided has fallen to what may be regarded as unacceptable levels and it is claimed that mistakes by junior staff flow from constraints and pressures resulting from underfunding by hospital management, then where should liability lie? One argument is that in such a situation an action may be brought for what is known as "corporate manslaughter". This involves prosecuting the officers of a company and holding them liable for the conduct of the organisation rather than imposing liability on an individual employee. (See *P&O*

Ferries (Dover) Ltd (1991) 93 Cr.App.R. 72.) Bringing an action for corporate manslaughter is fraught with difficulties. In the past the courts have indicated that it is necessary to show a "controlling mind" which, while feasible in a small company, may pose considerable difficulties in the context of a large organisation. (See C. Wells, *Corporations and Criminal Responsibility*, Oxford: Clarendon Press, 1993.) The Law Commission *op. cit.* has proposed reforms in this area. It recommends a new offence of "corporate killing, broadly corresponding to the individual offence of killing by gross carelessness" (para. 8.35).

QUESTION:

1. Is gross negligence a sufficient basis on which to convict a doctor of manslaughter? (For one view, see A. McCall-Smith, "Criminal Negligence and the Incompetent Doctor" (1993) 1 *Medical Law Review* 33.)

6. REFORM OF FAULT-BASED LIABILITY

As may be seen from the discussion in this chapter, bringing an action in the law of tort for compensation where malpractice has occurred is fraught with difficulties. Some of the general difficulties with the tort system as a mechanism for compensation and accountability were explored in a report published by the Kings Fund Institute in 1988.

C. Ham, R. Dingwall, P. Fenn and D. Harris, *Medical Negligence Compensation and Accountability*, Oxford: Kings Fund Institute, 1988

In parallel with the concern of health authorities and of the medical profession, organisations representing patients and their relatives have drawn attention to the shortcomings of the tort system. First, there is the lengthy and expensive procedure involved in pursuing a claim for damages. This means that cases are often brought only by the rich or those able to obtain legal aid. Cases take a considerable time to work their way through the courts: the average time for settling a claim is four years.

Second, the legal process is by definition adversarial. As such, it may cause doctors and health authorities to close ranks and not offer an adequate explanation to patients and their relatives when things go wrong. In addition, the legal process may itself be distressing in providing a constant reminder of painful or unhappy events.

Third, the emphasis on establishing fault and cause and effect in injury cases turns the tort system into a lottery. Compensation is based not on need but on the ability to prove that somebody was at fault. The rules of the legal process which put the burden of proof on those bringing a claim may create significant difficulties for plaintiffs. As a consequence, similar cases of injury may be compensated quite differently. For example, a child suffering brain damage after contracting encephalitis will receive no compensation, a child suffering brain damage as a result of vaccine damage will receive £20,000, and a child suffering brain damage following traumatic birth injury may receive hundreds of thousands of pounds compensation.

Fourth, only a small proportion of people suffering medical injuries are compensated through the tort system. This may mean that the losses incurred as a result of injury are inadequately compensated, although other sources of compensation are available.

Underlying these criticisms is a concern that maintaining high standards of medical practice and holding doctors to account for unacceptable standards of practice are inadequate. Action for the Victims of Medical Accidents (AVMA) established in 1982, has highlighted these issues, and has argued for much greater oppenness and accountability on the part of the medical profession in dealing with the consequences of accidents. One of the points emphasised by AVMA is that most people who suffer medical injuries are not seeking compensation but want an explanation of what went wrong. An adequate system for dealing with injuries needs to provide for this as well as to offer financial compensation.

Before considering these points more fully, it is worth noting a number of other criticisms levelled at the tort system as it applies to medical injury cases.

These are:

- those making a claim may find it difficult to obtain the services of a solicitor with relevant expertise
- there may be difficulty in obtaining the services of doctors willing to act as expert witnesses for patients
- the legal process causes distress and expense to doctors and health authorities as well as to patients
- the availability of legal aid may result in legal action being initiated in inappropriate cases, that is cases where those making a claim have little chance of success.

It is against this background that alternatives to existing arrangements come under scrutiny. One widely canvassed option is a no-fault compensation scheme. This has found favour with the British Medical Association (BMA) and the Association of CHC's in England and Wales (ACHCEW). Other possibilities include the introduction of differential premiums for doctors to reflect the risks involved in their work: shifting the cost of providing compensation to the NHS: reforming the tort law to overcome some of the shortcomings identified: providing more support to medical injury cases through the social security system: and extending first party insurance cover."

NOTES:

1. The delay in proceedings is noted by many commentators. It has been stated that there is an average delay from the commencement of legal proceedings to the ultimate hearing of three years in relation to county court hearings and of five years for High Court hearings (*Civil Justice Review* (n.394, (1988), para. 421). The appellate process may further lengthen delays. A notable example is that of the *Wilsher* litigation which commenced in 1978 with the final resolution of the matter being a decade later in 1988.

2. Since this report, there has been a trend towards greater specialisation by legal practitioners in medical negligence litigation, and a growth in the number of lawyers working in that area.

We consider a number of options for reform below.

(a) No-fault Compensation

The first and arguably most radical option would be to replace the tort action with a system of "no-fault compensation". (See S. McClean, "Can No Fault Analysis Ease the Problems of Medical Injury Litigation" and M. Brazier, "The Case for a No-Fault Scheme for Medical Accidents" in S. McLean (ed.), *Compensation for Damage: An International Perspective*, Aldershot: Dartmouth, 1993)). This could operate either as a general scheme applicable to all personal injury actions or as a scheme specific to medical injuries. The salient elements of such a system are that parties are not required to prove fault although they have to establish that the injury *caused* their loss. Instead of being awarded damages they awarded money from a central fund either established by the state or through private insurance. Such schemes have operated in Sweden and New Zealand for many years. In Sweden what is known as a "patient insurance scheme" applies. This is a no-fault scheme which is based on the rules of assessment for tort damages. The plaintiff may claim for injury from diagnosis and inappropriate medical treatment. A difficulty which plaintiffs may face is that they must show that the procedure was not medically justified. Payments under this scheme are relatively modest as they supplement the existing social security system. The basis for payment is that the injury must not be a consequence of original sickness, must not result from a risk taken to avert permanent disability or death. (The procedure which has caused injury must not be medically justified.) The scheme is funded by county councils, who in Sweden bear responsibility for health care. The councils are insured with private insurers.

A no-fault system was introduced in New Zealand in 1972 by the Accident Compensation Act. This allowed an individual to claim damages for "personal injury by accident". This was defined as "medical, surgical, dental or first aid misadventure". These were consequent upon the broader definition given to medical misadventure in the legislation as:

"(a) a person suffers bodily or mental injury or damage in the course of, and as part of, the administering to that person of medical aid, care or attention, and

(b) such injury or damage is caused by mischance or accident, unexpected and undesigned, in the nature of medical *error* or *mishap*."

Interpretation of the term "medical misadventure" has led to difficulties in practice and inhibited claims. (See K. Oliphant, "Defining Medical Misadventure: Lessons from New Zealand" (1996) 4 *Medical Law Review* 1.)

One problem with no-fault schemes is their cost. This was one reason for reform of the New Zealand scheme in 1992. The Accident Rehabilitation and Compensation Insurance Act 1992 provides that compensation may only be claimed where disability is severe and a rare occurence.

The adoption of a no-fault system in this country was examined by the Pearson Commission in their report in 1978 and ultimately rejected.

Royal Commission on Civil Liability and Compensation for Personal Injury (Pearson Commission) (1978) Cmnd. 7054.

1360 In considering the possibility of a no-fault scheme for this country we looked first at the question of cost. There are two aspects: the overall cost of any scheme and the machinery for financing it.

1361 It is difficult to be precise about cost. Minor injuries and complications of treatment could reasonably be excluded as in Sweden, where there has to be some incapacity for work for more than 14 days. If there were as many as 10,000 cases a year, and benefits were provided on the same lines as in our suggested work and road schemes, the total additional cost of compensation over the existing forms of compensation would be about 6 million a year. Some addition would have to be made for the cost of administration. This could well be substantial. Judging by the Swedish experience there would be at least two claims for every one that was successful.

1362 We think that it would be appropriate to finance any such scheme through the National Health Service. But the question of what to do about medical accidents in private practice would raise difficulties. Although it might be argued that many doctors have both National Health Service and private patients, that private doctors use National Health Service facilities and that all taxpayers contribute to the National Health Service, nevertheless we think that it is out of the question that a no-fault scheme provided by public funds should cover injuries received in the course of private treatment. There might be other ways of solving the problem. For example, such injuries could be covered by private no-fault insurance, or it might be possible to provide no-fault compensation through a levy on the subscription to medical defence societies. . . .

1363 Any attempt to devise a no-fault scheme would also run into the problem of whether, and if so how, treatment given by the "paramedical professions" should be covered. Most of those in such professions, for example, nurses and physiothera-pists, work with or mainly under the direction of doctors or dentists: but there would remain the problem of treatment not given by a medical team, for example, chiropody. Outside the National Health Service, there would be the further problem whether other practices, such as oseteopathy, should be covered.

Establishing causation

1364 The main problem with a no-fault scheme is how to establish causation, since the cause of many injuries cannot be identified. The Medical Research Council said that while future research was likely to establish more causal relationships it would also reveal increasingly complex interactions which would heighten the problems of proving causation in the individual case.

1365 Even with our definition of medical injury we were forced to conclude that in practice there would be difficulty in distinguishing medical accident from the natural progression of a disease or injury, and from a foreseeable side effect of treatment. It is quite normal for a patient not to recover completely for several weeks or months after a major operation: for complications to ensue after operations: and for a patient to find that the drugs prescribed cause serious side effects.

1366 How should words like 'expected' or 'foreseeable' be interpreted? Even rare side effects such as vaccine damage not caused by medical negligence are often foreseeable in the sense that they are well known to medical science. If such injuries were to be included in a no-fault scheme, where would the line be drawn between them and accepted risks of treatment? If they were to be excluded, the scheme would do little more than convert the negligence test of tort into a statutory formula, thereby making it easier for the victims of negligence to obtain compensation, but doing nothing for those suffering medical injury from other causes.

1367 In establishing causation, who should take the decision? We envisage that a no-fault scheme would be the responsibility of the DHSS. The use of its adjudication procedures however, would either place more burdens on the medical manpower available, or would put the onus of making the initial decision on the shoulders of junior officials who have neither the experience or training to determine those issues.

1368 To establish causation would involve deciding whether the condition was the result of the treatment and, if so, whether it was the result that might have been expected. This would have to be disentangled from the conditions resulting from the progress of the disease or advancing age or from some other purely fortuitous cicumstances.

1369 It is easy to distinguish the completely unexpected result from that which was expected. The gray areas in between pose serious difficulties in knowing where to draw the line.

NOTES:

1. The Pearson Commission did not recommend the adoption of a no-fault system although they did suggest that the issue should be kept under review.
2. The costs of a no-fault scheme were considered in a study in 1988 by C. Ham, R. Dingwall, P. Fenn and D. Harris (*Medical Negligence: Compensation and Accountability* London: Kings Fund Institute, 1988). They suggested that such a scheme would cost some £117 million per annum (at 1988 prices) as against an estimated cost of the tort system of £75 million.
3. One alternative to a no-fault scheme which does not depend upon civil litigation would be better provision through the social security system of a disability income, although it is suggested that the cost of such a system at present makes it a realistic possibility only on a long-term basis. (See Ham, Dingwall, Fenn and Harris (1988) *op. cit.*)

Though the Pearson Commission rejected the adoption of a comprehensive system of liability for medical injuries, it did recommend a limited scheme of this kind in relation to persons suffering vaccine-damage (paragraph 1407).

Vaccine Damage Payments Act 1979, s.1(1–4), s.2(1–3)

1.—(1) If, on consideration of a claim, the Secretary of State is satisfied:

(a) that a person is, or was immediately before his death, severely disabled as a result of vaccination against any of the diseases to which this Act applies; and
(b) that the conditions of entitlement which are applicable in accordance with section 2 below are fulfilled,

he shall in accordance with this Act make a payment of the relevant statutory sum to or for the benefit of that person or to his personal representatives.

(1A) In subsection (1) above 'statutory sum' means [£30,000] or such other sum as is specified by the Secretary of State for the purposes of this Act by order made by statutory instrument with the consent of the Treasury: and the relevant statutory sum for the purposes of that subsection is the statutory sum at the time when a claim for payment is first made.

(2) The diseases to which this Act applies are:

(a) diphtheria,
(b) tetanus,
(c) whooping cough,
(d) poliomyelitis,
(e) measles,
(f) rubella,
(g) tuberculosis,
(h) smallpox, and
(i) any other disease which is specified by the Secretary of State for the purposes of this Act by order made by statutory instrument.

(3) Subject to section 2(3) below, this Act has effect with respect to a person who is severely disabled as a result of a vaccination given to his mother before he was born as if the vaccination had been given directly to him and, in such circumstances, as may be prescribed by regulations under this Act, this Act has effect with respect to a person who is severely disabled as a result of contracting a disease through contact with a third person who was vaccinated against it as if the vaccination had been given to him and the disablement resulted from it.

(4) For the purposes of this Act a person is severely disabled if he suffers disablement to the extent of 80 per cent., or more, . . .

2.—(1) Subject to the provisions of this section, the conditions of entitlement referred to in section 1(1)(b) above are:

(a) that the vaccination in question was carried out:
    (i) in the United Kingdom or the Isle of Man, and
    (ii) on or after July 5, 1948, and
    (iii) in the case of vaccination against smallpox, before August 1, 1971;
(b) except in the case of vaccination against poliomyelitis or rubella, that the vaccination was carried out either at a time when the person to whom it was given was under the age of eighteen or at the time of the outbreak within the United Kingdom or Isle of Man of the disease against which the vaccination was given; and
(c) that the disabled person was over the age of two on the date when the claim was made or, if he died before that date, that he died after 9th May 1978 and was over the age of two when he died.

(2) An order under section 1(2)(i) above specifying a disease for the purposes of this Act may provide that, in relation to vaccination against that disease, the conditions of entitlement specified in subsection (1) above shall have effect subject to such modifications as may be specified in the order.

(3) In a case where this Act has effect by virtue of section 1(3) above, the reference in subsection 1(b) above to the person to whom a vaccination was given is a reference to the person to whom it was actually given and not the disabled person.

NOTES:

1. Section 1(3) extends compensation entitlement to two classes of person who have not themselves been vaccinated: those affected by

the vaccination of their mother prior to their birth and those who contract one of the specified diseases by virtue of contact with someone who has been vaccinated.

2. The Act embodies a causation requirement that the disease must be contracted "as a result" of vaccination. Under section 3(5) of the Act, the causal link, in common with the law of negligence, must be established on the balance of probabilities. This can be problematic, as illustrated by *Loveday v. Renton* [1990] 1 Med. L.R. 117 where the plaintiff failed to satisfy the court that pertussis vaccine was the cause of brain damage suffered. The effect of the decision in *Loveday* was dramatic. Following the case, the number of successful claims plummeted to almost nil.

   A further problem facing potential claimants under the scheme is that it was held in *DHSS v. Kinnear* (1984) 134 *N.L.J.* 886 that a policy decision of the Department of Health to promote vaccination is non-justiciable.

3. The "statutory sum" is currently fixed at £30,000 (Vaccine Damage Payments Act 1979 Statutory Sum Order 1991 S.I. 1991 No. 939).

QUESTION:

1. Can the threshold requirement of a minimum of 80 per cent disability (section 1(4)) be justified?

In 1991, Rosie Barnes M.P., put forward a Private Member's Bill which was intended to introduce a no-fault scheme into Britain.

National Health Service (Compensation) Bill 1991

1. The purposes of this Act are:

(a) to provide that compensation for injuries suffered due to mishaps during National Health Service care shall be available without proof of negligence;
(b) to secure that National Health Service patients have the benefit of the same implied terms as to quality and description in respect of goods (including medicines, blood and appliances) as private patients;
(c) to seek to ensure that public monies available for caring for and compensating patients during National Health Service care are spent on those purposes; and
(d) to minimise mishaps and compensation payments.

   3.—(1) There shall be a body corporate to be known as the Medical Injury Compensation Board.

   (2) The Board shall consist of a chairman and not fewer than 14 nor more than 16 other members, appointed by the Secretary of State.

   (3) The Chairman shall be a judge of the Supreme Court of England and Wales, appointed after consultation with the Lord Chancellor, or a judge of the Court of Session, appointed after consultation with the Lord Advocate.

   (4) Of the other members of the Board, who shall be appointed after consultation with such organisations as the Secretary of State considers appropriate —

(a) 3 shall be medical practitioners;
(b) 3 shall be practising solicitors, barristers or advocates;
(c) 2 shall have experience of management within the National Health Service;
(d) 2 shall be health care professionals (other than within (a) above); and
(e) not more than 6 nor fewer than 4 shall be persons other than those falling within (a) to (d) above.

4.—(1) The Board shall establish and maintain a separate medical injury compensation fund, into which shall be paid any money paid by the Secretary of State under section 10(1) below.

(3) On receiving a claim from:

(a) a person who has suffered injury; or, where that person has died or is a minor or is incapacitated, from his personal representative, guardian, or dependant; or
(b) a person acting on behalf of a person falling within paragraph (a) above,

the Board shall investigate the claim.

(4) A claim within subsection (3) is one which is made within 6 months of the patient becoming aware of the injury and of its relationship with National Health Service Care.

(5) Within 3 months of receiving the claim (or, where that is not practicable, at the earliest practicable opportunity), the Board shall notify the claimant of the results of its investigation.

(6) If the Board considers it appropriate it may offer and, subject to the other provisions of this Act, pay compensation to the claimant.

NOTES:

1. For the purposes of the Bill, "mishap" was defined as including (but not being restricted to) "any act or omission which gives rise to an action at common law (or for breach of contract or statutory duty) by a patient in respect of National Health Service care.

2. Funding for the envisaged scheme was to be provided by central government.

3. One aspect of a no-fault scheme is that it may not provide a sufficient deterrent for health professionals to avoid negligent conduct in the future (see further *Royal Commission on Civil Liability and Compensation for Personal Injury* (1978) Cmnd. 7054). It may be the case that an effective no-fault scheme needs to be accompanied by a revision of the system of professional discipline and accountability. (See further on this issue Chapter 4 below.)

QUESTIONS:

1. Would it be fair to grant compensation to patients regardless of whether their injury was caused by careless treatment, whilst others — for example, those injured in road accidents — would still need to prove negligence?

2. How adequately did Rosie Barnes' National Health Service (Compensation) Bill deal with the problems of proving causation and identifying the injuries for which compensation would be awarded (*cf* Vaccine damage scheme below)?

(b) Reforming the Existing Tort System

An alternative to no-fault compensation would be to simply amend the existing tort system.

(i) Strict Liability

Closely related to a system of no-fault compensation is one based on strict liability. The fact of having suffered harm, together with the ability to establish causation, would be the only pre-requisites to compensation. Such a scheme was considered in the Pearson Report 1978.

Report of the Royal Commission on Civil Liability and Compensation for Personal Injury 1978 (Cmnd. 7054)

1337 We also considered whether strict liability should be introduced. Whilst this would avoid the difficulties of proving or disproving negligence, there would remain the difficulty of proving that the injury was a medical accident, that is to say that it would not have occurred in any event. It would be necessary to define the area to be covered. For example, the foreseeable result of medical treatment such as amputation of a limb in a case of gangrene would not be included. The problems in defining the scope of medical injuries to be included would be the same as those we consider later in connection with the possibility of introducing a no-fault scheme.

1338 Even if it were possible to limit the scope satisfactorily, the imposition of strict liability, as with reversing the burden of proof, might well lead to an increase in defensive medicine. It would tend to imply rigid standards of professional skill beyond those which the present law requires to be exhibited, and beyond those which (in our view) can fairly be expected. We decided not to recommend that strict liability should be introduced.

NOTE:

1. Today, as we saw above at pages 188–193, a limited strict liability scheme operates under the auspices of the Consumer Protection Act 1987.

(ii) Payment for Legal Services — a Case for Contingency Fees?

Most individuals are unable to personally shoulder the costs of litigation. If their income falls within specified income and capital brackets then they may be able to claim legal aid (the state-funded assistance for litigation). However, the availability of legal aid has been curtailed in recent years. When it is appreciated that the majority of claims made for medical negligence are funded by legal aid — some 90 per cent. (See P. Hoyte, "Medical Negligence Litigation, Claims Handling and Risk Management" (1994) 1 *Medical Law International* 261) this indicates that there may be a substantial number of injured plaintiffs who may be unable to seek compensation. One alternative approach, for which provision was made under the Courts and Legal Services Act 1990, s.58 is the use of conditional fees (S.I. 1993 No. 2132). A lawyer takes on a case on a speculative basis with the client not being charged fees unless the case is successful, in which case the lawyer can charge up to double her normal fees. At present it appears that the conditional fee system has not been used in relation to medical negligence cases, due to difficulty in obtaining insurance to cover plaintiff's costs in the event of loss. A more radical alternative would be to introduce a "contingency fee". These are widely used in the United States. A lawyer takes on a client's case at no charge to the client but if the case is successful they will take a fixed percentage of the damages awarded. (This eventuality is reflected in the high damage awards made by juries in the United States). The existence of a contingency fee system would not necessarily lead to a major increase in medical negligence litigation. Lawyers "sieve" claims and are only likely to take on the risk of claim where there is a strong chance of success.

(iii) Alternative Dispute Resolution

Alternative dispute resolution has become increasingly popular in recent years in areas such as commercial and family disputes. The practice involves resolution of legal matters by reference to procedures such as conciliation and arbitration as opposed to reference to the courts. In 1991 the Department of Health published a consultation document outlining proposals for a voluntary arbitration scheme (see M. Jones, "Arbitration for Medical Claims in the NHS" (1992) 8 *Professional Negligence* 142). Such a scheme was regarded as having considerable advantages in the reduction of costs. An arbitration panel would be established consisting of two doctors (one chosen by each disputing party, and a lawyer specialising in medical negligence. The panel would operate largely applying the same tests as used by the courts in ascertaining negligence and in the award of damages.

Pilot schemes into another form of alternative dispute resolution, mediation, are in operation in the NHS. Mediation involves one person, who may be legally qualified attempting to bring the parties to an agreement. Unlike an arbitrator, a mediator has no power to impose a solution. A two-year pilot study which began in October 1995 is being operated in Oxford and Anglia, and Northern and Yorkshire areas. The first mediation case concerned Ruth McCall, who lost her foetus during pregnancy due to the negligence of the consultant caring for her. A settlement was reached in one day between Mrs McCall and the hospital representative in a case that Mrs McCall's solicitor estimated that, had it gone to litigation, would have normally taken three to four years to resolve. Two subsequent cases referred to mediation were also resolved in only one day (see J. Easterbrook, "Resolving Health Care Disputes" (1996) *Solicitors Journal* 140).

It is uncertain whether ADR will be generally adopted. There is widespread disagreement as to who should be mediators — lawyers or NHS managers (see J. Harris, "The Case for a Little Diplomacy" (1995)

Health Service Journal 1). Equally, how much cheaper ADR will prove to be, considering that it provides ample scope for (necessarily expensive) legal representation, also remains unclear. Furthermore, no matter how popular ADR becomes — and it is likely to become very popular given the support for it in the Woolf Report, *Access to Justice* (London: HMSO, 1996, below) — it is unlikely that litigation will be abandoned altogether as a means of dispute resolution.

(iv) Restructuring the Civil Justice System

The whole system of medical negligence has been considered as part of a wider study undertaken into the civil justice system by Lord Woolf. Lord Woolf consulted widely, holding seminars to which persons including lawyers, health professionals and representatives from patient organisations were invited. In July 1996 Lord Woolf published his report "Access to Justice" (London: HMSO, 1996). A number of proposals were made regarding medical negligence. These include the suggestion that a specialist court should be established to handle such cases. The judges handling such cases would be given medico-legal training. Judges would become trial managers monitoring speed of proceedings and costs. The report recommends that there should be an organisation to promote co-operation between plaintiffs and defendants. It also recommends that solicitors should advise individuals contemplating legal proceedings of alternatives such as reference to the Health Service Commissioner or the use of alternative dispute resolution.

The Woolf Report proposed a new "fast track" for smaller personal injury claims under £10,000. This would have a timescale of some 30 weeks and require written evidence to be given by expert witnesses. Woolf noted that this may not be as appropriate for medical negligence litigation and suggested a number of pilot schemes which could be put into operation. Three options were envisaged. First, a type of fast-track procedure with one expert chosen by both parties and one lawyer representing each party at trial along with a fixed limit of costs of £3,500. Alternatively, the proceedings could be brought along the lines of existing procedures with a budget limited to £4,000 per side. Finally, a tailor-made procedure, budget fixed in advance, an 18-month timescale and a joint expert who would act as an adviser to the court evaluating the evidence presented by each side. Proposals were made as to the use of multi-party actions. It was suggested that there should be a contingency legal aid fund for such cases which would be initially financed by the government and then may be funded through a levy on those who had brought a successful action. Such a fund would be available generally and not limited to those eligible for legal aid. The action would be handled by a single "managing" judge with assistance from a lawyer expert in that area as her deputy. It appears that these proposals are set for early implementation by the government. In October 1996 the Lord Chancellor stated his intention to implement the main aspects of the report by October 1998.

SELECT BIBLIOGRAPHY

A. Bell, "The Doctor and the Supply of Goods and Services Act 1982" (1984) 4 *Legal Studies* 175.

M. Brazier, "NHS Indemnity: The Implications for Medical Litigation" (1990) 6 *Professional Negligence* 88.

M. Brazier, "The Case for a No-Fault Compensation Scheme for Medical Accidents" in S. McLean (ed.), *Compensation for Damage: an International Perspective*, Aldershot: Dartmouth, 1993.

P. F. Ferguson, *Drug Injuries and the Pursuit of Compensation*, London: Sweet and Maxwell, 1996.

C. Ham, R. Dingwall, P. Fenn and D. Harris, *Medical Negligence: Compensation and Accountability*, Oxford: King's Fund Institute, 1988.

J. Harris, "The Case for a Little Diplomacy" (1995) 105 *Health Service Journal* 1

P. Hoyte, "Unsound Practice: The Epiderminology of Medical Negligence" (1995) 3 *Medical Law Review* 53.

M. Jones, *Medical Negligence* (2nd ed.), London: Sweet and Maxwell, 1996.

M. Jones, "Arbitration for Medical Claims in the National Health Service" (1992) 8 *Professional Negligence* 142.

K. McK. Norrie, "Common Practice and the Standard of Care in Medical Negligence" [1985] *Juridical Review* 145.

A. McCall-Smith, "Criminal Negligence and the Incompetent Doctor" (1993) 1 *Medical Law Review* 33.

J. Montgomery, "Medicine, Accountability and Professionalism" (1989) 16 *Journal of Law and Society* 319.

K. Oliphant, "Defining 'Medical Misadventure': Lessons from New Zealand" (1996) 4 *Medical Law Review* 1.

M. Stacey, "Medical Accountability: A Background Paper" in A. Grubb (ed.), *Challenges in Medical Care*, Chichester: John Wiley, 1992.

H. Teff, *Reasonable Care*, Oxford: OUP (1994).

4

PROFESSIONAL ACCOUNTABILITY II

1. INTRODUCTION

In the previous chapter we considered the means by which the healthcare professional may be held accountable for her behaviour in the courtroom. However, here also are a number of other ways in which a health professional may be held accountable. A patient may decide to lodge a complaint about the care he has received. The complaints procedures in operation in the NHS have been the subject of a major review, culminating with a total overhaul of complaints mechanisms in 1996. Where complaints are made in some instances the employer may decide to take disciplinary action against the employee. This is separate from the complaints system.

In addition to the internal systems for complaints within hospitals the Health Service Commissioner acts as an external regulator or Ombudsman. Patients will usually be expected to refer complaints through the established channels before going to the Commissioner. The Commissioner operates alongside the general complaints process. His jurisdiction has recently been extended to include, for example, the investigation of complaints regarding the exercise of clinical judgment.

The tort system is primarily concerned with affording patients compensation. But there may be instances in which the conduct of a health care professional is sufficiently grave to warrant punishment. In the previous Chapter we considered the use of the criminal law in the form of a prosecution for manslaughter when death occurs. However, criminal prosecutions against health care practitioners only occur in rare cases. A more realistic deterrent is afforded through the disciplinary powers of the health professions governing bodies. Today virtually all health care professionals are a member of a professional body. Some of these bodies are long established on a statutory basis such as the General Medical Council and the United Kingdom Central Council on Nursing and Midwifery. The changing nature of health care can be seen in the passage of recent legislation regulating other health care practitioners such as osteopaths and chiropractors. Health care services are also provided by health professionals, who are governed by their peers outside statute, such as psychotherapists. All these bodies possess some form of professional ethical code

211

(for examples of such codes see Chapter 2 above). There is usually provision for some form of professional sanctions in situations in which a professional infringes the provisions of her code. This Chapter considers these mechanisms of accountability. In section two we examine the operation of the NHS patient complaint systme. In section three the disciplinary procedures for health care professionals within the NHS are considered. Section four discusses the role of the health service commissioner. Section five considers professional self-regulation focusing on the disciplinary role of the General Medical Council.

2.   COMPLAINTS WITHIN THE NHS

The NHS complaints system was the subject of a major reconstruction in 1996. Traditionally there has been a division between the complaints systems operational in relation to family practitioners and those in relation to the hospital system. Hospital complaints were placed on a statutory footing by the Hospital Complaints Act in 1985. This Act was not implemented until 1988, when directions were introduced which stated that an officer within each hospital should be designated to receive complaints (H.C.(88)37). This was usually the unit general manager. Nevertheless, while the complaints system was subject to some reform, problems remained. Not least amongst these was the complexity of the system. There were a number of avenues through which complaints could be channelled. These were family health service procedures, hospital and community unit procedures, ambulance service procedures, parliamentary procedures such as complaints to a member of parliament or direct to the Department of Health, or the Health Service Commissioner (for further consideration of his role see below at pages 237–246). A separate procedure dealt with complaints concerning the exercise of clinical judgment.

In response to concerns expressed regarding the operation of the system the government established the Wilson Committee to consider the complaints system and, where appropriate, to recommend reforms. The Committee's report, *Being Heard*, London: DOH, 1994, was published in 1994. The Report highlighted the complexity of the existing system which was accompanied by difficulties for complainants such as lack of information about complaints procedures, delays and problems in obtaining a satisfactory response. It suggested radical reforms be introduced.

(a) The Aims of a Complaints Process

Being Heard: Report of a Review Committee on NHS Complaints Procedures (London: DOH, 1994) (Cross-references Omitted)

163 In the first place, complaints procedures should be responsive and aim to satisfy complainants. This does not mean that all complainants will be satisfied with

the outcome of their complaint, but the procedure should be directed to satisfying their objectives as well as those of the NHS.

164 As seen in both private and public sectors in Chapter V, complaints provide invaluable management information about the quality of services from the perspective of service users and their families and friends. They can help to identify problems and sometimes suggest solutions. The service improvements this can lead to may be to the benefit of all patients and of those involved in providing services for the NHS.

165 Procedures must be cost effective to operate. Although effective in theory, complaints systems which cannot be implemented because resources are not available benefit no one. Where cash limits apply, it is important that investment in complaint handling is not disproportionate to the resources available to improve services. Current information on costs of NHS complaints systems is poor. We have received some helpful information from the Department of Health which showed how costly complaint handling for family health services can be and that costs increase substantially the more formally complaints are investigated and considered. It is difficult to measure the costs of missed opportunities for service improvement, but the value of complaints in this respect should not be underestimated.

166 To satisfy complainants and for management information from complaints to be available, it must be as easy as possible for complainants to make their views known. This should include attempts to reduce potential barriers of class, race, language and literacy, and to recognise the needs of vulnerable groups such as children, people with mental health problems, and people with learning difficulties. Procedures must be well-publicised and understandable to all.

167 Once a complaint is made, both complainant and respondent should be able to expect the matter to be considered impartially. This means that procedures should ensure that different points of view are listened to and investigated without prejudice, and that support should be available to both parties involved. As the Institute for Health Services Management observes, 'Complaints are more likely to accept outcomes if they feel they have been treated fairly'.

168 A simple complaints procedure is desirable. It is likely to be more accessible for complainants and easier to use by those operating it. The simplicity of procedures may be constrained by other organisational elements (*e.g.* the independent contactor status of GPs within the NHS) or by the complexity of the issues involved (*e.g.* in relation to clinical judgment).

169 Complaints procedures should ensure that complaints receive as fast a response as is possible without jeopardising other principles. This can help to prevent dissatisfaction growing or further complaints arising about delays.

170 Complaints systems should encourage people to complain without fear that their current or future care will be compromised. This is of particular relevance to primary care, to priority care services (for people with learning disabilities, mental illness, long term handicap and so on), and for some patients detained under the Mental Health Act, who may receive long term care from certain staff members or from one particular organisation.

171 The NHS treats patient information as confidential and all those who work within the NHS are bound by a duty of confidence. Confidential information moves only on a need-to-know basis. This must equally apply to exchanges of information taking place within, or as a result of, complaints procedures.

172 It is important in relation to complaints that those bodies providing and purchasing services are accountable for what they do, and take responsibility at the most senior levels for the operation of complaints procedures. Chairmen and non-executive members of trusts are therefore to be held ultimately responsible for the operation of their complaints systems.

173 Accountability can also be furthered by openness in publication of complaints statistics by trusts, health authorities and health boards.

NOTES:

1. One of the reasons for the introduction of a complaints system is that the individual may seek an explanation of what has taken place and an apology rather than to pursue a remedy through the courts. But research has indicated that individuals may have other goals when they launch a complaint. Lloyd Bostock and Mulcahey who undertook an empirical study into the NHS complaints process identified a number of such goals. While patients may seek a specific remedy for themselves, they may also want changes in policy and changes to be introduced in order that such incidents do not arise in the future, or the patient may be simply seeking information. (See S. Lloyd Bostock and L. Mulcahey, "The Social Psychology of Making and Responding to Hospital Complaints: An Account of Model Complaints Processes" (1994) 16 *Law and Policy* 123.)

2. The Wilson Committee was influenced by complaints procedures operating in the private sector. But it has been questioned whether this approach is in fact directly analogous. (See J. Hanna, "Internal Resolution of NHS Complaints" (1993) 3 *Medical Law Review* 177.) The complaints process within the NHS differs from many external complaints processes, because of the heightened degree of public accountability — the NHS is a public body. An effective complaints process may be regarded as a method by which citizen grievances may be satisfied. Such an approach would require a complaints process to be assessed with reference to criteria such as openness, speed and impartiality.

(b) The Complaints Process

After the publication of *Being Heard* there was a period of formal consultation as to the conclusions/recommendations. The Government then produce a document setting out the proposed new complaints procedure "Acting on Complaints" in March 1995 (EL(95)37). Interim guidance was published in October 1995 followed by the final guidance in April 1996. Below are extracts from this guidance. This sets out and describes both the amendments which are being made in the form of statutory instruments along with the recommendations of the government as to how the complaints system should be structured.

Complaints, Listening . . . Acting . . . Improving: Guidance on Implementation of the NHS Complaints Procedure NHS Executive March 1996

4 PREPARATORY ACTION

Note: Some sections of the **Guidance** are reproduced in **bold/*italics*** indicating **mandatory requirements** of the new procedure, most of which will be established in **Directions** and **Regulations** other mandatory requirements arise from existing legislation and/or common law.

Formal Procedure

4.1 *Trust/health authority boards/family health services practitioners must establish a complaints procedure and take steps to publicise the arrangements.*

4.2 It will be a requirement for all trusts/health authorities to have a written complaints procedure, that has formally been adopted by the board, for complaints against themselves.

4.3 Family health services practitioners will be required by Regulations to establish and operate practice based complaints procedures that adhere to national criteria. This applies to all individuals, and public and private companies, who appear on the health authority's list of contractors and practitioners undertaking to provide family health services.

Grievance Procedures

4.4 It is important to recognise that the NHS complaints procedure is designed to address patients' complaints, not staff grievances, which will continue to be handled separately. *EL(93)51 and associated guidance* sets out the rights and responsibilities of NHS staff when raising issues of concern about health care matters. Local procedures will also cover more general grievances. Disputes on contractual matters between health authorities, family health services, practitioners should not be handled through the complaints procedure. Staff of trusts/health authorities may complain about the way they have been dealt with under the complaints procedure and provided they have exhausted the local grievance procedure, may complain to the Ombudsman. Family health services practitioners may complain to the Ombudsman about the way they have been dealt with under the complaints procedure.

Publicity

4.5 *Trusts and health authorities must ensure that the right to complain, advice about how to use the complaints procedure, the help available to complainants from staff, community health councils and other sources, is well publicised to all patients in their services, together with community health councils services for those patients, and to visitors and staff. (See paragraph 5.1 for family health services practitioners.)*

4.6 National publicity material in the form of a poster and leaflet will be now available. In addition, local information will also need to be available to cover:

- the arrangements for both Local Resolution and Independent Review of complaints
- how to refer a complaint to the complaints manager or the chief executive
- how to make a request to the convener for an Independent Review panel to be set up
- under what circumstances a complainant may approach a health authority with a complaint about a family health services practitioner
- the role of the community health council in giving individuals advice and support on making complaints
- the way to make a complaint to the Ombudsman [reference to Ombudsman here relates to the Health Service Commission]

Who may complain

4.7 *Trusts and Health Authorities**
Complainants will be existing or former patients using a trust's or health authority's NHS services and facilities. Complaints may be made on behalf of

existing or former patients by anyone who has the patient's consent. If the patient is unable to act, then consent is not needed. Where the complaints manager, or convener at the Independent Review stage, does not accept the complainant as a suitable representative of a patient who is unable to give consent, they may refuse to deal with the complainant, and may nominate another person to act on the patient's behalf.

*including special health authorities for special hospitals.

4.8 Family Health Services Practitioners

Complainants will be existing or former patients of a practitioner who has arrangements with a health authority to provide family health services. Complaints may be made on behalf of existing or former patients by anyone who has the patient's consent. If the patient is unable to act, then consent is not needed. Where the health authority's complaints manager, or convenor at the Independent Review stage, does not accept the complainant as a suitable representative of the patient, they may either refuse to deal with the complainant, or nominate another person to act on the patient's behalf.

4.9 The complaints procedure will apply to complaints made by or on behalf of patients, for example by their relatives. Trusts, health authorities and family health services practitioners should also, as a matter of good practice. ensure that they deal sensitively and effectively with complaints by visitors, contractors or other users of their facilities.

4.10 The question of whether a complainant is suitable to represent a patient who is unable to give consent depends in particular on the need to respect the confidentiality of the patient, and to any known wishes expressed by the patient that information should not be disclosed to third parties.

Time Limit on Initiating Complaints

4.11 *Normally a complaint should be made within six months from the incident that caused the problem, or within six months of discovering the problem, provided that this is within twelve months of the incident. There is discretion to extend this time where it would be unreasonable in the circumstances of a particular case for the complaint to have been made earlier, where it is still possible to investigate the facts of the case.*

4.12 Trusts, health authorities and family health services practitioners will encourage those who wish to complain to do so as soon as possible after an event. The discretion to vary the time limit should be used flexibly and with sensitivity. Wherever possible the complainant's concerns should be addressed constructively, while remaining scrupulously fair to staff. An example of where discretion should be exercised in favour of extending the time limit would be where the complainant has suffered such distress or trauma as to prevent him/her from making their complaint at an earlier stage.

4.13 When a complaint is made outside the time limit, it will be for the complaints manager, or appropriate family health service practitioner to take responsibility for considering an extension of the time limit.

4.14 If the discretionary extension of the time limit is rejected by the complaints manger, then the procedure will be as follows:

- the complainant may complain about the refusal to exercise discretion to waive the time limits:
- if the refusal is maintained, the complainant may request the convener to consider setting up a panel for Independent Review of the complaint about refusal to waive the time limit: the normal requirements as convening decisions will apply — including the time limit for a convening request;

- the convener may then decide
  —to take no further action, or
  —to refer the complaint back for Local Resolution, or
  —to set up a panel to consider the complaint.

If the convener decides to refer the complaint about the time limit before the trust/ health authority, the complaints manager — or chief executive referred specifically to him/her — should review very carefully the decision not to accept the complaint in the light of the convener's conclusion further action through Local Resolution is possible.

4.15 If the convener rejects the request, then the complainant may refer the complaint to the Ombudsman.

Complaints Manager

4.16 *The trust/health authority must have a designated complaints manager, who is readily accessible to the public: the complainant must be able to refer complaints to the complaints manager: The prime role of the complaints manager is to oversee the complaints procedure: The detailed role and functions of the complaints manager should be decided by the board.*

4.17 It is important to have one person in the organisation who has the overview of the whole complaints system.

The complaints manager may be

- the chief executive or
- a senior manager reporting directly to the chief executive, or
- particularly in large trusts, a senior manager reporting to the chief executive through another director, but with personal access to the chief executive when appropriate.

While it is not essential for the title to be used, it is nevertheless important that the individual with the role of complaints manager is easily identifiable to public and staff alike *(see paragraph 4.20 for equivalent role in family health services practices)*.

4.18 It is for the trust/health authority to decide the exact role of its complaints manager. This role may be either to investigate or advise, or both. He/she needs to have access to all relevant trust/health authority records which are essential for the investigation of a complaint referred to them. He/she should be ready to respond to complaints where the complainant does not wish to raise their concerns with those directly involved with their care, or where front-line staff are unable to deal with the complaint. He/she should always bear in mind the need to consult with those who have been complained against in advance of any response being made to the complainant. The complaints manager needs to be able to provide guidance, help, and sometimes to give direct support to other staff who are responding to complaints.

4.19 *Family health services practices must nominate one person to administer the complaints procedure and to identify that person to patients and clients.*

4.20 Family health services practices will decide who is most appropriate to be responsible for its complaints procedure, together with an alternative to act when that person is the subject of the complaint. Complainants may be unhappy at the prospect of having their complaint dealt with by someone who is already involved in their care and who may be the subject of the complaint. If contacted by a complainant, the health authority should be ready to provide assistance to both the complainant and the practitioner to resolve the complaint at practice level, bearing in mind the health authority may become formally involved if the decision is made to proceed to Independent Review (see paragraph 5.15).

Role of Community Health Councils and Patients' Advocates

4.21 Community health council staff have a very important role in assisting complainants at each stage of the process in both the hospital and community services and family health services. Trust and health authority chief executives as well as family health services practitioners, should ensure that advice on how to contact the local community health council assistance in making a complaint is well publicised and that community health councils are fully aware of the local arrangements for responding to complaints. The use of patients' advocates and interpreters to assist complainants either employed directly or through a contract with a local voluntary sector organisation is also commended. There can be positive advantages to both sides if a patient/complainant is encouraged to access the support of the community health council, or some other appropriate body or individual. The role of interpreting and explaining matters to and on behalf of a complainant may well help with the advancement of the process of Local Resolution.

Appointment of Convener

4.22 *Trusts/health authorities must appoint at least one person to act in the role of convener, who may not be one of its own employees at least one of the persons appointed must be a non-executive of the trust/health authority.*

4.23 Every trust/health authority must appoint one or more of its non-executive to act as conveners for considering requests by complainants for Independent Review panels to be set up. The discretion to appoint more than one convener to this function is so that the role can be shared and training of a successor or understudy can be organised more easily. It also provides for the possibility of an alternative convener representing the trust/health authority on the panel, if it is established, relieving the time pressures on the original convener, who may in any case have become involved in a second convening request. The concept of a 'lead' convener or 'convener's office' may be useful. The convener will need staff support in organising this, the trust/health authority will need to demonstrate impartiality — for example, where the remaining grievance relates in some way to the handling of the complaint during the Local Resolution.

4.24 Conveners may be appointed from any of the non-executive, although chairmen are recommended not to take on this role other than in exceptional circumstances. Trusts/health authorities should be very sensitive to any possible concerns about bias: the appointment to this role of non-executives who are practising or retired clinicians, or recently retired NHS staff, should be exceptional. Boards are required to appoint at least one of their non-executive directors as a convener, who should be fully appraised of guidance and issues relating to the role of the convener. It is recognised that some trust/health authority boards may wish to appoint additional people on a consultancy basis specifically to act as conveners in a similar manner to arrangements that are operated by some boards to help with Mental Health Act reviews of detention. Persons appointed to take on this task may act in the full role of the convener, including serving on the panel. Their terms of appointment by the board should ensure that their role is explicit and that they have appropriate indemnity cover.

4.25 It is suggested that these appointments be for an initial period of at least two years but, where more that one is designated, the appointments might be staggered. Trusts and health authorities should notify their regional office whenever new conveners are appointed.

4.26 Conveners will be indemnified for this duty in the same way as for the other duties of non-executive directors.

Complaints and Disciplinary Procedures to be Separated

4.27 *Trusts/health authorities must keep their complaints procedure separate from their disciplinary procedure. Disciplinary procedures for family health services practitioners will be separate from the complaints procedure.*

4.28 Policy remains firm on the need for the new complaints procedure to be concerned **only** with resolving complains and **not** with investigating disciplinary matters. The purpose of the complaints procedure is **not** to apportion blame amongst staff. It is to investigate complaints with the aim of satisfying complainants (while being scrupulously fair to staff) and to learn any lesson for improvement in service delivery. Inevitably, however, some complaints will identify information about serious matters which indicate a need for disciplinary investigation.

4.29 In hospital and community/ambulance services, a case for considering disciplinary investigation can be suggested at any˙ point during the complaints procedure, **but** consideration as to whether or not disciplinary action is warranted is a separate matter for management, outside the complaints procedure, and must be subject to a separate process of investigation. For family health services practitioners, local disciplinary procedures cannot be considered until after an Independent Review panel has investigated a complaint and reported to the chief executive.

Trusts/Health Authorities

4.30 In the case of trusts/health authorities' papers that have accumulated during the investigation of the complaint may be passed to the appropriate person in the trust/health authority who will be considering the need for a disciplinary or any other form of investigation (see paragraph 4.32 for other relevant forms of investigation). Information gathered in the complaints process can be made available for a disciplinary investigation.

Family Health Services Practitioners

4.31 . . . From April 1, 1996, complaints will be investigated using the new procedure and the need for local disciplinary action will only be considered after the handling of a complaint has been concluded. Only if action is necessary to protect patients, for example such as the need to involve the police, professional registration body, or the NHS Tribunal, would disciplinary investigation interrupt the handling of a family health services complaint. Information gathered on the complaints process by the practitioner, as part of Local Resolution, belongs to the practice. This information will be kept separate from the patient's health record. There the health authority has no right of access to it and will only be able to require that the practitioner concerned provides to the health authority **information** about action taken during Local Resolution. Information acquired during the Independent Review process cannot automatically be used in disciplinary investigations. However, the Ombudsman has wideranging powers which can be used, if necessary, to require the production of information and documents.

Hospital and Community Health Services

4.32 *If any complaint received by a member or employee of a trust/health authority indicates a prima facie need for referral to any of the following*

　　(i)　an investigation under the disciplinary procedure
　　(ii)　one of the professional regulatory bodies
　　(iii)　an independent inquiry into a serious incident under Section 84 of the National Health Service Act 1977
　　(iv)　an investigation of a criminal offence

*the person in receipt of the complaint should at once pass the relevant information
of the complaints manager, who will ensure that it is passed on to a suitable person
who can make a decision on whether and when to initiate such action: this
reference may be made at any point during any stage of the complaints procedure.*

*Neither the complaints manager nor the convener shall be responsible for
deciding whether to initiate any of the action referred to in i–iv above and they
should refer such cases to the person designated in the trust/health authority for
dealing with such matters.*

*Where it is decided to take action under any of i–iv above before a complaint
investigation has been completed, a full report of the investigation thus far should
be made available to the complainant.*

*The complainants procedure will not deal with matters relating to that part of
the original complaints which is currently the subject of disciplinary investigation.
If action is initiated under i or ii above, the complainant should be advised
accordingly so that appropriate action under the complaints procedure can be
pursued where there are other matters raised in the complaint which do not relate
to disciplinary investigation.*

*If any action is initiated under iii or iv above, the complaints procedure should
be similarly modified until such action is concluded.*

*Where any action under i–iv as set out above has been concluded that part of the
original complaint which has been referred to a different procedure should only
recommence through the complaints procedure where there are outstanding matters
in the complaint which have not been resolves through that action.*

(Note: as far as health authorities are concerned, *paragraphs 4.32 to 4.36* refer only
to complaints about their own services or staff and do not apply to complaints
about family health services practitioners.) . . .

4.34 If there are no outstanding issues from the original complaint to be
investigated, the complainant should be advised that no further action will be taken
other than that through the disciplinary procedure. The complainant may well ask
at this point to be informed of the outcome of the disciplinary inquiry. A judgment
will need to be made; on the one hand, in terms of reassuring the complainant, who
will be concerned that the matter complained about has been dealt with seriously
and satisfactory; and on the other, the protection of the confidentiality of the
member of staff. The guiding principle should be that, when the disciplinary
procedure is invoked, the complainant receives the same consideration and level of
information as if the matter had been dealt with through the complaints procedure.
The complainant should be able to understand what happened, why it happened,
and what action has been taken as a consequence to ensure that it does not happen
again. The complainant should be informed in general terms of any disciplinary
sanction imposed on any staff member.

4.35 It is most important that the complainant is satisfied with the action being
taken by the trust/health authority. If a referral for disciplinary investigation has
been made during the period of Local Resolution, then this part of the complaints
procedure should be rounded off with a formal written explanation of the action
taken by the trust/health authority. Where the referral is made later during the
Independent Review process, then a similar written explanation needs to be given
as part of the completion of this process. Within the context of the complaints
procedure, the overall consideration must be that, even if the investigation has been
moved into the disciplinary procedure, the complainant is not left dissatisfied, with
the feeling that their grievance has only been partially dealt with.

4.36 A similar approach will need to be adopted in a case which has indicated
the need for a referral to one of the professional regulatory bodies. A trust/health
authority has no control over what then happens and over what period. The
complainant should be similarly informed of this decision and, at this point, given
as full a response as possible to the complainant, making it clear that any
information obtained during the complaints investigation may need to be passed on

to the regulatory body. Those parts of the original complaint not included in the reference to the professional regulatory body should continue to be investigated under the complaints procedure.

Possible Claims for Negligence

4.37 *The complaints procedure should cease if the complainant explicitly indicates an intention to take legal action in respect of the complaint.*

4.38 If a complaint reveals a prima facie case of negligence, or if it is thought that there is a likelihood of legal action being taken, the person in receipt of the complaint should inform the person in the trust/health authority who is responsible for dealing with risk management and claims management. Even if a complainant's initial communication is via a solicitor's letter, the inference should not necessarily be that the complainant has decided to take formal legal action. A hostile, or defensive, reaction to the complaint is more likely to encourage the complainant to seek information and a remedy through the courts. In the early part of the process it may not be clear whether the complainant simply wants an explanation and apology, with assurances that any failures in service will be rectified for the future, or whether the complainant is in fact seeking information with formal litigation in mind. It may be that an open and sympathetic approach will satisfy the complainant. In a trust, where there is a prima-facie case of clinical negligence, the person dealing with the complaint should seek advice appropriately. This should not prevent a full explanation being given and, if appropriate, an apology offered to the complainant, an apology is not an admission of liability. If formal legal action has been instigated, the complaints procedure should be brought to an end, with the complainant and the complained against being advised appropriately in writing.

4.39 In all prima facie cases of negligence, or where the complainant has indicated the intention to start legal proceedings, the principles of good claims management and risk management should be applied. There should be a full and thorough investigation of the events. In any case where the trust/health authority accepts that there has been negligence, a speedy settlement should be sought.

5 LOCAL RESOLUTION

Trust and Health Authorities

5.1 *As part of its complaints procedure, the trust/health authority must establish a clear Local Resolution process. In the case of family health services, Local Resolution is the responsibility of the practitioner.*

5.2 The primary objective of Local Resolution is to provide the fullest possible opportunity for investigation and resolution of the complaint, as quickly as is sensible in the circumstances, aiming to satisfy the complainant while being scrupulously fair to staff. Trusts/health authorities' complaints procedures must therefore have a well-defined Local Resolution process, which lays emphasis on complaints being dealt with quickly and, where possible, by those on the spot. The intention of Local Resolution is that it should be open, fair, flexible, and conciliatory. The complainant should be given the opportunity to understand all possible options for pursuing the complaint, and the consequences of following any of these. This explanation should indicate that it might be necessary to look at the patient's health records. The community health council, and indeed any other patients' advocate, in advising and supporting the complainant, will be invaluable in this process *(see paragraph 4.21)*. The process should encourage communication on all sides. The aim should be to resolve complaints at this stage, and many should be capable of resolution orally. Local Resolution should not be seen simply as a run-up process to Independent Review: its primary purpose is to provide a comprehensive response that satisfies the complainant. The process of Local Resolution should provide for a range of different options for response to the complainant. Rigid, bureaucratic, and legalistic approaches should be avoided at all stages of the procedure, but particularly during Local Resolution. It is for trusts/health authorities to consider whether there would be advantage in offering access to conciliation *(see paragraph 5.16)*.

Role of Front-Line Staff in Trusts and Health Authorities

5.3 Complaints are most likely to be initiated with front-line staff on the wards, in clinics, at reception desks, or with departmental managers. Management needs to empower front-line staff to deal with complaints on the spot. Local guidance needs to assist front-line staff in distinguishing serious issues which need reference elsewhere, and when to refer complaints for fuller investigation by — or coordination through — the complaints manager. Steps need to be taken to ensure effective arrangements are in place for dealing with complaints that are received over the telephone. Steps should also be taken to ensure that complainants are made aware of the role of the community health council, and any other patients' advocate available to assist them in pursing complaints, and how they may be contacted.

5.4 The first responsibility of a recipient of a complaint is to ensure — before doing anything else — that the patient's immediate health care needs are being met. This may require urgent action before any matters relating to the complaint are tackled. Staff should, where possible, deal with the complaint rapidly and in an informal and sensitive manner. Complaints might also be made to clinical staff or to a member of the trust/health authority board. Whoever within the organisation receives the complaint should seek to understand the nature of the complaint and any nuances that are not immediately obvious. Where the recipient is unable to investigate the complaint adequately, or feels unable to give the assurances that the complainant is clearly looking for, then the complaint should be referred to the complaints manager, either for advice or for handling. Complainants should be encouraged to speak openly and freely about their concerns and should be reassured that whatever they may say will be treated with appropriate confidence and sensitivity.

5.5 Some complainants may prefer to make their initial complaint to someone who has not been involved in their case. In these circumstances they should be counselled to address their complaints manager or, if they prefer, to the chief executive. While front-line staff should always encourage complainants to be forthcoming in expressing their concern, apprehension and anxiety, particularly where they are dissatisfied with the care they have received, this should never be done at the expense of overriding the right of complainants to make their complaint to the complaints manager or the chief executive.

5.6 Front-line staff also need to be empowered to use the information they get from complaints to improve service quality, particularly oral comments or criticisms which are not actually complaints, where people want something put right or improved, not investigated. Mechanisms for achieving this can be agreed at team level and will be particularly important for sharing information relevant to the work of other teams, for example, those responsible for hotel services.

5.7 When deciding whether or not to pass an oral complaint on to the complaints manager, front-line staff, for example in trusts, will need to take into account the seriousness of the complaint and the possible need for more independent investigation and assessment. While an important role of the complaints manager is to investigate written complaints and to satisfy complainants, this must not preclude the complaints manager from advising front-line and other staff in the resolution of complaints.

Role of the Chief Executive

5.8 The chief executive of the trust/health authority must respond in writing to all written complaints and all oral complaints which are subsequently put in writing and signed by the complainant. In the case of an oral complaint, where the complainant is dissatisfied with the initial response and wants to pursue the matter further, the complaint should be put in writing and signed by the complainant.

5.9 The Citizen's Charter Complaints Task Force defined a complaint as 'an expression of dissatisfaction requiring a response'. In the majority of cases, complaints are made orally. All complaints, whether oral or written should receive a positive and full response, with the aim of satisfying the complainant that his/her concerns have been heeded, and offering an apology and explanation as appropriate, referring to any remedial action . . .

5.10 The Patient's Charter given patients the right to a written reply from the relevant trust/health authority chief executive in response to a written complaint. The Ombudsman has criticised chief executives of NHS bodies for failure to sign written responses to complainants who have made written complaints and the Chief Executive of the NHS has reaffirmed the importance which he and Ministers attach to performance in this area *(see EL(95)136)*. The reply might take the form of a full personally signed response or a shorter letter covering a full report from another member of staff, which the chief executive has reviewed and is content with. Some oral complaints are also sufficiently serious, or difficult to resolve, that they should be recorded in writing by the complaints manager. These complaints ought also receive a written response from the chief executive.

5.11 Consideration should be given to collecting data on oral complaints, even when they are not recorded in writing, so that lessons can be learned which may help in improving service delivery *(see paragraph 10.4 on the collection of data on complaints)*.

5.12 Any person handling a complaint, and particularly complaints managers handling written complaints, must ensure that any response given to a complainant which refers to matters of clinical judgment is agreed by the clinician concerned and in the case of medical care, by the consultant responsible for the care of the patient.

5.13 There may be occasions when a communication is critical of a service or the quality of care, but is not intended as a complaint. Chief executives will wish to ensure that their organisations are receptive to comments and suggestions, whether critical or positive, as well as to complaints. Such communications are often a useful form of feedback from patients and their relatives, which can be used to improve quality of service, and also to give encouragement to staff when they are doing well.

Family Health Services Practitioners

5.14 From April 1, 1996 there will be a term of service obligation on family health services practitioners to have in place and to operate practice-based complaints procedures which comply with minimum national criteria:

- administration of practice-based procedures will be practice-owned and managed entirely by the practice — the health authority will only become involved if the practice procedure does not appear to meet the national criteria
- health authorities will only become involved in an individual complaint if asked to do so by the complainant and/or the practitioner
- one person will be nominated by the practice to be responsible for overseeing the administration of the procedure
- practices must give the procedure publicity
- practices must ensure it is clear how to lodge a complaint and to whom

- an acknowledgement or initial response to a complaint should normally be made within two working days
- an explanation should normally be provided within two weeks (*i.e.* ten working days)

It is in everyone's interest that Local Resolution at practice level is successful *(see paragraph 1.6)*. General medical practitioners should keep records to help them bid to their health authority for additional funding under the reimbursement scheme to set up and operate new procedures, and health authorities are asked to consider reasonable bids favourably.

Action by the Health Authority

5.15 There are two roles for health authorities in the family health services Local Resolution process. Where, for example a complainant does not wish for some reason to have a complaint dealt with by the practice, or is having difficulty in getting the complaint dealt with by the practitioner, health authorities will, if both parties agree, act as 'honest broker' between the complainant and the practitioner to resolve the complaint at practice level. Health authorities will also make available lay conciliators as a service to complainants and practices. Arrangements for appointing lay conciliators and, when appropriate, professional advisers to the lay conciliators, are matters entirely for the health authority. Patients and family health service practitioners need to feel confident in the new complaints system. When an health authority is acting as intermediary between patient and practitioner in providing conciliation or dealing with a request for Independent Review it will be essential for health authorities to establish clear and constant lines of communication between patients and practitioners. This might be done via a named person in the health authority who can at all times give accurate information about a complaint's progress. Within the health authority, a 'need to know' procedure should be followed: only those who need to be involved in handling a complaint should be aware of its existence. Complaints about treatment provided under family health service arrangements may involve a statutory charge payable by the complainant. Health authorities will need to ensure that conciliators who may become involved fully understand the nature of such charges.

Family Health Services Conciliation

5.16 Conciliation may prove essential if complaints are to be resolved satisfactorily at practice level. Authorities should therefore continue to make conciliators available to practices where a conciliator's assistance is requested, either by the practice or the complainant *(see paragraph 5.15)*. Confidentiality must be strictly observed during the conciliation process. Conciliation is essentially a process of facilitating agreement between the practitioner and complainant. It is most effective when used as early in the complaints resolution process as possible. Confidentiality must be strictly observed during the conciliation process. Consequently, conciliators should never be required to report to health authorities the details of cases in which they are involved. Particularly, conciliators should not provide information which might then be used by the health authority should a complainant prove dissatisfied with Local Resolution and ask for Independent Review.

Completion of Local Resolution

5.17 There is a need to bear in mind that the right of the complainant to request the convener to set up an Independent Review panel is not a right to proceed automatically to Independent Review. The subtlety of this distinction may often be lost on complainants who may well be angry at the time as a result of their dissatisfaction with the outcome of Local Resolution. A clearly documented record of the events of Local Resolution — whether or not a final letter has been sent to the complainant — will assist in reducing the time the convener may have to spend researching the background of the complaint, in the event of an application by the complainant to proceed to Independent Review.

Trusts and Health Authorities

5.18 It may be appropriate for the entire process of Local Resolution to be conducted orally, without any written communication, leaving the complainant completely satisfied with the outcome. However, where for example

- the person dealing with the complaint suspects that the complainant may wish to consider taking the matter further
- the complainant is satisfied with the oral response but has expressed the wish for a formal response to close the case,

it is recommended that Local Resolution may best be rounded off with a letter to the complainant. Any letter concluding the Local Resolution stage (whether signed by the chief executive because it is written complaint, or by some other appropriate person) should indicate the right of the complainant to seek an Independent Review of the complaint, or any aspect of the response to it with which the complainant remains dissatisfied, and that the complainant has twenty-eight days from the date of that letter to make such a request. This communication should aim to satisfy the complainant that the complaint has been fully and fairly investigated, with an appropriately couched apology where things have gone wrong, and what is to be done to prevent a recurrence.

Family Health Service Practitioners

5.19 Guidance to family health services practitioners does not differentiate between the handling of written and oral complaints. In both cases practices are advised to round off the handling of the complaint by giving a written summary of the investigation and its conclusions to the complainant, also indicating the complainant's right to seek an Independent Review, and that the complainant has twenty-eight calender days from the date of the letter to make such a request. Local Resolution will end at this point. Practices have been advised to keep records of complaints handling — which should be separate from patients' health records — both for the purpose of using complaints to improve procedures and services, and in case they are needed to enable the practice to cooperate with later stages of the complaints procedure, including Independent Review.

5.20 Recognising that the primary purpose of Local Resolution is to satisfy the complainant whenever possible, while being scrupulously fair to staff, the following targets should be used with discretion. Where these targets are not being met, it is very important for the complainant to be informed of the delay and the reasons for it, as well as the likely revised timetable for dealing with the complaint. Similarly, where a complainant withdraws a complaint, it is important that the complained against and, in the case of family health services, the practitioner, are informed immediately.

Trusts and Health Authorities

5.21 Most oral complaints will be resolved on the spot or within two working days. Where this is not possible, and where there is a formal written complaint, trusts/health authorities should aim to make either an initial acknowledgement to the complainant with two working days or, if they are able to resolve the complaint fully within this time, to respond in five working days. For written complaints, and oral complaints recorded in writing acknowledgement should always be in writing. Full investigation and resolution of all types of complaints should be sought within twenty working days, recognising however that there is likely to be great variations in the nature of complaints and in the ability of complainants to cope with their part of the process. Given the complexity that arises in some complaints, a clear referencing and dating system is necessary for all communications with patients and family health services practitioners. First class post — or, exceptionally, special delivery mail — should be used in correspondence with complainants and practitioners. All communications should be marked 'Private and Confidential' and or 'Personal'.

Family Health Services Practitioners

5.22 The aim should be for family health services practitioners to complete the Local Resolution process within ten working days. The possibility however of the health authority being asked to provide support or conciliation *(see paragraph 5.15 and 5.16)* will inevitably extend the period of Local Resolution. In these cases it would not be unreasonable for the performance target to be extended.

NOTES:

1. The basic structure of the complaints process has been streamlined. The same pattern of complaints structure now applies both in the context of hospital care and in relation to complaints concerning general practitioners. The complaints procedure operates at two levels (following the Wilson recommendation), local resolution and independent review. The focus on informal resolution is indicative of the fact that in many situations the complainant's primary objective is obtaining an explanation and an apology rather than compensation. Where legal proceedings are to ensue the complaints procedure will cease (para. 4.37). Both clinical and non-clinical complaints are channelled under the one system. The complaints system maintains a separation of complaints from disciplinary processes (para. 4.27). A decision to stop the complaints procedure is only likely to be capable of legal challenge where a body can be shown to have acted unreasonably: *R v. Canterbury and Thanet DHA South East Thames RHA, ex p. Ford W.* [1994] 5 Med. L.R. 132.

2. Prior to the 1996 reforms, the complaints system for general practitioners had been separate from that of hospital complaints. This separation has continued post the NHS reforms. However, the procedures are designed along similar principles. Both schemes make provision for what is known as "independent review". While practices have considerable discretion with regards to the complaints process there are certain mandatory requirements as to the constituent elements of a complaints service. Specific guidance has been issued to G.P.s by the NHS management executive in the form of a document entitled "Practice — Based Complaints Procedures: Guidance for General Practitioners", NHS (February 1996).

3. The new procedures place considerable emphasis upon the role of Community Health Councils in the resolution of concerns. This has

the advantage of utilising a body independent from the health care provider but with sufficient expertise. When the internal market was introduced there was speculation as to whether the role of the CHCs would increase. (See D. Longley, "Diagnostic Dilemmas: Accountability in the Health Service" [1991] *Public Law* 527.) However, any anticipated expansion does not appear to have materialised. To expect expansion of the role of CHCs as presently constituted may be unrealistic. These bodies sit part time. For them to play a more active role in the complaints process would require the expenditure of considerable resources.

4. A six-month time limit is imposed in relation to complaints (para. 4.11). This may be particularly significant in that contracts between NHS purchasers and providers are normally of only 12 months duration. It may be important for information obtained from patient complaints to be fed into the contract monitoring process.

5. Complaints may be made regarding purchasing decisions. However, guidance states that where decisions regarding purchasing policy have been reached fairly and reasonably this is not a matter for the complaints process (para. 8.1). This should be compared with the approach which the courts have taken to actions brought by patients attempting to challenge decisions regarding NHS resource allocation. (See Chapter 1 above at pages 47–61.)

6. The complaints procedure operates alongside the existing procedure. Persons for instance wanting information regarding the NHS may still be channelled through the procedures set out in the NHS Code of Openness. (See Chapter 1 at page 46.)

7. In some instances care is provided to patients by a combination of health professionals and social services, as in relation to care of the elderly. The Government indicated that it intends in the future to examine procedures for "mixed sector" complaints. (See "Interim Guidance on Implementation of the NHS Complaints Procedure" October 1995, NHS Executive, at page 9.)

8. The guidance makes reference to the role of advocates acting for patients. Patient advocates are already used for example, in the context of the mentally ill. A number of hospitals have appointed persons as "patient representatives". Patient representatives are commonly used in United States hospitals (see generally S. McIver, "Investing in Patient Representatives" Birmingham: NAHAT, 1993 and S. McIver, "Establishing Patient Representatives; the 2nd Report of the Patient Representatives Project", Birmingham: NAHAT (1993)). In the United States their role varies, as does the extent of their perceived independence. Some patient representatives are a formal part of the complaints process within an individual hospital and are regarded as having a role in diffusing individual concerns (see further J. V. McHale, "Whistleblowing in the U.S." in G. Hunt (ed.), *Whistleblowing in the Health Service*, London: Edward Arnold, 1995).

Neither the Wilson Committee nor the government clarified the role of the nurse in the complaints process. The UKCC has recognised that part of the professional duty of the nurse is for her to act as an advocate for her patient. The government treat staff complaints and issues, such as the position of the member of staff who believes that she should "go public" about what she regards as an unacceptable standard of care, to be a matter separate from the complaints procedure (para. 4.4 above). Whether such an effective separation can, in practice, be made is questionable. (See further discussion Chapter 8 at pages 445–6.)

9. One criticism made of the old complaints system related to the fact that individuals were frequently unaware of the procedures. Longley notes the results of an empirical study which she had conducted: "Only a small number of health authorities provide any special leaflet or training for staff on how to handle complaints or where to refer patients so that matters can be dealt with appropriately." (Di Longley, *Public Law and Health Service Accountability*, Open UP: 1993, at page 71). The new complaints structure now emphasises the need for publicity (paras 4.5–4.6). In response to the Wilson Committee, the government stated that if procedures are to be effective in dealing with patient complaints, it will be necessary to provide proper training to enable practitioners and management staff to perform their functions as hoped and said that:

> "We will consult the professional regulatory and educational bodies on incorporating communications skills in training programmes. A new training package will be produced, in conjunction with interested parties, to improve complaints handling at all levels."

The guidance now includes a section on training. In addition to these complaints procedures a particular incident may also give rise to the appointment of an inquiry by a NHS Trust or Health Authority. This may be on an *ad hoc* basis or it may be a statutory inquiry. Section 89 of the National Health Service Act 1977 provides the Secretary of State with the power to establish an inquiry when he believes that it is advisable to do so. (See further M. Brazier, *Medicine, Patients and the Law*, (2nd ed.) Harmondsworth: Penguin 1992 at page 206).

The second stage of the complaints process is termed independent review.

Complaints, Listening . . . Acting . . . Improving: Guidance on Implementation of the NHS Complaints Procedure NHS Executive March 1996

Independent Review

Purpose of the Panel

7.1 The purpose of an Independent Review panel is to consider the complaint according to the terms of reference decided by the convener and in the light of the written statement provided to the convener by the complainant. The panel will investigate the facts of the case, taking into account the views of both sides. It will set out its conclusions, with appropriate comments and suggestions, in a written report.

Establishing the Panel

7.2 *Independent Review panels will be composed of three members*

- *independent lay chairman*
  (nominated by the Secretary of State for Health from the regional list)
- *convener*
  (non-executive of the trust/health authority or appointed person)
- *for trust panels, a representative of the purchaser*
  (either health authority non-executive or, of he/she wishes to be represented, a GP fundholder nominated by the fundholding practice which purchased the service concerned).

In the case of health authority panels or special hospital service panels, the third member of the panel will be another independent person nominated by the Secretary of State for Health.

Where the convener decides (after consultation with the prospective independent lay panel chairman, and after taking appropriate clinical advice) that the complaint is a clinical complaint the panel will be advised by at least two independent clinical assessors nominated by the regional office, following advice from the relevant professional bodies.

The panel is to be established as a committee of the trust/health authority and the assessors are to be appointed by the trust/health authority to advise the panel.

Appointment of Panel Members

7.3 Regional offices will be responsible for recruiting panel chairmen and lay panel members, except in the case of trust panels, when the third panel member will come from the health authority or GP fundholder as representative of the purchaser. Panel members should be chosen not only for their interest in the subject, but for their impartiality and judgmental skills and, where possible, experience in working in small groups, tasked with producing reports. Regional offices have collaborated in the preparation of an outline person specification for this role. Recruitment will be in accordance with the equal opportunities policy and the cultural make-up of local communities should be taken into account. The names held on the regional lists for the role of panel chairman and third panel members for health selection should be their independence and ability to act without bias only exceptionally will they be recently retired NHS staff, or lay non-executive other trusts/health authorities. Practising or retired members of the clinical professionals should not be chosen for this role. It is recognised that some health authority boards may wish to appoint additional people on a consultancy basis specifically to act as the third panel member role, in a similar manner to appointing additional people to act as conveners *(see paragraph 4.24)*. No panel member — other than the convener or alternatively should have any past or present links with the trust/health authority establishing the panel.

7.4 Regional directors are responsible for putting in place arrangements for holding the lists of independent lay chairmen and lay panel members. It will be for regional offices to organise access to broad training for independent lay chairmen and panel members and to decide their appropriate allocation to panels on request from trusts/health authorities. There is nothing to prevent regional offices assisting each other in finding an appropriate panel chairman or panel member, where circumstances demand a wider trawl. Call-off from these lists should be organised in a balanced, independent way, so that no one lay chairman or panel member becomes regularly linked with a particular trust/health authority.

7.5 It is for trusts/health authorities to issue formal letters covering the appointment of panel members to serve on a specific panel, including indemnity cover, and to ensure that arrangements are made to let panel members have appropriate background and briefing papers, together with the names of the assessors who have been appointed to assist a particular panel. Trusts/health authorities should inform the complainant of the panel members and assessors appointed to conduct the Independent Review.

Role of the Independent Lay Panel Chairman

7.6 The role of the independent lay panel chairman is in two parts . . .: first, to help the convener by providing independent advice and support during the convening period: second, to chair the panel where established. Regional offices will, on receiving a request, choose an appropriate person from their list for the trust/health authority conveners' to consult with. The trust/health authority will formally appoint the panel chairman, bearing in mind the need for indemnity cover in respect of the advice given to the convener during the convening period.

7.7 Once the convenor's decision has been made to establish an Independent Review panel, and he/she has set out the terms of reference for the panel, responsibility for leading the organisation of the panel's business then falls to its chairman.

Functioning of the Panel

7.8 *The function of the panel is to:*

- *investigate the aspect of the complaints set out in the convener's terms of reference, taking into account the complainant's grievance as recorded in writing to the convener*
- *make a report setting out its conclusions, with appropriate comments and suggestions.*

The panel will have no executive authority over any action by the trust/health authority, or family health services practitioner, and may not make any suggestion in its report that any person should be subject to disciplinary action or referred to any of the professional regulatory bodies.

7.9 The panel should be proactive in its investigations, always seeking to resolve the complainant's grievance in a conciliatory manner, while at the same time taking a view on the facts it has identified. The panel should be flexible in the way it goes about its business, choosing a method or procedure appropriate to the circumstances of the complaint. It should not allow confrontational situations to arise. Resolution of the complaint may be sought by the full panel, with its assessors, through separate meetings with the complainant and the complained against. It is a matter for the panel to decide whether the complainant and the complained against should be brought together at the same meetings: similarly whether smaller meetings involving say, any one member of the panel, with or without assessors, are appropriate in the circumstances.

7.10 *The panel will decide how to conduct its proceedings, having regard to Guidance issued by the NHS Executive, within the following rules:*

- *the panel's proceedings must be held in private*
- *the panel must give both the complainant and any person complained against a reasonable opportunity to express their views on the complaint*

- *if any of the panel members disagree about how the panel should go about its business, the chairman's decision will be final*
- *when being interviewed by any members of the panel or the assessors, the complainant and any other person interviewed may be accompanied by a person of their choosing, who may, with the agreement of the panel chairman, speak to the panel members/assessors, except that no person interviewed may be accompanied by a legally qualified person acting as an advocate.*

7.11 The panel will have access to all the records held by the trust health authority relating to the handling of the complaint; family health services practitioners will be asked to make available information about the handling of the complaint. If the complaint is a clinical complaint, the panel must have access to the relevant parts of the patient's health records.

Identification of Assessors

7.13 *Where the complaint is wholly or partly related to clinical matters, panels must be advised by at least two independent clinical assessors on relevant matters. The independent clinical assessors' role is to advise and make a report, or reports, to a panel on the clinical aspects of complaints. The assessors should decide in consultation with the panel, how to exercise their responsibilities, having regard to Guidance issued by the NHS Executive and their professional bodies.*

7.14 The role of an assessor is to advise the panel or its individual members. Assessors should not act independently to resolve a complaint. Where a complaint raises issues about more than one medical specialty or health care profession, at least one assessor for each relevant medical speciality/health care profession should be available to advise the panel. In cases where only one discipline is under scrutiny there will be two assessors for the relevant discipline. In some cases it may be appropriate for there to be more than two assessors and it will be for the panel chairman to make a decision.

7.15 The regional offices will hold national (England and Wales) lists of assessors for hospital and community health services and regional lists of assessors of family health services. GP fundholder complaints, and assessors with experience of exercising clinical judgment in a purchasing context.

7.16 The professional bodies' role in ensuring that lists of appropriate independent assessors, who are acceptable to the profession concerned to be kept up to date, is crucial to ensuring the general standing and efficacy of the assessor system . . .

Nomination of Assessors

7.17 On receipt of a request from a trust/health authority for assessors to advise a panel, the regional office will, on behalf of the Secretary of State for Health, nominate appropriate assessors from the national database. Trusts/health authorities will need to ascertain the availability of assessors before making formal appointments, notifying the regional office whether or not the assessor is able to accept the appointment. Normally assessors for hospital and community health services complaints will be selected from names of those working outside the region concerned, but regional offices have discretion on this point, particularly now that regions cover a wider area. In the case of family health services panels, assessors should be chosen from a list held by the regional office of assessors nominated by the local representative committees or, in the case of GP fundholders, by recognised local GP fundholding groups, working in conjunction with local medical committees. Family health services assessors should not come from within the health authority area of the practice or practitioner against whom the complaint is made.

When selecting assessors, it will be important to ensure that they have no connection with any of the parties to the complaint which might call in question their independence or objectivity in respect of a particular complaint. When there is doubt about the choice of an assessor, regional offices should contact the appropriate professional body.

Appointment of Assessors

7.18 Once notified by the regional office, responsibility for communicating with and ascertaining availability, and formally appointing the chosen assessors, will rest with trusts health authorities, who should issue formal letters covering their appointment to assist a specific panel, including indemnity cover. Trusts/health authorities will ensure that arrangements are made to let the assessors have appropriate documentation.

Release of Assessors

7.19 The role of the assessor is crucial to the success and impartiality of the complaints procedure. If the role is to be carried out thoroughly and successfully, then assessors will need to be granted prompt release from their commitments. Trusts and other employers are encouraged to recognise that the system will only work successfully if there is recognition that the release of assessors will need to be granted quickly, so that delays in the complaints process can be avoided *(see paragraph 7.51)*.

Role of Assessors

7.20 The role of the assessors is to advise the panel, as and when required of those aspects of the complaints involving clinical judgments . . .

7.21 *At least one assessor must be present when the panel, or a member of the panel, interviews either or both of the parties on occasions when matters relating to the exercise of clinical judgment are under consideration.*

7.22 The assessors must have access to all the patient's health records held by the trust/health authority/family health services practitioner together with information about the handling of the complaint. Assessors will need to acquaint themselves of any circumstances where a patient might be denied access to information in the health record, or where the patient has expressed the wish for personal information to be withheld from other parties.

7.23 Assessors may interview/examine complainants, who may if they wish have a person of their choosing present. Assessors should check whether the patient has ever been denied access to all or part of their health record. Where the complainant is not the patient, care must be taken not to discuss information which would breach the patient's confidence. Care must also be taken not to break third-party confidence. Assessors should not normally explain their findings to either the patient or complainant at this stage, before advising the panel of their views.

7.24 Similarly, assessors may interview any person complained against, who may have a person of their choosing present. Assessors should not normally explain their findings to the person complained against before advising the panel of their views.

7.25 There may be occasions when a patient's health record is no longer in the possession of the complained against (including a family health services practitioner against whom the complaint has been made). In these circumstances every effort should be made by the trust/health authority to provide the complained against with access to it for the purpose of framing a response. In the case of a family health services practitioner, if it is inappropriate to return the health record, then the whole or relevant part of the record might reasonably be photocopied or, alternatively, inspect at the health authority's premises.

Assessors' Reports

7.26 It will be open to assessors to provide combined or individual reports. The assessors' reports should **not** be made available to the complainant — or the consultant/clinician complained against — in advance of the reports being made available to panel members. The panel may decide, in consultation with the assessors, to release their reports to the complainant and the complained against, particularly if it is believed this will aid resolution of the complaint. Otherwise assessors' reports will only become accessible to them as part of the panel's final report, initially as a draft *(see paragraph 7.30)*.

7.27 Assessors should take care — since their reports may be made available at a later date to others than just panel members — to ensure their reports contain no information which might cause serious harm to the physical or mental health of the patient or of any individual, or contains information about, or provided by a third party (other than a health professional involved in the patient's care) who can be identified from the information, unless he/she has consented to its disclosure.

7.28 *The assessors' reports must be attached to the panel's final report when it is issued. If the panel disagrees with the assessors' reports it must state in its report the reasons for doing so.*

7.29 If the panel chairman finds it appropriate — for example, to meet the complainant as a way of rounding off resolution of the complaint — where the assessors are of different disciplines, each should be present in order to give a personal explanation to the complainant of any clinical findings.

Panel's Final Report

7.30 The panel may find it helpful to provide the complainant and any person(s) complained against with the opportunity to check a draft report — which may not necessarily include the final conclusions of the panel — for factual accuracy within a period of, say, fourteen days, before it is issued formally in its final form. The assessors' reports should be made available in time for their preliminary circulation with the panel's draft report. Those receiving the draft should be reminded that the report is confidential to them and the panel members. The complainant, and anyone complained against should be asked to inform the panel if he/she wishes to consult on the content of its draft report with an adviser who has not been previously involved in the complaint, *e.g.* the community health council. The responsibility for ensuring the panel finalises its report within the target time limit ultimately rests with the panel chairman.

7.31 *The panel's final report must be sent to:*

- *the complainant*
- *the patient, if a different person from the complainant and competent to receive it*
- *any person named in the complaint*
- *the clinical assessors*
- *the trust/health authority chairman and chief executive*
- *in the case of complaints against family health services practitioners/GP fundholders, the practitioner concerned*
- *the regional directors of public health and performance management*
- *the chairman and chief executive of the independent provider where the complaint is about services provided by the independent sector*
- *the health authority chairman and chief executive or GP fundholder who purchased the service concerned.*

The report will have a restricted circulation. The panel shall send it to any other person or body. The panel chairman has right to withhold any part of the panel's report and all or part the assessors' reports in order to ensure confidentiality of clinical information.

7.32 The panel's final report should set out the results of its investigation outlining its conclusion, with any appropriate comments or suggestions. The panel may **not** make any recommendations or suggestions in its report relating to disciplinary matters.

7.33 The complainant may wish to show the report to a representative of the community health council or other appropriate adviser. The chief executive may need to show the report, or sections of the report, to board members. A family health services practitioner may need to show the report, or part of the report, to colleagues in their practice. These, and any similar arrangements will need to protect the overall confidentiality of the report.

7.34 The requirement under the Patient's Charter (see HSG(92)4), that the Director of Public Health of the purchasing authority be notified of any formal complaint concerning the application of clinical judgment in the provision of the contracted service, is rescinded.

Follow-up Action by Trust/Health Authority Boards

7.35 *Following receipt of the panel's report, the chief executive must write to the complainant informing any action the trust/health authority is taking as a result of the panel's deliberations and the right of the complainant to take their grievance to the Ombudsman if they remain dissatisfied.*

7.36 Trust/health authority boards need to consider what arrangements are necessary for ensuring action is taken on the outcome of Independent Review panel reports, and that subsequent action in individual cases have been taken forward as agreed by the board. Boards are also responsible for ensuring that their decisions are communicated quickly and clearly to the complainant.

NOTES:

1. Where an independent review takes place and a report records an adverse finding it should be noted that compliance with the findings is not compulsory. The complainant may bring matters before the Health Service Commissioner although ultimately there is no legal sanction in relation to such findings. (The question of judicial enforcement of the Health Service Commissioners decisions is considered below.) The complaints system also does not provide any further right of appeal.

2. Independent review panels are intended to operate in an informal manner. The procedure adopted by the panel has been left to be determined on a discretionary basis by that individual panel, but it is not intended that it should operate in an adversarial manner (para. 7.12 of the guidance — not quoted above).

3. The professions and health authorities are to nominate appropriate individuals to act as assessors (para. 7.16)

4. Criticism has already been made of convenors who it has been said in a report issued by the Health Service Commissioner have blocked justifiable patients requests for independent review with the NHS guidance not being followed. Health Service Commissioner: second report for session 1996–7 (1996).

3. DISCIPLINARY PROCEDURES IN THE NHS IN RELATION TO HEALTH CARE PROFESSIONALS

As noted above, the Wilson Committee and the Government's restructuring of the system provided for a clear separation between complaints and the disciplinary system. These disciplinary procedures operate alongside the usual channels of redress in employment matters in the legal process through actions for unfair dismissal and wrongful dismissal. In some instances NHS employees have also sought to challenge action taken against them by their employer through judicial review (*R. v. East Berkshire HA, ex p. Walsh* [1985] Q.B. 152). Where disciplinary procedures have not been adhered to there is the possibility of a legal challenge as to its validity. (See *Irani v. Southampton and South-West Hampshire HA* [1985] IRLR 203.)

(a) Disciplinary Procedures in Relation to General Practitioners

National Health Service (Service Committees and Tribunal) Regulations 1992 (as amended)

The disciplinary system for general practitioners (G.P.s) is distinct from that applicable to other health service employees. Where a complaint concerns a G.P.'s terms of service, then it may be the subject of a formal hearing before the medical disciplinary committee (National Health Service Committee and Tribunal Regulations (S.I. 1992 No. 664) as amended). Full written particulars are required to be submitted and these are then forwarded by the HA to the chair of the disciplinary committee. Both parties are entitled to be represented. Lawyers can attended the hearing, although they are not allowed to actively present a parties case. Following the hearing the committee reports to the HA. This report contains details of the findings and any recommendations. If the HA reaches the conclusion that the terms of service have not been complied with then it can take one of a number of steps from warning the G.P. to recovering expenses from the G.P. The figure usually allowed is up to £500 although there is provision for a greater sum to be withheld with the permission of the Secretary of State. In very serious cases the HA may recommended removal of the doctors name from the General Medical List. Regulation 10 provides for appeals, in certain circumstances, to the Secretary of State against the decisions of the Family Health Service Appeal. In fact, this appellate function has been delegated, in England, to the Family Health Service Appeal Authority.

For criticism of operation of the disciplinary system see C. Newdick, *Who Should We Treat?* Oxford: OUP (1995) at page 260.

In addition cases may be referred to the National Health Service Tribunal — a national body which can suspend or state that practitioners are more fit to be engaged in Health Authority Services (section 46 and Schedule 9 of the National Health Service Act 1977).

(b) Disciplinary Procedures against Hospital Medical Staff

As with general practitioners, hospital medical staff are accountable to their employer, and poor performance may lead to disciplinary action being taken against them with the ultimate sanction of dismissal. The precise position regarding disciplinary procedures across the NHS as a whole appears somewhat uncertain. This is because the movement to trust status had led to a widespread renegotiation of contracts, though many contracts remain unaltered. Nevertheless we shall consider here the general procedures set out in Health Circular (90)9. There is a separate procedure applicable to senior medical practitioners such as consultants. Prior to 1990 there was one procedure to deal with grave allegations of misconduct which could result in dismissal. This procedure was subject to review by a Joint Working Party comprised of representatives from the NHS, the medical profession and the Department of Health. This led to the issuing of a Department of Health Circular H.C. (90)9. This provides guidance as to what should be followed. There is a "pre-disciplinary" procedure known as "professional review" used if it is claimed that a medical practitioner has failed to perform NHS contractual obligations, for example, a practitioner missing ward rounds. There is also an "intermediate procedure" used in circumstances in which allegations have been made against the doctor which are not sufficiently serious to warrant dismissal. Grave allegations are dealt with under a third category, the H.C. (90)(9) Annex B procedure. These are heard before a panel, comprised of a legally qualified chairman and two doctors where the claim is of incompetence or, where a claim concerns misconduct, a lay person. Professional misconduct is defined in the circular as being "Performance or behaviour of practitioner arising from the exercise of medical or dental skills". This category includes acting in a patronising and uncompromising manner to patients. Professional incompetence is to be assessed by reference to "Adequacy of performance of Practitioners related to the exercise of their medical or dental skills and professional judgment." (H.C. (90)(9)).

There are also separate procedures applicable in relation to personal misconduct. This is defined in H.C.(90)(9) as "Performance or behaviour of practitioners due to factors other than those associated with the exercise of medical or dental skills." This may be used in situations in which it is alleged that there has been fraudulent claiming of expenses or theft of NHS property. The disciplinary procedure for personal misconduct is set out in the General Whitley Council Terms and Conditions of Service — what is known as the "section 40" procedure. (See generally V. Du-Fen and O. Warnock, *Employment Law in the NHS*, London: Cavendish, 1995, and B. Raymond, "The Employment Rights of NHS Hospital Doctor" in C. Dyer (ed.), *Doctors, Patients and the Law*, Oxford: Blackwells Scientific Publications, 1992).) The "section 40" procedure is applicable to all employees. While there is an appeal to a committee of the health authority there is no right of appeal to the Secretary of State. (This was abolished in 1990.)

Consultants are however, subject to a special disciplinary procedure and there is the option of an appeal to the Secretary of State.

A further disciplinary sanction is that the decision may be taken to launch an inquiry (H.C. (90)(9) para. 5). The chairman of the Health Authority must ascertain whether an inquiry is warranted. An investigating panel is established. The panel chairman is generally a lawyer nominated by the Lord Chancellor; there are then usually two other persons drawn from both professional and lay groups. The procedure is formal, with rights pertaining to legal representation and the cross-examination of witnesses. At the end of the hearing the panel make recommendations which are then passed back to the Health Authority to take action. The panel itself has no disciplinary powers. For an account of an inquiry procedure in operation see the discussion of the inquiry in relation to consultant obstetrician Wendy Savage: *The Savage Inquiry*, London: Virago, 1986. There is also a procedure for a statutory enquiry under section 89 of the National Health Service Act 1977 (see above at page 228).

The employer has the power to suspend an employee pending disciplinary proceedings. This is a broad power. Average suspensions are usually around two years but on occasions an individual may be suspended for a very lengthy period indeed. In 1982 Dr O'Connell was suspended by North Thames RHA. In 1994 a settlement was finally reached and the Health Authority withdrew disciplinary proceedings while Dr O'Connell withdrew legal proceedings. The total costs arising out of this suspension totalled £600,000. The case was criticised by the House of Commons Public Accounts Committee (Fortieth Report 1994–5) (H.C. paper 322 10th July 1995). There are other drawbacks to suspension in addition to cost. As Samuels has commented the doctor may become "rusty" and need to be retrained. (See A. Samuel, "Suspension of Hospital Doctor" (1996) 64 *Medico-Legal Journal* 45.)

QUESTION:

1. Given that there is the avenue of redress through the courts or an industrial tribunal in the event of unfair or wrongful dismissal why should NHS employees be the subject of a complex series of disciplinary processes?

4. HEALTH SERVICE COMMISSIONER

The office of Health Service Commissioner or Ombudsman was originally established under the National Health Service (Reorganisation) Act 1973 (as amended). The current statutory framework establishing the Commissioner is contained in the Health Service Commissioner Act 1993. The Commissioner is the same person who acts as Parliamentary Commissioner for Administration and investigates complaints of maladministration in relation to central government. His functions are to consider complaints made by patients. Since the establishment of the office of Health Service Commissioner the number of complaints referred to him has increased considerably. In 1974–5 there were 400 complaints referred, by 1994–5 there were some 1,782 complaints. However, in that year the number of complaints accepted by the Commissioner for investigation was 233 (Report of the Select Committee on the Parliamentary Commissioner for Administration: Report of Health Service Ombudsman (1994–5) H.C. 39 1995–96). Many matters referred to him were outside his jurisdiction. The Commissioner's role has been expanded recently by the Health Service Commissioner (Amendment) Act 1996. Today the Commissioner operates alongside the existing complaints procedures described above.

Health Service Commissioner Act 1993 (as amended)
  2.—(1) The bodies subject to investigation by the Health Service Commissioner for England are
  (a) Health Authorities whose areas are in England
  (c) Special Health Authorities to which this section applies exercising functions only or mainly in England,
  (d) National Health Service trusts managing a hospital, or other establishment or facility, in England,
  (e) . . .
  (f) the Dental Practice Board, and
  (g) the Public Health Laboratory Service Board.
  (4) References in this Act to a "health service body" are to any of the bodies mentioned above.
  (5) The Special Health Authorities to which this section applies are those —
  (a) established on or before 1st April 1974, or
  (b) established after that date and designated by Order in Council as ones to which this section applies.
  (2) The bodies subject to investigation by the Health Service Commissioner for Wales are
  (a) Health Authorities whose areas are in Wales
  (b) Special Health Authorities to which this section applies exercising functions only or mainly in Wales, and
  (c) National Health Service Trusts managing a hospital, or other establishment or facility in Wales.

  2A.—(1) Persons are subject to investigation by the Health Service Commissioner for England if they are persons (whether individuals or bodies) undertaking to provide in England general medical services, general dental services, general ophthalmic services or pharmaceutical services under the National Health Service Act 1977.
  (2) Persons are subject to investigation by the Health Service Commissioner for Wales if they are persons (whether individuals or bodies) undertaking to provide in Wales general medical services, general dental services, general ophthalmic services or pharmaceutical services under the National Health Service Act 1977 . . .
  (4) In this Act —
  (a) references to a family health service provider are to any person mentioned in subsection (1), (2) or (3);
  (b) references to family health services are to any of the services so mentioned.

  2B.—(1) Persons are subject to investigation by the Health Service Commissioner for England if —

(a) they are persons (whether individuals or bodies) providing services in England under arrangements with health service bodies or family health service providers, and

(b) they are not themselves health service bodies or family health service providers.

(2) Persons are subject to investigation by the Health Service Commissioner for Wales if —

(a) they are persons (whether individuals or bodies) providing services in England under arrangements with health service bodies or family health service providers, and

(b) they are not themselves health service bodies or family health service providers.

(4) The services provided under arrangements mentioned in subsection (1)(a), (2)(a) may be services of any kind . . .

(5) In this Act references to an independent provider are to any person providing services as mentioned in subsection (1), (2) . . ."

3.—(1) On a complaint duly made to a Commissioner by or on behalf of a person that he has sustained injustice or hardship in consequence of

(a) a failure in a service provided by a health service body,

(b) a failure of such a body to provide a service which it was a function of the body to provide, or

(c) maladministration connected with any other action taken by or on behalf of such a body,

the Commissioner may, subject to the provisions of this Act, investigate the alleged failure or other action.

((1A) Where a family health service provider has undertaken to provide any family health services and a complaint is duly made to a Commissioner by or on behalf of a person that he has sustained injustice or hardship in consequence of —

(a) action taken by the family health service provider in connection with the services,

(b) action taken in connection with the services by a person employed by the family health service provider in respect of the services,

(c) action taken in connection with the services by a person acting on behalf of the family health service provider in respect of the services, or

(d) action taken in connection with the services by a person to whom the family health service provider has delegated any functions in respect of the services,

the Commissioner may, subject to the provisions of this Act, investigate the alleged action.

(1B) Where the family health service provider mentioned in subsection (1A) is a member of a recognised fund holding practice, references there to action taken by any person in connection with family health services include references to action taken by the person concerned in connection with any allotted sum paid to the members of the practice.

(1C) Where an independent provider has made an arrangement with a health service body or a family health service provider to provide a service (of whatever kind) and a complaint is duly made to a Commissioner by or on behalf of a person that he has sustained injustice or hardship in consequence of —

(a) a failure in the service provided by the independent provider,

(b) a failure of the independent provider to provide the service, or

(c) maladministration connected with any other action taken in relation to the service,

the Commissioner may, subject to the provisions of this Act, investigate the alleged failure or other action.

(1D) Any failure or maladministration mentioned in subsection (1C) may arise from action of —
(a) the independent provider,
(b) a person employed by the provider,
(c) a person acting on behalf of the provider, or
(d) a person to whom the provider has delegated any functions.

(2) In determining whether to initiate, continue or discontinue an investigation under this Act, a Commissioner shall act in accordance with his own discretion.

(3) Any question whether a complaint is duly made to a Commissioner shall be determined by him.

(4) Nothing in this Act authorises or requires a Commissioner to question the merits of a decision taken without maladministration by a health service body in the exercise of a discretion vested in that body.

(5) Nothing in this Act authorises or requires a Commissioner to question the merits of a decision without maladministration by —
(a) a family health service provider,
(b) a person employed by a family health service provider,
(c) a person acting on behalf of a family health service provider, or
(d) a person to whom a family health service provider has delegated any functions.

(6) Nothing in this Act authorises or requires a Commissioner to question the merits of a decision taken without maladministration by —
(a) an independent provider,
(b) a person employed by an independent provider,
(c) a person acting on behalf of an independent provider, or
(d) a person to whom an independent provider has delegated any functions.

(7) Subsections (4) to (6) do not apply to the merits of a decision to the extent that it was taken in consequence of the exercise of clinical judgment.

4.—(1) A Commissioner shall not conduct an investigation in respect of action in relation to which the person aggrieved has or had —
(a) a right of appeal, reference or review to or before a tribunal constituted by or under any enactment or by virtue of Her Majesty's prerogative, or
(b) a remedy by way of proceedings in any court of law,
unless the Commissioner is satisfied that in the particular circumstances it is not reasonable to expect that person to resort or have resorted to it.

(2) A Commissioner shall not conduct an investigation in respect of an action which has been, or is, the subject of an inquiry under section 84 of the National Health Services Act 1977.

(4) Subsection (5) applies where
(a) action by reference to which a complaint is made under section 3(1), (1A) or (1C) is action by reference to which a complaint be made under a procedure operated by a health service body, family health service provider or an independent provider,
(b) subsection (1), (2) or (3) does not apply as regards the action.

(5) In such a case a Commissioner shall not conduct an investigation in respect of the action unless he is satisfied that
(a) the other procedure has been invoked and exhausted, or
(b) in the particular circumstances it is not reasonable to expect procedure to be invoked or (as the case may be) exhausted.

7.—(1) A Commissioner shall not conduct an investigation in respect of action taken in respect of appointments or removals, pay, discipline, superannuation or other personnel matters in relation to service under the National Health Service Act

1977 or the National Health Service (Scotland) Act 1978 or the National Health Service and Community Care Act 1990.

(2) A Commissioner shall not conduct an investigation in respect of action taken in matters relating to contractual or other commercial transactions, except for —

(a) matters relating to NHS contracts (as defined by section 4 of the National Health Service and Community Care Act 1990 and, in relation to Scotland, by section 17A of the National Health Service (Scotland) Act 1978),

(b) matters arising from arrangements between a health service body and an independent provider for the provision of services by the provider and

(c) matters arising from arrangements between a family health service provider and an independent provider for the provision of service by the independent provider.

(3) In determining what matters arise from arrangements mentioned in subsection (2)(b) the Health Service Commissioners for England and for Wales shall disregard any arrangements for the provision of services at an establishment maintained by a Minister of the Crown mainly for patients who are members of the armed forces of the Crown.

(3A) A Commissioner shall not conduct an investigation in pursuance of a complaint if —

(a) the complaint is in respect of action taken in any matter relating to arrangements made by a health service body and a family health service provider for the provision of family health services.

(b) the action is taken by or on behalf of the body or by the provider, and

(c) the complaint is made by the provider or the body.

(3B) Nothing in the preceding provisions of this section prevents a Commissioner conducting an investigation in respect of action taken by a health service body in operating a procedure established to examine complaints.

NOTES:

1. The Commissioners role is to operate alongside existing complaints procedures. The legislation requires that complainants should, save in exceptional circumstances, exhaust alternative methods of complaint prior to the Commissioner accepting an investigation (s.4(5)). The Commissioner will usually also not investigate a complaint where this will be the subject of legal proceedings (s.4(2)). It has been suggested that the Commissioner, when deciding whether to accept a complaint for investigation, should take into consideration the increasing difficulty complainants may face in pursuing litigation. (See C. Newdick, *Who Should We Treat?*, Oxford: OUP, 1995, at page 250.)

2. The jurisdiction of the Health Service Commissioner was extended in 1996 by the Health Service Commissioners (Amendment) Act 1996 which inserted provisions into the 1993 Act. Complaints against general practitioners may now be investigated (section 2(1A)) as may also complaints against private health providers providing health services for health service bodies (section 2B). The extension of the jurisdiction to G.P.s follows recommendations in *Being Heard*, (London: DoH, 1994, para. 3.22), but does not apply to G.P. disciplinary proceedings (s.7(5)(b)).

3. Until 1996 there was a ban upon the Commissioner investigating complaints relating to clinical judgment. This resulted in a considerable number of complaints referred for investigation being turned away. For example, in 1992, some 25 per cent of complaints were turned away on this basis (Select Committee on the Parliamentary Commissioner for Administration "The Powers, Work and Jurisdiction of the Ombudsman" (H.C. 33–1; para. 101)). Nevertheless, this general exclusion did not mean that a doctor could simply allege that a matter was of a clinical nature and thus avoid investigation. The Commissioner was prepared to look behind this claim to ascertain whether it was truly a clinical matter. Some complaints with a clinical element were investigated. There was considerable debate as to whether this restriction upon his investigative powers was justifiable. It was finally removed by the Health Service Commissioner (Amendment) Act 1996 (s.6). The Act does not define clinical judgment. The Commissioner is to call upon specialist medical and nursing advice in investigating such complaints. These advisers will not act in a representative role and the advice given will generally only concern their professional discipline. It should be emphasised that the role of these professionals is one of providing *advice* and the Commissioner will compile the ultimate report. In a paper outlining his new powers (issued prior to the passage of the 1996 Act) the Commissioner stated that "Without seeking in any way to encourage or promote a 'blame culture' it is the ombudsman's responsibility to criticise where in his view the patient does not receive the service he is reasonably entitled to expect" (*Responsibilities of the Health Service Commissioner* Office of the Health Service Commissioner, 1996).

4. The Commissioner investigates failures in service and also "maladministration". The latter term is imported from the earlier legislation setting out the role of the Parliamentary Commissioner for Adminstration. As Richard Crossman, a former minister, stated when the Parliamentary Commissioner Act 1967 was being debated it encompasses "bias, neglect, inattention, delay, incompetence, ineptitude, perversity, turpitude". The Commissioner issues reports consequent upon investigations. In exceptional circumstances the Commissioner may decide to issue a special report about an individual case. For example, in 1996 the Commissioner published his investigation into the handling of complaints by Salford Royal Hospital. The report concerned investigations of 12 separate allegations made to the Commissioner concerning incidents over a four year period. The report identified poor communication, slow responses to complaints, records which had been mislaid and poor monitoring of procedures. (See "Investigation of Complaint Handling by Salford Royal Hospitals NHS Trust" Report of the Health Service Commissioner: HMSO, 1996.)

5. The Commissioner provides an outlet through which patients may highlight concerns in relation to NHS contracting (s.7(2)). The

Commissioner can consider complaints in relation to both NHS contracts and contracts made by NHS purchasers with private providers. The Commissioner has however been circumspect when investigating such claims (HSC Annual Report 93–94 HC 499 para. 3.8).

8.—(1) A complaint under this Act may be made by an individual or a body of persons, whether incorporated or not, other than a public authority.

(2) In subsection (1), "public authority" means

(a) a local authority or other authority or body constituted for the purposes of the public service or of local government,

(b) an authority or body constituted for the purposes of carrying on under national ownership any industry or undertaking or part of an industry or undertaking, and

(c) any other authority or body
    (i) whose members are appointed by Her Majesty or any Minister of the Crown or government department, or
    (ii) whose revenues consist wholly or mainly of money provided by Parliament.

9.—(1)The following requirements apply in relation to a complaint made to a Commissioner.

(2) A complaint must be made in writing.

(3) The complaint shall not be entertained unless it is made —

(a) by the person aggrieved, or

(b) where the person by whom a complaint might have been made has died or is for any reason unable to act for himself, by —
    (i) his personal representative,
    (ii) a member of his family, or
    (iii) some body or individual suitable to represent him.

(4) The Commissioner shall not entertain the complaint if it is made more than a year after the day on which the person aggrieved first had notice of the matters alleged in the complaint, unless he considers it reasonable to do so.

10.—(1) A health service body may itself refer to a Commissioner a complaint made to that body that a person has, in consequence of a failure or maladministration for which the body is responsible, sustained such injustice or hardship as is mentioned in section 3(1).

(2) A complaint may not be so referred unless it was made —

(a) in writing,

(b) by the person aggrieved or by a person authorised by section 9(3)(b) to complain to the Commissioner on his behalf, and

(c) not more than a year after the person aggrieved first had notice of the matters alleged in the complaint, or such later date as the Commissioner considers appropriate in any particular case.

(3) A health service body may not refer a complaint under this section after the period of one year beginning with the day on which the body received the complaint.

(4) Any question whether a complaint has been duly referred to a Commissioner under this section shall be determined by him.

(5) A complaint referred to a Commissioner under this section shall be deemed to be duly made to him.

11.—(1) Where a Commissioner proposes to conduct an investigation pursuant to a complaint under section 3(1), he shall afford —

(a) to the health service body concerned, and
(b) to any other person who is alleged in the complaint to have taken or authorised the action complained of,

an opportunity to comment on any allegations contained in the complaint.

(1A) Where a Commissioner proposes to conduct an investigation pursuant to a complaint under section 3(1A), he shall afford —

(a) to the family health service provider, and
(b) to any person by reference to whose action the complant is made (if different from the family health service provider),

an opportunity to comment on any allegations contained in the complaint.

(1B) Where a Commissioner proposes to conduct an investigation pursuant to a complaint under section 3(1C), he shall afford —

(a) to the independent provider concerned, and
(b) to any other person who is alleged in the complaint to have taken or authorised the action complained of,

an opportunity to comment on any allegations contained in the complaint."

(2) An investigation shall be conducted in private.

(3) In other respects, the procedure for conducting an investigation shall be such as the Commissioner considers appropriate in the circumstances of the case, and in particular —

(a) he may obtain information from such persons and in such manner, and make such inquiries, as he thinks fit, and
(b) he may determine whether any person may be represented, by counsel or solicitor or otherwise, in the investigation.

(4) A Commissioner may, if he thinks fit, pay to the person by whom the complaint was made and to any other person who attends or supplies information for the purposes of an investigation —

(a) sums in respect of expenses properly incurred by them, and
(b) allowances by way of compensation for the loss of their time.

Payments under this subsection shall be in accordance with such scales and subject to such conditions as may be determined by the Treasury.

(5) The conduct of an investigation pursuant to a complaint under section 3(1) shall not affect any action taken by the health service body concerned, or any power or duty of that body to take further action with respect to any matters subject to the investigation.

(5A) The conduct of an investigation pursuant to a complaint under section 3(1A) or (1C) shall not effect any action taken by the family health service provider or independant provider concerned, or any power or duty of that provider to take further action with respect to any matters subject to investigation.

(6) Where the person aggrieved has been removed from the United Kingdom under any order in force under the Immigration Act 1971 he shall, if the Commissioner so directs, be permitted to re-enter and remain in the United Kingdom, subject to such conditions as the Secretary of State may direct, for the purposes of the investigation.

12.—(1) For the purposes of an investigation pursuant to a complaint under section 3(1) a Commissioner may require any officer or member of the health service body concerned or any other person who in his opinion is able to supply information or produce documents relevant to the investigation to supply any such information or produce any such document.

(1A) For the purposes of an investigation into a complaint under section 3(1A) or (1C) a Commissioner may require any person who in his opinion is able to supply information or produce documents relevant to the investigation to supply any such information or produce any such document.

(2) For the purposes of an investigation a Commissioner shall have the same powers as the Court in respect of —

(a) the attendance and examination of witnesses (including the administration of oaths and affirmations and the examination of witnesses abroad), and

(b) the production of documents.

(3) No obligation to maintain secrecy or other restriction on the disclosure of information obtained by or supplied to persons in Her Majesty's service, whether imposed by any enactment or by any rule of law, shall apply to the disclosure of information for the purposes of an investigation.

(4) The Crown shall not be entitled in relation to an investigation to any such privilege in respect of the production of documents or the giving of evidence as is allowed by law in legal proceedings.

(5) No person shall be required or authorised by this Act —

(a) to supply any information or answer any question relating to proceedings of the Cabinet or of any Committee of the Cabinet, or

(b) to produce so much of any document as relates to such proceedings;

and for the purposes of this subsection a certificate issued by the Secretary of the Cabinet with the approval of the Prime Minister and certifying that any information, question, document or part of a document relates to such proceedings shall be conclusive.

(6) Subject to subsections (3) and (4), no person shall be compelled for the purposes of an investigation to give any evidence or produce any document which he could not be compelled to give or produce in civil proceedings before the Court.

13.—(1) A Commissioner may certify an offence to the Court where —

(a) a person without lawful excuse obstructs him or any of his officers in the performance of his functions, or

(b) a person is guilty of any act or omission in relation to an investigation which, if that investigation were a proceeding in the Court, would constitute contempt of court.

(2) Where an offence is so certified the Court may inquire into the matter and after hearing —

(a) any witnesses who may be produced against or on behalf of the person charged with the offence, and

(b) any statement that may be offered in defence,

the Court may deal with the person charged with the offence in any manner in which it could deal with him if he had committed the like offence in relation to the Court.

(3) Nothing in this section shall be construed as applying to the taking of any such action as is mentioned in section 11(5).

NOTES:

1. The Act sets out who can bring a complaint before the Commissioner in section 8 and 9(1). Health professionals may bring complaints on behalf of patients. One instance may be where the health professional is of the view that standards of care have fallen to unacceptable levels. (See further Chapter 8 below at pages 445–6.)

2. Where a Commissioner makes a finding against a health service body he issues a report. He is required to report to the complainant, health service body, family health service provider and any M.P. involved in the complaint (section 14). However, compliance with this report is not compulsory. This lack of mandatory powers is a feature of the office of Commissioners for Administration (see P. Birkinshaw, *Grievances, Remedies and the State*, London: Sweet and Maxwell, 1995, at page 209). There has been discussion in relation to other Commissioners of the need for judicial enforcement, although this has not been a major issue in the context of the NHS. There are a number of instances of authorities disregarding the Commissioners recommendations. In addition certain authorities appear to be repeatedly the subject of complaints — see J. Allsop and L. Mulcahy, *Regulating Medical Work*, Buckingham: Open UP (1997) at page 70.

   The Commissioner's decisions are subject to the courts. Both the parliamentary commissioner for administration and the local commissioners for administration (which examine maladministration in the context of central and local government respectively) have been the subject of judicial review and it is likely that the courts would be equally prepared to scrutinise the role of the Health Service Commissioner. (See *R. v. PCA, ex p. Dyer* [1994] 1 All E.R. 375.)

3. The Commissioner is now empowered by section 10 of the 1996 Act to lay reports directly before parliament. Prior to the enactment of this provision he was only under an obligation to report directly to the Secretary of State.

5. SELF-REGULATION OF THE HEALTH CARE PROFESSIONS

A Case Study: The Role of the General Medical Council

Health care professionals are not only accountable through the general law and also through their contracts of employment, but are frequently subject to regulation through a governing body of their profession. Common elements of self-regulation are the requirement that practitioners be placed upon a register and that they are bound by a professional ethical code/statement of practice. Failure to comply with this code may lead to disciplinary action being taken by the professional body. There has been an increase in the number of such bodies established under statute over the past two decades, with bodies such as chiropractors and osteopaths (see J. Stone and J. Matthews, *Complementary Medicine and the Law*, Oxford: OUP, 1996, at page 145 *et seq.*) now subject to regulation. In some respects statutory regulation can be seen as a sign of the maturity of a profession in the eyes of the public; a sign that it has been accorded general legitimacy.

While professional regulation, whether or not embodied in statute, may facilitate accountability it may bring certain problems. As was noted in

Chapter 2 above and is illustrated later in Chapter 8 when we consider the practice of "whistleblowing" in health care, in some situations the professional's obligations under her professional ethical code conflict with requirements set out in the contract of employment. One further problem with reliance upon professional self-regulation is the increasing proliferation of such professional bodies. These all have their own professional standards which do not necessarily correlate with one another. An example of this is the interpretation given to "serious professional misconduct" (see below at pages 251–257). Below we consider accountability through professional self-regulation in the context of the body governing the medical profession the General Medical Council.

The medical profession has a long history of professional self-regulation. A charter was given to the Royal College of Physicians in 1518. A body of surgeons — the College of Surgeons — split with the Company of Barbers with whom they had been previously associated in 1745. In addition to these two bodies a Society of Apothecaries was established. These practitioners provided health care to persons who had more limited financial means. Criticisms of the disputes between the three branches of the profession were made in the nineteenth century and around that time the professions themselves began to take a tougher stance upon "quack" practitioners. The Medical Act of 1858 introduced a statutory framework. Section 29 of that Act provided that doctors who were convicted of felonies or misdemeanours could be removed from the register. The GMC was described as having elements of a "gentleman's club" with poor behaviour being censored. Today the GMC is constituted in accordance with Schedule 1 to the Medical Act 1983. It comprises 25 doctors and 25 lay members appointed by the Privy Council and 54 elected doctor members (lay membership was increased in 1995). The Council performs three main functions: it maintains a register of qualified practitioners; it controls medical education and sets the standards for qualification as a doctor in the United Kingdom and it polices professional conduct and fitness to practise.

Disciplinary matters are first considered by a preliminary screener, assisted by five council members. Cases may then be referred to the Preliminary Proceedings Committee. The Preliminary Proceedings Committee is a body composed of 11 elected members which examines cases and considers whether they should be referred to the Professional Conduct Committee. A lay person is now a member of this committee.

Cases may then be referred to the Professional Conduct Committee. This is composed of 32 members, of whom 18 are elected members and six are lay representatives — 11 members sit on each case. (See GMC Blue Book, *Professional Conduct and Fitness to Practice*, London: GMC, 1993.) Only "serious" cases are referred. Stacey has argued that this can create difficulties because "what a patient may regard as 'serious' a GMC screener may not: medical and lay definitions can and do differ" (M. Stacey, "Medical Accountability" in G. Hunt (ed.), *Whistleblowing in the Health*

Services, London: Edward Arnold, 1995). In 1993–4, 195 cases were referred to the Preliminary Proceedings Committee. Of these only 83 were referred to the Professional Conduct Committee. Hearings before the committee are formal and lawyers play a major role. It should be noted that while the GMC and doctor who has been the subject of complaints are legally represented the complainant is not. Below we consider the disciplinary powers of the GMC in relation to serious professional misconduct.

Here, we are concerned only with its policing role which is performed by the Professional Conduct Committee of the GMC. The jurisdiction of this committee is set out in Part V of the Medical Act 1983. Professional practice is also influenced by statements issued by the doctors "trade union", the British Medical Association and the Royal Colleges — for example, the Royal College of Physicians.

Below we focus upon the accountability of doctors to the General Medical Council and the disciplinary procedures to which they are subject.

Medical Act 1983

36.—(1) Where a fully registered person —
(a) is found by the Professional Conduct Committee to have been convicted in the British Islands of a criminal offence, whether while so registered or not; or
(b) is judged by the Professional Conduct Committee to have been guilty of serious professional misconduct, whether while so registered or not;
the Committee may, if they think fit, direct —
    (i) that his name shall be erased from the register;
    (ii) that his registration in the register shall be suspended (that is to say, shall not have effect) during such period not exceeding twelve months as may be specified in the direction; or
    (iii) that his registration shall be conditional on his compliance, during such period not exceeding three years as may be specified in the direction, with such requirements so specified as the Committee think fit to impose for the protection of members of the public or in his interests.

(2) Where a fully registered person whose registration is subject to conditions imposed under subsection (1) above by the Professional Conduct Committee or under section 42(3)(c) below by the Preliminary Proceedings Committee [or the Professional Conduct Committee is judged by the Professional Conduct Committee] to have failed to comply with any of the requirements imposed on him as conditions of his registration the Committee may, if they think fit, direct —
(a) that his name shall be erased from the register; or
(b) that his registration in the register shall be suspended (that is to say, shall not have effect) during such period not exceeding twelve months as may be specified in the direction.

(3) Where the Professional Conduct Committee have given a direction for suspension under subsection (1) or (2) above, the Committee may —
(a) direct that the current period of suspension shall be extended for such further period from the time when it would otherwise expire as may be specified in the direction;
(b) direct that the name of the person whose registration is suspended shall be erased from the register; or

(c) direct that the registration of the person whose registration is suspended shall, as from the expiry of the current period of suspension, be conditional on his compliance, during such period not exceeding three years as may be specified in the direction, with such requirements so specified as the Committee think fit to impose for the protection of members of the public or in his interests;
but the Committee shall not extend any period of suspension under this section for more than twelve months at a time.

(4) Where the Professional Conduct Committee have given a direction for conditional registration, the Committee may —
(a) direct that the current period of conditional registration shall be extended for such further period from the time when it would otherwise expire as may be specified in the direction; or
(b) revoke the direction or revoke or vary any of the conditions imposed by the direction;
but the Committee shall not extend any period of conditional registration under this section for more than twelve months at a time.

(5) Subsection (2) above shall apply to a fully registered person whose registration is subject to conditions imposed under subsection (3)(c) above as it applies to a fully registered person whose registration is subject to conditions imposed under subsection (1) above, and subsection (3) above shall apply accordingly.

(6) Where the Professional Conduct Committee give a direction under this section for erasure, for suspension or for conditional registration or vary the conditions imposed by a direction for conditional registration the Registrar shall forthwith serve on the person to whom the direction applies a notification of the direction or of the variation and of his right to appeal against the decision in accordance with section 40 below.

(7) In subsection (6) above the references to a direction for suspension and a direction for conditional registration include references to a direction extending a period of suspension or a period of conditional registration.

(8) While a person's registration in the register is suspended by virtue of this section he shall be treated as not being registered in the register notwithstanding that his name still appears in it.

(9) This section applies to a provisionally registered person and to a person registered with limited registration whether or not the circumstances are such that he falls within the meaning in this Act of the expression "fully registered person".

38.—(1) On giving a direction for erasure or a direction for suspension under section 36(1) or (2) above in respect of any person the Professional Conduct Committee or the Health Committee [the Committee on Professional Performance], if satisfied that to do so is necessary for the protection of members of the public or would be in the best interests of that person, may order that his registration in the register shall be suspended forthwith in accordance with this section; and in this subsection the reference to section 36(2) includes a reference to that provision as applied in section 36(5) and the reference to section 37(2) includes a reference to that provision as applied by section 37(5).

(2) Where, on the giving of a direction an order under subsection (1) above is made in respect of a person, his registration in the register shall, subject to subsection (4) below, be suspended (that is to say, shall not have effect) from the time when the order is made until the time when the direction takes effect in accordance with paragraph 10 of Schedule 4 to this Act[or in accordance with rules made by virtue of paragraph 5A(3) of that Schedule or an appeal against it under section 40 below or paragraph 5A(2) of that schedule is (otherwise than by the dismissal of the appeal) determined.

(3) Where the Professional Conduct Committee [the Committee on Professional Performance] or the Health Committee make an order under subsection (1) above the Registrar shall forthwith serve a notification of the order on the person to whom it applies.

(4) If, when an order under subsection (1) above is made, the person to whom it applies is neither present nor represented at the proceedings, subsection (2) above shall have effect as if, for the reference to the time when the order is made, there were substituted a reference to the time of service of a notification of the order as determined for the purposes of paragraph 8 of Schedule 4 to this Act.

(5) While a person's registration in the register is suspended by virtue of subsection (1) above he shall be treated as not being registered in the register notwithstanding that his name still appears in it.

(6) The court may terminate any suspension of a person's registration in the register imposed under subsection (1) above, and the decision of the court on any application under this subsection shall be final.

NOTES:

1. Section 37 (not reproduced above) enables removal from the register on the basis of unfitness to practice due to illness, following consideration by a health screener and the health committee.

2. Conduct which may result in removal from the register includes drug and alcohol abuse, improper associations with patients, failures to visit, treat and refer patients. A notable example of the role played by the GMC can be seen in the "kidneys for cash" case. Here doctors involved in transplanting organs from persons from Turkey who were paid to come to England and have their organs removed so that they could be transplanted into patients were disciplined. This case resulted in legislation in the form of the Human Organ Transplants Act 1989 (see below Chapter 15). The GMC have also acted to discipline a doctor for scientific fraud (see S. Lock, "Lessons from the Pearce affair; handling scientific fraud" (1995) 311 *BMJ* 1547 and for an extensive discussion of the GMC in operation see M. Stacey, *Regulating British Medicine*, Chichester: Wiley, 1992).

3. Doctors are expected as part of their professional role to report colleagues who may be in breach of their professional duties. (See GMC, *Professional Conduct and Discipline: Fitness to Practice*, Blue Book, at paras. 63–67.)

4. The standard of proof required in establishing "serious professional misconduct" is the higher test of "beyond all reasonable doubt" as applied in the criminal law courts, rather than the lower civil liability test of "on the balance of probabilities".

5. While a doctor may be removed from the register, reforms introduced by the 1995 Act mean that she can now volunteer to be removed (section 2 of the 1995 Act). This may be seen as very much a "go quietly" provision. (See P. Marquand, "Protecting Patients" (1996) 140 *Solicitors Journal* 222.)

6. Under section 36 of the Medical Act, the Professional Conduct Committee is empowered to impose only three types of sanction:

suspension from the register, removal from the register and the imposition of conditional registration. The power to suspend or to make an order for conditional registration in disciplinary hearings has now been increased to a period of between two months to six months. Statutory committees may renew interim orders for three monthly periods or they may vary any conditions which have been imposed (section 3 of the Medical (Professional Performance) Act 1995). There is, in practice, a fourth sanction which exists outside the provisions of the Medical Act 1983. The "Chapter 15 procedure" (as it is known) is contained in the *Standing Orders* of the GMC. This procedure involves the GMC's Preliminary Proceedings Committee sending a letter of reprimand where "the doctor has behaved, or may have behaved in a manner which cannot be regarded as acceptable professional conduct and that matter is not trivial". (See further R. Smith, "Discipline II: The Preliminary Screener — A Powerful Gatekeeper" (1989) 298 *BMJ* 1569.)

7. The reliance upon self-regulation of the health care professions may be questioned. Stacey has argued that the GMC has consistently favoured the professionals over the public. As she notes, an investigation only results where a complaint has been made, as the GMC does not have its own inspectorate. (See M. Stacey, "Medical Accountability: A Background Paper" in A. Grubb (ed.), *Challenges in Medicine*, Chichester: Wiley, 1992.) Nor indeed does the GMC have the power to initiate its own investigations in contrast with other professional bodies such as the pharmaceutical society. While complaints may be made against doctors by members of the public, as Stone and Matthews note, there is little attempt to draw this to individuals' attention (J. Stone and J. Matthews, *Complementary Medicine and the Law*, Oxford: OUP, 1996, at p. 51). *Cf.* the role of the Patients' Charter and the new NHS complaints system discussed above (and see J. Allsop and L. Mulcahy, *Regulating Medical Work*, Buckingham: Open UP (1996) Chapter 4). While lay members are now involved in proceedings their involvement is somewhat limited. There is also little public information as to how proceedings are filtered and which are referred to the Health Committee.

QUESTIONS:

1. At present the composition of the General Medical Council is dominated by medical practitioners. To what extent is this satisfactory and should the membership be amended? (See J. Montgomery "Medicine, Accountability and Professionalism" (1989) 16 *Journal of Law and Society* 319).

The standards used to scrutinise professional conduct are serious professional misconduct and in the case of professional performance, seriously deficient conduct. In the past the test of serious professional misconduct has met with considerable criticism.

The meaning of serious professional conduct was considered in *Doughty v. General Dental Council*.

Doughty v. General Dental Council [1987] 3 All E.R. 843, [1988] 1 A.C. 164, [1987] 3 W.L.R. 769

A dentist was charged with serious professional misconduct before the Professional Conduct Committee of the General Dental Council under section 27(1) of the Dentists Act 1984. It was alleged (1) that he failed to retain the radiographs of 19 National Health Service patients for a reasonable period after completion of treatment and failed to submit them to the Dental Estimates Board when required to do so; (2) that he provided six patients with dental treatment in the course of which he failed to exercise a proper degree of skill and attention; and (3) that he provided four patients with dental treatment in the course of which he failed satisfactorily to complete the treatment required by the patient. The legal assessor advised the committee that in considering charge 3 they could take into account treatment which was not required as well as that which was not satisfactorily completed. The committee found the undisputed facts alleged in charge 1 proved, charge 2 proved with regard to five patients and charge 3 with regard to three patients. They judged the dentist to have been guilty of serious professional misconduct in relation to the facts proved against him in each charge, and directed that his name should be erased from the dentists' register.

LORD MACKAY OF CLASHFERN:
" . . . This is an appeal from a decision of the Professional Conduct Committee of the General Dental Council on 12 March 1987 that the appellant had been guilty of serious professional misconduct in relation to three charges and that his name should be erased from the Dentists' register. The three charges in question were:
'That being a registered dentist: 1. Between January 10 and October 26, 1984 you accepted 19 patients, whose names and addresses are shown on list 'A' (which is attached to the charge) for dental treatment as National Health Service patients, and thereafter provided them with dental treatment in the course of which, having obtained radiographs of these patients, you: (a) failed to retain those radiographs for a reasonable period of time after completion of the treatment; (b) failed to submit those radiographs to the Dental Estimates Board when required to do so by a letter from the board dated November 27, 1984. 2. Between June 5 and November 16, 1984 you accepted six patients, whose names and addresses are shown on list "B" (which is attached to the charge) for dental treatment as National Health Service patients and thereafter provided them with dental treatment in the course of which you failed to exercise a proper degree of skill and attention. 3. Between August 21 and October 5, 1984 you accepted four patients, whose names and addresses are shown on list "C" (which is attached to the charge) for dental treatment as National Health Service patients, and thereafter provided them with dental treatment in the course of which you failed satisfactorily to complete the treatment required by the patient. . . . And that in relation to the facts alleged in each of the above charges you have been guilty of serious professional misconduct.'

At the close of the case for the council submissions were made on behalf of the appellant. These were successful in relation to charge 4 which their Lordships have not narrated and with which this appeal is accordingly not concerned and also in relation to one of the patients mentioned in charge 2. At the conclusion of the evidence relating to the facts alleged the president of the Professional Conduct Committee announced the decision in the following terms:

'the Committee has decided, that the facts alleged against you in charge one, which you have admitted, in charge two, in relation to each of the five remaining patients and in charge 3 with the exception of those in relation to the patient Mr Goldberger, have been proved to the satisfaction of the Committee. In relation to the facts alleged against you in respect of Mr Goldberger, you have not been guilty of serious professional misconduct.'

Thereafter the committee went on to hear evidence led on behalf of the appellant directed to whether the facts found proved constituted serious professional misconduct and heard counsel on that matter. The committee announced their decision in the following terms:

'In relation to the facts alleged in head 1 of the charge which have been admitted, the Committee finds that you have been guilty of serious professional misconduct. In relation to the facts alleged against you in charge 2 in respect of the five remaining patients and in charge 3 in respect of the three remaining patients, the Committee finds that you have been guilty of serious professional misconduct.'

The committee directed that the appellant's name be erased from the Dentists' register.

As the committee decision records, the facts alleged in charge 1 were admitted on behalf of the appellant. The facts alleged in charge 2 in respect of two of the named patients were admitted on behalf of the dentist. On charge 2 evidence was led from the remaining patients and from Mr Taylor, a qualified dentist who was a member of the Dental Estimates Board and had been in general practice from 1958 until he took up his position with the Dental Estimates Board in August 1978. He gave evidence criticising root canal treatment that had been given by the dentist to the three remaining patients in respect of whom the facts alleged in the charge were found proved. The criticism was offered under two heads, first, that the root canal treatments were not necessary and second, that the root canal treatments were not properly carried out. In respect of one of the patients criticism was offered under both heads and in respect of the remaining patients under one head for each. In relation to charge 3, evidence was given by the three patients in respect of whom the facts alleged in the charge were found proved and also by Mrs Baker, an officer of the dental staff of the Department of Health and Social Security who qualified as a dentist in 1970 and took a diploma in orthodontics in 1977. She gave evidence in respect of two of these patients and evidence in respect of the third was given by Mr Davidson, a registered dental practitioner qualified in 1950 now employed as an officer of the dental staff of the Department of Health and Social Security. Again criticism was offered under the same two heads: under both heads in respect of two of the patients and under the second head in respect of the third.

At the hearing of this appeal counsel for the appellant in his clear and forceful submissions first pointed to the distinction in wording between charges 2 and 3. He submitted that charge 3 was not concerned with whether or not the treatment in question was necessary but only with whether it was satisfactorily completed. This question had been discussed at the hearing before the committee at the stage when counsel then appearing for the appellant was making submissions at the close of the evidence for the council. After discussion the legal assessor to the committee gave his view as follows:

'The word "required" is a simple English word which should be given a simple English meaning. It is wide enough to cover this aspect of the matter, namely, the provision of treatment which was not in fact necessary to be completed at all, although the patient may have agreed that it was; so that it is possible for you, under charge 3, to look at, as a head of the charge, the provision of root canal treatment which was not necessary as well as that which was poorly executed.' Counsel for the council submitted that the wording of charge 3 was wide enough to cover allegations that the treatment criticised was unnecessary.

Their Lordships cannot accept the counsel's submission. An allegation of failure 'satisfactorily to complete the treatment required by the patient' cannot, by any stretch of language be read as including an allegation of having administered treatment which was not necessary. It follows that the legal assessor's direction was erroneous but not necessarily that the committee's decision was thereby invalidated. In *Sivarajah v. General Medical Council* [1964] 1 All E.R. 504 at 507, Lord Guest said:

'Thus what might amount to a misdirection in law by a judge to a jury at a criminal trial does not necessarily invalidate the committee's decision. The question is whether it can "fairly be thought to have been of sufficient significance to the result to invalidate the committee's decision".'

This was followed in *McEniff v. General Dental Council* [1980] 1 All E.R. 461 at 465. In the present case there is not and could not have been any suggestion that the evidence given in relation to charge 2 was not covered by the words of that charge and it is difficult to see why the wording of charge 3 is different, since the evidence given criticising the appellant's treatment was broadly similar under both charges. No objection was taken to the evidence as it was being led and the appellant had full opportunity to meet it in his own evidence. In the whole circumstances of this appeal their Lordships are satisfied that the misdirection contained in the legal assessor's observations which have been quoted neither prejudiced the appellant nor caused any miscarriage of justice. It did not therefore invalidate the committee's decision.

The next point taken by counsel for the appellant was that in order to prove charges 2 and 3 it was necessary to show that the opinion held by the appellant in relation to the treatment was not honestly held by him and could not honestly be held by a dentist. This submission was founded principally on the observations of Lord Jenkins giving the judgment of this Board in *Felix v. General Dental Council* [1960] 2 All E.R. 391 at 400:

'With respect to the treatment alleged to have been unnecessary, the evidence (as their Lordships have already observed) showed that according to the appellant, he honestly believed it to be necessary (or likely to be found necessary), while the dentists who disagreed with him did not claim that the opinion expressed by the appellant was one which no dentist could honestly hold. In this state of the evidence their Lordships think it would be wrong to impute to the Disciplinary Committee an implied finding to the effect that the appellant did not honestly hold that opinion. And honestly held opinion, even if wrong, in their Lordships' view plainly cannot amount to infamous or disgraceful conduct.'

Counsel for the council submitted that the evidence was sufficient to entitle the committee both to hold the facts alleged in charges 2 and 3 proved so far as they had done so and also to hold that those facts constituted serious professional misconduct.

In considering the applicability of Lord Jenkins' observations to the circumstances of the present appeal, it has to be noted that Lord Jenkins was speaking of a case in which dishonesty was very much the issue and in the context of the statutory provision which was the basis of the proceedings in *Felix v. General Dental Council* namely, s.25 of the Dentists Act 1957. So far as relevant it was in these terms:

'(1) A registered dentist who either before or after registration . . . (b) has been guilty of any infamous or disgraceful conduct in a professional respect, shall be liable to have his name erased from the register.'

At that time this was the only penalty available in respect of such conduct. Section 15(1) of the Dentists Act 1983 provided:

'For section 25(1) of the principal Act [the Dentists Act 1957] (erasure from register for crime or infamous conduct) there shall be substituted — (1) A registered dentist who (whether before or after registration) . . . (b) has been guilty of serious professional misconduct, shall be liable to have his name erased from the register, or to have his registration in it suspended, in accordance with section 26(3) of this Act; . . .'

The suspension referred to is suspension for such period not exceeding 12 months as may be specified in the committee's determination. Counsel for the dentist suggests that this change in language was not intended to effect a change in substance. In *R. v. General Council of Medical Education and Registration of the United Kingdom* [1930] 1 K.B. 562, 569, referring to the statutory provision there applicable, namely 'infamous conduct in any professional respect', Scrutton L.J. said:

'It is a great pity that the word "infamous" is used to describe the conduct of a medical practitioner who advertises. As in the case of the Bar so in the medical profession advertising is serious misconduct in a professional respect and that is all that is meant by the phrase "infamous conduct"; it means no more than serious misconduct judged according to the rules written or unwritten governing the profession.'

In the General Medical Council's booklet entitled *Professional Conduct and Discipline: Fitness to Practise* (1985), the Council stated: 'In proposing the substitution of the expression "serious professional misconduct" for the phrase "infamous conduct in a professional respect" the Council intended that the phrases should have the same significance.'

Their Lordships readily accept that what was infamous or disgraceful conduct in a professional respect would also constitute serious professional misconduct but they consider that it would not be right to require the General Dental Council to establish now that the conduct complained of was infamous or disgraceful and therefore not right to apply the criteria which Lord Jenkins derived from the dictionary definitions of these words which he quoted in *Felix v. General Dental Council*. Their Lordships consider it relevant, in reaching a conclusion upon whether Parliament intended by the change of wording to make a change of substance, to notice that in addition to this change and in close conjunction with it the additional and much less severe penalty of suspension for a period not exceeding 12 months was provided. Further, in terms of s.1(2) of the Dentists Act 1984 which is the statute presently applicable: 'It shall be the general concern of the Council to promote high standards of dental education at all its stages and high standards of professional conduct among dentists . . .' In the light of these considerations in their Lordships' view what is now required is that the council should establish conduct connected with his profession in which the dentist concerned has fallen short, by omission or commission, of the standards of conduct expected among dentists and that such falling short as is established should be serious. On an appeal to this Board, the Board has the responsibility of deciding whether the committee were entitled to take the view that the evidence established that there had been a falling short of these standards and also entitled to take the view that such falling short as was established was serious.

In the present case the three charges of serious professional misconduct of which the appellant has been found guilty do not impute any dishonesty on his part. It was not suggested that he was carrying out unnecessary treatments for the purpose of enhancing his remuneration. What was suggested was that, judged by proper professional standards in the light of the objective facts about the individual patients that were presented in evidence to the committee, the dental treatments criticised as unnecessary would be treatments that no dentist of reasonable skill exercising reasonable care would carry out. It was for the committee with their expertise in this matter to judge as between the witnesses called by the council and the appellant, who had every opportunity to give his own reasons and explanations for what he did, and to judge whether the allegation was made out subject to the matter already dealt with in relation to charge 3. The point taken by counsel for the dentist at this stage of his submission was pressed primarily in relation to the criticisms of the dentist's treatment as unnecessary. With regard to the other criticisms it appears to their Lordships that the failures admitted in relation to charge 1 and admitted in part and proved to a further extent in relation to charge 2 and proved in relation to charge 3 amounted to professional misconduct. Whether the misconduct was serious depended on a number of factors, for example in relation to charge 1 on the number of patients in respect of whom the failure occurred and the importance of preserving the record for the well being of the patient and as a basis for decision on future treatment of the patient. In relation to charges 2 and 3 the seriousness of the conduct depended on the appreciation of such factors as the number of patients involved, the number of treatments criticised in relation to each patient and particularly in relation to unsatisfactory treatments, the nature and extent of the failure to complete the treatment properly. On all of these matters the committee were particularly well qualified to reach a view and their Lordships see no reason to disagree with their findings.

Counsel for the appellant stated that the appellant had ceased practising in the middle of 1986 and that he had no present intention to return to practice but he was prosecuting this appeal in order to clear his name. Their Lordships are happy to make clear that in their judgment the findings against the appellant do not import any moral stigma. All the failures found proved related only to work which the appellant carried out as a dentist but in their Lordships' opinion these were failures of a kind which the committee were entitled to hold rendered it right for them to direct erasure of the appellant's name from the Dentists Register. This is a matter very much for the professional judgment of the committee with which their Lordships see no cause to interfere.

For these reasons their Lordships will humbly advise Her Majesty that this appeal should be dismissed. The appellant must pay the council's costs before this Board."

NOTE:

1. The Privy Council operates as the highest appellate court for countries in the Commonwealth, but it also acts as a court of appeal from decisions of the Professional Conduct Committees of, *inter alia*, the General Medical Council and the General Dental Council. In view of the Privy Council's composition, its decisions can be treated as though they were decisions of the House of Lords.

QUESTION:

1. Do you agree with Lord Mackay's reasoning as to why "serious professional misconduct" ought not to be regarded as co-extensive with "infamous conduct in a professional respect"?

At one point in his speech, Lord Mackay stated that serious professional misconduct was conduct in which "the [practitioner] concerned has fallen short . . . of conduct expected among dentists and that such falling short as is established is serious". This begs the question of whether his Lordship considered that negligence could suffice to establish serious professional misconduct. The reference to standards one might normally expect of a practitioner might suggest as much. However, it seems that the Lord Chancellor had in mind conduct more akin to *gross* negligence (see Chapter 3) since he insisted that the failure to meet the established standard must be "serious".

The issue of whether "serious professional misconduct" includes serious deficiencies in the provision of medical treatment was explored in a subsequent case.

David Noel McCandless v. GMC. [1996] 1 W.L.R. 167

LORD HOFFMAN:
". . . Their Lordships think that some support can be found for Mr Mitting's submission in old cases on the meaning of 'infamous conduct in a professional respect' — the words which were used in 19th century Medical Acts and which continued to be used until replaced by the words 'serious professional misconduct' in the Medical Act 1969. For example, in *Felix v. General Dental Council* [1960] A.C. 704, 721, Lord Jenkins said of a dentist who was alleged to have given unnecessary treatment:
   'according to the appellant, he honestly believed it to be necessary . . . An honestly held opinion, even if wrong, in their Lordships' view plainly cannot amount to infamous or disgraceful conduct.'
Since *Felix v. General Dental Council*, however, much has changed. First, the words 'infamous conduct' in a professional respect were replaced by 'serious professional misconduct'. It is true that the General Medical Council's guide to 'Professional Conduct and Discipline: Fitness to Practice' stated (and continues to state — see the December 1993 ed. p. 7) that the new words were intended to mean the same as the old. On the other hand, it is by no means clear that the council accepted the *Felix* interpretation of what the old words meant. The guide also cites the dictum of Scrutton L.J. in *Rex v. General Council of Medical Education and Registration of the United Kingdom* [1930] 1 K.B. 562, 569: that 'infamous conduct' '. . . means no more than serious misconduct judged according to the rules written or unwritten governing the profession.'
This looks much more like an objective standard. Their Lordships think that the authorities on the old wording do not speak with one voice and that they are of little assistance in the interpretation of the new. Secondly, although there remains the single disciplinary offence now styled 'serious professional misconduct', the possible penalties available to the committee, which used to be confined to the ultimate sanction of erasure have been extended to include suspension and the imposition of conditions upon practise. This suggests that the offence was intended to include serious cases of negligence. Thirdly, the public has higher expectations of doctors and members of other self-governing porofessions. Their governing bodies are under a corresponding duty to protect the public against the genially incompetent as well as the deliberate wrongdoers. Fourthly, the meaning of the new wording has been authoratively stated by this Board in *Doughty v. General Dental Council* [1988] A.C. 164 or any of the earlier authorities.
This test appears to their Lordships to be *mutatis mutandis* equally applicable to treatment by doctors and in their Lordship's view should make it unnecessary in the future to revisit *Felix v. General Dental Council* [1960] A.C. 704 or any of the other earlier authorities.
Once it is accepted that seriously negligent treatment can amount to serious professional misconduct, then it seems to their Lordships that the appeal must fail. The eminent medical practitioners who sat on the committee came to the

conclusion that Dr McCandless's treatment of his three patients fell deplorably short of the standard to which patients are entitled to expect from general practitioners. In the circumstances, it is scarcely suprising that they concluded that Dr McCandless was guilty of serious professional misconduct. Their Lordships can see no basis for interfering with that conclusion. Nor can they see any ground for interfering with that committee's decision that the offences merited the penalty of erasion from the register."

NOTES:

1. The impact of this decision may be limited. It appears likely that in the future these cases will be channelled through the new procedure governing seriously deficient professional performance (see pages 259–260, below).
2. While the medical profession adheres to a standard of serious professional misconduct other professions have adopted different standards. Take, for example, the Chiropractors Act 1994;

Chiropractors Act 1994

   20.—(1) This section applies where any allegation is made against a registered chiropractor to the effect that —

   (a) he has been guilty of conduct which falls short of the standard required of a registered chiropractor; [or]
   (b) he has been guilty of professional incompetence.

   (2) In this Act conduct which falls short of the standard required of a registered chiropractor is referred to as "unacceptable professional conduct".

Section 22 of the Chiropractors Act makes provision for "admonition, suspension from the register, conditional registration and removal from the register in the event of unacceptable professional conduct". A similar approach is used in the context of osteopaths (Osteopaths Act 1993, s.20).

The UKCC, which governs nursing and the allied professions, is the equivalent to the GMC. It too has a disciplinary jurisdiction over its members which includes the power to remove their names from the professional register of qualified nurses, midwives and health visitors. This is set out in section 12 of the Nurses, Midwives and Health Visitors Act 1979 (as amended by the Nurses, Midwives and Health Visitors Act 1992).

Nurses, Midwives and Health Visitors Act 1979

   12.—(1) The Central Council shall determine circumstances in which, and the means by which —

   (a) a person may, for misconduct or otherwise, be removed from the register or a part of it, whether or not for a specified period;
   (b) a person who has been removed from the register or part of it may be restored to it;

(ba) a person's registration in the register or part of it may be directed to be suspended, that is to say, not to have effect during such period as may be specified in the direction;

(bb) the suspension of a person's registration in the register or a part of it may be terminated; and

(c) an entry in the register may be removed, altered or restored.

(2) Committees of the Council shall be constituted by the rules to hear and determine proceedings for a person's removal from, or restoration to, the register, for the suspension, or termination of the suspension, of a person's registration in the register or for the removal, alteration or restoration of any entry . . .

(3A) The rules shall so provide that the members of a committee constituted to adjudicate upon the conduct of any person are selected with due regard to the professional field where that person works.

(4) The rules shall make provision as to the procedure to be followed, and the rules of evidence to be observed, in such proceedings, whether before the Council itself or before any committee so constituted, and for the proceedings to be in public except in such cases (if any) as the rules may specify . . .

(6) Where a person's registration in the register or part of it is suspended under subsection (1)(ba), he shall be treated as not being registered in the register or part notwithstanding that his name still appears in it.

The sanctions of removal and suspension from the register are triggered by the commission of "misconduct". Misconduct is further defined in the Nurses, Midwives and Health Visitors (Professional Conduct) Rules Approval Order (S.I. 1987, No 2156). These rules elaborate upon the meaning of "misconduct" for which a nurse, midwife or health visitor may be removed or suspended from the professional register. Reg. 1(2)(i) "misconduct" means conduct unworthy of a nurse, midwife or health visitor, as the case may be, and includes obtaining registration by fraud. (See further the Nurses, Midwives and Health Visitors (Professional Conduct) Rules 1993 Approval Order 1993 and R. Pyne, "The Professional Dimension" in J. Tingle and A. Cribb (eds), *Nursing, Law and Ethics*, Oxford: Blackwell Science Ltd, 1995, and B. Dimmond, *Legal Aspects of Nursing* (2nd ed.), London: Prentice-Hall, 1995, Ch. 11.)

The difficulties with establishing serious professional misconduct in the past led to calls being made for reforms of the system.

In the early 1990s concern was expressed regarding a number of cases in which it was alleged that doctors' conduct was seriously deficient. Nigel Spearing M.P. attempted on a number of occasions to introduce reforms to the 1983 Act with the object of extending the Committee's jurisdiction to cases in which the doctor has "behaved in a manner which cannot be regarded as acceptable professional conduct" (see, *e.g.*, *Official Report of the House of Commons*, March 3, London: HMSO, 1987, cols 157–8). Spearing's action followed the death of a boy, in his constituency. The boy's G.P. had failed to satisfactorily treat or refer him, however the GMC were not prepared to find that this was sufficient to amount to serious professional misconduct. A Working Party established by the GMC under the chairmanship of Sir Douglas Black reported against the extension of the

GMC jurisdiction along the lines suggested by Spearing. The GMC then established a further working group. Following extensive consultation, finally in 1992, a document "Proposals for New Performance Procedures" was issued. The Government indicated it would be prepared to give parliamentary time to the matter and reforms were passed in the Medical Professional Performance Act 1995. A doctor's "professional performance" may now be formally reviewed if it is "seriously deficient". What constitutes such conduct is to be assessed against standards to be produced by the General Medical Council. An allegation of seriously deficient conduct will be referred to the Assessment Referral Committee. This will have extensive powers of investigation and obstruction of such investigations will constitute a criminal offence. The Assessment Referral Committee provides the option for a hearing in a situation in which the doctor either does not respond if contacted or where he disputes the allegation. This hearing is to be formal with legal representation allowed. Particularly serious cases or those where the doctor refuses to co-operate will be referred to the Committee on Professional Performance. At the time of writing these provisions are not yet in force (see P. Marquand "Protecting Patients" (1996) 140 *Solicitors Journal* 222).

The sanctions available here are as stated in s.36A, below:

36A.—[(1) Where the standard of professional performance of a fully registered person is found by the Committee on Professional Performance to have been seriously deficient, the Committee shall direct —
   (a) that his registration in the register shall be suspended (that is to say, shall not have effect) during such period not exceeding twelve months as may be specified in the direction; or
   (b) that his registration shall be conditional on his compliance, during such period not exceeding three years as may be specified in the direction, with the requirements so specified.

(2) Where a fully registered person, whose registration is subject to conditions imposed under any provision of this section by the Committee on Professional Performance, is judged by the Committee to have failed to comply with any of the requirements imposed on him as conditions of his registration the Committee may, if they think fit, direct that his registration in the register shall be suspended during such period not exceeding twelve months as may be specified in the direction.

(3) Where the Committee on Professional Performance have given a direction for suspension under any provision of this section the Committee may direct —
   (a) that the current period of suspension shall be extended for such further period from the time when it would otherwise expire as may be specified in the direction; or
   (b) that the registration of the person whose registration is suspended shall, as from the expiry (or termination under subsection (5)(b) below) of the current period of suspension, be conditional on his compliance, during such period not exceeding three years as may be specified in the direction, with such requirements so specified as the Committee think fit to impose for the protection of members of the public or in his interests;
but, subject to subsection (4) below, the Committee shall not extend any period of suspension under this section for more than twelve months at a time.

(4) The Committee on Professional Performance may make a direction extending a period of suspension indefinitely where —
   (a) the period of suspension will, on the date on which the direction takes effect, have lasted for at least two years, and
   (b) the direction is made not more than two months before the date on which the period of suspension would otherwise expire.

(5) Where the Committee on Professional Performance have made a direction for indefinite suspension, they —
   (a) shall review the suspension when requested to do so by the person whose registration is suspended (but not until two years after the date on which the direction takes effect and not more than once in any period of two years), and
   (b) having carried out such a review, may direct that the suspension be terminated.

(6) Where the Committee on Professional Performance have given a direction for conditional registration, the Committee may —
   (a) direct that the current period of conditional registration shall be extended for such further period from the time when it would otherwise expire as may be specified in the direction;
   (b) revoke the direction or revoke or vary any of the conditions imposed by the direction; or
   (c) direct that the registration shall be suspended during such period not exceeding twelve months as may be specified in the direction;

but the Committee shall not extend any period of conditional registration under this section for more than three years at a time.

(7) Where the Committee on Professional Performance give a direction under this section for suspension or for conditional registration, or vary the conditions imposed by a direction for conditional registration, the Registrar shall forthwith serve on the person to whom the direction applies a notification of the direction or of the variation and of his right to appeal against the decision in accordance with section 40 below.

(8) In subsection (7) above the references to a direction for suspension and a direction for conditional registration include references to a direction extending a period of suspension or a period of conditional registration.

(9) While a person's registration in the register is suspended by virtue of this section he shall be treated as not being registered in the register notwithstanding that his name still appears in it.

(10) This section applies to a provisionally registered person and to a person registered with limited registration whether or not the circumstances are such that he falls within the meaning in this Act of the expression "fully registered person".]

QUESTION:

1. Can, and indeed should, professional conduct be differentiated from professional performance? See Stacey in Grubb, *op. cit.*
2. Should Professional Practice be subject to this extra layer of accountability? — see J. Allsop and L. Mulcahy, *Regulating Medical Work*, Buckingham: Open UP (1996).

SELECT BIBLIOGRAPHY

J. Allsop and L. Mulcahy, *Regulating Medical Work: Formal and Informal Contracts*, Buckingham: Open UP [1996].

J. Carrier and I. Kendall, *Medical Negligence: Complaints and Compensation*, Aldershot: Avebury, 1990.

C. Christensen, "Complaints Procedures in the NHS: All Change" (1996) 2 *Medical Law International* 247.

B. Dimmond, *Legal Aspects of Nursing* (2nd ed.), London: Prentice-Hall, 1995.

J. Hanna, "Internal Resolution of NHS Complaints" (1995) 3 *Medical Law Review* 177.

J. Jacob, *Doctors and Rules: A Sociology of Professional Values*, London: Routledge, 1988.

L. Mulcahy, "From fear to fraternity: doctors' contract of accounts of complaints" (1996) 18 *Journal of Social Welfare and Family Law* 397.

J. Montgomery, "Medicine, Accountability and Professionalism" (1989) 16 *Journal of Law and Society* 319.

M. Moran and B. Wood, *States Regulation and the Medical Profession*, Buckingham: Open UP, 1993.

R. Palmer, "Accountability and Discipline" in C. Dyer (ed.), *Doctors, Patients and the Law*, Oxford: Blackwell, 1992.

J. Robinson, *A Patient Voice at the GMC: A Lay Member's View of the General Medical Council*, London: Health Rights, 1988.

R. Smith, "Discipline I: The Hordes at the Gates" (1989) 298 *BMJ* 1502.

R. Smith, "Discipline II: The Preliminary Screener — A Powerful Gatekeeper" (1989) 298 *BMJ* 1569.

R. Smith, "Discipline III: The Final Stages" (1989) 298 *BMJ* 1633.

R. Smith, *Medical Discipline — The Professional Conduct Committee Jurisdiction of the General Medical Council, 1858–1990*, Oxford: Clarendon Press, 1994.

M. Stacey, "Medical Accountability: A Background Paper" in A. Grubb (ed.), *Challenges in Medical Care*, Chichester: John Wiley, 1992.

M. Stacey, *Regulating British Medicine: The General Medical Council*, Chichester: John Wiley, 1992.

R. Pyne, "The Professional Dimension" in J. Tingle and A. Cribb (eds), *Nursing, Law and Ethics*, Oxford: Blackwell Science Ltd, 1995.

Wilson Committee, *Being Heard: The Report of the Wilson Committee*, London: Department of Health, 1994.

PART III

INTRODUCTION

Respect for the individual's autonomy or right to self-determination is a recurrent theme in health care ethics and practice. To exercise autonomy a patient requires knowledge - knowledge about himself, his current state of health and about the clinical options available. A fundamental basis of health care provision is that the patient should consent freely to clinical procedures. Failure to obtain consent may result in civil proceedings and in some circumstances a criminal prosecution may be brought. It is important to note that the patient's right to determine his own treatment is both facilitated and constrained by the reality of clinical practice. Furthermore the freedom to consent is limited by the choices which the health professional places before the patient. Indeed as we saw in Chapter 1 above, the patient cannot demand whatever treatment he wishes.

The *Bolam* test, applicable in the context of general liability in medical negligence, was adopted by the House of Lords in the context of the disclosure of information regarding treatment in *Sidaway v. Bethlem Royal Hospital Governors* [1985] 1 All E.R. 643. Thus, information about risks of treatment must be disclosed in accordance with the standard expected of a responsible body of professional practice. The implications of *Sidaway* are explored in Chapter 6 below. However while the basis of disclosure is the standard accepted by a body of professional practice this does not mean that in all situations the views of the defendant's medical experts will be accepted. Recently there have been indications that the court may be prepared to find against the body of professional opinion. There is some uncertainty as to whether application of the professional practice standard would be recognised in situations in which it is proposed to include persons in innovative therapy or a clinical trial. Clinical trial procedures, including information sheets supplied to patients are the subject of scrutiny by a research ethics committee (see Chapter 10 below). Clinical trials and procedures for obtaining consent under the Mental Health Act 1983 are the only situations in which there is routine external scrutiny over consent methods (see Chapter 9 below).

For various reasons, for instance, due to youth, temporary incapacity or mental handicap, patients may be unable to consent to treatment. This raises two issues; first, who should decide on their behalf and secondly, on what basis should the decision to give treatment be made. Where an adult patient is incompetent to decide, then it was confirmed by the House of Lords that treatment could be given by the health professional on the basis of "best interests" although no one had the power to act as "proxy" for that patient (*F. v. West Berkshire HA* [1989] 2 All E.R. 545). The child patient poses particular problems in that it is recognised today that a child's competence to consent to medical procedures is gradually acquired, and a decision relative test of capacity may prove acutely difficult to apply (*Gillick v. West Norfolk and Wisbech AHA* [1985] 3 All E.R. 402).

The right to consent to treatment usually also encompasses the right to refuse treatment. This is the case even if by refusing that treatment the patient is virtually accepting that he will die. This principle is not universally recognised. First, where patients are regarded as mentally ill and the powers of the Mental Health Act 1983 are employed, then they may be required to accept certain care and treatment regardless of their wishes (see Chapter 8). There are also a number of cases outside the provisions of the Mental Health Act where the patient's refusal has been, albeit controversially, overridden on application to the court, notably in the context of enforced Caesarian section (see Chapter 6, also Chapter 13 and appendices). One of the most controversial areas relates to judicial acceptance of the notion that the parental power of consent may trump treatment refusal by a competent minor (see Chapter 7).

The need to respect autonomy is also demonstrated in the protection given to patient information by health care professionals. They are required to maintain confidentiality and not to make unauthorised disclosures of patient information (see Chapter 8). Nevertheless confidentiality is not recognised as absolute, either in the law or by professional ethical codes. This can lead to a difficult balancing exercise being undertaken. When determining the legitimacy of disclosure the courts have made reference to guidelines set out by the General Medical Council. Conflicts may arise between the duty of confidentiality owed to the patient and the need to promote effective decision making. This is illustrated in relation to the child patient, when situations may arise in which a child seeks to withold from her parents information which the parents will require in order to override the child's refusal of treatment. A patient may also have a statutory right of access to his personal health information, though again this right is not absolute. (See, *e.g.* Access to Health Records Act 1990 at pages 490–492, below.) This may be seen as another instance where individual autonomy/self determination is limited by medical discretion

5

CAPACITY

---

1. Introduction

In a health care context, capacity refers to competence to make decisions with respect to medical treatment — usually competence to decide whether to consent to or refuse treatment. In Chapter 6 we will address the issue of consent. Before anyone can give a valid consent to medical treatment he must be deemed in law to possess the requisite capacity. First we deal with the hugely important question of capacity, which is a prerequisite for participation in our social and legal system. It involves issues central to health care ethics — concerning autonomy, power and choice, and raises important questions about the ability to make and effectuate decisions with regard to health care and treatment. (See S. Stefan, "Silencing the Different Voice: Competence, Feminist Theory and Law" (1993) 47 *University of Miami Law Review* 763.) Some commentators have criticised bioethicists and lawyers for focusing on the rights of competent patients to self-determination, at the cost of neglecting one of the most urgent and pervasive problems in bioethics — decision making for those who lack capacity. (See A. Buchanan and D. Brock, *Deciding For Others: The Ethics of Surrogate Decision Making*, Cambridge: Cambridge University Press, 1989). Buchanan and Brock's comment (at page 4) that American law and legal scholarship has failed to provide an adequate theory of decision making for the incompetent or a satisfactory analysis of competence, is equally true of English law. (See M. Gunn, "Treatment and Mental Handicap" (1987) 16 *Anglo-American Law Review* 242.) Our law presumes that, in the absence of evidence to the contrary, adult patients are capable of giving or withholding consent to treatment. It thus presumes capacity, rationality, autonomy and freedom. Where there is reason to believe that a patient is unable to understand the decision they are being asked to make, it is necessary to consider whether an adult presumption of capacity is rebutted in the particular case. Until 1992 no English case had directly addressed the issue of how to determine whether an adult patient is capable of consenting to medical care or treatment.

The failure to confront this issue is astonishing given the existence of vast numbers of people who are not legally competent — for instance, those who have not yet reached maturity, those suffering from dementia and those who are incompetent due to mental impairment or injury. Moreover, there is reason to believe that the number of incompetent patients is rising, as advances in health care have prolonged the lives of individuals who may become incompetent. Thus, issues of capacity are likely to be raised in a particularly acute form at the end of life (see Chapter 15). There has also been a series of cases in relation to the capacity of young people (see Chapter 7), and a line of cases which deals with decisions about sterilising or performing caesarian sections on women who are deemed to be incompetent (see Chapter 13).

Against this background there are now signs that English law and scholarship is beginning to develop more sophisticated reasoning on the issue of capacity. Broadly, however, the test of capacity is that the person concerned should have the ability to understand the nature and purpose of the proposed care (see *F v. West Berkshire Health Authority* [1989] 2 All E.R. 545). The cases of *Re T* [1992] 4 All E.R. 649 and *Re C* [1994] 1 All E.R. 819 supply additional guidance on applying this test. Some of the cases on children further illuminate the test for capacity, and you should compare the tests for capacity which may be derived from cases discussed in this Chapter with those discussed in Chapter 7.] However, it is noteworthy that the only comprehensive definition of capacity in a case involving an adult was that proposed by the High Court in the case of *Re C*, and that it has yet to be confirmed by any higher authority. The test of capacity has recently received considerable attention from the Law Commission. This Chapter begins with an exploration of the common law test for capacity and of the new statutory test proposed by the Law Commission. In section 3 we consider the position where no consent is available, and the basis on which incompetent patients may be treated. This is followed by an examination of the 'best interests' test and of the Law Commission's proposals to give substance to that test. Finally, we deal with the Commission's proposals for a statutory authority to treat the incompetent.)

2. CAPACITY TO CONSENT AT COMMON LAW

According to Lord Brandon in *F v. West Berkshire Health Authority* [1989] 2 All E.R. 545, (discussed below at page 287) to be competent to give a legally effective consent the patient must be able to understand the nature and purpose of the treatment, and must be able to weigh the risks and benefits of it. The importance of understanding had also been stressed in *Gillick v. West Norfolk and Wisbech AHA* [1985] 3 All E.R. 402 which established that a young person's capacity to consent to treatment is a matter of clinical judgment (see Chapter 7). The necessary degree of understanding varies with the nature of the treatment and competence may be affected by extraneous factors, such as the effect of medication. As

Buchanan and Brock point out, decision-making tasks vary substantially in the capacities they require of the decision-maker. Thus, some decisions will require a relatively low level of competence, while others will demand a much higher level of understanding. Buchanan and Brock emphasise that the crucial question is *how* defective an individual's capacity and skill to make a particular decision must be in order for that individual to be deemed to lack the capacity to make that decision. (See A. Buchanan and D. Brock, *Deciding For Others: The Ethics of Surrogate Decision Making*, Cambridge: Cambridge University Press, 1989 at page 19.) This was one of the issues addressed in *Re T* (below). Buchanan and Brock suggest that the patient must also possess the capacity to make a *choice* on the basis of his understanding, and be able to *communicate* that choice. They point out (at page 27) that the aim of determining competence is to categorise patients into two classes — those whose voluntary decisions must be respected by others and accepted as binding, and, those whose decisions may be set aside. The incompetent patient will thus effectively be denied any right of autonomy. Like most litigated cases, *Re T* arose out of a refusal of proffered medical treatment. This is an important point, as the reported cases on capacity to date suggest that, in practice, the competence of the patient is only likely to be questioned where the patient refuses treatment which the doctor thinks he should receive (see Chapter 6).

Re T (Adult: Refusal of Treatment) [1992] 4 All E.R. 649, [1993] Fam 95, [1992] 3 W.L.R. 782, [1992] 2 F.L.R. 458, 9 BMLR 46, [1992] 3 Med. L.R. 306.

T was pregnant. She was involved in a car accident and went into premature labour which necessitated a Caesarean section operation. T's mother was a Jehovah's witness, although T herself was not. Shortly after a conversation with her mother, T told the hospital staff that she did not want a blood transfusion and signed a form refusing one. Prior to that point she had not indicated any concern about a transfusion. In the event the Caesarean section was carried out without the need for a blood transfusion, although the baby was still-born. However, T's condition subsequently deteriorated and she was admitted to an intensive care unit, where it was decided that without a blood transfusion she would die. The Court of Appeal had to decide whether her earlier refusal of a transfusion, in relation to the Caesarean section, precluded the court from authorising a transfusion in the new situation. The case raised a number of issues. First, it was necessary to consider whether her refusal was legally valid. This involved examining the test for capacity to decide whether or not to accept treatment. It was the first English case squarely to confront this issue in relation to adults. The Court of Appeal also considered whether T's purported refusal of consent was invalidated due to her mother's influence. This issue is addressed in Chapter 6 at pages 370–371. Finally, the Court of Appeal discussed the law governing a patient's right to refuse, in advance, treatments that they envisaged might be imposed upon them at some time in the future when they had lost their capacity to consent. That aspect of the case is examined in Chapter 14.

LORD DONALDSON M.R.

". . . The law requires that an adult patient who is mentally and physically capable of exercising a choice *must* consent if medical treatment of him is to be lawful, although the consent need not be in writing and may sometimes be inferred from the patient's conduct in the context of the surrounding circumstances. Treating him without his consent or despite a refusal of consent will constitute the civil wrong of trespass to the person and may constitute a crime. If, however, the patient has made no choice and, when the need for treatment arises, is in no position to make one, the classic emergency situation with an unconscious patient, *e.g.* the practitioner can lawfully treat the patient in accordance with his clinical judgment of what is in the patient's best interest.

There seems to be a view in the medical profession that in such emergency circumstances the next of kin should be asked to consent on behalf of the patient and that, if possible, treatment should be postponed until that consent has been obtained. This is a misconception because the next of kin has no legal right either to consent or to refuse consent. This is not to say that it is an undesirable practice if the interests of the patient will not be adversely affected by any consequential delay. I say this because contact with the next of kin may reveal that the patient has made an anticipatory choice which, if clearly established and applicable in the circumstances — two major 'ifs' — would bind the practitioner. Consultation with the next of kin has a further advantage in that it may reveal information as to the personal circumstances of the patient and as to the choice which the patient might have made, if he or she had been in a position to make it. Neither the personal circumstances of the patient nor a speculative answer to the question 'What would the patient have chosen?' can bind the practitioner in his choice of whether or not to treat or how to treat or justify him in acting contrary to a clearly established anticipatory refusal to accept treatment but they are factors to be taken into account by him in forming a clinical judgment as to what is in the best interests of the patient. For example, if he learnt that the patient was a Jehovah's Witness, but had no evidence of a refusal to accept blood transfusions, he would avoid or postpone any blood transfusion so long as possible . . .

The right to decide one's own fate presupposes a capacity to do so. Every adult is presumed to have that capacity, but it is a presumption which can be rebutted. This is not a question of the degree of intelligence or education of the adult concerned. However a small minority of the population lack the necessary mental capacity due to mental illness or retarded development (see, for example, *F v. West Berkshire Health Authority* [1989] 2 All E.R. 545). This is a permanent or at least a long-term state. Others who would normally have that capacity may be deprived of it or have it reduced by reason of temporary factors, such as unconsciousness or confusion or other effects of shock, severe fatigue, pain or drugs being used in their treatment.

Doctors faced with a refusal of consent have to give very careful and detailed consideration to the patient's capacity to decide at the time when the decision was made. It may not be the simple case of the patient having no capacity because, for example, at that time he had hallucinations. It may be the more difficult case of a temporarily reduced capacity at the time when his decision was made. What matters is that the doctors should consider whether at that time he had a capacity which was commensurate with the gravity of the decision which he purported to make. The more serious the decision, the greater the capacity required. If the patient had the requisite capacity, they are bound by his decision. If not, they are free to treat him in what they believe to be his best interests.

This problem is more likely to arise at a time when the patient is unconscious and cannot be consulted. If he can be consulted, this should be done, but again full account has to be taken of his then capacity to make up his own mind.

As I pointed out at the beginning of this judgment, the patient's right of choice exists whether the reasons for making that choice are rational, irrational, unknown or even non-existent. That his choice is contrary to what is to be expected of the vast majority of adults is only relevant if there are other reasons for doubting his capacity to decide. The nature of his choice or the terms in which it is expressed may then tip the balance . . ."

NOTES:

1. The Court of Appeal unanimously decided that the doctors could disregard T's refusal of a blood transfusion because she was unable to make a genuine decision. The principal basis for this finding was that her apparent decision was invalidated by the undue influence exerted upon her by her mother. (See Chapter 6 at pages 370–371). The judges also indicated that it was unclear whether she had signed the refusal form under the erroneous impression that alternatives to a transfusion would be available and equally unclear whether she had intended to refuse all blood transfusions, or only those which were not necessary to keep her alive. Lord Donaldson was particularly critical of the layout of consent forms and the failure to clearly explain the consequences of refusing treatment.

2. Lord Donaldson's speech makes clear that capacity may vary depending on the gravity of the decision involved. Brazier illustrates this point with reference to the judgement in *In the Estate of Park* [1954] P. 122. In this case Mr Park had suffered a disabling stroke which left his memory and speech impaired. It was held that although he lacked the capacity to make a valid will on May 30, 1945, he retained sufficient understanding to marry validly on that same day. (See M. Brazier, "Competence, Consent and Proxy Consents" in M. Brazier and M. Loibjoit (eds) *Protecting the Vulnerable: Autonomy and Consent in Health Care*, London: Routledge, 1991 at page 37.) Stefan has argued that while such an approach may be attuned to the reality of people's lives, it is often used to ratify decisions with which judges agree, and to sweep aside choices that conflict with judges' values. (See S. Stefan, "Silencing the Different Voice: Competence, Feminist Theory and Law" (1993) 47 *University of Miami Law Review* 763 at page 774.)

3. Lord Donaldson also refers to the difficult issue of fluctuating capacity. It seems that the law may respond to the issue of fluctuating capacity differently depending on whether the patient is an adult or a minor. (For the position in relation to minors, see Lord Donaldson's judgment in *Re R (A Minor)* [1991] 4 All E.R. 177 extracted in Chapter 7.)

4. The law governing the position when no consent is available is considered in detail in *F v. West Berkshire Health Authority* [1989] 2 All E.R. 545 (extracted below at page 287).

5. The comments of Lord Donaldson on the role of the next of kin apply only to cases where the patient is over the age of eighteen. In

earlier cases there had been judicial dicta to the effect that next-of-kin could validly consent to treatment on behalf of their adult relatives. See, for example, the comments of Croom Johnson L.J. in *Wilson v. Pringle* [1986] All E.R. 440, at 447. (For the position in relation to children, see Chapter 7.)

6. In his judgment, Lord Donaldson went on to state that the only qualification to the absolute right of a competent adult to withhold consent to medical treatment was where the decision might result in the death of a viable foetus. For discussion of how this dictum and the subsequent case on forced caesareans might affect the presumed capacity of the pregnant woman, see Chapter 13 at page 782 and Appendix C.)

QUESTIONS:

1. What is the role of next of kin in relation to consent following this case? (See P. Fennell, "Statutory Authority to Treat, Relatives and Treatment Proxies" [1994] 2 *Medical Law Review* 30 at pages 43–5.)
2. How helpful is Lord Donaldson's judgment to a health professional trying to determine whether a patient is competent to consent to, or refuse, treatment?

More detailed guidance on determining whether a patient has the requisite capacity was provided in the case of *Re C* [1994] 1 All E.R. 819. Although only a High Court authority, this case is significant as the first English case to propose a detailed test for determining whether a patient is capable of consenting to, or refusing, medical care.

Re C (Adult: Refusal of Treatment) [1994] 1 All E.R. 819, [1994] 1 W.L.R. 290, [1994] 1 F.L.R. 31, 15 BMLR 77

C was a patient in Broadmoor Hospital. He was a 68-year-old chronic paranoid schizophrenic who expressed grandiose delusions of having been an internationally renowned doctor. C developed a gangrenous infection in one leg. His consultant surgeon believed that the leg should be amputated in order to save C's life, and that his chances of survival without amputation were no more than 15 per cent. C had stated that he would prefer to die with two feet than live with one. He believed that he might survive with the help of God, the doctors and the nurses, and that if he did die, his death would not be caused by his foot. Ultimately, the surgeon persuaded C to accept more conservative treatment, and the danger of death was averted without the need for amputation. However, the surgeon considered that C's leg might deteriorate and become life-threatening again in the future. C's solicitor therefore sought a declaration from the court that no amputation should take place in the future without C's written consent. The court had to decide whether his capacity was so reduced by chronic mental illness that he did not adequately understand the nature, purpose and effect of the proposed amputation, which would render his refusal invalid.

THORPE J.
". . . Dr Eastman [a consultant and senior lecturer in forensic psychiatry] saw C on 6 October, and reported comprehensively in writing on 7 October. In his oral evidence he emphasised that schizophrenia is an all-pervasive illness. Features present in C's case include grandiose and persecutory delusions as well as incongruity of affect, a technical term meaning mismatch between the words spoken and the accompanying emotional display. For the patient offered amputation to save life, there are three stages to the decision: (1) to take in and retain treatment information, (2) to believe it, and (3) to weigh that information, balancing risks and needs. C had, in Dr Eastman's opinion, achieved the first stage but not the second. Did his disbelief in the imminence of death arise out of his mental illness or other ordinary convictions, or a combination of both? Of course, if to others he showed greater appreciation of the risk of death, that was evidence that he had proceeded further in the progressive stages. It was significant that the persecutory delusions did not include the conviction that his present condition had been caused by agencies at Broadmoor or Heatherwood. For Dr Eastman, the ultimate conclusion should be reached by weighing in the scales the preservation of life against the autonomy of the patient. If the patient's capacity to decide is unimpaired, autonomy weighs heavier, but the further capacity is reduced, the lighter autonomy weighs. Plainly, C's capacity is reduced by his mental illness. But for him the decision as to whether it is sufficiently reduced remains marginal in the absence of any direct link between the persecutory delusions and his present condition . . .

Dr Gall assessed C at interviews on 22 September, and 5 October. He reported in writing on 6 October, with addendum on 7 October. He heard Dr Eastman's evidence and he agreed with it. He said that the differences between him and Dr Eastman were so fine as not to be worth expressing. Significantly, he also said that he agreed with Mr Rutter's [a consultant vascular surgeon, who had made it plain that he was not prepared to operate without C's unequivocal consent] assessment of the extent of C's deviation from the mean, certainly as C now is overall, mentally and physically.

Dr Ghosh [a consultant forensic psychiatrist and C's medical officer] has had responsibility for C since May 1992. She has seen him monthly since that date. In addition, she visits his ward weekly. She has developed a relationship within which she has C's trust and confidence. She reported on 15 September, and again on 6 October. She disagrees with Dr Eastman and Dr Gall. She considers C incompetent to decide major medical matters because of (1) his grandiose delusion that he was a doctor, and (2) his persecutory delusion that whatever treatment is offered is calculated to destroy his body. His capacity to decide is not absent but very seriously reduced. Far from being on the borderline, she regards the case as very clearcut.

Amongst the experts, my very clear conclusion is that the opinion of Dr Eastman and Dr Gall is to be preferred. They did not find any direct link between C's refusal and his persecutory delusions, nor was any to be found in C's oral evidence. Furthermore, it was clear to me that C was quite content to follow medical advice and to co-operate in treatment appropriately as a patient as long as his rejection of amputation was respected . . .

Unfortunately, Dr Ghosh had never discussed the case with Mr Rutter. When she wrote as she did on 6 October and testified on 11 October, she was unaware of the dramatic aversion of the risk of death over the preceding four weeks. On 11 October, she still regarded the limb as dead below the knee and death within a maximum of two years as certain without an amputation. She did not know that amputation carried a significant mortality risk. I have no doubt that this lack of information influenced her appraisal of the critical equation and of C's approach to it.

I was also impressed by the evidence of Mr Rutter, who had obviously considered his professional dilemma profoundly and had made a shrewd appraisal of C's capacity over the weeks in which their relationship had developed.

C himself throughout the hours that he spent in the proceedings seemed ordinarily engaged and concerned. His answers to questions seemed measured and generally sensible. He was not always easy to understand and the grandiose delusions were manifest, but there was no sign of inappropriate emotional expression. His rejection of amputation seemed to result from sincerely held conviction. He had a certain dignity of manner that I respect. The submissions of counsel were of a uniformly high standard. Much of the ground that they cover is common. Thanks to the recent decisions in *Re T (adult: refusal of medical treatment)* [1992] 4 All E.R. 649 and *Airedale NHS Trust v. Bland* [1993] 1 All E.R. 821, the legal principles applicable to this case are readily ascertained . . .

[S]ubmissions divide over the definition of the capacity which enables an individual to refuse treatment. Mr Gordon [the plaintiff's counsel] argues for what he calls the minimal competence test, which he defines as the capacity to understand in broad terms the nature and effect of the proposed treatment. It is common ground that C has the legal capacity to initiate these proceedings without a next friend, within the terms of R.S.C. Ord. 80. Mr Gordon contends that the capacity to refuse treatment is no higher and is equally no higher than the capacity to contract. I reject that submission. I think that the question to be decided is whether it has been established that C's capacity is so reduced by his chronic mental illness that he does not sufficiently understand the nature, purpose and effects of the proffered amputation.

I consider helpful Dr Eastman's analysis of the decision-making process into three stages: first, comprehending and retaining treatment information, secondly, believing it and, thirdly, weighing it in the balance to arrive at choice. The Law Commission has proposed a similar approach in paragraph 2.20 of its consultation paper 129, Mentally Handicapped Adults and Decision-Making. Applying that test to my findings on the evidence, I am completely satisfied that the presumption that C has the right of self-determination has not been displaced. Although his general capacity is impaired by schizophrenia, it has not been established that he does not sufficiently understand the nature, purpose and effects of the treatment he refuses. Indeed, I am satisfied that he has understood and retained the relevant treatment information, that in his own way he believes it, and that in the same fashion he has arrived at a clear choice . . ."

The court granted an injunction to prevent the hospital from amputating C's leg, thus giving binding effect to his 'anticipated refusal'.

NOTES:

1. This was the first English case to rule explicitly on the validity of advance directives. Douglas points out that the decision represents an important step in advancing patient autonomy. However, it also raises several potential problems, especially in relation to the effect of advance directives, which need to be clarified by legislation. (See her commentary [1994] *Family Law* 131.) The Law Commission has issued proposals for legislation on advance directives, which are discussed in Chapter 14 at pages 874–882.

2. Grubb notes that the case clarifies the nature of the 'understanding' needed for a valid consent, in the sense that "the patient's capacity to understand must be tied to that information which the patient must be informed of and understand in order for any touching not to be a battery: what other judges have referred to as 'in broad terms the nature of the procedure' (*Chatterton v. Gerson* [1981] Q.B. 432 at 433 *per* Bristow J.)" (See A. Grubb, "Treatment Without Consent: Adult" (1994) 2 *Medical Law Review* 92, and also M. Brazier, "Competence, Consent and Proxy Consents" in M. Brazier and M. Loibjoit (eds) *Protecting the Vulnerable: Autonomy and Consent in Health Care*, London: Routledge, 1991 at page 36. For discussion of *Chatterton v. Gerson*, see Chapter 6 at pages 328–332.) This case is also illustrative of how the mere fact that someone is mentally disordered does not necessarily render him incapable of making a decision pertaining to his treatment. (See P. Fennell, *Treatment Without Consent* London: Routledge, 1996 at page 257.)

3. Fennell suggests that the main practical difficulty with the test approved in *C* relates to the second criterion, *i.e.* that the patient must believe the relevant information. This criterion does not mean that the patient must accept the medical evaluation of the likely outcome of having the treatment or not having it and of the trade-off between risks and benefits. Thorpe J. clarified the test in his later judgment in *B v Croydon District Health Authority* [1995] 1 All E.R. 683 where he differentiated between outright disbelief, which meant being "impervious to reason, divorced from reality, or incapable of judgment after reflection", and "the tendency which most people have when undergoing medical treatment to self assess and then to puzzle over the divergence between medical and self assessment". This case was decided under the Mental Health legislation and is discussed in Chapter 9 at pages 546–547. (See P. Fennell, *op. cit.* at page 257.)

4. It is to be hoped that C will mark the end of the reliance placed by the courts on the concept of mental age. This tendency has been particularly marked in cases involving the sterilisation of mentally disabled women — see *F v. West Berkshire Health Authority* [1989] 2 All E.R. 545 at page 289 below, and Chapter 13 at pages 754–773). As commentators have noted, such standardised tests of intelligence have been largely discredited in professional circles. (See P. Mittler, "Competence and Consent in People with Mental Handicap" in M. Brazier and M. Loibjoit (eds), *Protecting the Vulnerable: Autonomy and Consent in Health Care*, London: Routledge, 1991. Note also the Law Commission's opposition to reliance on the concept of mental age at page 285 below.) Moreover, it is wrong to regard those who have been assigned the mental age of a child as though they really were children, given that they are biologically, and perhaps emotionally, adults. (See R. Lee and D. Morgan, "A Lesser Sacrifice?

Sterilisation and Mentally Handicapped Women" in R. Lee and D. Morgan (eds) *Birthrights: Law and Ethics at the Beginnings of Life*, London: Routledge, 1989 at pages 143–4.)

5. In *Secretary of State for the Home Dept v. Robb* [1995] 1 All E.R. 677 a prisoner who had been diagnosed as suffering from a personality disorder went on hunger strike. Thorpe J. issued a declaration that his physicians and nurses could lawfully observe and abide by his refusal to receive nutrition and could lawfully abstain from providing hydration and nutrition for as long as the prisoner retained capacity to refuse them. This confirmed that the effect of the decisions in *Re T* and *Airedale NHS Trust v. Bland* [1993] 1 All E.R. 281 had been to render forced feeding of a competent patient unlawful, unless he had been detained under the Mental Health Act 1983. (See the discussion of *B v Croydon District Health Authority* [1995] 1 All E.R. 683 in Chapter 9 at pages 546–547.) Furthermore Thorpe J. confirmed that capacity was to be determined according to the three-fold test "formulated by expert forensic psychiatry" which he had approved in *Re C*. Kennedy argues that *Robb* was inappropriately decided within the analytical framework of medical law, given that the prisoner concerned was not a patient and was not refusing medical treatment. He suggests it should have been decided as a straightforward civil liberties issue. (See I. Kennedy, "Consent: Force-feeding of Prisoners" (1995) 3 *Medical Law Review* 189.)

QUESTIONS:

1. How far can a general assessment of capacity help ascertain whether a patient is legally competent to consent to, or refuse, a particular treatment? (For criticism of existing legal definitions of capacity as based on the assumption that competence is an inherent, objective and measurable attribute of an individual, see S. Stefan, "Silencing the Different Voice: Competence, Feminist Theory and Law" (1993) 47 *University of Miami Law Review* 763.)

2. Was Thorpe J. justified in choosing between the expert assessments of C's capacity as he did? Which of the experts do you think was best placed to decide in C's best interests?

3. Dr Eastman had argued that the assessment of legal competence "should be reached by weighing in the scales the preservation of life against the autonomy of the patient. If the patient's capacity to decide is unimpaired, autonomy weighs heavier, but the further capacity is reduced, the lighter autonomy weighs." Do you think that this balancing act was the one performed by Thorpe J.?

4. How well do you think C understood his medical needs? Did he really satisfy the test endorsed by the court?

5. Do you think that Thorpe J.'s approach in *Re C* takes sufficient account of the comment by Lord Donaldson in *Re T* (above) that the

patient's capacity must be "commensurate with the gravity of the decision"?

6. Could an anorexic satisfy Thorpe J.'s test of capacity, given that compulsion to refuse treatment (i.e. feeding) is itself the major symptom of the condition? (See the discussion of anorexia in chapter 6 at pages 339–340.)

The following guidance to doctors attempting to assess capacity is offered in a joint publication by the British Medical Association and The Law Society:

Assessment of Mental Capacity: Guidance for Doctors and Lawyers, A Report of the British Medical Association and The Law Society, London: BMA, 1996

12.4 A systematic approach to assessing capacity

Once sure of the relevant legal test, the assessing doctor should become familiar with any background information about the person likely to be relevant to that particular test. The amount of information required will be determined by the complexity of the legal decision to be taken. For example, if the assessment relates to the capacity to make a will, the assessing doctor will need to have some idea about the extent and complexity of the person's estate and whether the person understands the claims of others to which consideration should be given in deciding about disposal of his or her assets. The doctor must therefore have some knowledge of the number and nature of the claims on the individual. Although the medical assessment should be carried out with an eye to the relevant legal criteria, there must be a clear distinction between the description of the disabilities and the interpretation of how they affect legal capacity. The doctor should, therefore, first define the diagnosis and the medical disabilities and then assess how these affect the person's ability to pass the relevant legal test.

Prior to undertaking the assessment, the doctor should try to have access to all relevant past medical and psychiatric records. An understanding of the progression of the person's disease will be relevant to prognosis, to any likely response to treatment, and thus to future potential capacity. Assessment of the permanence or transience of disabilities may be crucially important in offering a view about achievable capacity. Also, the medical records may give a different picture of a person's disabilities in general terms from that which the doctor gains at an individual assessment and it is important for the doctor to make an assessment on the basis of all of the information available. It is also important for the doctor to take full account of relevant information from other disciplines. An assessment by a clinical psychologist may already be available, or could be sought, and this may assist in giving a detailed, validated and systematic assessment of cognitive functioning. An occupational therapist might properly be consulted when information about daily functioning is of importance. Also, a report from a nurse or from an approved social worker may sometimes be helpful.

Information from friends, relatives or carers is often of great importance in the assessment of disability and its progression. However, great care must be taken when gaining information from such third parties, particularly if they have an interest in the outcome of the assessment of capacity. It is also important to take account of the person's known previous patterns of behaviour, values and goals. These may give clues as to whether current behaviour and thinking reflects an abnormal mental state. Aspects of a person's current thinking may derive not from a medical disability but from a normal personality, or from a particular cultural or ethical background, and this may be of great importance in determining capacity. It may even be necessary for the doctor to seek advice from others on such cultural issues, or to suggest that the patient be examined by a doctor of a cultural or ethical background similar to the person being assessed.

Where the person suffers from a mental disorder, it is good practice to express the diagnosis in terms of one of the accepted international classifications of mental disorders, the World Health Organisation International Classification of Diseases (WHO ICD 10), or the American Psychiatric Association, Diagnostic and Statistical Manual (DSM IV). This will ensure greater diagnostic consistency between doctors and minimise diagnostic confusion . . .

12.7 The duty to enhance mental capacity

Doctors should be aware both that medical disabilities can fluctuate and that there are many factors extraneous to a person's medical disorder which may adversely influence capacity. It is the duty of the assessing doctor to maximise capacity. The following points may assist.

- Any treatable medical condition which affects capacity should be treated before a final assessment is made.
- Incapacity may be temporary albeit for a prolonged period. For example, an older patient with an acute confusional state caused by infection may continue to improve for some time after successful treatment. If a person's condition is likely to improve, the assessment of capacity should, if possible, be delayed.
- Some conditions, for example, dementia, may give rise to fluctuating capacity. Thus, although a person with dementia may lack capacity at the time of one assessment, the result may be different if a second assessment is undertaken during a lucid interval. In cases of fluctuating capacity the medical report should detail the level of capacity during periods of maximal and minimal disability.
- Some mental disabilities may be untreatable and yet their impact can be minimised. For example, the capacity of a person with a short term memory deficit to make a particular decision may be improved if trained in suitable techniques by an occupational therapist or psychologist. If the assessing doctor believes that capacity could be improved by such assistance then this should be stated in any opinion.
- Some physical conditions which do not directly affect the mental state can *appear* to interfere with capacity. For example, disabilities of communication may not reflect an inability to understand relevant information or make a choice but may simply reflect an inability to communicate the person's wishes. Many communication difficulties which result from physical disabilities can be overcome and this emphasises the importance of recognising the true basis of what is only an apparent incapacity. There should, therefore, be careful assessment of speech, language functioning, hearing and (if appropriate) sight. Any disabilities discovered should, as far as possible (and if time allows), be corrected before any conclusion is reached about capacity.
- Care should be taken to choose the best location and time for the assessment. In someone who is on the borderline of having capacity, anxiety may tip that person into apparent incapacity. It may be appropriate to assess the person in his or her own home if it is thought that an interview at either a hospital or a GP's surgery would adversely affect the result. A relative or carer may be able to indicate the most suitable location and time for the assessment.
- The way in which someone is approached and dealt with generally can have a significant impact upon apparent capacity and the doctor should be sensitive to this.

- Educating the person being assessed as to the factors relevant to the proposed decision may enhance capacity. Indeed, the assessing doctor should always establish what the person understands about the decision he or she is being asked to undertake. It is important for the doctor to re-explain and, if necessary, write down those aspects of the decision which have not been fully grasped. The person being assessed should be allowed sufficient time to become familiar with concepts relevant to the decision. For example, people with learning disabilities may have difficulty in consenting to sexual relationships if they are ignorant about issues relating to sexuality and abuse. With a careful explanation of the relevant issues such people may be capable of consenting to personal and sexual relationships.
- The capacity of some people may be enhanced by the presence of a third party at the interview. Alternatively, the presence of such a person may increase the anxiety and thus reduce the capacity of the person. The person being assessed should be asked specifically whether he or she would feel more comfortable with some friend or other person present.
- Depression is common amongst those with other disabilities but is often not recognised. Its presence may profoundly affect capacity and yet it may be amenable to treatment. Making a diagnosis of depression in the presence of other disabilities affecting mental functioning can be particularly difficult, especially in patients with dementia. The opinion of a psychiatrist may be necessary in such cases. The low self-esteem of many patients whose capacity may be in question means that they are at particular risk of "going along with propositions" regardless of their own private views. The assessing doctor should be aware of this and structure the interview so as to avoid the use of leading questions.

QUESTION:

1. How helpful do you consider this guidance will be to doctors dealing with the reality of incapacity?

3. A STATUTORY TEST FOR CAPACITY?

Prior to *Re C* there was no comprehensive definition of capacity in English law. This is an issue which has concerned the Law Commission (the body charged with reviewing the law in England and Wales and proposing legal reform, see Chapter 2 at page 129–130) for a number of years. It has issued a number of consultation papers on the need for reform of this area of law, culminating in 1995 with the publication of its report on *Mental Incapacity* (Law Com. No. 231, 1995). The report contains proposals for legislative reform of the law on mental incapacity, and a draft bill intended as a basis for legislation. It was published to widespread academic acclaim and a general expectation that the draft bill on Mental Incapacity would be substantially implemented. However, on January 16, 1996 the Lord Chancellor announced that the Government did not intend to introduce legislation to enact the draft bill in its current form, largely due to expressions of public concern about its proposals on living wills (see Chapter 14 at pages 874–882). He announced the Government's intention of establishing a full public consultation process, with a view to issuing a consultation paper on mental incapacity in "due course". (See Press Release from Lord Chancellor's Department dated January 16, 1996 and "Government Announcement on Mental Incapacity" [1996] *Family Law* 246.) Nevertheless, in this Chapter we draw heavily upon the Law Commission's proposals for reform of the law on capacity, since its report represents the first fully informed consideration of this issue. In the following extract the Law Commission reviews a number of potential tests of capacity, and puts forward its own proposal for a statutory definition of capacity.

Law Commission, *Mental Incapacity*, Law Com. 231, 1995 (footnotes omitted)

(1) Capacity and Lack of Capacity

3.2   It is presumed at common law that an adult has full legal capacity unless it is shown that he or she does not. If a question of capacity comes before a court the burden of proof will be on the person seeking to establish incapacity, and the matter will be decided according to the usual civil standard, the balance of probabilities. We proposed in Consultation Paper No. 128 that the usual standard should continue to apply and the vast majority of our respondents agreed with this proposal. A number, however, argued that it would be helpful if the new statutory provisions were expressly to include and restate both the presumption of capacity and the relevant standard of proof.

> *We recommend that there should be a presumption against lack of capacity and that any question whether a person lacks capacity should be decided on the balance of probabilities. (Draft Bill, clause 2(6).)*

3.3   In our overview paper we described the variety of tests of capacity which already exist in our law, and we also discussed some medical and psychological tests of capacity. There are three broad approaches: the "status", "outcome" and "functional" approaches. A "status" test excludes all persons under eighteen from voting and used to exclude all married women from legal ownership of property. Under the present law, the status of being a "patient" of the Court of Prosecution is used in a variety of enactments to trigger other legal consequences. Case-law also suggests that the status of being a "patient" has the extremely significant effect of depriving the patient of all contractual capacity, whether or not as a matter of fact the patient actually had such capacity. The status approach is quite out of tune with the policy aim of enabling and encouraging people to take for themselves any decision which they have capacity to take.

3.4   An assessor of capacity using the "outcome" method focuses on the final content of an individual's decision. Any decision which is inconsistent with conventional values, or with which the assessor disagrees, may be classified as incompetent. This penalises individuality and demands conformity at the expense of personal autonomy. A number of our respondents argued that an "outcome" approach is applied by many doctors; if the outcome of the patient's deliberations is to agree with the doctor's recommendations then he or she is taken to have capacity, while if the outcome is to reject a course which the doctor has advised then capacity is found to be absent.

3.5   Most respondents to our overview paper strongly supported the "functional" approach. This also has the merit of being the approach adopted by most of the established tests in English law. In this approach, the assessor asks whether an individual is able, at the time when a particular decision has to be made, to understand its nature and effects. Importantly, both partial and fluctuating capacity can be recognised. Most people, unless in a coma, are able to make at least some decisions for themselves, and many have levels of capacity which vary from week to week or even from hour to hour.

3.6   In view of the ringing endorsement of the "functional" approach given by respondents to the overview paper, we formulated a provisional "functional" test of capacity and set this out in all three of our 1993 consultation papers. This test focused on inability to understand or, in the alternative, inability to choose. We also made specific provision for those unable to communicate a decision they might in fact have made. We were encouraged to find that many respondents approved our draft test, and we have been able to build on it while taking into account suggestions made on consultation. Although one respondent argued that the whole idea of a test of capacity was ill-conceived and unhelpful, many said that it was vital to have a clear test, and one which catered explicitly, for partial and fluctuating capacity. Professor Michael Gunn has referred to "the virtue of certainty" and written that our proposals for a statutory test of capacity will be welcomed, "if for no other reason than introducing certainty and clarity".

3.7   The present law offers a number of tests of capacity depending on the type of decision in issue. Case-law has offered answers to some problems put to it; individual statutes include occasional definitions; the Mental Health Act Code of Practice deals in some detail with capacity to make medical treatment decisions; and Part VII of the 1983 Act addresses capacity in relation to the management of "property and affairs". For the purposes of our new legislative scheme, a single statutory definition should be adopted. We turn now to consider the terms of such a definition.

3.8   In the consultation papers we suggested that a person (other than someone unable to communicate) should not be found to lack capacity unless he or she is first found to be suffering from "mental disorder" as defined in the Mental Health Act 1983. The arguments for and against such a diagnostic hurdle are very finely balanced and they are set out in full in Consultation Paper No. 128. In the event, most respondents agreed with our preliminary view that a diagnostic hurdle did have a role to play in any definition of incapacity, in particular in ensuring that the test is stringent enough not to catch large numbers of people who make unusual or otherwise unwise decisions. There may also be a small number of cases where a finding of incapacity could lead to action which could amount to "detention" as defined in the European Convention of Human Rights. The case-law of the European Court of Human Rights requires that any such detention should be pursuant to a finding of unsoundness of mind based on "objective medical expertise". Although we gave very careful consideration to the arguments against the inclusion of any diagnostic threshold, we have concluded that such a threshold would provide a significant protection and would in no sense prejudice or stigmatise those who are in need of help with decision-making.

3.9   That said, a significant number of respondents, including many who favoured a diagnostic threshold of some sort, expressed misgivings about the new legislation "coat-tailing" on the statutory shorthand of "mental disorder" and the definition set out in the Mental Health Act 1983. The full definition in the 1983 Act is that "'mental disorder' means mental illness, arrested or incomplete development of mind, psychopathic disorder and any other disorder or disability of mind". Although this definition is extremely broad and may well cover all the conditions which a diagnostic threshold should cover we no longer favour its incorporation into the new legislation. We learned at first hand in working party meetings how "mental disorder" is equated in many minds, both lay and professional, with the much narrower phenomenon of psychiatric illness or with the criteria for compulsory detention under the Mental Health Act 1983 . . .

3.12   We take the view that (except in cases where the person is unable to communicate) a new test of capacity should require that a person's inability to arrive at a decision should be linked to the existence of a "mental disability". The adoption of the phrase "mental disability" will distinguish this requirement from the language of the Mental Health Act 1983 and will stress the importance of a mental condition which has a disabling effect on the person's capacity.

We recommend that the expression "mental disability" in the new legislation should mean any disability or disorder of the mind or brain, whether permanent or temporary, which results in an impairment or disturbance of mental functioning. (Draft Bill, clause 2(2).)

3.13   We took the provisional view in the consultation papers that those who cannot communicate decisions should be included within the scope of the new jurisdiction. We had in mind particularly those who are unconscious. In some rare conditions a conscious patient may be known to retain a level of cognitive functioning but the brain may be completely unable to communicate with the body or with the outside world. In other cases, particularly after a stroke, it may not be possible to say whether or not there is cognitive dysfunction. It can, however, be said that the patient cannot communicate any decision he or she may make. In either case, decisions may have to be made on behalf of such people, and only two respondents expressed the purist view that they should be excluded from our new jurisdiction because they do not suffer from true "mental incapacity". It appears to us appropriate that they should be brought within the scope of our new legislation rather than being left to fend for themselves with the uncertain and inadequate principles of the common law.

The definition of incapacity

3.14   The functional approach means that the new definition of incapacity should emphasize its decision-specific nature. A diagnostic threshold of "mental disability" should be included, except in cases of inability to communicate.

We recommend that legislation should provide that a person is without capacity if at the material time he or she is:

(1) unable by reason of mental disability to make a decision on the matter in question, or
(2) unable to communicate a decision on that matter because he is unconscious or for any other reason.

3.15   It would defeat our aim of offering clarity and certainty were no further guidance given as to the meaning of the phrase "unable to make a decision". In the consultation papers we identified two broad sub-sets within this category, one based on inability to understand relevant information and the other based on inability to make a "true choice". Although many respondents expressed disquiet about the elusiveness of the concept of "true choice", there was broad agreement that incapacity cannot in every case be ascribed to an inability to understand information. It may arise from an inability to use or negotiate information which has been understood. In most cases an assessor of capacity will have to consider both the ability to understand information and the ability to use it exercising choice, so that the two "sub-sets" should not be seen as mutually exclusive. This was emphasised by Thorpe J. in the very important High Court case of *Re C (Adult: Refusal of Treatment)*, perhaps the first reported case to give any clear guidance on questions of capacity in relation to medical treatment decisions. Thorpe J. had to make a preliminary finding as to whether the patient concerned had capacity to refuse consent to amputation of his leg. He found it helpful to analyse decision-making capacity in three stages: first, comprehending and retaining information, second, believing it and, third, "weighing it in the balance to arrive at choice." He mentioned that we had proposed a similar approach to the question of capacity in the later case of *B v. Croydon District Health Authority*, while upholding a wide view of the scope of section 63 of the Mental Health Act 1983, which authorises treatment for mental disorder regardless of capacity and consent.

3.16   Respondents favoured our suggestion that it was more realistic to test whether a person can understand information, than to test whether he or she can understand "the nature of" an action or decision. It was, however, suggested that an ability to "appreciate" information about the likely consequences of a decision might be conceptually different from an ability to understand such information. We prefer to approach this question in a slightly different way, on the basis that information about consequences is one of the sorts of information which a person with capacity understands. Respondents supported the express mention of foreseeable consequences in our draft test, and we still see advantage in drawing attention to the special nature of information about likely consequences, as information which will in every case be relevant to the decision.

We recommend that a person should be regarded as unable to make a decision by reason of mental disability if the disability is such that, at the time when the decision needs to be made, he or she is unable to understand or retain the information relevant to the decision, including information about the reasonably foreseeable consequences of deciding one way or another or failing to make the decision. (Draft Bill, clause 2(2)(a).)

3.17   There are cases where the person concerned can understand information but where the effects of a mental disability prevent him or her from using that information in the decision-making process. We explained in Consultation Paper No. 128 that certain compulsive conditions cause people who are quite able to absorb information to arrive, inevitably, at decisions which are unconnected to the information or their understanding of it. An example is the anorexic who always decides not to eat. There are also some people who, because of a mental disability, are unable to exert their will against some stronger person who wishes to influence their decisions or against some *force majeure* of circumstances. As Thorpe J. said in *Re C*, some people can understand information but are prevented by their disability from being able to believe it. We originally suggested that such cases could be described as cases where incapacity resulted from inability to make a "true choice". Common to all these cases is the fact that the person's eventual decision is divorced from his or her ability to understand the relevant information. Emphasising that the person must be able to use the information which he or she has successfully understood in the decision-making process deflects the complications of asking whether a person needs to "appreciate" information as well as understand it. A decision based on a compulsion, the overpowering will of a third party or any other inability to act on relevant information as a result of mental disability is not a decision made by a person with decision-making capacity.

We recommend that a person should be regarded as unable to make a decision by reason of mental disability if the disability is such that, at the time when the decision needs to be made, he or she is unable to make a decision based on the information relevant to the decision, including information about the reasonably

*foreseeable consequences of deciding one way or another or failing to make the
decision. (Draft Bill, clause 2(2)(b).)*

3.18 In the draft test of incapacity which appeared in the consultation papers
we suggested that a person should be found to lack capacity if he or she was unable
to understand an explanation of the relevant information in broad terms and simple
language. Many respondents supported this attempt to ensure that persons should
not be found to lack capacity unless and until someone has gone to the trouble to
put forward a suitable explanation of the relevant information. This focus requires
an assessor to approach any apparent inability as something which may be dynamic
and changeable. As one commentator to our original draft test has written, we
chose "to import the patient's right to information by implication into the test of
capacity". Further guidance on the way the new statutory language may impinge on
the methods of assessing capacity in day to day practice should be given in a code of
practice accompanying the legislation.

*We recommend that a person should not be regarded as unable to understand the
information relevant to a decision if he or she is able to understand an explanation
of that information in broad terms and simple language. (Draft Bill, clause 2(3).)*

3.19 In the consultation papers we invited views on the need for a proviso
stipulating that a person should not be regarded as lacking capacity because the
decision made would not have been made by a person of ordinary prudence. We
provisionally doubted the need for any such proviso. Those we consulted, however,
overwhelmingly urged upon us the importance of making such an express stipula-
tion. This would emphasise the fact that the "outcome" approach to capacity has
been rejected, while recognising that it is almost certainly in daily use.

*We recommend that a person should not be regarded as unable to make a decision
by reason of mental disability merely because he or she makes a decision which
would not be made by a person of ordinary prudence. (Draft Bill, clause 2(4).)*

(2) Inability to communicate a decision

3.20 As most of our respondents appreciated, we intend the category of people
unable to communicate a decision to be very much a residual category. This test
will have no relevance if the person is known to be incapable of deciding (even if
also unable to communicate) but will be available if the assessor does not know, one
way or the other, whether the person is capable of deciding or not. Contrary to the
views of one expert commentator, "inability to communicate a decision" cannot be
paraphrased as "inability to express a view", nor should it be taken to apply to
persons with the most severe forms of mental disability. This second category is a
fall-back where the assessor cannot say whether any decision has been validly made
or made at all but nonetheless can say that the person concerned cannot
communicate any decision.

3.21 In relation to persons who are simply unconscious, many respondents
made the point that strenuous steps must be taken to assist and facilitate
communication before any finding of incapacity is made. Specialists with appropriate skills in verbal and non-verbal communication should be brought in where
necessary.

*We recommend that a person should not be regarded as unable to communicate his
or her decision unless all practicable steps to enable him or her to do so have been
taken without success. (Draft Bill, clause 2(5).)*

The assessment of incapacity: a code of practice

3.22 Many respondents who commented on our provisional tests of incapacity and were content with the broad outlines of the proposed test addressed themselves to technical questions about the methods of assessment and testing which should be applied. Some were insistent that outdates and discredited psychometric testing should not be used. There was grave concerns about the concept of "mental age". We found the arguments against the use of any such concept extremely compelling. It is unhelpful to discuss, for example, the merits of sterilisation as opposed to barrier contraception for a mature woman with a learning disability on the basis that she is somehow "equivalent" to a child of three. Particular professional bodies, for example the College of Speech and Language Therapists and the British Psychological Society, asserted that their members had the relevant skills to assess mental capacity. Others reminded us that cultural, ethnic and religious values should always be respected by any assessor of capacity. These are all very important matters, albeit not apt subjects for primary legislation. One of the matters which should certainly be covered by a code of practice is the way in which any assessment of capacity should be carried out.

We recommend that the Secretary of State should prepare and from time to time revise a code of practice for the guidance of persons assessing whether a person is or is not without capacity to make a decision or decisions on any matters. (Draft Bill clause 31(1)(a).)

NOTES:

1. As Fennell notes, there is no place in the Law Commission's scheme for the making of decisions which would protect other persons, but would not be in the best interests of the person lacking capacity. The Commission viewed the protection of others as the proper purview of the Mental Health Act 1983 (see Chapter 8). (See P. Fennell, *Treatment Without Consent* London: Routledge, 1996.)

2. Ian Kennedy and Andrew Grubb suggest that by opting for a functional or cognitive test of capacity, which places a premium on *understanding*, the Law Commission is basically endorsing the position adopted at common law. (See I. Kennedy and A. Grubb, "The Law Commission's Proposals: An Introduction" (1994) 2 *Medical Law Review*, 1 at page 4.) It is also very similar to the test for capacity propounded by Buchanan and Brock (see page 269), although it lacks any reference to choice.

3. Gunn notes that in formulating a test for capacity the Law Commission is treading a difficult path. On the one hand, the standard chosen must allow as many people as possible to take their own treatment decisions; but, on the other, it must be recognised that paternalism is justifiable up to a point, and that setting the standard too low could be harmful to the individual. (See M. Gunn, "The Meaning of Incapacity" (1994) 2 *Medical Law Review* 8.)

4. In response to criticism of its earlier proposals, the Law Commission dropped the formulation that an apparent consent may be disregarded if it does not represent a 'true choice' (see Consultation

Paper 128). Commentators were of the view that this could be invoked to override an irrational decision, thereby effectively reverting to an 'outcome' approach to capacity which the Commission had earlier rejected (see for example, P. Fennell, "Statutory Authority to Treat, Relatives and Treatment Proxies" (1994) 2 *Medical Law Review* 30, at page 41). As a result of this criticism, the Law Commission now proposes the formulation in paragraph 3.16.

5. At para 3.21 the Law Commission stresses the importance of communication, and states that all practicable steps should be taken to enable a person to communicate, before she is deemed incompetent. This is also stressed in the guidance for doctors prepared by the BMA and the Law Society (at pages 277–279, above). The significance of this issue is reinforced by Stefan, who argues that " . . . far from being an internal characteristic of an individual, competence is a value judgment arising from an individual's conversation or communication with individuals in positions of power or authority. Essentially, a judgment of incompetence is a judgment by those in power that the conversation has broken down . . . the whole focus of a competence inquiry centers on the alleged incompetent person to the exclusion of the powerful side of the dialogue. Therefore, incompetence is seen as an attribute of the less powerful person and all the failures of communication are attributed to her." (See S. Stefan, "Silencing the Different Voice: Competence, Feminist Theory and Law" (1993) 47 *University of Miami Law Review* 763 at pages 766–7.)

6. Although in paragraph 3.18 the Law Commission discuss the issue of the information required to be given to the patient, precise guidance on the details of the information to be disclosed are left to be fleshed out in a Code of Practice, rather than in the proposed legislation itself.

QUESTIONS:

1. Do you agree with the Law Commission that it is crucial to have a clear test, or was one critical respondent correct in arguing that the whole idea of a test for capacity is ill conceived and unhelpful? (See M. Gunn, "The Meaning of Incapacity" (1994) 2 *Medical Law Review*, 8 at page 13.)

2. Which of the three approaches to capacity — the status, outcome or functional approaches — identified in the Law Commission Report do you prefer? (See P. Fennell, "Statutory Authority to Treat, Relatives and Treatment Proxies" (1994) 2 *Medical Law Review* 30, at pages 33–37.)

3. How does the Law Commission's proposed statutory test of incapacity differ from, and how does it resemble the common law test approved in *Re C*? Which of these two tests do you prefer, and why?

4. Was the Law Commission right to depart from its earlier view that no-one should be found to lack capacity unless he is found to be suffering from a "mental disorder" as defined in the Mental Health Act 1983? (See Chapter 8 for discussion of that definition.) Will the alternative threshold of "mental disability" which it proposes avoid problems of stigma? (See M. Gunn, "Mental Incapacity — the Law Commission's Report" (1995) 17 *Child and Family Law Quarterly* 209.)

5. What makes 'senior members of the judiciary' the appropriate people to make these sort of medical decisions on behalf of the incapacitated?

6. Do you agree with the respondents to the earlier Law Commission papers that there was a need to expressly state that a person should not be regarded as unable to make a decision simply because it was not a prudent decision (paragraph 3.19)?

7. Is it justifiable to leave important details, such as the information to be disclosed, to be incorporated in a Code of Practice, as opposed to spelling out such details in the legislation? (Note the parallels between this proposed scheme and that implemented under the Human Fertilisation and Embryology Act 1990, where much of the detail was left to be implemented in a Code of Practice: see Chapter 11.)

8. Is the law able to fully protect the rights of those deemed to be incompetent given Stefan's argument that, "[c]ompetence is . . . relational and contextual and describes communication. It is not a fixed, inherent characteristic of an individual. The relationships and communications that provide the context in which competence is questioned and assessed are potentially unequal and hierarchial. The law, however, is not structured to take account of these differentials in power." (See S. Stefan, "Silencing the Different Voice: Competence, Feminist Theory and Law" (1993) 47 *University of Miami Law Review* 763 at page 790.)

4. TREATMENT WITHOUT CONSENT

The rules requiring the patient to consent apply only where a legally valid consent is possible. No one is in a position to consent on another adult's behalf, although those with parental responsibility are able to consent on behalf of their children who are under the age of 18 (see Chapter 7). Where a patient is unable to consent, and no one can give a valid consent on his behalf, then different rules apply. In this situation treatment will be lawful if it is in his best interests, as judged by responsible medical opinion.

F v. West Bershire Health Authority [1989] 2 All E.R. 545, [1990] 2 A.C. 1, [1989] 2 W.L.R. 938, [1989] 2 F.L.R. 476

F was a woman of 36 with serious learning difficulties. Her mental age was assessed at five, and her verbal capacity at two. She had been a voluntary in-patient at a mental hospital for over twenty years, and had formed a sexual relationship with a male patient. Expert evidence suggested that it would be disastrous for her to become pregnant. Furthermore, both her mother and the professionals caring for her thought it was best for her to be sterilised. As she was unable to consent, a declaration was sought that the operation would be lawful. The House of Lords held that it had no power to consent on her behalf, but considered whether it would be lawful for the operation to be performed without F's consent. Their Lordships also dealt with issues specific to sterilisation, which are discussed in Chapter 13. Their examination of the more general principles which permit certain types of treatment to be given without consent is extracted below.

LORD BRANDON
". . . At common law a doctor cannot lawfully operate on adult patients of sound mind, or give them any other treatment involving the application of physical force however small (which I shall refer to as 'other treatment'), without their consent. If a doctor were to operate on such patients, or give them other treatment, without their consent, he would commit the actionable tort of trespass to the person. There are, however, cases where adult patients cannot give or refuse their consent to an operation or other treatment. One case is where, as a result of an accident or otherwise, an adult patient is unconscious and an operation or other treatment cannot be safely delayed until he or she recovers consciousness. Another case is where a patient, though adult, cannot by reason of mental disability understand the nature or purpose of an operation or other treatment. The common law would be seriously defective if it failed to provide a solution to the problem created by such inability to consent. In my opinion, however, the common law does not fail. In my opinion, the solution to the problem which the common law provides is that a doctor can lawfully operate on, or give other treatment to, adult patients who are incapable, for one reason or another, of consenting to his doing so, provided that the operation or other treatment concerned is in the best interests of such patients. The operation or other treatment will be in their best interests if, but only if, it is carried out in order either to save their lives or to ensure improvement or prevent deterioration in their physical or mental health.

Different views have been put forward with regard to the principle which makes it lawful for a doctor to operate on or give other treatment to adult patients without their consent . . . The Court of Appeal in the present case regarded the matter as depending on the public interest. I would not disagree with that as a broad proposition, but I think that it is helpful to consider the principle in accordance with which the public interest leads to this result. In my opinion, the principle is that, when persons lack the capacity, for whatever reason, to take decisions about the performance of operations on them, or the giving of other medical treatment to them, it is necessary that some other person or persons, with the appropriate qualifications, should take such decisions for them. Otherwise they would be deprived of medical care which they need and to which they are entitled.

In many cases, however, it will not only be lawful for doctors, on the ground of necessity, to operate on or give other medical treatment to adult patients disabled from giving their consent: it will also be their common law duty to do so.

In the case of adult patients made unconscious by an accident or otherwise, they will normally be received into the casualty department of a hospital, which thereby undertakes the care of them. It will then be the duty of the doctors at that hospital to use their best endeavours to do, by way of either an operation or other treatment, that which is in the best interests of such patients . . .

The application of the principle which I have described means that the lawfulness of a doctor operating on, or giving other treatment to, an adult patient disabled from giving consent will depend not on any approval or sanction of a court but on the question whether the operation or other treatment is in the best interests of the patient concerned. That is, from a practical point of view, just as well, for, if every operation to be performed, or other treatment to be given, required the approval or sanction of the court, the whole process of medical care for such patients would grind to a halt . . .

There is one further matter with which I think that it is necessary to deal. That is the standard which the court should apply in deciding whether a proposed operation is or is not in the best interests of the patient. With regard to this Scott Baker J said:

'I do not think they [the doctors] are liable in battery where they are acting in good faith and reasonably in the best interests of their patients. I doubt whether the test is very different from that for negligence.'

This was a reference to the test laid down in *Bolam v. Friern Hospital Management Committee* [1957] 2 All E.R. 118, namely that a doctor will not be negligent if he establishes that he acted in accordance with a practice accepted at the time by a responsible body of medical opinion skilled in the particular form of treatment in question.

All three members of the Court of Appeal considered that the Bolam test was insufficiently stringent for deciding whether an operation or other medical treatment was in a patient's best interests. Lord Donaldson M.R. said:

'Just as the law and the courts rightly pay great, but not decisive, regard to accepted professional wisdom in relation to the duty of care in the law of medical negligence (the *Bolam* test), so they equally would have regard to such wisdom in relation to decisions whether or not and how to treat incompetent patients in the context of the law of trespass to the person. However, both the medical profession and the courts have to keep the special status of such a patient in the forefront of their minds. The ability of the ordinary adult patient to exercise a free choice in deciding whether to accept or to refuse medical treatment and to choose between treatments is not to be dismissed as desirable but inessential. It is a crucial factor in relation to all medical treatment. If it is necessarily absent, whether temporarily in an emergency situation or permanently in a case of mental disability, other things being equal there must be greater caution in deciding whether to treat and, if so, how to treat, although I do not agree that this extends to limiting doctors to treatment on the necessity for which there are "no two views" (per Wood J. in *T v. T* [1988] 1 All E.R. 613 at 621). There will always or usually be a minority view and this approach, if strictly applied, would often rule out all treatment. On the other hand, the existence of a significant minority view would constitute a serious contra-indication.'

Neill L.J. said:

'I have therefore come to the conclusion that, if the operation is necessary and the proper safeguards are observed, the performance of a serious operation, including an operation for sterilisation, on a person who by reason of a lack of mental capacity is unable to give his or her consent is not a trespass to the person or otherwise unlawful. It therefore becomes necessary to consider what is meant by "a necessary operation". In seeking to define the circumstances in which an operation can properly be carried out Scott Baker J said: "I do not think they are liable in battery where they are acting in good faith and reasonably in the best interests of their patients. I doubt whether the test is very different from that for negligence." With respect, I do not consider that this test is sufficiently stringent. A doctor may defeat a claim in negligence if he establishes that he acted in accordance with a practice accepted at the time as proper by a responsible body of medical opinion skilled in the particular form of treatment in question. This is the test laid down in *Bolam v. Friern Hospital Management Committee*. But to say that it is not negligent to carry out a particular form of treatment does not mean that that treatment is necessary. I would define necessary in this context as that which the general body of medical opinion in the particular specialty would consider to be in the best interests of the patient in order to maintain the health and to secure the well-being of the patient. One cannot expect unanimity but it should be possible to say of an operation which is necessary in the relevant sense that it would be unreasonable in the opinion of most experts in the field not to make the operation available to the patient. One must consider the alternatives to an operation and the dangers or disadvantages to which the patient may be exposed if no action is taken. The question becomes: what action does the patient's health and welfare require?'

Butler-Sloss L.J. agreed with Neill L.J.

With respect to the Court of Appeal, I do not agree that the *Bolam* test is inapplicable to cases of performing operations on, or giving other treatment to, adults incompetent to give consent. In order that the performance of such operations on, and the giving of such other treatment to, such adults should be lawful, they must be in their best interests. If doctors were to be required, in deciding whether an operation or other treatment was in the best interests of adults incompetent to give consent, to apply some test more stringent than the *Bolam* test, the result would be that such adults would, in some circumstances at least, be deprived of the benefit of medical treatment which adults competent to give consent would enjoy. In my opinion it would be wrong for the law, in its concern to protect such adults, to produce such a result . . .''

LORD GRIFFITHS
''. . . In a civilised society the mentally incompetent must be provided with medical and nursing care and those who look after them must do their best for them. Stated in legal terms the doctor who undertakes responsibility for the treatment of a mental patient who is incapable of giving consent to treatment must give the treatment that he considers to be in the best interests of his patient, and the standard of care required of the doctor will be that laid down in *Bolam v. Friern Hospital Management Committee* [1957] 2 All E.R. 118 . . .''

LORD GOFF
''. . . On what principle can medical treatment be justified when given without consent? We are searching for a principle on which, in limited circumstances, recognition may be given to a need, in the interests of the patient, that treatment should be given to him in circumstances where he is (temporarily or permanently) disabled from consenting to it. It is this criterion of a need which points to the principle of necessity as providing justification.

That there exists in the common law a principle of necessity which may justify action which would otherwise be unlawful is not in doubt. But historically the principle has been seen to be restricted to two groups of cases, which have been called cases of public necessity and cases of private necessity. The former occurred when a man interfered with another man's property in the public interest, for example (in the days before we could dial 999 for the fire brigade) the destruction of another man's house to prevent the spread of a catastrophic fire, as indeed occurred in the Great Fire of London in 1666. The latter cases occurred when a man interfered with another's property to save his own person or property from imminent danger, for example when he entered on his neighbour's land without his consent in order to prevent the spread of fire onto his own land.

There is, however, a third group of cases, which is also properly described as founded on the principle of necessity and which is more pertinent to the resolution of the problem in the present case. These cases are concerned with action taken as a matter of necessity to assist another person without his consent. To give a simple example, a man who seizes another and forcibly drags him from the path of an oncoming vehicle, thereby saving him from injury or even death, commits no wrong. But there are many emanations of this principle, to be found scattered through the books. These are concerned not only with the preservation of the life or health of the assisted person, but also with the preservation of his property (sometimes an animal, sometimes an ordinary chattel) and even to certain conduct on his behalf in the administration of his affairs. Where there is a pre-existing relationship between the parties, the intervener is usually said to act as an agent of necessity on behalf of the principal in whose interests he acts, and his action can often, with not too much artificiality, be referred to the pre-existing relationship between them. Whether the intervener may be entitled either to reimbursement or to remuneration raises separate questions which are not relevant to the present case.

We are concerned here with action taken to preserve the life, health or well-being of another who is unable to consent to it. Such action is sometimes said to be justified as arising from an emergency; in Prosser and Keeton *Torts* (5th edn, 1984) page 117 the action is said to be privileged by the emergency. Doubtless, in the case of a person of sound mind, there will ordinarily have to be an emergency before such action taken without consent can be lawful; for otherwise there would be an opportunity to communicate with the assisted person and to seek his consent. But this is not always so; and indeed the historical origins of the principle of necessity do not point to emergency as such as providing the criterion of lawful intervention without consent . . . But, when a person is rendered incapable of communication either permanently or over a considerable period of time (through illness or accident or mental disorder), it would be an unusual use of language to describe the case as one of 'permanent emergency', if indeed such a state of affairs can properly be said to exist. In truth, the relevance of an emergency is that it may give rise to a necessity to act in the interests of the assisted person without first obtaining his consent. Emergency is however not the criterion or even a prerequisite; it is simply a frequent origin of the necessity which impels intervention. The principle is one of necessity, not of emergency.

We can derive some guidance as to the nature of the principle of necessity from the cases on agency of necessity in mercantile law . . . . [F]rom them can be derived the basic requirements, applicable in these cases of necessity, that, to fall within the principle, not only (1) must there be a necessity to act when it is not practicable to communicate with the assisted person, but also (2) the action taken must be such as a reasonable person would in all the circumstances take, acting in the best interests of the assisted person.

On this statement of principle, I wish to observe that officious intervention cannot be justified by the principle of necessity. So intervention cannot be justified when another more appropriate person is available and willing to act; nor can it be justified when it is contrary to the known wishes of the assisted person, to the extent that he is capable of rationally forming such a wish. On the second limb of the principle, the introduction of the standard of a reasonable man should not in the present context be regarded as materially different from that of Sir Montague Smith's 'wise and prudent man', because a reasonable man would, in the time available to him, proceed with wisdom and prudence before taking action in relation to another man's person or property without his consent. I shall have more to say on this point later. Subject to that, I hesitate at present to indulge in any greater refinement of the principle, being well aware of many problems which may arise in its application, problems which it is not necessary, for present purposes, to examine. But as a general rule, if the above criteria are fulfilled, interference with the assisted person's person or property (as the case may be) will not be unlawful. Take the example of a railway accident, in which injured passengers are trapped in the wreckage. It is this principle which may render lawful the actions of other citizens, railway staff, passengers or outsiders, who rush to give aid and comfort to the victims: the surgeon who amputates the limb of an unconscious passenger to free him from the wreckage; the ambulance man who conveys him to hospital; the doctors and nurses who treat him and care for him while he is still unconscious. Take the example of an elderly person who suffers a stroke which renders him incapable of speech or movement. It is by virtue of this principle that the doctor who treats him, the nurse who cares for him, even the relative or friend or neighbour who comes in to look after him will commit no wrong when he or she touches his body.

The two examples I have given illustrate, in the one case, an emergency and, in the other, a permanent or semi-permanent state of affairs. Another example of the latter kind is that of a mentally disordered person who is disabled from giving consent. I can see no good reason why the principle of necessity should not be applicable in his case as it is in the case of the victim of a stroke. Furthermore, in the case of a mentally disordered person, as in the case of a stroke victim, the permanent state of affairs calls for a wider range of care than may be requisite in an emergency which arises from accidental injury. When the state of affairs is permanent, or semi-permanent, action properly taken to preserve the life, health or well-being of the assisted person may well transcend such measures as surgical operation or substantial medical treatment and may extend to include such humdrum matters as routine medical or dental treatment, even simple care such as dressing and undressing and putting to bed.

The distinction I have drawn between cases of emergency and cases where the state of affairs is (more or less) permanent is relevant in another respect. We are here concerned with medical treatment, and I limit myself to cases of that kind. Where, for example, a surgeon performs an operation without his consent on a patient temporarily rendered unconscious in an accident, he should do no more than is reasonably required, in the best interests of the patient, before he recovers consciousness. I can see no practical difficulty arising from this requirement, which derives from the fact that the patient is expected before long to regain consciousness and can then be consulted about longer term measures. The point has however arisen in a more acute form where a surgeon, in the course of an operation, discovers some other condition which, in his opinion, requires operative treatment for which he has not received the patient's consent. In what circumstances he should operate forthwith, and in what circumstances he should postpone the further treatment until he has received the patient's consent, is a difficult matter which has troubled the Canadian courts (see *Marshall v. Curry* [1933] 3 D.L.R. 260 and *Murray v. McMurchy* [1949] 2 D.L.R. 442), but which it is not necessary for your Lordships to consider in the present case.

But where the state of affairs is permanent or semi-permanent, as may be so in the case of a mentally disordered person, there is no point in waiting to obtain the patient's consent. The need to care for him is obvious; and the doctor must then act in the best interests of his patient, just as if he had received his patient's consent so to do. Were this not so, much useful treatment and care could, in theory at least, be denied to the unfortunate. It follows that, on this point, I am unable to accept the view expressed by Neill L.J. in the Court of Appeal, that the treatment must be shown to have been necessary. Moreover, in such a case, as my noble and learned friend Lord Brandon has pointed out, a doctor who has assumed responsibility for the care of a patient may not only be treated as having the patient's consent to act, but also be under a duty so to act. I find myself to be respectfully in agreement with Lord Donaldson M.R. when he said:

'I see nothing incongruous in doctors and others who have a caring responsibility being required, when acting in relation to an adult who is incompetent, to exercise a right of choice in exactly the same way as would the court or reasonable parents in relation to a child, making due allowance, of course, for the fact that the patient is not a child, and I am satisfied that that is what the law does in fact require.'

In these circumstances, it is natural to treat the deemed authority and the duty as interrelated. But I feel bound to express my opinion that, in principle, the lawfulness of the doctor's action is, at least in its origin, to be found in the principle of necessity. This can perhaps be seen most clearly in cases where there is no continuing relationship between doctor and patient. The 'doctor in the house' who volunteers to assist a lady in the audience who, overcome by the drama or by the heat in the theatre, has fainted away is impelled to act by no greater duty than that imposed by his own Hippocratic oath. Furthermore, intervention can be justified in the case of a non-professional, as well as a professional, man or woman who has no pre-existing relationship with the assisted person, as in the case of a stranger who rushes to assist an injured man after an accident. In my opinion, it is the necessity itself which provides the justification for the intervention.

I have said that the doctor has to act in the best interests of the assisted person. In the case of routine treatment of mentally disordered persons, there should be little difficulty in applying this principle. In the case of more serious treatment, I recognise that its application may create problems for the medical profession; however, in making decisions about treatment, the doctor must act in accordance with a responsible and competent body of relevant professional opinion, on the principles set down in *Bolam v. Friern Hospital Management Committee* [1957] 2 All E.R. 118. No doubt, in practice, a decision may involve others besides the doctor. It must surely be good practice to consult relatives and others who are concerned with the care of the patient. Sometimes, of course, consultation with a specialist or specialists will be required; and in others, especially where the decision involves more than a purely medical opinion, an inter-disciplinary team will in practice participate in the decision. It is very difficult, and would be unwise, for a court to do more than to stress that, for those who are involved in these important and sometimes difficult decisions, the overriding consideration is that they should act in the best interests of the person who suffers from the misfortune of being prevented by incapacity from deciding for himself what should be done to his own body in his own best interests . . ."

NOTES:

1. Since the passage of the Mental Health Act 1959 (which effectively codified state powers in relation to the mentally disordered but omitted to deal with the issue of consent to treatment) the old *parens patriae* jurisdiction of the court has been placed in abeyance, since no one has been entrusted with the power to exercise it. The earlier sterilisation cases of *Re B (a minor) (wardship: sterilisation)* [1987] 2 All E.R. 206 and *T v. T* [1988] 1 All E.R. 613 (see Chapter 13 at pages 754–773) marked the beginning of a dramatic development in the inherent jurisdiction of the High Court to make declarations. This process received the approval of the House of Lords in *F*, and has come to be used as a mechanism for authorising treatment of incompetent adults without their consent. One problem with the declaratory jurisdiction is that the possibility of using it only arises where there is some question of legality. Furthermore, the declaratory procedure does not alter the legal position of the parties — it

merely states what that position is. (See I. Kennedy, "Emerging
Problems of Medical Technology and the Law" in E. G. Baldwin (ed)
The Cambridge Lectures London: Butterworths, 1984; J. Bridgeman,
"Declared Innocent?" (1995) 3 *Medical Law Review* 117; P. Fennell,
Treatment Without Consent London: Routledge, 1996 at pages 242–
254.)

2. The House of Lords unanimously decided that sterilisation was in F's
best interests, and would therefore be lawful, even though no consent
had been given. The effect of the decison has been to give health care
professionals common law authority to treat incapacitated persons.
(See P. Fennell, "Statutory Authority to Treat, Relatives and Treatment Proxies" (1994) 2 *Medical Law Review*, 30.)

3. Following the decision in *F*, treatment is necessary in a patient's best
interests if it is carried out in order to save life, or to ensure
improvement or prevent deterioration in his health. If the doctor
believes that such treatment is not required in her patient's best
interests, to give it would amount to a battery. (See Chapter 6.)

4. One of the most disturbing features of this case is the fact that it
contains no debate on the presence or absence of capacity —
incapacity was simply assumed. (See M. Gunn, "The Meaning of
Incapacity" (1994) 2 *Medical Law Review* 8, at page 9.) McLean has
suggested that most of the decisions to sterilise young women start
from a similar presumption of incapacity (see S. McLean, *A Patient's
Right to Know*, Aldershot: Dartmouth, 1989 at page 67, and cases
discussed in Chapter 13 at pages 754–773).

5. Furthermore, as Grubb argues, even if the Law Lords were right that
F had never been competent, they should at least have contemplated
the possibility of tests other than that of "best interests". For
instance, they failed to consider the "substituted judgment" test (see
pages 304–306 below) which may be workable in the case of some
patients. (See A. Grubb, "Treatment decisions: keeping it in the
family" in A. Grubb (ed) *Choices and Decisions in Health Care*
Chichester: Wiley, 1993.)

6. Brazier identifies another major concern about the decision in *F*,
which derives from the suspicion that it (like some of the consent
cases in relation to children — see Chapter 7) protects doctors more
than patients. According to the House of Lords the courts are not
required to take an active role in investigating the propriety of the
medical treatment, which is measured against the *Bolam* standard.
(See M. Brazier, *Medicine, Patients and the Law* (2nd ed.), Harmondsworth: Penguin, 1992 at pages 98–100.)

7. One of the issues discussed in *F* was whether certain categories of
case should always be brought to court. The general view of the
House of Lords was that it would be advisable, although not
technically obligatory to bring sterilisation cases to court (see Chapter
13 at pages 754–773). In the Court of Appeal in *F*, it was suggested

that non-regenerative organ donation and abortion were in a similar category. However, it has since been held that abortions need not be considered by the courts in advance (*Re SG (a Patient)* [1991] 2 F.L.R. 329). With regard to sterilisation, the decision in *Re GF (medical treatment)* [1992] 1 F.L.R. 293 suggests that a second opinion which supports the intended operation may well provide a strong indication that it is lawful (see Chapter 13 at page 772). It would seem that sterilistion for therapeutic reasons are now routinely authorised. (See P. Fennell, *Treatment Without Consent* London: Routledge, 1996, pages 244–9.) (For the position in relation to organ transplantation, see Chapter 15, and for that pertaining to with-drawal of life sustaining treatment see Chapter 14.)

QUESTIONS:

1. Does the law as declared in *F* draw any distinction between cases where the unavailability of consent is temporary or permanent?

2. How far are the known wishes of a patient relevant to determining whether treatment is in his best interests?

3. Was the House of Lords right in *F* to devolve decision-making power to the medical carers rather than upon family members, especially given that it is the family who are entrusted with decision-making responsibility in the case of incompetent children? (See Chapter 7 and A. Grubb, "Treatment decisions: keeping it in the family" in A. Grubb (ed) *Choices and Decisions in Health Care* Chichester: Wiley, 1993.)

4. What should a surgeon do if she discovers an unexpected malignant cancerous growth during an operation, and she believes that it should be removed as soon as possible? May she ever proceed without the patient's consent?

5. What objections are there to applying the *Bolam* test to determine whether treatment without consent is lawful? (See P. Fennell, "Inscribing Paternalism in Law: Consent to Treatment and Mental Disorder" (1990) 17 *Journal of Law and Society* 29; D. Carson, "The Sexuality of People with Learning Difficulties" [1989] *Journal of Social Welfare Law* 335.)

6. How valid is Lord Brandon's point that the courts would be overwhelmed if they had to approve the treatment of every patient unable to give consent? Does this comment suggest the need to create some other mechanism to review such decisions?

7. Would a better test have been to adopt that proposed by Wood J. in *T v. T* [1988] 1 All E.R. 613 at 621 (and rejected by Lord Brandon at page 289 above), that doctors may only treat a patient unable to give consent if there are 'no two views' about what is in that patient's best interests? (See J. E. S. Fortin, "Sterilisation, The Mentally Ill and Consent to Treatment" (1988) 51 *M.L.R.* 634.)

The subsequent case of *Re S* [1995] 3 All E.R. 290 emphasises the inadequacy of the current law on decision-making by incompetent adults. It represents an important development in the evolution of the declaratory jurisdiction of the High Court. Although it is clear that the declaratory procedure has become the established procedure where private law questions arise in relation to medical treatment (See P. Fennell, *Treatment Without Consent* London: Routledge, 1996 at pages 242–254) this was the first time that the court has been faced with the question of the *locus standi* (legal standing) of interested parties to invoke the court's declaratory jurisdiction. The patient in this case was clearly incompetent. The issue for the court was whether there was some other legal justification for a proposed type of medical treatment, given that S. was unable to decide the matter for himself and communicate his decision. The judgment goes some way to redressing the problem, by holding that in exercising its jurisdiction to grant declaratory relief the court would not insist on the demonstration of a specific legal right by a party who sought a declaration which was relevant to the medical treatment which the patient would receive.

Re S (Hospital Patient: Court's Jurisdiction) [1995] 3 All E.R. 290

S was a wealthy Norwegian national who suffered a serious disabling stroke. At that time he was 74 and living in England with his companion Mrs A. Following his stroke he was admitted to a private hospital near their home. He was incapable of exercising his right to choose the nature and extent of his physical care. Mrs A visited him regularly and showed a close interest in his welfare. S's son, in collusion with S's wife (to whom S had not been close since the early years of his marriage), and with the knowledge of S's consultant, attempted to remove S from the hospital and fly him to Norway. Having heard of the plan, Mrs A secured an injunction to restrain the son from removing S from the jurisdiction, and then successfully sought a declaration that it would be unlawful to remove him. from the jurisdiction, because it was not in his best interests to do so. She argued that he wished to remain in England close to her — a claim supported by members of the nursing staff caring for him. S's wife and son appealed, contending that the court did not have the jurisdiction to grant declaratory and injunctive relief where there were no rights or obligations existing or likely to exist between the parties.

SIR THOMAS BINGHAM M.R.
". . . In her judgment ([1995] 1 All E.R. 449, [1995] 2 W.L.R. 38) Hale J reviewed the leading authorities on declarations and said:
'The position may be different in public law but this is a case about private rights. All of these authorities lead me to the conclusion that, although it is not necessary to establish a cause of action, it is necessary to show that the plaintiff's own legal position will in some way be resolved by the granting of the declaration. It is noteworthy that in *F v. West Berkshire Health Authority* [1989] 2 All E.R. 545, the plaintiff was the patient herself, suing by her mother as next friend. In *Airedale NHS Trust v. Bland* [1993] 1 All E.R. 821, the plaintiff was

the National Health Service Trust which was caring for the patient. It is argued by the Official Solicitor, however, that as the plaintiff is seeking to undertake the care of the patient in their own home, her own legal position will be affected by the relief she seeks. He also argues that there are sound policy reasons for allowing a person in her situation to invoke the court's jurisdiction. For it would be wrong if the legality of the actions of the current *de facto* carer could not be challenged by others, at least if they wished themselves to undertake the patient's care and had an arguable case for doing so. After all, if the parties' positions had been reversed and the defendant prevented from taking the patient away, he would now be seeking the assistance of this court in exactly the same way. Yet although his relationship to the patient is a close one, and his wishes are of course worthy of respect, he has no more legal right to decide the patient's future than has the plaintiff. Indeed, were this to be a Mental Health Act case, the facts might be such that the plaintiff (rather than the wife) would be the patient's nearest relative for the purposes of s.26 of the Mental Health Act 1983. For all these reasons I hold that, even if it is necessary for the proposed relief to concern the plaintiff's own legal position, the plaintiff was entitled to launch these proceedings in her own name. If that is not necessary and a 'sufficient interest' is all that is required, I hold that her relationship with the patient, extending over the past five years, their common home together for the six months before his stroke, the access he gave her to the funds which have financed his care for the past year, the concern she has shown by her regular and frequent visits, and her desire now to provide care for him herself outside hospital, all together amount to such an interest.' (See [1995] 1 All E.R. 449 at 457–458.)

Since the matter came before the judge at an interlocutory stage, she was not asked to and did not make a declaration. It is accepted that if the plaintiff had a standing which entitled her to ask the court in the exercise of its discretion to grant a declaration, it was appropriate for the court to preserve the position pending a final hearing by granting an injunction. If, on the other hand, the court lacked jurisdiction to grant a declaration, then it could have had no jurisdiction to grant an interlocutory injunction. Thus this appeal by the wife and son against the decision of Hale J. squarely raises the issue of jurisdiction.

III

On behalf of S's wife and son, Sir Louis Blom-Cooper Q.C. acknowledged that the court would have jurisdiction to grant declaratory relief on the application of the Official Solicitor as guardian *ad litem* representing S, or on the application of the private hospital in which S is a patient. He further accepted that if, as he contended, the court had no jurisdiction to grant relief on the application of a person such as the plaintiff, the law was seriously defective, since a course of action which might be inconsistent with S's best interests might be accomplished before it was practicable to invoke the aid of the court to prevent it. He none the less submitted that on existing authority the court had no jurisdiction to grant relief to the plaintiff. He described her action as 'misconceived'. He submitted that the grant of declaratory relief under R.S.C. Ord. 15, r.16 was unjustified. He submitted that the learned judge had seriously misunderstood some of the leading authorities, and he argued that the judge's decision represented an heroic but unjustified attempt to remedy a gap in the law. The basis of these submissions was that the court had no jurisdiction to grant declaratory and injunctive relief at the suit of the plaintiff against S's wife and son in circumstances (a) where there were no rights or obligations existing or likely to exist as between the parties to this private law suit (namely the plaintiff and S's wife and son), and (b) where the claim involved the inability of a mentally incapable adult to exercise his inalienable right to choose the nature and extent of his physical care.

Counsel for the plaintiff and for the Official Solicitor submitted that the jurisdiction of the court to grant declaratory relief was not so limited. They relied on a number of expansive judicial statements on the jurisdiction of the court, and, in particular, on a number of recent cases in which courts at all levels, confronted with the need to give guidance on questions of pressing and sometimes vital concern, had developed the declaratory judgment as a flexible and beneficial remedy without meticulous regard to the standing of a plaintiff who could show good reason for seeking the assistance of the court.

IV

The jurisdiction of the court to grant declaratory relief is not conferred, but is regulated by Ord. 15, r. 16 . . . The rule provides:
'No action or other proceeding shall be open to objection on the ground that a merely declaratory judgment or order is sought thereby, and the Court may make binding declarations of right whether or not any consequential relief is or could be claimed.'

The Master of the Rolls proceeded to discuss a number of these recent cases, including *Gouriet v. Union of Post Office Workers* [1977] 3 All E.R. 70, *Royal College of Nursing of the U.K. v. Dept of Health and Social Security* [1981] 1 All E.R. 545, *Gillick v. West Norfolk and Wisbech Area Health Authority* [1985] 3 All E.R. 402, *F. v. West Berkshire Health Authority* [1989] 2 All E.R. 545, *Re T (adult: refusal of medical treatment)* [1992] 4 All E.R. 649, and *Airedale NHS Trust v. Bland* [1993] 1 All E.R. 821.

He concluded:
. . . As observed in Zamir and Woolf, *The Declaratory Judgment* (2nd edn, 1993) p. 43, para. 3.008 with reference to the *Royal College of Nursing*, *Gillick*, *Re F* and *Bland* cases:
'Collectively, these cases appear to constitute the development of a new advisory declaratory jurisdiction.'

V

(1) The law respects the right of adults of sound mind to physical autonomy. Generally speaking, no one is entitled to touch, examine or operate upon such persons without their consent, express or implied. It is up to such persons to give or withhold consent as they wish, for reasons good or bad.
(2) This simple rule cannot be applied in cases of minors and those subject to serious mental illness, because they may be unable to form or express any, or any reliable, judgment of where their best interests lie. In such situations the law provides for parents or next friends or guardians to speak for the minor or the mental patient.
(3) Those rendered unconscious or inarticulate by accident, or sudden illness such as afflicted S, pose another but less familiar problem. I shall, for convenience and in no technical sense, refer to such persons as 'patients'. Patients cannot express preferences like rational, conscious adults.
(4) The consequence of this inability is not that the treatment of patients is regarded by the courts as a matter of indifference, nor that patients are regarded as having no best interests. Instead, in cases of controversy and cases involving momentous and irrevocable decisions, the courts have treated as justiciable any genuine question as to what the best interests of a patient require or justify. In making these decisions the courts have recognised the desirability of informing

those involved whether a proposed course of conduct will render them criminally or civilly liable; they have acknowledged their duty to act as a safeguard against malpractice, abuse and unjustified action; and they have recognised the desirability, in the last resort, of decisions being made by an impartial, independent tribunal.

(5) In none of the cases cited to us has an applicant for declaratory relief failed on purely procedural grounds. Thus the Royal College of Nursing, Mrs Gillick, doctors, hospital authorities and relatives (whether next friend of the patient or not) have all obtained relief or been held entitled in principle to do so. It cannot of course be suggested that any stranger or officious busybody, however remotely connected with a patient or with the subject matter of proceedings, can properly seek or obtain declaratory or any other relief (in private law any more than public law proceedings). But it can be suggested that where a serious justiciable issue is brought before the court by a party with a genuine and legitimate interest in obtaining a decision against an adverse party the court will not impose nice tests to determine the precise legal standing of that claimant.

(6) There is nothing in the existing evidence to suggest that the decision whether S should remain here or be returned to Norway is likely to have consequences as momentous and final as the decisions in issue in most of the decided cases. One may be confident that standards of medical treatment and nursing care will be of the highest in both countries. But the evidence does not suggest that S, like a patient in a persistent vegetative state, is immune from pain and incapable of emotion. So it would not be safe, certainly at this stage, to assume that S has no preferences about his future care and residence, even though he cannot express them. I have no doubt that the substantial issue in this case is a serious justiciable issue, involving as it potentially does the happiness and welfare of a helpless human being.

(7) When S suffered his stroke, it is plain that the plaintiff assumed the duty of ensuring that he was properly cared for. Having assumed that duty, she was at risk if she failed to discharge it: see *R v. Stone, R v. Dobinson* [1977] 2 All E.R. 341. She did discharge it. She arranged for S to be treated and cared for at the private hospital. If she made that contract as a principal, no one is prima facie entitled to vary or interfere with performance of it without the consent of either contracting party. If, perhaps more probably, she made the contract as an agent for S, deriving her authority from necessity, then she remains an agent authorised to safeguard the performance of the contract unless and until the best interests of S are shown to require a change in the arrangements. Although the wife and son of S have ties of affinity and blood with him which the plaintiff lacks, these ties confer no legal right to determine the course of S's treatment: see *Re T (adult: refusal of medical treatment)* [1992] 4 All E.R. 649 at 653 per Lord Donaldson of Lymington M.R. If it is necessary for the plaintiff to demonstrate in herself a specific legal right which is liable to be infringed by the proposed action of the wife and the son, then in my view the plaintiff does so. But to insist on demonstration of a specific legal right in this sensitive and socially important area of the law is, in my view, to confine the inherent jurisdiction of the court within an inappropriate straitjacket. The matters which the learned judge listed in her judgment are in my view quite enough to show that the plaintiff is far from being a stranger or an officious busybody, and that is in my view enough to give the court jurisdiction.

(8) I would be very reluctant to accept that the law is as defective as the argument of Sir Louis Blom-Cooper supposes. In practical terms neither the Official Solicitor nor the hospital management could have been expected to act in time to prevent the removal of S. The plaintiff could in theory have instituted proceedings to obtain a writ of habeas corpus, but a procedure designed to procure release from illegal imprisonment would scarcely have been appropriate to determine where S's best interests require him to be cared for. If the law were powerless to give practical help in cases such as this, the invitation to others similarly placed in future to take the law into their own hands, with the risk at least of unseemly tussles and at worst of violence, would be obvious. This is pre-eminently an area in which the common

law should respond to social needs as they are manifested, case by case. Any statutory rule, unless framed in terms so wide as to give the court an almost unlimited discretion, would be bound to impose an element of inflexibility which would in my view be wholly undesirable.

I would dismiss the appeal of S's wife and son and uphold the decision of the judge, very much for the reasons which she gave."

MILLETT L.J.

"This is not a case about medical treatment or the withdrawal of medical treatment, nor is it a case about the provision or withdrawal of care. It is in effect a custody dispute between two parties each of whom claims the right to look after an elderly gentleman (whom I will call 'the patient') in accordance with what each of them plausibly asserts he would wish if he were not by reason of incapacity unable to formulate or communicate his wishes. Formerly the court would have resolved the dispute by exercising its *parens patriae* jurisdiction, but as Lord Donaldson M.R. pointed out in *F v. West Berkshire Health Authority* [1989] 2 All E.R. 545 that jurisdiction was taken away from the courts in 1960, possibly in the mistaken belief that they had been given all the necessary powers by the Mental Health Act 1959.

It is clear from the authorities (and was conceded before us) that the court would have jurisdiction to determine the dispute if the proceedings were brought by the patient himself acting by the Official Solicitor; or by the hospital authority seeking guidance from the court as to the course it should take. The circumstances of the case did not admit of the former course, and the hospital authority cannot be compelled to adopt the latter. It follows, however, that it is a case about the plaintiff's standing, not about the court's jurisdiction save in the narrow sense that the court may be said to have no jurisdiction to grant relief to a person with no standing to seek it.

The increasing number of elderly and incapacitated dependants who are unable to formulate and articulate their wishes but who are expected to be cared for in the community, and the growing number of persons who for one reason or another have more than one family wishing to undertake responsibility for them, mean that disputes of the present kind are likely to recur with increasing frequency. They are justiciable in proceedings brought by the proper party, yet unless the court is willing to entertain proceedings brought by the parties who claim the responsibility for looking after the patient it will often not be possible to bring proceedings at all. In such circumstances the parties are likely to resort to self-help. This would be a lamentable state of affairs and would in my judgment represent a serious abdication of responsibility by the court.

On behalf of the patient's wife and son it was argued that, in private law proceedings like the present, it is not sufficient for a party who asks the court to grant a declaration to demonstrate that he has a legitimate interest in obtaining it. He need not assert a cause of action, but he must have a legal right to obtain relief. There must, it was submitted, be some legal relationship between the parties giving rise to mutual rights and obligations capable of being the subject matter of the declaration sought. In the present case there is no legal relationship between the plaintiff on the one hand and the patient's wife and son on the other. They have competing claims; but neither of them is asserting any legal right of its own. Each of them, no doubt for commendable reasons, wishes to undertake responsibility for the future welfare of the patient; and each of them may feel under a moral or social duty to assume such responsibility. But neither of them has any legal right or duty to do so; the legal right to choose where he should live and the nature and extent of his medical and other care is the right of the patient and no one else.

Millett L.J. then proceeded to examine cases which had considered the jurisdiction of the court to grant declaratory relief:

Since [*Gouriet v. Union of Post Office Workers* [1977] 3 All E.R. 70] the courts have developed the jurisdiction to grant declaratory relief in a number of cases which, though distinguishable from the present, are nevertheless not altogether dissimilar to it. We have now reached a position where the court is prepared in an appropriate case to fill much of the lacuna left by the disappearance of the parens patriae jurisdiction by granting something approaching an advisory declaration . . .

The layman would, I think, be astonished to be told that the plaintiff had sufficient legal standing to set in motion the process of medical treatment which the patient's condition required and to decide where he should be treated but lacked sufficient legal standing to set in motion the legal proceedings which later became necessary in order to decide where he should live. He would also be surprised to learn that, while the court had jurisdiction to decide that issue in proceedings brought by the patient himself joining the rival claimants as defendants, it had no jurisdiction to decide it in proceedings brought by either claimant joining the other claimant and the patient himself as defendants. He would conclude *inter alia* that the objection must be technical and procedural.

If the patient were a sack of potatoes, instead of a living person unable by reason of incapacity of making his wishes known, the court would have undoubted jurisdiction to resolve any dispute between rival claimants. It would do so by resort to considerations of legal title and possession. Why should it make a difference that the subject matter of the dispute is the right to look after a human being, and that the resolution of the dispute depends upon ascertaining his wishes or, if they cannot be ascertained, by determining what is in his best interest and inferring that that is what he would wish?

The answer given is that the so-called right is not a legal right at all, but rather a social or moral duty; and that the only legal rights which are in question are rights which belong to the patient. If necessary, I would hold that a claim to be allowed without interference to look after an elderly and incapacitated relative or other person in accordance with his presumed wishes is a legal right which the court will recognise and protect, and not merely a moral or social obligation.

But I do not think that it is necessary. The patient has a legal right to decide where and with whom he should live; he is incapable of making that decision or, if he can make it, of articulating it; there are two rival claimants each of whom wishes to care for him in accordance with his alleged wishes; and the court is asked to rule on which of them would be carrying out his wishes and which of them would be infringing his rights. The dispute raises a justiciable issue; it concerns the legal rights of the patient; all proper parties, including the patient, are before the court; and the determination of the issue affects the rival claimants and their rights and obligations to the patient. In my judgment the court is entitled and bound to decide it.

I would dismiss the appeal."

NOTES:

1. Kennedy L.J. agreed with the judgments of Sir Thomas Bingham M.R. and Millett L.J.
2. As Dewar comments, in this case the Court of Appeal followed the lead of earlier House of Lords decsions like *F v. West Berkshire Health Authority* and *Airedale NHS Trust v. Bland* [1993] 1 All E.R. 281 in taking a broad view of the use of the declaratory procedure. The Law Commission and others have doubted whether the declaration is a suitable way of developing the law in this area (see pages 310–312). However, as Dewar points out, unless the patient has made an advance directive concerning treatment (see Chapter 14), or

falls within the scope of the Mental Health Act 1983 (see Chapter 8), the declaratory procedure may be the only way of developing the law in the absence of legislation. (See J. Dewar, Comment, [1995] *Family Law* at pages 184–5.) Fennell notes that, with rare exceptions like *Re C* above, the declaratory jurisdiction has been primarily used by doctors or health authorities seeking authority to treat or withhold treatment in the absence of consent, and also to define the scope of "medical treatment". (See P. Fennell, *Treatment Without Consent* London: Routledge, 1996.) Bridgeman suggests that resort to the declaratory procedure may be valuable in clarifying the legal position prior to treating incompetent patients, and in allowing the courts to play a limited supervisory function. (See J. Bridgeman, "Declared Innocent?" (1995) 3 *Medical Law Review* 117.) It is, however, very expensive.

3. As Fennell points out, each time the declaratory procedure is extended it raises the question of whether a statutory *parens patriae* jurisdiction should be introduced to replace the old jurisdiction abolished by the Mental Health Act 1959 (see page 293, above, and Fennell, "Medical Law", *All E.R. Annual Review*, 1995, 354, at page 378). In *Airedale NHS Trust v. Bland* Lord Lowry also lamented the abolition of the prerogative power. Hoggett has doubted the value of reviving the jurisdiction. (See B. Hoggett, "The Royal Prerogative in Relation to the Mentally Disordered: Resurrection, Resuscitation, or Rejection?" in M. D. A. Freeman (ed.), *Medicine, Ethics and the Law*, London: Stevens, 1988.) Nevertheless, Brazier argues that its restoration would have a limited but beneficial effect in protecting the rights of the incompetent. However she suggests that the need for some residual jurisdiction in the courts must be coupled with a recognition that it can never resolve all the problems presented by incompetent patients. (See M. Brazier, "Competence, Consent and Proxy Consent" in M. Brazier and M. Loibjoit (eds), *Protecting the Vulnerable: Autonomy and Consent in Health Care*, London: Routledge, 1991, 37 at pages 44–5.) The Law Commission's proposal to introduce a new judicial forum for the incapacitated could have gone some way to resolving this issue (see pates 310–312 below).

4. Grubb contends that the court in this case should not have gone on to assert (per Sir Thomas Bingham M.R. and Millett L.J.) that the applicant did have a legal right. He suggests that the only relevant legal right at stake was that of S, to live as he chose. (See A. Grubb, Commentary, "Declaratory Jurisdiction: Locus Standi" (1995) 3 *Medical Law Review* 294)

5. At a subsequent hearing on the merits of the case, it was decided that it was in S's best interests to return to Norway — (see *Re S (Hospital Patient: Foreign Curator)* [1995] 4 All E.R. 30).

QUESTIONS:

1. In this case which of the parties do you think was best placed to ascertain S's wishes?
2. Do you agree with the Master of the Rolls that the ability of the common law to respond to social needs, as in this case, makes it a more appropriate mechanism than legislation for dealing with these sort of cases? If so, is that an argument against the type of legislative initiatives proposed by the Law Commission? For instance, compare the views of the Master of the Rolls with the Law Commission's opinion, in its Consultation Paper No. 119, that use of the declaratory procedure is not a satisfactory way of developing the law in this area.

5. THE BEST INTERESTS TEST

A number of the cases, principally *F v. West Berkshire Health Authority*, stress that the crucial issue in making treatment decisions is what is in the "best interests" of the patient. As will become apparent in this text the "best interests" test is widely adopted throughout medical law in relation to the incompetent patient (see Chapters 7 and 15 on children, neonates and those in a persistent vegetative state). It is also used to debar certain would-be parents from access to techniques of assisted conception on the grounds that it would not be in the interests of any resulting child (see Chapter 11). The "best interests" test was also accepted as appropriate by the Law Commission. Nothwithstanding this, the test has been subjected to a number of criticisms. The first problem is a definitional one. What precisely does the test mean? In particular, how are the best interests of a patient to be defined, given the vagueness of the test and the fact that no cases have yet produced an adequate definition? Even in the cases where most turns on the definition of 'best interests', such as *F v. West Berkshire* and *Re J (a minor) (wardship: Medical treatment)* [1990] 3 All E.R. 930 (see Chapter 15), little substance is given to the test.

Furthermore, aside from determining what is in the best interests of the patient, there is also the issue of how far the interests of others should be taken into account. Brazier points out that, although the courts have constantly reiterated that it is the best interests of the patient and the patient alone which determine what treatment may be provided, this rhetoric can be little more than a pious fiction. The interests of the patient and his carer may have become so closely intertwined that it is impossible to separate them out/Furthermore, in a context where much caring is done at home by relatives rather than at cost to the state, she questions whether it is fair to disregard the interests of the carer. (See M. Brazier, "Competence, Consent and Proxy Consents" in M. Brazier and M. Loibjoit (eds), *Protecting the Vulnerable: Autonomy and Consent in Health Care*, London: Routledge, 1992 at pages 46–9.)

The other major difficulty lies in deciding who is the appropriate body or person to determine what is in the best interests of the patient. In endorsing the *Bolam* test, the House of Lords in *F v. West Berkshire Health Authority* implied that doctors were best placed to determine the patient's best interests. However, the Law Commission has criticised the speeches by the Law Lords in that case for conflating the criterion for assessing complaints about professional negligence (the Bolam test — see Chapter 3) with the criterion for treating persons unable to consent, by suggesting that a doctor who acts in accordance with an accepted body of medical opinion is both (1) not negligent and (2) acting in the best interests of an incompetent person (Law Commission, *Mental Incapacity*, Law Com. 231, para. 3.26). Since the best interests of the patient are not simply a matter of clinical judgment, health professionals are not necessarily the best persons to determine the patient's best interests. Yet it is difficult to decide who else should determine or have an input into such decision-making. This issue may be particularly acute in relation to decisions taken at end of life (see Chapter 14). For instance, which relatives, if any, are well placed to determine the patient's best interests? What form would such input take? Would it simply amount to a right to be consulted, or a right to veto treatment? Should there be a test of proximity? A further issue is whether only the interests of family-carers should be taken into account, or those of professional carers as well. (See A. Grubb, Treatment decisions "Keeping it in the Family" in A. Grubb (ed.) Choices and Decisions in Health Care, Chichester: Wiley, 1993.)

Despite the lack of clarity concerning the best interests test, the Law Commission ultimately endorsed the test on the grounds that no viable alternative to it exists. In its report, however, it attempts to flesh out what the test means, by offering the guidance contained in the extract below on reform of the decision-making process.

Law Commission, *Mental Incapacity*, Law Com. 231, 1995

3.24 We will set out in later Parts of this report a graduated scheme for decision-making, designed to ensure that any substitute decision is taken at the lowest level of formality which is consistent with the protection of the person without capacity, both from the improper usurpation of his or her autonomy and from inadequate or even abusive decision-making. Although decisions are to be taken by a variety of people with varying degrees of formality, a single criterion to govern any substitute decision can be established. Whatever the answer to the question 'who decides?', there should only be one answer to the subsequent question 'on what basis?'.

3.25 We explained in our overview paper that two criteria for making substitute decisions for another adult have been developed in the literature in this field: 'best interests' on the one hand and 'substituted judgment' on the other. In Consultation Paper No. 128 we argued that the two were not in fact mutually exclusive and we provisionally favoured a 'best interests' criterion which would contain a strong element of substituted judgment. It had been widely accepted by respondents to the overview paper that, where a person has never had capacity, there is no viable alternative to the 'best interests' criterion. We were pleased to find that our arguments in favour of a 'best interests' criterion found favour with almost all our respondents, with the Law Society emphasising that the criterion as defined in the consultation papers was in fact 'an excellent compromise' between the best interests and substituted judgment approaches.

We recommend that anything done for, and any decision made on behalf of, a person without capacity should be done or made in the best interests of that person. (Draft Bill, clause 3(1).)

3.26 Our recommendation that a 'best interests' criterion should apply throughout our scheme cannot be divorced from a recommendation that statute should provide some guidance to every decision-maker about what the criterion requires. No statutory guidance could offer an exhaustive account of what is in a person's best interests, the intention being that the individual person and his or her individual circumstances should always determine the result . . .

3.28 In putting forward a 'best interests' criterion in our 1993 consultation papers, we linked it to a checklist of factors which should be taken into account by a substitute decision-maker . . . In considering the various fields of decision-making together, we have now developed a single check list which includes all the elements originally identified as important and commended by consultees. We take this opportunity to repeat some of the general comments made in our report on Guardianship and Custody . . . First, that a checklist must not unduly burden any decision-maker or encourage unnecessary intervention; secondly, that it must not be applied too rigidly and should leave room for all considerations relevant in a particular case; thirdly, that it should be confined to major points, so that it can adapt to changing views and attitudes . . .

We recommend that in deciding what is in a person's best interests regard should be had to:-

(1) *the ascertainable past and present wishes and feelings of the person concerned, and the factors that person would consider if able to do so;*
(2) *the need to permit and encourage the person to participate, or to improve his or her ability to participate, as fully as possible in anything done for and any decision affecting him or her;*
(3) *the views of other people whom it is appropriate and practicable to consult about the person's wishes and feelings and what would be in his or her best interests;*
(4) *whether the purpose for which any action or decision is required can be as affectively achieved in a manner less restrictive of the person's freedom of action. (Draft Bill, clause 3(2).)*

NOTES:

1. Under the "substituted judgment" test the proxy decision-maker is required to try and place herself in the position of the incapacitated patient, and seek to decide on the basis of what the patient himself would have decided if he possessed the requisite capacity. There are vestiges of this test in Lord Donaldson's judgment in *Re J* [1990] 3 All E.R. 930 (see Chapter 14). However it will only work where the patient has at some time had capacity. Even then, in *Airedale NHS Trust v. Bland* [1993] 1 All E.R. 821 the House of Lords rejected the substituted judgment test in favour of the best interests criterion (see Chapter 15).

2. Fennell suggests that the best interests test proposed by the Law Commission differs markedly from the common law best interests test. Certainly it involves much more than simply not being negligent. The Law Commission's proposal mandates a much more patient-centred consideration of best interests, and by requiring the patient's known past and present wishes to be carried out, it effectively imports an element of the substituted judgment test into the best interests test. (See P. Fennell, *Treatment Without Consent* London: Routledge, 1996 at page 259.)

3. Ultimately it can be argued that, despite the rhetoric of protecting the exclusive interests of the patient, the vagueness of the 'best interests' test allows public policy considerations to determine the course of action adopted. Public policy considerations seem implicit in judicial decisions authorising sterilisation of incompetent women (see Chapter 13) and withdrawal of treatment (see Chapter 15).

4. Some commentators have stressed the need for self-advocacy or substitute advocacy groups for those with a mental handicap, given that abilities within this group vary greatly. (See P. Mittler, "Competence and Consent in People with Mental Handicap" in M. Brazier and M. Loibjoit, *Protecting the Vulnerable: Autonomy and Consent in Health Care*, London: Routledge, 1991; see also Chapter 8.)

QUESTIONS:

1. Do you agree with the Law Commission in favouring the "best interests" test over that of "substituted judgment" in cases of persons who once were competent? Has the Commission effected an "excellent compromise" between the two competing tests?

2. Is the Law Commission's guidance on assessing the best interests of the patient sufficiently full? How useful is its attempt to draw up a check-list of factors which should be taken into account by the sustitute decision maker?

6. DECISIONS ON BEHALF OF THE INCOMPETENT

(a) The General Authority

In order to maximally enhance the rights of those who lack capacity, the Law Commission has proposed that patients should be able to make advance directives as to their future treatment, or appoint medical treatment attorneys to decide on their behalf. This issue is discussed in Chapter 14. For those who have never been competent, or who have failed to make advance provision, the Law Commission suggest that it is necessary to introduce a new mechanism to reach appropriate decisions in such cases. In its earlier consultation papers, it accepted that the decision in *F v. West*

Berkshire Health Authority did clarify the position in relation to the legality of health professionals taking action on behalf of those who lacked capacity. However, it argued that there was a strong case for clarifying by legislation the circumstances in which such decisions can be taken. In the extract below, the Commission suggest that certain routine medical treatment could be carried out without formal or juridical approval. Instead the decision could be made under a general authority conferred upon "treatment providers" by statute.

Law Commission, *Mental Incapacity*, Law. Com. 231, 1995

4.4   In the consultation papers we provisionally proposed a new statutory authority whereby "carers" and "treatment providers" might act reasonably to safeguard and promote the welfare and best interests of a person without capacity. Our original formulation provoked some misunderstanding on consultation, with respondents fearing that disagreement and disputes would arise as to the identity of "the carer" or "the treatment provider" in possession of the authority. In fact, reasonable action at the informal level can be taken by a variety of different people. On any one day it might be reasonable for the primary carer to dress the person concerned in suitable clothes, for the district nurse to give a regular injection and nursing care, for a worker from a voluntary organisation to take the person out on a trip and for another family member to bring round the evening meal and help the person to eat it. Just at the common law affords each person whose actions fall within the principle of/necessity a defence to a suit for trespass, so a statutory "general authority" should make the qualifying actions of any such person lawful. It is not, therefore, helpful to suggest that any one person can be defined and identified as the holder of the authority. We consider it preferable to refer to actions which are reasonable for the person doing them to do. This underlines the fact that number of people may have power to act on any one day. It also serves as a reminder that independent restrictions on who should be taking action are not superseded. Such restrictions might be imposed by employment contracts, by professional rules of conduct or by the law of negligence. In the example given, it would not be reasonable for the district nurse to administer treatment which requires prior authorization from a registered medical practitioner; nor for the voluntary organisation worker to take actions expressly prohibited by the terms and conditions of his or her employment.

> We recommend that it should be lawful to do anything for the personal welfare or health care of a person who is, or is reasonably believed to be, without capacity in relation to the matter in question if it is in all the circumstances reasonable for it to be done by the person who does it. (Draft Bill, clause 4(1).)

The obligation to act in the best interests of the person without capacity, having regard to the statutory factors, will immediately apply to anyone purporting to exercise this "general authority".

4.5   It would be out of step with our aims of policy, and with the views of the vast majority of the respondents to our overview paper, to have any general system of certifying people as "incapacitated" and then identifying a substitute decision-maker for them, regardless of whether there is any real need for one. In the absence of certifications or authorisations, persons acting informally can only be expected to have reasonable grounds to believe that (1) the other person lacks a capacity in relation to the matter in hand and (2) they are acting in the best interests of that person.

NOTES:

1. If the decision fails to be made in the "general authority", there is no limit upon who may act. The term 'treatment provider' is used to cover anyone providing medical treatment. It thus includes those without medical qualifications, such as relatives, or workers administering prescribed medication, as well as doctors and other health professionals. Hence it confers authority much more widely than did the decision in *F v. West Berkshire Health Authority*. (See P. Fennell, "Statutory Authority to Treat, Relatives and Treatment Proxies", (1994) 2 *Medical Law Review* 30, at page 42.) Reliance is placed on the requirement that it must be reasonable for the particular person to act in the patient's best interests. The Commission proposed that further guidance should be provided in the Code of Practice.

2. The Law Commission went on to propose certain restrictions on the "general authority". It concluded that no person should be able to make decisions on behalf of someone else regarding certain personal matters, such as voting at an election, consent to marriage or sexual relations, divorce on the basis of two years' separation, consent to adoption of a child or the discharge of parental responsibilities except in relation to a child's property. Moreover, if there is evidence that the incapacitated person objects to a particular course of action, a judicial forum (see pages 310–312 below) would have to approve it. The Commission also proposed that there should be a prohibition against confining a person who lacks capacity, where there is the possibility of immediate risk of serious harm to the incapacitated person or others. However, it recognises that the defence of necessity would apply if confinement was in the best interests of the person concerned.

3. The Law Commission proposed that the "treatment provider" should be placed under a statutory duty to consult relatives, but that the consent of those relatives would not be necessary before treatment could be provided. (See P. Fennell, *op. cit.*)

QUESTION:

1. Do you support the proposal for a statutory authority to treat? How, if at all, would it improve on the common law position established in *F v. West Berkshire Health Authority*?

(b) Independent supervision

In its report the Law Commission goes on to propose that certain types of treatment and research which raise special concern ought not to be authorised by a treatment provider but should always be independently approved. The draft bill lists the following 'serious medical interventions' which will require authorisation by the court, the donee of a continuing power of attorney or a manager appointed by the court — "court category" treatment.

Clause 7

(2)(a) any treatment or procedure intended or reasonably likely to render the person concerned permanently infertile except where it is for disease of the reproductive organs or for relieving existing detrimental effects of menstruation;

(b) any treatment or procedure to facilitate the donation of non-regenerative tissue or bone-marrow;

(c) such other treatments or procedures . . . as may be prescribed . . . by the Secretary of State.

A further category of cases — "second opinion category" treatments — would require certification by a second independent doctor. These cases are:

Clause 8

(3)(a) any form of treatment for the time being specified under section 58(1)(a) of the Mental Health Act 1983;

(b) the administration to the person concerned by any means of medicine for mental disorder if three months or more have elapsed since the first occasion when medicine was administered to him by any means for his mental disorder;

(c) abortion;

(d) any treatment or procedure intended or reasonably likely to render the person concerned permanently infertile where it is for relieving existing detrimental effects of menstruation;

(e) such other treatment or procedures a may be prescribed for the purposes of this section by regulations made by the Secretary of State.

NOTES:

1. Many respondents to the Law Commission expressed concern at the practice of performing abortion operations on young women with disabilities without sufficient investigation of their capacity. Similar concerns were expressed about sterilisation operations being performed on these women "for menstrual management". (See Law Commission, *Mental Incapacity*, paragraphs 6.9–6.10 and Chapter 13.)

2. In the case of some other treatments, the "best interests" criterion may not offer much effective guidance. For instance, for the position of a person in a persistent vegetative state, see Chapter 14 at pages 842–862.

3. Therapeutic research performed for the benefit of the incapable person himself is covered by the "general authority" to treat. For the position in relation to non therapeutic research see Chapter 10 at pages 589–593.

QUESTIONS:

1. In your view, should any other procedures have been included within these special categories?
2. Is certification by a second doctor a sufficient safeguard against abuse? Should performance of an abortion require court authorisation?

(c) A New Court Based Jurisdiction

In Part VIII of the Report the Law Commission recommended the introduction of a court-based jurisdiction to resolve the problems caused for carers where an individual lacks capacity. This proposed jurisdiction is designed to provide an integrated framework for the making of personal welfare decisions, health care decisions and financial decisions. It would replace the High Court's inherent jurisdiction to grant declarations in medical law cases, such as the declarations granted in *F v. West Berkshire Health Authority* and *Re S* (above). This Court would possess powers to make declarations as to the person's incompetence, the current validity of any earlier expressions of his wishes, and to approve or disapprove medical treatments which fall into one of the special categories. In paragraph 8.9 the Commission recommends that this court should have power to:

(1) make any decision on behalf of a person who lacks capacity to make that decision or
(2) appoint a manager to be responsible for making a decision on behalf of a person who lacks capacity to make it.

It adds that:

The decisions in question may extend to any matter relating to the personal welfare, health care, property or affairs of the person concerned, including the conduct of legal proceedings.

In relation to managers, the Commission emphasises that a specific decision by the court is preferable to the appointment of a manager, and that powers conferred on a manager should be as limited in scope and duration as possible (paras. 8.12–8.13).

The following extract deals with the court's jurisdiction on health care matters.

Law Commission, *Mental Incapacity*, Law. Com. 231, 1995

Health care matters

8.22 We suggested in Consultation Paper No. 129 that two kinds of orders would be required in relation to health care, namely an order approving (or not) a particular treatment and an order transferring the care of the patient to another person. Our consultees approved these suggestions, acknowledging that a power in the court to approve or disapprove proposed actions would be a great advance on the current declaration procedure. Attention could then focus on whether the thing *should* be done, rather than on its legality if it were to be done . . .

> *We recommend that the court's powers in relation to health care matters should cover (1) approving or refusing approval for particular forms of health care (2) appointing a manger to consent or refuse consent to particular forms of health care, (3) requiring a person to allow a different person to take over responsibility for the health care of the person concerned (Draft Bill, clause 26(1)(a) and (b).)*

8.23   We provisionally suggested that any proxy with health care powers should be able to exercise the rights of the person without capacity to access personal health records. Respondents agreed with this proposal, pointing out that access to records would often be essential to allow the manager to make a valid informed decision . . .

> *We recommend that the court's powers should cover obtaining access to the health records of the person concerned. (Draft Bill, clause 26(1)(c).)*

8.24   It follows from our policy in relation to advance refusals of treatment that neither the court nor a manager may approve any treatment which the patient has already refused. In that connection, however, it should also be made clear that, since no advance refusal of "basic care" by a patient who now lacks capacity can be effective, neither the court nor the manager may authorise the withholding of that type of care.

> *We recommend that the court may not approve, nor a manager consent to, (1) the withholding of basic care, or (2) any treatment refused by an advance refusal of treatment. (Draft Bill, clause 26(2)(b).)*

8.25   We have already recommended that certain kinds of medical decision should require independent supervision. In Consultation Paper No. 129 we suggested that no court-appointed manager should ever be able to reach such decisions. We no longer see the need for a blanket restriction of that type. It may be, for example, that the court has been asked whether sterilisation by hysterectomy would be in the patient's best interests, and it is then agreed to attempt a less intrusive method of contraception. Nonetheless, the court feels able to decide that the patient's sister is an appropriate person to make decisions about her health care, including any decision to consent to a sterilisation at a later stage. In such circumstances, there would be little merit in requiring everyone to return to court when that later stage is reached. Equally, the second opinion procedure is intended to ensure some supervision of serious decisions by someone independent of the responsible doctor. The court might sometimes be satisfied that a "health care manager" who was a family member, citizen advocate or friend was quite capable of providing the necessary independent input. Although we would not anticipate power over "court category" or "second opinion category" treatments being granted to managers as a matter of course, we are now persuaded that there could be cases where this was an appropriate step. Any such authority should be expressly granted by the court.

8.26   We have recommended the adoption of special procedures where it is proposed to carry out a procedure or a research project which will not bring direct benefit to the person without capacity. Again, there might be rare circumstances where the court may determine that a manager should in future have power to consent to such matters. Any such authority should, however, be expressly granted by the court. In relation to non-therapeutic research, no decision of the court could ever obviate the need for prior approval of the project by the statutory committee.

> *We recommend that the court may grant a manager express authority to consent to the carrying out of treatments which would otherwise require court approval or a certificate from an independent medical practitioner; or to consent to the carrying out of non-therapeutic procedures or research. (Draft Bill, clause 26(3).)*

NOTE:

1. For the court's power to order admission to hospital for assessment or treatment of mental disorder see Chapter 8.

QUESTIONS:

1. Do you think the Law Commission was right to retreat from its original opposition to granting managers the power to take decisions in relation to those medical treatments which require independent supervision? Is there a possibility of a conflict of interest here?
2. Should the manager (or the court) be able to consent to non-therapeutic research on incompetent patients? (See Chapter 10.)

In the extract above, the Law Commission simply referred to "the court" which would underpin its suggested framework of decision-making. In the extract which follows it makes it clear what this court or new 'judicial forum' might look like.

Law Commission, *Mental Incapacity*, Law Com. 231, 1995

10.4 Many respondents favoured an informal and inquisitorial approach to the issues which would arise under the new jurisdiction. There was also a very loud and clear call for the jurisdiction to be locally based and easily accessible. A number of respondents favoured tribunals for these reasons. Few, however, asserted that the Mental Health Review Tribunal could deal with the requisite range of issues. It is quite clear that the present expertise of the Mental Health Review Tribunal would have to be fundamentally altered and enormously extended before it could deal with the new jurisdiction.

10.5 There remains the option of a new and specially constituted tribunal, as suggested by various organisations over recent years and examined in our 1991 overview paper. Now that the scope of the new, unified jurisdiction has become clear, however, this option seems less compelling. The perceived advantages of informality and an inquisitorial approach could in fact be worked into a court-based system. It is true that a tribunal can include non lawyers with relevant expertise in the process of adjudication. However, the very wide range of decisions covered by the new 'incapacity' jurisdiction would make it very hard to identify which non-legal specialism was relevant in a particular case. Decisions about financial matters, personal and social matters and complex medical decisions will all fall to be made . . . [T]here was a widespread view on consultation that certain very serious medical decisions should continue to be taken by senior members of the judiciary. There is, moreover, little doubt that the type of property and finance issues currently being resolved in the Court of Protection will continue to be the major part of the workload. Jurisdiction over new-style Continuing Powers of Attorney should also be integrated with the broad decision-making powers of the judicial forum which is chosen. All these factors make the use of the court system seem increasingly appropriate.

10.6 We have benefitted from the deliberations of the House of Lords Select Committee on Medical Ethics. Although strongly attracted at first to the idea of using tribunals to decide difficult medical issues, the committee took account of the fact that we intended a new decision-making forum to discharge a wider range of functions. The committee acknowledged that "it would not be practical or desirable to establish two separate systems of decision-making, one for medical matters and another for dealing with, say, an incompetent person's financial affairs. Indeed it would no doubt sometimes be difficult to distinguish between different types of decision, or to separate one element of a person's affairs from others" . . .

10.8 We now consider that the use of existing court structures and personnel, albeit arranged so as to meet the needs of those without capacity, is the most responsible and practical way forward. The new statutory jurisdiction to make decisions on behalf of persons lacking capacity and to grant orders for the protection of vulnerable persons should be exercised by courts, both by an expanded and reconstituted Court of Protection and, in relation to the public law powers only, by magistrates courts.

10.9 . . . [A] single court should in future exercise jurisdiction in relation to Continuing Powers of Attorney; and in relation to personal, health care and financial decisions for a person who lacks capacity. The expertise of the existing Court of Protection, especially in relation to financial matters and powers of attorney, should be retained and built upon. At the same time, the opportunity should be taken to change the anomalous nature of the present Court of Protection, an 'office' of the Supreme Court with a single location in central London. The types of decisions which the judicial forum will be called upon to make are decisions which should be taken in a properly constituted court, whose decisions can contribute to a body of case-law.

We recommend that a new superior court of record called the Court of Protection should be established and that the office of the Supreme Court known as the Court of Protection should be abolished. (Draft Bill, clause 46(1).)

. . .

10.12 The new Court of Protection will have jurisdiction to deal with all of the matters with which this Report is concerned, including the same powers as magistrates' courts to issue entry warrants or make other orders for the care and protection of the vulnerable . . .

10.13 The Court of Protection should consist of an appropriate number of judges nominated by the Lord Chancellor to exercise the jurisdiction of the Court. These judges will build up special expertise in cases involving people who may lack mental capacity. The availability of a range of judicial personnel should mean that cases, depending on their subject matter or complexity, are heard at the appropriate level by a judge with the appropriate experience and expertise. The range of judges should include district and circuit judges, and judges from the Chancery and Family Divisions of the High Court. Judges of the Chancery Division are currently nominated to deal with cases concerning the property and affairs of patients under Part VII of the Mental Health Act 1983 and their experience in this area should be retained. Judges of the Family Division deal with such cases as arise at present concerning the personal welfare or medical treatment of persons without capacity to consent.

We recommend that the jurisdiction of the Court of Protection should be exercised by judges nominated by the Lord Chancellor, whether Chancery Division or

Family Division High Court judges, circuit judges or district judges. (Draft Bill, Clause 46(2).)

. . .

10.16

. . . *We recommend that the Court of Protection should be able to sit at any place in England and Wales designated by the Lord Chancellor. (Draft Bill, clause 46(6).) . . .*

10.20 Applications for public law orders may only be made by authorised officers of a local authority. In the consultation papers we suggested that some applicants for private law orders should be able to apply as of right, while others would require leave. Respondents supported the idea of a filtering mechanism, but tended to suggest more and more categories of persons who should be able to apply as of right. It became clear that it would be extremely difficult to create an acceptable list of relatives who should have an automatic right to apply. We have concluded that the category of persons with an automatic right to apply should be restricted to those who have *existing* decision-making powers, or who are mentioned in an *existing* order . . . The leave requirement can then be used in a positive and helpful way, to direct prospective applicants towards the factors which are likely to be relevant to the determination of any application for which leave is given.

We recommend that leave should be required before an application to the Court of Protection can be made. In granting leave the Court should have regard to:

(1) the applicant's connection with the person concerned,
(2) the reason for the application,
(3) the benefit to the person concerned of any proposed order,
(4) whether the benefit can be achieved in any other way.

No leave should be required for any application to the court by

(1) a person who is or is alleged to be without capacity, or, in respect of such a person who is under 18 years old, any person with parental responsibility for that person,
(2) a donee of a CPA granted by the person without capacity or a court-appointed manager [continuing Power of Attorney],
(3) the Public Trustee as respects any functions exercisable by virtue of an existing order, and
(4) any person mentioned in an existing order of the Court. (Draft Bill, clause 47.)

10.21 As in the case of Part VII of the Mental Health Act 1983 we consider that it would be useful for the Court of Protection to be able to make an order or give directions even if it cannot yet determine whether the person concerned actually lacks the capacity to take the decision in question. In exercising this emergency jurisdiction the court would only be able to make the order or give the directions sought if it is of the opinion that the order or direction is in the best interests of the person concerned.

We recommend that the Court of Protection should have power to make an order or give directions on a matter, pending a decision on whether the person concerned is without capacity in relation to that matter. (Draft Bill, clause 48.)

10.22

. . . We recommend that appeals should lie:

(1) *from a decision of a district judge to a circuit judge or a judge of the High Court;*
(2) *from a decision of a circuit judge or judge of the High Court given in exercise of his or her original or appellate jurisdiction to the Court of Appeal. (Draft Bill, clause 49(1).)*

. . .

10.25 Decisions taken by the court on behalf of a person without capacity must be taken in the person's 'best interests'. The court will be obliged to have regard to the wishes and feelings of the person concerned, and the factors he or she should have considered. It may not always be appropriate for the person concerned to be present in court, whether because of physical or mental frailty. Other parties and witnesses to the proceedings may offer conflicting assessments of the situation. It should be expected that an independent report should be prepared in such circumstances.

We recommend that, where the person concerned is neither present nor represented, the court should (unless it considers it unnecessary) obtain a report on his or her wishes. (Draft Bill, clause 52(2).)

10.26 The decisions which the court is asked to make may not depend purely on legal points. Arriving at the solution which is in the best interests of the person concerned might require evidence from expert professionals, and the House of Lords Select committee particularly urged that "some mechanism must be adopted whereby the new court will make full use of appropriate independent medical and ethical advice." The most appropriate mechanism, adapting existing procedures and personnel, is to involve court welfare officers and local authority officers where necessary.

We recommend that the Court of Protection should have power to ask a probation officer to report to the court, and power to ask a local authority officer to report or arrange for another person to report, on such matters as the court directs, relating to the person concerned.(Draft Bill, clause 52(1).)

NOTES:

1. On the powers of the existing Court of Protection see Chapter 8. As Fennell notes, there is some irony in the fact that, just as the Law Commission began its deliberations on this issue, the House of Lords in *F v. West Berkshire Health Authority* (above) rejected the argument that the Court of Protection's existing jurisdiction could extend to treatment decisions. (See P. Fennell, *Treatment Without Consent* London: Routledge, 1996 at page 252.)
2. The proposed judicial forum would have no powers other than those possessed by a competent person. Unlike the current Court of Protection, which is based in London, the new forum would have a base in each judicial circuit.
3. For the Law Commission's recommendations on Continuing Powers of Attorney and advance directives see Chapter 14 at pages 874–883.

QUESTION:

1. Do you think that the 'judicial forum' proposed by the Law Commission should take the form of a court? Would the introduction of a multi-disciplinary tribunal have been a better idea? In your view, who would be appropriate persons to sit on it? How would such a forum relate to institutional ethics committees discussed in Chapter 2 at page 136.

SELECT BIBLIOGRAPHY

M. Brazier and M. Lobjoit (eds), *Protecting the Vulnerable: Autonomy and Consent in Health Care*, London: Routledge, 1991.

A. Buchanan and D. Brock, *Deciding for Others: The Ethics of Surrogate Decision Making*, Cambridge: CUP, 1989, especially Chapter 1.

R. R. Faden and T. Beauchamp, *A History and Theory of Informed Consent*, New York: OUP 1986.

P. Fennell, "Inscribing Paternalism in the Law: Consent to Treatment and Mental Disorder" (1990) 17 *Journal of Law and Society* 29.

P. Fennell, "Statutory Authority To Treat, Relatives and Treatment Proxies" (1994) 2 *Medical Law Review* 30.

P. Fennell, *Treatment Without Consent*, London: Routledge, 1996.

M. Freeman, "Deciding for the Intellectually Impaired" (1994) 2 *Medical Law Review* 77

N. Glover and M. Brazier, "Ethical Aspects of the Law Commission Report on Mental Incapacity" (1996) 6 *Reviews in Clinical Gerontology* 365.

L. Gostin, "Consent to Treatment: the Incapable Person" in C. Dyer (ed) *Doctors, Patients and the Law*, Oxford: Blackwells, 1992.

A. Grubb, "Treatment decisions: Keeping it in the family" in A. Grubb (ed.) *Choices and Decisions in Health Care*, Chichester: Wiley, 1993.

M. Gunn, "Mental Incapacity: The Law Commissioner's Report" (1995) 7 *Child and Family Law Quarterly* 209.

M. Gunn, "The Meaning of Incapacity" (1994) 2 *Medical Law Review*

S. Hirsch and J. Harris (eds) *Consent and the Incompetent Patient: Ethics, Law and Medicine*, London: Gaskell, 1988.

B. Hoggett, "The Royal Prerogative in Relation to the Mentally Disordered: Resurrection, Resuscitation or Rejection" in M. Freeman (ed.) *Medicine, Ethics and the Law*, London: Sweet and Maxwell, 1988.

P. Skegg, *Law, Ethics and Medicine: Studies in Medical Law*, Oxford: OUP (1984/88) especially Chapters 2 and 3.

S. Stefan, "Silencing the Different Voice: Competence, Feminist Theory and Law" (1993) 47 *University of Miami Law Review* 763.

6

CONSENT

1. INTRODUCTION

Consent to medical procedures plays an extremely important role in the context of health care provision. The concept of consent operates as a unifying principle running through health care law. It represents the legal and ethical expression of the human right to have one's autonomy and self-determination respected. (See I. Kennedy, "Patients, Doctors and Human Rights" in Kennedy, *Treat Me Right: Essays in Medical Law and Ethics*, Oxford: Clarendon, 1988.) Although, as we have seen in Chapter 2, autonomy is regarded by many ethicists as the fundamental value in health care ethics, it has never been fully recognised as a legally protectable interest. Instead it has been vindicated as a by-product of two other interests which have been accorded legal protection. The first of these is bodily integrity. This is protected by rules prohibiting bodily contact unless the person consents. The second is bodily well-being, which is protected by rules governing professional competence that prohibit an unqualified person from practising medicine. (See M. M. Shultz, "From Informed Consent to Patient Choice: A New Protected Interest" (1985) 95 *Yale Law Journal* 219.) However, although respect for the patient's wishes will normally protect his welfare, tensions may arise if concerns for the patient's welfare leads to paternalism, which conflicts with the patient's right to make autonomous decisions (see Chapter 2 at pages 76–82).

The requirement that the patient's consent be obtained thus operates as a constraint on the power of the health care professional. It is particularly important that the law protects this right given that the health health professional, particularly the doctor, is in a powerful position *vis-à-vis* the patient (see Chapter 2 at pages 137–139), and that her role frequently involves touching, examining and operating upon patients. Given this power dynamic, control of information becomes a key feature in defining the balance of power between the health professional and the patient. (See J. Montgomery, "Patients First: the Role of Rights" in K. W. M. Fulford, *et al.* (eds), *Essential Practice in Patient-Centred Care*, Oxford: Blackwell Science, 1996.) For a patient to give a fully informed consent it is essential that he first have information about the benefits and risks of the proposed

317

course of treatment. (See S. McLean, *A Patient's Right to Know: Information Disclosure, the Doctor and the Law*, Aldershot: Dartmouth, 1989.)

Shultz notes the irony that the most significant threat to patient autonomy comes from doctors themselves who often pre-empt patient authority because of their greater knowledge and traditional role (*op. cit* at page 221). As she points out, attention has also focused upon the issue of patient autonomy because of the changing nature of medicine:

"Medical choice increasingly depends upon factors that transcend professional training and knowledge. As medicine has become able to extend life, delay and redefine death, harvest and transplant organs, correct abnormality within the womb, enable artificial reproduction, and trace genetic defect, questions about values have come to the fore in medical decision making. Health care choices involve profound questions that are not finally referable to professional expertise." (See M. M. Shultz, "From Informed Consent to Patient Choice: A New Protected Interest" (1985) 95 *Yale Law Journal* 219 at page 222.)

English law has focused upon the questions of (i) which risks should be disclosed to the patient, and (ii) according to whose standard should the materiality risk be assessed?

According to the *Patient's Charter* there is an established National Health Service right:

"to be given a clear explanation of any treatment proposed, including any risks and alternatives, before you decide whether you will agree to the treatment".

As we saw in Chapter 1 the Charter does not itself create rights. Instead those are derived from common law or statute. English common law does not appear fully to espouse a right to autonomy. The principles which can be derived from the common law establish two requirements. The first is that physical contact is permissible only where the health care professional has the patient's consent. This requirement is backed up by liability under both criminal and civil law (see section 2). The second is that health professionals are under a duty to provide patients with information about proposed treatment, and alternatives. The issue of capacity to consent has been considered in the previous Chapter. The need for consent is discussed in section 2 below, and the meaning of consent in section 3. Section 3 also explores the duty to inform patients, and the question of what happens when consent is refused or vitiated is addressed in section 4.

Because the law of consent, like much of health care law, has been developed by the courts, rather than Parliament, it follows that the rules have emerged in the context of specific disputes, rather than being drafted to deal with general issues. This sometimes makes it difficult to predict how they should be applied in different circumstances. Another problem with judge-made law is that it can be especially difficult to distil the principles on which the rules are based, especially when judges in the same case give different accounts of them. This is particularly problematic in relation to the principal case on disclosing information — *Sidaway v. Bethlem RHG* [1985] 1 All E.R. 643 (discussed fully below at page 341) — in which it is virtually impossible to establish any clear *ratio*.

2. THE NEED FOR CONSENT

If medical treatment is provided without consent having been obtained, the health professional is liable to be sued in tort. First, the patient may sue the health professional in tort for trespass to the person. Alternatively, the health professional may be sued in negligence. In certain extreme circumstances there exists the theoretical possibility of a criminal prosecution for assault or battery. Under this head of action, the patient alleges that the health professional negligently carried out her duty to advise him, so that he was not given sufficient information to make a fully informed choice.

Everybody has a right to bodily integrity, which is protected by the criminal and civil law of assault and battery. Medical procedures which involve touching the patient come within the potential scope of the crimes of battery or assault. In the criminal law context, the crimes of assault and battery are now treated as though they are synonymous, though historically at common law the technical meaning of assault was the threat of unlawful battery. The traditional definition of a battery is an act that directly and either intentionally or negligently causes some physical contact with the person of another without that person's consent. If a person has consented to the contact, expressly or impliedly, there is no battery, although it has been argued that battery would be better redefined as "an act that directly and either intentionally or negligently causes some physical contact with the person of another in circumstances in which such contact is not generally acceptable in the ordinary conduct of life". (See H. Brooke, "Consent to treatment or research: the incapable patient" in S. R. Hirsch and J. Harris (eds) *Consent and the Incompetent Patient* London: Gaskell, 1988.)

Together with false imprisonment, assault and battery comprise what the common law calls trespass to the person, which is any type of activity that infringes the bodily integrity or liberty of another. These actions are condemned by the common law as civil wrongs which are actionable in damages. In this Chapter we shall adopt the terminology of "trespass to the person" to refer to civil actions and "assault" to refer to criminal actions as those are the terms commonly adopted in case law. We deal first with the criminal law.

(a) The Criminal Law

As we shall see, it is extremely rare for a doctor to be charged with a criminal offence. It is much more likely that an aggrieved patient will pursue a civil law action with the aim of obtaining compensation. Thus, the criminal law plays only a secondary role in ensuring accountability for medical malpractice. This is because the criminal law is essentially concerned not with compensation but with punishment by the state, which has the power *inter alia* to fine or imprison those found guilty of criminal offences; but as most injuries occasioned in the course of medical treatment will be inflicted inadvertently or negligently (see Chapter 3), punishment by the state will generally be inappropriate. However, where a health carer deliberately or recklessly causes injury to a patient a criminal prosecution may be appropriate. In practice, this is most likely to occur where the patient dies and the doctor is charged with manslaughter (see Chapter 14). In this Chapter, for the sake of completeness, we consider non fatal offences against the person which may theoretically be committed by a health care professional.

(1) Assault Occasioning Actual Bodily Harm

The common law offence of assault is the basis of all the criminal law offences against the person.

Offences Against the Person Act 1861, s.47

47.—Whosoever shall be convicted on indictment of any assault occasioning actual bodily harm shall be liable to be imprisoned for any term not exceeding five years.

NOTES:

1. The Act is clear that actual bodily harm is required under section 47. According to Lyndsay J. in *R v. Miller* [1954] 2 Q.B. 282, citing Archbold, "actual bodily" includes "any hurt or injury calculated to interfere with health or comfort." This excludes emotional harm (unless it manifests as a recognisable medical condition: *R. v. Chan-Fook* [1994] 2 All E.R. 552).
2. Section 47 of the 1861 Act does not require malice on the part of the doctor, merely actual bodily harm to which the patient did not consent. So, just as with the civil law, consent will form a defence to any proceedings based on the infliction of actual bodily harm. This means, conceivably, that a health care professional might face prosecution in the following situations: (a) where no consent to the procedure undertaken was provided; (b) where consent has been extracted under duress; (c) where the patient is not competent to give a valid consent to treatment; (d) where the procedure is performed in spite of express refusal of consent; (e) where the patient was inadequately informed about the procedure proposed so as not to be able to provide an effective consent; and (f) where the doctor or nurse mistakes the scope of her authority.

QUESTIONS:

1. Where an interventionist medical procedure is on the whole beneficial to a patient, is it right to construe that procedure as "bodily harm" for the purposes of a section 47 offence?

2. What is the legal position where a nurse, rather than a specific surgeon (Dr X), performs an appendectomy given that when the patient consented to the procedure, he did not intend it to be performed by anyone other than Dr X? (See pages 336–337 below.)

(2) Offences Involving Grievous Bodily Harm and/or Wounding

Two further provisions of the Offences Against the Person Act 1861 are specifically concerned with causing more serious harm. These sections create very serious offences which, in practice, it would be rare for a doctor or nurse to commit (but which may be committed by a non-registered practitioner who masquerades as a fully qualified registered doctor).

Offences Against the Person Act 1861, s.18

18.—Whosoever shall unlawfully and maliciously by any means whatsoever wound or cause any grievous bodily harm to any person, with intent to do some grievous bodily harm to any person . . . shall be guilty of an offence, and being convicted thereof shall be liable to imprisonment for life.

NOTES:

1. The *actus reus* (or physical element) envisaged by section 18 is that the accused must either "wound" or cause "grievous bodily harm". In *C v. Eisenhower* [1983] 3 All E.R. 230 it was held that, for there to be a wound, both the outer and inner skin must be broken.

   In relation to the phrase "grievous bodily harm", the House of Lords held in *DPP v. Smith* [1960] 3 All E.R. 47 that the phrase simply meant "really serious harm". (Whether psychiatric injury may ever amount to grievous bodily harm was recently mooted in *R. v. Gelder*, (1994) *The Times*, December 16.)
2. The *mens rea* required is intention. This has not been clearly defined in the criminal law, but it seems that if a result is a virtually certain consequence of the defendant's action and the defendant foresees that consequence as virtually certain then the jury *may* infer that the result is intended (see *R v. Nedrick* [1986] 1 W.L.R. 1025; and generally C. Clarkson and H. Keating *Criminal Law: Text and Materials* (3rd edn), London: Sweet & Maxwell, 1994 at pages 134–158).

QUESTION:

1. In what circumstances would it be possible to charge a doctor or nurse under section 18?

Offences Against the Person Act 1861, s.20

20.—Whosoever shall unlawfully and maliciously wound or inflict any grievous bodily harm upon any person, either with or without any weapon or instrument, shall be guilty of an offence, and being convicted thereof shall be liable to a term of imprisonment not exceeding five years.

NOTES:

1. Section 20 resembles section 18 in that both sections are concerned with two types of outcome: wounding and grievous bodily harm. However, it is easier to secure a conviction under section 20 in that the *mens rea* requirement is less stringent: there is no need to prove the intention to cause the wound or grievous bodily harm. In *R. v. Savage*; *DPP v. Parmenter* [1991] 4 All E.R. 698 Lord Ackner explained the *mens rea* requirement for section 20 thus:

   " . . . I am satisfied that the decision in *Mowatt* [[1967] 3 All E.R. 47] was correct and that it is quite unnecessary that the accused should either have intended or have foreseen that his unlawful act might cause physical harm of the gravity described in section 20, *i.e.* a wound or serious physical injury. It is enough that he should have foreseen that some physical harm to some person, albeit of a minor character, might result."

   In other words, the *mens rea* for section 20 turns on a test of subjective foresight. This means that a doctor who undertakes a surgical procedure that she knows carries a risk of causing some harm, but who does not intend to inflict serious harm, may nonetheless be convicted under this provision. (See Clarkson and Keating, *op. cit.* at pages 526–566.)

2. Section 20 also differs from section 18 in that it stipulates that the wound or grievous bodily harm must be "inflicted" rather than, in the language of section 18, merely "caused". This means that criminal omissions, which seriously harm a patient to whom the accused doctor owed a duty of care, can only be prosecuted under section 18, and not section 20.

The absence of legally effective consent is an essential element of each of these criminal offences. Hence, if a legally effective consent is deemed to have been given, the medical touching will not constitute an assault. However, if the doctor is aware that no effective consent has been given, then even a therapeutic medical touching will amount to assault, unless some statutory or common law justification is available to the doctor. (See P. D. G. Skegg, *Law, Ethics and Medicine* Oxford: Clarendon Press, 1988, Chapter 2.) Moreover there are some forms of touching to which, it has been held no legally effective consent can be given. In these situations. The law has determined that, for reasons of public policy, a patient is not entitled to give a legally valid consent, even if he wishes to. This means that treatment may be unlawful even if a patient wants it. Consent will not normally render lawful the infliction of physical injury — *R. v. Donovan* [1934] 2 K.B. 498. The general position was considered by the Court of Appeal in *A.-G.'s Reference (No. 6 of 1980)* [1981] 2 All E.R. 1057. In this case, Lord Lane C.J. referred to the "accepted legality" of "reasonable surgical interference" and said that this, and other apparent exceptions to otherwise illegal conduct, were "needed in the public interest" (at page 1059). In *R. v. Brown* [1993] 2 All E.R. 65, which held that adults could not lawfully consent to the infliction of harm during sado-masochistic sex, it was suggested that consent to 'proper medical treatment' is valid, even though the bodily invasion involved may be extreme (*per* Lord Mustill at pages 109–110). In *Airedale NHS Trust v. Bland* [1993] 1 All E.R. 821 Lord Mustill stated that "bodily invasions in the course of proper medical treatment stand completely outside the criminal law" (at page 889). It is unlikely that treatment carried out in good faith, with the patient's consent, would be invalidated by public policy, but this poses the question of what is 'proper' medical treatment, or 'reasonable' surgery. The issue of whether it is reasonable to consent to one's death or the removal of one's organs is discussed in Chapters 14 and 15. Public policy limitations are sometimes specifically set out in statutes. For instance, the only circumstances in which the law permits the termination of pregnancy are described in the Abortion Act 1967 (see Chapter 12), and non-therapeutic female circumcision is outlawed by the Prohibition of Female Circumcision Act 1985.

Prohibition of Female Circumcision Act 1985

1.—(1) Subject to section 2 below, it shall be an offence for any person —

(a) to excise, infibulate or otherwise mutilate the whole or any part of the labia majora or labia minora or clitoris of another person; or
(b) to aid, abet, counsel or procure the performance by another person of any of those acts on that other person's own body.

(2) A person guilty of an offence under this section shall be liable —

(a) on conviction on indictment, to a fine or to imprisonment for a term not exceeding five years or to both; or
(b) on summary conviction, to a fine not exceeding the statutory maximum (as defined in section 74 of the Criminal Justice Act 1982) or to imprisonment for a term not exceeding six months, or to both.

2.—(1) Subsection (1)(a) of section 1 shall not render unlawful the performance of a surgical operation if that operation —

(a) is necessary for the physical or mental health of the person on whom it is performed and is performed by a registered medical practitioner; or

(b) is performed on a person who is in any stage of labour or has just given birth and is so performed for purposes connected with that labour or birth by —
    (i) a registered medical practitioner or a registered midwife; or
    (ii) a person undergoing a course of training with a view to becoming a registered medical practitioner or a registered midwife.

(2) In determining for the purposes of this section whether an operation is necessary for the mental health of a person, no account shall be taken of the effect on that person of any belief on the part of that or any other person that the operation is required as a matter of custom or ritual.

NOTES:

1. The exemptions for medical practitioners and midwives indicate the extent to which the law recognises the need for special provision to be made for the purposes of health care. Similar exemptions for medical practitioners are found in the Tattooing of Minors Act 1969.

2. Issues like female circumcision raise, in acute form, the problem of cultural relativism in judging the acceptability of medical practices (see Chapter 2 at page 141). The operation is required by certain traditions in order to accord with their ideal of feminine roles. It may be questioned how different this is from cosmetic surgery undergone by Western women in order to conform to our society's ideal of feminine beauty. (See K. Hayter, "Female Circumcision — Is there a Legal Solution?" [1984] *Journal of Social Welfare Law* 323; L. Bibbings, "Female Circumcision: Mutilation or Modification?" in J. Bridgeman and S. Millns (eds), *Law and Body Politics*, Aldershot: Dartmouth, 1995; M. Atoki "Should female circumcision continue to be banned?" (1995) 3 *Feminist Legal Studies* 223.) This in turn raises the issue of the extent to which women are making truly voluntary choices when they undergo forms of bodily modification (though see K. Davis, *Reshaping the Female Body: The Dilemma of Cosmetic Surgery*, London: Routledge, 1995.) Similar issues are raised in relation to whether the decision to undergo infertility treatment in a society where infertility is stigmatised can be truly voluntary (see Chapter 11).

3. More generally, there is an issue as to whether other operations should be outlawed, regardless of whether the patient consents, on the grounds of public policy. Although The Law Commission noted in its report, *Consent in the Criminal Law: A Consultation Paper*, Consultation Paper No. 139, London: HMSO, 1995, that conventional medical and surgical treatment for a therapeutic purpose by qualified practitioners gives rise to no particular difficulties, it did identify some areas related to medical practice which it perceived to be problematic. (For discussion of sterilisation operations see Chapter 13 at pages 754–773, on abortions see Chapter 12 and on organ transplantation see Chapter 15.) Gender reassignment surgery — commonly known as a sex change operation — which may entail

removal of sex organs is carried out on the National Health Service, and it seems accepted that such operations are lawful. (See G. Williams, "Consent and Public Policy" [1962] *Criminal Law Review*, 154; D. Meyers, *The Human Body and the Law* (2nd ed.), Edinburgh: Edinburgh University Press, 1990, Chapter 9.) Each of these issues may be differently regarded in different cultures.

4. For the purposes of clarifying the existing law, the following provision was proposed by the Law Commission:

> 8.50 We therefore provisionally propose that -
> (1) a person should not be guilty of an offence, notwithstanding that he or she causes injury to another, of whatever degree of seriousness, if such injury is caused during the course of proper medical treatment or care administered with the consent of the other person:
> (2) in this context "medical treatment or care" —
>   (a) should mean medical treatment or care administered by or under the direction of a duly qualified medical practitioner;
>   (b) should include not only surgical and dental treatment or care, but also procedures taken for the purposes of diagnosis, the prevention of disease, the prevention of pregnancy or as ancillary to treatment; and
>   (c) without limiting the meaning of the term, should also include the following:
>   (i) surgical procedures performed for the purposes of rendering a patient sterile;
>   (ii) surgical operations performed for the purposes of enabling a person to change his or her sex;
>   (iii) lawful abortions;
>   (iv) surgical operations performed for cosmetic purposes; and
>   (v) any treatment or procedure to facilitate the donation of regenerative tissue, or the donation of non-regenerative tissue not essential for life.

QUESTIONS:

1. Is the best solution to the problem of female circumcision to proscribe it by legislation? How else might this practice be eliminated? (See D. Pearl, "Legal issues arising out of medical provision for ethnic groups" in A. Grubb and M. Mehlman (eds), *Justice and Health Care: Comparative Perspectives*, Chichester: Wiley, 1995).

2. Is it an unjustifiable interference with the individual's liberty and autonomy to use law to restrain her from having an abortion or cosmetic surgery on public policy grounds if she consents to it?

3. Should the law deem invalid, on public policy grounds, consent to sexual intercourse with someone who deliberately conceals the fact that they are infected with the AIDS virus, thus making it easier to convict a person who intends to infect other people with the virus? (According to the old authority of *Clarence* (1888) 22 Q.B.D. 23 the fact that a woman consented to the act of intercourse with her husband meant that he was not guilty of inflicting grievous bodily

harm (contrary to section 18 of the Offences Against the Person Act 1861) or any assault when he infected her with gonorrhoea. Even though she would not have consented had she known of the disease, her consent was not negatived by his failure to tell her of his condition.) (See K. Smith, "Risking Death by Dangerous Sexual Behaviour and the Criminal Law" in R. Lee and D. Morgan (eds) *Death Rites: Law and ethics at the end of life*, London: Routledge, 1994; D. C. Omrerod and M. J. Gunn, "Criminal Liability for the Transmission of HIV" (1996) 1 Webb Journal of Current Legal Issues; M. Brazier and J. Harris, "Public Health and Private Lives" (1996) 4 *Medical Law Review* 171; S. Bronith, "Spreading Disease and the Criminal Law" [1994] *Criminal Law Review* 21.)

(b) The Civil Law

In a health care context it is much more likely that a civil action will be brought for trespass to the person, rather than a criminal action for assault. As Shultz notes, patient autonomy was initially identified with and subsumed under an interest in physical security, protected by the legal rules proscribing touching without consent. However it eventually became apparent that many aspects of the health care relationship did not fit comfortably into the trespass model. (See M. M. Shultz, "From Informed Consent to Patient Choice: A New Protected Interest" (1985) 95 *Yale Law Journal* 219 at pages 224–225.) For instance, treatments that involved no physical touching received no protection under trespass doctrine. Gradually, therefore, the dominant framework for litigation arising out of claims based in patient autonomy and self determination has become the negligence action for non-disclosure of information. Nevertheless, as Shultz argues, under negligence doctrine, choice remains encapsulated within the dominant interest in physical well-being (*op. cit.* at page 232.)

As we shall see below, the courts have been reluctant to countenance even civil actions for trespass against health care professionals. However, the availability of these legal provisions means that, in theory at least, patients are entitled to veto the care that health professionals wish to give them. The law only permits treatment to be forced upon patients in narrowly defined circumstances. The principal exception to the requirement that consent must be obtained is where the patient is unconscious and needs emergency treatment (see below, page 328). Other examples are: testing for certain infectious diseases (see Chapter 1 and pp. 337–339 below), in the context of mental health (see Chapter 9), in the case of children and immature young people (see Chapter 7), and possibly cases where a pregnant woman's refusal of consent to medical procedures during pregnancy or birth may have adverse consequences for the foetus (see Chapter 13). The focus in this Chapter is on the right of competent adult patients to give or refuse consent to medical care and treatment. However, as we shall see, even in the case of competent adults, the courts may readily find justification for overriding a purported refusal of consent.

F v. West Berkshire Health Authority [1989] 2 All E.R. 545, [1990] 2 A.C. 1, [1989] 2 W.L.R. 938, [1989] 2 F.L.R. 476

The facts of this case have been discussed in the previous Chapter at pages 287–288; this extract concerns the legal significance of consent:

LORD GOFF:
". . . I start with the fundamental principle, now long established, that every person's body is inviolate . . . [T]he effect of this principle is that everybody is protected not only against physical injury but against any form of physical molestation (see [*Collins v. Wilcock*] [1984] 3 All E.R. 374 at 378).

Of course, as a general rule physical interference with another person's body is lawful if he consents to it; though in certain limited circumstances the public interest may require that his consent is not capable of rendering the act lawful. There are also specific cases where physical interference without consent may not be unlawful: chastisement of children, lawful arrest, self-defence, the prevention of crime and so on. As I pointed out in *Collins v. Wilcock* [1984] 3 All E.R. 374 at 378, a broader exception has been created to allow for the exigencies of everyday life: jostling in a street or some other crowded place, social contact at parties and such like. This exception has been said to be founded on implied consent, since those who go about in public places, or go to parties, may be taken to have impliedly consented to bodily contact of this kind. Today this rationalisation can be regarded as artificial; and, in particular, it is difficult to impute consent to those who, by reason of their youth or mental disorder, are unable to give their consent. For this reason, I consider it more appropriate to regard such cases as falling within a general exception embracing all physical contact which is generally acceptable in the ordinary conduct of everyday life.

In the old days it used to be said that, for a touching of another's person to amount to a battery, it had to be a touching 'in anger' (see *Cole v. Turner* (1704) Holt KB 108 per Holt C.J.) and it has recently been said that the touching must be 'hostile' to have that effect (see *Wilson v. Pringle* [1986] 2 All E.R. 440 at 447). I respectfully doubt whether that is correct. A prank that gets out of hand, an over-friendly slap on the back, surgical treatment by a surgeon who mistakenly thinks that the patient has consented to it, all these things may transcend the bounds of lawfulness, without being characterised as hostile. Indeed, the suggested qualification is difficult to reconcile with the principle that any touching of another's body is, in the absence of lawful excuse, capable of amounting to a battery and a trespass. Furthermore, in the case of medical treatment, we have to bear well in mind the libertarian principle of self-determination which, to adopt the words of Cardozo J. (in *Schloendorff v. Society of New York Hospital* (1914) 211 N.Y. 125 at 126), recognises that:
'Every human being of adult years and sound mind has a right to determine what shall be done with his own body; and a surgeon who performs an operation without his patient's consent, commits an assault . . .'

NOTE:

1. Lord Goff's starting point in this extract is similar to the starting point taken by Lord Donaldson in *Re T* [1992] 4 All E.R. 649 (see Chapter 5 at pages 267–272). However, notwithstanding the emphasis placed on autonomy, like Lord Donaldson, he was ultimately prepared to sanction treatment without consent in certain circumstances, by holding that treatment was lawful provided it was judged necessary by doctors. (See I. Kennedy, "Patients, Doctors, and Human Rights" in *Treat Me Right: Essays in Medical Law and Ethics*, Oxford: Clarendon, 1988.)

3. THE MEANING OF CONSENT

Provided that the patient is capable of consenting, then no care or treatment will be lawful unless he has given a 'real consent'. This requires the patient to have been informed 'in broad terms' of the procedure in question and to have indicated his acceptance of it. The precise form in which consent must be given is not laid down by the law. Written consent is no more valid than oral consent or 'implied' consent (where it is clear from the actions of the patient that he is consenting, for example rolling up his sleeve to receive an injection). In each of these three situations what matters is that the patient did in fact consent. Consent may also be 'imputed', for example where the patient is unconscious, and it is argued that his tacit consent to treatment which is immediately necessary may be assumed. Less artificially, such treatment may be justified on the basis of necessity, as it is clearly in the public interest to come to the aid of a person needing medical treatment in an emergency. (See M. Brazier, *Medicine, Patients and the Law* (2nd edn.), Harmondsworth: Penguin, 1992 at pages 90–92; J. K. Mason and R. A. McCall Smith, *Law and Medical Ethics* (4th edn.), London: Butterworths, 1994, page 220.) However, in most situations it is much easier to prove that a patient consented if there is written evidence of consent, and patients are usually asked to sign a consent form for surgical and other major procedures. The NHS Executive has published a standardised consent form (see below page 335).

(a) The nature of "real consent"

The meaning of "real consent" is discussed in *Chatterton v. Gerson* [1981] 1 All E.R. 257, which considers the respective requirements of the torts of trespass and negligence (governing disclosure, and considered more fully later in this Chapter).

Chatterton v. Gerson [1981] 1 All E.R. 257, [1981] Q.B. 432, [1980] 3 W.L.R. 1003, (1990) 1 BMLR 80

Miss Chatterton suffered chronic intractable pain following a hernia operation. She was given an injection to block the pain. Initially the injection was successful, but the pain subsequently returned. She then had the procedure repeated, but this time the pain was not relieved and she was left gravely disabled — unable to feel anything in her right leg and foot. She sued Dr Gerson. She alleged first that she had not given a valid consent to the procedure because it had not been explained to her and, secondly, that Dr Gerson's explanation had been negligent. The judge considered the nature of these legal claims and discussed which was the most appropriate way to deal with allegations that a doctor has not properly informed her patients.

BRISTOW J.:

" . . . It was Dr Gerson's regular practice to explain to patients whom he intended to try to help by intrathecal phenol solution injection all about the process. His practice was to tell them that he hoped to relieve their pain by interrupting the nerve along which it was signalled to the brain, that this would involve numbness in the area from which the pain signals had been transmitted, numbness over an area larger than the pain source itself, and might involve temporary loss of muscle power. Sister Welch who worked with him at the clinic from 1973 says that he was very meticulous about his explanations. Neither she nor Dr Gerson pretend now to remember what he said to Miss Chatterton on the occasions in the summer of 1974 preceding the first intrathecal injection. Both remembered her very well as a charming, sensible, intelligent woman who did not make a fuss but complained, as Sister Welch remembers it, of desperate pain. There is no apparent reason why in Miss Chatterton's case Dr Gerson should have departed from his normal practice and not acted in accordance with the advice shortly to be published in his paper.

Miss Chatterton's recollection is that after the initial local injections at the scar site he told her about his pain block method and that it had been perfected in Boston, Massachusetts. It would be done under local anaesthetic and would not take very long. If you block the nerve which sends the pain message the brain does not receive it and so you do not have a pain. Dr Gerson told her what the clinic was all about. She does not remember him saying that the blocking injection would be near the spine. Her recollection is that he did not say she would have numbness and might have some muscle weakness. Is her evidence in this respect reliable? I have no doubt that she and all the other witnesses in this case have been entirely honest in their evidence, but that does not of itself mean that I can rely on her evidence that Dr Gerson did not explain that she would get numbness and possibly some muscle weakness as a result of the intrathecal block.

In the correspondence which followed the first operation there is no complaint by Dr Riddle that the numbness which she mentions on October 24 was unexpected or a matter of complaint by Miss Chatterton . . . It was not until the endorsement on the writ in this action, issued on July 22, 1976, as amended on June 8, 1978, that the averment of assault, which is based on a lack of proper explanation vitiating Miss Chatterton's consent to the intrathecal injections, first appears on our scene.

I am sure that if Miss Chatterton had not been told by Dr Gerson that she would get an area of numbness not confined to the scar site as a necessary concomitant of the interruption of the nerve passing the pain signals, she would have said both to Dr Gerson and Dr Riddle that she had not been told she would get the numbness she experienced following the first operation, and that Dr Riddle would have raised the matter with Dr Gerson if she had raised it with him.

I have come to the conclusion that on the balance of probability Dr Gerson did give his usual explanation about the intrathecal phenol solution nerve block and its implications of numbness instead of pain plus a possibility of slight muscle weakness, and that Miss Chatterton's recollection is wrong; and on the evidence before me I so find . . .

The claim

As I have said, there is no claim that Dr Gerson was negligent either in embarking on treatment of Miss Chatterton's chronic intractable pain by intrathecal phenol solution injection or in the performance of either of the operations which he carried out. The claim against him is put in two ways; (i) that her consent to operation was vitiated by lack of explanation of what the procedure was and what were its implications, so that she gave no real consent and the operation was in law a trespass to her person, that is, a battery; and (ii) that Dr Gerson was under a duty, as part of his obligation to treat his patient with the degree of professional skill and care to be expected of a reasonably skilled practitioner having regard to the state of the art at the time in question, to give Miss Chatterton such an explanation of the nature and implications of the proposed operation that she could come to an informed decision on whether she wanted to have it, or would prefer to go on living with the pain which it was intended to relieve; that such explanation as he gave was in breach of that duty; that if he had performed that duty she would have chosen not to have the operation; and that therefore the unhappy consequences resulting from the operation, however wisely recommended and skilfully performed it may have been, are damage to Miss Chatterton which flows from Dr Gerson's breach of duty and for which he is responsible . . .

Trespass to the person and consent

It is clear law that in any context in which consent of the injured party is a defence to what would otherwise be a crime or a civil wrong, the consent must be real. Where, for example, a woman's consent to sexual intercourse is obtained by fraud, her apparent consent is no defence to a charge of rape. It is not difficult to state the principle or to appreciate its good sense. As so often, the problem lies in its application . . .

In my judgment what the court has to do in each case is to look at all the circumstances and say 'was there a real consent?' I think justice requires that in order to vitiate the reality of consent there must be a greater failure of communication between doctor and patient than that involved in a breach of duty if the claim is based on negligence. When the claim is based on negligence the plaintiff must prove not only the breach of duty to inform but that had the duty not been broken she would not have chosen to have the operation. Where the claim is based on trespass to the person, once it is shown that the consent is unreal, then what the plaintiff would have decided if she had been given the information which would have prevented vitiation of the reality of her consent is irrelevant.

In my judgment once the patient is informed in broad terms of the nature of the procedure which is intended, and gives her consent, that consent is real, and the cause of the action on which to base a claim for failure to go into risks and implications is negligence, not trespass. Of course if information is withheld in bad faith, the consent will be vitiated by fraud. Of course if by some accident, as in a case in the 1940s in the Salford Hundred Court, where a boy was admitted to hospital for tonsillectomy and due to administrative error was circumcised instead, trespass would be the appropriate cause of action against the doctor, though he was as much a victim of the error as the boy. But in my judgment it would be very much against the interests of justice if actions which are really based on a failure by the doctor to perform his duty adequately to inform were pleaded in trespass.

In this case in my judgment even taking Miss Chatterton's evidence at its face value she was under no illusion as to the general nature of what an intrathecal injection of phenol solution nerve block would be, and in the case of each injection her consent was not unreal. I should add that getting the patient to sign a proforma expressing consent to undergo the operation 'the effect and nature of which have been explained to me', as was done here in each case, should be a valuable reminder to everyone of the need for explanation and consent. But it would be no defence to an action based on trespass to the person if no explanation had in fact been given. The consent would have been expressed in form only, not in reality.

Negligence

The duty of the doctor is to explain what he intends to do, and its implications, in the way a careful and responsible doctor in similar circumstances would have done; see *Bolam v. Friern Hospital Management Committee* [1957] 2 All E.R. 118, McNair J., and *Hatcher v. Black*, (1954) *The Times*, July 2, 1954, *per* Denning L.J. sitting as an additional judge of the Queen's Bench Division.

I am satisfied that Dr Gerson told the plaintiff what an intrathecal phenol solution injection nerve block was all about. I am satisfied that he told her that the concomitant of relief from pain would be numbness not confined to the scar but in the area served by the sensory nerves the injection would be intended to block, and that she might suffer from slight muscle weakness. Ought he to have done more?

The evidence before me on this was that of Dr Gerson himself, of Dr Mehta, an anaesthetist expert in pain relief, who would not have used the procedure except in a patient suffering from cancer pain, Mr. Currie, consultant neurosurgeon at St. Bartholomew's Hospital, who has used these procedures for the relief of intractable pain but confines his operations to the lumbar region where the insertion of the needle involves less risk than higher up, and Dr Bodley, a consultant anaesthetist, who would not have undertaken the procedure anyway, taking a gloomy view of it.

Dr. Mehta, if he had been talked into using the procedure as a last resort on someone suffering from chronic intractable pain other than that caused by terminal cancer, would have told the patient that there might be more loss of sensation than she would expect; that there might be loss of bladder control, though he agreed that at the level at which the plaintiff's injections were given it would be very unlikely; and there might be some muscle weakness. He would not have anticipated an effect on the leg from which Miss Chatterton subsequently suffered, and would not have warned her of the possibility of any such thing. Mr. Currie, apart from saying that the higher up the spine the injection is to be given the more closely you have to think about what warning to give, did not help on this aspect of the case. Dr Bodley would not have used this procedure anyway, but helped by saying that the risks involved in an anaesthetic given by the same means but without the use of phenol solution involves about as much danger as crossing Oxford Street, so that he would not volunteer any warning of risk in that case. None of these three, however distinguished, could really help over the adequacy of the explanation which as I have held Dr Gerson gave Miss Chatterton before the first operation, which he alone of those called thought right to do.

In my judgment there is no obligation on the doctor to canvass with the patient anything other than the inherent implications of the particular operation he intends to carry out. He is certainly under no obligation to say that if he operates incompetently he will do damage. The fundamental assumption is that he knows his job and will do it properly. But he ought to warn of what may happen by misfortune however well the operation is done, if there is a real risk of a misfortune inherent in the procedure, as there was in the surgery to the carotid artery in the Canadian case of *Reibl v. Hughes* (1978). In what he says any good doctor has to take into account the personality of the patient, the likelihood of the misfortune, and what in the way of warning is for the particular patient's welfare.

I am not satisfied that Dr Gerson fell short of his duty to tell Miss Chatterton of the implications of this operation, properly carried out. At the level at which he gave the injection there was on the evidence no real risk of damage to bladder control, and it is clear that the bladder difficulty of which Miss Chatterton now complains was wholly independent of the injections. There was no risk of significant damage to the motor nerves. There was no foreseeable risk that her leg and foot would be deprived of sensation or control, nor am I satisfied that anything done in the course of the second injection caused that result. In my judgment, on the expert evidence here that may be functional, just as the continuance of her scar pain is functional. The certain and intended result of the injections was to replace the pain at which they were aimed by numbness, numbness over an area larger than the scar area itself. This I am satisfied she was told before the first injection. Before the second injection she knew what to expect and in my judgment there was no need to spell it out again.

In my judgment the fact is that it is the lack of sensation in the leg and foot, which Dr Mehta would not have anticipated or warned of as a possibility, and failure of the second injection to relieve her pain which very naturally are Miss Chatterton's causes for complaint. As a result of the second injection there is no organic cause left for the pain still being there. The condition of her leg and foot was not a possibility inherent in the operation of which Dr Gerson should have warned her. Accordingly the claim of negligence fails.

I should add that if I had thought that Dr Gerson had failed in his duty to inform her of the implications inherent in the second injection, I would not have been satisfied that if properly informed Miss Chatterton would have chosen not to have it. The whole picture on the evidence is of a lady desperate for pain relief, who has just been advised by Mr Crymble to let Dr Gerson try again. When asked what she would have done she said that she would have refused because she knew her family was opposed to the second operation, because she knew how much it hurt and what it was like, and because she still had the pain and was beginning to learn to put up with it. She did not say she would have refused because the numbness following the first injection was unacceptable, or that she was not prepared to risk slight muscle weakness again. In my judgment the reasons which she did mention would all have been equally cogent whether she had been told again what she had been told before the first injection, or not."

NOTES:

1. This case illustrates the difficulties which confront a court attempting to assess what really happened. The patient and health professionals may well disagree about the true course of events, and the judge is faced with a choice of whom to believe. Bristow J.'s assessment of the credibility of the competing accounts is included to illustrate this problem. Once the judge has made a finding as to what probably happened, then the court treats the case as if those were the true facts, even though it may have been a very difficult decision.

2. Since the decision in *Chatterton v. Gerson*, English courts have consistently held that trespass actions should play only a very limited role in health care law. Bristow J's position has been endorsed by the High Court in *Hills v. Potter* [1983] 3 All E.R. 716; the Court of Appeal in *Freeman v. Home Office* [1984] 1 All E.R. 1036; and the House of Lords in *Sidaway v. Bethlem RHG* [1985] 3 All E.R. 643. (See G. Robertson, "Informed Consent to Medical Treatment"

(1981) 97 *Law Quarterly Review* 102 for the policy arguments which dictate the limited role of trespass actions.) One example of a recent successful trespass action is the case of *Bartley v. Studd* July 15, 1995. (Reported in *Medical Law Monitor* (1995) 2 page 1.) In this case the plaintiff, a 34-year-old woman, was being operated on for a hysterectomy to which she had consented. However, whilst she was under anaesthetic the gynaecologist removed her ovaries for what he considered to be justifiable clinical reasons.

3. Brazier points out that it is difficult to distinguish between an action which does constitute battery and one which does not on the *Chatterton* test. (See, for example, its application to the issue of blood tests for the HIV virus — discussed below at pages 337–339; M. Brazier, *Medicine, Patients and the Law* (2nd edn.), Harmondsworth: Penguin, 1992 at page 80.)

4. Pursuing his action in trespass as opposed to negligence carries certain advantages for the patient. First, in a trespass claim he need not establish any tangible injury, since the actionable injury is the unpermitted invasion of his body. Thus, the patient can succeed even if the battery actually improves his health, rather than causing him harm. By contrast, in a negligence action the patient must prove that damage resulted from the negligent behaviour of the health professional. Secondly, in the case of trespass all damage flowing from treatment imposed without consent will be recoverable, whether it was foreseeable or not, whereas in a negligence action unforeseeable damage will not be recoverable. Moreover, in some trespass cases punitive damages may be awarded if the patient's actions were particularly blameworthy. However, a major drawback is that a trespass claim may only be made where there is actual physical contact between patient and health professional. (See M. Brazier, *Medicine, Patients and the Law* (2nd ed.) Harmondsworth: Penguin, 1992, pp. 74–75.) Furthermore, in *Freeman v. Home Office* [1984] 1 All E.R. 1036 (discussed below at pages 368–370) the Court of Appeal held that where a patient alleges that he did not consent to treatment and sues in trespass, the onus of proof lies on the patient.

5. As far as the negligence action in this case was concerned, the test applied to determine whether Dr Gerson's explanation was negligent or not has now been elaborated by the House of Lords in *Sidaway v. Bethlem RHG* [1985] 1 All E.R. 643. Although the *ratio* of the latter case is not entirely clear, that decision seems to move away from a simple application of the *Bolam* test. The interpretation of *Sidaway* is considered in detail below at pages 352–356.

6. Note the important point at the end of Bristow J.'s judgment, which makes it clear that in negligence actions even if the doctor is guilty of failure to disclose material risks, the patient will only recover damages provided he is able to demonstrate that in the light of such risks he would have chosen to forego the treatment in question.

7. For any treatment received under the NHS the patient is required to sign a standard consent form.

Questions:

1. Consider the difficulties that Bristow J. had in determining what explanation was actually given by Dr Gerson. Do you think that judges are more likely to believe patients or doctors? Are judges entitled to place more reliance on evidence given by a health care professional? (On this point see also the case of *Smith v. Tunbridge Wells* [1994] 5 Med. L.R. 334, extracted below at pages 362–365.)
2. Would Miss Chatterton have succeeded if Dr Gerson's explanation had been unacceptable?
3. Why did Bristow J. believe that trespass was inappropriate for 'informed consent' cases? What types of case does Bristow J. think are appropriate for trespass?
4. Given the considerable advantages to the patient of framing his action in trespass, is the reluctance of the courts to countenance trespass actions justifiable? (See T. K. Feng, "Failure of medical advice: trespass or negligence?" (1987) 7 *Legal Studies* 149.)
5. In relation to the question of risks which the law requires a health professional to disclose, what does a "real risk of misfortune inherent in the procedure" mean?
6. Will the duty of disclosure be the same if the doctor is carrying out therapeutic research on the patient, rather than offering a tried and tested treatment? (See Chapter 10.)

NHS Consent Form HC(90)22 Appendix 1 as substituted in 1992

CONSENT FORM	APPENDIX
A(1)	

For medical or dental investigation, treatment or operation

Health Authority . . . . Patient's Surname . . . .

Hospital . . . . Other Names . . . .

Unit Number . . . . Date of Birth . . . .

Sex (*Please tick*) Male   Female

DOCTORS OR DENTISTS (*This part is to be completed by doctor or dentist*)
See notes on reverse

Type of operation, investigation or treatment for which written evidence of consent is considered appropriate

I confirm that I have explained the operation, investigation or treatment, and such appropriate options as are available and the type of anaesthetic, if any (general/local/sedation) proposed, to the patient in terms which in my judgment are suited to the understanding of the patient and/or to one of the parents or guardians of the patient

Signature. . . . .   Date. . . . .

Name of doctor or dentist . . . .

PATIENT/PARENT/GUARDIAN

1. Please read this form and the notes overleaf very carefully.
2. If there is anything that you don't understand about the explanation, or if you want more information, you should ask the doctor or dentist.
3. Please check that all the information on the form is correct. If it is, and you understand the explanation, then sign the form.

I am the patient/parent/guardian (*delete as necessary*)

I agree   ■ to what is proposed which has been explained to me by the doctor/dentist named on this form.

■ to the use of the type of anaesthetic that I have been told about.

I understand   ■ that the procedure may not be done by the doctor/dentist who has been treating me so far.

■ that the procedure in addition to the investigation or treatment described on this form will only be carried out if it is necessary and in my best interests and can be justified for medical reasons.

I have told   ■ the doctor or dentist about the procedures listed below I would *not* wish to be carried out straightaway without my having the opportunity to consider them first.

. . . .

. . . .

Signature . . . .

Name . . . .

Address . . . .

(*if not the patient*) . . . .

QUESTION:

1. How useful are consent forms? What is their legal effect? (Note the comments of Bristow J. in *Chatterton v. Gerson* (at page 331 above) and Lord Donaldson's criticisms of the layout of consent forms in *Re T.* (at page 271 above); see also I. Kennedy, "Consent to Treatment: the Capable Person" in C. Dyer (ed.) *Doctors, Patients and the Law*, Oxford: Blackwell, 1992, at page 49.)

(b) Current controversies in relation to consent

The following three situations have raised the question of whether the consent or purported refusal of consent is truly effective:

1. Treatment by students or nurses

An issue which has been much debated recently is whether consent is valid when a patient agrees to a doctor carrying out treatment or examination, but it is instead performed by a nurse or a student doctor. (For example, see the outrage occasioned by reports that a student on work experience at Bradford Hospital stitched a patient's wound, *The Guardian* November 2, 1995, and by exposure of the fact that a nurse had performed an appendectomy in 1994.) (see "Why I Picked Up the Surgeon's Knife', *The Sunday Telegraph*, June 23, 1996.) If the treatment is given by an incompetent person the patient may sue in negligence. Moreover, if the patient was not informed that the treatment was to be delivered by a nurse or student, this may give rise to a trespass action. (See M. Brazier, *Medicine, Patients and the Law* (2nd ed.), Harmondsworth: Penguin, 1992, pages 89–90.)

In response to the concerns which these reports occasioned, the Joint Consultants Committee — a representative forum of the medical Royal Colleges and the British Medical Association — agreed a set of safeguards designed to protect the safety of patients when invasive procedures are carried out by non-medically qualified people. Whilst acknowledging that delegation of duties can serve to reduce the hours of junior doctors, the committee states that there must be agreement by the doctors, nurses and patients concerned and that professional bodies must agree the precise definition of procedures; that adequate training and assessment must be provided; that the patient must be fully informed of the training and status of the person operating upon him and have given a fully informed consent; and surgical procedures must be supervised by a medical practitioner. (See "Safeguards for surgery for non-doctors produced" (1996) 313 *British Medical Journal* 190.)

Particular controversy has surrounded the case of vaginal examinations. Traditionally medical students have been taught how to carry out vaginal examinations by examining women who are anaesthetised. Such examinations are performed not for the benefit of that particular patient but for those of the students and future patients, and it is often unclear whether the woman in question has been asked for her consent. Again this raises the question of whether she could bring a action in trespass. (See S. Bewley, "The law, medical students and consent", (1992) 304 *British Medical Journal* 1551.)

The GMC offers the following guidance on this issue:

GMC, *Duties of a Doctor: Guidance from the General Medical Council*, October 1995

Delegating care to non-medical staff and students

28. You may delegate medical care to nurses and other health care staff who are not registered medical practitioners if you believe it is best for the patient. But you must be sure that the person to whom you delegate is competent to undertake the procedure or therapy involved. When delegating care or treatment, you must always pass on enough information about the patient and the treatment needed. You will still be responsible for managing the patient's care.

29. You must not enable anyone who is not registered with the GMC to carry out tasks that require the knowledge and skills of a doctor.

NOTE:

1. Given the constraints on NHS resources it is increasingly likely that experienced nurses will be called upon to perform minor routine operations. Concern has been expressed that nurses are outstripping their training and overstepping professional boundaries after it emerged that a nurse in Liverpool had performed over 200 such operations, including the removal of cysts and cancerous growths, with the knowledge of her employers and the consultants she worked with. (See "Nurse performs 200 operations", *The Sunday Telegraph*, June 23, 1996.)

QUESTION:

1. Is an experienced nurse likely to be more competent at performing routine operations than a student doctor? (See the discussion in the Court of Appeal in *Wilsher v. Essex Area Health Authority* [1986] 3 All E.R. 801 in Chapter 3 at pages 163–168.)

2. Consent to HIV tests

Another recent controversy pertaining to consent has been raised in the context of testing for the HIV virus. Debate has centred on the situation where a patient consents to giving blood in order for tests to be undertaken, but is not specifically told that one test will be to detect the presence of HIV virus. In this case it could be argued that the patient broadly understood the nature and purpose of the operation, in which case he would not succeed in a trespass action under the *Chatterton v. Gerson* test (see pages 328–334 above). This issue has not yet been litigated. In 1987 a majority of members of the BMA voted in favour of a proposal that non-consensual testing should take place at the discretion of the patient's physician, but the decision was not implemented owing to counsel's opinion that there was a possibility that it would give rise to legal difficulties. The GMC's stance on the matter is as follows:

GMC, *HIV and AIDS: The Ethical Considerations*, October 1995

Consent to investigation or treatment

11. It has long been accepted, and is well understood within the profession, that a doctor should treat a patient only on the basis of the patient's informed consent. Doctors are expected in all normal circumstances to be sure that their patients consent to the carrying out of investigative procedures involving the removal of samples or invasive techniques, whether those investigations are performed for the purposes of routine screening, for example in pregnancy or prior to surgery, or for the more specific purpose of differential diagnosis. A patient's consent may in certain circumstances be given implicitly, for example by agreement to provide a specimen of blood for multiple analysis. In other circumstances it needs to be given explicitly, for example before undergoing a specified operative procedure or providing a specimen of blood to be tested specifically for a named condition. As the expectations of patients, and consequently the demands made upon doctors, increase and develop it is essential that both doctor and patient feel free to exchange information before investigation or treatment is undertaken.

Testing for HIV infection: the need to obtain consent

12. The GMC believes that the above principle should apply generally, but that it is particularly important in the case of testing for HIV infection, not because the condition is different in kind from other infections but because of the possible serious social and financial consequences which may ensue for the patient from the mere fact of having been tested for the condition. These are problems which would be better resolved by a developing spirit of social tolerance than by medical action, but they do raise a particular ethical dilemma for the doctor in connection with the diagnosis of HIV infection or AIDS. They provide a strong argument for each patient to be given the opportunity, in advance, to consider the implications of submitting to such a test and deciding whether to accept or decline it.

13. In the case of a patient presenting with certain symptoms which the doctor is expected to diagnose, this process should form part of the consultation. Where blood samples are taken for screening purposes, as in ante-natal clinics, there will usually be no reason to suspect HIV infection but even so the test should be carried out only where the patient has given explicit consent. Similarly, those handling blood samples in laboratories, either for specific investigation or for the purpose of research, should test for the presence of HIV only where they know the patient has given explicit consent. Only in the most exceptional circumstances, where a test is operative in order to secure the safety of persons other than the patient, and where it is not possible for the prior consent of the patient to be obtained, can testing without explicit consent be justified.

14. A particular difficulty arises in cases where it may be desirable to test a child for HIV infection and where, consequently, the consent of a parent, or a person in loco parentis, would normally be sought. However, the possibility that the child may have been infected by a parent may in certain circumstances, distort the parent's judgment so that consent is withheld in order to protect the parent's own position. The doctor faced with this situation must first judge whether the child is competent to consent to the test on his or her own behalf. If the child is judged competent in this context, then consent can be sought from the child. If, however, the child is judged unable to give consent the doctor must decide whether the interests of the child should override the wishes of the parent. It is the view of the GMC that it would not be unethical for a doctor to perform such a test without parental consent, provided always that the doctor is able to justify that action as being in the best interests of the patient.

NOTE:

1. The general position in relation to consent by children is discussed in Chapter 7. However, particular issues are raised in relation to the testing of children for HIV. As the GMC guidelines make clear, there may be situations where it is in the best interests of the child to test him, but the parents are reluctant to consent.

QUESTIONS:

1. If a doctor suspects that a patient may be HIV+ and wishes to take a sample of blood for testing, does the doctor commit trespass if she merely tells the patient that the blood is required for testing, and does not disclose that she proposes to test it for the HIV virus? (See J. Keown, "The Ashes of AIDS and the Phoenix of Informed Consent" (1989) 52 *Modern Law Review* 790; J. Montgomery, "Victims or Threats? The Framing of HIV [1990] 12 *Liverpool Law Review* 25. C. d'Eca, "Medico-legal aspects of AIDS" in D. Harris and R. Haigh (eds.) *AIDS: A Guide to the Law* (2nd ed.), London: Routledge, 1996 at pages 114–116.)
2. Would it be preferable for health care professionals to simply assume that all patients are HIV+ and take the necessary precautions, thus avoiding the need to test anyone?
3. Would it be justifiable for a doctor to test a newly-born baby if she suspects his mother is HIV+, but the mother refuses to consent to a HIV test?

3. Force-feeding of anorexics

One of the most vexed questions relating to consent concerns the force-feeding of anorexics. Anorexia is an eating disorder. It manifests itself in an obsession with weight, a distorted perception of one's body size and shape and a compulsion to lose weight, resulting in a refusal to eat. The first medical description of anorexia as a discrete disorder dates from an address by W. Gull in 1868, but its incidence has risen dramatically in the last two decades. It disproportionately affects women, although there is now evidence that it is being diagnosed in young men with increasing frequency. (See R. Dresser, "Feeding the hungry artist: legal issues in treating anorexia nervosa" (1984) 2 *Wisconsin Law Review* 297; N. Frost, "Food for Thought: Dresser on Anorexia" (1984) 2 *Wisconsin Law Review* 375; J. Bridgeman, "They Gag Women, Don't They?" in J. Bridgeman and S. Millns (eds.) *Law and Body Politics: Regulating the Female Body* Aldershot: Dartmouth, 1995.)

QUESTIONS:

1. If an anorexic patient refuses to eat, is the court justified in authorising health professionals to feed and otherwise treat him against his will? This issue has been considered in cases involving young women (see Chapter 7) and women detained under the Mental Health Act 1983 (see Chapter 9).
2. Would the reasoning in *Re W (A Minor) (Medical Treatment: Court's Jurisdiction)* [1992] 4 All E.R. 627 (extracted in Chapter 7 at page 405) apply to a person aged over 18? (See J. Bridgeman, "Old enough to know best?" (1993) 13 *Legal Studies* 69.)

(c) Disclosure and the quality of consent

The obligations of a health professional to counsel her patients about decisions that the patient is required to make are governed by the tort of negligence. If a patient is improperly counselled and has suffered loss as a result, he may sue for compensation. To win a negligence case based on a failure to counsel properly, a patient must show that he was not given an explanation that responsible professionals would support; that had he been given a proper explanation he would have refused the care (see *Chatterton v. Gerson* (at pages 328–333 above)), and that he has been harmed by giving consent on the basis of improper advice. In effect he is alleging that the *quality* of consent which the health care professional obtained was not good enough. We begin by examining the general rules governing the health professional's obligation to disclose information to patients under-going treatment for therapeutic reasons. Two special circumstances are then examined: non-therapeutic procedures, and cases where the patient asks questions. Finally, in this section, we address the position of other health care professionals.

1. The Obligation to Disclose Information to the Patient: Therapeutic Cases

The leading case on the obligation to disclose information to patients as to the risks of a particular course of conduct is the House of Lords decision in *Sidaway v. Bethlem RHG* [1985] 1 All E.R. 643. Each of the four speeches in this case contain significant differences of approach. Identifying a majority view in order to provide a coherent statement of the law is therefore difficult.

Sidaway v. Bethlem RHG [1985] 1 All E.R. 643, [1985] 1 A.C. 871, [1985] 2 W.L.R. 480, 1 BMLR 132

Mrs Sidaway had undergone an operation on her spine to relieve pain. That operation involved two specific risks of injury over and above the more general risks of surgery. First, there was a possibility that a nerve root might be damaged in the area of the operation. Secondly, there was a risk that the spinal cord might be damaged. Neither risk was statistically large, estimated at between 1 per cent and 2 per cent by one expert witness. However, the consequences were very serious if either risk was to materialise. In the event, Mrs Sidaway was left severely disabled, with partial paralysis. She sued the doctor who had treated her, alleging that he had failed properly to warn her of the risks inherent in the operation, and that had she been so informed she would not have agreed to the operation. She did not suggest that the operation itself had been carried out negligently. The case was complicated by the fact that the doctor had died by the time it came to trial. He could not, therefore, give evidence about the precise nature of the warning that he had given Mrs Sidaway. Nevertheless, the judge felt able to infer that the doctor probably warned Mrs Sidaway about the risk of damage to the nerve root, but not that of damage to the spinal cord. Further, the judge found that the doctor did not explain to Mrs Sidaway that the operation was not absolutely necessary, but a matter of her choice. The case went to the House of Lords on appeal, on the basis that those were the true facts. The House of Lords had to decide whether the failure to advise Mrs Sidaway of the risk of injury to the spinal cord was negligent. In order to do so, they had to determine the standard of care that was applicable in this area of negligence.

LORD SCARMAN:
". . . The judge [in *Bolam v. Friern Hospital Management Committee* [1953] 2 All E.R. 118] clearly directed the jury to treat the test of negligence which he formulated as exclusively applicable in medical cases. The *Bolam* principle may be formulated as a rule that a doctor is not negligent if he acts in accordance with a practice accepted at the time as proper by a responsible body of medical opinion even though other doctors adopt a different practice. In short, the law imposes the duty of care, but the standard of care is a matter of medical judgment.
    The *Bolam* principle has been accepted by your Lordships' House as applicable to diagnosis and treatment: see *Whitehouse v. Jordan* [1981] 1 All E.R. 267, (treatment) and *Maynard v. West Midlands Regional Health Authority* [1985] 1 All E.R. 635 (diagnosis). It is also recognised in Scots law as applicable to diagnosis and treatment; indeed, McNair J. in the *Bolam* case cited a Scottish decision to that effect, *Hunter v. Hanley* 1955 SLT 213 at 217 per the Lord President (Clyde).
    But was the judge correct in treating the 'standard of competent professional opinion' as the criterion in determining whether a doctor is under a duty to warn his patient of the risk, or risks, inherent in the treatment which he recommends? Skinner J. and the Court of Appeal have in the instant case held that he was correct.

Bristow J. adopted the same criterion in *Chatterton v. Gerson* [1981] 1 All E.R. 257. The implications of this view of the law are disturbing. It leaves the determination of a legal duty to the judgment of doctors. Responsible medical judgment may, indeed, provide the law with an acceptable standard in determining whether a doctor in diagnosis or treatment has complied with his duty. But is it right that medical judgment should determine whether there exists a duty to warn of risk and its scope? It would be a strange conclusion if the courts should be led to conclude that our law, which undoubtedly recognises a right in the patient to decide whether he will accept or reject the treatment proposed, should permit the doctors to determine whether and in what circumstances a duty arises requiring the doctor to warn his patient of the risks inherent in the treatment which he proposes.

The right of 'self-determination', the description applied by some to what is no more and no less than the right of a patient to determine for himself whether he will or will not accept the doctor's advice, is vividly illustrated where the treatment recommended is surgery. A doctor who operates without the consent of his patient is, save in cases of emergency or mental disability, guilty of the civil wrong of trespass to the person; he is also guilty of the criminal offence of assault. The existence of the patient's right to make his own decision, which may be seen as a basic human right protected by the common law, is the reason why a doctrine embodying a right of the patient to be informed of the risks of surgical treatment has been developed in some jurisdictions in the United States of America and has found favour with the Supreme Court of Canada. Known as the 'doctrine of informed consent', it amounts to this: where there is a 'real' or a 'material' risk inherent in the proposed operation (however competently and skilfully performed) the question whether and to what extent a patient should be warned before he gives his consent is to be answered not by reference to medical practice but by accepting as a matter of law that, subject to all proper exceptions (of which the court, not the profession, is the judge), a patient has a right to be informed of the risks inherent in the treatment which is proposed. The profession, it is said, should not be judge in its own cause; or, less emotively but more correctly, the courts should not allow medical opinion as to what is best for the patient to override the patient's right to decide for himself whether he will submit to the treatment offered him. It will be necessary for the House to consider in this appeal what is involved in the doctrine and whether it, or any modification of it, has any place in English law . . .

It is, I suggest, a sound and reasonable proposition that the doctor should be required to exercise care in respecting the patient's right of decision. He must acknowledge that in very many cases factors other than the purely medical will play a significant part in his patient's decision-making process. The doctor's concern is with health and the relief of pain. These are the medical objectives. But a patient may well have in mind circumstances, objectives and values which he may reasonably not make known to the doctor but which may lead him to a different decision from that suggested by a purely medical opinion. The doctor's duty can be seen, therefore, to be one which requires him not only to advise as to medical treatment but also to provide his patient with the information needed to enable the patient to consider and balance the medical advantages and risks alongside other relevant matters, such as, for example, his family, business or social responsibilities of which the doctor may be only partially, if at all, informed.

I conclude, therefore, that there is room in our law for a legal duty to warn a patient of the risks inherent in the treatment proposed, and that, if such a duty be held to exist, its proper place is as an aspect of the duty of care owed by the doctor to his patient. I turn, therefore, to consider whether a duty to warn does exist in our law and, if it does, its proper formulation and the conditions and exceptions to which it must be subject.

Some American courts have recognised such a duty. They have seen it as arising from the patient's right to know of material risks, which itself is seen to arise from the patient's right to decide for himself whether or not to submit to the medical treatment proposed. This is the doctrine of informed consent, to which I have already briefly referred. The landmark case is a decision of the United States Court of Appeals, District of Columbia Circuit, *Canterbury v. Spence* (1972) 464 F 2d 772. This case, which has now been approved by the District of Columbia Appeal Court in *Crain v. Allison* (1982) 443 A 2d 558, is discussed learnedly and lucidly in an article by Mr Gerald Robertson 'Informed Consent to Medical Treatment' (1981) 97 L.Q.R. 102, on which I have drawn extensively in reaching my opinion in this appeal. I wish to put on record my deep appreciation of the help I have derived from the article. The author deals so comprehensively with the American, Canadian and other countries' case law that I find it unnecessary to refer to any of the cases to which our attention has been drawn, interesting and instructive though they are, other than *Canterbury v. Spence* and a case in the Supreme Court of Canada, *Reibl v. Hughes* (1980) 114 DLR (3d) 1, in which the judgment of the Supreme Court came too late to be considered by Mr Robertson in his article. I have also been greatly assisted by the note on the present case by Professor Ian Kennedy ((1984) 47 MLR 454).

It is necessary before discussing the doctrine to bear in mind that it is far from being universally accepted in the United States of America, or indeed elsewhere. Speaking of the position as it was in 1981 Mr Robertson said ((1981) 97 L.Q.R. 102 at 108):

'The present position in the United States is one of contrast between the minority of States which have chosen to follow the lead given by *Canterbury* by adopting the objective "prudent patient" test . . . and the majority of States which have been content to adopt the traditional test and determine the question of disclosure of risks by applying the "reasonable doctor" test.'

There can be little doubt that policy explains the divergence of view. The prolification of medical malpractice suits in the United States of America has led some courts and some legislatures to curtail or even to reject the operation of the doctrine in an endeavour to restrict the liability of the doctor and so discourage the practice of 'defensive medicine', by which is meant the practice of doctors advising and undertaking the treatment which they think is legally safe even though they may believe that it is not the best for their patient. The danger of defensive medicine developing in this country clearly exists, though the absence of the lawyer's 'contingency fee' (a percentage of the damages for him as his fee if he wins the case but nothing if he loses) may make it more remote. However that may be, in matters of civil wrong or tort courts are concerned with legal principle; if policy problems emerge, they are best left to the legislature: see *McLoughlin v. O'Brian* [1982] 2 All E.R. 298.

In *Canterbury v. Spence* the court enunciated four propositions. (1) The root premise is the concept that every human being of adult years and of sound mind has a right to determine what shall be done with his own body. (2) The consent is the informed exercise of a choice, and that entails an opportunity to evaluate knowledgeably the options available and the risks attendant on each. (3) The doctor must, therefore, disclose all 'material risks'; what risks are 'material' is determined by the 'prudent patient' test, which was formulated by the court (464 F 2d 772 at 787):

'[a] risk is . . . material when a *reasonable person*, in what the physician knows or should know to be the patient's position, would be likely to attach significance to the risk or cluster of risks in deciding whether or not to forego the proposed therapy.' (My emphasis.)

(4) The doctor, however, has what the court called a 'therapeutic privilege'. This exception enables a doctor to withhold from his patient information as to risk if it can be shown that a reasonable medical assessment of the patient would have indicated to the doctor that disclosure would have posed a serious threat of psychological detriment to the patient.

In Canada, in *Reibl v. Hughes* (1980) 114 D.L.R. (3d) 1, Laskin C.J.C. expressed broad approval of the doctrine as enunciated in *Canterbury v. Spence*, though it would seem that approval of the doctrine was not necessary to a decision in the case. I find no difficulty in accepting the four propositions enunciated in *Canterbury*'s case. But with two notable exceptions they have not yet been considered, so far as I am aware, by an English court. In *Chatterton v. Gerson* [1981] 1 All E.R. 257, Bristow J. did consider whether there is any rule in English law comparable with the doctrine of informed consent. He held that a doctor ought to warn of what may happen by misfortune however well the operation may be carried out 'if there is a *real* risk of a misfortune inherent in the procedure' (see [1981] 1 All E.R. 257 at 266; my emphasis). He held that whether or not a warning should have been given depended on what a reasonable doctor would have done in the circumstances and he applied the *Bolam* test to determine the reasonableness of what the doctor did. In *Hills v. Potter* [1984] 3 All E.R. 716, Hirst J., after discussing the doctrine, also applied the *Bolam* test.

In my judgment the merit of the propositions enunciated in *Canterbury v. Spence* (1972) 464 F 2d 772 is that without excluding medical evidence they set a standard and formulate a test of the doctor's duty the effect of which is that the court determines the scope of the duty and decides whether the doctor has acted in breach of his duty. This result is achieved, first, by emphasis on the patient's 'right of self-determination' and, second, by the 'prudent patient' test. If the doctor omits to warn where the risk is such that in the court's view a prudent person in the patient's situation would have regarded it as significant, the doctor is liable.

The *Canterbury* propositions do indeed attach great importance to medical evidence, though judgment is for the court. First, medical evidence is needed in determining whether the risk is material, *i.e.* one which the doctor should make known to his patient. The two aspects of the risk, namely the degree of likelihood of it occurring and the seriousness of the possible injury if it should occur, can in most, if not all, cases be assessed only with the help of medical evidence. And, second, medical evidence would be needed to assist the court in determining whether the doctor was justified on his assessment of his patient in withholding the warning.

My Lords, I think the *Canterbury* propositions reflect a legal truth which too much judicial reliance on medical judgment tends to obscure. In a medical negligence case where the issue is as to the advice and information given to the patient as to the treatment proposed, the available options and the risk, the court is concerned primarily with a patient's right. The doctor's duty arises from his patient's rights. If one considers the scope of the doctor's duty by beginning with the right of the patient to make his own decision whether he will or will not undergo the treatment proposed, the right to be informed of significant risk and the doctor's corresponding duty are easy to understand, for the proper implementation of the right requires that the doctor be under a duty to inform his patient of the material risks inherent in the treatment. And it is plainly right that a doctor may avoid liability for failure to warn of a material risk if he can show that he reasonably believed that communication to the patient of the existence of the risk would be detrimental to the health (including, of course, the mental health) of his patient.

Ideally, the court should ask itself whether in the particular circumstances the risk was such that this particular patient would think it significant if he was told it existed. I would think that, as a matter of ethics, this is the test of the doctor's duty. The law, however, operates not in Utopia but in the world as it is; and such an inquiry would prove in practice to be frustrated by the subjectivity of its aim and purpose. The law can, however, do the next best thing, and require the court to answer the question, what would a reasonably prudent patient think significant if in the situation of this patient? The 'prudent patient' cannot, however, always provide the answer for the obvious reason that he is a norm (like the man on the Clapham omnibus), not a real person; and certainly not the patient himself. Hence there is the need that the doctor should have the opportunity of proving that he reasonably believed that disclosure of the risk would be damaging to his patient or contrary to his best interest. This is what the Americans call the doctor's 'therapeutic privilege'. Its true analysis is that it is a defence available to the doctor which, if he invokes it, he must prove. On both the test and the defence medical evidence will, of course, be of great importance.

The 'prudent patient' test calls for medical evidence. The materiality of the risk is a question for the court to decide on all the evidence. Many factors call for consideration. The two critically important medical factors are the degree of probability of the risk materialising and the seriousness of possible injury if it does. Medical evidence will be necessary so that the court may assess the degree of probability and the seriousness of possible injury. Another medical factor, on which expert evidence will also be required, is the character of the risk. In the event of an operation is the risk common to all surgery, *e.g.* sepsis, cardiac arrest, and the other risks associated with surgery and the administration of an anaesthetic? Or is it specific to the particular operation under consideration? With the worldwide development and use of surgical treatment in modern times the court may well take the view that a reasonable person in the patient's situation would be unlikely to attach significance to the general risks; but it is not difficult to foresee circumstances particular to a patient in which even the general risks of surgery should be the subject of a warning by his doctor, *e.g.* a heart or lung or blood condition. Special risks inherent in a recommended operational procedure are more likely to be material. The risk of partial paralysis, as in this case where the purpose of the operation was not to save life but merely to relieve pain, illustrates the sort of question which may face first the doctor and later the court. Clearly medical evidence will be of the utmost importance in determining whether such a risk is material; but the question for the court is ultimately legal, not medical, in character . . ."

LORD DIPLOCK:
" . . . For the last quarter of a century the test applied in English law whether a doctor has fulfilled his duty of care owed to his patient has been that set out in the summing up to the jury by McNair J. in *Bolam v. Friern Hospital Management Committee* [1957] 2 All E.R. 118. I will call this the *Bolam* test. At any rate, so far as diagnosis and treatment are concerned, the *Bolam* test has twice received the express approval of this House . . .

The standard of skill and judgment in the particular area of the art of medicine in which the doctor practised that was called for . . . was the standard of ordinary skill and care that could be expected to be shown by a doctor who had successfully completed the training to qualify as a doctor, whether as general practitioner or as consultant in a speciality if he held himself out as practising as such, as the case might be. But, unless the art in which the artificer claims to have acquired skill and judgment is stagnant so that no improvement in methods or knowledge is sought (and of few is this less true than medicine and surgery over the last half-century), advances in the ability to heal resulting from the volume of research, clinical as well as technological, will present doctors with alternative treatments to adopt and a choice to select that treatment (it may be one of several) that is in their judgment likely at the time to prove most efficacious or ameliorating to the health of each particular patient committed to their care.

Those members of the public who seek medical or surgical aid would be badly served by the adoption of any legal principle that would confine the doctor to some long-established, well-tried method of treatment only, although its past record of success might be small, if he wanted to be confident that he would not run the risk of being held liable in negligence simply because he tried some more modern treatment, and by some unavoidable mischance it failed to heal but did some harm to the patient. This would encourage 'defensive medicine' with a vengeance. The merit of the *Bolam* test is that the criterion of the duty of care owed by a doctor to his patient is whether he has acted in accordance with a practice accepted as proper by a body of responsible and skilled medical opinion. There may be a number of different practices which satisfy this criterion at any particular time. These practices are likely to alter with advances in medical knowledge. Experience shows that, to the great benefit of humankind, they have done so, particularly in the recent past. That is why fatal diseases such as smallpox and tuberculosis have within living memory become virtually extinct in countries where modern medical care is generally available.

In English jurisprudence the doctor's relationship with his patient which gives rise to the normal duty of care to exercise his skill and judgment to improve the patient's health in any particular respect in which the patient has sought his aid has hitherto been treated as a single comprehensive duty covering all the ways in which a doctor is called on to exercise his skill and judgment in the improvement of the physical or mental condition of the patient for which his services either as a general practitioner or as a specialist have been engaged. This general duty is not subject to dissection into a number of component parts to which different criteria of what satisfy the duty of care apply, such as diagnosis, treatment and advice (including warning of any risks of something going wrong however skilfully the treatment advised is carried out). The *Bolam* case itself embraced failure to advise the patient of the risk involved in the electric shock treatment as one of the allegations of negligence against the surgeon as well as negligence in the actual carrying out of treatment in which that risk did result in injury to the patient. The same criteria were applied to both these aspects of the surgeon's duty of care. In modern medicine and surgery such dissection of the various things a doctor has to do in the exercise of his whole duty of care owed to his patient is neither legally meaningful nor medically practicable. Diagnosis itself may involve exploratory surgery, the insertion of drugs by injection (or vaccination) involves intrusion on the body of the patient and oral treatment by drugs, although it involves no physical intrusion by the doctor on the patient's body, may in the case of particular patients involve serious and unforeseen risks.

My Lords, no convincing reason has in my view been advanced before your Lordships that would justify treating the *Bolam* test as doing anything less than laying down a principle of English law that is comprehensive and applicable to every aspect of the duty of care owed by a doctor to his patient in the exercise of his healing functions as respects that patient. What your Lordships have been asked to do, and it is within your power to do so, is to substitute a new and different rule for that part only of the well-established test as comprises a doctor's duty to advise and warn the patient of risks of something going wrong in the surgical or other treatment that he is recommending.

The juristic basis of the proposed substitution, which originates in certain state court jurisdictions of the United States of America and has found some favour in modified form by the Supreme Court of Canada, appears to me, with great respect, to be contrary to English law. Its foundation is the doctrine of 'informed consent' which was originally based on the assumption made in the United States Court of Appeals, District of Columbia Circuit, in *Canterbury v. Spence* (1972) 464 F 2d 772, where the cynic might be forgiven for remarking that it enabled a defence under the state statute of limitations to be outmanoeuvred, that *prima facie* the cause of action in a case of surgery was trespass to the person unless 'informed consent' to the particular battery involved in the surgical operation could be proved. From a period long before American independence this, as I have pointed out, has never been so in English law. The relevant form of action has been based in negligence, *i.e.* in assumpsit, alone.

The Supreme Court of Canada, after some initial vacillation, rejected trespass to the person, *i.e.* battery, as the cause of action in cases of surgery but endeavoured to transfer the concept of 'informed consent' to a patient's cause of action in negligence, into which, in my opinion, it simply cannot be made to fit. Consent to battery is a state of mind personal to the victim of the battery and any information required to make his consent qualify as informed must be relevant information either actually possessed by him or which he is estopped from denying he possessed, because he so acted towards the defendant as to lead to the latter reasonably to assume the relevant information was known to him. There is no room in the concept of informed consent for the 'objective' patient (as he is referred to at one point by the Supreme Court of Canada) to whom the doctor is entitled, without making any inquiry whether it is the fact or not, to attribute knowledge of some risks but not of others. It may be that most patients, though not necessarily all, have a vague knowledge that there may be some risk in any form of medical treatment; but it is flying in the face of reality to assume that all patients from the highest to the lowest standard of education or intelligence are aware of the extent and nature of the risks which, notwithstanding the exercise of skill and care in carrying out the treatment, are inevitably involved in medical treatment of whatever kind it be but particularly surgical. Yet it is not merely conceded but specifically asserted in the Canadian cases that it is no part of the duty of care on the part of the doctor to go out of his way to draw the attention of his patient to these. On what logical or juristic basis can the need for informed consent be confined to some risks and not extended to others that are also real, and who decides which risk falls into which class?

My Lords, I venture to think that in making this separation between that part of the doctor's duty of care that he owes to each individual patient, which can be described as a duty to advise on treatment and warn of its risks, the courts have misconceived their functions as the finders of fact in cases depending on the negligent exercise of professional skill and judgment. In matters of diagnosis and the carrying out of treatment the court is not tempted to put itself in the surgeon's shoes; it has to rely on and evaluate expert evidence, remembering that it is no part of its task of evaluation to give effect to any preference it may have for one responsible body of professional opinion over another, provided it is satisfied by the expert evidence that both qualify as responsible bodies of medical opinion. But, when it comes to warning about risks, the kind of training and experience that a judge will have undergone at the Bar makes it natural for him to say (correctly) it is my right to decide whether any particular thing is done to my body, and I want to be fully informed of any risks there may be involved of which I am not already aware from my general knowledge as a highly educated man of experience, so that I may form my own judgment whether to refuse the advised treatment or not.

No doubt, if the patient in fact manifested this attitude by means of questioning, the doctor would tell him whatever it was the patient wanted to know but we are concerned here with volunteering unsought information about risks of the proposed treatment failing to achieve the result sought or making the patient's physical or mental condition worse rather than better. The only effect that mention of risks can have on the patient's mind, if it has any at all, can be in the direction of deterring the patient from undergoing the treatment which in the expert opinion of the doctor it is in the patient's interest to undergo. To decide what risks the existence of which a patient should be voluntarily warned and the terms in which such warning, if any, should be given, having regard to the effect that the warning may have, is as much an exercise of professional skill and judgment as any other part of the doctor's comprehensive duty of care to the individual patient, and expert medical evidence on this matter should be treated in just the same way. The *Bolam* test should be applied . . ."

LORD BRIDGE:
" . . . Broadly, a doctor's professional functions may be divided into three phases: diagnosis, advice and treatment. In performing his functions of diagnosis and

treatment, the standard by which English law measures the doctor's duty of care to his patient is not open to doubt. 'The test is the standard of the ordinary skilled man exercising and professing to have that special skill.' These are the words of McNair J. in *Bolam v. Friern Hospital Management Committee* [1957] 2 All E.R. 118 at 121, approved by this House in *Whitehouse v. Jordan* [1981] 1 All E.R. 276 at 277 *per* Lord Edmund-Davies and in *Maynard v. West Midlands Regional Health Authority* [1985] 1 All E.R. 635 *per* Lord Scarman. The test is conveniently referred to as the *Bolam* test. In *Maynard*'s case Lord Scarman, with whose speech the other four members of the Appellate Committee agreed, further cited with approval the words of the Lord President (Clyde) in *Hunter v. Hanley* 1955 SLT 213 at 217:

> 'In the realm of diagnosis and treatment there is ample scope for genuine difference of opinion and one man clearly is not negligent merely because his conclusion differs from that of other professional men . . . The true test for establishing negligence in diagnosis or treatment on the part of a doctor is whether he has been proved to be guilty of such failure as no doctor of ordinary skill would be guilty of if acting with ordinary care . . . '

The language of the *Bolam* test clearly requires a different degree of skill from a specialist in his own special field than from a general practitioner. In the field of neuro-surgery it would be necessary to substitute for the Lord President's phrase 'no doctor of ordinary skill', the phrase 'no neuro-surgeon of ordinary skill'. All this is elementary and, in the light of the two recent decisions of this House referred to, firmly established law.

The important question which this appeal raises is whether the law imposes any, and if so what, different criterion as the measure of the medical man's duty of care to his patient when giving advice with respect to a proposed course of treatment. It is clearly right to recognise that a conscious adult patient of sound mind is entitled to decide for himself whether or not he will submit to a particular course of treatment proposed by the doctor, most significantly surgical treatment under general anaesthesia. This entitlement is the foundation of the doctrine of 'informed consent' which has led in certain American jurisdictions to decisions and, in the Supreme Court of Canada, to dicta on which the appellant relies, which would oust the *Bolam* test and substitute an 'objective' test of a doctor's duty to advise the patient of the advantages and disadvantages of undergoing the treatment proposed and more particularly to advise the patient of the risks involved.

There are, it appears to me, at least theoretically, two extreme positions which could be taken. It could be argued that, if the patient's consent is to be fully informed, the doctor must specifically warn him of *all* risks involved in the treatment offered, unless he has some sound clinical reason not to do so. Logically, this would seem to be the extreme to which a truly objective criterion of the doctor's duty would lead. Yet this position finds no support from any authority to which we have been referred in any jurisdiction. It seems to be generally accepted that there is no need to warn of the risks inherent in all surgery under general anaesthesia. This is variously explained on the ground that the patient may be expected to be aware of such risks or that they are relatively remote. If the law is to impose on the medical profession a duty to warn of risks to secure 'informed consent' independently of accepted medical opinion of what is appropriate, neither of these explanations for confining the duty to special as opposed to general surgical risks seems to me wholly convincing.

At the other extreme it could be argued that, once the doctor has decided what treatment is, on balance of advantages and disadvantages, in the patient's best interest, he should not alarm the patient by volunteering a warning of any risk involved, however grave and substantial, unless specifically asked by the patient. I cannot believe that contemporary medical opinion would support this view, which would effectively exclude the patient's right to decide in the very type of case where it is most important that he should be in a position to exercise that right and, perhaps even more significantly, to seek a second opinion whether he should submit himself to the significant risk which has been drawn to his attention. I should perhaps add at this point, although the issue does not strictly arise in this appeal, that, when questioned specifically by a patient of apparently sound mind about risks involved in a particular treatment proposed, the doctor's duty must, in my opinion, be to answer both truthfully and as fully as the questioner requires . . .

I recognise the logical force of the *Canterbury* doctrine, proceeding from the premise that the patient's right to make his own decision must at all costs be safeguarded against the kind of medical paternalism which assumes that 'doctor knows best'. But, with all respect, I regard the doctrine as quite impractical in application for three principal reasons. First, it gives insufficient weight to the realities of the doctor/patient relationship. A very wide variety of factors must enter into a doctor's clinical judgment not only as to what treatment is appropriate for a particular patient, but also as to how best to communicate to the patient the significant factors necessary to enable the patient to make an informed decision whether to undergo the treatment. The doctor cannot set out to educate the patient to his own standard of medical knowledge of all the relevant factors involved. He may take the view, certainly with some patients, that the very fact of his volunteering, without being asked, information of some remote risk involved in the treatment proposed, even though he describes it as remote, may lead to that risk assuming an undue significance in the patient's calculations. Second, it would seem to me quite unrealistic in any medical negligence action to confine the expert medical evidence to an explanation of the primary medical factors involved and to deny the court the benefit of evidence of medical opinion and practice on the particular issue of disclosure which is under consideration. Third, the objective test which *Canterbury* propounds seems to me to be so imprecise as to be almost meaningless. If it is to be left to individual judges to decide for themselves what 'a reasonable person in the patient's position' would consider a risk of sufficient significance that he should be told about it, the outcome of litigation in this field is likely to be quite unpredictable . . .

Having rejected the *Canterbury* doctrine as a solution to the problem of safeguarding the patient's right to decide whether he will undergo a particular treatment advised by his doctor, the question remains whether that right is sufficiently safeguarded by the application of the *Bolam* test without qualification to the determination of the question what risks inherent in a proposed treatment should be disclosed. The case against a simple application of the Bolam test is cogently stated by Laskin C.J.C., giving the judgment of the Supreme Court of Canada in *Reibl v. Hughes* (1980) 114 DLR (3d) 1 at 13:

'To allow expert medical evidence to determine what risks are material and, hence, should be disclosed and, correlatively, what risks are not material is to hand over to the medical profession the entire question of the scope of the duty of disclosure, including the question whether there has been a breach of that duty. Expert medical evidence is, of course, relevant to findings as to the risks that reside in or are a result of recommended surgery or other treatment. It will also have a bearing on their materiality but this is not a question that is to be concluded on the basis of the expert medical evidence alone. The issue under consideration is a different issue from that involved where the question is whether the doctor carried out his professional activities by applicable professional standards. What is under consideration here is the patient's right to know what risks are involved in undergoing or foregoing certain surgery or other treatment.'

I fully appreciate the force of this reasoning, but can only accept it subject to the important qualification that a decision what degree of disclosure of risks is best calculated to assist a particular patient to make a rational choice whether or not to undergo a particular treatment must primarily be a matter of clinical judgment. It would follow from this that the issue whether non-disclosure in a particular case should be condemned as a breach of the doctor's duty of care is an issue to be decided primarily on the basis of expert medical evidence, applying the *Bolam* test. But I do not see that this approach involves the necessity 'to hand over to the medical profession the entire question of the scope of the duty of disclosure, including the question whether there has been a breach of that duty'. Of course, if there is a conflict of evidence whether a responsible body of medical opinion approves of non-disclosure in a particular case, the judge will have to resolve that conflict. But, even in a case where, as here, no expert witness in the relevant medical field condemns the non-disclosure as being in conflict with accepted and responsible medical practice, I am of opinion that the judge might in certain circumstances come to the conclusion that disclosure of a particular risk was so obviously necessary to an informed choice on the part of the patient that no reasonably prudent medical man would fail to make it. The kind of case I have in mind would be an operation involving a substantial risk of grave adverse consequences, as for example the 10 per cent risk of a stroke from the operation which was the subject of the Canadian case of *Reibl v. Hughes* (1980) 114 DLR (3d) 1. In such a case, in the absence of some cogent clinical reason why the patient should not be informed, a doctor, recognising and respecting his patient's right of decision, could hardly fail to appreciate the necessity for an appropriate warning.

In the instant case I can see no reasonable ground on which the judge could properly reject the conclusion to which the unchallenged medical evidence led in the application of the *Bolam* test . . . . [T]he appellant's expert witness's agreement that the non-disclosure complained of accorded with a practice accepted as proper by a responsible body of neuro-surgical opinion afforded the respondents a complete defence to the appellant's claim . . ."

LORD TEMPLEMAN:

" . . . On the assumption that Mr Falconer explained that it was necessary to remove bone and free a nerve root from pressure near the spinal cord, it seems to me that the possibility of damage to a nerve root or to the spinal cord was obvious. The operation was skilfully performed but by mishap the remote risk of damage to the spinal cord unfortunately caused the disability from which Mrs Sidaway is now suffering. However much sympathy may be felt for Mrs Sidaway and however much in hindsight the operation may be regretted by her, the question now is whether Mr Falconer was negligent in the explanation which he gave.

In my opinion, if a patient knows that a major operation may entail serious consequences, the patient cannot complain of lack of information unless the patient asks in vain for more information or unless there is some danger which by its nature or magnitude or for some other reason requires to be separately taken into account by the patient in order to reach a balanced judgment in deciding whether or not to submit to the operation. To make Mr Falconer liable for damages for negligence, in not expressly drawing Mrs Sidaway's attention to the risk of damage to the spinal cord and its consequences, Mrs Sidaway must show, and fails to show, that Mr Falconer was not entitled to assume, in the absence of questions from Mrs Sidaway, that his explanation of the nature of the operation was sufficient to alert Mrs Sidaway to the general danger of unavoidable and serious damage inherent in the operation but sufficiently remote to justify the operation. There is no reason to think that Mr Falconer was aware that, as Mrs Sidaway deposed, a specific warning and assessment of the risk of spinal cord damage would have influenced Mrs Sidaway to decline the operation although the general explanation which she was given resulted in her consenting to the operation.

There is no doubt that a doctor ought to draw the attention of a patient to a danger which may be special in kind or magnitude or special to the patient. In *Reibl v. Hughes* 114 DLR (3d) 1 a surgeon advised an operation on the brain to avoid a threatened stroke. The surgeon knew or ought to have known that there was a 4 per cent chance that the operation might cause death and a 10 per cent chance that the operation might precipitate the very stroke which the operation was designed to prevent. The patient ought to have been informed of these specific risks in order to be able to form a balanced judgment in deciding whether or not to submit to the operation.

When a patient complains of lack of information, the court must decide whether the patient has suffered harm from a general danger inherent in the operation or from some special danger. In the case of a general danger the court must decide whether the information afforded to the patient was sufficient to alert the patient to the possibility of serious harm of the kind in fact suffered. If the practice of the medical profession is to make express mention of a particular kind of danger, the court will have no difficulty in coming to the conclusion that the doctor ought to have referred expressly to this danger as a special danger unless the doctor can give reasons to justify the form or absence of warning adopted by him. Where the practice of the medical profession is divided or does not include express mention, it will be for the court to determine whether the harm suffered is an example of a general danger inherent in the nature of the operation and if so whether the explanation afforded to the patient was sufficient to alert the patient to the general dangers of which the harm suffered is an example. If a doctor conscientiously endeavours to explain the arguments for and against a major operation and the possibilities of benefiting and the dangers, the court will be slow to conclude that the doctor has been guilty of a breach of duty owed to the patient merely because the doctor omits some specific item of information. It is for the court to decide, after hearing the doctor's explanation, whether the doctor has in fact been guilty of a breach of duty with regard to information.

A doctor offers a patient diagnosis, advice and treatment. The objectives, sometimes conflicting, sometimes unattainable, of the doctor's services are the prolongation of life, the restoration of the patient to full physical and mental health and the alleviation of pain. Where there are dangers that treatment may produce results, direct or indirect, which are harmful to the patient, those dangers must be weighed by the doctor before he recommends the treatment. The patient is entitled to consider and reject the recommended treatment and for that purpose to understand the doctor's advice and the possibility of harm resulting from the treatment.

I do not subscribe to the theory that the patient is entitled to know everything or to the theory that the doctor is entitled to decide everything. The relationship between doctor and patient is contractual in origin, the doctor performing services in consideration for fees payable by the patient. The doctor, obedient to the high standards set by the medical profession, impliedly contracts to act at all times in the best interests of the patient. No doctor in his senses would impliedly contract at the same time to give to the patient all the information available to the doctor as a result of the doctor's training and experience and as a result of the doctor's diagnosis of the patient. An obligation to give a patient all the information available to the doctor would often be inconsistent with the doctor's contractual obligation to have regard to the patient's best interests. Some information might confuse, other information might alarm a particular patient. Whenever the occasion arises for the doctor to tell the patient the results of the doctor's diagnosis, the possible methods of treatment and the advantages and disadvantages of the recommended treatment, the doctor must decide in the light of his training and experience and in the light of his knowledge of the patient what should be said and how it should be said. At the same time the doctor is not entitled to make the final decision with regard to treatment which may have disadvantages or dangers. Where the patient's health and future are at stake, the patient must make the final decision. The patient is free to decide whether or not to submit to treatment recommended by the doctor and therefore the doctor impliedly contracts to provide information which is adequate to enable the patient to reach a balanced judgment, subject always to the doctor's own obligation to say and do nothing which the doctor is satisfied will be harmful to the patient. When the doctor himself is considering the possibility of a major operation the doctor is able, with his medical training, with his knowledge of the patient's medical history and with his objective position, to make a balanced judgment whether the operation should be performed or not. If the doctor making a balanced judgment advises the patient to submit to the operation, the patient is entitled to reject that advice for reasons which are rational or irrational or for no reason. The duty of the doctor in these circumstances, subject to his overriding duty to have regard to the best interests of the patient, is to provide the patient with information which will enable the patient to make a balanced judgment if the patient chooses to make a balanced judgment. A patient may make an unbalanced judgment because he is deprived of adequate information. A patient may also make an unbalanced judgment if he is provided with too much information and is made aware of possibilities which he is not capable of assessing because of his lack of medical training, his prejudices or his personality. Thus the provision of too much information may prejudice the attainment of the objective of restoring the patient's health. The obligation of the doctor to have regard to the best interests of the patient but at the same time to make available to the patient sufficient information to enable the patient to reach a balanced judgment if he chooses to do so has not altered because those obligations have ceased or may have ceased to be contractual and become a matter of duty of care. In order to make a balanced judgment if he chooses to do so, the patient needs to be aware of the general dangers and of any special dangers in each case without exaggeration or concealment. At the end of the day, the doctor, bearing in mind the best interests of the patient and bearing in mind the patient's right to information which will enable the patient to make a balanced judgment, must decide what information should be given to the patient and in what terms that information should be couched. The court will award damages against the doctor if the court is satisfied that the doctor blundered and that the patient was deprived of information which was necessary for the purposes I have outlined. In the present case on the judge's findings I am satisfied that adequate information was made available to Mrs Sidaway and that the appeal should therefore be dismissed."

NOTES:

1. Lord Keith agreed with Lord Bridge.
2. The difficulty of ascertaining the *ratio decidendi* — or binding principle of law — in this case has already been noted. The only points on which all five Law Lords seem to agree are that, first, Mrs Sidaway does not recover because of the difficulties in proving what actually was said; secondly, that the enquiring patient should be given the information which he requests; and thirdly that a subjective test for disclosure is untenable.
3. The major legal issue left to be decided following *Chatterton v. Gerson* (above at pages 328–334) was who ascertained the materiality of the risk in order to decide whether it should be disclosed — the doctor according to the professional medical standard, or the patient? All of the Law Lords rejected any suggestion that the test should be the subjective one of what the particular patient actually wanted to know. Do you agree with the rejection of a subjective patient test? Lord Scarman was of the view that in deciding whether something was a material consideration, the court should ask whether a reasonable person in the patient's position would have regarded it as being

significant — *i.e.* he adopted a "prudent patient" test. Note that such a test is subject to the doctor's "therapeutic privilege" to withhold information which she reasonably believes would be detrimental to the patient's health. The other Law Lords adopted the test of professional medical practice, though only Lord Diplock fully endorsed the application of the *Bolam* test in this context. (For examination of the glosses to that test introduced by Lords Bridge and Templeman, see S. Lee, "Towards a Jurisprudence of Consent" in J. Eekelaar and J. Bell, (eds) *Oxford Essays in Jurisprudence* (3rd series), Oxford: Oxford University Press, 1987.)

4. Kennedy has criticised the House of Lords decision on the basis that Lord Scarman was the only Law Lord who showed any awareness that he was dealing with the fundamental human right to control one's destiny by having sufficient information to make an informed choice whether to accept or refuse treatment. All the other Law Lords preferred to couch their opinions in the discourse of doctor's duties rather than patient rights. This led them to focus on narrower factual issues concerning what precisely was said and what doctors viewed as good practice. (See I. Kennedy, "Patients, Doctors, and Human Rights" in I. Kennedy, *Treat Me Right: Essays in Medical Law and Ethics*, Oxford: Clarendon, 1988, at page 389.)

5. A further criticism Kennedy makes of the *Sidaway* decision is its failure to explore why doctors should be in a special position compared to other professionals. As he points out, it is unimaginable, for example, that a solicitor should take action without her client's permission and be regarded as legally justified in doing so, on the basis that it saved her client from making hard decisions in times of distress (See I. Kennedy, "Patients, Doctors, and Human rights" in I. Kennedy, *op. cit.*, at page 391).

6. Although the Law Lords treated the case as being about whether or not to incorporate the North American doctrine of informed consent, there is no uniformity in the American approach. Mason and McCall-Smith note that although the majority of the 51 independent jurisdictions in the United States continue to invoke the professional standard, there is a 'recognisable national drift' towards the prudent patient standard. (See J. K. Mason and R. A. McCall Smith, *Law and Medical Ethics* (4th edn.), London: Butterworths, 1994, page 240.) They also suggest that the trend in favour of patient autonomy may have gone too far in the United States, thus encouraging malpractice litigation (*op. cit.*, page 246). As a result, in some states, the legislatures have been persuaded by the medical profession to impose statutory limitations on judicial development of the doctrine of informed consent. (See D. Meyers, *The Human Body and the Law* (2nd edn.), Edinburgh: Edinburgh University Press, 1990, page 127.)

7. The High Court of Australia adopted a significantly different approach to the issue of informed consent than that taken by the

majority in *Sidaway* a few years later. In *Rogers v. Whitaker* [1993] 4 Med. L.R. 78 the Australian court, in a joint judgment of five judges, referred to the dangers of applying the *Bolam* principle in the area of advice and information, and took the view that:

> "The law should recognise that a doctor has a duty to warn a patient of the material risk inherent in the proposed treatment. A risk is material if in the circumstances of the particular case a reasonable person in the patient's position if warned of the risk would be likely to attach significance to it; or if the medical practitioner is, or should reasonably be aware, that the particular patient, if warned of the risk, would be likely to attach significance to it."

(See D. Chalmers and R. Schwartz, "*Rogers v. Whitaker* and informed consent in Australia: a fair dinkum duty of disclosure" (1993) 1 *Medical Law Review* 139–159.) As Fennell notes, it seems likely that the United Kingdom will be the last bastion of *Bolam* type tests concerning information disclosure. (See P. Fennell, *Treatment Without Consent*, London: Routledge, 1996. Generally on comparative legal approaches to this issue see D. Giesen and J. Hayes, "The Patient's Right to Know — A Comparative View" (1992) 21 *Anglo-American Law Review* 101.)

8. McLean has argued that applied to the issue of consent to treatment

> "the *Bolam Test* sets hurdles for the patient which . . . make it relatively certain that no claim will succeed unless the failure to disclose information is so gross as in any event to merit consideration under assault analysis. If the important issue is patients' rights, however, then the relevant question is not whether or not the doctor is entitled to use the defence of *volenti*. For this to apply, the patient must have been informed of the type of risk(s) to which exposure was possible, and must have agreed to accept them. This is a test much more readily susceptible of proof, and in a sense much less objectionable, than that of reasonable or accepted medical practice."

(See S. McLean, *A Patient's Right to Know*, Aldershot: Dartmouth, 1989 at page 134.) In assessing this criticism of *Sidaway*, it is now important to take account of cases like *Smith v. Tunbridge Wells Health Authority* [1994] 5 Med.L.R. 334 and *Maynard v. West Midlands Regional Health Authority* [1985] 1 All E.R. 635 and *Joyce v. Merton, Sutton and Wandsworth Health Authority* [1996] 7 Med. L.R. 1 — see pages 362–365 below.

9. A further important distinction to bear in mind is that between informed consent and informed *choice*. Even if a greater obligation had been imposed upon doctors to disclose the risks of a particular treatment, this would frequently leave the patient only with a straightforward choice of whether to accept or reject that particular treatment. To make a fully informed choice, the patient must also be aware of a range of alternatives. (This became a crucially important issue in the Court of Appeal decisions subsequent to *Sidaway* which are discussed below). Moreover, as Freedman argues, whilst health

professionals are in a position to quantify the risk of an outcome, they cannot tell the patient what *value* to put on that risk, since the likelihood of it occurring is only one of many factors that will go into a patient's analysis of her own situation. (See L. Freedman, "Censorship and Manipulation of Reproductive Health Information" in S. Coliver (ed.) *The Right to Know: Human Rights and Access to Reproductive Health Information*, Pittsburg: University of Pennsylvania Press, 1995). For example, it will be the patient's own particular circumstances which dictate whether she would prefer treatment which would offer her a shorter period of high quality life, or a longer lifetime during which she will suffer pain and have restricted mobility.

10. On the importance of communication between health professional and patient in ensuring that information disclosure is adequate, see W. C. Wu and R. A. Pearlman, "Consent in Medical Decision Making: The Role of Communication" (1988) 3 *Journal of General Internal Medicine* 9.

11. In *Sidaway* two judges (Browne Wilkinson L.J. in the Court of Appeal and Lord Scarman in the House of Lords) rejected suggestions that a doctor's obligation to inform a patient of risks in a proposed course of treatment could be derived from any fiduciary duty she owed the patient to act for her benefit. However, Grubb has argued that the doctor-patient relationship displays many characteristics of a fiduciary relationship. He contends that it is likely in the future that the courts will have to re-examine the *Sidaway* decision, and that if the duty to disclose was to be regarded as an aspect of the doctor's fiduciary duty, this could well require the law to "heighten the standard of disclosure to require a doctor to disclose all information that would be material to the patient's decision". (See A. Grubb, "The Doctor as Fiduciary" [1994] *Current Legal Problems* 311 at page 337; for other situations where this analysis may be applied see Chapter 9 at page 500.) In this regard a QALY analysis could be helpful (see Chapter 2 at pages 99–101).

QUESTIONS:

1. Was there a majority of the House of Lords in favour of any of the following: (i) applying the *Bolam* test without modifications; (ii) using a modified *Bolam* test; or (iii) requiring the disclosure of 'material' risks?

2. What objections did their Lordships express to (i) the use of the *Bolam* test, and (ii) the legal doctrine of informed consent, as developed in Canada and the USA? How far do you accept their criticisms?

3. Do any of the speeches improve on the test for material risk propounded by Bristow J. in *Chatterton v. Gerson*? If so, how?

4. Do you agree with Lord Scarman that it is possible to split the doctor's duty into various component parts — diagnosis, treatment and counselling — and that different considerations apply in the case of disclosure, which may render the *Bolam* test inappropriate to a counselling role?

5. Do you think there is in practice a real difference between the *Bolam* test and the 'prudent patient' test?

6. Were the Law Lords justified in unanimously ruling out a subjective test of what the actual patient would have wanted to know, given Faulder's contention, that "The 'reasonable person' is you, me and every other adult, autonomous human being who normally expects to make decisions according to our own perceptions of what is reasonable for us"? (See C. Faulder, *Whose Body Is It? The Troubling Issue of Informed Consent*, London: Virago, 1984 at page 37.)

7. In what circumstances did the Law Lords envisage that judges would be entitled to disagree with the views of medical experts as to whether non-disclosure would be legitimate? (See further *Smith v. Tunbridge Wells Health Authority* [1994] 5 Med.L.R. 334 at pages 362–364 below.)

8. In your view, which of the four speeches should be taken as being most representative of the majority view in the case?

9. Does his endorsement of the doctrine of therapeutic privilege undermine even Lord Scarman's framework to vindicate the patient's right to self-determination?

2. The Obligation to Disclose Information to the Patient: Non-therapeutic Cases

The test for disclosure of information in *Sidaway* was later examined in the Court of Appeal decision of *Gold v. Haringey* [1987] 2 All E.R. 888, a case which on the face of it appeared to raise different issues. It was concerned with the provision of contraceptive advice and treatment rather than therapeutic care.

Gold v. Haringey Health Authority [1987] 2 All E.R. 888, [1988] 1 Q.B. 481, [1987] 3 W.L.R. 649, [1988] 1 FLR 55

Mrs Gold decided that she wished to have no further children. Her consultant obstetrician suggested that she should be sterilised. The operation went ahead, with Mrs Gold's consent, but was not successful, and she subsequently became pregnant again. It was found that the operation had been properly performed and was not guaranteed to succeed. However, Mrs Gold alleged that the consultant had been negligent in failing to discuss the treatment properly. Two mistakes were alleged: first, that he had failed to explain the risk of failure, and secondly, that he had not discussed any alternative method by which steps could be taken to avoid Mrs Gold becoming pregnant (namely by her husband undergoing a vasectomy). All the medical witnesses said that they would have warned Mrs Gold of the risk of failure, but that a sizeable proportion of doctors (estimated at up to 50 per cent) would not have done so at the time when she had the operation. However, the judge at first instance decided that the existence of this substantial body of medical opinion did not resolve the matter, because *Sidaway* only applied to therapeutic procedures, not to non-therapeutic procedures for contraceptive reasons. Thus, Mrs Gold was awarded £19,000 damages. The Health Authority appealed and the Court of Appeal offered its interpretation of the rule of law that *Sidaway* had established:

LLOYD L.J.:
" . . . The doctors were unanimous in their view that though they themselves would have warned of the risk of failure, nevertheless a substantial body of responsible doctors would not have given any such warning in 1979. One of the witnesses put the proportion of doctors who would not have given any such warning in 1979 as high as 50 per cent. How then did it come about that the judge convicted the defendants of negligence?
In directing the jury in *Bolam v. Friern Hospital Management Committee* [1957] 2 All E.R. 118 at 122 McNair J. said:
'[A medical man] is not guilty of negligence if he has acted in accordance with a practice accepted as proper by a responsible body of medical men skilled in that particular art . . . merely because there is a body of opinion that takes a contrary view.'
In *Maynard v. West Midlands Regional Health Authority* [1985] 1 All E.R. 635 at 638 the House of Lords applied the *Bolam* test to a case of wrongful diagnosis. Lord Scarman said:
'It is not enough to show that there is a body of competent professional opinion which considers that theirs' was a wrong decision if there also exists a body of professional opinion, equally competent, which supports the decision as reasonable in the circumstances. It is not enough to show that subsequent events show that the operation need never have been performed, if at the time the decision to operate was taken it was reasonable in the sense that a responsible body of medical opinion would have accepted it as proper.'
In *Sidaway v. Bethlem Royal Hospital Governors* [1985] 1 All E.R. 643 the House of Lords applied the same test to a case in which a doctor, before carrying out an operation, failed to warn his patient of a very small risk of very serious injury. It would have been open to the House of Lords to hold that the *Bolam* test applied to negligent diagnosis and negligent treatment, but not negligent advice. In other words, the House of Lords could have adopted the doctrine of 'informed consent' favoured in the United States of America and Canada. But the House of Lords declined to follow that path. . . .

Lloyd L.J. quoted from the speech of Lord Diplock:

How, then, I ask again, did it come about that the judge found the defendants guilty of negligence, when he accepted that there was a substantial body of responsible medical opinion in 1979 who would not have given any warning? The answer is that he drew a distinction between advice or warning in a therapeutic context and advice or warning in a contraceptive context. In a therapeutic context there was a body of responsible medical opinion which would not have warned of the failure rate. But in a contraceptive context there was no such body of responsible medical opinion. Even if there had been, he would still have found the defendants negligent, since in his view the *Bolam* test does not apply to advice given in a non-therapeutic context. He said:

'I accept that it was the view of the majority of the House of Lords that in the therapeutic context of that case [*Sidaway*] the duty to give advice was subject to the same test as the duty to diagnose and treat, and that this test, known as the *Bolam* test after an earlier case, was that a doctor is not negligent if he acts in accordance with a practice accepted as proper by a responsible body of medical opinion even though other doctors adopt a different practice. This test is different from the one generally applied in actions in respect of negligent advice. I see nothing in the reasons given for adopting the *Bolam* test in the sort of circumstances under consideration in *Sidaway* which compels me to widen the application of this exceptional rule so as to cause it to apply to contraceptive counselling.'

So the judge decided against the defendants on two grounds. First, he held that the *Bolam* test did not apply at all in a contraceptive context. Instead he applied his own judgment as to what should have been mentioned in that context. Second, if the *Bolam* test did apply, then he found as a fact that there was no body of responsible medical opinion which would not, in a contraceptive context, have warned of the risk of failure. I have reversed these two grounds, since the first ground raises a question of considerable general importance.

Was the judge right when he held that the *Bolam* test is an exception to the ordinary rule in actions for negligence? If by an 'exceptional rule' the judge meant that the *Bolam* test is confined to actions against doctors, then I would respectfully disagree. I have already quoted a passage from McNair J.'s summing up in *Bolam*'s case. In an earlier passage he had said ([1957] 2 All E.R. 118 at 121:

' . . . where you get a situation which involves the use of some special skill or competence, then the test whether there has been negligence or not is not the test of the man on top of a Clapham omnibus, because he has not got this special skill. The test is the standard of the ordinary skilled man exercising and professing to have that special skill.'

So far as I know that passage has always been treated as being of general application whenever a defendant professes any special skill . . . The *Bolam* test is not confined to a defendant exercising or professing the particular skill of medicine. If there had been any doubt on the question, which I do not think there was, it was removed by the speech of Lord Diplock in the *Sidaway* case [1985] 1 All E.R. 643 at 657 where Lord Diplock made it clear that the *Bolam* test is rooted in an ancient rule of common law applicable to all artificers. In *Saif Ali v. Sydney Mitchell & Co (a firm)* [1978] 3 All E.R. 1033 at 1043 Lord Diplock treated the same test as applicable to barristers, although he did not mention the *Bolam* case by name. The question in that case was whether a barrister is immune from an action in negligence in relation to advice given out of court. It was held that he is not. Lord Diplock said:

'No matter what profession it may be, the common law does not impose on those who practise it any liability for damage resulting from what in the result turned out to have been errors of judgment, unless the error was such as no reasonably well informed and competent member of that profession could have made.'

Counsel for the plaintiff did his best to argue that the *Bolam* test is confined to doctors. For the reasons I have given, I cannot accept that argument. I can see no possible ground for distinguishing between doctors and any other profession or calling which requires special skill, knowledge or experience. To be fair to the judge, it was not, I think, on this ground that he regarded the *Bolam* test as exceptional.

In passing, I should mention that the *Bolam* test is often thought of as limiting the duty of care. So in one sense it does. But it also extends the duty of care, as the second of the two passages I have quoted from McNair J.'s summing up in the *Bolam* case makes clear. The standard is not that of the man on the top of the Clapham omnibus, as in other fields of negligence, but the higher standard of the man skilled in the particular profession or calling.

Why then did the judge think that it would be an extension of the *Bolam* test to apply it in the present case? The reason can only have been that which I have already mentioned, namely the distinction between therapeutic and non-therapeutic advice. Counsel for the plaintiff took us through the *Sidaway* case speech by speech, and paragraph by paragraph, in order to point the distinction. But I remain unconvinced. In the first place the line between therapeutic and non-therapeutic medicine is elusive. A plastic surgeon carrying out a skin graft is presumably engaged in therapeutic surgery but what if he is carrying out a facelift, or some other cosmetic operation? Counsel found it hard to say.

In the second place, a distinction between advice given in a therapeutic context and advice given in a non-therapeutic context would be a departure from the principle on which the *Bolam* test is itself grounded. The principle does not depend on the context in which any act is performed, or any advice given. It depends on a man professing skill or competence in a field beyond that possessed by the man on the Clapham omnibus. If the giving of contraceptive advice required no special skill, then I could see an argument that the *Bolam* test should not apply. But that was not, and could not have been, suggested. The fact (if it be the fact) that giving contraceptive advice involves a different sort of skill and competence from carrying out a surgical operation does not mean that the *Bolam* test ceases to be applicable. It is clear from Lord Diplock's speech in *Sidaway* that a doctor's duty of care in relation to diagnosis, treatment and advice, whether the doctor be a specialist or general practitioner, is not to be dissected into its component parts. To dissect a doctor's advice into that given in a therapeutic context and that given in a contraceptive context would be to go against the whole thrust of the decision of the majority of the House of Lords in that case. So I would reject the argument of counsel for the plaintiff under this head, and hold that the judge was not free, as he thought, to form his own view of what warning and information ought to have been given, irrespective of any body or responsible medical opinion to the contrary.

So I turn to the second question, which assumes, as I have held, that the *Bolam* test applies. Here counsel for the plaintiff acknowledges that he is in some difficulty. For in the course of the defence evidence the judge observed to counsel for the plaintiff:

'You are in the happy position of being able to say, as I understand it, that all of the defence team, as it were, are all saying that they personally would have advised, and in one case they claim they did advise. You are in that happy position. You are in the unhappy position that they will say, as you have to accept, that there were squads of people who did not.'

To which counsel replied: 'Yes, if we apply the *Bolam* test, I have had it on this limb certainly'.

Indeed as late as counsel for the plaintiff's closing submission the judge observed that the defendants were 'home and dry' if *Sidaway* applied, as I have held it does. Yet when he came to give judgment, the judge had changed his mind. For the sake of convenience I repeat here verbatim the three relevant findings:

'(3) That in a non-contraceptive context, for instance if there had been a therapeutic reason for sterilising [the plaintiff], there was a responsible body of medical opinion which would not, unasked, have mentioned the fact that the operation involved an element of risk. (4) That in the context of someone seeking contraceptive advice there was such a body of medical opinion which would not, unasked, have mentioned that the failure rate of a post partum sterilisation operation was several times as high as the ultimate failure rate of a vasectomy. (5)

That in the context of someone seeking contraceptive advice there was no such body of medical opinion which would have failed to mention that there was a risk of failure of the post partum sterilisation or that vasectomy was an option or to make inquiries of the domestic situation of the party seeking advice.'

I can find nothing in the evidence which justifies the last of these findings. Counsel for the plaintiff relies on the documentary evidence, some of which is set out in the judge's judgment. I need not refer to it in detail. As was to be expected, it emphasises the importance of counselling before deciding on an operation, whether for male or female sterilisation. In addition, the documents published by the medical defence bodies, again as was only to be expected, discourage the giving of any sort of guarantee of success. But this evidence does not meet the point made by counsel for the defendants and by all the witnesses, including those called by the plaintiff, who said that though they would themselves have warned the plaintiff of the risk of failure, there was a body of responsible doctors in 1979 who would not have done so. The judge accepted in his judgment that the distinction between advising in a contraceptive and non-contraceptive context was not 'crystal clear' on the evidence. With respect, that is an understatement. The witnesses were never asked to distinguish between the two cases. There was therefore only one finding open on the evidence, namely that there was a body of responsible medical opinion which would not have given any warning as to the failure of female sterilisation, and the possible alternatives, in the circumstances in which the defendants actually found themselves. So I would not accept the second of the two grounds on which the judge decided against the defendants . . .

For the reasons I have given the plaintiff has failed to make good her claim for negligence. Accordingly, I would allow this appeal."

NOTES:

1. Watkins L.J. and Stephen Brown L.J. agreed.
2. The interpretation of the *Sidaway* decision which was adopted in *Gold* is the most protective of the medical profession and, in Lord Scarman's view, represented an abdication of the court's role to establish the limits of professional judgment.

QUESTIONS:

1. Was the interpretation of the *Sidaway* decision offered by the Court of Appeal a legitimate one? (See I. Kennedy, "The Patient on the Clapham Omnibus" in *Treat Me Right: Essays in Medical Law and Ethics*, Oxford: Clarendon, at pages 210–212.)
2. Do you think that it is possible to draw a distinction between therapeutic and non-therapeutic procedures? (You may like to consider the discussion of this matter in relation to sterilisation procedures, see Chapter 12, or in the context of clinical research, see Chapter 10.)
3. Does the whole tenor of Lloyd L.J.'s judgment undermine the significance of counselling in a contraceptive context? (For further discussion see Chapter 12 at pages 698–703.)

3. The Obligation to Disclose Information to the Patients: Where the Patient Asks Questions

In *Blyth v. Bloomsbury* [1993] Med. L.R. 151 it was argued that the *Sidaway* test should be limited to volunteering information; different rules applying where patients ask questions. Here too, the Court of Appeal proved resistant to forcing doctors to disclose information against their clinical judgment.

Blyth v. Bloomsbury Health Authority [1993] 4 Med. L.R. 151

The plaintiff, a nurse, claimed that she had asked her doctor about the side-effects of the injectable contraceptive drug Depo-Provera. At the time it was generally accepted medical opinion that Depo-Provera was well tolerated, and no significant side-effects had been reported. However, the doctor who treated her was aware that there might be a problem with irregular bleeding; and that another doctor in the hospital had carried out research (which was contained in the hospital files) which indicated that there may be other side effects. The patient subsequently experienced menstrual irregularity and bleeding. She brought an action for damages, alleging that as she had expressly enquired of the risks inherent in the contraceptive she should have been told of all the risks known to the hospital at that time. At first instance she was awarded £3,500 damages, as the judge held that she was entitled to receive *all* the information known to the hospital about the drug. In the Court of Appeal the judgment in her favour was reversed on the facts because it was found that she had not in fact requested the information. Two judges briefly discussed the law of consent in respect of cases where information has been requested. These dicta are set out below:

KERR L.J.:
" . . . In the light of these comments I conclude that the judge was in error in holding that there was any obligation to pass on to the plaintiff all the information available to the hospital; that is to say in this case the information contained in Dr Law's files. That conclusion could not properly be based upon the evidence. As regards the judge's repeated reference to the need to give a full picture in answer to a specific enquiry, it must be borne in mind, apart from the other matters already mentioned in that regard, that no specific enquiry was found to have been made in this case.

Secondly, I think the judge's conclusions equally cannot properly be based on the remarks of Lord Diplock and Lord Bridge in *Sidaway*. The question of what a plaintiff should be told in answer to a general enquiry cannot be divorced from the *Bolam* test, any more than when no such enquiry is made. In both cases the answer must depend upon the circumstances, the nature of the enquiry, the nature of the information which is available, its reliability, relevance, the condition of the patient, and so forth. Any medical evidence directed to what would be the proper answer in the light of responsible medical opinion and practice — that is to say, the *Bolam* test — must in my view equally be placed in the balance in cases where the patient makes some enquiry, in order to decide whether the response was negligent or not.

In that connection, apart from what was said by Lords Diplock and Bridge, I would also draw attention to the speech of Lord Templeman at page 903D onwards, which suggests to me that the *Bolam* test is all-pervasive in this context. Indeed I am not convinced that the *Bolam* test is irrelevant even in relation to the question of what answers are properly to be given to specific enquiries, or that Lord Diplock or Lord Bridge intended to hold otherwise. It seems to me that there may always be grey areas, with differences of opinion, as to what are the proper answers to be given to any enquiry, even a specific one, in the particular circumstances of any case. However, on the evidence in the present case this point does not arise, since no specific enquiry was found to have been made."

NEILL L.J.:
" . . . Furthermore, I do not understand that in the decision of the House of Lords in *Sidaway v. Governors of Bethlem Royal Hospital*, [1985] 1 All E.R. 643, in the passages to which my Lord has already drawn attention, either Lord Diplock or Lord Bridge were laying down any rule of law to the effect there where questions are asked by a patient, or doubts are expressed, a doctor is under an obligation to put the patient in possession of all the information on the subject which may have been available in the files of a consultant, who may have made a special study of the subject. The amount of information to be given must depend upon the circumstances, and as a general proposition it is governed by what is called the *Bolam* test. In 1978 irregular bleeding was the side-effect which was known and recognised. The plaintiff was told about it. In my judgment it was not established, either by means of evidence of some usual system, which broke down in this particular case, or by the application of some rule of law, that the plaintiff would, or should, have been put in possession of the material, or the bulk of the material, then in Dr Law's files."

NOTES:

1. The approach suggested by *dicta* in this case does not appear to be compatible with the comments in *Sidaway* regarding the proper response to a patient who asked questions. Even Lord Diplock, who came down most strongly in favour of the application of the *Bolam* test, was very clear that the enquiring patient has a right to be given the information which he requests.
2. The interpretation of *Sidaway* in the cases of *Gold* and *Blyth* would appear to confirm McLean's view that the United Kingdom is unlikely to develop a prudent patient standard for assessing materiality of risk. (See S. McLean, *A Patient's Right to Know*, Aldershot: Dartmouth, 1989, page 85.)

QUESTIONS:

1. Do approaches which would draw a distinction between the silent and enquiring patient discriminate in favour of the better educated patient?
2. Should a distinction be drawn between those cases where the patient asks a specific question, and those where he simply seeks more information in general terms?
3. Should the fact that the patient in this case was a nurse have had any impact on the degree of information which should have been disclosed to her?

4. The Obligation to Disclose Information: A More Pro-Patient Decision?

The interpretation of *Sidaway* offered by the Court of Appeal in *Gold* and *Blythe* has been heavily criticised by commentators like Kennedy for entrenching medical paternalism. However, more recent decisions on medical negligence have offered some evidence of the Court's readiness to question medical practice.

Smith v. Tunbridge Wells Health Authority [1994] 5 Med. L.R. 334

The plaintiff, Mr Smith, was a 28 year old married man with two children. His consultant, Mr Cook, had diagnosed a full thickness rectal prolapse, and advised surgery — an ivalon sponge rectopexy [the Wells operation] — which was generally performed on elderly women, and rarely upon men who generally have a narrower pelvis. The operation was successful in the sense that the rectum was repositioned in its correct anatomical place. However, due to nerve damage during surgery, the plaintiff was rendered impotent and suffered from significant bladder malfunction.

MORLAND J.:
" . . . the first issue . . . [is] whether or not Mr Cook [the plaintiff's consultant surgeon] was under a legal duty to inform the plaintiff of, in particular, the risk of impotence when on September 23, 1988, he recommended an ivalon sponge rectopexy . . .

Mr Cook in evidence said that although he had no recollection or note of giving a warning of the risk of impotence to the patient he would have done so because it was his duty as he saw it, to give that specific warning. If he had not given the warning he himself considered that he would have been in breach of duty.

I accept the defendant's submission that Mr Cook's personal view as to his duty is not definitive evidence that in law he owed that duty. In my judgment it is however cogent evidence that general surgeons in 1988 when faced with a patient with a similar condition and history to this plaintiff's, and recommending an ivalon sponge rectopexy, would have regarded it as the proper and accepted practice to warn such a patient of the risk of impotence . . .

In Mr Northover's [a distinguished colorectal surgeon called by the plaintiff] experience for ten years the proper practice had demanded warning of the risks about the type of operation recommended to the plaintiff. In his view by 1988 the general body of responsible medical opinion was that the patient had to be fully informed of the risks . . . [Mr Scurr] said he did not know of any surgeon who did not warn in similar circumstances. In his written report he said . . . "Operations on the rectum in young people are associated with a significant incidence of impotence . . ."

Mr Carroll, the neurologist called on behalf of the plaintiff, said that in all pelvic surgery warning is, and should be given of the risk of impotence and bladder malfunction.

Professor Golligher, the greatest of experts [author of *Surgery of the Anus, Rectum and Colon* (1984)], was called by the defendants. In his evidence in chief he frankly said that, considering his textbook to which I have referred:

'Perhaps we were slow and conservative. I should have been quicker. I was responsible for misleading surgeons. They look at standard text books. I did not then know. I now would definitely insert the risk in my text book.'

In his opinion quite a number of surgeons, because of his text book, would not have given a warning in 1988. He said the risk was not put in his book because he and his collaborators could not be sure that the risk existed. As he put it: "Now I regret to some extent the omission". However, as he made clear, that was hindsight. He said he became convinced of the risk in 1985 or 1986 when a patient was referred to him for a second opinion who was impotent following a rectal prolapse . . . He says that certainly since 1985 or 1986 he would give a warning of the risk of impotence, but he still believed that quite a lot of surgeons would not have adopted the attitude of Mr Cook in 1988 — Mr Cook's attitude being, of course, that he considered himself under a duty to give a warning . . .

Mr Kirkham [a consultant general surgeon with a special interest in colorectal surgery, called by the defendants] said that he canvassed the views of ten surgeons pointing out to them that the case involved a young male patient. He said they suggested to him, so far as eight of them were concerned, that they would not have given a warning of the risks to a young male patient, whereas two would have done so. However, as a result of the present case Mr Kirkham himself now warns in similar situations. He accepted that since the early 1980s the decision in *Sidaway* early in 1985 had resulted in more and more emphasis on informed consent, and that went back to the early 1980s.

In my judgment by 1988, although some surgeons may still not have been warning patients similar in situation to the plaintiff of the risk of impotence, that omission was neither reasonable nor responsible.

In my judgment Mr Cook, in stating that he considered that he owed a duty to warn, was reflecting not only the generally accepted standard practice, but also the only reasonable and responsible standard of care to be expected from a consultant in Mr Cook's position faced with the plaintiff's situation.

On this issue in my judgment the plaintiff succeeds applying the *Bolam* test as elucidated in *Sidaway* . . .

I now come to consider the second question: Did Mr Cook give an adequate warning to the plaintiff of the risks of the Wells operation when recommending it in appropriate language for understanding by the plaintiff? . . .

I prefer the evidence of the plaintiff to that of Mr Cook. I found the plaintiff truthful and fair. I have no doubt that Mr Cook, not unnaturally, is now convinced in his own mind that he did specifically mention the risk of impotence because he believes he would have done so as he felt it his duty. I suspect that Mr Cook omitted the mention of bladder damage because he was not clear in his own mind as to how and to what extent he should explain the risks of the surgery to the plaintiff. In human terms this is explicable. The plaintiff was his first sexually active man to whom he recommended rectopexy as a consultant. As Mr Cook was not clear in his own mind, his explanation to the plaintiff was confused, with the result the plaintiff misunderstood the message.

In my judgment the plaintiff has established on the balance of probabilities that Mr Cook failed to explain with sufficient clarity to be expected in 1988 of a consultant general surgeon with his interest in colorectal surgery the risk of impotence, and on this occasion was negligent.

I am entirely satisfied that if the risk of impotence had been explained to the plaintiff, he would have refused the operation.

It is worthwhile to consider the plaintiff and his condition. He was happily married, close to his wife, as he happily still is. His wife was outside in the waiting room. They lived within minutes of the hospital. In my judgment it is unlikely that this plaintiff at the age of 28 would there and then have consented to an operation for a condition which he had lived with for eight years without asking for further details and without asking whether there were any other methods of treatment which did not have this risk of impotence, if impotence had been mentioned.

In my judgment the very fact of consent and the speed of consent are indicative that a clear warning of the risk of impotence was not communicated clearly to the plaintiff . . ."

NOTES:

1. This case does seem to embody a more 'pro-patient' attitude than the cases of *Gold* and *Blyth*. However, it is worth noting that in those cases the plaintiff had also succeeded at first instance and judgment in favour of the plaintiff was overturned on appeal. It remains to be seen whether *Smith* represents a move towards stricter legal requirements for informing patients about their care, especially given that it is an unusual case on the facts, since the doctor admitted that he would normally give warnings.

2. Newdick takes the view that it can only be a matter of time before English law adopts the North American and Canadian approach with its presumption of openness and candour between health professional and patient. He suggests that the fact that failure to disclose risks in *Smith* was held to have been negligent on the court's own assessment of the facts may be indicative of an emerging more proactive approach on the part of the courts, rather than simply deferring to medical experts. (See C. Newdick, *Who Should We Treat? Law, Patients and Resources in the N.H.S.*, Oxford: Oxford University Press, 1995 at page 297; see also the cases of *Maynard v. West Midlands Regional Health Authority* [1985] 1 All E.R. 635, *Hotson v. East Berkshire Area Health Authority* [1987] 2 All E.R. 909 and *Bolitho v. City and Hackney Health Authority* (1992) 13 BMLR 111, and *Joyce v. Merton, Sutton and Wandsworth Health Authority* [1996] 7 *Med. L.R.* 1, discussed in Chapter 3.)

3. The decision in *Smith v Tunbridge Wells* may be regarded as out of line with the earlier decisions on information disclosure. It may also be limited to its particular factual situation. Nevertheless, developments at European Union level may impact on the test for information disclosure as enunciated in the cases subsequent to *Sidaway*. A recent European Union Directive (Dir. 92/27/EEC (L113/8)) requires medicinal products to be accompanied by a leaflet explaining their side effects. This development is likely to produce better informed patients who are more likely to question doctors about the risks involved in taking prescribed drugs.

QUESTIONS:

1. Do you think that the decision in *Smith v. Tunbridge Wells HA* is more in line with the spirit of *Sidaway* than that in *Gold*?

2. What do you think would have happened had the decision been appealed?

5.   The Obligation to Disclose Information to the Patient: The Position of Other Health Care Professionals

Sidaway and the subsequent line of cases on information disclosure were concerned with the doctor's duty to disclose risks, although the adoption of the *Bolam* test will clearly apply to other professionals involved in the patient's treatment. If, however, the patient is confused or uncertain about the doctor's explanation and his own treatment choice, he may well seek advice or clarification from a nurse or other carer. After talking with the patient, the nurse may be of the view that the patient has been provided with inadequate information. What should she do in this situation?

United Kingdom Central Council for Nursing, Midwifery and Health Visiting, Guidelines for professional practice (1996)

Truthfulness

24. Patients and clients have a legal right to information about their condition; registered practitioners providing care have a professional duty to provide such information. A patient or client who wants information is entitled to an honest answer. There may be rare occasions when a person's condition and the likely effect of information given at a specific time might lead you to be selective (although never untruthful) about the information you give. Any decision you make about what information to give must be in the best interests of the patient and client.

25. Any patient or client can feel relatively powerless when they do not have full knowledge about their care or treatment. Giving patients and clients information helps to empower them. For this reason, the importance of telling the truth cannot be over-estimated. If patients or clients do not want to know the truth it should not be forced upon them. You must be sensitive to their needs and must make sure that your communication is effective. The patient or client must be given a choice in the matter. To deny them that choice is to deny their rights and so diminish dignity and independence . . .

Consent

. . .

29. It is important that the person proposing to perform a procedure should obtain consent, although there may be some urgent situations where another practitioner can do so. Sometimes you may not be responsible for getting a patient's or client's consent as, although you are caring for the patient or client, you would not actually be carrying out the procedure. However, you are often best placed to know about the emotions, concerns and views of the patient or client and may be best able to judge what information is needed so that it is understood. With this in mind, you should tell other members of the health care team if you are concerned about the patient's or client's understanding of the procedure or treatment, for example, due to language difficulties.

NOTES:

1. Part of the UKCC Code of Professional Conduct is extracted in Chapter 2 at pages 134–136.
2. The UKCC Code states that it is the nurse's duty to remonstrate with the doctor who refuses to provide more information. Yet this begs the

question of what should happen if the doctor continues to refuse to do so. In such a case the nurse is torn between her professional ethical obligation and directions given to her in the course of her employment. There has, as yet, been no case to determine whether she is justified in disclosing information against a doctor's orders. Her options would appear to be: first, to obey orders having made her objections clear; secondly, to refuse to participate further in the treatment; thirdly, to proceed herself to provide the patient with more information. In the latter two cases the nurse runs the risk of disciplinary action and ultimately dismissal. She must therefore think carefully before taking such action. Moreover, if she does decide to disclose information, she must bear in mind that her assessment of risk may be wrong, in which case she would leave herself open to a negligence claim if the patient was unable to cope with the disclosure and suffered injury as a result. In this situation a court would have to determine whether the nurse, in disclosing, had acted in accordance with a responsible body of nursing opinion. If she opts to comply with the doctor's order it is unlikely that she could be successfully sued in negligence. (See J. McHale, "Consent and the Adult Patient: The Legal Perspective" in J. Tingle and A. Cribb (eds), *Nursing Law and Ethics*, Oxford: Blackwells, 1995.)

3. Note also the special position of midwives as advocates for the pregnant women.

QUESTION:

1. If a patient is diagnosed as suffering from terminal cancer, and the doctor exercises her therapeutic privilege not to disclose this diagnosis to the patient, does the nurse have a duty to tell the truth if the patient asks her directly?

4.   VITIATION OF CONSENT

Even if the patient has full capacity, and has been given adequate information on which to make a choice, this is not the end of the matter. In determining whether the consent was truly voluntary, a number of other factors which may vitiate consent must be taken into account. In some circumstances, an apparently valid consent to or refusal of treatment may be vitiated by the circumstances in which it was given. This might occur where it is obtained fraudulently (see *Chatterton v. Gerson* discussed at pages 328–331 above), by force (*Freeman v. Home Office* [1984] 1 All E.R. 1036, below), or otherwise as a result of undue influence (*Re T* [1992] 4 All E.R. 649, below). In these very rare circumstances it may appear that the patient has consented but there are policy reasons exist for invalidating that apparent consent.

Theoretically it would seem that there should be no difference in the legal analysis of consent and of refusal to consent to health care treatment. In practice, however, the consequences of withholding consent to treatment are usually much more significant and potentially dangerous than simply giving consent; thus it can be argued that refusing to give consent is a higher order of decision-making than merely giving consent. (See J. Pearce, "Consent to Treatment During Childhood: The Assessment of Competence and Avoidance of Conflict" (1994) 165 *British Journal of Psychiatry* 713.) As we shall see in Chapter 7, the different consequences of consenting to and refusing treatment may mean that this is not the case as far as young people are concerned, since even if they refuse their consent to treatment, their parents, guardians or the court itself may be able to consent. By contrast, if an adult patient refuses his consent to treatment, no-one else is in a position to give a proxy consent (*F v. West Berkshire Health Authority* [1989] 2 All E.R. 545). Not only is this troublesome in the case of the incapacitated (see Chapter 5), it may pose problems in the situation where the patient is deemed to be competent, but makes a decision which most people would judge irrational. (See, for example, the case of *Re C* [1994] All E.R. 819, extracted in Chapter 5 at pp. 272–274, and the cases on forced caesarean discussed in Chapter 13 at page 782). In these circumstances it has been suggested that judges too readily find excuses to justify vitiating the patient's refusal on the grounds that it is irrational. (See M. Brazier, "Patient Autonomy and Consent to Treatment: The Role of Law" (1987) 7 *Legal Studies* 169; C. Faulder, *Whose Body Is It? The Troubling Issue of Informed Consent*, London: Virago, 1985, Chapter 3.) Arguably this is what happened in *Re T* (see pp. 370–371 below), where the Court of Appeal stressed the importance of patient autonomy, which extended to the right to refuse life-saving treatment, only to find reasons to undercut that autonomy when it conflicted with the views of the doctors and posed a threat to her life. Reasons given for overriding a purported refusal of consent by a competent patient may relate to the public policy factors identified at pages 322–326 above.

One circumstance in which an apparently valid decision may not be effective in law is where, in reality, the consent of the patient was given only because he was under improper pressure to accept or refuse treatment. This possibility has been considered in two cases, *Freeman v. Home Office* and *Re T*.

Freeman v. Home Office [1984] 1 All E.R. 1036, [1984] 2 W.L.R. 802

Mr Freeman was a life prisoner. He was given drugs to alleviate a psychiatric condition. He claimed that those drugs had been forcibly administered against his consent. However, the judge found that he had in fact consented. Mr Freeman further contended that he had not given a real consent because the prison officers administering the drug had disciplinary authority over him and, consequently, he could not make a free choice.

Sir John Donalson M.R.:

" . . . Counsel appearing for the plaintiff has sought to argue that (a) his client never in fact consented to being injected (factual absence of consent), (b) his client, being a prisoner serving a life sentence, could not as a matter of law consent to such treatment (legal inability to consent), and (c) even if he could consent in fact and in law, such a consent was no defence to a claim for damages for trespass to the person unless, before he consented, he had been told (i) what he was suffering from, (ii) what was the precise nature of the treatment prescribed, and (iii) what, if any, were the side effects and risks involved in that treatment (uninformed consent). It may be convenient to deal with these contentions in reverse order.

Uninformed consent

This appeal was overtaken by a decision of a differently constituted division of this court, which held that the American doctrine of 'informed consent' has no place in the law of England: see *Sidaway v. Bethlem Royal Hospital Governors* [1984] 1 All E.R. 1018.

[NOTE: now upheld by the House of Lords, see pages 341–342 above].

If there was real consent to the treatment, it mattered not whether the doctor was in breach of his duty to give the patient the appropriate information before that consent was given. Real consent provides a complete defence to a claim based on the tort of trespass to the person. Consent would not be real if procured by fraud or misrepresentation but, subject to this and subject to the patient having been informed in broad terms of the nature of the treatment, consent in fact amounts to consent in law . . .

Legal inability to consent

Counsel for the plaintiff submitted that such were the pressures of prison life and discipline that a prisoner could not, as a matter of law, give an effective consent to treatment in any circumstances. This is a somewhat surprising proposition since it would mean that, in the absence of statutory authority, no prison medical officer could ever treat a prisoner. The answer of counsel for the plaintiff was in part that outside medical officers could be brought in, but I am not persuaded that this would reduce the pressures, whatever they may be. In support of this proposition, we were referred to the judgment of Scott L.J. in *Bowater v. Rowley Regis BC* [1944] 1 All E.R. 465. Scott L.J. there said:

'In regard to the doctrine *volenti non fit injuria*, I would add one reflection of a general kind. That general maxim has to be applied with especially careful regard to the varying facts of human affairs and human nature in any particular case, just because it is concerned with the intangible factors of mind and will. For the purpose of the rule, if it be a rule, a man cannot be said to be truly 'willing', unless he is in a position to choose freely and freedom of choice predicates, not only full knowledge of the circumstances upon which the exercise of choice is conditioned, in order that he may be able to choose wisely, but the absence from his mind of any feeling of constraint, in order that nothing shall interfere with the freedom of his will.'

The maxim *volenti non fit injuria* can be roughly translated as 'You cannot claim damages if you have asked for it', and 'it' is something which is and remains a tort. The maxim, where it applies, provides a bar to enforcing a cause of action. It does not negative the cause of action itself. This is a wholly different concept from consent which, in this context, deprives the act of its tortious character. Volenti would be a defence in the unlikely scenario of a patient being held not to have in fact consented to treatment, but having by his conduct caused the doctor to believe that he had consented.

The judge expressed his view on this aspect of the argument by saying ([1983] 3 All E.R. 589 at 597) 'The right approach, in my judgment, is to say that where, in a prison setting, a doctor has the power to influence a prisoner's situation and prospects a court must be alive to the risk that what may appear, on the face of it, to be a real consent is not in fact so.'

I would accept that as a wholly accurate statement of the law. The judge said that he had borne this in mind throughout the case. The sole question is therefore whether, on the evidence, there was a real consent.

Factual absence of consent

The case of counsel for the plaintiff was that he was forcibly restrained from resisting the administration of the injections by no less than four or five prison officers. It was *not* that, due to the constraints of prison life and discipline, his will to refuse the injections was overborne and what appeared to be consent was in reality merely submission. The judge rejected this allegation of forcible restraint. He saw and heard the plaintiff give evidence at length and concluded that if he had not been consenting, it would have been necessary for him physically to be held down and injected by superior force. He had no doubt that this did not happen and he therefore concluded that the plaintiff consented.

There was ample evidence to support this conclusion, the plaintiff having on at least two occasions refused to accept treatment."

QUESTIONS:

1. Can you imagine any circumstances when, following this decision, an apparently valid consent would be vitiated because the patient had no real choice? (See M. Brazier, "Prison Doctors and their Involuntary Patients" [1982] *Public Law* 282.)
2. Does the rule that consent must be freely given, not forcibly extracted, prevent a delirious patient being restrained while being given a sedative? Would such a patient be legally competent?

Re T [1992] 4 All E.R. 649, [1993] Fam. 95, [1992] 3 W.L.R. 782, [1992] 2 F.L.R. 458, 9 BMLR 46, [1992] 3 Med. L.R. 306.

The facts of this case were discussed in the preceding Chapter at pages 269–270. In summary, T was rushed to hospital following a car accident, and having talked with her mother who was a devout Jehovah's Witness, indicated for the first time that she did not wish to have a blood transfusion.

SIR JOHN DONALDSON M.R.:
" . . . A special problem may arise if at the time the decision is made the patient has been subjected to the influence of some third party. This is by no means to say that the patient is not entitled to receive and indeed invite advice and assistance from others in reaching a decision, particularly from members of the family. But the doctors have to consider whether the decision is really that of the patient. It is wholly acceptable that the patient should have been persuaded by others of the merits of such a decision and have decided accordingly. It matters not how strong the persuasion was, so long as it did not overbear the independence of the patient's

decision. The real question in each such case is 'Does the patient really mean what he says or is he merely saying it for a quiet life, to satisfy someone else or because the advice and persuasion to which he has been subjected is such that he can no longer think and decide for himself?' In other words 'Is it a decision expressed in form only, not in reality?'

When considering the effect of outside influences, two aspects can be of crucial importance. First, the strength of the will of the patient. One who is very tired, in pain or depressed will be much less able to resist having his will overborne than one who is rested, free from pain and cheerful. Second, the relationship of the 'persuader' to the patient may be of crucial importance. The influence of parents on their children or of one spouse on the other can be, but is by no means necessarily, much stronger than would be the case in other relationships. Persuasion based upon religious belief can also be much more compelling and the fact that arguments based upon religious beliefs are being deployed by someone in a very close relationship with the patient will give them added force and should alert the doctors to the possibility — no more — that the patient's capacity or will to decide has been overborne. In other words the patient may not mean what he says."

STAUGHTON L.J.:
" . . . The first reason [why a consent may be inoperative] is that the apparent consent or refusal was given as a result of undue influence. It is, I think, misleading to ask whether it was made of the patient's own free will, or even whether it was voluntary. Every decision is made of a person's free will, and is voluntary, unless it is effected by compulsion. Likewise, every decision is made as a result of some influence: a patient's decision to consent to an operation will normally be influenced by the surgeon's advice as to what will happen if the operation does not take place. In order for an apparent consent or refusal of consent to be less than a true consent or refusal, there must be such a degree of external influence as to persuade the patient to depart from her own wishes, to an extent that the law regards it as undue. I can suggest no more precise test than that."

NOTE:

1. Butler-Sloss L.J. expressed her agreement with the test for undue influence propounded by Staughton L.J.

QUESTIONS:

1. How can health professionals distinguish the situation where a patient has taken his own decision (having sought the advice of friends and relatives) from that where his ability to make a choice has been vitiated by undue influence?

2. Do you think that courts too readily categorise a refusal of consent as being not truly voluntary when it diverges from the views of the health professionals treating the patient, and thus appears to them irrational? (See M. Brazier, "Patient Autonomy and Consent to Treatment: The Role of Law" (1987) 7 *Legal Studies* 169; H. Teff, "Consent to Medical Procedures: Paternalism, Self-Determination or Therapeutic Alliance" (1985) 101 *Law Quarterly Review* 432.)

SELECT BIBLIOGRAPHY

M. Brazier, "Patient autonomy and consent to treatment: the role of law" (1987) 7 *Legal Studies* 169.

C. Faulder, *Whose Body Is It? The Troubling Issue of Informed Consent*, London: Virago, 1985.

S. R. Hirsch and J. Harris (eds) *Consent and the Incompetent Patient: Ethics, Law and Medicine* London: Gaskell, 1988.

I. Kennedy, "Consent to treatment: the capable person" in C. Dyer (ed.), *Doctors, Patients and the Law*, Oxford: Blackwells, 1992.

I. Kennedy, "The Patient on the Clapham Omnibus" in *Treat Me Right: Law and Medical Ethics*, Oxford: Oxford University Press, 1991.

J. Keown, "The Ashes of AIDS and the Phoenix of Informed Consent" (1989) 52 *Modern Law Review* 790.

S. Lee, "Towards a Jurisprudence of Consent" in J. Bell and J. Eekelaar (eds) *Oxford Essays in Jurisprudence* (3rd series) Oxford: OUP 1987.

S. A. McLean, *A Patient's Right to Know: Information Disclosure, the Doctor and the Law* Aldershot: Dartmouth, 1989.

D. Meyers, *The Human Body and the Law* (2nd ed.), Edinburgh: Edinburgh University Press, 1990, Chapter 5.

J. Montgomery, "Power/Knowledge/Consent: Medical Decisionmaking" (1988) 51 *Modern Law Review* 245.

G. Robertson, "Informed Consent to Medical Treatment" (1981) 97 *Law Quarterly Review* 102.

M. M. Shultz, "From Informed Consent to Patient Choice: A New Protected Interest" (1985) 92 *Yale Law Journal* 219.

P. D. G. Skegg, *Law, Ethics and Medicine*, Oxford: OUP, 1984 (revised 1988), Pt II.

H. Teff, "Consent to Medical Treatment: Paternalism, Self-determination or Therapeutic Alliance" (1985) 101 *Law Quarterly Review* 432.

C. Wells, "Patients, Consent and Criminal Law" [1994] *Journal of Social Welfare Law* 65.

7

CHILDREN

1. INTRODUCTION

In the previous two chapters we have examined the rights of adults to autonomy and self-determination, their competence to consent to or refuse medical treatment and what should happen in the case of the incapacitated adult. Particularly complex issues concerning capacity for medical decision-making arise in the case of children and adolescents. This issue must be viewed against a backdrop of increasing concern for the rights of children. Much of the impetus for a now extensive literature on children's rights derived from the leading case of *Gillick v. West Norfolk and Wisbech Area Health Authority and Another* [1985] 3 All E.R. 402 which endorsed the rights of the "mature minor" or "Gillick-competent" child to consent to her own medical treatment, the Cleveland Inquiry into Child Sexual Abuse (Report of the inquiry into Child Abuse in Cleveland 1987, Cm. 412 (1988)) and the passage of the Children Act 1989 which reflected the changing structure of the family and the philosophy of children's rights. (See generally, J. Eekelaar, "The Emergence of Children's Rights" (1986) 6 *Oxford Journal of Legal Studies* 161; M. Freeman, "Taking Children's Rights More Seriously" (1992) 6 *International Journal of Law and the Family* 52.) The ascription of rights to children is important if children are to be treated with equality and as autonomous beings. In 1989 the United Nations framed the International Convention on the Rights of the Child. It advocates the right of every child to self determination, dignity, respect, non-interference, and the right to make informed decisions. More specifically the European Charter for Children in Hospital states that "children and parents have the right to informed participation in all decisions involving their health care. Every child shall be protected from unnecessary medical treatment and investigation". (See P. Alderson, "European charter of children's rights" [1993] *Bulletin of Medical Ethics* 13.) It has been argued that United Kingdom law falls far short of the ideal the Convention sets out. Because children have lacked the moral coinage of rights it has been easy to brush their interests aside in a sweep of consequentialist thinking. As Freeman has argued, in an ideal world children may not need rights, but it is not an ideal world and certainly not for children. (See

Freeman, *op. cit.*) Nevertheless, the discourse of rights is particularly contentious when it is claimed by or on behalf of children, who historically have been viewed as lacking legal rights. Thus, O'Donovan has argued that the standard legal (rights-bearing) subject is constructed as rational and reasonable and that these are not qualities which law ascribes to children. She suggests that law's "ways of talking about children are paternalistic and predictive: the child's welfare is central to decisions . . . [b]ehind the word 'welfare' lies a claim to knowledge of what is in the child's interests." (See K. O'Donovan, "The Child as Legal Object" in *Family Law Matters*, London: Pluto, 1993, at page 90.) In her view, children constitute a site for struggle between the parents or between parents and various professional groups, including health care professionals. This is certainly one interpretation of the House of Lords decision in *Gillick*. Whilst the standard reading of the case was to hail it as a vindication of children's autonomy and judicial endorsement of children's rights, as O'Donovan argues, the "doctrine of the 'mature minor' enunciated in the *Gillick* case leaves scope for the assertion of autonomy, . . . [but] it is for adults with parental responsibility initially, and ultimately for the courts, to determine the child's welfare; this decision does not belong to the child" (at pages 95-6). In similar vein, O'Neill has argued that it is more appropriate to talk in terms of parental obligations than of children's rights. (See O. O'Neill, "Children's Rights and Children's Lives" (1981) 98 *Ethics* 445.)

The major issue is thus whether children are really able to exercise a right to autonomy. As was recognised by the majority in *Gillick*, the answer to this question is likely to depend upon the maturity of the individual child — it is impossible to set an age limit at which all children suddenly become capable of autonomous decision-making. If children are accorded rights, this entails being allowed to take risks and make choices. However, as we have seen in relation to case law on the capacity of adults in Chapter 5 the law may circumscribe those rights by questioning competence where a decision appears irrational, particularly if persisting in it will result in death. Understandably law is even more reluctant to countenance risky choices when they are made by minors. Thus much of the case-law justifies paternalistic decisions by determining that the young person lacks capacity, especially if he is refusing medical treatment. In the reported cases subsequent to *Gillick* it is note-worthy that the rhetoric of autonomy has been absent. Moreover, the judges have been reluctant to lay down clear guidance as to when a child is to be deemed sufficiently mature to make his own health care decisions. There is a failure to confront the issue of what it is that a child must understand in order to be able to exercise choice. As we saw in the case of adults who lack capacity, the question of whether medical treatment can lawfully be administered has been resolved by recourse to the doctrine of necessity. By contrast, in the case of children the solution has been to allow parents or guardians to supply the requisite consent. If there is no one with parental authority, the court can exercise such power under the Children Act, wardship or its inherent jurisdiction.

However, this still leaves open the crucial question of how the best interests of the child are to be determined, particularly where the parents wish to make risky choices in relation to their children, or include them in research (see Chapter 10 at pages 582–586).

We begin in section 2 by considering the position of the younger child. Case law pertaining to this issue has arisen out of disputes where parents and health professionals disagree over what is in the best interests of the child, rather than because of any conflict between the child and a third party. In section 3 we address the older child's capacity to consent to medical treatment, both under statute and at common law. Section 4 examines the parental right to consent, while section 5 addresses the issue of whether there are any limits to the parental power to consent. In section 6 we explore the impact of the Children Act 1989 upon the issue of health care decision-making. Section 7 considers the need for reform of this area of health care law.

2. THE LEGAL POSITION OF THE YOUNG CHILD

As we shall see in the remaining sections of this chapter, most of the decided legal cases tend to focus on adolescent children at the borderlines of capacity. It is, however, important to bear in mind that these issues rarely arise in the case of younger children. It simply is not meaningful to talk of very young children exercising rights to autonomy or self-determination. Brazier suggests that it may be said with reasonable certainty that a child under 12 years of age has virtually never achieved sufficient maturity to be entrusted with the power to make her own decisions about medical treatment, and that it would be rare for a 12 to 14-year-old to possess the requisite capacity. Thus the grey area revolves largely around the 14 plus age group who are the focus of most of the case law. (See M. Brazier, *Medicine, Patents and the Law* (2nd ed.), London: Penguin, 1992, at page 341.) Nevertheless, although this analysis may apply to major health care decisions, it is crucial to bear in mind that, as in the case of adults, there are many different levels of decisions to be made, and thus the requisite capacity will vary. For example, even a very young child may be competent to consent to bandages being applied to a wound, whilst a higher threshold of capacity would have to be reached before a child could validly consent to an organ transplant. Moreover, one study found that relevant experience of illness, treatment or disability was a far more salient factor than age for acquiring competence. (See L. Hammond *et al.*, *Children's Decisions in Health Care and Research*, London: Institute of Education, 1993.) This suggests that the crucial factor in assessing competence, as with the incapacitated adult (see Chapter 5 at pages 272–279) may be the way in which children are informed about their condition and treatments for it and supported in their decision-making. (See P. Alderson and J. Montgomery, "What about Me?" *Health Services Journal*,

April 11, 1996 at page 22.) However, where the child clearly lacks the competence to make choices about her health care, the position is less complex than with adults because the parents are in the position to act as proxy decision-makers. Thus, in the straightforward case of a sick child with caring parents, parental consent to treatment which is in the best interests of the child authorises the doctor to proceed without any risk of an action for trespass. In practice problems generally arise in the case of young children where the parents refuse consent to treatment which the health professionals treating him deem to be in the best interests of the child or where the parents disagree about treatment. The most common scenario is where parents elect to refuse treatment on behalf of the child due to their own moral or religious reasons.

Re R (A Minor) (Blood Transfusion) [1993] 2 FLR 757, [1993] Fam. Law 577, [1993] 2 F.C.R. 544

A 10-month-old girl was suffering from B-cell lymphoblastic leukaemia. The doctor had advised that she would require treatment for two years, which could necessitate the provision of blood transfusions. Her parents, both devout Jehovah's Witnesses, refused to consent to such treatment. The local authority therefore obtained leave to apply for a specific issue order under section 8 of the Children Act 1989 in order to gain judicial sanction for the use of blood products against the parents' wishes.

BOOTH J.:
" . . . The parents are extremely anxious that their daughter should receive the best possible medical care. Their primary objection to the proposed medical procedure is one of scriptural conscience. But the parents are also aware of the known hazards of blood transfusions and are anxious on this account. They further make the telling point that advances in medical science are so rapid that alternative blood management becomes possible in many procedures and as parents they want to be able to argue for their use whenever possible. If the court authorises the use of blood the parents are concerned to ensure that it is not a blanket authority to the doctors to do whatever they wish without consultation with them.

To obtain the court's authorisation for the use of blood products the local authority applied for a specific issue order under section 8 of the Children Act 1989. By definition a specific issue order means an order giving directions for the purpose of determining a specific question which has arisen, or which may arise, in connection with any aspect of parental responsibility for a child.

In the present case I am in no doubt that the application is well-founded under section 8 of the Act. The result which the local authority wishes to achieve, namely, the court's authorisation for the use of blood products, can clearly be achieved by the means of such an order. There is no need for the court otherwise to intervene to safeguard the little girl, so that I am satisfied that it is unnecessary and inappropriate for the court to exercise its inherent jurisdiction.

I therefore turn to consider the application and the matters to which the court must have regard under section 1 of the Act. The welfare of the little girl is the court's paramount consideration. At 10 months of age she is too young to express her wishes and feelings. The evidence is clear, however, that because of her medical condition the opinion of those who are responsible for her treatment supports the use of blood products. Without that treatment, the consensus is that the treatment will be unsuccessful and she will suffer harm. Only because they cannot give their consent to this treatment are her caring parents unable to meet her needs. But so overwhelming is her need for blood and so much is it in her best interests to have it in the light of current medical knowledge that, for her welfare, I am bound to override the parents' wishes and authorise the use of blood products, thus enabling the doctors to give her transfusions.

Mr Daniel, however, makes the powerful submission that such an order should not provide the medical consultants with a blanket authority to carry out such treatments without any further reference to the parents. They wish not only to be involved as far as possible in the care of their daughter but also to be able to draw attention to treatments alternative to the use of blood products and this is a field in which medical science is advancing rapidly and more such treatments are quickly becoming available. I consider this to be a perfectly proper approach. In a life-threatening emergency situation, the doctors clearly could not consult with the parents; but in the normal course of events it is reasonable that they should do so. Mrs Dangor, on behalf of the local authority, has been able to agree this and consequently the order which I made on Friday last provides for such consultation to take place."

NOTES:

1. This issue had been addressed in earlier cases. In *Re O (A Minor) (Medical Treatment)* [1993] 2 FLR 149 a baby was born prematurely, suffering from a respiratory distress syndrome, which would at some stage require a blood transfusion. Her parents were Jehovah's Witnesses, who were torn between their desire to preserve her life whilst wanting to avoid damaging her prospects in her next life. Other solutions were attempted, but the consultant paediatrician, who wished to anticipate the necessity for a blood transfusion, applied for an emergency protection order which was granted by the judge on the basis that "there is reasonable cause to suspect that the child is suffering or is likely to suffer significant harm because the parents are withholding their permission to give urgent medical treatment and unless this treatment is received the child may die". The effect of the order was to give the local authority parental responsibility for the baby. After weighing up the various considerations, including the religious principles which underlay the family's decision, Johnson J. concluded that the court's duty, acting as the judicial reasonable parent, was to give directions to ensure that whenever the need arose, the child would receive the blood transfusion that medical advice dictated.

2. In *Re S (A Minor) (Medical Treatment)* [1993] 1 FLR 396 a four-year-old boy suffered from T-cell leukaemia. The consultant paediatrician treating him considered blood transfusion to be an essential supplement to the child's continued treatment regime of intensified chemotherapy. However, the parents, who were Jehovah's Witnesses, refused consent to the transfusion of blood or blood products. Without the intensified treatment there was no prospect of a cure. In this case the local authority were prepared to invoke the inherent

jurisdiction of the High Court under section 100(3) of the Children Act (see page 425, below). However, the application was unopposed, and once again the court authorised this treatment in the best interests of the child.

3. These dilemmas are only likely to be resolved if blood substitutes are developed so as to provide an alternative to blood management in many procedures. This is one example of how scientific developments may alleviate ethical dilemmas rather than exacerbating them. Reference was made in *Re R* to such scientific advances.

4. If parents were to refuse *all* medical treatment for their child this would amount to a criminal offence, if the child was to suffer harm as a result. (See Chapter 14 at pages 824–827.) After *Re R*, it is likely that the case of a parent refusing only one form of treatment would be dealt with by way of a specific issue order under section 8 (for further discussion of the procedures by which a case may come to court see page 425 below and Appendix).

5. The only other case likely to cause similar problems for the court is when parents decide that they want to subject their child to a course of innovative medical treatment which may be onerous and which carries no guarantee of a cure. For instance in a case like *R v. Cambridgeshire Health Authority, ex parte B* (see Chapter 1 at pages 54–60), or that of Laura Davies a five year old girl from Manchester who had received repeated multiple organ transplants, the issue arises of whether parents should have the right to submit their children to aggressive invasive therapies which ultimately prove futile (see Chapter 15 at pages 905–908 and Appendix). The question of subjecting a child to innovative therapy also blurs into the right of parents to consent to the involvement of their child in clinical research programmes. (See Chapter 10 at pages 582–586.)

QUESTIONS:

1. A major difficulty in such cases is determining where the child's welfare lies if the parents genuinely believe that damage in a future life is likely to be occasioned by the preservation of life. Do you think that the courts have reached the right decision in consistently asserting that the child's welfare is served by preserving life in the face of parental objections? (See C. Bridge, "Parental beliefs and medical treatment of children" [1994] *Butterworth's Family Law Journal* 131.)

2. Does the welfare of the child require that he receive the most effective and painless course of treatment available, even if other riskier and less effective treatments provide an alternative?

3.   A CHILD'S CAPACITY TO CONSENT TO MEDICAL TREATMENT

(a) The Statutory Power of Consent

A potentially even more problematic situation is when the question for the court is whether a minor is sufficiently competent to decide upon his own medical treatment. For the purposes of English law, a child is only deemed to reach adulthood at 18 years of age. However, once he reaches the age of 16, the Family Law Reform Act 1969 validates his consent to certain forms of medical procedure, as though he was an adult.

Family Law Reform Act 1969, s.8(1–3)

8.—(1) The consent of a minor who has attained the age of sixteen years to any surgical, medical or dental treatment which, in the absence of consent, would constitute a trespass to his person, shall be as effective as it would be if he were of full age; and where a minor has by virtue of this section given an effective consent to any treatment it shall not be necessary to obtain any consent for it from his parent or guardian.

(2) In this section "surgical, medical or dental treatment" includes any procedure undertaken for the purposes of diagnosis, and this section applies to any procedure (including, in particular, the administration of an anaesthetic) which is ancillary to any treatment as it applies to that treatment.

(3) Nothing in this section shall be construed as making ineffective any consent which would have been effective if this section had not been enacted.

NOTES:

1. Subsection 2 fails to make clear whether the "surgical, medical or dental treatment" envisaged by subsection (1) must be therapeutic. This might place a limit on the medical procedures to which a 16-year-old may give a valid consent under the 1969 Act.
2. Notice that subsection 3 clearly preserves someone's power of consent but that it does not make clear whose power of consent that is. It could be the parents' power, the child's power or both parents' and the child's power — the provision is simply not explicit. This is a vital question when confronted with cases in which parents and children disagree about medical procedures. It is explored further in section 4 below.

(b) The Common Law Power of Consent

Section 8 deals only with a child's power to give consent where that child has attained 16 years of age. In relation to the younger child, any power to grant a valid consent to health care provision necessarily emanates from the common law. The leading case concerning a child's capacity to provide a valid consent at common law came before the House of Lords in 1985.

Gillick v. West Norfolk and Wisbech Area Health Authority and Another
[1985] 3 All E.R. 402, [1986] 1 A.C. 112, [1985] 3 W.L.R. 830, [1986] 1
FLR 224, 2 BMLR 11

The D.H.S.S. (as it then was) issued a circular to area health authorities
which contained advice effectively stating that if, at a family planning
clinic, a doctor was consulted by a girl under 16, she would not be acting
unlawfully if she prescribed contraceptives for the girl, as long as she was
acting in good faith to protect the girl from the harmful effects of sexual
intercourse. The plaintiff, Mrs Gillick, who herself had five daughters
under 16, sought an assurance from her local area health authority that her
own daughters would not be given any contraceptive advice or treatment
without her (Mrs Gillick's) prior knowledge and consent so long as those
girls were under 16. The authority refused to provide that assurance. In
consequence, Mrs Gillick brought an action seeking, against the area health
authority, a declaration that a doctor, or other professional employed by it
in its family planning service, could not give advice and treatment on
contraception to any of her children under 16 without her consent,
because to do so would be unlawful as being inconsistent with the
plaintiff's parental rights. At first instance, Woolf J. refused to grant the
declaration. Mrs Gillick appealed to the Court of Appeal where she was
successful and the judgments emphasised the parental right to control the
child. The health authority then appealed to the House of Lords.

LORD FRASER:
". . . The central issue in the appeal is whether a doctor can ever, in any
circumstances, lawfully give contraceptive advice or treatment to a girl under the
age of 16 without her parents' consent . . .
    The first statutory provision for contraceptive advice and treatment in the NHS
was made by s.1 of the National Health Service (Family Planning) Act 1967. That
section empowered local health authorities in England and Wales, with the
approval of the Minister of Health, to make arrangements for giving advice on
contraception, for medical examination of persons seeking such advice and for the
supply of contraceptive substances and appliances. There appears to have been no
similar provision applying to Scotland. The 1967 Act was repealed by the National
Health Service Reorganisation Act 1973, which, by s.4, replaced the power of local
health authorities to provide such advice and treatment with a duty on the
Secretary of State to do so. A similar duty was placed on the Secretary of State for
Scotland by s.8 of the National Health Service (Scotland) Act 1972. The 1973
provision for England and Wales has now been superseded by the National Health
Service Act 1977, which by s.5(1)(b) imposes a duty on the Secretary of State —
    'to arrange, to such extent as he considers necessary to meet all reasonable
    requirements in England and Wales, for the giving of advice on contraception,
    the medical examination of persons seeking advice on contraception, the
    treatment of such persons and the supply of contraceptive substances and
    appliances.'
These, and other, provisions show that Parliament regarded 'advice' and 'treatment'
on contraception and the supply of appliances for contraception as essentially
medical matters. So they are, but they may also raise moral and social questions on
which many people feel deeply, and in that respect they differ from ordinary
medical advice and treatment. None of the provisions to which I have referred

placed any limit on the age (or the sex) of the persons to whom such advice or treatment might be supplied . . .

There are some indications in statutory provisions to which we were referred that a girl under 16 years of age in England and Wales does not have the capacity to give valid consent to contraceptive advice and treatment. If she does not have the capacity, then any physical examination or touching of her body without her parents' consent would be an assault by the examiner. One of those provisions is s.8 of the Family Law Reform Act 1969, which is in the following terms:

> '(1) The consent of a minor who has attained the age of sixteen years to any surgical, medical or dental treatment which, in the absence of consent, would constitute a trespass to his person, shall be as effective as it would be if he were of full age; and where a minor has by virtue of this section given an effective consent to any treatment it shall not be necessary to obtain any consent for it from his parent or guardian . . .
> (3) Nothing in this section shall be construed as making ineffective any consent which would have been effective if this section had not been enacted.'

The contention on behalf of Mrs Gillick was that sub-s. (1) of s.8 shows that, apart from the subsection, the consent of a minor to such treatment would not be effective. But I do not accept that contention because sub-s. (3) leaves open the question whether consent by a minor under the age of 16 would have been effective if the section had not been enacted. That question is not answered by the section, and sub-s. (1) is, in my opinion, merely for the avoidance of doubt.

Another statutory provision which was referred to in this connection is the National Health Service (General Medical and Pharmaceutical Services) Regulations 1974 SI 1974/160, as amended by the National Health Service (General Medical and Pharmaceutical Services) Amendment Regulations 1975, SI 1975/719. The regulations prescribe the mechanism by which the relationship of doctor and patient under the NHS is created. Contraceptive services, along with maternity medical services, are treated as somewhat apart from other medical services in respect that only a doctor who specially offers to provide contraceptive or maternity medical services is obliged to provide them: see the definition of 'medical card' and 'treatment' in reg 2(1); see also regs 6(1)(a) and 14(2)(a) and Sch 1, para 13. But nothing turns on this fact. Two points in those regulations have a bearing on the present question although, in my opinion, only an indirect bearing. The first is that by reg 14 any 'woman' may apply to a doctor to be accepted by him for the provision of contraceptive services. The word 'woman' is not defined so as to exclude a girl under 16 or under any other age. But reg 32 provides as follows:

> 'An application to a doctor for inclusion on his list . . . may be made, either—(a) on behalf of any person under 16 years of age, by the mother, or in her absence, the father, or in the absence of both parents the guardian or other adult person who has the care of the child; or (b) on behalf of *any other person who is incapable* of making such an application by a relative or other adult person who has the care of such person . . . '

The words in para (b) which I have emphasised are said, by counsel for Mrs Gillick, to imply that a person under 16 years of age is incapable of applying to a doctor for services and therefore give some support to the argument on behalf of Mrs Gillick. But I do not regard the implication as a strong one because the provision is merely that an application 'may' be made by the mother or other parent or guardian and it applies to the doctor's list for the provision of all ordinary medical services as well as to his list for the provision of contraception services. I do not believe that a person aged 15, who may be living away from home, is incapable of applying on his own behalf for inclusion in the list of a doctor for medical services of an ordinary kind not connected with contraception.

Another provision, in a different branch of medicine, which is said to carry a similar implication is contained in the Mental Health Act 1983, s.131, which provides for informal admission of patients to mental hospitals. It provides by sub-s. (2):

'In the case of a minor who has attained the age of 16 years and is capable of expressing his own wishes, any such arrangements as are mentioned in subsection (1) above [for informal admission] may be made, carried out and determined notwithstanding any right of custody or control vested by law in his parent or guardian.'

That provision has only a remote bearing on the present question because there is no doubt that a minor under the age of 16 is in the custody of his or her parents. The question is whether such custody necessarily involves the right to veto contraceptive advice or treatment being given to the girl.

Reference was also made to the Education Act 1944, s.48, which dealt with medical inspection and treatment of pupils at state schools. Section 48(3), which imposed on the local education authority a duty to provide for medical and dental inspection of pupils, was repealed and superseded by the National Health Service Reorganisation Act 1973, s.3 and Sched. 5. The 1973 Act in turn was replaced by the National Health Service Act 1977, s.5(1)(a). Section 48(4) of the Education Act 1944, which has not been repealed, imposes a duty on the local education authority to arrange for encouraging pupils to take advantage of any medical treatment so provided, but it includes a proviso in the following terms:

'Provided that if the parent of any pupil gives to the authority notice that he objects to the pupil availing himself of any of the provision [for medical treatment etc.] so made the pupil shall not be encouraged . . . so to do.'

I do not regard that provision as throwing light on the present question. It does not prohibit a child under the stipulated age from availing himself of medical treatment or an education authority from providing it for him. If the child, without encouragement from the education authority, 'wishes to avail himself of medical treatment' the section imposes no obstacle in his way. Accordingly, in my opinion, the proviso gives no support to the contention from Mrs Gillick, but on the contrary points in the opposite direction.

The statutory provisions to which I have referred do not differentiate so far as the capacity of a minor under 16 is concerned between contraceptive advice and treatment and other forms of medical advice and treatment. It would, therefore, appear that, if the inference which Mrs Gillick's advisers seek to draw from the provisions is justified, a minor under the age of 16 has no capacity to authorise any kind of medical advice or treatment or examination of his own body. That seems to me so surprising that I cannot accept it in the absence of clear provisions to that effect. It seems to me verging on the absurd to suggest that a girl or a boy aged 15 could not effectively consent, for example, to have a medical examination of some trivial injury to his body or even to have a broken arm set. Of course the consent of the parents should normally be asked, but they may not be immediately available. Provided the patient, whether a boy or a girl, is capable of understanding what is proposed, and of expressing his or her own wishes, I see no good reason for holding that he or she lacks the capacity to express them validly and effectively and to authorise the medical man to make the examination or give the treatment which he advises. After all, a minor under the age of 16 can, within certain limits, enter into a contract. He or she can also sue and be sued, and can give evidence on oath. Moreover, a girl under 16 can give sufficiently effective consent to sexual intercourse to lead to the legal result that the man involved does not commit the crime of rape: see *R. v. Howard* [1965] 3 All E.R. 684 at 685, when Lord Parker C.J. said:

'. . . in the case of a girl under sixteen, the prosecution, in order to prove rape, must prove either that she physically resisted, or if she did not, that her understanding and knowledge were such that she was not in a position to decide whether to consent or resist . . . there are many girls under sixteen who know full well what it is all about and can properly consent.'

Accordingly, I am not disposed to hold now, for the first time, that a girl aged less than 16 lacks the power to give valid consent to contraceptive advice or treatment, merely on account of her age.

I conclude that there is no statutory provision which compels me to hold that a girl under the age of 16 lacks the legal capacity to consent to contraceptive advice, examination and treatment provided that she has sufficient understanding and intelligence to know what they involve . . .".

LORD SCARMAN:
" . . . The modern law governing parental right and a child's capacity to make his own decisions was considered in *R v. D* [1984] 2 All E.R. 449. The House must, in my view, be understood as having in that case accepted that, save where statute otherwise provides, a minor's capacity to make his or her own decision depends on the minor having sufficient understanding and intelligence to make the decision and is not to be determined by reference to any judicially fixed age limit. The House was faced with a submission that a father, even if he had taken his child away by force or fraud, could not be guilty of a criminal offence of any kind. Lord Brandon, with whom their other Lordships agreed, commented that this might well have been the view of the legislature and the courts in the nineteenth century, but had this to say about parental right and a child's capacity in our time to give or withhold a valid consent ([1984] 2 All E.R. 449 at 456):

'This is because in those times both the generally accepted conventions of society and the courts by which such conventions were buttressed and enforced, regarded a father as having absolute and paramount authority, as against all the world, over any children of his who were still under the age of majority (then 21), except for a married daughter. The nature of this view of a father's rights appears clearly from various reported cases, including, as a typical example, *Re Agar-Ellis, Agar-Ellis v. Lascelles* (1883) 24 Ch.D. 317. The common law, however, while generally immutable in its principles, unless different principles are laid down by statute, is not immutable in the way in which it adapts, develops and applies those principles in a radically changing world and against the background of radically changed social conventions and conditions.'

Later he said ([1984] 2 All E.R. 449 at 457):

'I see no good reason why, in relation to the kidnapping of a child, it should not in all cases be the absence of the child's consent which is material, whatever its age may be. In the case of a very young child, it would not have the understanding or the intelligence to give its consent, so that absence of consent would be a necessary inference from its age. In the case of an older child, however, it must, I think, be a question of fact for a jury whether the child concerned has sufficient understanding and intelligence to give its consent; if, but only if, the jury considers that a child has these qualities, it must then go on to consider whether it has been proved that the child did not give its consent. While the matter will always be for the jury alone to decide, I should not expect a jury to find at all frequently that a child under 14 had sufficient understanding and intelligence to give its consent.'

In the light of the foregoing I would hold that as a matter of law the parental right to determine whether or not their minor child below the age of 16 will have medical treatment terminates if and when the child achieves a sufficient understanding and intelligence to enable him or her to understand fully what is proposed. It will be a question of fact whether a child seeking advice has sufficient understanding of what is involved to give a consent valid in law. Until the child achieves the capacity to consent, the parental right to make the decision continues save only in exceptional circumstances. Emergency, parental neglect, abandonment of the child or inability to find the parent are examples of exceptional situations justifying the doctor proceeding to treat the child without parental knowledge and consent; but there will arise, no doubt, other exceptional situations in which it will be reasonable for the doctor to proceed without the parent's consent.

When applying these conclusions to contraceptive advice and treatment it has to be borne in mind that there is much that has to be understood by a girl under the age of 16 if she is to have legal capacity to consent to such treatment. It is not enough that she should understand the nature of the advice which is being given: she must also have a sufficient maturity to understand what is involved. There are moral and family questions, especially her relationship with her parents; long-term problems associated with the emotional impact of pregnancy and its termination; and there are the risks to health of sexual intercourse at her age, risks which contraception may diminish but cannot eliminate. It follows that a doctor will have to satisfy himself that she is able to appraise these factors before he can safely proceed on the basis that she has at law capacity to consent to contraceptive treatment. And it further follows that ordinarily the proper course will be for him, as the guidance lays down, first to seek to persuade the girl to bring her parents into consultation, and, if she refuses, not to prescribe contraceptive treatment unless he is satisfied that her circumstances are such that he ought to proceed without parental knowledge and consent.

Like Woolf J., I find illuminating and helpful the judgment of Addy J. of the Ontario High Court in *Johnston v. Wellesley Hospital* (1970) 17 D.L.R. (3d) 139, a passage from which he quotes in his judgment in this case ([1984] 1 All E.R. 365 at 374). The key passage bears repetition (17 D.L.R. (3d) 139 at 144-145):

'But, regardless of modern trend, I can find nothing in any of the old reported cases, except where infants of tender age or young children were involved, where the Courts have found that a person under 21 years of age was legally incapable of consenting to medical treatment. If a person under 21 years were unable to consent to medical treatment, he would also be incapable of consenting to other types of bodily interference. A proposition purporting to establish that any bodily interference acquiesced in by a youth of 20 years would nevertheless constitute an assault would be absurd. If such were the case, sexual intercourse with a girl under 21 years would constitute rape. Until the minimum age of consent to sexual acts was fixed at 14 years by a statute, the Courts often held that infants were capable of consenting at a considerably earlier age than 14 years. I feel that the law on this point is well expressed in the volume on *Medical Negligence* (1957) by Lord Nathan (page 176): "It is suggested that the most satisfactory solution of the problem is to rule that an infant who is capable of appreciating fully the nature and consequences of a particular operation or of particular treatment can give an effective consent thereto, and in such cases the consent of the guardian is unnecessary; but that where the infant is without the capacity, any apparent consent by him or her will be a nullity, the sole right to consent being vested in the guardian." '

I am, therefore, satisfied that the department's guidance can be followed without involving the doctor in any infringement of parental right. Unless, therefore, to prescribe contraceptive treatment for a girl under the age of 16 is either a criminal offence or so close to one that to prescribe such treatment is contrary to public policy, the department's appeal must succeed . . ."

NOTES:

1. Lord Bridge delivered a short speech of his own but, in it, he expressly agreed with both Lord Fraser and Lord Scarman, notwithstanding the fact that there are significant differences in their opinions. Both Lord Brandon and Lord Templeman dissented on the question of whether a doctor could ever give contraceptive advice or treatment to a girl under 16 without parental knowledge or consent. It is worth noting that overall a majority of the total of nine judges who heard the case would have found in favour of Mrs Gillick.

2. Various commentators have pointed out that the House of Lords failed to determine what exactly it is that the young person must understand in order to be deemed sufficiently mature to be entrusted with decision-making powers. Lord Fraser simply states without explanation that the girl must understand the doctor's advice. Lord Scarman does attempt to define the requisite capacity (at page 384 above), but this is problematic in that setting the threshold of understanding so high may mean that many adults would fail to satisfy his test. This is particularly evident when he speaks of "the attainment by a child of an age of sufficient discretion to enable him or her to exercise a wise choice in his or her own interests" and of the child achieving "a sufficient intelligence to enable him or her to understand fully what is proposed" (See S. Lee, *Judging Judges*, London: Faber & Faber, 1988, Chapter 11; J. Montgomery, "Children as Property?" (1988) 51 M.L.R. 323.)

QUESTIONS:

1. To be regarded as competent to consent to treatment, must a child understand merely in broad medical terms that which is proposed, or must she also understand the family and social implications of what is involved? Contrast the different views expressed by Lords Fraser and Scarman.

2. Is *"Gillick* competence" an absolute concept, representing a watershed beyond which a sufficiently mature minor is capable of consenting to all and any medical procedures? Or is it an incremental concept allowing a child to consent to simple operations — such as a tonsillectomy — at a relatively early stage in his development and then more complex medical procedures at a later stage, when he has matured even further? Also, can a child have fluctuating capacity (*i.e.* be *"Gillick* competent" one day but not the next)? (See *Re R (A Minor) (Wardship: Medical Treatment)* [1991] 4 All E.R. 177 at pages 398–403 below.)

3. Does the *Gillick* decision really emancipate children, or does it simply transfer the right to make paternalistic decisions from parents to doctors? (See J. Montgomery, *op. cit.*)

4. THE PARENTAL POWER OF CONSENT

Though the Family Law Reform Act 1969 confers an unequivocal power to consent to medical treatment upon a child when he reaches 16 years, the legislation does not address the power to refuse such treatment. This is by no means an academic point for, if the child of 16 is incapable of expressing a view or unwilling to grant consent, it raises the question as to whether the child's parents retain their power of consent (until the child's majority). If they do, then it becomes possible for parents to sanction treatment to which a *"Gillick* competent" child objects.

Whether parents do in fact retain their power to give consent to their child's treatment beyond 16 years of age or the attainment of *Gillick* competence was considered obliquely by their Lordships in the *Gillick* case.

Gillick v. West Norfolk and Wisbech Area Health Authority and Another [1985] 3 All E.R. 402, [1986] 1 A.C. 112, [1985] 3 W.L.R. 830, [1986] 1 FLR 224, 2 BMLR 11

The facts are set out in the preceding section of this chapter.

LORD FRASER:
". . . The amended [DHSS] guidance expressly states that the doctor will proceed from the assumption that it would be 'most unusual' to provide advice about contraception without parental consent. It also refers to certain cases where difficulties might arise if the doctor refused to promise that his advice would remain confidential and it concludes that the department realises that 'in such exceptional cases' the decision whether or not to prescribe contraception must be for the clinical judgment of a doctor. Mrs Gillick's contention that the guidance adversely affects her rights and duties as a parent must, therefore, involve the assertion of an absolute right to be informed of and to veto such advice or treatment being given to her daughters even in the 'most unusual' cases which might arise (subject, no doubt, to the qualifications applying to the case of court order or to abandonment of parents' duties).

It was, I think, accepted both by Mrs Gillick and by the DHSS, and in any event I hold, that parental rights to control a child do not exist for the benefit of the parent. They exist for the benefit of the child and they are justified only in so far as they enable the parent to perform his duties towards the child, and towards other children in the family. If necessary, this proposition can be supported by reference to *Blackstone's Commentaries* (1 Bl Com (17th edn, 1830) 452), where he wrote: 'The power of parents over their children is derived from . . . their duty.' The proposition is also consistent with the provisions of the Guardianship of Minors Act 1971, s.1, as amended, as follows:

'Where in any proceedings before any court . . . (a) the legal custody or upbringing of a minor . . . is in question, the court, in deciding that question, shall regard the welfare of the minor as the first and paramount consideration, and shall not take into consideration whether from any other point of view the claim of the father in respect of such legal custody, upbringing, administration or application is superior to that of the mother, or the claim of the mother is superior to that of the father.'

From the parents' right and duty of custody flows their right and duty of control of the child, but the fact that custody is its origin throws but little light on the question of the legal extent of control at any particular age. Counsel for Mrs Gillick placed some reliance on the Children Act 1975. Section 85(1) provides that in that Act the expression 'the parental rights and duties' means 'all the rights and duties which by law the mother and father have in relation to a legitimate child and his property', but the subsection does not define the extent of the rights and duties which by law the mother and father have. Section 86 of the Act provides:

'In this Act, unless the context otherwise requires, "legal custody" means, as respects a child, so much of the parental rights and duties as relate to the person of the child (including the place and manner in which his time is spent) . . . '

In the Court of Appeal Parker L.J. attached much importance to that section, especially to the words in brackets. He considered that the right relating to the place and manner in which the child's time is spent included the right, as he put it, 'completely to control the child' subject of course always to the intervention of the court. Parker L.J. went on thus ([1985] 1 All E.R. 533 at 540):

'Indeed there must, it seems to me, be such a right from birth to a fixed age unless whenever, short of majority, a question arises it must be determined, in relation to a particular child and a particular matter, whether he or she is of sufficient understanding to make a responsible and reasonable decision. This alternative appears to me singularly unattractive and impracticable, particularly in the context of medical treatment.'

My Lords, I have, with the utmost respect, reached a different conclusion from that of Parker L.J. It is, in my view, contrary to the ordinary experience of mankind, at least in Western Europe in the present century, to say that a child or a young person remains in fact under the complete control of his parents until he attains the definite age of majority, now 18 in the United Kingdom, and that on attaining that age he suddenly acquires independence. In practice most wise parents relax their control gradually as the child develops and encourage him or her to become increasingly independent. Moreover, the degree of parental control actually exercised over a particular child does in practice vary considerably according to his understanding and intelligence and it would, in my opinion, be unrealistic for the courts not to recognise these facts. Social customs change, and the law ought to, and does in fact, have regard to such changes when they are of major importance. An example of such recognition is to be found in the view recently expressed in your Lordships' House by Lord Brandon, with which the other noble and learned Lords who were present agreed, in *R v. D* [1984] 2 All E.R. 449 at 457. Dealing with the question of whether the consent of a child to being taken away by a stranger would be a good defence to a charge of kidnapping, Lord Brandon said:

'In the case of a very young child, it would not have the understanding or the intelligence to give its consent, so that absence of consent would be a necessary inference from its age. In the case of an older child, however, it must, I think be a question of fact for a jury whether the child concerned has sufficient understanding and intelligence to give its consent; if, but only if, the jury considers that a child has these qualities, it must then go on to consider whether it has been proved that the child did not give its consent. While the matter will always be for the jury alone to decide, I should not expect a jury to find at all frequently that a child under 14 had sufficient understanding and intelligence to give its consent.'

That expression of opinion seems to me entirely contradictory of the view expressed by Cockburn C.J. in *R. v. Howes* (1860) 121 E.R. 467 at 468–469:

'We repudiate utterly, as most dangerous, the notion that any intellectual precocity in an individual female child can hasten the period which appears to have been fixed by statute for the arrival at the age of discretion; for that very precocity, if uncontrolled, might very probably lead to her irreparable injury. The Legislature has given us a guide, which we may safely follow, in pointing out sixteen as the age up to which the father's right to custody of his female child is to continue; and short of which such a child has no discretion to consent to leaving him.'

The question for decision in that case was different from that in the present, but the view that the child's intellectual ability is irrelevant cannot, in my opinion, now be accepted. It is a question of fact for the judge (or jury) to decide whether a particular child can give effective consent to contraceptive treatment.

In times gone by the father had almost absolute authority over his children until they attained majority. A rather remarkable example of such authority being upheld by the court was *Re Agar-Ellis, Agar-Ellis v. Lascelles* (1883) 24 Ch.D. 317, which was much relied on by the Court of Appeal. The father in that case restricted the communication which his daughter aged 17 was allowed to have with her mother, against whose moral character nothing was alleged, to an extent that would be universally condemned today as quite unreasonable. The case has been much criticised in recent years and, in my opinion, with good reason. In *Hewer v. Bryant* [1969] 3 All E.R. 578 at 582 Lord Denning M.R. said:

'I would get rid of the rule in *Re Agar-Ellis* and of the suggested exceptions to it. That case was decided in the year 1883. It reflects the attitude of a Victorian parent towards his children. He expected unquestioning obedience to his commands. If a son disobeyed, his father would cut him off with 1 shilling. If a daughter had an illegitimate child, he would turn her out of the house. His power only ceased when the child became 21. I decline to accept a view so much out of date. The common law can, and should, keep pace with the times. It should declare, in conformity with the recent report on the Age of Majority (Report of the Committee on the Age of Majority (Cmnd 3342) under the chairmanship of Latey J., published in July 1967), that the legal right of a parent to the custody of a child ends at the eighteenth birthday; and even up till then, it is a dwindling right which the courts will hesitate to enforce against the wishes of the child, the older he is. It starts with a right of control and ends with little more than advice.'

I respectfully agree with every word of that and especially with the description of the father's authority as a dwindling right. In *J v. C* [1969] 1 All E.R. 788 Lord Guest and Lord MacDermott referred to the decision in *Re Agar-Ellis* as an example of the almost absolute power asserted by the father over his children before the Supreme Court of Judicature Act 1873 and plainly thought such an assertion was out of place at the present time: see *per* Lord MacDermott ([1969] 1 All E.R. 788 at 814–815). In *R v. D* [1984] 2 All E.R. 449 Lord Brandon cited *Re Agar-Ellis* as an example of the older view of a father's authority which his Lordship and the other members of the House rejected. In my opinion, the view of absolute paternal authority continuing until a child attains majority which was applied in *Re Agar-Ellis* is so out of line with present-day views that it should no longer be treated as having any authority. I regard it as a historical curiosity . . ."

LORD SCARMAN:

" . . . Mrs Gillick relies on both the statute law and the case law to establish her proposition that parental consent is in all other circumstances necessary. The only statutory provision directly in point is s.8 of the Family Law Reform Act 1969. Subsection (1) of the section provides that the consent of a minor who has attained the age of 16 to any surgical, medical or dental treatment which in the absence of consent would constitute a trespass to his person shall be as effective as if he were of full age and that the consent of his parent or guardian need not be obtained. Subsection (3) of the section provides:

'Nothing in this section shall be construed as making ineffective any consent which would have been effective if this section had not been enacted.'

I cannot accept the submission made on Mrs Gillick's behalf that sub-s. (1) necessarily implies that prior to its enactment the consent of a minor to medical treatment could not be effective in law. Subsection (3) leaves open the question whether the consent of a minor under 16 could be an effective consent. Like my noble and learned friend Lord Fraser, I read the section as clarifying the law without conveying any indication as to what the law was before it was enacted. So far as minors under 16 are concerned, the law today is as it was before the enactment of the section.

Nor do I find in the provisions of the statute law to which Parker L.J. refers in his judgment in the Court of Appeal (see [1985] 1 All E.R. 533) any encouragement, let alone any compelling reason, for holding that Parliament has accepted that a child under 16 cannot consent to medical treatment. I respectfully agree with the reasoning and conclusion of my noble and learned friend Lord Fraser on this point.

The law has, therefore, to be found by a search in the judge-made law for the true principle. The legal difficulty is that in our search we find ourselves in a field of medical practice where parental right and a doctor's duty may point us in different directions. This is not surprising. Three features have emerged in today's society which were not known to our predecessors: (1) contraception as a subject for medical advice and treatment; (2) the increasing independence of young people; and (3) the changed status of women. In times past contraception was rarely a matter for the doctor but with the development of the contraceptive pill for women it has become part and parcel of every-day medical practice, as is made clear by the department's *Handbook of Contraceptive Practice* (1984 revision) esp para. 1.2. Family planning services are now available under statutory powers to all without any express limitation as to age or marital status. Young people, once they have attained the age of 16, are capable of consenting to contraceptive treatment, since it is medical treatment; and, however extensive be parental right in the care and upbringing of children, it cannot prevail so as to nullify the 16-year-old's capacity to consent which is now conferred by statute. Furthermore, women have obtained by the availability of the pill a choice of life-style with a degree of independence and of opportunity undreamed of until this generation and greater, I would add, than any law of equal opportunity could by itself effect.

The law ignores these developments at its peril. The House's task, therefore, as the supreme court in a legal system largely based on rules of law evolved over the years by the judicial process is to search the overfull and cluttered shelves of the law reports for a principle or set of principles recognised by the judges over the years but stripped of the detail which, however appropriate in their day, would, if applied today, lay the judges open to a justified criticism for failing to keep the law abreast of the society in which they live and work.

It is, of course, a judicial commonplace to proclaim the adaptability and flexibility of the judge-made common law. But this is more frequently proclaimed than acted on. The mark of the great judge from Coke through Mansfield to our day has been the capacity and the will to search out principle, to discard the detail appropriate (perhaps) to earlier times and to apply principle in such a way as to satisfy the needs of his own time. If judge-made law is to survive as a living and relevant body of law, we must make the effort, however inadequately, to follow the lead of the great masters of the judicial art.

In this appeal, therefore, there is much in the earlier case law which the House must discard; almost everything I would say but its principle. For example, the horrendous *Agar-Ellis* decisions (see *Re Agar-Ellis, Agar-Ellis v. Lascelles* (1878) 10 Ch.D. 49) of the late nineteenth century asserting the power of the father over his child were rightly remaindered to the history books by the Court of Appeal in *Hewer v. Bryant* [1969] 3 All E.R. 578, an important case to which I shall return later. Yet the decisions of earlier generations may well afford clues to the true principle of the law: *e.g. R v. Howes* which I also later quote. It is the duty of this House to look at, through and past the decisions of earlier generations so that it may identify the principle which lies behind them. Even Lord Eldon (no legal revolutionary) once remarked, when invited to study precedent (the strength of which he never underrated):

' . . . all law ought to stand upon principle, and unless decision has removed out of the way all argument and all principle; so as to make it impossible to apply them to the case before you, you must find out what is the principle upon which it must be decided.'

(See *Queensberry Leases Case* (1819) 4 E.R. 127 at 179, quoted by Lord Campbell *Lives of the Lord Chancellors* (4th ed., 1857) vol. 10, Ch 213, p 244.)

Approaching the earlier law in this way, one finds plenty of indications as to the principles governing the law's approach to parental right and the child's right to make his or her own decision. Parental rights clearly do exist, and they do not wholly disappear until the age of majority. Parental rights relate to both the person and the property of the child: custody, care and control of the person and guardianship of the property of the child. But the common law has never treated such rights as sovereign or beyond review and control. Nor has our law ever treated the child as other than a person with capacities and rights recognised by law. The principle of the law, as I shall endeavour to show, is that parental rights are derived from parental duty and exist only so long as they are needed for the protection of the person and property of the child. The principle has been subjected to certain age limits set by statute for certain purposes; and in some cases the courts have declared an age of discretion at which a child acquires before the age of majority the right to make his (or her) own decision. But these limitations in no way undermine the principle of the law, and should not be allowed to obscure it.

Let me make good, quite shortly, the proposition of principle.

First, the guardianship legislation. Section 5 of the Guardianship of Infants Act 1886 began the process which is now complete of establishing the equal rights of mother and father. In doing so the legislation, which is currently embodied in s.1 of the Guardianship of Minors Act 1971, took over from the Chancery courts a rule which they had long followed (it was certainly applied by Lord Eldon during his quarter of a century as Lord Chancellor, as Parker L.J. in this case (see [1985] 1 All E.R. 533 at 541), quoting Heilbron J., reminds us) that when a court has before it a question as to the care and upbringing of a child it must treat the welfare of the child as the paramount consideration in determining the order to be made. There is here a principle which limits and governs the exercise of parental rights of custody, care and control. It is a principle perfectly consistent with the law's recognition of the parent as the natural guardian of the child; but it is also a warning that parental right must be exercised in accordance with the welfare principle and can be challenged, even overridden, if it be not.

Second, there is the common law's understanding of the nature of parental right. We are not concerned in this appeal to catalogue all that is contained in what Sachs L.J. has felicitously described as the 'bundle of rights' which together constitute the rights of custody, care and control (see *Hewer v. Bryant* [1969] 3 All E.R. 578 at 585). It is abundantly plain that the law recognises that there is a right and a duty of parents to determine whether or not to seek medical advice in respect of their child, and, having received advice, to give or withhold consent to medical treatment. The question in the appeal is as to the extent and duration of the right and the circumstances in which outside the two admitted exceptions to which I have earlier referred it can be overridden by the exercise of medical judgment.

As Parker and Fox L.JJ. noted in the Court of Appeal, the modern statute law recognises the existence of parental right: *e.g.* sections 85 and 86 of the Children Act 1975 and ss.2, 3 and 4 of the Child Care Act 1980. It is derived from parental duty. A most illuminating discussion of parental right is to be found in *Blackstone's Commentaries* (1 Bl Com (17th ed., 1830) vol I, Chs 16 and 17). He analyses the duty of the parent as the 'maintenance . . . protection, and . . . education' of the child (at p. 446). He declares that the power of parents over their children is derived from their duty and exists 'to enable the parent more effectually to perform his duty, and partly as a recompense for his care and trouble in the faithful discharge of it' (at p 452). In ch 17 he discusses the relation of guardian and ward. It is, he points out, a relation 'derived out of [the relation of parent and child]: the guardian being only a temporary parent, that is, for so long a time as the ward is an infant, or under age' (at p 460). A little later in the same chapter he again emphasises that the power and reciprocal duty of a guardian and ward are the same, pro tempore, as that of a father and child and adds that the guardian, when the ward comes of age (as also the father who becomes guardian 'at common law' if an estate be left to his child), must account to the child for all that he has transacted on his behalf (at pp 462–463). He then embarks on a discussion of the different ages at which for different purposes a child comes of sufficient age to make his own decision; and he cites examples, viz a boy might at 12 years old take the oath of allegiance; at 14 he might consent to marriage or choose his guardian 'and, if his discretion be actually proved, may make his testament of his personal estate'; at 18 he could be an executor: all these rights and responsibilities being capable of his acquiring before reaching the age of majority at 21 (at p 463).

The two chapters provide a valuable insight into the principle and flexibility of the common law. The principle is that parental right or power of control of the person and property of his child exists primarily to enable the parent to discharge his duty of maintenance, protection and education until he reaches such an age as to be able to look after himself and make his own decisions. Blackstone does suggest that there was a further justification for parental right, viz as a recompense for the faithful discharge of parental duty; but the right of the father to the exclusion of the mother and the reward element as one of the reasons for the existence of the right have been swept away by the guardianship of minors legislation to which I have already referred. He also accepts that by statute and by case law varying ages of discretion have been fixed for various purposes. But it is clear that this was done to achieve certainty where it was considered necessary and in no way limits the principle that parental right endures only so long as it is needed for the protection of the child.

Although statute has intervened in respect of a child's capacity to consent to medical treatment from the age of 16 onwards, neither statute nor the case law has ruled on the extent and duration of parental right in respect of children under the age of 16. More specifically, there is no rule yet applied to contraceptive treatment, which has special problems of its own and is a late comer in medical practice. It is open, therefore, to the House to formulate a rule. The Court of Appeal favoured a fixed age limit of 16, basing itself on a view of the statute law which I do not share and on its view of the effect of the older case law which for the reasons already given I cannot accept. It sought to justify the limit by the public interest in the law being certain. Certainty is always an advantage in the law, and in some branches of the law it is a necessity. But it brings with it an inflexibility and a rigidity which in some branches of the law can obstruct justice, impede the law's development and stamp on the law the mark of obsolescence where what is needed is the capacity for development. The law relating to parent and child is concerned with the problems of the growth and maturity of the human personality. If the law should impose on the process of 'growing up' fixed limits where nature knows only a continuous

process, the price would be artificiality and a lack of realism in an area where the
law must be sensitive to human development and social change. If certainty be
thought desirable, it is better that the rigid demarcations necessary to achieve it
should be laid down by legislation after a full consideration of all the relevant
factors than by the courts, confined as they are by the forensic process to the
evidence adduced by the parties and to whatever may properly fall within the
judicial notice of judges. Unless and until Parliament should think fit to intervene,
the courts should establish a principle flexible enough to enable justice to be
achieved by its application to the particular circumstances proved by the evidence
placed before them.

The underlying principle of the law was exposed by Blackstone and can be seen
to have been acknowledged in the case law. It is that parental right yields to the
child's right to make his own decisions when he reaches a sufficient understanding
and intelligence to be capable of making up his own mind on the matter requiring
decision. Lord Denning M.R. captured the spirit and principle of the law in *Hewer
v. Bryant* [1969] 3 All E.R. 578 at 582 [see above at p 388] . . .

But his is by no means a solitary voice. It is consistent with the opinion expressed
by the House in *J v. C* [1969] 1 All E.R. 788 where their Lordships clearly
recognised as out of place the assertion in the *Agar-Ellis* cases of a father's power
bordering on 'patria potestas'. It is consistent with the view of Lord Parker C.J. in *R
v. Howard* [1965] 3 All E.R. 684 at 685, where he ruled that in the case of a
prosecution charging rape of a girl under 16 the Crown must *prove* either lack of
her consent or that she was not in a position to decide whether to consent or resist
and added the comment that 'there are many girls who know full well what it is all
about and can properly consent'. And it is consistent with the views of the House in
the recent criminal case where a father was accused of kidnapping his own child, *R.
v. D.* [1984] 2 All E.R. 449 . . .

For the reasons which I have endeavoured to develop, the case law of the
nineteenth and earlier centuries is no guide to the application of the law in the
conditions of today. The *Agar-Ellis* cases (the power of the father) cannot live with
the modern statute law. The habeas corpus 'age of discretion' cases are also no
guide as to the limits which should be accepted today in marking out the bounds of
parental right, of a child's capacity to make his or her own decision and of a
doctor's duty to his patient. . . ."

LORD TEMPLEMAN [DISSENTING]:
" . . . An unmarried girl under the age of 16 does not, in my opinion, possess the
power in law to decide for herself to practice contraception. Section 6 of the Sexual
Offences Act 1956 makes it an offence for a man to have unlawful sexual
intercourse with a girl under the age of 16. Consent by the girl does not afford a
defence to the man or constitute an offence by the girl. Parliament has thus
indicated that an unmarried girl under the age of 16 is not sufficiently mature to be
allowed to decide for herself that she will take part in sexual intercourse. Such a girl
cannot therefore be regarded as sufficiently mature to be allowed to decide for
herself that she will practice contraception for the purpose of frequent or regular or
casual sexual intercourse. Section 6 of the Sexual Offences Act 1956 does not,
however, in my view, prevent parent and doctor from deciding that contraceptive
facilities shall be made available to an unmarried girl under the age of 16 whose
sexual activities are recognised to be uncontrolled and uncontrollable. Section 6 is
designed to protect the girl from sexual intercourse. But if the girl cannot be
deterred then contraceptive facilities may be provided, not for the purpose of aiding
and abetting an offence under s 6 but for the purpose of avoiding the consequences,
principally pregnancy, which the girl may suffer from illegal sexual intercourse
where sexual intercourse cannot be prevented. In general, where parent and doctor
agree that any form of treatment, including contraceptive treatment, is in the best
interests of the girl, there is, in my opinion, no legal bar to that treatment.

Difficulties arise when parent and doctor differ. The parent, claiming the right to decide what is in the best interests of a girl in the custody of that parent, may forbid the provision of contraceptive facilities. A doctor, claiming the right to decide what is in the best interests of a patient, may wish to override the parent's objections. A conflict which is express may be resolved by the court, which may accept the view of either parent or doctor or modify the views of both of them as to what is in the best interests of the girl. The present appeal is concerned with a conflict which is known to the doctor but is concealed from the parent and from the court. The girl, aware that the parent will forbid contraception, requests the doctor to provide and the doctor agrees to provide contraceptive facilities and to keep the parent in ignorance.

A parent is the natural and legal guardian of an infant under the age of 18 and is responsible for the upbringing of an infant who is in the custody of that parent. The practical exercise of parental powers varies from control and supervision to guidance and advice depending on the discipline enforced by the parent and the age and temperament of the infant. Parental power must be exercised in the best interests of the infant and the court may intervene in the interests of the infant at the behest of the parent or at the behest of a third party. The court may enforce parental right, control the misuse of parental power or uphold independent views asserted by the infant. The court will be guided by the principle that the welfare of the infant is paramount. But, subject to the discretion of the court to differ from the views of the parent, the court will, in my opinion, uphold the right of the parent having custody of the infant to decide on behalf of the infant all matters which the infant is not competent to decide. The prudent parent will pay attention to the wishes of the infant and will normally accept them as the infant approaches adulthood. The parent is not bound by the infant's wishes, but an infant approaching adulthood may be able to flout the wishes of the parent with ease.

A doctor tenders advice and offers treatment which the doctor considers to be in the best interests of the patient. A patient is free to reject the advice and refuse the treatment: see *Sidaway v. Bethlem Royal Hospital Governors* [1985] 1 All E.R. 643 at 665. Where the patient is an infant, the medical profession accept that a parent having custody and being responsible for the infant is entitled on behalf of the infant to consent to or reject treatment if the parent considers that the best interests of the infant so require. Where doctor and parent disagree, the court can decide and is not slow to act. I accept that if there is no time to obtain a decision from the court, a doctor may safely carry out treatment in emergency if the doctor believes the treatment to be vital to the survival or health of an infant and notwithstanding the opposition of a parent or the impossibility of alerting the parent before the treatment is carried out. In such a case the doctor must have the courage of his convictions that the treatment is necessary and urgent in the interests of the patient and the court will, if necessary, approve after the event treatment which the court would have authorised in advance, even if the treatment proves to be unsuccessful.

I accept also that a doctor may lawfully carry out some forms of treatment with the consent of an infant patient and against the opposition of a parent based on religious or any other grounds. The effect of the consent of the infant depends on the nature of the treatment and the age and understanding of the infant. For example, a doctor with the consent of an intelligent boy or girl of 15 could in my opinion safely remove tonsils or a troublesome appendix. But any decision on the part of a girl to practise sex and contraception requires not only knowledge of the facts of life and of the dangers of pregnancy and disease but also an understanding of the emotional and other consequences to her family, her male partner and to herself. I doubt whether a girl under the age of 16 is capable of a balanced judgement to embark on frequent, regular or casual sexual intercourse fortified by the illusion that medical science can protect her in mind and body and ignoring the danger of leaping from childhood to adulthood without the difficult formative transitional experiences of adolescence. There are many things which a girl under

16 needs to practise but sex is not one of them. Parliament could declare this view to be out of date. But in my opinion the statutory provisions discussed in the speech of my noble and learned friend Lord Fraser and the provisions of s.6 of the Sexual Offences Act 1956 indicate that as the law now stands an unmarried girl under 16 is not competent to decide to practise sex and contraception.

In the present case it is submitted that a doctor may lawfully make a decision on behalf of the girl and in so doing may overrule or ignore the parent who has custody of the girl. It is submitted that a doctor may at the request of a girl under 16 provide contraceptive facilities against the known or assumed wishes of the parent and on terms that the parent shall be kept in ignorance of the treatment. The justification is advanced that, if the girl's request is not met, the girl may persist in sexual intercourse and run the risk of pregnancy. It is not in the interests of a girl under 16 to become pregnant and therefore the doctor may, in her interests, confidentially provide contraceptive facilities unless the doctor can persuade the girl to abstain from sexual intercourse or can persuade her to ensure that precautions are taken by the male participant. The doctor is not bound to provide contraceptive facilities but, it is said, is entitled to do so in the best interests of the girl. The girl must be assured that the doctor will be pledged to secrecy otherwise the girl may not seek advice or treatment but will run all the risks of disease and pregnancy involved in sexual activities without adequate knowledge or mature consideration and preparation. The Department of Health and Social Security (DHSS) memorandum instructs a doctor to seek to persuade the girl to involve the parent but concludes that 'the decision whether or not to prescribe contraception must be for the clinical judgment of a doctor'.

There are several objections to this approach. The first objection is that a doctor, acting without the views of the parent, cannot form a 'clinical' or any other reliable judgement that the best interests of the girl require the provision of contraceptive facilities. The doctor at the family planning clinic only knows that which the girl chooses to tell him. The family doctor may know some of the circumstances of some of the families who form his registered patients but his information may be incomplete or misleading . . .

The second objection is that a parent will sooner or later find out the truth, probably sooner, and may do so in circumstances which bring about a complete rupture of good relations between members of the family and between the family and the doctor . . .

The third and main objection advanced on behalf of the respondent parent, Mrs Gillick, in this appeal is that the secret provision of contraceptive facilities for a girl under 16 will, it is said, encourage participation by the girl in sexual intercourse and this practice offends basic principles of morality and religion which ought not to be sabotaged in stealth by kind permission of the national health service. The interests of a girl under 16 require her to be protected against sexual intercourse. Such a girl is not sufficiently mature to be allowed to decide to flout the accepted rules of society. The pornographic press and the lascivious film may falsely pretend that sexual intercourse is a form of entertainment available to females on request and to males on demand but the regular, frequent or casual practice of sexual intercourse by a girl or a boy under the age of 16 cannot be beneficial to anybody and may cause harm to character and personality. Before a girl under 16 is supplied with contraceptive facilities, the parent who knows most about the girl and ought to have the most influence with the girl is entitled to exercise parental rights of control, supervision, guidance and advice in order that the girl may, if possible, avoid sexual intercourse until she is older. Contraception should only be considered if and when the combined efforts of parent and doctor fail to prevent the girl from participating in sexual intercourse and there remains only the possibility of protecting the girl against pregnancy resulting from sexual intercourse.

These arguments have provoked great controversy which is not legal in character. Some doctors approve and some doctors disapprove of the idea that a doctor may decide to provide contraception for a girl under 16 without the knowledge of the parent. Some parents agree and some parents disagree with the proposition that the decision must depend on the judgement of the doctor. Those who favour doctor power assert that the failure to provide confidential contraceptive treatment will lead to an increase in pregnancies amongst girls under 16. As a general proposition, this assertion is not supported by evidence in this case, is not susceptible to proof and in my opinion is of doubtful validity. Availability of confidential contraceptive treatment may increase the demand for such treatment. Contraceptive treatment for females usually requires daily discipline in order to be effective and girls under 16 frequently lack that discipline. The total number of pregnancies amongst girls of under 16 may, therefore, be increased and not decreased by the availability of contraceptive treatment. But there is no doubt that an individual girl who is denied the opportunity of confidential contraceptive treatment may invite or succumb to sexual intercourse and thereby become pregnant. Those who favour parental power assert that the availability of confidential contraceptive treatment will increase sexual activity by girls under 16. This argument is also not supported by evidence in the present case and is not susceptible to proof. But it is clear that contraception removes or gives an illusion of removing the possibility of pregnancy and therefore removes restraint on sexual intercourse. Some girls would come under pressure if contraceptive facilities were known to be available and some girls under 16 are susceptible to male domination.

Parliament could decide whether it is better to have more contraception with the possibility of fewer pregnancies and less disease or whether it is better to have less contraception with the possibility of reduced sexual activity by girls under 16. Parliament could ensure that the doctor prevailed over the parent by reducing the age of consent or by expressly authorising a doctor to provide contraceptive facilities for any girl without informing the parent, provided the doctor considered that his actions were for the benefit of the girl. Parliament could, on the other hand, ensure that the parent prevailed over the doctor by forbidding contraceptive treatment for a girl under 16 save by or on the recommendation of the girl's general medical practitioner and with the consent of the parent who has registered the girl as a patient of that general practitioner. Some girls, it is said, might pretend to be over 16 but a doctor in doubt could always require confirmation from the girl's registered medical practitioner.

This appeal falls to be determined by the existing law . . . The position seems to me to be as follows. A doctor is not entitled to decide whether a girl under the age of 16 shall be provided with contraceptive facilities if a parent who is in charge of the girl is ready and willing to make that decision in exercise of parental rights. The doctor is entitled in exceptional circumstances and in emergencies to make provision, normally temporary provision, for contraception but in most cases would be bound to inform the parent of the treatment. The court would not hold the doctor liable for providing contraceptive facilities if the doctor had reasonable grounds for believing that the parent had abandoned or abused parental rights or that there was no parent immediately available for consultation or that there was no parent who was responsible for the girl. But exceptional circumstances and emergencies cannot be expanded into a general discretion for the doctor to provide contraceptive facilities without the knowledge of the parent because of the possibility that a girl to whom contraceptive facilities are not available may irresponsibly court the risk of pregnancy. Such a discretion would enable any girl to obtain contraception on request by threatening to sleep with a man . . ."

NOTES:

1. The other dissenting Law Lord, Lord Brandon, based his decision on a perusal of statutory provisions governing the situation where a man

has sexual intercourse with a girl under the age of 16. As Lee points out, he thus not only evades the majority's search for legal principle, but is also in the curious position of having provided the principal legal authority for the majority judges — *i.e.* his landmark decision in *R v. D* [1984] 2 All E.R. 449. (See S. Lee, *Judging Judges*, London: Faber & Faber, 1988 at pages 80–82.) Moreover, Lord Brandon actually adopts a position which is more extreme than that advocated by Mrs Gillick in concluding that: " . . . on the view which I take of the law, making contraception available to girls under sixteen is unlawful whether their parents know of and consent to it or not."

2. The standard academic interpretation of Lord Scarman's opinion in the wake of the decision was that once a child has reached capacity there is no room for a parent to impose a contrary view (even if such a view seems to be more in accord with the child's best interests) because the parental right is extinguished once the child has reached full capacity. However, Eekelaar points out that Lord Fraser's judgment is much less firm on this matter. Whereas Lord Scarman suggests that the child assumes the power both to consent to and refuse treatment, Lord Fraser does not go beyond the issue of competence to assent to treatment and appears to contemplate that in some situations, parental rights survive the minor's acquisition of capacity (Eekelaar, "The Emergence of Children's Rights" (1986) 6 Oxford Journal of Legal Studies 161 at pages 180–181).

3. Parental responsibility rather than biological parenthood is, largely, the key to being able to provide a valid consent in respect of children. Accordingly, an unmarried father must obtain parental responsibility before he has a right to express an opinion on whether a child is to be treated. He may do this in one of three ways under the provisions of the Children Act 1989. First, under section 4(1)(b), parental responsibility may be acquired by agreement with the child's mother. Secondly, under section 4(1)(a), it can be conferred following an application to the court for a parental responsibility order. Finally, parental responsibility can be acquired incidentally to the making of a residence order in the unmarried father's favour.

4. The class of persons in whom parental responsibility may be vested is not limited to biological parents. Others who may possess it include adoptive parents, parents by means of assisted reproduction (see further Chapter 11), local authorities in whose care the child has been placed and anyone (who does not already possess it) who has a residence order made in their favour, *e.g.* a step-parent, foster parent or relative (section 12 of the Children Act 1989).

5. Aside from possessing parental responsibility, section 3(5) of the Children Act also provides that "A person who (a) does not have parental responsibility for a particular child; but (b) has care of the child, may . . . do what is reasonable in all the circumstances of the case for the purpose of safeguarding or promoting the child's welfare.

6. The result of the majority decision is that no criminal offence is committed by a doctor who give contraceptive advice or treatment to a young person under 16 without parental consent. The majority emphasised that criminal liability would depend upon intention, so that a doctor who provided contraceptive advice or treatment to a girl under the age of 16, honestly intending to act in the girl's best interests (by avoiding the consequences of an unwanted pregnancy) rather than with the intention of facilitating unlawful sexual intercourse would incur no criminal liability. (See J. Bridgeman, "Don't tell the children: The Department's guidance on the provision of information about contraception to individual pupils" in N. Harris (ed.) *Children, Sex Education and the Law: Examining the Issues*, London: National Children's Bureau, 1996 at page 53.

QUESTIONS:

1. Lord Fraser states that the solution to the issue in the *Gillick* case "depends upon a judgment of what is best for the child". Who do you think is best placed to make this judgment — the parents or the doctors — and why? (See J. Montgomery, "Children as property" (1988) 51 *M.L.R.* 323.) Is there a possibility that the decision in *Gillick* may simply store up future problems by suggesting that it is more appropriate for children's interests to be defined by the state, rather than by their parents? On what basis, if any, should the law circumscribe the power of the conscientious parent? (See J. Roche, "Children's rights: in the name of the child" (1995) 17 *Journal of Social Welfare and Family Law* 281.)

2. Do you agree with Lord Fraser's view that the nature of family structure has radically altered, and that cases decided at a time when the family was controlled by the father are no longer relevant? Does this only apply to western "nuclear" families? (See Roche, *op. cit.*)

3. Note that Lord Templeman would mitigate the practical effects of deeming young persons under 16 incompetent to consent to contraceptive treatment by invoking exceptional circumstances as a ground for dispensing with the requirement of parental consent. What precisely are the circumstances in which the court would sanction a health professional proceeding without parental consent, or at least permit the doctor to act as a proxy in giving consent? (See S. Lee, *Judging Judges* London: Faber & Faber, 1988, at pages 78–9.)

In the *Gillick* case, Lords Fraser and Scarman were equivocal on the question of whether the attainment of *Gillick* competence marked the extinction of the parental power to give consent. Instead, they simply refuted the suggestion that parents have *absolute* control over the health of their children until they reach majority. Neither of their Lordships offered a definitive interpretation of the problematic provision in section 8(3) of the Family Law Reform Act 1969 that: "Nothing in this section shall be construed as making ineffective any consent which would have been effective if this section had not been enacted." Two questions therefore remained unanswered. First, do a child's parents retain any power of consent after the child reaches 16 or acquires "*Gillick* competence" and secondly, where (assuming such power is retained), does the balance of power lie as between parents and their mature children? These issues were addressed by the then Master of the Rolls, Lord Donaldson, in two cases concerning adolescent girls:

Re R (A Minor) (Wardship: Medical Treatment) [1991] 4 All E.R. 177, [1992] Fam 11, [1991] 3 W.L.R. 592, [1992] 1 FLR 190

A 15-year-old girl, R, who had been on the local authority's at-risk register was received into voluntary care and was placed in a children's home after a fight with her father. While there, the state of her mental health grew progressively worse and she began to suffer hallucinations. Her behaviour also became more and more disturbed, to the point of threatening suicide and absconding to her father's house where she attacked him with a hammer. Following these episodes, the local authority obtained place of safety and interim care orders and placed her in an adolescent psychiatric unit. Whilst in the unit, her behaviour remained very disturbed and the unit sought the local authority's permission to administer anti-psychotic drugs to her. Her mental state fluctuated but the prognosis was that, despite her periodic lucidity, if the drugs were not provided, her psychotic state would return.

In lucid periods, during which R was capable of understanding the nature and effect of the medication, she objected to taking the drugs. To begin with, the local authority refused to authorise the administration of drugs against her will; but eventually the unit was unprepared to continue caring for her without authorisation to administer the proposed medication. The local authority then commenced wardship proceedings seeking permission for the unit to give R the anti-psychotic drugs, with or without her consent. The court had to consider, amongst other things, whether R was "*Gillick* competent", and if so whether, and in what circumstances, her refusal to consent to the drug treatment could be overridden.

LORD DONALDSON M.R.:
" . . . Mrs Gillick served notice on her local area health authority formally forbidding any medical staff employed by it from giving contraceptive or abortion advice to her four daughters, whilst they were under the age of 16, without her consent and invited the authority to advise the doctors employed by it accordingly. The health authority declined so to do and Mrs Gillick sought declarations against the department that the guidance given by it was unlawful and against the authority that no doctor or other professional person employed by it was entitled as a matter of law to give contraceptive advice and/or abortion advice and/or treatment to any of her children under the age of 16 without her consent. In a word she was asserting an absolute right of veto on the part of parents generally, and herself in

particular, on medical advice and treatment of the nature specified in relation to their children under the age of 16 (see [1985] 3 All E.R. 402 at 412 *per* Lord Fraser). She was not challenging the right of a wardship court to exercise its parens patriae jurisdiction. Indeed she accepted it in her printed case (see [1985] 3 All E.R. 402 at 406 *per* Lord Fraser). Nor was she concerned with how that jurisdiction should be exercised.

It is trite law that in general a doctor is not entitled to treat a patient without the consent of someone who is authorised to give that consent. If he does so, he will be liable in damages for trespass to the person and may be guilty of a criminal assault. This is subject to the necessary exception that in cases of emergency a doctor may treat the patient notwithstanding the absence of consent, if the patient is unconscious or otherwise incapable of giving or refusing consent and there is no one else sufficiently immediately available with authority to consent on behalf of the patient. However consent by itself creates no obligation to treat. It is merely a key which unlocks a door. Furthermore, whilst in the case of an adult of full capacity there will usually only be one keyholder, namely the patient, in the ordinary family unit where a young child is the patient there will be two keyholders, namely the parents, with a several as well as a joint right to turn the key and unlock the door. If the parents disagree, one consenting and the other refusing, the doctor will be presented with a professional and ethical, but not with a legal, problem because, if he has the consent of one authorised person, treatment will not without more constitute a trespass or a criminal assault.

If Mrs Gillick was to succeed in her claim to a declaration that the memorandum of guidance issued by the department was unlawful, she had to show that no child under the age of 16 could be a keyholder in respect of contraception advice and treatment or that the parents' key overrode the child's. As Lord Fraser put it ([1985] 3 All E.R. 402 at 412): 'She has to justify the absolute right of veto in a parent.' If she was to succeed in her claim against the area health authority, she had also to show that it was under a duty to inform all medical staff employed by it that Mrs Gillick was exercising that right of veto, but in the light of the House's finding that there was no such right, this additional factor can be ignored.

In the instant appeal Mr James Munby Q.C., appearing for the Official Solicitor, submits that (a) if the child has the right to give consent to medical treatment, the parents' right to give or refuse consent is terminated and (b) the court in the exercise of its wardship jurisdiction is only entitled to step into the shoes of the parents and thus itself has no right to give or refuse consent. Whilst it is true that he seeks to modify the effect of this rather startling submission by suggesting that, if the child's consent or refusal of consent is irrational or misguided, the court will readily infer that in the particular context that individual child is not competent to give or withhold consent, it is necessary to look very carefully at the *Gillick* decision to see whether it supports his argument and, if it does, whether it is binding upon this court.

The key passages upon which Mr Munby relies are to be found in the speech of Lord Scarman ([1985] 3 All E.R. 402 at 423–424):

'. . . as a matter of law the parental right to determine whether or not their minor child below the age of 16 will have medical treatment terminates if and when the child achieves a sufficient understanding and intelligence to enable him or her to understand fully what is proposed. It will be a question of fact whether a child seeking advice has sufficient understanding of what is involved to give a consent valid in law. Until the child achieves the capacity to consent, the parental right to make the decision continues save only in exceptional circumstances. Emergency, parental neglect, abandonment of the child or inability to find the parent are examples of exceptional situations justifying the doctor proceeding to treat the child without parental knowledge and consent; but there will arise, no doubt, other exceptional situations in which it will be reasonable for the doctor to proceed without the parent's consent.'

And ([1985] 3 All E.R. 402 at 421–422):

> 'The underlying principle of the law was exposed by Blackstone (1 Bl Com (17th ed, 1830) chs 16 and 17)] and can be seen to have been acknowledged in the case law. It is that parental right yields to the child's right to make his own decisions when he reaches a sufficient understanding and intelligence to be capable of making up his own mind on the matter requiring decision.'

What Mr Munby's argument overlooks is that Lord Scarman was discussing the parents' right 'to *determine* whether or not their minor child below the age of 16 will have medical treatment' (my emphasis) and this is the 'parental right' to which he was referring in the latter passage. A right of determination is wider than a right to consent. The parents can only have a right of determination if *either* the child has no right to consent, *i.e.* is not a keyholder, *or* the parents hold a master key which could nullify the child's consent. I do not understand Lord Scarman to be saying that, if a child was 'Gillick competent', to adopt the convenient phrase used in argument, the parents ceased to have an independent right of consent as contrasted with ceasing to have a right of determination, *i.e.* a veto. In a case in which the 'Gillick competent' child refuses treatment, but the parents consent, that consent *enables* treatment to be undertaken lawfully, but in no way determines that the child shall be so treated. In a case in which the positions are reversed, it is the child's consent which is the enabling factor and again the parents' refusal of consent is not determinative. If Lord Scarman intended to go further than this and to say that in the case of a 'Gillick competent' child, a parent has no right either to consent or to refuse consent, his remarks were obiter, because the only question in issue was Mrs Gillick's alleged right of veto. Furthermore I consider that they would have been wrong.

One glance at the consequences suffices to show that Lord Scarman cannot have been intending to say that the parental right to consent terminates with the achievement by the child of 'Gillick competence'. It is fundamental to the speeches of the majority that the capacity to consent will vary from child to child and according to the treatment under consideration, depending upon the sufficiency of his or her intelligence and understanding of that treatment. If the position in law is that upon the achievement of 'Gillick competence' there is a transfer of the right of consent from parents to child and there can never be a concurrent right in both, doctors would be faced with an intolerable dilemma, particularly when the child was nearing the age of 16, if the parents consented, but the child did not. On pain, if they got it wrong, of being sued for trespass to the person or possibly being charged with a criminal assault, they would have to determine as a matter of law in whom the right of consent resided at the particular time in relation to the particular treatment. I do not believe that that is the law.

I referred to a child who is nearing the age of 16, because at that age a new dimension is added by section 8 of the Family Law Reform Act 1969 to which Lord Fraser referred (see [1985] 3 All E.R. 402 at 407–408). This is in the following terms:

> '(1) The consent of a minor who has attained the age of sixteen years to any surgical, medical or dental treatment which, in the absence of consent, would constitute a trespass to his person, shall be as effective as it would be if he were of full age; and where a minor has by virtue of this section given an effective consent to any treatment it shall not be necessary to obtain any consent for it from his parent or guardian . . .
>
> (3) Nothing in this section shall be construed as making ineffective any consent which would have been effective if this section had not been enacted.'

Mr Munby submits, rightly as I think, that consent by a child between the ages of 16 and 18 is no more effective than that of an adult if, due to mental disability, the child is incapable of consenting. That is, however, immaterial for present purposes. What is material is that the section is inconsistent with Mr Munby's argument. If Mr Munby's interpretation of Lord Scarman's speech was correct, where a child over the age of 16 gave effective consent to treatment, not only would it 'not be necessary' to obtain the consent of the parent or guardian, it would be legally impossible because the parent or guardian would have no power to give consent and the section would, or at least should, have so provided. Furthermore sub-s. (3) would create problems since, if the section had not been enacted, a parent's consent would undoubtedly have been effective *as a consent*.

Both in this case and in *Re E* the judges treated *Gillick's* case as deciding that a 'Gillick competent' child has a right to refuse treatment. In this I consider that they were in error. Such a child can consent, but if he or she declines to do so or refuses, consent can be given by someone else who has parental rights or responsibilities. The failure or refusal of the 'Gillick competent' child is a very important factor in the doctor's decision whether or not to treat, but does not prevent the necessary consent being obtained from another competent source . . .

After considering the effect of R having been made a ward of court and whether she was *Gillick* competent, Lord Donaldson summed up as follows:

"(1) No doctor can be required to treat a child, whether by the court in the exercise of its wardship jurisdiction, by the parents, by the child or anyone else. The decision whether to treat is dependent upon an exercise of his own professional judgment, subject only to the threshold requirement that, save in exceptional cases usually of emergency, he has the consent of someone who has authority to give that consent. In forming that judgment the views and wishes of the child are a factor whose importance increases with the increase in the child's intelligence and understanding.

(2) There can be concurrent powers to consent. If more than one body or person has a power to consent, only a failure to, or refusal of, consent by all having that power will create a veto.

(3) A 'Gillick competent' child or one over the age of 16 will have a power to consent, but this will be concurrent with that of a parent or guardian. . . ."

STAUGHTON L.J.:
"The treatment centre which is most suitable to accommodate and care for the ward will not accept her unless either (i) she consents to such medication as may be necessary, or (ii) the court authorises that medication. This is not a one-off case, such as an abortion, sterilisation or some other surgical procedure. It is concerned with recurrent medication, which may or may not be desirable in the future but on the evidence probably will be.

The evidence shows that at times the ward has the capacity to make a rational and informed decision. But at other times she does not have that capacity, and those are the times when medication is desirable. The treatment centre wishes to have an assurance that the medication may then be lawfully administered; otherwise she will not be accepted as a patient.

I agree with the conclusion of Waite J. that, on those facts, the court can authorise medication, consistently with the decision of the House of Lords in *Gillick v. West Norfolk and Wisbech Area Health Authority*, even if it has no greater powers than a parent.

The alternative solution to this appeal, which gave rise to the bulk of the argument and perhaps to the appeal itself, depends on two questions of law. (1) Does the parent of a competent minor have power to override the minor's decision, either by granting consent when the minor has refused it or vice versa? (2) Does the court have power to override the decision of a competent minor who is a ward? In both questions I use the word 'competent' in the *Gillick* sense.

As to the first question, we were referred to the speech of Lord Scarman in *Gillick's* case [1985] 3 All E.R. 402 at 423:

' . . . I would hold that as a matter of law the parental right to determine whether or not their minor child below the age of 16 will have medical treatment terminates if and when the child achieves a sufficient understanding and intelligence to enable him or her to understand fully what is proposed.'

The hypothetical situation under consideration in *Gillick's* case was where a competent child did consent to medical treatment, but the parent either was not asked or expressly did not consent. The House of Lords decided, as it seems to me, that a doctor could lawfully administer treatment in such a case, although he would naturally take into account that the parent had not been asked or had expressly not consented.

Whether the doctor could lawfully administer treatment when the parent did consent but the competent child either did not consent or had not been asked — save in the case of emergency — was not a question for decision in *Gillick's* case. As Lord Donaldson M.R. points out, it may be putting a heavy burden on doctors if, having obtained the consent of the parent of a child under 16, they still have to consider whether the child is competent to give or refuse consent. Nevertheless the passage that I have quoted from Lord Scarman's speech, and particularly the words 'whether or not', suggests that the parent's consent is not sufficient in such a case. This is an important question. But it is not essential to the decision in this case, in my opinion, because I consider . . . that a wardship judge can validly consent to medical treatment even if the ward refuses her consent. In those circumstances I do not suppose that any opinion of mine as to the effect of consent by a natural parent would be of much assistance in resolving the difference between what appears to have been Lord Scarman's view and that of Lord Donaldson MR; so I express none . . ."

FARQUHARSON L.J.:
" . . . Mrs Gillick had objected to a circular published by the local health authority which contemplated medical advice about the use of contraceptives being given to children under the age of 16 without their parents being informed. Mrs Gillick sought a declaration that her own children — she was the mother of five girls, all under the age of 16 — should not be given advice of this nature without her consent. As already indicated, the House of Lords held that a girl under the age of 16 had the legal capacity to consent to medical examination and treatment including contraceptive treatment if she had sufficient maturity and intelligence to understand the nature and implications of the proposed treatment. Plainly the capacity to consent will vary with the treatment proposed but the House contemplated that as the child became equipped to make a decision of that nature the responsibility of the parent became less.

As Lord Denning M.R. put it in *Hewer v. Bryant* [1969] 3 All E.R. 578 at 582: '. . . it is a dwindling right [to custody] which the courts will hesitate to enforce against the wishes of the child, the older he is'.

It is to be emphasised that *Gillick's* case was not a wardship case and was concerned with mentally normal children. For my part I would find it difficult to import the criteria applied in *Gillick's* case to the facts of the present case. We are not here solely concerned with the developing maturity of a 15-year-old child but with the impact of a mental illness upon her. The *Gillick* test is not apt to a situation where the understanding and capacity of the child varies from day to day according to the effect of her illness. I would reject the application of the *Gillick* test to an on/off situation of that kind. The authority of a High Court judge exercising his jurisdiction in wardship is not constrained in this way. The judge's

well-established task in deciding any question concerning the upbringing of the
ward is to have regard to the welfare of the ward as the first and paramount
consideration. In some cases the decision might well be different if the *Gillick* test
were applied. That the two approaches are distinct is vividly illustrated in the
dramatic case of *Re E (a minor)* (September 21, 1990, unreported) [see pages 428–
431, below] by the decision of Ward J.

It is clear in the present appeal that, whether R's capacity to withhold consent to
medication was tested on the *Gillick* criteria or whether the court approached the
issue on the basis of her welfare being paramount, the result would have been the
same.

I would dismiss the appeal."

NOTES:

1. The opinion expressed by Lord Donaldson in this case that the
   parents of a "*Gillick* competent" child, or by a young person over the
   age of 16, retain their power of consent until the child reaches
   majority was strictly *obiter dictum*.

2. As Fennell has pointed out, in this line of cases on adolescent
   children, wardship and the inherent jurisdiction have been used in
   much the same way as the jurisdiction to grant declarations (discussed
   in Chapter 5 at pages 293–294) in order to establish a new body of
   judicial rules on the rights and duties of doctors and patients. (See P.
   Fennell, *Treatment Without Consent*, London: Routledge, 1996 at
   page 276.)

3. In *Re R* the Court of Appeal were unanimous that the *Gillick*
   reasoning had no direct application in wardship cases. The court
   decided that in exercising its wardship jurisdiction it could override
   the refusal of a minor to consent to medical treatment which was in
   his best interests, even if he was "*Gillick* competent". Staughton L.J.
   was prepared to go even further, stating that the wardship court also
   has the power to veto treatment to which a competent child has
   consented, although in this situation the parents of a "*Gillick*
   competent" child would have no right of veto. (See R. Thornton,
   "Multiple Keyholders — Wardship and Consent to Medical Treatment" [1992] *C.L.J.* 34; A. Bainham, "The Judge and the Competent
   Minor" (1992) 108 *L.Q.R.* 194.)

4. Grubb has criticised Lord Donaldson's reasoning in *Re R* as disingenuous. He argues that the Master of the Roll's statement that
   Gillick was not concerned with the question of whether a parent
   could validly consent to treatment in the face of a competent child's
   refusal is a remarkably narrow interpretation of *Gillick*. Furthermore,
   he is critical of how the judgment ignores the historical context in
   which the 1969 Act was passed, since the 1960s was very much the
   era of parental rights. (See A. Grubb, "Treatment decisions: keeping
   it in the family" in A. Grubb (ed), *Choices and Decisions in Health
   Care*, Chichester: Wiley, 1993 at pages 60–65.)

5. One problem with the view implicit in Lord Donaldson's judgment
   that R is to be assessed according to a measurement of her capacity

on her bad days, is that it is inconsistent with the law's usual approach to issues of capacity. Generally, the law recognises that it is capacity at the time of the act that is relevant, so that cases on fluctuating capacity recognise the validity of consents given in rational moments (see for example Chapter 5 at page 271). Furthermore, the adoption of such a stance entails a refusal to accept the autonomy of those suffering from mental disorders even when they are capable of making certain autonomous decisions. (See J. Montgomery, "Parents and children in dispute: who has the final word?" (1992) 4 *Journal of Child Law* 85.)

6. Bainham notes that, unless the administration of sedative drugs can be meaningfully distinguished from other medical or psychiatric procedures, *Re R* appears to conflict with many of the statutory provisions in the Children Act 1989, which would seem to endorse the *Gillick* principle by giving a child a right to refuse medical or psychiatric examination or treatment where he has "sufficient understanding to make an informed decision"; although he does concede that the Act is ambivalent on how decisive the views of a competent child are generally. (See A. Bainham, *op. cit.* at page 196: J. A. Devereaux *et al.*, "Can children withhold consent to treatment?" (1993) 306 BMJ 1459.) Similarly, in providing that where child patients are capable of consenting to an application to see their health records parental applications may only be made with the consent of that child (section 4(2) of the Access to Health Records Act 1990 discussed in Chapter 8 at page 493) Parliament appears to endorse the *Gillick* approach. (See J. Montgomery, *op. cit.*)

7. As to the power to determine health provision, recall that Lord Donaldson himself observed in the earlier case of *Re J* [1991] 3 All E.R. 930 at page 934 that:

> "No one can dictate the treatment to be given to any child, neither court, parents nor doctors ... The doctors can recommend treatment A in preference to treatment B. They can also refuse to adopt treatment C on the grounds that it is medically contra-indicated ... The court or parents for their part can refuse to consent to treatment A or B or both, but cannot insist on treatment C. The inevitable and desirable result is that choice of treatment is in some measure a joint decision of the doctors and the court or parents."

On this point see further *Re J (A Minor) (Wardship: Medical Treatment)* [1992] 4 All E.R. 614 and the discussion in J. Montgomery, "Consent to Health Care for Children" (1992) 4 *Journal of Child Law* 85.

QUESTIONS:

1 Do you agree with the Court of Appeal's unanimous conclusion that R was incompetent? Do you think that the doctors involved would have questioned R's competence if she had consented to the administration of the anti-psychotic drugs? (See A. Grubb, "Treatment

decisions: keeping it in the family" in A. Grubb (ed.), *Choices and Decisions in Health Care*, Chichester: Wiley, 1993 at page 58.) Do you accept Bainham's view that this decision "confirms the suspicion that the acquisition of capacity by children is capable of manipulation by adults"? (See Bainham, *op. cit.* at page 200.) For instance, is it significant in this case that the unit was not prepared to allow R to stay unless the anti-psychotic drugs could be administered to her?

2. Do you agree with Staughton L.J. that "the *Gillick* test is not apt to a situation where the understanding and capacity of the child varies from day to day according to the effect of her illness"? Contrast *Mason v. Mason* [1972] 3 All E.R. 315 (for the competency requirement of someone consenting to a divorce application).

3. Is it tenable to make a distinction, as Lord Donaldson does, between a right to *determine* treatment, and a right to give or withhold consent to treatment? (See J. Montgomery, "Parents and children in dispute: who has the final word?" (1992) 4 *Journal of Child Law* 85; J. A. Devereaux *et al., op. cit.*)

4. Do you concur with Grubb's view that the effect of Lord Donaldson's judgment, by giving the parents a right to veto, or at least to trump, the young person's refusal of treatment is giving them the very power to determine treatment which they were denied in *Gillick*? (See Grubb, *op. cit.* at page 64.)

5. Is this judgment unduly paternalistic in its emphasis on what others believe to be in the young person's best interests? Even if the court does technically possess the power to override the wishes of a mature adolescent, should it do so? (See A. Bainham, *op. cit.*)

6. How useful is Lord Donaldson's keyholder analogy?

The balance of power in child health decision making was again considered by the Court of Appeal in 1992. On this occasion closer analysis of the import of section 8(3) of the Family Law Reform Act 1969 was supplied.

Re W (A Minor) (Medical Treatment: Court's Jurisdiction) [1992] 4 All E.R. 627, [1993] Fam 64, [1992] 3 W.L.R. 758, [1993] 1 FLR 1, [1992] 9 BMLR 22, Fam. Law 541, [1992] 2 F.C.R. 785

W, a girl of 16, suffered from anorexia. She was admitted to a specialist adolescent residential unit. Her condition was deteriorating and, in consequence, it was proposed that she should be moved to a hospital specialising in the treatment of eating disorders. W wished to remain where she was and therefore objected to this proposal. Accordingly, the local authority applied to invoke the court's inherent jurisdiction under section 100(3), (4) of the Children Act 1989 for a direction that it should be permitted to move her to the specialist institution. At first instance, Thorpe J. held that although W was "*Gillick* competent" the court had inherent jurisdiction to make to order sought. W appealed contending that under section 8 of the

Family Law Reform Act 1969 she had an *exclusive* right to consent to
medical treatment or care.

LORD DONALDSON M.R.:

"... I turn therefore to section 8 and to the common law against the
background of which the section was enacted. The common law was author-
itatively considered and defined in *Gillick v. West Norfolk and Wisbech Area
Health Authority* and there is no suggestion that it had altered significantly since
1969 ...".

His Lordship set out section 8 of the 1969 Act and continued:

"In *Re R (A Minor) (Wardship: Treatment)* [1991] 4 All E.R. 177 this court was
concerned with a 15-year-old girl and accordingly the meaning and effect of
section 8 was not directly in issue. I did, however, express my views on the
construction and effect of the section which, it now appears, were at variance
with the views of academic and other writers (see Bainham, 'The judge and the
competent minor' (1992) 108 L.Q.R. 194 at 198; Thornton, 'Multiple Keyholders — Wardship and Consent to Medical Treatment' [1992] C.L.J. 34 at 36;
Kennedy, 'Consent to Treatment: the Capable Person'; Gostin, 'Consent to
Treatment: the Incapable Person' and Dodds-Smith, 'Clinical Research' in Dyer
(ed.) *Doctors, Patients and the Law* (1992) pp. 60–61, 156–157 and Brazier,
Medicine, Patients and the Law (2nd ed. (1992)) p. 346. Essentially what all are
saying is that a right to consent to medical treatment, whether required under the
common law (see *Gillick's* case) or under statute (section 8), must and does carry
with it a right not only to refuse consent to treatment, but to refuse the treatment
itself. As it is put by the Department of Health *Guidelines for Ethics Committee*
(August 1991):

'The giving of consent by a parent or guardian cannot override a refusal of
consent by a child who is competent to make that decision.'

Since my remarks were unnecessary for the decision, R not having yet attained
the age of 16, I am free to reconsider the matter and to reach an opposite
conclusion. Let me therefore start afresh by looking at the common law.

Gillick's case

In *Gillick's* case the central issue was *not* whether a child patient under the age of
16 could refuse medical treatment if the parents or the court consented, but
whether the parents could effectively impose a veto on treatment by failing or
refusing to consent to treatment to which the child might consent. Mrs Gillick
accepted that the court had such a power of veto and contended that the parents
had a similar power (see [1985] 3 All E.R. 402 at 406, 412, 418 *per* Lords Fraser,
Tullybelton and Scarman); Section 8 only came into the argument because it was
contended on behalf of Mrs Gillick that, but for s.8, no minor could ever consent to
medical treatment and that s.8 was designed only to lower the age of consent to
such treatment from 18 to 16 (see [1985] 1 All E.R. 533 at 539). The area health
authority and Department of Health and Social Security on the other hand
contended that under the common law a minor of sufficient intelligence and
understanding could always consent to treatment and that the effect of s.8 was to
produce an irrebuttable presumption that a child of 16 or 17 had such intelligence
and understanding.

The House of Lords decisively rejected Mrs Gillick's contentions and held that at
common law a child of sufficient intelligence and understanding (the 'Gillick

competent' child) could consent to treatment, notwithstanding the absence of the parents' consent and even an express prohibition by the parents. Only Lord Scarman's speech is couched in terms which might suggest that the refusal of a child below the age of 16 to accept medical treatment was determinative (see [1985] 3 All E.R. 402 at 423) because there could never be concurrent rights to consent:

> 'the parental right to determine whether or not their minor child below the age of 16 will have medical treatment terminates if and when the child achieves a sufficient understanding and intelligence to enable him or her to understand fully what is proposed.'

If the parental right terminates, it would follow that, apart from the court, the only person competent to consent would be the child and a refusal of consent to treatment would indirectly constitute an effective veto on the treatment itself. I say 'indirectly' because the veto would be imposed by the civil and criminal laws, rather than by the refusal of consent.

In the light of the quite different issue which was before the House in *Gillick's* case I venture to doubt whether Lord Scarman meant more than that the *exclusive* right of the parents to consent to treatment terminated, but I may well be wrong. Thorpe J. having held that 'there is no doubt at all that [W] is a child of sufficient understanding to make an informed decision,' I shall assume that, so far as the common law is concerned, Lord Scarman would have decided that neither the local authority nor W's aunt, both of whom had parental responsibilities, could give consent to treatment which would be effective in the face of W's refusal of consent. This is of considerable persuasive authority, but even that is not the issue before this court. That is whether *the court* has such a power. That never arose in *Gillick's* case, the nearest approach to it being the proposition, accepted by all parties, that the court had power to override any minor's consent (*not* refusal) to accept treatment.

The purpose of consent to treatment

There seems to be some confusion in the minds of some as to the purpose of seeking consent from a patient (whether adult or child) or from someone with authority to give that consent on behalf of the patient. It has two purposes, the one clinical and the other legal. The clinical purpose stems from the fact that in many instances the co-operation of the patient and the patient's faith or at least confidence in the efficiency of the treatment is a major factor contributing to the treatment's success. Failure to obtain such consent will not only deprive the patient and the medical staff of this advantage, but will usually make it much more difficult to administer the treatment. I appreciate that this purpose may not be served if consent is given on behalf of, rather than by, the patient. However, in the case of young children knowledge of the fact that the parent has consented may help. The legal purpose is quite different. It is to provide those concerned in the treatment with a defence to a criminal charge of assault or battery or a civil claim for damages for trespass to the person. It does not, however, provide them with any defence to a claim that they negligently advised a particular treatment or negligently carried it out.

Is s.8 ambiguous?

The wording of sub-s. (1) shows quite clearly that it is addressed to the legal purpose and legal effect of consent to treatment, namely, to prevent such treatment constituting in law a trespass to the person, and that it does so by making the consent of a 16- or 17-year-old as effective as if he were 'of full age.' No question of 'Gillick competence' in common law terms arises. The 16- or 17-year-old is conclusively presumed to be 'Gillick competent' or, alternatively, the test of 'Gillick competence' is bypassed and has no relevance. The argument that W, or any other 16- or 17-year-old, can by refusing to consent to treatment veto the treatment notwithstanding that the doctor has the consent of someone who has parental responsibilities, involves the proposition that section 8 has the further effect of depriving such a person of the power to consent. It certainly does not say so. Indeed if this were its intended effect, it is difficult to see why the subsection goes on to say that it is not *necessary* to obtain the parents' consent, rather than providing that such consent, if obtained, should be ineffective. Furthermore such a construction does not sit easily with subs. (3) which preserves the common law as it existed immediately before the Act which undoubtedly gave parents an effective power of consent for all children up to the age of 21, the then existing age of consent (see *Gillick's* case [1985] 3 All E.R. 402 at 408, 419 *per* Lords Fraser, Tullybelton and Scarman).

The most promising argument in favour of W having an exclusive right to consent to treatment and thus, by refusing consent, to attract the protection of the law on trespass to the person, lies in concentrating upon the words 'as effective as it would be if he were of full age.' If she were of full age her ability to consent would have two separate effects. First, her consent would be fully effective as such. Second, a failure or refusal to give consent would be fully effective as a veto, but only *because no one else would be in a position to consent*. If it is a possible view that s.8 is intended to put a 16- or 17-year-old in exactly the same position as an adult and there is thus some ambiguity, although I do not think that there is, it is a permissible aid to construction to seek to ascertain the mischief at which the section is directed.

The Latey Committee Report

It is common ground that the Family Law Reform Act 1969 was Parliament's response to the *Report of the Committee on the Age of Majority* (Cmnd 3342) (1967). The relevant part is contained in paras. 474 to 484. These show that the mischief aimed at was twofold. First, cases were occurring in which young people between 16 and 21 (the then age of majority) were living away from home and wished and needed urgent medical treatment which had not yet reached the emergency stage. Doctors were unable to treat them unless and until their parents had been traced and this could cause unnecessary suffering. Second, difficulties were arising concerning —

'operations whose implications bring up the question of a girl's right to privacy about her sexual life. A particularly difficult situation arises in the case of a girl who is sent to hospital in need of a therapeutic abortion and refuses point blank to enter the hospital unless a guarantee is given that her parents shall not be told about it.' (See para. 478.)

The committee had recommended that the age of majority be reduced to 18 generally. The report records that all the professional bodies which gave evidence recommended that patients aged between 16 and 18 should be able to give an effective consent to treatment and all but the Medical Protection Society recommended that they should also be able to give an effective refusal (see para. 480). The point with which we are concerned was therefore well in the mind of the committee. It did not so recommend. It recommended that —

'*without prejudice to any consent that may otherwise be lawful*, the consent of young persons aged 16 and over to medical or dental treatment shall be as valid as the consent of a person of full age.' (My emphasis.)

Conclusion on section 8

I am quite unable to accept that Parliament in adopting somewhat more prolix language was intending to achieve a result which differed from that recommended by the committee.

On reflection I regret my use in *Re R (a minor) (wardship: medical treatment)* [1991] 4 All E.R. 177 at 184 of the keyholder analogy because keys can lock as well as unlock. I now prefer the analogy of the legal 'flak jacket' which protects the doctor from claims by the litigious whether he acquires it from his patient who may be a minor over the age of 16 or a 'Gillick competent' child under that age or from another person having parental responsibilities which include a right to consent to treatment of the minor. Anyone who gives him a flak jacket (*i.e.* consent) may take it back, but the doctor only needs one and so long as he continues to have one he has the legal right to proceed.

The section extends not only to treatment, but also to diagnostic procedures (see sub-s. (2)). It does not, however, extend to the donation of organs or blood since, so far as the donor is concerned, these do not constitute either treatment or diagnosis. I cannot remember to what extent organ donation was common in 1967, but the Latey Committee expressly recommended that only 18-year-olds and older should be authorised by statute to consent to *giving* blood (see para. 485–489). It seems that Parliament accepted this recommendation, although I doubt whether blood donation will create any problem as a 'Gillick competent' minor of any age would be able to give consent under the common law.

Organ transplants are quite different and, as a matter of law, doctors would have to secure the consent of someone with the right to consent on behalf of a donor under the age of 18 or, if they relied upon the consent of the minor himself or herself, be satisfied that the minor was 'Gillick competent' in the context of so serious a procedure which could not benefit the minor. This would be a highly improbable conclusion. But this is only to look at the question as a matter of law. Medical ethics also enter into the question. The doctor has a professional duty to act in the best interests of his patient and to advise accordingly. It is inconceivable that he should proceed in reliance solely upon the consent of an under-age patient, however 'Gillick competent,' in the absence of supporting parental consent and equally inconceivable that he should proceed in the absence of the patient's consent. In any event he will need to seek the opinions of other doctors and may be well advised to apply to the court for guidance, as recommended by Lord Templeman in a different context in *Re B (a minor) (wardship: sterilisation)* [1987] 2 All E.R. 206 at 214–215.

Hair-raising possibilities were canvassed of abortions being carried out by doctors in reliance upon the consent of parents and despite the refusal of consent by 16- and 17-year-olds. Whilst this may be possible as a matter of law, I do not see any likelihood taking account of medical ethics, unless the abortion was truly in the best interests of the child. This is not to say that it could not happen. This is clear from the facts of *Re D (a minor) (wardship: sterilisation)* [1976] 1 All E.R. 326, where the child concerned had neither the intelligence nor understanding either to consent or refuse. There medical ethics did not prove an obstacle, there being divided medical opinions, but the wardship jurisdiction of the court was invoked by a local authority educational psychologist who had been involved with the case. Despite the passing of the Children Act 1989, the inherent jurisdiction of the court could still be invoked in such a case to prevent an abortion which was contrary to the interests of the minor.

Thus far I have, in the main, been looking at the problem in the context of a conflict between parents and the minor, either the minor consenting and the parents refusing consent or the minor refusing consent and the parents giving it. Although that is not this case, I have done so both because we were told that it would be helpful to all those concerned with the treatment of minors and also perhaps the minors themselves and because it seems to be a logical base from which to proceed to consider the powers of the court and how they should be exercised.

W's case

W is not in fact refusing all treatment. Her attitude is that she wishes to continue with the treatment which she was receiving when the hearing of this appeal began. Her reasons are not to be and were not dismissed lightly, but during the hearing the situation changed dramatically. The hearing began on 29 June at which time, so far as we knew, W's condition was stable or deteriorating only slowly, although there had been some further loss of weight. This accorded with information given to the court when the appeal was first set down. The Registrar of Civil Appeals appreciated that the issue could be one of extreme urgency, but was assured that it was not. Hence the fact that although Thorpe J. gave judgment on 12 May, more than a month elapsed before the appeal hearing began. However, on 30 June we were told in response to inquiries by the court that she had not taken solid food since 21 June and that, although she had maintained a fluid intake of 12 cups of tea a day, her weight had dropped from 39 kg on June 16 to 35.1 kg on 30 June. This represents a loss of weight of 8 lb in 14 days with a final weight of 5 stone 7 lb for a girl 5 feet 7 inches tall. More serious was the agreed medical opinion that should she continue in this way, within a week her capacity to have children in later life would be seriously at risk and a little later her life itself might be in danger.

In these circumstances, as we were agreed that we had power to do so, we made an emergency order enabling her to be taken to and treated at a specialist hospital in London, notwithstanding the lack of consent on her part. Later we were glad to hear that, whilst not consenting, W accepted that the order would have to be complied with. Thereafter we carried on with the hearing of the argument on whether Thorpe J. was or was not right to make the order which he did in the different circumstances which then existed and as to the more general issues raised by this appeal. It was this change of circumstances which led me in announcing the making of the emergency order to say that W's wishes were no longer of weight. At that stage they were completely outweighed by the threat of irreparable damage to her health and risk to her life. I was not purporting to consider, and was not considering, the importance of W's views at an earlier stage in the development of the illness or the importance of the views of patients under the age of 18 generally. They are matters to which I now turn.

As I say, W wished to continue with the same regime. She gave evidence before Thorpe J. and he recorded in his judgment:

'She looks very thin and very ill and I was equally impressed by her distress and the fervour with which she pleaded to be left where she is. She emphasised that she did not want to get better; that there was no reason or motive for her to get better; that she wished to remain in control; that she would cure herself when she decided that it was right to do so. She also stressed that she wanted to be parented within a family.'

In addition it is clear from the transcript that she, very naturally, attached great importance to the fact that she knew the staff at the unit, had two friends there and, perhaps even more important, had a great bond with a lady who was assisting in her treatment. Nevertheless it appears from the judgment of Thorpe J., and I do not doubt that he was right, that a dominant factor was W's desire to be in an environment where, as she thought, she was in control and could cure herself if and when she thought it right to do so. That she might leave it too late, does not seem to have occurred to her.

I have no doubt that the wishes of a 16- or 17-year-old child or indeed of a younger child who is 'Gillick competent' are of the greatest importance both legally and clinically, but I do doubt whether Thorpe J. was right to conclude that W was of sufficient understanding to make an informed decision. I do not say this on the basis that I consider her approach irrational. I personally consider that religious or other beliefs which bar any medical treatment or treatment of particular kinds are irrational, but that does not make minors who hold those beliefs any the less 'Gillick competent.' They may well have sufficient intelligence and understanding fully to appreciate the treatment proposed and the consequences of their refusal to accept that treatment. What distinguishes W from them, and what with all respect I do not think that Thorpe J. took sufficiently into account (perhaps because the point did not emerge as clearly before him as it did before us), is that it is a feature of anorexia nervosa that it is capable of destroying the ability to make an informed choice. It creates a compulsion to refuse treatment or only to accept treatment which is likely to be ineffective. This attitude is part and parcel of the disease and the more advanced the illness, the more compelling it may become. Where the wishes of the minor are themselves something which the doctors reasonably consider need to be treated in the minor's own best interests, those wishes clearly have a much reduced significance.

There is ample authority for the proposition that the inherent powers of the court under its *parens patriae* jurisdiction are theoretically limitless and that they certainly extend beyond the powers of a natural parent: see for example *Re R (a minor) (wardship: medical treatment)* [1991] 4 All E.R. 177 at 186, 189. There can therefore be no doubt that it has power to override the refusal of a minor, whether over the age of 16 or under that age but 'Gillick competent.' It does not do so by ordering the doctors to treat, which, even if within the court's powers, would be an abuse of them, or by ordering the minor to accept treatment, but by authorising the doctors to treat the minor in accordance with their clinical judgment, subject to any restrictions which the court may impose.

The remaining issue is how this power should be exercised in the context of a case in which a minor is refusing treatment or, whilst consenting to one form of treatment, is refusing to consent to another. Mr James Munby, appearing as amicus curiae, in his most helpful skeleton argument approached the matter as if 16- and 17-year-olds were in a special category. In a sense, of course, they are because s.8 applies to them. But Mr Munby so treated them because, in his submission, s.8 conferred complete autonomy on such minors, thus enabling them effectively to refuse medical treatment irrespective of how parental responsibilities might be sought to be exercised. That submission I have already rejected. This is not, however, to say that the wishes of 16- and 17-year-olds are to be treated as no different from those of 14- and 15-year-olds. Far from it. Adolescence is a period of progressive transition from childhood to adulthood and as experience of life is acquired and intelligence and understanding grow, so will the scope of the decision-making which should be left to the minor, for it is only by making decisions and experiencing the consequences that decision-making skills will be acquired. As I put it in the course of the argument, and as I sincerely believe, 'good parenting involves giving minors as much rope as they can handle without an unacceptable risk that they will hang themselves.' As Lord Hailsham of St Marylebone L.C. put it in *Re B (a minor) (wardship: sterilisation)* [1987] 2 All E.R. 206 at 212, the 'first and paramount consideration [of the court] is the well being, welfare or interests [of the minor]' and I regard it as self-evident that this involves giving them the maximum degree of decision-making which is prudent. Prudence does not involve avoiding all risk, but it does involve avoiding taking risks which, if they eventuate, may have irreparable consequences or which are disproportionate to the benefits which could accrue from taking them. I regard this approach as wholly consistent with the philosophy of s.1 of the Children Act 1989, and, in particular, subs. (3)(a). It was submitted that whilst this might be correct, such an approach is inconsistent with ss.38(6), 43(8) and 44(7) of that Act and with paras. 4 and 5 of Sched. 3. Here I disagree. These provisions all concern interim or supervision orders and do not impinge upon the jurisdiction of the court to make prohibited steps or specific issue orders under s.8 of the Act of 1989 in the context of which the minor has no right of veto, unless it is to be found in s.8 of the Act of 1969.

Thorpe J. was faced with having to choose between accepting one or other of two courses of action — leaving W where she was or transferring her to London — each of which was supported by responsible medical opinion. One of these doctors had consulted a Dr D, who was the pre-eminent expert in the treatment of anorexic cases. Initially Dr D was in favour of leaving W where she was, but he changed his mind when he came to give evidence. If ever there was a case for respecting the discretionary decision of the judge who had heard the witnesses, including W, this was it.

In seeking to escape from this conclusion it was submitted in argument that the reasoning of the judgment did not show, or show sufficiently, that Thorpe J. had given due weight to W's wishes and that accordingly he had misdirected himself. I regard this criticism as wholly misconceived. Although much of the argument before him and much of his judgment were devoted to the legal rights of a 16-year-old, the only reason for exploring this was that W was resisting a change of regime. W's wishes could therefore never have been out of his mind. Furthermore, in explaining that discretionary decision he said:

'The past year has not been a year of successful treatment or progress. There are a number of indications of this lack of success. There are the coercive measures of the gastro-nasal tubes and the plastering of the arms to which I have referred. There is the fact that her therapy was interrupted by fortuitous circumstances. There is the fact that consistent care by her consultant was interrupted by his illness. There is the fact that more recently the unit has promulgated stark rules including a drastic sanction in the event of breach. [W] has breached the rules, the sanction has not been applied, [W] is manifestly in control and the unit is reduced to proposing that they should move away from psychological coercion to offering reward for good behaviour. That announcement to [W] could, in my judgment, only serve to underline to her the extent to which she is in control. The management options for the immediate future have been considerably constricted by recent developments. Although I have great respect for [W's] consultant and for the dedication of the staff, it seems to me that they have been manoeuvred into a position from which a change is necessary, even if it is a change that carries the risk of interpretation by [W] as "yet another adult rejection and failure." Obviously there are pros for the solution urged by her consultant. As well as W's views and her vulnerability there is the fact that there is a quasi-family bonding where she is. There is also the consideration that she seems to be flirting with the possibility of committing herself to re-entering mainstream education locally. There is also the proximity of the proposed foster parents and her own siblings.'

In this passage Thorpe J. was quite clearly not only bearing [W's] wishes in mind, but looking behind them to see why [W] wished to remain where she was. Not only would I have refrained from interfering with Thorpe J.'s decision on the footing that he had properly directed himself and that it was for him to decide, but because, even on the facts as they then were, I consider that his decision was plainly right . . ."

His Lordship then summed up as follows:

"(1) No question of a minor consenting to or refusing medical treatment arises unless and until a medical or dental practitioner advises such treatment and is willing to undertake it.

(2) Regardless of whether the minor or anyone else with authority to do so consents to the treatment, that practitioner will be liable to the minor in negligence if he fails to advise with reasonable skill and care and to have due regard to the best interests of his patient.

(3) This appeal has been concerned with the treatment of anorexia nervosa. It is a peculiarity of this disease that the disease itself creates a wish not to be cured or only to be cured if and when the patient decides to cure himself or herself, which may well be too late. Treatment has to be directed at this state of mind as much as to restoring body weight.

(4) Section 8 of the Family Law Reform Act 1969 gives minors who have attained the age of 16 a right to consent to surgical, medical or dental treatment. Such a consent cannot be overridden by those with parental responsibility for the minor. It can, however, be overridden by the court. This statutory right does not extend to consent to the donation of blood or organs.

(5) A minor of any age who is 'Gillick competent' in the context of particular treatment has a right to consent to that treatment which again cannot be overridden by those with parental responsibility, but can be overridden by the court. Unlike the statutory right this common law right extends to the donation of blood or organs.

(6) No minor of whatever age has power by refusing consent to treatment to override a consent to treatment by someone who has parental responsibility for the minor and a fortiori a consent by the court. Nevertheless such a refusal is a very important consideration in making clinical judgments and for parents and the court in deciding whether themselves to give consent. Its importance increases with the age and maturity of the minor.

(7) The effect of consent to treatment by the minor or someone else with authority to give it is limited to protecting the medical or dental practitioner from claims for damages for trespass to the person . . ."

BALCOMBE L.J.:
" . . . The first issue before us, as it was before Thorpe J., was whether Parliament had, by s.8 of the Family Law Reform Act 1969, conferred on a minor over the age of 16 years an absolute right to refuse medical treatment, in which case the limitation of the court's inherent jurisdiction exemplified by *A v. Liverpool City Council* would have operated so as to preclude any intervention by the court . . .".

His Lordship then set out, so far as material, the provisions contained in section 8 of the Family Law Reform Act 1969. He then continued:

" . . . It will be readily apparent that the section is silent on the question which arises in the present case, namely whether a minor who has attained the age of 16 years has an absolute right to refuse medical treatment. I am quite unable to see how, on any normal reading of the words of the section, it can be construed to confer such a right. The purpose of the section is clear: it is to enable a 16-year-old to consent to medical treatment which, in the absence of consent by the child or its parents, would constitute a trespass to the person. In other words, for this purpose, and for this purpose only, a minor was to be treated as if it were an adult. That the section did not operate to prevent parental consent remaining effective, as well in the case of a child over 16 as in the case of a child under that age, is apparent from the words of sub-s. (3).

If there was any ambiguity as to the meaning of the section — and in my judgment there is not — it would be resolved by a glance at the *Report of the*

Committee on the Age of Majority (Cmnd. 3342 (1967)) (the Latey Report) to see what was the mischief which the section was intended to remedy. Paragraphs 474 to 489 of the Latey Report make it clear that doctors felt difficulty in accepting the consent of someone under 21 (the then age of majority) to medical treatment, even though parental consent might be unobtainable or, for reasons of the minor's privacy, undesirable. The nature of the problem is made apparent in para. 479 of the Latey Report:

'The legal position is in itself obscure. A cause of action to which a hospital authority or a member of its medical staff (or both) may be liable as the result of the performance of an operation is trespass to the person, and treatment administered without the patient's express or implied consent constitutes an assault which may lead to an action for damages. Until recent years the general rule has been to require the consent of a parent or guardian for an operation or an anaesthetic on a person of under 21, but increasingly at the present time it is becoming customary to accept the consent of minors aged 16 and over. There is no rigid rule of English law which renders a minor incapable of giving his consent to an operation but there seems to be no direct judicial authority establishing that the consent of such a person is valid.'

It was not until some 18 years after the publication of the Latey Report that the common law position on this topic was resolved by the decision of the House of Lords in *Gillick v. West Norfolk and Wisbech Area Health Authority*.

This interpretation of s.8 was given, *obiter*, by Lord Donaldson of Lymington M.R. in *Re R*. His judgment attracted a considerable degree of academic criticism. I have to say that I find this criticism surprising since, as I have already said, the section is in my judgment clear, unambiguous and limited in its scope. One writer went so far as to say that this construction 'flies in the face of the settled interpretation of this provision.' Counsel were unable to suggest any case which may have settled the interpretation of the section other than *Gillick's* case, and to that I now turn.

The issue in *Gillick's* case was stated by Lord Fraser of Tullybelton in the following terms [1985] 3 All E.R. 402 at 406:

'The central issue in the appeal is whether a doctor can ever, in any circumstances, lawfully give contraceptive advice or treatment to a girl under the age 16 without her parents' consent.'

To the like effect was Lord Scarman (see [1985] 3 All E.R. 402 at 418). To that issue the construction of section 8 was at best peripheral.

The section was mentioned by both Parker and Fox L.JJ. in the Court of Appeal (see [1985] 1 All E.R. 533 at 539), but neither attempted to give any definitive construction. In the House of Lords Lord Fraser of Tullybelton mentioned the section, but also did not attempt to define its meaning. Lord Bridge of Harwich, Lord Brandon of Oakbrook and Lord Templeman did not even mention the section. Lord Scarman did, however, mention the section at several points in the course of his speech, and after a consideration of its provisions and other matters said ([1985] 3 All E.R. 402 at 423):

'In the light of the foregoing I would hold that as a matter of law the parental right to determine whether or not their minor child below the age of 16 will have medical treatment terminates if and when the child achieves a sufficient understanding and intelligence to enable him or her to understand fully what is proposed.'

I accept that the words 'or not' in this passage suggest that Lord Scarman considered that the right to refuse treatment was co-existent with the right to consent to treatment. I also accept that if a 'Gillick competent' child under 16 has a right to refuse treatment, so too has a child over the age of 16. Nevertheless I share the doubts of Lord Donaldson of Lymington M.R. whether Lord Scarman was intending to mean that the parents of a 'Gillick competent' child had no right at all to consent to medical treatment of the child as opposed to no exclusive right to such consent. If he did so intend then, in the case of a child over the age of 16, his interpretation of the law was inconsistent with the express words of s.8(3) of the Act of 1969. It is also clear that Lord Scarman was only considering the position of the child vis-à-vis its parents: he was not considering the position of the child vis-à-vis the court whose powers, as I have already said, are wider than the parents'.

I am therefore satisfied that there is no interpretation of section 8 of the Act of 1969, and certainly no 'settled' interpretation, which persuades me that my view of the clear meaning of the section is wrong . . ."

NOTES:

1. Nolan L.J., who delivered a concurring judgment, did not directly consider whether reaching 16 or the attainment of "*Gillick* competence" extinguished the parental power to consent. He focused simply upon the balance of power between the child and the court in the exercise of its inherent jurisdiction.
2. Lord Donaldson hinted that anorexia nervosa was a condition that could destroy a patient's ability to make an informed choice. On this basis it could be argued that he did not regard W as "*Gillick* competent". (See J. Masson, "Re W: appealing from the golden cage" (1993) 5 *Journal of Child Law* 37.) This also raises the issue of whether the case should have been dealt with under the Mental Health legislation, as were the cases of *Riverside Mental Health NHS Trust v. Fox* [1994] 1 FLR 614 and *B. v. Croydon District Health Authority* [1995] 1 All E.R. 683. (See Chapter 9 at pages 546–547.)
3. Lord Donaldson expressed the view that no minor, whatever her age, could, by refusing treatment, override a consent to treatment given by someone with parental responsibility. This can be read as a fundamental incursion into the adolescent's right to self-determination. (See J. Bridgeman, "Old enough to know best?" (1993) 13 *Legal Studies* 69.)
4. It has been suggested that *Re W* should not be interpreted as being about the right of a teenager aged 16 or 17 to refuse life-saving treatment, but as concerning the right of a competent teenager to determine the medical treatment which she receives, *i.e.* whether to receive one form rather than another. (See J. Bridgeman, *op. cit.*)
5. Masson notes that, as in the case of *Re R*, the Court of Appeal in this case appeared to be less concerned with producing a clearly reasoned decision on the topic at issue, than with pronouncing on the general area of children and consent. Thus, once again, many of the dicta in the judgments are *obiter*. (See J. Masson, *op. cit.* at page 37.)

QUESTIONS:

1. Even if section 8(3) of the Family Law Reform Act 1969 preserved the common law power of a parent to grant consent, is it not possible

that "*Gillick* competent" children have the exclusive right to deter-
mine their health care by virtue of the actual *Gillick* decision? (See J.
Murphy, "W(h)ither Adolescent Autonomy?" [1992] *Journal of
Social Welfare and Family Law* 539; M. Brazier and C. Bridge,
"Coercion or Caring: analysing adolescent autonomy" (1996) 16
Legal Studies 84.)

2. In constructing the metaphor of consent as a "flak jacket", Lord
    Donaldson appears to have been more concerned with doctors'
    liberties (to undertake medical procedures immune from a trespass
    suit) than with adolescents' rights. Is this a proper way to approach
    such cases?

3. Lord Donaldson briefly considered the applicability of the Mental
    Health Act 1983 to this case, but he summarily dismissed the
    possibility of using that legislation on the grounds that the stigma
    associated with that Act meant that patients would be less prejudiced
    by compulsory treatment outside of that Act. Do you agree, especially
    in view of the fact that the 1983 Act contains statutory safeguards
    (discussed in Chapter 8) to protect those compulsorily treated under
    it? Does Lord Donaldson's attitude in itself reinforce the stigmatisa-
    tion of mental illness? (See P. Fennell, "Informal Compulsion"
    [1992] *Journal of Social Welfare and Family Law* 311; Masson, "*Re
    W*: appealing from the golden cage" (1993) 5 *Journal of Child Law*
    37; Brazier and Bridge, "Coercion or caring: analysing adolescent
    autonomy" (1996) 16 *Legal Studies* 84 at page 96.)

4. Should legislation be required to authorise coercive action by the
    state, such as the action taken in this case? (See A. Grubb, "Treat-
    ment decisions: keeping it in the family" in A. Grubb (ed.), *Choices
    and Decisions in Health Care*, Chichester: Wiley, 1993 at page 71.)

5. In this case do you agree with:
    (a) the outcome?
    (b) the reasoning?

5. LIMITS OF THE PARENTAL POWER OF CONSENT

In *Hewer v. Bryant* [1969] 3 All E.R. 578, Lord Denning stressed that
parental rights only exist for the benefit of the child. This assertion was
expressly approved by Lords Fraser and Scarman in the *Gillick* case.
However, one question which neither of those cases addressed was what
limits exist on the kinds of medical treatment to which an adult, as proxy,
may give consent. Lord Templeman did, however, consider the matter in a
case decided in 1987:

Re B (A Minor) (Wardship: Sterilisation) [1987] 2 All E.R. 206, [1988] 1
A.C. 199, [1987] 2 W.L.R. 1213, [1987] FLR 314, 2 BMLR 126, 86
L.G.R. 417

This case concerned a local authority which had received into its care a
mentally handicapped 17-year-old girl who suffered from epilepsy and had

a mental age of five or six. It was claimed that she lacked any understanding of the connection between sexual intercourse and pregnancy although she could understand the link between pregnancy and birth. It was also suggested that, were she to become pregnant, she would not be able to cope with giving birth or subsequent child care. On the other hand, she did exhibit a normal sexual drive for a girl of her age. Expert evidence declared it to be vital that she should not become pregnant but that certain contraceptive drugs would react with the drugs she needed to control her mental instability and epilepsy. In addition, evidence suggested that a course of oral contraception would be an impracticable means by which to avert a pregnancy. Accordingly the local authority applied to the High Court for her to be made a ward of court and for leave to be given for her to undergo a sterilisation operation. The application was supported by the girl's mother but not by the Official Solicitor, who was acting as guardian *ad litem*. At first instance, the judge granted the application. The Official Solicitor's appeal to the Court of Appeal was unsuccessful. He then appealed to the House of Lords.

LORD TEMPLEMAN:
" . . . In my opinion sterilisation of a girl under 18 should only be carried out with the leave of a High Court judge. A doctor performing a sterilisation operation with the consent of the parents might still be liable in criminal, civil or professional proceedings. A court exercising the wardship jurisdiction emanating from the Crown is the only authority which is empowered to authorise such a drastic step as sterilisation after a full and informed investigation. The girl will be represented by the Official Solicitor or some other appropriate guardian; the parents will be made parties if they wish to appear and where appropriate the local authority will also appear. Expert evidence will be adduced setting out the reasons for the application, the history, conditions, circumstances and foreseeable future of the girl, the risks and consequences of pregnancy, the risks and consequences of sterilisation, the practicability of alternative precautions against pregnancy and any other relevant information. The judge may order additional evidence to be obtained. In my opinion, a decision should only be made by a High Court judge. In the Family Division a judge is selected for his or her experience, ability and compassion. No one has suggested a more satisfactory tribunal or a more satisfactory method of reaching a decision which vitally concerns an individual but also involves principles of law, ethics and medical practice. Applications for sterilisation will be rare. Sometimes the judge will conclude that a sufficiently overwhelming case has not been established to justify interference with the fundamental right of a girl to bear a child; this was the case in *Re D (a minor) (wardship: sterilisation)* [1976] 1 All E.R. 326. But in the present case the judge was satisfied that it would be cruel to expose the girl to an unacceptable risk of pregnancy which could only be obviated by sterilisation in order to prevent child bearing and childbirth in circumstances of uncomprehending fear and pain and risk of physical injury. In such a case the judge was under a duty and had the courage to authorise sterilisation."

NOTES:

1. *Re B* is dealt with more fully in the context of non voluntary sterilisation (see Chapter 13 at pages 758–763).
2. In this case one needs to be particularly wary of accepting the stated facts at face value. As Lee and Morgan point out, what are treated as

settled facts in this case are actually highly selective and in reality constitute a series of assessments as to the girl's capabilities and prospects. (See R. Lee and D. Morgan, "A Lesser Sacrifice? Sterilisation and Mentally Handicapped Women" in R. Lee and D. Morgan (eds), *Birthrights: Law and Ethics at the Beginnings of Life*, London: Routledge, 1989 at pages 139–142.)

3. Note the similarity in the fundamental issues addressed in this case and *Gillick*, in that both are concerned with the extent to which individual autonomy can be over-ridden in the context of the reproductive autonomy of young women. Yet *Gillick* is not referred to by their Lordships. (See Lee and Morgan, *op. cit.* at page 134.)

4. Where sterilisation is a necessary incident of other, necessary treatment, it is not necessary to obtain the court's sanction. In *Re E* [1991] 2 FLR 585, for example, it was said that parents might give a valid consent to a hysterectomy operation on their daughter without first obtaining a declaration from the court.

5. Lord Templeman's opinion has been approved in *Re HG* [1993] 1 FLR 587.

QUESTION:

1. Which, if any, of the following medical procedures should also require judicial sanction in the case of a young person: abortion; cosmetic surgery; organ donation; medical research? In answering this question, is it necessary to be able to forge a distinction between therapeutic and non-therapeutic procedures? (See Chapter 6 at pages 356–360 and Chapter 13 at pages 764–765.) Are there matters of policy at stake which might circumscribe the remit of parental competence?

Though expressed *obiter*; Lord Templeman's opinion has since received judicial approval in the following case:

In Re P (a Minor) (1981) 80 LGR 301

P (Shirley) was a 15-year-old girl. Having been convicted of theft two years previously, she was committed to the care of the local authority under the provisions of the Children and Young Persons Act 1969. In November 1980 she gave birth to a baby boy. She and her son were placed in a mother and baby unit with educational facilities. During school hours her son was cared for in the nursery and outside school hours she cared for him. In August 1980 she again became pregnant and as with her first pregnancy her parents refused their consent to abortion, although on this occasion Shirley herself was anxious to have a termination. The local authority made her a ward of court and asked the court to make an order directing that her pregnancy be terminated. Her father suggested instead that she should carry her pregnancy to term and that he and his wife would bring up her first child.

BUTLER SLOSS J.:

". . . I would not like it to be thought that because she says she does not want the child her wishes should be given such paramount importance as to mean that for that reason only she should have an abortion. But where her wishes coincide with the facts that she is in danger of injury to her mental health; that she is undoubtedly — when I consider her interests, as I do, as the first and paramount consideration — unable to fulfil her own growing up as a child at her schooling as a consequence of this second pregnancy; where she is endangering the future of her current child; and where I take into account all the aspects of her actual and reasonably foreseeable environment, I have no doubt that this case comes within section 1(a) of the Abortion Act 1967. The continuance of the pregnancy would involve injury to the mental health of Shirley and her existing child who is the child of her family and that risk is undoubtedly much greater than the risk of the pregnancy being terminated. Indeed I am told by the consultants that the risks involved in terminating a pregnancy of under 12 weeks is minimal . . .

I now turn to the very considerable problem, and the very understandable approach, of Shirley's parents . . . They do not suggest that Shirley goes back to them, and they are aware that she had difficulties when she was at home. They, in fact, visit her regularly at weekends, and they are clearly attached to their grandson.

The grandfather puts his objections to the termination of the pregnancy on three grounds . . . First of all, that he is a Seventh Day Adventist, and that it is his religion and his own belief and that of his wife that is a criminal offence to take life. This is first and foremost in his view about this. He would not like, I think he told me on the last occasion last week, to be responsible for the child whom his daughter is bearing to have been prevented from living. That is an understandable approach to a moral question which exercises the minds of many people.

Secondly, he says, and understandably says, that Shirley will live to regret the decision that she has taken. Since she is a child I think he, by inference, is saying that she ought not to be allowed to take a decision like that that she will regret thereafter. Thirdly, he says that although he and his wife cannot care for Shirley he would like to take over the care of the boy, and relieve Shirley of that burden so that she can bring up the other child. There would be no problem, therefore, of the extra care of two children . . .

The consideration of grandparents as a stand-in for mother is too uncertain and vague, bearing in mind, firstly, the health of the grandmother; secondly, their ages of 46 and 43; and, thirdly, that there will be three people looking after this little boy instead of his own mother. Under the Abortion Act 1967 I have to consider existing children. This would be putting the unborn child in a position of benefit and depriving the existing boy of that benefit. Because however good the grandfather can be, and I am sure he is a very good grandfather, he could not be the boy's mother, nor could the grandmother be his mother, and the boy would be placed at a considerable disadvantage for the rest of his life if this particular decision was made that he should go to his grandparents . . .

I must take into account in considering the welfare of Shirley — and her welfare is what is paramount in my mind because she is the ward of court — and through her the effect on her son of having this unwanted child, the important aspect of her parents. I was helpfully reminded of what had been said in the House of Lords in *J v. C* [1970] A.C. 668 about the rights and obligations of parents. These parents are in certain difficulties in that they do not have the day to day care of Shirley since she is in care, and they are not able to offer to take over the day to day care of Shirley. In the circumstances, although I must give weight to their feelings as a factor in the case to be taken into consideration, and I must take into account their deeply and sincerely held religious objection, in considering the best interest of the minor as to whether she should have her pregnancy terminated I draw to some extent an analogy with Jehovah's Witnesses and blood transfusions; nevertheless, if

I am satisfied, as I am, that there is a risk of injury to the mental health of this minor, the factors raised by the grandfather on behalf of himself and his wife — which I have taken into account — cannot weigh in the balance against the needs of this girl so as to prevent the termination which I have decided is necessary in her best interests.

Therefore, I propose to direct that there shall be a termination of this pregnancy this week . . . "

Notes:

1. For the relevant provisions of the Abortion Act 1967 see Chapter 12.
2. This decision was followed in the case of *Re B (Wardship: Abortion)* [1991] 2 FLR 426. In that case L — a 12-year-old girl — wished to terminate her pregnancy. She was supported in her wish by the putative father, who was 16, and her maternal grandparents who had brought her up. However, her mother, who had maintained close contact with L, opposed an application by the local authority to have L's pregnancy terminated, on the ground that she didn't believe in abortion. Notwithstanding the mother's objection, Hollis J. held that it was in L's best interests to have the termination, given her age and small build, the trauma of an unwanted pregnancy and the disruption to her education.
3. For the limits of parental power to consent to other controversial treatments such as research, sterilisations and organ transplants see Chapters 10, 13 and 15.

Questions:

1. Was it justifiable for the court, in this case, to over-rule the parents' religious and other objections on the basis of the child's best interests?
2. Do you think that the court would ever deem it in the best interests of a minor to be compelled to have an abortion against her wishes?

6. The Children Act 1989 and Health Care Decisions

The cases of *Re R* and *Re W*, which have largely been seen as a retreat from the support for children's autonomy heralded by the House of Lord in *Gillick*, did not require the courts to directly address the impact of the Children Act 1989. Although the Act was seen as granting mature children statutory rights of self determination, it actually contains very little on the rights of minors/to make independent decisions about medical treatment. (See M. Brazier and C. Bridge, "Coercion or caring: analysing adolescent autonomy" (1996) 16 *Legal Studies* 84 at page 96.) However, section 1(3)(a) instructs the court to have regard to "the ascertainable wishes and feelings of the child concerned (considered in the light of his age and understanding)" and sections 38(6), 43(8) and 44(7) appear to grant a minor a statutory right to refuse to submit to medical or psychiatric examination or treatment where he "has sufficient understanding to make an informed decision". Thus, the young person able to make an informed decision was empowered to refuse a court-ordered assessment. This statutory right was largely a product of the deliberations of the Cleveland inquiry into child abuse, and was designed to allow a sexually abused adolescent to refuse an intimate medical examination. The extent of the right to veto was considered in the following case:

South Glamorgan County Council v. W and B [1993] 1 FLR 574

A was a 15-year-old girl. She and her two elder brothers had suffered severe psychiatric disturbance following her parents' divorce when she was aged seven, and she had rarely seen her mother since then. She lived with her father and eldest reclusive brother in the family home, along with an aunt who sometimes stayed with them. Her other brother was being helped by the local authority to live an independent life. A had received virtually no schooling since the age of 11, had been the subject of 22 former court appearances and was approaching the end of her first year as a recluse in a room in her home. She was verbally abusive to her family and effectively controlled them, dictating who could enter her room, cook her meals etc, and threatening suicide or harm to herself if they failed to comply. In a two year period she was seen by five child psychiatrists, one of whom, a Dr Darwish, had recommended her removal to an adolescent unit, where she had previously received psychiatric assessment and treatment, in her best interests, as she was clearly beyond parental control. However, at that point nothing was done to remove her. Eventually, when the medical evidence pointed to the immediate need for urgent and vigorous assessment and therapy, and a psychiatrist had stated that her behaviour was likely to "seriously impair her mental health in the future and limit her ability to function reasonably", the local authority applied to the court for an emergency protection order, which was refused. Subsequently, the local authority commenced care proceedings and sought various orders under the court's inherent jurisdiction, asking essentially for the court's consent to the proposed assessment and treatment, and for A to be removed from home for that purpose. A was represented by her guardian *ad litem* who was supported by her mother, with whom she had only had sporadic contact since her parents' divorce when she was seven. Her father opposed the application.

DOUGLAS BROWN J.:
" . . . The only doctor who has given evidence is Dr Ahmed Darwish . . . He was asked about her ability to understand her situation and to understand what was proposed and to consent to it. He was in this difficulty that he had not spoken with A or seen her since February 1992, but his evidence was this that, judging by the mental state she presented when he saw her then in the environment she was in, she might not be capable of making a wise decision of going for a psychiatric assessment as an in-patient.

The evidence being in that state, and bearing in mind the description of her mental powers given by Dr Darwish and indeed by other psychiatrists who have examined her, I am not prepared to find on that evidence that she is '*Gillick* incompetent' or that, to paraphrase the words of s 38(6) [of the Children Act 1989], she is not of sufficient understanding to make an informed decision about medical examination or psychiatric examination or other assessment.

In those circumstances, the local authority ask for leave for A to be conveyed to the Merrifield Unit in Taunton for the purpose of being assessed by Dr Cockett or his medical staff, for leave to the local authority to use such reasonable force as may be necessary to move her from her home and take her to that unit. That is, as I understand Mr Jenkins' submissions, insofar as the Children Act 1989 does not give the local authority those powers under the interim care order. He asks for leave that Dr Cockett or any medical practitioner at his direction have leave to administer such medication to A as is necessary to assist him in her assessment and to carry out any physical examination as is necessary by Dr Cockett or any other medical practitioner at his direction, in the performance of the assessment. Also, he asks for leave for the doctor and any other medical practitioner at his discretion to restrain by such reasonable means as are necessary to prevent A from — the word in the draft order is 'absconding' — from the Merrifield Unit and that the local authority have leave to return her to the unit, should she abscond therefrom.

Mr Jenkins submits that the inherent jurisdiction of the court provides the court with power to override the wishes of a girl of 15, even if she is '*Gillick* competent', even if she is of sufficient understanding to make an informed decision and refuses to submit to the examination or other assessment ordered by the court, last Thursday. He says that, in those circumstances, the court can use the inherent jurisdiction of the court and the powers given by it to supplement the powers given to the local authority under the Children Act 1989 and indeed the rights of the child which the Children Act 1989 gives her. That approach has the complete support of Mrs Mathews, solicitor for the guardian ad litem who, in effect, adopted Mr Jenkins' submission.

The position so far as the father is concerned is very different. Mr Dyson, whose submissions had all the appearances of being submissions on behalf of the child rather than of the father, assisted the court with the background to the Children Act 1989 and the effect, as he submitted it to be, of the Children Act provisions giving a veto to a child and the effect of that on the exercise of the court's inherent jurisdiction. What he said, and he is no doubt right about this, is that the moving spirit behind the Children Act 1989, in relation to children's rights, was the Cleveland report (Report of the Inquiry into Child Abuse in Cleveland 1987, 1988 Cm 412) and the factual circumstances which gave rise to Butler-Sloss L.J.'s inquiry, namely that children in care were being sent to doctors for medical examination without any opportunity for them to object. That situation, he says, was remedied by the Children Act 1989 and he referred particularly to the wording of s 38(6) which I have already in part referred to. I read the whole subsection.

'Where the court makes an interim order or interim supervision order, it may give such directions, if any, as it considers appropriate with regard to medical or psychiatric examination or other assessment of the child but, if the child is of sufficient understanding to make an informed decision, he may refuse to submit to the examination or other assessment.'

Mr Dyson makes the submission — if I may say so, a bold and startling submission in the circumstances of this case — and it is that the child's right to refuse, given in s.38(6), is the last step in the line. The court cannot go outside that and proceed to rely on the court's inherent jurisdiction. What Mr Dyson says is that implicitly, though he has to accept not expressly, the court's power under the inherent jurisdiction, exercising the parens patriae jurisdiction, to override in a proper case the wishes of a child and give consent for medical treatment, has been abrogated by the Children Act 1989. That power which has existed for centuries has gone.

I cannot accept that that is a correct statement of the law. The Children Act 1989 has specifically preserved the exercise by the High Court of its inherent jurisdiction with respect to children. It has circumscribed it and hedged it round but it has, as Mr Jenkins says, not abrogated the court's power to exercise that jurisdiction. Without any doubt, the position in law before the Act came into force was that the court, in an appropriate case, having considered all the circumstances, including the wishes of a child old enough to express a view, could nevertheless override the refusal of the child, even if the child was competent within the meaning ascribed to it in *Gillick v. West Norfolk Wisbech Area Health Authority and Another* [1985] 3 All E.R. 402. It would take very clear words, which cannot be found in the Act, to take away that power completely.

Mr Dyson submits that they exist in s 100(2)(d). That reads in this way:

'No court shall exercise the High Court's inherent jurisdiction with respect to children . . .
(d) for the purpose of conferring on any local authority power to determine any question which has arisen or which may arise in connection with any aspect of parental responsibility for a child.'

I do not think, with respect to him, that those words are apt to cover the situation in the instant case, and they certainly are not words which clearly can drive the court to the conclusion that the power, which without doubt did exist under the inherent jurisdiction to override a minor's wishes, has been abrogated. In my judgment, the court can in an appropriate case — and they will be rare cases — but in an appropriate case, when other remedies within the Children Act have been used and exhausted and found not to bring about the desired result, can resort to other remedies, and the particular remedy here is the remedy of providing authority for doctors to treat this child and authority, if it is needed, for the local authority to take all necessary steps to bring the child to the doctors so that she can be assessed and treated.

Mr Dyson, in a subsidiary argument, submitted that there was a difference between treatment and assessment and, in some ways, he is right. He said that there is all the difference between a case where a child has a broken leg, where there is really no need for any assessment and the child can be treated, and a case such as this where the first order of the court, at the request of the doctors, is that the child be made available so that she can be examined and assessed. I think the answer to that is that, in the case of problems which arise with the personality of the child, whether they amount to mental disorder or not, treatment begins with assessment and, as Dr Darwish says, the two are likely to go hand in hand. He would expect that that is what would happen with the Merrifield Unit under Dr Cockett. Therefore, the short answer to the contention, clearly and helpfully submitted by Mr Dyson, is that the court's powers under the inherent jurisdiction remain and they have not been affected by the Children Act 1989.

I was referred to *Re W (A Minor) (Medical Treatment: Court's Jurisdiction)* [1992] 4 All E.R. 627. Lord Donaldson, in the case of a 16 year old said this:

'There is ample authority for the proposition that the inherent powers of the court under its parens patriae jurisdiction are theoretically limitless and that they certainly extend beyond the powers of a natural parent (see, for example, *Re R (A Minor) (Wardship: Medical Treatment)* [1991] 4 All E.R. 177). There can therefore be no doubt that it has power to override the refusal of a minor, whether over the age of 16 or under that age but *Gillick*-competent. It does not do so by ordering the doctors to treat which, even if within the court's powers, would be an abuse of them, or by ordering the minor to accept treatment, but by authorising doctors to treat the minor in accordance with their clinical judgment, subject to any restrictions which the court may impose.'

It is clear that the principal decision before the court in that case involved consideration as to s 8 of the Family Law Reform Act 1969 and a girl of 16, and the remarks of Lord Donaldson MR are plainly *obiter*, but he was clearly dealing with the situation of a child in care, and a child in care under the Children Act 1989, and so his comments are a clear indication of judicial opinion in the Court of Appeal that the court's powers survive the Children Act, and I am reassured and confirmed in the opinion that I have formed when I read those words of Lord Donaldson MR.]

Therefore, if the court has the power, the question is, should the court exercise it? The child's welfare is the paramount consideration and there is a balancing exercise to be carried out in which the child's wishes are a very important factor. She has not given evidence before me, but her views have been represented, not only by a friend of the family, but also by her guardian.)It is clear that she will not leave the room and go to this centre. It may be that she was, on Friday, when she was seen, coming close to this at times but, at the end of the day, these experienced professionals were left with the clear view that she was not intending to leave the room. She was putting objections in the way of this. At times, when the situation was being explained to her, she was carrying on an irrational conversation with her family about the musical tapes which she was either playing or wanted to play, and she was obviously going through a show of ignoring the questions that were addressed to her and the advice that was given to her.

Her views, expressed in that way, are clear. She does not want to go to this unit. Her father is of the same state of mind and it may be — I do not know — that there is a connection between those two circumstances.

I give those wishes of this girl the fullest consideration, but I set against that the overwhelming view in combination of Dr Darwish, the views expressed in the written reports of the other doctors I referred to and the very experienced social workers involved in this case and the very experienced guardian ad litem, whose views, expressed through her solicitor to me today, are that this child must be admitted to this unit in her own interests and there must be no further delay. She accepts Dr Darwish's advice, as she invites the court to. The delay in this case has been quite extraordinary in coming to grips with this young girl's problems. The guardian, who has done the arithmetic, points to twenty-two previous court appearances in respect of this young girl. That, she says, cannot go on any longer.

The result of this balancing exercise is this, that in my judgment the court should give the leave to the local authority that they ask for. I was a little concerned at those parts of the draft order which dealt with keeping A in this unit. They undoubtedly stem from this part of Dr Cockett's report, which I have considered in addition to the other reports, a letter dated 20 October 1992 where he says this:

'Although Merrifield is not a secure unit, we would endeavour to prevent A from leaving the premises unaccompanied and it will be important that we have clear permission from the court to do this, otherwise it would not be possible to admit A to our unit without her consent.'

I was concerned that the local authority might be seeking to get the court to make a secure accommodation order under the inherent jurisdiction of the court. That, I think, would be a difficult road for the court to go down and I think that the order, as proposed by Mr Jenkins, falls just short of that and I regard it as a necessary leave to be given in order to achieve the best result for this unhappy young girl . . . "

NOTES:

    1. The inherent jurisdiction of the High Court subsumes, for the most part, and is wider than its wardship jurisdiction. The inherent

jurisdiction is, in practice, likely to be invoked by local authorities to whom it is, unlike wardship, still available providing three conditions are met. The three conditions are, first, that leave must be granted; secondly, that the result could not be obtained by way of a section 8 (specific issue) order and thirdly, that, in the absence of the court exercising its inherent jurisdiction, the child would probably suffer significant harm. These conditions are set out in section 100(3)–(5) of the Children Act. Had someone, such as A's father or brother, been prepared to seek a specific issue order under section 8(1) of the Children Act 1989, which empowers a court to make an order "giving direction for the purpose of determining a specific question which has arisen, or which may arise, in connection with any aspect of parental responsibility for a child" or had she been made a ward of court, she would have had no right of veto. (See M. Brazier and C. Bridge, "Coercion or Caring: Analysing Adolescent Autonomy" (1996) 16 *Legal Studies* 84 at page 101.)

2. Lyon argues of this case that the reasoning is less justifiable than the reasoning in *Re W* (above). She points out that in the earlier case the relevant statutory provision — section 8 of the Family Law Reform Act 1969 — was unclear, whereas there was no such lack of clarity in the provisions of the Children Act 1989, especially section 38(6), which fell to be construed in this case. She suggests that the judgment "conveys to children the message that they cannot trust that the clearly expressed 'rights' given by Parliament will be safe in the hands of the judges". (See C. Lyon, "What's happened to the child's right to refuse?" (1994) 6 *Journal of Child Law* 84 at page 87.)

3. In relation to the assessment of whether a minor is competent, it seems, following this case, that the young person only needs to be able to reach a considered choice. If she is capable of doing so, it is immaterial that she makes a "foolish" or irrational decision.

4. The judgment in this case echoes that of Lord Donaldson in *Re W* in its refusal to resort to the provisions of the Mental Health Act 1983.

QUESTIONS:

1. While statutory rights guaranteed by the Children Act 1989 may appear to have been eroded by this decision that, where other remedies under the Act had been exhausted and found not to bring about the desired result, the court could achieve its aim by resort to its inherent jurisdiction, had you been the judge in this case would you have felt justified in reaching a different decision? (Compare C. Lyon, *op. cit.* with M. Brazier and C. Bridge, *op. cit.*)

2. If you would have decided the case in the same way as Douglas Brown J., are you in effect arguing that A was not autonomous or are you really saying simply that something needed to be done? Do you think that A was rightly judged to be "*Gillick* competent"? Given

that she was deemed to be "*Gillick* competent", was this decision unduly paternalistic; or can it be justified on the grounds that the outcome of the case may ultimately promote her autonomy?

3. Brazier and Bridge note that had A been an adult the dilemma for her carers would have been stark. She could either have been left in her room or compulsorily admitted for assessment and treatment under the Mental Health Act 1983 (assuming that her disorder fell within the terms of the legislation — see Chapter 8) *(op. cit.* at page 99). In this event what do you think would have happened?

In the *South Glamorgan* case there was no dispute between A and anyone with parental responsibility for her. The following case raises the issue of how disputes between parents and older children over medical treatment should be resolved:

Re K, W and H (Minors) (Medical Treatment) [1993] 1 FLR 854

This case concerned three young people who were receiving specialist psychiatric treatment in a secure psychiatric unit — the John Clare unit — at St Andrews Hospital in Northampton. Prior to admitting children the unit required written consent to its treatment programme from a parent (or where appropriate a local authority). The programme included provision for the use of emergency medication. Following a number of complaints from children being treated at the unit, one of which concerned the administration of medication, the health authority established a committee to investigate./Its draft report included a recommendation that in circumstances of doubt regarding whether a minor had consented to treatment, a clinician should apply for a court ruling. Consequently, applications were made for a specific issues order under the Children Act 1989, section 8 to treat three young people, despite the existence of written parental consent. Two were 15 year olds suffering from unsocialised adolescent conduct disorder, the third was almost 15 and suffering from bipolar affective disorder.

THORPE J.:
" . . . [I]t is, in my judgment, unfortunate that the issue of this draft recommendation led St Andrews to issue applications under the Children Act 1989 for s 8 orders in relation to three patients who were currently on the John Clare unit. I say 'unfortunate' only in this sense — that the three children in question had been admitted to the unit after highly disturbed behaviour and each had been making commendable progress since admission. Inevitably, the issue of proceedings and the involvement in the proceedings of the children and their families has given rise to a good deal of anxiety and pressure which would otherwise have been avoided . . .

[H]aving read the papers, it seemed to me that the specific applications issued on 14 July, 1992 were misconceived and unnecessary. The law seems to me to be perfectly clear in this field and I do not accept the appraisal of the committee which described it as complex and confusing. The all-important judgment is the judgment of the Court of Appeal in the case of *Re R (A Minor) (Wardship: Medical Treatment)* [1991] 4 All E.R. 177. The fact that that authority arose out of a wardship application does not seem to me to distinguish it in any way from the case that I determine. It would have been perfectly open to St Andrews to have sought a ruling in wardship, and I do not think that the approach is any way different because these applications chance to have been brought under the Children Act 1989. The decision of the Court of Appeal in *Re R* (above) made it plain that a child with *Gillick* competence can consent to treatment, but that if he or she declines to do so, consent can be given by someone else who has parental rights or responsibilities. Where more than one person has power to consent, only a refusal of all having that power will create a veto. *Gillick* competence is a developmental concept and will not be lost or acquired on a day-to-day or week-to-week basis.

In the instant cases I am in no doubt at all that none of these three is *Gillick* competent. Even were they *Gillick* competent, it is manifest that their refusal of consent would not expose Dr Burnett to the risk of criminal or civil proceedings if he proceeded to administer medication in emergency and in the face of such refusal since in each instance he has a parental consent. I am in no doubt at all that the treatment methods that St Andrews have developed to deal with these extremely difficult and very important cases are not open to reasonable criticism or question, quite apart from a challenge to their legality. Dr Burnett established in evidence the statistics which show, in relation to the John Clare unit, that of the sixty-seven patients admitted to the unit and carried forward to discharge since January 1989, only twenty-six received tranquillising medication in emergency situations.

The suggestion of the committee constituted by the area health authority that the legality of a treatment programme which seems to me to have every medical justification has been threatened by the introduction of the Children Act 1989 is in my judgment completely misconceived. I do not think that that has been one of the consequential effects of the Children Act. I do not think that St Andrews should ever have been put in anxiety by this committee in the way that it was. I do not think that these applications were ever necessary and I have no hesitation at all in reaching the conclusion that no orders should be made on any of the three applications . . ."

Notes:

1. Bates points out that although Thorpe J. did not doubt that the young people in this case were not "*Gillick* competent", the basis of this finding is unclear, particularly since there is no reference to the opinion of the hospital's medical staff on this issue. (See P. Bates, "Children on secure psychiatric units: *Re K, W and H* — 'out of sight, out of mind'?" (1994) 6 *Journal of Child Law* 131 at page 135.)

2. The section 8 specific issue order is essentially a mechanism to enable disputes over any aspect of parental responsibility to be resolved. Rather than assuming parental responsibility, as it does in wardship, the court simply exercises control over a single issue affecting a child. As Brazier and Bridge note, it is a particularly useful mechanism for dealing with disputes over medical treatment. (See M. Brazier and C. Bridge, "Coercion or caring: analysing adolescent autonomy" (1996) 16 *Legal Studies* 84 at page 101.)

3. Thorpe J.'s statement that a specific issue order should never be sought where a parent has consented to treatment, even if the minor is "*Gillick* competent", denies the young person any forum in which to object to medical treatment. It also means that the doctor must

resolve alone any ethical reservations she has about proceeding
against the will of the minor. (See M. Brazier and C. Bridge, *op. cit.*
at page 102.)
4. Bates notes that if, as this case suggests, the law now permits
compulsory psychiatric treatment based upon parental consent (even
in non-emergency situations), it will rarely be necessary to detain
children under the Mental Health Act 1983 (see Chapter 8). Such
children will thus be denied the relevant statutory safeguards contained in that legislation. (See Bates *op. cit.* at pages 135–6; P.
Fennell, "Informal Compulsion" [1992] *Journal of Social Welfare and
Family Law* 311.)

QUESTIONS:

1. Do you agree with the appraisal of the Health Authority's committee,
   which was summarily dismissed by Thorpe J., that the law on
   children's power to refuse treatment is "complex and confusing"?
   How do you think it could be clarified?
2. Bates (*op. cit.*) argues that in the absence of clear and authoritative
   guidance as to when a young person's refusal of consent may be overridden, it is premature for the High Court to discourage applications
   for a ruling by way of a section 8 order under the Children Act 1989.
   Do you agree?
3. Contrast Thorpe J.'s ruling in this case and in *Re W* (above) with his
   decision in *Re C* discussed in Chapter 5 at pages 272–276.

7. REFUSAL OF TREATMENT BY BOTH MINORS AND PARENTS

The two recent cases discussed below serve to further demonstrate the
unsatisfactory state of the law concerning the young persons right to
consent to or refuse medical treatment. They present perhaps the most
difficult case at all — because in them the decision to refuse treatment is
made by intelligent adolescents suffering from no degree of mental
disorder, which arguably may differentiate them from the young people in
Re R, Re W, South Glamorgan, and *Re K, W and H.* Moreover, in these
cases the minors concerned had the support of at least one parent.

Re E (A Minor) (Wardship: Medical Treatment) [1993] 1 FLR 386

A was a young man aged fifteen-and-three-quarters, who suffered from
leukaemia. He and his parents were devout Jehovah's Witnesses, and
following his admission to hospital all three refused their consent to
conventional treatment for his condition, which required the administration of four drugs and of blood transfusions. Consent was given to a lesser
form of drug therapy, which avoided the need for blood transfusions, but

offered only a 40–50 per cent chance of full remission as compared to an 80–90 per cent chance where conventional treatment, including blood transfusions, was undertaken. Having successfully applied for A to be made a ward of court, the hospital authority sought the leave of the High Court to treat A conventionally, once it became apparent that in a matter of hours his haemoglobin and blood platelet levels would fall to dangerous levels, posing the risk of death from a heart attack or stroke. His parents contended that his decision should be respected, as he was so close to the age of 16, when his consent to treatment would be required under section 8 of the Family Law Reform Act 1969. However, since he was still three months short of his sixteenth birthday, the judge rejected this submission and instead considered whether he was "*Gillick* competent", so as to enable him to refuse treatment.

WARD J.:
" . . . In deference to the submissions made to me by counsel I will deal with the issue as to whether or not the refusal by A is a refusal taken in circumstances such as would, so it is submitted, enable him to override the parental choice. I find that A is a boy of sufficient intelligence to be able to take decisions about his own well-being, but I also find that there is a range of decisions of which some are outside his ability fully to grasp their implications. Impressed though I was by his obvious intelligence, by his calm discussion of the implications, by his assertion even that he would refuse well knowing that he may die as a result, in my judgment A does not have a full understanding of the whole implication of what the refusal of that treatment involves . . .

I am quite satisfied that A does not have any sufficient comprehension of the pain he has yet to suffer, of the fear that he will be undergoing, of the distress not only occasioned by that fear but also — and importantly — the distress he will inevitably suffer as he, a loving son, helplessly watches his parents' and his family's distress. They are a close family, and they are a brave family, but I find that he has no realisation of the full implications which lie before him as to the process of dying. He may have some concept of the fact that he will die, but as to the manner of his death and to the extent of his and his family's suffering I find he has not the ability to turn his mind to it nor the will to do so. Who can blame him for that?

If, therefore, this case depended upon my finding of whether or not A is of sufficient understanding and intelligence and maturity to give full and informed consent, I find he is not. Both, therefore, because s.8 does not apply and because, as I find, his veto is not a binding one, he not being in the position to take the decision, I reject the submission of Mr Daniel that this proceeding is an abuse of the process of the court . . .

In my judgment, whether or not he is of sufficient understanding to have given consent or to withhold consent is not the issue for me. In considering what his welfare dictates, I have to have regard to his wishes. What he wishes is an important factor for me to take into account and, having regard to the closeness to his attaining 16, a very important matter which weighs very heavily in the scales I have to hold in balance.

He is of an age and understanding at least to appreciate the consequence if not the process of his decision, and by reason of the convictions of his religion, which I find to be deeply held and genuine, he says 'no' to a medical intervention which may save his life. What weight do I place upon this refusal? I approach this case telling myself that the freedom of choice in adults is a fundamental human right. He is close to the time when he may be able to take those decisions. I should therefore be very slow to interfere. I have also to ask myself to what extent is that assertion of decision, 'I will not have a blood transfusion', the product of his full but his free informed thought? Without wishing to introduce into the case notions of undue influence, I find that the influence of the teachings of the Jehovah's Witnesses is strong and powerful. The very fact that this family can contemplate the death of one of its members is the most eloquent testimony of the power of that faith. He is a boy who seeks and needs the love and respect of his parents whom, he would wish to honour as the Bible exhorts him to honour them. I am far from satisfied that at the age of 15 his will is fully free. He may assert it, but his volition has been conditioned by the very powerful expressions of faith to which all members of the creed adhere. When making this decision, which is a decision of life or death, I have to take account of the fact that teenagers often express views with vehemence and conviction — all the vehemence and conviction of youth! Those of us who have passed beyond callow youth can all remember the convictions we have loudly proclaimed which now we find somewhat embarrassing. I respect this boy's profession of faith, but I cannot discount at least the possibility that he may in later years suffer some diminution in his convictions. There is no settled certainty about matters of this kind.

Putting the case at its highest as a considered wish to choose for oneself to die, is this choice of death one which a judge in wardship can find to be consistent with the welfare of the child? The father supplied the answer himself — life is precious. The risk of serious infection from a blood transfusion is infinitesimal and not a risk which would stand in the father's way but for his religious convictions because, as he said, life is too precious. When, therefore, I have to balance the wishes of father and son against the need for the chance to live a precious life, then I have to conclude that their decision is inimical to his well-being.

I am urged by Mr Daniel to say that this boy will suffer as the child in the Canadian case of *LDK* suffered, for there the court was satisfied upon the evidence that it had that the child would, if an attempt had been made to transfuse her with blood, 'fight that transfusion with all the strength she could muster. She would scream and struggle, pull the injecting device out of her arm and attempt to destroy the blood in the bag over her head'.

That may have been the finding in that case. It is not a finding I make in this. I find that A will protest, but I have no evidence before me which satisfies me that he will carry his protest to the point of pulling out the tubes or fighting the doctors as they endeavour to insert them or smashing the blood bags above his bed. On the contrary I find that, although he will protest, at the end of the day he will respect the decision of this court. In the Canadian case the court found that the emotional trauma of the blood transfusion would have a negative effect on the treatment. I have no such evidence to make that finding here. On the contrary, any emotional trauma in the immediate course of the treatment or in the longer term will not outweigh, in my judgment, the emotional trauma of the pain and the fear of dying in the hideous way he could die. On that scale the balance is wholly in favour of this treatment. In that case there was an alternative treatment plan. Here the only alternative available to A is the continuation of the administration of two of the four drugs with the likely prospect that his chances of success are seriously imperilled and his chances of death increasingly likely.

My jurisdiction is a protective one. It may be, as that very wise American judge, Justice Holmes, held in the case of *Prince v. Massachusetts* (1944) 321 US Reports 158, that:

'Parents may be free to become martyrs themselves, but it does not follow that they are free in identical circumstances to make martyrs of their children before they have reached the age of full and legal discretion when they can make choices for themselves.'

There is compelling and overwhelming force in the submission of the Official Solicitor that this court, exercising its prerogative of protection, should be very slow to allow an infant to martyr himself.

In my judgment, A has by the stand he has taken thus far already been and become a martyr for his faith. One has to admire — indeed one is almost baffled by — the courage of the conviction that he expresses. He is, he says, prepared to die for his faith. That makes him a martyr by itself. But I regret that I find it essential for his well-being to protect him from himself and his parents, and so I override his and his parents' decision. In this judgment — which has been truly anxious — I have endeavoured to pay every respect and give great weight to the religious principles which underlie the family's decision and also to the fundamental human right to decide things for oneself. That notwithstanding, the welfare of A, when viewed objectively, compels me to only one conclusion, and that is that the hospital should be at liberty to treat him with the administration of those further drugs and consequently with the administration of blood and blood products.

Therefore, I shall confirm the wardship. I will hear argument on the need for an order as to care and control and I shall make this direction and declaration, that the consent of the first and second defendants — that is today, the parents — and the consent of the third defendant — that is to say, A himself — to the transfusion of blood or blood products is dispensed with and that consequently leave is given to the plaintiff hospital to carry out such treatment as they deem to be appropriate including the transfusion of blood and blood products . . ."

NOTES:

1. When he reached adulthood E exercised his right to refuse medical treatment and died aged eighteen.
2. As Brazier and Bridge point out, E may well have had more understanding of death and less potential for regret than the average adult, for his adamant refusal was based on sincere religious belief. (See M. Brazier and C. Bridge, "Coercion or caring: analysing adolescent autonomy" (1996) 16 *Legal Studies* 84.)

QUESTIONS:

1. In your opinion, did Ward J. underestimate E's level of competence? Do you think that a court would ever deem a young person under the age of 16 competent to make a decision to refuse treatment where that decision is likely to result in the patient's death?
2. Given the strength of E's religious background, was he really in a position, even at 18, to exercise free choice?

Re S (A Minor) (Medical Treatment) [1994] 2 FLR 1065

S, a 15-year-old girl, had suffered from a life-threatening form of thalassemia from birth. Her condition had required her to endure daily injections and monthly blood transfusions since birth. As she had become irregular in administering her daily injections of an iron excreting drug, she had failed to grow normally, with the result that she suffered abuse from her peers. When S was 10 her mother converted to the Jehovah's Witness faith. She began to take S to religious meetings and began to influence her to stop her medical treatment. S subsequently failed to attend for her monthly blood transfusions and the local authority social services department requested the High Court to exercise its inherent jurisdiction and override S's refusal to consent to future transfusions.

JOHNSON J.:

" . . . Dr S [a consultant psychiatrist] says that at one level S knows the basic facts of her medical condition, but she also seemed to genuinely believe a mistake might have been made in the diagnosis. S said:

'They may have got it wrong all these years, and when I stop treatment they'll find it's something else and will treat it. I might not have thalassaemia. Who knows?'

Dr S found her surprisingly confused over many details. For example, she was very vague about the need for Desferal and said that if anyone had explained everything to her earlier she would have kept to the treatment more closely.

As to her death, she did not know how that would occur. She hoped she would die in her sleep but, she said, 'You never know, there could be a miracle and God might save me'. As to why God was against her having blood, she seemed uncertain, referring to the risk of HIV, and so on. Strikingly, she spoke to Dr S of "being free now, free from all these treatments". Dr S said it was as though she had drawn a line and was going to stick to it.

Dr S found the whole atmosphere in the home puzzling. There seemed to Dr S to be none of the gestures of affection or words of affection that one might have expected whatever one's beliefs. No less than nine times during the interview, S spoke about the possibility of a miracle saving her. Because she was faithful God might decide she should live, maybe she would not die, maybe she did not have thalassaemia.

Doctor S's conclusion was that S does not fully understand the implication of her decision. She doesn't know how death will occur; she certainly, in the view of Dr S, does not believe that a failure to have further transfusions will certainly result in death.

S is very fed up and negative and despondent about her illness, says Dr S. Like Dr J, she finds these feelings are always at their height in adolescence. In her oral evidence, Dr S said that she did not believe that S understood the implications of the decision:

'There were a lot of things that concerned me, the patness of her replies, some of her phrases. She and her mother were using exactly similar phraseology. S was not able to explain her thought except that, "it was said in the Bible". She had no understanding of the manner in which she might die.'

The most worrying thing for Dr S was that S seemed to have latched onto the idea that other Jehovah's Witnesses had thalassaemia and survived without transfusion. She said:

'I actually believe that she doesn't believe that she will die. Much of what she said is what I hear from other children who are chronically ill and who are fed up with their treatment. In age terms, this is the peak of such problems.'

Cross-examined on S's behalf, Dr S said that she did not consider that she had been tutored to give her answers. She was certainly very determined but she did not agree that S was expressing her own mind. Her feeling about being fed up with treatment makes her susceptible to influence.

I turn then to the manner in which the discretion of the court should be exercised. I start unhesitatingly from the position that S's wish should be given effect unless the balance is strongly to the contrary effect. S's right to determine what happens to her body should not be overridden lightly. If it is to be overridden it may be necessary for force to be used, and I proceed on the basis that it will be.

That is startling and to me, as to Dr J, extremely distasteful. But Dr J has had experience of the need to use force on patients in very many cases. He told me about anorexics and diabetics under his care whom he had forced to undergo treatment, in the case of anorexics, even forcing tubes down their throats. With the passage of time they come to recognise that what he has done has been right for them. None the less one must bear in mind the effect of all this on S who has surely troubles enough without being subjected to forced medication.

As Mr Daniel emphasised, whatever the decision of the court today, in 2 years' time S will be able to make up her own mind in the matter. He told me that the young man, the subject of Ward J.'s and the Court of Appeal's intervention in *Re E* had done precisely that and had now died. Against the background of the misery, for that is what she thinks it is, of this continuing treatment which she has sustained now for over 15 years, one may sensibly ask what is the point of forcing this young woman to have further treatment for what may be just 2½ years.

In contrast to many other cases which have come before the court, this is not a one-off transfusion of blood that is envisaged, it is a treatment that will be required regularly every month. As to the possibility of other options being available, there were broadly three. They are described in the medical literature that Mr Daniel showed me. One involves reactivation of the foetal haemoglobin switch and that, Mr Daniel told me this morning on further inquiries having been made, was thought by those who were experimenting with this possibility to be inappropriate for those of S's ethnic origin. As to the use of the erythropoietin referred to in the literature, those to whom Mr Daniel had spoken concluded that at this stage certainly it was appropriate only for patients suffering from sickle cell anaemia rather than thalassaemia. As to the use of the 5-azacytidine, the doctor who was experimenting with that treatment had told Mr Daniel that before that could be applied it would in any event be necessary for S to have a further transfusion of blood.

However, these options even if available would, in practical terms, seem to be available only in Toronto and there is now absolutely no question of S being able to get there.

However, there are obviously compelling reasons in favour of the court exercising the discretion to uphold S's rejection of treatment. On the other hand there are considerations the other way. This is a recent decision, S told me. Having had this treatment for over 15 years now and her mother having been a Jehovah's Witness since 1989, it was only when she read a particular Jehovah's Witness pamphlet in about April 1994 that she decided to reject the treatment.

As to the consequences of rejection, death is in my judgment inevitable and would be difficult and painful. The therapy is one that S has had for 15 years and it would surely seem a pity to stop it now. There is the possibility that, if it is forced upon her, her mind may change as Dr J and Dr S say children's minds do change in this situation, but of course those are not children who have the faith of Jehovah's Witnesses. Moreover, there is the possibility that within the next few years gene therapy will become available that will provide a complete cure for S's thalassaemia, so that blood transfusion will no longer be necessary.

As to her competence to make these decisions, because she is disillusioned with the treatment — one might say, fed up with it — she is susceptible to influence from outside. I do not believe that the mother or any Jehovah's Witnesses have overborne the wish of S in the matter, but I do believe that she has been influenced by them in the sense that she has come to share their faith. She does not understand the full implications of what will happen. It does not seem to me that her capacity is commensurate with the gravity of the decision which she has made. It seems to me that an understanding that she will die is not enough. For her decision to carry weight she should have a greater understanding of the manner of the death and pain and the distress.

Ward J. had said in *Re E* (above):

' . . . I find that he has no realisation of the full implications which lie before him as to the process of dying. He may have some concept of the fact that he will die, but as to the manner of his death and to the extent of his and his family's suffering I find he has not the ability to turn his mind to it nor the will to do so. Who can blame him for that?'

In *Re R* (above) Lord Donaldson M.R. spoke to the same effect.

Is S then '*Gillick*-competent' as to this? In approaching the case beforehand and having the advantage of reading some of the papers over the weekend, I had thought that this was a case of a child who was '*Gillick*-competent'. She is, after all, 15 years old. But having seen her and heard about her I have no doubt at all but that she is not '*Gillick*-competent'.

'When I was a child, I spoke as a child.' That seemed to me to be how S feels and speaks. There are those who are children and those who are adults and those who are in-between. I do not believe that S is in-between. She is still very much, in my view, a child. Whilst as she gave evidence I was so very strongly impressed by her integrity and her commitment, I believe they were the integrity and commitment of a child and not of somebody who was competent to make the decision that she tells me she has made. She hopes still for a miracle. My conclusion is, therefore, that she is not '*Gillick*-competent'.

I have thought anxiously about this case. I am grateful for the manner in which it has been conducted by counsel, the manner and restraint of their submissions, and I am grateful for the obvious effort that has been made to prepare skeleton arguments for my assistance.

In the event, and I have been particularly impressed by S herself, I am quite sure how I should exercise the discretion of the court. It is that I should override the expressed wish of S and give authority for Dr J if necessary, to force this treatment upon her . . ."

NOTES:

1. Note that S's decision not to undergo further treatment may have been influenced by other factors, particularly her low quality of life and the invasive nature of her treatment, in addition to her religious beliefs. (See M. Brazier and C. Bridge, "Analysing adolescent autonomy: coercion or caring" (1996) 16 *Legal Studies* 84, at page 106.)

2. As Grubb points out, one psychiatric witness doubted whether S was "seriously immature" for her age and, since she was 15-and-a-half years old, the finding of incompetence means that it is difficult to conceive of situations where a minor would be deemed legally competent to refuse such treatment. (See A. Grubb, "Treatment Without Consent: Child" (1995) 3 *Medical Law Review* 84.)

QUESTION:

1. Was Johnson J. right to conclude that S lacked the capacity to make an autonomous choice to discontinue blood transfusions? Did her lack of insight into her condition compromise her ability to make an autonomous choice? At age 18 will she be able to make such a choice?

8. REFORM OF THE LAW ON CHILDREN'S CONSENT TO MEDICAL TREATMENT

It should by now be apparent that the law in relation to children's powers to determine the medical treatment which they receive is in an unsatisfactory state. Arguably the decision in *Gillick* was unworkable in failing to lay down clear guidance for future judges; and both the judiciary and professionals dealing with young people who refuse medical treatment are conscious of the stigma attached to proceeding under Mental Health legislation. Even where the outcome of cases may be justifiable there is serious cause for doubt about the reasoning judges have employed in reaching their decisions. As Alderson and Montgomery argue, the rulings derived from extreme cases like *Re R* and *Re W* involving young people whose judgments may have been undermined by mental illness affect all minors, however informed and rational they may be. (See P. Alderson and J. Montgomery, "What about me?" *Health Service Journal*, April 11, 1996 at page 23.)

As the cases considered above demonstrate, one problem with the law relating to minors' consent to medical treatment is the emphasis on age. Brazier and Bridge note (*op. cit.* at page 107) that focusing on chronological age alone, and deeming rationality to be a factor acquired on a person's eighteenth birthday, ignores the development of the individual and flies in the face of notions of evolving autonomy. In order to surmount these problems and to ensure that children's rights are protected, Alderson and Montgomery have proposed a new framework for considering children's health law. The proposal is that children of compulsory school age should be presumed to be competent, so that the onus would lie upon adults to demonstrate the child's incompetence, rather than requiring the child to pass tests of competence which many adults might fail. This low age was chosen because the objective is that parents should be involved in decision-making and where appropriate the presumption would be rebutted, but in such cases detailed statutory safeguards such as those in the Mental Health Act 1983 would be necessary to protect the child's interests. (See Chapter 9.)

P. Alderson and J. Montgomery, *Health Care Choices: Making Decisions with Children*, London: Institute for Public Policy Research, 1996

Proposed children's code

We propose a code of practice for children's health care rights, to be established under an act of Parliament. The code would set out fundamental principles that:

- children should receive clear, detailed and relevant information;
- children should have the right to share in making decisions;
- children may grant or withhold consent to proposed treatment if they are competent to do so, subject to the supervisory role of the courts;
- children should have their privacy, dignity and confidentiality respected;

- doctors should always ascertain whether the child agrees with the views of the parents. Only if there is disagreement will it be necessary to make a formal assessment of the child's competence;
- children should be presumed competent from the age of five;
- for cases of irreversible choices, including those involving life-and-death decisions, the ultimate arbiter should be the courts;
- the basic rule must be that competent children should be entitled to refuse treatment. Parents and professionals should not merely be able to ignore such refusals, as the current law permits. If a child's refusal is to be overridden, there need to be mechanisms to ensure that a specific and valid justification for overriding the child's autonomy exists.

The meaning of competence should be specified in statutory form. Capacity would be defined as being present when a child understands:

- the type and purpose of the proposed treatment;
- in broad terms the nature and effects of the treatment;
- the principal benefits and risks;
- the consequences of not receiving treatment.

The code of practice would give guidance on assessing the abilities of young people.

A child's refusal would be legally binding on the health professionals if it were "competently" made on the tests for competence outlined above. The proposed statute makes it clear that to be competent the young person must understand the consequences of refusal of treatment.

The code of practice will also make it clear that a child's disagreement with a health professional cannot be evidence of incompetence.

Parents should not be able to veto treatment that children want. But where parents believe their child's competence has been wrongly assessed, a second opinion should be sought.

QUESTIONS:

1. In principle do you think it is a good idea to introduce a new framework along the lines suggested here?
2. Is five years of age an appropriate age at which to presumptively deem a child competent (see also G. Koren *et al*, "Maturity of Children to Convert to Medical Research: the Babysitter Test" [1993] 19 *Journal of Medical Ethics* 142)?
3. How does this proposal compare with the test for assessing an adult's capacity? (See Chapter 5 at pages 272–279.)

SELECT BIBLIOGRAPHY

A. Bainham, "The Judge and the Competent Minor" (1992) 108 L.Q.R. 194.

P. Bates, "Children in Secure Psychiatric Units: *Re K, W and H* — Out of Sight Out of Mind?" (1994) 6 *Journal of Child Law* 131.

M. Brazier and C. Bridge, "Coercion or Caring: Analysing Adolescent Authority" (1996) 16 *Legal Studies* 84.

C. Bridge, "Parental Religious Benefits and the Medical Treatment of Children" [1994] *Butterworth's Family Law Journal* 131.

J. Bridgeman, "Old Enough to Know Best?" (1993) 13 *Legal Studies* 69.

G. Douglas, "The Retreat from *Gillick*" (1992) 55 M.L.R. 569.

J. Eekelaar, "The Emergence of Children's Rights" (1986) 6 OJLS 161.

J. Eekelaar, "White Coats or Flak Jackets? Doctors, Children and the Courts — Again" (1993) 109 L.Q.R. 182.

P. Fennel, "Informal Compulsion" [1992] *Journal of Social Welfare and Family Law* 311.

A. Grubb, "Treatment Decisions: Keeping it in the Family" in A. Grubb (ed.), *Choices and Decisions in Health Care*, Chichester: Wiley, 1993.

I. Kennedy, "The Doctor, the Pill and the 15-year-old Girl" in M. Lockwood (ed.), *Moral Dilemmas in Modern Medicine*, Oxford: Oxford University Press, 1985.

R. Lavery, "Routine Medical Treatment of Children" [1990] *Journal of Social Welfare Law* 375.

S. Lee, "Towards a Jurisprudence of Consent" in J. Eekelaar and S. Ball (eds), *Oxford Essays in Jurisprudence* (3rd series), Oxford: OUP, 1987.

C. Lyon, "What's Happened to the Child's Right to Refuse?" (1994) 6 *Journal of Child Law* 84.

J. Masson, "Re W: appealing from the golden cage" (1993) 5 Journal of Child Law 37.

J. Montgomery, "Children as Property?" (1988) 51 M.L.R. 323.

J. Montgomery, "Consent to Health Care for Children" (1993) 5 *Journal of Child Law* 117.

J. Montgomery, "Parents and Children in Dispute: Who has the Final Word?" (1992) 4 *Journal of Child Law* 85.

J. Murphy, "Circumscribing the Autonomy of '*Gillick* Competent' Children" (1992) 43 *Northern Ireland Legal Quarterly* 60.

J. Murphy, "W(h)ither Adolescent Autonomy?" [1992] *Journal of Social Welfare and Family Law* 539.

8

CONFIDENTIALITY AND ACCESS TO RECORDS

1. INTRODUCTION

The requirement to protect patient confidentiality has long been included in the ethical codes of health care professionals. It has been argued that confidentiality is necessary to ensure that patients are willing to come forward to receive treatment. It is also claimed that confidentiality is part of the patient's right to control access to his own personal information, his right to privacy. There is no right to privacy explicitly recognised in English law (*Malone v. MPC* [1979] 2 All E.R. 620). However persons who believe that their privacy rights have been infringed may make an application to the European Commission of Human Rights in Strasbourg under Article 8 of the European Convention of Human Rights. This provides that:

"1. Everyone has the right to respect for his private and family life his home and correspondence.
 2. There shall be no interference by a public authority with the exercise of this right except such as is in accordance with the law and is necessary in a democratic society in the interests of national security, public safety or the economic well being of the country, for the prevention of disorder or crime, for the protection of health or morals, or for the protection of the rights and freedoms of others."

Article 8 has been interpreted by the European Court of Human Rights as affording protection to individual privacy (*Malone v. U.K.* Applications, No. 8691/79) (1984).

Today the obligation of a health care professional to maintain patient confidentiality frequently extends beyond her ethical codes. The terms and conditions of service of the NHS employee require her to keep patient information confidential. Unauthorised disclosure of confidential information may lead to an action under the equitable remedy of breach of confidence. In addition, certain specific statutory provisions safeguards confidentiality. Alternatively, breach of confidence may lead to the patient lodging a complaint under the NHS complaints procedure.

Protecting patient confidentiality may give rise to some very difficult moral and legal dilemmas, particularly at a time when health care practice has been shaken by the implications of the spread of AIDS. Medical care is more complex than it has ever been. The patient who enters hospital is cared for by many different health care practitioners, all with access to his records. In law the protection given to patient information is not absolute. In some situations the health professional may be required to break confidentiality by statute or at common law. In addition there is a grey area relating to information which, while generally protected by the obligation of confidentiality, may be disclosed in certain situations if, for example, it is in the public interest to do so.

While the patient has some means of redress where information is disclosed without his consent, until very recently the patient frequently faced considerable problems in obtaining access to his health care records. The position has gradually changed through the introduction of rights of access to computer records in the Data Protection Act 1984, with statutory rights of access to manual files being granted in the Access to Health Records Act 1990. Nevertheless these rights of access are not absolute. They can be restricted if, for example, disclosure is not in the patient's best interests because it would cause him significant physical or mental harm.

This chapter begins in section two with a consideration of the scope of confidentiality as highlighted in health care professions' ethical codes. It then examines the obligation of confidentiality as it arises in the employment context. In section four it deals with the legal obligation of confidentiality — at common law and discusses remedies for breach of confidence. Section five provides an examination of protection to patient confidentiality accorded by statute, while in section six those situations in which statute requires that confidence be broken are explored. Section seven considers disclosure of information and legal proceedings. Section eight discusses patients' access to records. Finally, the chapter concludes with a discussion of prospects for reform of the law in this area.

2. THE OBLIGATION OF CONFIDENTIALITY AND PROFESSIONAL ETHICAL CODES

All health professions include in their professional codes a requirement to preserve the confidentiality of health information. Below we provide some examples.

Confidentiality: Guidance from the General Medical Council (London: GMC 1995)

1. Patients have a right to expect that you will not disclose any personal information which you learn during the course of your professional duties, unless they give permission. Without assurances about confidentiality patients may be reluctant to give doctors the information they need in order to provide good care. For these reasons:

- When you are responsible for confidential information you must make sure that the information is effectively protected against improper disclosure when it is disposed of, stored, transmitted or received;
- When patients give consent to disclosure of information about them, you must make sure they understand what will be disclosed, the reasons for disclosure and the likely consequence;
- You must make sure that patients are informed whenever information about them is likely to be disclosed to others involved in their health care, and that they have the opportunity to withhold permission:
- You must respect requests by patients that information should not be disclosed to third parties, save in exceptional circumstances (for example, where the health of safety of others would otherwise be at serious risk):
- If you disclose confidential information you should release only as much information as is necessary for the purpose:
- You must make sure that health workers to whom you disclose information understand that it is given to them in confidence which they must respect;
- If you decide to disclose confidential information, you must be prepared to explain and justify your decision.

Disclosure of confidential information with the patient's consent

2. You may release confidential information in strict accordance with the patient's consent, or the consent of a person properly authorised to act on the patient's behalf.

Disclosure within teams

3. Modern medical practice usually involves teams of doctors, other health care workers, and sometimes people from outside the health care professions .The importance of working in teams is explained in the GMC's booklet " Good medical practice". To provide patients with the best possible care, it is often essential to pass confidential information between members of the team.

4. You should make sure — through the use of leaflets and posters as necessary — that patients understand why and when information may be shared between team members and any circumstances in which team members providing non-medical care may be required to disclose information to third parties.

5. Where the disclosure of relevant information between health care professionals is clearly required for treatment to which a patient has agreed, the patient's explicit consent would not be needed where a general practitioner, discloses relevant information to a medical secretary to have a referral letter typed, or a physician makes relevant information available to a radiologist when requesting an X-ray.

6. There will also be circumstances where, because of a medical emergency, a patient's consent cannot be obtained, but relevant information must in the patient's interest be transferred between health care workers.

7. If a patient does not wish you to share particular information with other members of the team, you must respect those wishes. If you and a patient have established a relationship based on trust the patient may choose to give you discretion to disclose information to other team members, as required.

8. All medical members of a team have a duty to make sure that other team members understand and observe confidentiality.

Disclosure to employers and insurance companies.

9. When assessing a patient on behalf of a third party (for example, an employer or insurance company) you must make sure, at the outset, that the patient is aware of the purpose of the assessment, of the obligation that the doctor has towards the third parties concerned, and that this may necessitate the disclosure of personal information. You should undertake such assessments only with the patient's written consent.

Disclosure of information without the patient's consent.

Disclosure in the patient's medical interests

10. Problems may arise if you consider that a patient is incapable of giving consent to treatment because of immaturity, illness or mental incapacity, and you have tried unsuccessfully to persuade the patient to allow an appropriate person to be involved in the consultation. If you are convinced that it is essential in the patient's medical interests, you may disclose relevant information to an appropriate person or authority. You must tell the patient before disclosing any information. You should remember that the judgment of whether patients are capable of giving or withholding consent to treatment or disclosure must be based on an assessment of their ability to appreciate what the treatment or advice being sought may involved, and not solely on their age.

11. If you believe a patient to be a victim of neglect or physical or sexual abuse, and unable to give or withhold consent to disclosure, you should usually give information to an appropriate responsible person or statutory agency, in order to prevent further harm to the patient. In these and similar circumstances, you may release information without the patient's consent, but only if you consider that the patient is unable to give consent, and that the disclosure is in the patient's best medical interests.

12. Rarely you may judge that seeking consent to the disclosure of confidential information would be damaging to the patient, but that the disclosure would be in the patient's medical interests. For example, you may judge that it would be in a patient's interests that a close relative should know about the patient's terminal condition, but that the patient would be seriously harmed by the information. In such circumstances information may be disclosed without consent.

Disclosure after a patient's death

13. You still have an obligation to keep information confidential after a patient dies. The extent to which confidential information may be disclosed after a patient's death will depend on the circumstances. These include the nature of the information, whether that information is already public knowledge, and how long it is since the patient died. Particular difficulties may arise when there is a conflict of interest between parties affected by the patient's death. For example, if an insurance company seeks information about a deceased patient in order to decide whether to make a payment under a life assurance policy, you should not release information without the consent of the patient's executor, or a close relative, who has been fully informed of the consequences of disclosure.

14. You should be aware that the Access to Health Records Act 1990 gives third parties right of access, in certain circumstances, to the medical records of a deceased patient.

Disclosure for medical teaching, medical research, and medical audit

Research

15. Where, for the purposes of medical research there is a need to disclose information which it is not possible to anonymise effectively, every reasonable effort must be made to inform the patients concerned, or those who may properly give permission on their behalf, that they may, at any stage withhold their consent to disclosure.
16. Where consent cannot be obtained, this fact should be drawn to the attention of a research ethics committee which should decide whether the public interest in the research outweighs patients' right to confidentiality. Disclosure to a researcher may otherwise be improper, even if the researcher is a registered medical practitioner.

Teaching and audit

17. Patients consent to disclosure of information for teaching and audit must be obtained unless the data have been effectively anonymised.

Disclosure in the interests of others

18. Disclosures may be necessary in the public interest where a failure to disclose information may expose the patient or others to risk of death or serious harm. In such circumstances you should disclose information promptly to an appropriate person or authority.
19. Such circumstances may arise, for example, where:

    - A patient continues to drive, against medical advice when unfit to do so. In such circumstances you should disclose relevant information to the medical adviser of the Driver and Vehicle Licensing Agency without delay . . .
    - A colleague, who is also a patient is placing patients at risk as a result of illness or another medical condition. Guidance on this issue, and on the rights of doctors who are ill, is contained in the GMC's leaflet HIV infection and AIDS: the ethical considerations" and in a separate note about the GMC's health procedures.
    - Disclosure is necessary for the prevention or detection of a serious crime.

Disclosure in connection with judicial or other statutory proceedings

20. You may disclose information to satisfy a specific statutory requirement, such as notification of a communicable disease or of attendance upon a person dependant upon certain controlled drugs. You may also disclose information if ordered to do so by a judge or presiding officer of a court or if you are summoned to assist a Coroner, Procurator Fiscal, or other similar officer in connection with an inquest or comparable judicial investigation. If you are required to produce patient's notes or records under a court order you should disclose only so much as is relevant to the proceedings. You should object to the judge or the presiding officer if attempts are made to compel you to disclose other matters which appear in the notes, for example matters relating to relatives or partners of the patient who are not parties to the proceeding.
21. In the absence of a court order, a request for the disclosure by a third party, for example, a solicitor, police officer or officer of a court, is not sufficient justification for disclosure without a patient's consent.

22. When a Committee of the GMC investigating a doctor's fitness to practice has determined that the interests of justice require disclosure information at the request of the Committee's Chairman, provided that every reasonable effort has been made to seek the consent of the patients concerned. If consent is refused the patient's wishes must be respected.

Disclosure to inspectors of taxes

23. If you have a private practice, you may disclose confidential information in response to a request from an inspector of taxes, provided you have made every effort to separate financial information from clinical records.
Doctors who decide to disclose confidential information must be prepared to explain and justify their decisions.

NOTES:

1. The courts have referred to the GMC guidelines when considering the scope of breach of confidence (See below *X v. Y* at pages 455–457, *W v. Edgell* at pages 458–467.
2. Breach of confidence may lead to disciplinary proceedings. (See further Chapter 4 above).
3. For further discussion regarding HIV/AIDS see below at pages 470–471.

A corresponding duty to maintain patient confidentiality is imposed upon members of the nursing profession.

United Kingdom Central Council of Nursing and Midwifery Code of Practice (1992)

As a registered nurse, midwife or health visitor you are personally accountable for your practice and in the exercise of your professional accountability, must:
10. protect all confidential information concerning patients and clients obtained in the course of professional practice and make disclosures only with consent, where required by order of a court and you can justify disclosure in the wider public interest.

NOTES:

1. The scope of this obligation is discussed further in the UKCC document "Guidance for Professional Practice" (London: UKCC, 1996).
2. Much of the debate in relation to the nurse's obligation of confidentiality in recent years has arisen in the context of the debate concerning "whistleblowing". (See below at pages 445–6.)

8.   CONFIDENTIALITY IN THE CONTRACT OF EMPLOYMENT

As noted above, health care professionals employed by the NHS are required by their contract of employment to maintain confidentiality.

Guidance regarding patient confidentiality was issued in Spring 1996 by the Department of Health: "The Protection and Use of Personal Informa-. tion" (DoH, 1996). In some situations this may conflict with other obligations contained in the health care professional's ethical code of conduct. This problem is graphically illustrated by the case of the "whistleblower" Grahame Pink.

Pink was employed as a night duty charge nurse on a ward for acutely ill patients. Having observed what he believed was an unacceptable reduction in standards of patient care, and having, in his opinion, received no satisfactory response to his expressed concerns he decided to "go public". He gave an interview to a local paper, which was subsequently reprinted in *The Guardian*. He was accused of breaching patient confidentiality. Relatives of the patients claimed they could recognise their relatives from the descriptions in the paper. Pink was eventually dismissed. He challenged his dismissal at an industrial tribunal He claimed that his disclosure was justified under Article 10 of the UKCC code because he was under a duty to bring to the attention of the appropriate authorities information which showed that standards of patient care had fallen. There is no special protection provided in employment law for a "whistleblowing employee". While an employee may assert before an industrial tribunal that his conduct was in the public interest, that does not by itself give rise to a claim for unfair dismissal. Mr Pink's case was settled out of court. Even if Mr Pink had won after a full hearing, any decision of such a tribunal would not set a precedent for subsequent cases. (See J. V. McHale "Whistleblowing in the NHS" (1992) 5 *Journal of Social Welfare Law* 363). Reinstatement is also very unlikely.

The response of the government to the Pink case was to publish the *Guidance for Staff on Relations With the Public and Media* (1993, DoH). The guidance states that Health Authorities should establish both formal and informal complaints systems for staff. They require that the complaints should be made internally, either through the existing management structure or to a complaints officer who would be the person appointed to receive patient complaints under the Hospital Complaints Act 1985. (See Chapter 4 above.)

The guidance has been the subject of considerable criticism (see J. V. McHale "Two Initiatives for Reform" in G. Hunt (ed) *Whistleblowing in the Health Services*, London: Edward Arnold, 1994). There is no provision for external appeal. While the guidance notes that staff may consult external bodies such as the Mental Health Act Commission or the Health Service Commissioner it emphasises the obligation of confidentiality and the fact that a member of staff who "goes public" risks disciplinary proceedings. There is no attempt to address the role of the nurse as advocate for her patient, nor the conflict which may face a health professional between her ethical code and contract of employment.

Attempts have been made to introduce legislation to safeguard the position of those who "go public" in the public interest.

In 1992 Derek Fatchett M.P. published a NHS Freedom of Speech Bill which attempted to introduce a general ethical code for all health care employees—a "Charter of Values". Clause 8 provided that there should be

"a duty and a right to report to any competent person any instruction, policy or practice which they would believe would result in inadequate or unsafe conditions which are likely to either harm the health and safety or well being of patients/clients or colleagues or be contrary to law or be to the detriment of the health service and public confidence in its operation."

The Bill also recommended that staff complaint procedures should be established, but it went beyond the Government proposals by providing for an external right of appeal. However it left open what form the appellate body should take. The Bill failed to obtain parliamentary time. An attempt was made in 1995 to introduce a Whistleblower Protection Bill, which applied generally to whistleblowers rather than exclusively within the NHS. The Bill was drafted by Maurice Frankel of the Freedom of Information campaign. Whether legislation will itself deal with the difficulty is perhaps questionable difficult disclosure dilemmas will remain: *cf.* the American eperience, J. V. McHale, "Whistleblowing in the USA" in G. Hunt, *op. cit.* In 1995 a charity — Public Concern at Work — was established with funding from the Joseph Rowntree foundation, to provide support for whistleblowers, including those within the health care professions.

4. Non-Statutory Protection in Law for Confidential Information: Breach of Confidence

(a) Basis for the action

English law provides protection for confidential information through the equitable remedy of breach of confidence. The basis in law for restraint of disclosure of confidential information is usually that of the equitable remedy of breach of confidence. The grounds on which an action for breach of confidence may be brought are stated in *A.-G. v. Guardian Newspapers (No. 2)* [1988] 3 All E.R. 545 at 658, [1990] 1 A.C. 109:

Lord Goff:
". . . a duty of confidence arises where confidential information comes to the knowledge of a person (the confidant) in circumstances where he has notice, or is held to have agreed, that the information is confidential with the effect that it would be just in all the circumstances that he should be precluded from disclosing the information to others. I have used the word 'notice' advisedly in order to avoid the . . . question of the extent to which actual notice is necessary, though I of course understand knowledge to include circumstances in which the confidant has deliberately closed his eyes to the obvious. The existence of this broad general principle reflects the fact that there is such a public interest in the maintenance of confidentiality that the law will provide remedies for this protection.

I realise that, in the vast majority of cases, in particular those concerned with trade secrets, the duty of confidence will arise from a transaction or relationship between the parties, often a contract, in which event the duty may arise by reason of an express or implied term of that contract. It is in such cases as these the expression 'confider' and 'confidant' are perhaps most aptly employed. But it is well settled that a duty of confidence may exist in equity independently of such cases . . ."

NOTES:

1. Today it is generally recognised that the doctor-patient relationship is one of the category of relationships protected by the equitable remedy of breach of confidence. It appears virtually certain that the courts would extend this protection to other health care relationships such as nurse-patient.

2. Alternative grounds for legal proceedings do exist. Actions may be brought in contract and in negligence. Negligence was held in a New Zealand case to be the basis on which an obligation of confidentiality arose (*Furniss v. Fitchett* [1958] N.Z.L.R. 396.) The action in contract, as we shall see below in the context of the child patient, may prove to be practically of some considerable importance.

3. Particular difficulties may arise if advice is sought from an occupational health doctor. An employer will have a vested interest in discovering information regarding the health of her employees. But at the same time the doctor owes an obligation of confidentiality to the patient. If the occupational health doctor intends to pass on information, then, as far as possible, this fact must be made clear to the employee and consent obtained. If information is to be disclosed without consent this must be justifiable in the public interest. (See generally D. Kloss, *Occupational Health Law* (2nd ed.), Blackwells: Oxford 1994).

   Difficulties may also arise in the context of the prisoner patient. He is cared for by the Prison Health Care Service. This organisation is not part of the NHS. While doctors are responsible for maintaining confidentiality there has in the past been erosion of confidentiality particularly in relation to prisoners diagnosed as HIV positive. These prisoners were kept segregated from other prisoners under what are known as Viral Infectivity restrictions thus effectively eliminating much of the confidentiality of their condition. (See J. McHale and A. Young "Policy, Rights and the HIV Positive Prisoner" in S. McVeigh and S. Wheelar (eds), *Law, Health and Medical Regulation*, Aldershot: Dartmouth, 1993).

4. Where the obligation of confidentiality arises other than from contract does a patient have to establish that some detriment has been suffered? There was disagreement on this point in the House of Lords in *A.-G. v. Guardian Newspapers*. In the later case of *X v. Y*]1988] 2 All E.R. 648 (see below at page 455) Rose J. seemed to recognise that this was not a requirement before an injunction was obtained.

(b) Who can bring an action for breach of confidence?

Usually an action for breach of confidence may be brought by the person to whom the confidence is owed (*Fraser v. Evans* [1969] 1 All E.R. 8). This may be a patient if where competent to do so, but it may equally be another person or body, for example, a health authority (see *X v. Y* [1988] 2 All E.R. 648 below.)

(i) Children

The leading case on the question of children and consent to treatment is that of *Gillick*. The facts of this case are set out in Chapter 7. Here we consider the question of confidentiality and the child patient.

Gillick v. West Norfolk and Wisbech Area Health Authority [1985] 3 All E.R. 402

Lord Fraser:
" . . . Once the rule of the parents' absolute authority over minor children is abandoned, the solution to the problem in this appeal can no longer be found by referring to rigid parental rights at any particular age. The solution depends on a judgment of what is best for the welfare of the particular child. Nobody doubts, certainly I do not doubt, that in the overwhelming majority of cases the best judges of a child's welfare are his or her parents. Nor do I doubt that any important medical treatment of a child under 16 would normally only be carried out with the parents' approval. That is why it would and should be 'most unusual' for a doctor to advise a child without the knowledge and consent of the parents on contraceptive matters. But, as I have already pointed out, Mrs Gillick has to go further if she is to obtain the first declaration that she seeks. She has to justify the absolute right of veto in a parent. But there may be circumstances in which a doctor is a better judge of the medical advice and treatment which will conduce to a girl's welfare than her parents. It is notorious that children of both sexes are often reluctant to confide in their parents about sexual matters, and the DHSS guidance under consideration shows that to abandon the principle of confidentiality for contraceptive advice to girls under 16 might cause some of them not to seek professional advice at all, with the consequence of exposing them to 'the immediate risks of pregnancy and of sexually-transmitted diseases'. No doubt the risk could be avoided if the patient were to abstain from sexual intercourse, and one of the doctor's responsibilities will be to decide whether a particular patient can reasonably be expected to act on advice to abstain. We were told that in a significant number of cases such abstinence could not reasonably be expected. An example is *Re P (A Minor)* (1981) 80 LGR 301, in which Butler-Sloss J. ordered that a girl aged 15 who had been pregnant for the second time and who was in the care of a local authority should be fitted with a contraceptive appliance because, as the judge is reported to have said (at 312):
    'I assume that it is impossible for this local authority to monitor her sexual activities, and, therefore, contraception appears to be the only alternative.'
There may well be other cases where the doctor feels that because the girl is under the influence of her sexual partner or for some other reason there is no realistic prospect of her abstaining from intercourse. If that is right it points strongly to the desirability of the doctor being entitled in some cases, in the girl's best interest, to give her contraceptive advice and treatment if necessary without the

consent or even the knowledge of her parents. The only practicable course is, in my opinion, to entrust the doctor with a discretion to act in accordance with his view of what is best in the interests of the girl who is his patient. He should, of course, always seek to persuade her to tell her parents that she is seeking contraceptive advice, and the nature of the advice that she receives. At least he should seek to persuade her to agree to the doctor's informing the parents. But there may well be cases, and I think there will be some cases, where the girl refuses either to tell the parents herself or to permit the doctor to do so and in such cases the doctor will, in my opinion, be justified in proceeding without the parents' consent or even knowledge provided he is satisfied on the following matters: (1) that the girl (although under 16 years of age) will understand his advice (2) that he cannot persuade her to inform her parents or to allow him to inform the parents that she is seeking contraceptive advice (3) that she is very likely to begin or to continue having sexual intercourse with or without contraceptive treatment (4) that unless she receives contraceptive advice or treatment her physical or mental health or both are likely to suffer (5) that her best interests require him to give her contraceptive advice, treatment or both without the parental consent.

That result ought not to be regarded as a licence for doctors to disregard the wishes of parents on this matter whenever they find it convenient to do so. Any doctor who behaves in such a way would, in my opinion, be failing to discharge his professional responsibilities, and I would expect him to be disciplined by his own professional body accordingly. The medical profession have in modern times come to be entrusted with very wide discretionary powers going beyond the strict limits of clinical judgment and, in my opinion, there is nothing strange about entrusting them with this further responsibility which they alone are in a position to discharge satisfactorily."

No authority has been cited which prevents an infant from seeking medical or any other advice or which forbids a doctor to advise an infant who has not been tendered by the parent as a patient. No authority compels a doctor to disclose to a parent, otherwise than in the course of litigation, any information obtained as a result of a conversation between the doctor and the infant. On the other hand, in my opinion, confidentiality owed to an infant is not breached by disclosure to a parent responsible for that infant if the doctor considers that such disclosure is necessary in the interests of the infant. A doctor who gave a pledge to a girl under 16 that he would not disclose the fact or content of a conversation would no doubt honour that pledge, but the doctor ought to hesitate before committing himself. A doctor who gave an unconditional pledge of confidentiality to a girl under 16 would, for example, be in a difficult position if the girl then disclosed information which made the doctor suspect that she was being introduced to sexual intercourse by a man who was also introducing her to drugs.

Although a doctor is entitled to give confidential advice to an infant, the law will, in my opinion, uphold the right of a parent to make a decision which the infant is not competent to make. The decision to authorise and accept medical examination and treatment for contraception is a decision which a girl under 16 is not competent to make. In my opinion a doctor may not lawfully provide a girl under 16 with contraceptive facilities without the approval of the parent responsible for the girl save pursuant to a court order, or in the case of emergency or in exceptional cases where the parent has abandoned or forfeited by abuse the right to be consulted. Parental rights cannot be insisted on by a parent who is not responsible for the custody and upbringing of an infant or where the parent has abandoned or abused parental rights. And a doctor is not obliged to give effect to parental rights in an emergency.

A girl under 16 is usually living with a parent and is usually attending school. It is sufficient for the doctor to obtain the consent of the parent or guardian with whom the girl is living. It seems to me to be contrary to law and offensive to professional standards that a doctor should provide contraceptive facilities against the known or presumed wishes of such a parent and that the doctor should conspire with the girl to keep the parent in ignorance of the fact that the girl intends to participate in frequent, regular or casual sexual intercourse in the belief that the only bar to sexual intercourse is the risk of pregnancy and in complacent reliance on the doctor's contraceptive facilities to obviate that risk.

But parental rights may have been abandoned. If the doctor discovers, for example, that the girl is not living with a parent but has been allowed to live in an environment in which the danger of sexual intercourse is pressing, the doctor may lawfully provide facilities for contraception until the parent has been alerted to the danger and has been afforded the opportunity to reassert parental rights and to protect the girl by means other than contraception. The court will uphold the doctor's actions if the doctor reasonably believes that parental rights have, for the time being at any rate, been abandoned.

Parental rights may have been abused. The dangers of sexual intercourse may emanate from the girl's home. The doctor would be entitled to provide the girl with contraceptive facilities but would then be bound to consider whether the local welfare authorities should be alerted to the possibility that the girl is in need of care and protection. Again, the doctor may be satisfied that the parent is a brute and that the girl has been driven to seek solace outside the family. The doctor might decide that it was necessary to provide contraceptive facilities for the girl without informing the parent but the doctor would be bound to consider the possible consequences if the parent, known to be brutal, discovered the truth.

The doctor may also be faced with circumstances which could properly be described as a medical emergency. The doctor may decide that the girl is unable to control her sexual appetite or is acting under an influence which cannot be counteracted immediately. The doctor would be entitled to provide contraceptive facilities as a temporary measure but would, in my opinion, be bound to inform the parent. A subsequent decision to continue contraceptive treatment would be open to the doctor and the parent acting jointly in default of agreement between them, the welfare authority or the court could be asked to intervene.

There may be other exceptional circumstances and emergencies which would impel the doctor to provide contraceptive facilities without the prior consent of the parent but in most cases the doctor would be bound to inform the parent as soon as possible in order that the parent might have the opportunity of exercising parental rights in such manner as to deter or prevent the girl from indulging in sexual intercourse."

NOTES:

1. Whether a child patient can restrain disclosure of information on the basis of breach of confidence has been a disputed issue. If a child is under 16 then he has no statutory right to consent to treatment (see Chapter 7). However, after *Gillick*, it is recognised that a child under 16 may be competent to consent but that this is dependant upon an assessment of the child's maturity. It appears that such an analysis would be applicable to the disclosure of personal health information. Where a child is of sufficient maturity he can determine the basis on which information could be disclosed. However, the position of the immature minor is less clear. Some have suggested that where a child is not *Gillick*-competent then questions regarding disclosure of information and consent to treatment are to be left to the child's parents (see A. Grubb and D. Pearl "Medicine, Health, Family and

the Law" (1986) *Family Law* 101). In contrast, Montgomery has argued that a child who approaches her doctor without telling her parents rightly expects that any disclosure which is made will be treated as confidential then the "very action evidences the maturity required before the law will recognise this expectation" (See J. Montgomery, "Confidentiality and the Immature Minor" (1987) *Family Law* 101).

2. An alternative basis for the obligation of confidence is that of contract. There are certain difficulties in establishing an obligation on the basis of contract in the context of the child patient. If treatment is being given privately rather than within the NHS then is the contract enforceable by the child? There is some authority to suggest that this may be the case if it can be shown that the contract was manifestly to the minor's advantage (*Clements v. London & North Western Railway Co* [1894] 2 Q.B. 482 and see Montgomery *op. cit.*). In the case of the NHS patient there is no direct contract between patient and practitioner. The existence of a contractual obligation in such a situation has been disputed, although one argument advanced is that an independent contract arises between patient and doctor regarding a promise to maintain confidentiality. (See Montgomery *op. cit. cf* Grubb and Pearl *op. cit.*).

3. Even if an obligation of confidence does arise then as we shall see this obligation is not absolute in nature. In law the obligation of confidentiality may be outweighed by the public interest in disclosure. In what situations may information regarding the child patient be disclosed to others and in particular his family? Essentially this is a question of where the public interest lies. A number of commentators have noted that sanctioning disclosure may have the effect of discouraging not only the particular patient from seeking treatment but also affect other patients. (See generally I. Kennedy "The Doctor, the Pill and the Fifteen Year Old Girl" in I. Kennedy (ed.) *Treat Me Right*, Oxford: OUP, 1989 and J. Montgomery, *op. cit.*). A further complication here is the Access to Health Records Act 1990 which states that where a child is competent then a parent cannot gain access to that information unless the child gives consent (section 4(2)). The tension between the legislative and the common law position remains to be resolved.

4. The decision in *Re R* casts further doubts upon the preservation of a minor's confidence(for general discussion of this case see Chapter 7 above). In this case the Court of Appeal indicated that a child's parents may be able to authorise treatment of a competent minor in the face of the minor's refusal. This has considerable potential implications for confidentiality. Put bluntly, how could parents overrule their child's refusal of treatment unless they had been informed of the refusal and surrounding circumstances in the first place? Does this mean that in any situation in which a refusal takes

place confidence may be broken? This is further complicated by the fact that, as was noted above, there are statutory limitations placed upon parental rights to see children's records. (See further A. Grubb "Treatment Decisions; keeping it in the family" in A. Grubb (ed.), *Choices and Decisions in Health Care*, Chichester: Wiley, 1994, at page 64). As Grubb notes, if the implications of the decision in *Re R* are followed through, then this would lead to a divergence between the common law and statutory position.

QUESTION

1. Should a doctor preserve the confidentiality of a 14-year-old boy who has contracted a sexually transmitted disease?

(ii) Incompetent Adults

There is no explicit authority stating the precise obligation of confidentiality which is owed to a mentally incompetent adult. Is there an obligation at all? Similar arguments arise here as in the context of the child patient. Does the fact that the patient lacks capacity mean that there is no obligation of confidentiality? It is submitted that the better view is that there is an obligation of confidence implied as a consequence of the doctor-patient relationship.

There is no decided authority as to whether information concerning an incompetent adult can be disclosed, for example, to his relatives. It would seem likely that the courts would adopt the same test as stated by the House of Lords in *F. v. West Berkshire Health Authority* [1989] 2 All E.R. 545 in relation to consent to treatment — namely that disclosure can take place if those treating the patient believe that it is necessary in the best interests of the patient. Adoption of this approach would require the doctors to exercise considerable discretion. It is submitted that the best interests of the patient would require that the information only be disclosed on a "need to know" basis.

(iii) Deceased Patients

The GMC professional ethical code requires a doctor to keep patient information confidential, even after the patient's death. Winston Churchill's physician, Lord Moran, was subject to considerable criticism after he published the book *Churchill — A Struggle For Survival* following the prime minister's death. (See J. K. Mason and R. A. McCall Smith, *Law and Medical Ethics* (4th edn.), Butterworths: London, 1994, at page 188; S. Lock and J. Loudan "A Question of Confidence" (1984) 288 *BMJ* 123.)

It is unclear whether a breach of confidence action could be brought to stop further publication of a patient's information after his death. It has been suggested that the courts may follow the approach taken in the tort of defamation, where an action cannot be brought after the person allegedly defamed has died because they have no interests in their reputation left to protect.

(b) Grounds for disclosure

(i) Consent

No action for breach of confidence will arise if the patient has consented to the disclosure. Consent must be given freely. Difficulties may arise in relation to patients in teaching hospitals, who may feel under considerable pressure to consent. (See J. K. Mason, R. A. McCall Smith *Law and Medical Ethics* (4th ed.), Butterworths: London, 1994, at page 169.) Consent includes both express and implied consent. Determining the scope/reality of implied consent may be very difficult. While a patient who enters hospital may impliedly consent to information being passed to other health care professionals where it is necessary for his treatment, he may be unaware of the extent to which his information will be passed on within the health care team. (See M. Siegler "Medical Confidentiality—a decrepit concept" (1982) 302 *New England Journal of Medicine* 1518.) This further illustrates the problematic nature of the GMC Code, which sanctions disclosure within the health care team. In the most recent guidance "The Protection and Use of Patient Information" (DoH, 1996), the Department of Health have commented that

"2.5 It is neither practicable nor necessary to seek a patient's (or other informant's) specific consent each time information needs to be passed on for a particular purpose. The public expects the NHS, often in conjunction with other agencies, to respond effectively to its needs; it can do so only if it has the necessary information. **Therefore, an essential feature of the relationship between patients and the NHS is the need for patients to be fully informed of the uses to which information about them may be put.**"

The Guidance goes on to state that

"3.1 All NHS bodies must have an active policy for informing patients of the kind of purposes for which information about them is collected and the categories of people or organisations to which information may need to be passed. Where other bodies are providing services for or in conjunction with the NHS, those concerned must be aware of each other's information policies.

3.2 Subject to some important common elements . . ., the precise arrangements for informing patients are for local decision, taking account of view expressed by community health councils, local patient groups, staff and agencies with which the NHS body is in close contact. However, those concerned, should bear in mind that:

    i. as a general rule, patients should be told how information would be used before they are asked to provide it and must have the opportunity to discuss any aspects that are special to their treatment or circumstances;

    ii. advice must be presented in a convenient form and be available both for general purposes and before a particular programme of care and treatment begins.

3.3 Methods of providing advice include;

- leaflets enclosed with patients' appointment letters or provided when prescriptions are dispensed;

- GP practice leaflets and/or notification on initial registration with a GP;
- routinely providing patients with necessary information as part of care planning;
- identifying someone to provide further information if patients want it."

The purposes for which information can be disclosed include management purposes (see below) and also on a "need to know" basis as stated in para 2.6 of the Guidance which includes NHS purposes where

"the recipient needs the information because he or she is or may be concerned with the patient's care and treatment (or that of another patient whose health may be affected by the condition of the original patient such as a blood or organ donor)."

QUESTION:

1. Does the DoH approach accord sufficient respect to the autonomy of the patient?

Certain disclosures for the purposes of management practice are widely recognised in the health service. An example is information collected for the purposes of medical audit. All doctors working in the NHS are required to participate in medical audit, which is the analysis of quality of health care, including diagnosis and treatment. It remains questionable whether such disclosures can be justified on the basis of implied consent by patients, and it is submitted that if it is sought to disclose information on such a ground a better approach would be to attempt to justify it on the basis of public interest. One further solution is to ensure that information disclosed is anomymised.

It should also be noted that maintainance of confidentiality is emphasised in contractual arrangements under the NHS internal market. (See guidance from the Department of Health — The Protection and Use of Patient Information, London: DoH, 1996, at para. 4.12.) Contractual requirements incorporate the so-called "safe haven" for the passage of contractual information involving patients. "Safe haven" includes the use of secure faxes to which there is limited access.

(ii) The public interest

The law of breach of confidence allows information to be disclosed where it is in the public interest to do so. No single definition of what amounts to the public interest exists. But in certain cases the courts have provided guidance as to what will be deemed to be disclosure in the public interest. It was said by Wood V.-C. in *Gartside v. Outram* ((1857) 26 L.J. Ch. (NS) 113, 114) "there is no confidence as to the disclosure of iniquity". Iniquity goes beyond, for example, the disclosure of information relating to a crime. In *Beloff v. Pressdram* [1973] 1 All E.R. 241, at page 260, Ungoed Thomas J. held that disclosure of information relating to "matters medically dangerous to the public" is justified. Nevertheless, while the public interest may justify disclosure that does not necessarily mean that all members of the public need to know the information in question. In *Initial Services v. Putterill* [1967] 3 All E.R. 145, Lord Denning held that disclosure would only be permitted if it was made to someone who had a proper interest in receiving the information. In *Lion Laboratories v. Evans* [1984] 2 All E.R. 47, Lord Wilberforce stated that there was a difference between something which was of interest to the public and which was in the public interest to know. This is a matter to be determined on a case by case basis.

X v. Y [1988] 2 All E.R. 648.

A national newspaper published details regarding two general practitioners (G.P.s) who had developed AIDS. The Health Authority brought proceedings to stop further publication of the health information of the G.P.s.

ROSE J.:
". . . Under the National Health Service (Venereal Disease) Regulations 1974 the plaintiffs and their servants have a statutory duty to take all necessary steps to secure that any information capable of identifying patients examined or treated for AIDS shall not be disclosed except to a medical practitioner, or a person under his direction, in connection with and for the purposes of treatment or prevention of the spread of the disease. Confidentiality is of paramount importance to such patients, including doctors. The plaintiffs take care to ensure it. Their servants are contractually bound to respect it. If it is breached, or if the patients have grounds for believing that it may be or has been breached they will be reluctant to come forward for and to continue treatment and, in particular counselling. If the actual or apprehended breach is to the press that reluctance is likely to be very great. If treatment is not provided or continued the individual will be deprived of its benefit and the public are likely to suffer from an increase in the rate of spread of the disease. The preservation of confidentiality is therefore in the public interest.

. . . [I]s publication of this confidential information [in relation to the two G.P.'s with AIDS] justified in the public interest?

Counsel for the second defendants accepted (as was indeed the evidence of every witness in the case) that public debate does not require the use of confidential information and he also accepted that in any publication the doctors should not be identified. But he submitted, as did counsel for the first defendant, that the public's right to know is not limited to theoretical debate; they submitted that the public is entitled to be told, at the very least, that two general practitioners with AIDS have practised in the United Kingdom. This form of proposed publication, first suggested in the final speech of counsel for the second defendants is the fifth or sixth version suggested by the defendants. Earlier versions, progressively diminishing the degree of identification, were put forward in paragraph 18 of the first defendant's defence and paragraph 12 of the second defendant's defence (which conflict as to whether the editor's intention was or was not to name the doctors), a letter from the second defendants' solicitors dated October 7, 1987 and the second defendants' amended defence (adopted by the first defendant). Not until October 7, did the second defendants purport to abandon their expressed intention to name both the doctors and the hospital where they were treated and even then (in the letter) they wished to identify the alleged specialities of both the doctors.

I accept the submission of counsel for the second defendants that the last version would not lead to identification; none of the evidence suggests that it would. With regard to the version in paragraph 10 of the amended defence (repeated in paragraph 19 of the amended counterclaim) there is a conflict of evidence between the physician who saw no danger of identification or breach of confidence attributable to the hospital and Sir Donald Acheson and Professor Adler who thought it presented a risk of identification. Essentially the question is one for me rather than for medical opinion. But I suspect that Professor Adler may be right in saying that this version narrows down the issue too much and would lead to further media investigation and, ultimately, tracing of the doctors; and that suspicion, in the absence of any evidence from the first defendant, the second defendants' editor or any other journalist, is a healthy one. But for the purpose of considering whether there should be an injunction I am prepared to assume, without finding, that the version in paragraph 10 of the amended defence would not lead to identification or attributable breach of confidence.

Counsel for the second defendants next submitted that, if the identities are not revealed, an injunction should not be granted even though the information has the necessary quality of confidentiality. There must (as is common ground) be a substantial, not trivial, violation of the plaintiffs' rights to justify the equitable relief. He accepted that what the plaintiffs' unfaithful servant did was not trivial but said that publication in the form suggested in paragraph 10 of the amended defence would be. Accordingly, he submitted that there was no discernible detriment to the plaintiffs and detriment is essential; he relied on the reference to detriment in *Seager v. Copydex Ltd* [1967] 2 All E.R. 415 at 417, 418, by Lord Denning M.R. and Salmon L.J. and suggested that, when in *Coco v. A. N. Clarke (Engineers) Ltd* [1969] RPC 41 at 48 Megarry V-C contemplates cases where the plaintiff may not suffer, that judgment has to be viewed in the light of the Court of Appeal judgments in *Seager v. Copydex Ltd*.

Counsel for the plaintiffs submitted that detriment is not a separate question but part of the balancing exercise. Furthermore, he said there is detriment, first, in the breach of contract, second, in the special arrangements which had to be made in order to continue treatment of one of the doctors (as described by the physician), third, in the pursuit of one of the doctors as appears from the first defendant's notes of conversation and unpublished draft article and in the information that the other doctor was 'very suicidal' and, fourth, in the apparent breach of the plaintiff's duties of medical confidentiality and under the National Health Service (Venereal Disease) Regulations 1974.

In my judgment detriment in the use of the information is not a necessary precondition to injunctive relief. Although in *Seager v. Copydex Ltd* the Court of Appeal held, by reference to the facts of the case, that the confidential information could not be used as a springboard for activities detrimental to the plaintiff, I do not understand any member of the court to have been saying that detrimental use is always necessary. I respectfully agree with Megarry V-C that an injunction may be appropriate for breach of confidence where the plaintiff may not suffer from the use of the information and that is borne out by more recent observations in the Court of Appeal and House of Lords, to which I will refer later (in particular in *Lion Laboratories v. Evans* [1984] 2 All E.R. 417, *Schering Chemicals v. Falkman Ltd* [1981] 2 All E.R. 321, and *British Steel v. Granada Television Ltd* [1981] 1 All E.R. 417), which contain no reference to the necessity for detriment in use and, indeed, point away from any such principle. In the present case, detriment occurred to the plaintiffs because patients' records were leaked to the press in breach of contract and breach of confidence, with the consequences, even without publication, to the plaintiffs and the patients listed by counsel for the plaintiffs. If use were made of that information in such a way as to demonstrate to the public (by identifying the hospital) the source of the leak, the plaintiffs would suffer further detriment. But use of the information (as the defendants now seek) in a way which identifies neither the hospital nor the patients does not mean that the plaintiffs have suffered no detriment. Significant damage, about which the plaintiffs are entitled to complain, has already been done. This is also the answer to the additional submission of counsel for the first defendant that, though there was a breach of confidence in obtaining the information there is, on the evidence, none in publishing it, if the doctors are not identified. In my judgment it is, in the present case, the initial disclosure and its immediate consequences, not subsequent publication, which found the plaintiffs' claim in breach of contract and breach of confidence.

The remaining, crucial, issue on the first question is public interest: does this require injunctive relief? . . .

On the one hand, there are the public interests in having a free press and an informed public debate; on the other, it is in the public interest that actual or potential AIDS sufferers should be able to resort to hospitals without fear of this being revealed, that those owing duties of confidence in their employment should be loyal and should not disclose confidential matters and that, *prima facie*, no one should be allowed to use information extracted in breach of confidence from hospital records even if disclosure of the particular information may not give rise to immediately apparent harm.

It is to be noted that in the present case the plaintiffs' cause of action lies not just (as in most of the authorities) in breach of confidence but also in procurement of breach of contract. The onus of proving justification once the tort of interference with contractual rights is established (as is not here disputed) is on the defendants (see *South West Wales Miners' Federation v. Glamorgan Coal Co. Ltd* [1904–7] All E.R. Rep. 211 at 214, 217, 219.

I keep in the forefront of my mind the very important public interest in freedom of the press. And I accept that there is some public interest in knowing that which the defendants seek to publish (in whichever version). But in my judgment those public interests are substantially outweighed when measured against the public interests in relation to loyalty and confidentiality both generally and with particular reference to AIDS patients' hospital records. There has been no misconduct by the plaintiffs. The records of hospital patients, particularly those suffering from this appalling condition should, in my judgment, be as confidential as the courts can properly keep them in order that the plaintiffs may 'be free from suspicion that they are harbouring disloyal employees'. The plaintiffs have 'suffered a grievous wrong in which the defendants became involved . . . with active participation'. The deprivation of the public of the information sought to be published will be of minimal significance if the injunction is granted; for, without it, all the evidence before me shows that a wide-ranging public debate about AIDS generally and about its effect on doctors is taking place among doctors of widely differing views, within and without the BMA, in medical journals and in many newspapers, including the Observer, the Sunday Times and the Daily Express. Indeed, the sterility of the defendants' argument is demonstrated by the edition of the second defendant's own newspaper dated on March 22, 1987. It is there expressly stated, purportedly quoting a Mr Milligan, that three general practitioners two of whom are practising (impliedly in Britain) have AIDS. Paraphrasing Templeman L.J. in the *Schering* case, the facts, in the most limited version now sought to be published, have already been made available and again be made available if they are known otherwise than through the medium of the informer. The risk of identification is only one factor in assessing whether to permit the use of confidential information. In my judgment to allow publication in the recently suggested restricted form, would be to enable both defendants to procure breaches of confidence and then to make their own selection for publication. This would make a mockery of the law's protection of confidentiality when no justifying public interest has been shown. These are the considerations which guide me, whether my task is properly described as a balancing exercise, or an exercise in judicial judgment, or both. No one has suggested that damages would be an adequate remedy in this case."

NOTES:

1. This case was the first breach of confidence case concerning disclosure of confidential medical information in recent times. (See J. V. McHale "Doctors with AIDS — Dilemmas of Confidentiality" (1988) 4 *Professional Negligence* 76.)

2. GMC guidelines state that "Only in the most exceptional circumstances, where the release of a doctor's name is essential for the protection of patients, may a doctor's HIV status be disclosed without his or her consent." (GMC *HIV Infection and AIDS: The Ethical Considerations*, Revised 1995). In only one case has it been shown that a patient contracted HIV from a health care professional. This related to a dentist in Florida, USA. (See M. Mulholland "AIDS, HIV and the Health Care Worker" (1993) 9 *Professional Negligence* 79.) In a number of cases in this country Health Authorities have published details of a health care professional with AIDS in an attempt to trace her patients.

QUESTIONS:

1. Would the decision of Rose J. to prevent further publication have been different had the doctors been surgeons as opposed to G.P.'s?

2. In view of the very small risk of transmission by medical practitioners to patients should disclosure be sanctioned at all?

3. How far should considerations of press freedom be taken into account in determining what protection should be given to patient confidentiality?

4. Should the fact that the doctor's identity was not disclosed be a relevant consideration in determining whether or not the article was in breach of confidence?

W v. Egdell [1990] 1 All E.R. 835, [1990] Ch. 359, [1990] 2 W.L.R. 471.

W was detained in hospital under a restriction order authorised by section 60 and section 65 of the Mental Health Act 1959, after being convicted of the manslaughter of five people. He applied to a Mental Health Review Tribunal for discharge from the hospital (section 41 of the Mental Health Act 1983). A psychiatrist, Dr Egdell, was commissioned to examine W and to compile a report on him. The report was unfavourable. Dr Egdell suggested that W had an abnormal personality which could be of a psychopathic nature and expressed his concern at W's interest in what W called fireworks, by which he meant such things as tubes of piping packed with explosive chemicals. On receipt of the report W's solicitors decided to withdraw his application to the tribunal. Dr Egdell asked W's solicitors for a copy of his report to be put in W's hospital file. They refused. Dr Edgell then decided to disclose the contents of the report to W's responsible medical officer. Subsequently the report was disclosed to the Home Office. The Home Secretary is periodically required to refer cases of patients such as W to a Mental Health Review Tribunal (Section 67 Mental Health Act 1983). After his own application to the tribunal had been withdrawn, W's case came up for review under this automatic procedure. W's solicitors obtained an injunction to restrain Dr Egdell from disclosing the contents of the report at the hearing. Unknown to them, however, the disclosure had already occurred. At the hearing the Home Secretary put forward the information obtained by Dr Egdell alleging breach of confidence.

SIR STEPHEN BROWN:
". . . In the course of his judgment Scott J said ([1989] 1 All E.R. 1089 at 1101–1102:

> 'The basis of W's case is that his interview with Dr Egdell on July 23, 1987 and the report written by Dr Egdell on the basis of that interview is, or ought to have been, protected from disclosure by the duty of confidence resting on Dr Egdell as W's doctor. It is claimed that Dr Egdell was in breach of his duty of confidence in telling Dr Hunter about the report, in sending a copy of the report to Dr Hunter and in urging the despatch of a copy to the Home Office . . . It is convenient for me first to ask myself what duty of confidence a court of equity ought to regard as imposed on Dr Egdell by the circumstances in which he obtained information from and about W and prepared his report. It is in my judgment plain, and the contrary has not been suggested, that the circumstances did impose on Dr Egdell a duty of confidence. If, for instance Dr Egdell had sold the contents of his report to a newspaper, I do not think any court of equity would hesitate for a moment before concluding that his conduct had been a breach of his duty of confidence. The question in the present case is not whether Dr Egdell was under a duty of confidence he plainly was. The question is as to the breadth of that duty. Did the duty extend so as to bar disclosure of the report to the medical director of the hospital? Did it bar disclosure to the Home Office? In the Spycatcher case [*A.-G. v. Guardian Newspaper Ltd (No.2)*] [1988] 3 All E.R. 545 at 658–659, in the House of Lords Lord Goff, after accepting "the broad general principle . . . that a duty of confidence arises when confidential information comes to the knowledge of a person (the confidant) in circumstances where he has notice, or is held to have agreed, that the information is confidential, with the effect that it would be just in all the circumstances that he should be precluded from disclosing the information to others", formulated three limiting principles. He said: 'The third limiting principle is of far greater importance. It is that, although the basis of the law's protection of confidence is that there is a public interest that confidences should be preserved and protected by the law, nevertheless that public interest may be outweighed by some other countervailing public interest which favours disclosure. This limitation may apply, as the learned judge pointed out, to all types of confidential information. It is this limiting principle which may require a court to carry out a balancing operation, weighing the public interest in maintaining confidence against a countervailing public interest favouring disclosure.' In *X v. Y* [1988] 2 All E.R. 648 at 653, a case which concerned doctors who were believed to be continuing to practise despite having contracted AIDS, Rose J. said: 'In the long run, preservation of confidentiality is the only way of securing public health otherwise doctors will be discredited as a source of education, for future individual patients will not come forward if doctors are going to squeal on them'. Consequently, confidentiality is vital to secure public as well as private health, for unless those infected come forward they cannot be counselled and self-treatment does not provide the best care . . . 'The question in

a particular case whether a duty of confidentiality extends to bar particular disclosures that the confidant has made or wants to make requires the court to balance the interest to be served by non-disclosure against the interest served by disclosure. Rose J. struck that balance. It came down, he held, in favour of non-disclosure. In the *Spycatcher* case that balance too was struck. In that case the balance did not come down in favour of non-disclosure. I must endeavour to strike the balance in the present case.'

Counsel for W agreed that the judge was required to carry out a balancing exercise. He said that it is a question of degree.

As a starting point Scott J. turned to 'Advice on Standards of Professional Conduct and of Medical Ethics' contained in the General Medical Council's 'Blue Book' on professional conduct and discipline. The judge said ([1989] 1 All E.R. 1089 at 1103,):

'These rules do not provide a definitive answer to the question raised in the present case as to the breadth of the duty of confidence owed by Dr Egdell. They seem to me valuable, however, in showing the approach of the General Medical Council to the breadth of the doctor/patient duty of confidence.'

These rules do not themselves have statutory authority. Nevertheless, the General Medical Council in exercising its disciplinary jurisdiction does so in pursuance of the provisions of the Medical Act 1983. Under the heading 'Professional Confidence', rr.79 to 82 provide as follows:

'79. The following guidance is given on the principles which should govern the confidentiality of information relating to patients.

80. It is a doctor's duty, except in the cases mentioned below, strictly to observe the rule of professional secrecy by refraining from disclosing voluntarily to any third party information about a patient which he has learnt directly or indirectly in his professional capacity as a registered medical practitioner. The death of the patient does not absolve the doctor from this obligation.

81. The circumstances where exceptions to the rule may be permitted are as follows:

(a) If the patient or his legal adviser gives written and valid consent, information to which the consent refers may be disclosed.

(b) Confidential information may be shared with other registered medical practitioners who participate in or assume responsibility for clinical management of the patient. To the extent that the doctor deems it necessary for the performance of their particular duties, confidential information may also be shared with other persons (nurses and other health care professionals) who are assisting and collaborating with the doctor in his professional relationship with the patient. It is the doctor's responsibility to ensure that such individuals appreciate that the information is being imparted in strict professional confidence.

(c) If in particular circumstances the doctor believes it undesirable on medical grounds to seek the patient's consent, information regarding the patient's health may sometimes be given in confidence to a close relative or person in a similar relationship to the patient. However, this guidance is qualified in paragraphs 83–85 below.

(d) If in the doctor's opinion disclosure of information to a third party other than a relative would be in the best interests of the patient, it is the doctor's duty to make every reasonable effort to persuade the patient to allow the information to be given. If the patient still refuses then only in exceptional cases should the doctor feel entitled to disregard his refusal.

(e) Information may be disclosed to the appropriate authority in order to satisfy a specific statutory requirement, such as notification of an infectious disease.

(f) If the doctor is directed to disclose information by a judge or other presiding officer of a court before whom he is appearing to give evidence, information may at that stage be disclosed. Similarly, a doctor may disclose information when he has been summoned by authority of a court in Scotland, or under the powers of a Procurator-Fiscal in Scotland to investigate sudden, suspicious or unexplained deaths, and appears to give evidence before a Procurator-Fiscal. Information may also be disclosed to a coroner or his nominated representative to the extent necessary to enable the coroner to determine whether an inquest should be held. But where litigation is in prospect, unless the patient has consented to disclosure or a formal court order has been made for disclosure, information should not be disclosed merely in response to demands from other persons such as another party's solicitor or an official of the court.

(g) Rarely, disclosure may be justified on the ground that it is in the public interest which, in certain circumstances such as, for example, investigation by the police of a grave or very serious crime, might override the doctor's duty to maintain his patient's confidence.

(h) Information may also be disclosed if necessary for the purpose of a medical research project which has been approved by a recognised ethical committee.

82. Whatever the circumstances, a doctor must always be prepared to justify his action if he has disclosed confidential information. If a doctor is in doubt whether any of the exceptions mentioned above would justify him in disclosing information in a particular situation he will be wise to seek advice from a medical defence society or professional association.'

The judge said that paragraph (b) and (g) of regulation 81 seemed to him to be particularly relevant. He then rehearsed the circumstances of the disclosure by Dr Egdell of his report and asked the question ([1989] 1 All E.R. 1089 at 1104):

'Did these circumstances impose on Dr Egdell a duty not to disclose his opinions and his report to Dr Hunter, the medical director at the hospital? In my judgment they did not. Dr Egdell was expressing opinions which were relevant to the nature of the treatment and care to be accorded to W at the hospital. Dr Egdell was, in effect, recommending a change from the approach to treatment and care that Dr Ghosh was following. He was expressing reservations about Dr Ghosh's diagnosis. The case seems to me to fall squarely within paragraph (b) of 81. But I would base my conclusion on broader considerations than that. I decline to overlook the background to Dr Egdell's examination of W. True it is that Dr Egdell was engaged by W. He was the doctor of W's choice. None the less, in my opinion, the duty he owed to W was not his only duty. W was not an ordinary member of the public. He was, consequent on the killings he had perpetrated, held in a secure hospital subject to a regime whereby decisions concerning his future were to be taken by public authorities, the Home Secretary or the tribunal. W's own interests would not be the only nor the main criterion in the taking of those decisions. The safety of the public would be the main criterion. In my view, a doctor called on, as Dr Egdell was, to examine a patient such as W owes a duty not only to his patient but also a duty to the public. His duty to the public would require him, in my opinion, to place before the proper authorities the result of his examination if, in his opinion, the public interest so required. This would be so, in my opinion, whether or not the patient instructed him not to do so.'

The judge then referred to the submission of counsel for W that the dominant public interest in the case was the public interest in patients being able to make full and frank disclosure to their doctors, and in particular to their psychiatrist, without fear that the doctor would disclose the information to others. The judge said ([1989] 1 All E.R. 1089 at 1104–1105):

'I accept the general importance in the public interest that this should be so. It justifies the General Medical Council's r.80 . . . In truth, as it seems to me, the interest to be served by the duty of confidence for which counsel for W contends is the private interest of W and not any broader public interest. If I set the private interest of W in the balance against the public interest served by disclosure of the report to Dr Hunter and the Home Office, I find the weight of the public interest prevails . . . In my judgment, therefore, the circumstances of this case did not impose on Dr Egdell an obligation of conscience, an equitable obligation, to refrain from disclosing his report to Dr Hunter, or to refrain from encouraging its disclosure to the Home Office.'

In this court counsel for W acknowledges that, in addition to the duty of confidence admittedly owed by Dr Edgell to W, it was necessary for the judge to consider the public interest in the disclosure by Dr Egdell of his report to the authorities. There are two competing public interest considerations. However, he submits that the dominant public interest was the duty of confidence owed by Dr Edgell to W. The burden of proving that duty was overridden by public interest considerations in disclosing his opinion to the public authorities rested fairly and squarely on Dr Edgell. He contended that, where the public interest relied on to justify a breach of confidence is alleged to be the real reduction or elimination of a risk to public safety it must be shown (a) that such a risk is real, immediate and serious, (b) that it will be substantially reduced by disclosure, (c) that the disclosure is no greater than is reasonably necessary to minimise the risk and (d) that the consequent damage to the public interest protected by the duty of confidentiality is outweighed by the public interest in minimising such a risk. He relied on the decision of Rose J. in *X v. Y* [1988] 2 All E.R. 648. He also acted a passage from the judgment of Boreham J. in *Hunter v. Mann* [1974] 2 All E.R. 414 at 417–418.

'The second proposition is this: that in common with other professional men, for instance a priest and there are of course others, the doctor is under a duty not to disclose, without the consent of his patient, information which he, the doctor, has gained in his professional capacity, save, says counsel for the appellant, in very exceptional circumstances. He quoted the example of the murderer still manic, who would be a menace to society. But, says counsel, save in exceptional circumstances, the general rule applies. He adds that the law will enforce that duty.'

He referred to the American case of *Tarasoff v. Regents of the University of California* (1976) 17 Cal 3d 358 as an example of extreme circumstances and submitted that only in the most extreme circumstances could a doctor be relieved from observing the strict duty of confidence imposed on him by reason of his relationship with his patient. In this instance, said counsel for W, there was no immediate prospect of W being released or of being detained other than under secure conditions and furthermore any change in his circumstances would be conditional on further expert analysis and recommendation.

The two interests which had to be balanced in this case were both public interests. The judge was wrong to refer to W's 'private' interest. The judge was also in error, said counsel for W, in saying: The case seems to me to fall squarely within paragraph (b) of regulation 81' (of the General Medical Council's rules). Dr Egdell did not have any clinical responsibility for W and accordingly that particular rule could not be relied on by Dr Egdell in the present circumstances.

With reference to 'legal privilege', counsel for W submitted that in the context of this case it was highly relevant that the report was commissioned by solicitors acting for W in the matter of his application to the tribunal. He argued that, if legal privilege did not strictly apply to the report of Dr Egdell as distinct from his instructions, nevertheless the context in which it was prepared added strength to the duty of confidence. He used the phrase 'accumulative effect'.

Counsel for Dr Egdell argued that Dr Egdell is acknowledged to be a responsible and experienced consultant psychiatrist having particular knowledge of the procedures relating to the management and treatment of restricted patients detained in secure conditions under the provisions of the Mental Health Act 1983. His evidence on matters of fact was not challenged. It must be accepted that he was genuinely seriously concerned by the revelation of what seemed to him to be entirely new facts relating to W's long-standing interest in guns and explosives. It is not challenged, he said, that he acted in good faith in disclosing his report to Dr Hunter and in urging its disclosure to the Home Secretary. He plainly believed that he was acting in the public interest.

The balance of public interest clearly lay in the restricted disclosure of vital information to the director of the hospital and to the Secretary of State who had the onerous duty of safeguarding public safety.

In this case the number and nature of the killings by W must inevitably give rise to the gravest concern for the safety of the public. The authorities responsible for W's treatment and management must be entitled to the fullest relevant information concerning his condition. It is clear that Dr Egdell did have highly relevant information about W's condition which reflected on his dangerousness. In my judgment the position came within the terms of r.81(g) of the General Medical Council's rules. Furthermore, Dr Egdell amply justified his action within the terms of r.82. The suppression of the material contained in his report would have deprived both the hospital and the Secretary of State of vital information, directly relevant to questions of public safety. Although it may be said that Dr Egdell's action in disclosing his report to Dr Hunter fell within the letter of r.81(b), the judge in fact based his conclusion on what he termed 'broader considerations', that is to say the safety of the public. I agree with him.

In so far as the judge referred to the 'private interest' of W, I do not consider that the passage in his judgment (see [1989] 1 All E.R. 1089 at 1105) accurately stated the position. There are two competing public interests and it is clear that by his reference to *X v. Y* [1988] 2 All E.R. 648 the judge was fully seised of this point. Of course W has a private interest, but the duty of confidence owed to him is based on the broader ground of public interest described by Rose J. in *X v. Y* . . .

BINGHAM L.J.:

'. . . The philosophy underlying the statutory regime which the judge described is in my view clear. A man who commits crimes, however serious, when subject to severe mental illness is not to be treated as if he were of sound mind. He requires treatment in hospital, not punishment in prison. So an order may be made committing him to hospital. He may, however, represent a great and continuing danger to the public. So his confinement in hospital may be ordered to continue until the Home Secretary, as guardian of the public safety, adjudges it safe to release him or relax the conditions of his confinement. But a decision by the Home Secretary adverse to the patient is not conclusive. The patient may have recourse to an independent tribunal which, if certain conditions are satisfied, must order his discharge either conditionally or absolutely and which may make non-binding recommendations. Lest an inactive patient be forgotten, his case must be reviewed by the tribunal at three-yearly intervals. These provisions represent a careful balance between the legitimate desire of the patient to regain his freedom and the legitimate desire of the public to be protected against violence. The heavy responsibility of deciding how the balance should be struck in any given case at any given time rests in the first instance on the Home Secretary and in the second instance on the tribunal. It is only by making a careful and informed assessment of the individual case that the potentially conflicting claims of humanity to the patient and protection of the public may be fairly and responsibly reconciled.

It has never been doubted that the circumstances here were such as to impose on Dr Egdell a duty of confidence owed to W. He could not lawfully sell the contents of his report to a newspaper, as the judge held. Nor could he, without a breach of the law as well as professional etiquette, discuss the case in a learned article or in his memoirs or in gossiping with friends, unless he took appropriate steps to conceal the identity of W. It is not in issue here that a duty of confidence existed.

The breadth of such a duty in any case is, however, dependent on circumstances. Where a prison doctor examines a remand prisoner to determine his fitness to plead or a proposer for life insurance is examined by a doctor nominated by the insurance company or a personal injury plaintiff attends on the defendant's medical adviser or a prospective bidder instructs accountants to investigate (with its consent) the books of a target company, the professional man's duty of confidence towards the subject of his examination plainly does not bar disclosure of his findings to the party at whose instance he was appointed to make his examination. Here, however, Dr Egdell was engaged by W, not by the tribunal or the hospital authorities. He assumed at first that his report would be communicated to the tribunal and thus become known to the authorities but he must, I think, have appreciated that W and his legal advisers could decide not to adduce his report in evidence before the tribunal.

The decided cases very clearly establish (1) that the law recognises an important public interest in maintaining professional duties of confidence but (2) that the law treats such duties not as absolute but as liable to be overridden where there is held to be a stronger public interest in disclosure. Thus the public interest in the administration of justice may require a clergyman, a banker, a medical man, a journalist or an accountant to breach his professional duty of confidence (*A.-G. v. Mulholland* [1963] 1 All E.R. 767 at 771, *Chantrey Martin & Co. v. Martin* [1953] 2 All E.R. 691,). In *Parry Jones v. Law Society* [1968] 1 All E.R. 177, a solicitor's duty of confidence towards his clients was held to be overridden by his duty to comply with the law of the land, which required him to produce documents for inspection under the Solicitors' Accounts Rules. A doctor's duty of confidence to his patient may be overridden by clear statutory language (as in *Hunter v. Mann* [1974] 2 All E.R. 414). A banker owes his customer an undoubted duty of confidence, but he may become subject to a duty to the public to disclose, as where danger to the state or public duty supersede the duty of agent to principal (*Tournier v. National Provincial and Union Bank of England* [1923] All E.R. Rep 550 at 554, 561). An employee may justify breach of a duty of confidence towards his employer otherwise binding on him when there is a public interest in the subject matter of his disclosure (*Initial Services Ltd v. Putterill* [1967] 3 All E.R. 145, *Lion Laboratories v. Evans* [1984] 2 All E.R. 417). These qualifications of the duty of confidence arise not because that duty is not accorded legal recognition but for the reason clearly given by Lord Goff in his speech in (*A.-G. v. Guardian Newspapers Ltd (No. 2)* [1988] 3 All E.R. 545 at 659, the Spycatcher case), quoted by Scott J. [1989] 1 All E.R. 1089 at 1102:

'The third limiting principle is of far greater importance. It is that, although the basis of the law's protection of confidence is that there is a public interest that confidences should be preserved and protected by the law, nevertheless that public interest may be outweighed by some other countervailing public interest which favours disclosure. This limitation may apply, as the judge pointed out, to all types of confidential information. is this limiting principle which may require a court to carry out a balancing operation, weighing the public interest in maintaining confidence against a countervailing public interest favouring disclosure.'

These principles were not in issue between the parties to this appeal. Counsel for W accepted that W's right to confidence was qualified and not absolute. But it is important to insist on the public interest in preserving W's right to confidence because the judge in his judgment concluded that while W had a strong private interest in barring disclosure of Dr Egdell's report he could not rest his case on any broader public interest (see [1989] 1 All E.R. 1089 at 1104–1105). Here, as I think, the judge fell into error. W of course had a strong personal interest in regaining his freedom and no doubt regarded Dr Egdell's report as an obstacle to that end. So he had a personal interest in restricting the report's circulation. But these private considerations should not be allowed to obscure the public interest in maintaining professional confidences. The fact that Dr Egdell as an independent psychiatrist examined and reported on W as a restricted mental patient under section 76 of the Mental Health Act 1983 does not deprive W of his ordinary right to confidence, underpinned, as such rights are, by the public interest. But it does mean that the balancing operation of which Lord Goff spoke falls to be carried out in circumstances of unusual difficulty and importance.

We were referred, as the judge was, to the current advice given by the General Medical Council to the medical profession pursuant to section 35 of the Medical Act 1983. Rule 80 provides:

'It is a doctor's duty, except in the cases mentioned below, strictly to observe the rule of professional secrecy by refraining from disclosing voluntarily to any third party information about a patient which he has learnt directly or indirectly in his professional capacity as a registered medical practitioner . . .'

I do not doubt that this accurately states the general rule as the law now stands, and the contrary was not suggested. A disclosure compelled by statute or court order is not voluntary. Rule 81 of the General Medical Council advice lists the exceptions. Our attention was drawn to paragraphs (b) and (d):

'(b) Confidential information may be shared with other registered medical practitioners who participate in or assume responsibility for clinical management of the patient. To the extent that the doctor deems it necessary for the performance of their particular duties, confidential information may also be shared with other persons (nurses and other health care professionals) who are assisting and collaborating with the doctor in his professional relationship with the patient. It is the doctor's responsibility to ensure that such individuals appreciate that the information is being imparted in strict professional confidence . . .

(d) If in the doctor's opinion disclosure of information to a third party other than a relative would be in the best interests of the patient, it is the doctor's duty to make every reasonable effort to persuade the patient to allow the information to be given. If the patient still refuses then only in exceptional cases should the doctor feel entitled to disregard his refusal.'

The judge regarded rule 81(b) as accurately stating the law and held that Dr Egdell's disclosure in the present case fell squarely within it. I have some reservations about this conclusion. It is true that the disclosure here may be said to fall within the letter of the first sentence of paragraph (b). But I think the paragraph is directed towards the familiar situation in which consultants or other specialised experts report to the doctor with clinical responsibility for treating or advising the patient, and the second sentence shows that the doctor whose duty is in question is regarded as having a continuing professional relationship with the patient. I rather doubt if the draftsman of paragraph (b) had in mind a consultant psychiatrist consulted on a single occasion —

'For the purpose of advising whether an application to a Mental Health Review Tribunal should be made by or in respect of a patient who is liable to be detained or subject to guardianship under Part II of this Act or of furnishing information as to the condition of a patient for the purposes of such an application . . .'(See section 76(1) of the Mental Health Act 1983). Nor do I think that Dr Egdell, in making disclosure, was primarily motivated by the ordinary concern of any doctor that a patient should receive the most efficacious treatment. Had that been his primary object, I think he would, consistently with the spirit of paragraph (d), have tried to reason with W to obtain his consent to disclosure in W's own interest. I need not, however, reach a final view. The judge preferred to rest his conclusion on a broader ground, which was in effect the exception set out in rule 81(g) of the General Medical Council advice, and I think that if the disclosure cannot be justified under that exception it would be unsafe to justify it under any other'.

Rule 81(g) provides:

'Rarely, disclosure may be justified on the ground that it is in the public interest which, in certain circumstances such as, for example, investigation by the police of a grave or very serious crime, might override the doctor's duty to maintain his patient's confidence.'

It was this exception which, as I understand, the judge upheld and applied when he held, in what is perhaps the crucial passage in this judgment ([1989] 1 All E.R. 1089 at 1104):

'In my view, a doctor called on, as Dr Egdell was, to examine a patient such as W owes a duty not only to his patient but also a duty to the public. His duty to the public would require him, in my opinion, to place before the proper authorities the result of his examination if, in his opinion, the public interest so required. This would be so, in my opinion, whether or not the patient instructed him not to do so.'

Counsel for W criticised this passage as wrongly leaving the question whether disclosure was justified or not to the subjective decision of the doctor. He made the same criticism of a passage where Scott J. said ([1989] 1 All E.R. 1089 at 1105,):

'If a patient in the position of W commissions an independent psychiatrist's report, the duty of confidence that undoubtedly lies on the doctor who makes the report does not, in my judgment, bar the doctor from disclosing the report to the hospital that is charged with the care of the patient if the doctor judges the report to be relevant to the care and treatment of the patient, nor from disclosing the report to the Home Secretary if the doctor judges the report to be relevant to the exercise of the Home Secretarys' discretionary powers in relation to that patient.'

In my opinion these criticisms are just. Where, as here, the relationship between doctor and patient is contractual, the question is whether the doctor's disclosure is or is not a breach of contract. The answer to that question must turn not on what the doctor thinks but on what the court rules. But it does not follow that the doctor's conclusion is irrelevant. In making its ruling the court will give such weight to the considered judgment of a professional man as seems in all the circumstances to be appropriate.

The parties were agreed, as I think rightly, that the crucial question in the present case was how, on the special facts of the case, the balance should be struck between the public interest in maintaining professional confidences and the public interest in protecting the public against possible violence. Counsel for W submitted that on the facts here the public interest in maintaining confidences was shown to be clearly preponderant. In support of that submission he drew our attention to a number of features of the case, of which the most weighty were perhaps these.

(1) Section 76 of the Mental Health Act 1983 shows a clear parliamentary intention that a restricted patient should be free to seek advice and evidence for the specified purposes from a medical source outside the prison and secure hospital system. Section 129 ensures that the independent doctor may make a full examination and see all relevant documents. The examination may be in private, so that the authorities do not learn what passes between doctor and patient.

(2) The proper functioning of section 76 requires that a patient should feel free to bare his soul and open his mind without reserve to the independent doctor he has retained. This he will not do if a doctor is free, on forming an adverse opinion, to communicate it to those empowered to prevent the patient's release from hospital.

(3) Although the present situation is not one in which W can assert legal professional privilege, and although tribunal proceedings are not strictly adversarial, the considerations which have given rise to legal professional privilege underpin the public interest in preserving confidence in a situation such as the present. A party to a forthcoming application to a tribunal should be free to unburden himself to an adviser he has retained without fearing that any material damaging to his application will find its way without his consent into the hands of a party with interests adverse to his.

(4) Preservation of confidence would be conducive to the public safety: patients would be candid, so that problems such as those highlighted by Dr Egdell would become known, and steps could be taken to explore and if necessary treat the problems without disclosing the report.

(5) It is contrary to the public interest that patients such as W should enjoy rights less extensive than those enjoyed by other members of the public, a result of his judgment which the judge expressly accepted (see [1989] 1 All E.R. 1089 at 1105,).

Of these considerations, I accept (1) as a powerful consideration in W's favour. A restricted patient who believes himself unnecessarily confined has, of all members of society, perhaps the greatest need for a professional adviser who is truly independent and reliably discreet (2) also I, in some measure, accept, subject to the comment that if the patient is unforthcoming the doctor is bound to be guarded in his opinion. If the patient wishes to enlist the doctor's wholehearted support for his application, he has little choice but to be (or at least convince an expert interviewer that he is being) frank. I see great force in (3). Only the most compelling circumstances could justify a doctor in acting in a way which would injure the immediate interests of his patient, as the patient perceived them, without obtaining his consent. Point (4), if I correctly understand it, did not impress me. Counsel's submissions appeared to suggest that the problems highlighted by Dr Egdell could be explored and if necessary treated without the hospital authorities being told what the problems were thought to be. I do not think this would be very satisfactory. As to (5), I agree that restricted patients should not enjoy rights of confidence less valuable than those enjoyed by other patients save in so far as any breach of confidence can be justified under the stringent terms of r.81(g) . .

When Dr Egdell made his decision to disclose, one tribunal had already recommended W's transfer to a regional secure unit and the hospital authorities had urged that course. The Home Office had resisted transfer in a qualified manner but on a basis of inadequate information. It appeared to be only a matter of time, and probably not a very long time, before W was transferred. The regional secure unit was to act as a staging post on W's journey back into the community. While W would no doubt be further tested, such tests would not be focused on the source of Dr Egdell's concern, which he quite rightly considered to have received inadequate attention up to then. Dr Egdell had to act when he did or not at all.

There is one consideration which in my judgment, as in that of the judge, weighs the balance of public interest decisively in favour of disclosure. It may be shortly put. Where a man has committed multiple killings under the disability of serious mental illness, decisions which may lead directly or indirectly to his release from hospital should not be made unless a responsible authority is properly able to make an informed judgment that the risk of repetition is so small as to be acceptable. A consultant psychiatrist who becomes aware, even in the course of a confidential relationship, of information which leads him, in the exercise of what the court considers a sound professional judgment, to fear that such decisions may be made on the basis of inadequate information and with a real risk of consequent danger to the public is entitled to take such steps as are reasonable in all the circumstances to communicate the grounds of his concern to the responsible authorities. I have no doubt that the judge's decision in favour of Dr Egdell was right on the facts of this case.

Counsel for W argued that even if Dr Egdell was entitled to make some disclosure he should have disclosed only the crucial paragraph of his report and his opinion. I do not agree. An opinion, even from an eminent source, cannot be evaluated unless its factual premise is known, and a detailed 10-page report cannot be reliably assessed by perusing a brief extract.

No reference was made in argument before us (or, so far as I know, before the judge) to the European Convention on Human Rights (Convention for the Protection of Human Rights and Fundamental Freedoms (Rome, November 4, 1950; TS 71 (1953) Cmd. 8969)), but I believe this decision to be in accordance with it. I would accept that art. 8(1) of the convention may protect an individual against the disclosure of information protected by the duty of professional secrecy. But art. 8(2) envisages that circumstances may arise in which a public authority may legitimately interfere with the exercise of that right in accordance with the law and where necessary in a democratic society in the interests of public safety or the prevention of crime. Here there was no interference by a public authority. Dr Egdell did, as I conclude, act in accordance with the law. And his conduct was in my judgment necessary in the interests of public safety and the prevention of crime.

NOTES:

1. This case differs from many doctor-patient encounters in that it involved a commissioned report by a specially appointed expert. The judgments in the Court of Appeal on the issue of disclosure can be usefully contrasted. Sir Stephen Brown followed the judgment of Scott J. at first instance. Bingham J., however, was more cautious. He stressed the obligation of confidentiality owed to a patient under a restriction order and that while, on the facts of this case, disclosure was warranted he indicated that such disclosure should not be made lightly. He emphasised the need to show that there was a "real risk" to the public. All the judges took note of what were then the current GMC guidelines regarding disclosure of confidential information. As has been noted, these professional guidelines, which have never undergone the test of wider public debate effectively became the legally enforced standard (see R. Lee "Deathly Silence" in R. Lee and D. Morgan, *Death Rites: Law and Ethics at the End of Life*, London: Routledge, 1994).

2. *W v. Egdell* was considered in the later case of *R. v. Crozier* (1990) *The Guardian*, May 8. In this case the defendant had pleaded guilty to attempted murder. The case had been adjourned for medical reports. Dr M was instructed to examine C (the defendant). The report did not reach defence counsel at the time of the hearing. The defendant was sentenced to nine years in prison. Dr M turned up late at the hearing by mistake. He approached the prosecution counsel and told him that in his opinion the defendant was suffering from a psychopathic disorder under the Mental Health Act 1983 and that another doctor who had originally been of the view that the defendant was not suffering from that mental disorder had changed his mind. The prosecution applied for and obtained variation of sentence. The judge quashed the original sentence and made an order under section 37 of the Mental Health Act 1983 and a restriction order under section 41. The defendant brought an appeal on the basis that disclosure was in breach of confidence. The defendant's appeal was rejected. The Court of Appeal said that Dr M had been in very much the same position as had Dr Egdell. Both doctors had believed that they were acting in the public interest.

3. In *W. v. Egdell* at first instance it was argued that the report compiled by Dr Edgell was subject to legal professional privilege and thus

immune from disclosure. This argument was rejected by Scott J., the judge at first instance. This point was not the subject of consideration by the Court of Appeal in that case. (For discussion of legal professional privilege see below at page 481.)

4. It appears that to establish public interest in disclosure it is not necessary to prove that there is danger to the public as a whole and that it will be sufficient to establish that there is a risk of harm to one specified individual. (See M. Jones "Medical Confidentiality and the Public Interest" (1990) 6 *Professional Negligence* 16).

5. We noted above that one of the circumstances in which the courts have been prepared to uphold disclosure of personal information as being in the public interest relates to the disclosure of information concerning iniquity. The Department of Health has recently issued guidance regarding certain situations in which such disclosure would be regarding as justifiable in their document *The Protection and Use of Patient Information, Guidance from the Department of Health* (DoH, 1996)

> "5.8 Passing on information to help tackle serious crime may be justified if the following conditions are satisfied:
> i. without disclosure, the task of preventing, detecting or prosecuting the crime would be seriously prejudiced or delayed;
> ii. information is limited to what is strictly relevant for a specific investigation;
> iii. there are satisfactory undertakings that the information will not be passed on or used for any purpose other than the present investigation."

6. In *Egdell* the court placed considerable emphasis upon the fact that it was in the *public* interest for information to be disclosed. However, it has been suggested that some patients, such as those who are HIV positive, have a considerable *private* interest in maintaining confidentiality. It has been argued that in the case of *Egdell* W had a strong private interest in personal liberty. (See R. Lee "Deadly Silence" in R. Lee and D. Morgan (eds) *Death Rites: Law and Ethics at the End of Life*, London: Routledge, 1994).

7. In the USA, courts have been prepared to find practitioners who did not disclose confidential information revealed to them by their patients to third parties, who subsequently suffered harm, liable in negligence. The leading case *Tarasoff v. Regents of the University of California* 551 p. 2d 334 131 Cal. R. 14 (1976) was cited in *Egdell*. It has been claimed that this case has had a considerable impact on the behaviour of psychiatrists in the United States, including greater willingness to breach confidentiality. The imposition of such a duty appears unlikely in this country. The English courts have been generally unwilling to impose duties on third parties. (*Smith v. Littlewood* [1987] All E.R. 710.)

8. Should a doctor decide to disclose medical information where she believes a patient to be at risk of harm she must take care to ensure that the disclosure of the information is accurate, otherwise she may find herself the subject of a defamation action. (See M. Brazier

Medicine, Patients and the Law (2nd ed.), Harmondsworth: Penguin, 1992, at page 56).

9. The scope of public interest disclosure in the health care context is still uncertain. Genetic screening and testing have given rise to a number of dilemmas. Increasingly, tests are available to enable a person to determine the probability that they will develop one or more genetic diseases. There may be instances in which it is sought to inform a third party where he may himself have inherited that condition and be either at risk of developing it or being a carrier. In most instances disclosure could be undertaken with consent. If disclosure is made without the patient's consent then a court would have to determine whether public interest justified disclosure. This may seem straightforward were a cure were to be available. Nevertheless, difficult issues could arise: for example, would disclosure to a woman, known to be contemplating pregnancy, of the fact that she is at risk of being a carrier of the lung disorder cystic fibrosis be in the public interest? The "harm" that she would be averting would be that of pregnancy. (*cf.* discussion of "wrongful life" actions in Chapter 13 below at page 792.) (See Nuffield Council on Bioethics Report *Genetic Screening* (1993 and P. Boddington "Confidentiality and Genetic Counselling" in A. Clarke (ed.) *Genetic Counselling: Practice and Principles*, London: Routledge, 1994). Disclosure to relatives in such circumstances may be deemed to be in the public interest.

QUESTIONS:

1. What is the duty owed to the patient by his examining psychiatrist? In what ways does this duty differ from that owed to the patient by other medical practitioners?
2. What did Scott J. mean when he said that there was a duty upon Dr Egdell to disclose? What would have been the consequences for Dr Egdell had he failed to disclose?
3. An important factor influencing the decision in *Egdell* was the harm which W might cause. In what situations may a health care professional break confidence on the grounds that harm may be caused to another?
   Consider the following situations:
   (a) A doctor discovers that his patient, who is epileptic, is working as a lorry driver (See Legal Correspondant "Doctors, Drivers and Confidentiality" (1974) 904 *BMJ* 399);
   (b) A patient tells the doctor that he has been shoplifting.

A major point of discussion regarding the scope of disclosure on the basis of public interest grounds relates to persons who are HIV positive.

HIV and AIDS: the ethical considerations (London: GMC, 1995)

15. Doctors are familiar with the need to make judgments about whether to disclose confidential information in particular circumstances and the need to justify their actions where such a disclosure is made. The GMC believes that, where HIV infection or AIDS has been diagnosed, any difficulties concerning confidentiality which arise will usually be overcome if doctors are prepared to discuss openly and honestly with patients the implications of their condition, the need to secure the safety of others, and the importance for continuing medical care of ensuring that those who will be involved in their care know the nature of their condition and the particular needs which they will have. The GMC takes the view that any doctor who discovers that a patient is HIV positive or suffering from AIDS has a duty to discuss these matters fully with the patient.

Informing other health care professionals

16. When a patient is seen by a specialist who diagnoses HIV infection or AIDS, and a general practitioner is or may become involved in that patient's care, then the specialist should explain to the patient that the general practitioner cannot be expected to provide adequate clinical management and care without full knowledge of the patient's condition. The GMC believes that the majority of such patients will readily be persuaded of the need for their general practitioners to be informed of the diagnosis

17 If the patient refuses consent for the general practitioner to be told, then the doctor has two sets of obligations to consider: obligations to the patient to maintain confidence, and obligations to other carers whose own health may be put unnecessarily at risk. In such circumstances the patient should be counselled about the difficulties which his or her condition is likely to pose for the team responsible for providing continuing health care and about the likely consequences for the standard of care which can be provided in the future. If, having considered the matter carefully in the light of such counselling, the patient still refuses to allow the general practitioner to be informed then the patient's request for privacy should be respected. The only exception to that general principle arises where the doctor judges that the failure to disclose would put the health of any of the health care team at serious risk. The GMC believes that, in such a situation it would not be improper to disclose such information as that person needs to know. The need for such a decision is, in present circumstances, likely to arise only rarely, but if it is made the doctor must be able to justify his or her action.

18. Similar principles apply to the sharing of confidential information between specialists or with other health care professionals such as nurses, laboratory technicians and dentists. All persons receiving such information must, of course, consider themselves under the same general obligation of confidentiality as the doctor principally responsible for the patient's care.

Informing the patient's spouse or other sexual partner

19. Questions of conflicting obligations also arise when a doctor is faced with the decision whether the fact that a patient is HIV positive or suffering from AIDS should be disclosed to a third party, other than another health care professional without the consent of the patient. The GMC has reached the view that there are grounds for such a disclosure only where there is a serious and identifiable risk to a specific individual who, if not so informed would be exposed to infection. Therefore, when a person is found to be infected in this

way, the doctor must discuss with the patient the question of informing a spouse or other sexual partner. The GMC believes that most such patients will agree to disclosure in these circumstances, but where such consent is withheld the doctor may consider it a duty to seek to ensure that any sexual partner is informed, in order to safeguard such persons from infection.

NOTES:

1. While the GMC appears to believe that there may be situations in which a doctor is under a duty to disclose to a third party the fact that a patient is HIV positive, it is questionable whether the courts would take this approach. (See *W v. Egdell* above.)
2. Imagine the situation where a patient of a G.P. refuses to tell his sexual partner that he is HIV positive. In such a situation both the GMC and a number of commentators would support disclosure to the sexual partner. (See, *e.g.* A. Grubb and D. Pearl, *AIDS and DNA Profiling*, Bristol: Jordan, 1990, though *cf.* R. Lee "Deathly Silence" in R. Lee and D. Morgan (eds) *Death Rites: Law and Ethics at the End of Life*, London: Routledge, 1994.)

QUESTIONS:

1. What amounts to a "serious risk" which would justify disclosure to third parties?
2. Would a health care professional be justified in breaking confidentiality under her professional ethical code and under the public interest exception to breach of confidence where a HIV carrier is known to be having unprotected sexual intercourse with numerous partners? This situation occurred in Birmingham in 1992 (see M. Brazier "At Large with a Lethal Weapon" *The Guardian* June 24, 1992).

5. REMEDIES FOR BREACH OF CONFIDENCE

A number of remedies may be available:

(a) Injunction

An injunction may be sought to prevent further publication. There has been some debate as to whether a court would be prepared to order an interlocutory injunction to prevent publication prior to the hearing (F. Gurny, *Breach of Confidence*, Oxford: OUP, 1986).

(b) Damages

If there is no contract between doctor and patient, as is the case in relation to most NHS patients, then it is questionable whether damages will be awarded for breach of confidence. Where the doctor-patient relationship is governed by a contract then the patient who brings an action for breach of confidence may seek damages for psychiatric harm and physical injury. In *W. v. Egdell* there was a contractual relationship. Dr Egdell had been commissioned to prepare the report for W's solicitors. In that case Scott J. expressed his doubt as to whether damages for nervous shock and personal injury could be awarded. To recognise such an action would be to go against the authority of *Addis v. Gramaphone Co* [1909] A.C. 488, which held that damages in contract could not be awarded for injured feelings. The Law Commission recommended reform of this area in their report *Breach of Confidence* ((1981) Report No. 110 Cmnd. 8388, paragraph 4.75). It suggested that the breach of confidence action be placed on a statutory footing and that damages for mental distress should be recoverable. (See D. Capper "Damages for breach of the equitable duty of confidence" (1994) 14 *Legal Studies* 313). At present although damages to injured feelings are unlikely to be recovered it appears that damage for any economic loss will be recoverable.

6. CONFIDENTIALITY REQUIREMENTS IMPOSED BY STATUTE

There is no general statutory protection for medical information. However certain statutory provisions require particular types of health information to be kept confidential. It is unsuprising that the statutory protection which does exists relates to areas of health care practice widely considered to be of a particularly sensitive nature, such as infertility treatment or treatment for venereal disease. By contrast, in certain other areas of health care practice, where confidentiality is regarded as being of paramount importance, such as psychiatry and psychotherapy there is no special statutory protection.

(a) Venereal Disease

National Health Service Venereal Disease Regulations (S.I. 1974 No. 29)

Every Regional Health Authority and every District Health Authority shall take all necessary steps to secure that any information capable of identifying any individual obtained by officers of the Authority with respect to persons examined or treated for any sexually transmitted disease shall not be disclosed except

(a) for the purpose of communicating that information to a medical practitioner or to a person employed under the direction of a medical practitioner in connection with the treatment of persons suffering from such disease or the prevention of the spread thereof, and
(b) for the purpose of such treatment or prevention.

NOTE:

1. For discussion of notifiable diseases and public health issues see Chapter 1 above. See also NHS Trusts (Venereal Diseases) Regulations 1991.

(b) Infertility Treatment

Human Fertilisation and Embryology Act 1990 (as amended),
s.33(1–7), (9)(a)

33.—(1) No person who is or has been a member of the Authority shall disclose any information mentioned in subsection (2) below which he holds or has held as such a member or employee.

(2) The information referred to in subsection (1) above is —

(a) any information contained or required to be contained in the register in pursuance of section 31 of this Act, and
(b) any other information obtained by any member or employee of the Authority on terms or in circumstances requiring it to be held in confidence.

(3) Subsection (1) above does not apply to any disclosure of information mentioned in subsection (2)(a) above made —

(a) to a person who is a member or employee of the Authority,
(b) to a person to whom a licence applies for the purpose of his functions as such,
(c) so that no individual to whom the information relates can be identified,
(d) in pursuance of an order of the court under section 34 or 35 of this Act or
(e) to the Registrar General in pursuance of a request under section 32 of this Act, or
(f) in accordance with section 31 of this Act.

(4) Subsection (1) above does not apply to any disclosure of information mentioned in subsection (2)(b) above —

(a) made to a person as a member or employee of the Authority,
(b) made with the consent of the person or persons whose confidence would otherwise be protected, or
(c) which has been lawfully made available to the public before the disclosure is made.

(5) No person who is or has been a person to whom a licence applies and no person to whom directions have been given shall disclose any information falling within section 31(2) of this Act which he holds or has held as such a person.

(6) Subsection (5) above does not apply to any disclosure of information made —

(a) to a person as member or employee of the Authority,
(b) to a person to whom a licence applies for the purposes of his functions as such,
(c) so far as it identified a person who, but for sections 27 to 29 of this Act, would or might be a parent of a person who instituted proceedings under section 1A of the Congenital Disabilities (Civil Liability) Act 1976, but only for the purpose of defending such proceedings, or instituting connected proceedings for compensation against that parent,
(d) so that no individual to whom the information relates can be identified,
(e) in pursuance of directions given by virtue of section 24(5) or (6) of this Act
(f) necessarily —
    (i) for any purpose preliminary to proceedings, or
    (ii) for the purposes of, or in connection with, any proceedings,

(g) for the purpose of establishing, in any proceedings relating to an application for an order under subsection (1) of section 30 of this Act, whether the condition specified in paragraph (a) or (b) of that subsection is met,

(h) under section 3 of the Access to Health Records Act 1990 (right of access to health records) [or]

(6A) Paragraph (f) of subsection (6) above, so far as relating to disclosure for the purposes of, or in connection with, any proceedings, does not apply —

(a) to disclosure of information enabling a person to be identified as a person whose gametes were used, in accordance with consent given under paragraph 5 of Schedule 3 to this Act, for the purposes of treatment services in consequence of which an identifiable individual was, or may have been, born, or

(b) to disclosure, in circumstances in which subsection (1) of section 34 of this Act applies, of information relevant to the determination of the question mentioned in that subsection.

(6B) In the case of information relating to the provision of treatment services for any identifiable individual —

(a) where one individual is identifiable, subsection (5) above, does not apply to disclosure with the consent of that individual;

(b) where both a woman and a man are treated together with her are identifiable, subsection (5) above does not apply —
   (i) to disclosure with the consent of them both, or
   (ii) if disclosure is made for the purpose of disclosing information about the provision of treatment services for one of them, to disclosure with the consent of that individual.

(6C) For the purposes of subsection (6B) above, consent must be to disclosure to a specific person, except where disclosure is to a person who needs to know —

(a) in connection with the provision of treatment services, or any other description of medical, surgical or obstetric services, for the individual giving the consent,

(b) in connection with the carrying out of an audit of clinical practice, or

(c) in connection with the auditing of accounts.

(6D) For the purposes of subsection (6B) above, consent to disclosure given at the request of another shall be disregarded unless, before it is given, the person requesting it takes reasonable steps to explain to the individual from whom it was requested the implications of compliance with the request.

(6E) In the case of information which relates to the provision of treatment services for any identifiable individual, subsection (5) above does not apply to disclosure in an emergency, that is to say, to disclosure made —

(a) by a person who is satisfied that it is necessary to make the disclosure to avert an imminent danger to the health of any individual with whose consent the information could be disclosed under subsection (6B) above, and

(b) in circumstances where it is not reasonably practicable to obtain that individual's consent,

(6F) In the case of information which shows that any identifiable individual was, or may have been, born in consequence of treatment services, subsection (5) above does not apply to any disclosure which is necessarily incidental to disclosure under subsections (6B) or (6E) above.

(6G) Regulations may provide for additional exceptions from subsection (5) above, but no exception may be made under this subsection —

(a) for disclosure of a kind mentioned in paragraph (a) or (b) of subsection (6A) above, or
(b) for disclosure, in circumstances in which section 32 of this Act applies, of information having the tendency mentioned in subsection (2) of that section.

(7) This section does not apply to the disclosure to any individual of information which —

(a) falls within section 31(2) of this Act by virtue of paragraph (a) or (b) of that subsection, and
(b) relates only to that individual or, in the case of an individual treated together with another, only to that individual and that other.

(9) In subsection (6)(f) above, references to proceedings include any formal procedure . . . for dealing with a complaint.)

NOTES:

1. Section 33 of the 1990 Act was amended by the Human Fertilisation and Embryology (Disclosure of Information) Act 1992. This Act was passed after protests from the medical profession that the original section 33 imposed undue restrictions upon disclosure. The Act protects information concerning treatment and storage of gametes and embryos of identifiable persons held in the register of information required to be established under the Act as well as any other information obtained in confidence. Unauthorised disclosure is expressly made a criminal offence.

2. Section 33 allows disclosure to be made in relation to "any proceedings". During the second reading debate upon the 1992 Act in the House of Lords the Lord Chancellor indicated that "proceedings" were not limited to legal proceedings but also included GMC and UKCC disciplinary procedures (H.L. Debates 1378, June 11, 1992). However, disclosure for these purposes does not include information relating to the donor of gametes. This may cause difficulties if such information is important for a doctor to establish his defence in civil proceedings.

3. Information may also be disclosed with the patient's consent. Section 33 states that a patient may consent to disclosure being made by the doctor to a specified person. This is in contrast to the original section which required the disclosure to be made personally by the patient. Consent may also be given to disclosure of information to a class of persons where this is necessary for medical treatment, clinical audit or accounts audit. Reasonable steps must be taken to explain to the patient the implications of giving consent.

4. Disclosure of information may take place in an emergency if the person disclosing the information is satisfied that the disclosure is

necessary to avert imminent danger to the patient's health and at the time it is not reasonably practicable to gain the patient's consent.

QUESTION:

1 What constitutes information which can be disclosed to other practitioners on the basis that it is information that they "need to know"?

7.   STATUTORY EXCEPTIONS

In certain situations statutes expressly require that patient confidentiality should be broken. For example, where information is required for the purposes of the investigation of crime or where disclosure is required on public health grounds. Medical records can be sought by the police when undertaking a criminal investigation. Such disclosure is regulated by the Police and Criminal Evidence Act 1984. This Act was amended during its passage to take account of the concerns expressed by the BMA that the reform of police powers rendered patient information unjustifiably vulnerable to access. Those seeking access to such records must now obtain a warrant from a circuit judge satisfying the provisions of sections 9–11 and Schedule 1.

Police and Criminal Evidence Act 1984, s.9(1), 11(1–2), 12

Special provisions as to access

9.—(1) A constable may obtain access to excluded material . . . for the purposes of a criminal investigation by making an application under Schedule 1 below and in accordance with that Schedule . . . (this schedule makes reference to the need to apply to a circuit judge).
   11.—(1) Subject to the following provisions of this section, in this Act, "excluded material" means —

(a) personal records which a person has acquired or created in the course of any trade or business, profession or other occupation or for the purposes of any paid or unpaid office or which he holds in confidence;
(b) human tissue or tissue fluid which had been taken for the purposes of diagnosis or medical treatment and which a person holds in confidence.

(2) A person holds material other than journalistic material in confidence for the purposes of this section if he holds it subject —

(a) to an express or implied undertaking to hold it in confidence or
(b) to a restriction on disclosure or any obligation of secrecy contained in any enactment including any enactment contained in an Act passed after this Act.

12.—In this Part of the Act "personal records" means documentary or other records concerning an individual (whether living or dead) who can be identified from them, and relating —

(a) to his physical or mental health

(b) to spiritual counselling or assistance given to him; or
(c) to counselling or assistance given or to be given to him for the purposes of his personal welfare, by any voluntary organisation or individual who —
    (i) by reason of his office or occupation has responsibilites for his personal welfare; or
    (ii) by reason of an order of the court has responsibilities for his supervision.

NOTES:

1. In *R. v. Cardiff Crown Court ex parte Kellam* (1994) 16 BMLR 762 the court held that both clinical and administrative records were capable of being classed as excluded material within section 11.
2. The requirement to obtain a search warrant from a circuit judge appears to have acted as a restraint. Judges have been prepared to deny unmeritorious applications. For example, in 1988 a circuit judge rejected an application for disclosure of more than 1000 names of men who shared the same blood group as blood stains found at the scene of a brutal murder. (See P. Schutte "Medical Confidentiality and Crime" (1992) *Journal of the Medical Defence Union* 68.)
3. Despite the fact that a special warrant is necessary for excluded material and special procedure material, once the police officer is lawfully present on premises (for example, having obtained a warrant from a magistrate under section 9 of the 1984 Act) she may seize anything on the premises which is evidence of the offence which she is investigating or of another offence, under section 19 of the Police and Criminal Evidence Act 1984.

Other statutes requiring information to be notified includes the Abortion Act 1967 see Abortion Regulations 1991, S.I. (1991) No. 499 and the Human Organ Transplants Act 1989, s.3, Human Organ Transplants (Supply of Information) Regulations 1989 S.I. (1989) No. 2108, Mental Health Act 1982, s.13(2), Public Health (Control of Disease) Act 1984 and Public Health (Infectious Disease) Regulations 1988.

8.   DISCLOSURE AND JUDICIAL PROCEEDINGS

Hunter v. Mann [1974] 2 All E.R. 414, [1974] Q.B. 767, [1974] 2 W.L.R. 742.

A car, taken without the owner's consent, was involved in an accident. After the accident both the driver and passenger left the scene and could not be traced. Later that day a doctor treated a man and a woman for injuries. The woman said that they had been involved in a car accident. The police later approached the doctor and asked for the names of those who had been treated. Section 168(3) of the Road Traffic Act 1972 provided that —

"Where the driver of a vehicle is alleged to be guilty of an offence to which this section applies.

    (b) any other person shall be required as aforesaid give any information which is in his power to give and which may lead to the identification of the driver.

BOREHAM J.:

" . . . The contentions of counsel for the appellant are directed towards a construction of section 168. His first contention is this. He says that the appellant does not fall within the limits of the expression in subsection (2)(b) 'any other person'. He says, and this is the basis of his submission on this aspect of the case, that it would not be right in the circumstances to give an unrestricted meaning to those words so as to include everyone except the driver or the keeper of the vehicle. He says that it would be wrong to give those words so unrestricted a meaning as to cause a doctor, or, as I understand it, any other professional man who stands in relation to his clients or patients in a position similar to a doctor, to act in breach of the duty of confidentiality on which a doctor's patient is entitled to rely.

He puts forward in support of that contention three propositions. He says first of all, and in effect this is a concession, that there is no absolute privilege in judicial proceedings for a doctor in respect of the disclosure of confidential information which was obtained by him in the course of his professional relationship with his patient. For my part at any rate I need no authority for that proposition; I accept it. The second proposition is this: that in common with other professional men, for instance a priest and there are of course others, the doctor is under a duty not to disclose, without the consent of his patient, information which he, the doctor, has gained in his professional capacity, save, says counsel for the appellant, in very exceptional circumstances. He quoted the example of the murderer still manic, who would be a menace to society. But, says counsel, save in such exceptional circumstances, the general rule applies. He adds that the law will enforce that duty.

I would accept that proposition if before the word 'disclosing' there were to be added the adverb 'voluntarily', as in the British Medical Association's handbook. I accept too counsel's cited authority for the proposition that the duty not to disclose information is enforceable at the behest of the patient in an action of contract or for breach of duty. But for my part at any rate I do not consider that that proposition covers the position where the doctor is compelled by law to disclose. In my judgment counsel for the appellant's second proposition relates only to voluntary disclosure. The third proposition is that protection is given to professional confidences to the extent that those who are bound by them are not ordinarily required to breach them and will only be compelled to do so by the order of a judge. Again counsel for the appellant has quoted authorities. I hope it will not indicate any lack of respect for him or for the authorities that he quoted if I do not cite them at this stage.

I would prefer to put the proposition in another way. I accept that the doctor, in accordance with the first proposition, has no right to refuse to disclose confidential information in the course of judicial or quasi-judicial proceedings; but I also accept that the judge in certain circumstances, and in the exercise of his, the judge's, judicial discretion, may refuse to compel him to do so. Further than this, in my judgment, the authorities which have been cited to us do not go. Moreover each one of those authorities was concerned with legal proceedings. In the present case it is important to bear in mind the distinction between privilege which is to be claimed in legal proceedings and a contractual duty not to disclose; that distinction is marked by a passage in the judgment of Diplock L.J. in *Parry-Jones v. the Law Society* [1968] 1 All E.R. 171 at 180,

'So far as the plaintiff's point as to privilege is concerned, privilege is irrelevant when one is not concerned with judicial or quasi-judicial proceedings because, strictly speaking, privilege refers to a right to withhold from a court, or a tribunal exercising judicial functions, material which would otherwise be admissible in evidence. What we are concerned with here is the contractual duty of confidence, generally implied though sometimes expressed, between a solicitor and client. Such a duty exists not only between solicitor and client, but, for example, between banker and customer, doctor and patient, and accountant and client. Such a duty of confidence is subject to, and overridden by, the duty of any party to that contract to comply with the law of the land. If it is the duty of such a party to a contract, whether at common law or under statute, to disclose in defined circumstances confidential information, then he must do so, and any express contract to the contrary would be illegal and void.'

With those words in mind I proceed to the conclusion drawn by counsel for the appellant from his contentions. He says that when one comes to construe the statute one should approach it thus; that Parliament must not be taken to have overridden or to have attempted to override the duty of confidence to which reference has been made, except by clear language or necessary implication. He says, and this is the burden of his whole contention, that 'any other person' in section 168 must be read in a restricted way so that that duty is not breached . . .

It seems to me that my first duty is to look at the section and give the words their ordinary natural meaning, and in the absence of equivocation or ambiguity to give effect to such meaning, unless of course there is something in the context of the section or of the Act itself which suggests that a special or restricted meaning should be given.

For my part I cannot find any ground for saying that a restricted meaning should be given. I find the words clear and unequivocal. I accept, as counsel for the appellant has suggested, that one should assume that Parliament has passed this Act, and this section in particular, with the existing law in mind. Accepting that, then it seems to me that Parliament must have been conscious of the use of very wide words here and, if it had been intended to create exceptions, it would have been easy enough to do so. It has not been done. Moreover I ask myself the question: if there is to be a restriction how far is it to go? Where is it to stop? I find it impossible to provide an answer to that question. In these circumstances I am driven to the conclusion that a doctor acting within his professional capacity, and carrying out his professional duties and responsibilities, is within the words 'any other person' in section 168(2)(b).

The next limb of counsel for the appellant's argument was directed to the words 'in his power' in the expression 'information which it is in his power to give'. He contends that power must include a legal right, that there is no legal right or power to disclose so far as a doctor is concerned and, therefore, that he is not caught by those words.

I am not going to attempt to define 'power'. It seems to me a word of fairly common understanding and reading it in its ordinary way I have no difficulty in coming to the conclusion that a doctor in the circumstances in which the appellant found himself had the power. It may be that but for the section in the Act he would not have exercised that power because of his duty to his patient, but that seems to me to beg the question, for that would have been in accordance with his duty not to make voluntary disclosure. Once it is decided that the appellant is a person to whom the statutory duty imposed by section 168 applies, then I have no doubt that he had the power. I think it would be no injustice to counsel for the appellant to say that this was the least strenuously argued of his points and I find it a point without substance.

In my view it is important when one is considering this section to have in mind that on many occasions serious accidents are caused by people who take away, without consent, other people's motor cars and who have no hesitation in leaving the scene as quickly as they possibly can so as to avoid detection. I therefore find it a comfort to think that the section gives the police a wide power for the purpose of detecting people who may cause damage to others.

May I say, before leaving this case, that I appreciate the concern of a responsible medical practitioner who feels that he is faced with a conflict of duty. That the appellant in this case was conscious of a conflict and realised his duty both to society and to his patient is clear from the finding of the justices, but he may find comfort, although the decision goes against him, from the following. First that he has only to disclose information which may lead to identification and not other confidential matters; secondly that the result, in my judgment, is entirely consistent with the rules that the British Medical Association have laid down . . ."

LORD WIDGERY C.J.:
". . . I agree also. With all deference to counsel for the appellant's argument, I felt that he was claiming a degree of medical confidence wider than that which his authorities would support. I would compliment the authors of the British Medical Association handbook to which reference has already been made, for a brief and, I think, effective statement of the position. I repeat it:
'A doctor should refrain from disclosing voluntarily to a third party information which he has learnt professionally or indirectly in his professional relationship with a patient, subject to exceptions, including the following . . .
    (2) the information is required by law.'
I would add one other point, namely, that if a doctor, giving evidence in court, is asked a question which he finds embarassing because it involves him talking about things which he would normally regard as confidential, he can seek the protection of the judge and ask the judge if it is necessary for him to answer. The judge, by virtue of the overriding discretion to control his court which all English judges have, can, if he thinks fit, tell the doctor that he need not answer the question. Whether or not the judge would take that line, of course, depends largely on the importance of the potential answer to the issues being tried."

NOTES:

1. The English courts have consistently rejected suggestions that a privilege be introduced allowing doctors to refuse to disclose confidential health information. (*Duchess of Kingston's case* (1776) 20 State Trials 355, and see J. V. McHale *Medical Confidentiality and Legal Privilege* London: Routledge, 1993). It also appears that the remedy of breach of confidence may not be used to restrain the disclosure of confidential information in a court of law (See P. Matthews "Legal Privilege and Breach of Confidence" (1980) 1 *Legal Studies* 77.)

2. Medical information may, however, be withheld from disclosure prior to or during a trial if protected by legal professional privilege or public interest immunity. Legal professional privilege protects information passed between lawyer and client. Public interest immunity is the term used to describe exclusion of evidence on public policy grounds. In *Morrow and Others v. DPP* (1993) 14 B.M.L.R. 54 abortion protestors were prosecuted under the Public Order Act 1986. They claimed in their defence that they had honestly believed that illegal abortions were to be undertaken at the Centre where they were protesting. They applied for production by the British Pregnancy Advisory Service of information relating to all the abortions which were to be undertaken that day at that clinic. This application was rejected. The judge held

that there was a strong public interest in maintaining confidentiality, illustrated by specific provisions contained in the Abortion Act 1967 and Abortion Regulations 1968. Disclosure of the documents was not essential to the defence — there was no need to show that the abortions which were to be undertaken were illegal — only that the defendant thought that they were. (For the operation of public interest immunity in relation to civil proceedings—see below at pages 495–496 and see C. Tapper (ed.) *Cross on Evidence*, (8th edn., 1995) London: Butterworths, Chapter XII.)

9. ACCESS TO HEALTH RECORDS

For many years the medical profession resisted calls for patients to be given rights of access to their medical records. It was argued that to allow the patient unrestricted access to his records may lead to harm because he may misunderstand their contents. In addition, if a doctor knew that the patient had a right of access this could result in the doctor being less candid in the information which is included in the record. However, others opposed these views. They argued that access could be regarded as part of recognising patient autonomy. Some health professionals also believed that disclosure could assist in patients decision-making.

In the past the Department of Health was of the view that records were the property of the health authority, with general practice records being owned by the Family Health Service Authority. The current position is uncertain in the light of the NHS reorganisation which took place in 1996 (see Chapter 1 above). While the patient does not appear to have rights of ownership, he does have various rights of control over access to records, through the action of breach of confidence and through statutory rights of access to the contents of his own records.

The Patient's Charter now notes the right to have access to one's own health records. The catalyst to change in the policy of access to patient records was the Data Protection Act 1984. This Act gives rights of access to information held on computer. A number of statutes following this legislation widened the rights of access to health care records culminating in the Access to Health Records Act 1990. However, none of these statutory rights are absolute in nature. A standard limitation is that access may be withheld where disclosure of the information may be harmful to the physical/mental health of the patient or would involve revealing details concerning the health of others. (See M. Gilhooley and S. M. McGhee "Medical records; practicalities and principles of patient possession" (1991) 17 *Journal of Medical Ethics* 138.)

(a) Health Care Records held on Computer

The Data Protection Act 1984 governs records held on computer. It provides certain safeguards for patient information. The operation of the legislation is overseen by the Data Protection Registrar. The legislation requires that persons who hold personal data on computer should register this information with the Data Protection Registrar (section 4(1)). The registration period lasts for three years (section 8(2)). Data users are required to comply with what are known as the "Data Protection principles". Information may be disclosed by the data user to persons named as recipients of such information when he registered as a data user. Unauthorised disclosure to persons other than registered recipients is a criminal offence (Data Protection Act 1984, s.5(5)).

Data Protection Act 1984, s.21(1–9)

21.—(1) Subject to the provisions of this section, an individual shall be entitled —

(a) to be informed by any data user whether the data held by him include personal data of which that individual is the data subject; and
(b) to be supplied by any data user with a copy of the information constituting any such personal data held by him;
and where any of the information referred to in paragraph (b) above is expressed in terms which are not intelligible without explanation the information shall be accompanied by an explanation of those terms.

(2) A data user shall not be obliged to supply any information under subsection (1) above except in response to a request in writing and on payment of such fee (not exceeding the prescribed maximum) as he may require; but a request for information under both paragraphs of that subsection shall be treated as a single request and a request for information under paragraph (a) shall, in the absence of any indication to the contrary, be treated as extending also to information under paragraph (b).

(3) In the case of a data user having separate entries in the register in respect of data held for different purposes a separate request must be made and a separate fee paid under this section in respect of the data to which each entry relates.

(4) A data user shall not be obliged to comply with a request under this section —

(a) unless he is supplied with such information as he may reasonably request in order to satisfy himself as to the identity of the person making the request and to locate the information which he seeks; and
(b) if he cannot comply with the request without disclosing information relating to another individual who can be identified from that information, unless he is satisfied that the other individual has consented to the disclosure of the information to the person making the request.

(5) In paragraph (b) of subsection (4) above the reference to information relating to another individual includes a reference to information identifying that individual as the source of the information sought by the request; and that paragraph shall not be construed as excusing a data user from supplying so much of the information sought by the request as can be supplied without disclosing the identity of the other individual concerned, whether by the omission of names or other identifying particulars or otherwise.

(6) A data user shall comply with a request under this section within forty days of receiving the request or, if later, receiving the information referred to in paragraph (a) of subsection (4) above and, in a case where it is required, the consent referred to in paragraph (b) of that subsection.

(7) The information to be supplied pursuant to a request under this section shall be supplied by reference to the data in question at the time when the request is received except that it may take account of any amendment or deletion made between that time and the time when the information is supplied, being an amendment or deletion that would have been made regardless of the receipt of the request.

(8) If a court is satisfied on the application of any person who has made a request under the foregoing provisions of this section that the data user in question has failed to comply with the request in contravention of those provisions, the court may order him to comply with the request; but a court shall not make an order under this subsection if it considers that it would in all the circumstances be unreasonable to do so, whether because of the frequency with which the applicant has made requests to the data user under those provisions or for any other reason.

(9) The Secretary of State may by order provide for enabling a request under this section to be made on behalf of any individual who is incapable by reason of mental disorder of managing his own affairs.

Rights of Access under the 1984 Act are not absolute in nature

Data Protection (Subject Access Modification) (Health) Order, art. 3(1–2), art. 4(1–6)

3.—(1) This Order applies to personal data consisting of information as to the physical or mental health of the data subject if —

(a) the data are held by a health professional; or
(b) the data are held by a person other than a health professional but the information constituting the data was first recorded by or on behalf of a health professional.

(2) This Order is without prejudice to any exemption from the subject access provisions contained in any provision of the Act or of any Order made under the Act.

4.—(1) The subject access provisions shall not have effect in relation to any personal data to which this Order applies in any case where either of the requirements specified in paragraph (2) below is satisfied with respect to the information constituting the data and the obligations contained in paragraph (5) below are complied with by the data user.

(2) The requirements referred to in paragraph (1) above are that the application of the subject access provisions —

(a) would be likely to cause serious harm to the physical or mental health of the data subject; or
(b) would be likely to disclose to the data subject the identity of another individual(who has not consented to the disclosure of the information) either as a person to whom the information or part of it relates or as the source of the information or enable that identity to be deduced by the data subject either from the information itself or from a combination of that information and other information which the data subject has or is likely to have.

(3) Paragraph (2) above shall not be construed as excusing a data user —

(a) from supplying the information sought by the request for subject access where the only individual whose identity is likely to be disclosed or deduced as mentioned in sub-paragraph (b) thereof is a health professional who has been involved in the care of the data subject and the information relates to him or he supplied the information in his capacity as a health professional; or

(b) from supplying so much of the information sought by the request as can be supplied without causing serious harm as mentioned in sub-paragraph (a) thereof or enabling the identity of another individual to be disclosed or deduced as mentioned in sub-paragraph (b) thereof, whether by the omission of names or other particulars or otherwise.

(4) In relation to data to which this Order applies, section 21 of the Act shall have effect as if subsections (4)(b) and (5) were omitted and as if the reference in subsection (6) to the consent referred to in the said section 21 (4)(b) were a reference to the consent referred to in paragraph (2)(b) above.

(5) A data user who is not a health professional shall not supply information constituting data to which this Order applies in response to a request under section 21 and shall not withhold any such information on the ground that one of the requirements specified in paragraph (2) above is satisfied with respect to the information unless the data user has first consulted the person who appears to the data user to be the appropriate health professional on the question whether either or both of those requirements is or are so satisfied.

(6) In paragraph (5) above 'the appropriate health professional' means – –

(a) the medical practitioner or dental practitioner who is currently or was most recently responsible for the clinical care of the data subject in connection with the matters to which the information which is the subject of the request relates; or

(b) where there is more than one such practitioner, the practitioner who is the most suitable to advise on the matters to which the information which is the subject of the request relates; or

(c) where there is no practitioner available falling within sub-paragraph (a) or (b) above, a health professional who has the necessary experience and qualifications to advise on the matters to which the information which is the subject of the request relates.

NOTES:

1. The 1984 Act allows access to health information which is held by a wide variety of health professionals, including doctors, dentists, nurses, pharmaceutical chemists, dieticians, occupational therapists and osteopaths.
2. The Act allows for damages to be awarded where the data held is inaccurate and also for rectification of the data held (sections 22–4).
3. It is a defence to establish that reasonable care had been taken to ensure the accuracy of the data: s.22(3).
4. The NHS is establishing a "NHS Wide Network" of computer access. The Data Protection Registrar has expressed her concern regarding data security in relation to computer networks: *Twelth Annual Report of Data Protection Registrar* (London: HMSO 1996).

(b) Access to Personal Files Act 1987

This Act allows access to certain files held by housing authorities and local authorities. These files may include information relating to health records.

Regulations provide for a right of access to information if an application is made in writing and contains sufficient information to allow the individual to be identified. If the person disagrees with information held, she may ask for it to be rectified and if the authority rejects rectification then a notice regarding the individual's objections should be put in the files. A person who is aggrieved by the decision of the authority can apply to have this decision reviewed by a committee of three members of the authority. Regulations allow the information to be withheld in certain situations, namely if the disclosure is likely to cause serious harm to the health of the person requesting the information or to another person, or if disclosure of the information would lead to the identification of third parties who have supplied the information. (Access to Personal Files (Social Services) Regulation 1989, S.I. 1989 No. 206 and Access to Personal Files (Housing) Regulations, S.I. 1989 No. 503).

(c) Access to Medical Reports Act 1988, s.2(1), s.3(1–2), s.4(1–4),
s.5(1–2), s.6(1–3), s.7(1–4)

This Act allows individuals a statutory right of access to medical records compiled for employment/insurance purposes.

2.—(1) In this Act —
"the applicant" means the person referred to in section 3(1) below;
"care" includes examination, investigation or diagnosis for the purposes of, or in connection with, any form of medical treatment;
"employment purposes", in the case of any individual, means the purposes in relation to the individual of any person by whom he is or has been, or is seeking to be, employed (whether under a contract of service or otherwise);
"health professional" has the same meaning as in the Data Protection (Subject Access Modification) (Health) Order 1987;
"insurance purposes", in the case of any individual, means the purposes in relation to the individual of any person carrying on an insurance business with whom the individual has entered into, or is seeking to enter into, a contract of insurance, and "insurance business" and "contract of insurance" have the same meaning as in the Insurance Companies Act 1982;
"medical practitioner" means a person registered under the Medical Act 1983;
"medical report", in the case of an individual, means a report relating to the physical or mental health of the individual prepared by a medical practitioner who is or has been responsible for the clinical care of the individual.
3.—(1) A person shall not apply to a medical practitioner for a medical report relating to any individual to be supplied to him for employment or insurance purposes unless —

(a) that person ("the applicant") has notified the individual that he proposes to make the application; and
(b) the individual has notified the applicant that he consents to the making of the application.

(2) Any notification given under subsection (1)(a) above must inform the individual of his right to withhold his consent to the making of the following rights under this Act, namely —

(a) the rights arising under sections 4(1) to (3) and 6(2) below with respect to access to the report before or after it is supplied,

(b) the right to withhold consent under subsection (1) of section 5 below, and

(c) the right to request the amendment of the report under subsection (2) of that section, as well as of the effect of section 7 below.

4.—(1) An individual who gives his consent under section 3 above to the making of an application shall be entitled, when giving his consent, to state that he wishes to have access to the report to be supplied in response to the application before it is so supplied; and, if he does so, the applicant shall —

(a) notify the medical practitioner of that fact at the time when the application is made, and (b) at the same time notify the individual of the making of the application; and each such notification shall contain a statement of the effect of subsection (2) below

(2) Where a medical practitioner is notified by the applicant under subsection (1) above that the individual in question wishes to have access to the report before it is supplied, the practitioner shall not supply the report unless —

(a) he has given the individual access to it and any requirements of section 5 below have been complied with, or

(b) the period of 21 days beginning with the date of the making of the application has elapsed without his having received any communication from the individual concerning arrangements for the individual to have access to it.

(3) Where a medical practitioner —

(a) receives an application for a medical report to be supplied for employment or insurance purposes without being notified by the applicant as mentioned in subsection (1) above, but

(b) before supplying the report receives a notification from the individual that he wishes to have access to the report before it is supplied, the practitioner shall not supply the report unless:
    (i) he has given the individual access to it and any requirements of section 5 below have been complied with, or
    (ii) the period of 21 days beginning with the date of that notification has elapsed without his having received (either with that notification or otherwise) any communication from the individual concerning arrangements for the individual to have access to it.

(4) References in this section and section 5 below to giving an individual access to a medical report are references to —

(a) making the report or a copy of it available for his inspection; or

(b) supplying him with a copy of it;

and where a copy is supplied at the request, or otherwise with the consent, of the individual the practitioner may charge a reasonable fee to cover the costs of supplying it.

5.—(1) Where an individual has been given access to a report under section 4 above the report shall not be supplied in response to the application in question unless the individual has notified the medical practitioner that he consents to its being so supplied.

(2) The individual shall be entitled, before giving his consent under subsection (1) above, to request the medical practitioner to amend any part of the report which the individual considers to be incorrect or misleading; and, if the individual does so, the practitioner —

(a) if he is to any extent prepared to accede to the individual's request, shall amend the report accordingly;

(b) if he is to any extent not prepared to accede to it but the individual requests him to attach to the report a statement of the individual's views in respect of any part of the report which he is declining to amend, shall attach such a statement to the report.

(3) Any request made by an individual under subsection (2) above shall be made in writing.

6.—(1) A copy of any medical report which a medical practitioner has supplied for employment or insurance purposes shall be retained by him for at least six months from the date on which it was supplied.

(2) A medical practitioner shall, if so requested by an individual, give the individual access to any medical report relating to him which the practitioner has supplied for employment or insurance purposes in the previous six months.

(3) The reference in subsection (2) above to giving an individual access to a medical report is a reference to —

(a) making a copy of the report available for his inspection; or

(b) supplying him with a copy of it;

and where a copy is supplied at the request, or otherwise with the consent, of the individual the practitioner may charge a reasonable fee to cover the costs of supplying it.

7.—(1) A medical practitioner shall not be obliged to give an individual access, in accordance with the provisions of section 4(4) or 6(3) above, to any part of a medical report whose disclosure would in the opinion of the practitioner be likely to cause serious harm to the physical or mental health of the individual or others or would indicate the intentions of the practitioner in respect of the individual.

(2) A medical practitioner shall not be obliged to give an individual access, in accordance with those provisions, to any part of a medical report whose disclosure would be likely to reveal information about another person, or to reveal the identity of another person who has supplied information to the practitioner about the individual, unless —

(a) that person has consented; or

(b) that person is a health professional who has been involved in the care of the individual and the information relates to or has been provided by the professional in that capacity.

(3) Where it appears to a medical practitioner that subsection (1) or (2) above is applicable to any part (but not the whole) of a medical report —

(a) he shall notify the individual of that fact; and

(b) references in the preceding sections of this Act to the individual being given access to the report shall be construed as references to his being given access to the remainder of it;

and other references to the report in sections 4(4), 5(2) and 6(3) above shall similarly be construed as references to the remainder of the report.

(4) Where it appears to a medical practitioner that subsection (1) or (2) above is applicable to the whole of a medical report —

(a) he shall notify the individual of that fact; but

(b) he shall not supply the report unless he is notified by the individual that the individual consents to its being supplied;

and accordingly, if he is so notified by the individual, the restrictions imposed by section 4(2) and (3) above on the supply of the report shall not have effect in relation to it.

NOTES:

1. A doctor may withold information if it may cause serious harm to a person's physical or mental health and it would reveal a practitioner's intentions towards his patient.
2. A person may be ordered by a court to comply with the Act (section 8).
3. A medical practitioner is not obliged to inform the patient of the fact that the contents of any report compiled might be serious or damaging to the patient (See H.C., Vol. 127, cols. 660–661).
4. Recently there has been considerable debate as to whether information that an individual has taken a HIV test should be withheld from his insurers. Evidence emerged that a positive answer to the question on an insurance form "have you ever had a HIV test" may lead to denial of insurance, although by taking the test itself an individual was not indicating that he had tested positive. The insurance industry have now indicated that such questions should be withdrawn. (See P. Roth and W. Gryk, "Aids and Insurance" in R. Haigh and D. Harris (eds) *AIDS and the Law*, London: Routledge, 1995, at page 96.) Should a medical practitioner be entitled to refuse to disclose such information on a medical report?
5. A further debate has arisen as to whether an individual is entitled to withhold from his medical report any information concerning a genetic screening test which he may have undertaken (see Nuffield Council on Bioethics Report *Genetic Screening*, 1993, Chapter 7). This is particularly problematic because even though an individual may have tested positive that does not necessarily mean that he will actually develop that condition; it may mean simply that he has an increased chance of developing a particular illness. This problem is likely to become acute in the future as testing becomes increasingly common. Discussions are currently being undertaken between the insurance industry and the government as to what information gained through genetic testing should be disclosed (see further on this issue J. Harris, *Wonderwoman and Superman*, Oxford: OUP, 1992, Chapter 10 and Science and Technology Committee, *Human Genetics: The Science and Its Consequences*, Third Report, H.C. 41–1 (1995), para. 243–250).

QUESTIONS:

1. Are reports which are compiled solely for the purposes of insurance within the provisions of the Act?
2. The Act refers to doctors who have the "clinical care" of the patient? Does this include occupational health physicians? (See J. Montgomery "Access to Medical Reports Act 1988" (1989) *Journal of Social Welfare Law* 129 at page 130.)

(d) Health Care Records Held as Manual Files

The Access to Health Records Act 1990 allows patients to gain access to their medical information where this is held on manual files. At present in contrast to the Data Protection Act, access to manual records is not overseen by an independent officer, such as the Data Protection registrar. This position may, however, change in the future. A recent E.U. directive (E.U. Directive 95/46/E.C.) has indicated that similar safeguards should be provided to data held on manual files as to data held on computer. Although it appears that the U.K. will not require manual records to be registered in the same form as computer records, some new requirements will be imposed upon holders of manual records. For example, the requirement that such manual data be processed fairly and lawfully and in a manner compatible with specified (Article 6) operations of the directive is to be under the supervision of the Data Protection Registrar. The Registrar will have powers to hear complaints from the subjects of manually held records as to their use. (See D. Bainbridge and G. Pearce, "Manual Processing, Access, Exemptions and the Registrar" (1995) *N.L.J.* 1656 and Data Protection Registrar *Questions to Answer: Data Protection and the E.U. Directive 95/46/E.C.* Wilmslow: Office of the Data Protection Registrar (1996)).

Access to manual records compiled by health professionals (including doctors, dentists and chemists) is provided under the 1990 Act:

Access to Health Records Act 1990, s.1(1–3), s.3(1–6), s.4(1–3),
s.5(1–5), s.7(1–3)

1.—(1) In this Act "health record" means a record which —

(a) consists of information relating to the physical or mental health of an individual who can be identified from that information, or from that and other information in the possession of the record; and
(b) has been made by or on behalf of a health professional in connection with the care of the individual;

but does not include any record which consists of information of which the individual is, or but for any exemption would be, entitled to be supplied with a copy under section 21 of the Data Protection Act 1984 (right of access to personal data).

(2) In this Act "holder", in relation to a health record, means:

(a) in the case of a record made by, or by a health professional employed by, a general practitioner —
    (i) the patient's general practitioner, that is to say the general practitioner on whose list the patient is included; or
    (ii) where the patient has no general practitioner, the Health Authority or Health Board on whose medical list the patient's most recent general practitioner was included;
(b) in the case of a record made by a health professional for purposes connected with the provision of health services by a health service body, the health service body by which or on whose behalf the record is held;

(c) in any other case, the health professional by whom or on whose behalf the record is held;

(3) In this Act "patient", in relation to a health record, means the individual in connection with whose care the record has been made.

3.—(1) An application for access to a health record, or to any part of a health record, may be made to the holder of the record by any of the following, namely —

(a) the patient;

(b) a person authorised in writing to make the application on the patient's behalf;

(c) where the record is held in England and Wales and the patient is a child, a person having parental responsibility for the patient;

(d) where the record is held in Scotland and the patient is a pupil, a parent or guardian of the patient;

(e) where the patient is incapable of managing his own affairs, any person appointed by a court to manage those affairs; and

(f) where the patient has died, the patient's personal representative and any person who may have a claim arising out of the patient's death.

(2) Subject to section 4 below, where an application is made under subsection (1) above the holder shall, within the requisite period, give access to the record, or the part of a record, to which the application relates —

(a) in the case of a record, by allowing the applicant to inspect the record or, where section 5 below applies, an extract setting out so much of the record as is not excluded by that section;

(b) in the case of a part of a record, by allowing the applicant to inspect an extract setting out that part or, where that section applies, so much of that part as is not so excluded; or

(c) in either case, if the applicant so requires, by supplying him with a copy of the record or extract.

(3) Where any information contained in a record or extract which is so allowed to be inspected, or a copy of which is so supplied, is expressed in terms which are not intelligible without explanation, an explanation of those terms shall be provided with the record or extract, or supplied with the copy.

(4) No fee shall be required for giving access under subsection (2) above other than the following, namely —

(a) where access is given to a record, or part of a record, none of which was made after the beginning of the period of 40 days immediately preceding the date of the application, a fee not exceeding the maximum prescribed under section 21 of the Data Protection Act 1984; and

(b) where a copy of a record or extract is supplied to the applicant, a fee not exceeding the cost of making the copy and (where applicable) the cost of posting it to him.

(5) For the purposes of subsection (2) above the requisite period is —

(a) where the application relates to a record, or part of a record, none of which was made before the beginning of the period of 40 days immediately preceding the date of the application, the period of 21 days beginning with that date;

(b) in any other case, the period of 40 days beginning with that date.

(6) Where —

(a) an application under subsection (1) above does not contain sufficient information to enable the holder of the record to identify the patient or, in the case of an application made otherwise than by the patient, to satisfy himself that the applicant is entitled to make the application; and
(b) within the period of 14 days beginning with the date of the application, the holder of the record requests the applicant to furnish him with such further information as he may reasonably require for that purpose,

subsection (5) above shall have effect as if for any reference to that date there were substituted a reference to the date on which that further information is so furnished.

4.—(1) Where an application is made under subsection (1)(a) or (b) section 3 above and

(a) in the case of a record held in England and Wales, the patient is a child; or
(b) in the case of a record held in Scotland, the patient is a pupil,

access shall not be given under subsection (2) of that section unless the holder of the record is satisfied that the patient is capable of understanding the nature of the application.

(2) Where an application is made under subsection (1)(c) or (d) of section 3 above, access shall not be given under subsection (2) of that section unless the holder of the record is satisfied either —

(a) that the patient has consented to the making of the application; or
(b) that the patient is incapable of understanding the nature of the application and the giving of access would be in his best interests.

(3) Where an application is made under subsection (1)(f) of section 3 above, access shall not be given under subsection (2) of that section if the record includes a note, made at the patient's request, that he did not wish access to be given on such an application.

5.—(1) Access shall not be given under section 3(2) above to any part of a health record —

(a) which, in the opinion of the holder of the record, would disclose:
    (i) information likely to cause serious harm to the physical or mental health of the patient or of any other individual; or
    (ii) information relating to or provided by an individual, other than the patient, who could be identified from that information; or
(b) which was made before the commencement of this Act.

(2) Subsection (1)(a)(ii) above shall not apply —

(a) where the individual concerned has consented to the application; or
(b) where that individual is a health professional who has been involved in the care of a patient;

and subsection (1)(b) above shall not apply where and to the extent that, in the opinion of the holder of the record, the giving of access is necessary in order to make intelligible any part of the record to which access is required to given under section 3(2) above

(3) Where an application is made under subsection (1)(c), (d), (e) or (f) of section 3 above, access shall not be given under subsection (2) of that section to any part of the record which, in the opinion of the holder of the record, would disclose -

(a) information provided by the patient in the expectation that it would not be disclosed to the applicant; or

(b) information obtained as a result of any examination or investigation to which the patient consented in the expectation that the information would not be so disclosed.

(4) Where an application is made under subsection (1)(f) of section 3 above, access shall not be given under subsection (2) of that section to any part of the record which, in the opinion of the holder of the record, would disclose information which is not relevant to any claim which may arise out of the patient's death.

(5) The Secretary of State may by regulations provide that, in such circumstances as may be prescribed by the regulations, access shall not be given under section 3(2) above to any part of a health record which satisfies such conditions as may be so prescribed.

7.—(1) A health service body or Health Authority shall take advice from the appropriate health professional before they decide whether they are satisfied as to any matter for the purposes of this Act, or form an opinion as to any matter for those purposes.

(2) In this section "the appropriate health professional", in relation to a health service body (other than a Health Authority or Health Board which is the holder of the record by virtue of section 1(2)(a) above), means —

(a) where, for purposes connected with the provision of health services by the body, one or more medical or dental practitioners are currently responsible for the clinical care of the patient, that practitioner or, as the case may be, such one of those practitioners as is the most suitable to advise the body on the matter in question;

(b) where paragraph (a) above does not apply but one or more medical or dental practitioners are available who, for purposes connected with the provision of such services by the body, have been responsible for the clinical care of the patient, that practitioner or, as the case may be, such one of those practitioners as was most recently so responsible; and

(c) where neither paragraph (a) nor paragraph (b) above applies, a health professional who has the necessary experience and qualifications to advise the body on the matter in question.

(3) In this section 'the appropriate health professional', in relation to a Health Authority or a Health Board which is the holder of the record by virtue of section 1(2)(a) above), means:

(a) where the patient's most recent general practitioner is available, that practitioner; and

(b) where that practitioner is not available, a registered medical practitioner who has the necessary experience and qualifications to advise the Board on the matter in question.

NOTES:

1. A child patient has a right of access to medical records if capable of understanding the application (section 4). Where an application is made on behalf of a child by a person with parental responsibility access may only be granted if either, the patient has consented or, where the child is incapable of giving consent, disclosure is in the

child's best interests (section 4(2)). In the latter situation information may still be withheld if, for example, if it records a doctor's concerns regarding parental care.

2. While an application may be made after a patient's death for disclosure of the patient's records no information may be disclosed if the patient has made an explicit request that he does not want the information disclosed (section 4(3)).

3. If a patient disagrees with an entry in his records then he may apply under section 6 for those records to be corrected. If the holder does not agree then she may refuse to amend the records but she must note the informant's views in the records and provide the patient with a copy.

4. The Act only grants access to medical records compiled after November 1, 1991. This means that in some situations it may be important for the applicant to establish a right of access at common law. (See below at page 496.)

5. The only remedy available under the Act is through an application to the High Court under section 8(1) to require that the 1990 Act has been complied with, *cf.* Data Protection Act 1984 above.

6. A fee may be charged for access to records. At present this is £10.

QUESTION:

1. What amounts to a record "made in connection with that patient's clinical care" under section 1(1)? (See C. Newdick, *Who Should We Treat?* Oxford: OUP, 1995, at page 236).

(e) Disclosure of Medical Records as a Preliminary to Legal Proceedings

Supreme Court Act 1981, s.34(1–4)

34.—(1) This section applies to any proceedings in the High Court in which a claim is made in respect of personal injuries to a person, or in respect of a person's death.

(2) On the application, in accordance with rules of court, of a party to any proceedings to which this section applies, the High Court shall, in such circumstances as may be specified in the rules, have power to order a person who is not a party to the proceedings and who appears to the court to be likely to have in his possession, custody or power any documents which are relevant to an issues arising out of the said claim —

(a) to disclose whether those documents are in his possession, custody or power;
(b) to produce such of those documents as are in his possession, custody or power to the applicant or, on such conditions as may be specified in the order:
  (i) to the applicant's legal advisers; or
  (ii) to the applicant's legal advisers and any medical or other professional adviser of the applicant; or
  (iii) if the applicant has no legal adviser, to any medical or other professional adviser of the applicant.

(3) On the application, in accordance with rules of court, of a party to any proceedings to which this section applies, the High Court shall, in such circumstances as may be specified in the rules, have power to make an order providing for any one or more of the following matters, that is to say —

(a) the inspection, photographing, preservation, custody and detention of property which is not the property of, or in the possession of, any party to the proceedings but which is the subject-matter of the proceedings or as to which any question arises in the proceedings;
(b) the taking of samples of any such property as is mentioned in paragraph (a) and the carrying out of any experiment on or which any such property.

(4) The preceding provisions of this section are without prejudice to the exercise by the High Court of any power to make orders which is exercisable apart from those provisions.

Provisions supplementary to sections 33 and 34

(1) The High Court shall not make an order under section 33 or 34 if it considers that compliance with the order, if made, would be likely to be injurious to the public interest.
(5) In Sections 32A, 33 and 34 and this section:
"property" includes any land, chattel or other corporeal property of any description;
"personal injuries" includes any disease and any impairment of a person's physical or mental condition

NOTES:

1. Although today the Access to Health Records Act 1990 enables the disclosure of many documents required for the purposes of litigation there may be circumstances in which it is sought to use section 31. Some health records are not compiled as part of "clinical care" and thus would fall outside the 1990 Act. Secondly, the 1990 Act applies only to those manual records created *after* November 1, 1991. Third, while information may be witheld under the 1990 Act on the basis that disclosure may cause serious physical or mental harm to the patient there are no such limitations upon disclosure under the 1981 Act. (See generally M. Jones *Medical Negligence* (2nd ed.), London: Sweet and Maxwell, 1996, at page 555.)
2. As a general rule, full disclosure of experts' reports prior to trial will be ordered. In *Naylor v. Preston AHA* [1987] 2 All E.R. 353 criticism was made of the approach taken in the *Wilsher* case in which it was stated that the earlier case was "fought in the dark" (see Chapter 3 above). R.S.C. Ord. 38 r.37 makes disclosure of expert evidence the norm, exceptions to this rule suggested in *Naylor* would be situations in which the particulars of negligence were inherently vague. Rules developed since *Naylor* support broader disclosure. For example, R.S.C. Ord. 38 r.2a(2) enables the court, at any stage in proceedings to order a party to serve on another a written summary of oral

evidence which they intend to use. The courts have indicated that disclosure should not be delayed in medical negligence cases (*Hall v. Wandsworth HA* (1985) 129 *S.J.* 181).

3. In both civil and criminal proceedings access to documents may be refused if the documents are covered by legal professional privilege or by public interest immunity. In *Lee v. South West Thames R.H.A.* [1985] 2 All E.R. 385 an infant suffered brain damage due to treatment in one of two hospitals — the first under the control of Hillingdon AHA and the second under the control of North East Thames AHA. Disclosure of reports compiled by the ambulance crew of South West Thames RHA for the purpose of Hillingdon obtaining legal advice was refused. The court held that they were covered by legal professional privilege. This was on the basis that a defendant should be able to obtain evidence without having to disclose the findings of the other party. In *W v. Egdell*, at first instance, Scott J. held that the report which Dr Egdell had compiled was not covered by legal professional privilege. He said that a distinction could be drawn between the situation in which instructions were given to experts for the making of a report, which were covered by legal professional privilege, and the ultimate opinion given by the expert which was not. Dr Egdell's report was not privileged. Whether such a distinction is justifiable is questionable. This matter was not discussed fully in the Court of Appeal, although Sir Stephen Brown appeared to agree with the approach taken by Scott J on this issue. (See J. V. McHale "Confidentiality — An Absolute Obligation?" (1989) 52 *Modern Law Review* 715.)

4. Discovery will also be refused if the documents are covered by public interest immunity. In deciding whether to disclose information on the basis of public interest immunity, the court will balance the public interest in preserving the confidentiality of the information against the public interest in ensuring that there is a fair hearing at the subsequent proceedings. In *Re HIV Haemophiliac Litigation* [1990] N.L.J.R. 1349, a large number of haemophiliacs had received blood infected with HIV. They sought to bring an action against the Department of Health on the grounds that the Department was negligent in failing to ensure that there was enough blood available for donation in the United Kingdom, and as a result having to obtain blood for donation from the USA. The government refused disclosure of certain documents. These documents concerned briefings for ministers as to whether a policy for self-sufficiency in blood products should be established and what resources would be required for such a policy, planning decisions relating to the Blood Products Laboratory and the decision whether and how to organise the National Blood Transfusion Service. The Court of Appeal held that discovery of the documents was necessary in order for the plaintiffs to make a thorough presentation of their case. (This litigation is further discussed in Chapter 1 above at pages 64–65.)

(f) Access to Health Records at Common Law

The Access to Health Records Act 1990 allows access to medical records compiled after November 1991. A patient seeking access to medical records compiled prior to that date has no automatic right of access. His only chance of obtaining the records, aside from undertaking litigation, is either to persuade his doctor to make a voluntary disclosure of the information or to attempt to claim that he has a right of access at common law.

R v. Mid Glamorgan Family Health Services Authority, ex p. Martin [1995] 1 All E.R. 356

M was diagnosed as being a catatonic schizophrenic suffering from depression, psychopathy and intellectual immaturity. He received psychotherapy. M fell in love with the consultant psychiatrist treating him. As a result of this she was withdrawn from treating him. M sought details of his records and of the decision to withdraw the psychiatrist. He was subsequently detained under the Mental Health Act 1959. He sought judicial review of the decision by Mid Glamorgan Family Health Services Authority to make consideration of disclosure of the records conditional upon an assurance from the applicant that no potential litigation was contemplated by him in respect of his treatment by South Glamorgan Health Authority. He also sought judicial review of the decision of South Glamorgan Health Authority on November 2, 1990 to refuse such disclosure to him.

At first instance the application was rejected by Popplewell J. He rejected the claim that there was a right of access and laid emphasis on the fact that legislation had been explicitly enacted for the purposes of granting access. He drew a distinction between treatment information, which the patient was entitled to receive in order to reach his decision regarding treatment and information which constituted a doctor's assessment of the patients condition to which the patient had no right of access. He said also that Article 8 of the European Convention of Human Rights was not applicable in this situation. (For a statement of Article 8 see at page 439 above.) Moreover Article 8 itself does not give unlimited access to medical records. Popplewell J. said that if he was wrong and there was a right of access at common law that still did not mean that Martin would be able to gain access since such rights were not absolute. Mr Martin appealed to the Court of Appeal.

NOURSE L.J.:
"Popplewell J. said that the claim was a public law claim and did not depend on private rights. Although both these propositions are correct, a public body, as the owner of medical records, can be in a position no different from that of a private doctor, whose relationship is governed by contract. In other words, a public body, in fulfilment of its duty to administer its property in accordance with its public purposes, is bound to deal with medical records in the same way as a private

doctor. In that regard the observations of Lord Templeman in *Sidaway v. Bethlem Royal Hospital Governors* [1985] 1 All E.R. 643 at 665–666 are pertinent:

'I do not subscribe to the theory that the patient is entitled to know everything nor to the theory that the doctor is entitled to decide everything. The relationship between doctor and patient is contractual in origin, the doctor performing services in consideration for fees payable by the patient. The doctor, obedient to the highest standards set by the medical profession, impliedly contracts to act at all times in the best interests of the patient. No doctor in his senses would impliedly contract at the same time to give to the patient all the information available to the doctor as a result of the doctor's training and experience and as a result of the doctor's diagnosis of the patient. An obligation to give a patient all the information available to the doctor would often be inconsistent with the doctor's contractual obligation to have regard to the patient's best interests. Some information might confuse, other information might alarm a particular patient Whenever the occasion arises for the doctor to tell the patient the result of the doctor's diagnosis, the possible methods of treatment and the advantages and disadvantages of the recommended treatment, the doctor must decide in the light of his training and experience and in the light of his knowledge of the patient what should be said and how it should be said.'

These observations provide a sensible basis for holding that a doctor, likewise a health authority, as the owner of a patient's medical records, may deny the patient access to them if it is in his best interests to do so, for example if their disclosure would be detrimental to his health. In the light of the offer made in the respondents' solicitor's letter of March 24, 1993, that is a complete answer to the appellant's application. I agree with Popplewell J. that the respondents have offered all that is necessary to comply with their duty to the appellant. The judge was entitled, in the exercise of his discretion, to refuse the appellant the relief that he sought and I would affirm his decision on that ground. Although the respondents have not taken this point, it might also, as a matter of discretion, have been affirmed on the ground that the appellant did nothing effective to pursue his rights against either of the respondents between 1981 and 1990.

It is inherent in the views above expressed that I do not accept that a health authority, any more than a private doctor, has an absolute right to deal with medical records in any way that it chooses. As Lord Templeman makes clear, the doctor's general duty, likewise the health authority's, is to act at all times in the best interests of the patient. Those interests would usually require that a patient's medical records should not be disclosed to third parties; conversely, that they should usually, for example, be handed on by one doctor to the next or made available to the patient's legal advisers if they are reasonably required for the purposes of legal proceedings in which he is involved. The respondents' position seems to be that no practical difficulty could arise in such circumstances, but that they would act voluntarily and not because they were under a legal duty to do so. If it ever became necessary for the legal position to be tested, it is inconceivable that this extreme position would be vindicated

On all the other points taken by the appellant I agree with Popplewell J. I would dismiss this appeal."

EVANS L.J.:
". . . Like Nourse L.J., I do not consider that the fact that these are public law proceedings alters the nature of the central issue which is the extent of the appellant's common law rights and of the respondent's correlative duties to provide access. Like him, also, I consider that the essential issue is whether they are entitled to deny access on the ground that their disclosure would be harmful to him

The statutory right under the 1990 Act is qualified in this way. Section 5(1) reads: '5(1)

Access shall not be given . . . to any part of a health record — (a) which, in the opinion of the holder of the record, would disclose — (i) information likely to cause serious harm to the physical or mental health of the patient or of any other individual . . .

Mr Allen submits that this restriction forms no part of the common law. He relied upon the fundamental right of self-determination which is expressed in art 8(1) of the Convention For the Protection of Human Rights and Fundamental Freedom (Rome, November 4, 1950 TS 71 (1953); Cmnd. 8969) as follows: 'Everyone has the right to respect for his private and family life, his home and his correspondence. . . .', and which is recognised, as he submits, by common law decisions including *Sidaway v. Bethlem Royal Hospital Governors* [1985] 1 All E.R. 643, regarding the patient's right to know sufficient of the relevant facts to enable him to make his own decision about medical treatment, and *Re T (adult: refusal of medical treatment)* [1992] 4 All E.R. 649 regarding the rights of a Jehovah's Witness to refuse medical treatment. The decision in *Re C (adult: refusal of medical treatment)* [1994] 1 All E.R. 819, demonstrates, he submits that the right of self-determination now outweighs the public interest in the sanctity of life. Therefore, the applicant is entitled to decide for himself whether or not to incur whatever risk of damage to his mental or physical health might accompany the disclosure of the records to him.

Mr Allen's reliance upon Art. 8 of the Convention, and on the decision of the European Court of Human Rights in *Gaskin v. U.K.* (1990) 12 E.H.R.R. 36, does not involve any contention that the Convention forms part of English law or that its provisions are directly enforceable here. Rather, he adopts the approach described in Sir John Laws' lecture to the Administrative Law Bar Association: "Is the High Court the Guardian of Fundamental Constitutional Rights?" [1993] *Public Law* 59. The fact that the convention does not form part of English law does not mean that its provisions cannot be referred to and relied upon as persuasive authority as to what the common law is, or should be. Article 8 therefore reflects the right of self-determination which now, he submits, forms part of the common law

For my part, I am prepared unreservedly to adopt this approach but I hope that it is not unduly insular, or even parochial, to remind oneself at the outset that the object of the inquiry is to establish the relevant rules of the common law. That inquiry in the present case reduces itself to the question whether the common law right of access, if there is one, is qualified in the same way as the statutory right now enacted is qualified by section 5(1)(a).

In my judgment, there is no good reason for doubting either that a right of access does exist or that it is qualified to that extent at least. The record is made for two purposes which are relevant here: first, to provide part of the medical history of the patient, for the benefit of the same doctor or his successors in the future; and secondly, to provide a record of diagnosis and treatment in case of future inquiry or dispute. Those purposes would be frustrated if there was no duty to disclose the records to medical advisers or to the patient himself, or his legal advisers, if they were required in connection with a later claim. Nor can the duty to disclose for medical purposes be limited, in my judgment, to future medical advisers. There could well be a case where the patient called for them in order to be able to give them to a future doctor as yet unidentified, *e.g.* in case of accident whilst travelling abroad

But the present case is not one where the records are required for medical purposes, or in connection with any dispute or projected litigation. Both are expressly disavowed. The applicant wishes to have a greater knowledge of his 'childhood, development and history' (see *Gaskin v. U.K.* (1989) 12 E.H.R.R. 36) and he seeks disclosure for this reason alone.

The respondents' solicitors' letter of March 24, 1993 offers to produce the records to a medical adviser who can assess their likely effect upon the mental or physical health of the applicant. It is more than 20 years since he was a patient of any doctor whose records they hold, and so they cannot assess this for themselves. The assessment can only be carried out by a medical adviser with knowledge of his present-day condition. To release the records to the applicant himself, when there are grounds for supposing that they might cause harm to his physical or mental health, would be to risk causing or aggravating the kind of injury which previously they undertook to prevent or cure. These are valid reasons, in my judgment, for holding that any common law right of access is limited to this extent."

Sir Roger Parker:
". . . I agree that this appeal must be dismissed for the reasons given in the judgment of Nourse L.J. I add only the following observations:

(1) I regard as untenable the proposition that, at common law, a doctor or health authority has an absolute property in medical records of a patient, if this means, which it appears to do, that either could make what use of them he or it chose. Information given to a doctor by a patient or a third party is given in confidence and the absolute property rights are therefore necessarily qualified by the obligations arising out of that situation.

(2) I regard as equally untenable the proposition that by reason of a 'right of self determination' a patient has an unfettered right of access to his medical records at all times and in all circumstances, indeed it is accepted for the applicant that this cannot be so.

(3) In my view the circumstances in which a patient or former patient is entitled to demand access to his medical history as set out in the records will be infinitely various, and it is neither desirable nor possible for this or any court to attempt to set out the scope of the duty to afford access or, its obverse, the scope of the patient's rights to demand access. Each case must depend on its own facts

(4) There can, I think, be no doubt, for example, that a doctor should, if requested by the patient, or perhaps by a patient's doctor for the time being, afford access to such doctor but not necessarily to the entire contents of the records. There may, however, be circumstances when direct access to the records or some part of them should be given to the patient himself. If, for example, he is about to emigrate and his condition is such that he might need treatment before he can nominate a successor doctor, it would, it seems to me, be probable that the doctor with the records would be obliged either to give access to the records or to provide his departing patient with a letter giving the information necessary to enable a doctor, faced with his collapse, for example, on board ship, to treat him properly.

Notes:

1. The Court of Appeal appeared to accept that there is a right of access to health care records, although this right is not absolute in nature. There has been some speculation as to the source of such a right. One possibility is that it may be grounded in the doctor's duty of care in negligence. This has however, been questioned. Grubb, for example, has argued that non-disclosure may be fully consistent with professional practice under *Bolam*. Secondly, there would be difficulties in some situations of establishing that non-disclosure constituted harm to the patient. (See A. Grubb " Access to Medical Records" (1994) 2 *Medical Law Review* 353.)

2. At first instance, before Popplewell J., it was argued that the doctor owed an obligation of disclosure as part of her general fiduciary duty

to her patient. This issue had arisen in the Canadian case of *McInerney v. MacDonald* (1992) 93 D.L.R. (4th edn.) 415 S.C.C. In that case the Canadian Supreme Court held that a right of access was derived from the doctor's fiduciary duty, because the doctor had a duty to act in the utmost good faith. A patient may not be able to establish that a doctor had acted in such a manner unless he was allowed access to information relating to his treatment. Popplewell J rejected the existence of a fiduciary duty. In reaching his decision he noted the rejection of a fiduciary duty in *Sidaway v. Bethlem Royal Hospital Governors* [1984] 1 All E.R. 1018 (see Chapter 6 above) and stated that the opinion reached by the doctor was the doctor's property and could be distinguished from the information which she had been provided by the patient.

QUESTIONS:

1. To what extent does the approach taken by Evans L.J. as to the basis on which information may be withheld differ from that adopted by Nourse L.J.?
2. What does Sir Roger Parker mean when he says that property rights in medical records are qualified?
3. Do you agree with the use made by Evans L.J. of Article 8 of the ECHR?
4. If the duty to disclose is derived from negligence then will the patient be able to suceed in a claim for damages based upon failure to disclose? (See further C. Newdick, *Who Shall We Treat?*, Oxford: OUP, 1995, at page 231.)

10. REFORMING THE LAW CONCERNING PATIENT INFORMATION

There is no comprehensive statutory protection accorded to personal health care information. Whilst, as we noted above particular statutes operate in certain areas to provide protection to confidential health information, such as the Human Fertilisation and Embryology Act 1990, their scope is limited. In 1981 in its report on Breach of Confidence the Law Commission recommended that the equitable remedy of breach of confidence should be placed on a statutory footing (Law Commission Report No. 110, *Breach of Confidence*, Cmnd. 8388 (1981)). More recently general privacy legislation was advocated by the National Heritage Committee (Fourth Report from the National Heritage Committee Session 1992–1993, *Privacy and Media Intrusion*, H.C. 294–1, paras. 47–59). It appears that at present such general legislation is unlikely. There may however, be a more realistic prospect of specific protection given to the privacy of health information. In 1996 a bill was introduced into the House of Lords and was given a second reading. This bill was modelled on a draft bill which had been published by the British Medical Association after widespread consultation with other health professionals in 1995. Extracts from this Bill are set out below.

Disclosure and Use of Personal Health Information Bill (1996)

2.—(1) Except as provided under sections 3 and 4, a health service body which holds a patient's health information, or information for the purpose of health care which includes information relating to a person other than the patient, shall not disclose that information.

(2) Except as provided under sections 3 and 4 and subsection (3) of this section, a qualified health professional shall not disclose a patient's personal health information, or information relating to a person other than the patient, for purposes other than the provision of health care to that individual.

(3) A qualified health professional may, in the course of providing health care to a patient, disclose to a health service body personal health information relating to that patient and such information shall not be disclosed by that health service body except in accordance with the provisions of this Act.

(4) Nothing in this Act prevents the disclosure of personal health information with the express consent of the person to whom it relates.

3.—(1) It shall be unlawful for a health service body which holds health information obtained in connection with one purpose to use this information for any other purpose unless —

(a) the use of the information for that purpose is authorised by-
    (i) the individual concerned or the individual's representative;
    (ii) a court: or
    (iii) statutory requirement
(b) the purpose for which the information is used is directly related to the purpose in connection with which the information was obtained and is not contrary to the express refusal of the individual;
(c) the source of the information is a publicly available publication;
(d) the source of the information for that purpose is necesary to prevent or lessen a serious and imminent threat to —
    (i) public health and safety
    (ii) the life or health of the individual concerned or another individual:
(e) the information —
    (i) is disclosed or used in a form in which the individual concerned is not identified:
    (ii) is disclosed, collected and used for audit purposes and will not be published in a form from which it can reasonably be expected that individual concerned can be identified; or
    (iii) is disclosed, collected and used for research purposes (for which approval by a research ethics committee, if required, has been given) and will not be published in a form from which it can reasonably be expected that the individual concerned can be identified and the individual has not registered an objection;
(f) non-compliance is necessary —
    (i) to avoid prejudice to the maintenance of the law by any public body, including the prevention, detection, investigation, prosecution or punishment of a serious offence; or
    (ii) for the conduct of proceedings before any court or tribunal (being proceedings that have been commenced or are reasonably in contemplation):

(iii) for any purpose authorised following application to the court.

4.—(1) Subject to subsection (2) it shall be unlawful for a health service body or for a health professional holding health information to disclose that information unless —

(a) the disclosure is to —
    (i) the individual concerned: or
    (ii) the individual's representative where the individual is dead or is an incompetent minor or is mentally incapacitated;
(b) the disclosure is authorised by —
    (i) the individual concerned: or
    (ii) the individual's representative where the individual is dead or is an incompetent minor or is mentally incapacitated:
(c) the disclosure of the information is one of the purposes in connection with which the information was obtained:
(d) the source of the information is a publicly available publication:
(e) the information is in general terms concerning the prescence, location and condition and progress of the patient in or on the premises of a health service body and the disclosure is not contrary to the express request of the individual:
(f) the information to be disclosed concerns only the fact of the death and the disclosure is by a health professional or by a person authorised by health service body to a person nominated by the individual concerned, or to the individual's representative, spouse, principal care giver or next of kin, close relative or other person whom it is in the opinion of the health professional reasonable in the circumstances to inform.

(2) Subsection (1) shall not apply where it is either not desirable or not practicable to obtain authorisation from the individual concerned and —

(a) the disclosure of the information is directly related to one of the purposes in connection with which the information was obtained;
(b) the information was disclosed by a registered health professional to a person nominated by the individual concerned, or to a social worker employed by the local authority or health service body, or to the principal care giver or a near relative of the individual concerned in accordance with the recognised professional practice and[that] the disclosure is not contrary to the express request of the individual, or where the individual is dead, his personal representative:
(c) the information is disclosed to protect the interests of a person who is unable to consent and is limited to recognised agencies who could act for that person, such as the Court of Protection or the individual's representative:
(d) the information is to be used —
    (i) in a form in which the individual concerned is not identified:
    (ii) for audit purposes and will not be published in a form from which it can reasonably be expected that the individual concerned will be identified: or
    (iii) for research purposes (for which approval by a research ethics committee, if required has been given) and will not be published in a form from which it can reasonably be expected that the individual concerned will be identified:
(e) the disclosure of the information is necessary to prevent or lessen a serious and imminent threat to —
    (i) public health and safety; or
    (ii) the life or health of the individual concerned or another individual:

(f) the disclosure of the information is in general terms and is essential to faciliate the sale or other disposition of a business as a going concern and is not contrary to the express request of the subject:

(g) the information to be disclosed briefly describes only the nature of the injuries of an individual sustained in an accident and that the individual's identity and the disclosure is —
  (i) by a person authorised by the person in charge of a hospital:
  (ii) a person authorised by the person in charge of a news medium;

for the purpose of publication or broadcast in connection with the news activities of that news medium and the disclosure is not contrary to the express request of the individual concerned or where that individual is dead, his personal representative:

(h) the disclosure of the information —
  (i) is required for the purposes of identifying whether an individual is suitable to be involved in health education and so that individuals may be identified may be asked to give their authority or, where they are incapable of doing so, so that the views may be sought of a person whom they have nominated or their representative, spouse, principal care giver, next of kin, close relative or other person whom it is in the opinion of the health professional reasonable in the circumstances to ask: and
  (ii) is by a person authorised by the health service body to a person authorised by a health training institution.

(j) the disclosure of the information is required for —
  (i) the purpose of a professionally recognised accreditation of a health service;
  (ii) a professionally recognised external quality assurance programme; or
  (iii) risk management assessment and the disclosure is solely to a person engaged by the health service body for the purposes of assessing that body's risk and the information will not be published in any form which could be expected to identify any individual nor disclosed by the accreditation or quality assurance or risk management organisation to third parties except as required by law:
  (iv) the purposes of examining and investigating any untoward event or side effect resulting from any medical prescription issued or procedure carried out by a registered medical practitioner employed by or in contract with a health service body:
  (v) the proper performance of any function imposed upon the health service body by the Mental Health Act 1983 or monitoring of patients for purposes ancillary to the Act:
  (vi) the investigation of a health service body or a Health Service Commissioner of any complaint or incident,

(k) non-compliance is necessary —
  (i) to avoid prejudice to the maintenance of the law by any public body, including the prevention, detection, investigation, prosecution and punishment of a serious offence: or
  (ii) for the conduct of proceedings before any court or tribunal (being proceedings that have been commenced or are reasonably in contemplation):
  (iii) for any purpose authorised following application to the court:
  (iv) for any purpose in connection with any disciplinary or legal proceedings against any qualified health professional or any person employed by or in contract with a health service body or any visitor to premises owned or occupied by a health service body:

(l) the individual concerned is or is likely to become dependant upon a controlled drug, prescription medicine or restricted medicine and the disclosure is by a health professional to a Medical Officer of Health for the purposes of the Misuse of Drugs Act 1971.

(3) For the avoidance of doubt it is hereby declared that it shall be lawful for a health professional to disclose health care information to another qualified professional, where he believes on reasonable grounds that it is necessary for the purpose of providing or assisting in the provision of health care to the patient to whom the information relates and the disclosure is not contrary to a valid and informed refusal by the patient.

(4) In any case where disclosure of personal health information is made by a qualified health professional under this section, it shall be lawfully disclosed only if he is satisfied that there are appropriate safeguards against the information being used for any other purpose than that for which it is disclosed, and in any proceedings where the lawfulness of the disclosure is in question it shall be presumed that the qualified health professional has verified this, unless the contrary is shown.

(5) Nothing in this section affects the operation of section 11
(excluded material) of the Police and Criminal Evidence Act 1984.

(6) Where information relates to the provision of health care to any patient, this section does not apply to disclosure made —

(a) by a person who is satisfied that it is immediately necessary to make the disclosure to avert an imminent danger to the health of the patient without whose consent that information could not otherwise have been lawfully divulged, and
(b) where it is not reasonably practicable to obtain that patient's consent.

5.—(1) Where the patient is a minor, disclosure shall not be made under the provisions of this Act without the consent of the patient or, in the case of an incompetent minor —

(a) one of his parents: or
(b) a person having parental responsibility for him, unless —
    (i) the health professional or the health service body proposing to make the disclosure has made such reasonable enquiry as may be practicable to obtain that consent: or
    (ii) disclosure is essential to ensure the protection and wellbeing of that minor.

(2) Where the patient is by reason of mental disorder unable to give valid consent to disclosure, disclosure shall not be made under the provisions of this Act unless—

(a) the disclosure is necessary for the treatment or continuing care and supervision of that patient: and
(b) the health professional or the health service body proposing to make the disclosure has made such reasonable enquiry as may be practicable to obtain the views as to disclosure from the patient's representative, or the disclosure has been authorised in writing by a Mental Health Review Tribunal, or the responsible medical officer certifies that the disclosure is authorised under the provisions of this Act: or
(c) the disclosure is essential for the patient's protection and well being.

NOTES:

1. The Bill also proposes that the primary responsibility for disclosure decisions will fall upon the health professional who has been caring for that patient (clause 6). In addition there would be procedures established governing the conduct of disclosure of information.

2. A statutory obligation would be placed on health service bodies to ensure that their employees were subject to such an obligation of confidentiality (clause 8). Unauthorised disclosure would be a criminal offence (clause 10).

QUESTIONS:

1. To what extent does the Bill set out above represent a radical departure from the present position in law regarding disclosure? Would it offer adequate safeguards for patient confidentiality?
2. Should all health care information be accorded the same degree of legislative protection or is it better to enact specific legislation targetting particular issues (such as section 33 of the Human Fertilisation and Embryology Act 1990) or legislation concerning genetic information?
3. Do the provisions regarding minors pay sufficient attention to their interests? (See discussion earlier at pages 448–451.)

SELECT BIBLIOGRAPHY

M. Beupré, "Confidentiality, HIV/AIDS and Prison Health Care Services [1994] 2 *Medical Law Reviews* 149.

J. Davis, "Patients' Rights of Access to their Health Records" [1996] 2 *Medical Law International* 189.

H. Emson, "Confidentiality; a modified value" (1988), 14 *Journal of Medical Ethics* 87.

F. Gurry, *Breach of Confidence*, Oxford: Clarendon, 1985.

G. Hunt (ed.), *Whistleblowing in the Health Services*, London: Edward Arnold, 1994.

M. Jones "Medical Confidentiality and the Public Interest" (1990) 6 *Professional Negligence* 16.

I. Kennedy "The Doctor, the Pill and the Fifteen Year Old Girl" in I. Kennedy (ed.), *Treat Me Right*, Oxford: OUP 1989.

M. H. Kottow "Medical confidentiality; an asbolute and intransigent obligation" (1986) 12 *Journal of Medical Ethics* 117.

R. Lee, "Deathly Silence" in R. Lee and D. Morgan (ed.) *Death Rites: Law and Ethics at the End of Life*, London: Routledge, 1994.

H. Lesser and Z. Pickup "Law, Ethics and Confidentiality" (1990) 17 *Journal of Law and Society* 17.

J. V. McHale, *Medical Confidentiality and Legal Privilege*, London: Routledge, 1993.

J. Montgomery "Confidentiality and the Immature Minor" [1987] *Family Law* 101.

9

MENTAL HEALTH

---

1. INTRODUCTION

As we saw in Chapter 6, above, the general rule for treatment of an adult is that he must consent to the treatment and that such consent cannot be overridden. Other than the special rules relating to people who are not able to consent to treatment and the regime in relation to children, the most obvious exception to this rule is where treatment is carried out under the Mental Health Act 1983. For a person to be compulsorily admitted it is not necessary that he be incompetent. Many, but by no means all, detained patients are competent, even if the concept of being able to make a "true choice" is part of the definition of compentency (see Chapter 5, above). The Act allows for the treatment of a competent detained patient even if he wishes not to have the treatment. The main focus of this Chapter is on treatment, but it is essential to consider the process of admission to hospital and also how such admission and subsequent detention may be challenged. These matters are considered by examining the law relating to what may be called "civil admission". The same treatment provisions exist in relation to patients detained as a result of contact with the criminal justice system, but they fall outwith the scope of this Chapter.

(a) Justification of Compulsory Admission

The two classic justifications for the compulsory detention of people with mental ill health are by reference to a *parens patriae* power in the State to ensure that people are treated for illnesses when necessary and/or the police power of the State to control people causing harm to others. The *parens patriae* justification operates on the basis that the State has the right, as the parent of its citizens, to take action for the benefit of citizens, even though the citizens may not perceive a need for help or indeed even wish to reject it. The major obstacle to the acceptability of such an approach was identified by John Stuart Mill in his *Essay on Liberty* (1859) where he argued that interference in the freedoms of others could only be justified where the action was designed to "prevent harm to others." The best interests of the citizen he argued would not be sufficient justification, though they would indicate the obligation to inform, advise or even remonstrate with the citizen. Nevertheless, this justification was part of the basis of the Percy Commission's proposals for reform of mental health law, which formed the basis of the Mental Health Act 1959 and, thus also, of the Mental Health Act 1983.

The Report of The Royal Commission on Mental Illness and Deficiency 1954–57 (Cmd. 169)

"In our view, individual people who need care because of mental disorder should be able to receive it as far as possible with no more restriction of liberty or legal formality than is applied to people who need care because of other types of illness. But mental disorder has special features which require special measures. Mental disorder makes any patients incapable of protecting themselves or their interests, so that if they are neglected or exploited it may be necessary to have authority to insist on providing them with proper care. In many cases, it affects the patient's judgment so that he does not realize he is ill, and the illness can only be treated against the patient's wishes at that time. In many cases too it affects the patient's behaviour in such a way that it is necessary in the interests of other people or of society to insist on removing him for treatment even if he is unwilling."

Barnes, Bowl and Fisher criticised this justification for compulsory hospitalisation on the basis that: (1) the fact that people do not know they are ill and may not seek help may appear to be attractive, but it begs the question of what degree of deviation from health is sufficient to justify compulsory powers; and (2) the fact that society has a right to protect itself is accepted, but its application in this context begs the question of exactly what behaviour patterns will justify compulsory powers. (M. Barnes, R. Bowl and M. Fisher, *Sectioned: Social Services and the 1983 Mental Health Act*, London: Routledge (1990). The latter concern is also reflected in the debate about mental illness (see below). If deviant behaviour is a sufficient grounding for the use of compulsory power, there are real risks: first, any deviance may be sufficient to warrant action; secondly, identification of deviant behaviour may be subjective and not objective, and, more particularly, identifying the 'norm' is culturally, racially and gender-based, thus allowing for, if not actively encouraging, discrimination in the use of compulsory powers.

The alternative to a *parens patriae* justification, which is also present in the extract from the Percy Commission, is the police power. This justification argues that where individuals present a danger or perhaps harm to others, the State is entitled to take action by interfering with that individual's freedoms, thereby protecting others from the danger or harm. This clearly is a justification for action taken through the criminal law, but it is also argued to be a justification for compulsory admission to hospital. The Mental Health Act 1983 clearly uses both justifications in establishing the criteria for admission to hospital.

QUESTIONS:

1. Is the rationale adopted by the Percy Commission an adequate basis for the compulsory hospitalisation of people? Is the *parens patriae*

justification sufficient on its own? If so, would you expect that it be demanded that the condition be curable or would it be sufficient that the person be offered some prospect of their condition being alleviated?

2. Would a clearer basis for interference on the basis of the police power of the state be a more appropriate basis for compulsory intervention?

3. If neither the *parens patriae* power nor the police power is sufficient justification for the use of compulsory powers, does this leave distressed and ill citizens to fend for themselves when help could easily be provided; if so, is that morally unacceptable? Do the answers to these questions assume that the individual is capable of exercising his rights? For a critical assessment of the basis of "civil commitment", see D. Price, "Civil commitment of the mentally ill: compelling arguments for reform" (1994) 2 *Medical Law Review* 321).

The critical balance is, as Fennell comments in "Inscribing Paternalism in the Law: Consent to Treatment and Mental Disorder" (1990) 17 *Journal of Law and Society* 29, between autonomy and paternalism. He notes that there are two important organising concepts: legalism (which emphasises "the need to put limits on the power of mental health professionals and the rights of patients to respect their autonomously expressed wishes) and medicalism (stressing "the need to ensure that the safeguards for the individual rights of patients are not so cumbersome as to impede medical interventions aimed at serving those same patients' best interests"). Fennell states that "there is now widespread acknowledgement of the folly of rigid insistence upon the ascendancy of patient autonomy over paternalism where the result would be to harm the patient."

It is not essential that a person be not competent prior to admitting him to hospital or providing him with treatment in hospital. However, it might be that a person with mental illness is not capable of making a "true choice" and so can be regarded as not competent (see B. Hoggett, *Mental Health Law*, London: Sweet & Maxwell, 4th edn., 1996, at pages 45–49. Still this is not required for admission to hospital or treatment.

QUESTIONS:

1. Do you agree with Fennell?

2. Is compulsory admission acceptable only when it is predicated on some form of incompetence, so that to exercise compulsory powers on the competent, mentally ill person should not be permitted?

3. The Mental Health Act 1983, as will be seen below, does not demand that a prospective patient be a "danger" to others nor does it demand that the condition be curable (though some alleviation or prevention

of deterioration may be necessary). Does this mean that compulsory admission may be justified on relatively flimsy grounds?

(b) The Significance of Safeguards

Despite the impact of the anti-psychiatry debate (for an introduction, see B. M. Hoggett, *Mental Health Law* (4th edn. 1996), pages 27–29 & 46–49), most people accept the need for a system of compulsory hospitalisation in some circumstances for people with mental illness. Since the restrictions on freedom of liberty are severe, it is essential that the means by which compulsory admission is imposed are and are seen to be fair and based upon clear evidence. Sir Thomas Bingham M.R. in *Re S-C* [1996] 1 All E.R. 532 said:

"Powers therefore exist to ensure that those who suffer from mental illness may, in appropriate circumstances, be involuntarily admitted to mental hospitals and detained. But, and it is a very important but, the circumstances in which the mentally ill may be detained are very carefully prescribed by statute. Action may only be taken if there is clear evidence that the medical condition of a patient justifies such action, and there are detailed rules prescribing the classes of person who may apply to a hospital to admit and detain a mentally disordered person. The legislation recognises that action may be necessary at short notice and also recognises that it will be impracticable for a hospital to investigate the background facts to ensure that all the requirements of the Act are satisfied if they appear to be so. Thus we find in the statute a panoply of powers combined with detailed safeguards for the protection of the patient. The underlying issue in the present appeal is whether those powers were properly exercised and whether the appellant was lawfully detained. One reminds oneself that the liberty of the subject is at stake in a case of this kind, and that liberty may be violated only to the extent permitted by law and not otherwise."

The European Convention on Human Rights also accepts the necessity of a system of compulsory hospitalisation, subject to necessary safeguards. Article 5 provides:

"Article 5

1. Everyone has the right to liberty and security of person. No one shall be deprived of his liberty save in the following cases and in accordance with a procedure prescribed by law:

. . .

(e) the lawful detention . . . of persons of unsound mind . . .

4. Everyone who is deprived of his liberty by arrest or detention shall be entitled to take proceedings by which the lawfulness of his detention shall be decided speedily by a court and his release ordered if the detention is not lawful."

The case law of the European Court of Human Rights has established that there are three minimum conditions which have to be satisfied for a State's law to comply with the requirements in Article 5. First, the prospective patient must be reliably shown by objective medical expertise to be of unsound mind; secondly, the patient's mental disorder must be of a kind or degree warranting compulsory confinement; and thirdly, the unsoundness of mind must continue throughout the period of detention. (See further, D. J. Harris, M. O'Boyle and C. Warbrick, *Law of the European Convention on Human Rights* (1995), Chapter 5 and M. G. Wachenfeld, *The Human Rights of the Mentally Ill in Europe* (1992).) MIND, the National Association for Mental Health, has taken the view that there are many areas in which mental health law fails to comply with these obligations (see, MIND and National Council of Civil Liberties, *People with Mental Illness and Learning Disabilities* (1993)). For a view that suggests there is rather greater compliance, see M. J. Gunn, "Mental Health Care" in D. J. Harris and S. Joseph (eds) *The International Convenant on Civil and Political Rights and United Kingdom Law* (Oxford: Clarendon Press, 1995).

QUESTIONS:

1. Do you accept that there must be a form of compulsory admission?
2. If so, is an element of professional discretion necessary? Can professional discretion be controlled by the procedure for admission ensuring that a multi-professional approach is adopted?
3. Would you involve lawyers and/or courts more in the decision-making process?

Re-consider these questions throughout the chapter and assess how close the Mental Health Act comes to your ideal approach.

The criteria and procedures for compulsory admission must be sufficient to avoid improper usage so that only those people for whom compulsory hospitalisation is necessary are indeed admitted (and this is the focus of some of this Chapter). The 1983 Act introduced many changes to the original provisions of the 1959 Act in a clear endeavour to meet the demands of civil libertarians (see, *e.g.* L. O. Gostin, *A Human Condition* (1975, London: MIND)). Thus, for example, the need for compulsory hospitalisation being the least restrictive alternative receives statutory recognition in section 3(2); provisions are introduced to regulate treatment (Part IV); an independent watchdog body was created (the Mental Health Act Commission); and a multi-disciplinary approach was used whenever possible (see, *e.g.*, the obligation on a responsible medical officer to consult others on renewal of detention and the involvement of two other professionals in advising the second opinion approved doctor in assessing the commencement or continuity of certain treatments).

A consequence of hospitalisation being the least restrictive alternative is that many people with mental disorder in need of some form of treatment and care will either not be detained in hospital, but be informal patients, or will be living in the community. The greatest need then is that the necessary support facilities are provided and this matter is further considered at the end of the Chapter.

Where a person is compulsory hospitalised, there is an argument that that person must have, as a consequence, a right to treatment. Indeed, such a right arguably exists for all those in contact with mental health services, whether living in hospital or not. No such legal right currently exists (but see the obligation to provide after-care under section 117; see below at page 560).

QUESTION:

1. If a person is compulsorily admitted to hospital would you agree that there should be an obligation to provide treatment to the patient? If so, should the patient be able to challenge the treatment with which he is provided? Keep this question in mind when examining the Act, and, in particular, when considering the implications of *R. v. Cannons Park MHRT, ex p. A* (below at page 522).

Finally, it is clear that resources for mental health services are inadequate. Bed occupancy rates are frequently reported as being over 100 per cent, thus resulting in some patients having to be out of hospital on leave so as to allow a bed to be made available to a more pressing case. One consequence of this is the high number of prisoners who have mental health problems. This is a major dilemma for those working in the mental health services.

QUESTION:

1. Should it be permissible to use coercive powers where there is no harm to others involved?

2. ADMISSION TO HOSPITAL

Admission to hospital may be either compulsory or informal. Section 131(1) of the Mental Health Act 1983 permits informal admission without any formal procedures. A person who has attained the age of 16 and is competent may also be admitted informally (section 131(2)). The *Mental Health Act Code of Practice* makes quite clear that preference is to be given to informal admission, where possible. An informal patient has the legal right to leave hospital at any time (subject to the use of compulsory powers) and to refuse treatment because the hospital has no right to stop him leaving and no right to treat, indeed such actions would amount to the tort of false imprisonment and assault and battery. It is arguable that the hospital and staff act in a tenuous legal situation if the informal patient is not competent to agree to stay in hospital or to be treated or is not expressing agreement. At the time of the amendments to legislation in 1982, it was proposed that informal patients should have a right of access to Mental Health Review Tribunals to seek their discharge. The proposal was swiftly rejected because a patient has a right to leave and refuse treatment. However, the Mental Health Act Commission has consistently drawn attention to the reality that informal patients often either cannot or will not exercise their own legal rights and some protection should be offered to them.

QUESTION:

1. Would you agree that the treatment position of an informal patient should continue to be governed by the common law?

3. COMPULSORY ADMISSION TO HOSPITAL

Hospitals and mental nursing homes (the latter being privately run institutions, including private hospitals, which are registered with the District Health Authority under the Registered Homes Act 1984 specifically for the purpose of admitting compulsory patients) may compulsorily admit patients under the Mental Health Act 1983. Section 145(1) defines hospital as meaning:
"(a) any health service hospital within the meaning of the National Health Service Act 1977; and
(b) any accommodation provided by a local authority and used as a hospital or on behalf of the Secretary of State under that Act . . . "

QUESTION:

1. From this definition, do you think that a hospital has to be a large institution or could a small building housing only a few patients be a hospital? If the latter, would it have to be staffed by nurses?

In 1992–93, 263,400 people were admitted to hospital both informally and compulsorily. Of these admission, only 21,356 were compulsorily admissions. Admissions under section 2 totalled 11,053 and those under section 3 totalled 157 (see Department of Health, *Statistical Bulletin* 1995/6).

(a) The main admission sections

2.—(2) An application for admission for assessment may be made in respect of a patient on the grounds that —

(a) he is suffering from mental disorder of a nature or degree which warrants the detention of the patient in a hospital for assessment (or for assessment followed by medical treatment) for at least a limited period; and

(b)   he ought to be so detained in the interests of his own health or safety or with a view to the protection of other persons.

(3) An application for admission for assessment shall be founded on the written recommendations in the prescribed form of two registered medical practitioners, including in each case a statement that in the opinion of the practitioner the conditions set out in subsection (2) above are complied with.

(4) Subject to the provisions of section 29(4) below, a patient admitted to hospital in pursuance of an application for admission for assessment may be detained for a period not exceeding 28 days beginning with the day on which he is admitted, but shall not be detained after the expiration of that period unless before it has expired he has become liable to be detained by virtue of a subsequent application, order or direction under the following provisions of this Act.

3.—(2) An application for admission for treatment may be made in respect of a patient on the grounds that —

(a)   he is suffering from mental illness, severe mental impairment, psychopathic disorder or mental impairment and his mental disorder is of a nature or degree which makes it appropriate for him to receive medical treatment in a hospital; and

(b)   in the case of psychopathic disorder or mental impairment, such treatment is likely to alleviate or prevent a deterioration of his condition; and

(c)   it is necessary for the health or safety of the patient or for the protection of other persons that he should receive such treatment and it cannot be provided unless he is detained under this section.

(3) An application for admission for treatment shall be founded on the written recommendations in the prescribed form of two registered medical practitioners, including in each case a statement that in the opinion of the practitioner the conditions set out in subsection (2) above are complied with; and each such recommendation shall include:

(a)   such particulars as may be prescribed of the grounds for that opinion so far as it relates to the conditions set out in paragraphs (a) and (b) of that subsection; and

(b)   a statement of the reasons for that opinion so far as it relates to the conditions set out in paragraph (c) of that subsection, specifying whether other methods of dealing with the patient are available and, if so, why they are not appropriate.

Section 3 may be renewed at the end of the first six months and thereafter at annual intervals, provided section 20 is satisfied. It demands that the responsible medical officer examine the patient within two months of the end of the detention period and, after consulting two people professionally concerned with the patient's medical treatment, make a report to the hospital managers if satisfied that:

(4)(a) the patient is suffering from mental illness, severe mental impairment, psychopathic disorder or mental impairment, and his mental disorder is of a nature or degree which makes it appropriate form him to receive medical treatment in a hospital; and

(b)   such treatment is likely to alleviate or prevent a deterioration of his condition; and

(c)   it is necessary for the health or safety of the patient or for the protection of others that he should receive such treatment and that it cannot be provided unless he continues to be detained;

but, in the case of mental illness or severe mental impairment, it shall be an alternative to the condition specified in paragraph (b) above that the patient, if discharged, is unlikely to be able to care for himself, to obtain the care which he needs or to guard himself against serious exploitation.

QUESTIONS:

1. What are the substantive requirements to be satisfied so that a person may be admitted to hospital under the two admission sections?
2. In what circumstances may section 3 be renewed, and how do the requirements differ from those for the original admission? (Particular attention should be paid to identifying whether dangerousness must be established and/or whether the condition must be treatable.)
3. What procedural requirements must be satisfied under these two sections?

NOTE:

1. Where there are compulsory powers, no common law powers continue to exist so either an admission is lawful because it satisfies the statutory criteria or it is not lawful. There is a common law power to "arrest the insane", nevertheless this is not available to fill in gaps in the legislation (see *Black v. Forsey* (1987) S.L.T. 681, D. Lanham, "Arresting the Insane" [1974] Crim. L.R. 515 and R. M. Jones, *Mental Health Act Manual* (4th edn., 1994), at page 19).

(b)   Mental Disorder

From sections 2 and 3, it is apparent that there are two broad categories of mental disorder to consider. First, a person may be admitted under section 2 if he or she is suffering from *mental disorder*, which means "mental illness, arrested or incomplete development of mind, psychopathic disorder and any other disorder or disability of mind" (section 1(2)).

Secondly, a person may be admitted under section 3 (and that admission be renewed under section 20) if he or she is suffering from one of four specific forms of mental disorder, that is mental illness, severe mental impairment, mental impairment and psychopathic disorder. "'Severe mental impairment' means a state of arrested or incomplete development of mind which includes severe impairment of intelligence and social functioning and is associated with abnormally aggressive or seriously irresponsible conduct on the part of the person concerned." "'Mental impairment' means a state of arrested or incomplete development of mind (not amounting to severe mental impairment) which includes significant impairment of intelligence and social functioning and is associated with abnormally aggressive or seriously irresponsible conduct on the part of the person concerned". "Psychopathic disorder" means a persistent disorder or disability of mind (whether or not including significant impairment of intelligence) which results in abnormally aggressive or seriously irresponsible conduct on the part of the person concerned . . . "

'Mental illness' is a central diagnosis and definition. This diagnosis will be that ascribed to at least 90 per cent of patients admitted to or resident in mental hospitals. In 1990–91, 17,781 of the 18,385 person compulsorily admitted were diagnosed as suffering from mental illness.

'Mental illness' is, however, a rather elusive concept because it bears no agreed definition. As Hoggett points out, the approach to the identification of mental illness can be made reliable by the adoption of standard criteria, but this does not answer the question of validity where there is a lack of agreement between three schools of thought which she identified: (1) all mental illnesses have an organic cause, though not all have yet been discovered; (2) the psychotherapeutic approaches are "aimed at the patient's individual psyche or at its interaction with family or societal pressures;" (3) the behavioural school which concentrates upon the identification of deviant behaviour. There are obvious dangers with all these schools, not least the problem that there is not necessarily any common ground upon which they might all agree, but also the organic school fails to allow that the patient's perceptions and rationality have a role to play; and labelling through these methods allows for the imposition of treatment upon "socially inconvenient people". The lack of agreement means that the ascription of the label 'mental illness' relies heavily upon the professional judgment and understanding of a psychiatrist, but this may be highly subjective and vary from one psychiatrist to another in a way which would not be acceptable with other doctors. However, it can be replied that this anti-psychiatry approach fails to recognise that some people are really ill and need care and treatment. (B. M. Hoggett, *Mental Health Law* (4th. edn.), London: Sweet & Maxwell, 1996, at pages 27–34); see also M. Cavadino, *Mental Health Law in Context: Doctor's Orders*, Aldershot: Gover, 1989, especially Chapters 4 & 5).

The reliability of the identification of mental illness can be achieved by all professionals using the various symptom descriptions provided by one of two manuals developed for statistical purposes: the Diagnostic and Statistical Manual IV of the American Psychiatric Association or the International Classification of Diseases and Disorders 10 of the World Health Organisation. Reliability, however, may not avoid the identification of some people as being mentally ill, for example, on inappropriate cultural or racial grounds.

QUESTIONS:

1. Does the lack of a clearly agreed definition of mental illness mean that the compulsory hospitalisation of people should not be possible? Alternatively does it mean that, whilst mental illness is generally recognised as existing, great care must be taken in ensuring that compulsory hospitalisation is carried out only when necessary and

with sufficient precautions being taken to avoid its usage on discriminatory or other unacceptable grounds? If the latter, assess whether the Mental Health Act provides sufficient protections for the person who is to be admitted to hospital as a detained patient. Note that a number of provisions of the *Mental Health Act Code of Practice* draw attention to and endeavour to avoid the risk of decisions being made when based upon assumptions above "a person's sex, social and cultural background or ethnic origin" (see, *e.g. Mental Health Act Code of Practice* (1993), paragraph 2.6).

2. Does the law provide sufficient clarity on the meaning of mental illness? Note that this is the one condition for which the Mental Health Act provides no definition. The question may be addressed by considering the following case.

W v. L (Mental Health Patient) [1974] Q.B. 711, [1973] 3 W.L.R. 859, (1973) 117 S.J. 757

The central issue in the case was whether a woman should be replaced as the nearest relative of a prospective patient on the basis that she had acted unreasonably in objecting to the making of an application. In the course of considering this matter, the court had to consider whether her husband might be suffering from mental illness. He was a young man aged 23. He had carried out a number of bizarre acts over roughly a two-year period. A series of acts occurred before he had any treatment: threatening his wife with a knife at her throat; putting a cat in a gas oven (it was rescued by his wife); forcing a cat to inhale ammonia and cutting its throat with a broken cup, eventually burying the body; hanging a Labrador puppy from the garage beams; strangling a terrier pup with a wire noose. After one week's stay voluntarily in a hospital, the husband discharged himself after which he stopped taking his medication and threatened to push his pregnant wife downstairs.

Lawton L.J.:
"... For the purpose of seeing what was the intention of the Act, the court has looked at the Report of the Royal Commission on the Law Relating to Mental Illness and Mental Deficiency [(1957) Cmnd 169]. The Royal Commission seem to have overlooked that their recommendations would not result in a definition of 'mental disorder' [Lawton L.J. must have meant 'mental illness']. The facts of this case show how difficult the fitting of particular instances into the statutory classification can be. Lord Denning M.R. and Orr L.J. have pointed out that there is no definition of 'mental illness'. The words are ordinary words of the English language. They have no particular medical significance. They have no particular legal significance. How should the court construe them? The answer in my judgment is to be found in the advice which Lord Reid recently gave in *Cozens v. Brutus* [1973] A.C. 854, 861, namely, that ordinary words of the English language should be construed in the way that ordinary sensible people would construe them. That being, in my judgment, the right test, then I ask myself, what would the ordinary sensible person have said about the patient's condition in this case if he had been informed of his behaviour to the dogs, the cat and his wife? In my

judgment such a person would have said: 'Well, the fellow is obviously mentally ill'. If that be right, then, although the case may fall within the definition of 'psychopathic disorder' in [section 1(2)], it also falls within the classification of 'mental illness'; and there is the added medical fact that when the EEG was taken there were indications of a clinical character showing some abnormality of the brain. It is that application of the sensible person's assessment of the condition, plus the medical indication, which in my judgment brought the case within the classification of mental illness and justified the finding of the county court judge."

QUESTIONS:

1. How helpful is this as a guide to anyone about the critical concept of mental illness? Note that Brenda Hoggett has described this as the "man must be mad test" (see B. Hoggett, *Mental Health Law*, 4th edn., London: Sweet & Maxwell (1996) at page 32). Do you agree with Hoggett that this approach "simply adds fuel to the fire of those who accuse the mental hygiene laws of being a sophisticated machine for the suppression of unusual, eccentric or inconvenient behaviour . . ."?

2. Would it have been more helpful to have adopted the proposed definition of mental illness in the D.H.S.S. Consultative Document on the 1959 Act? That document states:

"Mental illness means an illness having one or more of the following characteristics:

   (i) More than temporary impairment of intellectual functions shown by a failure of memory, orientation, comprehension and learning capacity;

 (ii) More than temporary alteration of mood of such degree as to give rise to the patient having a delusional appraisal of his situation, his past or his future, or that of others or to the lack of any appraisal;

(iii) Delusional beliefs, persecutory, jealous or grandiose;

(iv) Abnormal perceptions associated with delusional misinterpretation of events;

 (v) Thinking so disordered as to prevent the patient making a reasonable appraisal of his situation or having reasonable communication with others."

NOTES:

1. For further consideration of the definitions, see R. M. Jones, *Mental Health Act Manual* 4th edn., London: Sweet & Maxwell, 1994, at pages 16–19.

2. Whether the diagnosis is to be the generic "mental disorder" or one of the four specific forms of mental disorder, some things are stated not to fall within these terms, since section 1(3) provides:

"Nothing in subsection (2) above shall be construed as implying that a person may be dealt with under this Act as suffering from mental disorder, or from any form of mental disorder described in this section, by reason only of promiscuity or other immoral conduct, sexual deviancy or dependence on alcohol or drugs."

3. What amounts to sexual deviancy was briefly considered in *R. v. MHRT, ex p Clatworthy* [1985] 3 All E.R. 699:

"It may be at once observed that the effect of subsection (3) is apparently to prevent there being a condition of psychopathic disorder when the abnormally aggressive or seriously irresponsible conduct consequent on the persistent disorder or disability of mind is conduct which is a manifestation of sexual deviancy. It may also be observed that it can be contended that sexual deviancy does not mean tendency to deviation but means indulgence in deviation. That contention would achieve support from its context, the context being promiscuity or other immoral conduct and dependence on alcohol or drugs."

(c) Other Criteria for Admission

Whilst there are crucial differences between sections 2 and 3, the other criteria are considered together, with priority being given to a consideration of section 3. In *R. v. Wilson, ex. p. Williamson, The Independent*, April 19, 1995, the judge confirmed that admission:

"under section 2 is to be of short duration and for a limited purpose — assessment of the patient's condition with a view to ascertaining whether it is a case which would respond to treatment, and whether an order under section 3 would be appropriate . . . Although there is nothing to suggest that section 2 is a once and for all procedure, there is nothing in the Act which justifies successive or back to back applications under this section of the kind which occurred here. The powers under section 2 can only be used for the limited purpose for which they were intended, and cannot be utilised for the purpose of further detaining a patient for the purposes of assessment beyond the 28 day period, or used as a stop-gap procedure."

(i) The need for treatment in hospital

As will be seen later, there is no power to ensure that people take their treatment, usually medication, when living outside hospital. In an attempt to get around this problem "long leash treatment" was used. A patient would be admitted to hospital under section 3 with the intention of granting leave of absence on the following day. When on leave of absence a treatment regime could continue under Part IV of the Act, since that Part applies to patients on leave. The section would be renewed as and when necessary, and the patient would be recalled to hospital every six months so that the leave of absence could be renewed. It was argued that this satisfied the Act because the patient's condition and treatment needs demanded that he or she be on a section. However, the challenge to the use of this treatment was based upon the argument that the patient did not need treatment *in hospital* and so no section could be imposed nor renewed. These arguments have since been considered by the High Court.

R. v. Hallstrom, ex p. W; R. v. Gardner, ex p. L [1986] Q.B. 1090, [1985] 3 W.L.R. 1090, (1985) 129 S.J. 892

In this case W had been admitted to hospital under section 3 and granted leave of absence the following day, and L was a patient already in hospital who had been given leave of absence, and his section 3 was renewed under section 20 on being recalled to hospital over night.

McCullough J:
   ". . . Section 3 is concerned with admission to hospital and detention there. A person 'admitted' to hospital becomes an in-patient. This is the sense in which the word is ordinarily used . . . Detention follows admission. As, on admission, the patient becomes an in-patient, it must follow that his detention is *as an in-patient*, at any rate initially . . . The ordinary meaning of the words used in the Act of 1983 as a whole is to this effect. Section 3 and section 20 are about detention *in* a hospital. Section 3(2)(a) refers to treatment *in* a hospital. Section 17 deals with leave of absence *from* a hospital and recall (or return) *to* a hospital.
   The admission is 'for treatment'. Mr. Thorold submits that the treatment contemplated is treatment as an in-patient. But for the existence of section 17 this would certainly be so, since the treatment could only be given while the patient was detained, *i.e.* detained as an in-patient."

The argument [from counsel for the doctors] was that the mental disorder would have to require treatment in a hospital but not necessarily as an in-patient and that what was important was the use of the compulsory nature of the section rather than the hospitalisation.

   "Alternatively . . . if the meaning of section 3 is ambiguous, the construction for which [counsel] contends should be adopted because it enables doctors in such a situation to do what is, in accordance with good modern psychiatric practice, in the best interests of patients like W. *i.e.* treat them in the community, but compel them to accept the medication which their condition requires, but which, because of their illness, they do not think they need and therefore refuse.
   There is, however, no canon of construction which presumes that Parliament intended that people should, against their will, be subjected to treatment which others, however professionally competent, perceive, however sincerely and however correctly, to be in their best interests. What there is is a canon of construction that Parliament is presumed not to enact legislation which interferes with the liberty of the subject without making it clear that this was its intention.
   It goes without saying that, unless clear statutory authority to the contrary exists, no one is to be detained in hospital or to undergo medical treatment or even to submit himself to a medical examination without his consent. This is as true of a mentally disordered person as anyone else."

The judge recognised that there are various checks and controls within the legislation, such as: the various ways in which an authority to detain a patient may be discharged; the need for two doctors to give a reasoned opinion that the conditions of section 3 are met; the nearest relative's right to prevent a social worker from making an application for admission under section 3; the fact that a social worker who does so apply must first consult the nearest relative; and the fact that if the application is made by the nearest relative, a social worker must, as soon as practicable, interview the patient and report to the hospital managers on his social circumstances. But he concluded:

In my judgment, these provisions do not help to construe the sections with which this case is concerned. Each of these checks and controls is as compatible with [each argument].

In my judgment, the key to the construction of section 3 lies in the phrase "admission for treatment." It stretches the concept of "admission for treatment" too far to say that it covers admission for only so long as it is necessary to enable leave of absence to be granted, after which the necessary treatment will begin. "Admission for treatment" under section 3 is intended for those whose condition is believed to require a period of treatment as an in-patient. It maybe that such patients will also be thought to require a period of out-patient treatment thereafter, but the concept of "admission for treatment" has no applicability to those whom it is intended to admit and detain for a purely nominal period, during which no necessary treatment will be given.

The phrase "his mental disorder . . . makes it appropriate for him to receive medical treatment in a hospital" in section 3(2)(a) also leads to the conclusion that the section is concerned with those whose mental condition requires in-patient treatment. Treatment in a hospital does not mean treatment *at* a hospital . . . When it is remembered that the section authorises compulsory detention in a hospital it is at once clear why a distinction should be made between those whom it is appropriate to treat *in* a hospital, *i.e.* as in-patients, and those whom it is appropriate to treat otherwise, whether at the out-patient department of the hospital or at home or elsewhere.

It is true that the word "appropriate" rather than "necessary" is used in section 3(2)(a). This merely recognises the possibility that some forms of treatment required by a patient's mental disorder, although more appropriately given as an in-patient, might, as a matter of possibility be given elsewhere . . .

During the argument attention was focused on the word "detained" in the phrase "such treatment . . . cannot be provided unless he is detained under this section" in section 3(2)(c) . . . [This phrase should be read as meaning] "such treatment cannot be given unless he is then under detention" [and so] it is impossible without violation to the meaning of words to embrace those then liable to be detained but not then detained. [This interpretation] is consistent with the meaning of "admission for treatment" and of "treatment in a hospital" and with the intention of the section as a whole.

After referring to assistance in his approach from sections 13 and 2 and by comparison with the corresponding provision in the Mental Health Act 1959, section 26 and drawing upon the differences which must have been deliberate, the judge continued:

Even a night's detention is an infringement of personal liberty. Had Parliament intended to grant the power to overbear the refusal to consent of patients such as W, who could be maintained in the community provided they were given appropriate treatment, it would have so provided by a clear provision which involved no unnecessary detention. The differences between the Acts of 1959 and 1983 in relation to consent to treatment, to which I have already referred, underline the unlikelihood that Parliament intended in the later Act to provide for cases like W's in the indirect way contended for by counsel for the doctors.

For those various reasons, I conclude that section 3 only covers those whose mental condition is believed to require a period of in-patient treatment . . .

By similar process of argument, the judge arrived at the analogous position with regard to section 20, and stated:

The similarity of language between it and section 20 suggests that it too is concerned with those who are believed to require in-patient treatment. This tends to confirm that Parliament did not intend that the provisions for renewal would embrace those liable to be detained but not in fact detained . . . "

NOTE:

1. Since the treatment must be intended to take place in a hospital, it is possible that it means that the treatment to be offered must, in some way, be efficacious, and that this is a requirement separate from the treatability requirement.

QUESTION:

1. Do you agree with the interpretation given to the Act by McCullough J.? You might wish to revisit this question after considering matters related to treatment in the community.

(ii) The treatability requirement

The requirement in section 3(2)(b) (see also section 20) is often referred to as the "treatability test", although strictly speaking it is not necessary that the patient be likely to be cured. Some assistance as to the meaning of this requirement is proffered in the Court of Appeal's consideration of the same phrase appearing in the powers of discharge by a Mental Health Review Tribunal under section 72 in the following case.

R. v. Cannons Park MHRT, ex parte A [1994] 2 All E.R. 659

ROCH L.J.:
". . . I would suggest the following principles. First, if a tribunal were to be satisfied that the patient's detention in hospital was simply an attempt to coerce the patient into participating in group therapy, then the tribunal would be under a duty to discharge. Second, treatment in hospital will satisfy the treatability test although it is unlikely to alleviate the patient's condition, provided that it is likely to prevent a deterioration. Third, treatment in hospital will satisfy the treatability test although it will not immediately alleviate or prevent deterioration in the patient's condition, provided that alleviation or stabilisation is likely in due course. Fourth, the treatability test can still be met although initially there may be some deterioration in the patient's condition, due for example to the patient's initial anger at being detained. Fifth, it must be remembered that medical treatment in hospital covers nursing and also included are, habilitation and rehabilitation under medical supervision [this is a reference to the partial definition of 'medical treatment' in section 145]. Sixth, the treatability test is

satisfied if nursing care etc. are likely to lead to an alleviation of the patient's condition in that the patient is likely to gain an insight into his problem or cease to be uncooperative in his attitude towards treatment which would potentially have a lasting benefit."

The patient in this case was suffering from psychopathic disorder, the treatability of which is a matter of significant professional debate (see R. M. Jones, *Mental Health Act Manual* (4th edn., London: Sweet & Maxwell 1994 at pages 18–19 and 24–25) and B. M. Hoggett, Mental Health Law (4th edn., London: Sweet & Maxwell at pages 37–47) and E. Baker and J. Crichton, "*Ex parte A:* psychopathy, treatability and the law" (1995) 6 *Journal of Forensic Psychology*).

QUESTION:

1. If the environment in a given hospital is merely incarcerative or in another hospital merely a form of asylum and no therapeutic work is done by any staff would the treatability requirement be satisfied?

(iii) The least restrictive alternative

The latter part of section 3(2)(c) is a statutory expression of the least restrictive alternative. This is an internationally recognised principle demanding that detention should be used only when absolutely necessary and then imposing as little restriction on the freedom of the individual as possible.

QUESTION:

1. Does the Mental Health Act force approved social workers (ASWS) and doctors to consider whether sectioning is really necessary and what alternative facilities are available?

(iv) The nature or degree of the mental disorder

The first part of section 3(2)(c) does not demand that the prospective patient be dangerous. This criterion is satisfied if detention is for the prospective patient's health *or* safety *or* for the protection of others. That this is the correct interpretation had to be made clear in paragraph 2.6 of the *Mental Health Act Code of Practice* (2nd edn., 1993) since many professionals did not believe or accept, perhaps because they did not want to do so, that this was the force of section 3(2)(c).

QUESTIONS:

1. What will satisfy the requirement that the patient's "health or safety" be affected? Is it necessary that the person's mental health be at risk?

When is a person's safety sufficiently at risk to merit hospital detention?
2.   Is it right that it be possible for a person to be admitted compulsorily to hospital when he or she is not a danger to another, indeed presents no risk to others at all?

(d)   Procedural Issues

Since the power of compulsory admission is exercised without recourse to a court receiving evidence, the procedural issues are intended to establish sufficient safeguards to ensure that the power is used when, and only when, the statutory criteria are satisfied and that the then discretion whether to apply for the admission of a patient is exercised appropriately. This is achieved by identifying the people involved and setting procedural as well as substantive criteria:

(i) Applications for admission to hospital

An application for someone's admission to hospital is not made by a doctor, but is made by either an approved social worker (ASW) or the prospective patient's nearest relative (s.11). An ASW is an experienced social worker appointed to undertake this formal statutory work. Whilst employed by the social services department, an ASW is expected to exercise independent judgement to provide a non-medical view and to be aware of alternative facilities to compulsory admission to hospital. The details of the role of an ASW in admissions are to be found in sections 11 & 13 and in the *Code of Practice* at paragraphs 2.10–2.17.

Anyone could be a nearest relative. The Act provides, in section 26, a means of identifying both whether a person is a relative and whether they are the nearest relative. This is by no means always an easy task. Where an ASW applies for admission for assessment, he or she must inform the nearest relative (section 11(2)), and where an ASW applies for admission for treatment, he or she must consult the nearest relative who has the right of objection (section 11(3)). Laws J., in *R. v. South West Hospital Managers, ex p. M* [1993] Q.B. 683 (see also *Re S-C* [1996] 2 All E.R. 532, C.A.), made clear that the consultation must take place with the person the ASW genuinely believes, on the facts known, to be the nearest relative, but that such consultation may take place through another person when direct consultation is difficult. What is important is that the consultation be "full and effective". The nearest relative may be replaced as such by the county court on the application under section 29 of, amongst others, an ASW where the power of objection has been exercised unreasonably, as was the issue in *W v. L*, considered above. Where the nearest relative applies for admission of a person to hospital, the ASW will be asked to make a social circumstances report under section 14 when and if the patient is admitted to hospital. The *Code of Practice*, at paragraph 2.30, recommends that ordinarily the ASW ought to be the applicant

Whichever applies, they must have personally seen the patient within the previous 14 days (s 11(5)). This is an obligation which cannot be fulfilled through an intermediary according to Laws J. in *R. v. South West Hospital Managers, ex p. M* [1993] Q.B. 683.

Paragraph 2.6 of the Code of Practice offers guidance on the exercise of the discretion whether to use compulsory power. It suggests that factors to be taken into account include:

> "the patient's wishes and views of his own needs; his social and family circumstances; the risk of making assumptions based on a person's sex, social and cultural background or ethnic origin; the nature of the illness/behaviour disorder; what may be known about the patient by [others], assessing in particular how reliable this information is; other forms of care or treatment [available] . . . the impact that compulsory admission would have on the patient's life after discharge from detention; the burden on those close to the patient of a decision not to admit under the Act . . . "

(ii) Doctors Recommendations

Two doctors must make medical recommendations supporting the application. The Act seeks to secure their independence from one another in section 12. The *Code of Practice* at paragraph 2.19 makes clear that the doctors are expected to undertake a "direct personal examination of the patient's mental state, excluding any possible preconceptions based on the patient's sex, social and cultural background or ethnic origin" and considering all the relevant medical information. On the basis of an examination the doctor, as stated at in the *Code of Practice* at paragraph 2.18, must diagnose the patient with reference to the statutory concepts, decide whether the statutory criteria are satisfied, assess whether the person should be compulsorily admitted, and discover whether a hospital bed would be available.

(iii) Arrival at hospital

Once the patient arrives at the hospital, a decision must be taken whether to admit him. No hospital is obliged to accept a patient. The usual scenario is that the admission will have been sorted out prior to the patient's arrival, but a means of making or confirming decisions should be available at the actual time of admission.

6.—(1) An application for the admission of a patient to a hospital under this Part of this Act, duly completed in accordance with the provisions of this Part of this Act, shall be sufficient authority for the applicant, or any person authorised by the applicant, to take the patient and convey him to the hospital at any time within the following period, that is to say —

(a) in the case of an application other than an emergency application, the period of 14 days beginning with the date on which the patient was last examined by a registered medical practitioner before giving a medical recommendation for the purposes of the application;

(b) [for the case of emergency applications].

(2) Where a patient is admitted within the said period . . . the application shall be sufficient authority for the managers to detain the patient in hospital in accordance with the provisions of this Act.

(3) Any application for the admission of a patient under this Part of this Act which appears to be duly made and to be founded on the necessary medical recommendations may be acted upon without further proof of the signature or qualification of the person by whom the application or any such medical recommendation is made or given or of any matter of fact or opinion stated in it."

Notes:

1. Section 6(3) does not require a detailed examination of the issues behind the forms at the time of admission. Further, some errors in the forms may be amended within 14 days of the admission under section 15. Errors which may not be rectified include "a defect which arises because a necessary event in the procedural chain . . . has simply not take place at all" according to Laws J. in *R. v. South West Hospital Managers, ex p. M.* [1993] Q.B. 683 nor can this section enable "a fundamentally defective application to be retrospectively validated" according to Sir Thomas Bingham M.R. in *Re S-C* [1996] 2 All E.R. 532. So, for example, where personal interviews by ASWs and medical examinations do not take place, section 15 is of no avail to the hospital detaining the patient. See K. Keywood "Rectification of incorrect documentation under the Mental Health Act 1983" (1996) 7 *Journal of Forensic Psychology* 79.

2. Whether the hospital must institute any checks of the documentation was considered by Laws J. in *R. v. South Western Hospital Managers, ex p. M* [1994] 1 All E.R. 161. His Lordship said:

> "Section 6(1) and (2) confer authority to convey or detain the patient in hospital where the application is 'duly completed in accordance with the provisions of this Part of this Act'. In my judgment that is an objective requirement and means that the application must not only state that the relevant provisions (which include the requirements of s. 11(4)) have been fulfilled, but also that it be the case that they have actually been fulfilled . . .
>
> In my judgment, where an application on its face sets out all the facts which, if true, constitute compliance with the relevant provisions of Part II of the Act (again, including section 11(4)) it is an application which 'appears to be duly made' within section 6(3). If any of the facts thus stated are not true, then although the application appears to be duly made, it is not duly completed for the purposes of section 6(1) and 6(2). Here, Miss Stiller's application did state all the facts which, if true, constituted compliance with the relevant statutory provisions. Accordingly it was an application which appeared to be duly made. It follows that, although the managers were not authorised to detain the patient by section 6(2) standing alone, they were entitled to act upon the application, and thus to detain the patient, by virtue of section 6(3).
>
> Accordingly, the applicants detention is not unlawful.

That passage was considered by the Court of Appeal in *Re S-C* [1996] 2 All E.R. 532, where Sir Thomas Bingham M.R. said:

"Speaking for myself, I would accept almost everything in that passage as correct with the exception of the last sentence. The judge goes straight from a finding that the hospital managers were entitled to act upon an apparently valid application to the conclusion that the applicant's detention was therefore not unlawful. That is, in my judgment, a *non sequitur*. It is perfectly possible that the hospital managers were entitled to act on an apparently valid application, but that the detention was in fact unlawful. If that were not so the implications would, in my judgment, be horrifying. It would mean that an application which appeared to be in order would render the detention of a citizen lawful even though it was shown or admitted that the approved social worker purporting to make the application was not an approved social worker, that the registered medical practitioners whose recommendations founded the application were not registered medical practitioners or had not signed the recommendations, and that the approved social worker had not consulted the patient's nearest relative or had consulted the patient's nearest relative and that relative had objected. In other words, it would mean that the detention was lawful even though every statutory safeguard built into the procedure was shown to have been ignored or violated.

Bearing in mind what is at stake, I find that conclusion wholly unacceptable. I am, for my part, satisfied that on present facts an application for *habeas corpus* is an appropriate, and possibly even *the* appropriate, course to pursue."

QUESTIONS:

1. Why do you think that a hospital is obliged to have an admission process making clear, exactly, when the patient became a detained patient?
2. Do you agree with the analysis of Laws J. or that of Sir Thomas Bingham? What, if any, implications follow from their alternative conclusions?

(iv) The exercise of the doctor's discretion

As indicated above, the ASW and doctors must exercise their discretion, which must be based upon information and assessment. But they do not always know prospective patients nor have sufficient information to contemplate compulsory admission. If the prospective patient is at home, it can be particularly difficult to obtain sufficient information. If access is provided to the house by someone with the power to do so, so be it, but, according to the Divisional Court, there is no right of entry for doctors to undertake an examination (*Townley v. Rushworth* (1963) 62 L.G.R. 95). ASWs do have a power to enter and inspect premises under section 115, and this is supported by the offence of obstruction within section 129. But is any of this relevant to the function of the ASW in deciding whether or not to make an application?

Under section 135, an ASW has the power to seek a warrant from a magistrate for the police to enter the premises (by force if necessary) and remove certain people to a place of safety (such as a hospital, residential home, police station or other place where the occupier is willing to accept the patient), provided the necessary conditions are satisfied:

"that there is reasonable cause to suspect that a person believed to be suffering from mental disorder:

(a) has been, or is being, ill-treated, neglected or kept otherwise than under proper control, in any place within the jurisdiction of the justice, or

(b) being unable to care for himself, is living alone in any such place . . ."

(See P. Fennell, "The Beverley Lewis case: Was the Law to Blame?" (1989) 139 *New L.J.* 1559 and the Law Commission, *Mental Incapacity*, London: HMSO, Law Com. 231, for recommendation, 1995, for reform of this case.)

(e) Freedom of Movement

A patient's freedom of movement is severely restricted by detention in hospital. Further, his freedom to make decisions about treatment are dramatically altered. Whilst there are carefully worded criteria and an extensive process designed to ensure that detention only occurs where appropriate and necessary, it is important that a patient has the right to challenge that detention. Taking away freedom without providing the right to challenge is a severe breach of human rights, as recognised by Article 5(4) of the European Convention on Human Rights.

The patient may be discharged by decision of those with the relevant power (see later). This is not a formal means of challenge, but issues raised by the patient may result in his discharge. The patient has a right of appeal to a Mental Health Review Tribunal, but it appears that is not concerned with the initial decision to admit (see below).

The patient may seek to take an action for trespass to the person, particularly false imprisonment, or negligence. In view of the powers provided by the Mental Health Act, tortious actions would have to rely upon either a clear failure to comply with the statutory provisions or a failure properly to exercise discretion. If there was an unlawful admission, this might make the detention improper, and therefore provide the possibility of an action for false imprisonment. However, there is a major obstacle where an action is to be taken against an individual, though not where the action is against a health authority or trust. Section 139(1) provides that an individual cannot be liable in civil or criminal proceedings "in respect of any act purporting to be done in pursuance" of the legislation "unless the act was done in bad faith and without reasonable care." Further, section 139(2) provides that if proceedings are to be instituted, the patient must have the leave of the High Court in civil proceedings or the consent of the Director of Public Prosecutions in criminal proceedings. Leave will be given, on the materials immediately available to the court if "the applicant's complaint appears to be such that it deserves the fuller investigation which will be possible if the intended applicant is allowed to proceed": Lord Donaldson M.R. in *Winch v. Jones* [1985] 3 All E.R. 102. The objective of these provisions is to enable professionals to undertake their job of providing care and treatment whilst balancing that against the right of an individual to challenge any infringement in his freedoms. The only justification for these provisions can be that people with mental disorders who are detained are likely to take frivolous or vexatious legal action. There is some support for this approach in the speech of Lord Simon in *Pountney v. Griffiths* [1976] A.C. 314, but no supporting evidence. There is no major litigation problem concerning informal patients, to whom this provision does not apply as was decided in *R. v. Runighian* [1977] Crim. L.R. 361. It is confidently expected that a challenge to the propriety of this provision would fall foul of Articles 5(4) and 6 of the European Convention on Human Rights, although it appears the Commission was not enamoured with such a challenge in *Ashingdane v. U.K.*

QUESTIONS:

1. In view of the general power to restrict vexatious litigants in section 42 of the Supreme Court Act 1981, is there any reason why detained patients should have the automatic burden imposed by section 139(2)?
2. Why, if at all, do hospital staff need the protection of section 139(1) when similar provisions are not available to other staff facing difficult, perhaps violent, clients?

The most likely forms of challenge are either the writ of *habeas corpus* or an application for judicial review, to neither of which section 139 applies, since they are not "civil proceedings" (see *R. v. Hallstrom, ex parte W.* [1985] 3 All E.R. 775, C.A. and M. Gunn, "Judicial Review and Hospital Admissions and Treatment in the Community under the Mental Health Act 1983" (1986) *Journal of Social Welfare Law* 290.) A writ of *habeas corpus* may best deal with a clear failure to comply with the provisions of the legislation or where there is a matter of jurisdictional fact arising. In *Re S-C* [1996] 2 All E.R. 532, the Court of Appeal decided that seeking a writ of *habeas corpus* was the appropriate course of action where, in the words of Sir Thomas Bingham M.R., "there [was] not attempt to overturn any administrative decision. The object [was] simply to show that there was never jurisdiction to detain the patient in the first place, a fact which in agreed evidence appears to be plainly made out." The agreed evidence was that an application was made by an approved social worker after she had consulted with a person (the mother of the patient) whom she knew not to be the patient's nearest relative (who was the father and who would have objected to the making of an application for admission under section 3). Where the challenge is to the exercise of a discretion by an ASW, nearest relative, doctor or hospital, it is more likely that the appropriate challenge would be by way of an application for judicial review (see, *e.g.*, *R. v. Wilson and another, ex p. Williamson, The Independent*, April 19, 1995).

R. v. Managers of South Western Hospital, ex parte M. [1993] Q.B. 683

M. had been admitted to hospital under section 4, which was subsequently converted to a section 2 admission by the provision of the second medical recommendation. She appealed to the Mental Health Review Tribunal which concluded that her mental disorder did not warrant admission in hospital, but deferred discharge for arrangements to be made by social services. When her responsible medical officer received the decision of the tribunal, he recommended that she be admitted to hospital under section 3. He had not carried out an examination since the tribunal hearing, but took account of the tribunal's decision. A second, independent medical recommendation was provided by a general practitioner at M.'s practice, but who did not usually see M. She had been told by a nurse that M. was not taking her medication. The case was referred to an ASW. M. told the ASW that she was not taking her medication but was hiding it under her tongue. The ASW's professional assessment was that "if the applicant [were] allowed out of hospital without treatment, she would not take her medication: she did not take it in hospital. She would refuse out-patient treatment . . . I consider that she would until well continue to do bizarre things and threaten her neighbours. She would alienate herself further from the community and her family." There had been a consultation with M's uncle who was the nearest relative and he had no objection. M.'s uncle thought that the tribunal should not have ordered M.'s deferred discharge. The application made by the ASW was accepted by the hospital managers.

M. wished to challenge the decision by way of judicial review, but her application seeking leave was refused. She, therefore, instituted proceedings seeking a writ of *habeas corpus*.

LAWS J.:

". . . [The] major submission before me may be expressed in this way: once a tribunal has decided to discharge the patient, that decision must be respected to the extent at least that it cannot be nullified by a decision to detain the patient under section 3 which follows the tribunal decision after a short space of time and with no change of circumstances. He said that the section 3 decision here frustrates the tribunal decision, so that a writ of *habeas corpus* ought to go.

I shall deal with this part of the case out of deference to the general importance of the relationship between the section 3 regime and the tribunal's functions; but I can say at once that, in my judgment, it is a point which runs on the facts of the case not to *habeas corpus* but to judicial review, for reasons I shall explain . . .

In my judgment, the principal argument . . . must in the end depend upon the proposition that on the true construction of the Act the hospital managers have not the power to order or direct a detention under section 3 if a tribunal has recently decided that the patient be discharged (whatever the basis of the patient's original detention) and there has been no change of circumstances since that decision. So regarded, the question becomes one of pure statutory construction.

Mr Gordon for the hospital manager and Dr. Lawrence submits that the statute cannot be construed so as to produce such a consequence, not least since section 13, whose relevant parts I have read, imposes a duty on an approved social worker to make a section 3 application in the circumstances which that section specifies; the duty is not abrogated, or qualified, in a case where there has been a recent tribunal decision directing discharge; if it were to be abrogated or qualified, section 13 would say so. That being the case, the hospital managers must be obliged to consider on its merits an application made by the approved social worker in pursuance of his duty, and the existence of a recent tribunal decision can no more fetter this obligation than it can the social worker's own express duty under section 13. It is true (see section 13(5)) that there may be cases in which a section 3 application is made by the discretion, not pursuant to the duty, of the social worker; but in such a case the social worker's discretion cannot be any more fettered than can be the performance of his duty where that arises.

These submissions seem to me to be correct. Further, if the intention of the legislature was as Mr Buchan suggests, one would expect a clear qualification to have been imposed within the terms of section 3, or more likely section 6, on the discretion to admit a patient to hospital pursuant to a section 3 application. Or there might be a provision in section 13, analogous to section 13(5), to show that no application is to be made, even where otherwise it would be the approved social worker's duty to make it, where its being granted would conflict with an extant tribunal decision. There are no such provisions in any of these sections. The statute is careful to specify a rigorous procedure for the protection of the individual who may be liable to compulsory admission: not least, the requirement that there be two written medical recommendations.

I do not think that it can sensibly be suggested that if the intention were that a patient be not exposed to section 3 where there existed a recent tribunal decision to discharge and no change of circumstances, that would not be as clear and express on the face of the statute as are the other protections which it affords.

I also consider that Mr Buchan's submissions would require me to hold that the legality of section 3 detention may depend upon criteria which are subjective and elastic. In his initial skeleton argument he submitted that some period of time must be allowed to elapse after the tribunal decision, at least while there is no significant change in the patient's condition and circumstances, before the full force of section 3 is permitted to have effect . . . I cannot think this is right. Honest and responsible doctors will differ upon such questions as the significance of any apparent change in a patient's condition — even when there has been a change: to make the legality of a detention depend upon issues of that sort would be to abandon any claim in this area to a reasonable degree of legal certainty and would, likely as not, put the experts involved in individual cases in an invidious if not impossible position. More specifically, there is nothing whatever that I can find in the statute to suggest that such a state of affairs was an intended function or aspect of the regime of interlocking controls which the Act contains . . .

I can see no basis for construing the statute so as to produce the result that the duty and discretion of the approved social worker to make the section 3 application, and the function of the managers in considering it, are to any extent impliedly limited or abrogated by the existence of an earlier tribunal decision to discharge under section 72. Theoretically, this may produce an impasse: the tribunal directs a discharge; the patient is returned to or retained in hospital under section 3; there is a further application to the tribunal, which directs a further discharge; there follows a yet further successful application under section 3; and so on.

In reality this is highly unlikely to happen, given good faith on all hands and the procedures and safeguards which colour the section 3 process. As Mr Gordon submitted, the social worker must always conduct a personal interview before making a section 3 application; there must always be two separate medical recommendations; and there has to be a decision by the managers pursuant to section 6. Elementarily, the public law safeguards enshrined in the Associated

Provincial Pictures Houses Ltd *Wednesbury* corporates [1948] 1 K.B. 223 and *Padfield v. Ministry of Agriculture, Fisheries and Food* [1968] A.C. 997 apply to all exercises of administrative power by the bodies I have mentioned. In any event, there is no such impasse here . . .

I would therefore hold that there is no sense in which those concerned in a section 3 application are at any stage bound by an earlier tribunal decision. The doctors, social worker, and managers must under the statute exercise their independent judgment whether or not there is an extant tribunal decision relating to the patient. They will no doubt wish to have regard to any such decision, where they know of it, in order to ensure that they have the maximum information about the facts of the case. But in my judgment it cannot confine or restrict their own exercise of the functions which the Act confers on them.

If I am wrong, I would in any event hold that there was material here showing substantial grounds for supposing that the applicant would not abide by her undertaking to the Tribunal 'that she would co-operate with a programme of treatment organised for her by the hospital and would take medication as advised' . . . On the date when the section 3 application was made (December 16) there was every reason to suppose that the applicant would not cooperate with any programme or requirement arranged for her to take the medication that was prescribed . . . Thus, in my judgment, even if a section 3 application would only be good in the event of a change of circumstances, or fresh development in the face of an earlier tribunal decision to discharge that was sufficiently established here.

For all these reasons, I reject Mr Buchan's primary argument that the detention of the applicant under section 3 was flawed for a failure of consistency with the tribunal's decision to discharge.

I have said, however, that this point would in any event go to judicial review and not to *habeas corpus*. The reason is to be found in section 6(3) and may be shortly put [and has been considered earlier]. The applicant cannot, in my judgment, escape the effect of the provisions of section 6(3) demonstrating, were it the case, that the application should not have been made on grounds of conflict with the tribunal decision. In these circumstances, Mr Buchan's argument as to conflict with that decision cannot avail him on this application . . . ''

QUESTIONS:

1. Whilst it is not unlikely that a *habeas corpus* action failed, should leave to apply for judicial review have been granted?
2. Will an application for judicial review on the basis of *Wednesbury* unreasonableness succeed where a tribunal has ordered a discharge from one section and the doctor and an ASW immediately admit the patient under another section (section 3), without new facts or circumstances? Laws J. suggests the contrary but do you find his argument convincing?

(f)   Admission for Assessment in Emergency

Section 4 provides for the possibility of an admission for assessment in an emergency. The criteria for admission are the same as for admission under section 2 (section 4(2) & (3)), except that there must be a statement on the application that "it is of urgent necessity for the patient to be admitted and detained under section 2 above, and that compliance with the provisions of this Part of this Act relating to applications under that section would involve undesirable delay" (section 4(2)). Only one medical recommendation is needed (section 4(3)). If the patient is admitted, the section ceases to have effect after 72 hours unless a second medical recommendation is forthcoming to turn it into a section 2 admission (section 4(4)). In order to make an application, the patient must have been personally seen within the previous 24 hours (sections 11(5) and 4(5)).

(g) Admission of Patients Already in Hospital

Section 5 provides for the possibility of detaining a patient who is already in hospital but is not detained under a section of the Mental Health Act 1983. In considering the position of a patient informally resident in hospital, it is important to bear section 5 in mind, since it significantly affects the reality of the assertion that an informal patient is free to leave, exercising his freedom of movement.

There are two means whereby a patient in hospital informally (which is the meaning of in-patient in section 5(6)) may be prevented from leaving; one holding power may be used by a doctor, the other by a nurse. In 1990–91 the doctor's power was used on 7,788 occasions and the nurse's power on 1,053 occasions.

(i) The doctor's holding power

5.—(1) An application for admission of a patient to a hospital may be made under this Part of this Act notwithstanding that the patient is already an in-patient at that hospital or, in the case of an application for admission for treatment that the patient is for the time being liable to be detained in the hospital in pursuance of an application for admission for assessment; and where an application is so made the patient shall be treated for the purposes of this Part of the Act as if he had been admitted to the hospital at the time when that application was received by the managers.

Where the holding power is exercised by a report furnished or sent to the hospital managers, the patient may be detained in the hospital for 72 hours from the time the report is so furnished (s 5(2)).

QUESTIONS:

1. Must the in-patient be receiving treatment for a mental disorder? Compare the wording of section 5(4) below to assist you in considering this matter. If not, which doctor may institute this holding power?
2. What are the criteria for imposing this holding power? Are they clear and specific? If not, should they be?

The doctor in charge of the patient's medical treatment will not be on duty in the hospital at all times, so section 5(3) provides for the power to "nominate one (but not more than one) other" doctor on the hospital staff to exercise the power in his absence.

(ii) The nurses' holding power

5.—(4) If, in the case of a patient who is receiving treatment for mental disorder as an in-patient in a hospital, it appears to a nurse of the prescribed class:

(a) that the patient is suffering from mental disorder to such a degree that it is necessary for his health or safety or for the protection of others for him to be immediately restrained from leaving the hospital; and

(b) that it is not practicable to secure the immediate attendance of a practitioner for the purpose of furnishing a report under subsection (2) above,

the nurse may record that fact in writing; and in that event the patient may be detained in the hospital for a period of six hours from the time when that fact is so recorded or until the earlier arrival at the place where the patient is detained of a practitioner having power to furnish a report under that sub-section.

(5) A record made under subsection (4) above shall be delivered by the nurse (or by a person authorised by the nurse in that behalf) to the managers of the hospital as soon as possible after it is made; and where a record is made under that subsection the period mentioned in subsection (2) above shall begin at the time when it is made.

NOTE:

1. "Prescribed nurse" means, in old terminology, a nurse with a Registered Mental Nurse (RMN) or Registered Nurse of the Mentally Handicapped (RNMH) qualification and does not refer to seniority or any other such criteria.

QUESTIONS:

1. Would you expect section 5(4) to be interpreted so that the form must be furnished to the managers before a patient can be stopped from leaving?
2. Might section 5 operate on the mind of a person contemplating entering hospital as an in-patient to enter voluntarily or compulsorily?

4. IN HOSPITAL

Certain consequences flow from being a patient detained in a hospital. Of these, the most important, for present purposes, is the rules relating to treatment, but there are also other implications to be considered.

(a) Detention

The Mental Health Act 1983 permits the detention of a person in hospital. He or she can only be discharged if the procedures laid down in the Act are followed, and can only leave the hospital temporarily if granted leave of absence. If a patient is absent without leave, the Act provides for her or his return to hospital in section 18. Until the Mental Health (Patients in the Community) Act 1995, a patient who was absent without leave for 28 days or more could not be returned to hospital and so the detention came to an end. The 1995 Act introduced amendments which mean that the patient can be taken into custody and returned up until six months after going absent without leave (section 18(4) of the 1983 Act, as amended). Special provisions apply where the section would have terminated (but the termination is suspended under section 21) during the period of absence without leave and vary depending on whether the patient is returned within 28 days (section 21A) or six months (section 21B).

(b)   Leave of absence

Section 17(1) provides that a patient may be granted "leave to be absent from the hospital subject to such conditions (if any) as [the responsible medical officer] considers necessary in the interests of the patient or for the protection of other persons." Leave of absence may be granted "either indefinitely or on specified occasions or for any specified period; and where leave is so granted for a specified period, that period may be extended by further leave granted in the absence of the patient." The patient may be recalled from leave and the leave be revoked at any time if "it appears to the [RMO] that it is necessary to do so in the interests of the patient's health or safety or for the protection of others" (section 17(4)). Prior to the amendments introduced by the Mental Health (Patients in the Community) Act 1995, leave of absence could only last for six months. The effect of the amendments is that leave of absence can last until the section 3 comes up for renewal, in which case the patient must either be recalled to hospital or discharged (sections 17(5) and 20).

Great care has to be taken in the granting of leave of absence (as in discharge) because of the potential dangers presented by some, but by no means all, patients. The *Code of Practice* recommends in paragraph 20.5, that the "granting of leave and the conditions attached to it should be recorded in the patient's notes and copies given to the patient, any appropriate relatives/friends and any professionals in the community who need to know." Leave of absence is of real significance to a patient. It enables him to retain or obtain skills which will be necessary once he or she is discharged or allows him to retain contact with the "outside world." There are no limits imposed by the statute as to the purposes for which leave of absence may be granted. Further, when a patient is on leave of absence, he or she is liable to be detained and so the treatment regime provided for in Part IV of the Act applies. Therefore, if leave of absence can be renewed (and also the section 3 be renewed as necessary), it would be possible to provide treatment in the community, and the patient would not be able to refuse to take the medication, provided the criteria in section 58 of the Act were satisfied (see below). This forms of "long leash detention" was considered in the following case, aspects of which have already been considered. Note that when this case was decided leave of absence could only last for a maximum of six months.

R. v. Hallstrom and Another, ex p. W; R. v. Gardner and Another, ex p. L [1986] 1 Q.B. 1090

McCullough J.:

". . . The question . . . is whether it is lawful to recall to hospital a patient on indefinite leave of absence when the intention is merely to prevent him from being on leave of absence for six months continuously [Ed. now up to one year]. The short answer is that it is not because section 17(4) only empowers the responsible medical officer to revoke the leave of absence and recall the patient when "it is necessary so to do in the interests of the patient's health or safety or for the protection of other persons." If, upon revocation of leave of absence, the patient returns to hospital his status will once more be the same as it was before he was given leave of absence, *i.e.* that of an in-patient who is compulsorily detained . . . Thus, section 17(4) in effect says that leave of absence may only be revoked and the patient recalled when it is necessary in the interests of his health or safety or for the protection of other persons *that he again becomes an in-patient*. It was not necessary in the interests of L's health or safety or for the protection of others that L should again become an in-patient on September 25, 1985. In my judgment it is as simple as that.

Mr Thorold submitted, though not quite in these words, that a patient could not lawfully be recalled unless, in the opinion of the responsible medical officer, he required in-patient *treatment*. He argued that as a mental state of this quality was required for the purposes of section 3, it would be regarded as required for the revocation of leave of absence because such revocation then restored the patient to his status before he was granted leave of absence, *i.e.* one who had been admitted *for treatment*. I cannot accept this: first, because section 17(4) says no more than that the relevant considerations necessitate his recall to *hospital; second, because* Parliament may well have thought that many patients who on admission required inpatient treatment might progress to a state where, although further *detention* was *required, further treatment* was not. I am thinking, for example, of those being observed pending the taking of a decision to grant them leave of absence.

Once a patient has been on leave of absence for six months his liability to be recalled ends: section 17(5). To frustrate this provision by the device of recall for one night, for which recall there is no necessity, is to extend the duration of the liability to recall. Express provision for the extension of such liability has been made by section 20. To use section 17(5) in the way under consideration is to by-pass the requirements of section 20.

There can only be two intentions behind this device. One is to extend the period during which a patient may be treated compulsorily in the community. The other is to retain the power to recall him should considerations of his health or safety or the protection of others require this at some time in the future. In neither event could it truly be said that 'it is necessary so to do' (*i.e.* to detain him compulsorily as an in-patient) 'in the interests of [his] health or safety or for the protection of other persons'."

Questions:

1. Would you agree that, since the person is a detained patient, any absence from the hospital or its grounds must be authorised by a

leave of absence? If so, *e.g.*, every shopping trip must be covered by a leave of absence. Would you agree, then, that it is good practice to allow RMOs to provide fairly open-ended leave of absence for some patients whom it is known will be able to take regular journeys outside the hospital and for which the requirement to provide a fresh leave of absence on every occasion would be impracticable? If you disagree, can the power to grant leave of absence be delegated to overcome the problem that the RMO may not be available (on holiday, at the cinema, etc.)?

2. Do you agree with the analysis of McCullough J.? (See M. Gunn, "Judicial Review of Hospital Admissions and Treatment in the Community under the Mental Health Act 1983" [1986] *Journal of Social Welfare Law* 290.)

(c)   Restraint

There is nothing in the Act which indicates what can be done with patients on a day-to-day basis, unless it falls within the definition of "treatment", see below. There may, however, be some bodily interference which is necessary within the hospital, not as part of the therapeutic regime, but merely to ensure that the institution operates relatively efficiently including the exercise of necessary discipline and control. This appears to have been approved of by the House of Lords as a necessary implication of compulsory admission:

Pountney v. Griffiths [1976] A.C. 314

LORD EDMUND-DAVIES:
"... [sectioning] 'warrants the detention of the patient in a hospital for medical treatment', and that necessarily involves the exercise of control and discipline. Suitable arrangements for visits to patients by family and friends are an obvious part of a patient's treatment. Such visits inevitably involve the ushering of him back to his quarters when the permitted visiting time is ended. The respondent was accordingly acting in pursuance of the 1959 Act when the incident complained of occurred and, before civil or criminal proceedings for assault could properly be brought against him, the leave of the High Court should have been sought and obtained."

Restraint in a more technical sense may be justified or excused on the basis that it is the use of reasonable force in the defence of self or others (*i.e.* private defence). In this sense, it is considered in detail in Chapter 18 of the *Code of Practice*, which identifies that restraint may be necessary in some circumstances. Restraint includes physical restraint (paragraphs 18.9–18.13), medical restraint (paragraph 18.14) and seclusion (the "supervised confinement of a patient alone in a room which may be locked for the protection of others from significant harm": paragraph 18.15; on seclusion generally, see paragraphs 18.15–18.23). The basis for these actions is *not*, it is suggested, that they are treatment under Part IV of the Act or common law, despite what the *Code* suggests at paragraph 18.15.

(d) Treatment

The 1959 Act contained no provisions clarifying the treatment position of detained patients: Part IV of the 1983 Act does just that. If the justification for compulsory admission is either *parens patriae* or police powers, it would appear to follow that there is an obligation to provide treatment. Do you agree? If so, does it follow that it must be possible to provide that treatment compulsorily, even though this turns the common law on its head, in particular the assumption that a compulsorily detained patient is not capable of making her or his own treatment decisions?

Not all compulsory sections involve the patient being admitted for treatment (whether with assessment or not). Thus the treatment sections should and do not apply to patients in hospital under sections 5(2) and (4), 135 and 136. In addition, since section 4 is an emergency section, there is no good reason for applying the treatment provisions. It is easy to change it to a section 2, which is a treatment section. These objectives are achieved by section 56. For all these patients, the consent to treatment position is that under the common law (see *Mental Health Act Code of Practice*, Chapter 15). It is important to note that section 56 also applies the provisions of section 57 to informal patients, which is one of the very few provisions to apply to such patients (and which explains why the patient in *R. v. Mental Health Act Commission, ex p. X*, below, concerns an out-patient).

The phrase used in section 56(1)(a) is that a patient must be "liable to be detained" under of the sections which permits treatment (*i.e.*, sections 2 and 3 for our purposes).

QUESTION:

1. Using your knowledge gained so far, does a patient have to be detained in hospital to fall within this phrase? Refer back to *R. v. Hallstrom, ex p. W* (above at page 520).

The Mental Health Act separates treatment for mental disorder into three categories, covered by sections 57, 58 (and treatments covered by these section in an emergency under section 62) and 63. Note that treatment may include a plan of treatment (section 59). Note also that a patient may withdraw consent, if it had been provided, at any time (section 60).

57.—(1) This section applies to the following forms of medical treatment for mental disorder —

(a) any surgical operation for destroying brain tissue or for destroying the functioning of the brain tissue; and
(b) such other forms of treatment as may be specified for the purposes of this section by regulations made by the Secretary of State.

(2) Subject to section 62 below, a patient shall not be given any form of treatment to which this section applies unless he has consented to it and —

(a) a registered medical practitioner appointed for the purposes of this Part of this Act by the Secretary of State (not being the responsible medical officer) and two other persons appointed for the purposes of this paragraph by the Secretary of State (not being registered medical practitioners) have certified in writing that the patient is capable of understanding the nature, purpose and likely effects of the treatment in question and has consented to it; and

(b) the registered medical practitioner referred to in paragraph (a) above has certified in writing that, having regard to the likelihood of the treatment alleviating or preventing a deterioration of the patient's condition, the treatment should be given.

(3) Before giving a certificate under subsection (2)(b) above the registered medical practitioner concerned shall consult two other persons who have been professionally concerned with the patient's medical treatment, and of those persons one shall be a nurse and the other shall be neither a nurse nor a registered medical practitioner."

NOTES:

1. Section 57(1)(a) is concerned with psychosurgery. (For further consideration, see L. Gostin, "Psychosurgery: A Hazardous and Unestablished Treatment? A Case for the Importation of American Legal Safeguards to Great Britain" (1982) *Journal of Social Welfare Law* 83.) It is carried out very rarely. In 1993–1995 there were only 34 psychosurgery referrals to the Mental Health Act Commission (Mental Health Act Commission, *Sixth Biennial Report 1993–1995*, pages 181–183) and 24 operations took place. This includes both detained and informal patients.

2. Section 57(1)(b) is concerned with a treatment which is carried out even more rarely than psychosurgery (there were no referrals to MHAC in 1991–1995), and that is the surgical implantation of hormones to reduce male sexual drive (Mental Health (Hospital, Guardianship and Consent to Treatment) Regulations 1983, S.I. No. 893, reg. 16(1)(a)). It is interesting to note that this appears to be a treatment for sexual deviancy, placed in provisions relating to controlling consent to treatment for mental disorder. However, sexual deviancy is not a form of mental disorder and therefore it is doubtful whether it should be in the Act at all. In *R. v. Mental Health Act Commission, ex p X.* (1988) 9 BMLR 77, it was decided that this provision did not cover the administration of Goserelin, a drug the primary purpose of which was the treatment of prostrate cancer, but which had the side effect of reducing testosterone to castrate levels. Three Mental Health Act Commissioners had taken the view that the administration of the drug was covered by section 57. Stuart-Smith J. stated that: (a) it was not a hormone. The fact that it was a synthetic substance did not matter. It was a synthetic analogue, having the opposite effect of a hormone by obstructing the messages sent. (b) It was not surgically implanted. It was administered in a polymer cylinder which degraded so as to release the substance gradually and

was inserted subcutaneously via an injection, which did not comply with what would be regarded in common parlance as surgical implantation.

QUESTION:

1. If the administration of Goserelin does not fall within section 58, does it fall within any other provision of Part IV? If so, what consequences flow for what might be termed chemical castration? (You may wish to consider this question further after examining section 63 below. (See P. Fennell, "Sexual Suppressants and the Mental Health Act" [1988] *Crim. L.R.* 660, and Mental Health Act Commission (1989), *Third Biennial Report*, at page 22.))

58.—(1) This section applies to the following forms of medical treatment for mental disorder —

(a) such forms of treatment as may be specified for the purposes of this section by regulations made by the Secretary of State;
(b) the administration of medicine to a patient by any means (not being a form of treatment specified under paragraph (a) above or section 57 above) at any time during a period for which he is liable to be detained as a patient to whom this Part of the Act applies if three months or more have elapsed since the first occasion in that period when medicine was administered to him by any means for his mental disorder.

(3) Subject to section 62 below, a patient shall not be given any form of treatment to which this section applies unless —

(a) he has consented to that treatment and either the responsible medical officer or a registered medical practitioner appointed for the purposes of this Part of this Act by the Secretary of State has certified in writing that the patient is capable of understanding its nature, purpose and likely effects and has consented to it; or
(b) a registered medical practitioner appointed as aforesaid (not being the responsible medical officer) has certified in writing that the patient is not capable of understanding the nature, purpose and likely effects of that treatment or has not consented to it but that, having regard to the likelihood of its alleviating or preventing a deterioration of his condition, the treatment should be given.

(4) Before giving a certificate under subsection (3)(b) above the registered medical practitioner concerned shall consult two other persons who have been professionally concerned with the patient's medical treatment, and of those persons one shall be a nurse and the other shall be neither a nurse nor a registered medical practitioner."

(i) Medication

The three month rule, with regard to the continuation of medication (section 58(2)(b)), is often misunderstood and the *Code of Practice* attempts to clarify matters by providing that (in paragraph 16.11) the "period starts on the occasion when medication for mental disorder was first administered by any means during any period of continuing detention" and that the "medication does not necessarily have to be administered continuously throughout the three month period." This period allows (paragraph 16.13) "time for the doctor to create a treatment programme suitable for the patient's need. Although the patient can be treated in the absence of consent during this period no such treatment should be given in the absence of an attempt to obtain valid consent. The three month period is not affected by renewal of the detention order, withdrawal of consent, leave or change in or discontinuance of the treatment. A fresh period will only begin if there is a break in the patient's liability for detention." Where medication is continued beyond the three month period under section 58, it is important to note that the approval need not be for a particular drug, so the *Code of Practice* provides (at paragraph 16.12) that on the certificate indicating authorisation for continuation "the drugs proposed [should be indicated] by the classes described in the British National Formulary (BNF), the method of their administration and the dose range (indicating the dosages if they are above BNF advisory maximum limits)."

(ii) Electro-convulsive therapy

Electro-convulsive therapy was added by regulations (Mental Health (Hospital, Guardianship and Consent to Treatment) Regulations 1983, S.I. 893, reg. 16(2)). Some people object to the use of ECT. On the other hand, the indicators for its use have been carefully researched by psychiatrists, and the observations of its effect have been carefully identified, even if it is not quite clear how it works. It would appear that the active agent is the fit induced by ECT rather than the electricity itself. Many would regard it as a 'quick fix' treatment when other forms of treatment, though taking more time, would be as efficacious. In J. Cookson *et al*, *The Use of Drugs in Psychiatry*, there is a summary of guidance on the use of ECT. The purposes for which ECT may be used include severe depressive illness, mania, and catatonic stupor. Combined with a phenothiazine, a drug, it can assist in the short term treatment of schizophrenia. The treatment is safe provided a muscle relaxant is given and it is avoided, if possible, for people with aneurysms, recent cerebral haemorrhage or raised intracranial pressure. Brief confusion, restlessness, headache and nausea are common following ECT. A cup of tea, a lie-down and an aspirin may help these after-effects disappear. Assessment for therapeutic benefit should be made the next day, after each treatment. Amnesia for events immediately before ECT (anterograde) and patchy memory losses of memory after ECT (retrograde amnesia), most often for less important matters, is common. Memory difficulties usually subside in two or three weeks but may persist longer. Depressive illness does appear to be associated with memory impairment and distinguishing between this and an ECT effect may be impossible.

QUESTIONS:

1. When can ECT be given or drugs continued beyond the first three
    months?
2. What does the requirement with regard to consent in section 58(2)(a)
    mean? What is the procedural difference between section 57 and
    section 58 as regards validating the consent of the patient?

Consider the following view on the identical provision in section 57. Note
the different procedures for identifying that the substantive issues are
satisfied and read the following extract in that light.

R. v. Mental Health Act Commission, ex parte X. (1988) 9 BMLR 77

STUART-SMITH J.:
". . . A number of points should be made. First, all three commissioners have to
be satisfied before they can certify. [This does not apply to section 58] Secondly,
the subsection is concerned both with capacity and consent, and the commissioners have to be satisfied on both heads. Thirdly, the words are 'capable of
understanding' and not 'understands'. Thus the question is capacity and not
actual understanding. Fourthly, it is capacity to understand the likely effects of
the treatment and not possible side effects, however remote . . .
    No doubt the consent has to be an informed consent in that he knows the
nature and likely effect of the treatment. There can be no doubt that the
applicant knew this. So too in this case, where the treatment was not routinely
used for control of sexual urges and was not sold for this purpose, it was
important that the applicant should realise that the use on him was a novel one
and the full implications with use on young men had not been studied, since trials
had only been involved with animals and older men. Again it is perfectly clear
that the applicant knew this.
    [The judge then dealt with the issue that the Commissioners first assessed X to
be capable and then, three months later that his condition had so deteriorated
that he had no longer the capacity to understand] While I accept that there may
be cases where a patient's mental condition has so gravely deteriorated over three
months that his capacity to understand may have changed, I do not find the bald
assertion that it had done so in this case persuasive . . . I cannot accept that a
patient must understand the precise physiological process involved before he can
be said to be capable of understanding the nature and likely effects of the
treatment or can consent to it. In fact it is clear from his affidavit that the
applicant had a remarkably good understanding of the physiological process
involved. But I cannot accept that it is a necessary prerequisite.
    The second ground, that he denied the possibility of any medium or long term
side effects, is in contrast with his understanding in August. I think it is clear from
the applicant's own affidavit that he was adopting a somewhat cavalier and less
cooperative attitude to the questioning on November 17 as compared with that
on August 18. This is regrettable but not difficult to understand, since he knew
that the commissioners had already decided that he was capable of understanding
and had consented to the treatment he was anxious to have."

The judge concluded that, if the treatment had fallen within section 57, he
would have decided that "the decision to refuse a certificate under section
57(2) would have to be quashed on the grounds that the commissioners

took into account matters which they should not have taken into account, applied the wrong test and reached a decision that was unreasonable in the *Wednesbury* sense." Whilst the main critique was addressed to the question of capacity, the judge also considered whether the treatment was likely to alleviate or prevent a deterioration of the patient's condition and noted:

"In his report Professor Bluglass [a psychiatrist] has drawn attention to the problems involved in finding two people with whom the medically qualified commissioner must consult before he can certify under section 57(2)(b), when the patient is a voluntary outpatient. Both must have been professionally concerned with the patient's treatment, one must be a nurse, and the other neither a nurse nor a doctor . . . [P]sychologists, speech therapists, social workers and probation officers might come into the latter category. But it is obvious that many, if not most, voluntary outpatients will not have been involved with people in these disciplines. Moreover, there may even be difficulty in finding a nurse who is involved in his treatment. Quite apart from these practical difficulties . . . it is not entirely clear why it is appropriate for non-medically qualified people to be consulted on the desirability of medical treatment, having regard to the likelihood of it alleviating the patient's condition or preventing its deterioration . . . I am far from saying that in every case the medical commissioner must discuss every reservation that he may have with the responsible medical officer, but most, if not all, [the matters indicated by the medical commissioner] are criticisms of Dr Silverman's approach and treatment . . . [T]he medical commissioner does not have to have regard only to the likelihood of the treatment in alleviating the patient's condition or preventing its deterioration . . . [T]here are two matters that he must have regard to. The commissioner must first consider whether the proposed treatment is likely to alleviate the condition or prevent its deterioration. If he concludes that it is not so likely, then he must refuse a certificate. If he concludes that it is likely to do so, then no doubt he may balance the benefit against what he conceives to be the disadvantages . . . I am satisfied that whether it be put on the ground of unfairness or the failure to take relevant matters into consideration, or taking irrelevant matters into consideration, the refusal to certify under section 57(2)(b) could not stand in the event that I am wrong on the question of jurisdiction."

NOTE:

1. Every time the patient's detention is renewed, there must be a report on treatment provided under section 57(2)(b) only (section 61). It is, however, only good practice to review the position where the patient is consenting as provided in the *Code of Practice* (paragraphs 16.20–16.22).

QUESTIONS:

1. If the patient does not or cannot consent, can the treatment within section 58 still be given? If so, what are the requirements to be satisfied?
2. If the patient does not or cannot consent, what is the role of the Second Opinion Approved Doctor (known as a SOAD)? Consider the *Code of Practice* at paragraph 16.31:

"Every attempt should be made by the rmo and the SOAD to reach agreement. If the rmo and the SOAD are unable to reach agreement, the patient's rmo should be informed by the SOAD personally at the earliest opportunity. It is good practice for the SOAD to give reasons for his dissent. Neither doctor should allow a disagreement in any way to prejudice the interests of the patient. If agreement cannot be reached, the position should be recorded in the patient's case notes by the rmo who will continue to have responsibility for the patient's management. The opinion given by the SOAD is his personal responsibility. It cannot be appealed against to the Mental Health Act Commission."

3. Who is the nurse which the SOAD must consult? Should it be a qualified nurse, or can it be a nursing assistant? Must it be a nurse of a specific grade, *e.g.*, the nurse on charge of the ward on which the patient is currently resident? The Act offers no definition of "nurse", although the Mental Health Act Commission prefers that the nurse, where possible, be someone with an appropriate qualification, *i.e.* RMN or RNMH.

4. Who do you think is likely to be the other person consulted, and what might be their role?

In something like 80–90 per cent of cases the other person will be a social worker. However, increasingly there are problems. It is not appropriate to require that the consultee invariably be professionally qualified and on a professional register. "The Commission suggests that the appointed doctor should endeavour to meet with somebody whose qualifications, experience and knowledge of the patient should enable them to make an effective contribution to the work of the multi-disciplinary team. Appointed doctors are at liberty to consult with other members of staff if this is seen as helpful . . . " Mental Health Act Commission (1993), *Fifth Biennial Report 1991– 1993*, at paragraph 7.16. The Commission "has grave doubts about the validity of some certificates which, for example, refer to the 'ward clerk', 'gymnasium technician' and 'occupational therapy aid'. The *Code of Practice* states at paragraph 16.28 "consult with two other persons professionally concerned with the patient's care as statutorily required (*i.e.* the 'statutory consultees'). The SOAD should be prepared, where appropriate, to consult a wider range of persons professionally concerned with the patient's care than those required by the Act and (with the patient's consent) the patient's nearest relative or other appropriate relatives or supporters." (See also Mental Health Act Commission (1995), Sixth Biennial Report 1993–1995, at para. S.B.)

(iii) Treatment in an emergency

The need to contact the MHAC as required above and so satisfy the statutory criteria may delay necessary treatment. The need to follow the above procedures can be avoided if, in accordance with section 62, the treatment is:

62.—(1)(a) . . . immediately necessary to save the patient's life; or

(b) . . . (not being irreversible) . . . immediately necessary to prevent a serious deterioration of his condition; or

(c) . . . (not being irreversible or hazardous) . . . immediately necessary to alleviate serious suffering by the patient; or

(d) . . . (not being irreversible or hazardous) . . . immediately necessary and represent the minimum interference necessary to prevent the patient from behaving violently or being a danger to himself or others.

NOTE:

1. The Mental Health Act Commission remains concerned about the use of this section. Section 62 is alarmingly still used for non-detained patients, or patients under short term holding powers even though it clearly does not apply. The Commission expresses concern about treatments given under the common law (Mental Health Act Commission (1993), *Fifth Biennial Report*, at paragraph 7.12). In *Treatment Without Consent*, Fennell discovered that, in a sample of 1,009 statutory second opinions, "there were 114 cases where patients had been given emergency ECT under section 62 to save life or prevent a serious deterioration in health" (P. Fennell, *Treatment Without Consent*, London: Routledge (1996), at page 190.

2. Section 62(3) states that "treatment is irreversible if it has *unfavourable* physical or psychological consequences and hazardous if it entails *significant* physical hazard." [Emphasis added]

3. When the treatment proposed is carried out under section 57 or 58, there is a recording system and referral to the Mental Health Act Commission for treatment under section 62. However, there is no form which needs to be filled in (but it is good practice, see the *Code of Practice*, at paragraph 16.19).

QUESTIONS:

1. When is treatment "immediately necessary"? Note the time frame to which this refers must be affected by the speed with which the Commission can respond.

2. When is treatment irreversible or hazardous?

3. Would you propose any further protections for a patient provided treatment under section 62?

4. Is section 62 likely to be used very often? (See P. Fennell, "Statutory Authority to Treat, Relatives and Treatment Proxies" (1994) 2 *Medical Law Review* 30 and P. Fennell, *Treatment Without Consent*, London: Routledge, 1996, Chapters 12 and 13.)

(iv) Other Treatment

63. The consent of a patient shall not be required for any medical treatment given to him for the mental disorder from which he is suffering, not being

treatment falling within section 57 or 58 above, if the treatment is given by or under the direction of the responsible medical officer.

QUESTIONS:

1. If the drug Goserelin under consideration in *R. v. Mental Health Act Commission, ex p. X,* above, was not a treatment falling within section 57, did it fall within either section 58 or section 63? Is it a treatment for mental disorder, bearing in mind that section 1(3) rules out sexual deviancy from being a form of mental disorder? If the drug is for a form of mental disorder, is it possible that it could be given without the consent of the patient?
2. Would you accept that the following are typical forms of treatment within section 63: drugs for the first three months, behaviour modification and milieu therapy?
3. Might the forced feeding of a person suffering from anorexia nervosa be included within section 63?

Forced feeding is a matter which has come to the courts' attention. In considering these cases, assess whether the person did satisfy the admission criteria and whether the treatment proposed really was for the mental disorder (if there was one). The most recent consideration of the relevant issues is in the following case.

B. v. Croydon Health Authority [1995] 1 All E.R. 683

A woman, Miss B., was admitted to hospital under section 3 suffering from psychopathic disorder ("borderline personality disordered coupled with post traumatic stress disorder) and the treatment which she was to receive was psychotherapeutic psychoanalysis (the "core treatment"). In addition, she stopped eating as an "urge to punish herself". Although she had begun eating again at the time of the case, both Miss B. and the Health Authority wished to know whether feeding her by nasogastric tube would have been lawful.

HOFFMANN L.J.:
". . . I first consider s. 63 . . .
[The question is] whether tube feeding would have been treatment for the mental disorder from which Ms B. was suffering. My initial reaction was that it could not be. Ms B. suffers from a psychopathic disorder which, according to the evidence, is incapable of treatment except by psychoanalytical psychotherapy. How can giving her food be treatment for that disorder?
Mr Gordon says that it cannot. It may be a prerequisite to a treatment for mental disorder or it may be treatment for a consequence of the mental disorder, but it is not treatment of the disorder itself . . . Mr Gordon says that the patient cannot lawfully be detained unless the proposed treatment will alleviate or prevent a deterioration of his condition. No less should be required of the treatment which can be given without his consent under section 63.
This is a powerful submission. But I have come to the conclusion that it is too atomistic. It requires every individual element of the treatment being given to the

patient to be directed to his mental condition. But in my view this test applies only to the treatment as a whole. Section 145(1) gives a wide definition to the term 'medical treatment'. It includes 'nursing . . . care, habilitation and rehabilitation under medical supervision'. So a range of acts ancillary to the core treatment fall within the definition. I accept that by virtue of section 3(2)(b) a patient with a psychopathic disorder cannot be detained unless the proposed treatment, taken as a whole, is 'likely to alleviate or prevent a deterioration of his condition'. In my view, contrary to the submission of Mr Francis, 'condition' in this paragraph means the mental disorder on grounds of which the application for his admission and detention has been made. It follows that if there was no proposed treatment for Ms B.'s psychopathic disorder, s.63 could not have been invoked to justify feeding her by nasogastric tube. Indeed, it would not be lawful to detain her at all.

It does not however follow that every act which forms part of that treatment within the wide definition in section 145(1) must in itself be likely to alleviate or prevent a deterioration of that disorder. *Nursing and care concurrent with the core treatment or as a necessary prerequisite to such treatment or to prevent the patient from causing harm to himself or to alleviate the consequences of the disorder are, in my view, all capable of being ancillary to a treatment calculated to alleviate or prevent a deterioration of the psychopathic disorder.* [Emphasis added.] It would seem to me strange if a hospital could, without the patient's consent, give him treatment directed to alleviating a psychopathic disorder showing itself in suicidal tendencies, but not without such consent be able to treat the consequences of a suicide attempt. In my judgment the term 'medical treatment . . . for the mental disorder' in section 63 includes such ancillary acts.

I therefore agree with Ewbank J. in *Re KB (adult) (mental patient: medical treatment)* (1994) 19 B.M.L.R. 144 at 146 when he said of the tube-feeding of an anorexic: ' . . . relieving symptoms is just as much a part of treatment as relieving the underlying cause.' To similar effect is the judgment of Stuart-White J., quoted by Sir Stephen Brown P in *Riverside Mental Health NHS Trust v. Fox* [1994] 1 FLR 614 at 619. *Re C. (adult: refusal of medical treatment)* [1994] 1 All E.R. 819, in which a schizophrenic was held entitled to refuse treatment for gangrene, is distinguishable. The gangrene was entirely unconnected with the mental disorder.

Mr Gordon said that if the meaning of 'medical treatment for . . . mental disorder' was wide enough to include ancillary forms of treatment, section 63 would involve a breach of the Convention for the Protection of Human Rights and Fundamental Freedoms (the European Human Rights Convention (Rome, November 4, 1950; TS 71 (1953); Cmd 8969). He referred us to *Herczegfalvy v. Austria* (1992) 18 BMLR 48 at 68 in which the court said that a measure constituting an interference with private life and therefore *prima facie* contrary to article 8(1) (like involuntary tube feeding) can only be justified under article 8(2) if, among the other requirements of that article, its terms are sufficiently precise to enable the individual 'to foresee its consequences for him'. This requirement is necessary to prevent such measures from being a source of arbitrary official power, contrary to the rule of law. In my judgment section 63 amply satisfies this test. There is no conceptual vagueness about the notion of treating the symptoms or consequences of a mental disorder, although naturally there will be borderline cases. But there is no question of an exercise of arbitrary power.

I therefore think that the judge was right and would dismiss the appeal."

NOTE:

1. The decisions in *Riverside Mental Health NHS Trust v. Fox* [1994] 1 FLR 614 and *Re KB (adult)(mental patient: medical treatment)* (1994)

19 B.M.L.R. 144 are also of importance. (See also M. Gunn, "Treatment without consent" (1995) 6 *Journal of Forensic Psychiatry* 411.)

Tameside and Glossop Acute Services Trust v. CH (A Patient) [1996] 1 FCR 753

CH, the defendant was 41 and in her 38th week of pregnancy. She had two children, aged 18 and 14 respectively. She suffered from schizophrenia and had been admitted to hospital under s.3 of the Mental Health Act 1983. In January 1995 there was evidence that the foetus had inter-uterine growth retardation. A consultant obstretrician and gynaecologist gave evidence that unless labour was induced the foetus would die and there was the possibility that the patient would require a casearian section. Both these steps would require the patient's agreement. While at that stage the patient agreed the consultant was worried that she might change her mind. Evidence was also given by the psychiatrist who had initially seen the patient on her admission. He stated that she was a paranoid schizoprenic who was incapable of making a balanced rational decision about her treatment. He was of the view that she failed the three part test for competency, in *Re C* (see page 272). He noted that during her pregnancy she had resisted persons going near her and she had shown an adverse reaction to tranquillisers. He was of the view that it was in her optimum interest to bear a healthy child.

Mr Justice Wall examined the interpretation of section 63 of the Mental Health Act 1983. He considered three questions as raised by Mr Francis counsel for the patient. 1. Does the patient lack the capacity to consent or to refuse medical treatment in relation to the management of her pregnancy? 2. Is the proposed treatment necessary to save her life or prevent a deterioration in her physical or mental health? 3. Is the treatment in her best interests? His conclusions are set out below.

MR JUSTICE WALL:
"As to the first of the questions posed by Mr. Francis, the evidence is overwhelming that the defendant lacks the capacity to consent to, or to refuse medical treatment in relation to the management of her pregnancy. Mr Francis accepts this on her behalf. I agree with Dr M.'s evidence that she fails all three of the tests laid down in *Re C*. [1994] 2 FCR 151. In particular, she is suffering from the delusion that the doctors wish to harm her baby and is incapable of understanding the advice which she is given.

As to the second question, I accept the evidence of Dr M. that if the defendant is delivered of a still-born child this is likely to have a profound deliterous effect on the defendants mental health in both the short and the long-term. I will not repeat the evidence that I have already summarised.

As to the third question it is in my view plainly in the defendant's interests to give birth to a live baby . . .

Wall J. quoted section 63, above and noted the definition of "medical treatment" in section 145, above. He then referred to the decision in *B. v. Croyden HA* and continued. . . .

". . . Is the question of inducing the defendant's labour and/or causing her to be delivered of her child by Caesarian section "entirely unconnected" with her mental disorder? At first blush it might appear difficult to say that performance of a Caesarian section is medical treatment for the defendants mental disorder.

I am, however, satisfied that on the facts of this case so to hold would be "too atomistic a view" to use Hoffmann L.J.'s phrase in the passage from *B v. Croydon Health Authority* . . .

There are several strands in the evidence, which, in my judgment, bring the proposed treatment within s.63 of the Act. Firstly, there is the proposition that an ancillary reason for the induction and, if necessary the birth by Caesarian section is to prevent a deterioration in the defendant's mental state. Secondly, there is the clear evidence of Dr M. that in order for the treatment of the schizophrenia to be effective, it is necessary for her to give birth to a live baby. Thirdly, the overall structure of her treatment requires her to receive strong anti-psychotic medication. The administration of that treatment has been necessarily interrupted by her pregnancy and cannot be resumed until her child is born. It is not, therefore, I think stretching language unduly to say that achievement of a successful outcome of her pregnancy is a necessary part of the overall treatment of her mental disorder. In *Re C. (An Adult: Refusal of Treatment)* [1994] 2 FCR 151 treatment of C.'s gangrene was not likely to effect his mental condition: the manner in which the delivery of the defendant's child is treated is likely to have a direct effect on her mental state.

I am therefore satisfied that the treatment of the defendant's pregnancy proposed by Dr G. is within the broad interpretation of s63 of the Mental Health Act approved by the Court of Appeal in *B v. Croydon Health Authority*: it follows that since the defendant's consent is not required , Dr G is entitled, should he deem it clinincally necessary, to use restraint to the extent to which it may be reasonably required in order to achieve the delivery by the defendant of healthy baby.

In these circumstances it becomes unnecessary for me to consider whether or not I could make a declaration authorising the use of reasonable force outwith the provisions of s.63. Mr. Lloyd for the trust, was prepared on the facts of this case to accept a declaration under s.63. He made it quite clear, however, that he did not accept that my power to make such a declaration was limited to a case which fell within s.63 and wished to reserve for another occasion the argument that the court has the power at common law to authorise the use of reasonable force as a necessary incident of treatment. I make it clear that I express no opinion on whether or not the power for which Mr. Lloyd contends exists, which must await argument in another case . . ."

Note:

1. It seems that the declaration authorising the casearian section, if necessary, was based on the decision in *F. v. West Berkshire Health Authority* [1989] 2 All E.R. 545, although Wall J. seems to have been prepared to grant the declaration on the basis of section 63. Section 63 is clearly the basis for that part of the declaration authorising the use of restraint.

Questions:

1. Is anorexia nervosa a form of mental disorder?
2. Do you think that the *Croydon* case extends section 3 too far? Could it not be argued that almost any form of treatment falls within the criteria established in the case? If so, how does Hoffmann J. manage

to distinguish the scenario in *Re C*? Is it convincing? How can you be sure that the case falls within or outwith section 63?

3. Do you agree with Wall J. that restraint to enable a Caesarian section is a treatment for the mental disorder from which CH was suffering? Or do you think that the interpretation of section 63 extends the law too far? (See also Chapter 13 below at pages 782–784.)

4. If the decision in these two cases is correct, where will the dividing line between physical treatment (not covered) and treatment for mental disorder (covered) be drawn? In considering this question consider whether termination of pregnancy could fall within section 63 (note the conditions for lawful termination under the Abortion Act 1967 as amended — see Chapter 12) and whether the removal of a brain tumour might fall within the section.

(e) Information

Clearly a detained patient will be in a better position if he or she has information about the effect of the Mental Health Act. Section 132 requires the managers of the hospital to provide such information "as soon as practicable after the commencement of the patient's detention." The information must be provided "both orally and in writing" (section 132(3)). It is good practice to make "[p]eriodic checks . . . to ensure that patients continue to understand the information given to them" (*Code of Practice*, paragraph 14.1). Such information is also to be provided to the nearest relative, unless the patient objects (section 132(4)).

(f) Correspondence

Correspondence is not to be interfered with, unless such interference is permitted within section 134. Unless the person is detained in a special hospital when security factors are important, the restriction is that mail from the patient can only be stopped when it is addressed to someone who has requested that it should be withheld.

(g) Mental Health Act Commission

The Mental Health Act Commission has the broad remit to "keep under review the exercise of the powers and the discharge of the duties conferred or imposed by this Act so far as relating to the detention of patients or to patients liable to be detained under this Act" (section 120(1)). To that end it makes arrangements to visit all hospitals in which patients are detained and to meet with detained patients who make such a request. It has a complaints investigation jurisdiction (see section 120(1)(b)) when a complaint has been dealt with internally and the complainant wishes to pursue the matter further, has oversight of the correspondence limitations, and has specific roles within the consent to treatment provisions as mentioned earlier. It is a body which has a significant impact in providing an avenue for patients, and staff, to raise matters of concern about the operation of the legislation, other than the discharge of a patient, which is the remit of the Mental Health Review Tribunal.

5. DISCHARGE

The main focus of this Chapter is with admission to hospital (and how to challenge it) and treatment in hospital, but there must be at least brief consideration of the question of discharge. Issues relating to leave of absence and challenging the initial admission through judicial review or the writ of *habeas corpus* have already been considered. A person may be discharged from section by the section simply ending. The patient may not need to leave hospital (indeed, some patients will not wish to do so). A patient may be discharged at any time in accordance with section 23, which gives certain people the power of discharge.

23.—(2) An order for discharge may be made in respect of a patient:

(a) where the patient is liable to be detained in a hospital in pursuance of an application for admission for assessment or for treatment by the responsible medical officer, by the managers or by the nearest relative of the patient . . .

(3) Where the patient is liable to be detained in a mental nursing home in pursuance of an application for admission for assessment or treatment, an order for discharge may, without prejudice to subsection (2) above, be made by the Secretary of State and, if the patient is maintained under a contract with a National Health Service trust, Health Authority, . . . or special health authority, by that trust or authority."

NOTES:

1. The powers of discharge granted to a trust or Authority are exercisable by a committee of three members (section 23(4) & (5), as amended by the Mental Health (Amendment) Act 1994).
2. Where a nearest relative wishes to discharge the patient, he or she must provide 72 hours notice in writing of the decision to exercise the power (section 25). Within that time the discharge may be prevented if the RMO furnishes a report to the hospital managers stating that "the patient, if discharged, would be likely to act in a manner dangerous to other persons or himself". The nearest relative must be informed that a danger report has been issued (section 25(2)). The nearest relative has a right to apply to a Mental Health Review Tribunal seeking an order for discharge (section 66(1)(g)).

6. Mental Health Review Tribunals

Mental Health Review Tribunals were established under the 1959 Act to provide an independent body entitled to review the detention of a patient in hospital. Coincidentally their existence and jurisdiction also satisfies, broadly speaking, the requirements of Article 5 of the European Convention on Human Rights. Patients may seek their discharge by making an application to the tribunal office. The patient must make the application, which need not be made in any formal manner; mere indication of a desire to be discharged by the tribunal is sufficient. A patient (and, on occasion, others) has a right to apply to a MHRT if he or she falls within the provisions in section 66.

66.—(1) Where —

(a) a patient is admitted to a hospital in pursuance of an application for assessment; or
(b) a patient is admitted to a hospital in pursuance of an application for treatment; or . . .
(d) a report is furnished under section 16 above in respect of a patient; or
(e) a patient is transferred from guardianship to a hospital in pursuance of regulations made under section 19 above; or
(f) a report is furnished under section 20 above in respect of a patient and the patient is not discharged; or
(g) a report is furnished under section 25 above in respect of a patient who is detained in pursuance of an application for admission for treatment; or . . .
(h) an order is made under section 29 above in respect of a patient who is or subsequently becomes liable to be detained or subject to guardianship under Part II of this Act,
an application may be made to a Mental Health Review Tribunal within the relevant period:
  (i) by the patient (except in the cases mentioned in paragraphs (g) and (h) above) or, in the cases mentioned in paragraphs (d), (ga), (gb) and (gc) above, by his nearest relative if he has been (or was entitled to be) informed under this Act of the report or acceptance, and
  (ii) in the cases mentioned in paragraphs (g) and (h) above, by his nearest relative.

(2) In subsection (1) above "the relevant period" means —

(a) in the case mentioned in paragraph (a) of that subsection, 14 days beginning with the day on which the patient is admitted as so mentioned;
(b) in the case mentioned in paragraph (b) of that subsection, six months beginning with the day on which the patient is admitted as so mentioned . . .
(d) in the cases mentioned in paragraphs (d), (g) and (gb) of that subsection, 28 days beginning with the day on which the applicant is informed that the report has been furnished;
(e) in the case mentioned in paragraph (e) of that subsection, six months beginning with the day on which the patient is transferred;
(f) in the case mentioned in paragraph (f) of that subsection, the period for which authority for the patient's detention or guardianship is renewed by virtue of the report;
(g) in the case mentioned in paragraph (h) of that subsection, 12 months beginning with the date of the order, and in any subsequent period of 12 months during which the order continues in force.

QUESTIONS:

1. How frequently may a patient detained under section 3 apply?
2. What explanation can there be to allow a patient detained under section 2 only to apply to a MHRT within the first 14 days of the section?

NOTES:

1. The Act does not necessarily expect that a patient initiate the procedure, since in some circumstances there will be an automatic referral of the patient's case to a MHRT. Section 68 provides that a case will be automatically referred where the patient has been detained for six months under a new section 3 and has not applied to a MHRT; where a patient has been detained under a section 3 for three years and has not applied to a MHRT within that time; and where a patient has been transferred from guardianship to a section 3 and has not applied within six months of the transfer.
2. Patients before MHRTs may be represented and that representation may be paid for under the Advice By Way of Representation scheme for which there are no eligibility limits, so that all detained patients qualify. Representation may be from solicitor members of the Law Society's Mental Health Panel, but need not be.

An MHRT has certain specific statutory powers which are set out in section 72 of the Mental Health Act 1983.

72.—(1) Where application is made to a Mental Health Review Tribunal by or in respect of a patient who is liable to be detained under this Act, the tribunal may in any case direct that the patient be discharged, and:
  (a) the tribunal shall direct the discharge of a patient liable to be detained under section 2 above if they are satisfied:
      (i) that he is not then suffering form mental disorder or from mental disorder of a nature or degree which warrants his detention in a hospital for assessment (or for assessment followed by medical treatment) for at least a limited period; or
      (ii) that his detention as aforesaid is not justified in the interests of his own health or safety or with a view to the protection of other persons;
  (b) the tribunal shall direct the discharge of a patient liable to be detained otherwise than under section 2 above if they are satisfied:
      (i) that he is not then suffering from mental illness, psychopathic disorder, severe mental impairment or mental impairment or from any of those forms of disorder of a nature or degree which makes it appropriate for him to be liable to be detained in a hospital for medical treatment; or
      (ii) that it is not necessary for the health or safety of the patient or for the protection of other persons that he should receive such treatment; or
      (iii) in the case of an application by virtue of paragraph (g) of section 66(1) above, that the patient, if released would not be likely to act in a manner dangerous to other persons or to himself.

(2) In determining whether to direct the discharge of a patient detained otherwise than under section 2 above on a case not falling within paragraph (b) of subsection (1) above, the tribunal shall have regard:

  (a) to the likelihood of medical treatment alleviating or preventing a deterioration of the patient's condition; and
  (b) in the case of a patient suffering from mental illness of severe mental impairment, to the likelihood of the patient, if discharged, being able to care for himself, to obtain the care he needs or to guard himself against serious exploitation.

(3) A tribunal may under subsection (1) above direct the discharge of a patient on a future date specified in the direction; and where a tribunal do not direct the discharge of a patient under that subsection the tribunal may:

  (a) with a view to facilitating his discharge on a future date, recommend that he be granted leave of absence or transferred to another hospital or into guardianship; and
  (b) further consider his case in the event of any such recommendation not being complied with.

(3A) Where, in the case of an application to a tribunal by or in respect of a patient who is liable to be detained in pursuance of an application for admission for treatment or by virtue of an order or direction for his admission or removal to hospital under Part III of this Act, the tribunal do not direct the discharge of the patient under subsection (1) above, the tribunal may:

  (a) recommend that the responsible medical officer consider whether to make a supervision application in respect of the patient; and
  (b) further consider his case in the event of no such application being made . . .

(6) Subsections (1) to (5) above apply in relation to references to a Mental Health Review Tribunal as they apply in relation to applications made to such a tribunal by or in respect of a patient.

QUESTIONS:

  1. Section 72 indicates that a tribunal may discharge in any circumstances, but only has to discharge in the circumstances specifically stated in section 72(1) or (2), depending upon the section under which the patient is detained. In fact, it is only in these latter circumstances that the tribunal exercises the discharge power. Should the tribunal be prepared to exercise its power of discharge more generally? Would the general discretion allow the tribunal to take into account the legality of the original admission?
  2. Do you agree with Ackner L.J. in *R. v. Hallstrom, ex p. W* [1985] 3 All E.R. 775 that a tribunal, in particular because of the use of the phrase "not then" in section 72(1)(a)(i) and (b)(i), has no power to consider the original admission only whether, at the time seen by it, it has the power to consider whether the patient should continue to be detained? It is on the assumption that this view is correct that the ability to challenge the original admission by either judicial review or writ of *habeas corpus* is of particular significance.

NOTES:

1. A tribunal may defer discharge under section 72(3) for the purpose of ensuring that, *e.g.*, community support is provided to the patient. The discharge takes effect on the date stated by the MHRT even if the conditions are not fulfilled.
2. A tribunal has a new power to recommend the use of the after-care under supervision power (see below).
3. The tribunal is required to give reasons for the decision by virtue of rule 23(2) of the Mental Health Review Tribunal Rules (S.I. 1983 No. 942). The importance of reasons is explained in *Bone v. MHRT* [1985] 3 All E.R. 330 (see [1986] *Journal of Social Welfare Law* 177); *R. v. MHRT, ex p. Clatworthy* [1985] 3 All E.R. 699 (see [1986] *Journal of Social Welfare Law* 249); *R. v. MHRT, ex p. Pickering* [1986] 1 All E.R. 99 (see [1986] *Journal of Social Welfare Law* 258) as being so as to enable the patient and/or her or his legal advisor to be able to ascertain the reasons sufficiently so as to assess whether it is appropriate to challenge the decision through either the case stated process under section 78(8) and which was recommended as the appropriate route in *Bone v. MHRT* (above), and judicial review, which is the regularly used means of challenge, see, *e.g. R. v. MHRT, ex p. Clatworthy* and *R. v. MHRT ex p. Pickering*. There is no right of appeal against a decision by a tribunal.

7. COMMUNITY CARE AND TREATMENT

Most of the Mental Health Act 1983 is concerned with admission to, treatment and care in, and discharge from hospital. However, the vast majority of people with a mental disorder spend little, if any, time in a hospital, even as an informal patient. It is also government policy to provide for care in the community, as can be seen from the following extract from the White Paper which established the principles now enshrined in the National Health Service and Community Care Act 1990:

"Community care means providing the right level of intervention and support to enable people to achieve maximum independence and control over their own lives." ("Caring for People: Community Care in the Next Decade and Beyond" (HMSO, 1989)).

As regards mental health care, there is not only the general provision relating to community care, but also a specific obligation in the 1983 Act.

117.—(1) This section applies to persons who are detained under section 3 above, or admitted to a hospital in pursuance of a hospital order made under section 37 above, or transferred to a hospital in pursuance of a transfer direction under section 47 or 48 above, and then cease to be detained and (whether or not immediately after so ceasing) leave hospital.

(2) It shall be the duty of the Health Authority and of the local social services authority to provide, in co-operation with relevant voluntary agencies, after-care services for any person to whom this section applies until such time as the Health

Authority and the local social services authority are satisfied that the person concerned is no longer in need of such services, but they shall not be so satisfied in the case of a patient who is subject to after-care under supervision at any time while he remains so subject.

It would seem that these are not duties in the sense of a right enforceable by the patient, other than through the medium of judicial review, see *R. v. Ealing District Health Authority, ex parte Fox* [1993] 3 All E.R. 170. However, the new power of after-care under supervision (see below) builds upon this duty and its existence is of some value in forcing local delivery of services.

In the context of the present work, it is more important to consider the treatment position of a person in the community. The only directly relevant power to consider is that of guardianship, although the National Assistance Acts 1948 and 1951 provide for a power (exercisable also in an emergency) for the removal of certain categories of people, who are unable to cope or are living in insanitary conditions, to other accommodation.

(a) Guardianship

If the criteria of section 7 (see below) are satisfied an application may be made to the social services department for the reception of the person in question into the guardianship of either the social services department or of a private guardian. The procedure for making an application is similar to that for an admission to hospital for treatment. An application can be made by either an ASW or the nearest relative (section 11(1). If an ASW makes an application, the nearest relative has right to object (subject to replacement as such by the county court under section 29) and, in any case, must be consulted (section 11(4)). There must be two medical recommendations (sections 7(3) and 12). The applications must then be "forwarded to the local social services authority named in the application as guardian, or, as the case may be, to the local social services authority for the area in which the person so named resides" (section 11(2)). Applications must be forwarded within 14 days of the last medical examination (section 11(2)). The guardian will be either the social services department or a private guardian, that is "any other person (including the applicant himself)" (section 7(5)). If the guardian is not the social services, the application is "of no effect unless it is accepted . . . by the local social services authority for the area in which [the prospective guardian] resides" (section 7(5)). A private guardian must be willing to act, as impliedly must the authority.

7.—(1) A patient who has attained the age of 16 years may be received into guardianship, for the person allowed by the following provisions of this Act, in pursuance of an application (in this Act referred to as "a guardianship application") made in accordance with this section.

(2) A guardianship application may be made in respect of a patient on the grounds that:

(a) he is suffering from mental disorder, being mental illness, severe mental impairment, psychopathic disorder or mental impairment and his mental disorder is of a nature or degree which warrants his reception into guardianship under this section; and

(b) it is necessary in the interests of the welfare of the patient or for the protection of other persons that the patient should be so received.

Once received into guardianship, the guardian has the limited powers in section 8, known as the essential powers. The powers were dramatically reduced from those of a father of a child under the age of 14 because, it was thought, the extent of the powers was a major explanation for the lack of usage of the power since 1959.

8.—(1) Where a guardianship application [has been duly made and accepted by the social services department, it shall] confer on the . . . guardian, to the exclusion of any other person:

(a) the power to require the patient to reside at a place specified by the authority or person named as guardian;

(b) the power to require the patient to attend at places and times so specified for the purpose of medical treatment, occupation, education or training;

(c) the power to require access to the patient to be given, at any place where the patient is residing, to any registered medical practitioner, approved social worker or other person so specified.

Guardianship ends either because it is not renewed (for renewal, see section 20(6) & (7)) or because the patient is discharged by the RMO, the social services department or the nearest relative (section 23(2)(b)) or a Mental Health Review Tribunal orders discharge under section 72(4) (patients have the right of application at the end of the first six months and thereafter once during each period of renewal, see section 66(1)(c) & (f) & (2)(c) & (f)).

NOTE:

1. In fact, guardianship is rarely used. (See M. Fisher, "Guardianship under the Mental Health Legislation: a Review" (1988) *Journal of Social Welfare Law* 316.) It has been said (M. J. Gunn. "Mental Health Act Guardianship: Where Now?" (1986) *Journal of Social Welfare Law* 144) that guardianship is rarely used for the following reasons: (1) Some people are excluded by the choice of definitions, in particular many people with mental handicap or learning disabilities for whom it might have been extremely useful. Consider, therefore, the definitions of severe mental impairment and mental impairment, which exclude most people with learning disabilities because of the end phrase that the impairment "is associated with abnormally aggressive or seriously irresponsible conduct on the part of the person concerned . . . "; (2) The powers are not the essential powers, as they had been expected to be. In particular, the guardian does not have the power to consent to treatment. In the Mental Health Act 1959, a

guardian had the powers of a father of a child over the age of 14; (3) Institutional inertia and myth; that is social services believed that it was valueless, therefore it is valueless.

QUESTIONS:

1. Do you agree with the view of McCullough J. in R. v. Hallstrom, ex p. W [1986] 1 Q.B. 1090 that section 8 provides no power for the guardian to consent to treatment? Note that the comparable provision in the 1959 Act provide the guardian with the powers which a father would have a child under the age of 14.
2. Might guardianship be of some value in assisting people who are elderly and confused or people with learning disabilities to live in the community?

(b)   Community treatment

Since guardianship does not authorise treatment to be carried out without the consent of the "patient", a significant debate has been about the propriety of a compulsory treatment order. The debate is a response to the following: (a) "revolving door" admissions, *i.e.* where a person with a mental illness problem takes medication when in hospital, is then well enough to be discharged, perhaps takes the medication for a time, then stops taking it, deteriorates, and is re-admitted to hospital, only for the cycle to start again; (b) the need to protect the public from attacks by "patients" not taking medication. The first may be illustrated by the case of Ben Silcock who climbed into the Lion's enclosure in Regent's Park Zoo. He was severely injured by a lioness. It emerged that Ben Silcock was a schizophrenic. He had an individual care plan. He had been rejected from a day care centre because of his objectionable behaviour. The second may be illustrated by the case of Christopher Clunis. Jonathan Zito was making his way back home from Gatwick Airport, with his brother, who had just arrived, with the rest of the family, from Italy to spend Christmas with Jonathan and his new wife, Jayne. The rest of the family went by car, Jonathan and his brother by train. At Finsbury Park Tube Station Jonathan was attacked for no apparent reason and killed by Christopher Clunis. Clunis suffers from paranoid schizophrenia.

These problems have produced a demand for something to be done. The real danger is that these two incidents, amongst others, result in unnecessary action, including legislation, which, although indicating decisive and positive action, introduces new powers which affect the lives of many people living outside institutions and which will subsequently be difficult to review. Whilst not wishing in any way to minimise the tragedies for Ben Silcock, Jonathan Zito and his family and for Christopher Clunis (who is now detained in Rampton Hospital, Nottinghamshire), and recognising that all is not well with the mental health services, a careful, objective and non-emotional consideration of the issues is necessitated.

The proposals for some form of compulsory power in the community must be considered in the context of a commitment to care in the community as the preferred delivery of care and treatment to, for and with people with mental illness. At one time the only realistic form of care for people with mental illness was in institutions. Ever since the 1926 Royal Commission at least lip service has been paid to the ideal of care in the community. Implicit in the whole scheme established by the 1959 Act, and continued in the 1983 Act, was the ideal that hospitalisation would not be used unless necessary, giving a preference for treatment outside hospital. In addition, the number of beds available in hospitals has been significantly reduced, to the point where there is now, in many city areas, a crisis of lack of accommodation resulting in real difficulties in finding beds for all those who need them (see Mental Health Act Commission, *Fifth Biennial Report 1991–1993*, page 17). Cases such as that involving Silcock and Clunis raise questions as basic as whether community care can work for people who present serious challenges to services. It appears to be the case that for some people some form of hospital care needs to be retained. The compulsory admission of some people with mental health problems to hospital must remain as a realistic option. Some people with mental health problems are highly dangerous and unpredictable, some people cannot be treated except in hospital. For some people there is an increasing move to have recognised the possibility of asylum or safe haven. Indeed, the 1991 United Nations Principles for the Protection of Persons with Mental Illness and for the Improvement of Mental Health Care explicitly accept the continued existence of this form of care and treatment whilst giving priority to community care. For example, Principle 3 states, "Every person with a mental illness shall have the right to live and work, as far as possible, in the community." For people for whom community care services cannot and should not cope, hospitalisation is possible in appropriate cases. It is not a question of community care or nothing. Several proposals exist.

(i) Community Treatment Order

A Community Treatment Order involves creating a power whereby those admitted to it may be provided with treatment for their mental disorder whether or not they consent to it. No one in the recent debates appeared to be supporting such a power, although in some minds it would seem that the effect of other proposals might be to produce such a power, either explicitly or implicitly by the control and influence it would exercise over those within its remit.

(ii) Community Supervision Order

A Community Supervision Order is to what the Royal College of Psychiatrists turned in 1993 after the rejection of the earlier proposal for a CTO.

The purpose of a CSO is to "allow the compulsory supervision in the community of a patient previously compulsorily detained in hospital to prevent deterioration of his/her condition." To achieve this end, the potential supervisees would be people who have been detained under section 3 or section 37 of the Mental Health Act and "who have a history of frequent relapse and deterioration of their condition with subsequent compulsory admission as a consequence of failure or refusal to comply with treatment in the community." The supervisee would have to agree to accept treatment and to receive supervision. The application for the order would come from the individual's responsible medical officer and one other doctor, and a report by an a.s.w. would be obtained in support of the application. The application would then be presented to the Hospital Managers. The order would last initially for six months and then could be renewed annually by the responsible medical officer recommending so to the Hospital Managers. The sanction which would, it is presumed, ensure that the supervisee complies with the order is recall to hospital. Recall would be possible where "the patient refuses to accept supervision in the community [and as] a consequence of the patient's refusal, deterioration of his condition will not be prevented." Further, the patient "must be suffering from mental illness of a nature or degree such that it is necessary to recall him/her to hospital for treatment to prevent further deterioration of his/her condition." On recall, the supervisee would be regarded as a patient detained under section 3, and her/his case would be referred to a Mental Health Review Tribunal within 14 days.

(iii) Supervised Discharge Arrangement

The Department of Health Officials' Inquiry (*Legal Powers on the Care of Mentally Ill People in the Community*, 1993) rejected the plea for a Community Supervision Order but proposed, amongst other things, that a supervised discharge arrangement be introduced. The recommendation was that the Act be amended to provide for the supervised discharge of non-restricted patient, who would present a serious risk to their own health or safety or the safety of other people or of their being exploited by other people, unless care was supervised. A supervised discharge arrangement should encompass the principles of the Care Programme Approach, introduced in April 1991, and of guardianship under the Mental Health Act. This essentially means that the individual should have a named key worker, that there should be a clear treatment plan negotiated with the individual, that the individual could be required to reside at a specified place, that the individual could be required to attend places for medical treatment, occupation, education or training, and that the key worker and other named staff involved in the individual's care would be entitled to have access to her/him. The detail of the conditions would be agreed with the key worker, and others involved in the individual's care. The arrangement would last initially for six months, could be renewed for a further six months and thereafter could be renewed annually. No overall time-limit was proposed. If the patient did not comply with the conditions, an immediate review would take place which could consider whether the patient's condition had deteriorated so far as to meet the criteria for compulsory admission to hospital. A patient could apply to a Mental Health Review Tribunal to secure discharge without supervision, and thereafter the patient would have a right of application in each period of supervision, with an automatic reference of her/his case after three years.

(iv) After-care under supervision

Consequent upon the above proposals, after-care under supervision has been introduced by the Mental Health (Patients in the Community) Act 1995, which creates sections 25A-25H of the Mental Health Act 1983. It involves an application being made for a patient to be placed under supervision to secure that he or she receives the after-care services provided under section 117. The patient must be detained under sections 3 and be at least 16 years old (section 25A(1)). The further criteria for making a supervision application are contained in the following provision.

25A.—(4) A supervision application may be made in respect of a patient only on the grounds that —

(a) the patient is suffering from mental disorder, being mental illness, severe mental impairment, psychopathic disorder or mental impairment;

(b) that there would be a substantial risk of serious harm to the health or safety of the patient or the safety of other persons, or of the patient being seriously exploited, if he were not to receive the after-care services to be provided for him under section 117 below after he leaves hospital; and

(c) his being subject to after-care under supervision is likely to help to secure that he or she receives the after-care services to be so provided.

An application is made by the patient's RMO (section 25A(5)) after (a) consulting and taking into account the views of the patient, one or more persons professionally concerned with the patient's medical treatment in hospital, one or more persons who will be professionally concerned with the provision of the after-care services, and any person who the RMO believes will play a substantial part in the patient's care after leaving hospital but will not be professionally concerned (*i.e.* a carer) (section 25B(1) & (2)(b)) considering the after-care services to be provided, and (c) any requirements which may be imposed on the patient by the responsible after-care bodies (see below)(section 25B(1)&(3)). The application, which must make clear that the criteria are satisfied amongst other things (section 25B(4)), must be accompanied by a written medical recommendation from the doctor who will be professionally concerned with the patient after discharge and a written recommendation from an ASW (section 25B(5)). It must also be accompanied by a statement from the doctor who is to be the community RMO that he or she is to be in charge of the medical treatment provided under section 117, a statement in writing from the person who is to be the patient's supervisor, details of the after-care services and details of any requirements to be imposed (section 25B(8)). The RMO must inform the patient, the consultees and the nearest relative, unless the patient objects, of the making of an application, the after-care services to be provided, any requirements to be imposed, and the names of the community RMO and supervisor (section 25B(9) & (10). For other details relating to the application, see section 25C.

The application is addressed to the Health Authority with the section 117 duty to the patient (section 25A(6)). Before accepting it, the Authority must consult the relevant social services department (section 25A(7)). If the Authority accepts the application, it must inform the patient, the people consulted by the RMO and, except where the patient objects, the nearest relative (section 25A(8)).

The responsible after-care bodies (that is those bodies with the duty to provide after-care under section 117) may impose any of the requirements on a patient subject to after-care under supervision (section 25D(1)). The requirements referred to are contained in the following provision.
    25D.—(3) . . .

(a) that the patient reside at a specified place;
(b) that the patient attend at specified places and times for the purpose of medical treatment, occupation, education or training; and
(c) that access to the patient be given, at any place where the patient is residing, to the supervisor, any [doctor] or any approved social worker or to any other person authorised by the supervisor.

(4) A patient subject to after-care under supervision may be taken and conveyed by, or by any person authorised by, the supervisor to any place where the patient is required to reside or attend for the purpose of medical treatment, occupation, education or training.

The after-care services and any imposed requirements are to be kept under review and if necessary modified by the responsible after-care bodies (after a consultation process) where the patient refuses or neglects to receive any or all of the after-care services or to comply with any of the imposed requirements (section 25E(1)–(3), (5) & (6)). The amendments can include contemplating terminating the supervision or informing an ASW with a view to the patient being admitted to hospital (section 25E(4)). The patient, and others are to be informed of any modifications (section 25E(7)).

After-care under supervision begins on leaving the hospital and ends six months later (section 25G(1)), but it may be renewed for six months and thereafter annually (section 25G(2)). The process for renewal is similar to that for renewal of admission for treatment in demanding a report from the community RMO after a full consultation exercise (section 25G(3)-(10). The conditions which must be satisfied for renewal are set out in section 25G.
    25G.—(4) . . .

(a) the patient is suffering from mental disorder, being mental illness, severe mental impairment, psychopathic disorder or mental impairment;

(b) that there would be a substantial risk of serious harm to the health or safety of the patient or the safety of other persons, or of the patient being seriously exploited, if he were not to receive the after-care services to be provided for him under section 117 below after he leaves hospital; and

(c) his being subject to after-care under supervision is likely to help to secure that he or she receives the after-care services to be so provided.

After-care under supervision may be ended by the community RMO, after a consultation exercise, at any time (section 25H(1)-(3)). It is also ended if the patient is admitted to hospital for treatment or for assessment under section 2 (but not section 4) (section 25H(4)). Further, the patient has a right of application to a Mental Health Review Tribunal when a supervision application is accepted (the patient must apply within the first six months), when it is renewed (a patient has a right of application in every period of renewal) and if the patients' mental disorder is reclassified under section 25F (the patient must apply within 28 days of the report) (section 66(1), as amended). The nearest relative may also apply. The tribunal has the following power.

72.—(4A) . . . the tribunal may in any case direct that the patient shall cease to be so subject (or not become so subject) and shall so direct if they are satisfied:

(a) in a case where the patient has not yet left hospital, that the conditions set out in section 25A(4) above are not complied with; or

(b) in any other case, that the conditions set out in section 25G(4) above are not complied with.

We need to assess whether there is a convincing argument for any of the new powers and, in particular, for after-care under supervision.

NOTES:

1. Would it be permissible to have a community power which grants others powers of coercion? When a CTO was a serious proposal for consideration, one criticism was the graphic objection to Community Psychiatric Nurses having forcibly to inject patients on their own kitchen tables. At its heart there is a very serious objection here. Can treatment be provided in the community without an individual's consent without seriously breaching privacy and resulting in degrading treatment? Can the treatment be provided without consent but with appropriate safeguards? Where the patient is competent and refusing, there must come a point, if it is not with all treatments, that compulsory treatment should only take place in the privacy of a hospital with all the attendant health care safeguards and where abuses are more easily safeguarded against than in the community.

2. Why do people not follow a treatment/medication regime and so why might a power be necessary? The central issue is the value of medication in curing and/or controlling mental illness. Its value is

accepted by many, but even so there are doubts as to its efficacy and predictability. As was frequently pointed out in evidence to the House of Commons Health Select Committee (*Community Supervision Orders* (1993)), some people breakdown despite taking their medication and some people do not breakdown despite not taking their medication contrary to professional advice. Psychotropic medication may have severe side effects, some of which may be very long lasting. If an individual does not understand the drug or its effects or feels that information is being withheld, he or she is less likely to be willing to participate in a treatment regime involving the administration of medicine. There has been some success with Depot Clinics, where people are encouraged to attend for the administration of their medication via long term methods and whereby they present themselves to a supportive, information providing environment. The provision of greater information to patients might well result in greater treatment compliance. Not providing information is counterproductive. Further, it is entirely possible that the mere existence of power makes an individual less interested in engaging with the programme proposed. There is some evidence that the more client centred direction of the care programme approach, involving negotiation with the patient, is often effective with those people who have not traditionally engaged well with the ordinary services. Granting powers may not help.

3. The evidence available is unclear as to how many people might be subject to an order. Evidence before the Health Select Committee presented estimates which varied from 1,200 to 4,000. Of course, all estimates can only be guesses because saying that you will use a power and actually using it may be two very different things, exactly what the power would allow and its procedure may affect people's preparedness to be involved, and there was some confusion between prevalence and incidence, *i.e.* between how many people at any given time might be subject to an order and how many new orders might be imposed. The state of confusion is perhaps not surprising and is not, in itself, a major reason not to introduce a new power.

4. Is it likely to work, if anyone would agree to after-care under supervision (or a CSO) just to get out of hospital? It has been cogently suggested that any patient would agree to accept treatment and receive supervision if it meant getting out of hospital. So the essential prerequisite for the new power might well be fallacious.

5. Problems relate to whether a person may get off community based orders. In hospital cases, a calculated risk may be taken on discharging the individual. It seems quite clear that risk is likely to be exercised conservatively. This is certainly the outcome of the research into Tribunal decision-making by Peay (J. Peay, *Tribunals on Trial* (Oxford, Clarendon Press 1989)). If the individual is living in the community, there is nowhere for him to go but stay where he or she

already is. If one of the reasons for the imposition of the order is the 'revolving door syndrome', release becomes almost impossible since the history of the patient is bound to count against him. This is the group likely to be placed under such an order. The failure to impose an overall time limit upon a supervised discharge arrangement compounds the problems for the patient, even if the rationale for it may be compelling. There are however powers to terminate after-care under supervision.

QUESTIONS:

1. Why should a new power be introduced when powers similar to it have not been used in the past?
2. Review what is wrong with guardianship and assess whether this provides any improvements.

SELECT BIBLIOGRAPHY

E. Baker and J. Crichton, "*Ex parte A*: psychopathy, treatability and the law" (1995) 6 *Journal of Forensic Psychiatry* 101.

P. Bean, *Compulsory Admission to Mental Hospitals*, Chichester: Wiley & Sons, 1983.

W. Bingley, "The Mental Health Act Commission: An Audit" (1991) 2 *Journal of Forensic Psychiatry* 135.

M. Cavadino, *Mental Health Law in Context: Doctor's Orders*, Aldershot: Gower 1988.

M. Cavadino, "Commissions and Codes: A Case Study in Law and Public Administration" [1993] *Public Law* 333.

P. Fennell, "Detention and Control of Informal Mentally Disordered Patients" (1984) *Journal of Social Welfare Law* 345.

P. Fennell, "Sexual Suppressants and the Mental Health Act" [1988] *Criminal Law Review* 660.

P. Fennell, "The Beverley Lewis Case: Was the Law to Blame?" (1989) 139 *New Law Journal* 559.

P. Fennell, "Inscribing Paternalism in the Law: Consent to Treatment and Mental Disorder" (1990) 17 *Journal of Law and Society* 29.

P. Fennell, "Balancing Care and Control: Guardianship, Community Treatment Orders and Patient Safeguards" (1992) 15 *International Journal of Law and Psychiatry* 1.

P. Fennell, *Treatment without Consent*, London: Routledge, 1996.

M. Fisher, "Guardianship under the Mental Health Legislation: A Review" [1988] *Journal of Social Welfare Law* 316.

L. Gostin, "Psychosurgery: A Hazardous and Unestablished Treatment?" [1982] *Journal of Social Welfare Law* 83.

L. Gostin, *Mental Health Services: Law and Practice* (looseleaf), London: Shaw & Sons.

L Gostin and P. Fennell, *Mental Health: Tribunal Procedure* (2nd. edn.), London: Longman, 1992.

M. J. Gunn, "Mental Health Act Guardianship: Where Now?" (1986) *Journal of Social Welfare Law* 144.

M. J. Gunn, "Judicial Review of Hospital Admissions and Treatment in the Community under the Mental Health Act 1983" (1986) *Journal of Social Welfare Law* 290.

M. J. Gunn. "Mental Health Care" in D. J. Harris and S. Joseph (eds), *The International Covenant on Civil and Political Rights and United Kingdom Law*, Oxford: Clarendon Press, 1995.

B. M. Hoggett, *Mental Health Care* (4th edn.), London: Sweet & Maxwell, 1996.

R. M. Jones, *Mental Health Act Manual* (4th edn.), London: Sweet & Maxwell, 1994.

Mental Health Act Commission, *Biennial Reports*.

MIND and National Council on Civil Liberties, *People with Mental Illness and Learning Disabilities*, London: NCCL, 1993.

J. Peay, *Tribunals on Trial*, Oxford: Clarendon Press, 1989.

D. P. T. Price, "Civil Commitment of the Mentally Ill: Compelling Arguments for Reform" (1992) 2 *Medical Law Review* 321.

G. Richardson, *Law, Process and Custody: Prisoners and Patients*, London: Weidenfield and Nicholson, 1993.

10

CLINICAL RESEARCH

1. INTRODUCTION

Following the atrocities perpetrated by the Nazi regime scientists have been pressurised to be accountable for the conduct of clinical research. International ethical declarations were drawn up in the form of the Nuremburg Code in 1949 and the Declaration of Helsinki in 1964. In this country a movement towards the regulation of clinical research developed in the 1960s. In 1968 the Minister of Health, in response to a report issued by the Royal College of Physicians, sent a letter to Health Authorities requesting that they establish research ethics committees. These are non-statutory bodies composed of members drawn predominantly from the health professions who sit part time to consider proposals for clinical trials. It was not, however, until 1984 that the first extensive guidance was provided to researchers, in the form of a document issued by the Royal College of Physicians. General guidelines to research ethics committees were issued by the Department of Health in 1991 and these remain in force today. Whilst the guidelines issued by the Department of Health and by the Royal Colleges are non-statutory, nevertheless it is likely that they would be referred to in any judicial proceedings. There is little explicit guidance provided to researchers upon human subjects in the form of statutes and decided cases. This is perhaps ironic, since research upon animals is subject to a detailed statutory regulatory procedure under the Animals (Scientific Procedures) Act 1986.

Some statutory controls do exist in relation to pharmaceutical products. Generally, before drugs are used in a clinical trial, a clinical trial certificate (CTC) must be obtained from the Department of Health or Ministry of Food and Agriculture (sections 31–38 of the Medicines Act 1968). The use of the drug is subject to careful scrutiny from licensing authorities, who may have taken advice from an expert advisory committee. A special procedure is also set out in the Medicines (Exemption from Licences) Order 1981 (S.I. 1981 No. 1964). This allows trials to be undertaken without a clinical trial certificate for a period of three years as long as the licensing authority does not object and certain undertakings have been provided (CTX — clinical trial exemption). Finally, there are special provisions for trials undertaken by doctors and dentists (the DDX provisions — Medicines Exemptions From Licence (Special Cases and Miscellaneous Provisions) Order 1972, No. 1200). These also enable drugs to be used without a clinical trial certificate being granted.

One major difficulty concerns the overlap between research and innovative therapy. If a new surgical technique is used should this be subject to special regulation, as in the case of a new drug procedure? Particular controversy surrounds the use of such techniques as keyhole surgery. In response to this, the Government is now undertaking consultation. One suggestion which has been advanced is that a committee should be set up by the Medical Royal Colleges to regulate the question. This is presently under review by the Department of Health.

In section two we consider the mechanisms currently available for the scrutiny of clinical trials. In section three we examine the basis on which subjects are recruited into clinical trials and the information which they should be given before they participate. In section four the obligation placed on researchers to maintain the confidentiality of research information is discussed. Section five examines the question of fraudulent research. Section six considers scrutiny of decisions to approve a trial and section seven examines accountability of researchers. Section eight considers compensation for research subjects. In the final section of the Chapter we consider certain areas of research which are regarded as having given rise to particularly difficult dilemmas: embryo research, research on foetal tissue and gene therapy.

2. APPROVAL OF A CLINICAL TRIAL — THE RESEARCH ETHICS COMMITTEE.

Before a clinical trial is undertaken, it is standard practice for the trial to be referred to a research ethics committee for its approval. Failure to obtain such approval may mean that the researcher is subsequently unable to secure publication of his findings in an academic journal.

(i) Scope of review of clinical trials

Department of Health Guidelines to Local Research Ethics Committees (DOH 1991)

1.1 Medical research is important and the NHS has a key role in enabling it. The approval of research projects is an important management responsibility involving the availability of resources, financial implications and ethical issues. Such considerations are generally best left to the local management team, but on ethical issues they need to take into account independent advice. The purpose of a local research ethics committee is to consider the ethics of proposed research projects which will involve human subjects, and which will take place broadly within the NHS. The LREC's task is to advise the NHS body, under the auspices of which the research intended to take place. It is that NHS body which has the responsibility to decide whether or not the project should go ahead, taking account of the ethical advice of the LREC. For convenience, local research ethics committees are normally organised on a health district basis, but they exist to advise any NHS body. They are not in any sense management arms of the District Health Authority.

1.2 The NHS bodies which will look to an LREC for advice on the ethics of proposed research projects are therefore:

- district health authorities (in respect taking place within their hospitals or community health services or in private sector providers under contract to the DHA)
- special health authorities (in respect of research taking place within their units)
- family health service authorities (in respect of research involving general
- medical, general dental, or other family health services.)
- NHS trusts (in respect of research taking place within the units they control).

1.3 An LREC must be consulted about any research project involving

- NHS patients (*i.e.* subjects recruited by virtue of their past or present treatment by the NHS) including those treated under contracts with private sector providers fetal material and IVF involving NHS patients
- the recently dead, in NHS premises
- access to the records of past or present NHS patients
- the use of, or potential access to, NHS premises or facilities.

1.4 No NHS body should agree to such a research proposal without the approval of the relevant LREC body. No such proposal should proceed without the permission of the responsible NHS body. These requirements apply equally to researchers already working within the NHS and having clinical responsibility for the patients concerned, as they do to those who have no other association with the NHS and its patients beyond the particular research project.

1.5 The relevant LREC in each case is normally constituted in respect of the health district within the area of which the research is planned to take place. Special arrangements apply to multi-centre research . . .

1.6 By agreement an LREC may also advise on the ethics of studies not involving NHS patients, records or premises, carried out for example by private sector companies, the Medical Research Council or universities.

[These guidelines need now to be seen in the light of recent NHS reorganisation. DHA's and FHSA's have now been abolished and replaced with new Health Authorities (Health Authorities Act 1995, s.1).]

NOTES:

1. As the above terms of reference indicate, research ethics committees scrutinise diverse issues, ranging from patient questionnaires to major surgical trials. Although there is no requirement for trials undertaken outside the NHS to receive research ethics committee approval, some private organisations have established their own ethics committees.

2. Whilst local research ethics committees scrutinise clinical trials, they do not take decisions to include individual patients in trials. In this respect research ethics committees differ from bodies such as institutional ethics committees prevelant in the United States which do play a major role in the authorisation of treatment.

3. Trials are scrutinised on a local rather than a national basis. This may give rise to difficulties where it is proposed to operate trials in different parts of the country — what are known as "multi-centred trials" (for further discussion see page 571 below).

4. The committee is expected to provide an annual report to the body which established it setting out its operation over the past year. Research into the operation of research ethics committees discovered that many committees review a large number of projects — with a maximum per annum of 351 per committee. (See C. Gilbert Foster, "The annual reports of research ethics committees" (1995) 21 *Journal of Medical Ethics* 214.)

(ii) Membership of the committee

DOH Guidelines (1991)

2.4 An LREC should have eight to twelve members. This should allow for a sufficiently broad range of experience and expertise, so that the scientific and medical aspects of a research proposal can be reconciled with the welfare of research subjects and broader ethical implications.

2.5 Members should be drawn from both sexes and from a wide range of age groups. They should include:

- hospital medical staff
- nursing staff
- general practitioners
- two or more lay persons

2.6 Despite being drawn from groups identified with particular interests or responsibilities in connection with health issues, LREC members are not in any way the representatives of those groups. They are appointed in their own right, to participate in the work of LREC as individuals of sound judgement and relevant experience.

2.7 The health professionals should include those occupied chiefly in active clinical care as well as those experienced in clinical investigation and research. As well as consulting the relevant NHS bodies in connection with health professional appointments [D]HA's should consult local professional advisory committees and relevant health professional associations. Lay members should be appointed after consultation with the Community Health Council. At least one lay member should be unconnected professionally with health care and be neither an employee nor advisor of any NHS body.

Chairman and vice-chairman

2.8 After consultation with the relevant NHS bodies the [D]HA should appoint a chairman and vice chairman from amongst the members of the committee. At least one of these posts should be filled by a lay person.

Periods of appointment

2.9 Members should serve on LREC's for terms of three to five years. Terms of appointment may be renewed, but normally not more than two terms of office should be served consecutively.

Co-option

2.10 The LREC should, on its own initiative seek the advice of specialist referees or co-opt members to the committee so as to cover any aspect, professional, scientific, or ethical of a research proposal which lies beyond the expertise of existing members.

Confidentiality of proceedings

2.15 LREC members do not sit on the committee in any representative capacity and need to be able to discuss the proposals which come before them freely. For these reasons LREC meetings will normally be private and the minutes taken will be confidential to the committee.

QUESTIONS:

1. What is the ideal membership composition of a research ethics committee? Does it accord with that stated in the LREC guidelines?
2. Should the chair always be a lay member?

(iii) Multi-centred research

Occasionally it is proposed to undertake a number of trials across the country. At present the conduct of the trial would require approval by the research ethics committee in each area in which it is proposed to conduct the trial. This may lead to the trial receiving approval in certain areas of the country but not in others. For example, a study in 1995 noted that, in a situation in which the same proposal was submitted to 24 health authorities, in nine regions there was a wide range of variation in the manner in which the proposals were reviewed. Fourteen gave approval without modification, three rejected it and gave three different grounds for the rejection whilst six committees requested minor modifications. (See M. Redshaw, A. Harris, D. Baum,"Research Ethics, Committee Audit-Difference Between Committee" (1996) 22 *Journal of Medical Ethics* 78.) It has been argued that such diversity of approach is undesirable. The Department of Health guidelines suggested that one solution would be to nominate a particular ethics committee to consider multi-centered trial applications and that health authorities should encourage networks of co-operation between authorities. There may also be a case for a special committee to operate at national level. The functions of such a committee could extend beyond the operation of multi-centred trials to provide scrutiny of decision making by local committees. A recent Department of Health Consultation Paper has recommended that regional bodies should be established to scrutinise the operation of multi-centred trials (DoH: 1996). Each region would establish a multi-centre research ethics committee (MREC) to consider multi-centre research protocols. Where approval was given then this would be effective for research proposals generally, even outside the particular locality of the MREC. In addition to this specific procedure, approval for the conduct of the trial would still be required at LREC level. The consultation paper recommends that where a LREC reject a protocol they should inform the MREC of the reasons. In situations in which there are irresolvable differences between a MREC and a researcher then the matter could be referred to the MREC but only with agreement of both the MREC and the researcher. The consultation document notes that a standard procedure would have to be developed, with a common application form and agreed standards for MREC's. It remains to be seen whether such development will be extended to the establishment of a national committee. (See M. Warnock, "A National Research Ethics Committee" (1988) 297 *BMJ* 1626; M. Gelder, "A National Committee for the Ethics of Research" (1990) 16 *Journal of Medical Ethics* 146; Sir Michael Driver, "Symposium; Ethical Approval for Multi-Centred Trials" (1990) 16 *Journal of Medical Ethics* 148.)

(iv) Subject-matter of trials and those involving questions of public policy

DOH Guidelines (1991)

3.3 LRECs should consider the ethical implications of all research proposals which involve human subjects, including for example questionnaires. All proposals will belong to one of two categories, therapeutic or non-therapeutic research. Therapeutic research carries the prospect of direct benefit to the research subject. Non-therapeutic research, whilst designed to advance scientific knowledge and therefore be of collective benefit to the research subject. Non-therapeutic research may involve 'healthy' as well as 'patient' volunteers.

3.4 Where people volunteer to take part in non-therapeutic research they should know that they cannot expect to derive any direct benefit from that participation. The LREC will therefore want to be satisfied that the risk to which they are submitting themselves can be justified by the expected collective benefit.

NOTES:

1. It may be the case that the conduct of a particular trial involves a difficult issue of public policy; for example, a trial involving the controlled distribution of drugs, such as heroin, to drug abusers. It is arguable that issues of this nature should not be left for local resolution but should be determined by a national forum.

2. Controversy arose in relation to a video surveillance technique used in an attempt to detect whether child patients had been the victims of parental abuse, and particularly whether those who were harming the children were suffering from Munchausen's Syndrome by proxy. The researchers said that they had referred the practice to a research ethics committee, but that they had asked the committee to treat it as an accepted technique and not as a matter of research. The issue was subsequently referred to a special ethics committee. It has been suggested that such surveillance is not a matter for the research ethics committee and for the hospital but for the police. Interestingly, when these researchers first undertook a similar study in London the local

police were involved. However, in Staffordshire the police said that they would be unable to undertake such surveillance. Where a trial involves a difficult question of public policy it is arguable that reference should be made to some form of national forum to examine the ethics and legality of the procedure. (See D. Evans, "The Investigation of Life-threatening Child Abuse and Munchausen's Syndrome by Proxy" (1995) 21 *Journal of Medical Ethics* 9; D. P. Southall and M. P. Samuels, "Some ethical issues surrounding covert video surveillance — a response" (1995) 21 *Journal of Medical Ethics* 104; R. Gillon, "Editorial: 'Covert surveillance by doctor for life-threatening Munchausen's syndrome by proxy'" (1995) 21 *Journal of Medical Ethics* 131; and "Symposium on covert video surveillance" (1996) 22 *Journal of Medical Ethics* 16.)

3. The research ethics committee will be particularly concerned to examine the potential risk levels of participation in the trial. It has been noted in the past that the perception of risk levels by scientists may differ considerably from the research subject's perception of risk.

3. THE RESEARCH SUBJECT

(a) Obtaining consent

As with medical treatment, the consent of the research subject should be obtained before he is included in a clinical trial. Failure to obtain any consent at all will render the researcher liable to an action in trespass (see *Chatterson v. Gerson* [1981] 1 All E.R. 257 and Chapter 6. Even if some information is given this may be inadequate, thus leading to proceedings in battery and negligence (see below pages 574–5).

DOH Guidelines (1991)

3.7 The procedure for obtaining consent will vary according to the nature of each research proposal. The LREC will want to be satisfied on the level and amount of information to be given to a prospective research subject. Some methods of study such as randomised clinical trials need to be explained to subjects with particular care to ensure that valid consent is obtained. The LREC will want to look at such proposals particularly carefully. They will also want to check that all subjects are told that they are free to withdraw without explanation or hindrance at any stage of the procedure and with no detriment to their treatment.   An information sheet, to be kept by the subject should be required in the majority of cases.

3.8 Written consent should be required for all research (except where the most trivial of procedures is concerned). For therapeutic research, consent should be recorded in the patient's medical records.

3.9 Some research proposals will draw their subjects from groups of people who may find it difficult or impossible to give their consent, for example the unconscious the very elderly, the mentally disordered or some other vulnerable group. In considering these proposals the LREC should seek appropriate specialist advice and they will need to examine the proposal with particular care to satisfy themselves that proceeding without valid consent is ethically acceptable.

3.10 Further guidance on the issue of obtaining consent is available in a Department of Health circular H.C. (90) (22) 'Patient consent for examination or treatment'.

QUESTIONS:

1. Can a patient ever give voluntary consent to entry into a clinical trial? (See H. Thornton "Clinical Trials — A Brave New Partnership?" (1994) 20 *Journal of Medical Ethics* 19–22; M. Baum "Clinical Trials — a brave new partnership: a response to Mrs Thornton" (1994) 20 *Journal of Medical Ethics* 23–25.)

(b) Provision of information

The LREC guidelines state that an information sheet should be provided to subjects, but they do not stipulate the contents of such a sheet.

Royal College of Physicians, *Guidelines on the Practice of Ethics Committees in Medical Research Involving Human Subjects*, 3rd ed, London, 1996

7.28 Most research procedures should be the subject of an *information sheet* written in simple, easily comprehensible, language. It should set out the purpose of the investigation, the procedures, the risks (including distress), the benefits or their absence to the individual or to other or future individuals or society, a statement that the subjects may decline to participate (without incurring displeasure or any sort of penalty in the case of a dependent relationship, *e.g.* patient, student or employee), or withdraw at any time without giving a reason and without in any way impairing their care, and an invitation to ask questions. A statement about the arrangements and availability (or non-availability) of compensation for injury should be included wherever there is risk of physical injury. Approval by an REC or grant of a certificate by the Medicines Licensing Authority (MCA) should not be referred to in a way that may cause potential volunteers to think that the project is specially recommended or is specially safe.
7.29 The information sheet for the patient or healthy volunteer is an important part of the process of seeking consent. It should always form part of the application to the REC.
7.30 Information sheets should clearly state the name, address and telephone number of the investigator and, if appropriate, of the person supervising the research.

NOTES:

1. There are no decided cases or statutes regulating the quantity and content of information which should be disclosed to a subject in a clinical trial. At present it is uncertain whether the courts would follow the same approach in relation to therapeutic trials as they do in relation to medical treatment. (See Chapter 6 above.) It can be argued that in the context of a clinical trial the patient is entitled to a fuller explanation of the nature of the trial and of the risks than

would be the case in relation to medical treatment. As far as negligence is concerned as was noted in Chapter 6 (pages 341–360 above) the obligation of disclosure of the risks of a particular treatment was set out by the House of Lords in *Sidaway v. Bethlem Royal Hospital Governors* [1985] 3 All E.R. 643. It is perhaps questionable whether a court will require a different standard of disclosure in relation to therapeutic research as opposed to treatment. Nor would it necessarily be justified in doing so particularly in view of the very fine, line which exists between innovative treatment and research.

2. The position may be different in relation to non-therapeutic research. It is arguable that here the policy arguments weigh in favour of a broad duty of disclosure. The benefit of the trial is felt not directly by the individual participant but rather benefit the community as a whole. It is suggested that failure to disclose should give rise to liability in battery and in negligence. (See I. Kennedy, "The Law and Ethics of Informed Consent and Randomised Controlled Trials" in I. Kennedy (ed.), *Treat Me Right*, Oxford: OUP, 1989.) A Canadian case frequently cited in support of the approach which should be taken to disclosure to volunteers in clinical trials is *Halushka v. University of Saskatchewan* (1965) 53 D.L.R. (2d) 436. In this case Hall J. stated that: "The subject of medical experimentation is entitled to a full and frank disclosure of all the facts, probabilities and opinions which a reasonable man might be expected to consider before giving his consent". It has been suggested that such a rigorous standard should be employed in relation to both patients and volunteers. (See, *e.g.* M. Brazier, *Medicine, Patients and the Law*, (2nd edn.), Harmondsworth: Penguin, 1992, at pages 418–419.)

3. Failure to obtain the consent of an individual before including him in a clinical trial may give rise, not only to an action in battery, but also to a criminal prosecution. In addition, even if consent has been given to inclusion in a clinical trial it is possible that a clinical procedure may be held to be a criminal offence. As we noted earlier (see Chapter 6 at pages 322–323 there are certain types of harm to which the individual may not lawfully consent. If for example, a trial involved a very high risk of death or serious injury, a criminal prosecution might be brought. The Law Commission considered the question of clinical trials and consent in their consultation paper. (See *Consent in the Criminal Law*, Law Commission Consultation Paper No. 139, London: HMSO 1996, paras. 8.38–8.52.) The report states that

    8.51 "We provisionally propose that —
        (1) a person should not be guilty of an offence, notwithstanding that he or she causes injury to another, of whatever degree of seriousness, if such injury is caused during the course of properly approved medical research and with the consent of that other person; and

(2) in this context the term 'properly approved medical research' should mean medical research approved by a local research ethics committee or other body charged with the supervision and approval of medical research falling within its jurisdiction."

QUESTIONS:

1. In view of the fact that the law does not allow an individual to consent to the infliction of certain types of harm (see Chapter 6 at pages 322–323) should a volunteer be able to consent to involvement in a clinical trial?
2. Is it likely that a responsible body of professional medical opinions would support full disclosure to patients of the risk of entry into a clinical trial?

There is currently speculation as to how far the provision of information to persons in a clinical trial has been affected by requirements set out by the European Community regarding trials on medicinal products.

Notes for Guidance on Good Clinical Practice for Trials on Medicinal Products in The European Community (E.C.) 1990 III/3976/88–EN)

1.8 The principle of informed consent in the current revision of the Helsinki Declaration should be implemented in each clinical trial.

1.9 Information should be given in both oral and written form wherever possible. No. subject should be obliged to participate in the trial. Subjects, their relatives, guardians, or if necessary, legal representatives must be given ample opportunity to enquire about details of the trial. The information must make clear that refusal to participate or withdrawal from the trial at any stage is without any disadvantage for the subject's subsequent care. Subjects must be allowed enough time to decide whether or not they wish to participate.

1.10 The subject must be made aware and consent that personal information may be scrutinised during audit by competent authorities and properly authorised persons but that personal information will be treated as strictly confidential and not be publicly available.

1.11 The subject must have access to information about the procedures for compensation and treatment should he/she be injured/disabled by participating in the trial.

1.12 If a subject consents to participate after a full and comprehensive explanation of the study (including its aims, expected benefits for the subjects and/or others, reference treatments/placebo, risks and inconveniences — *e.g.* invasive procedures — and, where appropriate an explanation of alternative, recognised standard medical therapy), this consent should be appropriately recorded. Consent must be documented either by the subject's dated signature or by the signature of an independant witness who records the subject's assent. In either case the signature confirms that the consent is based on information which has been understood and that the subject has freely chosen to participate without prejudice to legal and ethical rights while allowing the possibility of withdrawal from the study without having to give any reason unless adverse events had occurred . . .

1.15 Any information becoming available during the trial which may be of relevance for the trial subject must be made known to them by the investigator.

NOTE:

1. The United Kingdom has passed the Medicines (Applications for Grant of Product Licences — Products for Human Use) Regulations S.I. 1993 No. 2538, which implements E.C. Directive 91/507/EEC. This provides that all phases of clinical investigations must be undertaken "in accordance with good clinical practice". It is uncertain whether this must be interpreted to read in accordance with the European Guidelines on Good Clinical Practice.

(c) Randomised clinical trials

An important part of medical research is the randomised clinical trial. Randomisation is used as a technique to reduce the possibility that the patient's positive response to a new treatment is simply because of the psychological effect of being given a new drug. In a randomised clinical trial, one group of subjects is given the drug, while another group is given the placebo, or dummy treatment. A variant upon the randomised controlled trial is the double blind trial in which the clinician is also unaware which drugs are being provided to the patient. Double blind trials are undertaken to avoid the patient being influenced by the clinician's enthusiasm for a particular treatment. Such trials are used almost exclusively in relation to pharmaceutical research.

Royal College of Physicians, *Research involving Patients* (1990)

Ethical problems with controlled trials

7.98 Double-blind and placebo-controlled trials have sometimes been the source of anxiety on the part of the public or of prospective participants, usually because an element of deception seems to be involved, or because patients who are allocated to the control group (which might for example, not receive a new treatment) may seem to be at an unfair advantage. Anxiety on both of these counts is quite proper if certain conditions fail to be met when the trial is proposed.

7.99 Where the administration of effective treatment is important for the future well being of the patient, it is ethical for a controlled trial to be undertaken only if, at the outset, the investigator does not know whether the trial treatment is more effective or less effective than the standard treatment with which it is to be compared (or than no treatment at all in the case of a placebo controlled study.) Obviously the fact that the study is initiated at all must mean that the investigator thinks that the question is worth asking. However, an investigator who holds the view that one treatment is known to be definitely superior to another is ethically unable to conduct a controlled study of this treatment and would also be unable to collaborate by inviting his patients to participate in such a trial arranged by another clinician. A different clinician who considered that there was no good evidence to indicate that either treatment was superior would be able to invite patients to participate in a controlled comparison of the new procedure with standard treatment. It is a matter of extending into the trial the same consideration for patient's interest which prevails in ordinary clinical practice.

Withholding effective treatment

7.100 Withholding effective treatment for a short time, whether or not it is substituted by a placebo, can sometimes be acceptable in order to validate a technique of measurement or confirm the sensitivity or discrimination of a therapeutic trial design. An investigator who proposes to do this should explicitly confirm his intention and the intended consent procedure to the Research Ethics Committee. Patient consent is necessary and the patient may agree that he need not know precisely when this will take place.

Use of placebos

7.101 The scientific justification for the use of placebo preparations is set out above. Their use is ethical if patients give consent in advance. Where consent is given there is no deception and the proper use of placebos constitutes a useful tool in evaluating treatment.

Giving consent for randomisation

7.102 Proper conduct of a randomised controlled trial requires the allocation of treatments to be conducted after the patient has given consent to participation in the study and has been enrolled. Otherwise, knowledge of which treatment would be allocated to a particular patient could influence recruitment to one or other treatment options and introduce a bias which could affect the outcome of the research.

7.103 Before making a choice about whether or not to participate, patients should be told of the alternative forms of treatment under study. It is sometimes difficult to ensure that patients understand that they are being invited to enrol in a study in which the treatment allocation will be determined by chance. If a patient expresses a strong preference for a particular treatment he is probably ineligible as a participant.

Randomisation of treatment without the consent of the patient.

7.104 In some circumstances it may be proposed that a random allocation should be made but that the random basis on which the doctor recommends a particular treatment should not be declared to the patient.

7.105 We consider that in general, randomisation of treatment without the consent of the patient is unethical. Exceptional circumstances may exist in some research where there is an argument for not telling patients. But acceptance of this should be a deliberate decision as part of an ethical review.

Randomisation before seeking consent

7.106 Randomised allocation of treatment *before* seeking consent to participation in the study is sometimes proposed in order to make it easier for patients to understand what is being offered to them and to facilitate recruitment. This may occasionally be ethically acceptable provided that the patient is told about the other option in the trial. However, in general, we think it is to be discouraged on both scientific and ethical grounds because of the risk of over-persuasion when inviting subjects to accept the allocated treatment.

NOTE:

1. One danger in informing patients that they are being involved in a randomised trial is that a group of patients who are suffering from a terminal condition might sabotage the trial by deciding to pool the drugs in order that they obtain at least some available treatment. Difficulties arose in the United States where patients with AIDS involved in AZT randomised trials, pooled the drugs and thus frustrated the trial. (See J. McHale and A. Young, "The Dilemmas of the HIV Positive Prisoner" (1992) 31 *Howard Journal of Criminal Justice* 89.)

(d) Ensuring consent is voluntary

As with medical treatment it is important that patients/volunteers in clinical trials give their consent voluntarily.

DOH Guidelines (1991)

3.5 No one should be made to participate in a research study against their will. Those recruiting participants should be careful to avoid exerting any undue influence. This is especially important where the recruits are drawn from a subordinate or dependant group, *e.g.* employees, students, junior hospital staff. The researcher should emphasise that participation is entirely voluntary; that refusal will attract no sanction; that if they agree to participate they are free to leave the study at any time with no detriment to their standing or employment, and that they will not be required to give reasons for declining to participate or leaving the study. Patients who refuse to participate in research studies should be reassured that they are free to do so with no detriment to their treatment.

(i) Financial inducements

Inducements may be offered to individual research subjects or to physicians to encourage participation in trials.

DOH Guidelines (1991)

3.15 The LREC should examine any financial aspect of a research project which may influence the patient's judgment in consenting or the researcher's judgment in his/her treatment of subjects, in such a way as to call the ethics of the research into question. Clearly any payments to subject or researcher must be considered, but it is also possible that benefits to an institution or department may raise similar ethical questions. Undue variations in payments between different sites in a multi-centre project may also raise questions. In general, however, the resource implications of a research project for the NHS body concerned are for consideration by the NHS management not by the LREC.

3.16 Payment in cash or kind to volunteers should only be for expense, time, and inconvenience reasonably incurred. It should not be at a level of inducement which would encourage people to take part in studies against their better judgement, or which would encourage them to take part in multiple studies.

QUESTION:

1. Is there anything inherently undesirable in volunteers being paid a high level of remuneration if they are prepared to take the risk of entry into a high risk trial? (Compare the position of women who undertake risks by acting as egg donors. See Chapter 11 below at pages 682–683.)

The issue of funding from drug companies is explored further in the following report

Report of The Royal College of Physicians: *The Relationship between Physicians and the Pharmaceutical Industry*, London, 1986

Physicians, pharmaceutical companies and ultimately our patients have much to benefit from the close cooperation of physicians with the officers of pharmaceutical companies in research projects and clinical trials of drugs. In providing opinions and services to companies the principles of honesty and decorum must prevail as in other professional activities. Formal arrangements are essential and should be negotiated through professional colleagues in the pharmaceutical companies not informally by loose arrangement with a company representative. The physician responsible for the project or trial is responsible for informing his employer, for ensuring that proper accounting procedures are adopted with independent audit and for fulfilling all legal requirements. We recommend that the financial arrangements should be made through the finance office of a Health Authority or a university and the accounts supervised by their finance officers.

The monies may be used to finance the execution of the studies which may include salaries of research workers, technicians, nurses or secretaries. They may be used to purchase equipment or expendables, to meet hospital or university overheads, to fund other research projects or to fund attendance of staff at scientific or educational meetings. It is undesirable for a physician to have any personal interest in studies carried out on patients under his care and it is reprehensible to advertise the availability of his own or his colleagues' patients for use as research subjects. Payments must be reasonable in terms of the time and effort given to the trial and openly declared.

NOTE:

1. Without commercial sponsorship many research projects could simply not be undertaken.

(ii) Trials including students

Royal College of Physicians: *Research on Healthy Volunteers*, London, 1986

Students are likely to volunteer as subjects for research for various reasons. Sometimes they are motivated by scientific interest and they may have much to gain in terms of knowledge and experience from taking part in the research. Financial reward may be an added incentive or even the sole motive. As students are normally young, healthy and have low incomes, they are easily recruited by university departments and other organisations. They are, however, particularly vulnerable to academic, personal and financial pressures. They may also be tempted to spend more time than is desirable away from their studies.

Unless the study is educational it is normally undesirable to recruit students who are in close contact with the investigator, *e.g.* on his medical teaching "firm" or in his class. This is because students are, or may feel, vulnerable to pressure from someone in a position to influence their careers, by assessment in an examination or otherwise. Ethics committees should be aware of and pay particular attention to this. When students of an institution are recruited for other than educational studies, the Deans of that institution or other designated person should be informed in writing and the student should be aware of this. The information given should include details of the research project, the names of those taking part and which Ethics Committee has approved the study.

NOTE:

1. There is a danger that persons may become involved in several trials simultaneously. For example, students may be tempted to enter a number of trials in order to alleviate financial pressures in relation to their education. Volunteers may put themselves at risk if drugs taken in different trials conflict. In addition, multiple participation may invalidate the success of a clinical trial. One possible way of dealing with the problem is for researchers to ask the subjects whether they are involved in another trial; it appears that some research ethics committees require that researchers include a question to that effect. The Royal College of Physicians *Guidelines on Research With Healthy Volunteers* (London, 1986) suggests that medical students involved in clinical trials should inform the Dean of the Medical School. However this does not deal with the problem of students from other disciplines who may seek to enter such trials. It is suggested that failure to ask the research subject whether he was involved in any other clinical trial, and if so to give details, would constitute negligence. Nevertheless, such a claim may fail because causation is not established or the student may be found contributorily negligent in participation or, have assumed that risk under the principle *volenti non fit injuria*. Of course cash strapped students may not tell the truth. Perhaps one way in which this problem could be addressed would be through the use of a national register listing all those who are currently included in a clinical trial perhaps by reference to their NHS number. Admittedly, the costs of this proposal may prove a deterrent to its establishment and it would not totally overcome the difficulty of the dubious researcher, although it may represent an improvement on the present position.

(iii) Trials including prisoners

Prisoners may be regarded as a vulnerable group of research subjects. Because of their position they are at risk of being coerced into participation in a trial. The Department of Health guidelines states that prisoners shall not be involved in a clinical trial without the explicit consent of the Director of the Prison Health Care Service (para. 4.6).

Royal College of Physicians *Research on Healthy Volunteers* (1986)

In the past, prisoners in Britain have not normally been invited to participate as healthy volunteers in research but we do not consider it as inherently unethical to carry out research on prisoners. There might be a reason to believe that a certain hormonal, genetic, psychological or other condition was associated with violence or other pattern of behaviour likely to lead to criminal action. It would be reasonable to study such a condition in prisoners as they constitute a group likely to be relevant to the study. All the usual safeguards, which include obtaining valid consent would apply and Ethics Committees might need to take special advice. Particular care need to be taken to avoid coercion in any form including any impression that inducements such a reduction of sentence or pardon or other favours could be given. Nevertheless we appreciate that there is no precise point where a recompense becomes an inducement. It should also be appreciated that for some prisoners the opportunity to contribute positively to the well being of society may be of help in re-establishing self-esteem and therefore in rehabilitation.

NOTE:

1. For the purposes of medical treatment prisoners are regarded as any other competent adult. (*Freeman v. Home Office* [1984] 1 All E.R. 1036.) It is presumed that they can also give consent to therapeutic medical research. (See further Chapter 6 at page 368.) As far as non-therapeutic research is concerned, it is suggested that were a prisoner to bring an action in battery claiming that he had not given valid consent much would depend upon whether his consent was given freely.

(e) Trials including women subjects

There has been considerable controversy as to whether women of child bearing age should be included at all in clinical trials because of risks to their child-bearing capacity. The Department of Health guidelines state that, if it is intended to use women as research subjects, the possibility of their being or becoming pregnant should always be considered, and the researcher should always justify the recruitment of women of child bearing age (para. 4.5). Inclusion of women in certain trials is unavoidable where the trial relates to, for example, contraceptive techniques. Even where the trial is not of that type, it is questionable whether women should be totally excluded. Firstly, such an exclusion would considerably reduce the potential pool of research subjects. Secondly, any research ethics committee which excluded women of child-bearing age as research subjects may be seen as paternalistic and sexist.

(f) Trials including child subjects

While much research can be undertaken using adult subjects, it is inevitable that there are situations in which the nature of the research dictates that child subjects must be used; for example, if it is proposed to undertake a trial into childhood diseases. In such cases the trials should be subjected to particularly careful scrutiny.

DOH Guidelines (1991)

4.1 Research proposals should only involve children where it is absolutely essential to do so and the information cannot be obtained using adult subjects.

4.2 When seeking consent to examination or treatment (which may include research which is intended to benefit the patient, *i.e.* therapeutic research) young people aged 16 and 17 are presumed (in the absence of indications to the contrary) to be able to give their full consent independently of their parents or guardians. Children who are under 16 years of age may also be able to give full consent-providing they have a sufficient understanding of what is proposed, as judged by the doctor attending them. Even for therapeutic research purposes it would however be unacceptable not to have the consent of the parent or guardian* where the child is under 16. Where the child is over 16 and under 18 generally parental consent should also be required-unless it is clearly in the child's best interests that the parents should not be informed.

4.3 Where the proposal is for non-therapeutic research, all of the above applies but in addition the child must be subject to no more than minimal risk as a result of his/her participation.

4.4 The LREC should note that those acting for the child can only legally give their consent provided that the intervention is for the benefit of the child. If they are responsible for allowing the child to be subjected to any risk (other than one so insignificant to be negligible) which is not for the benefit of that child, it could be said that they are acting illegally. It should also be noted that the giving of consent by a parent or guardian cannot override the refusal of consent by a child who is competent to make that decision.

* Persons other than parents or guardians may legally be in a position to give consent on behalf of a child to medical treatment. These include a local authority which has a care order, a person with a court order giving him legal custody and, after the Children's Act 1989 comes into force a person with a residence order.

NOTES:

1. Whether a child has the right to decide himself to be included in a clinical trial is uncertain. The courts may be willing to apply the test set out in *Gillick v. West Norfolk and Wisbech AHA* [1985] 3 All E.R. 402. (See Chapter 7 above at page 380). Where a child lacks sufficient maturity to give consent himself, then researchers would have to obtain consent from the person with the parental power of consent.

2. It is perhaps questionable whether courts would compel a child to be involved in a therapeutic trial. There is a remote possibility that a court may be asked to rule on such an issue, if the therapy offered the only chance of recovery from a terminal condition. The Department

of Health guidelines are not of particular help on this issue. (See paragraph 4.3–4.4.)

Whilst the legal position regarding non-therapeutic trials is equally uncertain, it is suggested the court would be most unlikely to compel an unwilling child to be involved in such a trial, even where it could be shown that the trial only involved a minimal risk.

Determining who has the power to decide who should be included in a clinical trial is only one issue; another equally important consideration is the basis on which clinical trials which involve child patients should be undertaken:

The British Paediatric Association *Guidelines for the Ethical Conduct of Research Involving Children* (1992)

"There are no general statutory provisions covering research on human beings. In the absence, also, of relevant case law, earlier cautions against research on minors that offers no direct benefit to the child subject have been replaced by qualified support. This has not been challenged in the courts. The attempt to protect children absolutely from the potential harms of research denies any of them the potential benefits. We therefore support the premise that research that is of no intended benefit to the child subject is not necessarily unethical or illegal. Such research includes observing and measuring normal development, assessing diagnostic methods, the use of "healthy volunteers" and of placebos in controlled trials.

The importance of evaluating potential benefits, harms and costs in research on human beings, and ways of doing so, have been discussed repeatedly. A summary of discussion points is included in these guidelines to illustrate how complex such evaluations can be. Our aim, rather than to provide answers, is to list questions for researchers and ethics committees to consider.

1. Assessment of potential benefit includes reviewing estimates of:

magnitude

- How is the knowledge gained likely to be used?
- In research into therapy how severe is the problem which the research aims to alleviate?
- How common is the problem?

probability

- How likely is the research to achieve its aims?

beneficiaries

- Is the research intended to benefit the child subjects and/or other children?

resources

- Will potential benefits be limited because they are very expensive, or require unusually highly trained professionals?

2. Assessment of potential harm includes estimates of;

types of intervention

- How invasive or intrusive is the research? (psychosocial research should be assessed as carefully as physical research.)

magnitude

- How severe may the harms associated with research procedures be?

probability

- How likely are the harms to occur?

timing

- Might adverse effects be brief or long-lasting, immediate or not evidence until years later?

equity

- Are a few children drawn into too many projects simply because they are available?
- Are researchers relying unduly on children who already have many problems?

interim finding

- If evidence of harm in giving or withholding certain treatment emerges during the trial, how will possible conflict between the interests of the child subjects and of valid research be managed?

3. Assessment of potential harm also includes reviewing personal estimates

Children's responses are varied, often unpredictable, and later as children develop, so that generalisations about risk tend to be controversial. A procedure which does not bother one child arouses severe distress in another. Researchers sometimes underestimate high risk or pain if the effects are brief, whereas the child or parents may consider the severe transient pain is not justified by the hoped for benefit. There is evidence that tolerance of pain increases with age and maturity when the child no longer perceives medical interventions as punitive.

Some potential harm may not be obvious without careful consideration of their consequences. For example, with research into serious genetic disorders which present in adult life, presymptomatic diagnosis in a child, while it may be beneficial, may also have very harmful effects and may affect the child's opportunities and freedom of choice.

4. Risks may be estimated as minimal, low or high

Minimal (the least possible) risk describes procedures such as questioning, observing and measuring children, provided that procedures are carried out in a sensitive way, and that consent has been given. Procedures with minimal risk include collecting a single urine sample (but not by aspiration), or using blood from a sample that has been taken as part of treatment.

Low risk describes procedures that cause brief pain or tenderness and small bruises or scars. Many children fear needles and for them low rather than minimal risks are often incurred by injections and venepuncture.

High risk procedures such as lung or liver biopsy, arterial puncture and cardiac catheterisation, are not justified for research purposes alone. It would be unethical to submit child subjects to more than minimal risk when the procedure offers no benefit to them, or only a slight or very uncertain one. Higher risks in research and novel treatments are accepted when children are enduring very harmful diseases. Illness and anxiety alone may put pressure on families to assent to heroic experimental procedures. In cases of severe or chronic disease therefore, the harms to the child of the condition of the medical treatment, and of the stress through taking part in research need to be assessed, so that all avoidable distress may be relieved.

Despite careful selection, children in clinical trials have social and emotional problems which are mainly unpredictable. Provision for the necessary continuing emotional support should be built in to the research design."

QUESTIONS:

1. Should inclusion of children in clinical trials be a matter for a local research ethics committee or should a special national committee be established for the conduct of trials on child subjects?
2. Should children be allowed to participate in non-therapeutic trials? Is it unethical to include a child in a non-therapeutic trial where there is more than a minimal risk? Parents allow their children to participate in risky activities for pleasure — why not allow them to include a child in a trial on the basis of the public interest? (See R. Nicholson, "The Ethics of Research With Children" in M. Brazier and M. Lobjoit (eds.), *Protecting the Vulnerable*, London: Routledge, 1991.)
3. Should a mature adolescent who is assessed as *"Gillick"* competent be able to include herself in a high risk trial despite her parents' objections? (See R. Nicholson, *Medical Research with Children*, Oxford: OUP, 1985.)
4. Should a child be deemed competent to refuse entry to a therapeutic clinical trial? Compare the position regarding refusal of treatment (see Chapter 7 above).

(g) Trials involving mentally disordered persons

Whilst clinical trials will usually be undertaken with competent adult volunteers there may be occasions in which research upon an incompetent adult is unavoidable because for instance, the trial is into a particular disorder/ mental disability. Again, as with the child patient, researchers are exhorted to have particular regard to the potential vulnerability of their subject group.

(i) General Issues

DOH Guidelines (1991)

4.7 Research on mentally disordered* people requires particular care and sensitivity bearing in mind that they are vulnerable and some may not be able to give consent. There is a need to weigh the rights of an individual to consent or refuse to take part in research and the particular status of those unable to consent against the need for research to advance the knowledge and treatment of mental disorders.

4.8 Consent must be freely given and based on information given in a form that is understandable to each individual. It is therefore necessary to take account of the capacity of the person to understand the information given and this in turn will depend upon their intellectual state, mental disorder and the possible variability of their mental state.

4.9 The prescence of mental disorder does not by itself imply incapacity, nor does detention under the Mental Health Act 1983.

4.11 Proposals for research where capacity to consent is impaired will need particularly careful consideration by the LREC, with regard to its acceptability in terms of the balance of benefits, discomforts and risks for the individual patient and the need to advance knowledge so that people with mental disorder may benefit.

4.12 The LREC and researchers will find the guidelines issued by the Royal College of Psychiatrists particularly useful in considering these issues.

* Mental disorder means mental illness, arrested or incompleted development of mind, psychopathic disorder and any other disorder or disability of mind and 'mentally disordered' shall be construed accordingly.

It is important to emphasise that patients suffering from a mental disorder may be capable of consenting to involvement in research.

Royal College of Psychiatrists, "Guidelines for Psychiatric Research involving Human Subjects" (1990) 14 *Psychiatric Bulletin* 48

Decision Making

Several factors can affect the ability to decide freely after having acquired appropriate information about the research. There may be covert pressures to take part, for example to please a doctor who has helped or who might help the person; this problem might arise between a patient and a doctor, or in forensic psychiatric research, between a prisoner and a research worker who is perceived as being able to influence the prisoners future; or between a senior member of staff and students or employees. It is good practice to allow a period for reflection between the explanation of the study and the final decision. Usually this period should be about a day, though in exceptional cases it may be impractical to wait so long. It is often appropriate to provide written information to remind the person of the discussion with the research worker. This written information should be accompanied by a spoken explanation and an opportunity for the person to ask questions. It is important to explain that consent can be withdrawn at any time, without affecting in any way the patient's usual treatment, the prisoner's sentence, or the career of a student or employee . . .

Features of the *mental state* are relevant to decision making. Delusions can affect a patient's ability to decide whether to take part in research, but neither delusions or other psychotic symptoms necessarily do so. There is no general state of incompetence to consent; the matter has to be decided knowing the nature of the decision to be taken and the influence that the delusional belief would be expected to have on the decision. Thus a patient with depressive delusions might consent to research that he considers unpleasant and hazardous because he believes that he is unworthy and should be punished. However, other kinds of delusion need not affect the person's decision . . .

Special problems

1. *Detained patients*

When a patient is detained in hospital under the Mental Health Act, particular care should be taken in relation to informed consent. However, it would not be ethical to deprive automatically all detained patients of the opportunity to contribute to research that could improve their own or other patient's care in the future. in these cases, the task of the Ethics Committee is to answer the same questions as apply to non-detained patients paying particular attention to the special circumstances of the detained patient the nature of the illness that led to detention, and the effect of both of these on the person's ability to give free informed consent.

2. *'Incompetent' patients*

Some patients, who may or may not be detained, are not competent to give free informed consent to research. They present particular problems since many suffer from conditions for which advances in knowledge are needed most, and cannot be obtained by studying other patients. Patients with severe mental handicap and severe dementia are examples of this group.

If the general points considered above are taken into account, this class of patients will be small; to suffer from severe dementia or mental handicap does not necessarily imply incompetence; and incompetence to make one kind of decision does not necessarily mean incompetence to make another kind. Although the group is small, the ethical problems related to research with these patients are very important and proposals for research involving them requires very careful consideration by the Ethics Committee.

When research with 'incompetent' patients involves physical contact (including the administration of drugs), the problems are greater because in these circumstances there is a potential legal problem as well as an ethical one. Procedures of this kind could be deemed a battery. However, legal opinion indicates that the law of battery is unlikely to be applied to such cases, provided due procedures of approval by an Ethics of Research Committee have been completed. (It is important to stress that many kind of psychiatric research do not involve physical contact.)

The problems of research with incompetent patients was addressed in the Declaration of Helsinki, which recommends that consent be obtained from a legal guardian. This recommendation is not helpful in the United Kingdom because the law does not recognise this kind of guardian except in cases where special steps have been taken to appoint a guardian in law. No person other than a legally appointed guardian can give consent on behalf of the patient, and there is no clear legal guidance about the best way of proceeding in cases in which none has been appointed. In the absence of such guidance, the following is a commonsense approach to the issues.

The Ethics Committee should decide in the usual way whether the research is acceptable in terms of the balance of benefits, discomforts and risks. Then it should consider the question of consent. No one else can consent on behalf of the patient. However, it would be good practice in most cases for the research worker to discuss the research with one or more close relatives, and discover their views. If there is no relative or the patient expresses the wish that his relative should not be consulted, it may be appropriate to consult an independent person who knows the patient well and will protect his interests (for example, a nurse). The choice of such a person should be approved by the Ethics of Research Committee. These people should attempt to form a judgement based on the patient's known previous opinions about research and on his recent behaviour, as to whether the patient would be likely to consent were he able to do so. Any patient who indicates refusal either in words or in actions should be excluded from the research whatever opinion is voiced by the others who have been consulted.

NOTES:

1. These guidelines preceded the decision of the House of Lords in *F. v. West Berkshire Area Health Authority* [1989] 3 All E.R. 545 which makes it clear that no one can give consent on behalf of a mentally incompetent person (See Chapter 5 above at pages 287–295.) Treatment may only be given if this is in the best interests of the patient. It is unclear as to whether this test applies in relation to research. It appears likely that the court will follow a "best interests" test in deciding whether an incompetent patient should be included in a therapeutic research project.
2. The Law Commission in its Report, *Mental Incapacity* (Law Com. 231, HMSO: 1995) suggested that the decision whether or not to include a mentally incompetent person in a therapeutic trial was one which could be left to the broad general authority to act reasonably in the best interests of the incompetent person which they propose earlier in the Report (para. 6.28), see Chapter 5 at pages 303–306. Whether this provides a sufficient check upon researchers is questionable. It is arguable that further safeguards are needed to protect the interests of the mentally incompetent adult in this area.
3. Care needs to be taken when it is proposed to include psychiatric patients in a clinical trial in view of the fact that such patients may be inherently emotionally vulnerable. (See K. W. M. Fulford and K. Howse, "Ethics of research with psychiatric patients: principles, problems and the primary responsibilities of researchers" (1993) 19 *Journal of Medical Ethics* 85.)

QUESTIONS:

1. Does the *Bolam* test provide an appropriate basis to determine whether a mentally incompetent person may be included in a therapeutic research project or should this task be entrusted to a third party decision maker? (See Chapter 5 at page 304.)

(ii) Non-therapeutic research and the mentally incompetent adult

It appears that undertaking non-therapeutic research upon the mentally incompetent adult is *prima facie* unlawful. *F. v. West Berkshire Area Health Authority* [1989] 2 All E.R. 545 indicated that therapeutic procedures could be undertaken if they were in the best interests of the patient. Nevertheless, it appears that this does not extend to non-therapeutic procedures. That does not mean, however, that non-therapeutic medical research should never be undertaken upon such a person. This matter has received extensive consideration by the Law Commission.

Law Commission, *Mental Incapacity*, Law Com. 231, 1995

6.29 'Non-therapeutic' research, on the other hand, does not claim to offer any direct or immediate benefit to the participant. Such procedures may well be scientifically and ethically acceptable to those who are qualified to decide such matters. If, however, the participant lacks capacity to consent to his or her participation, and the procedure cannot be justified under the doctrine of necessity, then any person who touches or restrains that participant is committing an unlawful battery. The simple fact is that the researcher is making no claim to be acting in the best interests of that individual person and does not therefore come within the rules of law set out in *Re F*. It was made abundantly clear to us on consultation, however, that non-therapeutic research projects of this nature are regularly taking place. We were told of a research project into the organic manifestations of Alzheimer's disease which involves the administration of radioactive isotopes to sufferers, followed by extensive testing of blood and bodily functions. Another project was said to involve the examination of written patients' records, although they are unable to consent to this examination. In some cases relatives are asked to 'consent' to what is proposed, and do so. It appears that some funding bodies and Ethics Committees stipulate for consent by a relative where the research participant cannot consent. As a matter of law, such 'consent' is meaningless. It appears that the question of the legality of non-therapeutic research procedures is regularly misunderstood or ignored by those who design, fund and approve the projects.
    6.30 A number of our respondents expressed concern about non-invasive research based on observations, photography or videoing of participants (sometimes covertly). We accept that questions of dignity and privacy arise in such situations where the project is not designed to benefit the research participant.
    6.31 We suggested in our consultation paper that the balance of expert opinion favours the participation of people unable to consent in even non-therapeutic research projects, subject to strict criteria. The majority of our consultees argued that there is an ethical case for such participation. This case turns on the desirability of eradicating painful and distressing disabilities, where progress can be achieved without harming research subjects. The wide range of guidance and expert commentary on this matter shows a striking degree of consensus over the factors which make non-therapeutic research ethical, and we remarked a similar consensus in the responses submitted to us on consultation. In summary, the consensus appears to be that non-therapeutic research involving participants who cannot consent is justifiable where (1) the research relates to the condition from which the participant suffers, (2) the same knowledge cannot be gained from research limited to those capable of consenting, and (3) the procedures involve minimal risk and invasiveness. The recommendations which follow are intended to resolve the unacceptable anomaly that projects of this type, assessed by those with appropriate scientific and ethical expertise as being important and meritorious, in fact involve

actionable unlawful conduct by the researchers. At the same time, our recommenda-tions will place necessary protections for the participant without capacity on a statutory footing.

We recommend that research which is unlikely to benefit a participant, or whose benefit is likely to be long delayed, should be lawful in relation to a person without capacity to consent if (1) the research is into an incapacitating condition with which the participant is or may be affected and (2) certain statutory procedures are complied with (Draft Bill, clause 11(1).)

6.32 Special considerations may apply in relation to the testing of medicinal products. The United Kingdom has implemented a European Directive on the licensing and testing of medicinal products. The Directive requires compliance with 'good clinical practice'. In 1991 the European Commission issued guidelines on "Good Clinical Practice for Trials on Medicinal Products in the European Community, one of the guidelines being that 'consent must always be given by the signature of the subject in a non-therapeutic study'. If 'good clinical practice' in the 1991 directive means good clinical practice as defined in the 1991 guidelines, then the directive forbids any non-therapeutic product research involving a participant without capacity to consent. One leading text book on medical law concludes that the meaning of 'good clinical practice' in the directive is a 'matter of conjecture'. Our own view is that it is not restricted to those matters set out in the 1991 guidelines and we understand that the Department of Health shares this view. In relation to those participants who lack capacity, our recommendations are designed to put good clinical practice on a proper legal footing.

A Mental Incapacity Research Committee

6.33 The Department of Health has instructed District Health Authorities to set up Local Research Ethics Committees (LRECs) 'to advise NHS bodies on the ethical acceptability of research proposals involving human subjects'. LRECs have no legal standing, a decision by a LREC does not make a researcher's actions lawful, and statute cannot enable a non-statutory body to achieve such an end. In the consultation paper we suggested that a judicial body should have power to make a declaration that proposed research involving persons without capacity would be lawful. Courts and adversarial process, however, are not well adapted to cases where there are no opposing parties to present evidence. Ordinary judges will have no relevant scientific expertise. Instead, therefore, we recommend that a new statutory committee should be established. This will supplement the "extra-legal" checks and balances which already exist, avoiding duplication of valuable time and effort.

We recommend that there should be a statutory committee to be known as the Mental Incapacity Research Committee (Draft Bill, clause 11(2)

6.34 A non-therapeutic research procedure should only be lawful in relation to a person who is without capacity to consent if the Mental Incapacity Research Committee approves the research. Although most research which would otherwise be unlawful will be 'medical' in the broadest sense, we do not suggest that the remit of the committee should be expressly limited to medical research. The criteria to be applied by the committee should be set out in statute. they all refer to the one particular issue of participants without capacity. Wider scientific questions will still be investigated by the relevant funding bodies. If NHS patients are involved, then the ethical advice of the LREC will be required before the Department of Health guidance will be satisfied.

We recommend that the committee may approve the proposed research if satisfied:

(1) that it is desirable to provide knowledge of the causes or treatment of, or of the care of people affected by, the incapacitating condition with which any participant is or may be affected,

(2) that the object of the research cannot be effectively achieved without the participation of persons who are or may be without capacity to consent and

(3) that the research will not expose a participant to more than negligible risk, will not be unduly invasive or restrictive of a participant and will not unduly interfere with a participant's freedom of action or privacy (Draft Bill, clause 11(3)).

The draft bill makes provision for the composition and procedures of the committee.

Protection for the individual participant

6.36 It is not realistic or practicable for the individual participation of a person without capacity in a particular project to be referred to the special statutory committee for approval. The committee's role is to approve the research protocol, and we anticipate this involving documentary submissions in most cases. There is, however, a need for a separate and individualised independent check to confirm whether any particular proposed participant should indeed be brought into the project. Our recommendations therefore involve a two-stage process. By way of example, researchers obtain the committee's approval to a project which envisages tests on those with advanced Alzheimer's Disease. The researchers should not then be under the impression that this approval means they may involve in their project all the residents of a particular nursing home who have been diagnosed as suffering from Alzheimer's Disease without the need for any further permission. They must approach each of these proposed participants as an individual. They must ask whether this particular person does indeed have the capacity to consent to what is proposed. It may be that an explanation in simpler or more appropriate terms would be quite comprehensible to the person, especially if given by a person familiar to him or her. If, however, it appears that the proposed participant is without capacity to consent to what is proposed then an independent check is required, and we describe the nature of this check below.

6.37 In most cases the appropriate person to carry out an independent check will be a registered medical practitioner who is not involved in the research project. This need not be an independent doctor appointed to consider such matters by the Secretary of State (as recommended in relation to "second opinion category" treatments). The important point is simply that this doctor should not be involved with the proposed research. The doctor who knows the person best, by virtue of having responsibility for his or her general medical care, will often be the best candidate. An attorney with express authorisation from a donor should be able to consent on the donor's behalf. Similarly, a court-appointed manager may have express authority to give such consent. In some cases the court itself may have made it clear whether the person concerned may participate in non-therapeutic research. In none of these situations need the 'second opinion' doctor be involved. There will also be some rare cases where the research protocol does not contemplate any direct contact between researcher and participant. These might involve covert observation or photographing, or the inspection of written records. In such cases, the broad ethical issues still have to be weighed by the committee but there is no purpose in anyone else looking at individual circumstances. The committee should therefore have the power to designate a project as one which does not involve direct contact with participants, with no second stage check then required.

We recommend that, in addition to the approval of the Mental Incapacity Research Committee, non-therapeutic research in relation to a person without capacity should require either:

(1) court approval,

(2) the consent of an attorney or manager,

(3) a certificate from a doctor not involved in the research that the participation of the person is appropriate, or

(4) the designation of the research not involving direct contact. (Draft Bill, clause 11(1)(c) and (4).

6.38 Where the court, an attorney, a manager or an independent doctor is considering the question of a particular individual participating in a project then regard should be had to the factors in the best interests checklist.

6.39 In accordance with the recommendations we have made elsewhere in this report, this should be a clear prohibition against anything being done to a research participant if he or she objects to what is being done. Equally, in the event that a person has made an effective advance refusal to participate in a non-therapeutic research project then no approval of the committee or third party's confirmation would have any effect.

NOTE:

1. The Law Commission recommends that trials undertaken upon a mentally incompetent adult should be subject to approval by one of four decision makers. The Commission does not, however, stipulate in which contexts which decison maker should operate. In addition it recommends that such clinical trials should not expose the participant to more than a "minimal risk". One of the possible approaches is to refer the decision to a judicial decision maker. But is judicial authorisation really required if, as the Law Commission suggests, the trial should never involve more than minimal risk? Furthermore, if judicial authorisation became the norm, regular referral of all intended research subjects to the courts would be expensive and time consuming.

QUESTIONS:

1. What are the advantages and disadvantages of establishing a national research committee to approve the conduct of trials upon those with mental incapacity?
2. Why should observational research be an exception to the "special consent" procedure proposed by the Law Commission?

4. CONFIDENTIALITY

Researchers will frequently obtain access to confidential patient information. If the researchers are NHS employees or health professionals then they will be bound by their legal and professional ethical obligation to maintain the confidentiality of that information. (See generally Chapter 9 above.) The local research ethics committee when approving a trial protocol may also make stipulations as to the confidentiality of research information.

DOH Guidelines (1991)

3.11 Researchers should be asked to confirm that personal health information will be kept confidential, that data will be secured against unauthorised access and that no individual will be identifiable from published results, without his or her explicit consent. All data from which an individual is identifiable should be destroyed when no longer required for the purposes of original research. If, exceptionally the researcher wishes to retain confidential information beyond the completion of the research, the LREC, the relevant NHS body and the research subject must first be made aware of the reasons for retaining the information and the circumstances in which this might be disclosed. The subject's consent to these arrangements must be recorded.

3.12 Epidemiological research through studies of medical records can be extremely valuable. Patients are, however, entitled to regard their medical records as confidential to the NHS and should in principle be asked if they consent to their own records being released to research workers. However there will be occasions when a researcher would find it difficult or impossible to obtain such consent from every individual and the LREC will need to be satisfied that the value of such a project outweighs in the public interest, the principle that individual consent should be obtained. Where a patient has previously indicated that he or she would *not* want their records released then this request should be respected.

3.13 The LREC will need to be assured that this kind of research will be conducted in accordance with current codes of practice and data protection. Wherever possible consent should also be sought from the health professional responsible for the relevant aspects of the subject's care. Once information has been obtained from the records no approach should be made to the patient concerned without the agreement of the health professional currently responsible for their care.

3.14 Certain enquiries and surveys, involving only access to patient records, such as the national morbidity surveys and the post-marketing surveillance of drugs, which are in the public interest, do not need prior approval of an LREC.

One important issue is the extent to which researchers should have access to patient records for research purposes without obtaining prior consent from the patient.

Royal College of Physicians, *Guidelines on the Practice of Ethics Committees in Medical Research Involving Human Subjects*, 3rd ed., London, 1996

"Use of medical records, registers or existing biological samples in research: the need for ethical reviews

A working party with a strong lay membership concluded that to require formal ethical review of research involving personal medical records or stored biological samples alone is likely to delay or even inhibit valuable research: they further recommended, provided that such research is provided with suitable confidentiality, it is by its nature harmless and does not require submission to a LREC. After careful consideration Council of the RCP agreed to publish this report which is summarised below and has been published in full.

Research involving access to medical records, registers or existing biological samples only, without direct patient contact or involvement, is not considered to require individual patient consent or independent ethical approval provided that:

- explicit consent to access a patient's records is obtained either from the official custodian of those records or from the patient's clinician: the decision to access personal medical information should not be left to the sole discretion of the investigator;
- confidentiality is assured through adherence to professional ethical codes of conduct;

- the recipient of the information is a senior professional person *e.g.* a consultant medical practitioner or a principal in general practice who is subject to an effective disciplinary code enforced by his or her professional body over any breach of confidentiality. *e.g.* by suspension from practice in a serious case . . ."

This statement is a summary of the report contained in Royal College of Physicians, "Independant Ethical Review of Studies involving Personal Medical Records: Report of a Working Group" (1994) 28 *Journal of Royal College of Physicians London* 429.

QUESTIONS:

1. Do the recommendations of the RCP working party accord with the guidelines of the DoH set out above?
2. Should patient's records be accessible for the purposes of research without patient consent? (Contrast the general approach taken to disclosure of patient information — see Chapter 8 above.)

5. REGULATING FRAUDULENT RESEARCHERS

Considerable pressures are placed upon those who are involved in clinical research to show results for the money spent. There are also pressures upon the researcher to publish numerous papers for career advancement. The temptation to falsify results is thus considerable. This may impact upon patient care if drugs/techniques are deemed "safe" from trials which are themselves inherently flawed. At present misconduct by a researcher may lead to her being struck off the register by the General Medical Council (C. Dyer, "GP Struck Off for Fraud in Drug Trials" (1996) 312 *BMJ* 798 and S. Lock (ed.), *Fraud and Misconduct in Medical Research* (2nd edn.), London: BMJ (1996). The Royal College of Physicians has stated that two measures are required to ensure ethical research practice. First, there should be adherence to good practice in research. Secondly, there should be some form of mechanism for investigating allegations into fraud. (See *Fraud and Misconduct in Medical Research*, Royal College of Physicians, London, 1991, Chapter 6.) They suggest measures such as limiting the number of papers research applicants can cite when applying for jobs. They also propose that consideration should be given to the American approach, namely that research grants are conditional upon an institution having a mechanisam in place to deal with scientific misconduct.

In 1995 a meeting was held, convened by the Royal College of Physicians and attended by representatives from the Royal Society, General Medical Council and Medical Research Council to consider the establishment of a central body, though this was not taken further. Recently there have been calls in both the *British Medical Journal* and the *Lancet* for this issue to be examined by the government. (See R. Smith, "Time to face up to research misconduct" (1996) 312 *BMJ* 789 and Editorial "Dealing with Deception" [1996] *Lancet* 843.)

6.   SCRUTINISING THE APPROVAL OF CLINICAL TRIALS

(a) Challenging the decision of a local research ethics committee to approve a clinical trial

A research ethics committee, as a public body, is liable to scrutiny of its action through judicial review. The decision of such a committee may be overturned on the basis that it had failed to act within the powers given to it by the Department of Health, failed to take into account relevant considerations when making the decision or failed to observe procedural proprieties when examining applications. There are no examples of such a challenge being brought. In both instances where judicial review actions have been brought against an ethics committee of an IVF unit the actions were unsuccessful (For example, *R. v. St Mary's Hospital Manchester ex p. Harriot* [1988] 1 FLR 51, *R. v. Sheffield H.A. ex p. Seale* (See Chapter 11 at pages 665–675.) Nevertheless the potential for an action against a research ethics committee remains. (See I. Kennedy, "Research Ethics Committees and the Law" in C. Gilbert Foster (ed.), *Manual for Research Ethics Committees* (2nd ed.), London: Centre of Medical Law and Ethics, 1991.)

(b) Liability of members of a research ethics committee to a research subject injured in a clinical trial

DOH Guidelines (1991)

2.11 Concern has been expressed by some LREC members that they may be legally liable for injury caused to patients participating in research projects. DHA's will wish to advise appointees on these matters. Legal advice available to the Department of Health is that there is little prospect of a successful claim against a LREC member for a mishap arising from research approved as ethical by the LREC. Any such claim would lie principally against the researcher concerned and against the NHS body under the auspices of which the research took place. The principal defendants should seek to have any claim against an LREC member struck out. Those members of an LREC who are employees of an NHS body are already covered by NHS indemnity arrangements. The DHA should also bear any costs in the case of other LREC members unless the member concerned is guilty of misconduct or gross lack of care in the performance of his or her duties and provided that, if any claim is threatened or made, the member notifies the DHA and assists it in all reasonable ways. If necessary the DHA may give the following undertaking to this effect to LREC members who are not employees of an NHS body:
'We confirm that the DHA will take full responsibility for all actions in the course of the performance of your duties as a member of the LREC other than those involving bad faith, wilful default or gross negligence; you should, however, notify the DHA if any action or claim is threatened or made, and in such an event be ready to assist the authority as required.'

NOTES:

1. The introduction of indemnity for members of NHS research ethics committees followed concern about the accountability of the members of the NHS committee were an action to be brought against them by injured research subjects. (See M. Brazier, "Liability of Ethics Committees and their Members" (1990) 6 *Professional Negligence* 186.)

2. While such a negligence action is theoretically possible it is likely that considerable practical difficulties would face a research subject bringing a negligence action against individual committee members. In the first place, the courts have indicated that they are unwilling to impose negligence liability upon regulatory bodies. (See *Yeu Keu-yen v. Att.-Gen. of Hong Kong* [1988] A.C. 175). Moreover, even if they were prepared to entertain such a claim, the case might well founder on the issue of causation. It would be difficult to establish that it was the negligence of the committee member which caused the ultimate injury that the research subject suffered.

7. ENSURING THAT RESEARCHERS ARE ACCOUNTABLE

DOH Guidelines (1991)

2.14 Once the LREC has approved a proposal, the researcher should be required to notify the committee, in advance, of any significant proposed deviation from the original protocol. Reports to the committee, should also be required once the research is underway if there are any unusual or unexpected results which raise questions about the safety of the research. Reports on success (or difficulties) in recruiting subjects may also provide the LREC with useful feedback on perceptions of the acceptability of the project among patients and volunteers.

NOTE:

1. While the Department of Health suggests notification procedures there is no requirement for systematic reporting regarding research subjects. The issue of whether there should be more extensive scrutiny of clinical trials has been considered further by Neuberger (see also J. V. McHale, "Guidelines for Medical Research: Some Ethical and Legal Problems" (1993) *Medical Law Review* 160).

J. Neuberger, *Ethics and Health Care: The Role of Research Ethics Committees in The United Kingdom*, Kings Fund Institute 1992

Enforcement and sanctions

REC's do not have adequate sanctions against those who ignore their advice. In some DHA's, it would be a disciplinary offence to conduct research on human subjects without getting ethics committee approval first. But that would by no means be the majority. Several clinicians cited the difficulty of getting work published in reputable journals if an approval letter from a research ethics committee could not be shown. But once again this is not universal. Several clinicians thought there might be no proper insurance cover for doctors involved in research who have not got approval from an REC. But it is not clear that this would be universally true. Some university departments would not provide insurance cover for researchers who had not sought the approval of an REC. Again it is by no means clear that this is universal.

The DOH guidelines state that:

'If it comes to the attention of a committee that research is being carried out which it has not been asked to consider or which it has considered and the advice has been ignored, then the REC should bring the matter to the attention of its appointing authority, the relevant NHS body and to the appropriate professional body (DOH, 1991,3.22).'

It is not, therefore, a matter for the RECs to take action themselves against those who do not bring their research for consideration, or ignore their advice. But they need to know what is going on. It is the DHA administrators more than anyone else, who look at the functions and constitution of the research ethics committee and ask questions about the degree to which there is, and should be, monitoring and enforcement.

There is a growing view amongst the members of DHA's that some kind of monitoring role is to be expected of them, though very few carry it out. The DOH guidelines merely require a follow-up by virtue of researchers being required to notify the Committee of changes, or of difficulty in recruiting subjects. But many REC's do not see themselves in a monitoring role at all. At the Royal College of Physicians' meeting for chairmen of REC's in February 1990, many chairmen argued that it was beyond their resources to monitor the research they had approved.

But there is a deeper concern than that, frequently expressed during this research. If the committee has no teeth, however hard it works, however carefully it comes to its decisions, it cannot fulfil its alleged task of protecting the public. It can perform a variety of valuable tasks. It can educate the medical and nursing and other health care staff about how to submit a research protocol. It can teach people how to consider the issues which might raise ethical doubts. It can chew over various issues beyond strict research, but have no locus in decision making. It can discuss the issues relating to IVF trials and to surrogacy. It can question the value of various trials and procedures. But it cannot enforce its decisions. The DHA's and Boards have an important role in increasing the status of REC's. It also became clear that the newly established REC's set up in the last few years, already have a higher status than many of the long established ones. This seems to have come about purely as a result of being set up with determination by the DHA's and Boards rather than having grown up somewhat randomly from a small committee of doctors in the 1960s or early 1970s.

Current practice

All the chairmen said that they rely heavily on the goodwill and honesty of colleagues or doctors. Some clearly felt that the role of the REC is more to educate than to police and others felt that the two roles are distinct and should both be carried out. Two chairmen were adamant in their view that it would be wrong for the REC to carry out any kind of policing role at all, since the committees were advisory rather than enforcement orientated. Nevertheless, the majority view was that there was a role for some kinds of enforcement. Policing is undoubtedly difficult, but all the REC administrators interviewed regarded policing of a sort as essential. That would clearly be the responsibility of the parent DHA concerned, but the REC would have a strong interest in any evidence that its advice was being ignored. Lay members also tended to take this view, as did two chairmen.

Only one REC had a computerised system which showed projects that were at the six months and one year stages and reminded researchers that the REC required a report. Only one REC had conducted spot checks, solely because the administrator felt that they were essential. Most required notification of changes in the protocol, or difficulty gaining subjects, but had no method of knowing whether they were being given the information. Yet adverse events do appear to be reported to REC's. On three occasions during this research, an adverse event was reported. It was felt most sensitively in committees where a death had taken place at any time, or where fraud had been recorded. All REC's observed have as part of their guidelines or as an ever present assumption the requirement that such events will be reported.

Policy options

It is clear that the sanctions RECs or their appointing authorities can impose and the degree to which RECs need to monitor research they have approved needs clarification. Although only advisory bodies, they are well placed to find out what is happening in an individual DHA and should be charged with some montoring function. They should also be empowered to make spot checks on the research in progress, to ensure it is being carried out in accord with their advice. This could range from checks on the consent arrangements to checks on the recruitment policy. Unless they do this, they cannot fulfil their public watchdog role adequately.

8.   COMPENSATION FOR RESEARCH SUBJECTS WHO SUFFER HARM THROUGH PARTICIPATION IN A CLINICAL TRIAL

The present position regarding compensation for subjects injured in a clinical trial is outlined in the Department of Health guidance. If a research subject is injured due to defective drugs or surgical appliances a strict liability action may be brought under the Consumer Protection Act 1987. (For general discussion of this Act see Chapter 3 at pages 188–193.)

The NHS does not provide specific undertakings to compensate those injured through involvement in clinical trials. However if the research is undertaken by a commercial company then undertakings for compensation may be given to the subject who is involved in the research. The Association of British Pharmaceutical Industry guidelines provide for contractually binding undertakings to be made in volunteer trials. Whilst it does not advocate such guarantees in therapeutic trials it suggests that the researcher should provide committees with assurances that if injury occurs compensation will be given. Such compensation does not cover injury incurred where the physician continues to administer the drug even though the trial is itself at an end. In addition it does not apply to trials carried out under the expedited "DDX" provisions (see above at page 568). There has been criticism of the operation of these guidelines. (See J. M. Barton *et al.*, "The Compensation of Patients Injured in Clinical Trials" (1995) 21

Journal of Medical Ethics 166.) Barton *et al* note that in some cases limits have been imposed at the maximum amount claimed along with a requirement that claims be brought within three years of the trial. The Medical Research Council has indicated that it will make *ex gratia* payments in appropriate circumstances to volunteers injured in clinical trials which it sponsors but there is no absolute right to compensation.

The eclectic state of compensation arrangements needs to be considered alongside the difficulties which may face a research subject in bringing a tort action. This poses the question whether there should be any special provision for compensation for those involved in clinical research. The matter was considered by the Pearson Commission in its wide ranging study of personal injury matters in 1978.

Royal Commission on Civil Liability and Compensation for Personal Injury (Cmnd. 7054) (1978)

Volunteers for medical research

1339 People may volunteer to take part in research or clinical trials of new forms of treatment or new drugs. Strict precautions are imposed, including the screening of experiments by medical ethics committees. Nevertheless the Medical Research Council stated in their evidence to us; despite the exercise of the highest degree of care and skill by the medical investigator concerned, death or personal injury which was quite unforeseen and indeed quite unforeseeable might be suffered by a person who volunteers to participate in such an investigation. For example, a volunteer taking part in a recent trial of live attenuated influenza vaccine developed a neurological lesion shortly after the administration of the vaccine — the first known neurological sequela to any attenuated influenza virus despite the fact that many hundreds of thousands of such innoculations had been given during the previous ten years : a causal connection between the administration of the vaccine and the neurological lesion could neither be proved or disproved. In such a situation, the Medical Research Council would seek authority to make an *ex gratia* payment from public funds to the volunteer or to his dependants and such a payment has been approved for the volunteer who developed the lesion in question.

Patients undergoing clinical trials

1340 Patients as well as healthy volunteers may be asked if they will agree to accept a new form of treatment in the interests of research. If a patient is given such treatment and through it suffers injury or a worsening of his condition which would not have been expected with conventional treatment, he is in the same position as a healthy person volunteering to take part in research.

1341 We think that it is wrong that a person who exposes himself to some medical risk in the interests of the community should have to rely on ex gratia compensation in the event of injury. *We recommend* that any volunteer for medical research or clinical trials who suffers severe damage as a result should have a cause of action, on the basis of strict liability, against the authority to whom he has consented to make himself available.

QUESTION:

1. Should the government be obliged to provide compensation for persons injured in government sponsored non-therapeutic clinical trials? (See R. Gillon "No-fault compensation for victims of non-therapeutic research — should government continue to be exempt?" (1992) 18 *Journal of Medical Ethics* 59.)

9.   PARTICULAR AREAS OF MEDICAL RESEARCH

(a) Embryo research

Experimentation on embryos has been the subject of much controversy. It has been claimed that embryo research is justified by scientific advantages such as the development of new contraceptive techniques, more effective IVF procedures and to an improve understanding of miscarriages. Some take the view that the conduct of embryo research does not give rise to any particular ethical difficulties arguing that the embryo is a clump of cells with no special status and that it does not require special protection. (For discussion of the status of the embryo foetus see Chapter 12.) Nevertheless embryo research has provoked considerable opposition. Some are of the view that research is unjustifiable because the embryo is a human being or a potential human being. Others perceive embryo research as sinister and are concerned as to the "slippery slope" to unjustifiable manipulation of the human race. (See Chapter 2 above at pages 115–119.) Some feminist critics who oppose new reproductive techniques also oppose embryo research, regarding it as a manifestation of the exploitation of procreative activity. (See generally — J. Harris and A. Dyson (eds.), *Experiments on Embryos*, London: Routledge, 1991).

The Warnock Committee which reported in 1984 considered embryo research.

Report of the Committee of Enquiry into Human Fertilisation and Embryology (Warnock Committee Report) Cmnd. 9314 (1984)

Arguments against the use of human embryos

11.11   It is obvious that the central objection to the use of human embryos as research subjects is a fundamental objection based on moral principles. Put simply, the main argument is that the use of human embryos for research is morally wrong because of the very fact that they are human and much of the evidence submitted to us strongly submits this. The human embryo is seen as having the same status as a child or an adult by virtue of its potential for human life. The right to life is held to be the fundamental human right and the taking of human life on this view is always abhorrent. To take the life of the innocent is an especial moral outrage. The first consequence of this line of argument is that since an embryo used as a research subject would have no prospect of fulfilling its potential for life, such research should not be permitted.

11.12   Everyone agrees that it is completely unacceptable to make use of a child or an adult as the subject of a research procedure which may cause harm or death. For people who hold the views outlined in 11.11 research on embryos would fall under the same principle. They proceed to argue that since it is unethical to carry out any research harmful or otherwise on humans without first obtaining their informed consent, it must be equally unacceptable to carry out research on a human embryo, which by its very nature, cannot give consent.

11.13   In addition to the arguments outlined above, and well represented in the evidence, many people feel an instinctive opposition to research which they see as tampering with the creation of human life. There is widely felt concern at the possibility of unscrupolous scientists meddling with the process of reproduction in order to create hybrids, or to indulge theories of selective breeding or eugenic selection.

11.14   Those who are firmly opposed to research on human embryos recognise that a ban on their use may reduce the volume not only of pure research but also research in potentially beneficial areas, such as the detection and prevention of inherited disorders, or the alleviation of infertility and that in some areas a ban would halt research completely. However, they argue that the moral principle outweighs any such possible benefits.

Arguments for the use of human embryos

11.15   The evidence showed that the views of those who support the use of embryos as research subjects cover a wide range. At one end is the proposition that it is only to *human persons* that respect must be accorded. A human embryo cannot be thought of as a person, or even as a potential person. It is simply a collection of cells which, unless it implants in a human uterine environment, has no potential for development. There is no reason therefore to accord these cells a protected status. If useful results can be obtained from research on embryos then such research should be permitted. We found that the more generally held position, however, is that though the human embryo is entitled to some added measure of respect beyond that accorded to other animal subjects that respect cannot be absolute and may be weighed against the benefits arising from research. Although many research studies in embryology and developmental biology can be carried out on animal subjects and it is possible in such cases to extrapolate these results and findings to man, in certain situations there is no substitute for the use of human embryos. This particularly applies to the study of disorders only occuring in humans, such as Downs syndrome, or research into the processes of human fertilisation or perhaps into the specific effect of drugs or toxic substances on human tissue.

The Warnock Committee went on to recommend that the human embryo should be given some special status in law.

11.19   The statutory body which we propose should issue licences for research will have as one of its main functions the regulation of research. First, it will have to be assured that no other research material is available for the particular project in mind, and second, it will have to limit the length of time for which an embryo can be kept alive *in vitro*. While as we have seen, the timing of the different stages of development is critical once the process has begun, there is no particular part of the developmental process that is more important than another: all are part of a continuous process, and unless each stage takes place normally at the correct time and in the correct sequence further development will cease.   Thus biologically there is no one single identifiable stage in the development of the embryo beyond which the *in vitro* embryo should not be kept alive.   However, we agreed that this was an area in which some precise decision must be taken in order to allay public anxiety.

11.20   The evidence showed a wide range of opinion on this question. One argument put forward may be termed the strictly utilitarian view. This suggests that the ethics of experiments on embryos must be determined by the balance of benefits over harm or pleasure over pain. Therefore, as long as the embryo is incapable of feeling pain, it is argued that its treatment does not weigh in the balance. According to this argument the time limit for some *in vitro* development and for research on embryos could be set at either when the first beginnings of the central nervous system can be identified or when functional activity first occurs. If the former is chosen then this would imply a limit of twenty two to twenty three days after fertilisation, when the neural tube begins to close. As to the latter, the present state of knowledge the onset of central nervous system functional activity could not be used to identify accurately the limits to research, because the timing is not known: however, it is generally thought to be considerably later in pregnancy. With either limit, proponents suggest subtracting a few days in order that there would be no possibility of the embryo feeling pain.

11.21   The Royal College of Obstretricians and Gynaceologists suggested that embryos should not be allowed to develop *in vitro* beyond a limit of seventeen days, as this is the point at which early neural development begins. The British Medical Association favoured a limit of fourteen days and a number of groups, including the Medical Research Council and the Royal College of Physicians suggested that the time limit should be at the end of the implantation stage. Again, some groups submitting evidence suggested that no embryo which had gone the beginning of the implantation stage should be used for research.

11.22   As we have seen, the objection to using human embryos in research is that each one is a potential human being. One reference point in the development of the human individual is the development of the human individuation in the performance of the primitive streak. Most authorities put this at fifteen days after fertilisation. This marks the beginning of individual development of the embryo. Taking such a time limit is consonant with the views of those who favour the end of the implantation stage as a limit. We have therefore regarded an earlier date than this as a desirable end-point for research. *We accordingly recommend that no live human embryo derived from in vitro fertilisation whether frozen or unfrozen, may be kept alive, if not transferred to a woman, beyond fourteen days after fertilisation. This fourteen day period does not include any time during which the embryo may have been frozen. We further recommend that it shall be a criminal offence to handle or to use as a research subject any live human embryo derived from in vitro fertilisation beyond that limit. We recommend that no embryo which has been used for research should be transferred to a woman.*

NOTES:

1. The Warnock Report noted the fact that the embryo has no specific legal status (see Chapter 12 above).
2. The Committee disagreed over whether embryos should be specially produced for research see para. 11–25–11.30. Four members of the Committee, while supporting research in general, were opposed to the creation of embryos specifically for use in research. (See J. Harris, *The Value of Life*, London: Routledge, 1985, page 129 onwards, and also Chapter 11 below.)

The Warnock Committee recommended that embryo research should continue but subject to regulation. This recommendation was accepted by the Government. In the period prior to legislation a voluntary regulatory regime was instituted in relation to new reproductive technologies (see Chapter 11 below). The Human Fertilisation and Embryology Act 1990 sets out the statutory framework within which treatment for infertility and embryo research are to be undertaken. The 1990 Act requires those proposing to undertake embryo research to obtain a licence from the Human Fertilisation and Embryology Authority, the regulatory body established under the statute. The grounds on which licences may be granted are set out below. (See generally on the passage of legislation D. Morgan and R. Lee, *Human Fertilisation and Embryology Act 1990*, London: Blackstone 1991, Chapter 3.)

Human Fertilisation and Embryology Act 1990, s.3(1–4)

3.—(1) No person shall:

(a) bring about the creation of an embryo, or
(b) keep or use an embryo

except in pursuance of a licence
(2) No person shall place in a woman —

(a) a live embryo other than a human embryo, or
(b) any live gametes other than human gametes.

(3) A licence cannot authorise —

(a) keeping or using an embryo after the appeerence of the primitive streak
(b) placing an embryo in an animal,
(c) keeping or using an embryo in any circumstances in which regulations prohibit its keeping or use, or
(d) replacing the nucleus of a cell of an embryo with a nucleus taken from a cell of any person, embryo or subsequent development of an embryo.

(4) For the purposes of subsection (3)(a) above, the primitive streak is to be taken to have appeared in an embryo not later than the end of the period of 14 days beginning with the day when the gametes are mixed, not counting any time during which the embryo is stored.

Human Fertilisation and Embryology Act 1990 Schedule 2, s.3(1–9)

3.—(1) A licence under this paragraph may authorise any of the following —

(a) bringing about the creation of embryos *in vitro*, and
(b) keeping or using embryos for the purposes of research specified in the licence.

(2) A licence under this paragraph cannot authorise any activity unless it appears to the Authority to be necessary or desirable for the purpose of —

(a) promoting advances in the treatment of infertility
(b) increasing the knowledge of congenital disease
(c) increasing knowledge about the cause of miscarriages,
(d) developing more effective means of contraception, or

(e) developing methods for detecting the prescence of gene or chromosome abnormalities in embryos before implantation, or for such other purposes as may be specified in regulations.

(3) Purposes may only be so specified with a view to the authorisation of projects of research which increase knowledge about the creation and development of embryos or about disease, or enable such knowledge to be applied.

(4) A licence under this paragraph cannot authorise altering the genetic structure of any cell while it forms part of an embryo, except in such circumstances (if any) as may be specified in or determined in pursuance of regulations.

(5) A licence under this paragraph may authorise mixing sperm with the egg of a hamster, or other animal specified in directions, for the purposes of developing more effective techniques for determining the fertility or normality of sperm, but only where anything which forms is destroyed when the research is completed, and in any event, not later than the two cell stage.

(6) No licence under this paragraph shall be granted unless the Authority is satisfied that any proposed use of embryos is necessary for the purposes of research.

(7) Subject to the provisions of this Act, a licence under this paragraph may be granted subject to such conditions as may be specified in the licence.

(8) A licence under this paragraph may authorise the performance of any of the activities referred to in sub paragraph (1) or (5) above in such a manner as may be so specified.

(9) A licence under this paragraph shall be granted for such period not exceeding three years as may be specified in the licence.

Human Fertilisation and Embryology Act 1990, s.15(1–4)

(1) The following shall be conditions of every licence under paragraph 3 of schedule 2 to this Act.

(2) The records maintained in pursuance of the licence shall include such information as the Authority may specify in directions about such matters as the Authority shall so specify.

(3) No information shall be removed from any records maintained in pursuance of the licence before the expiry of such period as may be specified in directions for records of the class in question.

(4) No embryo appropriated for the purposes of any project of research shall be kept or used otherwise than for the purposes of such a project.

NOTES:

1. During the debates upon the 1990 Act M.P.'s considered whether embryo research should be limited to spare embryos produced during infertility treatment and whether a ban should be placed upon specially created embryos. This proposal was however rejected.

2. The 1990 Act only authorises use of an embryo up until the appearance of the primitive streak (section 3(1)). Save where the embryo has been frozen, this period runs from when the gametes are mixed. At the appearence of the primitive streak it is possible to determine whether the embryo will develop into twins. However, some regard this limit as arbitrary. Other notable stages in the development of the foetus, which have been suggested as indicative of its development as a person do not occur until much later, for

example, it is not until at around 12 weeks that electrical activity can be detected in the brain of the foetus.

3. There is also a statutory ban on "cloning" — the replacement of the nucleus of one embryo with that of another person (section 3).

4. Human eggs can be mixed with hamster sperm but only up to the 2 cell stage. The value of this test is to assess male fertility levels. While there is a ban upon placing human embryos in an animal it appears to be possible to licence mixing human gametes inside an animal uterus. (See D. Morgan and R. Lee, *The Human Fertilisation and Embryology Act 1990*, London: Blackstones, 1991, at page 82.)

5. The Human Fertilisation and Embryology Authority regulates the conduct of research. Research proposals are submitted for approval to academic referees (paragraph 10.9, HEFA Code of Practice 1995). The Code of Practice provides that research projects will not be authorised if these involve embryo splitting (paragraph 10.5, HEFA Code of Practice 1995). In 1994 there were 34 licensed projects undertaken covering four broad areas — congenital disease, genetic abnormalities, general infertility problems and miscarriages. HEFA may also facilitate research through identification of patients who could be asked as to whether they would be prepared to take part in a follow up study.

6. Each IVF centre should have access to a research ethics committee. Some units have established their own committees. Such committees should not be comprised of more than one-third of the members who are employed by or have a financial interest in the Centre. The Code of Practice provides that research proposals should be referred to such a committee before a licence is obtained (paragraph 10.7, HEFA Code of Practice 1995).

7. As with abortion, embryo research is a subject on which certain persons hold strong ethical beliefs. The 1990 Act provides a right of conscientious objection in section 38 (see Chapter 11 at page 746.)

8. The 1990 Act also regulates experimental records (section 15).

QUESTIONS:

1. Is it justifiable to give statutory safeguards to embryos and animals while neglecting the human subject?

2. Does Schedule 2 paragraph 3 of the Human Fertilisation and Embryology Act 1990 give the Secretary of State unduly broad powers to make regulations.

The Human Fertilisation and Embryology Authority has issued a report explaining the use of ovarian tissue in treatment and embryo research. This debate is considered more fully in Chapter 11 below. Here we examine the recommendations in the context of research. There are three sources of such tissue: immature eggs from live donors or removed from cadavers, ovarian tissue grafting — a technique used on animals but which has not yet been used on human patients and ovarian tissue from aborted fetuses. Many of the ethical arguments which concern this area are considered in the Polkinghorne Report on use of fetal tissue (see pages 608–612 below).

Human Fertilisation and Embryology Authority, *Donated Ovarian Tissue in Embryo Research & Assisted Conception Report 1995*

14.   The Authority considers that the moral difficulties presented by using tissue from any of the proposed sources for embryo research permitted by licence under the HEF Act are not new. Donation of eggs and sperm for the purposes of embryo research are already permitted under the Act.

Live donors and cadavers

15.   The special status accorded to the embryo in the HFE Act requires informed specific written consent by the person providing eggs to their use to produce embryos. This can be obtained from live donors. Written decisions made before death or donor cards would be needed in the case of post mortem donation. There is no provision for proxy consent to the use of eggs and embryos in the HFE Act, and the Authority does not consider that next-of-kin should be able to give consent on behalf of a woman who has died or to override her consent. However, the Authority believes that it should be possible to develop a system for written informed consent by the woman before death which did not impinge on the existing donor card system for organ donation.

Minors

16.   The Authority is satisfied that at present, 18 is the age at which it can be confident that the full implications of donating ovarian tissue for the purposes of embryo research can be understood. This is the age limit set in the Code of Practice for live donors. However, the Authority recognises the concept of a child's maturity and understanding in relation to consent and intends to explore this further in relation to the use of ovarian tissue, including issues relating to post mortem donation.

Foetuses

17.   In the case of foetal tissue the woman undergoing an abortion is recognised in the Polkinghorne guidelines as having a special position with regard to the foetus so that her explicit consent should be obtained to the use of the foetus or foetal tissue for research. The use of eggs was not considered separately in the Polkinghorne report but consent to their use in embryo research could be obtained by an additional consent option.

NOTES:

1. Section 3A of the 1990 Act (inserted by the Criminal Justice and Public Order Act 1994, Commencement Order 1995, S.I. 1995 No. 721) which bans the use of foetal eggs in IVF treatment does not explicitly ban research using foetal eggs (see Chapter 11). Thus the practice may still be authorised by HEFA. Nonetheless this appears to

have restricted the likelihood that HEFA will authorise such research
as much of this research will be for the purposes of facilitating future
infertility treatment. (See A. Grubb, "Use of Foetal Eggs and Infertility Treatment" (1995) 3 *Medical Law Review* 203.)

2. HEFA recommends that a woman should be able to state her wishes
    as to the use of donated ovarian tissue. This is in accord with the
    general approach of the 1990 Act to control of gametes etc. This
    approach should be contrasted with the recommendations of the
    Polkinghorne Committee into the use of foetal tissue who recom-
    mended that a woman should only be able to give general consent to
    the use of such tissue rather than specifying how it should apply for
    particular purposes.

3. The use of ovarian tissue from cadavers is subject to the Human
    Tissue Act 1961. This Act does not impose an age limit upon
    donations. (See A. Plomer and N. Martin-Clement, "The limits of
    beneficience: egg donation under the Human Fertilisation and
    Embryology Act 1990" (1995) 15 *Legal Studies* 434.)

QUESTION:

1. Where a woman has not expressed her view prior to her death, is
    there anything inherently objectionable in use of ovarian tissue from a
    cadaver as long as enquiries are made of relatives? (Consider the
    operation of the Human Tissue Act 1961: see page 898 below and
    see A. Plomer and N. Martin Clement, *op. cit.*)

(b)   Research on foetal tissue

Foetal tissue may become available for use by researchers through spontaneous miscarriage or abortion. There are a number of potential advantages from the therapeutic use of foetal tissue. For example, foetal tissue
has been transplanted into brain cells of person's suffering from Parkin-
son's disease. As with embryo research, while scientists seeking to undertake such research emphasised the potential advantages, the use of foetal
tissue is controversial and has been the subject of much public debate.

The first major examination of foetal tissue research in this country was
undertaken by the Peel Committee in 1972. (*Report of the Advisory
Committee on the Uses of Foetuses and Foetal Tissue for Research*, London,
HMSO, 1972). The report was followed by the production of a Code of
Practice. The Peel Committee suggested that while there should be no
requirement to obtain the woman's consent to the use of foetal tissue for
research, parents should be given the opportunity to express their wishes as
to its use. The Warnock Report suggested that consideration should be
given to the introduction of legislation governing the use of foetal tissue
(Paragraph 11.18). Foetal tissue research was reconsidered by the Polkinghorne Committee in 1989. Polkinghorne noted that there had been no

breaches of the Peel Code and believed that it was best to proceed through informal guidance rather than statutory control. The Report did emphasise that the foetus was worthy of profound moral respect due to its potential to develop as a human being (para. 2.4). (For further discussion of the status of the foetus see Chapter 12 below.) The committee went on to consider the basis on which decisions concerning the use of foetal tissue should be made.

Review of The Guidance on Research Use of Fetuses and Fetal Material (Polkinghorne Committee Report) (Cmnd. 762, 1989)

Separation of the supply of foetal tissue from its use

4.1 We have taken the view that, whatever one's ethical opinion about abortion itself it does not follow that morally there is an absolute prohibition on the ethical use of foetuses or foetal material from lawful abortion. We have argued that the termination of pregnancy and the subsequent use of foetal tissue should be recognised as separate moral questions, and we regard it as of great importance that the separation of these moral issues should be reflected in the procedures employed. Accordingly we have recommended that great care should be taken to separate the decisions relating to abortion and to the subsequent use of foetal material. The prior decision to carry out an abortion should be reached without consideration of the benefits of subsequent use of foetal material. The generation or termination of pregnancy to produce material for research or therapy is unethical.

4.2 It has been argued that knowledge of the use of foetal tissue could influence mother's decisions to have their pregnancies terminated. It has been suggested that the use of foetal tissue could place women under pressure when reaching a decision or could result in more abortions taking place. It has even been put to us that someone could become pregnant in order to make a foetus available for medical use. In our view, pregnancy undertaken to such an end would be an ethically unacceptable use of the foetus as an instrument (treating it as a "thing"). It is not possible fully to discern people's motivations, but it is possible to limit the degree to which morally dubious wishes can be implemented. To this end we recommend, not only the separation of the decisions relating to abortion and the subsequent use of foetal tissue, but also procedures which will make it impossible for a mother to specify that foetal tissue which she makes available should be used in a particular way.

Method and timing of terminations and the use of fetal tissue

4.3 It has been put to us that knowledge of the potential use of fetal tissue could affect, not only the number of abortions taking place, but also their method and timing. For example, for transplantation purposes there might be a need for fetal tissue from second trimester fetuses, while it is normally in the mother's interest that termination be carried out as early as possible. It will often be the case that abortion by one method will be safer for the mother but abortion by a different method may be more suitable for certain research purposes. Such considerations have in our view no place in treatment or care. We recommend that the management of pregnancy of any mother should be dictated by her health care needs alone, and this will include the method and timing of an abortion. Similarly, we recommend that the clinical management of a mother whose fetus dies *in utero*, or who has a spontaneous abortion, should not be influenced by consideration of the use to which the fetus might be put.

Inducements

4.4 We consider that offering any kind of inducement to, or pressure on, a mother to let her fetal tissue be used is ethically unacceptable. The Peel Code prohibited "monetary exhange for fetuses or fetal material" but this is not quite enough. In the first place financial inducements can come in ways more subtle than simple monetary exchange (for example, by remission of fees.) Secondly, an inducement may be indirect, perhaps being offered to the institution where the abortion takes place rather than to the woman. For example, where extra facilities were offered to the clinic or staff at the same time as the fetal tissue being supplied, it would be equally difficult to resist the conclusion that an exchange was taking place. Equally there should be no pressure to supply associated items *e.g.* placentae . . .

We have taken the view that the effective way to prevent improper inducements is for potential recipients of fetal tissue to be unable to contact potential donors or exert influence in any way . . .

Women who wish to let the method and timing of termination be influenced by the use of foetal tissue

4.5 We concluded at 2.8 that a woman who has consented to an abortion should be consulted on whether her fetal tissue may be used. It has been suggested to us that the mother should similarly be able to control the manner of subsequent use, for the greatest public benefit. Separation, as described above, aims to put the mother beyond the influence of those, such as users of fetal tissue, whose interests may conflict with hers. However, it may be the mother herself who requests that the timing and method of her abortion should be dictated by factors other than her own health. It has been suggested that the distress of a woman undergoing an abortion might be alleviated by her knowledge that the fetal tissue was to be put to beneficial use.

4.6 We have given careful consideration to these points, but ultimately we are not persuaded by them. In our view our arguments for separation are of such ethical importance that they outweigh those for allowing the mother to make any direction concerning the use of her fetus or fetal tissue. Any system which made it possible for a mother to direct the specific use of fetal tissue could not be combined with the effective separation of the prior decision to terminate pregnancy and the process of abortion from the subsequent use of fetal tissue. Furthermore, a woman who has no actual knowledge of what will happen to the fetus or fetal tissue will be less likely to let the possibility of beneficial use of tissue influence her decision to have an abortion. In consequence, in addition to our recommendation that the mother should not be able to specify that fetal tissue which she makes available should be used in a particular way, we recommend that the mother should not know whether the fetus will be used at all and we incorporate a clause to that effect in our Code of Practice.

6.3 We recommend that positive explicit consent should be obtained from mothers to the use of the fetus or fetal tissue. We see the process of consent as requiring the mother to be counselled and given all the information, in a form that is comprehensible, to enable her to make a proper judgment of whether or not to allow the fetus to be used for research and therapy, including transplantation. This may take the form of an information sheet which might be supplemented with discussion. The information will have to be general because it must embrace all uses to which the fetus may be put.

The report goes on to consider the question of consent to use of foetal tissue.

6.5 In the case of therapeutic abortion, we recommend that consent to the use of fetal tissue should be distinct from, and subsequent to, consent to termination of pregnancy, although both consents could be obtained on the same occasion. It has been suggested that, for the two decisions to be separated in a genuine way, consent to the use of the fetus should take place after the termination. Otherwise, the very fact of asking the woman to consent to the use of the fetus or fetal material before she has actually undergone the abortion may override any final misgivings she may have and may persuade her to choose a method and timing of the abortion which maximises the potential for the use of the fetus or fetal material. We have given this careful consideration but we are not persuaded that this is desirable. It is impossible to prevent mothers giving thought to the possibility of research and transplantation before the abortion takes place, even if their consent is not sought until later. In many cases there would be no significant difference in separation by having consent after the operation. Furthermore, the validity of any consent the woman gave immediately following the termination of pregnancy would be seriously in doubt because of the effects of anaesthesia and other surrounding circumstances, such as the need for haste in making the material available. There would therefore be difficulty in obtaining consent which could be fairly be regarded as valid.

6.6 The subsequent use of the fetus must not be introduced by those responsible for counselling the mother until she has decided to have her pregnancy terminated and given her consent to that operation. It is, of course, impossible to prevent the mother introducing the subject and putting questions on the method and timing of abortion in relation to subsequent use. However, since it will not be permissible to give any indication of the use to which any particular fetus might be put, or even if it will be used at all, it will not be possible to give advice of this kind.

6.7 Having established the mother's position in this area, we considered whether the consent of anyone else was desirable or necessary. The father's case for being consulted would depend, as does the mother's, on respect rather than on the law. (It should be noted that his consent is not held necessary for the termination of pregnancy.) While the father's involvement may be desirable for a number of reasons-for example, he may know of some genetically transmitted disease or tests on fetal tissue may reveal a finding of potential significance to him — we believe that his relationship with the fetus is less intimate than the mother. We recommend that, although it may be desirable, the father's consent should not be a requirement for the use of fetal tissue and that he should not have the power to forbid research or therapy making use of fetal research.

Mothers who cannot give valid consent

6.8 In the case of mothers who are considered unable to give valid consent to the termination of pregnancy, consent to the use of the fetus or fetal material for research or transplantation should be sought from the person (usually a parent) who has authority to consent to termination. Again, this is out of respect for the feelings of the mother as represented by her proxy, rather than out of any requirement of law. The use of materials from such mothers should in general be avoided unless there are important and special reasons for doing so.

The use of the fetus or fetal tissue for specific purposes

6.10 Our attention has been drawn to the distress which may be caused by the use of the fetus or fetal tissue for teaching purposes without the mother having been consulted or having given her permission. We do not believe that this issue comes strictly within our terms of reference, but we think that it is a clear implication of the ethical attitude adopted in the Report that valid and appropriately informed consent should always be obtained.

6.11 We recognise that there may be patients who would be prepared to consent to the release of tissue either for research or transplantation, but not for both, or who would only object to the use of tissue for teaching purposes. We have concluded, however, that to allow for such preferences would be too great a breach of our principle that a mother should not be able to direct that the fetus should be used in a specific way. Explicit consent for all these purposes should, therefore, be obtained on all occasions.

Disposal of the fetus (mothers who do not wish to participate in research and transplantations)

6.12 Although this may be outside our terms of reference, we would like to put on record our belief that on general ethical grounds of respect, all mothers (whether participating in the provision of fetal tissue or not) should be given the opportunity clearly to express their wishes about the eventual disposal of the dead fetus, and that these wishes should, wherever possible, be respected.

NOTES:

1. The Polkinghorne Committee examined the question of research on both the living foetus and the cadavar. It stated that "The live foetus, whether *in utero* or *ex utero* . . . should be treated on principles broadly similar to those which apply to treatment and research conducted with children and adults" (para. 1.1). The question of the status of the foetus in law and ethics is discussed in Chapter 12 below at pages 704–707. It should be noted that the use of therapies are at a very early stage of development. Proposals to include a foetus in a clinical trial would involve difficult assessments of the risks and benefits of such procedures.
2. Use of tissue from the cadaver of a foetus must comply with the Human Tissue Act 1961. This Act requires that before organs are removed, death must be certified (section 1(6)) (see Chapter 15 below at pages 898–899.) It is not possible to use the brain stem death test, which would usually be employed to ascertain the point of death, in the case of foetal cadavers. The Polkinghorne Committee recommend that:

   ". . . death should be determined by reference to the absence of vital functions, *viz.* absence of spontaneous respiration and heartbeat after consideration of possible reversible factors such as the effects of hypothermia in the fetus, and of drugs or metabolic disorders in the mother. We derive further support for our conclusion from the fact that the presence or absence of heartbeat is already used as a test for determining death in the fetus *in utero* (paragraph 3.7)."

3. Polkinghorne did not treat placental tissue in the same manner as it dealt with other tissue. The committee stated that:

   "The special status which we attach to the fetus stems from its potential for development into a fully-formed human being. No such potential is present in material such as the placenta, and we consider that attempts to invest it with any notion of respect, which very properly attaches to the fetus itself." (paragraph 3.12).

It has been suggested that the placenta can be used for the purposes of research because it is *res nullis,* and becomes the property of the first person into whose hands it falls. (The question of ownership of body products is considered in Chapter 15 below at pages 928–934.) (See J. K. Mason and R. A. McCall Smith, *Law and Medical Ethics* (4th edn.), London: Butterworths, 1994, at page 378.) While the Polkinghorne Committee Report raised the issue of property in foetal tissue it considered fetal tissue largely in terms of consent to its use.

4. The Committee recognised that research on foetal tissue should be subject to research ethics committee approval (paragraph 2.3). A Code of Practice was issued following the Polkinghorne recommendations which is incorporated in the Department of Health guidelines to local research ethics committees.

5. The Polkinghorne Committee accepted that medical and nursing staff should be able to conscientiously object to participation in procedures involving foetal tissue/foetuses (paragraphs 2.10–2.11). This however, only applies to transplantation of such tissue and not to prior or subsequent care of the patient.

6. Polkinghorne recommended that there should be a strict separation between the role of the clinicians who were authorising the abortion and the clinicians using the foetal tissue, and that an intermediatory body should be established to facilitate this (Chapter 5 of the report).

QUESTIONS:

1. The Polkinghorne Committee talks in terms of the woman giving general rather than specific consent to use of foetal tissue. Should a woman be able to express her views as to the use of fetal material from her aborted foetus? (See generally J. Robertson, "Rights, Symbolism and Public Policy in Foetal Tissue Transplants" (1988) *Hastings Centre Report* 51).

2. Can foetal tissue from a mentally incompetent woman be used for the purposes of foetal research and transplantation? The Polkinghorne report was published before the decision of the House of Lords in *F v. West Berkshire Health Authority* [1989] 3 All E.R. 545. Contrast the Law Commission recommendations on *Mental Incapacity* (Law Commission No. 231, 1995). (See Chapter 15 below.)

3. Do you agree with the Committee's recommendation that a woman should not be able to determine the timing of her abortion to facilitate the subsequent proposed use of the foetal tissue?

4. Polkinghorne stated that the father should not be able to dictate the use of foetal tissue. Do you agree? (Compare the position as regards abortion — see Chapter 12. See J. Keown, "The Polkinghorne Report: Nice Recommendations: Shame About the Reasoning" (1993) 19 *Journal of Medical Ethics* 114.)

5. Should a woman be permitted to receive inducements for the use of her foetal tissue? (See paragraph 4.4.) Contrast the Human Fertilisation and Embryology Act 1990 which allows payment to be made to

donors of gametes at a fixed sum of £15 plus expenses (HEFA Third Annual Report 1994).

11. GENE THERAPY

The human genome project presently being undertaken has been established with the ultimate aim of mapping our genetic heritage (see S. McLean, "Science's 'Holy Grail' — Some Legal and Ethical Implications of the Human Genome Project" (1995) C.L.P. 23). In the future it is likely that it will be possible to identify each individual's propensity to develop a whole range of illnesses. Genetic diseases can be divided into three broad categories. The first is chromosonal. An example of such a disorder is Downs Syndrome. The second is unifactoral. Such conditions arise when there is a specific abnormal gene on a chromosome. Examples of such diseases are Huntingdon's Chorea and Cystic Fibrosis. There are also multi-factoral or "polygenic" conditions. These are the result of a combination of both environmental factors and a genetic defect. An example is coronary heart disease which is genetically determined up to a certain point but also may be influenced by other factors. Developments in the area of genetics have been regarded by many as a mixed blessing. While, for instance, genetic testing may facilitate diagnosis and ultimately possibly treatment, at the same time it throws up dilemmas pertaining to disclosure of genetic information (see Chapter 8 at pages 469–470).

One challenge for medical researchers is to determine whether it is possible to eradicate genetic illness through the use of what is known as "gene therapy". There are two types of gene therapy. First, somatic gene therapy. This involves gene therapy being undertaken on one particular patient. Secondly, germ-line gene therapy which would involve changing the gene line. Such therapy has implications for future generations. The ethics of research into gene therapy were considered by a government committee, the Clothier Committee, which reported in 1992.

The Clothier Committee, *Report of the Committee on the Ethics of Gene Therapy* (Cmnd. 1788) 1992

Somatic gene cell therapy research

4.6 A decision whether gene therapy research should proceed must depend on the careful prior assessment of the balance of potential benefits and risks for the individual patient. This assessment must draw upon knowledge of the genetic basis of the disorder, its pathological effects and clinical course. It will call for evidence of adequate experience of gene modification in experimental systems using isolated cells and laboratory animals, and must incorporate a judgment on the possible consequences of the proposed treatment. The risks to the patient will largely depend upon the safety of procedures for introducing genes into cells therapeutically, and the effects, both immediately and in the long term. Safety must be a foremost consideration when proposals to conduct gene therapy are made. Intrusions on privacy, too are an inevitable accompaniment of such pioneering procedures and the long term follow-up that is necessary.

4.7   In their joint statements the European Medical Councils brought out clearly the technical complexity of the procedures used in gene modification. Undesirable consequences . . . might include genetic modification of the germ line and its effects in progeny: modification of somatic cells other than those which have been targetted: interference with the normal workings of modified cells: cancerous changes in cells of the population modified; and changes induced by the insertion process.

4.8   The first crucial step in ethical review is a careful assessment of the scientific merits of the proposal, the competence of those wishing to carry out gene therapy and the potential benefits and risks in each particular instance for which a proposal is made. This assessment should include a critical examination of the arrangements to be made for the conduct of therapy and subsequent monitoring. It will necessarily call upon an uncommon degree and range of scientific and medical expertise, encompassing a deep knowledge of molecular biology, of experimental work in gene manipulation, and close familiarity with the molecular basis and clinical features of the disorder under consideration. No existing body is constituted for this task. Accordingly we *recommend* that a supervisory body with the necessary collective expertise, experience and authority be set up, having the responsibility for making such assessments in conjunction with ethical review. We also *recommend* that any proposal for gene therapy must be approved by this body as well as by a properly constituted local research ethics committee.

4.9   There is a duty to identify and assess promptly any adverse consequences of gene therapy for the patient, both in the aftermath of treatment and in the long term. This duty does not end with the death of the patient. To verify that therapy has not inadvertantly affected offspring and successive generations monitoring should continue over several generations. Therefore those conducting such research have a duty not only to maintain adequate records but also to ensure that an effective monitoring system is in place. It will require that a register be set up and carefully maintained with safeguards to protect confidentiality. We *recommend* that the necessary arrangements are made before the therapy begins. A complementary duty is to obtain a reliable commitment of patients, and their families, to participate in extended follow-up. During the process of informing and counselling and obtaining consent, the patient should also be made aware that although follow-up may be intrusive and burdensome the doctors accept a duty to minimise their effects.

4.10   Accordingly the conditions which must be satisfied when gene therapy research is proposed are that:

(a)   There must be sufficient scientific and medical knowledge together with knowledge of those proposing to undertake the research, to make sound judgments on:
   (i)   the scientific merit of the research
   (ii)   its probable efficacy and safety
   (iii)   the competence of those who wish to undertake the research, and
   (iv)   the requirements for effective monitoring.
(b)   The clinical course of the disorder must be known sufficiently well for the investigators and those entrusted with counselling to:
   (i)   give accurate information and advice: and
   (ii)   assess the outcomes of therapy.

Consent to research

4.11   A prior ethical requirement of research involving patients is the consent of the individual subject. Consent implies that sufficient information has been given, in a form that is understood, to enable that individual to make a voluntary decision to participate or not. Because gene therapy has novel, complex and possibly far reaching aspects, we are concerned to ensure that the patient is enabled to take these fully into account when giving consent. It is important that serious attention be given not only to the content of the information given to the patient but also to the way in which it is conveyed. Above all, care must be taken to ensure that the patient has understood the risks, benefits and obligations and has the fullest possible information. Independant advice, not aimed at obtaining consent, should ideally be provided by someone unconnected with the research or therapeutic team and well versed in the implications of gene therapy.

4.12   We foresee the possibility that a competent adult, in whom the disorder had progressed to a stage at which there was little prospect of direct benefit from therapy, might nevertheless consent to participate in non-therapeutic research — for the collective human benefits that the research should be designed to yield. For such research to be ethical it must be to assess the consequences of the procedure, by measurement or detection of changes within the body, or their absence, even if there were to no discernible clinical benefit. We conclude that participation by a competent adult in such research is acceptable.

4.13   Children with genetic diseases are likely to be among the first candidates for gene therapy. The special problems to be faced where children are the subjects of research have been examined in existing guidelines. The foremost consideration must be the best interests of the child and in this respect somatic gene therapy raises no new ethical issue.

Germ line gene therapy

5.1   The purpose of gene modification of sperm or ova or cells which produce them would be to prevent the transmission of defective genes to subsequent generations. Gene modification at an early stage of development, before differentiation of the germ line, might be a way of correcting gene defects in both germ line or somatic cells. However, we share the view of others that there is at present insufficient knowledge to evaluate the risks to future generations, to which we have already pointed.

5.2   We *recommend* therefore, that gene modification of the germ line should not yet be attempted. For couples identified as being at risk of bearing a child with a serious genetic disorder, embryonic diagnosis and selective implantation of an unaffected embryo would provide another way of achieving the same end without incurring the known risks of germ line modification. Moreover this approach offers the prospect of avoiding genetic disorders which result in structural fetal abnormalities.

The concept of germ line gene therapy was considered further by the House of Common Select Committee on Science and Technology:

House of Commons Select Committee on Science and Technology Third Report: *Human Genetics the Science and its Consequences* (HC 41–1)

113. The Clothier Committee recommended that 'gene modification of the germ-line should not yet be attempted.' In fact, the Human Fertilisation and Embryology Act 1990 forbids manipulation of the nucleus of an embryonic cell; since the chromosomes are contained in the nucleus, this would rule out germ-line manipulation on embryos, although it would, in theory be possible to change the gametes of an adult.

114. Even before the Human Fertilisation and Embryology Act there was a voluntary moratorium on research into human germ-line manipulation. However germ-line manipulation of animals is routine and, earlier this year, a researcher filed

for a patent in a method of maipulating the sperm of mice which extended to the use of the technique in other animals, including humans.

115. The practical difficulties which would have to be overcome before such germ-line manipulation became routine are manifold. The control mechanisms of the genome would have to be far better understood than they are now, and researchers would need the ability to insert material at precise points in the genome rather than almost randomly as is now done with animals. Moreover, we would need to know enough about the genes to be altered or replaced to be sure they were unequivocally harmful; as we have seen, many genetic disorders come from combinations of genes which could be beneficial if only a single copy of a particular variation were present. Nonetheless, there was suprising confidence that such manipulation would, in time, become possible- Professor Modell guessed that this would be within three generations.

117. Germ line manipulation rouses great controversy. The Council of Europe draft Bioethics Convention would prohibit it completely, and some of our witnesses agreed. However most were less certain; a sizeable group felt the question should be postponed until more was known about the long term effects of somatic gene therapy and about germ-line manipulation in animals. Others, like the Biochemical Society, found it 'hard to think of something as "wrong" if it could stop future generations suffering the misery of a genetic disease'. The Genetic Interest Group (GIG) said "GIG does not see any objections in principle to making decisions for future generations through germ-line intervention." Our witnesses from the Church of England agreed that if germ-line intervention were shown to be safe then it would be right to use it.

119. One benefit advanced for germ-line manipulation was that it would remove deleterious genes from the gene pool. Dr Sydney Brenner considered this " an unreasonable, fantastic way of doing something which we could already do by non-technical means", but had chosen not to.

120. Another advantage was that it would enable couples at risk of producing a child with a genetic disease to have normal children. Dr King, the Editor of *GenEthics News*, did not consider this a sufficient justification;

"Although there is a strong moral imperative to medically intervene to reduce individual physical, and in some cases mental, suffering, I do not believe the suffering of a couple who may not be able to have children without producing a disabled child, in any way justifies the crossing the barrier into a new era of human histroy, with its incalculable consequences"

Other opponents of germ-line therapy felt that selective termination or diagnosis of embryos could be used to help those at risk of producing a disabled child. Professor Modell pointed out the drawbacks of selective termination: "statistics can be very unkind, because you may terminate the pregnancy . . . but then you may be unlucky the next time . . . we have . . . several ladies who have been unlucky five times in a row"; she identified carriers of fragile X mental handicap, who had a 50 per cent chance of carrying an affected foetus or a female carrier of the condition as having a "major problem". While she thought that both pre-implantation diagnosis and germ line therapy would offer hope for those in such situations, some religious groups oppose the destruction of embryos implicit in pre-implantation diagnosis. The Linacre Centre, a Roman Catholic research centre, suggested that manipulation of a gamete before it was fertilised would, in principle, avoid such destruction.

121. There were objections to germ-line intervention on the ground that it would be impossible to test it before it was used: this would involve extensive research on embryos (which those opposed to pre-implantation diagnosis are also likely to oppose) and could create a class of "experimental human beings". The Linacre Centre considered that this was likely to prove an insurmountable hurdle to such intervention.

122. Another objection was that such intervention was taking decisions for future generations. This premise was attacked by those who suggested selective termina-tion was, in essence an extreme case of germ- line manipulation, and GIG which

claimed "if we have the scientific capacity to alter the germ-line and do not do so, we are also making a decision about the health of future generations".

123. A further fear was that germ-line manipulation would not be confined to the avoidance of serious disease but would be used to give embryos desirable characteristics. As GIG says "much of the discussion bears no relationship to what is ever likely to be possible" but there were suggestions that it could be difficult to draw a distinction between "enhancement" and "cure". This should not necessarily preclude research; Professor Ruth Chadwick suggested that the "slippery slope" arguments themselves are rather suspect" and each case should be considered on its own merits.

124. Germ-line intervention would arouse such great controversy if it were proposed as a practical development that other, currently uncontroversial uses of genetic science might become unacceptable. Geneticists have acted responsibly in imposing a moratorium on such manipulation. Nonetheless, matters of such importance ought not be left to the conscience of individual geneticists. The United Nations Educational, Scientific and Cultural Organisation Bioethics Committee set up a sub committee to consider Human Gene Therapy. It concluded:

"those who suggest the desirability of germ-line therapy have not . . . made a plausible case for any near term substantial use for it, and certainly no case that the gains would be worth the extraordinary efforts required."

We agree. However, the Sub-Committee considered that although "Germline gene therapy is indefensible at present . . . it should not be categorically disallowed." There was debate amongst our witnesses about the extent to which research should be curtailed; however, there was agreement that "publicly funded scientists may properly be required to uphold the values and limitations set by society." We accept that as the science moves on perceptions may change, but there are many urgent research projects which do not present the moral dilemmas involved in germ-line manipulation. In spite of our profound sympathy for those whose reproductive choices are curtailed by genetic diseases we consider the advantages of germ-line intervention are outweighed by its potential risks and we see no use for it at present.

The current prohibition on manipulating the genetic structure of a human embryo should remain, and there should be no manipulation of a human germ-line at any stage (including manipulation of gametes) without the approval of GTAC.

NOTES:

1. The Clothier Committee recommended the establishment of an expert advisory body to oversee the operation of gene therapy. The proposed body would advise on the conduct of gene therapy, recommend whether proposals should be approved and act in accordance with local research ethics committees (paragraph 6.2). The Government accepted the Committee's recommendations and in 1993 established a new non-statutory body — the Gene Therapy Advisory Committee. Certain elements of the Committee's operation have been criticised. The Committee meets in private and does not publish its recommendations. It has been argued that this level of secrecy is necessary to enable full consultation to go ahead. However the House of Commons Select Committee in its report *Human Genetics, Science and Its Consequences* (1995) HC 41–1 were of the view that the Committee should at the very least make public the proposals approved, in so far as this was consistent with protection of

patient confidentiality (para. 110). Guidelines were subsequently issued for the conduct of such research. These Guidelines state that the Committee is required to "consider and advise on the acceptability of proposals for gene therapy research on human subjects on ethical grounds taking account of the scientific merits of proposals and the potential benefits and risks."

2. One element of the Guidelines is that researchers should ensure that patients receive independent counselling. This can be contrasted with the appraisal of research protocols by LREC's. These Guidelines stipulate more rigid follow up requirements than those required by the Department of Health Guidelines to Local Research Ethics Committees.

> "7.5 Follow up arrangements.
> A detailed description of the monitoring programme should be provided and should include the duration of follow-up. How will subjects be monitored to assess specific effects of treatment, how frequently and for how long?
>
> It is the opinion of GTAC that monitoring should continue for the lifetime of the subject and, in certain cases where the subjects of the research subsequently have children, should extend to the next generation. It is essential that the reasons are a firm commitment to such monitoring and that the reasons are sufficiently explained to subjects. Consent should be obtained to their names being entered into a register and to any future approaches which might be made to them in connection with monitoring.
>
> 7.6 Reporting requirements
> (a) Any adverse effects should be reported promptly to the GTAC, the LREC and to the MCA. It is not envisaged that such reports to the GTAC will need to identify patients other than by reference to a GTAC number.
> (b) Progress reports should be filed with the GTAC within six months of the commencement of the study and at six month intervals thereafter. In the event of a subject's death, GTAC and MCA should be notified promptly. The findings at post mortem including those of special studies, together with a statement of the cause of death should be submitted as soon as possible."

3. Early research has not involved children, as was first envisaged but has concerned the use of genes to enhance the response of the immune system to cancer (see Gene Therapy Advisory Committee 1st Annual Report November 1993–December 1994).

4. The Clothier Committees rejection of germ line therapy is reflective of much concern expressed as to the implications of such a technique (See J. K. Mason and R. A. McCall Smith, *Law and Medical Ethics* (4th edn.), Butterworths: 1994, at page 145 and W. French Anderson, "Human Gene Therapy, Scientific and Ethical Considerations" in R. Chadwick (ed.) *Ethic Reproductionism and Genetic Control*, London: Routledge, 1987.

SELECT BIBLIOGRAPHY

M. Baum, "The Ethics of Clinical Research" and S. Bottros, "Equipoise, consent and the ethics of randomised clinical trials" in P. Byrne (ed.), *Ethics and Law in Health Care and Research*, Chichester: Wiley, 1990.

S. Bottros, "Abortion, embryo research and foetal transplantation; their moral interrelationship" in P. Byrne (ed.) *Medicine, Medical Ethics and the Value of Life*, Chichester: Wiley, 1989.

M. Brazier, "Embryos 'Rights': Abortion and Research" in M. Freeman, *Medicine, Medical Ethics and Law*, London: Sweet & Maxwell, 1990.

I. Dodds-Smith, "Clinical Research" in C. Dyer (ed.), *Doctors, Patients and the Law*, Blackwells: Oxford, 1992.

C. Gilbert Foster, "The development and future of research ethics committees in Britain", in A. Grubb (ed.), *Choices and Decisions in Health Care*, Chichester: Wiley, 1993.

D. Giesen, "Civil Liability of Physicians for New Methods of Treatment and Experimentation Comparative Examination" (1995) 3 *Medical Law Review* 22.

J. M. Goldenring, "The Brain Life Theory" (1985) *J. of Medical Ethics* 198.

J. Harris and A. Dyson (eds.), *Experiments on Embryos*, London: Routledge, 1990.

J. Harris, *Wonderwoman and Superman*, Oxford: OUP, 1992.

C. Hodge, "Harmonisation of European Controls Over Research Ethics Committees: Consent, Compensation and Indemnity" in A. Goldberg and I. Dodds-Smith (eds.), *Pharmaceutical Medicine and the Law*, London: Royal College of Physicians, 1991.

I. Kennedy, "The Law and Ethics Informed Consent and Randomised Controlled Trials" in I. Kennedy, *Treat Me Right*, Oxford: OUP, 1988.

J. V. McHale, "Guidelines for Medical Research, Some Ethical and Legal Problems" (1993) 1 *Medical Law Review* 160.

J. K. Mason, *Medico-Legal Aspects of Reproduction and Parenthood*, Aldershot: Dartmouth, 1993.

D. Morgan and R. Lee, *Human Fertilisation and Embryology Act 1990*, London: Blackstones, 1991.

P. Muccullagh, *The Foetus as Transplant Donor*, Chichester: Wiley, 1987.

M. Shea, "Embryonic Life and Human Life" (1985) *Journal of Medical Ethics* 205.

P. Singer, *et al.*, *Embryo Experimentation: Ethical, Legal and Social Issues*, Cambridge: CUP, 1990.

PART IV

INTRODUCTION

This section of the book is concerned with reproductive choices, and the constraints, legal and otherwise, which limit those choices. Chapter 11 explores the rights of those who are infertile or single or in gay relationships to assisted conception. By contrast, Chapter 12 focuses on the rights of the fertile woman to control her fertility through access to contraception and legal abortion. Whilst contraception and abortion may be viewed as private choices, requiring only that others (for instance, the state or the health care and legal professions) should not interfere with the right in question; many commentators have argued that there is also a positive obligation on the state to provide abortion and contraceptive services. Increasingly similar claims are being made by and on behalf of the infertile, asserting rights to avail of assisted conception techniques financed by the NHS. In Chapter 13 we focus on issues which arise once a prenancy has been established and the woman has chosen to carry her child to term. We examine the right of the pregnant woman to manage her pregnancy and birthing process without state or medical interference. In this context we explore the impact of medical developments such as ultrasound, amniocentesis and fetal surgery. On one level such innovations increase the choices open to the pregnant woman, but they may also impose obligations upon her to undergo screening, tests or medical procedures for the benefit of the foetus, and possibly even lead to pressure to abort if it emerges that the foetus is handicapped. We go on to examine whether the foetus has a right of action if it is injured during pregnancy, either as a result of the actions of the pregnant woman or of a third party.

Taken as a whole, these three chapters focus on the extent to which English law promotes reproductive choices in practice. In British law there would appear to be no clearly established right to reproduce. The only statement to the effect that there is such a right dates from the High Court judgment of Heilbron J. in *Re D (a minor) (wardship: surrogacy)* [1976] 1 All E.R. 326 (see Chapter 13 at page 755) in which she stated that a woman's right to reproduce was a basic human right. Significantly, Heilbron J.'s statement was confined to the right of the *woman* to reproduce, and presumably she envisaged any such right as a negative one prohibiting interference by the state with the rights of those who are naturally fertile. Subsequent sterilisation cases, however, would appear to have undermined even this limited recognition of reproductive rights (see Chapter 13). Indeed, reproductive issues offer a good illustration of the limitations of rights discourse, and the difficulties which law faces in trying to resolve competing rights. Whilst no law may ever satisfactorily resolve the competing moral claims of the pregnant woman and the foetus, it is becoming apparent that soon law will have to grapple with even more vexed issues. For instance, the reproductive rights of men are now being asserted in the context of surrogacy (see Chapter 11), abortion (see Chapter 12) and sterilisation (see Chapter 13). Moreover, against a backdrop of increased pressure on scarce resources, in the future it is likely that lawyers will have to squarely confront the issue of whether the state has positive obligations to promote reproductive health.

As yet, no British cases have considered the potential implications of international human rights law in relation to reproductive choice, despite the view expressed by some commentators in Chapters 1 and 2 that medical law is best viewed as a branch of human rights law. In a reproductive context the general problems of vagueness and enforceability which plague human rights law are compounded by the way in which women's concerns have been systematically marginalised by human rights law. (See R. Cook, *Human Rights of Women: National and International Perspectives*, Philadelphia: University of Pennsylvania Press, 1994; F. Beveridge and S. Mullally, "International Human Rights and Body Politics" in J. Bridgeman and S. Millns, *Law and Body Politics: Regulating the Female Body*, Aldershot: Dartmouth, 1995.) Nevertheless, human rights law has considerable potential to protect and enhance reproductive choices. This renders it particularly disappointing that our judges have failed to address the issue of the United Kingdom's obligations under international law. The most significant international provisions from a British perspective are those contained in the European Convention on Human Rights (ECHR). Although the Convention has not been incorporated into British law, the United Kingdom is a signatory to the ECHR. Thus, whilst it does not directly provide a remedy in British courts, a United Kingdom citizen who believes her rights under the Convention have been violated may petition the European Commission of Human Rights in Strasbourg. It will decide whether her case should be heard by the European Court of Human Rights. If it holds that United Kingdom has infringed the ECHR, the United Kingdom is obliged by the ECHR to secure to its citizens an adequate remedy. Article 8 of the ECHR provides that "Everyone has the right to respect for his private and family life", while Article 12 states that "Men and women of marriageable age have the right to marry and found a family, according to the national laws governing the exercise of this right". Similar commitments are found in Article 16 of the Universal Declaration of Human Rights, and Article 23 of the International Covenant on Civil and Political Rights. It is significant that these all link the right to found a family with the right to marry — women in international documents tend to be constructed as married mothers. More progressively, article 12 of the Convention on the Elimination of All Forms of Discrimination Against Women obliges states to take:

> "all appropriate measures to eliminate discrimination against women in the field of health care in order to ensure, on a basis of equality of men and women, access to health care services, including those related to family planning."

Some substance was given to this provision following the adoption of a Programme of Action at the 1994 International Conference on Population and Development in Cairo, under which approximately 180 countries have committed themselves to realising the concept of "reproductive health":

> 7.2 Reproductive health is a state of complete physical, mental and social well-being and not merely the absence of disease or infirmity, in all matters relating to

the reproductive system and to its functions and processes. Reproductive health therefore implies that people are able to have a satisfying and safe sex life and that they have the capability to reproduce and the freedom to decide if, when and how often to do so. Implicit in this last condition is the right of men and women to be informed and to have access to safe, effective, affordable and acceptable methods of family planning of their choice.

The adoption of this provision is indicative of an emerging trend which suggests that reproductive rights are best conceptualised as a health care issue, combining the discourses of public health and human rights. (See N. Whitty, "The Mind, The Body, and Reproductive Health Information" (1996) 18 *Human Rights Quarterly* 224.) Such a conceptualisation makes it easier to argue that the state has positive obligations to promote reproductive health and choice. It also links in to feminist arguments that reproductive rights must be grounded in equality. (See C. MacKinnon, "Reflections on Sex Equality under Law" (1991) 100 *Yale Law Journal* 1309.) However, it remains to be seen whether such arguments will prove productive in enhancing real reproductive choice than arguments based on rights to privacy (see C. MacKinnon, "Abortion: On Public and Private" in *Towards a Feminist Theory of the State*, Cambridge, Masachusetts: Harvard University Press, 1989) or rights to self-determination (see J. Stone, "Infertility Treatment: A Selective Right to Reproduce" in P. Byrne (ed.), *Ethics and Law in Health Care and Research*, Chichester: John Wiley, 1990).

Overall, it is apparent that English law currently lacks a clear commitment to reproductive rights, and that existing legislation is piecemeal and complex. Despite the fact that much of the current legislation relating to reproductive issues resulted from the deliberations by the Warnock Committee, commentators have contended that it is not based on a set of coherent ethical principles. This is reflected in the way in which English law has effectively ducked fundamental questions about the status of the embryo/foetus (see Chapter 12), and avoided the issue of how reproductive rights should be conceptualised. Yet, notwithstanding the lack of consideration of these issues, it has sought to define parental roles within the family (see pages 675–682 below).

Furthermore, although English legislators and judges have never squarely addressed the fundamental issues at stake in formulating a right to reproduce, the expectations of patients (fuelled by developments in medical technology and the role of the media in publicising them) are becoming ever greater. Increasingly, what is being asserted is not simply a right to reproduce, but a right to produce a perfect baby. The reproductive technologies discussed in Chapter 11, which permit more control over the reproductive process than was ever previously possible, have paved the way for potential parents to select the characteristics they believe it is desirable for their child to possess. Once such techniques are available it is inevitable that persons seek to avail themselves of them. In turn this raises the issue of whether a woman should be able to terminate a pregnancy if tests reveal some characteristic which is not regarded as desirable. Demand for "designer babies" has further consequences. The premium placed on perfect children raises the issue of whether it is justifiable to prevent people conceiving (for example, for eugenic reasons), if it is thought that their offspring will be less then perfect. It also poses the question of whether the parents of a child who is born handicapped, or the child herself, posses a right to sue anyone for their misfortune. These issues are addressed in Chapter 13.

11

REPRODUCTIVE CHOICE I: ASSISTED CONCEPTION

---

1. Introduction

This Chapter focuses upon the reproductive choices available to those who are infertile, or who decide not to have children via heterosexual intercourse. Infertility may leave persons feeling defective in an area central to personal identity and fulfilment and has caused debate about whether it may properly be regarded as an illness. The alternative methods of reproduction discussed in this Chapter have flourished in a social context where it is alleged that levels of infertility have risen to the point where approximately one in six couples in the United Kingdom are infertile. Whilst there is much debate about whether total levels of infertility have increased, it is clear that whereas the problem used to be concentrated amongst older, poorer people it is now becoming highly visible amongst educated middle-class couples in their 20s and 30s. (It should be noted that recently more attention has been devoted to post-menopausal women asserting rights to reproduce in their 40s and 50s.) The causes of such decreased fertility have been variously located. One factor is changing patterns of sexual behaviour, which carry an increased incidence of sexually-transmitted diseases, especially pelvic inflammatory disease. Decreasing fertility levels are also linked to contraceptive methods. The oral contraceptive pill, IUD and injectable and implantable forms of contraception like Depo Provera and Norplant — which along with abortion, carry some risk of infertility (see Chapter 12 at pages 698–703). Changes in the roles of women which have entailed postponement of child-bearing have also played a role. More generally, fertility problems may be connected with a range of workplace hazards and environmental oestrogens. Allied with a decrease in the number of healthy babies available for adoption all these factors have contributed to the high visibility of infertility. Simultaneously, medical technology has developed new methods of alleviating infertility over the last couple of decades. There is, however, much debate as to whether these methods offer a real solution to the problem. Critics argue that they are a technological fix which mask the real causes of infertility. Moreover they suggest that conceptive technologies are a product of the same ideology which is blamed for exacerbating infertility problems. Their criticisms are compounded by the fact that this new menu of options is frequently only available to those with the resources to pay for them privately. Thus, like all the reproductive choices discussed in this part of the book, such choices operate under certain constraints. Furthermore, as individuals and couples other than those who are infertile have increasingly sought to use reproductive technologies, limits have been imposed on who may have access to them. This has served to make the issue of access politically controversial. Another reason why assisted conception has been so contentious is that resort to the methods discussed in this Chapter — artificial insemination, surrogacy and *in vitro* fertilisation — renders the whole process of reproduction more visible and hence more open to medical control. Furthermore, in frequently separating out the processes of sex and reproduction, these conceptive techniques have called into question the extent to which traditional family structures can be regarded as natural, and fundamentally questioned our notions of maternity and paternity. For the first time a number of new variables have to be considered by law. These include such issues as who can donate gametes and under what conditions; how and where fertilisation and gestation will take place; who will assume parental responsibility for the products of the new reproduction and what is meant by the "family". We begin in section 2 by exploring the nature and causes of infertility. In section 3 we consider techniques for alleviating infertility and the extent to which they are regulated by law. Section 4 addresses the impact of assisted conception on the family and how it has necessitated a redefinition of the legal status of mother, father and child. In section 5 we examine issues arising out of the donation and storage of gametes and embryos.

2. INFERTILITY

(a) Defining Infertility

The definition of infertility is contested. Some commentators suggest that it is not properly regarded as a health care issue at all. Such definitional problems can have legal consequences. For example, as we saw in Chapter 1, section 128 of the National Health Service Act 1977 states that "'illness' includes . . . any injury or disability requiring medical or dental treatment or nursing". Under section 3 of that Act a duty is imposed upon the Secretary of State for Health to provide services for the diagnosis and treatment of illness. Whether someone will have a right to treatment for infertility under the Act will therefore depend upon whether fertility constitutes an "illness" for the purpose of the section (see further Chapter 1; S. Elliston and A. Britton, "Is infertility an illness?" (1994) 145 *New Law Journal Practitioner* 1552; J. Montgomery, "Rights, Restraints and Pragmatism: The Human Fertilisation and Embryology Act 1990" (1991) 54 *M.L.R.* 524.) Certain commentators have argued that the problem of infertility is really concerned with socially constructed desires and choices, which medical science should not necessarily meet. It is unclear, however, whether needs and desires can be clearly distinguished in this way, since it could be argued that (apart from life-threatening diseases), all calls for medical treatment are desires rather than needs. However, some (mainly feminist) commentators have argued that for those advocating assisted conception it was necessary to define infertility as a disease in order to promote conceptive technologies like *in vitro* fertilisation as the cure (see P. Spallone, *Beyond Conception: The New Politics of Reproduction*, London: Macmillan, 1989). It has been suggested that if the real problem is cultural conditioning with regard to infertility, then the solution lies in social responses (like shared parenting), rather than the application of medical technology. (See N. Pfeffer, "Artificial Insemination, In-vitro Fertilization and the Stigma of Infertility" in M. Stanworth (ed.) *Reproductive Technologies: Gender, Motherhood and Medicine,* Cambridge: Polity Press, 1987.) Moreover, the medicalisation of infertility has encouraged a focus on the interests of "sick" parents, arguably at the expense of the interests of resulting children (see page 689 below).

G. Douglas, *Law, Fertility and Reproduction*, London: Sweet & Maxwell, 1991, pages 104–5 (footnotes omitted)

"There are different definitions of infertility. Dickens summarises some of the alternatives.
'Infertility includes infecundity, meaning inability to conceive or impregnate, and pregnancy wastage, meaning failure to carry a pregnancy to term through spontaneous abortion and stillbirth. Infertility includes primary infertility, where a couple has never achieved conception, and secondary infertility, where at least one conception has occurred but the couple is currently unable to achieve pregnancy.'
To constitute a problem, such inability to produce a child must have continued for a certain length of time. It has been estimated that 63 per cent. of normally fertile women having unprotected sexual intercourse with a fertile partner will conceive within six months, and 80 per cent. will conceive by the end of one year. A failure to conceive within a year may therefore indicate a potential problem, and here we shall take infertility to mean this. But the World Health Organisation takes two years as the cut-off point, and demographers may take five years as significant. This variety of definitions shows that infertility is not an absolute, objectively determined state, but has a flexible content."

NOTES:

1. As Douglas notes, commentators have disagreed over the period which must elapse before a couple may properly be regarded as infertile. However, the trend in clinics which treat infertility is towards defining infertility as an inability to conceive after one year.
2. The incidence of infertility should also be addressed in a global context. Although all reproductive decisions may directly lead to burdens for others, and for society at large (for instance, if children

are born disabled), there have been few efforts to address the issue of reproductive responsibility in countries which are not perceived to have a "population problem". Yet, at the same time that infertility is perceived to be endemic in western countries, women's fertility is seen as rampant and out of control in non-western nations. Thus, in contrast to the technologies and drugs promoting fertility in the "first" world, third world women receive drugs designed to decrease fertility and governments in these countries are debating policies which promote sterilisation and infanticide. (See A. Griffiths and A. Fink, "Policy and Procreation: The Regulation of Reproductive Behaviours in the Third World" in S. McLean (ed.) *Law Reform and Human Reproduction*, Aldershot: Dartmouth, 1992; L. Freedman, "Censorship and Manipulation of Reproductive Health Information: An Issue of Human Rights and Women's Health" in S. Coliver (ed.), *The Right to Know: Human Rights and Access to Reproductive Health Information*, Pittsburg: University of Pennsylvania Press, 1995.

The problem of defining infertility is compounded by the difficulty of establishing numbers who are actually infertile. The low priority then accorded to the provision of infertility services in Britain was deplored by the Warnock Committee — a Government Committee established to examine the social, ethical and legal implications of developments in the field of human assisted conception (see also Chapter 10 at page 600–607).

Warnock Committee: *Report of the Committee of Inquiry into Human Fertilisation and Embryology* (1984) Cmnd. 9314

2.14 We recognise the difficulty of providing reliable statistics on infertility because of the number of infertile couples who do not seek treatment or are voluntarily childless. Nevertheless we were surprised at how few data there were on the prevalence of infertility, the extent of available services, their location and the numbers treated. Where figures were available, they were often out of date and of dubious relevance. Quite often, people with an infertility problem seek professional advice about other symptoms. Thus any estimate of the extent of infertility treatment within the NHS understates the present level of provision; the primary diagnosis may reflect the symptoms about which advice was first sought, rather than infertility. We believe that these data deficiencies should be remedied so that policy makers and planners can make decisions against a background of objectively assessed facts. *We recommend that funding should be made available for the collection of adequate statistics on infertility and infertility services . . .*
2.16 We find the present haphazard organisation of services unsatisfactory. While we can appreciate that all gynaecologists want to offer help to their own patients, we nonetheless believe that a greater degree of specialisation is necessary. A working party of the Royal College of Obstetricians and Gynaecologists (RCOG) has recommended the creation of a new sub-specialty of reproductive medicine which would include infertility, and though we regard an assessment of the merits of this proposal as outside our terms of reference, we see some advantages in it. *We recommend that each health authority should review its facilities for the investigation and treatment of infertility and consider the establishment, separate from routine gynaecology, of a specialist infertility clinic with close working relationships with*

specialist units, including genetic counselling services, at regional and supraregional level. Where it is not possible to have a separate clinic we recommend that infertility patients should be seen separately from other types of gynaecological patient wherever possible. The husband and wife should be seen together and it would then be possible for the necessary expertise to be available to deal with problems in the man as well as the woman. It would allow numbers of infertile couples to meet each other, and would offer scope for developing informal arrangements for mutual support. A more specialised service would, we believe, make the best use of available expertise and resources.

(b) Causes of Infertility

There are a number of causes of infertility. In approximately a third of cases the fertility problem lies with the man, in a third with the woman, and in the remaining third the cause is unknown (idiopathic infertility). As we shall see, most medico-legal attention has focused upon female fertility. One reason for the comparative invisibility of male infertility was that "remedies" for the problem have hitherto been open to unsupervised use and thus lacked medical scrutiny. However, this is also changing, in response to new technologies. The most common known causes of male infertility are blockage of the vasa deferentia which may be surgically treated, and low sperm count or low motility which may be treated through artificial insemination. Female infertility problems are more likely to require application of sophisticated medical technology. The most common known source of female infertility is abnormalities in the fallopian tubes which inhibit the ovum's journey from the ovary to the uterine cavity. Usually, of course, this will also block the movement of sperm, though there is the risk of an ectopic pregnancy. Other causes include inability to ovulate, or the development of antibodies to a partner's sperm. A woman may also be capable of pregnancy, but unable to carry a child because of repeated miscarriages or risks to her physical health.

3. TECHNIQUES FOR ALLEVIATING INFERTILITY

There are a variety of means by which the infertility of an individual, or a couple, can be overcome. Here, we explore the range of possibilities.

(a) Assisted Insemination

Assisted insemination (AI) has a long history, having originated for use by humans in the nineteenth century. It has been a standard procedure for the last four decades and available on the NHS since 1968. AI can be used to overcome both female infertility problems (where the cervix or fallopian tubes pose barriers to normal insemination) and male infertility problems (by concentrating sperm before insemination). The process involves the collection of sperm outside the body and its introduction into the uterus for the purpose of inducing conception. Sperm is procured either from the partner of the woman who is to be inseminated (Artificial Insemination by Husband (AIH) or Partners (AIP)), or from an anonymous donor who will not normally be legally related to the resulting offspring (Donor Insemination (DI) (formerly referred to as Artificial Insemination by Donor (AID)). In the former case, artificial insemination may be necessary because the partner's sperm count is abnormally low. A male's sperm count may be increased by laboratory manipulation of sperm density in a given sample. AIH may also be used where the male partner predicts damage to his testicles, *e.g.* because of workplace hazards, and deposits semen in a "sperm bank". (For more detail on the technique see R. Snowden and G. Mitchell, *The Artificial Family: A Consideration of Artificial Insemination by Donor*, London: Allen and Unwin, 1981.) Some commentators have argued that DI is not truly a therapy for male infertility; rather it is a way of enabling a woman whose male partner is unable to impregnate her to have a child. (See R. Hull, *Ethical Issues in the New Reproductive Technologies*, 1990, Belmont, California: Wadsworth Publishing Co., at page 54.) In most cases, unlike some of the reproductive technologies discussed below, assisted insemination is a fairly low-tech procedure. It can be accomplished with nothing more sophisticated than a syringe, turkey baster or drinking straw. Under subsection 4(1)(a) of the Human Fertilisation and Embryology Act 1990 DI is brought within the regulatory framework. However, subsection 4(1)(b) of the Act (see below at page 658 effectively excludes AIH/AIP from the statutory scheme of regulation since no donation of sperm is involved, and thus a doctor performing AIH/AIP is not required to be licensed by the Act. Assisted insemination is the most widely accepted of the alternative methods of reproduction, although it continues to be shrouded in secrecy. (See J. Dewar, "Fathers in Law? The Case of AID" in R. Lee and D. Morgan (eds) *Birthrights: Law and Ethics at the End of Life*, London: Routledge, 1989.) However, when it was first introduced it created exactly the same moral panic about its threat to the family and society that are currently evoked by surrogacy and IVF. (See C. Smart, "'There is of course the distinction dictated by nature': Law and the Problem of Paternity" in M. Stanworth (ed.) *Reproductive Technologies: Gender, Motherhood and Medicine*, Cambridge: Polity Press, 1987.) Since, in the past DI was shrouded in secrecy, many of the ethical dilemmas it poses have only been debated fairly recently. Objections have been based mainly on concern for the impact on the child produced as a result of DI, particularly where the sperm donor is genetically related to the male infertile partner. Historically, the main source of opposition to the practice comes from the Roman Catholic Church. (See Congregation for the Doctrine of the Faith, *Instruction on Respect for Human Life in Its Origin and on the Dignity of Procreation* reprinted at pages 21–39 in R. Hull, *op. cit.*; on changing attitudes to AI see J. Dewar, *op cit.*) The current widespread social acceptance of DI as a means of alleviating infertility in heterosexual couples may simply be due to the fact that it has been available as a form of treatment on the NHS for so long. Legally, the main issue is whether DI should be regulated by the medical profession and that the focus has switched to new areas of assisted conception. The issue of regulation, and consequently of the availability of the technique, has proven particularly contentious where single and lesbian women have sought to inseminate themselves, thus creating 'fatherless' children. (See K. Harrison, "Lesbian Mothers, Sperm Donors and Limited fathers" in M. Fineman and I. Karpin, *Mothers-in-Law: Feminist Theory and the Legal Regulation of Motherhood*, New York: Columbia University Press, 1995.)

Warnock Committee: Report of the Committee of Inquiry into Human Fertilisation and Embryology (1984) Cmnd. 9314:

4.16 We have concluded that AID [DI] should no longer be left in a legal vacuum but should be subject to certain conditions and safeguards, and receive the protection of the law. It is certain that, for some people, AID will always remain unacceptable. Nevertheless we cannot accept their objections as a reason for denying the opportunity for treatment to those infertile couples who do not share their beliefs. Moreover the practice of AID will continue to grow, with or without official sanction and its clandestine practice could be very harmful. It is therefore desirable that AID should be available as a treatment for the alleviation of infertility, in a form subject to all possible safeguards. We regard it as a legitimate form of treatment for those infertile couples for whom it might be appropriate. Therefore *we recommend that AID should be available on a properly organised basis and subject to . . . licensing arrangements . . . to those infertile couples for whom it might be appropriate. Consequently we recommend that the provision of AID services without a licence for the purpose should be an offence.*

NOTE:

1. The Warnock proposals on DI were incorporated in statute by the Human Fertilisation and Embryology Act 1990 (see pages 656–659 below).
2. Since the passage of the legislation, any man who willingly donates sperm in an agreement *not* sanctioned under the NHS or by a licensed infertility clinic will be regarded in law as the father of the child, and thus liable to maintenance. (On the status of the father under the 1990 Act see pages 676–680 below.)
3. The medically sanctioned form of DI raises issues concerning storage of, and property rights in, sperm. It also poses the question of what screening procedures should apply to donated gametes (ova and sperm). (These issues are discussed at pages 682–691 below.)
4. A further issue currently generating some controversy is the imposition of appropriate age limits for sperm donors. While the 1990 Act does not address this question, the current *Code of Practice* issued by the Human Fertilisation and Embryology Authority (HFEA) suggests that, unless there are exceptional circumstances, donors of sperm should be aged between 18 and 55. (See HFEA, *Code of Practice*, 1995, paragraphs 3.35–3.39; and pages 685–686 below.) In December 1995 the HFEA issued a consultation document inviting comments on

whether the Code of Practice should be revised to restrict the upper age limit for semen donors to 40, in the light of a 1991 academic paper which concluded that there was a correlation between paternal age and the incidence of serious non chromosomal birth defects, especially those arising from new autosomal mutations. As a result the American Fertility Society reduced the age limit to 40 in its guidelines on sperm donations, and the British Andrology Society is now considering whether to issue a similar recommendation.

Section 12(e) of the Human Fertilisation and Embryology Act prohibits payment for gametes (sperm or eggs) or embryos except in accordance with HFEA directions. Under a direction issued in 1991 (as amended in February 1996) donors may be paid up to £15, plus "reasonable expenses" or benefits in kind. A Working Party has been established by HFEA to consider whether donors should continue to receive payment other than expenses incurred. (See HFEA, *Fifth Annual Report*, July 1996 at pages 22–24.)

QUESTIONS:

1. Do you agree with Warnock's conclusion that AID should only be legally permissible when conducted through a statutorily licensed organisation?
2. Should sperm donors be paid for their services? If so, what level of payment is appropriate? If sperm donors should be paid, what would be appropriate payment for egg donation? (See discussion below; and compare this with the issue of payment for body parts in Chapter 15.)
3. Should the number of donations from any one sperm donor be limited? The Warnock Committee (at paragraph 4.26) suggested that any single sperm donor should only be permitted to 'father' up to ten children as a result of donor insemination. Whilst this recommendation was not incorporated in the 1990 Human Fertilisation and Embryology Act, it is inserted in the *Code of Practice* issued by the Authority (paragraph 7.18.) Is this an appropriate limit?
4. Warnock states that DI is a "legitimate form of treatment" for couples. Should this include lesbian couples? What about single women? Is it ethically wrong for the medical profession to assist in the creation of fatherless children (see further pages 678–679 below)? If single women and lesbians are not permitted access to DI, should use of this technique by them constitute a criminal offence?
5. In what way could the clandestine practice of DI be "harmful" to the health of the couple and/or child(ren)?

(b) Surrogacy

(i) Definitions and Attitudes

Of all the alternative methods of conception, it is surrogacy which has provoked the most intense passion and the greatest public hostility, probably due to its very visible splitting of motherhood into genetic, gestational and social components. A surrogate pregnancy may be established through a variety of methods. "Partial surrogacy", which is currently the most common form of arrangement, is where the carrying woman is fertilised with the commissioning man's sperm either as a result of sexual intercourse or assisted insemination. Thus, she not only carries and gives birth to the baby, she also has a genetic link to it. "Full surrogacy" is where the commissioning couple provide both sperm and ovum so that the child is genetically entirely theirs, although carried by another woman. It necessarily involves the use of *in vitro* fertilisation (see section (c) below). "Full surrogacy" can thus be regarded as a form of womb leasing. (See G. Douglas, *Law, Fertility and Reproduction*, London: Sweet & Maxwell, 1989, pages 141–167). Surrogacy can help alleviate infertility, where a woman suffers from severe pelvic disease, has no uterus, experiences repeated miscarriages, or where pregnancy is medically undesirable for other reasons. The Warnock Committee has neatly summarised the arguments both for and against surrogacy.

Warnock Committee: *Report of the Committee of Inquiry into Human Fertilisation and Embryology* (1984) Cmnd. 9314.

8.10 There are strongly held objections to the concept of surrogacy, and it seems from the evidence submitted to us that the weight of public opinion is against the practice. The objections turn essentially on the view that to introduce a third party into the process of procreation which should be confined to the loving partnership between two people, is an attack on the value of the marital relationship . . . Further, the intrusion is worse than in the case of AID, since the contribution of the carrying mother is greater, more intimate and personal, than the contribution of a semen donor. It is also argued that it is inconsistent with human dignity that a woman should use her uterus for financial profit and treat it as an incubator for someone's else's child. The objection is not diminished, indeed it is strengthened, where the woman entered an agreement to conceive a child, with the sole purpose of handing the child over to the commissioning couple after birth.

8.11 Again, it is argued that the relationship between mother and child is itself distorted by surrogacy . . . It is also potentially damaging to the child, whose bonds with the carrying mother, regardless of genetic connections, are held to be strong, and whose welfare must be considered to be of paramount importance. Further it is felt that a surrogacy agreement is degrading to the child who is to be the outcome of it, since, for all practical purposes, the child will have been bought for money.

8.12 It is also argued that since there are some risks attached to pregnancy, no woman ought to be asked to undertake pregnancy for another, in order to earn money. Nor, it is argued should a woman be forced by legal sanctions to part with a child, to which she has recently given birth, against her will.

8.13 If infertility is a condition which should, where possible, be remedied, it is argued that surrogacy must not be ruled out, since it offers to some couples their only chance of having a child genetically related to one or both of them. In particular, it may well be the only way that the husband of an infertile woman can have a child. Moreover, the bearing of a child for another can be seen, not as an undertaking that trivialises or commercialises pregnancy, but, on the contrary, as a deliberate and thoughtful act of generosity on the part of one woman to another. If there are risks attached to pregnancy, then the generosity is all the greater.

8.14 There is no reason, it is argued, to suppose that carrying mothers will enter into agreements lightly, and they have a perfect right to enter into such agreements if they so wish, just as they have a right to use their own bodies in other ways, according to their own decision . . .

8.15 As for intrusion into the marriage relationship, it is argued that those who feel strongly about this need not seek such treatment, but they should not seek to prevent others from having access to it.

8.16 On the question of bonding, it is argued that as very little is actually known about the extent to which bonding occurs when the child is *in utero*, no great claims should be made in this respect. In any case the breaking of such bonds, even if less than ideal, is not held to be an overriding argument against placing a child for adoption, where the mother wants this.

Having outlined the pros and cons of surrogacy the Warnock Committee reached the following conclusion:

8.17 The question of surrogacy presented us with some of the most difficult problems we encountered. The evidence submitted to us contained a range of strongly held views and this was reflected in our own views. The moral and social objections to surrogacy have weighed heavily with us. In the first place we are all agreed that a surrogacy for convenience alone, that is, where a woman is physically capable of bearing a child but does not wish to undergo pregnancy, is totally ethically unacceptable. Even in compelling medical circumstances the danger of exploitation of one human being by another appears to the majority of us far to out weigh the potential benefits, in almost every case. That people should treat others as a means to their own ends, however desirable the consequences, must always be liable to moral objection. Such treatment of one person by another becomes positively exploitative when financial interests are involved. It is therefore with the commercial exploitation of surrogacy that we have been primarily, but by no means exclusively, concerned.

8.18 We have considered whether the criminal law should have any part to play in the control of surrogacy and have concluded that it should. We recognise that there is a serious risk of commercial explosion surrogacy and that this would be difficult to prevent without the assistance of the criminal law. We have considered whether a limited, non-profit making surrogacy service, subject to licensing and inspection, could have any useful part to play but the majority agreed that the existence of such a service would in itself encourage the growth of surrogacy. *We recommend that legislation be introduced to render criminal the creation or the operation in the United Kingdom of agencies whose purposes include the recruitment of women for surrogate pregnancy or making arrangements for individuals or couples who wish to utilise the services of a carrying mother; such legislation should be wide enough to include both profit and non-profit making organisations. We further recommend that the legislation be sufficiently wide to render criminally liable the actions of professionals and others who knowingly assist in the establishment of a surrogate pregnancy.*

8.19 We do not envisage that this legislation would render private persons entering into surrogacy arrangements liable to criminal prosecution, as we are anxious to avoid children being born to mothers subject to the taint of criminality. We nonetheless recognise that there will continue to be privately arranged surrogacy agreements. While we consider that most, if not all, surrogacy arrangements would be legally unenforceable in any of their terms, we feel that the position should be put beyond any possible doubt in law. We recommend that it be provided by statute that all surrogacy agreements are illegal contracts and therefore unenforceable in the courts.

NOTE:

1. Commentators are virtually unanimous that the Warnock Committee's recommendations on surrogacy represent the weakest stage

of the report, since the conclusions appear to have been based on public opposition to the practice rather than any considered philosophical position. (See M. Freeman, "Is surrogacy exploitative?" in S. McLean (ed.) *Legal Issues in Human Reproduction*, Aldershot: Gower, 1989; S. Lee, "Re-reading Warnock" in P. Byrne (ed.) *Rights and Wrongs in Medicine*, London: King Edward's Hospital Fund, 1986; M. Lockwood, "The Warnock Report: a philosophical appraisal" in M. Lockwood (ed.) *Modern Dilemmas in Modern Medicine*, Oxford: Oxford University Press, 1985; S. Roberts, "Warnock and Surrogate Motherhood: Sentiment or Argument" in P. Byrne (ed) *Rights and Wrongs in Medicine*, Oxford: Oxford University Press, 1986. For a considered philosophical argument against surrogacy, see R. Hursthouse, *Beginning Lives*, Oxford: Blackwells, 1987.)

QUESTIONS:

1. Do you agree with the Warnock Committee's conclusions on this issue? Compare and contrast the Warnock proposals on surrogacy with those on *in vitro* fertilisation (discussed at pages 653–654 below) and embryo research — see Chapter 10 at pages 600–607.

2. Do you think that the case against surrogacy is really grounded in arguments which oppose *commercial* surrogacy rather than the practice *per se*? Can commercial and non commercial surrogacy be distinguished? (Compare S. McLean, "Mother and others: the case for surrogacy" in E. Sutherland and A. McCall Smith (eds), *Family Rights: Family Law and Medical Advance*, Edinburgh: Edinburgh University Press, 1990 with U. Narayan, "The Gift of a Child: Commercial Surrogacy, Gift Surrogacy and Motherhood" in P. Boling (ed.) *Expecting Trouble: Surrogacy, Foetal Abuse and New Reproductive Technologies*, Boulder, Colorado: Westview Press, 1995.)

3. Do you agree with Freeman that, whereas Warnock strongly endorses the principles of autonomy and self-determination on issues like AI, IVF and egg and embryo donation, on the issue of surrogacy it reverts to the paternalism and moralism which it had elsewhere eschewed, citing public opinion as justification? (See M. Freeman, "Is surrogacy exploitative?" in S. McLean (ed.), *Legal Issues in Human Reproduction*, Aldershot: Dartmouth, 1989.) If you agree that Warnock was overly paternalistic on this issue, who do you think was the object of such paternalism? Was its paternalism directed at the woman who wants a child, or the carrying mother, or the child?

4. Is the "work" involved in pregnancy and birth analogous to other forms of human labour which are the subject of contracts of employment? (See M. L. Shanley, "Surrogate Mothering and Women's Freedom: A Critique of Contracts for Human Reproduction" in P. Boling, *op. cit.*)

(ii) Judicial Attitudes Towards Surrogacy

Although surrogacy is commonly discussed as part of a package of "reproductive technologies" it can, of course, like DI, be performed very simply with no professional intervention. However, as with DI, its use has been shrouded in secrecy, making it difficult to establish the extent to which it has been practised. (See D. Morgan, "Surrogacy: An Introductory Essay" in R. Lee and D. Morgan (eds), *Birth Rights: Law and Ethics at the Beginnings of Life*, London: Routledge, 1989.) The first surrogacy case to be litigated was heard in 1978, at a time when reproductive techniques were becoming a subject of public controversy. Compare judicial attitudes to surrogacy in the following two cases:

A v. C [1985] F.L.R. 445, [1984] Fam. Law 241

This case concerned an unmarried couple in which the woman, who had children from a previous relationship, was unable to have any further children. Her partner, A, had a very strong desire to raise his own biological child. He found a woman, C, who was prepared to be artificially inseminated by him and agreed to hand the baby over at birth for adoption by him and his partner in return for a payment of £3,000. However, after the birth she decided to keep the child and forego the money. A commenced wardship proceedings seeking custody of the child. In court proceedings, Conwyn J. held that the child should remain a ward of court until majority or further order. C was given care and control of the child, the father was granted access, and a supervisory order was made in favour of the local authority.

ORMROD L.J.:
" . . . It is very unfortunate for both men and women when they find themselves in a situation where they are unable to have that very natural satisfaction [of having their own children]. The only difference between this father and the others is that the others try to accept it, whereas this father embarked upon the most extraordinary naive plan to achieve his object . . . It is unnecessary to make any more comment on the irresponsibility shown by all three of the adults in this case, which is perhaps only rivalled by the irresponsibility of the person who performed the insemination on the mother . . . We are dealing here with two people who have never had any sort of relationship together at all, not even a relationship amounting to one single isolated act of intercourse taking place casually on some occasion and never to be repeated. Here we have nothing but the clinical fact that the father has contributed the necessary male sperm to the conception of this child. That is the sum total of his contribution to this child.

He now finds himself reluctantly in the position of having to accept — and we are told that he only accepted it with difficulty before the judge — that there could be no possible question in the circumstances of his having care and control of this very small child, and it may well be that he finds difficulty now in accepting that situation . . .

The judge very properly directed himself in accordance with the law, particularly as it is laid down in *J v. C* [1970] A.C. 668 in the House of Lords, that the first and paramount consideration was the welfare of the child, bearing in mind, of course, the wishes and feelings and so on of the respective parents and other people concerned with the child, but always bearing in mind that the decision must rest in terms of the best interests of the child, having taken all these other factors into account. That is exactly as the judge put it.

The only possible criticism of his judgment, so far as the law is concerned, occurs — and I think this may be more a matter of expression than anything else — where he said: 'Prima facie (this is the next proposition, I would have thought), a parent should have access to his child'. I would differ from that only to this extent: while it is a correct statement of the general practice, it is always a little dangerous in these cases when judges talk in terms of presumption and burden of proof. It leads to many very false conclusions if it is pressed too far. It is simply a statement of common sense that in the ordinary way, as society today is constituted, both parents should be in contact with their children, even if they have parted. It is no more than that and I would deprecate any idea that there is a presumption either way in these matters or an onus either way . . .

The main point put forward by counsel for the mother and the Official Solicitor was: 'Access can only trouble the mother and progressively the child also. It would endanger care and control all through the minority'. The background, they say, is such that the father should yield up the child completely to the mother. It shows him and his now wife to have been, and to be, 'unstable, unreliable, unsuitable and obsessive'. He noted the gulf between the respective environments of the father and the mother and the child which could only unsettle the child . . .

The question of access as between mother and child, and father and child, raises different considerations. There is always a close physical bond between mother and child which tends to get closer from the time of birth onwards for some considerable time and then, perhaps, to slacken off a little as the child gets older. The bond between father and child operates in the opposite direction. At first it is very slight indeed, but gradually, as association between father and child increases and lengthens in time, the bond becomes more and more real and lasts, sometimes, longer — not always. In this case we have a situation where there is no bond between the father and the child except the mere biological one. There has never been any association, except of the most exiguous character, between the father and the mother. There has never been anything between them except a sordid commercial bargain. The father has only had the intermittent contact provided by access to a very young child over the past year. He has been very assiduous in maintaining that access, bringing with him his present wife, whose role in this case, as I have said before, fills me with sympathy. What her position can be in that house during periods of access, I find very hard to imagine. Her emotions must be very mixed and I feel sorry for her.

But what is the future? The mother is 21. She is almost certain, given the chance and a little peace from litigation or the strain of access, to marry and set up a family of which this child will be part. By far the best thing that can happen to this child is that he should become a member of a family just like other children. This will give him as normal a life as possible . . .

So what is the good of keeping this wholly artificial, painful tie going? My answer is: No good will be done whatever. It may be gratifying in some ways to the father. I suppose, in some ways, it might be said that it will enable him to deal with his guilt sense, which I hope he has in regard to this case. But there are many other ways in which he can assuage his guilt. To my mind, to permit access to continue in the circumstances of this case is to perpetuate the most artificial situation that one can possibly imagine.

Speaking for myself, I do not find comparisons very useful, but if we are to make comparisons we might as well make them accurately. There is a world of difference between the father of an illegitimate child who has been living with the mother for 2 years or 6 months, and this case. There is some difference, but not much, between this case and that of a man who gets a girl pregnant in a casual act of intercourse on the way home from a pub one night. But such fathers do not, even in these days, often apply for access to their children and, when they do, they do not as a rule find a very sympathetic court. There is a slightly romantic notion about these days that even the most casual of fathers is better than none, but that is a matter on which I think there may be room for more than one view.

I can see absolutely no advantage to this child in continuing to be in contact with the father, except possibly a financial advantage to which I attach no significance whatever, in this case.

NOTES:

1. This was the first surrogacy case to be litigated in the U.K. Although it was not fully reported until 1985 it was actually decided in 1978.
2. Stamp and Cumming-Bruce L.JJ. delivered concurring judgments. Cumming-Bruce L.J. added that the fact that a child was conceived through artificial means, as compared to natural methods of conception, could have no effect on the duty of a court to seek to afford the child a life that would best promote the child's welfare.

QUESTIONS:

1. It seems that Ormrod L.J.'s attitude to infertility in 1978 was simply that the infertile person or couple should learn to accept it. Do you think that many judges would adopt the same attitude today? Do you think judicial views on such contested issues reflect public opinion?
2. Do you think it would have made any difference to the decision if the parties had actually had sexual intercourse; or indeed if they had some sort of continuing relationship? Should it?
3. Do you agree with the manner in which Ormrod L.J. dismissed the claims of the commissioning father — effectively reducing his status to that of a sperm donor? In what ways, if any, can a man who commissions a surrogate pregnancy be distinguished from a sperm donor, given that his biological involvement is the same in both cases?
4. What assumptions about the welfare of children and family structures does Ormrod L.J. make in his judgment? Do you agree?
5. Do you think the outcome would have been different if the mother had been 30, already had children of her own, was a close friend of the family, and there had never been any question of her receiving payment?

Re C (A Minor) (Wardship: Surrogacy) [1985] F.L.R. 846

Re C concerned a married couple, Mr and Mrs A, where Mrs A was infertile. The couple were of Asiatic origin. They contacted a North American agency which secured a British woman to bear Mr A's child in return for payment. A nurse performed the artificial insemination, and the commissioning couple never met the woman who had agreed to carry the child. The couple came to England for the birth and on the day of the birth the local authority obtained a place of safety order. Mr A commenced wardship proceedings and asked that care and control of the child be committed to him and his wife. The surrogate mother voluntarily left the baby in hospital in the care of nurses while its future was determined. The local authority carried out inquiries into the suitability of the prospective parents and concluded by fully endorsing the application that the baby be given into the care of Mr and Mrs A.

LATEY J.:
" . . . First and foremost, and at the heart of the prerogative jurisdiction in wardship, is what is best for the child or children concerned. That and nothing else. Plainly, the methods used to produce a child as this baby has been, and the commercial aspects of it, raise difficult and delicate problems of ethics, morality and social desirability. These problems are under active consideration elsewhere.

Are they relevant in arriving at a decision on what now and, so far as one can tell, in the future is best for this child? If they are relevant, it is incumbent on the court to do its best to evaluate and balance them.

In my judgment, however, they are not relevant. The baby is here. All that matters is what is best for her now that she is here and not how she arrived. If it be said (though it has not been said during these hearings) that because the father and his wife entered into these arrangements it is some indication of their unsuitability as parents, I should reject any such suggestion. If what they did was wrong (and I am not saying that it was), they did it in total innocence.

It follows that the moral, ethical and social considerations are for others and not for this court in its wardship jurisdiction.

So, what is best for this baby? Her natural mother does not ask for her. Should she go into Mr and Mrs A's care and be brought up by them? Or should some other arrangement be made for her, such as long-term fostering with or without adoption as an end?

The factors can be briefly stated. Mr A is the baby's father and he wants her, as does his wife. The baby's mother does not want her. Mr and Mrs A are a couple in their 30s. They are devoted to each other. They are both professional people, highly qualified. They have a very nice home in the country and another in a town. Materially they can give the baby a very good upbringing. But, far more important-antly, they are both excellently equipped to meet the baby's emotional needs. They are most warm, caring, sensible people, as well as highly intelligent. When the time comes to answer the child's questions, they will be able to do so with professional advice if they feel they need it. Looking at this child's well-being, physical and emotional, who better to have her care? No one.

Accordingly, the orders which I made on Friday evening are that the wardship will continue until further order . . . "

NOTE:

1. The above was perhaps the most high profile of the British surrogacy cases, decided around the time of the "*Baby M*" case in the United States (see P. Chessler, *Sacred Bond: Motherhood Under Seige*, London: Virago, 1988) and popularised in the media as the "Baby Cotton" case (see K. Cotton and D. Winn, *Baby Cotton: For Love or Money*, London: Dorling Kindersley, 1985.)

QUESTIONS:

1. What factors explain the shift in judicial opinion which this case seems to indicate? Is the different outcome solely due to the fact that there was no dispute in this case?
2. How relevant was the commercial aspect of the agreement which the parties had entered into in the two cases considered above?
3. In the latter case the judge stresses the "innocence" of the parties to the transaction. Is it meaningful to talk of entering a surrogacy arrangement "innocently"?

(iii) The Legislative Approach

In 1985 the United Kingdom became the first country to legislate on surrogacy, acting remarkably quickly in this instance on the Warnock proposals to ban commercial surrogacy. However the Act did not go so far as to endorse Warnock's suggestion that the actions of any third party who facilitated the arrangement should be banned regardless of whether they received money. (See S. Sloman, "Surrogacy Arrangements Act 1985" (1985) 135 *New L.J.* 978.)

Surrogacy Arrangements Act 1985, s.1(1–1A) and s.2(1–4)

1.—(1) The following provisions shall have effect for the interpretation of this Act.

(2) 'Surrogate mother' means a woman who carries a child in pursuance of an arrangement —

(a) made before she began to carry the child, and
(b) made with a view to any child carried in pursuance of it being handed over to, and parental responsibility being met (so far as practicable) by, another person or other persons.

(3) An arrangement is a surrogacy arrangement if, were a woman to whom the arrangement relates to carry a child in pursuance of it, she would be a surrogate mother.

(4) In determining whether an arrangement is made with such a view as is mentioned in subsection (2) above regard may be had to the circumstances as a whole (and, in particular, where there is a promise or understanding that any payment will or may be made to the woman or for her benefit in respect of the carrying of any child in pursuance of the arrangement, to that promise or understanding).

(5) An arrangement may be regarded as made with such a view though subject to conditions relating to handing over of any child.

(6) A woman who carries a child is to be treated for the purposes of subsection (2)(a) above as beginning to carry it at the time of the insemination or of the placing in her of an embryo, of an egg in the process of fertilisation or of sperm and eggs, as the case may be, that results in her carrying the child.

(7) "Body of persons" means a body of persons corporate or unincorporated.

(8) "Payment" means payment in money or money's worth.

(9) This Act applies to arrangements whether or not they are lawful.

1A.—No surrogacy arrangement is enforceable by or against any of the persons making it.

2.—(1) No person shall on a commercial basis do any of the following acts in the United Kingdom, that is —

(a) initiate or take part in any negotiations with a view to the making of a surrogacy arrangement;
(b) offer or agree to negotiate the making of a surrogacy arrangement, or
(c) compile any information with a view to its use in making, or negotiating the making of, surrogacy arrangements;

and no person shall in the United Kingdom knowingly cause another to do any of those acts on a commercial basis.

(2) A person who contravenes subsection (1) above is guilty of an offence; but it is not a contravention of that subsection —

(a) for a woman, with a view to becoming a surrogate mother herself, to do any act mentioned in that subsection or to cause such an act to be done, or
(b) for any person, with a view to a surrogate mother carrying a child for him, to do such an act or to cause such an act to be done.

(3) For the purposes of this section, a person does an act on a commercial basis (subject to subsection (4) below) if —

(a) any payment is at any time received by himself or another in respect of it, or
(b) he does it with a view to any payment being received by himself or another in respect of making, or negotiating or facilitating the making of, any surrogacy arrangement.

In this subsection "payment" does not include payment to or for the benefit of a surrogate mother or prospective surrogate mother.

(4) In proceedings against a person for an offence under subsection (1) above, he is not to be treated as doing an act on a commercial basis by reason of any payment received by another in respect of the act if it is proved that —

(a) in a case where payment was received before he did the act, he did not do the act knowing or having reasonable cause to suspect that any payment had been received in respect of the act; and
(b) in any other case, he did not do the act with a view to any payment being received in respect of it.

NOTES:

1. Section 1A above was inserted by section 36(1) of the Human Fertilisation and Embryology Act 1990. This amendment provides legislative endorsement for the position adopted in *A v. C* (above). Section 36(2) extends the meaning of a surrogacy arrangement to cover the placing in the woman of sperm and eggs, or of an egg in the process of fertilisation as well as embryo transfer.
2. Section 3 of the 1985 Act prohibits advertisements in relation to surrogacy arrangements.
3. The 1985 Act proscribes only the actions of commercial agencies or individuals seeking to profit from surrogacy. Thus, the commissioning couple and the surrogate mother do not commit any offence, even if

she is paid. However they may be guilty of an offence under section 6 of the Adoption Act 1976 which makes it a criminal offence to give or receive any payment in relation to the adoption of a child, the grant of consent to adoption or the handing over of a child with a view to its adoption, unless such payment is authorised by a court.

4. In *Re: An Adoption Application* [1987] 2 All E.R. 826, the third case concerning surrogacy to come before the British courts and the first to be considered after the passage of the 1985 Act, the High Court indicated a willingness to assist a couple who wished to adopt a surrogate baby born as a result of intercourse between the surrogate and the husband. Even though the couple had paid £10,000 to the surrogate mother, thus appearing *prima facie* to have breached the prohibition on payment in the Adoption Act 1976, Latey J. held that the payment was for expenses rather than to procure the gestational mother's consent to adoption. Moreover, he added that even if he was wrong on that point, the court could authorise such payments retrospectively, in the interests of the child. This case thus represents another step in the progressive liberalisation of judicial attitudes towards surrogacy arrangements. A similar approach has been adopted in subsequent cases. In these the courts have been prepared to sanction retrospectively breaches of adoption law, where the child's interests are deemed to lie with the commissioning parents. (See G. Douglas, "Commentary on *Re MW*" [1995] *Fam Law* 666.) In the most recent of these cases — *Re MW (Adoption) (Surrogacy)* [1995] 2 F.L.R. 759 — the court retrospectively authorised payments to the surrogate mother even though it acknowledged such payments to be unlawful.

5. Even legislative policy would appear to be softening. Section 30 of the 1990 Human Fertilisation and Embryology Act, which came into force in 1995, appears to run counter to the discouragement of surrogacy in the 1985 Act (see pages 680–682 below).

6. Another recent case provides further evidence of the judiciary's increasing willingness to facilitate surrogacy arrangements. Even though section 30 of the 1990 Human Fertilisation and Embryology Act (which provides for the grant of a court order that the commissioning couple should be regarded in law as the parents of the child, discussed further below at pages 680–682) was not then in force in *Re W (minors) Surrogacy* [1991] 1 F.L.R. 385, Scott Baker J. was prepared to treat twins born as a result of a "total" surrogacy arrangement as the children of the commissioning couple. In his view the paramount issue was how to facilitate any steps which would ensure that the child would bond with the genetic parents.

7. The choice of statutory language is significant. Notice how the gestational mother is labelled the surrogate (substitute) mother although she is what most people would have regarded as the "natural" mother. What are the political and legal consequences of using such language? (See Chapter 2 at page 115.)

8. There have been no prosecutions under the 1985 Act, and many babies have been born to surrogate mothers. An organisation called COTS ("Childlessness Overcome Through Surrogacy") was formed to bring together potential surrogates and infertile couples. Under the Act it cannot charge for its services, but as a consequence it fails to screen surrogates or commissioning couples. A Bill aimed at strengthening this legislation, sponsored by the Earl of Halsbury failed (Surrogacy Arrangements (Amendment) Bill 1986).

QUESTIONS:

1. Why do you think that the United Kingdom Government was so quick to act on surrogacy, whereas it procrastinated for a further six years on the issue of embryo research? Also, why do you think it failed to accept fully the recommendations of the Warnock Committee on surrogacy, whereas ultimately Warnock's proposals on embryo research were enacted (see Chapter 10 at pages 600–607)?

2. Would you agree with Freeman that the Act represents "an ill-considered and largely irrelevant panic measure"? (See M. Freeman, "Is surrogacy exploitative?" in S. McLean (ed.), *Legal Issues in Human Reproduction*, Aldershot: Dartmouth, 1989, at page 165.) Does it demonstrate the dangers of legislating too early before some sort of social/moral/public consensus has built up? Is such a consensus likely to accrue on an issue like surrogacy?

3. Is the strategy of applying criminal penalties only to the "middle-men" involved in surrogacy transactions morally and rationally consistent? (Compare M. Gibson, "Contract Motherhood: Social Practice in Social Context" in C. Feinman (ed.), *Criminalization of a Woman's Body*, New York: The Haworth Press, 1992 with U. Narayan, "The 'Gift' of a Child: Commercial Surrogacy, Gift Surrogacy and Motherhood" in P. Rolling (ed.), *Expecting Trouble: Surrogacy, Foetal Abuse and New Reproductive Technologies*, Boulder, Colorado: Westview Press, 1995.)

4. Would it have been a better policy to stop short of banning commercial arrangements altogether and have regulated them instead? If so, in what ways would you seek to regulate the practice?

5. Does the legislative failure to enforce surrogacy contracts violate the commissioning party's "right to procreate"? (Compare J. Robertson "Embryos, Families and Procreative Liberty: The Legal Structure of the New Reproduction" (1986) 59 *Southern California Law Review* 942 with M. Lyndon Shanley, "'Surrogate Mothering' and Women's Freedom: A Critique of Contracts for Human Reproduction" in P. Rolling (ed.) *op. cit.*)

Although the 1985 Act made the position of commercial agencies clear, it failed to provide any ethical guidelines for doctors who might be approached to facilitate the establishment of a surrogate pregnancy. In 1990 the British Medical Association published the report of a Working Party on Surrogacy it had established in response to a resolution passed at its Annual Representative Meeting calling for the production of ethical guidelines in relation to surrogacy. The report was extremely hostile to the practice of surrogacy and discouraged medical professionals from facilitating it. (See BMA, *Surrogacy: Ethical Considerations*, Report of the Working Party on Human Infertility Services (1990). However, in recognition of the increased prevalence of surrogacy the BMA it has recently issued the following guidance:

Changing Conceptions of Motherhood: The Practice of Surrogacy in Britain, London: BMA, 1996

Guidelines for Health Professionals

1. Surrogacy is an acceptable option of last resort in cases where it is impossible or highly undesirable for medical reasons for the intended mother to carry a child herself. In all cases the interests of the potential child must be paramount and the risks to the surrogate mother must be kept to a minimum.
2. Health professionals consulted about a surrogacy arrangement should inform themselves about the legal position before offering advice. In particular, health professionals should be aware of the non-enforceability of surrogacy arrangements and the legal position with regard to parentage of the child.
3. In surrogacy arrangements the level of the health professionals' ethical responsibilities will vary depending on the degree of involvement in the arrangement. The BMA has divided these into three broad categories: (i) health professionals consulted about an established pregnancy; (ii) those consulted by women considering self-insemination; and (iii) those professional teams providing assisted conception techniques for the establishment of a pregnancy involving a surrogacy arrangement. Health professionals have responsibilities to all their patients. However, where health professionals are providing treatment services to assist people to have children they have additional responsibilities to the potential child.
4. Once a surrogate pregnancy has been established, the practitioner's ethical obligations to the surrogate mother and child are no different from those owed to any other pregnant woman except that additional support may be required. The duty of the health care team is to provide the appropriate level of support and guidance both during and after the pregnancy.
5. Practitioners approached by people considering self-insemination should encourage those concerned to consider the issues and implications very carefully and should ensure that they are aware of how to obtain accurate information about the medical, psychological, emotional and legal issues involved with the surrogacy.
6. Before agreeing to provide licensed treatment services aimed at establishing a surrogate pregnancy, for example through in vitro fertilisation or donor insemination, the health care team must take all reasonable steps to ensure that the medical, emotional and legal issues have been carefully considered and must, in all cases, take account of the welfare of the child who may be born as a result of the treatment. Such treatment services may only be provided in clinics licensed by the Human Fertilisation & Embryology Authority (HFEA) and in compliance with the HFEA's Code of Practice.

Before proceeding with treatment, health professionals should also satisfy themselves that the intended parents have tried all other reasonable treatment options.

7. Some health professionals who are not providing treatment services or advising on surrogacy may nonetheless be aware that a woman is, or a couple are, considering surrogacy. In such cases, the practitioner should seek to persuade them to share relevant information which might be important to the overall assessment of the interests of the potential child. It is particularly important to divulge information, such as a history of child abuse or neglect, to the medical team providing the treatment services. If such information highlights an *exceptional* risk to the parties involved, the person should be informed that the practitioner might, in a rare and particularly serious case, consider disclosing such details without his or her consent. In such cases the person should first be advised of this intention and be given the opportunity to divulge the relevant information voluntarily, or to challenge the disclosure.

8. Health professionals providing treatment services or advice about surrogacy, should actively encourage those considering this option to seek counselling and testing for infectious diseases.

9. Health professionals providing advice or treatment services should also emphasise the importance of discussing with all parties, in advance, the decisions which may need to be made before, during and after the pregnancy. These include decisions about the number of embryos to be replaced in surrogacy using IVF, the level of prenatal testing, the preferred method of delivery and decisions about care in the immediate postpartum period. Ideally these decisions should be reached by mutual agreement but in all cases of dispute, the surrogate mother, in conjunction with the health professionals, should make the final decision.

10. There should be mutual trust and openness between the health professionals and their patients as much as between the individual parties to the arrangement.

11. It is important that care and treatment are provided non-judgmentally.

12. The surrogate mother should usually have successfully borne at least one child prior to the surrogacy arrangement and preferably will have completed her own family and have a partner, family or friends to provide support throughout and after the pregnancy. In some cases, particular attention may be necessary where family support is to be given to the surrogate mother and the intended mother from the same family.

13. In view of the potential risks to the surrogate mother's health, the intended parents should be advised of the importance of ensuring that proper insurance cover has been arranged for the surrogate mother.

14. All of the health professionals involved should understand clearly who has overall management of the pregnancy.

15. After birth, the surrogate mother, her family and the intended parents are likely to need additional support and advice. These needs should be recognised by the health team. Midwives and health visitors have a particularly important role to play at this stage.

16. Health professionals providing treatment services aimed at establishing a surrogate pregnancy should ensure, before proceeding, that consideration has been given to the long-term medical and psychological needs of those participating in the arrangement.

17. Openness and truth-telling between parents and children is generally to be encouraged.

18. Health professionals with a conscientious objection to surrogacy are not obliged to participate in the arrangement but have an ethical duty to refer that patient to another practitioner who would be prepare to consider offering help and advice.

QUESTIONS:

1. What factors do you think account for the change of attitude towards surrogacy on the part of the BMA?
2. Is it right that the final say in relation to the matters identified in guideline 9 is left to the surrogate mother in conjunction with the health professionals? What if they disagree?

(iv) Disputes Between Commissioning Couple And The Surrogate Mother

One of the risks of surrogacy highlighted by the BMA Working Party in 1990 was that of disputes between the parties. We have already seen that in *A v. C* the Court of Appeal was not prepared to enforce a surrogacy arrangement when a dispute arose between the surrogate mother and the commissioning couple. A similar issue was raised in the following case.

Re P (Minors) (Wardship: Surrogacy) [1987] 2 F.L.R. 421

Mrs P offered her services as a surrogate mother to Mr and Mrs B who were seeking a woman to bear his biological child, as Mrs B was unable to carry a child to term. Mr and Mrs B contracted to pay Mrs P sums of money by instalment throughout the pregnancy, which was brought about by artificial insemination. It was agreed that following the birth of twins Mrs P should take them home for a couple of months and hand them over to the commissioning couple for adoption on an agreed date. Mrs P had doubts throughout her pregnancy about her willingness to hand over the children, which crystallised after bringing the twins home. She expressed such doubts in a letter to Mr B but wrote that despite her willingness she still intended to give up the children. Both parties then approached the local authority which applied to make the children wards of court.

SIR JOHN ARNOLD P.:
" . . . In this, as in any other wardship dispute, the welfare of the children, or child, concerned is the first and paramount consideration which the court must, by statute, take into account and that is what I do.
   These children have been, up to their present age of approximately 5 months, with, quite consistently, their mother and in those circumstances there must necessarily have been some bonding of those children with their mother and that is undoubtedly coupled with the fact that she is their mother, a matter which weighs predominantly in the balance in favour of leaving the children with their mother, but there are other factors which weigh in the opposite balance and which, as is said by Mr B through his counsel, outweigh the advantages of leaving the children with their mother and it is that balancing exercise which the court is required to perform . . . [The Wardship Jurisdiction] is a jurisdiction in which, as I have already indicated, the court's duty is to decide the case, taking into account as the first and paramount consideration, the welfare of the child or children concerned and if that consideration leads the court to override any agreement that there may be in the matter, then that the court is fully entitled to do. It is, therefore, not of great importance in this case to rule upon the validity, or otherwise, of the agreement

which was made. One possible view about that matter is that there is, or may in certain circumstances be, an element concerning the surrogacy agreement which is repellent to proper ideas about the procreation of children, so as to make any such agreement one which should be rejected by the law as being contrary to public policy. It is not necessary in this case, for the reasons which I have indicated, to come to any conclusion upon that point. The existence of the agreement is relevant to this extent, that plainly one of the factors which has to be taken into account in determining where the welfare of the children lies, is the factor of the character of the rival custodians who were put forward for consideration and it might be that the willingness of those persons to enter into a surrogacy agreement would reflect upon their moral outlook so adversely as to disqualify them as potential custodians at all, but I do not think that that factor enters into the present case . . .

What then are the factors which the court should take into account? I have already mentioned on the side of Mrs P the matters which weigh heavily in the balance are the fact of her maternity, that she bore the children and carried them for the term of their gestation and that ever since she has conferred upon them the maternal care which they have enjoyed and has done so successfully. The key social worker in the case who has given evidence testifies to the satisfactory nature of the care which Mrs P has conferred upon the children and this assessment is specifically accepted by Mr B as being an accurate one. I start, therefore, from the position that these babies have bonded with their mother in a state of domestic care by her of a satisfactory nature and I now turn to the factors which are said to outweigh those advantages, so as to guide the court upon the proper exercise of the balancing function to the conclusion that the children ought to be taken away from Mrs P, and passed over, under suitable arrangements, to Mr and Mrs B. They are principally as follows. It is said, and said quite correctly, that the shape of the B family is the better shape of a family in which these children might be brought up, because it contains a father as well as a mother and that is undoubtedly true. Next, it is said that the material circumstances of the B family are such that they exhibit a far larger degree of affluence than can be demonstrated by Mrs P. That, also, is undoubtedly true. Then it is said that the intellectual quality of the environment of the B's home and the stimulus which would be afforded to these babies, if they were to grow up in that home, would be greater than the corresponding features in the home of Mrs P. That is not a matter which has been extensively investigated, but I suspect that that is probably true. Certainly, the combined effect of the lack of affluence on the part of Mrs P and some lack of resilience to the disadvantages which that implies has been testified in the correspondence to the extent that I find Mrs P saying that shortage of resources leads to her sitting at home with little E and overeating, because she has no ability from a financial point of view to undertake anything more resourceful than that. Then it is said that the religious comfort and support which the B's derive from their Church is greater than anything of that sort available to Mrs P. How far that is true, I simply do not know. I do know that the Bs are practising Christians and do derive advantages from that circumstance, but nobody asked Mrs P about this and I am not disposed to assume that she lacks that sort of comfort and support in the absence of any investigation by way of cross-examination to lay the foundations for such a conclusion. Then it is said, and there is something in this, that the problems which might arise from the circumstance that these children who are, of course, congenitally derived from the semen of Mr B and bear traces of Mr B's Asiatic origin would be more easily understood and discussed and reconciled in the household of Mr and Mrs B, a household with an Asiatic ethnic background than they would be if they arose in relation to these children while they were situated in the home of Mrs P, which is in an English village and which has no non-English connections. Obviously that is expressed contingently as a factor, although there is no means by which the court can measure the likelihood or otherwise of the contingency which has regard to racial discrimination. The situation in which Mrs P lives is not, as it seems to me, likely to breed that sort of intolerance. She lives in a smallish country community, large in terms of a village but small in terms of a town, where there is very little penetration by any immigrant citizens, which does not seem to me to be a community in which racial discrimination is very likely, but it is a factor which contingently at least may have some importance.

Those are the particular matters which are put forward as counter-weights to the advantages to which Mrs P can point, and additionally there is the matter to which I have already referred, that it is said that in the letter of mid-November 1986, Mrs P was, herself, recognizing that the balance of advantage, which the court is required to consider for the reason that I have indicated, operated in favour of the solution of placing the children with the Bs and taking them away from Mrs P, but I do not think that that last factor is of substantial importance. At the time when that letter was written there was, as independent evidence testifies, a prevalent state of things in which Mrs P was suffering from post-natal depression, or at least post-natal stress, so that her expressions of opinion were not likely to have been very reliable at that time. Secondly, any such opinion was expressed at a stage when the children were 1 month old and might not be valid in the circumstance such as now prevails. They are five months old and have consistently been looked after by their mother during that five months period and, thirdly, the court is not only not bound, although it might be influenced, by such an expression of opinion, but is required in the due exercise of the jurisdiction to come to its own conclusion upon that topic.

As regards the other factors, they are, in the aggregate, weighty, but I do not think, having given my very best effort to the evaluation of the case dispassionately on both sides, that they ought to be taken to outweigh the advantages to these children of preserving the link with the mother to whom they are bonded and who has, as is amply testified, exercised over them a satisfactory level of maternal care, and accordingly it is, I think, the duty of the court to award the care and control of these babies to their mother . . .''

NOTE:

1. The stance taken by the British judges in *A v. C* and *Re P* may be contrasted with the approach adopted in many North American cases. Feminist scholars in the United States have argued that the reasoning in North American cases has generally been detrimental to the "surrogate" mother, as it has focused on the material advantages of the commissioning couple, under the guise of promoting the best interests of the child. (See, for example, M. A. Field, *Surrogate Motherhood* (2nd ed.), Cambridge, Massachusetts: Harvard University Press, 1994.)

QUESTIONS:

1. Of the factors outlined above by the President, which weighed heaviest upon the Court? Do you agree with its assessment?
2. Are surrogacy cases more analogous to adoption cases or residence cases? In adoption cases the interests of the child is only the first consideration (Adoption Act 1976, section 6), whereas in surrogacy cases it is the paramount consideration (Children Act 1989, section 1). Should decisions in cases of disputed surrogacy arrangements be made primarily on the grounds of the welfare of the child?

3. Is the "best interests" test a meaningful test where a child is unaware of its genetic origins? Would it not be better to have a presumption that the gestational mother is the best person to look after the child? Do you think this was the criterion which the President was actually using in this case? (On the best interests test generally, see Chapter 5 at pages 303–306.)

4. Is the President right in suggesting that the courts have no business dealing with the morality of surrogacy contracts? Can law and morality be so easily separated? (See Chapter 2 at pages 103–119.)

5. Can any conclusions about the motives of surrogate mothers be drawn from the British cases which have been litigated, or are they, by definition, unusual cases? (See K. Cotton and D. Winn, *Baby Cotton: For Love or Money*, London: Dorling Kindersley, 1985.) In your view, does the "surrogate" mother generally freely consent to enter into the contract?

6. Given that the surrogacy arrangement in English law cannot be regarded as a contract for the sale of a commodity, is it more appropriately viewed as a gift? (See J. Dolgin, "Status and Contract in Surrogate Motherhood", (1990) 38 *Buffalo Law Review* 515.)

7. In April 1996 it was revealed that the NHS had funded a surrogate pregnancy for the first time, and was considering funding other cases. The first case cost Yorkshire Health Authority £5,000. ("Surrogate grandmother wants twins", *The Guardian*, April 15, 1996.) Is this a justifiable use of NHS resources?

(v) The Terms of The Surrogacy Arrangement

Theoretically there are no limits to the type of clauses which may be inserted into surrogacy contracts. This raises the question of what terms it is justifiable to mandate in a surrogacy contract. For instance the commissioning couple could insert a clause prohibiting the surrogate mother from smoking or drinking during her pregnancy, or indeed compelling her to take certain forms of exercise or undergo medical tests in the interests of the foetus. The insertion of such clauses also raises the issue of what should happen in the event of breach of contractual conditions. Would breach entitle the commissioning couple to refuse payment or reject the baby? Could they compel the surrogate mother to abort the pregnancy? The issue is becoming more vexed as ultra sound, amniocentesis and other forms of screening throughout pregnancy are becoming more common (see Chapter 13). Although all pregnancies are increasingly subject to medical scrutiny and legal regulation, the ability of the commissioning couple to dictate terms raises the question of the exploitative nature of surrogacy. It is unlikely that women in well paid occupations would agree to become surrogate mothers, which suggests that it may be a form of commercial exploitation of women to expect them to undertake womb-leasing arrangements for other women. (See M. Radin, "Market-Inalienability" (1987)

100 *Harvard Law Review* 1849.) On the other hand, this suggestion may deny the agency and choice of the woman concerned. (See C. Shalev, *Birth Power*, New Haven: Yale University Press, 1989.) Since many feminists would argue that male/female sexual relationships are inherently unequal economic bargains, perhaps relations which are explicit in surrogacy arrangements are simply pervasive in women's condition. (See M. Freeman, "Is surrogacy exploitative?" in S. McLean (ed.), *Legal Issues in Human Reproduction*, Aldershot: Gower, 1989; U. Narayan, "The Gift of a Child: Commercial Surrogacy, Gift Surrogacy and Motherhood" in P. Boling (ed.), *Expecting Trouble: Surrogacy, Fetal Abuse and New Reproductive Technologies*, Boulder, Colorado: Westview Press, 1995.) It would, however, be easier to avoid the charge of exploitation if there was some sort of statutory regulation of the contents of surrogacy arrangements — for instance, if it could be provided that the gestational mother be allowed the same sort of revocation period available to a woman who offers her baby for adoption. A further issue is whether there is anything to prevent the insertion of a clause permitting the commissioning couple to reject the child — for example, if it is born disabled. So far, all the British cases have involved disputes where both parties want the child. An even more distressing case would be where neither party to the couple wanted the child. (The impact of surrogacy and other forms of assisted conception on the family will be considered below at pages 689–690.)

(c) *In Vitro* Fertilisation

(i) Definitions And Attitudes

Whilst AI and surrogacy are relatively low-tech procedures, which have been available in some form for years, *in vitro* fertilisation (IVF) is a recent development in the treatment of infertility, dating from the birth of the first "test-tube baby" — Louise Brown — in 1978. It is a unique form of reproductive technique in that fertilisation occurs outside the body. It thus brings the formerly invisible processes of fertilisation and early embryonic development into view, greatly extending the potential for medico-legal control of the reproductive process. IVF involves a three stage process. First, multiple ovulation is induced in the woman by hormonal treatment and ovarian stimulation. This will usually involve the administration of fertility drugs for several days from days 3–7 of a woman's menstrual cycle. In August 1996 ethical controversy was generated by the case of Mandy Allwood who allegedly became pregnant with octuplets as a result of fertility treatment which was administered without her partner's knowledge. (See "Octuplet woman's boyfriend 'not told of drugs'", *The Times*, August 12, 1996.) Following drug treatment, one or more follicles containing eggs will generally develop. Oocytes (immature eggs) or ova (mature eggs) are removed from ovarian follicles through a surgical technique known as laparoscopy. A laparoscope is a thread-like device, composed of quartz fibres, capable of transmitting light and images. Alongside a hollow needle, the laparoscope is inserted into the woman's abdomen. The ovarian follicles are located and aspirated in order to obtain the eggs. The eggs are then drawn out through the needle attached to the laparoscope. This is a surgical procedure carried out under anaesthetic. Increasingly, egg retrieval is now being undertaken through transvaginal aspiration with a local anaesthetic. Following removal, oocytes are first placed in a specially prepared culture and incubated to develop into mature eggs. Secondly, the ova are incubated with the sperm in a petri dish. A capacitating chemical may be used to endow sperm with the ability to pierce the egg's cellular wall. Thirdly, when the resulting zygote has developed to the 4–8 cell stage, it is transferred to the woman's uterine cavity in the hope that it will implant. At this stage hormonal preparation of the woman and timing of the transfer are crucial in securing a successful implantation. If it is successful, pregnancy should be detectable 10–14 days later. As will be apparent, this treatment is extremely invasive and may have a significant impact on the health of the woman undergoing it. (See J. Raymond, *Women as Wombs: Reproductive technologies and the battle over women's freedom*, New York: Harper Collins, 1994 at pages 9–14.)

Warnock Committee: *Report of the Committee of Inquiry into Human Fertilisation and Embryology* (1984) Cmnd. 9314, 1984 (footnotes omitted)

5.1 *In vitro* fertilisation (IVF) is very much a new development. Of those women who are infertile a small proportion can produce healthy eggs but, although they have a normal uterus, have damaged or diseased fallopian tubes which prevent the egg passing from the ovary to the uterus. A certain proportion of these women can be helped by tubal surgery. Until IVF became a reality, the possibility of achieving a pregnancy for women with tubal problems was not great. IVF may be appropriate perhaps for 5 per cent of infertile couples. Recently claims have been made for IVF as a treatment for other forms of infertility including its use in the treatment of oligospermia and unexplained infertility . . .

5.5 Despite the technical difficulties of IVF, at the time we write, there have been some hundreds of such births throughout the world. These births continue to exercise considerable fascination. At the same time, this public interest creates, in itself, difficulties, adding to the pressure on doctors practising in this field who are not only trying to provide a new treatment for their patients, but are also constantly working in the public eye . . .

5.10 We have reached the conclusion that IVF is an acceptable means of treating infertility and *we therefore recommend that the service of IVF should continue to be available subject to the same type of licensing and inspection as we have recommended with regard to the regulation of AID* . . . For the protection and reassurance of the public this recommendation must apply equally to IVF within the NHS and in the private medical sector. At the present time IVF is available on a limited scale within the NHS and *we recommend that IVF should continue to be available within the NHS*. One member of the Inquiry would not like to see any expansion of NHS IVF services until the results obtained in using this technique are more satisfactory. IVF requires a concentration of skilled medical and scientific expertise, and it is appropriate for only a small proportion of infertile couples. Therefore we would not argue that it should be available at all district general hospitals, or even at all university teaching hospitals. However in order to minimise travelling and other inconvenience to patients, we believe that ultimately NHS centres should be distributed throughout the United Kingdom We recognise that there will be those who will press for at least one in every region.

5.11 We are conscious that such specialised units with their distinctive organisational features, would have considerable cost implications. We are also mindful that IVF is only one of a range of treatments for infertility and . . . [that] there is scope for improvement in the provision of infertility services generally. We would not want to see IVF with its present relatively low success rate, cream off all the resources available for the treatment of infertility just because it has the glamour of novelty. Details of the financing of the service are outside our terms of reference, but these factors make it desirable that the early development of the service within the NHS be carefully monitored. *We recommend that one of the first tasks of the working group, whose establishment we recommend . . . should be to consider how best an IVF service can be organised within the NHS.*

NOTES:

1. There are a number of variations on the basic IVF procedure. In gamete intrafallopian transfer (GIFT) eggs harvested from a woman and sperm from her partner or a donor are injected into the woman's fallopian tube to enable fertilisation to occur *in vivo.* In some cases it appears to have a higher success rate than IVF, but it is not appropriate where a woman's fallopian tubes are damaged. As with IVF, ovarian hyperstimulation is a problem as is a higher risk of multiple pregnancy since it is not open to the same degree of monitoring as IVF. ZIFT is a variation of GIFT in which the fertilised egg/zygote is transferred into the fallopian tube at the pronuclear stage when it is one day old. ICSI (Intra Cytoplasmic Sperm Injection) is a technique in which a sperm is injected into an egg using a fine glass needle. The technique was pioneered in Belgium, and the Human Fertilisation and Embryology Authority in England has issued licences for clinical research into the technique.

2. It would appear that GIFT and ZIFT fall outside the regulatory scheme of the 1990 Act, as section 1(3) states that the Act "applies only to keeping or using an embryo outside the human body". However, the difficulty of determining precisely when fertilisation takes place means that there is a possibility with GIFT that fertilisation could occur outside the body, thus bringing it within the regulatory scheme of the Act. (See G. Douglas, *Law, Fertility and Reproduction* London: Sweet and Maxwell, 1991, at pages 117–8, and D. Morgan, "Assisted conception and clinical practice: whose freedom is it?" (1990) 140 New L.J. 600.

3. On the prevalence of GIFT see the 1995 Annual Report of the Human Fertilisation and Embryology Authority. It reported results of a survey undertaken to ascertain the extent to which GIFT was being carried out in unlicensed clinics. It concluded that virtually all GIFT treatments were carried out in licensed clinics where there was no evidence of inappropriate use. However, the issue is being kept under

review, and the Secretary of State has power to make it a licensable activity by regulation. For an argument that GIFT should be regulated, see D. Morgan and R. Lee, *Blackstone's Guide to the Human Fertilisation and Embryology Act 1990*, London: Blackstone Press, 1991, at pages 126–136.)

4. A much contested issue is the success rate of IVF. Even proponents of the technologies have to admit that success rates for IVF are low, and that they vary tremendously from one clinic to another. As rates of miscarriage are high (c. 28 per cent) the most satisfactory measure is the "live birth" rate. 1995 figures show that, on average, licensed clinics in Britain had a live birth rate of 14.2 per cent. The live birth rate in clinics providing more than 100 courses of treatment per year varied from 4.8 per cent to 23.3 per cent. (See the Human Fertilisation and Embryology Authority, *The Patient's Guide to AI and IVF Clinics*, London: HFEA, 1995.) A number of commentators note that the popularity of and huge demand for IVF is surprising, since it is stressful, expensive if carried out privately, necessitates an invasive surgical technique, has a number of side-effects ranging from dizziness to ovarian hyperstimulation and cysts and the possibility of ovarian cancer, and its success rates are low. (See J. Raymond, *Women as Wombs: Reproductive Technologies and the Battle over Women's Freedom*, San Francisco: HarperCollins, 1993, Chapter 1.)

5. A further problem with IVF, fuelled by concern about success rates, has been the issue of multiple order births. Under the HFEA Code of Practice (paragraph 7.9) clinics are limited to implanting three embryos, in order to reduce the problems of selective reduction (see Chapter 13). However, a clinic's success rate can be enhanced if several women have two or three babies as a result of a single IVF treatment. This introduces a potential conflict between the interests of the woman and clinic, as pressure to publish high success rates may lead clinics to downplay the adverse consequences which multiple pregnancy may have for the health of the pregnant woman.

QUESTIONS:

1. To what extent should societal resources be devoted to developing techniques for the alleviation of infertility? (Bear in mind the question, mooted at page 628, above, whether infertility can be classified as a disease for the purposes of section 128 of the National Health Service Act 1977.) Is such expense justified when the "solutions" work only for a relatively small percentage of those seeking treatment? Given the low success rates and risks to health would there ever be any justification for preventing people who are willing to pay for such treatment themselves from doing so?

2. In the light of factors like the low success rate, expense and risks of IVF treatment, what factors do you think account for its popularity?

Given these factors do you think that there is a problem in ensuring that consent to IVF treatment is truly voluntary? (See Chapter 6, pages 367–371 and B. J. Berg, "Listening to the Voices of the Infertile" in J. C. Callaghan (ed.), *Reproduction, Ethics and the Law: Feminist Perspectives*, Bloomington and Indianapolis: Indiana University press, 1995.)

3. Is IVF sufficiently proven to qualify as medical treatment or ought it more properly to be regarded as research? (See Chapter 10.)

(ii) Statutory Control of In Vitro Fertilisation

THE HUMAN FERTILISATION AND EMBRYOLOGY AUTHORITY:
A crucial aspect of the 1990 Act was the establishment of a new statutory licensing authority — the Human Fertilisation and Embryology Authority (HFEA) — to monitor and control research and the provision of infertility services. It replaced the Voluntary (later Interim) Licensing Authority which had operated since the publication of the Warnock report. (For further detail see J. Gunning and V. English, *Human* In Vitro *Fertilisation: A Case Study in the Regulation of Medical Innovation*, Aldershot: Dartmouth, 1993.) Its principal duty is to license and monitor, by means of a licensing system, any research or treatment which involves the creation, keeping and using of human embryos outside the body, or the storage or donation of human eggs and sperm. Its other duties include maintaining a register of information about gamete and embryo donors, and children born as a result of such treatment. It also provides advice to the Secretary of State for Health on developments concerning infertility services and embryology and the formulation of a Code of Practice. The Act aimed to ensure that there would be substantial lay representation on the Authority. The HFEA currently licenses 123 clinics for treatment (IVF and DI) and/or storage of gametes and embryos. Of these, 73 are licensed for IVF treatment, 38 for donor insemination only and 11 for the storage of sperm only. There are 25 research projects undertaken at 12 licensed clinics. (See Human Fertilisation and Embryology Authority, *Fourth Annual Report*, 1995.) (On the significance of the Authority's role, see D. Morgan and R. Lee, *Blackstone's Guide to the Human Fertilisation and Embryology Act*, London: Blackstone Press, 1991, Chapter 4.)

Human Fertilisation and Embryology Act 1990, s.5(1–3)

5.—(1) There shall be a body corporate called the Human Fertilisation and Embryology Authority.
(2) The Authority shall consist of —

(a) a chairman and deputy chairman, and
(b) such number of other members as the Secretary of State appoints.

(3) Schedule 1 to this Act (which deals with membership of the Authority, etc) shall have effect.

Schedule 1

4.—(1) All the members of the Authority (including the chairman and deputy chairman who shall be appointed as such) shall be appointed by the Secretary of State.

(2) In making the appointments the Secretary of State shall have regard to the desirability of ensuring that the proceedings of the Authority, and the discharge of its functions, are informed by the views of both men and women.

(3) The following persons are disqualified from being appointed as chairman or deputy chairman of the Authority —

(a) any person who is, or has been, a medical practitioner registered under the Medical Act 1983 (whether fully, provisionally or with limited registration), or under any repealed enactment from which a provision of that Act is derived,

(b) any person who is, or has been, concerned with keeping or using gametes or embryos outside the body, and

(c) any person who is, or has been, directly connected with commissioning or funding any research involving such keeping or use, or has actively participated in any decision to do so.

(4) The Secretary of State shall secure that at least one-third but fewer than half of the other members of the Authority fall within sub-paragraph (3)(a), (b) or (c) above, and that at least one member falls within each of paragraphs (a) and (b).

THE LEGISLATIVE FRAMEWORK:

The introductory sections of the Act lay down the basic framework of the regulatory scheme.

Human Fertilisation and Embryology Act 1990, ss.1–4

1.—(1) In this Act, except where otherwise stated —

(a) embryo means a live human embryo where fertilisation is complete, and

(b) references to an embryo include an egg in the process of fertilisation and, for this purpose, fertilisation is not complete until the appearance of a two cell zygote.

(2) This Act, so far as it governs bringing about the creation of an embryo, applies only to bringing about the creation of an embryo outside the human body; and in this Act —

(a) references to embryos the creation of which was brought about *in vitro* (in their application to those where fertilisation is complete) are to those where fertilisation began outside the human body whether or not it was completed there, and

(b) references to embryos taken from a woman do not include embryos whose creation was brought about *in vitro*.

(3) This Act, so far as it governs the keeping or use of an embryo, applies only to keeping or using an embryo outside the human body.

(4) References in this Act to gametes, eggs or sperm, except where otherwise stated, are to live human gametes, eggs or sperm but references below in this Act to gametes or eggs do not include eggs in the process of fertilisation.

2.—(1) In this Act —

"the Authority" means the Human Fertilisation and Embryology Authority established under section 5 of this Act, . . .

"licence" means a licence under Schedule 2 to this act and, . . .

"treatment services" means medical, surgical or obstetric services provided to the public or a section of the public for the purpose of assisting women to carry children.

(2) Reference in this Act to keeping, in relation to embryos or gametes, include keeping while preserved, whether preserved by cryopreservation or in any other way; and embryos or gametes so kept are referred to in this Act as "stored" (and "store" and "storage" are to be interpreted accordingly).

(3) For the purpose of this Act, a woman is not to be treated as carrying a child until the embryo has become implanted.

3.—(1) No person shall —

(a) bring about the creation of an embryo or
(b) keep or use an embryo, except in pursuance of a licence.

(2) No person shall place in a woman:

(a) a live embryo other than a human embryo, or
(b) any live gametes other than human gametes.

(3) A licence cannot authorise:

(a) keeping or using an embryo after the appearance of the primitive streak,
(b) placing an embryo in any animal,
(c) keeping or using an embryo in any circumstances in which regulations prohibit its keeping or use, or
(d) replacing a nucleus of a cell of an embryo with a nucleus taken from a cell of any person, embryo or subsequent development of an embryo.

(4) For the purpose of subsection (3)(a) above, the primitive streak is to be taken to have appeared in an embryo not later than the end of the period of 14 days beginning with the day when the gametes are mixed, not counting any time during which the embryo is stored.

3A.—No person shall, for the purposes of providing fertility services for any woman, use female germlines taken or derived from an embryo or a foetus or use embryos created by using such cells.

4.—(1) No person shall —

(a) store any gametes, or
(b) in the course of providing treatment services for any woman, use the sperm of any man unless the services are being provided for the woman and the man together or use the eggs of any other woman, or
(c) mix gametes with the live gametes of any animal,
except in pursuance of a licence.

(2) A licence cannot authorise storing or using gametes in any circumstances in which regulations prohibit their storage or use.

(3) No person shall place sperm and eggs in a woman in any circumstances specified in regulations except in pursuance of a licence.

(4) Regulations made by virtue of subsection (3) above may provide that, in relation to licences only to place sperm and eggs in a woman in such circumstances, sections 12 to 22 of this Act shall have effect with such modifications as may be specified in the regulations.

(5) Activities regulated by this section or section 3 of this Act are referred to in this Act as "activities governed by this Act".

Schedule 2

1.—(1) A licence under this paragraph may authorise any of the following in the course of providing treatment services —

(a) bringing about the creation of embryos *in vitro*,
(b) keeping embryos,
(c) using gametes,
(d) practices designed to secure that embryos are in a suitable condition to be placed in a woman or to determine whether embryos are suitable for that purpose
(e) placing any embryo in a woman
(f) mixing sperm with the eggs of a hamster, or other animal specified in directions, for the purpose of testing the fertility or normality of the sperm, but only where anything which forms is destroyed when the test is complete and, in any event, not later than the two cell stage, and
(g) such other practices as may be specified in, or determined in accordance with, regulations.

(2) Subject to the provisions of this Act, a licence under this paragraph may be granted subject to such conditions as may be specified in the licence and may authorise the performance of any of the activities referred to in sub-paragraph (1) above in such manner as may be so specified.

(3) A licence under this paragraph cannot authorise any activity unless it appears to the Authority to be necessary or desirable for the purpose of providing treatment services.

(4) A licence under this paragraph cannot authorise altering the genetic structure of any cell while it forms part of an embryo.

(5) A licence under this paragraph shall be granted for such period not exceeding five years as may be specified in the licence.

NOTES:

1. Sections 3 and 4 define actions which cannot be licensed, whereas Schedule 2 lists activities which may be the subject of licences.
2. Subsections 3(2) and (3) are designed to dispel fears about the creation of a *Brave New World* scenario. Section 3A was inserted by section 156 of the Criminal Justice and Public Order Act 1994, in response to fears that the shortage of donated eggs for treatment of infertile women would lead to the use of eggs obtained from aborted female foetuses. The provision bans the use of foetal eggs, or embryos derived from foetal germlines (eggs), in fertility treatment. (See Commentary by A. Grubb, [1995] 3 *Medical Law Review*, pages 203–4; A. Plomer and N. Martin Clement, "The limits of beneficence: egg donation under the Human Fertilisation and Embryology Act 1990" (1995) 15 *Legal Studies* 434.) The fact that this provision was introduced as a late amendment to a criminal justice statute which otherwise had nothing to do with infertility treatment illustrates the vagaries of the legislative process in this area.

(iii) Sanctions for Breach of the 1990 Act

A breach of any of the provisions of the 1990 Act is punishable as a criminal offence. Sections 16–22 of the Act deal with the procedure for granting licences and the situations in which licences may be revoked, varied, refused or suspended. Under section 25(6) failure to observe provisions of the *Code of Practice* may be taken into account by the licence committee in deciding whether to vary or revoke a licence. Where there is an alleged or apparent breach of the Act, or of a Direction issued by the Authority, or of its *Code of Practice*, the HFEA makes preliminary enquiries to establish whether there is *prima facie* evidence of a breach. Information will then be referred to a licence committee which will decide what further action, if any, needs to be taken. Where there is the possibility that a criminal offence may have been committed, a decision will be taken whether to refer the matter to the Director of Public Prosecutions. Since its establishment the HFEA has revoked one licence and refused to renew two others. It has also refused to grant several applications for new licences or to vary existing ones. (See Human Fertilisation and Embryology Authority, *Fourth Annual Report*, London: HFEA, 1995, pages 9–10.)

Human Fertilisation and Embryology Act 1990, s.41(1–4), (10–11), s.25(6)

41.—(1) A person who —

(a) contravenes section 3(2) or 4(1)(c) of this Act, or
(b) does anything which, by virtue of section 3(3) of this Act, cannot be authorised by a licence,

is guilty of an offence and liable on conviction on indictment to imprisonment for a term not exceeding ten years or a fine or both.
　(2) A person who —

(a) contravenes section 3(1) of this Act, otherwise than by doing something which, by virtue of section 3(3) of this Act, cannot be authorised by a licence,
(b) keeps or uses any gametes in contravention of section 4(1)(a) or (b) of this Act,
(c) contravenes section 4(3) of this Act . . .

is guilty of an offence.
　(3) If a person:

(a) provides any information for the purposes of a grant of a licence, being information which is false or misleading in a material particular, and
(b) either he knows the information to be false and misleading in a material particular or he provides the information recklessly,
he is guilty of an offence.

(4) A person guilty of an offence under subsection (2) or (3) above is liable —

(a) on conviction on indictment, to imprisonment for a term not exceeding two years or a fine or both, and

(b) on summary conviction, to imprisonment for a term not exceeding six months or a fine not exceeding the statutory maximum or both . . .

[Sub-sections 41(5)-(9) deal with offences in relation to failure to comply with provisions of the Act relating to confidentiality, inspections and appeals.]

(10) It is a defence for a person ("the defendant") charged with an offence of doing anything which, under section 3(1) or 4(1) of this act, cannot be done except in pursuance of a licence to prove —

(a) that the defendant was acting under the direction of another, and
(b) that the defendant believed on reasonable grounds —
  (i) that the other person was at the material time the person responsible under a licence, a person designated by virtue of section 17(2)(b) of this Act as a person to whom a licence applied, or a person to whom directions had been given by virtue of section 24(9) of this Act, and
  (ii) that the defendant was authorised by virtue of the licence or directions to do the thing in question.

(11) It is a defence for a person charged with an offence under this Act to prove —

(a) that at the material time he was a person to whom a licence applied or to whom directions had been given, and
(b) that he took all such steps as were reasonable and exercised all due diligence to avoid committing the offence.

25.—(6) A failure on the part of any person to observe any provision of the [*Code of Practice*] shall not of itself render the person liable to any proceedings, but —

(a) a licence committee shall, in considering whether there has been any failure to comply with any conditions of a licence and, in particular, conditions requiring anything to be "proper" or "suitable", take account of any relevant provision of the code, and
(b) a licence committee may, in considering, where it has power to do so, whether or not to vary or revoke a licence, take into account any observations of or failure to observe the provision of the code.

(iv) Conscientious Objection

Health care professionals who object on moral grounds to being involved in the provision of treatment services are provided, under the Act, with a basis on which to object to such participation.

Human Fertilisation and Embryology Act 1990

38.—(1) No person who has a conscientious objection to participating in any activity governed by this Act shall be under any duty however arising, to do so.
(2) In any legal proceedings the burden of proof of conscientious objection shall rest on the person claiming to rely on it.

The Human Fertilisation and Embryology Authority, Code of Practice (Revised December 18, 1995)

1.15 Anyone who can show a conscientious objection to any of the activities governed by the Act is not obliged to participate in them.

1.16 Prospective employees should be provided with a full description of all the activities carried out at the centre. Interviewers should raise the issue of conscientious objection during the recruitment process and explain the right of staff to object.

NOTE:

1. A similar right of conscientious objection applies in the case of abortion (see Chapter 12; generally on the ethics of conscientious objection see Chapter 2 at pages 139–141).

(v) Access to IVF Services

The test of child welfare has been used to limit access to IVF treatment. In this area of the law, as in general with laws concerning children (see Chapter 7) the policy has been to declare the best interests of the potential child to be paramount. Those seeking access to treatment services will be screened by treatment centres to assess their suitability. In practice access is also governed by the individual policies of each clinic, operating under the guidance of Ethics Committees. They are also put into practice by individual consultants. This question of access has proven to be one of the most controversial aspects of debates concerning the right to reproduce. Views on this issue were canvassed in the two reports which follow.

Warnock Committee: *Report of the Committee of Inquiry into Human Fertilisation and Embryology* (1984) Cmnd. 9314

2.5 It is sometimes suggested that infertility treatment should be available only to married couples, in the interests of any child that may be born as a result. While we are vitally aware of the need to protect these interests, we are not prepared to recommend that access to treatment should be based exclusively on the legal status of marriage.

2.6 In discussing treatment for infertility, this report takes the term *couple* to mean a heterosexual couple living together in a stable relationship, whether married or not. We use the words *husband and wife* to denote a relationship, not a legal status (except where the context makes differentiation necessary, for example in relation to legitimacy) . . .

2.9 . . . the various techniques for assisted reproduction offer not only a remedy for infertility, but also offer the fertile single woman or lesbian couple the chance of parenthood without the direct involvement of a male partner. To judge from the evidence, many believe that the interests of the child dictate that it should be born into a home where there is a loving, stable, heterosexual relationship and that, therefore, the *deliberate* creation of a child for a woman who is not a partner in such a relationship is morally wrong. On the other side some expressed the view that a single woman or lesbian couple have a right under the European Convention to have children even though those children may have no legal father. It is further argued that it is already accepted that a single person, whether man or woman, can in certain circumstances provide a suitable environment for a child, since the existence of single adoptive parents is specifically provided for in the Children Act 1975.

2.10 In the same way that a single woman may believe she has a right to motherhood, so a single man may feel he has a right to fatherhood. Though the feminist position is perhaps more frequently publicised, we were told of a group of single, mainly homosexual, men who were campaigning for the right to bring up a child. Their primary aim at present is to obtain in practice equal rights in the adoption field, but they are also well aware of the potential of surrogacy for providing a single man with a child that is genetically his. There have been cases in other countries of surrogacy in such circumstances. It can be argued that as a matter of sex equality if single women are not totally barred from parenthood, then neither should single men be so barred.

2.11 We have considered these arguments, but nevertheless, we believe that as a general rule it is better for children to be born into a two-parent family, with both father and mother, although we recognise that it is impossible to predict with any certainty how lasting such a relationship will be.

2.12 We have considered very carefully whether there are circumstances where it is inappropriate for treatment which is solely for the alleviation of infertility to be provided. In general we hold that everyone should be entitled to seek expert advice and appropriate investigation. This will usually involve referral to a consultant. However, at the present time services for the treatment of infertility are in short supply, both for initial referral and investigation and for the more specialized treatments considered in this report. In this situation of scarcity some individuals will have a more compelling case for treatment than others. In the circumstances, medical practitioners will, clearly, use their clinical judgment as to the priority of the individual case bearing in mind such considerations as the patient's age, the duration of infertility and the likelihood that treatment will be successful. So far this is not contentious. However, notwithstanding our view that every patient is entitled to advice and investigation of his or her infertility, we can foresee occasions where the consultant may, after discussion with professional health and social work colleagues, consider that there are valid reasons why infertility treatment would not be in the best interests of the patient, the child that may be born following treatment, or the patient's immediate family.

Compare the approach adopted by the Warnock Committee with that adopted in the following report:

"Fertility and the Family": The Glover Report on Reproductive Technologies to the European Commission, London: Fourth Estate, 1989

3. Some people think that reproductive technology should only be available in the 'standard' case of the infertile couple. Others disagree. A doctor who wants to stick to helping the infertile couple should of course be free to follow his or her conscience. But what should we say about a doctor or clinic deciding to give help in the non-standard cases? Are they doing good by helping satisfy the need for children in women who would previously have been denied them? Or are they doing something to which there are ethical objections?

The non-standard cases are not all the same, and it may be consistent to take one view of the widow and a different one of the lesbian couple. We will here briefly take the case of the lesbian couple as an example. This is an interesting case for its possible impact on how the family is to evolve . . .

. . . it is surely right to be predisposed in favour of anything that removes some of the barriers against homosexuals having a fulfilled family life. Lesbians who want to have children are not different in their needs from heterosexual women. Like many other women, lesbians may care about what adoption does not provide: having a child genetically theirs and to whom they give birth. They may care as much about having *their* children as an infertile wife, and their lives may be as much enriched by such children as anyone else's.

4. Removal of discrimination against homosexuals in such a fundamental matter would be a great gain. But obviously there are strong grounds for unease about reproductive help where the family circumstances may impose a serious handicap on the child. The anxieties are based partly on the child's own interests, and partly on the social impact of the spread of such families. Everything depends on how well founded these anxieties are. People differ over the hypothesis that children born through AID to one of a lesbian couple are likely to be at a disadvantage. Some think that, in the light of what we know of human nature, the hypothesis is very plausible, while others think there is no such presumption in favour of it.

The fullest study we have been able to find is suggestive, but not conclusive (Golombok, Spencer and Rutter: *Journal of Child Psychology and Psychiatry*, 1983). Thirty-seven children aged between five and seventeen, being brought up in twenty-seven lesbian households, were compared with thirty-eight children in twenty-seven single-parent families, being brought up by a heterosexual mother. Psychosexual and psychiatric appraisals were based on interviews with the children, on interviews with the mothers, and on questionnaires given to the mothers and to teachers. The two groups did not differ in gender identity: all the children said they were glad to be the sex they were. (But gender identity is usually established at an early age, and in some cases *could* have been established before the lesbian partnership was set up). The two groups did not differ in sex-role behaviour. And there were no signs of differences in sexual orientation between the two groups . . .

These negative findings suggest that anxieties about the effects of being brought up in a lesbian family may be unfounded. But they cannot completely exclude the hypothesis of disadvantage . . .

Rather little is known with certainty of the effects of lesbian parenthood. On the one hand, this is an argument for caution. But, on the other hand, it can be an argument for letting the future shape of the family evolve experimentally. No doubt people should be discouraged from taking high risks of major family disasters. And it goes without saying that new forms of family life must only be tried voluntarily. But, subject to these qualifications, we prefer a society predisposed in favour of 'experiments in living' to one in which they are stifled.

We may find that *not* all happy families are alike.

QUESTIONS:

1. Could Articles 8 and 12 of the European Convention on Human Rights (see page 624 above) be interpreted as affording a right to provision of infertility services by the state? (See G. Douglas, *Law, Fertility and Reproduction*, London: Sweet & Maxwell, 1991, Chapter 2.) Are resources more likely to be devoted to infertility services if they are conceptualised as health care issues, rather than being concerned with rights to privacy or to found a family? (See pages 623–626 above.)

2. Should the provision of fertility services be available only to those who are proven to be infertile? Would such a position unacceptably discriminate against fertile lesbians and single women? (See K. Dawson and P. Singer, "Should fertile people have access to *in vitro* fertilisation?" (1990) 300 *British Medical Journal* 167.)

3. The Warnock Committee referred to "the feminist position" on single motherhood. Is single motherhood only a feminist issue? What is "the feminist position" on single motherhood and how adequately did Warnock address it?

4. Should decisions about who will receive infertility treatment services be left in the hands of medical practitioners? Given that the Warnock Committee accepted that such judgments were not purely medical, was it justifiable to leave responsibility to doctors? (See S. Millns, "Making 'social judgments that go beyond the purely medical': The Reproductive Revolution and Access to Fertility Treatment Services" in J. Bridgeman and S. Millns (eds), *Law and Body Politics,* Aldershot: Dartmouth, 1995; I. Kennedy, "What is a Medical Decision" in *Treat Me Right: Essays in Medical Law and Ethics,* Oxford: Oxford University Press, 1988.)

The following action for judicial review of the decision-making process was brought by a candidate who was not selected for IVF treatment. It arose out of the criteria then used at St Mary's hospital in Manchester.

R v. Ethical Committee of St Mary's Hospital (Manchester), ex p. Harriott, [1988] 1 F.L.R. 512, [1988] Fam. Law. 165

Mrs H was experiencing difficulty in becoming pregnant and had applied to her local authority's social services department to adopt or foster a child. Her application was turned down, because of the applicant's criminal record (which included soliciting for prostitution) and her allegedly poor understanding of the role of a foster-parent. She subsequently applied for IVF under the National Health Service and once again her application was refused. She unsuccessfully sought judicial review of the decision to refuse her treatment alleging that it was reached by the wrong body, and that she was not given adequate opportunity to make representation.

SCHIEMANN J.:
" . . . In the spirit of [the Warnock] report, a local committee exists at St Mary's Hospital, Manchester. Its constitution and functions were decided in June 1985, although it evolved from separate committees of those individuals providing IVF and AID/AIH . . . services at the hospital . . . It is clear that the committee, with its wide range of expertise, is intended as an advisory rather than a decision-making body . . .
    The Notice of Application . . . seeks amongst other things to quash an alleged decision of the committee . . . to remove the applicant from the hospital's IVF programme. The applicant also seeks relief against the managers of the regional IVF unit. The operational policy of that unit is in evidence before me. Although I am about to read from a document which was not approved until November 18, 1985, it embodied what was already the practice of the IVF unit.   Under the heading 'Operational Policy' there are four subheadings. The first is 'Waiting List', the second, 'Treatment', the third 'Future Development' and the fourth 'Ethical Committee'. Paragraphs 1 and 4 under the heading 'Waiting List' read as follows:
    '1. Couples are accepted on to the waiting list to be considered for treatment only after referral via the recognized medical channels (in practice, their general practitioner or gynaecological consultant). Acceptance on to this waiting list is based on the available medical/social information and the unit reserves the right to remove a couple's names from the waiting list and to decline treatment at any subsequent stage should any further information indicate the need to do so.

4. (1) Couples accepted on to the waiting list must, in the ordinary course of events, satisfy the general criteria established by adoption societies in assessing suitability for adoption. (2) There must be no medical, psychiatric or psychosexual problems which would indicate an increased probability of a couple not being able to provide satisfactory parenting to the offspring or endanger the mother's life or health if she became pregnant.'

The part dealing with the Ethical Committee reads as follows:

'An Infertility Services Ethical Committee exists within the hospital. The committee was established in the spirit of the Warnock Report on Human Fertilization and Embryology. The committee provides a forum for those who provide infertility services to discuss issues of concern and seek advice and guidance. The committee meets quarterly.'

It is important to note at the outset that no complaint is made by Mr Blom Cooper on behalf of the applicant as to the policy that couples accepted on to the waiting list must, in the ordinary course of events, satisfy the general criteria established by adoption societies in assessing suitability for adoption.

I turn now to deal with the main dates with which I am concerned. On 26 January, 1983 the applicant was put on the waiting list for in vitro fertilisation.

In March 1984 a laparoscopy was performed upon the applicant.

On 18 July, 1984, she was seen for the first time in the IVF unit. On that date Dr Buck became aware that the applicant had in the past sought to adopt children, but had been refused, although the reasons for such refusals were not then given to Dr Buck. The length of time between being put on the waiting list and this first interview is explained in an affidavit sworn on behalf of the respondent as follows:

' . . . the mere fact of being placed upon the waiting list did not mean that the applicant had been accepted for treatment: given the necessarily limited resources of the IVF unit and the demands upon it, a waiting list was (and is) inevitable and persons on it were (and are) not able to be seen immediately in relation to their suitability for treatment.'

On 29 August, 1984 the applicant was seen by Mrs Schryber, a counsellor attached to the IVF unit. At that interview, the applicant for the first time disclosed her past convictions in relation to prostitution and running a brothel. Following that interview Dr Buck understood the reason for the past refusal of permission to adopt to be these convictions. It appears that while the convictions played a part in persuading the authority not to grant permission, they were not the only matters. In any event, before 11 December, 1984 Dr Buck decided that the applicant should not be given the IVF treatment and should be taken off the waiting list.

On 11 December, 1984 Dr Buck saw the applicant and informed her that she would be unable to treat her because of some infection in her husband's semen. The true reason for the refusal to treat her was, perhaps, out of a sense of delicacy, not revealed to the lady. In that interview the applicant complained of various symptoms which caused Dr Buck to carry out, inter alia, liver function tests and to consider whether the applicant might be consuming excessive amounts of alcohol. The results of those liver function tests were abnormal.

On 10 January, 1985, Dr Buck saw the applicant to discuss the same to ask the applicant about her consumption of alcohol. Dr Buck then gave the liver abnormality as another reason for the applicant not being able to have IVF treatment. Again she failed to mention the real reason. On 15 March, 1985 the Ethical Committee met for the first time. On 20 June, 1985 Dr Buck saw the applicant again, and again told her that she would not be given treatment, but again the true reason was not revealed.

On 16 September, 1985 the committee met once more. It seems probable that the case of the applicant was mentioned . . .

On 20 September, 1985 or about this time in any event, the applicant and her husband were, for the first time, informed of the actual reason for the decision of Drs Lieberman and Buck. They were advised that the unit was unable to offer them treatment in view of the refusal by adoption agencies to consider placing children with them . . .

With that background, it is convenient to consider separately the position of the committee and that of Dr Buck. So far as the committee is concerned, Mr Blom Cooper accepts that there was no statutory duty on anyone to set up the committee and that there was no statutory duty imposed on the committee either to decide or advise. He accepts that in fact the committee have no power to decide whether or not a particular treatment should be offered to a particular individual. He does not suggest that the general policy pursued by the regional IVF unit, namely, that 'couples accepted on to the waiting list must, in the ordinary course of events, satisfy the general criteria established by adoption societies in assessing suitability for adoptions' is in any way illegal. He submits, however, that once the committee had been asked for advice on whether a treatment should be given to a particular individual, the committee was obliged itself to investigate the matter and give advice following such investigation. He points out that the membership of the committee was such that it was well placed to give advice and perhaps better placed than an obstetrician and a gynaecologist.

I do not accept Mr Blom Cooper's submission. In my judgment, the committee's function was to provide a forum for discussion amongst professionals. It is essentially an informal body. If the committee in a particular case refuses to give advice or does not have a majority view as to what advice should be given, then I do not consider that the courts can compel it to give advice or to embark upon a particular investigation.

Mr Bell, for the committee, submitted that judicial review does not lie to review any advice given by the committee. As at present advised, I would be doubtful about accepting that submission in its full breadth. If the committee had advised, for instance, that the IVF unit should in principle refuse all such treatment to anyone who was a jew or coloured, then I think the courts might well grant a declaration that such a policy was illegal . . . But I do not need to consider that situation in this case. Here the complaint is that the committee's advice was that the consultant must make up her own mind as to whether the treatment should be given. That advice was, in my judgment, unobjectionable.

Mr Blom Cooper's second complaint about the committee is a procedural one. He submits that the committee should have given the applicant an opportunity to put evidence and submissions before the committee. I also reject that submission. If I am right in holding that the committee was entitled not to give advice and that it was set up to provide a forum for professionals to talk things over and to provide general guidelines, then I think the court should be slow, if indeed it has the power, to force such a committee to receive representations before it decides not to give advice . . .

I turn now to consider the position of the consultant. The complaint against her is entirely a procedural one. Mr Blom Cooper submits that when a consultant is making a decision removing a woman from the IVF list and is taking that decision on social grounds, either exclusively or mainly where those social grounds involve issues of contested fact, then the doctor has a duty to act fairly.

Mr Bell submits that the doctor/patient relationship is outside the purview of administrative law. I am prepared for the purposes of this judgment to assume that Mr Blom Cooper's submission is correct in law. But even on that assumption, I am not prepared to grant his client any relief. I can see arguable grounds for criticism of Dr Buck's decision in December 1984 not to treat the applicant. That decision was made without first giving her an opportunity to try to establish that the case was an extraordinary one in some way and that, therefore, the applicant should be accepted for treatment notwithstanding that she did not satisfy the general criteria established by adoption societies in assessing suitability for adoptions. I can see further arguable grounds for criticism of Dr Buck's decision not to inform the applicant of the true reason for refusal until September 1985. She was misled and is understandably furious that time went by in what now appears to have been shadow-boxing. However, it must be remembered that decisions by doctors as to whether to give or refuse treatment are not ones which, once made, render the doctor powerless to change her view in the light of new arguments and new facts. I consider that the applicant has since that time had opportunities to put more information in front of Dr Buck and the Health Authority. She has used those opportunities. I have no reason to suppose that they have acted unfairly in the matter or shut their ears to her representations in the sense of being unwilling to entertain them. It is not, and could not be, suggested that no reasonable consultant could have come to the decision to refuse treatment to the applicant.

In those circumstances, I see no reason to grant the applicant the relief she seeks against the consultant, namely, an order requiring the consultant to consider her case after giving her a further opportunity to make representations. In consequence, I do not need to decide the question whether or not in principle judicial review will lie in respect of such a decision."

NOTE:

1. This case demonstrates that issues of resource allocation must always be addressed on a number of levels. At the macro level, decisions are taken regarding whether particular services should be provided at all. It is only when the decision is made to provide a service that micro allocation questions arise as to whether particular patients should be given treatment. Thus, but for the fact that Manchester was one of the first areas in the United Kingdom that has fully funded IVF services on the NHS, this question might never have arisen.

QUESTIONS:

1. Is it meaningful to talk of the welfare of an unborn child, or is the welfare test too artificial to be workable in this context?
2. In what ways, if any, is the welfare of a child threatened by the fact that his mother has convictions for prostitution? Does the thrust of the judgment imply that workers in the sex industry should not be allowed to become parents?
3. Is the model of adoption an appropriate one to use in assessing the suitability of persons seeking infertility services? (See G. Douglas, *Law, Fertility and Reproduction*, London: Sweet and Maxwell, 1991, Chapter 6.)
4. As a result of the decision in *ex p. Harriott*, it would seem that an IVF clinic which denies treatment to an ex-prostitute is acting reasonably; but one which denies treatment to members of ethnic minorities is introducing unlawful and irrelevant considerations. Would a reasonable IVF clinic debar a white couple from having a black or mixed race child?
5. Does the *ex p. Harriott* decision offer any solace to parties aggrieved by the decision to deny them treatment? (See D. Longley, *Public Law and Health Service Accountability*, Buckingham: Open University Press, 1993.)

6. Although the case was decided before the 1990 Act came into force, do you think there would be any significant difference in how the case would be decided now? Should there have been provision in the Act for a review mechanism, so that aggrieved parties could appeal against a decision to deny them treatment? (See Chapter 1 on the issue of the right to treatment.)

Perhaps surprisingly, very little mention was made in the 1990 Act of eligibility for treatment or the best interests of the resultant child.

Human Fertilisation and Embryology Act 1990

13.—(5) A woman shall not be provided with treatment services unless account has been taken of the welfare of any child who may be born as a result of the treatment (including the need of that child for a father), and of any child who may be affected by the birth.

QUESTIONS:

1. Does section 13(5) provide adequate guidance about how to assess the best interests of the child? Should fuller guidance have been contained in the statute or was it appropriate to leave it to the *Code of Practice*?
2. Is the need of a child for a father so significant that it should be the only factor specifically referred to in the legislation with regard to child welfare?

When the HFEA Code of Practice was revised in December 1995 the guidelines on the welfare of the child were reviewed to give fuller guidance on assessing the future child's welfare and require that centres have clear written procedures.

HFEA, *Code of Practice* (1995)

3.14 Centres should have clear written procedures to follow for assessing the welfare of the potential child and of any other child who may be affected. The HFE Act does not exclude any category of woman from being considered for treatment. Centres should take note in their procedures of the importance of a stable and supportive environment for any child produced as a result of treatment.

3.15 Centres should take all reasonable steps to ascertain who would be legally responsible for any child born as a result of the procedure and who it is intended will be bringing up the child. When clients come from abroad, centres should not assume that the law of the country relating to the parentage of a child born as a result of donated gametes is the same as that of the United Kingdom.

3.16 People seeking treatment are entitled to a fair and unprejudiced assessment of their situation and needs, which should be conducted with the skill and sensitivity appropriate to the delicacy of the case and the wishes and feelings of those involved.

3.17 Where people seek licensed treatment, centres should bear in mind the following factors:

(a) their commitment to having and bringing up a child or children;
(b) their ability to provide a stable and supportive environment for any child produced as a result of treatment;
(c) their medical histories and the medical histories of their families;
(d) their ages and likely future ability to look after or provide for a child's needs;
(e) their ability to meet the needs of any child or children who may be born as a result of treatment, including the implications of any possible multiple births;
(f) any risk of harm to the child or children who may be born, including the risk of inherited disorders, problems during pregnancy and of neglect or abuse; and
(g) the effect of a new baby or babies upon any existing child of the family.

3.18 Where people seek treatment using donated gametes, centres should also take the following factors into account:

(a) a child's potential need to know about their origins and whether or not the prospective parents are prepared for the questions which may arise while the child is growing up;
(b) the possible attitudes of other members of the family towards the child, and towards their status in the family;
(c) the implications for the welfare of the child if the donor is personally known within the child's family and social circle; and
(d) any possibility known to the centre of a dispute about the legal fatherhood of the child . . .

3.18 Further factors will require consideration in the following cases:

(a) where the child will have no legal father. Centres are required to have regard to the child's need for a father and should pay particular attention to the prospective mother's ability to meet the child's needs throughout their childhood. Where appropriate, centres should consider particularly whether there is anyone else within the prospective mother's family and social circle willing and able to share the responsibility for meeting those needs, and for bringing up, maintaining and caring for the child.
(b) where it is the intention that the child will not be brought up by the carrying mother. In this case, centres should bear in mind that *either* the carrying mother and in certain circumstances her husband or partner, *or* the commissioning parents may become the child's legal parents. Centres should therefore consider the factors listed in paragraphs 3.17 and 3.18 as applicable in relation to all those involved, and any risk of disruption to the child's early care and upbringing should there be a dispute between them. Centres should also take into account the effect of the proposed arrangement on any child of the carrying mother's family as well as its effect on any child of the commissioning parent's family.

3.20 The application of assisted conception techniques to initiate a surrogate pregnancy should only be considered where it is physically impossible or undesirable for medical reasons for the commissioning mother to carry the child . . .

3.22 When selecting donated gametes for treatment, centres should take into account each prospective parent's preferences in relation to the general physical characteristics of the donor. This does not allow the prospective parents to choose for social reasons alone, a donor of different ethnic origin(s) from themselves. Clients should be advised that the result of any attempt at matching physical characteristics cannot be guaranteed.

NOTE:

1. The most significant amendments to the earlier Code of Practice are the introduction of the requirement for clinics to have written

procedures, the emphasis upon the fact that the legislation does not exclude any category of woman from treatment, the stress upon the need for a stable and supportive environment, and the prominence given to the age of the patient.

QUESTION:

1. How adequate is this guidance in relation to child welfare? Should any other factors have been explicitly referred to in the legislation?

In addition to this general legal guidance, clinics providing IVF draw up their own criteria for selecting those it will treat. It is instructive to look at the criteria employed by one major centre providing IVF treatment. St Mary's Hospital in Manchester was the first National Health Service clinic to provide IVF services. As we saw above, its decision to refuse treatment services to an applicant was the subject of judicial review. The following criteria are those which it currently employs:

St Mary's Hospital (Manchester): IVF Unit Guidelines

1. We are only able to offer treatment to couples who have been living together for at least three years.
2. We only *list* women less than the age of 36 and/or couples where the male is less than 46 years old. We only *treat* couples where the female is less than 40 years old and the male is less than 50.
3. Prior to the April 1, 1993 we were only able to accept couples who resided within the geographical boundaries covered by the North West Regional Health Authority. As of April 1, 1993, we are able to accept couples who reside elsewhere in the United Kingdom by way of extra contractual referrals, provided they meet the other existing criteria.
4. If you are overweight, it is difficult to see the ovaries on the scan and dangerous to undertake a laparoscopy or have a general anaesthetic. We treat women who are close to their ideal body weight for their height.
5. Once accepted (*i.e.* after the clinic visit), each couple is offered a *maximum* of three complete courses of treatment.
   A complete course of IVF treatment is one ending in the replacement of one or more embryos or the transfer of eggs and sperm into the tube with GIFT. Completed courses of treatment at other centres are included in the calculation.
6. Only childless couples are accepted onto the waiting list for possible treatment. Since October 1984 we are unable to accept couples who have a child living with them by the current or previous relationships or by adoption.

The treatment by IVF, of couples with known genetic disorders is only undertaken after detailed consideration.

If you adopt a child whilst on the waiting list or after being accepted, we will be unable to offer you treatment.

NOTES:

1. There is no guarantee that those admitted to a waiting list will eventually be treated.

2. The use of such criteria by infertility clinics once again raises the question of whether there is a right to infertility treatment. Ultimately the decision to treat seems to turn on the discretion of the individual consultant. (Note that this appears analogous to the discretion accorded to doctors to determine whether a woman has satisfied the statutory criteria for abortion — see Chapter 12 at pages 713–718.)

QUESTIONS:

1. Is it right in principle for those administering IVF programmes to screen parents as to their suitability? What is the difference between screening them in order to assess their suitability to benefit medically from the procedures, and screening them to assess their suitability as parents *per se*? Which is the more important?
2. Is it not absurd to attempt to deny single persons the right to assisted conception when unmarried sexual relations are common and single women cannot be forced to use contraception or to abort after pregnancy has occurred? (See J. Harris, *Wonderwoman and Superman*, Oxford: Oxford University Press, 1992, at pages 73–8.)
3. The criteria used by St Mary's Hospital refers to the age of both parents as a relevant criterion. Do you agree that this is a relevant criterion, and do you agree with the ages fixed upon?

R. v. Sheffield Health Authority, ex p. Seale, 1994, unreported

Having experienced difficulty in conceiving, Mrs Seale, who was aged 36, applied to Sheffield Area Health Authority for IVF treatment. The authority rejected her application. In a letter to her husband it was explained that because of competing health priorities only £200,000 could be allocated to the provision of assisted reproduction services. In rationing these limited resources the authority had decided that age was a relevant criterion because such treatments are generally less effective in women aged over 35 years.

AULD J.:
" . . . The issue raised by that response to Mrs Seale's request and by this application must be one that is likely to be repeated in various of the medical services provided by the health authorities at their different levels and ultimately through the Secretary of State under the National Health Service Act 1977, having regard to the tension between demand for medical services and the money to pay for them. The scheme of the legislation and subordinate legislation to which Mr Straker has helpfully referred me has as its starting point section 3 of the 1977 Act. That provides, in subsection (1), so far as material: 'It is the Secretary of State's duty to provide throughout England and Wales, to such extent as he considers necessary, to meet all reasonable requirements . . .' Then the subsection goes on to list medical services in the various forms, among which Mr Straker says can be found, not expressly but by clear implication, the provision of *in vitro* fertilisation.

Mr Straker challenges the decision made in this case, based on the criteria set out in the letter of April 22, 1994, under three heads. The first is illegality. As I understand his submission, it is that as the Secretary of State has given no directions or imposed no limitations on the provision of *in vitro* fertilisation, and it is not for the district health authority, once it has committed itself to providing such a service, to restrict that provision if in the case of any patient there is a chance, a reasonable probability, a possibility — I do not quite know where the line is to be drawn — of the treatment being effective. As I understand Mr Straker's argument, it is that if any such qualification beyond efficacy is to be introduced, that is for the Secretary of State, and she has not done it here. In my view, it is not possible to erect out of the absence of a direction by the Secretary of State, or of the imposition by her of a limitation on the provision of such a service, a denial to the regional or district health authority of itself determining the circumstances in which such a service can be provided. It is not arguable, in my view, that it is bound, simply because it has undertaken to provide such a service, to provide it on demand to any individual patient for whom it may work, regardless of financial and other constraints upon the authority. Accordingly, I reject as unarguable any submission based on illegality here. In my view it is clear that if the Secretary of State has not limited or given directions as to the way in which such a service once undertaken should be provided, the authority providing it is entitled to form a view as to those circumstances and when they justify provision and when they do not.

The second argument of Mr Straker is that the decision here is irrational, that is, absurd. That is what he has to show as arguable to succeed on this application for leave. He says it is irrational because it is not founded on any sustainable, clinical approach. The basis of that argument appears to be that there is more than one view of the appropriate "cut-off" age for such treatment. In short, he submits, and refers me to the views of other doctors, that 35 years old is too low an age. It is possible to achieve success certainly up to the age of 42. I cannot, nor could the Court when deciding the matter as a substantive issue, if it came to that, form a view as to the rightness or wrongness of competing medical views on the effective cut-off date for the utility of such treatment. The decision letter does not say that the treatment cannot be effective after the age of 35, but merely that it is "generally less effective in women aged over 35 years". If that is so, can Mr Straker challenge the decision as irrational on the basis that it is absurd to apply the age of 35 years as a blanket cut-off point, taking no account of individual circumstances? His submission is that every case should be considered individually. Clinically speaking, there is no doubt good sense in such a submission. And a clinical decision on a case by case basis is clearly desirable and, in cases of critical illness, a necessary approach. However, it is reasonable, or it is at least not *Wednesbury* unreasonable, of an authority to look at the matter in the context of the financial resources available to it to provide this and the many other services for which it is responsible under the National Health Service legislation. I cannot say that it is absurd for this Authority, acting on advice that the efficacy of this treatment decreases with age and that it is generally less effective after the age of 35, to take that as an appropriate criterion when balancing the need for such a provision against its ability to provide it and all the other services imposed upon it under the legislation.

The third matter upon which Mr Straker relied as part of his argument based on irrationality was a reference to a particular condition from which this applicant suffers for which pregnancy is said to be a cure. However, that matter does not appear to have loomed large, or at all, in the circumstances giving rise to the decision of 22 April. Nor does it appear to have been particularly prominent as a reason for special treatment in this case in the correspondence that followed that decision. Under the heading of "Irrationality" Mr Straker relies upon the fact that privately paying patients can secure such treatment until the age of 42. It seems to me that that argument does not meet the central problem here of an authority coping with a finite budget and a myriad of services which it is bound to provide under it. I am, therefore, of the view that there is no arguable case that this decision was irrational, applying the high test that that word imports under the *Wednesbury* decision."

NOTES:

1. In 1996 Mrs Seale gave birth to a baby boy as a result of IVF treatment paid for privately by an anonymous business person (*The Independent*, June 21, 1996).
2. Nothing in the 1990 Act imposes an age limit on recipients of IVF treatment. However, age is a factor which ethics committees may take into account in reviewing applications for this treatment. Many clinics do include age limits in their own guidelines, and, as noted above, the latest HFEA Code of Practice highlights the importance of parental age when assessing the best interests of any potential children.
3. According to a survey by the National Association of Health Authorities, 11 Health Authorities, including Hertfordshire and Northamptonshire, refuse to purchase IVF treatment at all. ("Health ration decisions must be made public", *The Independent*, June 21, 1996.)

QUESTIONS:

1. Should the Human Fertilisation and Embryology Act 1990 have set an upper age limit beyond which access to IVF services would have been barred? On what grounds would you support or oppose the inclusion of such a provision? If you support such a measure, what should the upper age limit be? Should it apply equally to fathers (especially in the light of the recent HFEA consultation document floating the issue of whether upper age-limits for sperm donors should be reduced — see pages 633–634 above)?
2. If a couple have been diagnosed to be HIV+ should they be allowed access to IVF treatment? Does it make a difference if only the male partner is HIV+? (See J. R. Smith *et al.*, "Infertility management in HIV positive cases: a dilemma" (1991) 302 *British Medical Journal* 1447; L. Delaney and K. Doyle, "The childless HIV couple" [1995] *New L.J.* 1517.) In May 1996 Hammersmith hospital's IVF unit decided to give IVF treatment to a HIV+ woman in her 30s. The woman was a former heroin addict who had had the virus for 10 years. For five years she had been in what was described as a "completely supportive" relationship, but was unable to conceive naturally because of damaged Fallopian tubes. It was estimated that there was a 10–15 per cent chance of the baby being infected by the virus, although a Caesarian section delivery, and administration to the woman of anti-viral drugs during pregnancy would probably reduce the risk to about 7 per cent. ("Fertility treatment for HIV woman sparks controversy", *The Guardian*, May 13, 1996.) Do you think that this decision can be squared with the decision of St Mary's Hospital in Manchester not to treat Mrs Harriott?
3. More widespread use of IVF has made pre-implantation diagnosis (PID) more common. This allows embryos to be screened, and not

used if they carry genetic diseases. But, supposing that a couple have four daughters and seek to pay for IVF services with the aim of implanting only male embryos to ensure that they have a son. Would that be ethical? (See Human Fertilisation and Embryology Authority, *Sex Selection: Public Consultation Document*, January 1993; H. Bequaert Holmes, "Choosing Children's Sex: Challenges to Feminist Ethics" in J. C. Callaghan (ed.), *Reproduction, Ethics and the Law: Feminist Perspectives*, Bloomington and Indianapolis: Indiana University Press, 1995.)

4. Should parents ever be given the right to select offspring characteristics, such as sex and race? What other characteristics might parents want to select? (See R. Chadwick, "The Perfect Baby: Introduction" in R. Chadwick (ed.), *Ethics, Reproduction and Genetic Control*, London: Routledge, 1989.) What would justify the medical profession or the government stepping in to limit such choices? When do the interests of resulting offspring or society justify regulation of reproductive decisions made by freely consenting persons in the private sector? (See J. Harris, *Wonderwoman and Superman*, Oxford: Oxford University Press, 1992, Chapter 7.)

4. THE IMPACT OF ASSISTED CONCEPTION: STATUS PROVISIONS

Many commentators have argued that the·most profound effect of reproductive technologies may well be their impact on the legally defined family. The ability to separate and recombine the various factors of reproduction as necessary to produce a child seriously undermines the integrity of the family unit. Also, because recent developments have occurred so quickly there has been little opportunity to assess the impact upon children born as a result of the "reproductive revolution". (See P. Singer and D. Wells, *The Reproduction Revolution: New Ways of Making Babies*, Oxford: Oxford University Press, 1984.) Because the methods of assisted conception discussed above have the potential to alter our definition of the family and the role of·family members (see D. Morgan, "Technology and the Political Economy of Reproduction" in M. Freeman (ed.), *Medicine, Ethics and the Law*, London: Stevens, 1988) it is convenient at this point to consider together the provisions in the legislation defining the status and responsibilities of mothers and fathers and the status of children born as a result of assisted conception.

(a) Mothers

The much publicised cases on surrogacy and "test-tube babies" in the 1970s and 1980s focused attention on the fact that procreative roles can now be divided up into various components. We can no longer rely on the presumption that the mother is the woman who gave birth to the child.

(See D. Morgan, "Surrogacy: An Introductory Essay" in R. Lee and D. Morgan (eds), *Birthrights: Law and Ethics at the Beginnings of Life*, London: Routledge, 1989.) The genetic mother is the woman who provides the ova, the gestational mother is the woman who bears and gives birth to the child, and the social mother is the woman who assumes parental responsibility for the child after birth. As we saw above, in relation to the early surrogacy cases, the courts were faced with the difficult issue of adjudicating on the competing claims of gestational mothers and those of genetic fathers and their partners. The issue of which 'mother' is to be regarded in law as the mother of the child has now been settled by the 1990 Act.

Human Fertilisation and Embryology Act 1990, s.27(1)–(3)

27.—(1) The woman who is carrying or has carried a child as a result of the placing in her of an embryo or sperm and eggs, and no other woman, is to be treated as the mother of the child.

(2) Subsection (1) above does not apply to any child to the extent that the child is treated by virtue of adoption as not being the child of any person other than the adopter or adopters.

(3) Subsection (1) above applies whether the woman was in the United Kingdom or elsewhere at the time of the placing in her the embryo or the sperm and eggs.

QUESTION:

1. What policy arguments do you think were instrumental in the decision to define the gestational mother as the legal mother of the child she carries? Do you agree with those policy arguments? See R. Tong, "Feminist Perspectives and Gestational Motherhood: The Search for a Unified Legal Focus" and P. Smith, "The Metamorphosis of Motherhood" in J. C. Callaghan (ed.), *Reproduction, Ethics and the Law: Feminist Perspectives*, Bloomington and Indianapolis: Indiana University Press, 1995.

(b) Fathers

The issue of paternity was always more contested, as a man could never be absolutely sure of his status as father. This, combined with the fact that inheritance of property and privilege was dependent upon descent through the male line ensured that, unlike motherhood, the issue of establishing fatherhood has always posed problems for the legal system. This led to the introduction of a common law presumption that children of a marriage were the legitimate children of the husband. Thus it is marriage, rather than any blood tie which confers automatic paternity upon men. The advent of conception in a petri dish has given men a firmer guarantee that they are the genetic fathers of their future children. (See C. Smart, "'There is of course the distinction dictated by nature': Law and the Problem of Paternity" in M. Stanworth (ed.), *Reproductive Technologies: Gender, Motherhood and Medicine*, Cambridge: Polity Press, 1987.)

Human Fertilisation and Embryology Act 1990, s.28(1)–(9)

28.—(1) This section applies in the case of a child who is being or has been carried by a woman as the result of the placing in her of an embryo or of sperm and eggs or her artificial insemination.

(2) If —

(a) at the time of the placing in her of the embryo or the sperm and eggs or of her insemination, the woman was a party to a marriage, and

(b) the creation of the embryo carried by her was not brought about with the sperm of the other party to the marriage,

then, subject to subsection (5) below, the other party to the marriage shall be treated as the father of the child unless it is shown that he did not consent to the placing in her of the embryo or the sperm and eggs or to her insemination (as the case may be).

(3) If no man is treated, by virtue of subsection (2) above, as the father of the child but —

(a) the embryo or the sperm and eggs were placed in the woman, or she was artificially inseminated, in the course of treatment services provided for her and a man together by a person to whom a licence applies, and

(b) the creation of the embryo carried by her was not brought about with the sperm of that man,

then, subject to subsection (5) below, that man shall be treated as the father of the child.

(4) Where a person is to be treated as the father of the child by virtue of subsection (2) or (3) above, no other person is to be treated as the father of the child.

(5) Subsections (2) and (3) above do not apply —

(a) in relation to England and Wales and Northern Ireland, to any child who, by virtue of the rules of common law, is treated as the legitimate child of the parties to a marriage,

(b) in relation to Scotland, to any child who, by virtue of any enactment or other rule of law, is treated as the child of the parties to a marriage, or

(c) to any child to the extent that the child is treated by virtue of adoption as not being the child of any person other than the adopter or adopters.

(6) Where —

(a) the sperm of a man who had given such consent as is required by paragraph 5 of Schedule 3 to this Act was used for a purpose for which such consent was required, or

(b) the sperm of a man, or any embryo the creation of which was brought about with his sperm, was used after his death,

he is not to be treated as the father of the child.

(7) The references in subsection (2) above to the parties to a marriage at the time there referred to —

(a) are to the parties to a marriage subsisting at that time, unless a judicial separation was then in force, but

(b) include the parties to a void marriage if either or both of them reasonably believed at that time that the marriage was valid; and for the purpose of this subsection it shall be presumed, unless the contrary is shown, that one of them reasonably believed at the time that the marriage was valid.

(8) This section applies whether the woman was in the United Kingdom or elsewhere at the time of the placing in her of the embryo or the sperm and eggs or her artificial insemination.

(9) In subsection (7)(a) above, "judicial separation" includes a legal separation obtained in a country outside the British Islands and recognised in the United Kingdom.

NOTES:

1. Sub-section 28(2) effectively re-enacts and expands section 27 of the Family Law Reform Act 1987, which provided that a child born to a married couple as a result of DI should be treated as a legitimate child of the marriage, *unless* the husband proves that he did not consent to her being inseminated. The burden of proof is an onerous one since acquiescence in, or ignorance of, his wife's insemination will result in him being treated as the father of the child.

2. Sub-section 28(5)(a) states that the common law presumption of paternity attaching to the man to whom the woman is married at the time of the birth, takes precedence over either of the statutory presumptions contained in subsections 28(2) or (3). Accordingly, the first step for any man denying the paternity of a child born to his wife by virtue of treatment services is to rebut the common law presumption of paternity. This may now be done by recourse to DNA testing (which may raise difficult issues in relation to consent if he wishes the child to be tested). The fact that he can rebut the *common law* presumption of paternity merely allows the statutory presumption in subsection 28(2) to operate. Thus, the husband who denies paternity must also show that he did not consent to his wife receiving treatment.

3. Sub-section 28(3) provides that where an unmarried heterosexual couple seek treatment together the male partner will be regarded in law as the child's father, with the same limited legal rights as any other unmarried father. Thus he can agree with the mother to share parental rights or seek a court order to that effect under the Children Act 1989, section 4. Furthermore subsection 29(1) provides that he is to be treated in law as the father of the child for all purposes, except transmission of titles of honour.

4. Sub-section 28(6) creates a new legal class of child: the "fatherless child". Sub-section 28(6)(a) operates to protect men who act as sperm donors. Provided DI is performed in a licensed clinic all legal links between the sperm donor and any resulting child are severed. Thus if a woman presents for treatment by herself, or if she is married and her husband has not consented, any resulting child is legally fatherless. A second type of legally fatherless child is created by subsection 28(6)(b), which provides that where a woman is

inseminated with frozen sperm or implanted with an embryo created from such sperm after her partner's death he is not to be treated posthumously as the father. The Warnock Committee had recommended the insertion of such a provision to ensure that estates could be administered with some degree of finality. However, the same end would have been achieved had Warnock recommended that he be regarded as the legal father, but excluded succession by the child. Smart argues that this provision effectively means that the woman's pregnancy can only occur with patriarchal grace and that she is to be kept in order by the patronage of her husband. Moreover, she notes that with the introduction of this provision, the law has, for the first time, created a category of illegitimacy which ignores both the biological links between the child and the father and the marital status of the parent. (See C. Smart, *Law, Crime and Sexuality: Essays on Feminism*, London: Sage, 1995, pages 226–7.) See *Re Q (Parental Order)* [1996] 1 FLR 369, at page 682 below (see also Appendix B).

5. According to section 29 of the Act, sections 27 and 28 apply for all legal purposes except succession to dignities or transmission of titles of honour. (See D. Morgan and R. Lee, *Blackstone's Guide to the Human Fertilisation and Embryology Act 1990*, London: Blackstone Press, 1991, pages 160–162.) Since section 29 allows women who have received treatment services to be treated as the mother for all practical purposes, the combined effect of sections 27 and 29 is to endorse egg and embryo donation, at least for heterosexual couples. Although subsection 28(3) deals with the position of unmarried couples, there is no provision for the single woman.

6. One issue which has recently arisen before the courts is the extent to which a man who is deemed by law to be a father under section 28 is protected once the marriage breaks up. In the case of *Re CH (Contact: Parentage)* [1996] 1 FLR 569, the parties had been married for eight years. The husband had a daughter from a previous marriage and had been sterilised subsequent to her birth. It proved impossible to have the vasectomy reversed when he and his second wife decided that they wanted children. Eventually they decided to have a child by donor insemination. The husband gave his written consent to the procedure, was present at the birth of the child in April 1993, and was registered as the father at the time of birth. The parties separated in March 1994 as a result of the husband's drunkenness and violence. Having remarried, the wife sought to deny contact to her former husband on the basis that he was not the biological father and consequently there was no presumption in his favour that contact should take place.

However, Callman J. held that the mother's wish to sever the legal ties between her child and her ex-husband on the grounds that he was not the biological father was contrary both to the express wishes of Parliament in the 1990 Act and to principles of justice. He stated that without the father's consent to and participation in treatment there would have been no child, and that he could see no reason why the father should be denied contact given that he had displayed no violence to the child. The case is interesting for its dissection of the concept of fatherhood into three components — social fatherhood (the mother's new husband); legal fatherhood (her ex-husband); and biological fatherhood (the sperm donor).

QUESTIONS:

1. Do you agree with the legal definitions of parents in the 1990 Act?
2. Does section 28 place the burden of proof in the right place? In theory the following scenario could occur, if checks by the clinic were not sufficiently thorough:
   A married woman has an affair and seeks infertility treatment with her lover. If her husband knows nothing of the fact that she has sought such treatment he is unable to object to it, and is therefore presumed by law to be the father, since subsection 28(3) only operates when subsection 28(2) does not apply.
   Can this be right, especially in view of child support legislation which makes the husband liable to pay maintenance in such a case?
3. Should the legislation have banned a woman from being posthumously inseminated with her husband's frozen sperm, rather than simply discouraging the practice by providing that the child will be legally fatherless (unless she has subsequently remarried)?
4. Why do you think that the Act failed to make provision for motherhood in relation to single women who avail themselves of licensed services under the Act?

(c) Children

Until 1987 a sperm donor was regarded in law as the father of any ensuing child. In 1987 the status of children born as a result of artificial insemination was clarified by the Family Law Reform Act which removed the taint of illegitimacy from children born as a result of AID. As noted above, section 27 of that Act provided that where the woman's husband had not refused consent to her insemination, any child born to her was to be treated also as the child of her husband. Section 30 of the 1990 Act extends the approach of section 27 of the Family Law Reform Act 1987 to children born via surrogacy involving egg or embryo donation.

Human Fertilisation and Embryology Act 1990, s.30(1–7)

30.—(1) The court may make an order providing for a child to be treated in law as the child of the parties to a marriage (referred to in this section as "the husband" and "the wife") if —

(a) the child has been carried by a woman other than the wife as the result of the placing in her of an embryo or sperm and eggs or her artificial insemination,

(b) the gametes of the husband or the wife, or both, were used to bring about the creation of the embryo, and

(c) the conditions in subsections (2) to (7) below are satisfied.

(2) The husband and the wife must apply for the order within six months of the birth of the child or, in the case of a child born before the coming into force of this Act, within six months of the coming into force.

(3) At the time of the application and of the making of the order —

(a) the child's home must be with the husband and the wife, and

(b) the husband or the wife, or both of them, must be domiciled in a part of the United Kingdom or in the Channel Islands or the Isle of Man.

(4) At the time of the making of the order both the husband and the wife must have attained the age of eighteen.

(5) The court must be satisfied that both the father of the child (including a person who is the father by virtue of section 28 of this Act), where he is not the husband, and the woman who carried the child have freely, and with full understanding of what is involved, agreed unconditionally to the making of the order.

(6) Subsection (5) above does not require the agreement of a person who cannot be found or is incapable of giving agreement and the agreement of the woman who carried the child is ineffective for the purposes of that subsection if given by her less than six weeks after the child's birth.

(7) The court must be satisfied that no money or other benefit (other than for expenses reasonably incurred) has been given or received by the husband or the wife for or in consideration of —

(a) the making of the order,

(b) any agreement required by subsection (5) above,

(c) the handing over of the child to the husband and the wife, or

(d) the making of any arrangements with a view to the making of the order,

unless authorised by the court.

NOTES:

1. The effect of section 30, which came into force in 1995, is that where a married couple have commissioned a woman (the "surrogate mother"), to carry a child, the couple may apply for a court order (a "parental order"), that they shall be regarded as the child's parents under this section provided one or both of them have donated gametes. The section was added as a late amendment arising out of the case of *Re W (minors) (surrogacy)* [1991] 1 F.L.R. 385, discussed above at page 644.) This provision will only be of use in uncontested cases, where both the surrogate mother and her partner consent to the handing over of the child. The effect of a 'parental order' under this section is that the child will be regarded in law as the child of the commissioning married couple. It thus effectively reverses the provisions of sections 27–29 above, which would deem the surrogate to be the mother and her partner to be the father. The procedure is considerably less cumbersome than procedures under the adoption legislation, which would produce the same end result.

2. The Parental Orders (Human Fertilisation and Embryology) Regulations 1994 (S.I. 1994 No. 2767) amend and apply certain provisions in the Adoption Act 1976 to parental order cases under section 30. The regulations specify that hearings should be in private and that the paramount consideration is "the need to safeguard and promote the welfare of the child throughout his childhood". The effect of a parental order under section 30 is to extinguish any 'parental responsibility' on the part of the surrogate mother and her partner. The Registrar General is required to maintain a distinct 'Parental Order Register' to record the effects of parental orders made by the court. A person who is the subject of a parental order will be allowed to obtain details of their birth once they have reached the age of 18. (See A. Grubb, Commentary (1995) 3 *Medical Law Review* 204.)

3. In the case of *Re Q (Parental Order)* [1996] 1 F.L.R. 369 the question arose as to who was to be treated as a father for the purpose of giving consent to the making of a parental order under section 30. The facts of the case were that an unmarried woman had acted as a surrogate mother for a married couple, and she carried a child created from the egg of the wife of the commissioning couple fertilised by sperm from a licensed donor. Johnson J. held that as the surrogate mother was not married, she had no husband who could be treated as the father under sub-section 28(2); and that as the husband of the commissioning couple had not presented himself for "treatment services" with the surrogate mother he could not be deemed to be the father under sub-section 28(3). The sperm donor was excluded because he had donated via a licensed clinic. Thus the child was legally fatherless (see note 4 at page 678 above) and only the surrogate mother's consent was needed before a parental order could be made.

QUESTIONS:

1. Is section 30 out of line with the general legislative policy of discouraging surrogacy? If so, what explains this provision? (See D. Morgan and R. Lee, *Blackstone's Guide to the Human Fertilisation and Embryology Act 1990*, London: Blackstone Press, 1991, pages 153–4; E. Blythe, "Section 30 — The Acceptable Face of Surrogacy?" [1993] *Journal of Social Welfare and Family Law* 248.)

2. Why does section 30 only operate in favour of *married* couples? Is it inconsistent with section 28 which allows an unmarried man to be treated as a father where his partner receives treatment?

5.   DONATION OF GAMETES AND EMBRYOS

(a) Donating and Storing Gametes and Embryos

The issue of sperm donation was discussed above in relation to artificial insemination. There it seemed that, aside from the issue of access by single or lesbian women, few objections have been raised to the use of donated sperm. It is also generally accepted that sperm donors should be paid expenses. Egg donation differs in a number of ways from sperm donation. First, since eggs are naturally much less plentiful than sperm, egg donation will require the donor to take superovulatory drugs. Secondly, egg retrieval requires the donor to undergo a surgical procedure, as eggs are "harvested" through the abdominal wall. This may be carried out when the woman is undergoing another surgical procedure such as sterilisation. A third difference is that, whereas freezing of sperm is relatively straightforward, thus permitting cyropreservation or "spermbanking", it is much harder to successfully freeze eggs. However, it has recently been reported that scientists in Australia have developed a new technique for successfully freezing and thawing eggs, and have established an "egg bank" at the Royal Women's Hospital in Melbourne). The result is that spare eggs tend to be fertilised and the resulting embryo is frozen. (See F. Price, "The donor, the recipient and the child — human egg donation in U.K. licensed centres" (1995) 7 *Child and Family Law Quarterly* 145. Given the low success rates and the expense of IVF treatment every effort must be taken to ensure that such treatment is as effective as possible. In order to avoid repeated courses of egg retrieval scientists will fertilise a number of eggs at once. However, under the HFEA *Code of Practice* no more than three eggs or embryos should be placed in a woman in any one cycle (paragraph 7.9). This raises the thorny problem of what happens to any "spare" embryos which are not implanted. The issue of ownership or property rights in an embryo was discussed in Chapter 10 at pages 603–607, and the subject of property is more fully explored in Chapter 14 at pages 928–934. Similar issues are raised by the issue of whether gametes may be donated or sold. The 1990 Act contains provisions on the storage of gametes and embryos and also on the extent to which donors can control the subsequent use of 'their' sperm, eggs or embryos.

Human Fertilisation and Embryology Act 1990, s.14(1–5)

14.—(1) The following shall be conditions of every licence authorising the storage of gametes or embryos —

(a) that gametes of a person or an embryo taken from a woman shall be placed in storage only if received from that person or woman or acquired from a person to whom a licence applies and that an embryo the creation of which has been brought about *in vitro* otherwise than in pursuance of that licence shall be placed in storage only if acquired from a person to whom a licence applies,

(b) that gametes or embryos which are or have been stored shall not be supplied to a person otherwise than in the course of providing treatment services unless that person is a person to whom a licence applies,

(c) that no gametes or embryos shall be kept in storage for longer than the statutory storage period and, if stored at the end of the period, shall be allowed to perish, and

(d) that such information as the Authority may specify in directions as to the persons whose consent is required under Schedule 3 to this Act, the terms of their consent and the circumstances of the storage and as to such other matters as the Authority may specify in directions shall be included in the records maintained in pursuance of the licence.

(2) No information shall be removed from any record maintained in pursuance of such a licence before the expiry of such period as may be specified in directions for records of the class in question.

(3) The statutory storage period in respect of gametes is such period not exceeding ten years as the licence may specify.

(4) The statutory storage period in respect of embryos is such period not exceeding five years as the licence may specify [see now note 1, below].

(5) Regulations may provide that subsection (3) or (4) above shall have effect as if for ten years or, as the case may be, five years there were substituted —

(a) such shorter period, or
(b) in such circumstances as may be specified in the regulations, such longer period as may be specified in the regulations.

Schedule 3: Consent to use of Gametes or Embryos

1. A consent under this Schedule must be given in writing and, in this Schedule, "effective consent" means a consent under this Schedule which has not been withdrawn.

2.—(1) A consent to the use of any embryo must specify one or more of the following purposes —

(a) use in providing treatment services to the person giving consent, or that person and another specified person together,
(b) use in providing treatment services to persons not including the person giving consent, or
(c) use for the purposes of any project of research,

and may specify the conditions subject to which the embryo may be so used.

(2) A consent to the storage of any gametes or any embryo must —

(a) specify the maximum period of storage (if less than the statutory storage period), and
(b) state what is to be done with the gametes or embryo if the person who gives the consent dies or is unable because of incapacity to vary the terms of the consent or to revoke it,

and may specify conditions subject to which the embryos or gametes may remain in storage . . .

5.—(1) A person's gametes must not be used for the purposes of treatment services unless there is an effective consent by the person to their being so used and they are used in accordance with the terms of the consent.

(2) A person's gametes must not be received for use for those purposes unless there is an effective consent by that person to their being so used.

(3) This paragraph does not apply to the use of a person's gametes for the purposes of that person, or that person and another together, receiving treatment services.

6.—(1) A person's gametes must not be used to bring about the creation of any embryo *in vitro* unless there is an effective consent by that person to any embryo the creation of which may be brought about with the use of those gametes being used for one or more of the purposes mentioned in paragraph 2(1) above.

(2) An embryo the creation of which was brought about *in vitro* must not be received by any person unless there is an effective consent by each person whose

gametes were used to bring about the creation of the embryo to the use for one or more of the purposes mentioned in paragraph 2(1) above of the embryo.

(3) An embryo the creation of which was brought about *in vitro* must not be used for any purpose unless there is an effective consent by each person whose gametes were used to bring about the creation of the embryo to the use for that purpose of the embryo and the embryo is used in accordance with those consents.

(4) Any consent required by this paragraph is in addition to any consent that may be required by paragraph 5 above.

7.—(1) An embryo taken from a woman must not be used for any purpose unless there is an effective consent by her to the use of the embryo for that purpose and it is used in accordance with the consent.

(2) An embryo taken from a woman must not be received by any person for use for any purpose unless there is an effective consent by her to the use of that embryo for that purpose.

(3) This paragraph does not apply to the use, for the purpose of providing a woman with treatment services, of an embryo taken from her.

8.—(1) A person's gametes must not be kept in storage unless there is an effective consent by that person to their storage and they are stored in accordance with the consent.

(2) An embryo the creation of which was brought about *in vitro* must not be kept in storage unless there is an effective consent, by each person whose gametes were used to bring about the creation of the embryo, to the storage of the embryo and the embryo is stored in accordance with those consents.

(3) An embryo taken from a woman must not be kept in storage unless there is an effective consent by her to its storage and it is stored in accordance with the consent.

HFEA, Code of Practice *(1995)*

3.35 Gametes should not be taken from the treatment of others from female donors over the age of 35, and from male donors over the age of 55, unless there are exceptional reasons for doing so. If there are exceptional reasons, these should be explained in the treatment records.

3.36 Gametes taken from women over 35 and men over 55 may be used for their own treatment, or the treatment of their partner. They should be offered clinical advice and counselling before deciding whether to proceed with treatment.

3.37 Gametes should not be taken for the treatment of others from anyone under the age of 18.

3.38 In exceptional circumstances, gametes may be taken from people under the age of 18 if it is the intention to use them for their own treatment or that of their partner, provided that the centre is satisfied that the person from whom the gametes are taken is capable of giving a valid consent and has done so. It is not necessary also to obtain the consent of their parent or guardian.

3.39 Sperm taken from a male under 18 may only be stored for the purpose of research if he is capable of giving a valid consent, and that consent had been obtained.

3.40 Eggs should not be taken from females under 18 either to be stored for the purpose of research or to be used for research requiring a licence without first referring to the authority.

3.41 Sperm or eggs *must not* be taken from anyone who is not capable of giving a valid consent or who has not given a valid consent.

NOTES:

1. Under the Act the maximum storage period for gametes was 10 years and for embryos was 5 years. Where the gametes were supplied by a

person under the age of 45 for their own subsequent use and their fertility has since become or is likely to become impaired, the Human Fertilisation and Embryology (Statutory Storage Period) Regulations 1991 (S.I. 1991 No. 1540) provides for those periods to be extended. In May 1996, the Government introduced regulations to extend the storage period for embryos to 10 years (S.I. 1996 No. 375). However, in order for this to happen the person(s) storing the embryo must have communicated their consent to the five-year extension by August 2, 1996. The failure of many persons to communicate the requisite consent to the clinic where the embryos were stored by the deadline resulted in the destruction of over 3,300 frozen embryos. The anti-abortion group LIFE called upon the Official solicitor to intervene to stop the destruction, but he rejected such appeals on the ground that his jurisdiction extends only to legal persons and that embryos are not recognised by English law as persons. (See Chapter 12 at pages 704–708; "Clinics start destruction of embryos", *The Guardian*, August 2, 1996.)

2. The consent provisions in Schedule 3 are unusually stringent in requiring all consent to be in writing, following "proper" counselling. See Appendix B.

3. When the HFEA Code of Practice was revised in December 1995, a new section was added to the code (Part 9) drawing together all the guidance relevant for clinics which store embryos and gametes for cancer patients. Part 9 stresses the special importance of counselling in such cases and the fact that a female cancer patient storing embryos produced using her eggs *must* specify the purpose for which they may be used, and that the terms of her consent *must* be compatible with the consent of the man who provided the sperm. It makes clear that, whereas insemination of a woman with her husband's or partner's sperm while he is alive is not covered by the 1990 Act, insemination using the sperm of her late husband or partner is regulated under the Act. For this to take place the man *must* have given consent to the posthumous use of his sperm to treat the woman [Schedule 3 paragraph 2(2)(b) and 5(1)] and the licensed treatment centre must take account of the welfare of the potential child in deciding whether to treat the woman. Similarly, when a woman who has stored an embryo as a cancer patient wishes to have the embryo transferred in treatment the centre must consider her for treatment in the normal way, taking into account the welfare of the potential child.

4. The HFEA *Code of Practice* provides that, unless there are exceptional reasons, donors of eggs should be aged between 18 and 35 (paragraphs 3.33–3.35).) Note the proposal to reduce the upper age limit for donation of sperm to 40 years of age — see pages 633–634 above. Note that no age limit for recipients of eggs is stipulated in the HFEA guidelines.

5. Because an embryo created *in vitro* may only lawfully be kept in storage with the consent of both partners it seems that if one partner dies the other has no *right* to insist on treatment. Morgan and Lee argue that the effect of reading together sections 14(1)(b) and 4(1)(b) renders it a matter for the exercise of clinical judgment and discretion if the clinic decides to honour the wishes of the deceased partner, as expressed in the written consent s/he was required to give. (See D. Morgan and R. Lee, *Blackstone's Guide to the Human Fertilisation and Embryology Act 1990*, London: Blackstone Press, 1991.)

QUESTIONS:

1. Should there be a duty to transfer all embryos to a uterus? If so, whose uterus? Does it make a difference to the moral and/or legal status of the embryo whether or not it is one which is intended to be transferred to a uterus or one which is essentially a "spare" embryo — a by-product of the IVF process? Does its potential to come into existence as a person make a difference? (See J. Harris, *The Value of Life*, London: Routledge and Kegan Paul, 1985, Chapter 6; Chapter 2, above.)
2. If spare eggs are produced as a result of administering fertility drugs, and are not donated or sold, how should they be disposed of?
3. What age limits, if any, would you place on those willing to donate (or sell) eggs? Should there be an upper age limit for recipients of donated eggs? (See F. Price, "The donor, the recipient and the child: human egg donation in U.K. licensed centres" (1995) 7 *Child and Family Law Quarterly* 145.)
4. On June 14, 1996 the federal government in Ottawa, Canada announced new laws — known as Bill C–47 — to control reproductive technology. The proposed law would make it a criminal offence to buy, sell or trade in human eggs, sperm or embryos. Should the United Kingdom Government follow suit?
5. What criminal offence is committed, or what property rights violated, in destroying surplus embryos? (See A. Capron, "Alternative Birth Technologies: Legal Challenges" (1987) 20 *University of California at Davis Law Review* 679.)
6. What do you think should happen to spare embryos or gametes where one of the partners dies or the couple separate? (See A. Grubb, "The legal status of the frozen embryo" in *Challenges in Medical Care*, Chichester: Wiley 1992.)

(b) The Sale of Gametes

Given apparent acceptance of the fact that gametes and embryos may be donated for use in the infertility treatment of others, or for research, this raises the further question of whether they may be sold. The problem is particularly acute since there is a shortage of donated eggs. It is estimated that over 1,000 women in Britain each year seek treatment with donor eggs. (See *The Guardian*, August 24, 1994.) One of the general conditions for the granting of a licence is that, under section 12(e) of the 1990 Act no money or other benefit shall be given or received in respect of any supply of gametes or embryos unless authorised by directions. As noted above at page 634 current HFEA directions permit donors to be paid up to £15 per donation plus reasonable expenses. Although this has been most commonly applied to sperm donors, the direction also allows women to be offered benefits, in the form of treatment services or free sterilisation, in exchange for donating eggs. The direction regularised the position which existed when the HFEA was established. Controversy erupted in Britain over an advertisement by the Genetics and IVF Institute in Fairfax, Virginia, United States, which appeared in (1994) *The Times* August 23, claiming that it had a supply of donor eggs and no waiting lists for treatment. In November 1995 further controversy was generated when it emerged that the Hope Agency in Cornwall was paying egg donors. White donors were paid £850, while Asian, Chinese and Afro Caribbean donors received up to £1,000. Childless couples seeking to avail themselves of the service were required to pay a £250 registration fee and £4,000 for a successful implantation (See A. Neustatter, "Psst. Wanna buy a baby?", *The Guardian*, November 6, 1995.) Such practices raise the issue of what sort of screening is appropriate to women willing to donate eggs. More broadly, the questions raised by selling gametes relate to issues of autonomy, the market and paternalism which recur throughout this text.

QUESTIONS:

1. Is it justifiable to offer treatment, such as sterilisation, in return for a donation of eggs, or to offer infertile women IVF on condition that they donate eggs? Is this really distinguishable paying women to donate eggs?
2. Given the shortage of donor eggs, was it justifiable for Parliament to ban the retrieval of ova from aborted female foetuses, in the Criminal Justice and Public Order Act? Are different issues raised if eggs could be extracted from cadavers? (See the discussion of research on foetal tissue in Chapter 10 at pages 607–613.)

Human Fertilisation and Embryology Authority, *Donated Ovarian Tissue in Embryo Research and Assisted Conception* (July 1994)

17. The deep distress felt by people who are unable to have children in the normal way is widely acknowledged. In some cases this could be alleviated but for the fact that there is a shortage of donated eggs. The Authority therefore believes that it is acceptable to seek to increase the supply of eggs for infertility treatment.
18. The Authority has concluded that it would be acceptable to use ovarian tissue in infertility treatment from adult live donors provided informed specific written

consent has been given. This can be carried out in accordance with the current provisions of the HFE Act and *Code of Practice*, which sets an age limit of 18. The Authority is satisfied that it is possible to control the number of offspring from one donor. Only a limited amount of ovarian tissue would be available from a single donor. Control would be in line with the Authority's policy on gamete donors set out in its *Code of Practice*, *i.e.* the limit of 10 offspring.

19. In the case of the use of ovarian tissue in infertility treatment from females under 18 who have died, the same concerns about obtaining specific informed consent from minors . . . lead the Authority to the view that tissue form this source should not currently be used. In the case of an adult women who has died, there is no objection in principle. This is provided that the woman has given informed consent specifically to donate her tissue for the treatment of others, for example, by means of a special donor card or a will. However, more can and should be done to find out about the psychological consequences for the recipient couple and particularly for the prospective child. The Authority will then reconsider licensing treatment using ovarian tissue from women or girls who have died.

20. The use of foetal ovarian tissue raises difficult social, medical, scientific and legal concerns. No arguments emerging from consultation have convinced the Authority that these can be put aside. The Authority considers that the issue of possible psychological consequences for the offspring is most difficult. There is widespread and fundamental objection to using foetal tissue in this way. Accordingly, it would be particularly difficult for a child to come to terms with being produced from a foetus because of prevailing social attitudes. The HFEA, therefore, does not consider the use of tissue from this source to be acceptable in infertility treatment. Other developments are taking place involving ovarian tissue from adults which look likely to reduce the need to consider the use of foetal ovarian tissue in infertility treatment.

NOTES:

1. This report was superseded by the passage of the Criminal Justice and Public Order Act 1994 and its insertion into the Act of section 3A (see page 658 above). That legislation referred to female germlines rather than eggs because of doubt about whether the term 'gametes' covered immature eggs.

QUESTIONS:

1. Are children born of donated gametes and embryos, or of surrogates, or as a result of IVF likely to be harmed in physical or psychosocial ways by collaborative reproduction, which involves a mixture of genetic, gestational and social parental roles? In what ways might such harms manifest themselves?
2. Were HFEA right to place such stress on prevailing social attitudes?
3. Is egg donation to organ or tissue donation? (See F. Price, "The donor, the recipient and the child — human egg donations in U.K. licensed centres" (1995) 7 *Child and Family Law Quarterly* 145.
4. Are there any ethical problems raised by the following case:

    A 27-year-old woman suffering from chronic leukaemia was accepted for IVF treatment in the knowledge that the disease would render her infertile. She produced several eggs following administration of ovary stimulating drugs. These were fertilised with her husband's sperm and the resulting three embryos were implanted four years later, after her condition had been treated. (See case reported in *The Times*, September 23, 1993.)

5. Supposing the woman had contracted leukaemia prior to puberty, so that she could no longer produce her own eggs, is there a problem with her sister donating her eggs in order to produce genetically related embryos? (See F. Price, "Establishing Guidelines: Regulation and the Clinical Management of Infertility" in R. Lee and D. Morgan (eds), *Birthrights: Law and Ethics at the Beginning of Life*, London: Routledge, 1989.)

6. Are there valid ethical objections to permitting any woman who wishes to delay child-bearing to have her eggs frozen during her 20s when they are in peak condition, and re-implanted when she decides that she wishes to have a child?

7. Is there a moral difference between selling or donating gametes and selling or donating embryos?

(c) Screening Donors, Gametes and Embryos

The HFEA Code of Practice requires licensed clinics to test donors for HIV and other infections.

HFEA, Code of Practice *(1995)*

3.46 Centres should give careful consideration to the suitability of individual donors before accepting or using their gametes for the treatment of others. The views of all those at the centre who have been involved with the potential donor should be taken into account. Centres should consider in particular:

(a) any personal or family history of heritable disorders;
(b) any personal history of transmissible infection;
(c) the level of potential fertility indicated by semen analysis;
(d) whether the donor has children of their own; and
(e) the attitude of the donor towards the donation.

3.47 Centres should adopt whatever is current best practice in the scientific testing of semen samples and of donors of gametes and embryos.

3.48 In relation to HIV testing, centres should adopt as a minimum the procedure set out in "HIV Screening for Gamete Donors" by the Human Fertilisation Authority and the Department of Health . . .

3.49 In relation to the testing of donors for other infections and of semen samples, centres should as a minimum follow the guidelines of the British Andrology Society. It is for centres to ensure that the most up-to-date guidance is followed.

3.50 Centres should also re-screen potential donors where appropriate, and adopt any other test which may come to be regarded as a matter of good practice by the standards of professional colleagues in relevant specialities or may be indicated in a particular case while this Code is in force.

NOTES:

1. The guidance referred to in paragraph 3.48 above suggests that the blood of donors should be tested for HIV antibody at the time the

donation is made and that semen donors should be tested a second time for HIV antibody at least 180 days after the first test. As donated eggs must be used immediately, the guidance acknowledges that there is a slight risk that donor infection will not be identified. This small risk should be explained to recipients of donated eggs. All donors should give an informed consent to HIV testing and should be advised of the practical consequences of a test, and given counselling if tests prove positive.

2. Paragraph 3.49 requires clinics to follow the British Andrology Society (BAS) guidelines on screening of semen donors for donor insemination. The BAS guidelines do not make screening for cystic fibrosis mandatory. The HFEA in December 1995 issued a consultation document seeking views on screening of donors for cystic fibrosis (which is not currently mandatory), following media coverage of the birth of a baby conceived through donor insemination and affected by cystic fibrosis and the fact that a firm is now marketing a mail-order test for cystic fibrosis.

3. Although gene surgery, or actual interference with, or manipulation of, the embryo, is regulated by the 1990 Act, there is nothing in the legislation to prevent screening of embryos for genetic diseases. In its 1995 Annual Report the HFEA stated that it would be monitoring the issue of preimplantation diagnosis whereby cells are removed from embryos *in vitro* and tested in order to detect their sex or the presence of a genetic disorder. This would allow a woman at risk of having a child with a life-threatening disorder to have only unaffected embryos implanted. Similarly, in the case of a sex-linked disorder it would permit only male or female embryos to be implanted. Part 6 of the *Code of Practice* contains provisions on counselling donors, including counselling about screening. Nothing in the 1990 Act prohibits sex selection which does not involve interference with the embryo. Thus, for example, the London Gender Clinic which offers a technique based on sperm selection, does not come within the regulatory scheme of the Act.

QUESTIONS:

1. In your view should donors be tested for cystic fibrosis, bearing in mind the principle of screening for a genetic disease, the implications for donors who are screened and the availability of a test which is estimated to only detect 85 per cent of carriers?

2 In general, should donors be screened for genetic disorders to determine whether they are an unwitting carrier of a genetic disease? Would this be likely to lead to a decrease in potential donors? (See Chapter 10 at pages 613–619.)

3. Is it morally wrong for parents to reject embryos which carry a genetic disorder? If not, should they be given a similar right to reject embryos of the "wrong" sex?

(d) Liability for Disability

If a child born as a result of IVF or DI suffers from a disability at birth which is due to the negligence of the licensed clinic the parents will have a right to sue the clinic. In such a situation the trauma that the parents will suffer is clearly foreseeable. However, there may be difficulties in establishing who was the negligent party. If the treatment is undertaken on the NHS, the health authority or NHS trust will owe a direct duty to the parents. (See Chapter 3.) If the treatment is undertaken privately patients should ensure that the clinic is under a contractual duty to underwrite the whole course of treatment. (See M. Brazier, *Medicine, Patients and the Law* (2nd ed.), London: Penguin, 1992, page 278.) As far as actions by the child are concerned section 44 of the 1990 Human Fertilisation and Embryology Act 1990 amends the Congenital Disabilities (Civil Liability) Act 1976 to allow for an action resulting from negligence in the course of providing infertility treatment. (See Chapter 13 at pages 786–791.)

One issue which has not been resolved by the Act is whether gametes or embryos could ever amount to a "product" for the purposes of the Consumer Protection Act 1987. (This legislation is discussed in Chapter 2.) Morgan and Lee point out that, although subsection 6(3) of the Consumer Protection Act specifically incorporates claims for congenital disability, this was probably intended to cover only claims based on pharmaceutical products. Given judicial hostility to "wrongful life" claims (see Chapter 13 at pages 791–798), they suggest that courts are unlikely to countenance claims under the 1987 Act alleging that gametes or embryos were defective. (See D. Morgan and R. Lee, *Blackstone's Guide to the Human Fertilisation and Embryology Act 1990*, London: Blackstone Press, 1991.) By contrast, Stern has argued that, by applying the Consumer Protection Act, courts may award compensation in cases where donated gametes cause injury, provided it was possible to detect the risk that injury would be so caused. (See K. Stern, "Strict Liability and the Supply of Donated Gametes" (1994) 2 *Medical Law Review* 261.)

In the case of gametes, Stern has argued that a screening process may enable some assessment of safety. Where gametes are taken from a donor who has been screened and found to be healthy, the gametes can be deemed to be safe as the risk has been screened out. However, liability would be imposed in a situation in which gametes were used from unhealthy donors who should have been screened out. She suggests that because the courts are required to assess the risk of disease, taking into account public policy considerations, they would probably find some risk of disease transmission to be acceptable (Stern, *op. cit.*)

QUESTION:

1. Is it appropriate to seek to apply the language of property, contract and consumer law in this context? Can you think of any alternative language that could be adopted?

(e) Tracing Genetic Origins

The decision what to tell children born of assisted conception has proven to be problematic. Some commentators have asserted that children born as a result of DI (and by implication as a result of egg or embryo donation) should be able to trace their conceptual origins. Such a contention is rooted in the general moral convention that all persons wish to and have a right to know their family history, and that by analogy with adoption, children conceived through DI should be granted the same rights to counselling and information concerning ethnic origin and genetic health that are available to adopted children. The Warnock Committee addressed this issue briefly.

Warnock Committee: *Report of the Committee of Inquiry into Human Fertilisation and Embryology* (1984) Cmnd. 9314

4.21 As a matter of principle we do not wish to encourage the possibility of prospective parents seeking donors with specific characteristics by the use of whose semen they hope to give birth to a particular type of child. We do not therefore want detailed descriptions of donors to be used as a basis for choice, but we believe that the couple should be given sufficient relevant information for their reassurance. This should include some basic facts about the donor such as his ethnic group and his genetic health. A small minority of the Inquiry, while supporting the principle set out above, and without compromising the principle of anonymity, consider that a gradual move towards making more detailed descriptions of the donor available to prospective parents, if requested, could be beneficial to the practice of AID, provided this was accompanied by appropriate counselling. *We recommend that on reaching the age of eighteen the child should have access to the basic information about the donor's ethnic origin and genetic health and that legislation should be enacted to provide the right of access to this* . . .

Warnock's recommendation was partially adopted in the 1990 Act.

Human Fertilisation and Embryology Act 1990, s.31(1–4)

31.—(1) The Authority shall keep a register which shall contain any information obtained by the Authority which falls within subsection (2) below.
(2) Information falls within this subsection if it relates to —

(a) the provision of treatment services for any identifiable individual, or
(b) the keeping or use of the gametes of any identifiable individual or of an embryo taken from any identifiable woman,
or if it shows that any identifiable individual was, or may have been, born in consequence of treatment services.

(3) A person who has attained the age of eighteen ("the applicant") may by notice to the Authority require the Authority to comply with a request under subsection (4) below, and the Authority shall do so if -

(a) the information contained in the register shows that the applicant was, or may have been, born in consequence of treatment services, and

(b) the applicant has been given a suitable opportunity to receive proper counselling about the implications of compliance with the request.

(4) The applicant may request the Authority to give the applicant notice stating whether or not the information contained in the register shows that a person other than a parent of the applicant would or might, but for sections 27 to 29 of this Act, be a parent of the applicant and, if it does show that -

(a) giving the applicant so much of that information as relates to the person concerned as the Authority is required by regulations to give (but no other information), or
(b) stating whether or not that information shows that, but for sections 27 to 29 of this Act, the applicant, and a person specified in the request as a person who the applicant proposes to marry, would or might be related . . .

NOTE:

1. No regulations have yet been issued under this section specifying what information may be divulged to a child conceived using donated materials.
2. A person who is the subject of a "parental order" under section 30 of the 1990 Act will be allowed details of their birth at 18 years of age. They thus have the same rights as adopted children under section 51 of the Adoption Act 1976, but are the only children born as a result of assisted conception who have been granted this right.
3. Section 33 of the 1990 Act imposes limits on disclosure of registered information under section 31 and of other information obtained in confidence by the HFEA. (For discussion of this provision see Chapter 9.)

QUESTIONS:

1. Does section 31 strike an acceptable balance between respecting privacy whilst simultaneously disclosing necessary information to children born as a result of assisted conception?
2. Should all children be able to trace their genetic origins? Should parents have a duty to tell their children if they were born as a result of gamete donation? (Compare J. Mason, *Medico-legal Aspects of Reproduction and Parenthood*, Aldershot: Dartmouth 1990, at pages 196–198 with K. O'Donovan, "'What shall we tell the children?' Reflections on Children's Perspectives and the Reproductive Revolution" in R. Lee and D. Morgan (eds), *Birthrights: Law and Ethics at the Beginnings of Life*, London: Routledge, 1989.)
3. To what extent should the interets of gamete donors be taken into account? (See F. Price, "The donor, the recipient and the child — human egg donation in U.K. licensed centres" (1995) 7 *Child and Family Law Quarterly* 145.) How should those be weighed against the interests of the children who may be born? (See S. Maclean and M. Maclean, "Keeping secrets in assisted reproduction — the tension

between donor anonymity and the need of the child for information"
(1996) 8 *Child and Family Law Quarterly* 243.)

SELECT BIBLIOGRAPHY

R. Arditti *et al.*, (eds), *Test-Tube Women: What Future for Motherhood?*,
London: Pandora Press, 1989.

J. C. Callaghan (ed.), *Reproduction, Ethics and the Law: Feminist Perspectives*, Bloomington and Indianapolis: Indiana University Press, 1995.

R. Chadwick (ed.), *Ethics, Reproduction and Genetic Control*, London:
Routledge, 1990.

G. Corea, *The Mother Machine: Reproductive Technologies from Artificial Insemination to Artificial Wombs*, London: The Women's Press,
1988.

D. Cuisine, *New Reproductive Techniques*, Aldershot: Gower, 1989.

G. Douglas, *Law, Fertility and Human Reproduction*, London: Sweet and
Maxwell, 1991.

J. Harris, *Wonderwoman and Superman: The Ethics of Human Biotechnology*, Oxford: Oxford University Press, 1992.

R. Lee and D. Morgan (eds.), *Birthrights: Law and Ethics at the Beginning of Life*, London: Routledge, 1989.

S. McLean (ed.), *Legal Issues in Human Reproduction*, Aldershot: Gower,
1989.

S. McLean (ed.), *Law Reform and Human Reproduction*, Aldershot:
Dartmouth, 1992.

D. Morgan and R. Lee, *Blackstone's Guide to the Human Fertilisation and Embryology Act 1990*, London: Blackstone Press, 1991.

D. Morgan, "Technology and the Political Economy of Reproduction" in
M. Freeman, (ed.), *Medicine, Law and Ethics*, London: Stevens,
1988.

L. Purdy, *Reproducing Persons: Issues in Feminist Bioethics*, Ithaca and
London: Cornell University Press, 1996.

J. Raymond, *Women as Wombs: Reproductive Technologies and the Battle over Women's Freedom*, 1994.

J. Robertson, "Embryos, Families and Procreative Liberty: The Legal Structure of the New Reproduction" (1986) 59 *Southern California Law Review* 942.

P. Rolling (ed.), Expecting Trouble: Surrogacy, Foetal Abuse and New Reproductive Technologies, Boulder, Colorado: Westview Press,
1995.

P. Spallone, *Beyond Conception: The New Politics of Reproduction*,
London: Macmillan, 1989.

M. Stanworth, *Reproductive Technologies: Gender, Motherhood and Medicine*, Cambridge: Polity Press, 1987.

1. INTRODUCTION

As we saw in the preceding chapter a host of legal, ethical and political issues are raised when individuals or couples seek to assert a positive right to reproduce. These issues have become increasingly contentious in the past couple of decades as health care professionals have become more involved in the provision of assisted conception. Equally complex issues, of somewhat longer standing, are raised by the assertion of a right *not* to reproduce by women claiming rights to bodily autonomy, privacy and equality. Each of these rights have been asserted by women in the context of family planning decisions. Although contraceptive choices have proven controversial, it is abortion which is probably the most contentious issue in health care law. The intractable nature of the abortion debate is reflected in the strategy adopted by legislators throughout the world, which is to avoid, if at all possible, having to legislate on such a divisive social issue in which there are no votes to be won (see M. Fox and T. Murphy, "Irish Abortion: Seeking Refuge in Jurisprudence of Doubt and Delegation" (1992) *Journal of Law and Society*). This is certainly true in the United Kingdom where the main legislation — the 1967 Abortion Act — resulted from a private member's bill introduced by the Liberal M.P. David Steele. As a result, the drafting has been the subject of judicial criticism (see pages 720–725 below). The refusal of the British government to squarely confront the abortion issue is further evidenced by its failure to extend the 1967 legislation to Northern Ireland and the reluctance of both main political parties to reform the 1967 law (despite 22 attempts to amend or repeal it) until forced to do so when abortion became linked with the issues addressed by the Human Fertilisation and Embryology Act 1990. (For discussion of proposed amendments to the law between 1967 and 1990 see J. Keown, *Abortion, Doctors and the Law*, Cambridge: CUP, 1988.) In section 2 we consider the law on contraception. We start our consideration of abortion in section 3 with a discussion of the moral and legal status of the foetus and the ethics of abortion. Given the divergence of views on abortion, as with most contested issues legislators adopted what may be regarded as a pragmatic compromise. In section 4 we consider in detail the law on abortion, which in the United Kingdom is very much subject to medical control. We examine the criminal prohibitions on procuring a miscarriage, the grounds on which abortion may be lawfully carried out, and legal regulation of where and how abortions may be performed. We then consider in section 5 the interests of other parties affected by the decision whether or not to abort. We conclude in section 6 with a discussion of conscientious objection and its impact on the choice to terminate.

2.   CONTRACEPTION

In Great Britain in recent years the provision of contraceptive advice and treatment has not been legally contentious, except in the context of providing such advice and treatment to minors (see Chapter 7) and to persons incapable of consenting by reason of mental disability or severe learning difficulties (see Chapter 13 at pages 754–773). While there has never been a general ban in English law on the use of contraceptive devices, in the past the availability of contraception has been indirectly regulated under obscenity legislation and through the scrutiny of the Divorce Court. (See G. Douglas, *Law, Fertility and Reproduction*, London: Sweet & Maxwell, 1991, at pages 42–46; K. McK Norrie, *Family Planning Practice & the Law*, Aldershot: Dartmouth, 1991, at pages 7–15, and for an account of opposition to birth control in the last century see M. Thomson, "Women, Medicine and Abortion in the Nineteenth Century" (1995) 3 *Feminist Legal Studies* 159.) The subject continues to be a contentious issue in Northern Ireland where the opening of a Brook Advisory Centre (one of a network of clinics providing contraceptive advice and treatment targeted at young people) in Belfast in 1992 attracted sustained opposition, notwithstanding the high rates of teenage pregnancies in the jurisdiction (See the Medico Legal Enquiry Group, *The Brook Clinic in Northern Ireland — An Agenda for Debate*, Belfast, 1992; "Brook in Belfast: Why did it take a year?" (1992) 1(2) *Women's Choice* 27.) Elsewhere in the United Kingdom the major issue has been that of access to adequate contraceptive advice and treatment, especially since a crucial factor in the take up of contraceptive advice and services is the manner in which treatment is provided. Contraception has been available on NHS prescription since the passage of the NHS (Family Planning) Act 1967. In 1974 the NHS assumed responsibility for the provision of family planing clinics, which generally offer a much broader range of advice and services than GPs are able to offer. The current legislation places the Secretary of State for Health under a statutory duty to arrange:

National Health Service Act 1977, s.5(1)(b)

. . . to such extent as he considers necessary to meet all reasonable requirements in England and Wales, for the giving of advice on contraception, the treatment of such persons and the supply of contraceptive substances and appliances.

However, despite government policy consistently emphasising the importance of ensuring the development and effective provision of family
planning services in order to maximise uptake, in recent years many clinics
have been closed. (See F. Godlee, "Regions co-ordinate family planning
services" [1992] *British Medical Journal* 304, 401.) Following concerns
expressed by the Family Planning Service in relation to the closure of
family planning clinics, DHSS guidance issued in 1989 urged health
authorities to take account of the following factors —

- the need to give choice to encourage full uptake of services;
- the need for separate, more informal arrangements for young
  people;
- the wider health role of family planning services, such as the
  provision of cervical cytology screening facilities. (NHSME, H.C.
  (89)24, LAC89(11), H.N. (FP)(89)17, Department of Health, 1989.)

The provision of contraceptive services by GPs has grown substantially
over the last 20 years, reflecting both increased contraceptive availability
within general practice and reduced availability of family planning clinic
services. While the range of contraceptive services available within general
practice varies substantially, such surgeries rarely provide a full range of
contraceptive methods. In particular GPs are usually unable to provide free
condoms for financial reasons. Moreover, staff in family planning clinics
will have more experience and training in fitting contraceptive devices.
Available research suggests that there is a demand for provision of less
"medicalised" contraceptive services, although it is unlikely that this
demand will be met. (See Contraceptive Education Service, *Contraceptive
choices: supporting effective use of methods*, London: Family Planning
Association, 1996.)

Constraints on contraceptive choices are not limited to control of the
service by medical professionals. Although the seemingly constant proliferation of contraceptive drugs and devices appears to have led to an
increased menu of choice in the field of family planning, Douglas warns
that:

> "the provision of effective contraception may have been a mixed blessing for
> women. While it may have freed them from the fear of an unplanned pregnancy,
> this has been at the cost of having to face new potential health risks, and of
> surrendering effective control over the decision of when and how to use
> contraception to the medical profession, thanks to the way the judiciary and
> legislature have dealt with contraceptive issues" (G. Douglas, *Law, Fertility and
> Reproduction* London: Sweet & Maxwell, 1991, at page 41).

Available contraceptive methods can be divided into two broad categories
— surgical and non-surgical. Surgical sterilisation offers the most permanent form of contraception. Female sterilisation may be undertaken by
clipping the fallopian tubes which carry the eggs from the ovaries to the
uterus. A more radical operation is the hysterectomy which involves the
complete removal of the womb. This may be used in the case of women
suffering from heavy periods, although doctors have been criticised for

performing the operation too readily. Male sterilisation or vasectomy is effected by cutting and tying back the vas deferens — the tube which leads through the testes epidemus to the urethra and enables the sperm to pass through. As we noted in Chapter 6 at pages 324–326 a person does not have absolute freedom to consent to any surgical operation. The legality of sterilisation was formerly contested on public policy grounds:

Bravery v. Bravery [1954] 3 All E.R. 59:

LORD DENNING:
". . . when there is no just cause or excuse for an operation it is unlawful even though a man consents to it. Likewise with a sterilisation operation. When it is done with the man's consent for a just cause or excuse, it is quite lawful: as for instance when it is done to prevent the transmission of a hereditary disease. But when it is done without just cause or excuse it is unlawful even though the man consents to it. Take a case where a sterilisation operation is done so as to enable a man to have the pleasure of sexual intercourse without shouldering the responsibilities attaching to it. The operation is then plainly injurious to the public interest. It is degrading to the man himself. It is injurious to his wife and any woman he may marry to say nothing of the way it opens to licentiousness, and unlike contraception it leaves no room for any change of mind by the other side."

NOTES:

1. In this case a woman sought to divorce her husband on the grounds of his cruelty in having undergone a vasectomy contrary to her wishes. Although Lord Denning was in the minority, and the majority view was that there is no legal obligation to obtain spousal consent for a sterilisation operation, the court did consider that it was good medical practice to obtain a partner's consent. In the past the form which requested consent for sterilisation contained a clause for spousal consent. It appears that such clauses are no longer used, although the BMA suggests that it remains good practice to obtain the consent of both parties. It is, however, unlikely that the courts would be prepared to accord the partner a legal right to be consulted, particularly since a sexual partner has no right in law to be consulted regarding abortion (see pages 737–746 below).
2. As we shall see in Chapter 13, the fact that courts have been prepared to compensate for failed sterilisations and to sanction the sterilisation of the allegedly mentally disabled women in their best interests has removed any taint of illegality attaching to the procedure.

Non-surgical contraceptive techniques include barrier methods such as the male condom, the female condom (Femidom) and the diaphragm or cap, which is inserted in the vagina so as to cover the cervix prior to intercourse. Barrier methods have an important role to play in preventing sexually transmissible diseases and have thus featured heavily in health promotional materials. Such methods have no medical side effects although they may not be as effective as other methods, and also require a high degree of motivation on the part of those using them. Non-barrier methods include the intrauterine device. This is a ring placed in the uterus which releases a copper irritant, thus rendering the uterus inhospitable to fertilised eggs. It has been linked to pelvic inflammatory disease and other infections. The most common form of non-barrier contraceptive is the oral contraceptive pill. Whilst highly effective if properly used, it does carry the risk of side effects. The combined oral contraceptive pill in particular can cause side-effects ranging from headaches, nausea, breast tenderness, acne or weight gain through poor menstrual cycle control to more serious side-effects such as thrombosis, breast cancer and infertility. Longer lasting contraceptives which give protection for up to five years have recently been developed. These include Depo Provera — an injectable contraceptive — and Norplant which involves the insertion of capsules or rods containing the progestin levonorgestrel into the arm. The rods require surgical insertion and removal. These long-term methods have proven controversial because of their increased risk of side effects and the delayed return of fertility after use.

Thus, although a variety of contraceptive methods are available, choice is limited by either their safety or effectiveness or both. Indeed it has been suggested that "[t]he methods of fertility regulation from which most couples choose represent a choice among unpleasant alternatives" (R. Snowden, *Consumer Choices in Family Planning*, London, Family Planning Association, 1985). This unsatisfactory position underlines the need for care in prescribing, the necessity of adequate disclosure of risks and counselling as to alternatives. To this end, a recent report by the Contraceptive Education Service emphasised the importance of communication between doctor and patient, stressing the need for the doctor to listen to the client and to "provide information, verbally and in writing, about the method, how effective it is and about any concerns that the client may have about its use" (see Contraceptive Education Service *Contraceptive choices: supporting effective use of methods*, London: Family Planning Association, 1996 at page 19.) A significant proportion of the women surveyed by the Contraceptive Education Service would have liked more information about their contraceptive options. The report also stressed the significance of health promotion strategies in this context, finding that by the time a woman approaches a health professional for contraceptive treatment she has usually already reached a decision on the method she intends to use, based for the most part on negative perceptions of these she has chosen not to use. This finding highlights the importance of health promotion information in ensuring that women's contraceptive choices are also informed by the positive characteristics of methods which they could use. The report stressed that positive information about the advantages of different contraceptive methods must be made available to women before they take active steps to choose or change a contraceptive method. It concluded that:

"[p]oorly informed or misinformed contraceptive choices are associated with reduced user-satisfaction, lower user-effectiveness and discontinuation of method use while still at risk of unintended pregnancy. By the consistent and co-ordinated provision of information which is standardised, accurate, appropriately targeted, and impartially presented, all members of the health care team can promote and support informed contraceptive choices, and improve user-satisfaction and user-effectiveness" (Contraception Education Service, *op. cit.* at page 34).

In the light of these findings, it is unfortunate that English law (as we have seen in Chapter 6 at pages 356–362) has regarded the provision of such information as a clinical matter totally within the doctor's discretion. The attitude that "doctor knows best" may be queried in view of the readiness of GPs to prescribe the oral contraceptive pill — a factor which significantly limits contraceptive choices. Foster suggests that doctors are predisposed to prescribe methods of contraception which leave them in control and are simple to prescribe. Moreover, she suggests that pharmaceutical companies have a vested interest in persuading doctors to prescribe their products. (See P. Foster, "Contraception and Abortion" in *Women and the Health Care Industry: An Unhealthy Relationship?*, Buckingham: Open University Press, 1995). The prescription of long-lasting contraceptives, such as the Mirena IUD (which may require a general anaesthetic for insertion and removal) and Norplant may also be influenced by doctors' perception of certain woman as feckless and unable to manage their own contraceptive regimes. In such cases the consent of the woman is questionable. (See J. Hoyal and M. Dutton, "The Right to Reproduce — Sterilisation and the Mirena IUD" [1996] *Family Law* 376.) More controversial still has been use of sterilisation, which may be very difficult to reverse, in the case of mentally disabled women (see Chapter 13 at pages 754–773). As the cases discussed in Chapter 6 demonstrate (except, it seems, to appellate level judges), social factors are as significant as medical ones in the choice of contraceptives, and hence in this field there is a particular need for full disclosure of risks and benefits, as well as advice and counselling on alternatives. Unfortunately United Kingdom law has failed to endorse such a position. (See the cases of *Gold v. Haringey* and *Blyth v. Bloomsbury Health Authority* discussed in Chapter 6 at pages 356–362.)

The side effects of contraceptive products have led to litigation. The most notorious example was the Dalkon Shield IUD which was heavily marketed in the United States in the early 1970s before it was withdrawn having caused at least 20 deaths in the United States alone and injured and rendered infertile tens of thousands of women worldwide, as well as failing to prevent pregnancy. (See P. Foster, *Women and the Health Care Industry: An Unhealthy Relationship?* Buckingham: Open University Press, 1995 at page 19). Other types of IUD have also caused side effects (see P. Ferguson, *Drug Injuries and the Pursuit of Compensation*, London: Sweet & Maxwell, 1996, at pages 6–8). In 1995 an action group was established in Britain to sue the manufacturers of Norplant for serious problems that have occurred in removing the implants. (See J. Burne, "Protection Racket", *Sunday*

Telegraph, June 23, 1996.) As with any other drugs or medical products a person who suffers side effects may seek legal redress (see Chapter 3 at pages 187–193). A private patient may be able to sue for breach of contract, under section 13 of the Supply of Goods and Services Act 1982. Where contraceptives are obtained under the NHS the patient's remedy will be in negligence — for instance if she suffered a perforated uterus because a doctor fell below the expected standard in inserting an IUD. Both private and NHS patients may also have a remedy against the manufacturer of defective products under the Consumer Protection Act 1987 (see Chapter 3 at pages 187–193). Liability for failure of contraceptive measures is considered in the context of failed sterilisation in Chapter 13 at pages 798–807. As Douglas argues, doubts about the safety of female contraceptives and criticism of the cavalier attitude taken to women's concern about side effects are increasing, especially in the light of the recent scare about the link between certain bands of the oral contraceptive pill and an increased incidence of thrombosis and breast cancer. (See "What every woman knows", *The Guardian*, October 21, 1995; Burne, *op. cit.*) Furthermore, she contends that all women who wish to use contraceptives are effectively treated as guinea pigs, given the fact that information about long-term side effects of prolonged contraceptive use is still unavailable. (G. Douglas, *Law, Fertility and Reproduction*, London: Sweet & Maxwell, 1991, at pages 62–66).

QUESTIONS:

1. Is the provision of contraceptive treatment of such importance that it should be the only medical product supplied free to all users without any form of means-testing or financial contribution? If it is so important, would it make economic sense for doctors, as well as family planning clinics, to provide free condoms?

2. Should the provision of contraceptives be limited to specialist family planning clinics, especially given the numerous demands on the time of GPs, the fact that adequate advice and counselling is essential to the effective use of contraception, and that doctors are not actually obliged to provide contraceptive services?

3. Should post-coital contraception be available over the counter, as was suggested by an internal report of the Royal Pharmaceutical Society (Annual Report, 1995, at page 6)? Indeed, should oral contraceptives be available without prescription?

4. Should the administration of oral and injectable/implantable contraception be viewed as a form of research on women? If it were to be regarded as such by the courts, what consequences would that have for the type of information a doctor would have to disclose to a woman seeking contraceptive advice? (See Chapter 10.)

5. Why do you think that research on contraceptive drugs and devices has largely focused on women?

3. THE ETHICS OF ABORTION

(a) The Construction of the Ethical Debate

As we shall see below (at pages 725–729) there is no clear dividing line between certain forms of contraception on the one hand and abortifacients on the other. However, notwithstanding the continuity between methods of contraception and abortion, abortion has provoked much greater controversy. In the last two decades, the debate on abortion has become increasingly polarised around the world. Although Britain has escaped the excesses witnessed elsewhere (particularly in the United States — see R. Dworkin, *Life's Dominion: An Argument about Abortion and Euthanasia*, London: HarperCollins, 1993, Chapter 1) the abortion debate has nevertheless continued to be construed as a debate between two polarised camps — one claiming to be "pro-life" and the other as "pro-choice". "Pro-life" pressure groups such as LIFE and SPUC (the Society for the Protection of the Unborn Child) maintain that the life of the human embryo/foetus is sacrosanct and consequently that termination of pregnancy cannot be tolerated unless the life of the pregnant woman is at serious risk. For proponents of this position, life begins at conception when the sperm and ovum merge to create a (potential) human being with her or his own unique genetic pattern. (Though note the problems in defining the point of conception — see R. Lee and D. Morgan, *Blackstone's Guide to the Human Fertilisation and Embryology Act 1990*, London: Blackstone Press, 1991 at pages 63–67). "Pro-choice" advocates, on the other hand, see pregnancy as a uniquely female experience which must be controlled by the individual woman concerned. They view the life of the foetus as subordinate to the needs of the pregnant woman. For them the real issue at stake is the right of the pregnant woman to control her own body free from intrusion by third parties, including the state, which may seek to intervene on behalf of the foetus. However, although these competing moral and political positions seem logically irreconcilable, they encompass many different shades of opinion, which lead us to the conclusion that the abortion issue is best viewed as a spectrum encompassing a range of opinions. As McLean points out, it is likely that most people who reflect on the abortion issue are not necessarily or inevitably committed to the extreme positions (see S. McLean, "Abortion Law: Is Consensual Reform Possible?" (1990) 17 *Journal of Law and Society* 106 at page 107).

(b) The moral status of the foetus

There is an extensive philosophical literature on the moral status of the foetus, which mainly focuses on the point at which personhood may be attributed to the foetus. Commentators variously argue for conception, implantation, the development of a nervous system or acquisition of humanness, viability, birth or when personhood is acquired. A detailed philosophical discussion of foetal status is beyond the scope of this text. Nevertheless, the issue arises in various contexts — in relation to arguments about personhood in Chapter 2; the morality of embryo research and the use of foetal tissue in Chapter 10, and in terms of its impact on the management of pregnancy in Chapter 13. (For a full philosophical discussion of the issue see R. Hursthouse, *Beginning Lives*, Oxford: Basil Blackwell, 1987). In recent years there has been increased recognition of the necessity of finding some common ground on the abortion issue. (See R. Colker, *Abortion and Dialogue: Pro-choice, Pro-life and American Law*, Bloomington: Indiana University Press, 1992). In this regard various suggestions have been made to find ways out of the moral and political impasse. For example, Dworkin has suggested that each side may lack a clear grasp of what they are disagreeing about, and that common ground between the two groups and a basis for dialogue may be found in the fact that "[a]lmost everyone shares, explicitly or intuitively, the idea that human life has objective, intrinsic value that is quite independent of its personal value for anyone, and disagreement about the right interpretation of that shared idea is the actual nerve of the great debate about abortion" (Dworkin, *op. cit.* at page 67). He contends that in practice no one holds the belief that from conception a human life is of the same value as that of a child or adult, and from this it follows that the foetus cannot have rights until it is born and thus that it is a nonsense to attempt to balance its rights against the rights of the pregnant woman. However, he does concede that the foetus has value, and argues that there is general agreement, albeit from different perspectives, on the intrinsic value of human life. Thus, he suggests that from the moment of conception a foetus embodies a form of human life which is sacred, although he maintains that this claim need not imply that a foetus has interests of its own. Roberston adopts a similar position. He argues for an intermediate position of special respect for prenatal life on the basis that it is "genetically unique, living, human tissue that, as pregnancy progresses, increases in capacity, and eventually becomes a newborn infant". He suggests that adopting this view of the embryo/foetus is symbolically significant of our membership in the human community, although that does not require that everyone must find the same symbolic meaning or that everyone must act according to the meaning that others find. (See J. Robertson, *Children of Choice: Freedom and the New Reproductive Technologies*, Princeton, New Jersey: Princeton University Press, 1994, at pages 50–57.) Many British commentators also share this view that the foetus grows in moral worth. (See G. Douglas, *Law, Fertility and Reproduction* London: Sweet & Maxwell, 1991, Chapter 3; J. Glover, *Causing Death and Saving Lives*, Harmondsworth: Penguin, 1977, Chapter 9; J. Harris, *The Value of Life*, London: Routledge & Kegan Paul, 1985, Chapter 1; I. Kennedy, 'The Moral Status of the Embryo' in I. Kennedy, *Treat Me Right*, Oxford: Oxford University Press, 1988.) Such a view was translated into law in the landmark United States Supreme Court case of *Roe v. Wade* 410 U.S. 113 (1973), in which the

United States Supreme Court decided that the constitutional right to privacy enshrined in the United States Constitution was broad enough to encompass a woman's right to terminate her pregnancy. The Supreme Court adopted a trimester framework for analysing pregnancy. It held that the pregnant woman's right to privacy must prevail in the first trimester, but suggested that by the third trimester the state's interest in protecting foetal life should prevail unless there was a risk to the life or health of the pregnant woman. Although the trimester framework was subsequently invalidated in *Planned Parenthood of S.E. Pennsylvania v. Casey* (1992) 112 St. 2791 it did seem to accord with the intuitive views of many commentators that the foetus grows in moral worth throughout the pregnancy. The notion that the foetus has some sort of 'intermediate' moral status, which is less than that of a person but more than a body part, and of its complex relationship to the pregnant woman has also been recognised in much feminist writing. (See C. MacKinnon, "Reflections on Sex Equality under Law" (1991) 100 *Yale Law Journal* 1281; B. Steinbock, *Life Before Birth*, New York: Oxford University Press, 1992, Chapter 1.)

Such a position, commanding as it does a widespread consensus at least amongst legal and philosophical scholars, has led McLean to suggest that the issue of late abortions provides one example of common ground, since all parties to the debate can agree that late terminations should be avoided. (See McLean, *op. cit.*). There may also be space for progressive dialogue on the need to reduce the number of abortions through the provision of better education and improved access to contraception, although many "pro-life" advocates are almost equally vehemently opposed to these developments.

A few other factors are worth noting about the abortion debate. First, it provides a good illustration of the political importance of terminology (see further Chapter 2 at pages 115), since all the available language in which the issue may be debated is morally loaded. Even the terms "pro-life" and "pro-choice", in which the debate is normally couched, are morally loaded. Moreover, we recognise that speaking in terms of the "pregnant woman" and "foetus", as we have elected to do, rather than using the words "mother" and "unborn child" skews the debate in particular ways. We have chosen this language to reflect the fact that law has traditionally accorded the foetus a different status from a human being, and in order to avoid the ideology of maternity that comes with adopting the term "mother" (see E. Fegan, "'Fathers' Foetuses and Abortion Decision-making: The Reproduction of Maternal Ideology" (1996) 5 *Social and Legal Studies* 75). Secondly, the abortion debate exemplifies the problematic nature of rights-based arguments and their tendency to lead to a political and moral impasse, as in this situation where the pregnant woman's right to autonomy is pitted against the right to life of the foetus. Rights arguments also have a tendency to represent the debate in a way which is at odds with the experiences of the pregnant woman. (See C. Smart, *Feminism and the Power of Law*, Routledge: London, 1989 at pages 138–159; E. Kingdom, *What's Wrong with Rights: Problems for a Feminist*

Politics of Law, Edinburgh: Edinburgh University Press, 1991, Chapter 3). Thirdly, it is worth noting that many leading commentators on the abortion law issue are North American, and that "solutions" to complex social issues like abortion may not be easily transplanted to other jurisdictions. (See S. Gibson, "Continental Drift: The Question of Context in Feminist Jurisprudence" (1990) I *Law and Critique* 173.)

(c) The relationship between ethics and law

In practice, legislators in Britain have largely sidestepped the ethical debate by opting for the pragmatic course of permitting abortion in a limited range of circumstances. Our legislators have thus failed to address the status of the foetus, or indeed the rights of any of the parties concerned (see below at pages 730–746). In part this is a result of the main statute's origin as a private member's bill, the form of which was dictated largely by the medical profession who were concerned about the uncertainty of the common law regarding the circumstances in which abortion was permissible. (See T. Newburn, *Permission and Regulation: Law and Morals in Post-War Britain*, London: Routledge, 1989, at pages 136–157.) For the most part, the 1967 Abortion Act (which like most legislation on contentious social issues was the subject of a free vote in parliament), was a compromise premised largely on two pragmatic arguments. The first is that unless law tolerates abortions performed by doctors we would face the spectre of backstreet abortions, since prior to the passage of the 1967 legislation unlawful terminations were frequently carried out by medically untrained persons in unhygienic conditions and at extortionate rates. A further pragmatic argument in favour of abortion rests on the principle of "double-effect", which operates to permit terminations where the intention of the physician is to save the life of the woman and the destruction of the foetus is an unintended side-effect of the overall good end of preserving the life of the woman (see further Chapter 2 at pages 114–115; and T. Beauchamp and R. Childress, *Principles of Biomedical Ethics*, 4th ed., 1994 at pages 205–7 on the applicability of the doctrine to the issue of abortion).

The lack of sustained discussion of the moral and legal status of the foetus has served to medicalise and consequently depoliticise the issue of abortion in the United Kingdom. (See S. Sheldon, "Subject Only to the Attitude of the Surgeon Concerned: The Judicial Protection of Medical Discretion" (1996) 5 *Social and Legal Studies* 95.) One consequence of the pragmatic stance adopted by English law is that the legal status of the foetus may be inconsistent. In Chapter 10 we saw that the law permits embryo experimentation only up to 14 days, yet as we shall see, provided the 1967 Act is satisfied, abortions may be performed up to 24 weeks, or in certain circumstances right up to birth. (See J. Harris, "Should we experiment on embryos?" in R. Lee and D. Morgan, *Birthrights: Law and ethics at the beginning of life*, London: Routledge, 1989). What is clear is that English law has not recognised the foetus as a person to whom rights may be attributed. Any rights which the foetus has are contingent on it being born alive (see pages 731–737 below). However, it has been argued that attempts to vindicate foetal rights in law by pro-life individuals and groups, even though they have not been successful to date, have shifted the moral terrain in favour of pro-life forces. (See S. Sheldon, "The Law of Abortion and the Politics of Medicalisation" in J. Bridgman and S. Millns (eds), *Law and Body Politics*, Aldershot: Dartmouth, 1995). Indeed, even to focus on the debate about foetal status and personhood as means of deciding the debate may be misdirected. (See C. Wells and D. Morgan "Whose Foetus Is It?" (1991) 81 *Journal of Law and Society* 431.) Such a focus may obscure both the role of the woman and "important connections between unwanted pregnancies and broader social factors. Moreover, it fosters a climate where it seems possible to deal with the problem of unwanted pregnancy merely by the provision of abortion without ever listening to women in order to explore the problems which lead to unwanted pregnancy itself" (S. Sheldon, "Subject only to the Attitude of the Surgeon Concerned: The Judicial Protection of Medical Discretion" (1996) 5 *Social and Legal Studies* 95). Furthermore, as we shall see in Chapter 13, the effect of technological interventions during pregnancy which have rendered the foetus *in utero* increasingly visible, has been to construct the foetus as a separate individual and "second patient" in medical and scientific discourse (see R. Petchesky, "Foetal images: the power of visual culture in the politics of reproduction" in M. Stanworth (ed.), *Reproductive Technologies*, Cambridge: Polity Press, 1987; A. Young, "Decapitation or Feticide: The Fetal Laws of the Universal Subject" (1993) 4 *Women: A Cultural Review* 288).

QUESTION:

1. The abortion debate provides a good context in which to explore the relationship between law and morality addressed in Chapter 2. Thus, whatever your view of the morality of abortion and the moral status of the foetus, can you make a convincing case for your arguments to be translated into law? (See M. Brazier, "Embryo's 'Rights': Abortion and Research" in M. D. A. Freeman (ed.), *Medicine, Ethics and the Law*, London: Stevens & Sons, 1988.)

4. THE LAW OF ABORTION

The law of abortion forms part of the criminal law: those who unlawfully terminate (or, in some circumstances, attempt to terminate) a pregnancy are liable to be convicted of an offence. So too may those who procure the means of unlawfully terminating a pregnancy. These offences are contained in the Offences Against the Person Act 1861 and centre on the notion of procuring a miscarriage.

(a) The criminal prohibition on procuring a miscarriage

Offences Against the Person Act 1861, ss.58–59

58 Every woman being with child, who, with intent to procure her own miscarriage, shall unlawfully administer to herself any poison or other noxious thing, or shall unlawfully use any instrument or other means whatsoever with the like intent and whosoever, with intent to procure the miscarriage of any woman whether she be or be not with child, shall unlawfully administer to her or cause to be taken by her any poison or other noxious thing, or shall unlawfully use any instrument or other means whatsoever with the like intent, shall be guilty of an offence, and being convicted thereof shall be liable . . . to be kept in penal servitude for life . . .

59 Whosoever shall unlawfully supply or procure any poison or other noxious thing, or any instrument or thing whatsoever, knowing that the same is intended to be unlawfully used or employed with intent to procure the miscarriage of any woman, whether she be or not be with child, shall be guilty of an offence, and being convicted thereof shall be liable . . . to be kept in penal servitude for a term not exceeding five years.

[Note: words omitted were repealed by the Statute Law Revision Act 1892 and the Statute Law Revision (No. 2) Act 1893]

NOTES:

1. The 1861 Act proscribes three kinds of conduct: the self-induction of miscarriage, things done by a second person to procure the miscarriage of a woman (whether or not she is in fact pregnant), and the supply or procurement of an abortifacient (*i.e.* an implement or drug designed to bring about a miscarriage).
2. A woman cannot be convicted of attempting to self-induce a miscarriage where she is not in fact pregnant: the act makes any offence by her conditional upon her "being with child".

QUESTION:

1. Is it necessary that the act of a person other than the woman should be successful in producing a miscarriage so long as the act in question was done with the intent to procure a miscarriage? (Re-read section 59 carefully!)

In 1929 Parliament passed another statute which is relevant to the law on abortion — the Infant Life Preservation Act of 1929. This Act was introduced for two main reasons. The first was to fill a lacuna in the law. As we have seen, the 1861 Act affords protection to the foetus *in utero*. The law of homicide (see Chapter 14 at pages 821–827) protects a child once it has been born. However, no legal protection was afforded to the baby whilst it was in the process of being born. In 1928 a defendant charged with procuring a miscarriage had been acquitted on the grounds that the child was in the process of being born, and the legislation was introduced to close this loophole. The second reason for the passage of the 1929 Act was to protect a doctor who performed a craniotomy — an operation in which the impacted head of a foetus was crushed in order to save the mother's life. This operation was commonly practised before Caesarean sections became routine.

Infant Life (Preservation) Act 1929, s.1(1)–(2)

1.—(1) Subject as hereinafter in this subsection provided, any person who, with intent to destroy the life of a child capable of being born alive, by any wilful act causes a child to die before it has an existence independent of its mother, shall be guilty of felony, to wit, of child destruction, and shall be liable on conviction thereof on indictment to penal servitude for life.

Provided that no person shall be found guilty of an offence under this section unless it is proved that the act which caused the death of the child was not done in good faith for the purpose only of preserving the life of the mother.

(2) For the purposes of this Act, evidence that the woman had at any material time been pregnant for a period of twenty-eight weeks or more shall be *prima facie* proof that she was at that time pregnant with a child capable of being born alive.

NOTE:

1. The crucial threshold criterion for the operation of the 1929 Act is the attainment, by the foetus, of the capacity to be born alive. However this phrase is not clearly defined? This is a crucial question since section 1(2) of the Act simply provides a (rebuttable) presumption that a child attains this capacity at 28 weeks' gestation. (For the position at present see pages 715–718 below.)

Just as the 1929 Act rendered craniotomies lawful, so section 58 of the 1861 Act, by using the word "unlawful" seemed to envisage some situations in which abortion would be lawful. This issue was addressed in the leading case prior to the passage of the 1967 legislation.

R v. Bourne [1938] 3 All E.R. 615; [1939] 1 K.B. 687

This case concerned the prosecution of Mr Bourne, a distinguished gynaecologist, who deliberately challenged the English law on abortion in order to clarify the scope of defences available to doctors who performed abortions. Having performed an abortion on a 14-year-old girl who had been subjected to gang rape by a group of soldiers and become pregnant as a result, he presented himself to the authorities and was charged with unlawfully procuring a miscarriage, contrary to section 58.

MACNAUGHTEN J.:

". . . The charge against Mr Bourne is the very grave charge under the Offences Against the Person, 1861, s.58, that he unlawfully procured the abortion of the girl . . . [J]udging by the cases that come before the court, it is a crime by no means uncommon. This is the second case at these July sessions at this court where a charge of an offence against that section has been preferred, and I mention that case only to show you how different the case now before you is from the type of case which usually comes before a criminal court. In that case, a woman without any medical skill or any medical qualifications did what is alleged against Mr Bourne here: she unlawfully used an instrument for the purpose of procuring the miscarriage of a pregnant girl. She did it for money . . . The case here is very different. A man of the highest skill, openly, in one of our great hospitals, performs the operation. Whether it was legal or illegal you will have to determine, but he performs the operation as an act of charity, without fee or reward, and unquestionably believing that he was doing the right thing, and that he ought, in the performance of his duty as a member of a profession devoted to the alleviation of human suffering, to do it . . .

The question that you have got to determine is whether the Crown has proved to your satisfaction beyond reasonable doubt that the act which Mr Bourne admittedly did was not done in good faith for the purpose only of preserving the life of the girl . . .

There has been much discussion before you as to the meaning of the words 'preserving the life of the mother' . . . [The Infant Life (Preservation) Act 1929] provides that no one is to be found guilty of the offence created by the Act — namely, 'child destruction' — unless it is proved that:

> . . . the act which caused the death of the child was not done in good faith for the purpose only of preserving the life of the mother.

Those words express what, in my view, has always been the law with regard to the procuring of an abortion, and although not expressed in s.58 of the Act of 1861, they are implied by the word 'unlawful' in that section. No person ought to be convicted under s.58 of the Act of 1861 unless the jury are satisfied the act was not done in good faith for the purpose only of preserving the life of the mother. My view is that it has always been the law that the Crown have got to prove the offence beyond reasonable doubt, and it has always been the law that, on a charge of procuring abortion, the Crown have got to prove that the act was not done in good faith for the purpose of preserving the life of the mother. It is said — and I think, rightly — that this is a case of great importance to the public, and more especially to the medical profession, but you will observe that it has nothing to do with ordinary cases of procuring abortion, to which I have already referred. In those cases, the operation is performed by a person of no skill, with no medical qualifications, and there is no pretence that it is done for the preservation of the mother's life. Cases of that sort are in no way affected by the consideration of the question that is put before you. In the ordinary cases, no question of that sort can arise. It is obvious that that defence could not be available to the professional abortionist. As I say, you have heard a great deal of discussion as to the difference between danger to life and danger to health . . .

But is there a perfectly clear line of distinction between danger to life and danger to health? I should have thought not. I should have thought that impairment of health might reach a stage where it was a danger to life . . . If that is a view which commends itself to you, so that you cannot say that there is this division into two separate classes with a dividing line between them, then it may be that you will accept the view that Mr Oliver put forward when he invited you to give to the words 'for the purpose of preserving the life of the mother' a wide and liberal view of their meaning. I would prefer the word 'reasonable' to the words 'wide and liberal'. Take a reasonable view of the words 'for the preservation of the life of the mother'. I do not think that it is contended that those words mean merely for the preservation of the life of the mother from instant death. There are cases, we were told — and indeed I expect you know cases from your own experiences — where it is reasonably certain that a woman will not be able to deliver the child with which she is pregnant. In such a case, where the doctor expects, basing his opinion upon the experience and knowledge of the profession, that the child cannot be delivered without the death of the mother, in those circumstances the doctor is entitled — and, indeed, it is his duty — to perform this operation with a view to saving the life of the mother, and in such a case it is obvious that the sooner the operation is performed the better. The law is not that the doctor has got to wait until the unfortunate woman is in peril of immediate death and then at the last moment to snatch her from the jaws of death. He is not only entitled, but it is his duty, to perform the operation with a view to saving her life . . .

[I]f the doctor is of opinion, on reasonable grounds and with adequate knowledge, that the probable consequence of the continuance of the pregnancy will be to make the woman a physical or mental wreck, the jury are quite entitled to take the view that a doctor, who, in those circumstances, and in that honest belief, operates, is operating for the purpose of preserving the life of the woman . . ."

NOTES:

1. As the jury acquitted Mr Bourne, this authority was never confirmed by an appellate court. The uncertainty of the parameters of the *Bourne* decision gave impetus to the movement to reform the law on abortion.

2. Keown has pointed out that it was unnecessary for Macnaughten J. to complicate matters by referring to the 1929 Act, since a number of cases before and after the 1861 Act had made it quite clear that there were circumstances in which abortion was lawful. (See J. Keown, *Abortion, Doctors and the Law*, Cambridge: CUP, 1988, Chapter 3.) On this view the summing up to the jury on the circumstances in which abortion is lawful may have been more restrictive than earlier cases had indicated.

3. It has recently been confirmed in three unreported cases that the precedent of *Bourne* governs the law on abortion in Northern Ireland, where the Abortion Act 1967 has never applied. (See S. Lee, "An A to K to Z of abortion law in Northern Ireland: abortion on remand" in A. Furedi (ed.), *The Abortion Law in Northern Ireland: Human Rights and Reproductive Choice*, Belfast: Family Planning Association, 1995; T. McGleenan, "*Bourne* again? Abortion Law in Northern Ireland from *Re K* to *Re A*" (1994) 46 *Northern Ireland Legal Quarterly* 389. As Lee notes, although most abortions in Northern Ireland are performed on the basis of foetal disability, it is difficult to see how *Bourne* can be stretched to encompass terminations on the ground of foetal disability. (See S. Lee, "Abortion law in Northern Ireland: the twilight zone" in Furedi, *op. cit.* at page 21.)

QUESTIONS:

1. Was Macnaughten J.'s summing up to the jury unduly favourable to Mr Bourne? (See Chapter 3 at page 156 for the argument that tests propounded by the courts may favour the medical profession.)

2. Do you agree with the way in which Macnaughten J. interpreted the relevant statutes?

3. Are medical qualifications needed to perform an abortion? (See *Royal College of Nursing v. Department of Health and Social Security* [1981] 1 All E.R. 545 at pages 720–725 below; R. Chalker and C. Dovner, *A Woman's Book of Choices*, Four Walls and Eight Windows, 1992.)

4. Is it justifiable not to allow women in Northern Ireland the same right to abortion as their counterparts elsewhere in the United Kingdom?

(b) The statutory grounds for lawful termination

The circumstances in which a termination can lawfully be performed were significantly extended by the enactment of the Abortion Act 1967. This statute, as has already been observed, was intended in large part to eradicate the problem of "back street" abortions. It thus required that except in emergencies, a termination performed under the Act must be performed in an NHS (Trust) hospital or other approved place. This was clearly intended to minimise the effects of a medical mishap during termination as well as to reduce the likelihood of infection.

The statutory pre-conditions for a lawful termination are contained in section 1 of the 1967 Act (as amended by the Human Fertilisation and Embryology Act 1990).

Abortion Act 1967, ss.1(1–2), 5, 6

1.—(1) Subject to the provisions of this section, a person shall not be guilty of an offence under the law relating to abortion when a pregnancy is terminated by a registered medical practitioner if two registered medical practitioners are of the opinion, formed in good faith —

(a) that the pregnancy has not exceeded its twenty-fourth week and that the continuance of the pregnancy would involve risk, greater than if the pregnancy were terminated, of injury to the physical or mental health of the pregnant woman or any existing children of her family; or

(b) that the termination is necessary to prevent grave permanent injury to the physical or mental health of the pregnant woman; or

(c) that the continuance of the pregnancy would involve risk to the life of the pregnant woman, greater than if the pregnancy were terminated; or

(d) that there is a substantial risk that if the child were born it would suffer from such physical or mental abnormalities as to be seriously handicapped.

(2) In determining whether the continuance of a pregnancy would involve such risk of injury to health as is mentioned in paragraph (a) or (b) of subsection (1) of this section, account may be taken of the pregnant woman's actual or reasonably foreseeable environment . . . [For the remaining provisions of this section see page 718 below.]

5.—(1)No offence under the Infant Life (Preservation) Act 1929 shall be committed by a registered medical practitioner who terminates a pregnancy in accordance with the provisions of this Act.

(2) For the purposes of the law relating to abortion, anything done with intent to procure a woman's miscarriage (or, in the case of a woman carrying more than one

foetus, her miscarriage of any foetus) is unlawfully done unless authorised by section 1 of this Act and, in the case of a woman carrying more than one foetus, anything done with intent to procure her miscarriage of any foetus is authorised by that section if — (a) the ground for termination of the pregnancy specified in subsection (1)(d) of that section applies in relation to any foetus and the thing is done for the purpose of procuring the miscarriage of that foetus, or (b) any of the other grounds for termination of the pregnancy specified in that section applies.

6.—In this Act, the following expressions have meanings hereby assigned to them:

"the law relating to abortion" means sections 58 and 59 of the Offences against the Person Act 1861, and any rule of law relating to the procurement of abortion; . . .

NOTES:

1. Perhaps the most significant omission in the 1967 Abortion Act, prior to its amendment in 1990 was that it set no time limit as to when abortions could lawfully be performed. However, the 1967 Act did contain a provision that nothing in it which affected the operation of the 1929 Infant Life (Preservation) Act. As we have seen that statute provided that if a woman had been pregnant for 28 weeks that was prima facie evidence that the child was capable of being born alive. Thus, it was assumed that abortions under the 1967 Act were lawful if they were performed before the foetus was 28 weeks old. However, the 1967 Act did not preclude the possibility that a foetus could be deemed capable of being born alive at some earlier gestational age. This possibility received judicial consideration in two cases before the 1990 amendments. In *C v. S* [1987] 1 All E.R. 1230 (considered further below). A single woman wished to terminate her pregnancy which was dated at between 18 and 21 weeks. Two medical practitioners were satisfied that continuance of the pregnancy would involve a risk of injury to her physical or mental health greater than if the pregnancy was terminated. They certified their view in accordance with the Abortion Act 1967. The putative father nevertheless sought to restrain the proposed termination on the basis that it would in fact be in contravention of the Infant Life (Preservation) Act 1929. Crucial to his claim was that a foetus of between 18 and 21 weeks is capable of being born alive (in which case a termination could only lawfully be performed to preserve the life of the pregnant mother). The meaning of the phrase therefore fell for judicial consideration both at first instance, and on appeal to the Court of Appeal.

   In both the High Court and Court of Appeal judgments the judges stated that they need not provide an authoritative interpretation of what the phrase "capable of being born alive" meant, since they accepted that a foetus of 19–21 weeks gestation was not capable of being born alive. The later case of *Rance and another v. Mid-Downs Health Authority and Another* [1991] 1 All E.R. 801. This case concerned an action for negligence brought by a husband and his wife who gave birth to a baby boy suffering from spina bifida. The gist of their action was that the defendant health authority's employees ought to have diagnosed the disability and to have availed to plaintiffs of the possibility of having the pregnancy legally terminated. The defendant authority, however, contended that their failure to diagnose the foetal disability was immaterial since, as Mrs Rance was about 26 weeks pregnant a legal termination could not have been performed in any event. It followed, the health authority argued, that no action for failure to advise of the possibility of an abortion could possibly lie. In this case Brooke J. held that a 26-week-old foetus was capable of being born alive, so that it would be too late for a lawful abortion to be performed and consequently the claim for damages failed. (See J. Murphy, "Grey Areas and Green Lights: Judicial Activism in the Regulation of Doctors" (1991) 42 *Northern Ireland Legal Quarterly* 260.) Since the insertion of the 24-week time limit into the 1967 Act by the 1990 Human Fertilisation and Embryology Act these cases are of historical interest only. (See D. Morgan and R. Lee, *Blackstone's Guide to the Human Fertilisation and Embryology Act 1990* London: Blackstone Press, 1991, at page 49 for the complicated pattern of voting in the House of Commons on the time-limits issue.)

2. There is no time-limit on the grounds in section 1(1)(b)–(d) which may all be invoked until the point of birth.

3. The justification for abortion enshrined in section 1(1)(a) is sometimes referred to as the "social grounds". This is because in assessing the risk to the woman's health (or that of any existing children), or the threat to her life, account may be taken of her home environment, pursuant to section 2. Usually, this provision will be invoked to sanction a termination, and the vast majority of abortions are on this basis. Indeed statistics would appear to demonstrate that the risks of continuing with the pregnancy and birth are always greater than the risk of abortion within the first 12 weeks. However, in the case of a pregnant teenage girl from an ethnic minority or strict religious denomination, the social ground might well necessitate consideration of the fact that, if the girl undergoes a termination, she is likely to be shunned or ostracised within her community or by her family. The fact that there is external pressure on her may also affect the validity of her consent to the termination. (See further, D. Pearl, "Legal Issues arising out of Medical Provision for Ethnic Groups" in A. Grubb (ed.), *Justice and Health Care: Comparative Perspectives*, Chichester: John Wiley, 1995.)

4. Particular problems arise with respect to dating pregnancies for the purposes of section 1(1)(a). Doctors date pregnancies from the last menstrual period, which means that by the time the fusion of sperm and ovum takes place, the pregnancy is already two weeks old. It can also be argued, however, that fertilisation or implantation are the

critical dates (assuming in 28 day cycle). (See J. Murphy, "Cosmetics, Eugenics and Ambivalence: the Reform of the Abortion Act 1967" [1991] *Journal of Social Welfare and Family Law* 375.)

5. Sub-section 1(1)(b) is a new ground for abortion inserted by the 1990 Act. "Grave permanent injury" to the woman's physical or mental health must mean something less serious than either "a risk to her life greater than if the pregnancy was terminated" (the ground specified in sub-section 1(1)(c)), or "an immediate risk to her life" dealt with in sub-section 1(4). Morgan and Lee suggest that this puts into statutory form the reading given to the Infant Life (Preservation) Act 1929 in *Bourne*; and would include conditions such as mild pre-eclampsia or uncontrolled diabetes in which the risk to the woman increases during pregnancy due to hormonal changes. (See Morgan and Lee, *Blackstone's Guide to the Human Fertilisation and Embryology Act 1990*, London: Blackstone Press, 1991 at pages 50–51.)

6. The ground in section 1(1)(c) — that a termination is justified where the pregnant woman's life is at risk — is largely a codification of the principle expounded in *R. v. Bourne* [1938] 3 All E.R. 615.

7. The meaning of the foetal handicap ground in section 1(1)(d) is not settled under English law. Some discussion of its possible import — that in some circumstances it is better not to be born than to suffer disabilities — was supplied by Stephenson L.J. in *McKay v. Essex AHA* [1982] 2 All E.R. 771. (For academic discussion, see D. Morgan, "Abortion: the Unexamined Ground" [1990] *Criminal Law Review* 687; J. Murphy, "Cosmetics, Eugenics and Ambivalence: the Reform of the Abortion Act 1967" [1991] *Journal of Social Welfare and Family Law* 375.)

8. Though the Act is explicit in requiring the approval of two medical practitioners, it is also implicit that a legal termination will not be performed against the wishes of the pregnant woman. Ordinarily this presents no difficulties since doctors will not normally become involved until they are approached by a woman who seeks a termination. Nonetheless, a real problem is encountered where the pregnant woman is over 18-years-old and, owing to mental disability, unable to form the requisite capacity to give her consent to the termination. Here the question arises whether her pregnancy can lawfully be terminated. The answer — according to *T v. T* [1988] 1 All E.R. 613, where the matter was litigated — appears to be that an abortion is not unlawful provided it is (a) in the woman's best interests and (b) in accordance with good medical practice. (On the legal definition of capacity to consent see Chapter 5.) The Law Commission in its report, *Mental Incapacity*, Law Com. 231, recommended (at paragraph 6.10) that before an abortion is performed, an independent medical practitioner should issue a certificate that the abortion would be in her best interests.

9. Related problems can be encountered in relation to teenage girls. Once again, the courts will adopt the "patient's best interests

approach", but they must be cautious to examine the girl's best interests from a suitably wide perspective, and not focus simply upon whether an abortion is desirable purely in medical terms. (See Chapter 7 at pages 418–420.)

10. The "selective reduction" of pregnancy — that is, termination of one or more foetuses in the case of multiple pregnancy — is now permissable where the woman (a) has a multiple pregnancy (*i.e.* twins, triplets etc) and (b) the terms specified in section 5(2) are met. This provision was inserted by the Human Fertilisation and Embryology Act 1990, in recognition of the high increase of multiple pregnancies resulting from *in vitro* fertilisation. It permits the destruction of one or more foetuses in the interests of the one or more which will survive. (See J. Keown, "Selective Reduction of Multiple Pregnancy" (1987) *New L.J.* 1165; D. Price, "Selective Reduction and Feticide: The Parameters of Abortion" [1988] *Criminal Law Review* 199.) It is estimated that approximately 100 selective terminations are performed every year on women who have undergone IVF treatment. In August 1996 a national debate on the ethics of selective termination erupted when it emerged that a 28-year-old woman who was 16 weeks pregnant with healthy twins had aborted one foetus on the ground that she could not cope with twins. It was initially suggested that she was a single mother in "socially straitened" circumstances, although it later became apparent that she was in fact a married professional woman. (See " 'No new issue' in abortion of twin", *The Guardian*, August 5, 1996.) Later in the same month the issue was aired again when a woman who was pregnant with octuplets as a result of taking ovulatory drugs rejected medical advice that some of the foetuses should be aborted. (See "Pregnancy that should be viewed as a catastrophe for all involved", *The Times*, August 12, 1996.) Both cases raise important issues about the parameters of acceptable reproductive choices.

11. Whereas the original 1967 Abortion Act had specifically preserved the effect of the Infant Life Preservation Act; that saving is removed by section 37(4) of the 1990 Act which inserts a new section 5(1) into the Abortion Act. Hence, since 1990 when an abortion is carried out in accordance with section 1 no prosecution will lie even if the foetus destroyed is "capable of being born alive" within the meaning given to that phrase in the *Rance* decision (above at pages 714–715).

QUESTIONS:

1. If the point of viability can change through time (and from one part of the world to another depending on the level of medical technology available) can viability be regarded as a point of moral significance in the development of the foetus?

2. Do you think that the statutory provisions as to the circumstances in which abortion is lawful are more workable than the test in *Bourne*? If so, is this an argument for further statutory regulation of health care law as opposed to leaving such issues to be settled by the judiciary?

3. What, for the purposes of section 1, amounts to the absence of good faith on the part of the two registered medical practitioners who certify a termination? How would one prove the absence of good faith. (See *Paton v. British Pregnancy Advisory Service and Another* [1978] 2 All E.R. 987 at page 738 below.)

4. Certain ethnic minorities place great emphasis on the importance of having a male son and heir. It follows that a woman who seems able only to give birth to daughters might find herself pressurised (even ostracised) within her community to the extent that her mental or physical health begin to suffer. Would it be possible, in such circumstances, to provide abortions as a means of sex selection? Is sub-section 1(1)(a) — read in the light of sub-section 2 — wide enough to permit such terminations? (See D. Morgan, "Foetal sex identification, abortion and the law" (1988) 18 *Family Law* 355.)

5. Would the risk of harm to the psychological health suffice for the purposes of sub-section 1(1)(b)?

6. Would sub-section 1(1)(b) (construed in accordance with sub-section 1(2)) entitle a doctor to take account of risks to mental health caused by the effects of child rearing if the pregnancy were not terminated?

7. Is it wrong in principle to allow terminations on the basis of foetal disability? Can aborting a very mature foetus be justified on this, or any other, ground where, if the foetus was born, it would probably survive? Is it right to compel the mother of a severely disabled foetus to give birth only to let the child die later as a severely disabled neonate? (See further Chapter 14.)

8. What is the level of (a) risk and (b) disability necessary for a termination on the basis of sub-section 1(1)(d)? Would a termination on the basis of a "hare-lip" suffice? Who is to decide the meaning of the sub-section? The doctors, the courts or the pregnant woman? (See D. Morgan, "Abortion: The Unexamined Ground" [1990] *Criminal Law Review* 687.)

(c) Where and how may lawful abortions be performed?

One of the objectives of the 1967 Act was to eradicate "back-street" abortions, performed by persons who frequently were not medically qualified, and carried out in unhygienic conditions. The Act therefore requires that, in addition to satisfying one of the grounds in section 1(1) that terminations must, save in emergencies, be carried out in a hospital or other suitably hygienic environment.

Abortion Act 1967, s.1(3), (3A), (4), s.2(1), (2), (4)

1.—(3) Except as provided by subsection (4) of this section, any treatment for the termination of pregnancy must be carried out in a hospital vested in the Secretary of State for the purposes of his functions under the National Health Service Act 1977 or the National Health Service (Scotland) Act 1978 or in a hospital vested in a National Health Service trust or in a place approved for the purposes of this section by the Secretary of State.

(3A) The power under subsection (3) of this section to approve a place includes power, in relation to treatment consisting primarily in the use of such medicines as may be specified in the approval and carried out in such manner Abortion Act 1967, section 1 as may be so specified, to approve a class of places.

(4) Subsection (3) of this section, and so much of subsection (1) as relates to the opinion of two registered medical practitioners, shall not apply to the termination of a pregnancy by a registered medical practitioner in a case where he is of the opinion, formed in good faith, that the termination is immediately necessary to save the life or to prevent grave permanent injury to the physical or mental health of the pregnant woman.

Section 3A was clearly inserted (by the Human Fertilisation and Embryology Act 1990) in anticipation of the abortion pill — see page 726, below.

Before a termination will be lawful, proper certification that the terms of the 1967 Act have been met must take place in accordance with section 2 of the Act.

Abortion Act 1967, s.2(1–2, 4)

2.—(1) The Minister of Health in respect of England and Wales, and the Secretary of State in respect of Scotland, shall by statutory instrument make regulations to provide:

(a) for requiring any such opinion as is referred to in section 1 of this Act to be certified by the practitioners or practitioner concerned in such form and at such time as may be prescribed by the regulations, and for requiring the preservation and disposal of certificates made for the purposes of the regulations;

(b) for requiring any registered medical practitioner who terminates a pregnancy to give notice of the termination and such other information relating to the termination as may be so prescribed;

(c) for prohibiting the disclosure, except to such persons or for such purposes as may be so prescribed, of notices given or information furnished pursuant to the regulations.

(2) The information furnished in pursuance of regulations made by virtue of paragraph (b) of subsection (1) of this section shall be notified solely to the Chief Medical Officer of the Department of Health, or of the Welsh Office, or of the Scottish Home and Health Department.

(3) Any person who wilfully contravenes or wilfully fails to comply with the requirements of regulations under subsection (1) of this section shall be liable on summary conviction to a fine not exceeding level 5 on the standard scale.

(4) Any statutory instrument made by virtue of this section shall be subject to annulment in pursuance of a resolution of either House of Parliament.

The requisite certification must be on one of two prescribed forms. The first relates to the ordinary case where two doctors' testimonies are required. The second covers those cases where a doctor treats a woman on his own in an emergency to save her life or prevent her suffering irreparable, grave ill-health. Since 1967 there has only been one successful prosecution of a doctor owing to failure to comply with the terms of the Act. The doctor in question performed an abortion without examining the woman or enquiring about her medical history (*R v. Smith* [1974] 1 All E.R. 376).

One important question concerning the draftsmanship of section 1 of the Abortion Act is how wide a construction ought to be placed on the phrase "when a pregnancy is terminated by a registered medical practitioner". The significance of this question stems from the fact that medically induced terminations are usually in fact performed by nurses since it is they who actually administer the hormone which induces labour (*i.e.* a series of uterine contractions which culminates in the birth of the child).

Royal College of Nursing v. Department of Health and Social Security [1981] 1 All E.R. 545; [1981] A.C. 800

The Royal College of Nursing brought the proceedings out of which this case arose-seeking to clarify the lawfulness of the nurses involvement in terminations obtained by medical induction. The College was unconvinced by the contents of a Department of Health and Social Security Circular which had stated that no offence was committed by nurses who administer fluids to a pregnant woman with the result that premature birth would be induced and that the foetus would be born dead.

The College sought a declaration that the advice contained in the circular was wrong and that the administration by a nurse of prostaglandin (or some other such substance) was contrary to section 58 of the Offences Against the Person Act 1861.

LORD KEITH:
" . . . My Lords, this appeal is concerned with the question whether s.1(1) of the Abortion Act 1967 applies, so as to relieve the participants from criminal liability, to the procedures normally followed in operating a modern technique for inducing abortion by medical means.

The technique, which has been evolved and become common practice over the past ten years for the purpose of terminating pregnancy during the third trimester, is considered in medical circles to involve less risk to the patient than does surgical intervention. The details of the procedure have been fully described in the judgments of the courts below. Its main feature is the introduction via a catheter into the interspace between the amniotic sac and the wall of the uterus of an abortifacient drug called prostaglandin. The purpose of this is to induce uterine contractions which in most cases, but not in all, result in the expulsion of the foetus after a period of between 18 and 30 hours. The process is assisted by the introduction into the blood stream, via a cannula inserted in a vein, of another drug called oxytocin. Responsibility for deciding on and putting the procedure into operation rests with a registered medical practitioner who himself inserts the catheter and the cannula. The attachment of the catheter and the cannula to a supply of prostaglandin and of oxytocin respectively and the initiation and regulation of the flow of these drugs are carried out by a nurse under the written instructions of the doctor, who is not normally present at those stages. He or a colleague is, however, available on call throughout.

Section 1(1) of the 1967 Act can operate to relieve a person from guilt of an offence under the law relating to abortion only 'when a pregnancy is terminated by a registered medical practitioner'. Certain other conditions must also be satisfied, but no question about these arises in the present case. The sole issue is whether the words I have quoted cover the situation where abortion has been brought about as a result of the procedure under consideration.

The argument for the Royal College of Nursing is, in essence, that the words of the subsection do not apply because the pregnancy has not been terminated by any registered medical practitioner but by the nurse who did the act or acts which directly resulted in the administration to the pregnant woman of the abortifacient drugs.

In my opinion this argument involves placing an unduly restricted and unintended meaning on the words 'when a pregnancy is terminated'. It seems to me that these words, in their context, are not referring to the mere physical occurrence of termination. The side-note to section 1 is 'Medical termination of pregnancy'. 'Termination of pregnancy' is an expression commonly used, perhaps, rather more by medical people than by laymen, to describe in neutral and unemotive terms the bringing about of an abortion. So used, it is capable of covering the whole process designed to lead to that result, and in my view it does so in the present context. Other provisions of the Act make it clear that termination of pregnancy is envisaged as being a process of treatment. Section 1(3) provides that, subject to an exception for cases of emergency, 'treatment for the termination of pregnancy' must be carried out in a national health service hospital or a place for the time being approved by the minister. There are similar references to treatment for the termination of pregnancy in section 3, which governs the application of the Act to visiting forces. Then by section 4(1) it is provided that no person shall be under any duty 'to participate in any treatment authorised by this Act to which he has a conscientious objection'. This appears clearly to recognise that what is authorised by section 1(1) in relation to the termination of pregnancy is a process of treatment leading to that result. Section 5(2) is also of some importance. It provides:

'For the purposes of the law relating to abortion, anything done with intent to procure the miscarriage of a woman is unlawfully done unless authorised by section 1 of this Act.'

This indicates a contemplation that a wide range of acts done when a pregnancy is terminated under the given conditions are authorised by section 1, and leads to the inference that, since all that section 1 in terms authorises is the termination of pregnancy by a registered medical practitioner, all such acts must be embraced in the termination.

Given that the termination of pregnancy under contemplation in section 1(1) includes the whole process of treatment involved therein, it remains to consider whether, on the facts of this case, the termination can properly be regarded as being 'by a registered medical practitioner'. In my opinion this question is to be answered affirmatively. The doctor has responsibility for the whole process and is in charge of it throughout. It is he who decides that it is to be carried out. He personally performs essential parts of it which are such as to necessitate the application of his particular skill. The nurse's actions are done under his direct written instructions. In the circumstances I find it impossible to hold that the doctor's role is other than that of a principal, and I think he would be very surprised to hear that the nurse was the principal and he himself only an accessory. It is true that it is the nurse's action which leads directly to the introduction of abortifacient drugs into the system of the patient, but that action is done in a ministerial capacity and on the doctor's orders. Even if it were right to regard the nurse as a principal, it seems to me inevitable that the doctor should also be so regarded. If both the doctor and the nurse were principals, the provisions of the subsection would be still satisfied, because the pregnancy would have been terminated by the doctor notwithstanding that it had also been terminated by the nurse.

I therefore conclude that termination of pregnancy by means of the procedures under consideration is authorised by the terms of section 1(1). This conclusion is the more satisfactory as it appears to me to be fully in accordance with that part of the policy and purpose of the Act which was directed to securing that socially acceptable abortions should be carried out under the safest conditions attainable. One may also feel some relief that it is unnecessary to reach a decision involving that the very large numbers of medical practitioners and others who have participated in the relevant procedures over several years past should now be revealed as guilty of criminal offences.

My Lords, for these reasons I would allow the appeal, and restore the declaration granted by Woolf J."

LORD WILBERFORCE [DISSENTING]:
". . . Section 1 of the 1967 Act created a new defence, available to any person who might be liable under the existing law. It is available (i) '*when a pregnancy is terminated by a registered medical practitioner*' (these are the words of the Act), (ii) when certain other conditions are satisfied, including the expressed opinion of two registered medical practitioners as to the risks (specified in paragraphs (a) and (b)) to mother, or child, or existing children, and the requirement that the treatment for the termination of pregnancy must be carried out in a national health service hospital or other approved place. The present case turns on the meaning to be given to condition (i).

The issue relates to a non-surgical procedure of medical induction by the use of a drug called prostaglandin. This operates on the mother's muscles so as to cause contractions (similar to those arising in normal labour) which expel the foetus from the womb. It is used during the second trimester. The question has been raised by the Royal College of Nursing as to the participation of nurses in this treatment, particularly since nurses can be called on (subject to objections of conscience which are rarely invoked) to carry it out. They have felt, and express grave concern as to the legality of doing so and seek a declaration, that a circular issued by the Department of Health and Social Security, asserting the lawfulness of the nurses' participation, is wrong in law.

There is an agreed statement as to the nature of this treatment and the part in it played by the doctors and the nurses or midwives. Naturally this may vary somewhat from hospital to hospital, but, for the purpose of the present proceedings, the assumption has to be made of maximum nurse participation, *i.e.* that the nurse does everything which the doctor is not required to do. If that is not illegal, participation of a lesser degree must be permissible.

1. The first step is for a thin catheter to be inserted via the cervix into the womb so as to arrive at, or create, a space between the wall of the womb and the amniotic sac containing the fetus. This is necessarily done by a doctor. It may, sometimes, of itself bring on an abortion, in which case no problem arises: the pregnancy will have been terminated by the doctor. If it does not, all subsequent steps except no. 4 may be carried out by a nurse or midwife. The significant steps are as follows (I am indebted to Brightman L.J. for their presentation):

2. The catheter (*i.e.* the end emerging from the vagina) is attached, probably via another tube, to a pump or to a gravity feed apparatus. The function of the pump or apparatus is to propel or feed the prostaglandin through the

catheter into the womb. The necessary prostaglandin infusion is provided and put into the apparatus.

*3. The pump is switched on, or the drip valve is turned, thus causing the prostaglandin to enter the womb.

4. The doctor inserts a cannula into a vein.

*5. An oxytocin drip feed is linked up with the cannula. The necessary oxytocin (a drug designed to help the contractions) is supplied for the feed.

6. The patient's vital signs are monitored; so is the rate of drip or flow.

*7. The flow rates of both infusions are, as necessary, adjusted.

*8. Fresh supplies of both infusions are added as necessary.

9. The treatment is discontinued after discharge of the fetus, or expiry of a fixed period (normally 30 hours) after which the operation is considered to have failed.

The only steps in this process which can be considered to have a direct effect leading to abortion (abortifacient steps) are those asterisked. They are all carried out by the nurse, or midwife. As the agreed statement records 'the causative factor in inducing . . . the termination of pregnancy is the effect of the administration of prostaglandin and/or oxytocin and not any mechanical effect from the insertion of the catheter or cannula'.

All the above steps 2 to 9 are carried out in accordance with the doctor's instructions, which should, as regards important matters, be in writing. The doctor will moreover be on call, but may in fact never be called.

On these facts the question has to be answered: has the pregnancy been terminated by the doctor; or has it been terminated by the nurse; or has it been terminated by doctor and nurse? I am not surprised that the nurses feel anxiety as to this.

In attempting to answer it, I start from the point that in 1967, the date of the Act, the only methods used to produce abortions were surgical methods; of these there were several varieties, well enough known. One of these was by intra-amniotic injection, *i.e.* the direct injection of glucose or saline solutions into the amniotic sac. It was not ideal or, it appears, widely used. Parliament must have been aware of these methods and cannot have had in mind a process where abortifacient agents were administered by nurses. They did not exist. Parliament's concern must have been to prevent existing methods being carried out by unqualified persons and to insist that they should be carried out by doctors. For these reasons Parliament no doubt used the words, in section 1(1), 'termination of pregnancy by a registered medical practitioner'.

Extra-amniotic administration of prostaglandin was first reported in 1971, and was soon found to have advantages. It involves, or admits, as shown above, direct and significant participation by nurses in the abortifacient steps. Is it covered by the critical words?

In interpreting an Act of Parliament it is proper, and indeed necessary, to have regard to the state of affairs existing, and known by Parliament to be existing, at the time. It is a fair presumption that Parliament's policy or intention is directed to that state of affairs. Leaving aside cases of omission by inadvertence, this being not such a case when a new state of affairs, or a fresh set of facts bearing on policy, comes into existence, the courts have to consider whether they fall within the parliamentary intention. They may be held to do so if they fall within the same genus of facts as those to which the expressed policy has been formulated. They may also be held to do so if there can be detected a clear purpose in the legislation which can only be fulfilled if the extension is made. How liberally these principles may be applied must depend on the nature of the enactment, and the strictness or otherwise of the words in which it has been expressed. The courts should be less willing to extend expressed meanings if it is clear that the Act in question was designed to be restrictive or circumscribed in its operation rather than liberal or permissive. They will be much less willing to do so where the new subject matter is different in kind or dimension from that for which the legislation was passed. In any event there is one course which the courts cannot take under the law of this country: they cannot fill gaps; they cannot by asking the question, 'What would Parliament have done in this current case, not being one in contemplation, if the facts had been before it?', attempt themselves to supply the answer, if the answer is not to be found in the terms of the Act itself.

In my opinion this Act should be construed with caution. It is dealing with a controversial subject involving moral and social judgments on which opinions strongly differ. It is, if ever an Act was, one for interpreting in the spirit that only that which Parliament has authorised on a fair reading of the relevant sections should be held to be within it. The new (post-1967) method of medical induction is clearly not just a fresh species or example of something already authorised. The Act is not one for 'purposive' or 'liberal' or 'equitable' construction. This is a case where the courts must hold that anything beyond the legislature's fairly expressed authority should be left for Parliament's fresh consideration.

Having regard particularly to the Act's antecedents and the state of affairs existing in 1967, which involved surgical action requiring to be confined to termination by doctors alone, I am unable to read the words 'pregnancy terminated by a registered medical practitioner' as extended or extensible to cover cases where other persons, whether nurses, or midwives, or even lay persons, play a significant part in the process of termination. That a process in which they do so may be reliable, and an improvement on existing surgical methods, may well be the case, we do not in fact even know this. It may be desirable that doctors' time should be spared from directly participating in all the stages of the abortifacient process; it may be (though there are very many hospitals and nursing homes in the United Kingdom, not all with the same high standards) that nurses, midwives, etc. may be relied on to carry out the doctor's instructions accurately and well. It may be that doctors, though not present, may always be available on call. All this may, though with some reservation, be granted, but is beside the point. With nurse, etc. participation, to the degree mentioned, a new dimension has been introduced; this should not be sanctioned by judicial decision, but only by Parliament after proper consideration of the implications and necessary safeguards.

The Department contend that the Act is framed in sufficiently wide terms to authorise what they say is lawful.

Their contention, or that which they were willing to accept as their contention during argument, was that the words 'pregnancy is terminated by a registered medical practitioner' means 'pregnancy is terminated by treatment of a registered medical practitioner in accordance with recognised medical practice'. But, with all respect, this is not construction: it is rewriting. And, moreover, it does not achieve its objective. I could perhaps agree that a reference to treatment could fairly be held to be implied; no doubt treatment is necessary. But I do not see that this alone carries the matter any further: it must still be treatment by the registered medical practitioner. The additional words, on the other hand, greatly extend the enactment, and it is they which are supposed to introduce nurse participation. But I cannot see that they do this. For a nurse to engage in abortifacient acts cannot, when first undertaken, be in accordance with recognised practice, when it is the legality of the practice that is in question. Nor can the recognised practice (if such there is, though the agreed statements do not say so) by which nurses connect up drips to supply glucose or other life-giving or preserving substances cover connecting up drips etc. giving substances designed to destroy life, for that is what they are. The added words may well cover the provision of swabs, bandages or the handing up of instruments; that would only be common sense. They cannot be used as cover for a dimensional extension of the Act.

The argument for the department is carried even further than this, for it is said that the words 'when a pregnancy is terminated by a registered medical practitioner' mean 'when treatment for the termination of pregnancy is carried out by a registered medical practitioner'. This is said to be necessary in order to cover the supposed cases where the treatment is unsuccessful, or where there is no pregnancy at all. The latter hypothesis I regard as fanciful; the former, if it was Parliament's contemplation at all in 1967 (for failures under post-1967 methods are not in point), cannot be covered by any reasonable reading of the words. Termination is one thing; attempted and unsuccessful termination wholly another. I cannot be persuaded to embark on a radical reconstruction of the Act by reference to a fanciful hypothesis or an improbable casus omissus.

It is significant, as Lord Denning M.R. has pointed out, that recognised language exists and has been used, when it is desired that something shall be done by doctors with nurse participation. This takes the form 'by a registered medical practitioner or by a person acting in accordance with the directions of any such practitioner'. This language has been used in four Acts of Parliament (listed by Lord Denning M.R.), three of them prior to the 1967 Act, all concerned with the administration of substances, drugs or medicines which may have an impact on the human body. It has not been used, surely deliberately, in the present Act. We ought to assume that Parliament knew what it was doing when it omitted to use them.

In conclusion, I am of opinion that the development of prostaglandin induction methods invites, and indeed merits, the attention of Parliament. It has justly given rise to perplexity in the nursing profession. I doubt whether this will be allayed when it is seen that a majority of the judges who have considered the problem share their views. On this appeal I agree with the judgments in the Court of Appeal that an extension of the 1967 Act so as to include all persons, including nurses, involved in the administration of prostaglandin is not something which ought to, or can, be effected by judicial decision. I would dismiss the appeal."

NOTES:

1. Lords Diplock and Roskill delivered speeches concurring with Lord Keith; whilst Lord Edmund Davies delivered a dissenting judgment.

2. Kingdom has argued that the issue of competence to perform abortions is of crucial significance, and that had the Law Lords upheld the Court of Appeal's ruling it would have represented a setback to feminists' hopes that trained personnel other than medical practitioners might, in the future, lawfully terminate pregnancies. (See E. Kingdom, *What's Wrong with Rights? Problems for Feminist Politics of Law*, Edinburgh: Edinburgh University Press, 1991 at pages 52–3.)

3. The outcome of the *RCN* case is indicative of the reluctance of courts to interfere with "good medical practice". (See S. Sheldon, "Subject Only to the Attitude of the Surgeon Concerned: The Judicial Protection of Medical Discretion" (1996) 5 *Social and Legal Studies* 95 at pages 102–3.)

QUESTIONS:

1. Do you prefer the reasoning employed by the majority, or the powerful dissent in the *RCN* case?

2. Does the outcome of the *RCN* case reinforce the hierarchal relationship between doctors and nurses? (See Chapter 2 at pages 137–139 and J. Montgomery, "Doctors' Handmaidens: The Legal Contribution" in S. McVeigh and S. Wheeler (eds), *Law, Health and Medical Regulation*, Aldershot: Dartmouth, 1992.)

The *RCN* case was concerned with the legality of one method of performing abortion, and its outcome seemed to entrench medical control of abortion. This has been a feature of abortion provision in the United Kingdom and has led to calls from some feminist commentators for women to be given more control over abortion, which need not be a highly technical medical procedure. The other main issue raised by the various techniques for performing abortion is whether some of the methods can be meaningfully distinguished from contraceptive techniques.

(i) Menstrual extraction

This method involves the contents of the uterus being emptied by suction (or aspiration) when the menstrual period is less than 14 days overdue. Because it is impossible to establish with certainty that a woman is pregnant at this stage, it poses similar problems of legality as the insertion of an IUD when a woman fears she may be pregnant (see page 728 below).

(ii) Aspiration termination [surgical abortion]

In the early stages of pregnancy (during the first 12 weeks), most abortions are performed using this technique. The cervix is first dilated in proportion to the size of the uterus, which is then evacuated with a suction curette. Up to eight weeks the procedure can be done using only a local anaesthetic.

(iii) Prostaglandin termination

After 12 weeks aspiration termination is hazardous. Thus, after this point abortions are induced through the administration of prostaglandins either extra amniotically (introduced through a cervical catheter) or intra-amniotically (introduced by amniocentesis).

(iv) Anti-progestin terminations

The most significant recent innovation in abortion techniques has been the development of anti-progestin abortions. The "abortion pill", commonly referred to as RU486 (and marketed under the names mifepristone and mifegyne), is an anti-progestin drug. It works by preventing progesterone (a reproductive hormone necessary to maintain a pregnancy) from entering the cells in the lining of the uterus, and thus stops the uterine wall from thickening. This means that it is not receptive to implantation by the fertilised ovum. Even if an ovum is implanted in the uterine wall, the lack of progesterone will cause it to be discharged in the menstrual flow. Thus the drug has a double action — both rendering the uterus inhospitable and dislodging any implantations that have not been prevented. It was discovered in the early 1970s, tested on human volunteers in Switzerland in

1982, and marketed in France in 1988 in the face of huge anti-abortion opposition which led to its temporary withdrawal. It was licensed in the United Kingdom on July 3, 1991 having been approved for abortions up to a maximum of 63 days. The drug has been used on the NHS since September 1991 and was approved for use in the private sector by the Department of Health in December 1991. (See "What is happening about RU486" (1993) 1 *Women's Choice* 2).

RU486 is used in combination with a prostaglandin pessary administered 48 hours later, which induces uterine contractions. Within a few hours 90 per cent of women have completed their termination, and the remainder will usually do so within a few days. The success rate of the method is approximately 96 per cent. For those who fail to abort, a surgical abortion is required. Side effects include bleeding, pain (which varies greatly in severity), nausea, vomiting and diarrhoea. About one per cent of women bleed severely enough to require a blood transfusion. (On side effects of RU486, see J. Raymond, "RU486: Progress or Peril?" in J. Callaghan (ed.), *Reproduction, Ethics and the Law: Feminist Perspectives*: Bloomington and Indianapolis: Indiana University Press, 1995.) The woman must return to the clinic within 12 days to check whether the abortion is complete and the severity of side effects. Sub-section 37(3) of the Human Fertilisation and Embryology Act 1980 gives the Secretary of State the power to authorise classes of places for the administration of such drugs. The enactment of this provision indicates that, in the future, GP's surgeries or family planning clinics may be licensed to supply at least some of the treatment.

The major advantage of RU486 over existing forms of abortion is that, in addition to obviating the need for surgery and anaesthetic, it can be administered as soon as the woman knows she is pregnant, whereas with a surgical abortion she has to wait until at least six weeks after her last menstrual period. It thus facilitates the performance of terminations at an early stage in pregnancy, which many people are prepared to concede is at least a lesser evil. (See S. McLean, "Abortion Law: Is Consensual Reform Possible?" (1990) 17 *Journal of Law and Society* 106.) Conversely its disadvantage in comparison to surgical abortion is that it takes more time for the process of abortion to be completed.

It is significant that in the United Kingdom, not only has the introduction of RU486 attracted less debate and opposition than it did in France and the United States, but it appears to have been significantly under-used in this jurisdiction. For instance, in the first two years of availability, only 2 per cent of NHS abortions were performed using this method, whereas in France RU486 accounts for approximately one third of abortions. To date, it still only accounts for about five per cent of the total number of abortions in Britain, and most RU486 abortions are performed within the private or charitable sector. This may be explained by the bureaucratic nature of the NHS which has frequently led to delays in performing abortions. Since RU486 is only effective up to nine weeks, it is particularly important that delays are minimised.

Legally, anti-progestin abortions fall within the terms of the Abortion Act 1967 and are subject to the same regulations as surgical abortions (see pages 718–719). Thus, RU486 abortion must be approved by two doctors and administered on licensed premises. Sheldon has argued that the comparative underuse of the drug in England is due to the fact that discussion of RU486 has taken place within a highly medicalised framework. She suggests that, although the drug "embodies the potential to place more control in the hands of women . . . this potential seems not to have been realised in the way the drug has been introduced in practice" (S. Sheldon, "Anti-progestin Terminations: Issues of Access and Control", University of Liverpool: *Feminist Legal Research Unit Working Paper, 1997).* Medical control of the drug is further tightened by the fact that the manufacturers of the drug, Roussel-Uclaf, have required any doctor to whom the drug is supplied to attend training seminars, which it started running in July 1991. The manufacturers also issue specific instructions on how the drug must be stored, delivered and returned if not used, in order to prevent the drug becoming more widely available.

In relation to the ethics of abortion and contraception, RU486 drug is interesting in that it offers the potential to irrevocably change the nature of the abortion debate, since the earlier abortion is performed, the less convincing may be the opposition of "pro-life" groups, and the line between post-coital contraception and abortion becomes more blurred. It thus has the potential to undermine the entire "pro-life" campaign. (See L. A. Cole, "The End of the Abortion Debate" (1989) 138 *University of Pennsylvania Law Review* 217; M. J. Lees, "I Want a New Drug: RU486 and the Right to Choose" (1990) 63 *Southern California Law Review* 1113.)

NOTES:

1. Although many commentators have objected to the tight controls on its use, it is likely that RU486 would not be available at all but for the fact that it is subject to such strict regulation, given the fear of manufacturers of being sued for side effects or harm. (See Lees, *op. cit.*)

2. Menstrual extraction offers similar theoretical possibilities for women to assert control over the process of abortion. (See R. Chalker and C. Dovner, *A Woman's Book of Choices*, Four Walls and Eight Windows, 1992.)

3. The issue of the blurring between contraception and abortifacient is a longstanding one. A question which has received little judicial attention is whether "interceptive" methods of post-coital birth control are legal. In *R. v. Price* [1968] 2 All E.R. 282 a prosecution was brought under section 58 of the 1861 Act against a doctor who had fitted a patient with an intra-uterine device while she was pregnant. So doing caused the woman to suffer a miscarriage shortly

afterwards. Ultimately, the prosecution brought against the doctor failed because it was not proven that he knew that the woman concerned was pregnant.

4. In 1981 pro-choice campaigners urged the Director of Public Prosecutions to prosecute a doctor for inserting a coil as an abortifacient, in the hope of obtaining a ruling that this was lawful. However the view of the Government's Law Officers — the DPP and the Attorney-General — seems to be that a prosecution would be inappropriate. (See written answer by the Attorney-General, Parl. Deb., H.C., Vol. 142 (May 1983), 238 at page 239; L. Clarke, "Abortion — A Rights Issue?" in R. Lee and D. Morgan (eds.) *Birthrights: Law and Ethics at the Beginnings of Life*, London: Routledge, 1989.)

QUESTIONS:

1. The decision in *Price* seems to suggest that the use of interceptive methods of post-coital birth control — *i.e.* those designed to destroy, or prevent the implantation of, the fertilised ovum — are contrary to section 58. If there has been no implantation, then there can have been no "carriage"; does it not follow, therefore, that it is impossible in such circumstances to procure a "miscarriage" contrary to the 1861 Act?

2. The French health minister described RU486 as the "moral property of women". Given the fact that so few British women who have abortions on the NHS have RU486 abortions, is this an unjustifiable restriction on women's choice in relation to abortion?

3. Do you think women having an abortion would prefer to use this treatment, in which they play a more active role in the process of abortion, rather than having a surgical operation which is performed on them?

4. Are the controls which the manufacturer has imposed on the distribution and use of RU486 justifiable?

5. Should the Secretary of State utilise her powers under the Abortion Act 1967 section 3A, which was clearly introduced with the future use of anti-progestins in mind, to issue regulations permitting RU486 to be administered in a GP's surgery, rather than in a hospital or licensed clinic?

6. Given that the termination process is ongoing from the point at which the woman takes RU486, through the administration of prostaglandin until the foetus is expelled, does this breach the terms of the legislation, which requires the abortion to be performed on licensed premises?

7. If, as seems likely, it emerges that RU486 abortions are considerably cheaper to perform than surgical abortions, would the medical profession be justified in encouraging women to undergo this form of abortion in order to conserve resources?

8. Some commentators have argued that early abortion should be promoted as a form of contraception to be used as a back up method where barrier methods fail. They suggest that this would be preferable to the negative effects on women's health of more "effective" forms of contraception. Do you agree? (See P. Foster, *Women and the Health Care Industry: An Unhealthy Relationship?*, Buckingham: Open University Press, at pages 24–6.)

(d) Emergency abortions

Much feminist opposition to the medicalisation of abortion has questioned the need for *two* registered medical practitioners to certify that one or more of the specified grounds for abortion exist. As Douglas points out, this requirement adds to the delay in abortion being performed (G. Douglas, *Law, Fertility and Reproduction*, London: Sweet and Maxwell, 1991, at page 87). Section 1(4) of the Act (at page 719 above) provides a defence for the doctor who terminates a pregnancy without such second opinion only in an emergency situation where he considers the termination to be immediately necessary. This issue came before the courts in the unreported case of Reginald Dixon in 1995. Mr Dixon is a consultant gynaecologist and obstetrician who performed a hysterectomy on Barbara Whitten, a 35-year-old woman who suffered from a painful and chronic disease of the womb. Having tried for several years to become pregnant, she believed that the disease had left her unable to conceive and thus opted for a hysterectomy. During the operation Mr Dixon noticed that Mrs Whiten's uterus was enlarged, which could have been an indication of pregnancy. Rather than delaying the hysterectomy operation so that a scan could determine the cause of the swelling, he elected to go ahead with the operation. The following day he informed her that she had been pregnant and that he had, in accordance with "the usual practice", removed a healthy 11 week old foetus. Dixon was charged under section 58 of the Offences against the Person Act 1861 with unlawfully procuring a miscarriage. Although it was accepted that he had failed to obtain a second signature as required by the 1967 Act, he was acquitted of the offence on the grounds that he had acted within the terms of sub-section 1(4) of the Act which permits a registered medical practitioner to carry out a termination in 'emergency' situations without complying with certain formalities. (See *The Guardian*, December 22, 1995.) Sheldon points out that, as the *Dixon* case demonstrates, the crucial ethical issue of whether or not the pregnant woman had consented to abortion is deemed legally irrelevant under the Abortion Act. Its emphasis instead is on protecting the medical relationship from outside challenge. As she notes, the only other potential criminal action — a charge of battery — has never been sustained against a doctor acting in good faith. (See S. Sheldon, "Subject Only to the Attitude of the Surgeon Concerned: The Judicial Protection of Medical Discretion" (1996) 5 *Social and Legal Studies* 95.)

QUESTIONS:

1. Should the test of whether the situation constitutes an emergency be judged subjectively according to what the doctor believed in good faith, or should the test be the objective one of whether the reasonable doctor would have judged it to be an emergency?
2. Do you agree with Sheldon (*op. cit.*) that in the case law on abortion medical paternalism is actively enforced and condoned by law?

5.　CONFLICTING INTERESTS AT STAKE IN ABORTION DECISIONS

There are a number of parties affected by any decision to abort, and as noted above, English law has failed to fully address the competing claims at stake in making abortion decisions, or the legal weight to be given to those competing interests. The parties most intimately affected by the decision to abort are as follows:

(a) The pregnant woman

Although the pregnant woman has been recognised in other jurisdictions as the person most directly affected by the abortion decision (see, for instance, *Planned Parenthood of SE Pennsylvania v. Casey* (1992) 112 St 2791; *R v. Morgantalor* [1988] 44 DLR (4th) 385), the Abortion Act does not accord the woman any legal right to decide that she will have an abortion, not even in the very early stages of pregnancy. (For a comparison with other European jurisdictions see D. Morgan and R. Lee, *Blackstone's Guide to the Human Fertilisation and Embryology Act 1990*, London: Blackstone Press, 1991.) It is clear from the decision in *Re T (adult: refusal of medical treatment)* [1992] 4 All E.R. 649 (see Chapter 5 at pages 272–277) that an adult woman has a right to refuse treatment, so that no third party would be able to compel an adult woman to undergo a termination against her will. However, she has no right to demand an abortion. Rather, English law has accorded rights only to doctors, who have the right to decide whether a woman's situation falls within the terms of the 1967 Act. (See L. Clarke, "Abortion: A Rights Issue?" in R. Lee and D. Morgan, *Birthrights: Law and Ethics at the Beginnings of Life*, London: Routledge, 1989.) Ironically, however, as we shall see at pages 737–746 below, this may have protected the abortion decision from interference by any third party — it is purely a matter for the woman and her doctor. However, the vast discretion accorded to doctors by the 1967 Act has resulted in huge regional variations in the provision of abortion.

　　Foster cites statistics which show that in 1984, whilst the NHS performed 86 per cent of all abortions in the northern region, it performed only 35 per cent in Yorkshire and only 20 per cent in the West Midlands. Since 1984, the total percentage of abortions performed on the NHS has declined from 50 per cent to 47 per cent.

QUESTIONS:

1. Should the decision whether to abort be entrusted to the woman alone, given the impact of pregnancy and becoming a parent on her life?
2. What factors do you think explain regional variations in the numbers of abortion performed in the public sector?

(b) The foetus

Since virtually no one would dispute that the foetus is a form of human life, which deserves some consideration, the real question is whether the foetus should be accorded any legal rights independent of the pregnant woman who is carrying it. This issue was addressed in the following case:

Attorney-General's Reference (No. 3 of 1994) [1996] 2 All E.R. 10

The defendant stabbed his girlfriend whom he knew to be 22–24 weeks pregnant with their child. Initially no injury to the foetus was detected and the woman appeared to make a good recovery. However, six weeks later she was admitted to hospital and gave birth to a grossly premature baby. It was then apparent that when she was stabbed the knife had penetrated the uterus and injured the foetus. It lived for 120 days. Prior to the child's death the defendant had been charged with wounding his girlfriend with intent to do her grievous bodily harm, to which he pleaded guilty. Following the child's death he was charged with murdering the child. The trial judge upheld a defence submission that the facts could not give rise to a homicide conviction, and therefore directed the jury to acquit. The Attorney General referred the following questions to the Court of Appeal:

(i) whether, subject to proof of the requisite intent, the crimes of murder or manslaughter could be committed where unlawful injury was deliberately inflicted to a child *in utero* or to a mother carrying a child *in utero* where the child was subsequently born alive, existed independently of the mother and then died, the injuries *in utero* either having caused or made a substantial contribution to the death, and

(ii) whether the fact that the child's death was caused solely as a consequence of injury to the mother rather than as a consequence of direct injury to the foetus could remove any liability for murder or manslaughter in those circumstances.

LORD TAYLOR C.J.:
". . . The classic definition of murder at common law was given by Coke (3 Co Inst 47):

'Murder is when a man of sound memory, and of the age of discretion, unlawfully killeth within any county of the realm any reasonable creature *in rerum natura* under the king's peace, with malice fore-thought, either expressed by the party, or implied by law, so as the party wounded, or hurt, &c die of the wound, or hurt, &c within a year and a day after the same.'

Leaving aside such matters as provocation and diminished responsibility, which have no bearing upon the issues presently under consideration, the prosecution must prove the following elements: (1) that the defendant did an act; (2) that the act was deliberate and not accidental; (3) that the act was unlawful; (4) that the act was a substantial cause of a death; (5) that the death was of a person in being; (6) that death resulted within a year and a day; and (7) that at the time of doing the act the defendant intended either to kill or to cause really serious bodily injury to the victim or, subject to the extent of the doctrine of transferred malice, to some other person.

Elements 1 to 6 represent the actus reus of murder and if any is absent the actus reus will not be established. Element 7 is the mens rea of murder for which the old expression, malice aforethought, was used.

The actus reus of murder

Clearly in a case such as that being considered the first and second elements are simply a matter of evidence and present no particular problem of law. The third element of unlawfulness does require further discussion in the light of a submission made by Mr Hawkesworth that to cause injury to a foetus is not in itself unlawful. He argues that since the foetus has no separate existence, causing an injury to it is not unlawful unless it comes within the scope of one of the statutory offences such as child destruction or abortion. We reject that submission. In law the foetus is treated as a part of the mother until it has a separate existence of its own. Thus to cause injury to the foetus is just as unlawful as any assault upon any other part of the mother.

Mr Hawkesworth cautioned us that conclusions adverse to the respondent's submissions might render a doctor who carried out a lawful abortion liable to conviction if the foetus was born alive as a result of a lawful abortion and then died thereafter. His reasoning was that the Abortion Act 1967, as subsequently amended, only provides that a registered medical practitioner shall not be guilty of an offence under the law 'relating to abortion' and says nothing about not being liable on a charge of murder.

In our judgment, Mr Hawkesworth's concerns in this regard are misplaced. A doctor who carries out an abortion in accordance with the 1967 Act is not acting unlawfully and hence, were such a doctor to be charged with murder, the charge would fail because the element that the act must be unlawful could not be made out. Just as a doctor who causes death in a bona fide surgical operation is not guilty because he does nothing unlawful, so would a doctor carrying out a lawful abortion be similarly protected. In the course of argument, the situation of a foetus being born alive consequent upon a lawful abortion and subsequently being neglected or killed was touched upon, but such questions have no relevance to the issues which are raised by this reference and we make clear that we have given no consideration to them.

The fourth element to be established on a charge of murder is that the act was a substantial cause of death. This was the element that Hale doubted could ever be established, but clearly on medical evidence today a jury might properly be so satisfied. In the instant case there was a submission that the evidence was inadequate for a jury to reach a conclusion to that effect. The judge ruled against that submission and although the matter has not been argued before us he was, in so far as we can judge, right so to do.

The fifth element is that the death must be of a person in being. In its simplest form this means that to cause the death of a foetus in the womb cannot be murder. However, the situation under consideration raises the question whether the child needs to be in being at the time when the act causing death is done by the defendant. Clearly, when the respondent stabbed his girlfriend the child was not a person in being. It is at this point of the argument and for this purpose alone that Mr Smith places reliance upon the pre-1957 common law in support of his third principle, namely that the fact that the foetus is not a person in being at the time of the unlawful act which is proved to have caused death is no impediment to a successful prosecution for murder or manslaughter provided the child is subsequently born alive and achieves an existence independent of the mother. He argues that in this respect the 1957 [Homicide] Act did not change the law and that if the cases of *Senior* (1832), 168 E.R. 1298 and *West* (1848) 175 E.R. 329 correctly represented the law, the law in this respect remains unaltered.

We have concluded that there is no requirement that the person who dies needs to be a person in being at the time that the act causing death is perpetrated. That, we are satisfied, was the position at common law and to hold otherwise would produce anomalies of an unacceptable kind. For example, a defendant who poisoned the water of a pregnant woman intending her to drink it and be killed, would not be guilty of murder if the woman gave birth to a child and then made up a bottle for the baby using the poisoned water which killed the child. On the other hand, if at the time of the poison being added, the child had already been born, and the mother for whom it was intended used the poisoned water in precisely the same way with the same consequences, it would amount to murder.

The sixth element, that death must result within a year and a day, provided an arbitrary time limit, which no doubt was introduced as a safeguard at a time when proof of causation was far from easy. Consideration of the desirability of retaining such a provision is currently the subject of debate but it has no relevance to our considerations.

The mens rea of murder

Thus we turn to the mental element of the crime of murder. It is argued on behalf of the Attorney General that the Crown can succeed in one of two ways. If the jury are satisfied that the defendant at the time when he did the act intended to kill or cause serious bodily injury to the foetus, then it is said that this will suffice provided 'the intention is directed to a child capable of becoming a person in being' at a later date. In the alternative it is argued that an intention to kill or cause really serious bodily injury to the mother will suffice by reason of the doctrine of transferred malice.

In Smith and Hogan *Criminal Law* (7th ed., 1992) p. 329, the authors' view of the position is stated as follows:

'In modern law, however, a person who intends to kill or cause serious injury to an unborn child does not have the *mens rea* for murder — he does not intend to kill or cause serious injury to a person in being — and should not be liable to conviction of that offence. If the child is born alive and dies of the injury inflicted with that intent he might be guilty of manslaughter if there was an obvious and serious risk . . . that this might occur. If D's intention was to cause the death or serious injury to the mother he would, by 'transferred malice', be guilty of murder of the child who was born alive and died of the injury so inflicted.'

In so far as that passage, by implication if not expressly, rejects the concept of an intention directed towards a child capable of becoming a person in being, we agree. The concept is a wholly new one that it is sought to introduce and we do not see it as either necessary or desirable to add this gloss to the law.

That is not to say that we think if an intention is directed towards the foetus a charge of murder must fail. In the eyes of the law the foetus is taken to be a part of the mother until it has an existence independent of the mother. Thus an intention to cause serious bodily injury to the foetus is an intention to cause serious bodily harm to a part of the mother just as an intention to injure her arm or her leg would be so viewed. Thus consideration of whether a charge of murder can arise where the focus of the defendant's intention is exclusively the foetus falls to be considered under the head of transferred malice, as is the case where the intention is focused exclusively or partially upon the mother herself.

Transferred malice

It is, therefore, necessary to consider the concept of transferred malice in order to answer the questions posed in this reference. At its simplest the concept is that if a defendant intends to kill or cause really serious injury to A but instead kills B, he is guilty of the murder of B as if the object of his intentions had been B rather than A.

Mr Hawkesworth mounts his principal challenge to Mr Smith's contentions in this regard. He raises three arguments. (1) In applying the doctrine of transferred malice there is plainly a distinction to be drawn between transferring the malice of an offence of stabbing the mother, where the actus reus is the infliction of a stab wound, and the offence of murder here alleged, which is causing the death of the child by bringing about its birth at such a premature stage that it could not survive. The actus reus of the two crimes does not coincide, so that malice cannot be transferred. (2) All such cases proceed upon the assumption that at the time of the assault or blow aimed at A there is *at the same time* another person in being, B, namely the person who is the unintended victim. Since at the time of the stabbing the foetus was not a person in being, it *could not* be the subject of an offence contrary to s 18 of the 1861 Act. (3) In terms of causation the birth and eventual death of the baby was so far removed from the event of stabbing that malice cannot be transferred.

It is perhaps convenient to deal first with the second of those contentions, that malice cannot be transferred to a person who is not in being at the time of the act causing death. It is important to observe that malice cannot in any event be transferred until such time as the act affects the victim. For example, if a defendant sends a box of poisoned chocolates to A but B eats them and dies, it can only be at the moment when B places a chocolate in his mouth that any question of transfer of malice can arise. That time would in such circumstances of necessity be significantly after the act done by the sender.

We can see no reason to hold that malice can only be transferred where the person to whom it is transferred was in existence at the time of the act causing death. It is perhaps pertinent to observe that a sufficient intention may be directed at no individual but rather there may be an indiscriminate intention which will suffice. Thus a defendant who introduces poison into baby food on a supermarket shelf with an intention to kill some wholly unidentified child is clearly guilty of murder if a child later dies from eating the poisoned food. It would be a remarkable state of affairs if such a person was only guilty of murder if the child had already been born at the date when the poison was introduced to the food. If in such cases of general malice there is no requirement that the child should already have been born, it is not easy to see why there should be a distinction drawn when malice is instead transferred from an intended victim to an unintended one. The example given earlier of poisoned water intended for the pregnant woman but used to make a bottle for the child demonstrates the possible unsatisfactory conclusions that would arise from such a rule.

In support of his first and third contentions, Mr Hawkesworth has directed our attention to passages in Professor Glanville Williams *Criminal Law — The General Part* (2nd ed., 1961) pp. 125–127, 132–134. The author contends (pp. 125, 132–133):

'Although the decided cases do not show it, there can be no doubt that an unexpected difference of mode will be regarded as severing the chain of causation if it is sufficiently far removed from the intended mode . . . There is another way in which it seems that the rule may be circumscribed. Hitherto it has been applied only in gross cases, and although there are no clear authorities on the bounds to be set to it, the rule should be confined to cases where it appears to conform to the plain man's view of justice, and so should be limited to cases where the consequence was brought about by negligence in relation to the actual victim.'

To illustrate the second proposition Professor Williams says:

'Thus suppose that D shoots at O intending to kill him; the shot misses O and kills P, who, unknown to D was behind a curtain at the time. If P's presence could not possibly have been foreseen by D, it may be thought to be going too far to convict him of the murder of P.'

We, for our part, do not find Professor Williams' exoneration of D in respect of murder to be self-evidently 'the plain man's view of justice' in the example he poses.

Professor Williams, as appears from the quoted passages, found no authority in support of either of his propositions. The only authority to which he makes reference in respect of the second proposition is *R v. Latimer* [1886–90] All E.R. Rep 386, which he acknowledges to be against his contention.

In *R v. Mitchell* [1983] 2 All E.R. 427, decided after the date of Professor Williams' quoted work, this court considered a conviction for manslaughter arising where a defendant in the course of a quarrel in a queue hit another man, causing him to fall against an elderly woman who suffered a broken leg, an injury from which it appeared she was recovering until she suffered a pulmonary embolism which caused her death. No qualification of the sort contended for was introduced in that case. The headnote of the case records the decision of the court as follows:

'*Held*, dismissing the appeal, that to constitute the offence of manslaughter it was not necessary to establish that the unlawful and dangerous act was aimed at, or involved a direct attack or impact upon, the person who died; and that, accordingly, although the appellant had aimed no blow and had no physical contact with the woman who died, she was injured as a direct and immediate result of his act and died thereafter, and it was open to the jury to conclude that her death was caused by the appellant's act.'

Mr Hawkesworth has highlighted the words 'direct and immediate result' but the context in which those words were used by Straughton J. in giving the judgment of the court was as follows ([1983] 2 All E.R. 427 at 432):

'Although there was no direct contact between Mitchell and Mrs Crafts, she was injured as a direct and immediate result of his act. Thereafter her death occurred. The only question was one of causation: whether her death was caused by Mitchell's act. It was open to the jury to conclude that it was so caused; and they evidently reached that conclusion.'

We do not understand that the court was intending thereby to make the 'immediate' causing of injury a requirement of a conviction in such circumstances. In that particular case it was the fact that the injury was caused immediately and the relevance of that fact was that the court did not have to consider any questions of causation that might have arisen in different circumstances.

Although not directly to the point, we find the approach of suggesting that such matters go to causation of assistance. It is clear from *Mitchell's* case that it is unnecessary for the precise mechanism of death to be foreseen in manslaughter and we are satisfied that the same is true for murder. We do not think it is right or necessary to reintroduce any question of causation at the stage when mens rea falls to be considered. Provided that the jury are satisfied that the death was caused by the defendant's act, then we see no reason why the concept of transferred malice should not operate.

Obviously, if the mode of death is utterly remote, there may be circumstances in which this could be regarded as severing the chain of causation, but in the instant case we cannot see that it should matter whether the child dies after birth as a result of a stab wound suffered by the foetus before birth or as a result of premature birth induced by the stabbing.

Equally, we can see no justification for the proposed qualification that some degree of negligence towards the intended victim is required. Thus we can see no reason to conclude that the doctrine of transferred malice is excluded in a situation such as falls to be considered in the reference.

Manslaughter

The focus of our attention so far has been on the law relating to a charge of murder. The reference also raises questions relating to a charge of manslaughter. In the light of our conclusions relating to murder, we cannot see that any different approach is required and none has ben suggested to us in argument . . ."

NOTES:

1. This case confirms existing precedent that the foetus is not to be regarded as a person for the purposes of the criminal law. (See *R. v. Tait* [1989] 3 All E.R. 682.) However, by ruling that the foetus is effectively part of the pregnant woman, the Court of Appeal established that an intention to kill or cause grievous bodily harm to the foetus constitutes the requisite mens rea for murder. If the intention is to kill or cause serious harm to the foetus, and the mother dies, that is a straightforward case of murder. If the intention is to kill or seriously harm the mother and instead the child dies after birth, the doctrine of transferred malice is invoked to transfer the mens rea from woman to foetus. (See J. C. Smith, Commentary, [1996] *Criminal Law Review* 269.)

2. Lord Taylor considered, *obiter*, the impact of the ruling on the law of abortion. The Court of Appeal's view was that a doctor who performed an abortion in accordance with the 1967 Act could not be guilty of murder if the child was born alive but subsequently died. The Court of Appeal stated that provided the doctor's action in terminating the pregnancy complied with the 1967 Act his action would be lawful. Grubb argues that the court's reasoning could be extended to put all medical treatment outside the scope of the criminal law of violent offences. (See A. Grubb, Commentary (1995) 3 *Medical Law Review* 302 at pages 308–9.)

3. Grubb notes that the "unity of persons" doctrine espoused in this case would justify the artificial ventilation of a pregnant woman, who, owing to an accident, was in a state of coma and had no hope of recovery, for long enough to allow the foetus to be born by Caesarean section. (See Chapter 13 at page 784.)

QUESTIONS:

1. Do you think that the Court of Appeal in this case was right to regard the foetus "as a part of the mother until it has a separate existence of its own", so that "an intention to cause serious bodily harm to the foetus is an intention to cause serious bodily harm to a part of the mother just an intention to injure her arm or leg would be so viewed"? (See C. MacKinnon, "Reflections on Sex Equality under Law" (1991) 100 *Yale Law Journal* 1281.)

2. Can this decision be reconciled with the earlier decision in *Re S (Adult: Refusal of Medical Treatment)* [1992] 4 All E.R. 671 (discussed in Chapter 13 at pages 782–784 and Appendix D)? (See A. Grubb, Commentary (1995) 3 *Medical Law Review* 302 at page 306.)

(c) The putative father

As we have seen, the Court of Appeal in the *Attorney-General's Reference* case has effectively decided that the interests of the pregnant woman and the foetus are the same — there is only one legal person in existence. It has also been decided that it is ultimately up to the pregnant woman's doctor to determine whether she qualifies for an abortion under the criteria laid down in the 1967 Act. This raises the issue of whether any third party could veto the woman's decision to have an abortion if a doctor certifies that the terms of the 1967 Act are fulfilled. The third party most likely to be affected is the putative father of the child, who may seek to intervene on behalf of the unborn child.

Paton v. Trustees of The British Pregnancy Advisory Service and Another
[1978] 2 All E.R. 987; [1979] Q.B. 276; [1978] 3 W.L.R. 687

The second defendant (the plaintiff's wife) consulted two medical practitioners with a view to obtaining a termination under the provisions of the Abortion Act 1967. Following the consultation, the two doctors were of the opinion, formed in good faith, that the continuance of the pregnancy would constitute a sufficient threat to her physical and mental health to justify a termination under section 1 of the Act. Her husband sought an injunction to restrain the first defendants (the British Pregnancy Advisory Service) from proceeding with the operation.

In effect, since his allegation was that the abortion could not be undertaken without his consent, his claim was that he possessed a right to veto the termination. The case was heard by Sir George Baker P. sitting as an additional judge of the Queen's Bench Division. His Lordship first made plain the basis on which injunctive relief is available in English law.

SIR GEORGE BAKER P:
" . . . In considering the law the first and basic principle is that there must be a legal right enforceable at law or in equity before the applicant can obtain an injunction from the court to restrain an infringement of that right. That has long been the law . . . The law relating to injunctions has been considered recently in the House of Lords, in *Gouriet v. Union of Post Office Workers* [1977] 3 All E.R. 70. Many passages from their Lordships' speeches have been cited. I do not propose to go through them because it is now as clear as possible that there must be, first, a legal right in an individual to found an injunction and, second, that the enforcement of the criminal law is a matter for the authorities and for the Attorney-General . . ."

Sir George Baker then went on to consider whether the father of an unborn child possessed any right to veto a termination.

"The first question is whether this plaintiff has a right at all. The foetus cannot, in English law, in my view, have any right of its own at least until it is born and has a separate existence from the mother. That permeates the whole of the civil law of this country (I except the criminal law, which is now irrelevant), and is, indeed, the basis of the decisions in those countries where law is founded on the common law . . .

The husband's case must therefore depend on a right which he has himself. I would say a word about the illegitimate, usually called the putative, but I prefer myself to refer to the illegitimate, father. Although American decisions to which I have been referred concern illegitimate fathers, and statutory provisions about them, it seems to me that in this country the illegitimate father can have no rights whatsoever except those given to him by statute. That was clearly the common law.

One provision which makes an inroad into this is s.14 of the Guardianship of Minors Act 1971, and s.9(1) and some other sections of that Act applicable to illegitimate children, giving the illegitimate father or mother the right to apply for the custody of or access to an illegitimate child. But the equality of parental rights provision in s.1(1) of the Guardianship Act 1973 expressly does not apply in relation to a minor who is illegitimate: see s.1(7).

So this plaintiff must, in my opinion, bring his case, if he can, squarely within the framework of the fact that he is a husband. It is, of course, very common for spouses to seek injunctions for personal protection in the matrimonial courts during the pendency of or, indeed, after divorce actions, but the basic reason for the non-molestation injunction often granted in the family courts is to protect the other spouse or the living children, and to ensure that no undue pressure is put on one or other of the spouses during the pendency of the case and during the breaking-up of the marriage . . .

The law is that the court cannot and would not seek to enforce or restrain by injunction matrimonial obligations, if they be obligations such as sexual intercourse or contraception (a non-molestation injunction given during the pendency of divorce proceedings could, of course, cover attempted intercourse). No court would ever grant an injunction to stop sterilisation or vasectomy. Personal family relationships in marriage cannot be enforced by the order of a court. An injunction in such circumstances was described by Judge Marger in *Jones v. Smith* (1973) 278 So 2d 339 (at 344) in the District Court of Appeal of Florida as 'ludicrous'.

I ask the question 'If an injunction were ordered, what could be the remedy?' And I do not think I need say any more than that no judge could even consider sending a husband or wife to prison for breaking such an order. That, of itself, seems to me to cover the application here; this husband cannot by law by injunction stop his wife having what is now accepted to be a lawful abortion within the terms of the Abortion Act 1967.

The case which was first put forward to me a week ago, and indeed is to be found in the writ, is that the wife had no proper legal grounds for seeking a termination of her pregnancy and that, not to mince words, she was being spiteful, vindictive and utterly unreasonable in seeking so to do. It now appears I need not go into the evidence in the affidavits because it is accepted and common ground that the provisions of the 1967 Act have been complied with, the necessary certificate has been given by two doctors and everything is lawfully set for the abortion.

The case put to me finally by counsel for the husband (to whom I am most indebted for having set out very clearly and logically what the law is) is that while he cannot say here that there is any suggestion of a criminal abortion nevertheless if doctors did not hold their views, or come to their conclusions, in good faith, which would be an issue triable by a jury (see *R v. Smith (John)* [1974] 1 All E.R. 376), then this plaintiff might recover an injunction. That is not accepted by counsel for the first defendants. It is unnecessary for me to decide that academic question because it does not arise in this case. My own view is that it would be quite impossible for the courts in any event to supervise the operation of the 1967 Act. The great social responsibility is firmly placed by the law on the shoulders of the medical profession: *per* Scarman L.J., in *R v. Smith (John)* [1974] 1 All E.R. 376 at 378.

I will look at the 1967 Act very briefly. Section 1 provides:

'(1) . . . a person shall not be guilty of an offence under the law relating to abortion when a pregnancy is terminated by a registered medical practitioner if two registered medical practitioners are of the opinion, formed in good faith, (a) that the continuance of the pregnancy would involve risk . . . of injury to the physical or mental health of the pregnant woman . . . [Then there are other provisions which I need not read].

(2) In determining whether the continuance of pregnancy would involve such risk of injury to health as is mentioned in paragraph (a) of subsection (1) of this section, account may be taken of the pregnant woman's actual or reasonably foreseeable environment . . ."

That does not now arise in this case. The two doctors have given a certificate. It is not and cannot be suggested that that certificate was given in other than good faith and it seems to me that there is the end of the matter in English law. The 1967 Act gives no right to a father to be consulted in respect of the termination of a pregnancy. True, it gives no right to the mother either, but obviously the mother is going to be right at the heart of the matter consulting with the doctors if they are to arrive at a decision in good faith, unless, of course, she is mentally incapacitated or physically incapacitated (unable to make any decision or give any help) as, for example, in consequence of an accident. The husband, therefore, in my view, has no legal right enforceable at law or in equity to stop his wife having this abortion or to stop the doctors from carrying out the abortion . . .

This certificate is clear, and not only would it be a bold and brave judge (I think counsel for the husband used that expression) who would seek to interfere with the discretion of doctors acting under the 1967 Act, but I think he would really be a foolish judge who would try to do any such thing, unless possibly, there is clear bad faith and an obvious attempt to perpetrate a criminal offence. Even then, of course, the question is whether that is a matter which should be left to the Director of Public Prosecutions and the Attorney-General. I say no more for I have stated my view of the law of England . . ."

NOTE: The effect of the *Paton* decision has been to completely entrench medical control over the abortion decision (see L. Clarke, "Abortion: A Right's Issue?" in R. Lee and D. Morgan (eds) *Birthrights: Law and Ethics at the Beginnings of Life*, London: Routledge 1989, S. Sheldon, "Subject only to the Attitude of the Surgeon Concerned: The Judicial Protection of Medical Discretion" (1996) and *Social and Legal Studies* 95.)

The decision in *Paton*, that the putative father had no right, simply because of his paternity, to prevent the doctors and mother from proceeding with a termination, was later indirectly endorsed in another decision of the Queen's Bench Division of the High Court.

When he was refused an injunction by the British courts — Paton took his case to the European Commission of Human Rights. One of his arguments before the commission was that he had standing to protect the right to life of his unborn child.

Paton v. United Kingdom (1980) 3 EHRR 408 (From the Opinion of the European Commission)

6. Article 2(1), first sentence, provides: 'Everyone's right to life shall be protected by law'.

7. The Commission first notes that the term 'everyone' ('toute personne') is not defined in the Convention. It appears in Article 1 and Section I, apart from Article 2(1), in Articles 5, 6, 8 to 11 and 13. In nearly all these instances the use of the

word is such that it can apply only postnatally. None indicates clearly that it has any possible prenatal application, although such application in a rare case — *e.g.* under Article 6(1) — cannot be entirely excluded.

8. As regards, more particularly, Article 2(1), it contains the following limitations of 'everyone's' right enounced in the first sentence of paragraph (1):

- a clause permitting the death penalty in paragraph (1), second sentence: 'No one shall be deprived of his life save in the execution of a sentence of a court following his conviction of a crime for which this penalty is provided by law'; and
- the provision, in paragraph (2), that deprivation of life shall not be regarded as inflicted in contravention of Article 2 when it results from 'the use of force which is no more than absolutely necessary' in the following three cases: 'In defence of any person from unlawful violence'; 'in order to effect a lawful arrest or to prevent the escape of a person lawfully detained'; 'in action lawfully taken for the purpose of quelling a riot or insurrection'.

All the above limitations, by their nature, concern persons already born and cannot be applied to the foetus.

9. Thus both the general usage of the term 'everyone' ('toute personne') of the Convention (paragraph 7 above) and the context in which this term is employed in Article 2 (paragraph 8 above) tend to support the view that it does not include the unborn.

10. The Commission has next examined, in the light of the above considerations, whether the term 'life' in Article 2(1), first sentence, is to be interpreted as covering only the life of persons already born or also the 'unborn life' of the foetus. The Commission notes that the term 'life', too, is not defined in the Convention.

11. It further observes that another, more recent international instrument for the protection of human rights, the American Convention on Human Rights of 1969, contains in Article 4(1), first and second sentences, the following provisions expressly extending the right to life to the unborn:

Every person has the right to have his life respected. This right shall be protected by law and, in general, from the moment of conception.

12. The Commission is aware of the wide divergence of thinking on the question of where life begins. While some believe that it starts already with conception others tend to focus upon the moment of nidation, upon the point that the foetus becomes 'viable', or upon live birth.

13. The German Federal Constitutional Court, when interpreting the provision 'everyone has a right to life' in Article 2(2) of the Basic Law, stated as follows:

Life in the sense of the historical existence of a human individual exists according to established biological and physiological knowledge at least from the 14th day after conception (Nidation, Individuation) . . . The process of development beginning from this point is a continuous one so that no sharp divisions or exact distinction between the various stages of development of human life can be made. It does not end at birth: for example, the particular type of consciousness peculiar to the human personality only appears a considerable time after the birth. The protection conferred by Article 2(2) first sentence of the Basic Law can therefore be limited neither to the 'complete' person after birth nor to the foetus capable of independent existence prior to birth. The right to life is guaranteed to every one who 'lives'; in this context no distinction can be made between the various stages of developing life before birth or between born and unborn children. 'Everyone' in the meaning of Article 2(2) of the Basic Law is 'every living human being', in other words: every human individual possessing life; 'everyone' therefore includes unborn human beings.

14. The Commission also notes that, in a case arising under the constitution of the United States, the State of Texas argued before the Supreme Court that, in

general, life begins at conception and is present throughout pregnancy. The Court, while not resolving the difficult question where life begins, found that, 'with respect to the State's important and legitimate interest in potential life, the "compelling" point is at viability'.

15. The Commission finally recalls [a] decision of the Austrian Constitutional Court above which, while also given in the framework of constitutional litigation, had to apply, like the Commission in the present case, Article 2 of the European Convention on Human Rights.

16. The Commission considers with the Austrian Constitutional Court that, in interpreting the scope of the term 'life' in Article 2(1), first sentence, of the Convention, particular regard must be had to the context of the Article as a whole. It also observes that the term 'life' may be subject to different interpretations in different legal instruments, depending on the context in which it is used in the instrument concerned.

17. The Commission has already noted, when discussing the meaning of the term 'everyone' in Article 2 (paragraph 8 above), that the limitations, in paragraphs (1) and (2) of the Article, of 'everyone's' right to 'life', by their nature, concern persons already born and cannot be applied to the foetus. The Commission must therefore examine whether Article 2, in the absence of any express limitation concerning the foetus, is to be interpreted:

- as not covering the foetus at all;
- as recognising a 'right to life' of the foetus with certain implied limitations; or
- as recognising an absolute 'right to life' of the foetus.

18. The Commission has first considered whether Article 2 is to be construed as recognising an absolute 'right to life' of the foetus and has excluded such an interpretation on the following grounds.

19. The 'life' of the foetus is intimately connected with, and cannot be regarded in isolation from, the life of the pregnant woman. If Article 2 were held to cover the foetus and its protection under this Article were, in the absence of any express limitation, seen as absolute, an abortion would have to be considered as prohibited even where the continuance of the pregnancy would involve a serious risk to the life of the pregnant woman. This would mean that the 'unborn life' of the foetus would be regarded as being of a higher value than the life of the pregnant woman. The 'right to life' of a person already born would thus be considered as subject not only to the express limitations mentioned in paragraph 8 above but also to a further, implied limitation.

20. The Commission finds that such an interpretation would be contrary to the object and purpose of the Convention. It notes that, already at the time of the signature of the Convention (4 November 1950), all High Contracting Parties, with one possible exception, permitted abortion when necessary to save the life of the mother and that, in the meanwhile, the national law on termination of pregnancy has shown a tendency towards further liberalisation.

21. Having thus excluded, as being incompatible with the object and purpose of the Convention, one of the three different constructions of Article 2 mentioned in paragraph 17 above, the Commission has next considered which of the two remaining interpretations is to be regarded as the correct one — *i.e.* whether Article 2 does not cover the foetus at all or whether it recognises a 'right to life' of the foetus with certain implied limitations.

22. The Commission here notes that the abortion complained of was carried out at the initial stage of pregnancy — the applicant's wife was ten weeks pregnant — under section 1(1)(*a*) of the Abortion Act 1967 in order to avert the risk of injury to the physical or mental health of the pregnant woman. It follows that, as regards the second of the two remaining interpretations, the Commission is in the present case not concerned with the broad question whether Article 2 recognises a 'right to life'

of the foetus during the whole period of the pregnancy but only with the narrower issue whether such a right is to be assumed for the initial stage of pregnancy. Moreover, as regards implied limitations of a 'right to life' of the foetus at the initial stage, only the limitation protecting the life and health of the pregnant woman, the so-called 'medical indication', is relevant for the determination of the present case and the question of other possible limitations (ethic indication, eugenic indication, social indication, time limitation) does not arise.

23. The Commission considers that it is not in these circumstances called upon to decide whether Article 2 does not cover the foetus at all or whether it recognises a 'right to life' of the foetus with implied limitations. It finds that the authorisation, by the United Kingdom authorities, of the abortion complained of is compatible with Article 2(1), first sentence because, if one assumes that this provision applies at the initial stage of the pregnancy, the abortion is covered by an implied limitation, protecting the life and health of the woman at that stage, of the 'right to life' of the foetus.

24. The Commission concludes that the applicant's complaint under Article 2 is inadmissible as being manifestly ill-founded within the meaning of Article 27(2).

NOTE:

1. As in the *Attorney-General's Reference* case (see page 732, above), the Commission stresses as the inseparability of the interests of the woman and the foetus.

QUESTIONS:

1. Could a putative father prevent a termination any more successfully if he based his argument on Article 12 of the European Convention which invests adults of marriageable age with "the right to marry and *found a family*"?
2. In the absence of any threat to the life or health of the pregnant woman, does the European Convention confer upon the unborn child an absolute right to life, a qualified right to life or no right to life at all?

The discontented putative father in *Paton* then proceeded to argue before the European Commission of Human Rights that his right to 'respect for his private and family life' guaranteed by Article 8 of the European Convention of Human Rights had been violated by British law.

Paton v. United Kingdom (1980) 3 EHRR 408 (From the Opinion of the European Commission)

25. In its examination of the applicant's complaints concerning the Abortion Act 1967 and its application in this case, the Commission has next had regard to Article 8 of the Convention which, in paragraph (1), guarantees to everyone the right to respect for his family life. The Commission here notes, apart from his principal complaint concerning the permission of the abortion, the applicant's ancillary submission that the 1967 Act denies the father of the foetus a right to be consulted, and to make applications, about the proposed abortion . . .

26. As regards the principal complaint concerning the permission of the abortion, the Commission recalls that the pregnancy of the applicant's wife was terminated in accordance with her wish and in order to avert the risk of injury to her physical or mental health. The Commission therefore finds that this decision, in so far as it interfered in itself with the applicant's right to respect for family life, was justified under paragraph (2) of Article 8 as being necessary for the protection of the rights of another person.

The Commission also considered briefly, the argument that the putative father has a right to be consulted, and equally briefly rejected.

27. The Commission has next considered the applicant's ancillary complaint that the Abortion Act 1967 denies the father of the foetus a right to be consulted, and to make applications, about the proposed abortion. It observes that any interpretation of the husband's and potential father's right, under Article 8 of the Convention, to respect for his private and family life, as regards an abortion which his wife intends to have performed on her, must first of all take into account the right of the pregnant woman, being the person primarily concerned in the pregnancy and its continuation or termination, to respect\fro her private life. The pregnant woman's right to respect for her private life, as affected by the developing foetus, has been examined by the Commission in its Report in the BRUGGEMANN AND SCHE-UTEN case (1978) 10 D. & R. 100. In the present case the Commission, having regard to the right of the pregnant woman, does not find that the husband's and potential father's right to respect for his private and family life can be interpreted so widely as to embrace such procedural rights as claimed by the applicant, *i.e.* a right to be consulted, or a right to make applications, about an abortion which his wife intends to have performed on her.

NOTE:

1. Van Dijk and Van Hoof have argued that the reasoning of the European Commission in this case is ambiguous, and that the Commission seems too easily to extend the exceptional case in which abortion is necessary to save the life of the pregnant woman to situations where abortion is considered *desirable* form some other medical reason. (See P. van Dijk and G. van Hoof, *Theory and Practice of the European Convention of Human Rights* (2nd edn.), Deventer, The Netherlands: Kluwer, 1990 at page 386.)

QUESTION:

1. Do you think the Commission might reach a different decision if it was confronted by an abortion at a later stage in the woman's pregnancy?)See M. Brazier, *Medicine, Patients and the Law* (2nd edn.), London: Penguin, 1992, at page 309.)

C v. S [1987] 1 All E.R. 1230; [1988] 1 Q.B. 135; [1987] 2 W.L.R. 1108; [1987] 2 FLR 5

In this case, it was the woman's boyfriend rather than her husband who applied for an injunction to prevent the proposed termination. (An account of the facts has already been given above.)

HEILBRON J.:

" . . . The first plaintiff, Mr C, a single man and a postgraduate student, is the father of the second plaintiff, who is named as 'a child en vèntre sa mere' and sues by his father and next friend.

Mr C applies on his own behalf, and on behalf of the second plaintiff for orders restraining Miss S from having an abortion and the area health authority, the second defendants, from causing or permitting, by itself or its servants or agents, the abortion to be performed . . .

Counsel's case on behalf of Mr C is that he has the *locus standi* to bring these proceedings, based on his personal interest, which he does not put as high as a legal right, and because the proposed termination encompasses, he submits, a threatened crime concerning the life of his child.

If it were to be decided that there were no such threat, he concedes that he has no standing qua father, for he does not contend that as a father he has any special right. He concedes too that a husband has no special rights qua husband, and he accepts the correctness of the decision in *Paton v. Trustees of BPAS* . . .

The question of the plaintiff's *locus standi* both as husband and father was also considered in *Paton's* case by Baker P., who decided that, since an unborn child had no rights of his own and since a father had no rights at common law over his illegitimate child, the plaintiff's right to apply for an injunction had to be made on the basis that he had the status of a husband and had rights of consultation and consent under the 1967 Act. But the judge pointed out that the Act gives the husband no such rights and, in his view, therefore, the husband had no legal right enforceable at law or in equity (a necessary basis for issuing the injunction) to stop his wife having the abortion or to stop the doctors from carrying it out.

Counsel for Mr C does not seek to argue for the contrary; but he submits that the instant case is distinguishable, because no suggestion was made in *Paton's* case, as here, that there is a potential criminal abortion and that, if it is carried out, the doctor would be contravening the provisions of s1 of the 1929 Act and would be guilty because he would be aborting a foetus of 18 weeks. Indeed, he further submitted that any doctor who since 1967 had aborted, or who proposed to abort, a foetus of that duration must be found guilty of the offence.

Having decided that the weight of expert evidence indicated that a foetus of 18–21 weeks was not viable, Heilbron J. continued:

I now, finally, come to consider the alleged criminality and to decide, as I am asked to do, whether or not I should grant the injunction which is sought . . .

Counsel for Mr C no longer claims *qua* father, but it is not unimportant to point out, as Baker P. did in *Paton v. Trustees of BPAS* [1978] 2 All E.R. 987 at 990 that, apart from a right to apply for custody of or access to an illegitimate child, the father has no other rights whatsoever, and the equality of parental rights provision in s1(1) of the Guardianship of Minors Act 1971 and s1(7) of the Guardianship Act 1973 expressly does not apply to an illegitimate child; parental rights are exclusively vested in the mother.

An injunction of the nature sought is rare. Indeed, a case of this sort is rare. The *Paton's* case was, I understand, the first to be heard in this country. Such an injunction should not issue, in any event, on evidence which is conflicting, or uncertain, as here, and, in my opinion, for such an injunction to issue there must, most importantly, be strong evidence against the proposed defendant and virtual certainty that what is being complained of constitutes a defined criminal offence. Every case depends on its own facts and circumstances and none more so than this, for the graver the offence the more vital it is that, before an injunction issues to interfere with the operative procedures because of the risk to the health of Miss S, it is shown that an offence is virtually certain to be committed if no injunction issues.

Moreover, the statute whose terms have to be interpreted in order to found this alleged offence is a penal one and the offence which it is said will be committed is one which attracts a penalty, as I have indicated, of life imprisonment. Such a statute must be strictly construed . . .

In my view, there is no sufficient basis for saying that there is a threatened crime and, if a case were brought, the judge would in my judgment be bound to stop the case, as I would. I have no hesitation in coming to the conclusion that counsel for Mr C has not made out his case for an injunction.

In view of of my conclusion, which disposes of the matter, I have not thought it necessary to add to this already long judgment by considering another hurdle that counsel might have encountered by reason of the decisions with regard to a private individual seeking to prevent the commission of an offence by way of an injunction, following the *Gouriet* line of cases (see *Gouriet v. Union of Post Office Workers* [1977] 3 All E.R. 70).

The applications are dismissed."

NOTE:

1. Heilbron J.'s decision was upheld by the Court of Appeal, see [1987] 1 All E.R. 1241; and the Appeal Committee of the House of Lords refused leave to appeal.
2. In *C v. S* the court conveniently "medicalised" the issue before it. That is, it side-stepped the difficult question of whether a putative father has the right to parenthood on the basis of it being a hypothetical, and therefore unnecessary question given that the pregnancy in *C v. S* could lawfully be terminated. (On the avoidance of this difficult question, see C. Smart, *Feminism and the Power of Law*, London: Routledge, 1989, pages 17-19)

QUESTION:

1. If the pregnant woman was acting as a surrogate mother on behalf of the father and his wife, and she had become pregnant by virtue of *in vitro* fertilisation using an embryo created using that couple's gametes, would (or should) the father have any greater say in any termination decision in this case? (For one possible solution see C. Farsides, "Body Ownership" in S. McVeigh and S. Wheeler (eds.) *Law, Health and Medical Regulation* (Aldershot: Dartmouth, 1992)

(d) The parents of an underage girl

A further interest which may need to be considered is whether the parents of a girl under the age of 16 have a right to veto her decision to have abortion or to be consulted about it; or indeed to compel her to undergo a termination if they considered it to be in her best interests. This question is addressed in Chapter 7 at pages 418–420.)

6. CONSCIENTIOUS OBJECTION

As we observed in the first part of this Chapter, the liberalisation of abortion in England under the 1967 Act represented a compromise: it allowed for medically certified terminations but did not confer an absolute right on pregnant women to demand abortion on request. Furthermore, it conferred a right to abstain from participation upon those persons who hold a conscientious objection to abortion.

Abortion Act 1967, s.4(1)–(2)

4.—(1) Subject to subsection (2) of this section, no person shall be under any duty, whether by contract or by any statutory or other legal requirement, to participate in any treatment authorised by this Act to which he has a conscientious objection:
Provided that in any legal proceedings the burden of proof of conscientious objection shall rest on the person claiming to rely on it.
(2) Nothing in subsection (1) of this section shall affect any duty to participate in treatment which is necessary to save the life or to prevent grave permanent injury to the physical or mental health of a pregnant woman.

The main issue raised by subsection 4(1) is the meaning of the words "participate in any treatment authorised by this Act"? Do they simply cover those who actually perform the termination or are they of broader compass?

Janaway v. Salford Area Health Authority [1988] 3 All E.R. 1079; [1989] A.C. 537; [1988] 3 W.L.R. 1350; [1989] 1 F.L.R. 1

Mrs Janaway was a doctor's receptionist who refused to type a letter of referral for an abortion on the grounds of conscientious objection. She was dismissed from her position for her alleged breach of the health authority's disciplinary rules. According to the authority she was guilty of an "unjustified refusal of a lawful and reasonable instruction". She then sought, by way of judicial review, to obtain both a declaration that she was not (because of her conscientious objection) obliged to type the letter, and an order of certiorari to quash the authority's decision. She pursued her contention all the way to the House of Lords seeking to rely on section 4(1) of the 1967 Act.

LORD KEITH:
" . . . The applicant claims the protection of s4(1). The issue in the case turns on the true construction of the words in that subsection 'participate in any treatment authorised by this Act'. For the applicant it is maintained that the words cover taking part in any arrangements preliminary to and intended to bring about medical or surgical measures aimed at terminating a pregnancy, including the typing of letters referring a patient to a consultant. The health authority argues that the meaning of the words is limited to taking part in the actual procedures undertaken at the hospital or other approved place with a view to the termination of a pregnancy.

The argument for the applicant proceeds on the lines that the acts attracting the protection afforded by s4(1) are intended to be coextensive with those which are authorised by s1(1) [*i.e.* actual terminations] and which in the absence of that provision would be criminal. The criminal law about accessories treats one who aids and abets, counsels or procures a criminal act as liable to the same extent as a principal actor. In the absence of s1(1) the applicant by typing a letter of referral would be counselling or procuring an abortion, or at least helping to do so, and subject to a possible defence on the principle of *R v. Bourne* [1938] 3 All E.R. 615, would be criminally liable. Therefore any requirement to type such a letter is relieved, in the face of a conscientious objection, by s4(1).

The majority of the Court of Appeal (Slade and Stocker L.JJ) accepted the main thrust of the applicant's argument, to the effect that ss1(1) and 4(1) are coextensive, but decided against her on the ground that her intention in typing a letter of referral would not be to assist in procuring an abortion but merely to carry out the obligations of her employment. In their view the typing of such a letter by the applicant would not be a criminal offence in the absence of s1(1).

Nolan J., however, and Balcombe L.J. in the Court of Appeal rejected the applicant's main argument. They accepted the argument for the health authority that on a proper construction the word 'participate' in s4(1) did not import the whole concept of principal and accessory residing in the criminal law, but in its ordinary and natural meaning referred to actually taking part in treatment administered in a hospital or other approved place in accordance with s1(3), for the purpose of terminating a pregnancy.

In my opinion Nolan J. and Balcombe L.J. were right to reach the conclusion they did. I agree entirely with their view about the natural meaning of the word 'participate' in this context. Although the word is commonly used to describe the activities of accessories in the criminal law field, it is not a term of art there. It is in any event not being used in a criminal context in s4(1). Ex hypothesi treatment for termination of a pregnancy under s1 is not criminal. I do not consider that Parliament can reasonably have intended by its use to import all the technicalities of the criminal law about principal and accessory, which can on occasion raise very nice questions about whether someone is guilty as an accessory. Such niceties would be very difficult of solution for an ordinary health authority. If Parliament had intended the result contended for by the applicant, it could have procured it very clearly and easily by referring to participation 'in anything authorised by this Act' instead of 'in any treatment [so] authorised'. It is to be observed that s4 appears to represent something of a compromise in relation to conscientious objection. One who believes all abortion to be morally wrong would conscientiously object even to such treatment as is mentioned in sub-s (2), yet the subsection would not allow the objection to receive effect.

The applicant's argument placed some reliance on a passage in the speech of Lord Roskill in *Royal College of Nursing of the U.K. v. Dept. of Health and Social Security* [1981] 1 All E.R. 545 at 577:

'My Lords, I read and reread the 1967 Act to see if I can discern in its provisions any consistent pattern in the use of the phrase "a pregnancy is terminated" or "termination of a pregnancy" on the one hand and "treatment for the termination of a pregnancy" on the other hand. One finds the former phrase in s1(1) and (1) (a), the latter in s1(3), the former in ss1(4) and 2(1)(b) and the latter in s3(1)(a) and (c). Most important to my mind is s4, which is the conscientious objection section. This section in two places refers to "participate in treatment" in the context of conscientious objection. If one construes s4 in conjunction with s1(1), as surely one should do in order to determine to what it is that conscientious objection is permitted, it seems to me that s4 strongly supports the wider construction of s1(1). It was suggested that acceptance of the department's submission involved rewriting that subsection so as to add words which are not to be found in the language of the subsection.

My Lords, with great respect to that submission, I do not agree. If one construes the words "when a pregnancy is terminated by a registered medical practitioner" in s1(1) as embracing the case where the "treatment for the termination of a pregnancy is carried out under the control of a doctor in accordance with ordinary current medical practice" I think one is reading "termination of pregnancy" and "treatment for termination of pregnancy" as virtually synonymous and as I think Parliament must have intended they should be read. Such a construction avoids a number of anomalies as, for example, where there is no pregnancy or where the extra-amniotic process fails to achieve its objective within the normal limits of time set for its operation.'

That case was concerned with a particular process of treatment for the termination of pregnancy carried out in hospital, important parts of which were performed not by a registered medical practitioner but by a nurse acting under his instructions. The issue was whether the actions of the nurse were unlawful, and it was held that they were not, on the ground that what was authorised by the Act was the whole medical process resulting in termination of pregnancy and that the process was carried out by a registered medical practitioner when that was done under his supervision and in accordance with his instructions, notwithstanding that certain parts of the process were carried out by others. The House was not concerned with the meaning of the word 'participate' in s4(1) in relation to anything other than the actual medical process carried out in the hospital, and then only indirectly. So Lord Roskill's words cannot be read as having any bearing on the decision of the present case . . ."

NOTE:

1. The other Law Lords agreed with the judgment of Lord Keith.
2. The narrow construction of "participate in any treatment" supplied by Lord Keith gives rise to the following question. If a G.P. considers that one of the grounds in section 1(1) is satisfied, is he obliged to sign the requisite certificate (known as 'the green form') himself, or is he entitled to rely upon section 4(1)? The question was acknowledged but not conclusively dealt with by Lord Keith, who observed:

   "The regulations do not appear to contemplate that the signing of the certificate would form part of treatment for the termination of pregnancy, since reg. 3(2) provides:
   'Any certificate of an opinion referred to in section 1(1) of the Act shall be given before the commencement of the treatment for the termination of the pregnancy to which it relates.'

   It does not appear whether or not there are any circumstances under which a doctor might be under any legal duty to sign a green form, so as to place in difficulties one who had a conscientious objection to doing so. The fact that during the 20 years that the 1967 Act has been in force no problem seems to have surfaced in this connection may indicate that in practice none exists. So I do not think it appropriate to express any opinion on the matter."

QUESTIONS:

1. Where the risk of continuing the pregnancy is that the woman concerned would suffer psychological harm, is this a sufficient basis

to trigger section 4(2) — which compels assistance in emergency
cases — thus debarring a doctor from invoking the conscience clause?

2. Could an anaesthetist, or a pharmacist who refuses to dispense an
abortifacient drug, invoke the conscientious objection clause?

In *Janaway* Lord Keith might usefully have considered the question of
whether, if the GP refuses to sign the certificate, he is obliged to refer the
pregnant woman to either another GP or a consultant whom he knows has
no moral objection to abortion. The matter is governed by the GP's
contractual duties which are set out in her terms of service. Although
patients do not pay for the services provided by their GP, it is nonetheless
the case that her professional obligations are to be discharged in favour of
such patients. For this reason, the duty (if any) to make referrals turns
upon the construction of the relevant terms of service.

*National Health Service (General Medical Services) Regulations 1992 (S.I.
1992 No. 635), Schedule 2:*

3.—Where a decision whether any, and if so what, action is to be taken under
these terms of service requires the exercise of professional judgment, a doctor shall
not, in reaching that decision, be expected to exercise a higher degree of skill,
knowledge and care than—

. . .

   (b) . . . that which general practitioners as a class may reasonably be expected to
exercise.

12.—(1) Subject to paragraphs 3, 13 and 44, a doctor shall render to his patients
all necessary and appropriate personal medical services of the type usually provided
by general medical practitioners.

   (2) The services which a doctor is required by sub-paragraph (1) to render shall
include the following:

. . .

   (d) arranging for the referral of patients, as appropriate, for the provision of
     any services under the [National Health Services] Act [1977].

QUESTIONS:

1. Where, for the purpose of Schedule 2 to the regulations, is it
"appropriate" for a GP, with a moral objection to abortion, to refer a
pregnant woman to another GP without such an objection? Where
the woman's life is at risk? Where her health is at risk? Or where the
fetal handicap ground is satisfied?

2. Is the effect of Schedule 2, paragraph 3 of the regulations to make the
doctor liable for failure to observe the terms of service only where
she would be negligent according to the *Bolam* standard of care? (On
the *Bolam* standard, see further Chapter 3.)

SELECT BIBLIOGRAPHY

M. Brazier, "Embryos 'Rights': Abortion and Research" in M. D. A. Freeman (ed.), Medicine, Ethics and Law, London: Stevens, 1988.

L. Clarke, "Abortion: A Rights issue?" in R. Lee and D. Morgan (eds), *Birthrights: Law and Ethics at the Beginnings of Life*, London: Routledge, 1989.

L. S. Colliver (ed.), *The Right to Know: Human Rights and Access to Reproductive Health Information*, Pittsburg: University of Pennsylvania Press, 1985.

R. Dworkin, *Life's Dominion: An Argument about Abortion and Euthanasia*, London: HarperCollins, 1993.

J. Fortin, "Legal Protection for the Unborn Child" (1988) 51 *Modern Law Review* 54.

P. Foster, "Contraception and abortion" in *Women and the Health Care Industry: An Unhealthy Relationship*, Buckingham: OUP, 1995.

A. Grubb, "The New Law of Abortion: Clarification or Ambiguity" [1991] *Criminal Law Review* 659.

J. Hadley, *Abortion: Between Freedom and Necessity*, London: Virago, 1991.

I. Kennedy, *Treat Me Right*, Oxford: OUP, 1991, Chapters 3 and 4.

J. Keown, *Abortion, Doctors and the Law*, Cambridge, CUP, 1988.

J. Keown, "The Scope of the Offence of Child Destruction" (1988) 104 *Law Quarterly Review* 120.

E. Kingdom, "Legal Recognition of a Woman's Right to Choose" in *What's Wrong with Rights? Problems for Feminist Policies of Law*, Edinburgh: Edinburgh University Press, 1991.

E. Kingdom, "Body Politics and Rights" in J. Bridgeman and S. Millns (eds), *Law and Body Politics: Regulating the Female Body*, Aldershot: Dartmouth, 1995.

S. McLean, "Abortion Law: is Consensual Reform Possible?" (1990) 17 *Journal of Law and Society* 106.

C. Mackinnon, "Reflections on Sex Equality under Law" (1991) 100 *Yale Law Journal* 1281.

J. K. Mason and A. McCall-Smith, *Law and Medical Ethics* (4th ed.), London: Butterworths, 1994, Chapter 5.

D. Morgan, "Abortion: the Unexamined Ground" [1990] *Criminal Law Review* 687.

D. Munday et al., "Twenty-one Years of Legal Abortion" (1989) 298 *British Medical Journal* 1231.

J. Murphy, "Cosmetics, Eugenics and Ambivalence: the Reform of the Abortion Act 1967" [1991] *Journal of Social Welfare and Family Law* 375.

J. Murphy, "Grey Areas and Green Lights: Judicial Activism in the Regulation of Doctors" (1991) 42 *Northern Ireland Legal Quarterly* 260.

S. Sheldon, "Who is the Mother to Make the Judgment? The Constructions of Women in English Abortion Law" (1993) 1 *Feminist Legal Studies* 3.

S. Sheldon, "Subject Only to the Attitude of the Surgeon Concerned: The Judicial Protection of Medical Discretion" (1996) 5 *Social and Legal Studies* 95.

S. Sheldon, "The Law of Abortion and the Politics of Medicalisation" in J. Bridgeman and S. Millns (eds), *Law and Body Politics: Regulating the Female Body*, Aldershot: Dartmouth, 1995.

P. Skegg, *Law, Ethics and Medicine*, Oxford: OUP, 1988, Chapter 1.

M. Thomson, "Women, Medicine and Abortion in the Nineteenth Century" (1995) 3 *Feminist Legal Studies* 159.

C. Wells and D. Morgan, "Whose Foetus Is It?" (1992) 18 *Journal of Law and Society* 43.

13

REPRODUCTIVE CHOICE III

1. INTRODUCTION

The debates surrounding reproductive choices and rights are frequently associated with the issues of assisted conception and abortion, which we have considered in the previous two chapters. But while the question of choices and rights provided the backdrop to the enactment of legislation such as the Abortion Act 1967 and the Human Fertilisation and Embryology Act 1990, the most extensive judicial consideration of the issue is to be found in the context of sterilisation of the mentally incompetent patient. The reality of choices is predicated upon the ability to make that choice. Does this mean that it is then otiose to talk in terms of "reproductive choice" in relation to the mentally incompetent? This issue needs to be seen in the light of more general changes in attitude towards the mentally handicapped in the last half-century with a greater willingness to, wherever possible, promote their autonomy (see C. Heginbotham, "Sterilising People With Mental Handicaps" in S. McLean (ed.), *Legal Issues in Human Reproduction*, Aldershot: Dartmouth, 1989. While the discourse of choice may be problematic in this context what then of rights? In the introduction to this part of the book (above at pages 763–766 we explored what was meant by reproductive rights. Below we consider the approach taken by the judiciary to claims of reproductive rights in the context of the mentally incompetent.

Reproductive choices may be facilitated by technological developments, as we saw in the context of assisted conception. During the period of pregnancy a wider range of choices are available. Techniques of pregnancy management have grown in sophistication and variety and there is increasing availability of techniques such as screening. But alongside the greater awareness of information in relation to care of woman and foetus during pregnancy, the knowledge that by adopting a certain lifestyle or undertaking particular behaviour such as smoking or taking drugs may harm the foetus puts into sharp focus the question, has a woman any obligations to the foetus in her womb during pregnancy? To what extent should a woman be free to manage her own pregnancy free of medical intervention? In the United States, where there has been extensive discussion of this issue, there

have been attempts to use criminal sanctions against women who place
themselves and the foetus at risk of harm during pregnancy. Indeed, the
management of pregnancy may be seen as the greatest threat to reproductive choice. In contrast in England the judiciary has largely refused to
intervene in regulating behaviour during pregnancy. Legal regulation of
pregnancy has been largely confined to the regulation of the conduct of
childbirth itself.

Scientific advances enhancing certain choices have led to discussion of
the search for the "designer baby". Sex may be chosen, handicaps may be
screened out. Nevertheless, this process may go wrong and we explore
below the potential for litigation where this occurs. Particular issues of
policy arise. Should an action be capable of being brought on behalf of a
child who is born handicapped? Should a woman be able to claim damages
for the birth of a healthy child on the basis that her chosen option to
refrain from conception had been undermined by medical negligence?
Furthermore, obstetrics and gynaecology is an area where practitioners are
particularly at risk of negligence suits in view of the nature of the clinical
practice not least sensitivity of the birth process.

In section two of the chapter we discuss the issue of the sterilisation of
the incompetent patient. In section three we explore the management of
pregnancy, the choices which are available and the extent to which a
woman is subject to pressures which may operate as constraints upon those
choices. In the final section we consider the question of litigation subsequent upon the failures of reproductive choices.

2. AUTHORISATION OF STERILISATION AND THE INCOMPETENT
PATIENT

(a) General Principles

Where it is proposed to undertake a sterilisation operation upon a
mentally incompetent person, whether child or adult, it is usually (though
not invariably) the case that this decision will be referred to the courts. A
number of such cases have come before the courts during the last two
decades. The cases discussed in this section involve both child and adult
patients, but are dealt with together because similar questions of principle
arise in them.

The need to safeguard the best interests of an incompetent person
involves a particularly sensitive calculation where a sterilisation operation
is proposed. Such procedures give rise to issues in relation to the eugenics
debate. Advocates of eugenics argued that traits such as intellectual
disability, epilepsy, criminality, alcoholism and pauperism were hereditary.
In the early years of this century some schools of thought, both in England
and abroad, advocated sterilisation of the mentally incompetent. Unsuccessful attempts were made to introduce legislation regarding sterilisation

of the mentally unfit by Major Archibald Church in 1931. (See further P. Fennell, *Treatment Without Consent*, London: Routledge, 1996, Chapter 6.) In examining the cases that follow you may wish to consider how far eugenic considerations have affected judicial approaches (see Chapter 2 above at pages 118–119).

Re D [1976] 1 All E.R. 326; [1976] Fam. 185

D was an 11-year-old child from a poor background. She suffered from Sotos syndrome which is accelerated growth during infancy, epilepsy, generalised clumsy appearance, behaviour problems and certain aggressive tendencies. She had reached puberty and though she hadn't shown any marked interest in the opposite sex her mother was concerned about the consequences should she become pregnant and wanted her daughter sterilised, an opinion supported by her doctor.

HEILBRON J.:
" . . . I have first of all to decide whether this is an appropriate case in which to exercise the court's wardship jurisdiction. Wardship is a very special and ancient jurisdiction. Its origin was the sovereign's feudal obligation as parens patriae to protect the person and property of his subjects, and particularly those unable to look after themselves, including infants. This obligation, delegated to the chancellor, passed to the Chancery Court, and in 1970 to this division of the High Court.

The jurisdiction in wardship is very wide, but there are limitations. It is not in every case that it is appropriate to make a child a ward, and counsel for Mrs B has argued with his usual skill and powers of persuasion that, as this case raises a matter of principle of wide public importance, and is a matter which affects many people, continuation of wardship would be inappropriate.

In his powerful argument, counsel for the Official Solicitor, on the other hand, submitted that the court in wardship had a wide jurisdiction which should be extended to encompass this novel situation, because it is just the type of problem which this court is best suited to determine when exercising its protective functions in regard to minors. As Lord Eldon L.C. said many years ago in *Wellesley v. Duke of Beaufort* [(1827) 2 Russ 1, at 20]:
'This jurisdiction is founded on the obvious necessity that the law should place somewhere the care of individuals who cannot take care of themselves,   particularly in cases where it is clear that some care should be thrown around them.'
It is apparent from the recent decision of the Court of Appeal in *Re X (A Minor)* [[1975] 1 All E.R. 697] that the jurisdiction to do what is considered necessary for the protection of an infant is to be exercised carefully and within limits, but the court has, from time to time over the years, extended the sphere in the exercise of this jurisdiction.

The type of operation proposed is one which involves the deprivation of a basic human right, namely the right of a woman to reproduce, and therefore it would, if performed on a woman for non-therapeutic reasons and without her consent, be a violation of such right. Both Dr Gordon and Miss Duncan seem to have had in mind the possibility of seeking the child's views and her consent, for they asked that this handicapped child of 11 should be consulted in the matter. One would have thought that they must have known that any answer she might have given, or any purported consent, would have been valueless. Nevertheless Dr Gordon did ask Mrs B to discuss the proposed operation with D, and Miss Duncan did intend, she said, to seek the child's consent prior to the operation.

Mrs B therefore discussed the proposed operation with the child, and asked her if she would like to have babies when she was old enough to have them. I do not think any useful purpose would be served by referring to this unfortunate episode in any further detail, but I express surprise that such a request should have been made, or such a discussion thought fitting. As the evidence showed, and I accept it, D could not possibly have given an informed consent. What the evidence did, however, make clear was that she would almost certainly understand the implications of such an operation by the time she reached 18. This operation could, if necessary, be delayed or prevented if the child were to remain a ward of court, and as Lord Eldon L.C., so vividly expressed it in *Wellesley's* case: 'It has always been the principle of this Court, not to risk the incurring of damage to children which it cannot repair, but rather to prevent the damage being done.'

I think that is the very type of case where this court should 'throw some care around this child', and I propose to continue her wardship which, in my judgment, is appropriate in this case. The operation — should it be performed?

In considering this vital matter, I want to make it quite clear that I have well in mind the natural feelings of a parent's heart, and though in wardship proceedings parents' rights can be superseded, the court will not do so lightly, and only in pursuance of well-known principles laid down over the years. The exercise of the court's jurisdiction is paternal, and it must be exercised judicially, and the judge must act, as far as humanly possible, on the evidence, as a wise parent would act. As Lord Upjohn pointed out in *J v. C*, the law and practice in relation to infants 'have developed, are developing and must, and no doubt will, continue to develop by reflecting and adopting the changing views, as the years go by, of reasonable men and women, the parents of children, on the proper treatment and methods of bringing up children; for after all that is the model which the judge must emulate for . . . he must act as the judicial reasonable parent.'

It is of course beyond dispute that the welfare of this child is the paramount consideration, and the court must act in her best interests.

The question of the sterilisation of a minor is one aspect of a sensitive and delicate area of controversy into which I do not propose to enter. I am dealing here with the case of this particular young girl, but the evidence, including that which disclosed that Dr Gordon has recommended and Miss Duncan had performed two prior operations of this nature on handicapped children in Sheffield, indicates the possibility that further consideration may need to be given to this topic, consideration which would involve extensive consultation and debate elsewhere.

Dr Gordon's reason for wishing this operation to be performed was, of course, to prevent D ever having a child. He recognised, as did Mrs B, that there are other methods of achieving that objective, but his view was that D could not satisfactorily manage any form of contraception. Mrs B was concerned lest D might be seduced and become pregnant. She too was against all forms of contraception.

A good deal of evidence was directed to ascertaining whether Mrs B.'s fears were soundly based or not. The answer is in the nature of things somewhat speculative, but it was common ground that D had as yet shown no interest in the opposite sex, and that her opportunities for promiscuity, if she became so minded, were virtually non-existent, as her mother never leaves her side and she is never allowed out alone. Much of the evidence, which I found convincing, was to the effect that it was premature even to consider contraception, except possibly to allay the mother's fears.

Mrs B's genuine concern, however, cannot be disregarded. A body of evidence was produced, therefore, to indicate the advantages and disadvantages of various forms of contraception. I shall not, however, burden this judgment with any detailed examination of it, save to say that I do not accept on the evidence Dr Gordon's contention that this young girl, if and when the time arrived, would not be a suitable subject for one of the various methods described by the doctors. I think it is only necessary to refer to the fact that Miss Duncan herself stated in evidence that if Mrs B had been willing to accept one of the methods of contraception, she would have advised one before sterilisation, and I entirely accept Professor Huntingford's evidence that there were certainly two methods, either one of which could be safely and satisfactorily used. I think it was a pity that both Dr Gordon and Mrs B were so reluctant to accept this possibility, or even the alternative of abortion, if, unhappily, it ever proved necessary, rather than the proposed use of such an irrevocable procedure.

It was common ground that D had sufficient intellectual capacity to marry, in the future of course, and that many people of a like kind are capable of, and do so. Dr Gordon agreed that this being so, she and her future husband would then be the persons most concerned in any question of sterilisation, and such an operation might have a serious and material bearing on a future marriage and its consequences. The purpose of performing this operation is permanently to prevent the possibility of reproduction. The evidence of Professor Huntingford, consultant and professor of obstetrics and gynaecology at the University of London and at St Bartholomew's Hospital and the London Hospital Medical Colleges, was that in his view such an operation was normally only appropriate for a woman who consented to it, possibly at the conclusion of child-bearing, and then only after careful and anxious consideration by her and her husband of many factors and, what is most important, with full knowledge of all its implications.

Professor Huntingford, Dr Snodgrass and Dr Newton were all agreed that such an operation was not medically indicated in this case, and should not be performed. Dr Snodgrass said he was firmly of the view that it was wrong to perform this operation on an 11-year-old, on the pretext that it would benefit her in the future. Dr Newton said: 'In my opinion sterilisation of a child before the age of consent can only be justified if it is the treatment for some present or inevitable disease. In this case, sterilization is not a treatment for any of the signs or symptoms of Sotos Syndrome, from which she suffers. I am totally against this operation being performed on D.' Professor Huntingford stated: 'In my considered opinion it will not be in the best interests of the ward to be sterilized having regard to her age and all other relevant factors.' He had never ever heard of a child of this age being sterilised. Dr Snodgrass, with his great experience of handicapped children of all types, had never known anyone suffering from epilepsy to be sterilised for that reason, nor would he consider recommending such an operation, even if a child was mentally retarded. D was only one of at least a hundred thousand people of a similar degree of dull normal intelligence. If it ever became necessary he would, he said, be prepared to recommend abortion, not sterilisation. Dr Gordon, however, maintained that, provided the parent or parents consented, the decision was one made pursuant to the exercise of his clinical judgment, and that no interference could be tolerated in his clinical freedom. The other consultants did not agree. Their opinion was that a decision to sterilise a child was not entirely within a doctor's clinical judgment, save only when sterilisation was the treatment of choice for some disease, as, for instance, when in order to treat a child and to ensure her direct physical well-being, it might be necessary to perform a hysterectomy to remove a malignant uterus. Whilst the side effect of such an operation would be to sterilise, the operation would be performed solely for therapeutic purposes. I entirely accept their opinions. I cannot believe, and the evidence does not warrant the view, that a decision to carry out an operation of this nature performed for non-therapeutic purposes on a minor, can be held to be within the doctor's sole clinical judgment.

It is quite clear that once a child is a ward of court, no important step in the life of that child, can be taken without the consent of the court, and I cannot conceive of a more important step than that which was proposed in this case.

A review of the whole of the evidence leads me to the conclusion that in a case of a child of 11 years of age, where the evidence shows that her mental and physical condition and attainments have already improved, and where her future prospects are as yet unpredictable, where the evidence also shows that she is unable as yet to understand and appreciate the implications of this operation and could not give a valid or informed consent, but the likelihood is that in later years she will be able to make her own choice, where, I believe, the frustration and resentment of realising (as she would one day) what had happened, could be devastating, an operation of this nature is, in my view, contra-indicated."

NOTE:

1. One perceived difficulty in safeguarding the interests of the mentally incompetent has been the fact that until relatively recently these concerns were not the subject of widespread public discussion.

Re B [1987] 2 All E.R. 206; [1988] A.C. 109; [1987] 2 W.L.R. 1212

B was 17-years-old but with a mental age of 5-6 and was epileptic. It was alleged that she did not understand and was unable to learn the causal connection between intercourse, pregnancy and the birth of children. It was, however, claimed that she had the sexual inclinations of a normal 17-year-old. If oral contraceptives were given to her they would only have a 40 per cent chance of establishing an acceptable regime and had serious side effects. Furthermore, her swings of mood and considerable physical strength, might prevent administration of a daily dose. She was also obese and because of the irregularity of her periods it was not obvious that, should she become pregnant, this would be detected sufficiently early. B's mother and the local authority advised by the social worker, gynaecologist and physician applied for sterilisation to be authorised.

LORD HAILSHAM OF ST MARYLEBONE L.C.:
" . . . There is no doubt that, in the exercise of its wardship jurisdiction, the first and paramount consideration is the well-being, welfare or interests (each expression occasionally used, but each, for this purpose, synonymous) of the human being concerned, that is the ward herself or himself. In this case I believe it to be the only consideration involved. In particular there is no issue of public policy other than the application of the above principle which can conceivably be taken into account, least of all (since the opposite appears to have been considered in some quarters) any question of eugenics. The ward has never conceived and is not pregnant. No. question therefore arises as to the morality or legality of an abortion.

The ward in the present case is of the mental age of five or six. She speaks only in sentences limited to one or two words. Although her condition is controlled by a drug, she is epileptic. She does not understand and cannot learn the causal connection between intercourse and pregnancy and the birth of children. She would be incapable of giving a valid consent to contracting a marriage. She would not understand, or be capable of easily supporting, the inconveniences and pains of pregnancy. As she menstruates irregularly, pregnancy would be difficult to detect or diagnose in time to terminate it easily. Were she to carry a child to full term she would not understand what was happening to her, she would be likely to panic, and would probably have to be delivered by Caesarian section, but, owing to her emotional state, and the fact that she has a high pain threshold she would be quite likely to pick at the operational wound and tear it open. In any event, she would be 'terrified, distressed and extremely violent' during normal labour. She has no maternal instincts and is not likely to develop any. She does not desire children, and, if she bore a child, would be unable to care for it.

In these circumstances her mother, and the local authority under whose care she is by virtue of a care order, advised by the social worker who knows her, a gynaecologist, and a paediatrician, consider it vital that she should not become pregnant, and in any case she would not be able to give informed consent to any act of sexual intercourse and would thus be a danger to others. Notwithstanding this, she has all the physical sexual drive and inclinations of a physically mature young woman of 17, which is what in fact she is. In addition, she has already shown that she is vulnerable to sexual approaches, she has already once been found in a compromising situation in a bathroom, and there is significant danger of pregnancy resulting from casual sexual intercourse. To incarcerate her or reduce such liberty as she is able to enjoy would be gravely detrimental to the amenity and quality of her life, and the only alternative to sterilisation seriously canvassed before the court is an oral contraceptive to be taken daily for the rest of her life whilst fertile, which has only a 40 per cent chance of establishing an acceptable regime, and has serious potential side effects. In addition, according to the evidence, it would not be possible in the light of her swings of mood and considerable physical strength to ensure the administration of the necessary daily dose. As her social worker put it, 'If she [the ward] is . . . in one of her moods . . . there is no way' she would try to give her a pill.

In these circumstances, Bush J. and the Court of Appeal both decided that the only viable option was sterilisation by occlusion of the Fallopian tubes (not hysterectomy). Apart from its probably irreversible nature, the detrimental effects are likely to be minimal. For my part, I do not myself see how either Bush J. or the Court of Appeal could sensibly have come to any other possible conclusion applying as they did as their first and paramount consideration the correct criterion of the welfare of the ward.

The ward becomes of age (18) on May 20 next. There seems some doubt whether some residual parens patriae jurisdiction remains in the High Court after majority (*cf.* Hoggett, *Mental Health Law* (2nd ed., 1984) p. 203 and 8 *Halsbury's Laws* (4th ed.) para. 901, note 6). I do not take this into account. It is clearly to the interest of the ward that this matter be decided now and without further delay. We should be no wiser in 12 months' time than we are now and it would be doubtful then what legal courses would be open in the circumstances.

We were invited to consider the decision of Heilbron J. in *Re D (a minor) (wardship: sterilisation)* [1976] 1 All E.R. 326 at 332, when the judge rightly referred to the irreversible nature of such an operation and the deprivation, which it involves, of a basic human right, namely the right of a woman to reproduce. But this right is only such when reproduction is the result of informed choice of which this ward is incapable. I have no doubt whatsoever that that case was correctly decided, but I venture to suggest that no one would be more astonished than that wise, experienced and learned judge herself if we were to apply these proper considerations to the extreme and quite different facts of the present case.

We were also properly referred to the Canadian case of *Re Eve* (1986) 31 DLR (4th) 1. But whilst I find La Forest J.'s history of the *parens patriae* jurisdiction of the Crown (at 14–21) extremely helpful, I find, with great respect, his conclusion (at 32) that the procedure of sterilisation 'should never be authorised for non-therapeutic purposes' (my emphasis) totally unconvincing and in startling contradictions to the welfare principle which should be the first and paramount consideration in wardship cases. Moreover, for the purposes of the present appeal I find the distinction he purports to draw between 'therapeutic' and 'non-therapeutic' purposes of this operation in relation to the facts of the present case above as totally meaningless, and, if meaningful, quite irrelevant to the correct application of the welfare principle. To talk of the 'basic right' to reproduce of an individual who is not capable of knowing the causal connection between intercourse and childbirth, the nature of pregnancy, what is involved in delivery, unable to form maternal instincts or to care for a child appears to me wholly to part company with reality . . . "

LORD BRIDGE OF HARWICH (AGREEING WITH LORD HAILSHAM AND LORD OLIVER): " . . . It is unfortunate that so much of the public comment on the decision should have been based on erroneous or, at best, incomplete appreciation of the facts and on mistaken assumptions as to the grounds on which the decision proceeded. I can only join with others of your Lordships in emphasising that this case has nothing whatever to do with eugenic theory or with any attempt to lighten the burden which must fall on those who have the care of the ward. It is concerned, and concerned only, with the question of what will promote the welfare and serve the best interests of the ward.

There is no reason to doubt that the Canadian decision in *Re Eve* was correct on its own facts. La Forest J., delivering the judgment of the Supreme Court, emphasised (at 9) that 'there is no evidence that giving birth would be more difficult for Eve than for any other woman'. The supposed conflict between the views of the Supreme Court in Canada and of the Court of Appeal in England arises from the passage where it is said (31 DLR (4th) 1 at 32):
  'The grave intrusion on a person's rights and the certain physical damage that ensues from non-therapeutic sterilization without consent, when compared to the highly questionable advantages that can result from it, have persuaded me that it can never safely be determined that such a procedure is for the benefit of that person. Accordingly, the procedure should never be authorised for non-therapeutic purposes under the *parens patriae* jurisdiction.'
This sweeping generalisation seems to me, with respect, to be entirely unhelpful. To say that the court can never authorise sterilisation of a ward as being in her best interests would be patently wrong. To say that it can only do so if the operation is 'therapeutic' as opposed to 'non-therapeutic' is to divert attention from the true issue, which is whether the operation is in the ward's best interest, and remove it to an area of arid semantic debate as to where the line is to be drawn between 'therapeutic' and 'non-therapeutic' treatment. In *Re D (A Minor) (Wardship: Sterilisation)* [1976] 1 All E.R. 326 at 332, Heilbron J. correctly described the right of a woman to reproduce as a basic human right. The Supreme Court of Canada in *Re Eve* 31 DLR (4th) 1 at 5 refer, equally aptly, to 'the great privilege of giving birth'. The sad fact in the instant case is that the mental and physical handicaps under which the ward suffers effectively render her incapable of ever exercising that right or enjoying that privilege. It is clear beyond argument that for her pregnancy would be an unmitigated disaster. The only question is how she may best be protected against it. The evidence proves overwhelmingly that the right answer is by a simple operation for occlusion of the Fallopian tubes and that, quite apart from the question whether the court would have power to authorise such an operation after her eighteenth birthday, the operation should now be performed without further delay. I find it difficult to understand how anybody examining the facts humanely, compassionately and objectively could reach any other conclusion."

LORD TEMPLEMAN (AGREEING WITH LORD HAILSHAM AND LORD OLIVER): " . . . In my opinion sterilisation of a girl under 18 should only be carried out with the leave of a High Court judge. A doctor performing a sterilisation operation with the consent of the parents might still be liable in criminal, civil or professional proceedings. A court exercising the wardship jurisdiction emanating from the Crown is the only authority which is empowered to authorise such a drastic step as sterilisation after a full and informed investigation. The girl will be represented by the Official Solicitor or some other appropriate guardian the parents will be made parties if they wish to appear and where appropriate the local authority will also appear. Expert evidence will be adduced setting out the reasons for the application, the history, conditions, circumstances and foreseeable future of the girl, the risks and consequences of pregnancy, the risks and consequences of sterilisation, the practicability of alternative precautions against pregnancy and any other relevant information. The judge may order additional evidence to be obtained. In my opinion, a decision should only be made by a High Court judge. In the Family Division a judge is selected for his or her experience, ability and compassion. No. one has suggested a more satisfactory tribunal or a more satisfactory method of reaching a decision which vitally concerns an individual but also involves principles of law, ethics and medical practice. Applications for sterilisation will be rare. Sometimes the judge will conclude that a sufficiently overwhelming case has not been established to justify interference with the fundamental right of a girl to bear a child this was the case in *Re D (A Minor) (Wardship: Sterilisation)* [1976] 1 All E.R. 326. But in the present case the judge was satisfied that it would be cruel to expose the girl to an unacceptable risk of pregnancy which could only be obviated by sterilisation in order to prevent child bearing and childbirth in circumstances of uncomprehending fear and pain and risk of physical injury. In such a case the judge was under a duty and had the courage to authorise sterilisation.

LORD OLIVER OF AYLMERTON:
" . . . My Lords, none of us is likely to forget that we live in a century which, as a matter of relatively recent history, has witnessed experiments carried out in the name of eugenics or for the purpose of population control, so that the very word 'sterilisation' has come to carry emotive overtones. It is important at the very outset, therefore, to emphasise as strongly as it is possible to do so, that this appeal has nothing whatever to do with eugenics. It is concerned with one primary consideration and one alone, namely the welfare and best interest of this young woman, an interest which is conditioned by the imperative necessity of ensuring, for her own safety and welfare, that she does not become pregnant . . .

Here then is the dilemma. The vulnerability of this young woman, her need for protection, and the potentially frightening consequences of her becoming pregnant are not in doubt. Of the two possible courses, the one proposed is safe, certain but irreversible, the other speculative, possibly damaging and requiring discipline over a period of many years from one of the most limited intellectual capacity. Equally it is not in doubt that this young woman is not capable and never will be capable herself of consenting to undergo sterilisation operation. Can the court and should the court, in the exercise of its wardship jurisdiction, give on her behalf that consent which she is incapable of giving and which, objectively considered, it is clearly in her interests to give?

My Lords, I have thought it right to set out in some detail the background of fact in which this appeal has come before your Lordships' House because it is, in my judgment, essential to appreciate, in considering the welfare of this young woman which it is the duty of the court to protect, the degree of her vulnerability, the urgency of the need to take protective measures and the impossibility of her ever being able at this age or any later age either to consent to any form of operative treatment or to exercise for herself the right of making any informed decision in matters which, in the case of a person less heavily handicapped, would rightly be thought to be matters purely of personal and subjective choice.

My Lords, the arguments advanced against the adoption of the expedient of a sterilisation operation are based almost entirely (and, indeed, understandably so) on its irreversible nature. It was observed by Dillon L.J. in the Court of Appeal that the jurisdiction in wardship proceedings to authorise such an operation is one which should be exercised only in the last resort and with that I respectfully agree. What is submitted is that, in concluding as it did that instant case was one in which, as the last resort, that jurisdiction ought to be exercised, the Court of Appeal was in error and had not given sufficient weight to the alternative course of experimentation with the progestogen pill. That submission has been reinforced before your Lordships by a further submission not made in either court below that there lies in the court an inherent jurisdiction in the case of a mentally handicapped subject of any age to sanction, as *parens patriae*, an operation such as that proposed whenever it should be considered necessary. Thus, it is argued, some of the urgency is taken out of the case, for a further application can be mounted at any time should alternative methods of contraception prove ineffective. My Lords, speaking for myself, I should be reluctant to express any view regarding the correctness of this submission without very much fuller argument than it has been possible for counsel in the time available to present to your Lordships. But in fact I do not consider that in the instant case the point is of more than of academic interest for I am, for my part, prepared to assume for present purposes that the *parens patriae* jurisdiction continues into full age. Making that assumption, I remain wholly unpersuaded that the Court of Appeal failed to give full weight to the alternative proposed or that it erred in any way in the conclusion to which it came. It was faced, as your Lordships are faced, with the necessity of deciding here and now what is the right course in the best interests of the ward. The danger to which she is exposed and the speculative nature of the alternative proposed are such that, on any footing, the risk is not one which should properly be taken by the court. For my part I have not been left in any doubt that Bush J. and the Court of Appeal rightly concluded that there was no practicable alternative to sterilisation and that the authority sought by the council should be given without further delay.

Your Lordships' attention has, quite properly, been directed to the decision of Heilbron J. in *Re D (A Minor) (Wardship: Sterilisation)* [1976] 1 All E.R. 326, a case very different from the instant case, where the evidence indicated that the ward was of an intellectual capacity to marry and would in the future be able to make her own choice. In those circumstances Heilbron J. declined to sanction an operation which involved depriving her of her right to reproduce. That, if I may say so respectfully, was plainly a right decision. But the right to reproduce is of value only if accompanied by the ability to make a choice and in the instant case there is no question of the minor ever being able to make such a choice or indeed to appreciate the need to make one. All the evidence indicates that she will never desire a child and that reproduction would in fact be positively harmful to her. Something was sought to be made of the description of the operation for which authority was sought in *Re D* as 'non-therapeutic', using the word 'therapeutic' as connoting the treatment of some malfunction or disease. The description was, no doubt, apt enough in that case, but I do not, for my part, find the distinction between 'therapeutic' and 'non-therapeutic' measures helpful in the context of the instant case, for it seems to me entirely immaterial whether measures undertaken for the protection against future and foreseeable injury are properly described as 'therapeutic'. The primary and paramount question is only whether they are for the welfare and benefit of this particular young woman situate as she is situate in this case.

Your Lordships have also been referred to *Re Eve* (1986) 31 DLR (4th) 1, a decision of the Supreme Court of Canada which contains an extremely instructive judgment of La Forest J. in which he considered the extent of the *parens patriae* jurisdiction over mentally handicapped persons. His conclusion was that sterilisation should never be authorised for non-therapeutic purposes under the parens patriae jurisdiction. If in that conclusion the expression 'non-therapeutic' was intended to exclude measures taken for the necessary protection from future harm of the person over whom the jurisdiction is exercisable, then I respectfully dissent from it for it seems to me to contradict what is the sole and paramount criterion for the exercise of the jurisdiction, *viz.* the welfare and benefit of the ward. La Forest J. observed (at 32–33):

'If sterilisation of the mentally incompetent is to be adopted as desirable for general social purposes, the legislature is the appropriate body to do so.'

With that I respectfully agree but I desire to emphasise once again that this case is not about sterilisation for social purposes it is not about eugenics it is not about the convenience of those whose task it is to care for the ward or the anxieties of her family and it involves no general principle of public policy. It is about what is in the best interests of this unfortunate young woman and how best she can be given the protection which is essential to her future well-being so that she may lead as full a life as her intellectual capacity allows. That is and must be the paramount consideration as was rightly appreciated by Bush J. and by the Court of Appeal. They came to what, in my judgment, was the only possible conclusion in the interests of the minor. I would accordingly dismiss the appeal."

NOTES:

1. Lord Brandon agreed with Lords Bridge and Oliver.
2. *Re B* was decided prior to the House of Lords decision in *F v. West Berkshire Health Authority* [1989] 2 All E.R. 545 (see below at pages 767–770). There was some urgency in *B* to perform the sterilisation before her eighteenth birthday as the legality of the performance of a sterilisation operation upon a mentally incompetent adult was unclear. After the decision of the House of Lords in *F v. West Berkshire Health Authority* it is clear that the performance of a sterilisation operation upon a mentally incompetent adult may be authorised where it is in her best interests. This at least should afford more opportunity to "wait and see" how a girl may develop and then, if necessary, undertake sterilisation when she is older.
3. While sterilisation may protect against the risk of pregnancy it will not protect against the risk of sexual abuse. Sterilisation may leave a mentally handicapped person vulnerable to seduction. The vulnerability may relate to the adequacy of supervision of the mentally handicapped person. This in turn may depend on what resources are devoted to supervision. (See R. Lee and D. Morgan, "A Lesser Sacrifice: Sterilisation and the Mentally Handicapped Woman" in R. Lee and D. Morgan (eds.), *Birthrights: Law and Ethics at the Beginning of Life*, London: Routledge 1987.)
4. It has also been questioned whether decisions to sterilise are gender biased. It is notable that those cases which have come before the court concern female patients. (See M. Freeman, "For Her Own Good" (1987) 84 *L.S.Gaz.* 949.) However, as Gillian Douglas points out, one difficulty regarding sterilising a mentally incompetent man is that it cannot be regarded as in his best interests (see G. Douglas, *Law, Fertility and Reproduction*, London: Sweet & Maxwell, 1991, at page 89).
5. Emphasis was laid in *Re B* upon B's mental age. Yet it has been argued that mental age is not a static concept. Heginbotham comments:
   > "People with mental handicaps have complex personalities like everyone else. To talk of a mental age of two or three is meaningless. Although intellectually he/she may only function at that level, life skills may approximate to those of a child of five or six or eight or nine) and, socially, the person may be capable of adolescent or adult interaction."

(C. Heginbotham, "Sterilising people with mental handicaps" in S. McLean (ed.), *Legal Issues in Human Reproduction*, Aldershot: Dartmouth, 1989, and see also M. Freeman, "Sterilising the Mentally Handicapped" in M. Freeman (ed.), *Medicine, Ethics and Law*, London: Sweet & Maxwell, CLP, 1988).

6. One difficulty identified in this case was B's lack of comprehension of the information given. Keywood has suggested that the lack of comprehension by B of the link between intercourse and pregnancy may be the product of poor sex education. (See K. Keywood, "Sterilising the Woman with Learning Disabilities" in J. Bridgeman and S. Millns (eds.), *Law and Body Politics*, Aldershot: Dartmouth, 1995.)

7. One worrying element is the extent to which eugenics plays a part in the decision making process whether covertly or overtly (on eugenics generally see Chapter 2 above at pages 118–119). In *Re M* (discussed later in *Re P*, at pages 765–766) Bush J. took into account the fact the woman had a 50 per cent chance should she become pregnant of giving birth to a handicapped child. (See M. Brazier, "Down the Slippery Slope" (1990) 6 *Professional Negligence* 25.)

8. A further complication, and an issue hardly discussed in the decided cases, is that section 7 of the Sexual Offences Act 1956 provides that sexual intercourse with a mental defective is a criminal offence. The difficulty here is to establish whether an individual is a mental defective. Section 45 of the Sexual Offences Act 1956 states that a defective is a "person suffering from a state of arrested or incomplete development of mind which includes severe impairment of intelligence and social functioning." Severe impairment is to be ascertained by reference to the standard of a normal person (*R. v. Hall* [1977] Crim. L.R. 831).

In contrast to the approach in *Re Eve* and the English sterilisation cases is the approach taken in the Australian courts in the case of *Department of Health v. JWB and SWB* (1992) 66 A.L.J.R. 300. (See N. Cica, "Sterilising the Intellectually Disabled" (1993) 1 *Medical Law Review* 186.) This case concerned the decision to sterilise an intellectually disabled girl of 14. Here the majority of the court accepted the existence of a distinction between therapeutic and non-therapeutic sterilisations. The court addressed human rights issues although the majority did indicate that they were not focusing upon a right to reproduce. The majority stated that non-therapeutic sterilisations were capable of authorisation where they were in the patient's best interests, but that they required judicial approval (there was, however, a strong dissent from Brennan J., who supported the view expressed in *Re Eve*). The judges noted that such procedures might be costly and time-consuming and it was suggested that this may be an area in which there should be legislative reform, enabling these matters to be considered by an informal board or tribunal.

QUESTIONS:

1. Do you agree with the House of Lords rejection of the approach taken in *Re Eve?* Is it correct to say that a distinction between therapeutic and non-therapeutic sterilisation is meaningless? (See R. Lee *op. cit.* and I. Kennedy *loc. cit.* and G. Douglas at pages 56–71.)
2. Is sterilisation of an incompetent person for contraceptive purposes ever justifiable? (See I. Kennedy, "Patients, Doctors and Human Rights" in I. Kennedy, *Treat Me Right*, Oxford: OUP, 1989.)
3. Examine the judgments in *Re B* and consider whether a mentally incompetent person could ever be said to have a "right to reproduce".

In reaching its decision the Court in *Re B* considered the fact that a sterilisation operation was irreversible in nature. In more recent cases evidence has been brought before the court as to the possibility that a sterilisation operation may be reversed.

Re P (A Minor) (Wardship: Sterilisation) [1989] 1 F.L.R. 182; [1989] Fam. Law 102

Mrs P sought sterilisation of her daughter T. T was made a ward of court to facilitate this. The father supported the application. T was 17, of attractive appearance, but with a mental age of six. Depo Provera had been attempted but was discontinued because of its considerable side-effects. The girl was due to go to an adult training centre.

EASTHAM J.:
" . . . In opening, Mr Ward referred me to an unreported decision of Bush J. [now reported *sub nom. Re M (A Minor) (Wardship: Sterilisation)* [1988] 2 FLR 497], which he heard in Manchester in December 1987, where the judge attached considerable importance to the fact that the mother in that case would not be allowed to keep any child that she might have. The case is, however, of interest from another point of view, and that is that there was a professor at some unidentified university (unidentified because the name of the university has been struck out) who said that the operation of sterilization by occlusion of the Fallopian tubes, which involves the placing of clamps on the Fallopian tubes, is not necessarily irreversible. The evidence before Bush J. was that, indeed in 50 per cent to 75 per cent of the cases, by the use of micro-surgery it is possible successfully to reverse the operation. Professor X says that he regards the operation as more one of contraception than of sterilization, with all the emotive feelings that the use of the word 'sterilization' arouses. The judge went on to say quite rightly:
'I do not think that in *Re B* that was part of the evidence. Indeed I think, reading the opinions of the House of Lords, that they seem to have proceeded on the basis that the operation itself was probably irreversible.'
In the present case one of the witnesses who has deposed to an affidavit and has attended to give evidence is Professor Robert Winston. He is a consultant obstetrician and gynaecologist. He is willing to carry out the necessary operation of sterilization with clips applied bilaterally over each Fallopian tube. He deals with that operation in his affidavit. He says that the operation can be done under a short

15 minute anaesthetic through a very small incision inside the navel. The post-operative pain is negligible. He says:

'But the crucial fact (and one not previously debated by the Law Lords) is that this method of sterilization is highly reversible. There is now overwhelming evidence that this method of sterilization can be reversed if a patient's circumstances change. Micro-surgical reversal of sterilization was first described by Winston.'

Then he deals with various works, but, more importantly, in his own team the situation is that clip sterilization, which is the operation he is prepared to carry out, followed by subsequent micro-surgical anastomosis, carries a 95 per cent chance of reversal with a resulting term pregnancy.

It is right, however, to say that the reversal operation is not the very minor operation so far as time, anaesthetic and post-operative pain are concerned that the sterilization operation is: it involves a longer operation, it involves a larger surgical wound, it involves a longer period in hospital, but there is the high rate, certainly at [X] Hospital, of successful reversal operations. In the old days, before reversal became seriously considered in the profession, not a great deal of care was taken in the sterilization operation, but now, as medical practitioners and experts are coming to realize that people change their minds and want the sterilization reversed, providing that care is taken to minimize the damage on the sterilization operation, there is a very good chance, albeit with a much more serious operation, of a successful reversal operation. I say all that because in *Re B (A Minor) (Wardship: Sterilisation)* (above) there is the passage in the speech of Lord Oliver at page 328 when he says:

'My Lords, the arguments advanced against the adoption of the expedient of a sterilization operation are based almost entirely — and, indeed, understandably so — upon its irreversible nature. It was observed by Dillon L.J. in the Court of Appeal that the jurisdiction in wardship proceedings to authorize such an operation is one which should be exercised only in the last resort and with that I respectfully agree.'

The situation today is that the operation is not irreversible, although it is still the current ethical practice to tell patients that it is an irreversible operation as part of the information to be given to them when they are giving consent for the operation to be carried out, although if such a patient changes her mind, no doubt it would be explained to her that the more serious reversal operation could be contemplated.

It seems to me that, although the question of sterilization is a very important question, in view of the advance of the medical profession in the reversal field, perhaps the comment of Dillon L.J., approved of by Lord Oliver of Aylmerton, does not carry quite so much weight, but in any event I have come to the conclusion that the test that I have to apply is as stated by all the Lords of Appeal, namely that the welfare or interests of T are my first and paramount consideration."

NOTE:

1. In this case the court regarded the possibility of reversal of sterilisation operation as an important factor. However, it has been noted that success rates for reversals may not accord with those quoted by the leading experts and that furthermore the mentally incompetent patient may not be at the head of the queue for an operation for the reversal of sterilisation. (See M. Brazier, "Down the slippery slope" (1990) 6 *Professional Negligence* 25.)

QUESTION:

1. Do you think that the judiciary in these sterilisation cases can be criticised for undue deference to the opinion of medical experts?

(b) Sterilisation of The Mentally Incompetent Adult Patient

Sterilisation of the adult patient was addressed by the House of Lords in *F. v. West Berkshire Health Authority* [1989] 2 All E.R. 545. In that case the House of Lords indicated that before undertaking sterilisation it would be desirable for the approval of the court to be sought through application of a declaration.

F. v. West Berkshire Health Authority [1989] 2 All E.R. 545; [1990] 2 A.C. 1; [1989] 2 W.L.R. 938

F was a 36-year-old mentally handicapped woman who lived as a voluntary "in patient" in a mental hospital. She had the mental age of a small child. Concern arose when she formed a sexual relationship with a male patient. The opinion of the hospital medical staff was that she would be unable to cope with pregnancy. As was seen in Chapter 5 above the House of Lords held that unlike the case of the child patient they had no jurisdiction to decide whether medical treatment of a mentally incompetent adult should be undertaken. Nevertheless, treatment could be given where it was in the patient's best interests to do so.

LORD GRIFFITHS:
" . . . My Lords, the argument in this appeal has ranged far and wide in search of a measure to protect those who cannot protect themselves from the insult of an unnecessary sterilisation. Every judge who has considered the problem has recognised that there should be some control mechanism imposed on those who have the care of infants or mentally incompetent women of child bearing age to prevent or at least inhibit them from sterilising the women without approval of the High Court. I am, I should make it clear, speaking now and hereafter of an operation for sterilisation which is proposed not for the treatment of diseased organs but an operation on a woman with healthy reproductive organs in order to avoid the risk of pregnancy. The reasons for the anxiety about sterilisation which it is proposed should be carried out for other than purely medical reasons, such as the removal of the ovaries to prevent the spread of cancer, are readily understandable and are shared throughout the common law world.
    We have been taken through many authorities in the United States, Australia and Canada which stress the danger that sterilisation may be proposed in circumstances which are not truly in the best interests of the woman but for the convenience of those who are charged with her care. In the United States and Australia the solution has been to declare that, in the case of a woman who either because of infancy or mental incompetence cannot give her consent, the operation may not be performed without the consent of the court. In Canada the Supreme Court has taken an even more extreme stance and declared that sterilisation is unlawful unless performed for therapeutic reasons, which I understand to be as a life-saving measure or for the prevention of the spread of disease: see *Re Eve* (1986) 31 DLR (4th) 1. This extreme position was rejected by this House in *Re B (A Minor) (Wardship: Sterilisation)* [1987] 2 All E.R. 206, which recognised that an operation might be in the best interests of a woman even though carried out in order to protect her from the trauma of a pregnancy which she could not understand and with which she could not cope. Nevertheless Lord Templeman stressed that such an operation should not be undertaken without the approval of a High Court judge of the Family

Division. In this country *Re D (A Minor) (Wardship: Sterilisation)* [1976] 1 All E.R. 326, stands as a stark warning of the danger of leaving the decision to sterilise in the hands of those having the immediate care of the woman, even when they genuinely believe that they are acting in her best interests.

. . . I agree that an action for a declaration is available as a mechanism by which a proposed sterilisation may be investigated to ensure that it is in the woman's best interests.

But I cannot agree that it is satisfactory to leave this grave decision with all its social implications in the hands of those having the care of the patient with only the expectation that they will have the wisdom to obtain a declaration of lawfulness before the operation is performed. In my view the law ought to be that they must obtain the approval of the court before they sterilise a woman incapable of giving consent and that it is unlawful to sterilise without that consent. I believe that it is open to your Lordships to develop a common law rule to this effect. Although the general rule is that the individual is the master of his own fate the judges through the common law have, in the public interest, imposed certain constraints on the harm that people may consent to being inflicted on their own bodies. Thus, although boxing is a legal sport, a bare knuckle prize fight in which more grievous injury may be inflicted is unlawful (see *R v. Coney* (1882) 8 Q.B.D. 534), and so is fighting which may result in actual bodily harm (see *Re Att.-Gen.'s Reference of 1980)* [1981] 2 All E.R. 1057). So also is it unlawful to consent to the infliction of serious injury on the body in the course of the practice of sexual perversion (see *R v. Donovan* [1934] All E.R. Rep 207). Suicide was unlawful at common law until Parliament intervened by the Suicide Act 1961.

The common law has, in the public interest, been developed to forbid the infliction of injury on those who are fully capable of consenting to it. The time has now come for a further development to forbid, again in the public interest, the sterilisation of a woman with healthy reproductive organs who, either through mental incompetence or youth, is incapable of giving her fully informed consent unless such an operation has been inquired into and sanctioned by the High Court. Such a common law rule would provide a more effective protection than the exercise of *parens patriae* jurisdiction which is dependent on some interested party coming forward to invoke the jurisdiction of the court. The *parens patriae* jurisdiction is in any event now only available in the case of minors through their being made wards of court. I would myself declare that on grounds of public interest an operation to sterilise a woman incapable of giving consent on grounds of either age or mental incapacity is unlawful if performed without the consent of the High Court. I fully recognise that in so doing I would be making new law. However, the need for such a development has been identified in a number of recent cases and in the absence of any parliamentary response to the problem it is my view that the judges can and should accept responsibility to recognise the need and to adapt the common law to meet it. If such a development did not meet with public approval it would always be open to Parliament to reverse it or to alter it by perhaps substituting for the opinion of the High Court judge the second opinion of another doctor as urged by counsel for the Mental Health Act Commission.

As I know that your Lordships consider that it is not open to you to follow the course I would take I must content myself by accepting, but as second best, the procedure by way of declaration proposed by Lord Brandon and agree to the dismissal of this appeal."

LORD GOFF OF CHIEVELEY:
" . . . In the present case, your Lordships have to consider whether the foregoing principles apply in the case of a proposed operation of sterilisation on an adult woman of unsound mind, or whether sterilisation is (perhaps with one or two other cases) to be placed in a separate category to which special principles apply. Again,

counsel for the Official Solicitor assisted your Lordships by deploying the argument that, in the absence of any *parens patriae* jurisdiction, sterilisation of an adult woman of unsound mind, who by reason of her mental incapacity is unable to consent, can never be lawful. He founded his submission on a right of reproductive autonomy or right to control one's own reproduction, which necessarily involves the right not to be sterilised involuntarily, on the fact that sterilisation involves irreversible interference with the patient's most important organs, on the fact that it involves interference with organs which are functioning normally, on the fact that sterilisation is a topic on which medical views are often not unanimous and on the undesirability, in the case of a mentally disordered patient, of imposing a 'rational' solution on an incompetent patient. Having considered these submissions with care, I am of the opinion that neither singly nor as a whole do they justify the conclusion for which counsel for the Official Solicitor contended. Even so, while accepting that the principles which I have stated are applicable in the case of sterilisation, the matters relied on by counsel provide powerful support for the conclusion that the application of those principles in such a case calls for special care. There are other reasons which support that conclusion. It appears, for example, from reported cases in the United States that there is a fear that those responsible for mental patients might (perhaps unwittingly) seek to have them sterilised as a matter of administrative convenience. Furthermore, the English case of *Re D (Minor) (wardship: sterilisation)* [1976] 1 All E.R. 326, provides a vivid illustration of the fact that a highly qualified medical practitioner, supported by a caring mother, may consider it right to sterilise a mentally retarded girl in circumstances which prove, on examination, not to require such an operation in the best interests of the girl. Matters such as these, coupled with the fundamental nature of the patient's organs with which it is proposed irreversibly to interfere, have prompted courts in the United States and in Australia to pronounce that, in the case of a person lacking the capacity to consent, such an operation should only be permitted with the consent of the court. Such decisions have of course been made by courts which have vested in them the *parens patriae* jurisdiction, and so have power, in the exercise of such jurisdiction, to impose such a condition. They are not directly applicable in this country, where that jurisdiction has been revoked for that reason alone I do not propose to cite passages from the American and Australian cases although, like my noble and learned friend Lord Brandon, I have read the judgments with great respect and found them to be of compelling interest. I refer in particular to *Re Grady* (1981) 85 N.J. 235 in the United States and, in Australia, to the very full and impressive consideration of the matter by Nicholson C.J. in *Re Jane* (December 22, 1988, unreported), who in particular stressed the importance of independent representation by some disinterested third party on behalf of the patient (there a minor).

Although the *parens patriae* jurisdiction in the case of adults of unsound mind is no longer vested in courts in this country, the approach adopted by the courts in the United States and in Australia provides, in my opinion, strong support for the view that, as a matter of practice, the operation of sterilisation should not be performed on an adult person who lacks the capacity to consent to it without first obtaining the opinion of the court that the operation is, in the circumstances, in the best interests of the person concerned, by seeking a declaration that the operation is lawful. (I shall return later in this speech to the appropriateness of the declaratory remedy in cases such as these.) In my opinion, that guidance should be sought in order to obtain an independent, objective and authoritative view on the lawfulness of the procedure in the particular circumstances of the relevant case, after a hearing at which it can be ensured that there is independent representation on behalf of the person on whom it is proposed to perform the operation. This approach is consistent with the opinion expressed by Lord Templeman in *Re B (A Minor) (Wardship: Sterilisation)* [1987] 2 All E.R. 206 at 214-215, that, in the case of a girl who is still a minor, sterilisation should not be performed on her unless she has first been made a ward of court and the court has, in the exercise of its wardship jurisdiction, given its authority to such a step. He said:

'No one has suggested a more satisfactory tribunal or a more satisfactory method of reaching a decision which vitally concerns an individual but also involves principles of law, ethics and medical practice.'

I recognise that the requirement of a hearing before a court is regarded by some as capable of deterring certain medical practitioners from advocating the procedure of sterilisation but I trust and hope that it may come to be understood that court procedures of this kind, conducted sensitively and humanely by judges of the Family Division, so far as possible and where appropriate in the privacy of chambers, are not to be feared by responsible practitioners.

It was urged before your Lordships by counsel for the Mental Health Act Commission (the commission having been given leave to intervene in the proceedings) that a court vested with the reponsibility of making a decision in such a case, having first ensured that an independent second opinion has been obtained from an appropriate consultant of the appropriate speciality, should not, if that second opinion supports the proposal that sterilisation should take place, exercise any independent judgment but should simply follow the opinion so expressed. For my part, I do not think that it is possible or desirable for a court so to exercise its jurisdiction. In all proceedings where expert opinions are expressed, those opinions are listened to with great respect but, in the end, the validity of the opinion has to be weighed and judged by the court. This applies as much in cases where the opinion involves a question of judgment as it does in those where it is expressed on a purely scientific matter. For a court automatically to accept an expert opinion, simply because it is concurred in by another appropriate expert, would be a denial of the function of the court. Furthermore, the proposal of the commission is impossible to reconcile with the American and Australian authorities which stress the need for a court decision after a hearing which involves separate representation on behalf of the person on whom it is proposed to perform the operation. Having said this, I do not feel that the commission need fear that the opinions of the experts will in any way be discounted. On the contrary, they will be heard with the greatest respect and, as the, present case shows, there is a high degree of likelihood that they will be accepted."

NOTES:

1. The test of best interests employed in *F v. West Berkshire Health Authority* has been the subject of considerable criticism. The House of Lords stated that "best interests" is to be determined with reference to the standard set by a responsible body of medical practitioners (see Chapter 5 at pages 287–293). Contrast now the recommendations of the Law Commission in their report *Mental Incapacity*, Law Com. No. 231, London: HMSO, 1995 (see above at pages 303–306).

2. Following *F v. West Berkshire Health Authority*, a Practice Note was issued. This provides guidance for subsequent courts in making orders, although it is not binding upon the court (*Practice Note (Official Solicitor: Sterilisation)* [1996] Fam. Law 439). This Note suggests that the position of the patient be safeguarded by her being made a party to the application, and in addition that the Official Solicitor should be involved in the proceedings. (The role of the Official Solicitor is to act as an independent person and to represent the patient's interests.) It proposes a number of criteria to be taken

into account: these include the patient's ability to make an informed judgement now or in the future; the fact that a sterilisation operation is required because the patient is fertile and the patient is engaging in sexual conduct, the risk of trauma from pregnancy, and the fact that there is no practical less intrusive alternative to sterilisation.

3. In *Re W (Mental Patient)* [1993] 1 FLR 381, W was a 20-year-old woman with the mental age of a young child, who also suffered from severe learning disabilities, mild epilepsy and mobility problems related to dislocation of the hips which had resulted from a congenital disability. Sterilisation was sought on the grounds that were she to become pregnant this would aggravate her epilepsy. While she showed limited understanding of issues such as pregnancy and childbirth, it appeared that there was little immediate chance of her becoming pregnant because she was under good supervision. Medical opinion on the question was divided. Hollis J. in granting a declaration authorising sterilisation noted that it would be undesirable for her to become pregnant and that contraception was unsuitable. He stated that he did not regard sterilisation as being to W's detriment. This decision may be seen as consistent with earlier cases in providing judicial endorsement of medical opinion.

4. It has been suggested in the context of sterilisation decisions generally that "the courts somewhat misplaced concern for the woman's vulnerability seems to be at the expense of recognising her sexual needs and desires." (See K. Keywood, "Sterilising the Woman with Learning Disabilities" in J. Bridgeman and S. Millns (eds.), *Law and Body Politics*, Aldershot: Dartmouth, 1995.)

(c) Undertaking Sterilisation Without Judicial Order

Re E (A Minor) (Medical Treatment) [1991] 2 F.L.R. 585

J, a 17-year-old mentally handicapped girl, suffered from severe menstrual problems. She was overweight and any attempt to deal with the menstrual problem through the use of hormones would have only worsened the obesity factor. The only other method available to deal with the condition was surgery in the form of a hysterectomy.

Sir Stephen Brown P.:
" . . . Mr Nicholls, for the Official Solicitor, submits that it is not necessary for the formal consent of the court to be granted in this case in order that the operation in question can be carried out. In a detailed skeleton argument, he has analysed what he submits is the correct legal position. This is a case where the operation is required for therapeutic reasons; it is in order to treat J therapeutically that the operation is said to be required. This is not a case where the objective is sterilisation. This is not a case where the doctors are saying that this young girl should be sterilised because it would be wrong for her to become pregnant. That is not the issue in this case, and I make that very clear. In this case, the submission is made to the court that it ought not be necessary for a responsible doctor to have to

seek the formal consent of the court for the carrying out of an operation which is required in order to treat the patient therapeutically.

It is quite clear that, in recent times, the medical profession has become very anxious about its legal position and possible legal liabilities. It was because of this climate of concern, if I may so describe it, that the Medical Defence Union advised Mr Robinson, the consultant in this case, that he should not swear an affidavit or take any step in this matter unless the court made an order in the wardship proceedings. Mr Nicholls, in an attempt to clarify the legal position of doctors and, indeed, of parents placed in a similar position to the parents of J, decided that this matter should be clarified by an application to the court.

The case of *Re F* [1990] 2 A.C. 1, recently decided in the House of Lords, is, of course, the basis of the Medical Defence Union's position in this matter. However, that was a wholly different case on its facts, and it is to be observed that the House of Lords did not rule that the consent of the court was required by law. It stated that, as a matter of good practice, it would be wise for consent to be sought.

It is important that the medical profession should be clear about the position in such cases. I am satisfied, after the careful analysis which Mr Nicholls has presented to the court, that there is a clear distinction to be made between cases where an operation is required for genuine therapeutic reasons and those where the operation is designed to achieve sterilisation. That position was recognised by Lord Bridge in *Re F* (above), and I believe that it is the correct position in the present case. I think that J's parents are in a position to give valid consent to the proposed operation. I am not dealing in this instance with the case of an adult; I am dealing with the case of a minor, and it is plainly desirable that in order to relieve the particular symptoms of her distressing condition, J should undergo this particular treatment. Accordingly, in this case, I rule that the consent of the court is not required for this operation to be carried out. It is necessary for therapeutic reasons. In any event, if it were to be considered necessary, I would have no hesitation in granting the court's consent.

This is a case where, after careful deliberation and consideration of all the medical factors, the consultant has come to the conclusion that this treatment is necessary for the relief of the condition from which this unfortunate girl suffers. Accordingly the court will rule and declare that on the facts of this case no formal consent is necessary."

NOTE:

1. This decision was followed in *Re GF* [1992] 1 F.L.R. 293, [1993] 4 Med. L.R. 77. In that case Sir Stephen Brown held that a declaration for approval of a sterilisation operation was unnecessary provided two doctors agreed first that an operation was necessary for therapeutic purposes, secondly, that it was in the patient's best interests and thirdly, that no practicable less intrusive treatment was available.

QUESTION:

1. Did the court in *Re E* recognise a distinction between therapeutic and non-therapeutic sterilisation operations? How does this approach equate with that taken by the court in *Re B*? (See G. Douglas, *Law, Fertility and Reproduction*, London: Sweet & Maxwell at page 58.)

(d) Reform

The issue of sterilisation of the mentally incompetent was examined by the Law Commission in its 1995 report.

Law Commission, *Mental Incapacity* Law Com. No. 231, London, HMSO 1995

Paragraph 6.4. We suggested in our consultation paper that sterilisation operations could be divided into three sub-sets: those intended to treat a disease of the reproductive organs; those intended for 'menstrual management'; and those intended for contraceptive purposes. None of our respondents suggested that statutory supervision should be applied to those in the first category which can properly be carried out under the general authority, with access to the court if there is a dispute or difficulty. A number of respondents confirmed, however that the need for 'menstrual management' can too easily be invoked to avoid the judicial supervision which should currently apply to any operation intended to sterilise the patient as a method of contraception. We were greatly assisted by discussions with those in the Official Solicitors Department who have experience of representing patients in actions involving proposed sterilisations. We are persuaded that there is a valid distinction to be drawn between an operation which is intended to address an existing harmful condition associated with menstruation and one intended to guard against any future distress which might arise from an unintended pregnancy. The phrase 'menstrual management' may obfuscate this crucial distinction instead of emphasising it. We take the view that sterilisation operations designed to relieve the immediate and genuine harmful effects of menstruation can be distinguished from those intended to prevent conception and need not attract supervision by the court. In view of the concern expressed by the respondents however, we suggest a different form of independant supervision for such cases.

We recommend that any treatment or procedure intended or reasonably likely to render the person permanently infertile should require court authorisation unless it is to treat a disease of the reproductive organs or relieve existing detrimental effects of menstruation (Draft Bill clause 7(2)(a)).

6.9. Although we have concluded that a sterilisation operation designed to relieve a patient of any existing pain and harmful effects connected with menstruation should not require authorisation by the court, many of our respondents expressed concern about operations being labelled 'menstrual management', with the result that no independant supervision at all is required. A consultant in developmental psychiatry who has made a special study of the sterilisation of people with learning difficulties suggested that the level of menstrual distress is often misrepresented, and that further investigation can reveal less drastic means of coping with the problem than a sterilisation operation. There is a clear need for independent supervisions in such circumstances.

We recommend that any treatment or procedure intended or reasonably likely to render the person concerned permanently infertile should require a certificate from an independent medical practitioner where it is for relieving the detrimental effects of menstruation. (Draft Bill, clause 8(3)(d).)

QUESTIONS:

1. Would referral of the sterilisation decision to judicial authority provide a sufficient safeguard?
2. Do the "best interests" criteria set out in the proposals provide adequate guidance? (See Chapter 6 above.)

3. MANAGEMENT OF PREGNANCY

There is increasing medical intervention in the management of pregnancy.

A woman may have the option of discovering whether or not she or her partner are carriers of a genetic condition which could result in a child suffering a disability. Prior to conception she may decide to undertake a genetic test with/without her partner in order to ascertain whether there is a risk that a hereditary condition may emerge in the child and on the result of this test she may base her decision whether or not to attempt to conceive. During pregnancy a woman may be offered tests to determine whether the foetus she is carrying is suffering from, or will later develop, a handicap. A range of tests are available for conditions such as Rubella and Downs Syndrome.

These tests have increased a woman's choice whether that of termination of pregnancy or to be given the information which will enable her to plan for the birth of a handicapped child. (See generally for discussion of screening techniques in the context of genetic diagnosis Nuffield Council on Bioethics Report, *Genetic Screening*, London, 1993, paras. 3.32–3.43.) It appears likely that in the future it will be possible to undertake tests for the propensity to develop a whole range of genetic conditions. Failure to offer ante-natal tests may lead to a subsequent negligence action.

Such tests have potentially very wide ramifications. A genetic test may not only impact on decisions concerning pregnancy, but, in addition, the person tested may as a result discover their own propensity to develop a particular illness. There may be implications for other family members who may themselves be also carriers of a particular gene. This may lead to difficult issues regarding patient confidentiality and disclosure of information (see Chapter 8 at pages 469–470 and Nuffield Council on Bioethics, *Genetic Screening: Ethical Issues*, 1993). A difficulty with screening procedures during pregnancy is they may not be risk free. Ultrasound is a technique which enables the detection of malformation of the foetus and is undertaken at around 16–20 weeks into pregnancy. Claims have been made that the use of ultrasound has been linked to changes in body cells and lowbirth weight. (See P. Foster, *Women and the Health Care Industry*, Buckingham: Open UP, 1995, at p. 34.) Tests used to detect Downs Syndrome — amniocentesis (involving taking amniotic fluid from the sac surrounding the foetus by means of a needle) and chorus villus sampling (involving the removal of a small sample of placental tissue) have been linked to an increased risk of miscarriage. There is also the possibility of misdiagnosis from procedures such as ultra sound.

QUESTION:

1. Should a woman be legally obliged to undertake all possible tests during pregnancy to reveal any genetic defects in the foetus she is carrying in her womb?

The management of pregnancy increasingly incorporates elements of health promotion with women being encouraged to adopt healthy lifestyles (see Chapter 1). Since the early 1970s there have been campaigns targetting pregnant women regarding the dangers of smoking. (See P. Foster, *Woman and the Health Care Industry: An Unhealthy Relationship?*, Buckingham: Open UP, 1995, page 131.) Studies have found links between smoking during pregnancy and low birth rates. Alcohol consumption by the pregnant mother may result in "Foetal alcohol syndrome", which is linked to disabilities such as mental retardation and learning difficulties. But while strong encouragement may be given to a woman to adopt a particular lifestyle during her pregnancy, to what extent should this extend to legal compulsion?

Re F (In Utero) [1988] 2 All E.R. 193; [1988] 2 W.L.R. 1288

F's mother had a history of mental disturbance and drug abuse. She gave birth to a child in 1977. This child was placed in care. Later mother and child went to live a nomadic existence around Europe. Finally they returned to England and the child was placed with foster parents. The mother subsequently became pregnant. Concern was expressed as to the welfare of the unborn child. The mother had left her flat and the local authority did not know her whereabouts. As a result, an attempt was made to make the unborn child a ward of court. This involved first an order directed to the tipstaff who could involve the police to search for the mother; an order requiring the mother to live at a particular place and attend a particular hospital; thirdly, orders relating to the care and control of the child once it was born. At first instance the judge rejected the application, but leave to appeal was granted.

Balcombe L.J.:
" . . . Of particular significance in the present case is that there is no recorded instance of the courts having assumed jurisdiction in wardship over an unborn child. Indeed, the whole trend of recent authority is to the contrary effect. In *Paton v. Trustees of BPAS* [1978] 2 All E.R. 987, Baker P. refused an application by a husband for an injunction to restrain his wife from having an abortion. In the course of his judgment Baker P. said ([1978] 2 All E.R. 987 at 989-990):
'The first question is whether this plaintiff has a right at all. The foetus cannot, in English law, in my view, have any right of its own at least until it is born and has a separate existence from the mother. That permeates the whole of the civil law of this country (except the criminal law, which is now irrelevant), and is, indeed, the basis of the decisions in those countries where law is founded on the common law, that is to say, in America, Canada, Australia, and, I have no doubt, in others. For a long time there was great controversy whether after birth a child could have a right of action in respect of pre-natal injury. The Law Commission considered that and produced a working paper (Law Com. No. 47) in 1973, followed by a final report (Report on Injuries to Unborn Children, Law Com. No. 60 (Cmnd. 5709)), but it was universally accepted, and has since been accepted, that in order to have a right the foetus must be born and be a child. There was only one known possible exception which is referred to in the working paper (Law Com. no. 47, page 3), an American case, *White v. Yup* (1969) 458 P

2d 617, where a wrongful death of an eight month old viable foetus, stillborn as a consequence of injury, led an American court to allow a cause of action, but there can be no doubt, in my view, that in England and Wales, the foetus has no right of action, no right at all, until birth. The succession cases have been mentioned. There is no difference. From conception the child may have succession rights by what has been called a "fictional construction" but the child must be subsequently born alive. See *per* Lord Russell of Killowen in *Elliot v. Joicey* [1935] All E.R. Rep 578 at 589. The husband's case must therefore depend on a right which he has himself.'

To the like effect is the judgment of Heilbron J. in *C. v. S.* [1987] 1 All E.R. 1230. This was another attempt by a father to prevent the mother of his unborn child having an abortion, but in this case the unborn child was named as the second plaintiff, suing by his father and next friend (the first plaintiff). On this aspect of the case the judge said ([1987] 1 All E.R. 1230 at 1234–1235):

'The authorities, it seems to me, show that a child, after it has been born, and only then in certain circumstances based on his or her having a legal right, may be a party to an action brought with regard to such matters as the right to take, on a will or intestacy, or for damages for injuries suffered before birth. In other words, the claim crystallises on the birth, at which date, but not before, the child attains the status of a legal persona, and thereupon can then exercise that legal right. This also appears to be the law in a number of Commonwealth countries. In *Medhurst v. Medhurst* (1984) 46 O.R. (2d) 263 Reid J. held in the Ontario High Court that an unborn child was not a person and that any rights accorded to the foetus are held contingent on a legal personality being acquired by the foetus on its subsequent birth alive. Nor could its father, the husband in that case, act as the foetus's next friend. A similar decision was taken in *Dehler v. Ottawa Civic Hospital* (1979) 25 O.R. (2d) 748, quoted with approval by Reid J., and affirmed by the Ontario Court of Appeal (see (1980) 29 O.R. (2d) 677n).'

The judge then cited with approval the last portion of the passage from the judgment of Baker P. in *Paton v. Trustees of BPAS* and continued ([1987] 1 All E.R. 1230 at 1235):

'In his reply, counsel's final position was summarised in this way: (1) he no longer relied on the numerous succession cases but he wished to retain some reliance on the position of the unborn child in *Thellusson v. Woodford* (1799) 4 Ves 227, 31 E.R. 117(2) he did not claim that a child had either a right to be born or a right to life in view of the terms of the [Abortion Act 1967] but (3) he maintained that the unborn child had a right to be a party because it was the subject of a threatened crime, that is to say, that of child destruction. If there was no such threat, then this claim too failed. In my judgment, there is no basis for the claim that the foetus can be a party, whether or not there is any foundation for the contention with regard to the alleged threatened crime, and I would dismiss the second plaintiff from this suit and the first plaintiff in his capacity as next friend.'

That case came before this court, but the part of the appeal relating to the rights of the unborn child was dismissed by consent, without a ruling of this court (see [1987] 1 All E.R. 1230 at 1243).

However, these decisions only relate directly to the legal rights of the foetus: they are not decisive of the question before us, namely has the court power to protect a foetus by making it a ward of court?

The statutory provisions relating to wardship afford no assistance in answering this question as they are negative in character. Section 41 of the Supreme Court Act 1981 refers to a minor being made a ward of court and section 1(1) of the Family Law Reform Act 1969 provides that minority ends on the attainment of the age of 18; neither Act contains anything to indicate whether it is possible for a person to be a minor before birth. The Rules of the Supreme Court are likewise silent on this point: see Ord 90, r.3(1) and (2).

Counsel, who appeared for the local authority before us, in the course of a persuasive argument referred us to the Infant Life (Preservation) Act 1929. Section 1(1) of that Act provides that, subject to an exception for an act done in good faith for the purpose only of preserving the life of the mother, 'any person who, with intent to destroy the life of a child capable of being born alive, by any wilful act causes a child to die before it has an existence independent of its mother' shall be guilty of a criminal offence. Section 1(2) provides that, for the purposes of the Act, 'evidence that a woman had at any material time been pregnant for a period of twenty-eight weeks or more shall be *prima facie* proof that she was at that time pregnant of a child capable of being born alive'. Counsel conceded that, if the jurisdiction in wardship existed, it was likewise limited to a child capable of being born alive. Whilst I can understand the practical reasons for this concession, it does not appear to me to rest on any logical basis. If there is jurisdiction to protect a foetus by making it a ward of court, I do not see why that jurisdiction should start only at a time when the foetus is capable of being born alive. A foetus at an earlier stage of pregnancy is protected by the criminal law by ss.58 and 59 of the Offences against the Person Act 1861, although the extent of that protection has been greatly reduced by the provisions of the Abortion Act 1967. However, I do not find these provisions of the criminal law of assistance in answering the question before us.

Counsel also sought to rely on art 2(1) of the European Convention for the Protection of Human Rights and Fundamental Freedoms (Rome, November 4, 1950; TS 71 (1953) Cmd. 8969): 'Everyone's right to life shall be protected by law.' However, in *Paton v. U.K.* [1980] 3 EHRR 408, on a complaint by the unsuccessful plaintiff in *Paton v. Trustees of BPAS* the European Commission of Human Rights ruled that on its true construction art. 2 is apt only to apply to persons already born and cannot apply to a foetus (at 413 (para. 8)). They continued (at 415 (para. 19)):

'The "life" of the foetus is intimately connected with, and cannot be regarded in isolation from, the life of the pregnant woman. If Article 2 were held to cover the foetus and its protection under this Article were, in the absence of any express limitation, seen as absolute, an abortion would have to be considered as prohibited even where the continuance of the pregnancy would involve a serious risk to the life of the pregnant woman. This would mean that the "unborn life" of the foetus would be regarded as being of a higher value than the life of the pregnant woman. The "right to life" of a person already born would thus be considered as subject not only to the express limitations mentioned in paragraph 8 above but also to a further, implied limitation.'

Thus, far from assisting counsel's submission, art. 2 of the convention, as interpreted by the European Commission, is in my judgment against him.

We were also referred to s.1 of the Guardianship of Minors Act 1971, which (as amended) provides:

'Where in any proceedings before any court . . . (a) the legal custody or upbringing of a minor . . . is in question, the court, in deciding that question, shall regard the welfare of the minor as the first and paramount consideration . . .'

'Legal custody' is defined by s.86 of the Children Act 1975 as 'so much of the parental rights and duties as relate to the person of the child', and this definition is incorporated by reference in the 1971 Act by s.20(2) of that Act see also s.85 of the 1975 Act for a definition of 'parental rights and duties'. I do not derive any assistance from these provisions. They do not contain anything to suggest that they contemplate minority commencing before birth in any event, the legal custody or upbringing of a minor is not in question when the subject matter of the proposed proceedings is an unborn child.

In the end it seems to me that the question is one of first principles on which there is no direct authority. However, the question has been the subject of academic discussion. Phillips 'Wardship and Abortion Prevention' (1979) 95 L.Q.R. 332 at 333 suggests that the courts should be prepared to extend jurisdiction in wardship to an unborn child. Lyon and Bennett 'Abortion-Whose Decision' (1979) 9 Fam. Law 35 at 37 suggest that, while an extension of the notion of wardship would be required to make it applicable to a foetus, that would be 'a logical and natural development'. Radevsky 'Wardship and Abortion' (1980) 130 NLJ 813 and Lowe 'Wardship and Abortion Prevention-Further Observations' (1980) 96 L.Q.R. 29 and 'Wardship and Abortion-A Reply' (1981) 131 NLJ 561 are to the opposite effect. Both these latter make the point that any such extension of the law should be left to Parliament, while Lowe stresses the point that any such extension of wardship would necessarily involve controlling the mother. In the latest edition of his work on *Wards of Court* (2nd ed., 1986) p. 18 Lowe partially resiles from his previous attitude, suggesting that 'since the court is occasionally faced with novel circumstances the door should, possibly, be left open for the future development of the jurisdiction in this respect'.

Approaching the question as one of principle, in my judgment there is no jurisdiction to make an unborn child a ward of court. Since an unborn child has, ex hypothesi, no existence independent of its mother, the only purpose of extending the jurisdiction to include a foetus is to enable the mother's actions to be controlled. Indeed, that is the purpose of the present application. In the articles already cited Lowe gives examples of how this might operate in practice (96 L.Q.R. 29 at 30):

'It would mean, for example, that the mother would be unable to leave the jurisdiction without the court's consent. The court being charged to protect the foetus' welfare would surely have to order the mother to stop smoking, imbibing alcohol and indeed any activity which might be hazardous to the child. Taking it to the extreme were the court to be faced with saving the baby's life or the mother's it would surely have to protect the baby's.'

Another possibility is that the court might be asked to order that the baby be delivered by Caesarian section: in this connection see Fortin 'Legal Protection for the Unborn Child' (1988) 51 M.L.R. 54 at 81 and the United States cases cited in note 16, in particular *Jefferson v. Griffin Spalding County Hospital Authority* (1981) 274 S.E. 2d 457. Whilst I do not accept that the priorities mentioned in the last sentence of the passage cited above are necessarily correct, it would be intolerable to place a judge in the position of having to make such a decision without any guidance as to the principles on which his decision should be based. If the law is to be extended in this manner, so as to impose control over the mother of an unborn child, where such control may be necessary for the benefit of that child, then under our system of parliamentary democracy it is for Parliament to decide whether such controls can be imposed and, if so, subject to what limitations or conditions. Thus, under the Mental Health Act 1983, to which we were also referred, there are elaborate provisions to ensure that persons suffering from mental disorder or other similar conditions are not compulsorily admitted to hospital for assessment or treatment without proper safeguards: see ss.2, 3 and 4 of that Act. If Parliament were to think it appropriate that a pregnant woman should be subject to controls for the benefit of her unborn child, then doubtless it will stipulate the circumstances in which such controls may be applied and the safeguards appropriate for the mother's protection. In such a sensitive field, affecting as it does the liberty of the individual, it is not for the judiciary to extend the law."

NOTES:

1. Staughton L.J. and May L.J. agreed.
2. The effect of the action, had it succeeded, would have been to impose constraints on the mother during pregnancy. The court was of the

view that the imposition of such controls should be left to parliament. But this should now be contrasted with the later case of *Re S* [1992] 4 All E.R. 671 (see below at pages 782–783).

3. In *Re F* the court emphasised the fact that the foetus is not a legal person for the purposes of English civil or criminal law. This was confirmed most recently in *Attorney-General's Reference (No. 3 of 1994)*. (See Chapter 12 above at pages 732–737.)

4. Judicial unwillingness to impose constraints on the pregnant woman in this country can be contrasted with the approach in the United States. (See J. Robertson, *Children of Choice*, Princeton, New Jersey: University of Pennsylvania Press, 1995, Chapter 8 and see also B. Steinbock, "Maternal-Foetal Conflict" in D. R. Brahamet, *et al.* (eds.), *Ethics in Reproductive Medicine*, London: Springer-Verlag, 1992.) Women have been subject to prosecutions after birth, for example, for taking drugs during pregnancy.

5. Although, as we saw in *Re F* the courts are not prepared to impose controls on a mother during pregnancy, nevertheless her conduct during pregnancy may lead health professionals to conclude that it is in the child's best interests for him to be taken away from the mother at birth. An example of this was provided by the case of *D (A Minor) v. Berkshire County Council* [1987] 1 All E.R. 20, in which a child was born suffering from drug withdrawal symptoms. The mother was a registered drug addict and had been taking drugs for 10 years. She continued to take drugs during pregnancy, although she knew that this could harm the foetus. The child was kept in intensive care in hospital for several weeks immediately following the birth. A place of safety order was obtained by Berkshire social services on April 23 and successive interim care orders were in force from May 13, 1985 to the date of the hearing. At the time of the hearing the child had not been in the care or control of either the mother or father since birth. Her parents continued to be drug addicts. The House of Lords upheld the care order as valid. This is, of course, an extreme situation. Removal of a child from its parents on the basis of what is deemed to be an unacceptable lifestyle is highly controversial and is unlikely to receive widespread endorsement.

6. If a woman is reckless as to her conduct during pregnancy and as a result the foetus dies this could result in a prosecution for manslaughter. A prosecution might also be attempted under the Infant Life Preservation Act 1929. This makes it an offence to destroy the life of a child capable of being born alive. Nevertheless, establishing liability under this statute is improbable. It has been noted that it would be exceedingly difficult to establish a wilful act causing the ultimate injury. (See P. Glazebrook, "What Care Must be Taken of an Unborn Baby?" (1993) 52 *Cambridge Law Journal* 20 and I. Kennedy, "A Woman and Her Unborn Child" in P. Byrne (ed.), *Ethics and Law in Health Care and Research*, Chichester, Wiley: 1990). (For further

discussion of the imposition of criminal liability where a foetus is injured by a third party during pregnancy see Chapter 12, at pages 732–737.)

7. The judicial unwillingness to coerce lifestyle choices during pregnancy is linked with the general unwillingness to regulate this area. One of the limited respects in which such choices are constrained is through the employment process. In the past there were considerable legislative restrictions upon women's hours of work: while these have been repealed, an employer may impose certain constraints consequent upon a woman's pregnancy. In *Page v. Freight Hire* [1981] I.C.R. 299 a woman employed as a tanker driver was told by her employer that she could not drive lorries because they contained chemicals which could potentially damage her reproductive capacity. She objected, saying that she did not want children. However, she ultimately lost her job. It was held that the dismissal was valid because the Sex Discrimination Act 1975 under which her action at the industrial tribunal was brought, allowed discriminatory behaviour where sanctioned under earlier statutes and here the employers relied upon a defence under the Health and Safety at Work Act 1974. This provision is still in force. (See further M. Thompson, "Employing the Body: The Reproductive Body and the Employment Exclusion" (1996) *Social Legal Studies* 243.)

QUESTIONS:

1. Is it appropriate for the wardship jurisdiction to be used to resolve conflicts between mother and foetus? (See A. Bainham, *Parents, Children and the State*, London: Sweet & Maxwell, 1988, Chapter 6 and *cf.* G. Douglas, *Law, Fertility and Reproduction*, London: Sweet & Maxwell, 1991, at page 188.)
2. Should a woman's partner be held responsible for his conduct during the pregnancy and any injury that may result to the foetus? (See J. Robertson, *Children of Choice*, Princeton: Pennsylvania University Press, 1994, at page 191.)

4. CHILDBIRTH

(a) The Choice Where to Give Birth

A woman may wish to choose where to give birth and also to choose the manner of the birth. One issue is whether she should have the right to choose to give birth at home rather than in hospital. Last century, as a general rule, women who had the means gave birth at home with only the poor going into hospital. Before the First World War births in homes, hospitals or institutions established under the Poor Law only amounted to

1 per cent of the total number of births. (See P. Foster, *Women and the Health Care Industry: An Unhealthy Relationship*, Buckingham: Open UP, 1995, at page 29.) During the last 10 years not only have women been encouraged to give birth in hospital but there has also been a trend towards "managed" pregnancy, induced births and a growth in the number of caesarian sections. Such procedures may be medically necessary, they may facilitate pregnancy and indeed they may enhance a woman's control over her body. There has, however, been criticism of the emphasis placed upon hospital births (see generally P. Foster, *Women and the Health Care Industry*, Buckingham: Open UP, 1995, at page 38 onwards). Caesarian sections are an interventionist procedure. It has been argued that the therapeutic benefit of such Procedures is questionable. Some evidence has suggested that women with caesarean sections are at an increased risk of post-natal depression and they may suffer impaired bonding with their infant. (See further L. Miller, "Two Patients or One: Problems of Consent in Obstetrics" (1993) 1 *Medical Law International* 97.) The growth of Caesarean sections is also seen as an indication of the practice of "defensive medicine" by obstetricians and gynaecologists who wish to minimise risk in what is a very high risk area of clinical practice. Around 98 per cent of births now take place in hospital. A House of Commons Committee on Maternity Services in 1992 came to the conclusion that the policy of encouraging women to give birth in hospitals could not be justified on safety grounds. (*The Winterton Report*, H. Committee 2nd Report H.C. Maternity Services, Vol. 1, 1992, paragraph 25.) This approach was given support by the Report of the Expert Maternity Group *Changing Childbirth* (London: Department of Health, 1993, and see I. Walton, *Midwives and Changing Childbirth*, Hale: BFM, 1995). This report stated that moreover, safety was not the only consideration in determining birth policy. It did emphasise, however, that high risk births should be undertaken in hospitals.

(b) Nurses, Midwives and Health Visitors Act 1979

Attendance by Unqualified Persons at Childbirth, s.17

17.—(1) A person other than a registered midwife or a registered medical practitioner shall not attend a woman in childbirth.
 (3) Subsection(1) does not apply:

(a) where the attention is given in a case of sudden or urgent necessity; or
(b) in the case of a person who, while undergoing training with a view to becoming a medical practitioner or to becoming a midwife, attends a woman in childbirth as part of a course of practical instruction in midwifery recognised by the General Medical Council or one of the National Boards

(4) A person who contravenes subsection (1) . . . shall be liable on summary conviction to a fine of not more than [level 4 on the standard scale].

Notes:

1. The requirement that a midwife be present may itself limit the choice of birth place. If a particular health authority is not in favour of home births then they may not make NHS midwives available. A woman who wanted a home birth would be left with the choice of paying a private midwife or of breaking the law. In 1985 a consultant obstetrician, Wendy Savage, faced a disciplinary hearing after it was alleged that she had let her enthusiasm for natural childbirth override what was suitable for patient care. This case was seen by many as a debate over the rights of the woman in relation to natural childbirth (See W. Savage, *A Savage Enquiry*, London: Virago, 1986.)
2. To "attend" is not defined in the legislation (See J. Finch, "Paternalism in Childbirth" (1982) 132 *New L.J.* 1012).
3. According to Eeeklaar and Dingwall, "At the end of the day parents should not ultimately be free to dictate the terms under which their children are born": J. Eeeklar and R. Dingwall, "Some Legal Issues in Obstetric Practice" [1984] *Journal of Social Welfare Law* 258. Consider this quote in the light of the 1979 Act and of the section on enforced Caesarians, below.

(c) Control over Childbirth — Enforced Caesarians

A woman will routinely agree with her midwife what is known as a "birthing plan". This will include, for example, what pain relief method the woman has chosen to be used during the birth. Difficulties may arise if departure from the birth plan appears to be appropriate. In some situations a woman's opinion as to the conduct of her pregnancy may differ from that of the health professional. Such difficulties may be acute if it is proposed to undertake medical procedures which the health care professional regards as being in the interests of both mother and child but to which the woman expresses a "conscientious objection". An example of such a situation arose in the case of *Re S*.

Re S (Adult: Refusal of Treatment) [1992] 4 All E.R. 671

Sir Stephen Brown P.:
" . . . This is an application by a health authority for a declaration to authorise the surgeons and staff of a hospital to carry out an emergency Caesarian operation upon a patient, who I shall refer to as 'Mrs S'.

Mrs S is 30 years of age. She is in labour with her third pregnancy. She was admitted to a London hospital on October 10, 1992 with ruptured membranes and in spontaneous labour. She has continued in labour since. She is already six days overdue beyond the expected date of birth, which was October 6, 1992, and she has now refused, on religious grounds, to submit herself to a Caesarian section operation. She is supported in this by her husband. They are described as 'born again Christians' and are clearly quite sincere in their beliefs.

I have heard the evidence of P a fellow of the Royal College of Surgeons, who is in charge of this patient at the hospital. He has given, succinctly and graphically, a description of the condition of this patient. Her situation is desperately serious, as is also the situation of the as yet unborn child. The child is in what is described as a position of 'transverse lie'; with the elbow projecting through the cervix and the head being on the right side. There is the gravest risk of a rupture of the uterus if the section is not carried out and the natural labour process is permitted to continue. The evidence of the surgeon is that we are concerned with 'minutes rather than hours' and that it is a 'life and death' situation. He has done his best, as have other surgeons and doctors at the hospital, to persuade the mother that the only means of saving her life, and also I emphasise the life of her unborn child, is to carry out a Caesarian section operation. The surgeon is emphatic. He says it is absolutely the case that the baby cannot be born alive if a Caesarian operation is not carried out. He has described the medical condition. I am not going to go into it in detail because of the pressure of time.

I have been assisted by Mr Munby Q.C., appearing for the Official Solicitor as *amicus curiae*. The Official Solicitor answered the call of the court within minutes and, although this application only came to the notice of the court officials at 1.30 p.m. it has come on for hearing just before 2 p.m. and now at 2.18 p.m. I propose to make the declaration which is sought. I do so in the knowledge that the fundamental question appears to have been left open by Lord Donaldson of Lymington M.R. in *Re T (adult: refusal of medical treatment)* [1992] 4 All E.R. 649, and in the knowledge that there is no English authority which is directly in point. There is, however, some American authority which suggests that if this case were being heard in the American courts the answer would be likely to be in favour of granting a declaration in these circumstances: see *Re A.C.* (1990) 573 A. 2d 1235, 1240, 1246–1248, 1252.

I do not propose to say more at this stage, except that I wholly accept the evidence of P as to the desperate nature of this situation, and that I grant the declaration as sought.

NOTES:

1. This case took the form of an expedited hearing and the judgment was very brief.

2. Sir Stephen Brown emphasised the fact that the operation would save the life of the unborn child. However, English courts have in the past expressly rejected the notion that a foetus has explicit rights. Sir George Thomas in *Paton v. British Pregnancy Advisory Service Trustees* stated that "The foetus cannot, in English law, in my view, have a right on its own at least until it is born and has a separate existence from its mother." (See above Chapter 12 at pages 738–747.)

3. Reference was made to the case of *Re AC* (1990) 573 A. 2d 1235. In the case of *Re AC* a 27-year-old woman was 26 weeks pregnant and was dying of cancer. The woman, her husband and her parents were opposed to a Caesarian section. Her own doctor was also opposed to the surgery being undertaken. However, the court authorised the operation. The child died within a few hours of the operation and the mother also died two days afterwards. The parents' subsequent appeal was granted by the Appeals Court in Washington. (See G. Annas, "She's going to die: the case of Angela C" (1988) *Hastings Center Report* 23.) This case is widely regarded as having stemmed the tide of enforced caesarian sections in the United States.

4. It has also been suggested that it is difficult to equate the decision in *Re S* with the approach taken in the Congenital Disabilities (Civil Liability) Act 1976. The child's ability to bring an action under that statute is derivative upon a duty owed to the parents rather than according the child independent rights as such. (See M.Thompson "After *Re S*" (1994) 2 *Medical Law Review* 127).

5. Although some might regard *Re S* as an exceptional case it may have far reaching applications. Barbara Hewson commented, "Some women in ante-natal classes in England are now told that they have no longer the right to refuse surgical intervention": (B. Hewson "Mother Knows Best" (1992) New L.J. 1538).

6. In *Tameside v Glossop* [1996] 1 F.C.R. 753, the court issued a declaration to the effect that a pregnant woman suffering from schizophrenia, sectioned under the Mental Health Act 1983, could undergo procedures consequent upon birth including a Caesarian section if required as this constituted necessary treatment under section 63 of the 1983 Act (see further Chapter 9 above). See Appendix 3.

QUESTIONS:

1. Was it justifiable to operate on S. in the public interest, despite her opposition? If so: what constitutes "public interest" the interests of the child, of the mother or both? (See K. Stern, "Court Ordered Caesarians — Whose Interests?" (1993) 56 *Modern Law Review* 238.)

2. Does a pregnant woman have any right to control the manner in which the birth is conducted?

3. If you are of the view that a woman has a *moral* obligation to submit to medical treatment in a case in which a caesarian section is required to save the life of the foetus, should this be a legally enforceable obligation? (See Chapter 2 above at pages 103–111.)

4. Is it justifiable to maintain a woman on a life support system after death has been diagnosed with the aim of ensuring that the child in her womb is brought to full term? (See in relation to a situation in which this issue arose in the United States, K. De Gama, "A Brave New World? Rights Discourse and the Politics of Reproductive Autonomy" (1995) *Journal of Law and Society* 114 and D. Lamb, *Death, Brain Death, and Ethics*, Beckenham: Croom Helm, 1985, at pages 99–102.)

5. If a woman can be compelled to have a caesarian section, does that also mean that she could be compelled to receive foetal surgery? (See G. Annas, "Forced Caesarian sections: the unkindest cut of all" (1982) 12 *Hastings Center Report* 16 and *cf. Re F (In utero)* above.)

5. Liability for Injury in Connection with Failed Sterilisation and Childbirth

If a sterilisation operation proves unsuccessful or if the child is damaged during birth, an action may be brought seeking damages. These actions fall into two broad categories, actions brought on behalf of a child patient and those brought by the parents. (Actions concerning defective drugs are considered fully at pages 187–193.)

Before we begin this section we must note the conceptual difficulties that surround analysis of many of those actions. A number of different terms have been used to describe the actions brought. Dickens has explained them as follows.

B. Dickens, *"Wrongful Birth and Life, Wrongful Death Before Birth and Wrongful Law"* in S. McLean (ed.), *Legal Issues in Human Reproduction*, Aldershot: Dartmouth, 1989)

" • *Wrongful pregnancy* is a claim that another's negligence resulted in a plaintiff's unplanned conception of a child, whether or not the pregnancy was carried to term.
 • *Wrongful conception* is a narrower claim that negligent performance of a sterilisation procedure resulted in a conception which the purportedly sterilized plaintiff intended should not occur, but no child was born due to spontanaeous or induced abortion:
 • *Wrongful birth* is a claim that a health care provider violated a legal duty owed to a parent to give information or to perform a medical procedure with due care, resulting in the birth of a defective child.
 • *Wrongful life* is a claim by, or on behalf of, a person born with predictable physical or mental handicaps that, but for the defendants negligence, the person would not have been conceived or, having been conceived, would not have been born alive;
 • *Dissatisfied life* is a claim by, or on behalf of, a person that he or she was born with disadvantages of a non-medical nature due to a defendant's wrong, such as the disadvantage of being illegitimate."

Note:

1. The latter claim has not been yet recognised by the English courts. It should be noted that these terms are not used consistently by commentators. (For general comment on these heads of liability see A. Grubb (ed.), "Conceiving: A New Cause of Action" in M. Freeman, *Medicine, Ethics and Law*, London: Sweet and Maxwell, 1988, and H. Teff, "The Action for Wrongful Life in England" (1985) 34 *ICLQ* 432.)

(a) Actions Brought on Behalf of the Child

(i) Where a child is born dead

It appears that an action brought claiming that the birth of a still born child was due to the defendant's negligence is not sustainable after the passage of the Congenital Disabilities (Civil Liability) Act 1976. This statute requires a child to be born alive (section 4(2)(a)). It was suggested by Dillon L.J. in *B v. Islington AHA* [1992] 3 All E.R. 832, that such an action may have been available at common law.

(ii) Actions under the Congenital Disabilities (Civil Liability) Act 1976

An action brought on behalf of a child claiming damages for negligent conduct resulting in handicap will today lead to proceedings under the Congenital Disabilities (Civil Liability) Act 1976.

In the 1960s a drug called "Thalidomide" was given to pregnant women to treat morning sickness. It was claimed that the effects of the drug led to these women giving birth to handicapped children. Legal actions were brought against the manufacturer. Although settlements were eventually reached with the drug company, Distillers, concern was expressed as to what was seen as inadequate avenues for legal redress. The question of compensation for injuries to a child prior to birth was referred to the Law Commission. Following its Report, the Congenital Disabilities (Civil Liability) Act was passed in 1976.

Congenital Disabilities (Civil Liability) Act 1976, s.1(1–7), s.1A(1–4), s.2, s.3(1–5), s.4(1–6)

1.—(1) If a child is born disabled as the result of such an occurrence before its birth as is mentioned in subsection (2) below, and a person (other than the child's own mother) is under this section answerable to the child in respect of the occurrence, the child's disabilites are to be regarded as damage resulting from the wrongful act of that person and actionable accordingly at the suit of the child.

(2) An occurrence to which this section applies is one which—

(a) affected either parent of the child in his or her ability to have a normal, healthy child; or
(b) affected the mother during her pregnancy, or affected her or the child in the course of its birth, so that the child is born with disabilities which would not otherwise have been present.

(3) Subject to the following subsections, a person (here referred to as 'the defendant') is answerable to the child if he was liable in tort to the parent or would, if sued in due time, have been so; and it is no answer that there could not have been such liability because the parent suffered no actionable injury, if there was a breach of legal duty which, accompanied by injury, would have given rise to the liability.

(4) In the case of an occurrence preceding the time of conception, the defendant is not answerable to the child if at that time either or both of the parents knew the risk of their child being born disabled (that is to say, the particular risk created by

the occurrence); but should it be the child's father who is the defendant, this subsection does not apply if he knew of the risk and the mother did not.

(5) The defendant is not answerable to the child, for anything he did or omitted to do when responsible in a professional capacity for treating or advising the parent, if he took reasonable care having due regard to then received profesional opinion applicable to the particular class of case; but this does not mean that he is answerable only because he departed from received opinion.

(6) Liability to the child under this section may be treated as having been excluded or limited by contract made with the parent affected, to the same extent and subject to the same restrictions as liability in the parent's own case; and a contract term which could have been set up by the defendant in an action by the parent, so as to exclude or limit his liability to him or her, operates in the defendant's favour to the same, but no greater, extent in an action under this section by the child.

(7) If in the child's action under this section it is shown that the parent affected shared the responsibility for the child being born disabled, the damages are to be reduced to such extent as the court thinks just and equitable having regard to the extent of the parent's responsibility.

1A.—(1) In any case where-

(a) a child carried by a woman as the result of the placing in her of an embryo or of sperm and eggs or her artificial insemination is born disabled,

(b) the disability results from an act or omission in the course of the selection, or the keeping or use outside the body, of the embryo carried by her or of the gametes used to bring about the creation of the embryo, and

(c) a person is under this section answerable to the child in respect of the act or omission,

the child's disabilities are to be regarded as damage resulting from the wrongful act of that person and actionable accordingly at the suit of the child.

(2) Subject to subsection (3) below and the applied provisions of section 1 of this Act, a person (here referred to as 'the defendant') is answerable to the child if he was liable in tort to one or both of the parents (here referred to as "the parent or parents concerned") or would, if sued in due time, have been so; and it is no answer that there could not have been such liability because the parent or parents concerned suffered no actionable injury, if there was a breach of legal duty which, accompanied by injury, would have given rise to the liability.

(3) The defendant is not under this section answerable to the child if at the time the embryo, or the sperm and eggs, are placed in the woman or the time of her insemination (as the case may be) either or both of the parents knew the risk of their child being born disabled (that is to say, the particular risk created by the act or omission).

(4) Subsections (5) to (7) of section 1 of this Act apply for the purposes of this section as they apply for the purposes of that but as if references to the parent or the parent affected were references to the parent or parents concerned.

2.—A woman driving a motor vehicle when she knows (or ought reasonably to know) herself to be pregnant is to be regarded as being under the same duty to take care for the safety of her unborn child as the law imposes on her with respect to the safety of other people; and if in consequence of her breach of that duty her child is born with disabilities which would not otherwise have been present those disabilities are to be regarded as damage resulting from her wrongful act and actionable accordingly at the suit of the child.

3.—(1) Section 1 of this Act does not affect the operation of the Nuclear Installations Act 1965 as to liability for, and compensation in respect of, injury or damage caused by occurrences involving nuclear matter or the emission of ionising radiations.

(2) For the avoidance of doubt anything which —

(a) affects a man in his ability to have a normal, healthy child; or
(b) affects a woman in that ability, or so affects her when she is pregnant that her child is born with disabilities which would not otherwise have been present,

is an injury for the purposes of that Act.

(3) If a child is born disabled as the result of an injury to either of its parents caused in breach of a duty imposed by any of sections 7 to 11 of that Act (nuclear site licensees and others to secure that nuclear incidents do not cause injury to persons, etc.), the child's disabilities are to be regarded under the subsequent provisions of that Act (compensation and other matters) as injuries caused on the same occasion, and by the same breach of duty, as was the injury to the parent.

(4) As respects compensation to the child, section 13(6) of that Act (contributory fault of person injured by radiation) is to be applied as if the reference there to fault were to the fault of the parent.

(5) Compensation is not payable in the child's case if the injury to the parent preceded the time of the child's conception and at that time either or both of the parents knew the risk of their child being born disabled (that is to say, the particular risk created by the injury).

4.—(1) References in this Act to a child being born disabled or with disabilities are to its being born with any deformity, disease or abnormality, including predisposition (whether or not susceptible of immediate prognosis) to physical or mental defect in the future.

(2) In this Act —

(a) "born" means born alive (the moment of a child's birth being when it first has a life separate from its mother), and "birth" has a corresponding meaning; and
(b) "motor vehicle" means a mechanically propelled vehicle intended or adapted for use on roads

[and references to embryos shall be construed in accordance with section 1 of the Human Fertilisation and Embryology Act 1990].

(3) Liability to a child under section 1 [1A] or 2 of this Act is to be regarded —

(a) as respects all its incidents and any matters arising or to arise out of it; and
(b) subject to any contrary context or intention, for the purpose of construing references in enactments and documents to personal or bodily injuries and cognate matters,

as liability for personal injuries sustained by the child immediately after its birth.

(4) No damages shall be recoverable under [any] of those sections in respect of any loss of expectation of life, nor shall any such loss be taken into account in the compensation payable in respect of a child under the Nuclear Installations Act 1965 as extended by section 3, unless (in either case) the child lives for at least 48 hours.

(4A) In any case where a child carried by a woman as the result of the placing in her of an embryo or of sperm and eggs or her artificial insemination is born disabled, any reference in section 1 of this Act to a parent includes a reference to a person who would be a parent but for sections 27 to 29 of the Human Fertilisation 'and Embryology Act 1990.]

(5) This Act applies in respect of births after (but not before) its passing,and in respect of any such birth it replaces any law in force before its passing, whereby a person could be liable to a child in respect of disabilities with which it might be born; but in section 1(3) of this Act the expression "liable in tort" does not include

any reference to liability by virtue of this Act, or to liability by virtue of any such law.

(6) References to the Nuclear Installations Act 1965 are to that Act as amended; and for the purposes of section 28 of that Act (power by Order in Council to extend the Act to territories outside the United Kingdom) section 3 of this Act is to be treated as if it were a provision of that Act.

NOTES:

1. The Act allows recovery for pre-conception injuries. An example, given by the Law Commission of the type of injury it was envisaged should lead to recovery was that of a defective contraceptive pill which was not only ineffective but also damaging to the foetus. (See "Report on Injuries to Unborn Children" Law Commission Report No. 60, Cmnd. 5709, 1974.) The statute also applies to injuries *in utero* (section 1(2)(b)) and during childbirth. The statute refers to "parents" and thus it appears that liability is excluded in relation to the second generation.

2. For liability to accrue it must be shown that the defendant is liable in tort to the parents. It is not necessary to show that the parents had suffered an "actionable injury" (section 1(3)).

3. The Act rules out an action being brought against the mother for negligent conduct against the foetus *in utero*, the only exception being a situation in which a child is injured due to the negligent driving of the mother. This exception is due to the fact that it was perceived as unfair to deny compensation to a child where the cost was borne by insurers due to compulsory third party insurance. The Law Commission recommended that claims should not be brought against the child's mother on the grounds that it could harm relationships within families and that it would raise problematic issues regarding conduct during pregnancy. (Law Com. No. 60, Cmnd. 5709.)

4. A claim may only be brought in connection with a child who has been born alive (subsection 4(2)). Objections were voiced by the Law Commission and during the passage of the Bill through parliament, to the idea that a child who had only had a very brief existence could bring a claim for lost expectation of life. This needs to be seen in the context of a wider debate being undertaken at that time as to whether damages for lost expectation of life should be replaced by a claim by relatives for damages for bereavement. (See, *e.g.* Ian Gow M.P., *Hansard*, Vol. 910, cols. 730–740 (1976).). Section 4(4) precludes an action for damages for loss of expectation of life where the child had lived for up to 48 hours after birth.

5. Section 1A, which was inserted by the Human Fertilisation and Embryology Act 1990, gives a right of action to children born disabled where harm had been caused for example, to the embryo in the course of infertility treatment. This would, it appears, cover both

harm caused during storage of gametes and also during embryo selection. There are however, some question marks as to the application of the section where an embryo has been obtained by lavage from one woman and implanted in another. In certain situations when bringing proceedings under section 1A it may be necessary to trace the donor of gametes. Section 31 of the Human Fertilisation and Embryology Act 1990 provides that an application may be made to the court for an order to require disclosure of persons who may be parents of the child.

6. Liability generally does not arise if the parents knew of the risk of harm to the child. But an exception exists in a situation in which the father did have such knowledge but the mother was unaware that her partner had been affected by the defendant's negligence.

7. There is a possibility that an action may be brought under the Act on the basis that the child's parents were given negligent genetic counselling. It has been argued that an action may be successful if the consequence of the genetic advice is that measures could have been taken during pregnancy to prevent harm to that child, by, for example, averting the onset of a disease. However, if the result of the screening was diagnosis of a foetal abnormality with a decision to undergo an abortion an action would not be possible because this would constitute a "wrongful life" action. (See further M. Jones, *Medical Negligence* (2nd ed.), London: Sweet and Maxwell, 1995, at para. 2–045.

8. A potential problem in establishing liability may arise if a child is injured due to delivery procedures, *e.g.* inexpert manipulation of forceps or monitoring equipment. In such a situation Dingwall and Eeklaar suggest that although there is a duty owed to the *child* it may be difficult to establish a duty owed to the *mother*. (See J. Eeklaar and R. Dingwall, "Some Legal Issues in Obstetric Practice" [1984] *Journal of Social Welfare Law* 258.)

9. Where a child has been damaged due, for example, to the administration of a defective drug during pregnancy this may, in addition, give rise to an action under the Consumer Protection Act 1987. However, establishing a claim under this statute may be difficult. The manufacturer may choose to rely upon the "development risk defence" (see discussion in Chapter 3 above at pages 192–193).

10. Damages awarded may be reduced if it can be shown that the parents were contributorily negligent in relation to the harm which was suffered (section 1(7)). This reflects the earlier recommendations of the Law Commission, who stated:

> "Paragraph 65
> Our provisional conclusion as to a mother's liability to her own child led us, almost inevitably, to the opinion that a mother's contributory negligence ought not to effect any reduction in her child's damages. On consultation many have expressed the opinion that such a rule would be grossly unfair to tortfeasors and their insurers in a fault based tort

system, and that the physical fact of identification between mother and foetus during pregnancy ought to mean that the mother's own negligence should reduce the damages payable by a tortfeasor. The medical treatment and medication of a pregnant woman depends so much on the cooperation and care for herself that the possibility of joint liability (perhaps with the mother herself most to blame) is one which cannot be ignored. In such circumstances we think it would be wrong if, perhaps for very slight carelessness in comparison with the mother's own negligence, a doctor, chemist or drug manufacturer had to compensate the child in full for his disability."

Thus, while explicit obligations, as we saw above, are not placed upon the mother to take care of herself during pregnancy it appears that some obligations are implicit.

QUESTIONS:

1. Does the 1976 Act allow actions to be brought by the genetic parents where a child was born under a surrogacy arrangement and the parents have been granted a section 30 order under the Human Fertilisation and Embryology Act 1990? (See D. Morgan and R. Lee, *Human Fertilisation and Embryology Act 1990*, London: Blackstones, 1991, at page 172 and Chapter 11 above at pages 680–682.)

2. Section 4(2)(a) provides that an action accrues when a child has a life separate from that of its mother. When does this point arise? (See C. Pace, "Civil Liability for Pre-natal Injuries" (1977) 40 *Modern Law Review* 141.)

3. If a woman refuses a caesarian section despite medical advice and during a prolonged labour the child suffers brain damage then can an action be brought under the 1976 Act? (Consider J. Eeklaar and R. Dingwall, "Some Legal Issues in Obstetric Practice" [1984] *Journal of Social Welfare Law* 258.)

4. Is there a distinction between "disability" and "injury" thus allowing actions for the latter at common law while rejecting the former? (See J. Murphy, "The tortious liability of physicians for injuries sustained in childbirth" (1995) 10(2) *Professional Negligence* 82.)

The position at common law was considered in the case of *B. v. Islington AHA*, a case in which the action accrued prior to the 1976 Act coming into force. We noted earlier (see Chapter 12 at pages 738–747) that a foetus is not a legal person. In *B* the court held that an action could be brought at common law claiming damages for injury which occurred *in utero*. In addition it appears that such an action would have been sustainable for a pre-conception injury for example, where a woman's pelvis is harmed and this causes injury when a child is subsequently conceived and develops in the uterus. (See A. Whitfield, "Common Law Duties to Unborn Children" (1993) 1 *Medical Law Review* 28.) The harm was foreseeable and the cause of action arose at birth. As we shall see below, the courts have expressed the view that no residual common law action applies to claims arising after the 1976 Act.

(iii) Wrongful life

A child who is born handicapped due to negligence may seek to bring an action claiming that but for the defendant's negligence she would have never been born — a so called "wrongful life" action. It appears that today such an action would be unsuccessful.

McKay v. Essex Area Health Authority [1982] 2 All E.R. 771; [1982] Q.B. 1160

Mary McKay was born in 1975. She had been infected in the womb with rubella (german measles). As a result she was born partially blind and deaf. The allegation was made that one doctor had acted negligently in failing to treat rubella infection on being told it was suspected by the mother. It was claimed that another doctor had *either* negligently mislaid a blood sample which the mother had given or had failed to interpret test results correctly. Mary McKay claimed that the doctor owed her a duty of care when she was *in utero*, which involved advising her mother as to the desirability of having an abortion, advice which the mother said she would have accepted.

STEPHENSON L.J.:
" . . . I have come, at the end of two day's argument, to the same answer as I felt inclined to give the question before I heard argument, namely that plainly and obviously the claims disclose no reasonable cause of action. The general importance of that decision is much restricted by the Congenital Disabilities (Civil Liability) Act 1976, and in particular s.4(5) to which counsel for the doctor called our attention. That enactment has the effect explained by Ackner L.J. of depriving any child born after its passing on 22 July, 1976 of this cause of action. Section 1(2)(b) repeats the same clause of the draft bill annexed as an appendix to the Law Commission's *Report on Injuries to Unborn Children* (Law Com. no. 60, August 1974: Cmnd. 5709), and was intended to give the child no right of action for 'wrongful life' and to import the assumption that, but for the occurrence giving rise to a disabled birth, the child would have been born normal and healthy (not that it would not have been born at all) (see pp. 46–47 of the report). I reject counsel for the plaintiff's submission that it did not carry out that intention, which, in my judgement, the language of the paragraph plainly expresses. But the Act went further than the draft Bill in replacing, by s.4(5), 'any law in force before its passing, whereby a person could be liable to a child in respect of disabilities with which it might be born'.
    The importance of this cause of action to this child is somewhat reduced by the existence of her other claim and the mother's claims, which, if successful, will give her some compensation in money or in care.
    However, this is the first occasion on which the courts of this country or the Commonwealth have had to consider this cause of action, and I shall give my reasons for holding that it should be struck out.
    If, as is conceded, any duty is owed to an unborn child, the authority's hospital laboratory and the doctor looking after the mother during her pregnancy undoubtedly owed the child a duty not to injure it, if she had been injured as a result of lack

of reasonable care and skill on their part after birth, she could have sued them (as she is suing the doctor) for damages to compensate her for injury they have caused her in the womb. (*cf.* the thalidomide cases, where it was assumed that such an action might lie: *e.g. Distillers Co. (Biochemical) Ltd v. Thompson* [1971] 1 All E.R. 694.) But this child has not been injured by either defendant, but by the rubella which has infected the mother without fault on anybody's part. Her right not to be injured before birth by the carelessness of others has not been infringed by either defendant, any more than it would have been if she had been disabled by disease after birth. Neither defendant has broken any duty to take reasonable care not to injure her. The only right on which she can rely as having been infringed is a right not to be born deformed or disabled, which means, for a child deformed or disabled before birth by nature or disease, a right to be aborted or killed; or, if that last plain word is thought dangerously emotive, deprived of the opportunity to live after being delivered from the body of her mother. The only duty which either defendant can owe to the unborn child infected with disabling rubella is a duty to abort or kill her of that opportunity.

It is said that the duty does not go as far as that, but only as far as a duty to give the mother an opportunity to choose her abortion and death. That is true as far it goes. The doctor's alleged negligence in misleading the mother as to the advisability of an abortion, failing to inform or advise her of its advisability or desirability; the laboratory's alleged negligence is not so pleaded in terms but the negligence pleaded against them in failing to make or interpret the tests of the mother's blood samples or to inform the doctor of their results must, like the doctor's negligence, be a breach of their duty to give the doctor an opportunity to advise the mother of the risks in continuing to let the foetus live in the womb and be born alive. But the complaint of the child, as of the mother, against the health authority, as against the doctor, is that their negligence burdened her (and her mother) with her injuries. That is another way of saying that the defendants' breaches of their duties resulted not just in the child's being born but in her being born injured or, as the judge put it, with deformities. But, as the injuries or deformities were not the result of any act or omission of the defendants, the only result for which they were responsible was for her being born. For that they were responsible because if they had exercised due care the mother would have known that the child might be born injured or deformed, and the plaintiffs' pleaded case is that, if the mother had known that, that she would have been willing to undergo an abortion, which must mean she would have undergone one or she could not claim that the defendants were responsible for burdening her with an injured child. If she would not have undergone an abortion had she known the risk of the child being born injured, any negligence on the defendants' part could not give either plaintiff a cause of action in respect of the child being born injured.

I am accordingly of opinion that, though the judge was right in saying that the child's complaint is that she was born with deformities without which she would have suffered no damage and have no complaint, her claim against the defendants is a claim that they were negligent in allowing her, injured as she was in the womb, to be born at all, a claim for 'wrongful entry into life' or 'wrongful life'.

This analysis leads inexorably on to the question: how can there be a duty to take away life? How indeed can it be lawful? It is still the law that it is unlawful to take away the life of a born child or of any living person after birth. But the Abortion Act 1967 has given mothers a right to terminate the lives of their unborn children and made it lawful for doctors to help to abort them.

That statute (on which counsel for the plaintiffs relies) permits abortion in specified cases of risks to the mothers interests, but there is one provision relevant to the interests of the child. Section 1(1) provides:

'Subject to the provisions of this section, a person shall not be guilty of an offence under the law relating to abortion when a pregnancy is terminated by a registered medical practitioner if two registered medical practitioners are of the opinion, formed in good faith . . . (b) that there is a substantial risk that if the child were born it would suffer from such physical or mental abnormalities as to be seriously handicapped.'

That paragraph may have been passed in the interests of the mother, the family and the general public, but I would prefer to believe that its main purpose, if not its sole purpose, was to benefit the unborn child; and, if and in so far as that was the intention of the legislature, the legislature did not make a notable inroad on the sanctity of human life by recognising that it would be better for a child, born to suffer from such abnormalities as to be seriously handicapped, not to have been born at all. That inroad, however, seems to stop short of a child capable of being born alive, because the sanctity of human life by recognising that it would be better for a child, born to suffer from such abnormalities as to be seriously handicapped, not to have been born at all. That inroad, however, seems to stop short of a child capable of being born alive, because the sanctity of the life of a viable fetus is preserved by the enactment of s.5(1) that 'Nothing in this Act shall affect the provisions of the Infant Life (Preservation) Act 1929 (protecting the life of the viable foetus).'

Another notable feature of the 1967 Act is that it does not directly impose any duty on a medical practitioner or anyone else to terminate a pregnancy, though it relieves conscientious objectors of a duty to participate in any treatment authorised by the Act in all cases with one exception: see s.4 of the Act. It is, however, conceded in this case that a medical practitioner is under a duty to the mother to advise her of her right under the Act to have her pregnancy terminated in cases such as the present. There was, on the pleaded facts of this case, a substantial risk that if the child were born it would suffer from such physical or mental abnormalities as to be seriously handicapped. And, from what we have been told without objection of her present mental and physical condition, that risk has become tragically actual.

There is no doubt that this child could legally have been deprived of life by the mother's undergoing an abortion with the doctor's advice and help so the law recognises a difference between the life of a fetus and the life of those who have been born. But, because a doctor can lawfully by statute do to a fetus what he cannot lawfully do to a person who has been born, it does not follow that he is under a legal obligation to a fetus to do it and terminate its life, or that the foetus has a legal right to die.

Like this court when it had to consider the interests of a child born with Down's syndrome in *Re B (A Minor) (Wardship Medical Treatment* [1981] 1 WLR 1421, I would not answer until it is necessary to do so the question whether the life of a child could be so certainly 'awful' and 'intolerable' that it would be in its best interests to end it and it might be considered that it had a right to be out to death. But that is not this case. We have no exact information about the extent of this child's serious and highly delibitating congenital injuries; the judge was told that she is partly blind and deaf, but it is not and could not be suggested that the quality of her life is such that she is certainly better dead, or would herself wish that she had not been born or should now die.

I am therefore compelled to hold that neither defendant was under any duty to the child to give the child's mother an opportunity to terminate the child's life. That duty may be owed to the mother, but it cannot be owed to the child.

To impose such a duty towards the child would, in my opinion, make a further inroad on the sanctity of human life of a handicapped child as not only less valuable than the life of a normal child, but so much less valuable that it was not worth preserving, and it would even that a doctor would be obliged to pay damages to a child infected with rubella before birth who was in fact born with some mercifully trivial abnormality. These are the consequences of the necessary basic assumption that a child has a right to be born whole or not at all, not to be born unless it can be born perfect or 'normal', whatever that may mean.

Added to that objection must be the opening of the courts to claims by children born handicapped against their mothers for not having an abortion. For the reasons given by the Royal Commission on Civil Liability and Compensation for Personal Injury (report, vol. I; Cmnd 7054-1), cited by Ackner L.J., that is, to my mind, a graver objection than the extra burden on doctors already open to actions for negligent treatment of a fetus, which weighed with the Law Commission.

Finally, there is the nature of the injury and damage which the court is being asked to ascertain and evaluate.

The only duty of care which court of law can recognise and enforce are duties owned to those who can be compensated for loss by those who owe the duties, in most cases, including cases of personal injury, by money damages which will as far as possible put the injured party on the condition in which he or she was before being injured. The only way in which a child injured in the womb can be compensated in damages is by measuring what it has lost, which is the difference between the value of its life as whole and healthy normal child and the value of its life as an injured child. But to make those who have not injured the child pay for that difference is to treat them as if they injured the child, when all they have done is not taken steps to prevent its being born injured by another cause.

The only loss for which those who have not injured the child can be held liable to compensate the child is the difference between its condition as a result of their allowing it to be born alive and injured and its condition if its embryonic life had ended before its life in the world had begun. But how can a court of law evaluate that second condition and so measure the loss to the child? Even if a court were competent to decide between the conflicting views of theologians and philosophers and to assume an 'afterlife' or non-existence as the basis for the comparison, how can a judge put a value on the one or the other, compare either alternative with the injured child's life in this world and determine that the child has lost anything, without the means of knowing what, if anything, it has gained?

Judges have to pluck figures from the air in putting many imponderables into pounds and pence. Loss of expectation of life, for instance, has been difficult that the courts have been driven to fix for it a constant and arbitrary figure. Counsel for the plaintiffs referred us to what judges have said on that topic in *Rose v. Ford* [1937] 3 All E.R. 359 and *Benham v. Gambling* [1941] 1 All E.R. 7. But in measuring the loss caused by shortened life, courts are dealing with a thing, human life, of which they have some experience; hence the court is being asked to deal with consequences of death for the dead, a thing of which it has none. And the statements of judges on the necessity for juries to assess damages and their ability to do so in cases of extreme difficulty do not touch the problem presented by the assessment of the claims we are considering. To measure loss of expectation of death would require a value judgment where a crucial factor lies altogether outside the range of human knowledge and could only be achieved, if at all, by resorting to the personal beliefs of the judge who has the misfortune to attempt the task. If difficulty in assessing damages is a bad reason for refusing the task, impossibility of assessing them is a good one. A court must have a starting point for giving damages for a breach of duty. The only means of giving a starting point to a court asked to hold that there is the duty on a doctor or a hospital which this child alleges is to require the court to measure injured life against uninjured life, and that is to treat the doctor and the hospital as responsible not for the child's birth but for its injuries. That is what in effect counsel for the plaintiffs suggests that the court should do, tempering the injustice to the defendants by some unspecified discount.
· This seems almost as desperate an expedient as an American judge's suggestion that the measure of damages should be the 'diminished childhood' resulting from the substantial diminution of the parent's capacity to give the child special care: see the dissenting judgment of Handler J. in *Berman v. Allan* (1979) 404 A. 2d 8 at 15, 19, 21. If there is no measure of damage which is not unjustified and indeed unjust, courts of law cannot entertain claims by a child affected with prenatal damage against those who fail to provide its mother with the opportunity to end its damaged life, however careless and unskilful they may have been and however liable they may be to the mother for the negligent failure.

If a court had to decide whether it were better to enter into life maimed or halt than not to enter it at all, it would, I think, be bound to say it was better in all cases of mental and physical disability, except possibly those extreme cases already mentioned, of which perhaps the recent case of *Croke v. Wiseman* [1981] 3 All E.R. 852 is an example, but certainly not excepting such a case as the present. However that may be, it is not for the courts to take such a decision by weighing life against death or to take cognisance of a claim like this child's. I would regard it on principle as disclosing no reasonable cause of action and would accordingly prefer the master's decision to the judge's.

I am happy to find support for this view of the matter in the Law Commission's Report and the Congenital Disabilities (Civil Liability) Act 1976, to which I have already referred, and in the strong current of American authority, to which we have been referred. Direct decisions of courts in the United States of America on the same topic are of no more than persuasive authority but contain valuable material and with one exception would rule out the infant plaintiff's claims in our case.

The first of the American cases is a decision of the Supreme Court by New Jersey in 1967: *Gleitman v. Cosgrave* 227 A. 2d 689. It was preceded by an article by G. Tedeschi, 'On Tort Liability for Wrongful Life' [1966] Israel L.R. 513. That article treated of earlier cases mainly concerned with illegitimate children and of the acts of parents in producing a child likely to be diseased, but concentrated on the impossibility of comparing the two alternatives of non-existence and existence with the disease. *Gleitman's* case has been followed in New Jersey and in other jurisdictions of the United States of America, all but one finally approving the decision on this point that the child has no claim for wrongful life against medical advisers for incompetent advice about the risks of being born severely disabled.

The facts in *Gleitman's* case are very like the facts of this case. The infant plaintiff was born handicapped as a result of the mother's 'German measles' during pregnancy. Dr Cosgrove and another doctor, who was also a defendant, had advised the mother (though they denied it) that the disease would have no effect on her unborn child. The doctor agreed that, if the mother had told him of the disease, his duty as a physician required him to inform her of the possibility of birth defects. The boy sued the doctors for his birth defects, the mother on the effects on her emotional state caused by her son's condition, the father for the costs incurred in caring for him the trial judge dismissed the boy's complaint at the close of the plaintiff's case and the parents' complaint after all the evidence was heard. The Supreme Court, by a majority, affirmed the judge's decision. Proctor J., delivering the judgment of the court, held that the boy's complaint was not actionable because the conduct complained of, even if true, did not give rise to damages cognisable at law (see 227 A. 2d 689 at 692). Both Proctor J. and Weintraub C.J., assenting on this point, stated that the boy's complaint involved saying that he would have been better off not to have been born at all. 'Man, who knows nothing or death or nothingness, cannot possibly know whether that is so.' (See 227 A 2d 689 at 711.)
. . .

Judicial opinion expressed in the American decisions can, I think, be summarised in the following propositions: (1) though which gives rise to the cause of action is not just life with defects, the real cause of action is negligence in causing life; (2) negligent advice or failure to advise is the proximate cause of the child's life (though not of its defects); (3) a child has no right to be born as a whole, functional being (without defects); (4) it is contrary to public policy, which is to preserve human life, to give a child a right not to be born except as a whole, functional being, and to impose on another a corresponding duty to prevent a child being born except without defects, that is, a duty to cause the death of an unborn child with defects; (5) it is impossible to measure the damages for being born with defects because it is impossible to compare the life of a child born with defects and non-existence as a human being; (6) accordingly, by being born with defects a child has suffered no injury cognisable by law and if it is to have a claim for being so born the law must be reformed by legislation.

The current opinion has run in favour of the fourth consideration and against the fifth consideration even to the point of dismissing it altogether. Authority for that, and for the consideration which I have formulated, is to be found in particular in the judgment of the Supreme Court of New Jersey given by Pashman J. in *Beman v. Allan* (1979) 404 A 2d 8, at 11–13, in the judgments of Presiding Judge Cercone and Judge Spaeth in *Speck v. Finegold* (1979) 408 A 2d 496 at 508, 512 and in the judgment of Judge Blatt in *Phillips v. USA* (1980) 508 F Supp 537 at 543 which I have already mentioned.

There are indications, to which counsel for the plaintiffs called to our attention that some of the judges's opinions on the sanctity of human life were influenced by the illegality of abortion in some states; but those indications do not in my opinion play a decisive part in their decisions or weaken their persuasive force in considering the right answer to the same question in a jurisdiction where abortion has some statutory sanction.

I do not think it matters whether the injury is not an injury recognised by the law or the damages are not damages that the law can award. Whichever way it is put, the objection means that the cause of action is not cognisable or justiciable or 'reasonable' and I can draw no distinction between the first two terms and the third as it is rather artificially used in RSC. Ord. 18 r. 19.

The defendants must be assumed to have been careless. The child suffers from serious disabilities. If the defendant had not been careless, the child would not be suffering now because it would not be alive. Why should the defendants not pay the child for its suffering? The answer lies in the implications and the consequences of holding that they should. If public policy favoured the introduction of this novel cause of action, I would not let the strict application of logic or the absence of precedent defeat it. But as it would be, in my judgment, against public policy for the courts to entertain claims like those which are the subject of this appeal, I would for this reason and for other reasons which I have given, allow the appeal, set aside the judge's order and restore the master's order."

NOTES:

1. Ackner and Griffiths L.J. agreed. It is questionable whether a wrongful life action should be rejected on the basis that the damages are difficult to evaluate. Difficulty of assessment has not stopped the award of damages elsewhere in the law of tort. (See, for example, *Lim Po Chew v. Camden Area Health Authority* [1989] A.C. 176.) It is worthy of note that when the action in *McKay* was brought, establishment of a wrongful birth action would have been more difficult than it subsequently became.

2. One argument advanced in *McKay* for the rejection of the claim was that it was wrong for a child plaintiff to be able to bring a tortious action against her mother. Such a policy is reflected in the Congenital Disabilities (Civil Liability) Act 1976 where generally a child cannot sue her mother (see page 789 above). However it has been suggested that this consideration should not debar actions for "wrongful life": "whatever reasons for the mother's wish to bear a handicapped child, it seems improbable in the extreme that her failure to prevent birth will result from negligence." (See R. Lee, "To be or Not to Be: Is that the Question? The Claim of Wrongful Life" in R. Lee and D. Morgan (eds.), *Birthrights: Law and Ethics at Beginning of Life*, London: Routledge, 1989).

3. Fortin suggests that section 4(5) of the 1976 Act does not preclude a wrongful life action if the basis for the claim is that the health professional was negligent in failing to advise the woman of the quality of life which the child was likely to have in the light of the disabilities (J. Fortin, "Is the wrongful life action really dead?" (1987) *Journal of Social Welfare Law* 306).
4. *McKay* also illustrates the problems with selective use of overseas judicial authority. While the Court of Appeal stressed the absence of authority supportive of the wrongful birth action in other jurisdictions and emphasised the decision in *Gleitman*, the decision in that case had been overruled by *Berman v. Allan* 80 N.J. 421 404 A 2d 8 (1979). Indeed, New Jersey subsequently developed the wrongful life action. (See R. Lee, "To Be or Not to Be: Is that the Question; The Claim of Wrongful Life" in R. Lee and D. Morgan (eds.), *op. cit.*)
5. The Law Commission had as a basis for the rejection of wrongful life the fact that it could motivate doctors to advise an abortion. This was questioned by Griffiths L.J. in *McKay* on the basis that no liability would arise as long as the doctor explains the risk in the continuation of pregnancy.

QUESTIONS:

1. In the light of the *Bland* case is it correct to say that today life is worth preserving at all costs?
2. Is it possible to reject a wrongful life action but at the same time accept a "wrongful" birth action? (See discussion below at pages 805–811.)

(b) Actions Brought by Parents

Claims in Contract

Sterilisation operations are frequently undertaken privately. If the operation proves unsuccessful this may lead to an action for breach of contract. It may be claimed that the defendant was in breach of an express warranty that the plaintiff would be rendered permanently sterile. Alternatively it may be alleged that he gave an implied warranty to that effect. The existence of an implied warranty is assessed by the courts applying the test laid down in the *The Moorcock* [1886-90] All E.R. Rep 530. This test is to the effect that even if no words were expressly spoken by the parties a term could be implied if it could be said that if someone had asked the contracting parties what would happen in a certain case they would confidently reply — "of course so and so will happen we did not trouble to say that because it is obvious". Finally, an action may be brought claiming negligent misrepresentation.

Eyre v. Measday [1986] 1 All E.R. 488

The plaintiff was a 35-year-old woman who had three children. She had been taking the contraceptive pill for some years but was then advised that continued use was potentially harmful. She and her husband did not want any more children. The plaintiff saw her doctor and he put her and her husband in contact with Mr Measday, a well-known gynaecologist. The sterilisation operation was carried out privately under a budget scheme which meant it was a low-cost private operation. However, in April 1979, she discovered to her amazement that she was pregnant and in October 1979 she gave birth to a healthy boy. The plaintiff decided to let the pregnancy run full term. She decided not to go back to work until her child was about 10 years old. She brought an action claiming negligence and breach of contract. By the time the case reached the Court of Appeal the negligence claim had been abandoned.

SLADE L.J.:

" . . . It is, I think, common ground that the relevant contract between the parties in the present case was embodied as to part in the oral conversations which took place between the plaintiff and her husband and the defendant at the defendant's consulting rooms, and as to the other part in the written form of consent signed by the plaintiff, which referred to the explanation of the operation which had been given in that conversation. It is also common ground, I think, that, in order to ascertain what was the nature and what were the terms of that contract, this court has to apply an objective rather than a subjective test. The test thus does not depend on what either the plaintiff or the defendant *thought* were the terms of the contract in her or his own mind. It depends on what the court objectively considers that the words used by the respective parties must be reasonably taken to have meant. It would, therefore, be of no assistance to the defendant to say that he did not intend to enter into a contract which absolutely guaranteed the plaintiff 's future sterility. It would likewise be of no assistance to the plaintiff to say that she firmly believed that she was being offered a contract of this nature.

I now turn to the first of the two principal issues which I have indicated. At the start of his argument for the plaintiff counsel indicated that his primary ground of appeal would be that the effect of the contract between the plaintiff and the defendant was one by which the defendant contracted to render the plaintiff absolutely sterile. Nevertheless, on the facts of this case, I, for my part, find this contention quite impossible to sustain. It seems to me quite clear from the evidence which we have as to the conversation which took place between the plaintiff and her husband and the defendant at the defendant's consulting rooms that he explained to them that the operation which he would propose to perform on the plaintiff was an operation by way of *laparoscopic sterilisation* and that was the method he intended to adopt and no other. Equally, that was the nature of the operation to which the plaintiff herself agreed, as is shown by the form of consent which she signed. The contract was, to my mind, plainly a contract by the defendant to perform that particular operation.

The matter may be tested in this way. Suppose that when the plaintiff had been under anaesthetic the defendant had formed the view that an even more effective way of sterilising her would be to perform a hysterectomy and had carried out that operation, the plaintiff would, of course, have had the strongest grounds for complaint. She could have said:

'I did not give you a general discretion to perform such operation as you saw fit for the purpose of sterilizing me. I gave my consent to one particular form of operation. That was the operation I asked you to do and that was the operation you agreed to do.'

In the end, as I understood him, counsel for the plaintiff did not feel able to press his argument on the first issue very strongly. The nature of the contract was, in my view, indubitably one to perform a laparoscopic sterilisation.

That, however, is by no means the end of the matter. The question still arises: did the defendant give either an express warranty or an implied warranty to the effect that the result of the operation when performed would be to leave the plaintiff absolutely sterile? In response to our inquiry counsel for the plaintiff helpfully listed the two particular passages in the evidence on which he relied for the purpose of asserting that there was an express warranty. The first was a passage where, in the course of examination by her counsel, the plaintiff said:

'We went to the consulting rooms and we saw Mr Measday and we discussed sterilisation. He told us the method that he used for sterilising was the clip. He told us once I had had it done it was irreversible.'

Counsel for the plaintiff also relied on a passage in which the plaintiff was asked in chief:

'Q. Did he show you a clip?

A. He showed us a clip and he also showed us the diagram and told us where the the clips would go on the tubes. He said once I had the operation done there was no turning back, I could not have it reversed.'

Counsel for the plaintiff referred us to paragraph 2 of the defence in the action which read as follows:

'On the October 30, 1978 the Plaintiff consulted the Defendant about an operation of sterilisation. The Defendant examined her and agreed to carry out the operation and advised her that it must be regarded as a permanent procedure. He did not warn the Plaintiff of the slight risk of failure, nor did he guarantee success.'

There was thus a specific admission in the defence that the defendant advised the plaintiff that it must be 'regarded as a permanent procedure'.

In the light of these various representations or statements by the defendant, counsel for the plaintiff submitted that it was being expressly represented to the plaintiff that the effect of the operation would be to render her sterile absolutely and for ever. I, for my part, cannot accept that submission. There has been some discussion in the course of argument on the meaning of the phrase 'irreversible' and as to the relevance of the statement, undoubtedly made by the defendant to the plaintiff, that the proposed operation must be regarded as being irreversible. However, I take the reference to irreversibility as simply meaning that the operative procedure in question is incapable of being reversed, that what is about to be done cannot be undone. I do not think it can reasonably be construed as a representation that the operation is bound to achieve its acknowledged object, which is a different matter altogether. For my part, I cannot spell out any such express warranty as is asserted from the particular passages in the evidence and in the pleadings relied on by counsel for the plaintiff to support it, or from any other parts of the evidence.

In the alternative, however, counsel for the plaintiff relies on an implied warranty . . .

The test to be applied by the court in considering whether a term can or cannot properly be implied in a contract is that embodied in what is frequently called the doctrine of *The Moorcock* [1886–90] All E.R. Rep 530. It is conveniently set out in 9 Halsbury's Laws (4th edn) para. 355:

'A term can only be implied if it is necessary in the business sense to give efficacy to the contract that is if it is such a term that it can confidently be said that if at the time the contract was being negotiated someone had said to the parties, "What will happen in such a case", they would both have replied, "Of course, so and so will happen we did not trouble to say that it is too clear." '

Counsel for the plaintiff, in the light of the passage in cross-examination which I have just read and in the light of all the other background of the case to which I have referred, submitted that if someone had said to the parties, 'Is it intended that the defendant should warrant that the operation will render the plaintiff absolutely sterile?', the answer of both parties must have been, 'Yes.' This, he submitted, is really the only possible inference from what had been said on both sides in the defendant's consulting rooms. He particularly drew attention to the question that he had put to the defendant, 'Would it have been reasonable for her to have gone away from your consulting rooms thinking that she would be sterilised and that would be the end of the matter?', To which the defendant had replied, 'Yes, it would.' Counsel for the plaintiff submitted that the defendant himself was thus acknowledging that the reasonable inference would have been as he suggested.

Applying *The Moorcock* principles, I think there is no doubt that the plaintiff would have been entitled reasonably to assume that the defendant was warranting that the operation would be performed with reasonable care and skill. That, I think, would have been the inevitable inference to be drawn, from an objective stand-point, from the relevant discussion between the parties. The contract did, in my opinion, include an implied warranty of that nature. However, that inference on its own does not enable the plaintiff to succeed in the present case. She has to go further. She has to suggest, and it is suggested on her behalf, that the defendant, by necessary implication, committed himself to an unqualified guarantee as to the success of the particular operation proposed, in achieving its purpose of sterilising her, even though he were to exercise all due care and skill in performing it. The suggestion is that the guarantee went beyond due care and skill and extended to an unqualified warranty that the plaintiff would be absolutely sterile.

On the facts of the present case, I do not think that any intelligent lay bystander (let alone another medical man), on hearing the discussion which took place between the defendant and the other two parties, could have reasonably drawn the inference that the defendant was intending to give any warranty of this nature. It is true that in cross-examination he admitted that it would have been reasonable for the plaintiff to have gone away from his consulting rooms thinking that she would be sterilised. He did not, however, admit that it would have been reasonable for her to have left his consulting rooms thinking that he had given her a *guarantee* that after the operation she would be absolutely sterile this, I think, is the really relevant point. She has to say that this would have been the reasonable inference from what he said to her and from what she and her husband said to him. But, in my opinion, in the absence of any express warranty, the court should be slow to imply against a medical man an unqualified warranty as to the results of an intended operation, for the very simple reason that, objectively speaking, it is most unlikely that a responsible medical man would intend to give a warranty of this nature. Of course, objectively speaking, it is likely that he would give a guarantee that he would do what he had undertaken to do with reasonable care and skill but it is quite another matter to say that he has committed himself to the extent suggested in the present case."

NOTE:

1. Purchase L.J. and Cummings Bruce L.J. agreed with Slade L.J.

Thake v. Maurice [1986] 1 All E.R. 497; [1986] Q.B. 644

Mr and Mrs Thake had a family of four children. Mrs Thake became pregnant aagain. The family were short of money and did not want more children. Mr Thake therefore underwent a vasectomy — performed by the defendant. The defendant made it clear that they must regard the decision as final. Although there was an operation which would restore fertility, the defendant did not guarantee that it would succeed. The defendant held both arms horizontally with clenched fists together, he pulled his arms apart to indicate the gap that is formed when the piece of the vas deferens is removed. He bent his wrists backwards to show how the ends of the vas are tied back to face in the opposite direction. The defendant alleged that his usual warning about the possibility of an operation being reversed had been given, but the judge rejected this. The operation appeared to be a success. The couple resumed sexual intercourse. However, in 1978, three years later, Mrs Thake began to miss her periods. Initially she thought it could be the early onset of the menopause. Subsequently she saw her doctor and discovered that she was four months pregnant. Her husband was tested. It was discovered that he had become fertile again. The Thakes brought an action against the defendants both in contract and in negligence.

KERR L.J. (DISSENTING):
" . . . The judge reached the conclusion that in the unusual circumstances of this case the plaintiffs had established that the revival of Mr Thake's fertility gave rise to the breach of the contract concluded between the defendant and the plaintiffs. He expressed this in the following terms ([1984] 2 All E.R. 512 at 519–520):
'I have hesitated before arriving at this conclusion. It is a decision which surgeons will regard with alarm. I accept that they would not deliberately guarantee any result which depended on the healing of human tissue; but there is no reason in law why a surgeon should not contract to produce such a result. I have to ascertain what the terms of the contract were on the unusual facts of this case. I have been driven by the logic if the argument which counsel presented for the plaintiffs to the conclusion that the contract was to make the male plaintiff irreversibly sterile.'
I have certainly shared the judge's hesitation on this difficult aspect. In the ultimate analysis, however, I have reached the same conclusion, though not in quite the same way as the judge. I have reached it on the basis of the cogency of the evidence alone, all of which the judge accepted. I do not found myself on the construction of the consent form, whether contra proferentum or otherwise, to which the judge referred immediately before the passage quoted, nor merely on the logic of the argument presented on behalf of the plaintiffs. I also respectfully differ from the judge in his conclusion in the next following passage of his judgment that the defendant had given a collateral warranty to the effect that Mr Thake would be rendered permanently sterile by the operation. This aspect was not permanently abandoned, but not pursued, on this appeal, as well as a claim for misrepresentation under the Misrepresentation Act 1967. I cannot see that there was anything collateral to the terms of the contract itself. The problem is to determine what these terms were, on a correct assessment of the whole of the evidence.

He then referred to the judgment of Slade L.J. in *Eyre v. Measday* and went on to say . . .

On this appeal it was common ground that the court's task was to determine objectively the terms of the contract whereby the defendant offered and agreed to operate on the male plaintiff. What would a reasonable person in the position of Mr and Mrs Thake have concluded in that regard? Was it merely that the defendant would perform a vasectomy operation subject to the duty implied by law that he would do so with reasonable skill and care? Or was it that the defendant would perform this operation so as to render Mr Thake permanently sterile? Counsel for the defendant submitted that, even if the latter was the correct objective construction of the terms of the offer made by the defendant, it was nevertheless not so understood by Mr and Mrs Thake. He said that this was merely what they believed would be the result of the operation, not what they believed the defendant had undertaken to do, and he relied on the decision of this court in *Allied Marine Transport Ltd v. Vale do Rio Doce Narvegacao SA The Leonardis D* [1985] 2 All E.R. 796 at 804–805. But in my view no such further question arised here, since it is plain on the evidence that Mr and Mrs Thake intended that Mr Thake should be rendered permanently sterile and believed that this is what the defendant had agreed to do. No. submission on these lines was made below, and it would clearly have been rejected by the judge. The only issue is as to the objective interpretation of the offer made by the defendant once he had agreed to perform the operation.

On this issue I have reached the same conclusion as the judge. Having regard to everything that passed between the defendant and the plaintiffs at the meeting, coupled with the absence of any warning that Mr Thake might somehow again become fertile after two successful sperm tests, it seems to me that the plaintiffs could not reasonably have conclude anything other than that his agreement to perform the operation meant that, subject to successful sperm tests, he had undertaken to render Mr Thake permanently sterile. In my view this follows from an objective analysis of the undisputed evidence of what passed between the parties, and it was also what the plaintiffs understood and intended to be the effect of the contract with the defendant.

The consideration which led to this conclusion can be summarised as follows. First, we are here dealing with something in the nature of an amputation, not treatment of an injury or disease with inevitable uncertain results. The nature of the operation was the removal of parts of the channels through which sperm has to pass to the outside in such a way that the channels could not reunite. This was vividly demonstrated to the plaintiffs by the defendant pulling apart his arms and fists and turning back his wrists, as well as by a sketch. The defendant repeatedly and carefully explained that the effect of the operation was final, as the plaintiffs said again and again in this evidence, subject only to a remote possibility of surgical reversal, and that was the only warning which the defendant impressed on them. Subject to this and the two sperm tests of which the plaintiffs were told, designed to make sure that the operation had in fact been successful, I cannot see that one can place any interpretation on what the defendant said and did other than that he undertook to render Mr Thake permanently sterile by means of the operation. Nor can I see anything in the transcripts of the evidence which leads to any other conclusion, and the defendant himself agreed that in the context of the discussion as a whole, the word 'irreversible' would have been understood by the plaintiffs as meaning 'irreversible by God or man'. On the evidence in this case the position is quite different, in my view, from what was in the mind of Lord Denning M.R. in *Greaves & Co (Contractors) Ltd v. Baynham Meikle & Partners* [1975] 3 All E.R. 99 at 103–104 when he said: 'The surgeon does not warrant that he will cure the patient.' That was said in the context of treatment or an operation designed to cure, not in the context of anything in the nature of an amputation. The facts of the present case are obviously extremely unusual, but I do not see why the judge's and my conclusion on these unusual facts should be viewed by surgeons with alarm, as mentioned by the judge. If the defendant had given his usual warning, the objective analysis of what he conveyed would have been quite different . . ."

NEILL L.J.:
" . . . The question for consideration is whether in the circumstances of the instant case the defendant further undertook that he would render Mr Thake permanently sterile by means of this operation.

On behalf of the plaintiffs it is conceded that the defendant never used the word 'guarantee' in relation to the outcome of the operation, but it is submitted that what the defendant said and did at the consultation on or about 25 September, 1975 would have led a reasonable person in the position of the plaintiffs to the conclusion that the defendant was giving a firm promise that the operation would lead to permanent sterility.

It is not in dispute that the task of the court is to seek to determine objectively what conclusion a reasonable person would have reached having regard to (a) the words used by the defendant, (b) the demonstration which he gave and (c) the form which Mr and Mrs Thake were asked to sign.

Counsel for the plaintiffs placed particular reliance on the following matters: (1) that on more than one occasion the defendant explained to the plaintiffs that the effect of the operation was 'irreversible', subject to the remote possibility of later surgical intervention, and counsel pointed out that his explanation was reinforced by the statement in the form: 'I understand that the effect of the operation is irreversible'; (2) that the defendant agreed in evidence that the word 'irreversible' would have been understood by the plaintiff as meaning 'irreversible by God or man'; (3) that the demonstration which the defendant gave with his hands and arms and the sketch which he drew would have led the plaintiffs to believe that, because a piece of the vas was to be severed and the severed ends were to be turned back, there was no possibility whatever of the channels being reunited unless some further surgery took place; (4) that the defendant stated that two sperm tests were required to ensure that the operation was successful; this statement would have strengthened the impression given to his listeners that the operation when completed would render the patient sterile.

I recognise the force of the submissions put forward on behalf of the plaintiffs and I am very conscious of the fact that both the trial judge and Kerr L.J. have reached the conclusion that the case in contract has been established. For my part, however, I remain unpersuaded. It seems to me that it is essential to consider the events of 25 September, 1975 and the words which the defendant used against the background of a surgeon's consulting room. It is the common experience of mankind that the results of medical treatment are to some extent unpredictable and that any treatment may be affected by the special characteristics of the particular patient. It has been well said that 'the dynamics of the human body of each individual are themselves individual'.

I accept that there may be cases where, because of the claims made by a surgeon or physician for his method of treatment, the court is driven to the conclusion that the result of the treatment is guaranteed or warranted. But in the present case I do not regard the statements made by the defendant as to the effect of his treatment as passing beyond the realm of expectation and assumption. It seems to me that what he said was spoken partly by way of warning and partly by way of what is sometimes called 'therapeutic reassurance'.

Both the plaintiffs and the defendant expected that sterility would be the result of the operation the defendant appreciated that that was the plaintiff's expectation. This does not mean, however, that a reasonable person would have understood the defendant to be giving a binding promise that the operation would achieve its purpose or that the defendant was going further than he expected and believed that it would have the desired result. Furthermore, I do not consider that a reasonable person would have expected a responsible medical man to be intending to give a guarantee. Medicine, though a highly skilled profession, is not, and is not generally regarded as being, an exact science. The reasonable man would have expected the defendant to exercise all the proper skill and care of a surgeon in that speciality; he would not in my view have expected the defendant to give a guarantee of 100 per cent success.

Accordingly, though I am satisfied that a reasonable person would have left the consulting room thinking that Mr Thake would be sterilised by the vasectomy operation, such a person would not have left thinking that the defendant had given a *guarantee* that Mr Thake would be absolutely sterile."

NOTES:

1. Nourse L.J. agreed with Neill L.J.
2. In the context of failed sterilisation there is the possibility of bringing a claim under section 2(1) of the Misrepresentation Act 1967 for negligent misrepresentation, on the basis that a claim that the procedure was "irreversible" had the effect of negligently misrepresenting the nature of the procedure. A duty arises at common law if there is a special relationship between the parties and a number of conditions are satisfied. First, it must be reasonably foreseeable by the representor that the representee would rely upon the statement made to him. Secondly, there must be sufficient proximity between the parties. Thirdly, it must be just and reasonable for the law to impose such a duty. However, following the approach taken in *Eyre v. Measday* the imposition of such a duty appears unlikely. Furthermore in *Gold v. Haringey* (see Chapter 6 at pages 356–360) Lloyd L.J. stated that the fact that the plaintiff was told that the operation was irreversible did not mean that it was bound to succeed.

QUESTION:

1. Is it reasonable to assume that in all such cases the surgeon would not have guaranteed the success of the operation?

(c) Claims in Negligence

(i) Basis for the Action

Claims in negligence regarding pregnancy and childbirth relate to issues ranging from inadequate provision of information concerning clinical procedures to negligent conduct of such procedures.

Thake v. Maurice [1986] 1 All E.R. 497; [1986] Q.B. 644

The facts of this case are as stated at pages 801–802 above.

KERR L.J.:
" . . . The evidence relevant to this issue can be summarised as follows. In the course of the defendants evidence he was taken through medical publications dealing with 'late recanalisation' and he agreed that he was aware that there was a slight risk that this might occur. The opening part of his cross-examination was then in the following terms:
Q. Mr Maurice, I take it from your evidence (and please tell me whether this is right or wrong) that in 1975 you considered it necessary to give a warning about the risk of recanalisation.

A. Yes.

Q. Thank you. I would understand from that (and again would you tell me whether this is right or wrong) that if it was necessary to give a warning it had to be such a warning that it was going to be understood and sufficiently clear to be understood.

A. Yes.'

In addition to this evidence it must be remembered that the defendant agreed that, if he had failed to give any warning on these lines, then the plaintiffs would have been left with the mistaken impression that, subject only to confirmation by the two sperm tests, Mr Thake had been rendered permanently sterile, and, as discussed hereafter, that if Mrs Thake nevertheless became pregnant again, she might not realise that this had happened, having regard to her age, until it was too late for her to have the pregnancy terminated.

The submission made on behalf of the defendant was that this material was not sufficient to entitle the judge to conclude, as he did, that the defendant's failure to give his usual warning amounted to an inadvertent negligent omission on his part. The ground for this submission was that no independent expert evidence had been called on either side on the question whether the absence of any such warning in these circumstances would have been regarded as breach of professional duty, by applying the test laid down in *Bolam v. Friern Hospital Management Committee* [1957] 2 All E.R. 118, as approved by the House of Lords in *Sidaway v. Bethlem Royal Hospital Governors* [1985] 1 All E.R. 643. The judge rejected this and I entirely agree with his reasoning (see [1984] 2 All E.R. 513 at 512–522). There was no appeal against his refusal to allow a urologist to be called on behalf of the defendant after the completion of his evidence, but it should be mentioned that it was explained to us, as I accept, that the failure to disclose his evidence in advance in the form of a written report, as had been ordered in relation to any expert that either side might wish to call, was merely due to inadvertence. In the event, therefore, no independent medical evidence was called by either party. But I cannot accept that in these circumstances the judge was not entitled to conclude that the defendant's failure to give his usual warning amounted to an inadvertent breach on his part of the duty of care which he owed to the plaintiffs. Unless and until rebutted, which they never were, the defendants own evidence and the surrounding circumstances to which I have referred speak for themselves. It would have been open to the defendant to qualify the answers which he gave, either in cross-examination, by saying that he did not believe that it was general practice to give any such warning or that the other surgeons might not consider this to be necessary. He was given the opportunity of doing so in a later part of his cross-examination when it was suggested to him that he might not have given the warning because this might have caused worry or concern to the plaintiffs, but he did not accept this. Accordingly, unlike the situations considered in *Bolam v. Friern Hospital Management Committee* and *Sidaway v. Bethlem Hospital Governors*, in the present case there was nothing to be placed in the balance against the need for the warning which the defendant himself recognised in his evidence. He was a general surgeon with high professional qualifications whose competence was not in question, and I think that the plaintiffs were entitled to rely on his evidence just as if it had been given by an independent expert with the same qualifications. Since there is nothing to be placed against it, I consider that the judge was entitled to conclude, as he did, that the plaintiffs had established an inadvertent breach of duty on the part of the defendant sufficient to amount to negligence both in contract and in tort."

NOTES:

1. As with other medical negligence cases, the level of information given must be in accordance with that proposed by a responsible body of

professional practice. The Court of Appeal in *Gold v. Haringey AHA* [1987] 2 All E.R. 888 stated clearly, but controversially, that no distinction should be drawn between the level of information disclosed whether the procedure was for therapeutic or for non-therapeutic purposes (see Chapter 6 above).

2. The revised NHS consent forms spell out the risk that an operation may be unsuccessful, although, of course the fact that a consent form has been signed is only evidence that consent has been given. Failure to provide an adequate explanation may still lead to a claim in damages. In *Lybart v. Warrington AHA* (1995) 25 BMLR 91, a woman was sterilised after having given birth to her third child by Casearean section. She was informed prior to sterilisation that the procedure was irreversible and she signed a NHS consent form. Subsequently she became pregnant. She brought an action in negligence claiming damages. Her claim succeeded. In the Court of Appeal it was held that she had not been given an adequate warning. The Court stated that the gynaecologist had not taken reasonable steps to ensure that the information given had been understood. (See further A. Grubb, "Failed Sterilisation: Duty to provide adequate warning" (1995) 3 *Medical Law Review* 297.)

3. In *Goodwill v. British Pregnancy Advisory Service* [1996] 2 All E.R. 161, the Court of Appeal stated that a duty was not owed to a pregnant woman who had commenced a sexual relationship with M three years after a vasectomy had been performed and who having been told by M that he had undergone a vasectomy did not take further contraceptive precautions.

(ii) Causation

An important part of a negligence action is to establish that the defendant's conduct caused the harm suffered. The plaintiffs must show either that had they known of the risks they would not have undergone the sterilisation operation or that the woman once she became pregnant would have chosen an abortion. As we saw in Chapter 6 the test of causation appears to be subjective rather than objective (*Chatterson v. Gerson* and Chapter 6, page 333).

But if an abortion is an option, must the woman take it? If she refuses, will her refusal constitute a *novus actus interveniens* breaking the chain of causation? This issue came before the Court of Appeal in the following case:

Emeh v. Chelsea and Kensington Area Health Authority [1984] 3 All E.R. 1044, C.A.; [1985] Q.B. 142

The plaintiff was sterilised but the operation was carried out negligently and she became pregnant again. She found out she was around 24 weeks pregnant. She refused to have an abortion. The issue before the court was whether her refusal to have an abortion was justifiable. It was claimed by the defence that this refusal amounted to a *novus actus interveniens* breaking the chain of causation.

WALLER L.J.:

" . . . The plaintiff, in her evidence, gave her views about those matters; she was saying she did not consider an abortion because she was afraid. Then she described her husband's reaction by saying: 'My husband did try to talk to me and we went back over all our previous talks of not wanting any more children.' She said her husband was trying to persuade her to have an abortion, and then gave this explanation:

'I said, "I do not want any more operations. I cannot go through an operation like that again. I could be 26 weeks pregnant, I am not going to risk my life. I will manage. We will manage."

Quite clearly there was no justification for thinking there was a 26 weeks pregnancy at that stage, but what she was clearly saying was that she would reject an abortion, but that her husband would have wished she should have one.

The judge went on to find:

'I am sure that, within a few days of realising that she was pregnant, she made a firm decision to have the baby and abandoned any thought of obtaining an abortion, if ever she had entertained such an idea.'

That may well be so because she in fact was saying she decided she would not have an abortion.

Our attention has also been drawn to the comparative risks of an abortion, evidence of which was given by Sir John Dewhurst. He divided such risks into three categories: 12 weeks under, over 12 weeks and up to 22 weeks. While he was saying that from 12 to 22 weeks the risks were not all that great, however it did require going into hospital for a few days and there could be a risk connected with breathing, and so on.

It may well be that if the judge had taken a different view about that first question, he might have been prepared to take more notice of the view expressed by the plaintiff, namely, that she was frightened to have an abortion.

In my judgment Mr Green is right in saying that that particular finding of the judge was based on a wrong assumption; and it also appears that the judge gave no consideration to the fact that there is a considerable difference between someone who is six to eight weeks pregnant, and someone who is something of the order of 20 weeks pregnant, which was the fact in this particular case, although the plaintiff said (and she laid great emphasis on this) that she thought she was between 26 to 28 weeks pregnant. However, the fact is she was about 20 weeks pregnant.

It is sufficient to say that in my opinion the judge might not have taken such a hard view of the plaintiff's conduct if he had appreciated the point which I have just made. In my opinion, while the plaintiff might well have been less than frank in relation to the circumstances surrounding her original abortion and sterilisation operation, the judge may well have found it necessary to reject all answers which the plaintiff gave in her evidence, those answers which I have already mentioned.

He held that the plaintiff's conduct in refusing to consider an operation for an abortion was so unreasonable as to eclipse the breach of contract, and in that connection he was considering *Scuriaga v. Powell* (1979) 123 S.J. 406, where Watkins J. held, in a not dissimilar case, that there was no break in the chain of causation. However, the judge then said:

'In the instant case, on very different evidence, I hold that there was such a break, as the plaintiff's act in failing to obtain an abortion was, in the circumstances of this case, so unreasonable as to eclipse the defendants' wrongdoing.'

He held that the conduct in fact was a novus actus; or alternatively, as was put before us, her conduct was a failure to minimise the damage.

Can it be said that the plaintiff's conduct was so unreasonable as to eclipse the defendants' wrongdoing? In *McKew v. Holland & Hannen & Cubitt (Scotland) Ltd* [1969] 3 All E.R. 1621, Lord Reid, dealing with rather different facts but considering an argument concerning the chain of causation, said, at p. 1624:

'But I think it is right to say a word about the argument that the fact that the appellant made to jump when he felt himself falling is conclusive against him. When his leg gave way the appellant was in a very difficult situation. He had to decide what to do in a fraction of a second. He may have come to a wrong decision: he probably did. But if the chain of causation had not been broken before this by his putting himself in a position where he might be confronted with an emergency, I do not think that he would put himself out of court by acting wrongly in the emergency unless his action was so utterly unreasonable that even on the spur of the moment no ordinary man would have been so foolish as to do what he did.'

And that speech of Lord Reid was concurred in by Lord Guest and Lord Upjohn. So the degree of unreasonable conduct which is required is, on Lord Reid's view, very high.

In my opinion, on the findings of the judge, even as they were, I would be disposed to say that this conduct on the part of the plaintiff was not so reasonable as to eclipse the defendants' wrongdoing. But when there is taken into account, first of all the judge's misunderstanding of the earlier part of the plaintiff's evidence concerning dates, when she was in fact entirely truthful; and secondly when one sees no reference was made by the judge to the difference between a 20-week pregnancy and eight-week pregnancy, it would seem that when the plaintiff decided to have the baby and, having made that decision, she then decided to sue the defendants, her conduct could not be described as utterly unreasonable. Especially when one bears in mind that she had an argument with her husband about it, he apparently wanted her to have an abortion; and the judge accepted that evidence, that makes decision all the more understandable. I would therefore come to the conclusion that that finding of the judge, namely her failure to undergo an abortion was so unreasonable as to eclipse the defendants' wrongdoing is incorrect, and that the plea of novus actus, or the failure to take steps to minimise the damage, in whatever way the matter is put — fails."

Slade L.J.: (agreeing with Waller L.J.)

" . . . I respectfully agree with the judgment which has just been delivered, but will add something of my own, since we are differing from the judge in the court below . . . I would, for my part, be prepared to proceed on the basis of the judge's finding that the plaintiff did make a conscious decision to keep the child soon after she learned of her pregnancy. On this footing, the judge held that, apart from the cost of her second sterilisation operation, she was not entitled to any damage accruing after she had learned of her pregnancy in late January 1977. His reason was that she had, by her own conduct in refusing to seek an abortion, interfered with the chain of causation. The judge referred to a passage from *Clerk and Lindsell on Torts*, 15th ed. (1982), p. 561:

'Although *novus actus* is generally regarded as the act of a third party, the act of the plaintiff himself will be sufficient. This is connected with the principle *volenti non fit injuria*, or almost invariably nowadays contributory negligence, or the duty to minimise damage, which have all been discussed. Where the *novus actus* is that of the plaintiff himself the same considerations apply as above, principally whether his act is so unreasonable as to eclipse the defendant's wrongdoing.'

Echoing the guidance given by this passage, the judge held that the plaintiff's act in failing to obtain an abortion was, in the circumstances, so unreasonable as to eclipse the defendants' wrongdoing. With the greatest respect to the judge, I find myself in profound disagreement with him in this criticism of the plaintiff's conduct. The hospital authority had performed on her an operation which led her reasonably to believe it had rendered her incapable of having children. They had performed the operation is inefficiently that only some months later she discovered that she was again pregnant; nor did she make this discovery in the early stages of her pregnancy. She discovered it when the pregnancy had continued for some $17\frac{1}{2}$ to 20 weeks. By that time the foetus would inevitably have grown to a considerable extent; according to the evidence of Sir John Dewhurst, an operation would not have been entirely without risk, and would no doubt have involved her in considerable pain and discomfort. Furthermore the child in this instance was that of her husband, and only some seven months before she had had to undergo a similar operation in hospital, which had no doubt been very disagreeable.

I am quite prepared to infer that she made a conscious decision not to have the pregnancy terminated a second time, but have no doubt that in the circumstances a large number of mixed motives would have influenced her in reaching this decision.

The judge, in saying that her failure to obtain an abortion was so unreasonable as to eclipse the defendants' wrongdoing, was, I think, really saying that the defendants had the right to expect that, if they had not performed the operation properly, she would procure an abortion, even if she did not become aware of its existence until nearly 20 weeks of her pregnancy had elapsed.

I do not, for my part, think that the defendants had the right to expect any such thing. By their own negligence, they faced her with the very dilemma which she had sought to avoid by having herself sterilised.

For the reasons which I have attempted to give, I think that they could, and should have reasonably foreseen that if, as a consequence of the negligent performance of the operation she should find herself pregnant again, particularly after some months of pregnancy, she might well decide to keep the child. Indeed for my part I would go even a little further. Save in the most exceptional circumstances, I cannot think it right that the court should ever declare it unreasonable for a woman to decline to have an abortion in a case where there is no evidence that there were any medical or psychiatric grounds for terminating the particular pregnancy. And no such evidence has been drawn to our attention relating to this particular pregnancy of the plaintiff in the present case."

PURCHAS L.J.:
"I find it unacceptable that the court should not be invited to consider critically in the context of a defence of *novus actus interveniens* the decision of a mother to terminate or not her pregnancy which has been caused by the defendants' negligence. I am satisfied that taking the features of this case as highly as one can against the plaintiff, namely that on January 19 she knew or had reason to suspect she was pregnant, her decision cannot be questioned. Although the judge put her term of pregnancy at as short a period as $16\frac{1}{2}$ weeks, it must be recalled from the notes of her general practitioner that he recorded and communicated to her a pregnancy period of 18 to 20 weeks. The judge, in coming to his conclusion on a break in the chain of causation, studied the professional evidence of Sir John Dewhurst, and considered the risks and inconvenience and discomfort of a further operation, matters which would not have been in the mind of the plaintiff at all in fact, and discounted her evidence, which he quoted in his judgment and then found not to be established because of his view of the motive of the plaintiff. Those were matters which, in my judgment, were not relevant to the decision within the objective test which the judge had taken from the textbook. They are decisions as to whether or not the plaintiff might have acted reasonably, or not in mitigation of damage, but in my judgment they certainly have no relevance to the more formal decision as to whether or not the chain of causation has been broken at all.

So for those reasons, having disposed of the one feature in this case, namely the conclusion which the judge in my judgment, with great respect, was not entitled to reach on the established evidence (namely, that the plaintiff's motivation was totally incorrect and "commercial") it is clear that she did have reasons and reasons, if I may say so, only too obvious to anyone who reads the facts of this case, for hesitation. Whether or not the risks are to be placed at the 14th, 16th or 20th week of pregnancy, to my mind, does not carry the matter any further.

This mother was entitled to take the decision which she did in all the circumstances of the case."

QUESTION:

1. In what situations, if any, would a court be prepared to question the decision of a woman to refuse to have an abortion and hold that as a result her conduct broke the chain of causation?

(iii) Award of Damages

In negligence actions consequent upon management of pregnancy and childbirth claims may be brought for both pecuniary and non-pecuniary loss. In the past there was debate as to whether recovery should be allowed for the cost of upkeep of a healthy child (see *Udale v. Bloomsbury AHA* [1983] 2 All E.R. 522). It was suggested that public policy might militate against such damages on the grounds that it would be unwise for a child to discover that he had been "unwanted". However today it seems clear that such damages will be awarded in recognition of the costs of bringing up such a child. (Peter Pain J. in *Thake v. Maurice* [1984] 2 All E.R. 513, approved by the Court of Appeal in *Emeh v. Chelsea and Kensington AHA* [1985].) The principles for awarding damages in negligence cases in relation to failed sterilisations were summarised by Brooke J. in *Allen v. Bloomsbury AHA* [1993] 1 All E.R. 65. First, the mother can recover damages for pain or discomfort during her pregnancy. However, this must be set off against the pain and suffering which she would have avoided had she decided not to continue with her pregnancy and had an abortion. Secondly, she may recover economic loss in the form of financial loss, the cost of feeding, clothing, or education of the child and also lost earnings. The tiredness which she may have experienced in bringing up a healthy child is offset against the advantages of bringing a healthy child into the community. In addition Brooke J. stated that she may recover damages for the additional stress and burden of bringing up a handicapped child. This particular head of damages has been the subject of criticism. Grubb has commented that damages for stress and anxiety are not recoverable in tort and therefore it is difficult to see how they could be recovered on the basis that they are psychiatric injury (see A. Grubb, "Damages for Birth of a Healthy Child" (1993) 1 *Medical Law Review* 238). Other losses may be recovered such as costs of private education if, for example, other children in the family had been sent to boarding schools (*Bennarr v. Kettering AHA* (1979) *New L.J.* 179). The court will not award damages for both loss of earnings and the cost of nursing care in the case of a handicapped child (*Fish v. Wilcox* (1993) 13 BMLR 134).

SELECT BIBLIOGRAPHY

M. Brazier, *Medicine, Patients and the Law*, (2nd edn.), Harmondsworth: Penguin, 1992, Chapters 11 & 17.

M. Brazier, "Down the slippery slope" (1990) 6 *Professional Negligence* 25.

N. Cica, "Sterilising the Intellectually Disabled" (1993) 1 *Medical Law Review* 186.

B. Dickens, "Wrongful birth and life, wrongful death before birth and wrongful law", S. McClean (ed.), *Legal Issues in Human Reproduction*, Aldershot: Dartmouth, 1989.

H. Draper, "Women and Sterilisation Abuse" in M. Brazier and M. Lobjoit (eds.), *Protecting the Vulnerable*, London: Routledge, 1991.

G. Douglas, *Law, Fertility and Reproduction*, London: Sweet & Maxwell, 1991.

J. Fortin, "Legal Protection for the Unborn Child" (1988) 51 *Modern Law Review* 54.

J. Fortin, "Can you ward a Foetus?" (1988) 51 *Modern Law Review* 768.

M Freeman, "Sterilising the Mentally Handicapped" in M. Freeman, *Medicine, Ethics and Law*, London: Sweet & Maxwell.

A. Grubb, "Conceiving — a new course of action" in M. Freeman, *Medicine Ethics and Law, op. cit.*

C. Heginbotham, "Sterilising people with mental handicaps" in S. McLean (ed.), *Legal Issues in Human Reproduction*, Aldershot: Dartmouth, 1989.

R. Lee, "To be or not to be: Is That the Question? The Claim of Wrongful Life" and R. Lee, D. Morgan, "A Lesser Sacrifice, Sterilisation and the Mentally Handicapped Woman", in R. Lee and D. Morgan (eds.), *Birthrights: Law and Ethics at the Beginning of Life*, London: Routledge, 1987.

J. Montgomergy, "Rhetoric and Welfare" (1989) 9 Oxford J. Leg. Stud. 395.

K. McNorrie, *Family Planning Practice and the Law*, Aldershot: Dartmouth, 1991.

J. Shaw, "Regulating Sexuality: A Legislative Framework for Non-Consensual Sterilisation" in S. McVeigh and S. Wheelar (eds.), *Law, Health and Medical Regulation*, Aldershot: Dartmouth 1993.

A. Whitfield, "Common Law Duties to Unborn Children" (1993) 1 *Medical Law Review* 28.

PART V

PART V

Medical technology has wrought many changes at the end of life. The very concept of death itself has altered over time, from the recognition of death as being cessation of the heart to the current position in which death is brain stem death (irreversible degeneration of the brain stem). Today, life support systems through the provision of artificial ventilation and nutrition and hydration offer the potential for life to be sustained and considerably prolonged. However, such technologies bring with them costs. Almost invariably not all patients can be sustained in such a manner. Health professionals are left to choose when therapies should be given or withdrawn. In the past many of these choices were left hidden, but the position has changed and the issue is now the subject of heated public debate. We noted in Chapter 6 above that a competent patient has the right to consent or refuse consent to medical treatment even if death results. The law supports the autonomy of the patient to refuse treatment, but at the same time there is no "right to die" as such recognised in law. In the absence of a Bill of Rights, the English courts, unlike their United States counterparts, have not been faced with the argument that individual choice in dying can be said to derive from a fundamental right to privacy: *Cruzan v. Department of Health of Missouri* 497 U.S. 281. However, a health professional may not deliberately end the patients life. Should she do so then if she is liable to be prosecuted for murder.

Difficulties arise if it is sought to withdraw treatment from an incompetent patient. This dilemma is particularly acute when the patient is being sustained through the provision of nutrition and hydration through artificial means. The medical profession have for many years expressed adherence to the principle set out in Arthur Hough's satirical piece "The Latest Decalogue", "thou shalt not kill but needst not strive officiously to keep alive". Euthanasia has been consistently rejected by legislators and health care professionals alike. The courts have recently affirmed their support for the principle of the sanctity of life. Yet some commentators are of the view that in many situations there is a very fine line between the withdrawal of treatment resulting in death and taking active steps to bring a person's life to an end (see Chapter 2 above at pages 111–115). Over a number of years the courts have shown themselves willing to sanction courses of non-active treatment, initially in a series of cases concerning newly born infants with severe handicaps and subsequently in relation to adult patients in a persistent vegetative state, that is to say those lacking cognitive functions. The most notable case in recent years has been perhaps the decision in *Airedale NHS Trust v. Bland* [1993] 1 All E.R. 821, in which the House of Lords authorised the withdrawal of artificial nutrition and hydration from Tony Bland who had been injured during the disaster at the Hillsborough football ground and left in a persistent vegetative state. The courts have now confirmed that such decisions are to be made on the basis of "best interests". Consistent with the decision in *F v. West Berkshire*

Health Authority [1989] 2 All E.R. 545, which we examined in Chapter 5 above, "best interests" is to be determined with reference to what a responsible body of professional practice would deem to be in a patient's best interests. Difficulties in decision making regarding treatment withdrawal may also concern problems of diagnosis. More recently questions have been raised as to the conclusiveness of the diagnosis of patients in persistent vegetative state (see Chapter 14 below). The courts are likely to be faced with decisions relating to whether treatment should be continued on the basis that the patient's quality of life is likely to be poor.

The individual may have the right to control actions taken with regard to his body during his lifetime but what is the position after his death? To what extent can he, and indeed should he be able to stipulate use of bodily products? At one extreme it could be argued that he has no rights, claims or interests. Such an approach would allow an individual's organs (where clinically suitable) to be routinely salvaged and used for the purposes of transplantation. English law does not follow such an approach. The Human Tissue Act 1961 provides that organs may be removed from the deceased where there has been an expression of willingness prior to their death for this removal to occur or where such enquiries have been made of the relatives as are reasonably practicable. We explore the uncertainties surrounding this legislation in Chapter 15. At present there is a serious shortage of organs, and amongst the alternatives advanced is the introduction of new legislation allowing automatic removal of organs, save where the deceased had expressed an indication to the contrary. The deceased are not the only potential source of organs. Organs may be transplanted from living donors. Such donations are subject both to general principles of consent to treatment and in addition compliance is required with a series of criteria set out in statute and regulations. The shortage of organs for transplantation has led to a number of proposals to increase the supply, from legislative reform to the development of new scientific techniques such as the use of organs transplantated from animals. As with many such technologies, the efficacy of transplantation has been questioned not least in the light of the costs entailed. In addition, as we noted earlier in this book, treatment options may be influenced by personal ethical and religious beliefs and this is particularly the case in relation to organ transplantation where mutilation of the body after death has met with some opposition.

The use of organs and tissue after death raise questions of ownership. This is particularly important at a time in which the use of such bodily products may prove lucrative for scientists. There are many uncertainties as to the law in this area and they are presently the subject of an active debate. This Part ends with an examination of these issues at pages 928–934 below.

14

END OF LIFE

1. INTRODUCTION

In 1993 the House of Lords was asked to make a declaration approving the withdrawal of artificial feeding from Tony Bland, a young man who was in a persistent vegetative state resulting from being crushed in the Hillsborough Football Stadium disaster. A year before, Dr Cox had stood trial for murder of an elderly female patient. The woman, who had pleaded with him to put her out of her misery, was suffering from rheumatoid arthritis, gastric ulcers and body sores and was in great pain. He eventually gave her a lethal dose of potassium chloride. These two cases illustrate some of the most difficult dilemmas in health care practice. Medical technology enables life to be prolonged but at what point should such treatment cease? Is it ever justifiable to take steps to deliberately end a person's life on their request, as in the *Cox* case. English law has never sanctioned "mercy killing" and yet a patient may be given a high dosage of pain-killing drugs even if the incidental effect is that the patient's death is hastened. An individual patient may bring their own life to an end — suicide is not a crime — yet patient autonomy here does not extend to an incompetent patient being allowed assistance in dying.

This Chapter examines English law as it regulates decisions at the end of life. In section two, the position in criminal law is considered. At present deliberate termination of the life of the patient is likely to result in a prosecution for murder. The courts have nevertheless recognised that it may in some situations be legitimate to withhold treatment or to take the decision not to recommence therapy. Judicial approaches to making such orders are considered in section three. The final section of the chapter concerns the proposals advanced for reform of the present position. These include the recognition of active euthanasia, the reform of the grounds on which treatment may be withdrawn and the enactment of legislation governing living wills or recognition of proxy decision-makers for the mentally incompetent.

The use of advance directives stating the basis on which individuals would wish treatment to be withdrawn is explored.

2. ENDING THE LIFE OF A PATIENT — CRIMINAL LAW

(a) Suicide

Until relatively recently English law did not recognise a right to suicide. To take your own life was a crime. This position was changed by section 1 of the Suicide Act 1961 which legalised suicide. Nevertheless, the 1961 Act provides that assistance in suicide is a criminal offence.

Suicide Act 1961

Section 2

(1) A person who aids, abets, counsels or procures the suicide of another, or an attempt by another to commit suicide, shall be liable on conviction on indictment to imprisonment for a term not exceeding fourteen years . . .

(2) If on the trial on an indictment for murder or manslaughter it is proved that the accused aided, abetted, counselled or procured the suicide of the person in jury may find him guilty of that offence.

NOTE:

1. Persons who have assisted in ending the life of a terminally ill relative have been prosecuted under this section. In the case of *R v. Beecham* (1988) the defendant assisted the suicide of his daughter who was suffering from cancer, multiple sclerosis and persistent severe pain. The daughter had previously made two suicide attempts. The defendant was convicted of aiding and abetting suicide. The judge gave him a suspended prison sentence of 12 months (see D. Meyer, *The Human Body and the Law* (2nd ed.) Edinburgh University Press: Edinburgh, 1990, at page 285).

What constitutes aiding and abetting suicide?

A.G. v. Able [1984] 1 All E.R. 277; [1984] Q.B. 795

The defendants were members of the Voluntary Euthanasia Society. They published a booklet entitled *A guide to self-deliverance* to be distributed to members of the society, subject to certain qualifications. The booklet was supplied on payment of a fee and only to members of the society who were 25 and over and who had been members for at least three months. The booklet set out five different ways in which suicide could be committed. There was evidence that in the eighteen months after the booklet had been first distributed 15 suicide cases were linked to it. In a further nineteen cases documents had been found which indicated that the deceased was a member, or had corresponded with, the Society. The Attorney General sought for a declaration that future supply of the booklet constituted an offence under section 2(1) of the 1961 Act.

WOOLF J.:

'. . . The fact that the supply of the booklet could be an offence does not mean that any particular supply is an offence. It must be remembered that the society is an unincorporated body and there can be no question of the society committing an offence. Before an offence under s.2 can be proved, it must be shown that the individual concerned 'aided, abetted, counselled or procured' an attempt at suicide or a suicide and intended to do so by distributing the booklet. The intention of the individual will normally have to be inferred from facts surrounding the particular supply which he made. If, for example, before sending a copy of the booklet, a member of the society had written a letter, the contents of which were known to the person sending the booklet, which stated that the booklet was required because the member was intending to commit suicide, then, on those facts, I would conclude that an offence had been committed or at least an attempted offence contrary to s.2 of the 1961 Act. However, in the majority of cases, a member requesting the booklet will not make clear his intentions and the supply will be made without knowledge of whether the booklet is required for purposes of research, general information, or because suicide is contemplated. Is it, therefore, enough that in any particular case the person responsible for making the supply would appreciate that there is a real likelihood that the booklet is required by one of the substantial number of members of the society who will be contemplating suicide? It is as to this aspect of the case that there is the greatest difficulty and little assistance from the authorities.

Counsel on behalf of the respondents contends that before a person can be an accessory, there must be a consensus between the accessory and the principal, and there can be no consensus where the alleged accessory does not even know whether the principal is contemplating (in this case) suicide. As, however, is pointed out in Smith & Hogan *Criminal Law* (4th edn. 1978), while counselling implies consensus, procuring and aiding do not. The authors say (p. 116).

'the law probably is that: (i) "Procuring" implies causation "but not consensus" (ii) "abetting" and "counselling" imply consensus but not causation and (iii) "aiding" requires actual assistance but neither consensus nor causation.'

As a matter of principle, it seems to me that as long as there is the necessary intent to assist those who are contemplating suicide to commit suicide if they decide to do so, it does not matter that the supplier does not know the state of mind of the actual recipient. The requirement for the necessary intent explains why in those cases where, in the ordinary course of business a person is responsible for distributing an article, appreciating that some individuals might use it for committing suicide, he is not guilty of an offence. In the ordinary way such a distributor would have no intention to assist the act of suicide. An intention to assist need not however, involve a desire that suicide should be committed or attempted.

In this connection, I must refer to *R v. Fretwell* (1862) 9 Cox C.C. 152. In that case the Court of Criminal Appeal decided that the mere provision of the means of committing a crime is not sufficient to make the provider guilty as an accessory. In giving the judgment of the court, Erle C.J. (said, at p. 154):

'In the present case the prisoner was unwilling that the deceased should take the poison; it was at her instigation and under the threat of self-destruction that he procured it and supplied it to her; but was found that he did not administer it to her or cause her to take it. It would be consistent with the facts of the case that he hoped she would change her mind; and it might well be that the prisoner hoped and expected that she would not resort to it.'

While I accept that this reasoning does not accord with mine. I do not regard the case as requiring me to come to a different conclusion from that which I have indicated. That case is inconsistent with *National Coal Board v. Gamble* [1958] 3 All E.R. 203, and I regard it as confined to its own facts, for the reasons indicated in Smith & Hogan, *Criminal Law* (4th edn, 1978 pp. 120, 121). Counsel for the respondents points out, and this I accept that in some cases the booklet, far from precipitating someone to commit suicide might have the effect of deterring someone from committing suicide when they might otherwise have done so. In such circumstances, he submits it would be quite nonsensical to regard the supply of the booklet as being an attempted offence contrary to s.2 of the 1961 Act. I agree, though I recognise that on one approach the result would be different. The reason why I agree with the submission is because, in such a case, the booklet has not provided any assistance with a view to a contemplated suicide. Such assistance is necessary to establish the actus reus for even the attempted offence.

There will also be cases where, although the recipient commits or attempts to commit suicide, the booklet has nothing to do with the suicide or the attempted suicide; for example, a long period of time may have elapsed between the sending of the booklet and the attempt. In such a case, again, I would agree with counsel for the respondents that there would not be a sufficient connection between the attempted suicide and the supply of the booklet to make the supplier responsible. This does not mean that it has to be shown that the suicide or attempted suicide would not have occurred but for the booklet. However, if "procuring" alone is relied upon, this may be the case. As Lord Widgery C. J. stated in *Attorney-General's Reference (No. 1 of 1975)* [1975] 2 All E.R. 684 at 686–687:

'To procure means to produce by endeavour. You procure a thing by setting out to see that it happens and taking the appropriate steps to produce that happening. You cannot procure an offence unless there is a causal link between what you do and the commission of the offence.'

However, you do not need to procure to be an accessory and the same close causal connection is not required when what is being done is the provision of assistance.

I therefore conclude that to distribute the booklet can be an offence.' But, before an offence can be established to have been committed, it must at least be proved: (a) that the alleged offender had the necessary intent, that is, he intended the booklet to be used by someone contemplating suicide and intended that person would be assisted by the booklet's contents, or otherwise encouraged to attempt to take or to take his own life; (b) that while he still had that intention he distributed the booklet to such a person who read it; and, (c) in addition, if an offence under s.2 is to be proved, that such a person was assisted or encouraged by so reading the booklet to attempt to take or to take his own life, otherwise the alleged offender cannot be guilty of more than an attempt.

If these facts can be proved, then it does not make any difference that the person would have tried to commit suicide anyway. Nor does it make any difference, as the respondents contend, that the information contained in the booklet is already in the public domain. The distinguishing feature between an innocent and guilty distribution is that in the former case the distributor will not have the necessary intent, while in the latter case he will.

However, in each case it will be for a jury to decide whether the necessary facts are proved. If they are, then normally the offence will be made out. Nevertheless, even if they are proved, I am not prepared to say it is not possible for there to be some exceptional circumstance which means that an offence is not established.

NOTES:

1. This action took the form of an action for a declaration by the Attorney General to clarify the law in this area. (See J. Bridgeman, "Declared Innocent" (1993) 1 *Medical Law Review* 117.)
2. Assisting in suicide may also be charged as attempted murder. For example, see *R v. Hough* (1984) 6 Cr.App.R.(S) 404 where the

defendant pleaded guilty to attempted murder after she had assisted an elderly woman who was blind and deaf to commit suicide.

QUESTION:

1. What is meant by 'almost certainly know that a significant number of those to whom the booklet would be sent would be contemplating suicide'? (See K. J. M. Smith, "Assisting in Suicide — The Attorney General and the Voluntary Euthanasia Society" [1983] Crim.L.R. 579.)

(b) Murder/Manslaughter

(i) Basic principles

Deliberate termination of the life of the terminally ill patient will constitute murder or manslaughter. One of the most celebrated cases was that of *R v. Arthur* in 1981. In *R v. Arthur* (*The Times*, November 6, 1981) a baby, John Pearson, was born with Down's Syndrome but apparently no other complications. Dr Arthur was a paediatrician caring for the child. He wrote in the notes "Parents do not wish it to survive, nursing care only." Dr Arthur also prescribed a strong pain-killing drug, DF118, which was a drug not normally given to infants. Some 69 hours later the baby died. Dr Arthur was charged initially with murder but this was later reduced to a charge of attempted murder. He was eventually acquitted. The judge asked the jury to consider whether Dr Arthur's actions amounted to a holding operation:

> "setting a condition where the child could if it contradicted pneumonia die peacefully? Or was it a positive act on behalf of Dr Arthur which was likely to kill the child and represented an attempt accompanied by an intent on his part that it should as a result of the treatment that he prescribed die."

The concept used of a "holding operation" has been the subject of much criticism. It is argued that administration of the drug DF118 was a positive act causing death. The issues discussed in *Arthur* have now been largely superseded by the approach taken by the House of Lords in *Bland*. (See M. J. Gunn and J. C. Smith, "Arthur's Case and the Right to Life of a Down's Syndrome Child" [1985] Crim.L.R. 705. See also comments by D. Poole, D. Brahams and reply by Gunn and Smith [1986] Crim.L.R. 383. For discussion of *Bland* see below at pages 854–856) The case of *R v. Arthur* can usefully be contrasted with the contemporaneous decision in *Re B* (see below at page 828).

There have been a number of prosecutions of doctors who have deliberately ended the life of a terminally ill adult patient. In *R v. Carr*, *Sunday Times*, November 1986, Dr Carr was charged with murder. He had injected a massive dose of phenobarbitone into a patient with inoperable lung cancer. He was acquitted of the charge but Mars Jones J., emphasised that the patient was entitled to every hour that God had given him however seriously ill he might be. In *R v. Lodwig, The Times*, March 16, 1990 the doctor was on an 80-hour shift for the last 18 hours of which he had been continuously on duty. The relatives of a patient terminally ill with cancer of the pancreas who was writhing in pain begged the doctor to put him out of his misery. The doctor eventually said that there was something that he could do but that it might put the patient "over the top". He gave the patient a dose of an anaesthetic to kill the pain. Five minutes later the patient died peacefully. The doctor was charged with murder but this charge was dropped when the main prosecution witness admitted it was possible that the man might have died from natural causes as opposed to a potassium overdose. In *R v. Cox* (*The Times*, September 22, 1992; (1992) 12 BMLR 38) a doctor was convicted of attempted murder. His patient, a 70-year-old woman, was terminally ill with rheumatoid arthritis and this was complicated by gastric ulcers, gangrene and body sores. He gave her a dose of potassium chloride after repeated doses of heroin had failed to ease her agony. The doctor was given a sentence of one year's imprisonment, suspended for 12 months. The General Medical Council admonished him. They noted that his actions had been taken in good faith. (See C. Dyer "Rheumatologist Convicted of Attempted Murder" (1993) 305 *BMJ* 731). It is possible that if the death appears to be a "mercy killing" by a relative then the prosecution may decide to accept a plea of manslaughter rather than prosecute for murder. There is, however, no specific defence of mercy killing in English law, something which was confirmed recently by the House of Lords in *Airedale NHS Trust v. Bland* see below page 842.

(It is interesting to note that the prosecutions of both Dr Arthur and of Dr Cox resulted from a nurse alerting the authorities to what had transpired.)

(ii) Administration of pain-killing drugs

Deliberate termination of life through administration of a drug may lead to a prosecution under section 23 of the Offences Against the Person Act 1861 which makes it an offence to "unlawfully administer to or cause to be administered to or taken by any other person any poison or other destructive or noxious thing, so as to thereby endanger the life of such a person . . ." This section carries a penalty of up to 10 years' imprisonment. However, while a doctor may not deliberately end the life of her patient, she may administer pain killing drugs, even at a high dosage which may result in the patient's death.

R v. Bodkin Adams (1957)

Dr Bodkin Adams, who had treated many elderly patients and had been rewarded by many in their wills, was tried for murder. He had been treating an 81-year-old lady who had suffered from a stroke. She was prescribed heroin and morphia by Dr Adams and subsequently died. She had left Dr Adams a chest of silver and a Rolls Royce in her will. Dr Adams was acquitted.

H. Palmer, "Adam's Trial for Murder" [1957] Crim.L.R. 365

"Devlin J., summing up to the jury, said that murder was an act or series of acts, done by the prisoner, which were intended to kill, and did in fact kill. It did not matter whether Mrs Morell's death was inevitable and that her days were numbered. If her life were cut short by weeks or months it was just as much murder as if it was cut short by years. There had been a good deal of discussion as to the circumstances in which doctors might be justified in administering drugs which could shorten life. Cases of severe pain were suggested and also cases of helpless misery. The law knew of no special defence in this category, but that did not mean that a doctor who was aiding the sick and dying had to calculate in minutes or even hours, perhaps not in days or weeks, the effect on a patient's life of the medicines which he would administer. If the first purpose of medicine, the restoration of health, could no longer be achieved, there was still much for the doctor to do, and he was entitled to do all that was proper and necessary to relieve pain and suffering even if the measures he took might incidentally shorten life by hours or perhaps even longer. The doctor who decided whether or not to administer the drug could not do his job if he were thinking in terms of hours or months of life. The defence in the present case was that the treatment given by Dr Adams was designed to promote comfort, and if it was the right and proper treatment, the fact that it shortened life did not convict him of murder."

NOTES:

1. A detailed account of the trial is provided in a book written by the trial judge Lord Patrick Devlin, *Easing the Passing* (1985).
2. The question of the administration of pain killing drugs was also addressed in *Bland* see below at page 846.
3. In *Re C (A Minor)* the court approved a direction "to treat the ward in such a way that she might end her life peacefully." (See further below at page 829.)
4. It has been suggested that this case introduces the doctrine of double-effect into English law. (See M. Brazier (2nd edn.) *Medicine, Patients and the Law,* Harmondsworth: Penguin, 1992, (2nd edn.) page 447). (See discussion in Chapter 2 above at page 114).
5. In February 1995 Dr Richard Nicholson (the editor of the *Bulletin of Medical Ethics*) commented publicly that 20 years previously, while working as a junior paediatrician, he had increased the dosage of pain killers given to two new born infants with severe hydrocephalus and spina bifida. The infants died within three days. The doctor claimed that it could not be said whether death was a result of the drug or from natural causes (*The Guardian,* February 15, 1995).

QUESTION:

1. Is the use of the "doctrine of double effect" in this context justifiable? (See Chapter 2 above at page 114). Would a better approach be to acknowledge that the morally right action in these circumstances is the action which hastens death?

(iii) Infanticide

If a mother kills a newly-born handicapped child who is gravely suffering then, as with any so-called "mercy killing", she is liable to be prosecuted for murder. But in some instances a prosecution may be brought for the alternative offence of infanticide. This offence can be seen to reflect medical evidence that a high proportion of women following pregnancy suffer from depression and thus, in this situation, a charge other than murder would be appropriate.

Infanticide Act 1938, s.1(1)(3)

Section 1—(1) Where a woman, by any wilful act or omission causes the death of her child, being a child under the age of twelve months, but at the time of the act or omission the balance of her mind was disturbed by reason of her not having fully recovered from giving birth to the child or by the reason of the effect of lactation consequent upon the birth of the child, then, notwithstanding that the circumstances were such that but for this Act the offence would have amounted to murder, she should be guilty of infanticide or may, for such offence be dealt with and punished as if she had been guilty of the manslaughter of the child.

NOTE:

1. This offence was introduced at a time when there was no partial defence of diminished responsibility to murder. The Criminal Law Revision Committee advocated the retention of the offence of infanticide because it avoided the necessity of charging the mother with murder (Criminal Law Revision Committee *Offences Against the Person* Working Paper No. 26). These recommendations were followed by the Law Commission in its draft criminal code in 1988. Clause 64(1) of this provides that:

   "A woman who, but for this section, would be guilty of murder or manslaughter of her child is not guilty of murder or manslaughter but is guilty of infanticide, if her act is done where the child is under the age of twelve months and when the balance of her mind is disturbed by reason of the effect of giving birth or of circumstances consequent upon the birth." (Law Com. No. 177.)

2. The proposals of the Law Commission may be seen as reflecting the fact that the decision to charge a woman with infanticide is not necessarily primarily related to the fact that her mental capacity is

unduly impaired. Instead tacit it may be seen as a recognition that the death has arisen in a situation in which the mother is unable to cope because the child is severely handicapped or because of straitened financial circumstances. (See further K. O'Donovan, "The Medicalisation of Infanticide" [1984] Crim. L.R. 259.)

(iv) Liability for Failure to Provide Care

While there is generally no obligation to act for the benefit of another in English law, in some situations the law imposes a positive duty. For example, such an obligation may be imposed by statute. As we saw above, liability under the Infanticide Act 1938 can be established by an ommission. Furthermore section 1 of the Children and Young Persons Act 1933 provides that:

> "(1) If any person who has attained the age of sixteen years and has the custody, charge, or care of any young person under that age, wilfully assaults, ill treats, neglects, abandons, or exposes him . . . in a manner likely to cause him unnecessary suffering or injury to health . . . that person shall be guilty of a misdemeanour."

Liability under the 1933 Act would extend to a parent who failed to seek medical assistance resulting in the death of the child. In *R v. Senior* [1899] 1 Q.B. 283 the defendant was a member of a sect who had religious objections to the use of medical assistance and medicines. His child fell ill and medical aid was not sought. The child died of diarrhoea and pneumonia. Evidence was given to the effect that had medical help been given the child would probably have lived. Except for the non-provision of medical help the child was treated well by its parents. It was held that the action of the parents constituted neglect under the Prevention of Cruelty to Children Act 1896 section 1 (the statutory predecessor of the 1933 Act). In addition, the fact that the defendant had caused or accelerated death, meant that he was rightly convicted of manslaughter. A successful prosecution for manslaughter as a result of non-compliance with the 1933 Act now appears to be unlikely. In *R v. Lowe* [1973] Q.B. 702, the court indicated that neglect by itself will not necessarily mean that a prosecution for manslaughter will succeed. In that case Phillimore L.J. suggested that while, for example, striking a child in a manner likely to cause it harm would lead to a prosecution for manslaughter, a simple failure to act with the consequence that death results would not inevitably result in a manslaughter prosecution. In 1993 a child's parents were prosecuted and convicted of manslaughter consequent upon negligence in care of their child. The couple, who were vegans and believed in homeopathic remedies, discharged their diabetic daughter from hospital. They treated her with homeopathic remedies but the girl subsequently died. (*The Independent*, October 29, 1993).

What constitutes "wilful neglect" within section 1 was considered in *R v. Sheppard* [1981] A.C. 394.

R v. Sheppard [1981] A.C. 394

A 16-month-old child died of hypothermia and malnutrition. The child had suffered from gastroenteritis but the parents who were poor and of low intelligence had not sought medical attention. The parents were convicted, the judge having directed the jury that to establish liability under the section it was necessary to show that a reasonable parent with knowledge of these facts would have appreciated that this was likely to cause the child unnecessary suffering or injury to health. In the House of Lords the appeal was allowed.

LORD DIPLOCK:

" . . . the verb 'neglect' cannot, in my view, of itself import into the criminal law the civil law concept of negligence. The *actus reus* in a case of wilful neglect is simply a failure for whatever reason, to provide the child whenever it in fact needs medical aid with the medical aid it needs. Such a failure as it seems to me could not properly be described as 'wilful' unless the parent *either* (1) had directed his mind to the question whether there was some risk (though it might fall far short of a probability) that the child's health might suffer unless he was examined by a doctor and provided with such curative treatment as the examination might reveal as necessary, and had made a conscious decision, for whatever reason, to refrain from arranging for such medical examination, or (2) had so refrained because he did not care whether the child might be in need of medical treatment or not.

. . . The section speaks of an act or an omission that is 'likely' to cause unnecessary suffering or injury to health. This word is imprecise. It is capable of covering a whole range of possibilities from 'its on the cards' to 'its more probable than not'; but having regard to the ordinary parent's lack of skill in diagnosis and to the very serious consequences which may result from failure to provide a child with timely medical attention, it should, in my view be understood as excluding only what would fairly be described as highly unlikely . . . "

LORD KEITH:

" . . . This appeal is concerned solely with a failure to provide adequate medical care. The word 'adequate' as applied to medical care may mean no more than 'ordinarily competent'. If it is related to anything, I think it is related to the prevention of unnecessary suffering an injury to health as mentioned in section 1(1) where the adjective 'unnecessary' qualifies both 'suffering' and 'injury to health'. There could be no question of a finding of neglect against a parent who provided ordinarily competent medical care, but whose child nevertheless suffered further injury to its health, for example paralysis in a case of poliomyelitis, because the injury to health would not in the circumstances be unnecessary, in the sense that it could have been prevented by the provision by the parent of adequate medical care. Failure to provide adequate medical care may be deliberate as when the child's need for it is perceived yet nothing is done, negligent, as where the need ought reasonably to have been perceived but was not, or entirely blameless as when the need is not perceived but ought to have been perceived by the ordinary reasonable parent. I would say that in all three cases the parent has neglected the child in the sense of the statute, since I am of the opinion that in a proper construction of section 1(2)(a) it is to be ascertained objectively and in the light of events whether the parent failed to provide ordinarily competent medical care which as a matter of fact the child needed in order to prevent unnecessary suffering or injury to its health."

Note:

1. Lord Edmund Davies agreed with Lords Diplock and Keith. Lords Scarman and Fraser dissented.

In addition, if a person undertakes care of another then abandonment of care may lead to liability at common law. In *R v. Gibbins & Proctor* (1918) 13 Cr.App.R. 134, Gibbins, along with Proctor, the woman with whom he was living, were convicted of murdering Gibbin's child by withholding food. The child died of starvation. By living with the man and receiving money from him for food the woman had also assumed a duty to care for the man's child. In this case the jury reached the conclusion that the defendants were liable for murder because there was evidence that the woman had deliberately witheld food. In *R v. Stone* [1977] 2 All E.R. 341, Stone's sister, F came to live with Stone and his mistress. The sister suffered from anorexia nervosa. Her condition deteriorated. Stone (who was 67, of low intelligence, partly deaf and nearly blind) and his mistress took certain measures to care for F but these were largely ineffectual. F subsequently died and a manslaughter charge was brought against Stone and his mistress. The Court of Appeal held that the judge at first instance had been correct to direct the jury that the minimal attention given by Stone and his mistress was sufficient to give rise to a duty of care and that they had been grossly negligent in the performance of that duty. A doctor who takes on the duty to care for a sick child and neglects that child also risks prosecution at common law. For the scope of doctor's duties to their patients see Chapter 3, above.

3. Judicial Sanctioning of the Removal of Life Support Systems from an Incompetent Patient

While active termination of life is a criminal offence, and in certain situations criminal liability will also arise for failure to provide care, in some cases the courts have been prepared to authorise withdrawal of treatment. In order to ascertain whether cessation of treatment is lawful, it has become increasingly common for an application to be made to the court for a declaration approving a course of treatment. Indeed, in the case of withdrawal of treatment from an incompetent adult patient in a state of PVS, such referral seems mandatory. The ethics of recognising withdrawal of treatment ("passive" euthanasia) while rejecting active euthanasia are a source of dispute. The medical profession recognise passive euthanasia as being acceptable while active euthanasia is not. However, it has been questioned as to whether it is possible for a satisfactory distinction to be drawn between the two (see Chapter 2 at page 111.) One final point is that the cases largely concern removal of treatment, but in some situations extend to decisions not to recommence therapy should a particular incident occur.

(a) Role of the court in approving the discontination of medical treatment of neonates

The first cases which came before the courts in relation to non-treatment concerned handicapped infants.

Where a child is born gravely handicapped, some argue it is better not to pursue aggressive treatment, particularly in a situation in which life expectancy is short. In the past this view was reflected in medical practice in certain hospitals, in Sheffield in the 1970s under the paediatrician John Lorber (for the Lorber-Harris debate see Chapter 2, above), for example. It was only after some time that the issue of withdrawal of treatment from a handicapped infant came before the courts. Today the decision whether to continue treatment of a neonate may be brought before the court by use of the inherent jurisdiction of the court or by one of the orders available under the Children Act 1989 such as a specific issue order (see Chapter 7 at page 420).

Re B [1990] 3 All E.R. 927; [1981] 1 W.L.R. 1421

B was a baby girl born suffering from Downs Syndrome who also had an intestinal blockage which would be fatal unless operated on. Her parents took the view that it would be better for her simply not to have the operation and to die within a few days. In the interval before her death she could be kept from pain and suffering by sedation. The doctors informed the local authority of the parents decision and applied for the child to be made a ward of court. The Court authorised the operation, but then the child was moved to another hospital. There, differences of medical opinion developed. The surgeon who was to carry out the operation declined to do so. He did not want to override the wishes of the parents. The case came eventually before the Court of Appeal.

TEMPLEMAN L.J.:
" . . . The parents say that no one can tell what will be the life of a mongoloid child who survives during that 20 or 30 years, but one thing is certain she will be very handicapped mentally and physically and no one can expect that she will have anything like a normal existence. They make that point not because of the difficulties which will be occasioned to them but in the child's interest. This is not a case in which the court is concerned with whether arrangements could or could not be made for the care of this child, if she lives, during the next 20 or 30 years; the local authority is confident that the parents having for good reason decided that it is in the child's best interests that the operation should not be performed, nevertheless good adoption arrangements could be made and that in so far as any mongol child can be provided with a happy life then such a happy life can be provided.

The question which this court has to determine is whether it is in the interests of this child to be allowed to die within the next week or to have the operation in which case if she lives she will be a mongoloid child, but no one can say to what extent her mental or physical defects will be apparent. No one can say whether she will suffer or whether she will be happy in part. On the one hand the probability is that she will not be a 'cabbage' as it is called when people's faculties are entirely destroyed. On the other hand it is certain that she will be very severely mentally and physically handicapped.

On behalf of the parents counsel for the parents has submitted very movingly, if I may say so, that this is a case where nature has made its own arrangements to terminate a life which would not be fruitful and nature should not be interfered with. He has also submitted that in this kind of decision the views of responsible and caring parents, as these are, should be respected and that their decision that it is better for the child to be allowed to die should be respected. Fortunately or unfortunately, in this particular case the decision no longer lies with the parents or with the doctors, but lies with the court. It is a decision which of course must be made in the light of the evidence and views expressed by the parents and the doctors, but at the end of the day it devolves on this court in this particular instance to decide whether the life of this child is demonstrably to be so awful that in effect the child must be condemned to die, or whether the life of this child is still so imponderable that it would be wrong for her to be condemned to die. There may be cases, I know not, of severe proved damage where the future is so certain and where the life of the child is so bound to be full of pain and suffering that the court might be driven to a different conclusion, but in the present case the choice which lies before the court is this: whether to allow an operation to take place which may result in the child living for 20 or 30 years as a mongoloid or whether (and I think this must be brutally the result) to terminate the life of a mongoloid child because she also has an intestinal complaint. Faced with that choice I have no doubt that it is the duty of this court to decide that the child must live. The judge was much affected by the reasons given by the parents and came to the conclusion that their wishes ought to be respected. In my judgment he erred in that the duty of the court is to decide whether it is in the interests of the child that an operation should take place. The evidence in this case only goes to show that if the operation takes place and is successful then the child may live the normal span of a mongoloid child with the handicaps and defects and life of a mongoloid child, and it is not for this court to say that life of that description ought to be extinguished."

NOTE:

1. The trial of Dr Arthur (noted above at page 821) took place after the case. As Mason and McCall Smith note, *Re B* and *Arthur* are virtually impossible to reconcile and yet *Re B* was not referred to in the criminal trial. (See J. K. Mason and R. A. McCall Smith, *Law and Medical Ethics* (4th ed.), London: Butterworths, 1994 page 151).

QUESTIONS:

1. Does an assessment of whether the life of the child is "intolerable" provide a workable test?
2. Would this case be decided the same way today, in view of the fact that the Abortion Act 1967 (as amended), now sanctions termination on the basis of serious foetal handicap up until full term. (See Chapter 12 above at page 716.)
3. In the *Bland* case Lord Goff talked in terms of "futility" of treatment as a basis for the withdrawal of treatment (see below at page 847.) Is this a preferable test to that of demonstrably awful as sanctioned by Templeman?

Re C [1989] 2 All E.R. 782

Baby C was made a ward of court when it was found that her parents
would have great difficulty in caring for her. She was born prematurely
with severe hydrocephalus. She had what were described as massive
handicaps as a result of a permanent brain lesion. The handicap was
apparently a mixture of severe mental handicap, blindness, probable
deafness and spastic cerebral palsy of all four limbs. She was thin and did
not gain weight. Without constant doses of sedative cholral she cried as if
in pain. The medical experts agreed that there was no prospect of
improvement. The judge at first instance had referred to the earlier case of
Re B but said that the facts in that case were very different. In that case B.
had the chance of the lifespan of a normal child. The first instance judge
therefore made an order to the effect that:

> "Putting the interests of this child first and putting them foremost so that they
> override all else, and in fulfilment of the awesome responsibility which Parlia-
> ment has entrusted upon me, I direct that leave be given to the hospital
> authorities to treat the ward to die; to die with the greatest dignity and the least
> of pain, suffering and distress."

He then later revised this, after receiving the draft from the shorthand
writers to read:

> "I direct that leave be given to the hospital authorities to treat the ward in such a
> way that she may end her life and die peacefully with the greatest dignity and the
> least of pain, suffering and distress."

The local authority then appealed.

LORD DONALDSON OF LYMINGTON M.R.:
" . . . All concerned accept that the judge correctly directed himself that the first
and paramount consideration was the well-being, welfare and interests of C as
required by the decision of this court in *Re B (a minor) (wardship: medical
treatment)* and by the House of Lords in a later and different case with the same
name *Re B (a minor) (wardship: sterilisation)* [1987] 2 All E.R. 206 at 211, *per* Lord
Hailsham L.C.

Counsel for the local authority nevertheless felt it his duty to direct our attention
to a decision of the British Columbia Supreme Court in *Re SD* [1983] 3 WWR 618,
while submitting that the facts were very different. In so doing he was fulfilling the
fundamental duty of members of the legal profession to assist the courts in the
administration of justice, regardless of the views or interests of their client. He was
wholly right to do so. In the event, I am fully satisfied that it does nothing to cast
doubts on the correctness of his client's and the judge's, view that the advice of the
professor should be accepted. It was another case in which a child suffered from
hydrocephalus, but the child concerned was very much older. The child had twice
been operated on to implant a shunt and the question was whether he should now
undergo a third operation.

He was undoubtedly severely handicapped, but not as severely as some in his
class at the hospital school. If a third operation were to be performed he would
probably continue to live as he had done before and would do so for some years.
The parents thought that there should be no operation and that he should be
allowed to die at once. The higher court authorised the operation, saying that it was

too simplistic to say, as did the parents, that the child would be allowed to die in peace. There was a real possibility that, without the operation, the child would endure in a state of progressive disability and pain. That is a wholly different case.

The Official Solicitor in bringing this appeal had three objectives. The first was to question the propriety of an order expressed to be 'liberty to treat the minor to die'. As I hope I have made clear, neither Ward J. nor anyone else would uphold such phraseology and he has himself amended it. Secondly, the Official Solicitor wished to question that part of the order of the judge which appeared to provide that in no circumstances should certain treatment be undertaken. To that I will return in a moment. Third, the Official Solicitor wished to allay anxieties in some quarters that the hospital staff were treating C in a way designed to bring about her death. These anxieties, whilst no doubt sincerely felt, were wholly without foundation and, when expressed, were deeply wounding to the dedicated staff caring for C who, as the professor said, were providing C with devoted care which could not be replicated in many children's units.

Let me make it clear that, in my judgment, the Official Solicitor has been quite right to adopt this course. His first objective was achieved by the judge himself, but the Official Solicitor was not to know that this would occur. His third objective has, I hope, now been achieved. There remains only the second objective.

In para. (4) of his order the judge ordered that:

'The hospital authority do continue to treat the minor within the parameters of the opinion expressed by [the professor] in his report of 13.iv.1989 which report is not to be disclosed to any person other than the hospital authority.'

However, in para. (3) he had ordered:

'. . . but it shall not be necessary either, (a) to prescribe and administer antibiotics to treat any serious infection which the minor might contract; or (b) to set up intravenous fusions or nasal gastric feeding regimes for the minor.'

These two parts of the order are inconsistent with one another because the professor did not wholly rule out these steps if the local nurses and carers took a different view when the question arose for decision. He merely said that he did not think that such measures were correct if the object was simply to prolong a life which had no future and appeared to be unhappy for C I have no doubt that he would have considered revising his opinion, and indeed would have revised it, if the local nurses and carers had thought that such treatment would relieve C's suffering during such life as remained for her.

The second difficulty which arises out of this part of the order is the ban on any publication of the professor's advice. This was one of those comparatively rare cases of special difficulty and sensitivity in which the public interest requires that, subject to maintaining the privacy of those concerned, the courts decision and the reasons for it shall be open to public scrutiny. The formal order itself will not be likely to be very informative, and in any event it would require considerable editing to remove any clues as to the identity of those concerned. What is required in such cases is that the judge should give judgment in open court, taking all appropriate measures to preserve the personal privacy of those concerned. However, such a judgment can set out all the relevant facts and the medical and other considerations of which the judge has taken into account. Thus, in this judgment I have quoted extensively from the professors advice without I hope, giving any clue as to his identity or that of C, her parents or the authority involved.

No new principle is involved in this appeal. I would allow the appeal to the extent of deleting the whole of paragraph (3) of the judge's order. I do so for two reasons. First, the inclusion of specific instructions as to treatment is potentially inconsistent with paragraph (4) which adopts the professors advice. Second, paragraph (3) of the order as amended starts with these words:

'The hospital authority be at liberty to treat the minor to allow her life to come to an end peacefully and with dignity and, act pursuant to such leave, it is directed that the hospital authority shall administer such treatment to the minor as might relieve her from pain, suffering and distress *inter alia* by sedation.'

Now, the specific references to treatment are, of course amply covered by the
professor's advice. But the opening words seem to me to have a potential for giving
rise to misunderstanding and are, therefore, much better avoided and now deleted.
To that extent I would allow the appeal."

NOTES:

1. Balcombe and Nicholls L.J. agreed with Lord Donaldson M.R.
2. In *Re C* the Court of Appeal made explicit reference to the fact that
   the decision to withdraw active treatment where it proved necessary
   was one which had received the support of the medical staff, nurses
   and other carers. This is an important recognition of the fact that
   many health care decisions are made in "teams" composed of a wide
   variety of personnel including persons other than medical practitioners. But should such a decision be left to the treatment team? One
   option is for such decisions to be referred to an institutional ethics
   committee. (See R. Weir, *Selective Non-Treatment of Severely
   Damaged Neonates,* Oxford: OUP, 1979.) Contrast this with the
   judgment of Lord Mustill in *Bland,* below at page 851.

QUESTION:

1. What amounts to treatment which is in the best interests of the child?
   Is the test subjective or objective? (See C. Wells *et al.,* "An unsuitable
   case for treatment" [1990] *New L.J.* 1544.)

Re J [1990] 3 All E.R. 930; [1991] Fam. 33.

J was born nearly 13 weeks premature weighing only 1.1kg. He was not
breathing, and was immediately placed on a ventilator to assist survival. He
was drip fed, and given antibiotics to counteract infection. At four weeks J
was removed from the ventilator but, on several occasions relapses
occurred and further use of the ventilator was necessary. The medical
evidence showed that J was very severely brain damaged, apparently blind
and probably deaf. It was likely that he would be paralysed in all his limbs.
It appeared that, while he would be unable to communicate or understand
what was happening to him, he would experience pain. The judge at first
instance held that if J were to stop breathing he should not be reventilated.

LORD DONALDSON OF LYMINGTON M.R.:
" . . . The Official Solicitor submits that there are two justifications for an appeal.
(i) *Re C (a minor) (wardship: medical treatment)* [1989] 2 All E.R. 782 gives
guidance on the approach which it is appropriate to adopt in relation to the medical
treatment of children who are dying and whose deaths can only be postponed for a
short while, *Re B (a minor) (wardship: medical treatment)* (1981) [1990] 3 All E.R.
927, gives similar guidance in relation to severly but not grossly handicapped
children with a shortened, but nevertheless substantial expectation of life. In the
Official Solicitor's view, the present case illustrates a different category falling

between these two on which guidance should be given. (ii) Whilst Scott Baker rightly directed himself that he must act in what he considered to be the best interests of the child, in the Official Solicitor's submission he erred in that a court is never justified in withholding consent to treatment which could enable a child to survive a life threatening condition, whatever the quality of life which it would experience thereafter. This is the absolutist approach. Alternatively, he submits that the judge erred in that a court is only justified in withholding consent to such treatment if it is certain that the quality of the child's subsequent life would be 'intolerable' to the child, 'bound to be full of pain and suffering' and 'demonstrably . . . so awful' that in effect the child must be condemned to die (see *Re B* [1990] 3 All E.R. 927 at 929, 930 per Dunn and Templeman L.J.). In this case, in the Official Solicitor's submission, this has not been shown . . .

Against this background I return to the submissions of counsel for the Official Solicitor. His first, or absolutist, submission is that a court is never justified in withholding consent to treatment which could enable a child to survive a life threatening condition, 'what'er the pain or other side effects inherent in the treatment and whatever the quality of the life which it would experience thereafter. In making this submission, he distinguishes a case such as that of *Re C (A Minor) (Wardship: Medical Treatment)* [1989] 2 All E.R. 782, where the child was dying and no amount of medical skill or care could do more than achieve a brief postponement of the moment of death. He submits, rightly, that in such a case neither the parents nor the court, in deciding whether to give or to withhold consent, nor the doctors in deciding what treatment they recommend or would be prepared to administer, are balancing life against death. In such a case death is inevitable, not in the sense that it is inevitable for all of us, but in the sense that the child is actually dying. What is being balanced is not life against death, but a marginally longer life of pain against a marginally shorter life free from pain and ending in death with dignity. He also distinguished and excepted from his proposition the case of the child whose faculties have been entirely destroyed, the so-called 'cabbage' case.

In support of this submission counsel for the Official Solicitor draws attention to the decision of this court in *McKay v. Essex Area Health Authority* [1982] 2 All E.R. 771. There a child suffered severe and irreversible damage before birth, as a result of her mother contracting rubella (German measles). She sued the health authority claiming damages under two heads. First, she claimed that if her mother had received appropriate treatment her disabilities would have been less. She therefore claimed damages based on the difference between the quality of her life as it was and the quality of life which she would have enjoyed if her mother had received that treatment. That claim was allowed to proceed. However, the child also claimed damages on a different basis. This was founded on the proposition that her mother should have been advised to seek an abortion and that, if this advice had been given and accepted, she would never have been born at all. The damages claimed under this head were necessarily based on a comparison between her actual condition and her condition if, as a result of an abortion, she had never been born at all.

This court struck out the second claim as disclosing no cause of action and it is on the reasoning which underlay this decision that counsel for the Official Solicitor relies. Stephenson L.J. said ([1982] 2 All E.R. 771 at 781):

'To impose such a duty towards the child (to give the child's mother an opportunity to terminate the child's life) would, in my opinion, make a further inroad on the sanctity of human life which would be contrary to public policy. It would mean regarding the life of a handicapped child as not only less valuable than the life of a normal child, but so much less valuable that it was not worth preserving . . .'

Later he said [1982] 2 All E.R. 771 at 781–782:

'But how can a court of law evaluate that second condition [where "the child's embryonic life has been ended before its life in the world had begun"] and so measure the loss to the child? Even if a court were competent to decide between the conflicting views of theologians and philosophers and to assume an "after-life" or non-existence as the basis for the comparison, how can a judge put a value on the one or the other, compare either alternative with the injured child's life in this world and determine that the child has lost anything, without the means of knowing what, if anything, it has gained?'

Ackner L.J. said [1982] 2 All E.R. 771 at 787,):

'But how can a court begin to evaluate non-existence,"This undiscovered country from whose bourn no traveller returns?" No comparison is possible and therefore no damage can be established which a court could recognise. This goes to the root of the whole cause of action.'

Similarly, Griffiths L.J. said: [1982] 2 All E.R. 771 at 790.

'To my mind, the most compelling reason to reject this cause of action is the intolerable and insoluble problem it would create in the assessment of damage.'

I do not regard this decision as providing us with either guidance or assistance in the context of the present problem. The child was claiming damages and the decision was that no monetary comparison could be made between the two states. True it is that it contains an assertion of the importance of the sanctity of human life, but that is not in issue.

Counsel for the Official Solicitor then turns to the decision of the Supreme Court of British Columbia in *Re Superintendent of Family and Child Service and Dawson* (1983) 145 DLR (3d) 610, which is also reported and referred to in *Re C. sub nom Re SD* [1983] 3 WWR 618. There the issue was whether a severely brain damaged child should be subjected to a relatively simple kind of surgical treatment which would assure the continuation of his life or whether, as the parents considered was in the child's best interests, consent to the operation should be refused with a view to the child being allowed to die in the near future with dignity rather than to continue a life of suffering. Counsel for the Official Solicitor relies on the first paragraph of the judgment of McKenzie J., but I think that paragraph read in isolation is capable of being misleading. The full quotation is (145 DLR (3d) 610 at 620–621):

'I do not think that it lies within the prerogative of any parent or of this court to look down upon a disadvantaged person and judge the quality of that person's life to be so low as not to be deserving of continuance. The matter was well put in an American decision *Re Weberlist* ((1974) 360 NYS 2d 783 at 787), where Justice Asch said: "There is a strident cry in America to terminate the lives of *other* people — deemed physically or mentally defective . . . Assuredly, one test of a civilization is its concern with the survival of the 'unfittest', a reversal of Darwin's formulation . . . In this case, the court must decide what its ward would choose, if he were in a position to make a sound judgment." This last sentence puts it right. It is not appropriate for an external decision maker to apply his standards of what constitutes a liveable life and exercise the right to impose death if that standard is not met in his estimation. The decision can only be made in the context of the disabled person viewing the worthwhileness or otherwise of his life in its own context as a disabled person-and in that context he would not compare his life with that of a person enjoying normal advantages. He would know nothing of a normal person's life having never experienced it.'

I am in complete agreement with McKenzie J. that the starting point is not what might have been, but what is. He was considering the best interests of a severely handicapped child, not of a normal child, and the latter's feelings and interests were irrelevant. I am also in complete agreement with his implied assertion of the vast importance of the sanctity of human life. I cavil mildly, although it is a very important point, with his use of the phrase 'the right to impose death'. No such right exists in the court or the parents. What is in issue in these cases is not a right to impose death, but a right to choose a course of action which will fail to avert death. The choice is that of the patient, if of full age and capacity, the choice is that of the parents or court if, by reason of his age, the child cannot make the choice and it is a choice which must be made solely *on behalf of* the child and in what the court or parents conscientiously believe to be his best interests.

In my view the last sentence of the passage which I have quoted from the judge's judgment shows that he was rejecting a particular comparison as a basis for decision rather than denying that there was a balancing exercise to be performed. I do not therefore think that this decision supports the absolutist approach which I would in any event unhesitatingly reject. In real life there are presumptions, strong presumptions and almost overwhelming presumptions, but there are few, if any, absolutes.

I turn, therefore, to the alternative submission of counsel for the Official Solicitor that a court is only justified in withholding consent to treatment which could enable a child to survive a life-threatening condition if it is certain that the quality of the child's subsequent life would be 'intolerable to the child', 'bound to be full of pain and suffering and 'demonstrably so awful that in effect the child must be condemned to die'. As I have already mentioned, this submission owes much to the decision of this court in *Re B* (1981) [1990] 3 All E.R. 927."

The judge referred to the judgments of Templeman J. and Dunn L.J. in that case and then said:

"Again I have to cavil at the use of such an expression as 'condemn to die' and 'the child must live' in Templeman L.J.'s judgment, which, be it noted, was not a reserved judgment. 'Thou shalt not kill' is an absolute commandment in this context. But, to quote the well-known phrase of Arthur Hugh Clough in *The Latest Decalogue*, in this context it is permissible to add 'but need'st not strive officiously to keep alive', The decision on life and death must and does remain in other hands. What doctors and the court have to decide is whether, in the best interests of the child patient, a particular decision as to medical treatment should be taken which as a *side effect* will render death more or less likely. This is not a matter of semantics. It is fundamental. At the other end of the age spectrum, the use of drugs to reduce pain will often be fully justified, notwithstanding that this will hasten the moment of death. What can never be justified is the use of drugs or surgical procedures with the primary purpose of doing so.

Re B seems to me to come very near to being a binding authority for the proposition that there is a balancing exercise to be performed in assessing the course to be adopted in the best interests of the child. Even if it is not, I have no doubt that this should be and is the law.

This brings me face to face with the problem of formulating the critical equation. In truth it cannot be done with mathematical or any precision. There is without doubt a very strong presumption in favour of a course of action which will prolong life, but, even excepting the 'cabbage' case to which special considerations may well apply, it is not irrebuttable. As this court recognised in *Re B* account has to be taken of the pain and suffering and quality of life which the child will experience if life is prolonged. Account has also to be taken of the pain and suffering involved in the proposed treatment itself. *Re B* was probably not a borderline case and I do not think that we are bound to, or should, treat Templeman L.J.'s use of the words 'demonstrably so awful' or Dunn L.J.'s use of the word 'intolerable' as providing a quasi-statutory yardstick.

For my part I prefer the formulation of Asch J. in *Re Weberlist* (1974) 360 NYS 2d 783 at 787 as explained by McKenzie J. in the passage from his judgment in Dawson's case (1983) 145 DLR (3d) 610 at 620–621 which I have quoted, although it is probably merely another way of expressing the same concept. We know that the instinct and desire for survival is very strong. We all believe in and assert the sanctity of human life. As explained, this formulation takes account of this and also underlines the need to avoid looking at the problem from the point of view of the decider, but instead requires him to look at it from the assumed point of view of the patient. This gives effect, as it should, to the fact that even very severely handicapped people find a quality of life rewarding which to the unhandicapped may seem manifestly intolerable. People have an amazing adaptability. But in the end there will be cases in which the answer must be that it is not in the interests of the child to subject it to treatment which will cause increased suffering and produce no commensurate benefit, giving the fullest possible weight to the child's, and mankind's, desire to survive . . .

The issue here is whether it would be in the best interests of the child, to put him on a mechanical ventilator and subject him to all the associated processes of intensive care, if at some future time he could not continue breathing unaided. Let me say at once that I can understand the doctors wishing to ascertain the court's wishes at this stage, because it is an eventuality which could occur at any time and, if it did, an immediate decision might well have to be made. However, the situation is significantly different from being asked whether or not to consent on behalf of the child to particular treatment which is more or less immediately in prospect. The judge has found that the odds are about even whether the need for artificial ventilation, whether mechanical or manual, will ever arise. If it does arise, the very fact that it has arisen will mean that the more optimistic end of the range of prognoses, pessimistic though the whole range is, will have been falsified. On the other hand, the child's state of health might change at any time for the better as well as for the worse, even though there are distinct limits to what could be hoped for, let alone anticipated.

The doctors were unanimous in recommending that there should be no mechanical reventilation in the event of his stopping breathing, subject only to the qualifications injected by Dr W and accepted by the judge that in the event of a chest infection short term manual ventilation would be justified and that in the event of the child stopping breathing the provisional decision to abstain from mechanical ventilation could and should be revised, if this seemed appropriate to the doctors caring for him in the then prevailing clinical situation.

There can be no criticism of the judge for indorsing this approach on the footing that he was thereby abdicating his responsibility and leaving it to the doctors to decide. He had reviewed and considered the basis of the doctors' views and recommendations in the greatest detail and with the greatest care. Nothing could be more inimical to the interests of the child than the judge should make an order which restricted the doctors' freedom to revise their present view in favour of more active means to preserve the life of the child, if the situation changed and this then seemed to them to be appropriate.

The basis of the doctors' recommendations, approved by the judge, was that mechanical ventilation is itself an invasive procedure which, together with its essential accompaniments, such as the introduction of a nasogastric tube, drips which have to be resited and constant blood sampling, would cause the child distress. Furthermore, the procedures involve taking active measures which carry their own hazards, not only to life but in terms of causing even greater brain damage. This had to be balanced against what could possibly be achieved by the adoption of such active treatment. The chances of preserving the child's life might be improved, although even this was not certain and account had to be taken of the extremely poor quality of life at present enjoyed by the child, the fact that he had already been ventilated for exceptionally long periods, the unfavourable prognosis with or without ventilation and a recognition that if the question of reventilation ever arose, his situation would have deteriorated still further.

I can detect no error in the judge's approach and in principle would affirm his decision. This is subject to two qualifications. (i) Although all concerned have, as they know, liberty to apply to the judge at any time and he had arranged to review his decision in December, I think that he should have asked for periodic reports meanwhile on J's condition, so that he could, if he thought it appropriate, review the matter before then of his own motion. (ii) I do not think that his order should have been in the form of 'The [local authority] shall direct the relevant health authority to continue to treat' because neither the court in wardship proceedings nor, I think, a local authority having care and control of the baby is able to require the authority to follow a particular course of treatment. What the court can do is to withhold consent to treatment of which it disapproves and it can express its approval of other treatment proposed by the authority and its doctors. There is ample precedent for the judge's formula, but I think that it is wrong and obscures the cooperative nature of the relationship between court and medical authorities. I would prefer 'Approval is given to this continuance of the treatment of . . .'

Subject to the minor variations in his order which I propose, I would dismiss the appeal."

TAYLOR L.J.:

" . . . The plight of baby J is appalling and the problem facing the court in the exercise of its wardship jurisdiction is of the greatest difficulty. When should the court rule against the giving of treatment aimed at prolonging life?

Three preliminary principles are not in dispute. First, it is settled law that the court's prime and paramount consideration must be the best interests of the child. That is easily said but not easily applied. What it does involve is that the views of the parents, although they should be heeded and weighed, cannot prevail over the court's view of the ward's best interests. In the present case the parents, finding themselves in a hideous dilemma, have not taken a strong view so that no conflict arises.

Second, the court's high respect for the sanctity of human life imposes a strong presumption in favour of taking all steps capable of preserving it, save in exceptional circumstances. The problem is to define those circumstances.

Third, and as a corollary to the second principle, it cannot be too strongly emphasised that the court never sanctions steps to terminate life. That would be unlawful. There is no question of approving, even in a case of the most horrendous disability, a course aimed at terminating life or accelerating death. The court is concerned only with the circumstances in which steps should not be taken to prolong life . . . "

The judge referred to *Re C* and to the dicta of Templeman L.J. in *Re B* and to the statements of the Court of Appeal in *McKay v. Essex Area Health Authority* and then continued.

" . . . Despite the court's inability to compare a life afflicted by the most severe disability with death, the unknown, I am of the view that there must be extreme cases in which the court is entitled to say: 'The life which this treatment would prolong would be so cruel as to be intolerable.' If, for example, a child was so damaged as to have negligible use of its faculties and the only way of preserving its life was by the continuous administration of extremely painful treatment such that the child either would be in a continuous agony or would have to be so sedated continuously as to have no conscious life at all, I cannot think counsel's absolute test should apply to require the treatment to be given. In those circumstances, without there being any question of deliberately ending the life or shortening it, I consider the court is entitled in the best interests of the child to say that deliberate steps should not be taken artificially to prolong its miserable lifespan.

Once the absolute test is rejected, the proper criteria must be a matter of degree. At what point in the scale of disability and suffering ought the court to hold that the best interests of the child do not require further endurance to be imposed by positive treatment to prolong its life? Clearly, to justify withholding treatment, the circumstances would have to be extreme. Counsel for the Official Solicitor submitted that if the court rejected his absolute test, then at least it would have 'to be certain that the life of the child, were the treatment to be given, would be intolerably awful'.

I consider that the correct approach is for the court to judge the quality of life the child would have to endure if given the treatment and decide whether in all the circumstance such a life would be so afflicted as to be intolerable to that child. I say 'to that child' because the test should not be whether the life would be tolerable to the decider. The test must be whether the child in question, if capable of exercising sound judgment, would consider the life tolerable. This is the approach adopted by McKenzie J. in *Re Superintendent of Family and Child Service and Dawson* (1983) 145 DLR (3d) 610 at 620–621 in the passage cited with approval by Lord Donaldson MR. It takes account of the strong instinct to preserve one's life even in circumstances which an outsider, not himself at risk of death, might consider unacceptable. The circumstances to be considered would, in appropriate cases, include the degree of existing disability and any additional suffering or aggravation of the disability which the treatment itself would superimpose. In an accident case, as opposed to one involving disablement from birth, the child's pre-accident quality of life and its perception of what has been lost may also be factors relevant to whether the residual life would be intolerable to that child.

Counsel for the Official Solicitor argued that, before deciding against treatment, the court would have to be *certain* that the circumstances of the child's future would comply with the extreme requirements to justify that decision. Certainly as to the future is beyond human judgment. The courts have not, even in the trial of capital offences required certainty of proof. But, clearly the court must be satisfied to a high degree of probability.

In the present case the doctors were unanimous that in his present condition J should not be put back onto a mechanical ventilator. That condition is very grave indeed. I do not repeat the description given of it by Lord Donaldson M.R. In reaching his conclusion, the judge no doubt had three factors in mind. First, the severe lack of capacity of the child in all his faculties which even without any further complication would make his existence barely sentient. Second, that, if further mechanical ventilation were to be required, that very fact would involve the risk of a deterioration in B's condition, because of further brain damage flowing from the interruption of breathing. Third, all the doctors drew attention to the invasive nature of mechanical ventilation and the intensive care required to accompany it. They stressed the unpleasant and distressing nature of that treatment. To add such distress and the risk of further deterioration to an already appalling catalogue of disabilities was clearly capable in my judgment of producing a quality of life which justified the stance of the doctors and the judge's conclusion."

NOTES:

1. The court in this case appeared to support a "substituted" judgment test when considering authorisation of non-treatment. However the use of such a test is fraught with its own difficulties, particularly in the case of infants where the court will not have any previously expressed views. It is perhaps instructive that the substituted judgments test was rejected by the Law Commission in considering the basis on which the mentally incompetent patient should be given treatment. (Law Commission, *Mental Incapacity,* Law Com. No. 231. London: HMSO, 1995, and see Chapter 3, *supra.*)

2. In *Re J* the court made reference to the invasive nature of continued therapy.

QUESTION:

1. *Re J* differs from *Re C* in that the evidence stated that C was dying. How far is it open to the court to sanction non – intervention in relation to a condition which if left untreated, is life threatening, but would not automatically lead to the death of the patient? (See R. Thornton, "Wardship – Witholding Medical Treatment" [1991] *Cambridge Law Journal* 238.)

The issue of treatment of a damaged infant was raised in the later case of:

Re J [1992] 4 All E.R. 614

J was 16 months old. He was severely handicapped having hit his head after an accidental fall when only one month old. He suffered from cerebral palsy, severe epilepsy and was largely fed by a naso-gastric tube. Medical opinion was that he was unlikely to develop beyond his present level of functioning. The local authority had placed him with foster parents. They sought an order to determine whether life-saving measures should be given to J if he suffered a life threatening event. At first instance the judge made an interim order granting an injunction requiring the health authority to use intensive therapeutic measures (including artificial ventilation) for so long as such measures were capable of prolonging his life. The Health Authority supported by the Official Solicitor acting as guardian *ad litem,* and the local authority (which had changed its views) appealed against the order. The child's natural mother supported the continuation of treatment.

LORD DONALDSON M.R.:
" . . . The fundamental issue in this appeal is whether the court in the exercise of its inherent power to protect the interests of minors should ever require a medical practitioner or health authority acting by a medical practitioner to adopt a course of treatment which in the bona fide clinical judgement of the practitioner concerned is contra indicated as not being in the best interests of the patient. I have to say that I cannot at present conceive of any circumstances in which this would be other than an abuse of power as directly or indirectly requiring the practitioner to act contrary to the fundamental duty which he owes to his patient. This, subject to obtaining any necessary consents is to treat the patient in accordance with his best clinical judgment, notwithstanding that other practitioners who are not called upon to treat the patient may have formed a quite different judgment or that the court, acting on expert evidence, may disagree with him.
    It is said that the views which I expressed in my judgments in *Re J (A Minor)* [1990] 3 All E.R. 930 and *Re R (A Minor)* [1991] 4 All E.R. 177, which are relevant to this were obiter and did not receive the express assent of those sitting with me. So be it but, remaining as I am of the view that they were a correct expression of the law, I repeat them as part of the *ratio* of my decision in this case. From *Re J* [1990] 3 All E.R. 930 at 934.
    'No one can *dictate* the treatment to be given to the child, neither court, parents or doctors. There are checks and balances. The doctors can recommend treatment A in preference to treatment B. They can also refuse to adopt

treatment C on the grounds that it is medically contra-indicated or for some other reason is a treatment which they could not conscientiously administer. The court or parents for their part can refuse to consent to treatment A or B or both but cannot insist on treatment C. The inevitable and desirable result is that the choice of treatment is in some measure a joint decision of the doctors and the court or parents. This co-operation is reinforced by another consideration. Doctors nowadays recognise that their function is not a limited technical one of repairing or servicing a body. They are treating real people in a real life context. This at once enhances the contribution which the court or parents can make towards reaching the best possible decision in all the circumstances.' (My original emphasis.)

From *Re R* [1991] 4 All E.R. 177 at page 184:

'It is trite law that in general a doctor is not entitled to treat a patient without the consent of someone who is authorised to give that consent . . . However consent by itself creates no obligation to treat. It is merely a key which unlocks a door . . . No. doctor can be required to treat a child, whether by the court in the exercise of its wardship jurisdiction, by the parents, or by anyone else. The decision whether to treat is dependent upon an exercise of his own professional judgment, subject only to the threshold requirement that, save in exceptional cases usually of emergency, he has the consent of someone who is authorised to give that consent.'

The order of Waite J. was wholly inconsistent with the law as so stated and cannot be justified on the basis of any authority known to me. Furthermore it was, in my judgement, erroneous on two other substantive grounds, only slightly less fundamental than that to which I have just averted. The first is its lack of certainty as to what was required of the health authority. The second is that it does not adequately take account of the sad fact of life that health authorities may on occasion find that they have too few resources, either human or material or both, to treat all patients whom they would like to treat in the way in which they would like to treat them. It is then their duty to make choices.

The court when considering what course to adopt in relation to a particular child has no knowledge of competing claims to a health authority's resources and is in no position to express any view as to how it should elect to deploy them. Although the order is subject to the condition precedent that the required drugs and equipment are or could reasonably have been made available it makes no reference to the availability of staff and it has to be born in mind that artificial ventilation of a young child in an intensive care unit is highly intensive of highly skilled staff. It gives no guidance as to what is meant by the concept of being reasonably available, yet it is not difficult to imagine circumstances in which there could be bona fide differences of opinion as to whether equipment or staff was reasonably available. The health authority is entitled to object and does object to being subject to an order of the court with penal consequences in the event of disobedience when it does not know precisely what is required of it.

There remains the very real problem of what is to happen if it appears that Professor B or some other suitably qualified practitioner was willing should the need arise to subject J to mechanical ventilation and had the facilities for doing so. What should then happen would depend upon a number of considerations upon which I am in no position to speculate or express a view. The local authority exercising parental responsibility would certainly have to consider very carefully whether it accepted that practitioners' advice and any advice as to the risks of the transfer of J from one hospital to another before giving its consent to such different treatment. So too would the parents and, in the event of a difference of opinion, the local authority would have to consider whether or not to exercise its powers under section 33(b) of the Children Act 1989. The health authority would have a legitimate interest in the decision in the light of its currrent responsibilities towards J and towards other patients for whose care its necessarily limited resources have to be used. I would hope that each would adopt an understanding attitude towards the other's problems in circumstances in which the checks and balances of consent and willingness and ability to treat of which I spoke in *Re J (a minor) (Wardship: Medical Treatment)* [1990] 3 All E.R. 930 could come under considerable strain.

In announcing the decision of the court at the conclusion of the argument stressed and I repeat that the effect of setting aside the order leaves the health authority and its medical staff free subject to consent not being withdrawn to treat J in accordance with their best clinical judgment. This does not mean that we thought and still less required that in no circumstances should J be subjected to mechanical ventilation. The view expressed by Dr I in April 1992 that this should not happen was supported by independent medical opinion, but I have no doubt that all the doctors concerned would agree that situations can change and that if and when a decision whether or not to use mechanical ventilation has been taken it must be taken in the light of the situation as it then exists. That is what clinical judgment is all about. What we were saying is that so long as those with parental responsibilities consent to J being treated by the medical staff of the health authority, he must be treated in accordance with their clinical judgment."

BALCOMBE L.J.:
" . . . I can conceive of no situation where it would be a proper exercise of the (inherent) jurisdiction to make such an order as was made in the present case; that is to order a doctor whether directly or indirectly to treat a child in a manner contrary to his or her clinical judgment. I would go further, I find it difficult to conceive of a situation where it would be a proper exercise of the jurisdiction to make an order positively requiring a doctor to adopt a particular course of treatment in relation to a child unless the doctor himself or herself was asking the court to make such an order. Usually all the court is asked or needs to do is to authorise a particular course of treatment where the person or body whose consent is required is unable or unwilling to do so."

He went on to say that he supported the judgment of Lord Donaldson M.R. in *Re R* and *Re J* and then continued . . .

"The court is not or certainly should not be in the habit of making orders unless it is prepared to enforce them. If the court orders a doctor to treat a child in a manner contrary to his or her clinical judgment it would place a conscientious doctor in an impossible position. To perform the courts order could require a doctor to act in a manner which he genuinely believed not to be in the patient's best interests; to fail to treat the child as ordered would amount to a contempt of court. Any judge would be most reluctant to punish the doctor for such a contempt, which seemed to me to be a very strong indication that such an order could not be made.

I would also stress the absolute undesirability of the court making an order which may have the effect of compelling a doctor or health authority to make available scarce resources (both human and material) to a particular child without knowing whether or not there are other patients to whom those resources might more advantageously be devoted. Lord Donaldson M.R. has set out in his reasons the condition of J and his very limited future prospects. The effect of the order of Waite J. had it not been immediately stayed by this court might have been to require the health authority to put J on a ventilator in an intensive care until and possibly to deny those limited resources to a child who was much more likely than J to benefit from them. At the very least it would in those circumstances have required the health authority to make a further application to the court to vary or discharge the injunction . . . "

LEGATT L.J.:
". . . For present purposes it does not matter whether the court has no power to order specific treatment to be given contrary to the doctor's will or has power but

will in practice not exercise it in such circumstances. Before Waite J. the doctors were unanimous that mechanical ventilation should not be provided if the occasion for it arose. Now Professor B would be prepared to provide it. But the essential distinction remains: whether the court should positively order treatment to be given or whether it should do no more than consider whether or not to authorise it, where authority is needed. I can myself envisage no circumstances in which it would be right directly or indirectly to require a doctor to treat in a way that was contrary to the doctor's professional judgment and duty to the patient.

A court can give or withold a consent or authority such as might be given or withheld by a patient or a child's parent. But no reported case has been cited to the court in which any judge in any jurisdiction has ever purported to order a doctor to treat a patient in a particular way contrary to that doctor's will until Waite J. made the order in the present case. The order which he in fact made was against the health authority requiring it to ('cause such (including if so required to prolong his life'). That was an order with which it was probably impossible for the health authority to comply, because it had no power contractual or otherwise to require doctors to act in a way which they do not regard as medically appropriate. If it could comply it would be obliged to accord to this priority over others to patients to whom the health authority owes the same duties, but about whose interests the court is ignorant."

NOTES:

1. The court recognised that it may not always be in the patient's best interests for aggressive therapy to be pursued. This approach was followed in the later case of *Airedale NHS Trust v. Bland* [1993] 1 All E.R. 521. (Note that the court also ordered that treatment be discontinued in the face of opposition from J's mother.)
2. Judicial unwillingness to make statements in relation to medical resources is inconsistent with other cases involving resource allocation (See Chapter 1 at pages 47–60.)

QUESTIONS:

1. Is it ever possible to judge whether an individual has an adequate quality of life? In any event, should quality of life be the standard that is used when determining whether treatment should be withdrawn? (See Chapter 2 above at pages 99–101.)
2. Do you agree that a court should never compel a doctor to administer a particular type of treatment?

(b) Withdrawal of treatment from adult patients

The cases which concern non-treatment of the handicapped infant now need to be read in the light of the approach taken by the courts to applications for orders in relation to withdrawal of treatment from the incompetent adult patient. Particular difficulties may arise in relation to adult patients in a persistent vegetative state, who have no prospect of recovery and who are supported through artificial nutrition and hydration. (For further discussion as to the meaning of persistent vegetative state see

Chapter 15 below.) The leading case on this issue of the House of Lords in *Airedale NHS Trust v. Bland*: The reader is encouraged to examine the law reports.

Airedale NHS Trust v. Bland [1993] 1 All E.R. 521; [1993] A.C. 879

Tony Bland was a spectator at the Hillsborough football ground in April 1989. He suffered a severely crushed chest during a stampede of spectators and this gave rise to hypoxic brain damage. He entered a persistent vegetative state. He remained in this state and showed no signs of recovery. He was fed through a naso-gastric tube. The hospital, the Airedale NHS Trust, which was caring for him, sought a declaration authorising the discontinuation of all life sustaining treatment and medical support mechanisms. Sir Stephen Brown in granting the declaration said that it was in the patient's best interests that the feeding regime be withdrawn. He said that while Mr Bland's life would come to an end as a consequence, the true cause of death was the injuries suffered at Hillsborough. In the Court of Appeal the appeal of the Official Solicitor was dismissed. There was an appeal to the House of Lords. The judgments in the House of Lords in *Bland* present a rich analysis of the problems in relating to withdrawal of treatment. Here the extracts are largely drawn from the judgment of Lord Goff which can be regarded as the leading judgment in the case.

LORD GOFF OF CHIEVELEY:
" . . . The central issue in the present case has been aptly stated by Sir Thomas Bingham M.R. to be whether artificial feeding and antibiotic drugs may lawfully be withheld from an insensate patient with no hope of recovery when it is known that if that is done the patient will shortly thereafter die. The Court of Appeal, like Sir Stephen Brown P., answered this question generally in the affirmative, and (in the declarations made or approved by them) specifically also in the affirmative in relation to Anthony Bland. I find myself to be in agreement with the conclusions so reached by all the judges below, substantially for the reasons given by them. But the matter is of such importance that I propose to express my reasons in my own words.
      I start with the simple fact that, in law, Anthony is still alive. It is true that his condition is such that it can be described as a living death; but he is nevertheless still alive. This is because, as a result of developments in modern medical technology, doctors no longer associate death exclusively with breathing and heart beat, and it has come to be accepted that death occurs when the brain, and in particular the brain stem, has been destroyed (see Professor Ian Kennedy's Paper entitled 'Switching off Life Support Machines: The Legal Implications,' reprinted in *Treat Me Right, Essays in Medical Law and Ethics* (1988), esp. at 351–352, and the material there cited). There has been no dispute on this point in the present case, and it is unnecessary for me to consider it further. The evidence is that Anthony's brain stem is still alive and functioning and it follows that, in the present state of medical science, he is still alive and should be so regarded as a matter of law.
      It is on this basis that I turn to the applicable principles of law. Here, the fundamental principle is the principle of the sanctity of human life — a principle long recognised not only in our own society but also in most, if not all, civilised societies throughout the modern world, as is indeed evidenced by its recognition both in art. 2 of the European Convention for the Protection of Human Rights and

Fundamental Freedoms (1953) (Cmd 8969), and in art. 6 of the International Covenant of Civil and Political Rights 1966 (New York 19 December 1966, TS 6 (1977) Cmnd. 6702).

But this principle, fundamental though it is, is not absolute. Indeed there are circumstances in which it is lawful to take another man's life, for example by a lawful act of self-defence, or (in the days when capital punishment was acceptable in our society) by lawful execution. We are not however concerned with cases such as these. We are concerned with circumstances in which it may be lawful to withhold from a patient medical treatment or care by means of which his life may be prolonged. But here too there is no absolute rule that the patient's life must be prolonged by such treatment or care, if available, regardless of the circumstances.

First, it is established that the principle of self-determination requires that respect must be given to the wishes of the patient, so that if an adult patient of sound mind refuses, however unreasonably, to consent to treatment or care by which his life would or might be prolonged, the doctors responsible for his care must give effect to his wishes, even though they do not consider it to be in his best interests to do so (see *Schloendorf v. Society of New York Hospital* (1914) 211 N.Y. 125 at 129-30, *per* Cardozo J.; *S v. S; W. v. Official Solicitor* [1970] 3 All E.R. 107 at 111, *per* Lord Reid; and *Sidaway v. Board of Governors of Bethlem Royal Hospital and the Maudsley Hospital* [1985]1 All E.R. 643 at 649, *per* Lord Scarman). To this extent, the principle of the sanctity of human life must yield to the principle of self-determination (see *ante,* pages p. 851 *ante,* per Hoffmann L.J.), and, for present purposes perhaps more important, the doctor's duty to act in the best interests of his patient must likewise be qualified. On this basis, it has been held that a patient of sound mind may, if properly informed, require that life support should be discontinued: see *Nancy v. Hotel Dieu de Quebec* (1992) 86 DLR (4th) 385. Moreover the same principle applies where the patient's refusal to give his consent has been expressed at an earlier date, before he became unconscious or otherwise incapable of communicating it; though in such circumstances especial care may be necessary to ensure that the prior refusal of consent is still properly to be regarded as applicable in the circumstances which have subsequently occurred: see, e.g., *Re T (Adult: refusal of medical treatment)* [1992] 4 All E.R. 649. I wish to add that, in cases of this kind, there is no question of the patient having committed suicide, nor therefore of the doctor having aided or abetted him in doing so. It is simply that the patient has, as he is entitled to do, declined to consent to treatment which might or would have the effect of prolonging his life, and the doctor has, in accordance with his duty, complied with his patient's wishes.

But in many cases not only may the patient be in no condition to be able to say whether or not he consents to the relevant treatment or care, but also he may have given no prior indication of his wishes with regard to it. In the case of a child who is a ward of court, the court itself will decide whether medical treatment should be provided in the child's best interests, taking into account medical opinion. But the court cannot give its consent on behalf of an adult patient who is incapable of himself deciding whether or not to consent to treatment. I am of the opinion that there is nevertheless no absolute obligation upon the doctor who has the patient in his care to prolong his life, regardless of the circumstances. Indeed, it would be most startling, and could lead to the most adverse and cruel effects upon the patient, if any such absolute rule were held to exist. It is scarcely consistent with the primacy given to the principle of self-determination in those cases in which the patient of sound mind has declined to give his consent that the law should provide no means of enabling treatment to be withheld in appropriate circumstances where the patient is in no condition to indicate, if that was his wish, that he did not consent to it. The point was put forcibly in the judgment of the Supreme Judicial Court of Massachusetts in *Superintendent of Belchertown State School v. Saikewicz* (1977) 373 Mass 728 at 747, as follows:

'To presume that the incompetent person must always be subjected to what many rational and intelligent persons may decline is to downgrade the status of the incompetent person by placing a lesser value on his intrinsic human worth and vitality.'

I must however stress, at this point, that the law draws a crucial distinction between cases in which a doctor decides not to provide, or to continue to provide, for his patient treatment or care which could or might prolong his life, and those in which he decides, for example by administering a lethal drug, actively to bring his patient's life to an end. As I have already indicated, the former may be lawful, either because the doctor is giving effect to his patient's wishes by withholding the treatment or care, or even in certain circumstances in which (on principles which I shall describe) the patient is incapacitated from stating whether or not he gives his consent. But it is not lawful for a doctor to administer a drug to his patient to bring about his death, even though that course is prompted by a humanitarian desire to end his suffering, however great that suffering may be: see *Reg v. Cox* (unreported, September 18, 1992, *per* Ogden J. in the Crown Court at Winchester). So to act is to cross the Rubicon which runs between on the one hand the care of the living patient and on the other hand euthanasia — actively causing his death to avoid or to end his suffering. Euthanasia is not lawful at common law. It is of course well known that there are many responsible members of our society who believe that euthanasia should be made lawful; but that result could, I believe, only be achieved by legislation which expresses the democratic will that so fundamental a change should be made in our law, and can, if enacted, ensure that such legalised killing can only be carried out subject to appropriate supervision and control. It is true that the drawing of this distinction may lead to a charge of hypocrisy; because it can be asked why, if the doctor, by discontinuing treatment, is entitled in consequence to let his patient die, it should not be lawful to put him out of his misery straight away, in a more humane manner, by a lethal injection, rather than let him linger on in pain until he dies. But the law does not feel able to authorise euthanasia, even in circumstances such as these; for once euthanasia is recognised as lawful in these circumstances, it is difficult to see any logical basis for excluding it in others.

At the heart of this distinction lies a theoretical question. Why is it that the doctor who gives his patient a lethal injection which kills him commits an unlawful act and indeed is guilty of murder, whereas a doctor who, by discontinuing life support, allows his patient to die, may not act unlawfully — and will not do so, if he commits no breach of duty to his patient? Professor Glanville Williams has suggested (see his *Textbook of Criminal Law* (2nd edn.), (1983), p. 282) that the reason is that what the doctor does when he switches off a life support machine 'is in substance not an act but an omission to struggle,' and that 'the omission is not a breach of duty by the doctor, because he is not obliged to continue in a hopeless case.'

I agree that the doctor's conduct in discontinuing life support can properly be categorised as an omission. It is true that it may be difficult to describe what the doctor actually does as an omission, for example where he takes some positive step to bring the life support to an end. But discontinuation of life support is, for present purpose, no different from not initiating life support in the first place. In each case, the doctor is simply allowing his patient to die in the sense that he is desisting from taking a step which might, in certain circumstances, prevent his patient from dying as a result of his pre-existing condition; and as a matter of general principle an omission such as this will not be unlawful unless it constitutes a breach of duty to the patient I also agree that the doctor's conduct is to be differentiated from that of, for example, an interloper who maliciously switches off a life support machine because, although the interloper may perform exactly the same act as the doctor who discontinues life support, his doing so constitutes interference with the life-prolonging treatment then being administered by the doctor. Accordingly, whereas the doctor, in discontinuing life support, is simply allowing his patient to die of his pre-existing condition, the interloper is actively intervening to stop the doctor from prolonging the patient's life, and such conduct cannot possibly be categorised as an omission.

The distinction appears, therefore, to be useful in the present context in that it can be invoked to explain how discontinuance of life support can be differentiated from ending a patient's life by a lethal injection. But in the end the reason for that difference is that, whereas the law considers that discontinuance of life support may be consistent with the doctor's duty to care for his patient, it does not, for reasons of policy, consider that it forms any part of his duty to give his patient a lethal injection to put him out of his agony.

I return to the patient who, because for example he is of unsound mind or has been rendered unconscious by accident or by illness, is incapable of stating whether or not he consents to treatment or care. In such circumstances, it is now established that a doctor may lawfully treat such a patient if he acts in his best interests, and indeed that, if the patient is already in his care, he is under a duty so to treat him: see *F v. West Berkshire Health Authority* [1989] 2 All E.R. 545, in which the legal principles governing treatment in such circumstances were stated by this House. For my part I can see no reason why, as a matter of principle, a decision by a doctor whether or not to initiate, or to continue to provide, treatment or care which could or might have the effect of prolonging such a patient's life, should not be governed by the same fundamental principle. Of course, in the great majority of cases, the best interests of the patient are likely to require that treatment of this kind, if available, should be given to a patient but this may not always be so. To take a simple example given by Thomas J. in the High Court of New Zealand in *Auckland Area Health Board v. Att.-Gen.* [1993] 1 NZLR 235 at 253, to whose judgment in that case I wish to pay tribute, it cannot be right that a doctor, who has under his care a patient suffering painfully from terminal cancer, should be under an absolute obligation to perform upon him major surgery to abate another condition which, if unabated, would or might shorten his life still further. The doctor who is caring for such a patient cannot, in my opinion, be under an absolute obligation to prolong his life by any means available to him, regardless of the quality of the patient's life. Common humanity requires otherwise, as do medical ethics and good medical practice accepted in this country and overseas. As I see it, the doctor's decision whether or not to take any such step must (subject to his patient's ability to give or withhold his consent) be made in the best interests of the patient. It is this principle too which, in my opinion, underlies the established rule that a doctor may, when caring for a patient who is, for example, dying of cancer, lawfully administer painkilling drugs despite the fact that he knows that an incidental effect of that application will be to abbreviate the patient's life. Such a decision may properly be made as part of the care of the living patient, in his best interests; and, on this basis, the treatment will be lawful. Moreover, where the doctor's treatment of his patient is lawful, the patient's death will be regarded in law as exclusively caused by the injury or disease to which his condition is attributable.

It is of course the development of modern medical technology, and in particular the development of life support systems, which has rendered cases such as the present so much more relevant than in the past. Even so, where (for example) a patient is brought into hospital in such a condition that, without the benefit of a life support system, he will not continue to live, the decision has to be made whether or not to give him that benefit, if available. That decision can only be made in the best interests of the patient. No doubt, his best interests will ordinarily require that he should be placed on a life support system as soon as necessary, if only to make an accurate assessment of his condition and a prognosis for the future. But if he neither recovers sufficiently to be taken off it nor dies, the question will ultimately arise whether he should be kept on it indefinitely. As I see it, that question (assuming the continued availability of the system) can only be answered by reference to the best interests of the patient himself, having regard to established medical practice. Indeed, if the justification for treating a patient who lacks the capacity to consent lies in the fact that the treatment is provided in his best interests, it must follow that the treatment may, and indeed ultimately should, be discontinued where it is no longer in his best interests to provide it. The question which lies at the heart of the present case is, as I see it, whether on that principle the doctors responsible for the treatment and care of Anthony Bland can justifiably discontinue the process of artificial feeding upon which the prolongation of his life depends.

It is crucial for the understanding of this question that the question itself should be correctly formulated. The question is not whether the doctor should take a course which will kill his patient, or even take a course which has the effect of accelerating his death. The question is whether the doctor should or should not continue to provide his patient with medical treatment or care which, if continued, will prolong his patient's life. The question is sometimes put in striking or emotional terms, which can be misleading. For example, in the case of a life support system, it is sometimes asked: should a doctor be entitled to switch it off, or to pull the plug? And then it is asked: can it be in the best interests of the patient that a doctor should be able to switch the life support system off, when this will inevitably result in the patient's death? Such an approach has rightly been criticised as misleading, for example by Professor Ian Kennedy in his paper in *Treat Me Right, Essays in Medical Law and Ethics*, (1988) and by Thomas J. in *Auckland Health Board v. Att.-Gen.* [1993] NZLR 235 at 247. This is because the question is not whether it is in the best interests of the patient that he should die. The question is whether it is in the best interests of the patient that his life should be prolonged by the continuance of this form of medical treatment or care.

The correct formulation of the question is of particular importance in a case such as the present, where the patient is totally unconscious and where there is no hope whatsoever of any amelioration of his condition. In circumstances such as these, it may be difficult to say that it is in his best interests that the treatment should be ended. But if the question is asked, as in my opinion it should be, whether it is in his best interests that treatment which has the effect of artificially prolonging his life should be continued, that question can sensibly be answered to the effect that it is not in his best interests to do so.

Even so, a distinction may be drawn between (I) cases in which, having regard to all the circumstances (including, for example, the intrusive nature of the treatment, the hazards involved in it, and the very poor quality of the life which may be prolonged for the patient if the treatment is successful), it may be judged not to be in the best interests of the patient to initiate or continue life-prolonging treatment, and (II) cases such as the present in which, so far as the living patient is concerned, the treatment is of no benefit to him because he is totally unconscious and there is no prospect of any improvement in his condition. In both classes of case, the decision whether or not to withhold treatment must be made in the best interests of the patient. In the first class, however, the decision has to be made by weighing the relevant considerations. For example, in *Re J (A Minor) Wardship: Medical Treatment)* [1990] 3 All E.R. 930 at 945, the approach to be adopted in that case was stated by Taylor L.J. as follows:

'I consider that the correct approach is for the court to judge the quality of life the child would have to endure if given the treatment and decide whether in all the circumstances such a life would be so afflicted as to be intolerable to that child.'

With this class of case, however, your Lordships are not directly concerned in the present case; and though I do not wish to be understood to be casting any doubt upon any of the reported cases on the subject, nevertheless I must record that argument was not directed specifically towards these cases, and for that reason I do not intend to express any opinion about the precise principles applicable in relation to them.

By contrast, in the latter class of case, of which the present case provides an example, there is in reality no weighing operation to be performed. Here the condition of the patient, who is totally unconscious and in whose condition there is no prospect of any improvement, is such that life-prolonging treatment is properly regarded as being, in medical terms, useless. As Sir Thomas Bingham M.R. pointed out, in the present case, medical treatment or care may be provided for a number of different purposes. It may be provided, for example, as an aid to diagnosis; for the treatment of physical or mental injury or illness; to alleviate pain or distress, or to make the patient's condition more tolerable. Such purpose may include prolonging the patient's life, for example, to enable him to survive during diagnosis and treatment. But for my part I cannot see that medical treatment is appropriate or requisite simply to prolong a patient's life, when such treatment has no therapeutic purpose of any kind, as where it is futile because the patient is unconscious and there is no prospect of any improvement in his condition. It is reasonable also that account should be taken of the invasiveness of the treatment and of the indignity to which, as the present case shows, a person has to be subjected if his life is prolonged by artificial means, which must cause considerable distress to his family — a distress which reflects not only their own feelings but their perception of the situation of their relative who is being kept alive. But in the end, in a case such as the present it is the futility of the treatment which justifies its termination. I do not consider that, in circumstances such as these, a doctor is required to initiate or to continue life-prolonging treatment or care in the best interests of his patient . . .

In *F v. West Berkshire Health Authority* [1989] 2 All E.R. 545 it was stated that, where a doctor provides treatment for a person who is incapacitated from saying whether or not he consents to it, the doctor must, when deciding on the form of treatment, act in accordance with a responsible and competent body of relevant professional opinion, on the principles set down in *Bolam v. Friern Hospital Management Committee* [1957] 2 All E.R. 118. In my opinion, this principle must equally be applicable to decisions to initiate, or to discontinue, life support, as it is to other forms of treatment. However, in a matter of such importance and sensitivity as discontinuance of life support, it is to be expected that guidance will be provided for the profession; and, on the evidence in the present case, such guidance is for a case such as the present to be found in a Discussion Paper on Treatment of Patients in Persistent Vegetative State, issued in September 1992 by the medical ethics committee of the British Medical Association. Anybody reading this substantial paper will discover for himself the great care with which this topic is being considered by the profession. Mr Francis, for the respondents, drew to the attention of the Appellate Committee four safeguards in particular which, in the committee's opinion, should be observed before discontinuing life support for such patients. They are: (1) every effort should be made at rehabilitation for at least six months after the injury; (2) the diagnosis of irreversible PVS should not be considered confirmed until at least 12 months after the injury, with the effect that any decision to withhold life-prolonging treatment will be delayed for that period; (3) the diagnosis should be agreed by two other independent doctors; and (4) generally, the wishes of the patient's immediate family will be given great weight.

In fact, the views expressed by the committee on the subject of consultation with the relatives of PVS patients are consistent with the opinion expressed by your Lordships' House in *F v. West Berkshire Health Authority* [1989] 2 All E.R. 545 that it is good practice for the doctor to consult relatives. Indeed the committee recognises that, in the case of PVS patients, the relatives themselves will require a high degree of support and attention. But the committee is firmly of the opinion that the relatives' views cannot be determinative of the treatment. Indeed, if that were not so, the relatives would be able to dictate to the doctors what is in the best interests of the patient, which cannot be right. Even so, a decision to withhold life-prolonging treatment, such as artificial feeding, must require close co-operation with those close to the patient; and it is recognised that, in practice, their views and the opinions of doctors will coincide in many cases.

Study of this document left me in no doubt that, if a doctor treating a PVS patient acts in accordance with the medical practice now being evolved by the Medical Ethics Committee of the BMA, he will be acting with the benefit of guidance from a responsible and competent body of relevant professional opinion, as required by the *Bolam* test. I also feel that those who are concerned that a matter of life and death, such as is involved in a decision to withhold life support in case of this kind, should be left to the doctors, would do well to study this paper. The truth is that, in the course of their work, doctors frequently have to make decisions which may affect the continued survival of their patients, and are in reality far more experienced in matters of this kind than are the judges. It is nevertheless the function of the judges to state the legal principles upon which the lawfulness of the actions of doctors depend; but in the end the decisions to be made in individual cases must rest with the doctors themselves. In these circumstances, what is required is a sensitive understanding by both the judges and the doctors of each other's respective functions, and in particular a determination by the judges not merely to understand the problems facing the medical profession in cases of this kind, but also to regard their professional standards with respect. Mutual understanding between the doctors and the judges is the best way to ensure the evolution of a sensitive and sensible legal framework for the treatment and care of patients, with a sound ethical base, in the interest of the patients themselves . . .

I wish however to refer at this stage to the approach adopted in most American courts, under which the court seeks, in a case in which the patient is incapacitated from expressing any view on the question whether life-prolonging treatment should be withheld in the relevant circumstances, to determine what decision the patient himself would have made had he been able to do so. This is called the substituted judgment test, and it generally involves a detailed inquiry into the patient's views and preferences: see, *e.g.* Re *Quinlan* (1976) 50 N.J. 10, and *Belchertown State School Superintendent v. Saikewicz* (1977) 373 Mass 728. In later cases concerned with PVS patients it has been held that, in the absence of clear and convincing evidence of the patient's wishes, the surrogate decision-maker has to implement as far as possible the decision which the incompetent patient would make if he was competent. However, accepting on this point the submission of Mr Lester, I do not consider that any such test forms part of English law in relation to incompetent adults, on whose behalf nobody has power to give consent to medical treatment. Certainly, in *F v. West Berkshire Health Authority* [1989] 3 All E.R. 545 your Lordships' House adopted a straightforward test based on the best interests of the patient; and I myself do not see why the same test should not be applied in the case of PVS patients, where the question is whether life-prolonging treatment should be withheld. This was also the opinion of Thomas J. in *Auckland Area Health Board v. A.G.* [1993] NZLR 235, unreported, August 13, 1992, a case concerned with the discontinuance of life support provided by ventilator to a patient suffering from the last stages of incurable Guillain-Barre syndrome. Of course, consistent with the best interests test, anything relevant to the application of the test may be taken into account; and if the personality of the patient is relevant to the application of the test (as it may be in cases where the various relevant factors have to be weighed), it may be taken into account, as was done in *Re J (A Minor) (Wardship: Medical Treatment)* [1990] 3 All E.R. 930. But, where the question is whether life support should be withheld from a PVS patient, it is difficult to see how the personality of the patient can be relevant, though it may be of comfort to his relatives if they believe, as in the present case, and indeed may well be so in many other cases, that the patient would not have wished his life to be artificially prolonged if he was totally unconscious and there was no hope of improvement in his condition.

I wish to add however that, like the courts below, I have derived assistance and support from decisions in a number of American jurisdictions to the effect that it is lawful to discontinue life-prolonging treatment in the case of PVS patients where there is no prospect of improvement in their condition. Furthermore, I wish to refer to the section in Working Paper No. 28 (1982) on Euthanasia, Aiding Suicide and Cessation of Treatment published by the Law Reform Commission of Canada concerned with cessation of treatment, to which I also wish to express my indebtedness. I believe the legal principles as I have stated them to be broadly consistent with the conclusions summarised at pages 65-66 of the Working Paper, which was substantially accepted in the Report of the Commission (1983), pages 32–35. Indeed, I entertain a strong sense that a community of view on the legal principles applicable in cases of discontinuing life support is in the course of development and acceptance throughout the common law world.

In setting out my understanding of the relevant principles, I have had very much in mind the submissions advanced by Mr Munby on behalf of the Official Solicitor, and I believe that I have answered, directly or indirectly, all his objections to the course now proposed. I do not, therefore, intend any disrespect to his argument if I do not answer each of his submissions seriatim. In summary, his two principal arguments were as follows. First, he submitted that the discontinuance of artificial feeding would constitute an act which would inevitably cause and be intended to cause, Anthony's death; and as such, it would be unlawful and indeed criminal. As will be plain from what I have already said, I cannot accept this proposition. In my opinion, for the reasons I have already given, there is no longer any duty upon the doctors to continue with this form of medical treatment or care in his case, and it follows that it cannot be unlawful to discontinue it. Second, he submitted that discontinuance of the artificial feeding of Anthony would be a breach of the doctor's duty to care for and feed him; and since it will (as it is intended to do) cause his death, it will necessarily be unlawful. I have considered this point earlier in this opinion, when I expressed my view that artificial feeding is, in a case such as the present, no different from life support by a ventilator, and as such can lawfully be discontinued when it no longer fulfils any therapeutic purpose. To me, the crucial point in which I found myself differing from Mr Munby was that I was unable to accept his treating the discontinuance of artificial feeding in the present case as equivalent to cutting a mountaineer's rope, or severing the air pipe of a deep sea diver. Once it is recognised, as I believe it must be, that the true question is not whether the doctor should take a course in which he will actively kill his patient, but rather whether he should continue to provide his patient with medical treatment or care which, if continued, will prolong his life, then, as I see it, the essential basis of Mr Munby's submissions disappear. I wish to add that I was unable to accept his suggestion that recent decisions show that the law is proceeding down a 'slippery slope', in the sense that the courts are becoming more and more ready to allow doctors to take steps which will result in the ending of life. On the contrary, as I have attempted to demonstrate, the courts are acting within a structure of legal principle, under which in particular they continue to draw a clear distinction between the bounds of lawful treatment of a living patient, and unlawful euthanasia.

I turn finally to the extent to which doctors should, as a matter of practice, seek the guidance of the court, by way of an application for declaratory relief, before withholding life-prolonging treatment from a PVS patient. The President considered that the opinion of the court should be sought in all cases similar to the present. In the Court of Appeal, Sir Thomas Bingham M.R. expressed his agreement with Sir Stephen Brown P. in the following words. (See p 842 *ante*.)

'This was in my respectful view a wise ruling, directed to the protection of patients, the protection of doctors, the reassurance of patients' families and the reassurance of the public. The practice proposed seems to me desirable. It may very well be that with the passage of time a body of experience and practice will build up which will obviate the need for application in every case, but for the time being I am satisfied that the practice Sir Stephen Brown P. described should be followed.'

Before the Appellate Committee, this view was supported both by Mr Munby, for the Official Solicitor, and by Mr Lester, as *amicus curiae*. For the respondents, Mr Francis suggested that an adequate safeguard would be provided if reference to the court was required in certain specific cases, *i.e.* (1) where there was known to be a medical disagreement as to the diagnosis or prognosis, and (2) problems had arisen with the patient's relatives — disagreement by the next of kin with the medical recommendation; actual or apparent conflict of interest between the next of kin and the patient; dispute between members of the patient's family; or absence of any next of kin to give their consent. There is, I consider, much to be said for the view that an application to the court will not be needed in every case, but only in particular circumstances, such as those suggested by Mr Francis. In this connection I was impressed not only by the care being taken by the medical ethics committee to provide guidance to the profession, but also by information given to the Appellate Committee about the substantial number of PVS patients in the country, and the very considerable cost of obtaining guidance from the court in cases such as the present. However, in my opinion this is a matter which would be better kept under review by the President of the Family Division than resolved now by your Lordships' House. I understand that a similar review is being undertaken in cases concerned with the sterilisation of adult women of unsound mind, with a consequent relaxation of the practice relating to applications to the court in such cases. For my part, I would therefore leave the matter as proposed by Sir Thomas Bingham M.R.; but I wish to express the hope that the President of the Family Division, who will no doubt be kept well informed about developments in this field, will soon feel able to relax the present requirement so as to limit applications for declarations to those cases in which there is a special need for the procedure to be invoked.

I wish to add one footnote. Since preparing this opinion, I have had the opportunity of reading in draft the speech of my noble and learned friend, Lord Browne-Wilkinson, in which he has expressed the view that a doctor, in reaching a decision whether or not to continue, in the best interests of his patient, to prolong his life by artificial means, may well be influenced by his own attitude to the sanctity of human life. The point does not arise for decision in the present case. I only wish to observe that it has implications not only in the case of a patient who, like Anthony Bland, is totally unconscious, but also one who may be suffering from great physical pain or (as in the case of one suffering from Guillain-Barré syndrome) extreme mental distress; and it would in theory fall to be tested if the patient's relatives, dismayed by the artificial prolongation of the agony of their loved one, were to seek to restrain by injunction a doctor who was persisting in prolonging his life. I cannot help feeling, however, that such a situation is more theoretical than real. I suspect that it is unlikely to arise in practice, if only because the solution could be found in a change of medical practitioner. It is not to be forgotten, moreover, that doctors who for conscientious reasons would feel unable to discontinue life support in such circumstances can presumably, like those who have a conscientious objection to abortion, abstain from involvement in such work. For present purposes, however, it is enough to state that the best interests test is broad and flexible in the sense that room must be allowed for the exercise of judgment by the doctor as to whether the relevant conditions exist which justify the discontinuance of life support."

LORD MUSTILL:
" . . . An alternative approach is to develop the reasoning of *F v. West Berkshire Health Authority* [1989] 2 All E.R. 545, by concentrating on the best interests, not of the community at large, but of Anthony Bland himself. Just as in *F v. West Berkshire Health Authority*, so the argument runs, the best interests of the patient demand a course of action which would normally be unlawful without the patient's consent. Just as in *F v. West Berkshire Health Authority* the patient is unable to decide for himself. In practice, to make no decision is to decide that the care and treatment shall continue. So that the decision shall not thus be made by default it is necessary that someone other than Anthony Bland should consider whether in his

own best interests his life should now be brought to an end, and if the answer is affirmative the proposed conduct can be put into effect without risk of criminal responsibility.

I cannot accept this argument which, if sound, would serve to legitimate a termination by much more direct means than are now contemplated. I can accept that a doctor in charge of a patient suffering the mental torture of Guillain-Barré syndrome, rational but trapped and mute in an unresponsive body, could well feel it imperative that a decision on whether to terminate life could wait no longer and that the only possible decision in the interests of the patient, even leaving out all the other interests involved, would be to end it here and now by a speedy and painless injection. Such a conclusion would attract much sympathy, but no doctrine of best interests could bring it within the law.

Quite apart from this the case of Anthony Bland seems to me quite different. He feels no pain and suffers no mental anguish. Stress was laid in argument on the damage to his personal dignity by the continuation of the present medical regime, and on the progressive erosion of the family's happy recollections by month after month of distressing and hopeless care. Considerations of this kind will no doubt carry great weight when Parliament comes to consider the whole question in the round. But it seems to me to be stretching the concept of personal rights, beyond breaking point to say that Anthony Bland has an interest in ending these sources of others distress. Unlike the conscious patient he does not know what is happening to his body, and cannot be affronted by it; he does not know of his family's continuing sorrow. By ending his life the doctors will not relieve him of a burden become intolerable, for others carry the burden and he has none. What other considerations could make it better for him to die now rather than later? None that we can measure, for of death we know nothing. The distressing truth which must not be shirked is that the proposed conduct is not in the best interests of Anthony Bland, for he has no best interests of any kind.

6. Best interests: the termination of treatment

After much expression of negative opinions I turn to an argument which in my judgement is logically defensible and consistent with the existing law. In essence it turns the previous argument on its head by directing the inquiry to the interests of the patient, not in the termination of life but in the continuation of his treatment. It runs as follows. (i) The cessation of nourishment and hydration is an omission not an act. (ii) Accordingly the cessation will not be a criminal act unless the doctors are under a present duty to continue the regime. (iii) At the time when Anthony Bland came into the care of the doctors decisions had to be made about his care which he was unable to make for himself. In accordance with *F v. West Berkshire Health Authority* [1989] 2 All E.R. 545 these decisions were to be made in his best interests. Since the possibility that he might recover still existed his best interests required that he should be supported in the hope that this would happen. These best interests justified the application of the necessary regime without his consent. (iv) All hope of recovery has now been abandoned. Thus, although the termination of his life is not in the best interests of Anthony Bland, his best interests in being kept alive have also disappeared, taking with them the justification for the non-consensual regime and the co-relative duty to keep it in being. (v) Since there is no longer a duty to provide nourishment and hydration a failure to do so cannot be a criminal offence.

My Lords, I must recognise at once that this chain of reasoning makes an unpromising start by transferring the morally and intellectually dubious distinction between acts and omissions into a context where the ethical foundations of the law are already open to question. The opportunity for anomaly and excessively fine distinctions, often depending more on the way in which the problem happens to be stated than on any real distinguishing features, has been exposed by many commentators, including in England the authors above-mentioned, together with Smith and Hogan *Criminal Law* (6th ed., 1988), p. 51, H. Beynon 'Doctors as Murderers' [1982] Crim.L.R. 17 and M. J. Gunn and J. C. Smith '*Arthurs* case and the right to life of a Downs Syndrome Child" [1985] Crim.L.R. 705. All this being granted we are still forced to take the law as we find it and try to make it work. Moreover, although in cases near the borderline the categorisation of conduct will be exceedingly hard, I believe that nearer the periphery there will be many instances which fall quite clearly into one category rather than the other. In my opinion the present is such a case, and in company with Compton J. in *Barber v. Superior Court of Los Angeles County* (1983) 147 Cal. App. 3d 1006 at 1017, amongst others I consider that the proposed conduct will fall into the category of omissions.

I therefore consider the argument to be soundly-based. Now that the time has come when Anthony Bland has no further interest in being kept alive, the necessity to do so, created by his inability to make a choice, has gone; and the justification for the invasive care and treatment, together with the duty to provide it have also gone. Absent a duty, the omission to perform what had previously been a duty will no longer be a breach of the criminal law.

In reaching this conclusion I have taken into account the fact that whereas for almost all concerned the adoption of the proposed course will be a merciful relief, this will not be so for the nursing staff, who will be called on to act in a way which must be contrary to all their instincts, training and traditions. They will encounter the ethical problems, not in a court or in a lecture room, but face to face. As the United Kingdom Council for Nursing, Midwifery and Health Visiting has emphasised, for the nurses involved the interval between the initiation of the proposed conduct and the death of Anthony Bland will be a very stressful period. Acknowledging this I hope that the nurses will accept, as I believe, that sadly it is for the best.

For these reasons I would uphold the declarations. Whilst there is no need to go further it is better to mention one further point. The reasoning which I propose is, I believe, broadly in line with that of your Lordships. But I venture to feel some reservations about the application of the principle of civil liability in negligence laid down in *Bolam v. Friern Hospital Management Committee* [1957] 2 All E.R. 118 to decisions on best interests in a field dominated by the criminal law. I accept without difficulty that this principle applies to the ascertainment of the medical raw material such as diagnosis, prognosis and appraisal of the patient's cognitive functions. Beyond this point, however, it may be said that the decision is ethical, not medical, and that there is no reason in logic why on such a decision the opinions of doctors should be decisive. If there had been a possibility that this question might make a difference to the outcome of the appeal I would have wished to consider it further, but since it does not I prefer for the moment to express no opinion upon it.

IV. The ethical question

After discussing the legal issues at length I will deal only briefly with the ethical question which must be for most lay people what the case is really about. With the general tenor, if not with the details, of what was said in the courts below I respectfully agree. But I prefer to advance on a narrower front. In law, if my conclusion is right, the way is clear for the doctors to proceed as they and the family think best. If the principle of *Bolam* applies that is the end of the matter, since nobody could doubt that a body of reasonable medical opinion would regard the proposed conduct as right. But even if *Bolam* is left aside, I still believe that the proposed conduct is ethically justified, since the continued treatment of Anthony Bland can no longer serve to maintain that combination of manifold characteristics which we call a personality. Some who have written on this subject maintain that this is too narrow a perspective, so I must make it clear that I do not assert that the human condition necessarily consists of nothing except a personality, or deny that it may also comprise a spiritual essence distinct from both body and personality. But of this we can know nothing, and in particular we cannot know whether it perishes with death or transcends it. Absent such knowledge we must measure up what we do know. So doing, I have no doubt that the best interests of Anthony Bland no longer demand the continuance of his present care and treatment. This is not at all to say that I would reach the same conclusion in less extreme cases, where the glimmerings of awareness may give the patient an interest which cannot be regarded as null. The issues, both legal and ethical, will then be altogether more difficult. As Mr Munby has pointed out, in this part of the law the court has moved a long way in a short time. Every step forward requires the greatest caution. Here however I am satisfied that what is proposed, and what all those who have considered the matter believe to be right, is in accordance with the law.

Anthony Bland died on March 3, 1993 of renal failure.

NOTES:

1. The decision of the House of Lords in *Bland* confirms the existence of the act/omission distinction in English law. (See discussion of this in Chapter 2 above at page 111). The House of Lords stated that the removal of the tube was not to be classed as an action causing death rather it could be categorised as an omission. As we saw above, the fact that conduct constitutes an omission does not mean that there is no liability in criminal law. Some omissions are culpable. In *Bland* the House of Lords held that withdrawal of treatment would not be a culpable omission if it was in the patient's best interests. The approach taken in *F v. West Berkshire Health Authority* was followed and the "substituted judgment" test used in certain other jurisdictions was rejected. (See further Chapter 5, above at pages 305–306.) The majority of the court in *Bland* (four out of five law lords) stated that what amounted to best interests was to be determined by reference to the *Bolam* test although Lord Mustill was not prepared to accept the *Bolam* approach.

2. In the past there has been much discussion as to the distinction between ordinary and extra-ordinary treatment. It was suggested that while failure to provide a basic level of care would be culpable in criminal law failure to continue more advanced types of medical treatment – "extraordinary treatment" – would not lead to liability. But whether such a clear cut distinction can be drawn between the categories has been questioned, since advancing medical technology may make today's extraordinary measures commonplace within a short period of time. The House of Lords in *Bland* did not base their decision on such a distinction.

3. In *Bland* the application was made for the removal of artificial nutrition/hydration. Two members of the House of Lords, (Lords Keith and Lowry) referred to this as medical treatment, Lord Goff stated that it was medical treatment or "part of the medical care of the patient". One difficult issue to be resolved in the future is

whether "spoon feeding" would be classed as medical treatment. It could be argued that the distinction between spoon feeding and artificial nutrition/hydration is that the latter is invasive. Moreover the insertion of a feeding tube may lead to greater complications. This approach has been questioned by some commentators. "At one extreme spoon feeding of a reluctant ament can be regarded as invasive and, accordingly, improper treatment; at the other, the installation of fluid through a tube can be seen as simple care involving no risk but can be done only as a *result* of invasion" (See J. K. Mason and R. A. McCall Smith, *Law and Medical Ethics*, (4th ed.) London: Butterworths, 1994, at page 341).

4. Lord Browne Wilkinson suggested that not only was withdrawal of treatment lawful but that in a situation in which continued treatment was not in the patient's best interests it would be actually unlawful to continue with treatment.

LORD BROWNE WILKINSON:
" . . . What then is the extent of the right to treat Anthony Bland which can be deduced from *F v. West Berkshire Health Authority?* Both Lord Brandon of Oakbrook, and Lord Goff, make it clear that the right to administer invasive medical care is wholly dependent upon such care being in the best interests of the patient. Moreover, a doctor's decision whether invasive care is in the best interests of the patient falls to be assessed by reference to the test laid down in *Bola v. Friern Hospital Management Committee* [1957] 2 All E.R. 118 *viz* is the decision in accordance with a practice accepted at the time by a responsible body of medical opinion ([1989] 2 All E.R. 545 at 559, 567 per Lord Brandon and Lord Goff). In my judgment it must follow from this that if there comes a stage where the responsible doctor comes to the reasonable conclusion (which accords with the views of a responsible body of medical opinion) that further continuance of an intrusive life support system is not in the best interests of the patient, he can no longer lawfully continue that life support system: to do so would constitute the crime of battery and the tort of trespass to the person. Therefore he cannot be in breach of any duty to maintain the patient's life. Therefore he is not guilty of murder by omission."

This statement by Lord Browne Wilkinson has implications for any attempt to undertake a non-therapeutic procedure on an incompetent patient and is one reason why procedures for the harvesting of organs such as elective ventilation may be unlawful. (See Chapter 15 below at pages 915–916). Furthermore were life to be prolonged at the relatives request where this was not in the patient's best interests then it appears that this would be unlawful.

5. The question of withdrawal of treatment from patients who are not in a peristent vegetative state remains open after *Bland*. In the earlier case of *Re J* [1990] 3 All E.R. 930 there was discussion of J's quality of life when considering withdrawal of treatment. Whether such an approach will be followed is questionable. In *Bland* Lord Mustill rejected such a balancing test while Lords Browne Wilkinson and Goff left the question open.

6. In *Bland* Lord Goff appeared to follow the approach in *Bodkin Adams* — namely that the administration of pain-killing drugs is lawful even though the incidental effect may be to shorten a patient's life.

7. If the patient is being supported upon a ventilator but is conscious then would switching off the ventilator be justifiable? This issue would presumably turn upon whether a court would be prepared to regard the support provided by a ventilator as medical treatment. (See below page 864.)

8. The proceedings in *Bland* took the form of a declaration. Whilst this by itself does not preclude subsequent criminal proceedings, as Lord Goff noted, the fact that a declaration has been obtained will normally have the effect of inhibiting prosecution. In addition the Attorney General could enter a *nolle prosequi* to stop later proceedings. The court emphasised the exceptional nature of the case and the fact that cases concerning withdrawal of treatment from patients in PVS should be referred to the courts. (See J. Bridgeman, "Declared Innocent" (1995) 3 *Medical Law Review* 117.) After the *Bland* case a minister, the Revd Morrow, attempted to start criminal proceedings against Bland's doctor for murder and he laid an information before Bingley magistrates to that effect. (*R v. Bingley Magistrates Court, ex p. Morrow*, April 13, 1994, Q.B.D., and see A. Grubb "Declaration: Effect on Subsequent Criminal Proceedings" (1995) 3 *Medical Law Review* 86.) They refused and Mr Morrow brought an application for judicial review of the magistrates decision. His application was rejected. The court agreed with the statement by Lord Goff in *Bland* that a civil declaration would normally preclude a subsequent criminal prosecution.

9. In the *Bland* case the Law Lords suggested that there was a need for the issues raised in the case to receive further consideration by parliament. Subsequently a House of Lords Select Committee on Euthanasia was established (H.L. Paper 21–2, London: HMSO, 1994). The conclusions of this Committee are considered more fully in the section on reform below. The Select Committee recommended that a definition of PVS be drawn up and a Code of Practice for the management of PVS patients be developed. Guidance has now been issued by the Royal College of Physicians and in the form of a Practice Note by the Official Solicitor — see appendices.

QUESTIONS:

1. Should the question of withdrawal of a patient from artificial nutrition/ventilation be referred automatically to the courts?

2. Why did the court grant the declaration in *Bland*? What is the effect of such a declaration in criminal and in civil law?

3. Why is the conduct of a doctor who discontinues nutrition/hydration not murder? (See J. M. Finnis, "Bland — Crossing the Rubicon" (1993) 109 *Law Quarterly Review* 329.)

4. Should the appropriate test to apply in such cases be whether an accepted body of medical opinion would be of the view that treatment should be withheld?
5. Is it correct to say that in a case, such as that of Tony Bland, death can be in the patient's best interests? Examine Lord Mustill's judgment.
6. The weighing up of medical resources in reaching the decision was rejected by the House of Lords in the *Bland* case, but should medical resources be a factor taken into consideration?
7. Lord Goff suggests that doctors who have a conscientious objection could probably abstain from work in this area. However there are only two specific statutory provisions which allow for conscientious objection in health care, neither of which relate to the end of life. (See Chapter 2 at pages 139–141.) Should the doctor or other health professional be allowed to opt out on an ad hoc basis? Examine Lord Mustill's judgment above at page 853 in relation to the role of the nurse.
8. What are the implications of the *Bland* case for cases involving the withdrawal of treatment from neonates? (See Lord Goff's judgment above at page 847.)
9. Lord Goff talks in terms of not being appropriate to prolong care where treatment is "futile". But what constitutes "futility"? Is it "futile" to treat a 10-year-old suffering from leukaemia where there is a success rate of 1-4 per cent. (See C. Newdick, *Who Should We Treat?*, Oxford: OUP pages 280–285 and also Chapter 1 above at pages 54–60.)

The issue of whether treatment should be withdrawn from a patient in a PVS state has come before the courts in later cases.

Frenchay Healthcare National Health Service Trust v. S [1994] 2 All E.R. 403; [1994] 1 W.L.R. 601; [1994] 1 F.L.R. 485

S took a drug overdose. As a consequence he suffered brain damage. He was treated in hospital where he was diagnosed as being in a persistent vegetative state. He was fed via a naso-gastric tube in his stomach. The tube became disconnected. The consultant surgeon treating him did not believe that the tube could be reconnected and thought that the only alternative was to insert another tube. The doctor took the view that continued treatment was not in the best interests of S. The hospital sought an order from the court that it would be lawful not to reinsert the tube. On appeal to the Court of Appeal.

SIR THOMAS BINGHAM M.R.:
" . . . the doctors were confronted on Monday with this appalling decision as to whether they should authorise a further surgical procedure to insert a gastrostomy tube or whether they should desist with the prospect that the patient would shortly

thereafter die. Advice was taken and late on Wednesday of this week an application to the judge sitting in Bristol was mounted. Notice was given to the Official Solicitor that the application was being made but it was very short notice, through no fault of the plaintiffs. Thus it was that the matter came before Swinton Thomas J. yesterday afternoon, 13 January, in Bristol when he was invited to make a declaration, the effect of which was to authorise the plaintiff hospital trust not to replace the gastrostomy tube. The Official Solicitor was represented by counsel, but it is of course right to observe that the Official Solicitor himself had very little time to give instructions and counsel herself had very little time to prepare her submissions. However, the matter was heard before the judge yesterday afternoon and having heard argument on both sides, and having been referred in some detail to *Airedale NHS Trust v. Bland* [1993] 1 All E.R. 821 case, particularly the House of Lords' decision, the judge concluded that he should in all the circumstances grant the declaration which the hospital were seeking.

Today, and still at short notice, the Official Solicitor appeals to this court against that decision and the case has been argued, with his customary skill and erudition, by Mr Munby on his behalf.

I am conscious that in the course of this judgment I have already referred on a number of occasions to the authority of *Airedale NHS Trust v. Bland*. That is a very well-known decision, young though it is, involving a young Hillsborough victim who had been in a persistent vegetative state for a period of over three years, and who gave rise to an application to the court on behalf of the hospital trust responsible for his treatment for leave to discontinue feeding and providing liquid to him. The case began with Sir Stephen Brown P., passed through this court and ended in the House of Lords, Lord Keith, Lord Goff, Lord Browne-Wilkinson and Lord Mustill being unanimous in their view that the leave which the hospital sought should be given. It is right to observe that it was an extreme case of the persistent vegetative state. There was no hope of recovery whatever. There was no division of medical opinion. The ethical guidelines which were before the court all pointed the same way. There was, despite this unamity of judicial opinion, widespread and understandable concern, both among lawyers and amongst the public, at the implications of the decision. This is not in any way surprising since it touched on values which are literally fundamental to our view of society and of the world. The courts were of course alive to, and I would hope responsive to, this concern. They were certainly anxious that their decision should not be in any way misunderstood or misapplied. So it was that various rules and principles were laid down in that case to try and prevent abuse and reassure the public. First of all, it was suggested, at any rate in the short term, that those seeking to discontinue treatment in what I may call the *Bland* situation should come to court and obtain a declaration from the court that it was proper to do so. Secondly, it was envisaged that such applications should be preceded by full investigation with an opportunity for the Official Solicitor, as the representative of the unconscious patient, to explore the situation fully, to obtain independent medical opinions of his own, and to ensure that all proper material was before the court before such a momentous decision was taken. Thirdly, the courts made plain that their decisions were to be understood as strictly applying to the *Bland* situation and no other. A number of judges were at pains to emphasise that they should not be taken as approving anything falling outside the factual situation which was then before the court.

It is against that background that we have heard the submissions made on behalf of the Official Solicitor today. So far as the first of those safeguards is concerned, namely the application to the court, that has indeed been satisfied because despite the compressed timetable it has been possible for the plaintiff trust to apply to the court, to put medical reports and opinions before the court, and to enable the court to consider the matter, albeit at short notice. It is however to be observed that cases must from time to time arise in which this procedure simply cannot be practicable. I have in mind the acute emergency when a decision has to be taken within a matter of minutes, or at most hours, as to whether treatment should be given or not, whether one form of treatment should be given or another, or as to whether treatment should be withheld. In such situations it is of course impossible that doctors should be obliged or able to come to the court and seek a decision. I think it is therefore inevitable that there must be emergencies in which application to the court is simply not possible, even though this case is not one of them. That consideration does however lead on to Mr Munby's first major submission of the three which he has made to us, which is that the procedure which has been adopted in this case has in effect deprived S, and his representative, the Official Solicitor, of a fair and full opportunity to explore the matter fully and make sure that all relevant material is before the court. There is inevitably a measure of truth in that. If the court were to allow the appeal and withhold a declaration, it may be that the surgical procedure would be undertaken and that there would then be an opportunity for a full investigation with the prospect of an application such as was made in *Bland's* in some months' time. It does not however seem to me that we should regard that consideration as conclusive. Just as there will be some situations in which it will be impracticable for the plaintiff to apply to the court at all, so there will be other situations, such as the present, in which although it is possible to come to court, it is not possible to present the application in the same leisurely way as in a case where there is no pressure of time at all. For my part, therefore, I think it important to take note of Mr Munby's submission and to look very critically at the facts and at the material which is before the court, but I do not consider that it would be right to allow the appeal simply on the basis that there has not been an opportunity on behalf of S for there to be a full exploration of the facts which in other circumstances would be desirable.

I go on then to what is Mr Munby's second major submission which is that on the face of the plaintiffs' own evidence there is reason to question the diagnosis of PVS. This is of course an important submission because, as I have emphasised, in *Bland's* case the courts were at pains to emphasise that their decision applied only to the facts which were before them. Mr Munby raises an important question as to whether the facts of *Bland's* case are the facts of the present case for legal purposes. He draws attention to a number of features of the evidence which in his submission raise doubts as to whether the cases are truly comparable. He draws attention, for example, to the fact that the consultant in charge of S made his original diagnosis after only four months, and he reminds us of BMA guidelines which suggest that a diagnosis of PVS should not be confirmed until twelve months has expired. For my part I see little force in that point since the initial diagnosis was clearly provisional. There is no doubt at all that it has been confirmed by the consultant with a very much more detailed knowledge of S's case. Mr Munby draws attention to the fact that rehabilitation was pursued for a period of two years and this again, he suggests, throws doubt on the confidence with which the consultant made his diagnosis, since this would have been futile had the diagnosis been made with complete confidence. Again, I cannot for my part regard that as undermining the acceptability of the consultant's diagnosis since, however sure one was that the prospects of recovery were nil one would still wish to leave no possible stone unturned and no doubt it would be necessary to satisfy members of the family that every possible chance was being explored. More significantly, attention is drawn to suggestions in the medical reports of what might be interpreted as volitional behaviour: that is, not mere spasm or reflex reaction, but voluntary behaviour on the part of the patient. There is reference at one point to pulling at the nasogastric tube and indeed to the pulling out of the gastrostomy tube Monday of this week. There are references to the possibility that S may feel distress and may be suffering. Indeed, it is pointed out that one of the reasons why the nurses are so gravely distressed by S's condition is that they are convinced that at times he seems to suffer.

It is commented that the consultant neuro-psychiatrist does little more than endorse the consultant's report and it is suggested in respect of the professor of neurology that he does not diagnose PVS. It is true, I think, that that is not an expression that he uses and he expresses doubt as to whether S can recognise his family rather than expressing a concluded opinion that he cannot. He makes a reference to S appearing to suffer pain. Again, it is pointed out that the consultant at Putney does not unequivocally diagnose PVS but refers to resistance by S on some occasions and to certain forms of response, and expresses her views on his ability to communicate in a somewhat equivocal way. In contrast again to the neuro-psychiatrist, who thought that S's quality of life was nil, she thought that there were respects in which it could be improved.

I think it is plain that the evidence in this case is not as emphatic and not as unanimous as that in *Bland's* case. That certainly causes one to look critically and anxiously at the evidence that is before us. In particular we have to ask ourselves whether the respects in which the evidence is not the same throws doubt on the decision which the consultant has taken and invited the court to approve. For my part there appears to be very little doubt in the evidence, particularly the evidence of the doctors who know S best, that he is in a persistent vegetative state, that there is no prospect of recovery, and that he has no cognitive function worth the name. It is not suggested that one is dealing here with a brain-damaged patient who has some significant cognitive function. The evidence to which I have already referred in some detail presents S as a person who has no conscious being at all. That being the case it does not seem to me that in the acute emergency which has arisen the court should attach great weight to the points of distinction that have been raised between the two cases.

I come on, therefore, to the third major submission that Mr Munby has laid before the court which is this. Mr Munby is at pains to make plain that he is anything but critical of the judge who was faced with a difficult decision to be made at short notice and with very little opportunity for thought, certainly for prolonged thought. Mr Munby does, however, submit that the judge erred in attaching too much importance to the judgment of doctors as to what was in the patient's best interests. Mr Munby submits that the House of Lords' decision in *Airedale NHS Trust v. Bland* [1993] 1 All E.R. 121 left open whether the judgment was finally to be made by the doctors or by the court, his submission being that in the last resort it must be made by the court, albeit with great regard to the opinions of responsible medical men. It is true that the judge paid close attention to what members of the House of Lords had said about the subject in the course of their speeches in Bland's case and did express the view that the conclusion at which S's consultant had arrived was reasonable and bona fide. He regarded the judgments which had been expressed by the doctors in this case as being fully in accord with criteria which their Lordships had laid down. It is, I think, important that there should not be a belief that what the doctor says is the patient's best interest is the patient's best interest. For my part I would certainly reserve to the court the ultimate power and duty to review the doctor's decision in the light of all the facts. But in a case such as this the question which must be asked is, I think, clear, and the question is: what is in the best interests of the patient? The plaintiffs' answer to that question is clear, and it is that given by the consultant to whom I have repeatedly referred. The answer given on behalf of S, through the Official Solicitor, is that a declaration should not be made. That would leave the doctors in this position: either they would feel obliged to embark upon the surgical procedure necessary to reinsert the tube, which the consultant has made quite clear is contrary in a profound sense to his judgment of what is in the patient's best interests, and which he is himself unwilling to authorise, or they would simply do nothing and persist in the course of conduct on which they have embarked, uncertain whether at the end of the day the law would condemn that decision or not. That may sometimes be the right course for the court to adopt, but it seems to me a highly unsatisfactory position into which one should be reluctant to lead doctors unless the court has real doubt about the reliability, or bona fides, or correctness of the medical opinion in question. Here we have, as it seems to me, a careful, professional and clearly very thoughtful conclusion expressed by a consultant of the highest standing with a knowledge of this patient acquired over a period of years. It is an opinion shared by other doctors who have had the opportunity of seeing the patient, again over a period of years. It is an opinion which no medical opinion contradicts. It is strictly correct, as Mr Munby points out, that there are not two independent medical opinions supporting that of the consultant who in effect makes this application. That is partly a reflection of the emergency which has given rise to the application. But we have, as I have said, two opinions, both to the same effect as the consultant's, and no contrary opinion.

NOTES:

1. Waite L.J. and Peter Gibson L.J. agreed.
2. In *Frenchay* the issue of treatment was urgent because the tube had become dislodged. The judge also noted that the diagnosis was not as conclusive as in the *Bland* case. The case illustrates some of the difficulties which are likely to arise in the future because these applications will frequently be made as emergency orders (See A. Palmer, "Withdrawal of Medical Treatment: The Emergency Case" [1995] *Family Law* 195). This may be seen as particularly problematic in view of the fact that recently there has been some concern expressed as to practices in relation to the diagnosis of PVS. A study undertaken at the Royal Hospital for Neurodisability in Putney found that out of 40 patients referred to the hospital with a diagnosis of persistent vegetative state between 1992 and 1995 some 17 had been wrongly diagnosed. (See K. Andrew, L. Murphy, R. Munday, C. Littlewood, "Misdiagnosis of the vegetative state: retrospective study in a rehabilitation unit" (1996) 313 *BMJ* 13.) The BMA have indicated that it is updating its guidelines on the diagnosis of PVS (*The Independent* March 18, 1996).
3. The extent to which the wishes of relatives should be considered in determining the treatment of PVS patients was considered in the later case of *Re G* [1995] 2 FLR 528). Following a motorcycle accident in 1991 G had been in a persistent vegetative state. G's wife, along with the doctors treating him, supported the withdrawal of treatment. However, his mother wanted treatment continued. The matter was referred to the court. Sir Stephen Brown P. said that while relatives should be consulted these views could not be conclusive and that in this case the opinion of the consultant orthopaedic surgeon that further treatment was not in the best interests of G should be followed. (See A. Grubb, "Incompetent Patient in PVS: Views of Relatives; Best Interests" (1995) 3 *Medical Law Review* 80.)
4. In *Swindon & Marlborough NHS Trust v. S* [1995] Med. Law Rev. 84) S, a 48-year-old married woman in a PVS state, was being cared for primarily by her family at home, although there were also certain periods of care in hospital. She was receiving nutrition through a gastrostomy tube. The tube became blocked and an operation was

required to insert a new tube. An application was made to the court
for an order that further treatment should not be pursued. The court
granted the order. Waite J. made the point that in a situation in
which the patient was being cared for at home proceedings regarding
the withdrawal of treatment should be brought either by the hospital
caring for the patient or by the GP to avoid the burden of bringing
such proceedings falling on the family. (See J. Stone, "Withholding of
Life Sustaining Treatment" (1995) *New L.J.* 354 and M. Hinchliffe,
"Vegetative State Patients" (1996) 146 *NLJ* 1579.)

4. The issue of withdrawal of treatment from newly born infants may
   need reconsideration in the light of the *Bland* decision. The case of a
   three-month-old girl, severely damaged by meningitis was referred to
   the court in April 1996. The girl, who was blind, deaf and unable to
   respond to her parents, was unable to breathe without ventilator
   assistance. Sir Stephen Brown authorised the withdrawal of ventilation. The judge refused to set out principles as guidance in future
   cases. He indicated that such withdrawal of treatment matters should
   be referred to the courts. (News: "Judge allows baby to die in peace"
   (1996) 312 *BMJ* 928. *Re C (a baby)* [1996] 2 FLR 43.)

QUESTIONS:

1. Contrast the "best interests" approach taken in *Frenchay* with the
   approach of the majority of the House of Lords in *Bland*. Which
   approach is preferable?
2. S's condition was due to a failed suicide attempt. Should this be a
   factor influencing the decision whether or not to withdraw treatment?

There may be some situations in which it is sought to discontinue
treatment but it cannot be said to be in the best interests of the patient to
take that course of action. The question of withdrawal of treatment has
been considered by the Law Commission. (See general discussion of this
report in Chapter 5.)

Law Commission, *Mental Incapacity*, Law Com. No. 231 (1995)

6.20 Respondents with experience in intensive care made it clear to us that
decisions to terminate artificial feeding often have to be taken in acute cases. It does
not follow from our analysis of the difficulty where a patient is in persistent
vegetative state that *any* decision to discontinue artificial nutrition should have to
go to court. In an acute case, it may very well be obvious that it is in the best
interests of the patient for sustenance to be withdrawn, so that he or she does not
recover consciousness to live in temporary pain and distress and then die shortly
afterwards of severe and incurable injuries or illness. The recommendation below is
directed to those cases where the 'best interests' criterion cannot be invoked to
resolve the dilemmas of treatment providers. Those cases are where (1) artificial
sustenance is being provided and (2) the patient's condition is such that it cannot be

said to be in his or her best interests to discontinue the sustenance. The defining characteristic of such a condition is a complete inability to have any physical or emotional experience of whatever kind whether in the present or at any future time. This can be established by assessing whether there is any activity in the cerebral cortex. In our view, a lawful route to the discontinance of artificial sustenance in such circumstances should be provided. There should, however, be a very high level of independent supervision.

We recommend that discontinuing the artificial nutrition and hydration of a patient who is unconscious, has no activity in the cerebral cortex and no prospect of recovery should be lawful if certain statutory requirements are met (Draft Bill, clause 10(1)).

6.21 We agree with the majority of our consultees that, as at present, the discontinuance of artificial sustenance to a patient in PVS should in every case require the prior approval of the court, unless an attorney or court-appointed manager already has express authority to make that decision. Equally if the patient has made an advance refusal of artificial sustenance in the circumstances that have arisen then that would resolve the matter and there would be no obligation to seek court approval. It was, however, suggested by the Master of the Rolls in *Bland's* case that there might come a time when a body of experience and practice had built up, such that a prior court declaration might not be necessary in every case. This suggestion was reiterated in four of the five speeches in the House of Lords. If, as we recommended, the matter is placed on a statutory footing then the primary legislation would require amendment if it were decided that no court approval was necessary. This would be a laborious process. In view of the comments made in *Bland's* case we have therefore made provision for the Secretary of State by order to replace the need for court approval with a requirement of a certificate from an independent medical practitioner duly appointed for that purpose to the effect that it is appropriate for artificial nutrition to be discontinued. Before making any such order, the Secretary of State should consult with relevant organisations and with the Official Solicitor and any order should be subject to an affirmative resolution by each House of Parliament. In cases of dispute or difficulty it would of course still be possible for the decision to be referred to the court, even if the alternative of a second opinion procedure were to be brought into force.

We recommend that the discontinuance of artificial sustenance to an unconscious patient with no activity in cerebral cortex and no prospect of recovery should require either (1) the approval of the court, (2) the consent of an attorney or manager or (3) if an order of the Secretary of State so provides, a certificate by an independent medical practitioner.

6.22 Not all of our consultees agreed with Lord Mustill's view that decisions to discontinue artificial nutrition for a patient in PVS cannot be justified by reference to the patient's 'best interests'. We prefer to avoid any semantic argument and confusion by disapplying the general rule where such decisions are concerned and concentrating instead on the individual factors in the best interests check list. Some of these are equally applicable to any decision as to whether cessation of feeding and hydration should occur. This is especially true of the first factor, namely the wishes and the feelings of the person and the factors he or she would have taken into account if able to do so. Equally important may be the third factor, namely the views of any of the persons who should be consulted as to the patient's wishes and best interests.

We recommend that where the court, an attorney or manager or an independent medical practitioner decides on discontinuation of artificial sustenance for an unconscious patient with no activity in the cerebral cortex and no prospect of recovery, then regard must be had to the factors in the best interests checklist (Draft Bill Clause 10(3)).

NOTES:

1. Factors in the best interests checklist provided by the Law Commission which are likely to be of relevance in making a decision relating to withdrawal of treatment include any ascertainable past wishes of the patient, the views of other persons whom it is practicable to consult in relation to the person's wishes and feelings and to what decision is in his best interests. See Chapter 5, pages 303–306.

2. The Law Commission also considered whether there were circumstances in which a patient's life should be prolonged in the interests of others. An example of such a situation is the procedure of elective ventilation which facilitates organ transplantation (see Chapter 15 below at pages 915–916). The Law Commission suggested that although at present such a procedure should not be included in legislation, provision should be made in the draft bill for the Secretary of State to make an order. This could provide that certain procedures may be undertaken on incapacitated persons which, while not for their benefit, would not cause them significant harm and would be of significant benefit to others.

QUESTIONS:

1. The Law Commission regarded the "best interests" test which they advocate as the basis for the treatment of the mentally incompetent as being unworkable in relation to end of life decisions. If this is the case then on what basis should treatment be discontinued?

2. To what extent would delegation of decisions concerning treatment to one independent medical practitioner would provide an appropriate solution?

(c) Withdrawal of ventilator support

If a patient is supported on a ventilator can it be withdrawn? If the patient is conscious then he may be able to disengage mechanical support himself by flicking a switch. (The situations in which a patient is competent while supported on a ventilator are limited, examples including a patient with motor neurone disease.) If it is deemed to be treatment then, arguably, it could, although reference to a court for a declaration would be justifiable. But there are particularly emotive connotations in the removal of ventilator support. As Mason and McCall Smith have commented, "The practical difference must lie in the immediacy and the certainty of death when the respirator is turned off; the health care team is, effectively, being asked to suffocate their patient" (J. K. Mason, R. A. McCall Smith, *Law and Medical Ethics* (4th ed. London: Butterworths 1994, at page 333). Examples in other jurisdictions exist of judicial approval being given to the withdrawal of treatment in such situations. (See, *e.g. Nancy B. v. Hotel*

Dieu de Quebec (1992) 86 DLR (4th) 385, (1992) 1 BMLR 95). It should be noted that withdrawal of ventilation may not result in death.

A celebrated instance of such a case is the United States case of Karen Quinlan, a case that led to a heated debate regarding the right to die in the United States. It should be noted that in Quinlan's case, although ventilator support was withdrawn, Quinlan herself lived on (*Re Quinlan* 355 A 2d 664 (N.J., 1976).

(d) Do not resuscitate orders

Most of the cases which we have considered up until now concern the withdrawal of treatment once begun. But difficult issues also concern the commencement of therapy. The decision whether to treat at all is a medical decision and one made initially when the patient is brought in to hospital. This difficult assessment, known as "triage", is a rationing decision and is a matter of relatively low public visibility, which has not been the subject of judicial or legislative consideration. (See S. F. Spicker, "ICU triage: the ethics of scarcity, the ideal of impartiality and the inadvertent endorsement of evil" in R. Lee and D. Morgan (ed.), *Deathrites: Law and Ethics at the End of Life,* London: Routledge, 1994.) Once therapy has commenced then in some situations the decision may arise as to whether therapy should be continued if, for example, a feeding tube becomes dislodged—as we saw in the *Frenchay* case above (at page 857). Another issue is not whether a particular therapy should be continued but whether therapy should be initiated at all. A patient may be made the subject of what is known as a "Do Not Resuscitate Order". These are directions given that, should a particular event occur, this patient should not be given one or more types of treatment. The directions are given by health practitioners. These directives were the subject of consideration in the following case.

Re R [1996] 2 FLR 99

R was a man of 23 with cerebral palsy, brain malformation and consequent learning difficulties. He was unable to walk or sit upright without help. While he was not in PVS he was in what was termed a low awareness state. He was totally dependent upon professional care and evidence was given to the effect that he was deteriorating neurologically and physically. The consultant stated that it was in R's best interests to let nature take its course when a "life threatening crisis" took place. The parents agreed that if R suffered a cardiac arrest he should not be resuscitated. A doctor caring for R signed a "Do Not Resuscitate" (DNR) direction. The staff of the day centre where R was being cared for, challenged this order. They sought judicial review claiming that the DNR policy was irrational and unlawful because it allowed treatment to be withheld on the basis of an assessment of a patient's quality of life. The NHS trust also went to court seeking a declaration to the effect that their actions were lawful. In the proceedings eventually heard before Sir Stephen Brown the Trust sought a declaration to the effect that it would be lawful to withhold cardio-pulmonary resuscitation of the patient and the administration of antibiotics in the event of the patient developing of potentially life-threatening infection which would otherwise call for the administration of antibiotics.

SIR STEPHEN BROWN P.:
". . . In March 1993 the British Medical Association and the Royal College of Nursing published a joint statement entitled 'Cardio-Pulmonary Resuscitation: A Statement from the R.C.N. and the B.M.A.' A copy of the statement is to be found in the documents before the court. The introduction reads

'Cardio-Pulmonary Resuscitation (C.P.R.) can be attempted on any individual in whom cardiac or respiratory function ceases. Such events are inevitable as part of dying and thus C.P.R. can theoretically be used on every individual prior to death. It is therefore essential to identify patients for whom Cardio-pulmonary arrest respresents a terminal event in their illness and in whom C.P.R. is inappropriate.'

Under the heading 'Background' appears the following:

Do not resuscitate (DNR) orders may be a potent source of misunderstanding and dissent amongst doctors, nurses and other involved in the care of patients. Many of the problems in this, difficult area would be avoided if communication and explanation of the decision were improved . . .

These guidelines therefore should be viewed as a framework providing basic principles within which decisions regarding local policies on CPR may be formulated. Further assistance for doctors and nurses where individual problems arise, can be obtained from their respective professional organisations.

Guidelines

'It is appropriate to consider a do-not-resuscitate (D.N.R.) decision in the following circumstances:
(a) where the patient's condition indicates that effective cardio-pulmonary resuscitation (C.P.R.) is unlikely to be successful;
(b) where C.P.R. is not in accord with the recorded sustained wished of the patient who is mentally competent;
(c) where successful C.P.R. is likely to be followed by a lengthened quality of life which would not be acceptable to the patient.

2. Where a D.N.R. order has not been made and the express wishes of the patient are unknown, resuscitation should be initiated if cardiac or pulmonary arrest occurs. Anyone initiating C.P.R. in such circumstances, should be supported by their senior and medical nursing colleagues.

3. The overall responsibility for a D.N.R. decision rests with the consultant in charge of the patient's care. This should be be made after appropriate consultation and consideration of all aspects of the patients condition. The perspectives of other members of the medical and nursing team, the patient, and with due regard to patient confidentiality, the patient's relatives or close friends, may all be valuable in forming the consultants's decision.

5. Although responsibility for C.P.R. policy rests with the consultant, he or she should be prepared always to discuss the decision for an individual patient with other health professionals involved in the patient's care.

Paragraph 9 states:

'when the basis for a D.N.R. Order is the absence of any likely medical benefit, discussion with the patient, or others close to the patient, should aim at securing an understanding and acceptance of the clinical decision which has been reached.

If a D.N.R. decision is based on quality of life considerations, the views of the patient where these can be ascertained are particularly important. If the patient cannot express a view, the opinion of others close to the patient may be sought regarding the patient's best interests.'

In December 1993 the NHS Trust in question published its own version of the statement issued jointly by the BMA and the RCN. Its wording was slightly different and in particular in para. 2(c) used the phrase 'because of unacceptable quality of life'. That differed slightly from the wording of the joint BMA/RCN guidance which referred to 'the length of and quality of life which would not be acceptable to the patient'. However, the document issued by this NHS Trust made it clear in the first paragraph that 'the overall responsibility for such a D.N.R. decision rests with the consultant in charge of the patient's care. This should be made after appropriate consultation and consideration of all aspects of the patient's condition'.

. . . Dr Andrews points out that a 'do not resuscitate' policy is a well-recognised procedure in health care. He draws attention to the joint statement of the British Medical Association and the Royal College of Nurses to which I have already referred . . . He points out that (b) and (c) involve the views of the patient and therefore are not appropriate to this particular situation. It is (a) where the guideline deals with the effectiveness of CPR which is particularly relevant in the present case. Dr Andrews said that even in hospital settings, on average, only about 13 per cent of patients receiving CPR survive to discharge. In a residential home without medical staff present the chances of a successful resuscitation would be almost nil. There would also be a very real risk in the case of someone with deformities of the kind which the patient R has of his receiving injuries, such as broken ribs, from the procedure. Dr Andrews, gave it as his considered opinion that in the light of the extremely small potential for success and the distress which injuries would cause it would be wholly inappropriate to give this treatment to R. Accordingly, a 'do not resuscitate' policy in his view is appropriate based on the likely futility of attempts to resuscitate R successfully in a residential setting . . ."

The judge noted the unanimous view of the medical expert that to undertake resuscitation was inappropriate here and evidence to the effect that it could result in further brain damage and harm by excessive pressure being applied to an already fragile bone structure and continued . . .

"So far as the withholding of antibiotics is concerned Dr Andrews stated that this is a matter which can only properly be decided at the time when a potentially life threatening situation from infection arises. There should not be, as it were, a global 'Do Not Treat' policy. The plaintiff trusts has indicated that it is content to accept that position. The decision as to the withholding of the administration of antibiotics in a potentially life threatening situation is a matter fully within the responsibility of the consultant having the responsibility for treating the patient. It is a matter which should be considered in conjunction with the general practitioner and, futhermore, in the case of R, with his parents. The Official Solicitor submits that it would be appropriate for the court at this stage to make a declaration that it would be lawful to withhold the administration of antibiotics in the event of the patient developing a potentially life-threatening infection which would otherwise call for the administration of antibiotics but only if immediately prior to withholding the same.

(a) The trust is so advised both by the general medical practitioner and by the consultant psychiatrist having the responsibility at the time of the patient's treatment and care and

(b) One or other or both of the parents first give their consent thereto.

Such a declaration would recognise the ultimate and effective responsibility of the consultant having responsibility at the time for the patient's treatment and care. A declaration in these terms would be a modification of the declaration which was initially sought in the originating summons

In this case there is no question of the Court being the phrase 'because of unacceptable quality of life'. That differed slightly from the wording of the joint BMA/RCN guidance which referred to 'the length and quality of life which would not be accepted to the patient'. However, the document issued by this NHS Trust made it clear in the first paragraph on page 2 that the overall responsibility for such a DNR decision rests with the consultant in charge of the patient's condition.

. . . The court is concerned with circumstances in which steps should be taken to prolong life. The facts are very different from those in the case of *Airedale NHS Trust v. Bland* [1993] A.C. 789. The principle of law to be applied in this case is that of the "best interests of the Patient" as made clear by the Court of Appeal in *Re J* [1991] Fam. 33 . . ."

The judge referred to the facts in *Re J* and continued

"In the course of his judgment Taylor L.J. said:
    'The plight of baby J is appalling and the problem facing the court in the exercise of its wardship jurisdiction is of the greatest difficulty. When should the court rule against the giving of treatment aimed at prolonging life?' . . .
    At 55F and 383M respectively Taylor L.J. said:
    'I consider the correct approach is for the court to judge the quality of life the child would have to endure if given the treatment and decide whether in all circumstances such a life would be so afflicted as to be intolerable to that child.'
Although this present case concerns a handicapped adult and not a child who is a ward of court the overriding principle in my judgment is the same. The operative words in this passage from the judgment of Taylor L.J. to which I have referred are 'so afflicted as to be intolerable'. The extensive medical evidence in this case is unanimous in concluding that it would not be in the best interests of R to subject him to cardio-pulmonary resuscitation in the event of his suffering a cardiac arrest. The conclusions of the doctors are supported by R's parents. The Official Solicitor on behalf of R agrees that this is an appropriate course to be followed. He submits that in the context of the facts of this case it would be appropriate for the Court to make a declaration that it shall be lawful as being in the patient's best interests for the Trust and/or the responsible medical practitioners having the responsibility at the time for the patient's treatment and care to withhold cardio-pulmonary resuscitation of the patient. I agree that this declaration should be made.

    The withholding in the future of the administration of antibiotics in the event of the patient developing a potentially life-threatening infection which would other-wise call for the administration of antibiotics is a decision which can only be taken at the time by the patient's responsible medical practitioners in the light of the prevailing circumstances. This requires a clinical judgment in the light of the prevailing circumstances. Mr Munby Q.C. on behalf of the Official Solicitor has referred to a passage in the speech of Lord Goff of Chieveley in the case of *Airedale NHS Trust v. Bland* [1993] A.C. 789. Lord Goff said:
    'I turn finally to the extent to which doctors should, as a matter of practice, seek the guidance of the Court, by way of an application for declaratory relief, before withholding life prolonging treatment from a PVS patient. The President considered that the opinion of the Court should be sought in all cases similar to the present. In the Court of Appeal, Sir Thomas Bingham M.R. expressed his agreement with Sir Stephen Brown P. in the following words:
        "This was in my respectful view a wise ruling, directed to the protection of patients, the protection of doctors, the reassurance of patients': families and the reassurance of the public. The practice proposed seems to me to be desirable. It may very well be that with the passage of time a body of experience and practice will build up which will obviate the need for application in every case, but for the time being I am satisfied that the practice which the President described should be followed."

Before the Appellate Committee, this view was supported both by Mr Munby for the Official Solicitor, and by Mr Lester, as *amicus curiae*. For the Respondents Mr Francis suggested that an adequate safeguard would be provided if reference to the Court was required in certain specific cases.'

Lord Goff then gave certain examples [and] . . . then said:

'For my part, I would therefore leave the matter as proposed by the Master of the Rolls; but I wish to express the hope that the President of the Family Division, who will no doubt be kept well informed about developments in this field, will soon feel able to relax the present requirement so as to limit applications for declarations to those cases in which there is a special need for the procedure to be invoked.'

Mr Munby, relying upon that passage in Lord Goff's speech, submits that in the light of the medical evidence and all the factual material in this case it would be appropriate for the Court to make a declaration in terms which would not require a future application to the Court. He suggests a declaration in the following terms:

'To withhold the administration of antibiotics in the event of the patient developing a potentialy life threatening infection which would otherwise call for the administration of antibiotics but only if immediately prior to withholding the same

(a) the trust is so advised both by the general medical practitioner and by the consultant psychiatrist having the responsibility at the time for the patient's treatment and care and

(b) one or other or both of the parents first give their consent thereto.

Counsel for the plaintiff trust agrees with that proposal. In my judgment it would reflect the reality of the situation. The decision to withhold antibiotics in a given situation falls fairly and squarely within the clinical responsibility of the consultant treating the patient. I am quite satisfied on the evidence in this case that the consultant and the general practitioner having the responsibility for R's treatment do have R's best interests in mind. They are fully supported by the parents. I am accordingly satisfied that it would be in the best interests of R to make a declaration in these terms . . ."

NOTES:

1. This case represents the first judicial consideration of "do not resuscitate orders". The use of such orders was considered by the House of Lords Select Committee on Euthanasia, who were opposed to the enactment of legislation on this subject (H.L. Paper 21–2, London: HMSO, 1994).

2. A number of reasons have been advanced as to why cardio-pulmonary resuscitation should be withheld from patients. CPR is costly, even if resuscitated the patient may then suffer a relapse, and furthermore it is an invasive procedure. (See further J. Saunders, "Medical Futility: CPR" in R. Lee and D. Morgan (eds.), *Deathrites: Law and Ethics at the End of Life,* London: Routledge, 1994.)

3. In situations in which patient approval has been obtained for a DNR it may be regarded as being a "living will" or "advance directive" (see further below at pages 876–881).

QUESTIONS:

1. Sir Stephen Brown rejected the use of the term "because of an unacceptable quality of life" but is such an assessment implicit in the order made?

2. Consider the above cases concerning non-treatment of the newly-
   born infant. To what extent is this case analogous and how far are
   the principles applied in those cases of assistance in a case of this type
   with regard to the issues of both resuscitation and administration of
   antibiotics?

4. ENGLISH LAW REFORM

(a) Active Termination of Life

It has been argued that just as an individual who has the means and
necessary physical strength can end his own life, so a person unable to end
his own life should be able to request another to assist him in that process.
"Euthanasia" is the term used to describe the deliberate ending of the life
of a person suffering from a painful illness. Several different categories of
euthanasia have been recognised: voluntary euthanasia: life terminated at
the patient's request; non-voluntary euthanasia: termination of life of an
incompetent patient; involuntary euthanasia: ending of life of the patient
on paternalistic or other grounds disregarding any wishes expressed by the
patient. The latter category is almost universally regarded as unacceptable
not least because it overrides the individual's autonomy and their right to
life. The other two categories have been the source of considerable
controversy. Two further distinctions should be noted: "active euthanasia"
which, as the name suggests, is positive action terminating life; and
"passive euthanasia" which concerns the shortening of life through an
omission to act. English law, as we have already seen, rejects active
euthanasia while accepting passive euthanasia.

A series of unsuccessful attempts have been made to introduce legislation
permitting euthanasia into English law. Proposed legislation falls into two
broad categories. First, it may take the form of prior authorisation through
for example, approval for euthanasia being given by two doctors or by a
tribunal. Secondly, a reporting procedure requiring the doctor to report to
an official body the fact that euthanasia has been given and that certain
criteria have been complied with.

The Euthanasia Bill 1936 provided that if a patient who was over 21 and
suffering from an incurable and fatal illness would be able to sign a form in
the presence of two witnesses asking to be put to death. The form and
certificates were to be submitted to a euthanasia referee who was to have
the task of interviewing the patient and other interested parties. The matter
was then to go to a court which had the right to consider the case, review
evidence and if they were satisfied then to issue a certificate authorising a
doctor to perform euthanasia in the presence of an official witness. The
Voluntary Euthanasia Bill 1969 authorised doctors to end the life of a
patient who was over 21, who requested it and who was certified by two
doctors as suffering from "serious physical illness or impairment reasonably thought in the patients case to be incurable and expected to cause him

severe distress or render him incapable of rational existence." The patient was to execute a declaration requesting euthanasia. A series of Incurable Patients Bills were introduced during the 1970s. One such Bill would have granted an incurable patient a right to receive whatever quantity of drugs he might need to get full relief from pain or physical distress and to be rendered unconscious if there was no treatment which could give him such relief. More recently a euthanasia Bill allowing a doctor to provide euthanasia where this was requested by an incurably ill patient has been given publicity by a parliamentary euthanasia group. (See (1991) 303 BMJ 1422.) The first instance of statutory recognition being given to the practice of euthanasia recently took place in Australia. The Australian Rights of the Terminally Ill Act 1995 provides that a person can request assistance to terminate life. A request must be voluntary, the patient must be of sound mind and over 18, the patient must be suffering from an illness that the medical practitioner believes will result in the patient's death. The assessment of the need for euthanasia must also be confirmed by a second medical practitioner. The request is not to be effective where medically acceptable pallative care options exist. The legislation requires there to be notification that the criteria under the statute have been complied with. This statute has proved controversial and is presently the subject of legal challenge in the Australian Federation.

(See also C. J. Ryan and M. Kaye, "Euthanasia in Australia — the Northern Territory Rights of the Terminally Ill Act 1995" (1996) *New England Journal of Medicine* 326.)

Those who oppose active euthanasia argue that it is not possible to either satisfactorily enact a euthanasia statute or provide legal defences to euthanasia which will provide sufficient safeguards against abuse. Some regard the introduction of voluntary euthanasia as one step down the slippery slope to involuntary euthanasia. Critics of euthanasia point to the experience in the Netherlands. In the Netherlands doctors are not prosecuted as long as they follow certain guidelines in administering euthanasia. The guidelines state that the request for euthanasia must be voluntary, durable and well considered, the patient must be experiencing intolerable suffering with no prospect of improvement; euthanasia must be a last resort; euthanasia must be performed by a physician who must consult with an independent physician colleague who has experience in the field. It has been claimed that these safeguards do not provide — satisfactory protection against abuses. (For strong support of active voluntary euthanasia see L. Kennedy, "Euthanasia" in A. Grubb (ed.), *Choices and Decisions in Health Care*, Chichester: Wiley 1993; G. Williams, "Euthanasia" (1973) 41 *Medico-Legal Journal* 4. The dangers of the "slippery slope" are discussed in D. Lamb, *Down the Slippery Slope,* Croom Helm: 1988, Chapter 2, "It started from small beginnings"; J. Keown, "Law and Practice of Euthanasia" (1992) 108 *L.Q.R.* 51; H. Jochemsem "Euthanasia in Holland: an ethical critique of the new law" (1994) 20 *Journal of Medical Ethics* 212.) It has also been argued that active euthanasia is less of an issue today in view of the extensive development of pallative care along with the administration of pain-killing drugs.

Alongside this has been the growth of the hospice movement. (See R. G. Twycross, "Where there is hope, there is life: a view from the hospice" in J. Keown (ed.), *Euthanasia Examined*, Cambridge: CUP (1995).) In 1967 Dame Cecily Saunders funded St Christophers Hospice to care for dying patients and their families at home and on the wards — it was aimed at teaching and research. Her initiative led subsequently to the development of a network of hospices across the country, (see N. James "From Vision to System" in R. Lee and D. Morgan, (eds), *Deathrites: Law and Ethics at the End of Life,* (London: Routledge, 1994. Finally, some health care professional bodies such as the British Medical Association have argued that recognition of active euthanasia would result in the doctor acquiring a function which was at odds with her traditional role as healer.

The issue of euthanasia received consideration by a House of Lords Select Committee established following the *Bland* case (H.L. Paper 21–2, London: HMSO, 1994). The Committee, who received an extensive quantity of evidence from leading experts, recommended that there should be no change in the law to allow active euthanasia. They were motivated in their decision by a concern to prohibit intentional killing, the slippery slope argument, the position of the elderly and others who may feel vulnerable and the availability of pallative care. (See further L. Gormally, "Walton, Davies, Boyd and the legalisation of euthanasia" in J. Keown (ed.) *Euthanasia Examined*, Cambridge: CUP (1995).

(b) Defence to those Prosecuted for Active Cessation of Life of a Neonate

In the aftermath of *R v. Arthur* it was suggested that a doctor who terminated the life of a neonate should not be prosecuted for murder but rather for some alternative offence. Diana and Malcolm Brahams proposed a Limitation of Treatment Bill. No criminal offence would be committed where a doctor refused or stopped treatment of an infant under 28 days old subject to two conditions being satisfied. First, the parents must give their written consent. Secondly, two doctors, both of at least seven years standing and one of them being a paediatrician, must certify in writing that the infant suffered from a severe mental or physical handicap which was either irreversible or of such gravity that after receiving all available treatment the child would enjoy no worthwhile quality of life. In determining the issue of quality of life the doctors were to take into account various factors. These would include the degree of pain and suffering likely to be endured, the child's potential to communicate, the extent to which the parents were willing to care for the child and the effect that the child may have on the parent's physical and mental health. (See D. and M. Brahams, "*R. v. Arthur*" (1981) 78 L.S.Gaz. 1342.) Legislative reform has also been proposed by J. K. Mason and R. A. McCall Smith, *Law and Medical Ethics* (4th ed.), 1994, page 162. They suggest that:

"In the event of positive treatment being necessary for a neonate's survival, it will not be an offence to withhold such treatment if two doctors, one of whom is a consultant paediatrician, acting in good faith and with the consent of both parents if available, decide against treatment in the light of reasonably clear medical prognosis which indicates that the infant's further life would be intolerable by virtue of pain or suffering or because of severe cerebral incompetence."

QUESTIONS:

1. Is legislation necessary in order to safeguard the position of medical practitioners?
2. Do you think that the safeguards built into the legislative proposals outlined above are adequate?
3. Who should make decisions to cease treatment of neonates? What qualities are required in such a decision maker? (See R. Weir, *Selective Non Treatment of the Handicapped Newborn,* Oxford: OUP, 1979, Chapter 9.)

(c) Statutory Recognition of Mercy Killing

Murder carries a mandatory life sentence. It can be argued that a person who kills another out of compassion for her suffering should not be classed in the same way as other murderers. One alternative approach to recognition of euthanasia would be the legislative recognition of mercy killing. This could take one of several forms. First, there could be a special offence of "mercy killing". Such an option was considered by the Criminal Law Revision Committee:

Criminal Law Revision Committee, 14th Report, *Offences Against The Person,* Cmnd 7844 (1980), page 53, Section F.

115. In our Twelfth Report we suggested that even if the mandatory life sentence is retained the judge in such cases should be given a discretion not to pass a custodial sentence. In our Working Paper we went much further. We suggested tentatively that there should be a new offence which would apply to a person who, from compassion, unlawfully kills another person who is or is believed by him to be:

(1) permanently subject to great bodily pain or suffering, or
(2) permanently helpless from bodily or mental incapacity, or
(3) subject to rapid and incurable bodily or mental degeneration.

We suggested that 2 years imprisonment would be an appropriate maximum penalty. When making this suggestion we appreciated that grave problems of definition would have to be solved — problems for which the Royal Commission on Capital Punishment had been unable to find a solution. Our suggestion aroused much interest and led to discussions in the press and elsewhere: it was not well received. Of those who wrote to us the great majority were against it. Some lawyers supported it. This was probably because they were aware of the difficulty judges are now in when dealing with genuine cases of compassionate killing. No one connected with the case wants to see the defendant convicted of murder. The result is that legal and medical consciences are stretched to bring about a verdict of manslaughter by reason of diminished responsibility. Some lawyers think that is bad for the law; others and probably the majority of laymen, are pleased that the law can bend enough to deal with hard cases. The majority of our correspondents opposed our suggestion both in principle and on pragmatic grounds. We were reminded that we were dealing with a fundamental ethical problem and that as lawyers we had no special qualifications or experience for solving it; and it was said that our suggestion would not prevent suffering but would cause suffering, since the weak and the handicapped would receive less effective protection from the law than the fit and well because the basis of the suggested new offence would rest upon the defendant's evaluation of the condition of the victim. That evaluation might be made in ignorance of what medicine would do for the sufferer. We were reminded too of the difficulties of definition. When we came to examine our suggestion again for the purposes of this report, we decided unanimously that we should withdraw it, if only on the ground that it is too controversial for the exercise in law reform on which we are engaged. We do not recommend that there should be an offence of mercy killing or that any special sentencing discretion should be given to judges when trying these cases.

NOTES:

1. The approach of the Criminal Law Revision Committee has been criticised, not least because of its unwillingness to deal with an issue on the basis that that it controversial. It has been suggested that reliance on the plea of diminished responsibility in the case of mercy killers may be unsatisfactory because the courts have taken a more restrictive approach to the definition of diminished responsibility requiring at least some evidence of mental imbalance. (See R. Leng, "Mercy Killing and the CLRC" (1982) 132 *New L.J.* 76.)

2. An alternative approach is for mercy killing to operate as a defence to a prosecution for murder. A plea of mercy killing could reduce a charge of murder to manslaughter or alternatively operate as a total defence. The House of Lords Select Committee on Euthanasia considered this option (H.L. Paper 2–1, London: HMSO, 1994). Evidence was presented to the Committee to the effect that there was not a pressing case at that time for such a defence. Home Office statistics revealed that between 1982 to 1991 "mercy killing" was an issue in 22 cases of homicide; none of those cases concerned health professionals. Although in all cases a prosecution was begun for murder only one conviction and sentence of life imprisonment eventually resulted. In all other cases other sentences were substituted. The House of Lords Select Committee did suggest that the mandatory penalty of life imprisonment for murder should be abolished. (See M. Otlowski, "Active Voluntary Euthanasia" (1994) 2 *Medical Law Review* 161.) A final option would be that in a situation in which a judge determines that a mercy killing has taken place he should have the power to reduce the sentence imposed. This would require a departure from the existing mandatory life sentence for murder.

QUESTIONS:

1. What are the difficulties facing a legislative draftsman attempting to define a mercy killing offence?
2. Would a mercy killing offence place a patient in an unduly vulnerable position?

(d) Advance Directives

Advance directives (also known as living wills) are documents which allow a person to state the criteria on which they would wish treatment to be given should they become incapable of making their own decisions (see further J. Montgomery, "Power over death: the final sting" in R. Lee and D. Morgan (eds), *Death Rites: Law and Ethics at the end of Life,* London: Routledge, 1994). Use of advance directives has become increasingly common. Draft living wills have been drawn up by a number of organisations, including the Terence Higgins Trust, an organisation which assists persons who are HIV positive or who have AIDS. We noted in Chapter 6 that patients have the right to refuse treatment where competent to do so, even if it means that death results. The courts have now confirmed that an advance refusal of treatment should be respected:

Re T [1992] 4 All E.R. 649; [1992] W.L.R. 782

For the facts of this case see page 269 above.

LORD DONALDSON M.R.:
" . . .

1. Prima facie every adult has the right and capacity to decide whether or not he will accept medical treatment even if a refusal may risk permanent injury to his health or even lead to premature death. Furthermore it matters not whether the reasons for the refusal were rational or irrational, unknown or even none existent. This is so not withstanding the very strong public interest in preserving the life and health of all citizens. However, the presumption of capacity to decide which stems from the fact that the patient is an adult is rebuttable.
2. An adult patient may be deprived of his capacity to decide either by long term mental incapacity or retarded development or by temporary factors such as unconsciousness or confusion or the effects of fatigue, shock, pain or drugs.
3. If an adult patient did not have the capacity to decide at the time of the purported refusal and still does not have that capacity, it is the duty of the doctors to treat him in whatever way they consider in the exercise of his clinical judgement to be their best interests.
4. Doctors faced with a refusal of consent have to give very careful and detailed consideration to what was the patient's capacity to decide at the time when the decision was made. It may not be a case of capacity or no capacity. It may be a case of reduced capacity. What matters is whether at the time the patient's capacity was reduced below the level needed in the case of a refusal

of that importance for refusals can vary in importance. Some may involve a risk to life or of irreparable damage to health. Others may not.

5. In some cases doctors will not only have to consider the capacity of the patient to refuse treatment but also whether the refusal has been vitiated because it resulted not from the patient's will, but from the will of others. It matters not that those others sought however strongly, to persuade the patient to refuse so long as in the end the refusal represented the patient's independent decision. If, however his will was overborn the refusal would not have represented the patient's true decision. In this context the relationship of the persuader to the patient — for example, spouse, parents or religious adviser will be important, because some relationships more readily lend themselves to overbearing the patient's independent will than others.

6. In all cases doctors will need to consider what is the true scope and basis of the refusal? Was it based upon assumptions which in the end have not been realised? A refusal is only effective within its true scope and vitiated if it is based upon false assumptions.

7. Forms of refusal should be redesigned to bring the consequences of a refusal forcibly to the attention of patients.

8. In cases of doubt as to the effect of a purported refusal of treatment where failure to treat threatens the patient's life or threatens irreparable damage to his health, doctors and health authorities should not hesitate to apply to the courts for assistance."

NOTES:

1. This case emphasises the general principle that competent patient has the right to both consent and refuse consent to treatment. Indeed failure to respect a valid refusal of consent may give rise to an action in battery. (For general discussion of *Re T* see Chapter 5 at page 269.) The approach taken in *Re T* was reinforced by the decision of the Court of Appeal in *Re C* (see Chapter 5 at page 272). Support was also given to advance directives by the Court of Appeal and the House of Lord in *Airedale NHS Trust v. Bland* (see page 842 above). In *Bland* the court indicated that it would be unlawful to ignore a valid refusal of treatment. That of course does not mean that a doctor would always be bound by an advance directive. She would have to consider the scope and applicability of the directive.

2. In *Re T* itself the patient's refusal of treatment was overidden. Subsequent to *Re T*, in *Re S* [1992] 4 All E.R. 671 a treatment refusal was also overridden in the case of a pregnant woman (see Chapter 13 above). This perhaps illustrates the fact that the right to die is by no means absolute. It should be noted that the Law Commission in their consideration of advance treatment refusals examine situations in which the decision to overrule treatment refusal may be displaced.

3. There are now a number of draft living wills which can be obtained by the general public. For example, draft living wills have been published by the Terence Higgins Trust in conjunction with Kings College London (2nd ed.) (1994) in M. Molloy and V. Mepham, *Let Me Decide,* Harmondsworth: Penguin, 1993 and in "The Patients Association *Advance Statements about Future Medical Treatment*"

1996 Guidance on advance directives has also been published by the British Medical Association, *Advance Statements about Medical Treatment,* London: BMA, 1995.

Advance directives have been the subject of extensive consideration by the Law Commission. While the government have now stated that it is not their intention to enact these proposals and that they intend to undertake further discussion, this report provides a useful basis for consideration of these issues.

Law Commission Report, *Mental Incapacity,* Law Com. No. 23 (1995)

Advance refusals of treatment

5.16 To maintain the effect of the present law is consistent with our policy aim of enabling people to make such decisions as they are able to make for themselves. In order to give full effect to this aim, special provision is now required for cases where a person makes an anticipatory refusal of treatment which is intended to remain in effect even when the maker no longer has capacity to review the decision made.

We recommend that an 'advance refusal of treatment' should be defined as a refusal made by a person aged eighteen or over with the necessary capacity of any medical, surgical or dental treatment or any other procedure and intended to have effect at any subsequent time when he or she may be without capacity to give or refuse consent.

5.17 'The right to decide one's own fate presupposes a capacity to do so'. It should therefore be an essential characteristic of an advance refusal that it was made at a time when the maker had capacity to make it. The new statutory definition of incapacity will be applied in any case where a doubt about capacity needs to be resolved.

Age

5.18 There would be little point in our recommending that an anticipatory refusal of treatment can be made by persons under the age of eighteen since it is now settled if controversial law that the court in the exercise of its statutory and/or inherent jurisdiction (and possibly also any person who has parental responsibility) may overrule the refusal of a minor, competent or not, to accept medical treatment.

Terminal conditions

5.19 None of our respondents disagreed with our preliminary view that it would be wrong to stipulate that advance decisions can only apply when a patient is in a 'terminal condition'. Such stipulations were common in early statutes in the United States which laid down strict formalities for the making of 'living wills', but they would be out of place in a scheme which seeks to build upon and clarify the fundamental legal principle that patients with capacity can refuse *any* treatment.

5.20 If an 'advance refusal' has been made then a treatment provider cannot rely on the authority which would otherwise be available to enable a patient without capacity to be treated reasonably and in his or her best interests. Obviously, the treatment provider will not be liable for proceeding with treatment unless he or she knows or has reasonable ground for believing that there is an advance refusal.

We recommend that the general authority should not authorise any treatment or procedure if an advanc refusal of treatment by the person concerned applies to that treatment or procedure in the circumstances of the case.

Validity and applicability

5.21 The recommendation made in paragraph 5.20 above will effectively take the place of the proposition in *Re T* that an advance refusal of treatment must be 'clearly established' and 'applicable in the circumstances'. As was made clear in *Re T*, 'doctors will need to consider what is *the true scope* and basis of the decision'. They must ask whether the patient has refused consent to the treatment or procedure which it is now desired to carry out, in the circumstances in which it would now be carried out. Inevitably, problems of evidence will sometimes arise. Equally, however, it can be seen from certain model forms that patients are already able to make the terms of their refusals absolutely clear. A Jehovah's Witness might have stated that 'my express refusal of blood is absolute and is not to be overridden in ANY circumstances'. Someone else might have provided that 'if I become permanently unconscious with no likelihood of regaining consciousness . . . I wish medical to be limited to keeping me comfortable and free from pain, and I REFUSE all other medical treatment'.

5.22 Statutory provisions cannot resolve the problems and questions which may arise in relation to the validity and applicability of advance refusals. The development of a code of practice and of model forms which direct patients towards making the terms of any refusal clear will help to address the most likely problems. In the words of Lord Donaldson, 'what really matters' is 'the declaration by the patient of his decision with a full appreciation of the possible consequences, the latter being expressed in the simplest possible terms'. It may be that the most effective format will be one which uses succinct and non-technical language, and avoids detailed provisions about particular ailments or conditions or particular treatments or procedures. As a matter of evidence, a document which refers to particular circumstances, but not to those which have arisen, may be found not to apply to the present circumstances. Similarly, a document which does not mention, expressly or impliedly, the particular treatment which is now proposed would not be an effective refusal of that treatment. The technique (adopted by the THT/King's College model form) of referring to treatments with particular purposes rather than any particular treatments may be one way of avoiding some of the difficulties. We do not believe that primary legislation can elucidate the many questions which can arise about the 'applicability' of a particular advance refusal. Our respondents consistently raised with us two matters in particular in relation to questions about applicability and we would expect to see these points addressed in any code of practice. First, many respondents were anxious to ensure that treatment which has become available since the time the refusal was made should not be withheld unless it was clear that the patient intended to refuse this treatment as well. Secondly, it was said of any discussion with a health care professional might often be based on erroneous ideas and information. This is not to suggest that any refusal made without such a discussion would always be 'inapplicable'; a Jehovah's Witness would be unlikely to be swayed by any such discussion. These are, however, two of the many matters which will be relevant to the determination of whether any advance refusal 'applies to' the treatment or procedure now proposed 'in the circumstances of the case'.

Life-sustaining treatment

5.23 A number of north America cases indicate the great reluctance of both doctors and courts to approve the withholding of treatment which is imperative to prevent death, unless any refusal of such treatment expressly contemplates the possibility of such an avoidable death. This was also an issue in the leading English case of *Re T*. The public interest in preserving the life and health of citizens does not prevent an adult patient from refusing life-sustaining treatment, although any doubt will be resolved in favour of the preservation of life. Patients should therefore be aware that they should address their minds to the possibility of dying if they wish any refusal of treatment to apply notwithstanding this possibility. Some model forms already make express reference to the danger of death.

Pregnant women

5.24 The case of *Re S* involved a refusal by a pregnant woman to consent to a Caesarian section. The woman's refusal was effectively overruled by the High Court, which declared (after a brief hearing arranged at very short notice) that it would be lawful to perform the operation in the circumstances. Either this decision is in conflict with the later decision in *Re C* or its *ratio* is limited to cases where the life of an unborn viable foetus is in danger. It has been heavily criticised and a number of respondents urged us to address the problem of principle it appears to pose, namely that a pregnant woman may lawfully be subjected to what would otherwise be an unlawful battery.

5.25 The majority of the U.S. states with living will legislation set statutory limits to the effectiveness of any declarations during the maker's pregnancy. Similarly, it has been suggested here that '[i]f a living will comes into operation in relation to a woman who is pregnant, any instructions to forego life-sustaining treatment should be regarded as invalid during the course of the pregnancy'. We do not, however, accept that a woman's right to determine the sorts of bodily interference which she will tolerate somehow evaporates as soon as she becomes pregnant. There can, on the other hand, be no objection to acknowledging that many women do in fact alter their views as to the interventions they find acceptable as a direct result of the fact that they are carrying a child. By analogy with cases where life might be needlessly shortened or lost, it appears that a refusal which did not mention the possibility that the life of a foetus might be endangered would be likely to be found not to apply in circumstances where a treatment intended to save the life of the foetus was proposed. Women of child-bearing age should therefore be aware that they should address their minds to this possibility if they wish to make advance refusals of treatment.

A presumption of non-applicability

5.26 There are likely to be particular problems in relation to questions of applicability where life-sustaining treatment or treatment which would save the life of a foetus are at issue. The best way of balancing the continuing right of the patient to refuse such treatment with the public interest in preserving life is to create a statutory presumption in favour of the preservation of life.

We recommend that in the absence of any indication to the contrary it shall be presumed that an advance refusal of treatment does not apply in circumstances where those having the care of the person who made it consider that the refusal (a) endangers that person's life or (b) if that person is a woman who is pregnant the life of the foetus.

Conscientious objections

5.28 We have experienced some difficulty with the notion, put forward by a very small number of our respondents, that special provisions should cater for the fact that doctors may have a 'conscientious objection' to withholding treatment which a patient has refused. The law, clearly stated in *Re T*, is that treating a patient despite a refusal of consent 'will constitute the civil wrong of trespass to the person and may constitute a crime'. The majority of our respondents were keen to see statutory force given to this clear principle and we ourselves fail to see the significance of the fact that some doctors may disagree with a patient's motives in making a refusal or advance refusal of treatment. If the principle of self-determination means anything, the patient's refusal must be respected. There is therefore no need for any specific statutory provision. We note the clear view of the BMA that it is unethical for a doctor to flout a competent refusal of treatment, including one made in advance; and that a doctor placed in difficulties by such an advance directive 'should relinquish the patient's management to colleagues'.

Formalities

5.29 In the consultation paper we discussed the possible merits of a prescribed form for anticipatory decisions. We suggested that the importance of flexibility was such that there should simply be a presumption that a written, signed and witnessed decision was 'clearly established'. Our respondents generally favoured maximum flexibility, although a number of them told us that a model form would often be very helpful to patients. Some model forms are already widely available and more seem always to be being produced. Both the BMA and the Law Society expressed misgivings about any rules which would invalidate a patient's genuine choices simply because those choices were made in ways which fell short of formalities laid down in statute. To disregard valid decisions on that account would be contrary to our aims of policy. Matters of form and execution are essentially questions of evidence in any particular case. We have said that the present common law position is that the issue is the 'true scope and basis' of the decision, rather than the way it has been recorded. The existence of a formal document is no guarantee of either validity or applicability, nor is the absence of such a document any guarantee that a valid and applicable advance refusal has not been made. Although we gave careful consideration to the introduction of statutory requirements prescribing the form and contents of any advance refusal, we concluded that these would benefit no-one.

5.30 We do, however, see merit in at least encouraging patients to express any advance refusals of treatment in writing, to sign the document and to have their signature witnessed. Such a step would be likely to furnish some definite proof that the refusal was made by the patient and intended to have effect in the future. We take the view that a rebutable presumption is the best way to balance the need for flexibility and the desirability of formal writing. It would not, of course, answer the questions the doctor must ask as to whether (1) the patient had capacity to make the refusal and whether (2) the refusal applies to the treatment now proposed and in the circumstances which now exist.

> *We recommend that in the absence of any indication to the contrary it should be presumed that an advance refusal was validly made if it is in writing signed and witnessed.*

We would certainly expect any code of practice to recommend the making of any refusal in writing.

Withdrawing or altering an advance refusal

5.31 The consultation paper suggested that it should be possible to revoke an anticipatory decision at any time when the maker has capacity to do so. Consultees favoured a flexible approach to 'revocation', although some concern was expressed about the possibility of claims being made that a carefully considered refusal had been revoked in the privacy of a doctor's consulting room. This, again, is inevitably a question of fact and evidence in any particular case. It would seem entirely wrong to stipulate that an advance refusal must stand until, for example, paper and pencil and an independent witness can be found.

5.32 Some respondents pointed out that disputes could arise as to whether a 'revocation' was intended to be permanent, or only to apply to a particular proposed procedure. This led us to conclude that 'revocation' was an unhelpful term in the context of a policy favouring maximum flexibility. The essential point is that the maker should retain power, commensurate with his or her capacity, to depart from the terms of an advance refusal.

We recommend that an advance refusal of treatment may at any time be withdrawn or altered by the person who made it, if he or she has capacity to do so.

5.33 Respondents generally agreed with our provisional view that automatic revocation after a period of time would be unduly restrictive. We would expect any code of practice to give guidance to patients on updating any refusal on a regular basis, so as to reduce the risk of it being found not to apply to circumstances which arise many years later.

Exclusion of 'basic care'

5.34 In the consultation paper we proposed that an advance directive should never be effective in refusing either pain relief or basic care. On consultation, there was general agreement to the proposition that a patient's right to self-determination could properly be limited by considerations based on public policy. A number of respondents highlighted the effect on staff and other patients if patients were to have power to refuse in advance even the most basic steps to ensure comfort and cleanliness. One respondent argued that since a patient with capacity can refuse all types of treatment the same rule should apply to those making anticipatory refusals, but this minority view did not appeal to us. We were grateful for the assistance of the BMA on the details of the proposed exclusion clause. We accept that patients with capacity regularly refuse certain types or levels of pain relief because they prefer to maintain alertness, and we prefer now to refer only to the alleviation of severe pain. We have also replaced reference to 'spoon-feeding' with reference to direct oral feeding, to cater for the administration of nutrition and hydration by syringe or cup. Our proposed definition of 'basic care' reflects a level of care which it would be contrary to public policy to withhold from a patient without capacity.

We recommend that an advance refusal of treatment should not preclude the provision of basic care, namely care to maintain bodily cleanliness and to alleviate severe pain, as well as the provision of direct oral nutrition and hydration.

Accident and emergency situations

5.35 One of our respondents suggested that any provision restricting the power or duty to treat should not be applicable in accident and emergency situations. The House of Lords Select Committee stated that 'there should be no expectation that treatment in an emergency should be delayed while enquiry is made about a possible advance directive'. The broad scheme of general authority based on reasonable treatment in a patient's best interests appear to us quite flexible enough to cover any distinction there might be between emergency situations and others. There is no need for any special provision exempting accident and emergency personnel from the broad terms of that scheme.

The role of the court

5.36 Most respondents agreed with our provisional proposal that the court should not have power to override a valid and applicable anticipatory decision in the exercise of its 'best interests' jurisdiction. Although some respondents appeared to favour such a power, it was apparent on close reading that they were concerned about out-of-date refusals (where new treatments had become available), or those made in a state of depression or mental frailty. These issues go to applicability and validity respectively and do not necessitate any power to 'override'. Resort to the court will only be available and necessary where a decision is required about the validity of the refusal (including any issue as to whether it has been withdrawn or altered) or its applicability. Where there is any doubt about such matters and an application to the court is made, treatment provided should have authority to take minimum steps to prevent the patient's death or deterioration in the interim.

We recommend that an advance refusal should not preclude the taking of any action necessary to prevent the death of the maker or a serious deterioration in his or her condition pending a decision of the court on the validity or applicability of an advance refusal on the question whether it has been withdrawn or altered.

NOTES:

1. The Law Commission do not accept that a person should be able to execute an advance directive refusing all types of care including spoon feeding. To adopt such an approach would be to create a division between the approach taken in law to a competent patient who is refusing all treatment including feeding and the patient expressing his views through an advance directive. It has been suggested that such a restriction is justifiable because it protects the sensibilities of the medical staff and indeed that such an exception should be extended to the competent patient. (See A. Grubb (1993) 1 *Medical Law Review* 84.)

2. Recognition of the patient's right to refuse treatment should not, the Law Commission emphasised, mean that a person could require through the use of an advance directive that a doctor undertake an illegal positive action or an action contrary to the doctor's clinical judgment (paragraph 5.6).

3. The Law Commission recommend that there should be a new offence of concealing/destroying an advance directive (paragraph 5.38). In addition they recommend that a Code of Practice for the use of advance directives should be drawn up.

4. It was suggested that there should be a presumption that an advance directive should not apply in the case of treatment of a pregnant woman. (For discussion of treatment in face of opposition from a pregnant woman see Chapter 13 above and Appendix 3, below.)

5. The Law Commission recommend that a treatment provider who has acted in the reasonable belief that an advance directive applies in that situation shall be exempt from liability in future legal proceedings. (Paragraph 5.27.)

6. The House of Lords Select Committee on Medical Ethics favoured advance directives but opposed legislation on the basis that doctors were recognising the ethical obligation to act in accordance with advance directives and that judicial support had been given to this. They proposed the development of a Code of Practice. (See D. Morgan had been given to this "Odysseus and the binding directive" (1994) 14 *Legal Studies* 411.)

QUESTIONS:

1. Do you agree with the Law Commission's rejection of the use of advance directives by those under 18 years of age? (see paragraph 5.18 above). Is the Law Commission endorsement of the policy of the

present law regarding the ability to overule expressed wishes of patients under 18 justifiable? (See Chapter 7 above.)

2. Should an individual be able to make an advance refusal of treatment where there is a chance that if treatment were given, some health may be restored? (See C. Ryan, "Betting your life: an argument against certain advance directives" (1996) 22 *Journal of Medical Ethics* 95 and S. Luttrell and A. Somerville, "Limiting risks by curtailing rights: a response to Dr Ryan" (1996) 22 *Journal of Medical Ethics* 100.)

(e) Power of Attorney

As was made clear by the House of Lords in *F. v. West Berkshire Health Authority* [1989] 2 All E.R. 545, no one has the power to consent on behalf of an incompetent patient. Nevertheless, there may be situations in which an individual would wish another to have powers to make decisions about medical treatment. If a living will exists it may be that some provisions may be unclear and require interpretation. It is equally unlikely that a living will would be sufficiently comprehensive to cover all situations. Where a living will is unclear a proxy decision-maker may be of considerable benefit. The Enduring Power of Attorney Act 1985 allowed an individual to appoint a proxy to make decisions regarding financial matters once they became incapacitated, but such powers were not extended in relation to medical treatment. In its report *Mental Incapacity*, (Report No. 231, 1995) the Law Commission state that a scheme should be established allowing for the appointment of a proxy decision-maker by persons over 18. (See Part VII of the Report.) The Law Commission recommend that a proxy should be able to act only in the patient's "best interests" (See Chapter 5.) They recommend that only persons over 18 should be able to appoint a power of attorney. The document containing the power of attorney should contain a statement by the donee that she understands that it is her duty to act in the best interests of the donor. This power should be registered by a registration authority appointed by the Lord Chancellor. The donor would have the right to revoke the power while he has capacity to do so. The Law Commission also suggest that the donee's powers should be capable of being modified by court order save where a contrary intention has been expressed by the donor. Consistent with its recommendations regarding living wills it proposes limitations upon the power which a proxy would be able to exercise. Thus while a proxy may facilitate the process there are still likely to be situations in which the wishes of the incompetent person will be unascertainable with the ultimate decision being thrown back onto medical discretion.

SELECT BIBLIOGRAPHY

British Medical Association, *Euthanasia,* London: BMA, 1988.

British Medical Association, *Advance Statements about Medical Treatment,* London: BMA, 1995.

M. Brazier, *Medicine, Patients and the Law* (2nd ed.) Harmondsworth: Penguin, 1992, Chapter 13.

A. G. M. Campbell, "The Right to be Allowed to Die" (1985) 11 *Journal of Medical Ethics* 136.

R. Dworkin, *Life's Dominion,* London: HarperCollins, 1993.

M. Freeman, *Medicine, Ethics and the Law,* London: Sweet and Maxwell.

J. K. Gevers, "Legislation on euthanasia; recent developments in the Netherlands" (1992) 18 *Journal of Medical Ethics* 138.

J. Glover, *Causing Death and Saving Lives,* Oxford: OUP, 1987.

R. Goff, "A Matter of Life and Death" (1995) 3 *Medical Law Review* 1.

H. Jochemsem "Euthanasia in Holland: an ethical critique of the new law" (1994) 20 *Journal of Medical Ethics* 212.

I. Kennedy, *Treat Me Right*, Oxford: OUP 1991, Chapters 7, 8, 15 and 17.

J. Keown (ed.), *Euthanasia Examined: Ethical, Clinical and Legal Perspectives*, Cambridge: CUP, 1995.

P. Key, "Euthanasia, Law and Morality" (1989) 16 (2) *Auckland University Law Review* 224.

M. Khuse & P. Singer, *Should the baby live?*, Oxford: OUP, 1985.

R. Lee and D. Morgan (eds), *Deathrites: Law and Ethics at the End of Life,* London: Routledge, 1994.

J. K. Mason & R. A. McCall Smith, *Law and Medical Ethics* (4th ed.), London: Butterworths, 1994, Chapters 7, and 15.

S. A. M. McLean (ed.), *Death, Dying and the Law*, Aldershot: Dartmouth (1996).

D. Meyers, *The Human Body and the Law,* (2nd edn.), Edinburgh: EUP 1990, Chapters 10 and 11.

J. Montgomery, "Power over Death — The Final Sting" in R. Lee and D. Morgan (eds.), *Deathrites: Law and Ethics at the End of Life,* Routledge, 1994, Chapter 3.

D. Morgan, "Odysseus and the binding directive; only a cautionary tale" (1994) 14 *Legal Studies* 411.

M. Otlowski, "Active Voluntary Euthanasia: Options for Reform" (1994) 2 *Medical Law Review* 161.

J. Rachels, *The End of Life*, Oxford: OUP, 1985.

P. Singer, *Rethinking Life and Death: The Collapse of our Traditional Ethics,* Oxford: OUP, 1995.

P. Skegg, *Law, Ethics and Medicine,* Oxford: OUP, 1984.

P. Skegg, "The Edges of Life" [1988] *Otago Law Review* 517.

R. G. Twycross, "Euthanasia — a Physicians' Viewpoint" (1982) 8 *Journal of Medical Ethics* 86.

R. Weir, *Selective Non-Treatment of Handicapped New Borns* Oxford: OUP, 1985.

15

DEATH AND ORGAN TRANSPLANTATION

---

1. INTRODUCTION

Medical technology, with its potential to redefine the boundaries of life, has forced radical reconsideration of what is meant by death. Traditionally, death was classified as cardiac death. But this definition became outdated as life could be prolonged through artificial ventilation. A new definition of death was formulated, the irreversible degeneration of the brain stem, although it was only after some time that brain stem death became generally accepted by the medical profession. Ascertaining the point at which death occurs may be of considerable practical importance, not least in relation to the law of succession, where it may be crucial for determining who succeeds under a will. (See, *e.g.* M. Brazier, *Medicine, Patients and the Law* (2nd ed.) London: Penguin at page 434.) Today brain stem death is recognised, both by the medical profession and by the courts, as the point of death. Nevertheless the debate has not ended. Some have argued that the definition of death should be extended to encompass those persons in a state of cognitive death or upper brain death. Such reclassification would allow the person in a persistent vegetative state to be recognised as "dead". But, as we shall see below, such an extension is likely to meet considerable opposition.

Death is not simply a legal but is also a philosophical concept raising many issues, *e.g.* of personhood (see Chapter 2 and D. Lamb, *Death, Brain Death and Ethics* (1985)).

Scientific advances have meant that after the death of a person, parts of his body or tissue may be used by others. Transplantation of organs and tissue is common today. The range and sophistication of such transplants has dramatically increased over past decades (see D. Lamb, *Organ Transplants and Ethics*, London: Routledge (1990). The conduct of transplantation surgery is inhibited by a considerable shortage in the availability of organs for transplantation. Some proposals advanced to increase the supply of organs are discussed.

Use of tissue, organs and other body products gives rise to the question, what rights has a person to control the use of such bodily products? We noted in Chapter 13 that where for example, it is sought to use foetal tissue then consents should be obtained from the mother and that similar provisions regarding consents apply to gametes and embryos. To what extent if at all we possess any property rights over bodily products is an issue of increasing importance at a time when it is possible for certain bodily products to be used to produce substances of commercial value. Section two considers the issue of death. The legal regulation of transplantation is considered in section three. The chapter concludes in section four with a discussion of the question of organ and tissue ownership.

2. DEATH

The definition of death has been the source of much academic commentary. (See further C. Pallis, *An ABC of Brain Stem Death*, (2nd ed.) London: *BMJ*, 1996.) A summary of the background to the current scientific exposition of death is provided by Lamb in the following extract:

D. Lamb, *Organ Transplants and Ethics*, London: Routledge, 1990, (references ommitted).

Until the early 1960s and the advent of techniques for taking over the functions of the lungs and heart, the public had shown almost complete acceptance of medical practice concerning the diagnosis of death. This has not always been the case. Distrust of the profession's competence had been evident in scores in pamphlets and tracts written in the eighteenth and nineteenth centuries. In 1740 it had been suggested by Jacques Béenigne Winslow that putrefaction was the only sure sign of death. Such a proposal reflected a total loss of public confidence in their doctors. Yet putrefaction has never been seriously advanced as a definition of death by either physicians or philosophers.

The prestige of physicians increased however, during the mid-nineteenth century as health care sought to become more scientific and professional, although distrust of the kind expressed in Edgar Allan Poe's novel, *The Tell-Tale Heart*, continued throughout the century. Nevertheless, the development of certain technological aids, such as the stethoscope, enabled a more accurate detection of heart beat and respiration, and was an important factor in the growth of public confidence in the ability to diagnose death. In the twentieth century scepticism has returned in some areas. It will be argued that this scepticism is without foundation, and that refinements in diagnostic criteria have reached the point where public acceptance is justified.

The earliest references in the neurological literature to states resembling brain death go back to the 1890s. In 1898 Sir Dyce Duckworth reported on four cases with structural brain lesions in which "the function of respiration had earlier ceased for some hours before that of the circulation." Then in 1902 Harvey Cushing described a patient whose spontaneous respiration ceased as a result of an intracranial tumour, but whose heart was kept beating for 23 hours with artificial respiration.

The concept of brain death really emerged in France in 1959. Early that year a group of French neurosurgeons described a condition which they termed "death of the central nervous system". The characteristics of that state were "persistent apnoeic coma, absent brain stem and tendon reflexes, and an electrically silent brain." These patients had no detectable electrophysiological activity in either the superficial or deeper parts of their brains. Whilst they looked like cadavers a regular pulse could be discerned as long as ventilation was maintained. Although the authors did not directly address the issue of whether this state was equivalent to death, they concluded that the persistence of this condition for 18 to 24 hours warranted disconnection from the ventilator. Later that year a more complete account of the condition was published by two Parisian neurologists, Mollaret and Goulon who called it *coma dépassé* (a state beyond coma). They were not prepared to equate *coma dépassé* with death and, unlike their predecessors, they did not advocate the withdrawal of ventilatory support. The patients had all sustained massive, irreversible structural brain damage. Patients in a state of *coma dépassé* were in a state of irreversible coma associated with an irreversible loss of the capacity to breathe. They had not only lost all capacity to respond to external stimuli, they could not even cope with their internal mileu: they were poikilothermic, had diabetes insipidus, and could not sustain their own blood pressure. The cardiac prognosis of the condition was at most a few days, but sometimes as little as a few hours.

Outside France the term *coma dépassé* never really caught on. The condition as of course encountered wherever resuscitation was sufficiently well organised and intensive care units adequately equipped, to prevent irreversible apnoea immediately resulting in the cessation of cardiac action. During this period there was no attempt to relate observations of this condition to any well founded concept of death. Neither of the two French groups discussed the meaning of death (which is probably why they suggested different courses of action for what is essentially the same condition). By the late 1960s an increasing rate of organ transplantation and greater successes in resuscitation provided a background to the need for greater philosophical clarity concerning what it meant to be dead. The lack of such clarity was reflected in the ambiguous and often confusing terminology used at the time.The term "irreversible coma" was sometimes employed to refer to a condition which was equivalent to *"coma dépassé"*. The term "brain death" referred to the same state. Although the terminology was in a state of flux, the construct "brain death" achieved a degree of precision that allowed it to be used in a popular way. The term *coma dépassé* survived in France until May 24, 1988 when it was rejected in favour of "brain death" by the French Academy of Medicine, who commented that their decision "ends semantic ambiguity which leads to clinical ambiguity".

In 1968 the Ad Hoc Committee of the Harvard Medical School to Examine the Definition of Brain Death published its report and brain death (which was exactly what the French had described as *coma depasse*) achieved world wide recognition (Ad Hoc Committee of the Harvard Medical School, 1968). The Harvard criteria for brain death were fourfold:

    (1) absence of cerebral responsiveness;
    (2) absence of induced or spontaneous movement;
    (3) absence of spontaneous respiration;
    (4) absence of brain stem and deep tendon reflexes.

An isolectric EEG was deemed to be of "great confirmatory value" but the performance of an EEG was not considered mandatory. The report specified two conditions which were capable of mimicking the state of brain death and which had to be excluded in each case: hypothermia and drug intoxication. Finally, the report recommended that tests be repeated over a period of 24 hours to document the persistence of the condition. Since then numerous patients throughout the world have been diagnosed as brain dead, maintained on ventilators and observed until their hearts stopped. No patient meeting the Harvard criteria has ever recovered despite the most heroic management.

In the years following the publication of the Harvard report it was gradually realised that the clinically testable component of brain death was the death of the brain stem (brain stem death). In 1971 the work of two neurosurgeons Mohandas and Chouc, in Minneapolis, had a profound influence on thinking and practice regarding the diagnosis of death on neurological grounds. From detailed observations of patients who has sustained massive intracranial damage they concluded that irreversible damage to the brain stem was the "point of no return in the dying process," and that a diagnosis of this state "could be based on clinical judgment". Their recommendations became known as the Minnesota criteria, which were significant in that they introduced aetilogical preconditions to the diagnosis of brain death. A valid diagnosis of a dead brainstem, they held, was context dependant in the sense that an essential precondition was knowledge of "irreparable intracranial lesions".

This point about context dependency has not been fully appreciated by critics of brainstem death in the popular media, who frequently assume that tests are conducted in ignorance of the causes of the coma. Later guidelines stress that the all-important characteristic of irreversibility can only be established with reference to crucial preconditions. Not only must there be a known primary diagnosis which accounts for the cause of the coma, there must also be evidence that all reversible causes of brainstem dysfunction (such as hypothermia and drug intoxication) have been excluded. This of course, may take time, which is why it is misleading to speak simply of tests for brain stem death.

The basis for brain stem death test in England was set out in guidance published in 1976.

(a) Diagnosing death

"The Diagnosis of Brain Death" (1976) *British Medical Journal* 1187 [References omitted]

With the development of intensive-care techniques and their wide availability in the United Kingdom it has become commonplace for hospitals to have deeply comatose patients with severe brain damage who are maintained on artificial respirators by means of mechanical ventilators.

This state had been recognised for many years and it has been the concern of the medical profession to establish diagnostic criteria of such rigour that on their fulfilment the mechanical ventilator can be switched off, in the secure knowledge that there is no possible chance of recovery.

There has been much philosophical argument about the diagnosis of death which has throughout history been accepted as having occurred when the vital functions of respiration and circulation have ceased. However, with the technical ability to maintain these functions artificially the dilemma of when to switch off the ventilator has been the subject of much public interest. It is agreed that permanent functional death of the brain stem constitutes brain death and that once this has occurred further artificial support should be withdrawn. It is good medical practice to recognise when brain death has occurred and to act accordingly, sparing relatives from the further emotional trauma of sterile hope.

Codes of practice such as the Harvard criteria (1968) have been devised to guide medical practitioners in the diagnosis of brain death. These have provided considerable help with the problem and they have been refined by the knowledge gained from the experience which has been collated.

More recently Forrester has written on established practice in Scotland and Jennnett has made useful observations. The diagnostic criteria presented for brain death here have been written with the advice of the subcommittee of the Transplant Advisory Panel and the working party of the Faculty of Anaesthetists and the Royal College of Surgeons and have been approved by the Conference of Medical Royal Colleges and their Faculties in the United Kingdom. They are accepted as being sufficient to distinguish between those patients who retain the functional capacity to have a chance of even partial recovery and those where no such possibility exists.

Conditions under which the diagnosis of brain death should be considered

1. The patient is deeply comatose

  (a) There should be no suspicion that this state is due to depressant drugs (*Note 1*).

Note 1:

Narcotics, hypnotics and tranquillisers may have prolonged duration particularly when some hypothermia exists. The benzodiazepines are markedly cumulative and persistent in their actions and are commonly used as anti-convulsants or to assist synchronisation with mechanical ventilations. It is therefore recommended that the drug history should be carefully reviewed and adequate intervals allowed for the persistence of drug effects to be excluded. This is of particular importance in patients where the primary cause of coma lies in the toxic effects of drugs followed by anoxic cerebral damage.

  (b) Primary hypothermia as a cause of coma should be excluded (*Note 2*).

Note 2:

Metabolic and endocrine factors contributing to the persistence of coma must be subject to careful assessment. There should be no profound abnormality of the serum-electrolytes, acid-base balance or blood glucose.

  (c) Metabolic and endocrine disturbances which can be responsible for or can contribute to coma should have been excluded.

  2. The patient is being maintained on a ventilator because spontaneous respiration had previously become inadequate or had ceased altogether.

    Relaxants (neuromuscular blocking agents) and other drugs should have been excluded as a cause of respirator inadequacy or failure (*Note 3*).

Note 3:

Immobility, unresponsiveness and lack of spontaneous respiration may be due to the use of neuromuscular blocking drugs and the persistence of their effects should be excluded by elicitation of spinal reflexes (flexion or stretch) or by the demonstration of adequate neuro-muscular condition with a conventional nerve stimulation. Equally persistent effects of hypnotics and narcotics should be excluded as the cause of respiratory failure.

  3. There should be no doubt that the patient's condition is due to irremediable structural brain damage. The diagnosis of a disorder which can lead to brain death should have been fully established (*Note 4*).

Note 4:

It may be obvious within hours of a primary intercranial event such as severe head injury, spontaneous inter cranial haemorrhage or following neurosurgery that the condition is irremediable. However, when a patient has suffered primarily from cardiac arrest, hypoxia or severe circulatory insufficiency with an indefinite period of cerebral anoxia or is suspected of having cerebral air or fat embolism then it may take much longer to establish the diagnosis and to be confident of the prognosis. In some patients the primary pathology may be a matter of doubt and a confident diagnosis may only be reached by a continuity of clinical observation and investigation.

Diagnostic tests for the confirmation of brain death

All brain-stem reflexes are absent

    (a) The pupils are fixed in diameters and do not respond to sharp changes in the intensity of incident light.

    (b) There is no corneal reflex.

    (c) The vestibulo-ocular reflexes are absent (*Note (a)*).

    (d) No. motor responses within the cranial nerve distribution can be elicited by adequate stimulation of any somatic area.

    (e) There is no gag relex or reflex response to bronchial stimulation by a suction catheter down the trachea.

    (f) No respiratory movements occur when the patient is disconnected from the mechanical ventilator for long enough to ensure that the arterial carbon dioxide tension rises above the threshold for stimulation of respiration.

Note (a)

Vestibulo-ocular reflexes. These are absent when no eye movement occurs during or following the slow injection of 20 ml of ice-cold water into each external auditory meatus in turn, clear access to the tympanic membrane having been established by direct inspection. This test may be contra-indicated on one or other side by local trauma.

Other considerations

Repetition of testing

It is customary to repeat the tests to ensure that there has been no observer error. The interval between tests must depend upon the primary pathology and the clinical course of the disease. Note 4 indicates some conditions where it would be unnecessary to repeat them since a prognosis of imminent brain death can be accepted as being obvious. In some conditions the outcome is not so clear cut and in these it is recommended that the tests should be repeated. The interval between tests depends upon the progress of the patient and might be as long as 24 hours. This is a matter for medical judgement and repetition time must be related to the signs of improvement, stability, or deterioration which present themselves.

Integrity of spinal reflexes

It is well established that spinal cord function can persist after insultya which irretrievably destroy brain stem function. Reflexes of spinal origin may persist or return after an initial absence in brain dead patients.

Confirmatory investigations

It is now widely accepted that electro-encephalography is not necessary for the diagnosis of brain death. Indeed this view was only expressed from Harvard in 1969 only a year after the publication of their original criteria.

    Electro-encephalography has its principal value at earlier stages in the care of patients, in whom the original diagnosis is in doubt. When electro-encephalography is used the strict criteria recommended by the Federation of EEG Societies must be followed.

Other investigations such as cerebral angiography or cerebral blood flow measurements are not required for the diagnosis of brain death.

Body temperature

The body temperature in these patients may be low because of depression of central temperature regulation by drugs or by brain stem damage and it is recommended that it should not be less than 35°C before the diagnostic tests are carried out. A low reading thermometer should be used.

Specialist opinion and the status of the doctors concerned

Experienced clinicians in intensive care units, acute medical wards and accident and emergency departments should not normally require specialist advice. Only when the primary diagnosis is in doubt is it necessary to consult with a neurologist or neurosurgeon.

Decision to withdraw artificial support should be made after all the criteria presented above have been fulfilled and can be made by any one of the following combination of doctors:

(a) A consultant who is in charge of the case and one other doctor
(b) In the absence of a consultant, his deputy, who should have been registered for 5 years or more *and* who should have had adequate previous experience in the care of such cases and one other doctor.

"Memorandum on the Diagnosis of Death" (1979) 1 *British Medical Journal* 332.

(1) In October 1976 the Conference of the Royal College and their Faculties (U.K.) published a report unanimously expressing the opinion that "brain death" when it had occurred, could be diagnosed with certainty. The report has been widely accepted.

The conference was not at that time asked whether or not it believed that death itself should be presumed to occur when brain death takes place or whether it would come to some other conclusion. The present report examines this point and should be considered as an addendum to the original report.

(2) Exceptionally, as a result of massive trauma, death occurs instantaneously or near-instantaneously. Far more commonly, death is not an event, it is a process, the various organs and systems supporting the continuation of life failing and eventually ceasing altogether to function, successively and at different times.

(3) Cessation of respiration and cessation of heart beat are examples of organic failure occurring during the process of dying and since the moment that the heart beat ceases is usually detectable with simplicity by no more than clinical means, it has for centuries been accepted as the moment of death itself, without any serious attempt being made to assess the validity of this assumption.

(4) It is now universally accepted by the lay public as well as by the medical profession, that it is not possible to equate death itself with cessation of heart beat. Quite apart from the elective cardiac arrest of open-heart surgery spontaneous cardiac arrest followed by successful resuscitation is today commonplace and although the more sensational accounts of occurrences of

this kind still refer to the patient being "dead" until restoration of the heart beat the use of the quote marks usually demonstrate that this word is not to be taken literally, for to most people the one aspect of death that is beyond debate is irreversibility.

(5) In the majority of cases, in which a dying patient passes through the processes leading to the irreversible state we call death, successive organ failures eventually reach a point at which brain death occurs and this is the point of no return.

(6) In a minority of cases, brain death does not occur as a result of the failure of other organs or systems but as a direct result of severe damage to the brain itself from, perhaps, a head injury or a spontaneous intracranial haemor-rhage. Here the order of events is reversed; instead of the failure of such vital functions as heart beat and respiration eventually resulting in brain death, brain death results in the cessation of spontaneous respiration; this is normally followed within minutes by cardiac arrest due to hypoxia. If, however, oxygenation is maintained by artificial ventilation the heart beat can continue for some time and haemoperfusion will for a time be adequate to maintain function in other organs such as the liver and kidneys.

(7) Whatever the mode of its production, brain death represents the stage at which a patient becomes truly dead, because by then all functions of the brain have permanently and irreversibly ceased. It is not difficult or illogical in any way to equate this with the concept in many religions of the departure of the spirit from the body.

(8) In the majority of cases, since brain death is part of or the culmination of a failure of all vital functions, there is no necessity for a doctor specifically to identify brain death individually before concluding that the patient is dead. In a minority of cases in which it is brain death that causes failure of other organs and systems, the fact that these systems can be artificially maintained even after brain death has made it important to establish a diagnostic routine which will identify with certainty the existence of brain death.

Conclusion

(9) It is the conclusion of the Conference that the identification of brain death means that the patient is dead, whether or not the function of some organs such as heartbeat, is maintained by artificial means.

[Author's Note: These guidelines have now been superceded by a new set of Criteria for the Diagnosis of Brain Stem Death by a Working Group Convened by the Royal College of Physicians endorsed by the Conference of Medical Royal Colleges and their Faculties of the U.K. 1996). These are substantially based on the existing guidelines.]

Notes:

1. What constitutes death must be seen in the context of cultural and religious traditions. (See further D. Lamb, *Death, Brain Death and Ethics*, Beckenhem: Croom Helm, 1985).

2. Despite the widespread acceptance of brain stem death amongst the medical profession it has some critics, (See M. Evans "Against the definition of brain stem death" in R. Lee and D. Morgan (eds), *Deathrites*, London: Routledge, 1994. It has been suggested that considerable moral significance can be placed upon the fact that an

individual is still breathing, both from intuition and traditional medical widsom. It is perhaps worthy of note that while brain stem death is recognised in many countries it does not command universal acceptance. For example, there has been a movement back towards recognition of cardiac death in Denmark. (See M. Evans, "Death in Denmark" (1990) 16 *Journal of Medical Ethics* 191 and D. Lamb, "Death in Denmark — A Reply" (1991) 17 *Journal of Medical Ethics* 100.)

3. The procedure used to detect brain stem death in the United Kingdom is not standard worldwide. In certain countries it is also necesssary to show that there is a negative electroencephalogram (EEG) test to ascertain blood flow in the brain although it may be that such tests are redundant if the brain stem death test is accurately employed. (See J. K. Mason and R. A. McCall Smith, *Law and Medical Ethics* (4th ed), London: Butterworths, 1994, at page 285 and see generally P. McCullagh, *Brain Death, Brain Absent, Brain Donors*, Chichester: Wiley, 1993).

(b) Deciding the point of death — the law

(i) Defining death — common law

While the medical profession had reached consensus as to the point of death, for a considerable period of time the legal definition of death was unclear. In *R. v. Malcherek and Steel* [1981] 2 All E.R. 422 the defendants were charged with murder. The defence claimed that the chain of causation was broken because after the assault the victims had been supported on a ventilator, and it was only when they were subsequently removed from the ventilator that brain stem death was diagnosed. Lord Lane stated that:

"Where the medical practitioner using generally acceptable methods, came to the conclusion that the patient was, for all practical purposes dead and that such vital functions as remained were being maintained solely by mechanical means and accordingly discontinued treatment, that did not break the chain of causation between the initial injury and death."

This statement appeared to amount to judicial acceptance of recognition of brain stem death as death. Nevertheless, the precise position remained uncertain for over a decade before finally being confirmed in *Re A*:

Re A [1992] 3 Med. L.R. 303

A was a young child just under 2 years of age. He was taken to hospital where he was found to have no heartbeat. He was suffering from non-accidental injuries including blood on the brain. He was put on a ventilator. There were no signs of recovery. The court considered the question of whether the child had died and thus could be removed from the ventilator.

JOHNSON J.:

"... The present criteria of death has been the subject of recommendations by both the Royal College of Surgeons and the Royal College of Physicians and a working party of the British Paedeatric Association. Applying the criteria laid down by her profession the consultant concluded on January 20 that A was not brain stem dead. On the following day she again carried out the tests which are necessary to determine whether the necessary criteria are satisfied. The consultant described each test to me and she explained to me that each one was satisfied. The tests lasted overall about half an hour.

Describing the criteria and her observations of A and expressing myself in lay terms, her evidence was to the following effect. A's pupils were fixed and dilated. On movement of the head his eyes moved with his head. What is called a 'dolls eye response' was absent. On his eye being touched with a piece of cotton wool there was no response. On cold water being passed into his ear there was no reflex reaction neither was there reaction to pain being applied to his central nervous system. Finally, on his temporary removal from the ventilator to enable the carbon dioxide content of his body to increase there was no respiratory response. All in all the consultant was satisfied that A was brain stem dead ...

On the same day the consultant had arranged for a colleague consultant paediatrician neurologist to carry out the same tests that she had, herself, carried out the previous day with a view to confirming or otherwise the validity of her professional conclusions. Under professional guidelines it was not necessary for her to seek a second opinion in that way, but she decided that in the particular circumstances of the case it would be a wise thing for her to do. Accordingly the tests were carried out again on Wednesday of last week, January 22, by this colleague who reached the same conclusion as had been reached by the first consultant.

Both doctors were at pains to exclude other possibilities for A's state, including the possibility of his suffering from extreme hypothermia or some abnormality of his biochemistry. Moreover, they tested for drug, lest his brain-stem functions should have been suppressed by the administration of some drug of which they had not been aware, although he had, in fact, been under the consultants supervision for three days in Guy's hospital and they would have been aware had drugs been administered to him. Nonetheless they carried out the necessary checks and satisfied themselves that no such drug was present.

Both doctors concluded that A was brain stem dead ...

It is now Monday January 27. I have no hesitation at all in holding that A has been dead since Tuesday of last week January 21 ...".

NOTES:

1. This approach also received the support of the House of Lords in *Airedale NHS Trust v. Bland* [1993] 1 All E.R. 821. (See Chapter 15.)
2. If a doctor fails to follow the accepted professional criteria for the diagnosis of brain stem death this may result in a civil action or criminal prosecution although in the absence of a statutory definition of death there is otherwise no specific sanction.

(ii) No statutory definition of death

The existing definition of death is dependent upon the common law. The question of whether there should be a statutory definition of death was examined by the Criminal Law Revision Committee in 1980.

Criminal Law Revision Committee, *Fourteenth Report: Offences Against the Person* Cmnd. 7844 (1980), HMSO

Paragraph 37

We have considered whether there should be a statutory definition of death. A memorandum issued by the honorary secretary of the Conference of Medical Royal Colleges and Faculties in the United Kingdom on January 15, 1979 refers to an earlier report of the Conference which expressed their unanimous opinion that 'brain death' could be diagnosed with certainty. The memorandum states that the report published by the Conference has been widely accepted and says that the identification of brain death means that a patient is truly dead, whether or not the function of some organs. such as a heart beat, is still maintained by artificial means. Brain death is said to be when all the functions of the brain have permanently and irreversibly ceased. We are however extremely hesitant about embodying in a statute (which is not always susceptible of speedy amendment) an expression of present medical opinion and knowledge derived from a field of science which is continually progressing and inevitably altering its opinions in the light of new information. If a statutory definition of death were to be enacted there would, in our opinion, be a risk that further knowledge would cause it to lose the assent of the majority of the medical profession. In that event, far from assisting the medical profession, for example, in cases of organ transplants, the definition might be a hindrance to them. Moreover while there might be agreement that the statutory definition was defective there might be differences of view about the proper content of any new definition. An additional reason for not recommending a definition of death is that such a definition would have wide repercussions outside offences against the person and the criminal law. A legal definition of death would also have to be applicable in the civil law. It would be undesirable to have a statutory definition confined only to offences against the person, which is the extent of our present remit. For these reasons therefore we are not recommending the enactment of a statutory definition of death.

QUESTION:

1. Should the issue of brain stem death be subject to consideration in Parliament rather than left to judicial and clinical determination? (See P. D. G. Skegg, "The Case for a Statutory Definition of Death" (1976) *Journal of Medical Ethics* 190; while for a contrasting view see I. Kennedy, "Alive or Dead" (1969) 22 *Current Legal Problems* 102.)

(c) Extending the definition of death — cognitive death

Whilst support has been given by courts and the medical profession to the concept of brain stem death, some have suggested that the definition of death could be extended still further to encompass cognitive death. This is death of upper hemispheres of the brain while the brain cells are still functioning. The status of cognitive death was considered in the *Bland* case.

Airedale NHS Trust v. Bland [1993] 1 All E.R. 821; [1993] A.C. 789.

For the facts of this case see pages 842–843, above.

LORD KEITH:

". . . Anthony Bland has for over three years been in the condition known as persistent vegetative state (PVS). It is unnecessary to go into all the details about the manifestations of this state which are already set out in the judgment of the courts below. It is sufficient to say that it arises from the destruction, through prolonged deprivation of oxygen, of the cerebral cortex, which has resolved into a watery mass. The cortex is that part of the brain which is the seat of cognitive function and sensory capacity. Anthony Bland cannot see, hear or feel anything. He cannot communicate in any way. The consciousness which is the essential feature of individual personality has departed for ever. On the other hand the brain stem, which controls the reflexive functions of the body, in particular heartbeat, breathing and digestion, continues to operate. In the eyes of the medical world and of the law a person is not clinically dead so long as the brain stem retains its function. In order to maintain Anthony Bland in his present condition, feeding and hydration are achieved artificially by means of a nasogastric tube and excretionary functions are regulated by a catheter and by enemas. The catheter from time to time gives rise to infections which have to be dealt with by appropriate medical treatment. The undisputed consensus of eminent medical opinion is that there is no prospect whatever that Anthony Bland will ever make any recovery from his present condition, but that there is every likelihood that he will maintain his present state of existence for many years to come, provided that the medical care which he is now receiving is continued."

NOTES:

1. Recognition of a cognitive definition of death would be in line with those commentators who define humans in terms of personhood and afford them rights accordingly (see Chapter 2 above). Destruction of the ability to reason could be seen as commensurate with the destruction of personhood. Nevertheless recognition of cognitive death would create considerable problems. As the judgments in *Bland* illustrate, one such problem concerns a patient who is in a persistent vegetative state. Should such a patient be recognised as dead? (See I. Kennedy and A. Grubb, "Withdrawal of Artificial Nutrition and Hydration: Incompetent Adult" (1993) 1 *Medical Law Review* 359.) Note the American case of *Re Quinlan*, 70 N.J. 10 353A 2d 647 (1976), a patient in PVS who, after ventilation was withdrawn continued to live for several years.

2. Recognition of cognitive death would also require clarification of the position of anencephalic infants. Anencephalic infants are born with some or all of the upper hemispheres of the brain absent. They are capable of living for some days. Recognition of cognitive death would result in such infants being declared "dead" at birth. This would mean that for example, their organs could be used immediately for the purposes of transplantation. Whether this approach should be adopted has been questioned. (See P. McCullagh, *Brain Dead, Brain*

Absent Brain Donors, Chichester: Wiley, 1993, Chapters 4 and 5. There are also varying degrees of anencephaly combined with a risk of misdiagnosis (see A. D. Shewman, "Anencephaly: selected medical aspects" (1988) 11 *Hastings Centre Report* and D. Lamb, *Organ Transplants and Ethics,* London: Routledge, 1990).

3. ORGAN AND TISSUE TRANSPLANTATION

There was no statutory regulation of the medical use of cadaver tissue until the Anatomy Act 1832. This statute was passsed following the prosecution for murder of the "body snatchers" Burke and Hare who supplied corpses for payment to the medical schools of Edinburgh. The 1832 Act allowed a person to make a declaration donating their body after their death for the purposes of medical science. The Corneal Grafting Act in 1952 allowed individuals to donate the use of their eyes for therapeutic purposes after their death. This was followed in 1961 by the Human Tissue Act. This legislation, which governs the transplantation of cadaver tissue, is still in force. In addition, statute now also governs the use of organs from live donors in the form of the Human Organ Transplants Act 1989. Information concerning transplantation procedures and donation is available through a statutory body, the U.K. Transplant Support Services. (U.K. Transplant Support Services Authority Regulations S.I. 1992 No. 408).

Over the last few decades the number and sophistication of transplantation procedures undertaken for therapeutic purposes has increased. Today transplants are undertaken of many organs and tissues from hearts to corneas to bone marrow. Currently research is being undertaken into the use of substitutes for human organs in the form of artificial organs and animal organs/tissue — which are known as xenographs. However, these alternative forms have not reached a stage at which they will supplant the use of human tissue. The use of xenographs also poses some acute ethical dilemmas. There is a further question, namely whether transplantation technology should be increasing as fast as it is or whether medical resources should be expended in other ways. We do not enter into that debate here. (See Chapter 2 above.)

The difficulty facing health professionals involved in transplant surgery at present is that there is a discrepancy between the number of organs available for transplantation and the number of organs required. For example, in 1994 1,744 kidneys were transplanted. But in 1994 (U.K. Transplant Support Services Authority statistics 1995) some 4,970 persons were waiting for a kidney. This shortage of organs has led to considerable debate as to the means by which the supply can be improved. In this section we consider the existing legal regime for undertaking organ transplants (in relation to both cadaver and live organ donors) and the legal implications of various proposals which have been put forward for increasing the supply. Many ethical issues arise regarding other transplantation procedures which we do not have the space to consider here, see R.

Gills, "Editorial: Brain transplantation, personal identity and medical ethics" (1996) 22 *Journal of Medical Ethics* 131.

(a) Cadaver transplants

(i) Authorisation of the use of cadaver organs for transplantation

Human Tissue Act 1961 (as amended by the Corneal Tissue Act 1986)

1.—(1) If any person, either in writing at any time or orally in the presence of two or more witnesses during his last illness, has expressed a request that his body or any specified part of his body be used after his death for therapeutic purposes or for purposes of medical education or research, the person lawfully in possession of his body after his death may, unless he has reason to believe that the request was subsequently withdrawn, authorise the removal from the body of any part or, as the case may be, the specified part, for use in accordance with the request.

(2) Without prejudice to the foregoing subsection, the person lawfully in possession of the body of the deceased person may authorise the removal of any part from the body for use for the said purposes if, having made such reasonable enquiry as may be practicable, he has no reason to believe —

(a) that the deceased had expressed an objection to his body being so dealt with after his death, and had not withdrawn it; or
(b) that the surviving spouse or any surviving relative of the deceased objects to the body so being dealt with.

(3) Subject to subsections (4) (4a) and (5) of this section, the removal and use of any part of a body in accordance with an authority given in pursuance of this section shall be lawful.

(4) No such removal, except of eyes or parts of eyes, shall be effected except by a registered practitioner, who must have satisfied himself by personal examination of the body that life is extinct.

(4A) No such removal of an eye or part of an eye shall be effected except by —

(a) a registered medical practitioner, who must have satisfied himself by personal examination of the body that life is extinct; or
(b) a person in the employment of a health authority or NHS trust acting on the instructions of a registered practitioner who must, before giving those instructions, be satisfied that the person in question is sufficiently qualified and trained to perform the removal competently and must also either —
   (i) have satisfied himself by personal examination of the body that life is extinct, or
   (ii) be satisfied that life is extinct on the basis of a statement to that effect by a registered practitioner who has satisfied himself by personal examination of the body that life is extinct.

(5) Where a person has reason to believe that an inquest may be required to be held on anybody or that a post-mortem examination of any body may be required by the coroner, he shall not, except with the consent of the coroner —

(a) give an authority under this section in respect of the body; or
(b) act on such an authority given by any other person.

(6) No authority shall be given under this section in respect of any body by a person entrusted with the body for the purpose only of its interment or cremation.

(7) In the case of a body lying in the hospital, nursing home or other institution, any authority under this section may be given on behalf of the person having the control and management thereof by any officer or person designated for that purpose by the first-mentioned person.

(8) Nothing in this section shall be construed as rendering unlawful any dealing with, or with any part of, the body of a deceased person which is unlawful apart from this Act.

NOTES:

1. The Act does not state who the person in lawful possession of the body is. Where a person dies in hospital it will usually be the hospital authorities. (See P. D. K. Skegg, *Law, Ethics and Medicine*, Oxford: OUP (1984) at pages 235–239; Section 1(7) and NHS Circular (1975) Gen DHSS). However, the hospital's right to possession may be displaced by a person who has a better right to possession, such as the executors. (See D. Lanham "Transplants and the Human Tissue Act 1961" (1971) 11 *Medicine, Science and the Law* 16.) The undertakers are not persons "lawfully in possession" for the purposes of the Act (section 1(6)).

2. There is no limit on the age at which a declaration under section 1(1) can be made. Thus the position regarding child donors is unclear. (See D. Lanham 'Transplants and the Human Tissue Act 1961' (1971) 11 *Medicine, Science and the Law* 16.) It appears that children may donate if competent to do so. The DHSS in its booklet "Code of Practice Cadaveric Organs for Transplantation (1993) states that

   > "Approaches to the parents of a dead child (not defined) need a particularly high standard of sensitivity and tact; while the law does not demand parental consent, it should always be obtained in the case of a child."

   In practice organs will almost invariably only be removed with the relatives' consent.

3. A declaration executed by the deceased does not bind the hospital to use the organs. The hospital authorities may, for example, decide not to go ahead with transplantation because the organs are unsuitable. One further difficulty with written declarations is that the declaration — usually taking the form of a signed organ donor card — may not be found on the deceased at the time of death.

4. Whether or not a declaration has been executed by the deceased the person lawfully in possession of the body can authorise the transplantation of organs, (section 1(2)). Transplantation should not be undertaken if the deceased had expressed an objection (the legislation does not make clear whether this must be written or whether an oral expression is sufficient).

   Enquiries should be made of relatives under section 1(2). This does not take into account a situation in which a person is estranged from their relatives but has been living with another person for a long time as their "common law spouse". Care needs to be taken in making such enquiries at a time when the relatives are coming to terms with their bereavement.

5. The transplant process may be held up by the coroner's investigations (section 1(5)). However, the government has indicated that, wherever possible, the coroner should not inhibit transplantation (H.C. (77) August 28, 1975). The coroner should only reject a request for an organ to be removed in a situation in which the organ would be needed in evidence, where the organ might be the cause/partial cause of death, or where removal might inhibit further investigations. It has been suggested that one method of facilitating transplantation would be to follow the Scottish system of allowing the coroner to be present when the transplantation operation was undertaken. The operation itself also constitutes the post mortem (See J. K. Mason, "Organ Donation and Transplantation" in C. Dyer (ed.), *Doctors, Patients and the Law,* Oxford: Blackwells, 1992).

6. The statute remains silent as to the legality of maintaining the corpse in a suitable condition to facilitate organ removal for example ventilating the corpse and keeping the heart operational — the 'beating heart donor'. (See further J. K. Mason and R. A. McCall Smith, *Law and Medical Ethics* (4th ed.) London: Butterworths, 1994, at pages 302–303).

QUESTIONS:

1. Section 1(2) refers to "such enquiries as are reasonably practicable in the time available". What amounts to such an enquiry? (See P. D. K. Skegg, "Human Tissue Act 1961" (1976) 16 *Medicine, Science and Law* ,197.)

2. If the organs are needed sufficiently urgently is it justifiable to go ahead without having made any enquiries? (See G. Dworkin, "The Law Relating to Organ Transplantation in England" (1970) 30 *Modern Law Review* 353.)

3. Why should enquiries be made of the surviving spouse/relative?

(ii) Enforcement of the Human Tissue Act 1961

The 1961 Act contains no specific penalty for breach of the statute. A number of suggestions have been put forward as to how failure to comply with the statute may give rise to liability in criminal law.

Criminal law

R v. Lennox Wright [1973] Crim. L.R. 529

H.H. JUDGE LAWSON Q.C.:
". . . The defendant, who had taken and failed two medical examinations abroad, gained admission to the ophthalmic department of an English hospital by means of

false representations and a forged document which purported to show that he had qualified as an M.D. of Louvain University in Belgium.

In the course of his work at the hospital he removed the eyes from a dead body for their further use in a different hospital. He was charged, *inter alia* with (after amendment) 'Doing an act in disobedience of a statute by removing parts of a dead body, contrary to section 1(4) of the Human Tissue Act 1961.'

The Human Tissue Act 1961, makes provision for the use of parts of bodies of deceased persons for therapeutic purposes and purposes of medical education and research and with respect to the circumstances in which the removal of parts of a body may be carried out . . .

On a motion to quash the count it was contended by the defence that the Act was merely regulatory and created no offence, and that the Act provided no punishment for contravening section 1(4).

Held:

(1) The law was well settled that if a statute prohibits a matter of public grievance to the liberties and securities of the subject or commands a matter of public convenience (such as repairing of highways or the like) all acts or omissions contrary to the prohibitions or command of the statute are misdemeanours at common law punishable by indictment unless such method manifestly appears to be excluded by statute (2 Hawkins c.25 section 4, *R v. Hall* [1891] 1 Q.B. 747, *R v. Wright* (1841) 9 C. & P. 754). See paragraph 6 of *Archbold*.

(2) It followed that the punishment was governed by the common law and therefore an unlimited term of imprisonment or an unlimited fine could apply.

Note:

1. This decision has been criticised on the grounds that it goes against a line of established authority to the effect that had Parliament intended to create a criminal offence it would have done so expressly. (See I. Kennedy, "Liability and the Human Tissue Act 1961" in I. Kennedy, *Treat Me Right,* Oxford, OUP, 1989.)

It now appears that if there is a statute which deals with the issue of liability and does not explicitly make conduct a criminal offence, then a court is unlikely to hold that a breach of statute gives rise to criminal liability at common law.

R v. Horseferry Justices, ex p. IBA [1987] Q.B. 54

The facts of this case do not concern the question of organ donation and thus they have been omitted. The extract is simply included because of the question of law which it raises.

LLOYD J.:
". . . In 1976 the Law Commission in their Report on Conspiracy and Criminal Law Reform H.C. Paper (1975–76) described the "doctrine" of contempt of statute as obsolete but not dead. They recommended that the doctrine be abolished.

'In essence [they said] this is a matter for statutory construction: and the modern approach would, we think, be to ask whether, in the absence of an express provision making a particular conduct an offence, there was any intent by Parliament to penalise that conduct. The answer today, we suggest, would always be in the negative . . . .'

In *Maxwell on the Interpretation of Statutes* (12th ed. 1969) pp. 334–335 it is said that the procedure by way of indictment for breach of statutory duty is never used today.

How then does the matter stand? The one thing which to my mind emerges clearly from all of the above authorities to which I have referred and in particular from the qualification in Hawkins 'unless such method of proceeding do manifestly appear to be excluded' is that it is a question of construction in each case whether a breach of statutory duty for which Parliament has provided no remedy creates an offence or not. Among the factors which will be considered are (i) whether the duty is mandatory or prohibitory; (ii) whether the statute is ancient or modern; for in ancient statutes it was far more common than it is today for no offence to be defined, but to leave enforcement, for example, to a common informer; and (iii) whether there are any other means of enforcing the duty. In the case of mandatory duty imposed by a modern statute, enforceable by way of judicial review, the inference that Parliament did not intend to create an offence in the absence of an express provision to that effect is nowadays almost irresistable.

Mr Kemp urged us to hold that *R v. Price* (1840) 11 Ad & E 727, 113 E.R. 590 *Rathbon v. Bundock* [1962] 2 All E.R. 257 and *R v. Lennox Wright* [1973] *Crim. L.R.* 529 were wrongly decided, if they cannot be distinguished. He argued that the rule as stated in Hawkins, *Pleas of the Crown*, has ceased to exist; *cessante ratione legis; cessat lex ipsa.* I do not find it necessary to go that far; for as I have said, the 'rule' or 'doctrine' never was more than a rule of construction. It is not a substantive rule of law. The only difference between today and 1716 when *Hawkins* was first published, is that it is easier to infer in the case of a modern statute that Parliament does not intend to create an offence unless it says so. There is no longer any presumption, if indeed there ever were, that a breach of duty imposed by statute is indictable. Nowadays the presumption, if any, is the other way; although I would prefer to say that it requires clear language, or a very clear inference to create a crime."

QUESTIONS:

1. Is there a common law offence of breach of statutory duty?
2. What is the status of *R v. Lennox Wright* after this case?

Liability in tort

While it appears that there is no property interest in a corpse as such, the courts have held that a person under a duty to dispose of the body has a right of possession for that purpose. There are a number of possible actions which could be brought by such a person if organs are removed contrary to his wishes. It has been suggested that any unauthorised intereference with the right to possession of a dead body, for example, an unauthorised post mortem will constitute a trespass to the person. Such an action could be brought without having to show actual damage (See P. D. K. Skegg, "Liability for the unauthorised regard of Cadaveric Transplant Material" (1974) *Medicine, Science and Law* 53). An action may be brought for the tort of intentional infliction of nervous shock (*Wilkinson v. Downton*

[1897] 2 Q.B. 57; *Janvier v. Sweeney* [1919] 2 K.B. 316). However, it appears that in practice establishing such a claim would be exceedingly difficult. This is because one element of this tort — the necessary intention to inflict harm — would be almost impossible to prove. A spouse or other close relative may bring an action in negligence claiming damages for psychiatric injury caused due to the mutilation of the body by transplantation. In principle such an action may succeed if it could be shown that some recognisable psychiatric illness has been caused. However the law in this area is unclear. While the courts have stated that they are prepared to recognise a bystanders claim for psychiatric injury if they are sufficiently closely connected (*Alcock v. Chief Constable of South Yorkshire Police* [1991] 4 All E.R. 907), in a later case, (*McFadden v. EE Caledonian* [1994] 2 All E.R. 1) the court stated that such a claim cannot be made (see further J. Murphy, "A Reappraisal of Negligently Inflicted Psychiatric Harm" [1995] *Legal Studies* 415).

It has been suggested that failure to comply with the Human Tissue Act 1961 may give rise to breach of statutory duty. This is because the statute imposes a duty to make such reasonable enquiry as may be practicable. Nevertheless there would be difficulties in establishing the action. The duty contained in the 1961 Act is not absolute — it depends on reasonableness. However, if such a duty were recognised it has been argued that that there would be little difficulty in showing that section 1(2) was designed to prevent psychiatric harm to relatives where tissue was removed without enquiry being made (See I. Kennedy, "Liability and the Human Tissue Act 1961" in I. Kennedy, *Treat Me Right*, Oxford: OUP 1989.)

(iii) Obstruction of a coroner in the execution of his duties

If a coroner's enquiry is being undertaken and organs are removed without the coroner's consent this may amount to the offence of obstructing a coroner in the execution of his duties. However it appears that if the organ removed is a kidney, such removal is unlikely to constitute an actual obstruction of the coroner's investigations. (See J. K. Mason "Organ Donation and Transplantation" in C. Dyer (ed.), *Doctors, Patients and the Law*, Oxford: Blackwells 1992.)

(b) Live organ donation

Most organ transplantation operations are undertaken using cadaver organs. The extent to which organs from live organ donors are used varies between transplant centres. The transplantation of organs from living persons is governed both by the common law and the Human Organ Transplants Act 1989.

(I) Common law — consent to organ donation

(i) The competent adult

Law Commission, *Consent in the Criminal Law: A Consultation Paper,* Law Commission Consultation Paper No. 139 (1996)

Although the practice of taking kidneys and other tissue material from live donors has been an established therapeutic procedure for decades, the principles that make it lawful to remove organs from living donors have never been set out clearly in any English case. In 1969 Lord Justice Edmund Davies said, extra-judicially, that he would be surprised if any liability, civil or criminal, attached to the surgeon who performed a transplant operation on a competent donor who freely consented to the operation, provided that it did not present an unreasonable risk to the donor's life or health. The existence of the risk to the donor has led to a distinction being drawn between the use of regenerative tissue (such as blood or bone marrow), non-regenerative tissue that is essential for life (such as the heart or the liver), and other non-regenerative tissue.

There are no special principles relating to the nature of the consent that must be obtained, although when the donor is closely related to the potential donee, the doctor in performing the operation needs to be conscious of the psychological pressure on the donor and to ensure that consent is indeed freely given. What is more difficult is to identify the principles on which English law sanctions these operations, since they do not confer any therapeutic benefit on the donors.

Professor Dworkin has suggested that legal justification might be derived from treating a volunteer donor as favourably as the courts have traditionally treated rescuers. Professor Skegg has argued that the shortage of organs available for transplantation means that the courts may be expected to accept that there is a just cause or good reason for transplant operations on living donors. Whatever the true legal analysis, there can be no doubt that, once a valid consent has been forthcoming, English law now treats as lawful operative procedures designed to remove regenerative tissue and also non-regenerative tissue that is not essential for life.

NOTES

1. As noted, an individual is not able to consent to removal of an organ where death would be the inevitable consequence. In such a situation the surgeon would also be liable to be prosecuted for murder.
2. It has also been suggested that it would be unlawful to accept organs, such as an animal organ (see below at pages 922–927) where there is a high probability that such an organ will be rejected. (See J. K. Mason in, "Organ Transplantation" in C. Dyer (ed.), *Doctors, Patients and the Law,* Oxford: Blackwells, 1992.) The legality of the performance of organ transplant procedures is considered more fully in relation to the discussion on consent to treatment in Chapter 5 above.

(ii) The incompetent adult

It is unclear whether mentally incompetent adults may act as organ donors. While the House of Lords in *F v. West Berkshire Health Authority* [1989] 2 All E.R. 454, made it clear that medical treatment may be undertaken where it is in the person's best interests (see Chapter 5 at pages 267–295) the person who is an organ donor is not being "treated" for an illness; rather, by donating an organ he is acting as a means to cure another. It is questionable whether the donation of an organ by a mentally incompetent person could ever be regarded as being in his best interests. In its recent report, *Mental Incapacity*, Law Commission Report No. 231, 1995, the Law Commission stated that

> "Para 65 . . . Respondents supported our suggestion that an operation to facilitate the donation of non-regenerative tissue or bone marrow by a person without capacity should automatically be referred to the court. The need for any such decision will not stem from any existing distressing condition of the person without capacity but from the illness of some other person. Organ donation will only rarely, if ever, be in the best interests of a person without capacity, since the procedures and their aftermath often carry considerable risk to the donor. There is however authority from another jurisdiction that where a transplant would ensure the survival of a close family member it may be in the best interests of the person without capacity to make such a donation.
> *We recommend that any treatment or procedure to facilitate the donation of non-regenerative tissue or bone marrow should require court authorisation* (Draft Bill, clause 7(2)(b))."

NOTE:

1. The Law Commission referred here to the United States case of *Strunk v. Strunk* (1969) 35 A.L.R. (3d) 683. In that case the court sanctioned the donation of a kidney from a 26-year-old mentally handicapped man to his brother who was dying of kidney disease. In making the order the court emphasised the strong emotional bond in existence between the two brothers. See *Re Y* (1996) discussed in Appendix.

(iii) Children

Re W (A Minor) (Medical Treatment: Court's Jurisdiction), [1992] 4 All E.R. 627, [1993] Fam. 64, [1992] 3 W.L.R. 758, [1993] 1 F.L.R. 1, [1992], 9 BMLR 22, Fam. Law 541, [1992] 2 F.C.R. 785

The facts of this case are stated in Chapter 7 above at page 405.

Organ donation involving child patients raises a number of difficult legal and ethical issues. First, whether the child can actually consent at all to become the recipient of an organ. Transplantation is a major procedure. In the case of an older child it can be questioned whether such a child would be *Gillick* competent to give consent herself. In most situations it is arguable that a child would be required to have a high degree of competence before being capable of giving consent to such a major surgical procedure. In practice it would appear that parental consent would, in effect, be required before the transplantation operation could be undertaken. Difficulties may arise in a situation in which a child's parents refuse to give consent to a transplantation operation being undertaken on the basis that the child had "suffered enough" and they do not believe it appropriate to take therapy further. It may be also the case that a transplant procedure is of a pioneering nature and the parents do not wish to take the risk of including their child in such a therapy. An example of such parental opposition which came before the courts in 1996 was the case of *Re T* (1996) (discussed in Appendix A). Here parents refused consent to their child undergoing a liver transplant. This case is however highly exceptional in its nature and may in the future be seen as distinguishable upon its unusual facts. An analogy can be drawn here with clinical research and the performance of therapeutic research procedures, is it legitimate to subject children to a procedure where there may be a high degree of risk in the face of parental opposition? (See Chapter 10 at pages 583 onwards.) Where a dispute arises between health care professionals and parents as to the efficacy of the transplantation procedure this is a matter which should be referred to the court under one of the available orders (see Chapter 7 above at pages 425).

The second issue relates to whether a child may lawfully act as an organ donor. Where a child is very young this would again be a matter for parental consent. Can a parent authorise such a procedure? Parents may consent to clinical procedures on the basis that this clinical procedure is in the child's best interests. But can the donation of an organ be truly said to be in a child's best interests? Similar problematic issues arises here as in the context of the mentally incompetent adult (and also see further discussion of *Re Y* (1996) in the appendix). Much uncertainty surrounds the basis on which parents may legitimately consent to the inclusion of their children in non-therapeutic procedures in general (see Chapter 7 at page 378). (It is worthy of note that some jurisdictions prohibit donation of organs by minors, *e.g.* Human Tissue and Transplant Act 1982, Western Australia, sections 12 and 13.)

What of a situation in which it is proposed to use an older child as an organ donor? Can such a child herself give consent to such a procedure? This matter received some judicial discussion by the Court of Appeal in the case of *Re W* [1992] 4 All E.R. 627. This case was discussed in Chapter 7 above at page 405 onwards in connection with the refusal of treatment by a competent minor. Here we extract statements from the judgment of Lord Donaldson.

The facts of the case are as stated at page 405, above. Lord Donaldson discussed the scope of the Family Law Reform Act 1969 section 8 of which provides that persons over 16 could give consent to "surgical, medical or dental treatment" as if they were of full age. The section provided that

8(2)—"In this section "surgical, medical or dental treatment" includes any procedure undertaken for the purposes of diagnosis and this section applies to any procedure (including, in particular the administration of an anaesthetic) which is ancillary to any treatment as it applies to that treatment."

Lord Donaldson considered the report of the Latey Committee (Report of the Committee on the Age of Majority (1967) (Cmnd. 3342) which formed the basis for the 1969 Act and then continued:

LORD DONALDSON M.R.:

The section extends not only to treatment, but also to diagnostic procedures: see subsection (2). It does not, however, extend to the donation of organs or blood since, so far as the donor is concerned, these do not constitute either treatment or diagnosis. I cannot remember to what extent organ donation was common in 1967, but the Latey Committee expressly recommended that only 18-year-olds and older should be authorised by statute to consent to giving blood: see paragraphs 485–489. It seems that Parliament accepted this recommendation, although I doubt whether blood donation will create any problem as a 'Gillick competent' minor of any age would be able to give consent under the common law.

Organ transplants are quite different and, as a matter of law, doctors would have to secure the consent of someone with the right to consent on behalf of a donor under the age of 18 or, if they relied upon the consent of the minor himself or herself, be satisfied that the minor was 'Gillick competent' in the context of so serious a procedure which could not benefit the minor. This would be a highly improbable conclusion. But this is only to look at the question as a matter of law. Medical ethics also enter into the question. The doctor has a professional duty to act in the best interests of his patient and to advise accordingly. It is inconceivable that he should proceed in reliance solely upon the consent of an under-age patient, however 'Gillick competent,' in the absence of supporting parental consent and equally inconceivable that he should proceed in the absence of the patient's consent. In any event he will need to seek the opinions of other doctors and may be well advised to apply to the court for guidance, as recommended by Lord Templeman in a different context in *Re B (A Minor) (Wardship: Sterilisation)* [1987] 2 All E.R. 206 at 214–215.

NOTES:

1. The Court of Appeal in *Re W* clearly state that the 1969 Act does not cover donation of organs or blood and thus who is and who is not able to consent is a matter for the common law.
2. One difficulty relating to live organ donation, which may be particularly acute in the case of children, is ensuring that the donation is voluntary. The emotional pressure placed upon a child by relatives to donate to a sibling may be considerable. There may be a case for the introduction of some special procedure for independent supervision of child donors. Nevertheless, it appears that this matter may be of

more theoretical than practical import because removal of organs from living child donors would be undertaken only in very rare cases. (See M. Brazier, *Medicine, Patients and the Law,* 2nd (ed.), Harmondsworth: Penguin, 1992 at page 398; J. K. Mason, "Organ Transplantation" in C. Dyer (ed.), *Doctors, Patients and the Law,* Oxford: Blackwells, 1992). Donations of other body products from child patients are more common. Bone marrow donations involve tests, with the child being admitted to hospital for up to two nights and the administration of a general anaesthetic. There is also the risk of severe pain and discomfort consequent upon the transplantation. Sibling donations may lead to considerable pressure being placed upon the child donor. It has been argued that the donation of bone marrow by a child patient should be subject to regulation. Delaney has suggested that donation should be only authorised where these are in the best interests of the child determined by reference to a check list of factors. In addition an independant forum should authorise each graft. (See L. Delaney "Protecting Children from Forced Altruism; The Legal Approach" (1996) *BMJ* 240). This view has been disputed by those who argue that it is a safe procedure. (S. Month, "Preventing children from donating may not be in their best interests" J. Savulescu, "Substantial harm but substantial benefit", P. Browett, S. Palmer, "Legal barriers might have catastrophic effects" (1996) 312 *BMJ* 242).

3. The Council of Europe Resolution on the Harmonization of Transplantational Legislation provides that the removal of organs from minors and other legally incapacitated persons should be allowed if the donor and his legal representative are given information about consequences of donating, *e.g.* the medical, social and psychological consequences of so doing (Resolution (78) 29 Art. 6.).

(iv) Could a person ever be forced to donate?

We noted earlier in relation to consent to treatment that in certain exceptional situations the courts have authorised treatment despite the patient's expressed objections (see, for example, *Re T* [1992] 4 All E.R. 649, *Re S* [1992] 4 All E.R. 671). But those two cases are, in many respects exceptional. In both these cases authorisation of treatment enabled the life of the patient to be prolonged. It would thus appear inconceivable that an individual would be compelled to undergo a transplant operation.

(v) The anencephalic infant

There has been considerable debate as to whether it is appropriate to harvest organs from anencephalic infants. Such infants are born with all or part of the upper hemispheres of the brain missing. They live usually for only some 24 hours, though in rare cases this has extended to weeks or months.

Working Party of the Medical Royal Colleges on Organ Transplantation in Neonates (1988)

Tests of brain stem functions are applied in adults because the absence of such function establishes that the brain is dead: they are clearly inapplicable when the forebrain is missing. Such infants clearly have a major neurological deficiency incompatible with life for longer than a few hours. A view which commended itself to the Working Party was that organs could be removed from an anencephalic infant when two doctors (who are not members of the transplant team) agreed that spontaneous respiration had ceased. In the adult the diagnosis of brain death plus apnoea is recognised as death. The Working Party felt by analogy that the absence of a forebrain in these infants plus apnoea would similarly be recognised as death.

NOTES:

1. Some believe that it is justifiable to harvest organs from anencephalic infants because they are not "persons" since they lack cognitive functions. However, such reasoning throws into question the status of those individuals who are in a persistent vegetative state. Could they too be made available as organ donor banks? Others are strongly critical of such an approach, questioning, for example, the adverse effect which the use of anencephalic infants would have upon the status of handicapped infants generally. (See A. Shewman and A. Capron *et al.*, "Use of Anencephalic Infants as Organ Sources: A Critique" (1989) 261 *Journal of the American Medical Association* 12; A. Davies, "The status of anencephalic babies: should their bodies be used as donor banks?" (1988) 14 *Journal of Medical Ethics* 150).

2. It may be the case that the debate regarding the use of anencephalics becomes in the future one of simply historical interest. The increased use of screening during pregnancy and other medical developments have led to a steady fall in the number of anencephalic infants being born.

QUESTIONS:

1. Is treating the anencephalic infant as a donor currently lawful?
2. Should a specific statutory provision allow anencephalics to be used as organ donors?
3. In view of the limited availability of organs for transplantation should patients in a persistent vegetative state whose relatives agree be used as organ donors? (Refer back to the discussion of PVS earlier at page 897 and also to the decision in *Airedale NHS Trust v. Bland*— discussed in Chapter 15 below at page 892.)

(II) Statutory regulation of live organ transplantation

Human Organ Transplants Act 1989, s.2(1–6), s.7(2)

2.—(1) Subject to subsection (3) below, a person is guilty of an offence if in Great Britain he —

   (a) removes from a living person an organ intended to be transplanted into another person; or

   (b) transplants an organ removed from a living person into another person,

unless the person into whom the organ is to be or, as the case may be, is transplanted is genetically related to the person from whom the organ is removed.

   (2) For the purposes of this section a person is genetically related to —

   (a) his natural parents and children;

   (b) his brothers and sisters of the whole or half blood of either of his natural parents; and

   (c) the natural children of his brothers and sisters of the whole or half blood or of the brothers and sisters of the whole or half blood of either of his natural parents

but persons shall not in any particular case be treated as related in any of those ways unless the fact of the relationship has been established by such means as are specified by regulations made by the Secretary of State.

   (3) The Secretary of State may by regulations provide that the prohibition in subsection (1) above shall not apply in cases where —

   (a) such authority as is specified in or constituted by the regulations is satisfied —

      (i) that no payment has been or is to be made in contravention of section 1 above; and

      (ii) that such other conditions as are specified in the regulations are satisfied and;

   (b) such other requirements as may be specified in the regulations are complied with.

   (4) The expenses of any such authority shall be defrayed by the Secretary of State out of money provided by Parliament.

   (5) A person guilty of an offence under this section is liable on summary conviction to imprisonment for a term not exceeding three months or a fine of not exceeding level 5 on the standard scale or both.

   (6) The power to make regulations under this section shall be exercisable by statutory instrument . . .

   7.—(2) In this Act "organ" means any part of a human body consisting of a structured arrangement of tissues which, if wholly removed, cannot be replicated by the body.

NOTES:

1. The definition of "organ" in section 7 is very narrow, referring as it does to solid organs. There is no general statutory prohibition on the use of other bodily tissues/fluids.

2. The authority provided for in section 2(3) is the Unrelated Live Transplants Authority (ULTRA) established under the (Human Organs Transplants (Unrelated Persons) Regulations 1989 (S.I. 1989 No. 2480). ULTRA is a body of 7–11 members, with a chairman appointed by the Secretary of State. At least three members of the Authority and the chairman, are to be registered medical practitioners whilst at least four members of the Authority must be drawn from outside the medical profession.

3. What amounts to a genetic relationship under the Act is to be ascertained in accordance with DNA tests. (Human Organ (Establishment of Relationship) Regulations (1989) S.I. 1989 No. 2107.)

The 1989 Regulations provide that transplants may take place between donors who are not genetically related if the issue of donation is referred to ULTRA by the doctor clinically responsible for the donor and a number of criteria have been satisfied.

Human Organ Transplants (Unrelated Persons) Regulations (1989) S.I. 1989 No. 2480

3.—(1) The prohibition in section 2(1) of the Act shall not apply in cases where a registered medical practitioner has caused the matter to be referred to the Authority and where the Authority is satisfied —

(a) that no payment has been made or is to be in contravention of contrary to section 1 of the 1989 Act
(b) that the registered medical practitioner who has caused the matter to be referred to the Authority has clinical responsibility to the donor; and
(c) except in a case where the primary purpose of removal of an organ from a donor is the medical treatment of that donor, that the condition specified in paragraph (2) of this regulation are satisfied.

(2) The conditions referred to in paragraph (1)(c) of this regulation are —

(a) that a registered medical practitioner has given the donor an explanation of the nature of the medical procedure for, and the risk involved in, the removal of the organ in question;
(b) that the donor understands the nature of the medical procedure and the risks, as explained by the registered medical practitioner, and consents to the removal of the organ in question;
(c) that the donor's consent to the removal of the organ in question was not obtained by coercion or the offer of an inducement;
(d) that the donor understands that he is entitled to withdraw his consent if he wishes, but has not done so;
(e) that the donor and the recipient have both been interviewed by a person who appears to the Authority to have been suitably qualified to conduct such interviews and who has reported to the Authority on the conditions contained in subparagraphs (a) to (d) above and has included in his report an account of any difficulties of communication with the donor or the recipient and an explanation of how those difficulties were overcome.

NOTES:

1. Regulation 3 requires comprehension of information regarding organ donation. This presumably means that a mentally incompetent donor who is not genetically related to the recipient cannot donate an organ.
2. Some transplants take the form of "domino transplants", *e.g.* in the case of a person with cystic fibrosis a heart and a lung may be transplanted together rather than simply transplanting the lung. The patient's heart is thus capable of being used for subsequent transplantation.

3. Interviews under paragraph 2(e) will usually be conducted by a hospital consultant or a person of equivalent standing.
4. There is an appeal structure. Non urgent cases are considered by the next meeting of the Authority. In urgent cases a case committee is set up to approve applications.

Regulations require certain information to be supplied to the authority (section 3). Failure to provide this information is an offence.

QUESTIONS:

1. Is the test of capacity under the regulations the same as that recognised in *Re C* [1992] All E.R. (See Chapter 5 at pages 272–276.)
2. Why are un-related donors regarded as requiring the special protection provided by ULTRA while genetically related donors are not? (See M. Evans "Organ Donation Should Not be Restricted to Relatives" (1989) 15 *Journal of Medical Ethics* 17.)
3. Should children ever be allowed to donate organs to members of their family?

(III) Accountability for defective organs/tissue

An action in negligence may be brought by a person who has received a defective organ or defective tissue during a transplant operation. A claim may be brought on the basis of negligence at common law or strict liability under the Consumer Protection Act 1987. In some situations an action may be brought for breach of statutory duty. An example of such an action brought in relation to defective bodily products was in *Re Haemophiliac Litigation* [1990] NLJR 1349. The plaintiffs were haemophiliacs who had been infected with HIV after they had been given a clotting agent — "Factor 8" — contaminated with the virus which had been imported from the United States. The hearing was an application for discovery of documents (this is discussed further in Chapter 1 above). In determining whether to order disclosure, the Court of Appeal considered the substantive merits of the plaintiff's case. The Court said that there was an arguable case both in negligence and for breach of statutory duty. As far as the action for breach of statutory duty was concerned the plaintiffs had relied upon section 1 of the National Health Service Act 1977. However, both at first instance and in the Court of Appeal, the judges noted that bringing such an action involved considerable practical difficulties. Ralph Gibson L.J. stated that the duties under the 1977 Act did not clearly demonstrate that Parliament had intended to impose a duty enforceable by civil action. The action in negligence may have met with more success. The basis for the claim was that the Department of Health was negligent in not ensuring adequate provision of blood supplies in England and Wales which had resulted in the importation of contaminated blood from the United States.

The Court of Appeal stated that such an action was sustainable in principle.

This case illustrates the difficulties in establishing an action where the courts are faced with a dilemma which involves policy making and the allocation of medical resources. (See Chapter 1 at pages 47–60.) The case was settled prior to trial. It is questionable whether the plaintiffs would have succeeded at the full hearing of the action.

The supply of a defective organ may lead to an action being brought under the Consumer Protection Act 1987. The difficulty facing the plaintiff will be to establish that the organ/tissue is a product for the purposes of the legislation. There are defences under the Act, for example the state of scientific and technical knowledge at the time (section 4). An action may also be brought against a donor where a donee was affected by diseased organs/tissue. Nonetheless establishment of such an action may be difficult. Even were a duty of care to be established in that the donor should have made the donee aware of the prospect of disease transmission, causation may not be established because the organ would be subject to screening prior to transplantation.

(IV) Commercial dealing in organs

There is no general ban upon commercial dealing in bodily products in this country. Nonetheless in certain areas there are statutory limitations upon the extent to which that commercial dealing may be undertaken. We noted in Chapter 11 above the ban on commercial surrogacy agreements. Similarly in other areas considerations of public policy have led to Government action, largely as an ad hoc response to a particular incident. An excellent illustration of such a response is provided by the Turkish Organ sale scandal. During the 1980's there was much public controversy regarding trading in organs. Persons brought to the United Kingdom from Turkey were paid to donate organs. This practice contravened the GMC guidelines which stated that doctors could not give treatment if organ donors were paid. Three doctors were found guilty of serious professional misconduct and one was struck off the Medical Register. Prior to the enactment of the 1989 Act it was suggested that trading in organs was illegal at common law. Brahams suggested that the courts might have been prepared to hold that such contracts were unenforceable because that they were contrary to public policy. In addition if it is illegal to sell organs then the courts would not uphold a contract to sell such organs on the basis that this was unlawful. (See D. Brahams, "Kidneys for Sale by Living Donors" (1989) *Lancet* 285 and "Kidneys for Sale" (1989) *New L.J.* 159). The law regarding commercial dealing in organs is now as stated in the Human Organ Transplant Act 1989, passed shortly after the "kidneys for sale" incident. It should be noted that this statute applies to solid organs not to other bodily parts.

Human Organ Transplants Act 1989, s.1(1–4)

1.—(1) A person is guilty of an offence if in Great Britain he —

(a) makes or receives any payment for the supply of or for an offer to supply an organ which has been or is to be removed from a dead or living person and is intended to be transplanted into another person whether in Great Britain or elsewhere;
(b) seeks to find a person willing to supply for payment such an organ as is mentioned in paragraph (a) above or offers to supply such an organ for payment;
(c) initiates or negotiates any arrangement involving the making of any payment for the supply of or an offer to supply, such an organ; or
(d) takes part in the management or control of a body of persons corporate or incorporate whose activities consist of or include the initiation or negotiation of such arrangements.

(2) Without prejudice to paragraph (b) of subsection (1) above, a person is guilty of an offence if he causes to be published or distributed or knowingly publishes or distributes in Great Britain an advertisement —

(a) inviting persons to supply for payment any such organs as are mentioned in paragraph (a) of that subsection or offering to supply any such organs for payment; or
(b) indicating that the advertiser is willing to initiate or negotiate any such arrangement as is mentioned in paragraph (c) of that subsection.

(3) In this section "payment" means payment in money or money's worth but does not include any payment for defraying or reimbursing —

(a) the cost of removing, transporting or preserving the organ to be supplied; or
(b) any expenses or loss of earnings incurred by a person so far as reasonably and directly attributable to his supplying an organ from his body.

(4) In this section "advertisement" includes any form of advertising whether to the public generally, to any section of the public or individually to selected persons.

NOTES:

1. The World Health Organisation Resolution (WH40.13) provides that commercial dealing with organs is inconsistent with the most basic human values and contravenes the Universal Declaration of Human Rights and the spirit of the World Health Organisation Constitution. This view itself is controversial and also raises wider questions regarding dealings with human body parts. (See I. Davies, "Live Donation of Human Body Parts: A Case for Negotiability?" (1991) *Med. Legal Journal* 100.)
2. While providing donors with monetary payment has been rejected other incentives may be offered such as funeral expenses to a deceased donor's family. (See R. Jarvis, "Join the club: a modest proposal to increase the availability of donor organs" (1995) 21 *Journal of Medical Ethics* 199.).

(c) Increasing the supply of organs for transplantation — measures for reform

We noted above the fact that there is a chronic shortage of organs available for transplantation. A number of suggestions have been put forward suggestions to alleviate the shortage. Some of these relate to improvements in medical practice such as the methods for harvesting organs, others concern proposals for the reform of legislation. (See R. Hoffenberg, *Report of the Working Party on Supply of Donor Organs for Transportation*, London: DHSS, 1987.) We consider below a number of initiatives advanced.

(i) Opting-in registry

B. New, M. Soloman, R. Dingwall, J. McHale *"A Question of Give and Take": Improving the Supply of Donor Organs for Transplantation*, London: Kings Fund Institute, 1994.

An opting-in registry operates on the same principle as the donor card; it is an explicit statement of consent by a potential donor while he or she is still alive. Such an explicit statement is in accord with section 1(1) of the Human Tissue Act 1961, the difference being that it would take the form of a record on a centralised computer register to which all relevant hospital units could have instant access. Such a proposal is claimed to hold significant advantages over the donor card. Once the statement is made, it cannot be "lost" nor can the statement fail to be found simply because the donor did not have it about his or her person at the time of death. A computer register should be cheaper to administer, involving only electronically recorded information (although the publicity needed to achieve a substantial response may be expensive). And it would be extremely flexible with anyone able to add or to remove their name at any time.

The United Kingdom has some experience of such schemes as do other European countries with rather disappointing results. The United Kingdom scheme "Lifetime Wales", was established in Cardiff in 1986. A computer database is held at the Cardiff Royal Infirmary and ICU units can phone in to see if a brain dead patient is on the registry. It is currently claimed that, about 300, 000 names are held on the computer, from a population of approximately 2.8 million. Although donor rates improved significantly in the year following the introduction of the scheme to approximately 20 pmp [per million of population] it was suspected that this was due in large measure to the publicity surrounding its launch. Donor rates have now settled to their pre-1987 levels of around 14 pmp. Furthermore, those who run the scheme report that no donors have been obtained via the scheme in circumstances when the donor's family would otherwise have refused consent' because [every registered person] who had died had been carrying a donor card and his or her name was already known . . .

NOTES:

1. The authors in the conclusions to the report expressed the view that opting-in registers had not demonstrated their effectiveness. However, the government did introduce an NHS Organ Donor Register in 1994. It is held by the United Kingdom Transplant

Support Services in Bristol where the national database of patients who are waiting for organ transplants is kept. Transplant co-ordinators can contact the service 24 hours a day to identify the wishes of the deceased person and pass this information on to the relatives (*The Guardian*, October 7, 1994).

2. Persons can now also register their intention to become donors by ticking a box on their driving licence application form. This information is also registered with the NHS Organ Donor Registry.

(ii) Altering clinical procedures to facilitate transplantation

Controversy surrounded a technique called "elective ventilation". This is a practice whereby patients who were brought into hospital suffering from intra-cranial haemorrhage and regarded as suitable as potential organ donors were moved from a general ward to the intensive care unit. Before they were moved to intensive care, the consent of the relatives was obtained. The patient was then placed on a ventilator until brain stem death is diagnosed. The practice was halted in 1994 after the view was expressed that it was illegal. First, the procedure could not be regarded as simply part of the process of transplantation in relation to cadavers because the patient had not been declared brain stem dead. In addition it was argued that it was a non-therapeutic procedure which could not be said to be in the patient's best interests. It appears also that the practice of elective ventilation conflicts with suggestions made by the House of Lords in the *Bland* case that it would be unlawful to prolong life where this not in the best interests of the patient. (See J. V. McHale, "Elective Ventilation — Pragmatic Solution or Ethical Minefield?" (1995) 10 *Professional Negligence* 28.) For general discussion on clinical options see further S. M. Gore, 'Organ Donation from Intensive Care Units in England and Wales Two Year Confidential Audit of Deaths in Intensive Care (1992), 349 *BMJ* 304, and New, Soloman, Dingwall and McHale, *op. cit.* at pages 47–52.

(iii) Amending existing legislation

A further option would be to amend the existing transplantation legislation. The Human Tissue Act 1961, in particular, has been criticised for impeding transplantation. Statutory amendments could be introduced to clarify what amounts to "reasonable enquiries" and of whom the enquiries should be made.

(iv) Presumed consent

A more radical alternative would be the introduction of presumed consentor "opting-out" scheme. This is the reverse of the present system. It enables organs to be removed automatically subject to expressions to the contrary.

B. New, M. Soloman, R. Dingwall, J. McHale, *A Question of Give and Take*, London: Kings Fund Institute 1994

Presumed consent schemes have been introduced into many countries, although attempts to enact such legislation in the United Kingdom have always failed, the latest being the Transplantation of Human Organs Bill 1993. The international legislation falls into several categories. The purest version of the law allows automatic removal except in a situation in which the deceased has expressed an objection during his or her lifetime. This 'strict' type of presumed consent procedure applies in Austria where organs can be removed

> 'provided in his or her life, the person concerned had not expressed an objection. The views of close relatives are not taken into account.'

A slightly less strict version of presumed consent operates in Belgium where, if there is no explicit objection by the deceased, the relatives are allowed to object but the medical profession are under no obligation to seek their views. The relatives must initiate the process under these circumstances.

Other, still weaker, schemes allow removal unless the deceased has made an explicit or informal objection at any time. Such a formulation of the law effectively requires that the relatives are consulted in order to glean the wishes of the deceased. Although it is formally the views of the deceased whilst alive which are being sought, such schemes allow the relatives to object on the deceased's behalf. France and Spain operate presumed consent legislation of this kind.

Finally, a scheme in operation in Singapore provides for the automatic exclusion of certain categories of potential donor, including non-citizens and Muslims. Muslims can, however, donate their organs if they wish, by pledging their organs whilst alive or if their relatives consent . . .

Does presumed consent work? Belgium

Belgium enacted presumed consent legislation in June 1986 in the middle of a period of sustained and steady growth in kidney transplantation in Europe . . .

Belgium did increase the number of available kidneys by a significant margin during 1987, a rise of 37 per cent over the year before — and this does not seem to be simply the continuation of an earlier trend. Furthermore neither the United Kingdom, Germany nor the Netherlands experienced a similar increase in the same year. On the other hand Austria did not introduce similar legislation in the same year having done so in 1982 formalising a 200 year tradition of routinely utilising the corpse for medical purposes). For instance the publicity devoted to the organ donation issue whilst the law was being debated could itself have promoted a greater willingness to donate on the part of the public and a more informed attitude on behalf of ICU staff. It has been noted that the number of transplant co-ordinators increased around this time, and that the law formalised systems of reimbursement so that donating hospitals could be sure that they would receive the appropriate payment for managing the donor.

These objections are inconclusive, however. One would expect a 'publicity effect' to subside. The increase in the number of co-ordinators was likely to be as much a result of the increased number of donors as the cause of it. And the law merely formalised payment systems which operated successfully for the majority of hospitals beforehand.

It is clear that the influence of publicity, co-ordinators and payment systems had no effect in those centres where relatives' permission is always sought. It certainly seems as though the law had an independent effect on kidney retrieval where its provisions were adopted.

In any time series — analysis 'concurrent interventions' such as those described above will make it difficult to prove the causal influence of the intervention of the intervention in question, in this case a law. On balance, though, the evidence suggests that the introduction of presumed consent in Belgium had a significant impact on the availability of organs.

Does presumed consent work? Singapore

Singapore also introduced presumed consent legislation after a long period of transplant activity under an 'opting-in' system. The number of transplants under-taken in Singapore are relatively small and so were not included in the international analysis. Nevertheless, the development of kidney transplantation over time has some interesting features . . .

Between 1970 and 1982 only 30 cadaervic kidneys were transplanted, constitut-ing an average of approximately 0.9 pmp per year, clearly inadequate by any international standards. In an attempt to increase this level of activity, kidneys were imported from Europe and North America . . . The initial success of this policy was short lived when it became clear that the one year graft survival of these kidneys was poor probably as a result of the prolonged 'cold ischaemia times' involved.

In 1987, the Human Organ Transplant Act was introduced incorporating the provisions described above. The number of transplants undertaken in 1989–1990 increased significantly over the 'non-import' totals of the previous years, imports being discontinued in 1988. Some analyses . . . have attempted to isolate exactly the number of kidneys procured under the new law compared with the number obtained under the old opting-in legislation, which still applied for those wishing to pledge their organs. However, such analysis will underestimate the number of voluntary pledges since it cannot be known for certain how many families would have consented given the chance. Nevertheless the evidence from Singapore adds to that of Belgium as to the efficacy of presumed consent legislation.

The Kings Fund Report went on to consider the ethical issues relating to the introduction of opting out legislation.

The wishes of the individual

Most commonly, individuals are given the opportunity to 'opt-out' under presumed consent legislation. Although less serious, the concern remains that individual wishes would be ignored. The Hoffenburg Committee commented that there was a danger that organs would be removed when this was not the wish of the person. Whilst alive persons may feel pressurised into not opting-out because it might be seen as socially unacceptable. Others may be ignorant of the law or unable to understand it — vulnerable groups would be most at risk. In a multi-cultural society, the risk of ignoring the implicit wish of individuals with strong religious beliefs is particularly serious. No presumed consent legislation can possibly guaran-tee that the wishes of all concerned will be respected.

The sensibilities of the relatives

If concern would be felt by those now living with strong beliefs about the proper procedure for their body after death, distress could certainly be caused to family members who wished to wished to grieve without the knowledge or suspicion that the body of the loved one was being 'mutilated' — particularly if donation was conducted only under a 'presumption' that the deceased had given consent. The Committee of European Health Ministers commented that,

'the role of the family in deciding on organ removal is much more important in cases of presumed consent than in cases of express consent. In the latter case the

sentimental objections of the family have to be weighed against the legal rights of the deceased who has willed the organ donation. In the case of presumed consent the family's express objection weighs more heavily against the presumed consent of the deceased . . . In practice therefore whether consent is express or presumed, the final decision rests to a very large extent with the family of the deceased.'
It is worth noting however that the sensibilities of the family are not taken into consideration in the case of a coroner's autopsy. In England in the early 1980s 'some 20 per cent of persons dying . . . [were] subject to a medico-legal autopsy.' In other words a large number of deceased individuals are subjected to invasive surgery, without the need for consent, to satisfy social imperatives. What is more, society sanctions such investigations only as a means of establishing cause of death or to help the solving of a crime — lives are not directly at stake. The ethical distinction which supports the coroner's autopsy but denies the donation of organs unless consent is provided, is by no means clear.

Trust in the medical profession

Both these possible consequences — ignoring individual rights and offending the family's feelings — could have an impact on trust and respect for the medical profession. Whilst presumed consent may, in the short run, furnish more organs for transplants, in the long run its systematic effect on the institutions of medical care, could be depressing and corrosive of that trust upon which the doctor-patient relationship depend. And, even in the short run, public controversy can adversely affect donation rates. Furthermore, doctors may be unwilling to override the wishes of nearest relatives regarding organ donation, blunting the impact of the schemes.

Good medical practice

There may also be certain risks in removal without consent. In October 1979 a woman who died suddenly in France had her corneas transplanted. Unfortunately the patient who received her eyes contracted rabies. It was later revealed that the donor had contracted rabies when bitten by a dog in Eygpt where she had been shortly before her death. Her family knew this and had they been asked they would have been able to pass on this information to the medical team.

Can presumed consent legislation be ethical?

If a presumed consent scheme were to be introduced certain questions would need to be addressed. Would all organs be covered by the presumed consent scheme? Should organs be made available simply for clinical transplant or also for experimentation purposes? Should certain vulnerable groups of patients be excluded from routine removal? The 1969 Renal Transplantation Bill, an attempt to introduce a limited form of opting out, provided exclusions for persons who, at the time of death were suffering from mental illness or mental handicap, minors, those over 65, prisoners and permanent residents in institutions for the aged, disabled or handicapped.
It may also be necessary for a statutory definition of death to be enacted. This would, as was noted earlier, prove a difficult and controversial task. Presumed consent would also have to be accompanied by massive publicity in order that members of the public are made aware of their opportunity to opt out. In addition the legislators would need to address themselves to the question of who should have ownership and control of the cadaver and of the organs.
However, it may be that many of these ethical objections can be overcome by sufficiently carefully drafted legislation . . . Individual rights can be safeguarded by means of computer registries and exclusions of certain categories of individual. The sensibilities of the relatives can be safeguarded by allowing them to initiate an

objection which must be respected. The position of the medical profession is protected by allowing the individual clinician to decide how and when to utilise the laws provisions. Such a law would also allow for donation under circumstances whereby the relatives at a moment of grief, do not wish to discuss the possibility, but would otherwise normally be in favour of donation.

Nevertheless, unless the medical profession broadly supports the implementation of presumed consent legislation there is a serious danger that transplantation will be brought into disrepute by the controversy which would ensue. This in turn may corrode the public's trust in doctors and medicine. The best way forward is for the debate to continue until those who would have to work within a new law are satisfied that those reservations have been addressed.

NOTES:

1 One question surrounding the introduction of any opting-out legislation is whether it would command sufficient public support. The Report contained results of a specially commissioned opinion poll. Forty per cent were in favour of presumed consent, 48 per cent were against presumed consent, whilst 12 per cent didn't know.

2. The Report did not finally recommend that opting-out legislation should be introduced into this country although it was suggested that there should be continued debate regarding the concerns which were caused by presumed consent legislation. (See generally in support of opting-out I. Kennedy "The Donation and Transplantation of Kidneys: Should the Law be Changed?" in I. Kennedy, *Treat Me Right,* Oxford: OUP, 1989, and in opposition to such a scheme R. A. Sells, "Let's Not Opt-Out; Kidney Donation and Transplantation" (1979) 5 *Journal of Medical Ethics* 165.)

3. There is a divergence of opinion amongst certain religious/cultural groups, for example, certain parts of the Jewish community (see R. P. Bulka, "Jewish Perspectives on Organ Transplantation" (1990) 22(3) *Transplantation Proceedings* 945), as to the removal of organs without consent having been obtained from the deceased or to a definition of brain stem death. These concerns would need to be addressed before any change in the law was introduced to allow opting-out. (See further New, Solomon, Dingwall and McHale *op. cit.* at pages 35–37).

(v) Required request and routine enquiry

An alternative approach to the opting-out legislation commonly adopted in Europe is routine enquiry/required request which is used in the United States.

B. New, M. Solomom, R. Dingwall, J. McHale, *A Question of Give and Take*, London: Kings Fund Institute, 1994

Required request and routine enquiry are used extensively in the United States with the aim of increasing the supply of organs. The Uniform Anatomical Gift Act 1987 which forms the model for many state statutes makes provision for required request and routine enquiry. The development of required request policies by hospitals was encouraged by the Omnibus (Budget) Reconciliation Act 1986. This Act provides that failure on the part of hospitals to adopt routine enquiry or required request policies will lead to the denial of Medicare and Medicaid reimbursements from the Health Care Finance Authority.

Required request is a procedure in which enquiries are made of the families of potential donors to see whether they would allow their relatives' organs to be used. Twenty six U.S. states have this type of policy. The legislation in some states incorporates exceptions to the general duty of enquiry where for example, the wishes of the deceased are already known the medical staff are unable to locate the family in a timely manner and where enquiry would exacerbate mental or emotional distress.

Routine enquiry is the procedure of informing individuals and families of the option of organ donation. Eighteen states have legislation on this question. Some states do not require hospitals to directly approach families but stipulate that they must establish organ and tissue donation committees to design policies which would result in prompt identification of donors and prompt referral to the Organ Procurement Agency.

How successful have the required request and routine enquiry schemes been? While there was an initial increase in the availability of organs over time the schemes do not appear to have had a major impact. One reason for this, it is suggested is the lack of institutional commitment to ensuring that the required request procedures are followed. The United States experience illustrates that simply to enact required request legislation is not enough. It is vital to have adequately trained and qualified personnel.

'As one organ procurement official observed "if you simply ask relatives about organ donation by simply citing the law the consent rate is zero." '

Another reason suggested for the lack of dramatic impact of required request is that doctors find organ procurement time consuming and emotionally demanding. It is perhaps questionable as to whether statutory enactment of required request would have a significant impact. The national audit found that only 6 per cent of relatives in the U. K. are not approached when an otherwise potential donor is on a ventilator, and many of these would probably have communicated their unwillingness to consider donation by other means.

The Report also considers the ethics of this procedure;

A. L. Caplan has been one of the strongest advocates of the required request procedure. He argues that institutional required request means that opportunities for obtaining consent will not be missed. Required request standardises enquiry and thus places less strain on health care professionals and family members at a time of great stress and emotional upheaval. It also preserves the right of the individual to refuse consent since voluntary choice remains the ethical foundation upon which required request is based.

However others disagree, making a number of criticisms of the required request procedure Doctors and relatives may find the system distressing, though for rather different reasons than those relating to presumed consent. Doctors may be put under pressure to find that donors are suitable candidates for donation with implications for the diagnosis of brain stem death. Unlike presumed consent legislation, required request prescribes actions. It does not in general allow for the doctor to decide on a case by case basis the proper approach. In some circumstances it may be quite clear that requesting organ donation may be insensitive to the needs of the family. To suggest to relatives that organ donation is a gift of life is to play upon their emotions and guilt feelings at the time of their loved one's death.

There is also a danger that respect for donors may be eroded in the constant search for organs and this may have long term implications for public confidence in the medical team and the organ donation process. In general it seems clear that required request's prescriptive nature, and the associated problems of enforceability, mean that it is ethically unsustainable. There is also little evidence that it would be effective in improving the supply.

(vi) A market in organs

A further option is to remove the statutory ban on commercial dealing in organs and tissue. There has been considerable debate as to whether individuals should be allowed to trade in bodily products, in particular in organs/tissue. (See Lori Andrews, "My Body My Property" (1986) *Hastings Centre Report* 28; C. Errin and J. Harris, "A Monopsonistic Market; or how to buy and sell human organs, tissues and cells ethically" in I. Robinson (ed.) *Life and Death under High Technology Medicine* Manchester: MUP, 1994). In the context of organs and tissue it has been suggested that creation of a market may facilitate an increase in supply with individuals being more willing to donate organs if given payment. It can be seen as part of individual autonomy. Against this it is argued that individuals do not have an unfettered ability to deal with their body as they choose and that there is a weighty public policy argument that may be deployed against the commercialisation of bodily products in such a situation. It has also been argued that commercialisation degrades humanity. (See further J. Harris, *Wonderwoman and Superman: The Ethics of Human Biotechnology*, London: Routledge, 1992 page 118 and N. Duxbury, "Law, Markets and Valuation" [1995] *Brooklyn Law Review* 657.) Some see it as a "slippery slope" and that undue pressure may be placed upon the poor and disadvantaged to donate. Particular concern has been expressed that rich nations may prey upon poor nations to obtain donors. It has also been suggested that the existence of a market may actively discourage some persons who would otherwise come forward to make a voluntary donation. (See generally D. Lamb, *Organ Transplants and Ethics*, London: Routledge, 1990, at pages 133–140.) The legalisation of a market in organs seems unlikely at least in the near future. A variant could be the provision of increased non-financial incentives (see R. Javis, *op. cit.*).

(vii) Xenotransplantation

An alternative method which has been suggested for increasing the supply of available organs for transplantation is to use animal organs. Researchers are developing technology to enable the transplantation of animal organs into humans. While the use of animal organs and tissues provides one potential solution to the organ shortage, there are, however, difficulties in such transplantation. The first is scientific. Human immune systems frequently reject the introduction of animal substances. At present this limits the use of such technologies, although scientists have had some success in the transplantation of pig heart valves. In addition there are fears that the use of animal body products in this way may lead to transmission of disease from animals to humans. The second is ethical. Should animals be used in this way? Objections have been voiced that this is a morally unacceptable approach to take (see M. Fox, "Animal Rights and Wrongs" in R. Lee and D. Morgan (ed.) *Deathrites: Law and Ethics at the End of Life,* London: Routledge, 1995 and A. Capron, "Is xenografting morally wrong?" (1992) 24 *Transplantation Proceedings* 722). As a means of reducing the possibility of rejection scientists have been developing transgenic animals. The United Kingdom company, Imutran Ltd, has stated its intention to transplant hearts from transgenic pigs into human recipients.

The subject of xenotransplantation has recently been under consideration at a national level. In spring 1996 the Nuffield Council on Bioethics issued a report on the subject. The issue is also the subject of an inquiry by the Department of Health under the chairmanship of Professor Ian Kennedy.

Nuffield Council on Bioethics, *Animal to Human Transplants: The Ethics of Xenotransplantation*, London 1996

Animal concerns: principles

10.7　One line of thought holds that when judging whether it is acceptable to use animals for medical purposes it is necessary to consider whether the pain and suffering of the animals is justified by the potential benefit to human beings. Another line of thought suggests that animals, like human beings, have rights that must be respected when considering their use for such purposes. Whether the argument is framed in terms of the interests or the rights of animals, the crucial point is the extent to which animals share the features supposed to be important to human interests and rights. The feature to which most importance has generally been attached is that of self-awareness. To be self-aware requires a high degree of intelligence, the capacity to make comparisons and judgments, and a language with which to articulate them. It has been argued that suffering and death are uniquely painful to a self-aware being who not only senses pain but can also perceive the damage being done to his or her self and future.

10.8　The Working Party accepted that some use of animals for medical purposes is '*an undesirable but avoidable necessity*' and that '*in the absence of any scientifically and morally acceptable alternative, some uses of animals . . . can be justified as necessary to safeguard and improve the health and alleviate the suffering of human beings.*' Not every benefit to human beings will justify the use of animals, and in some cases, the adverse effects on the animals will be so serious as to preclude their use. This conclusion drew on the position set out by the Institute of Medical Ethics towards biomedical research using animals.

The use of primates for xenotransplantation

10.9　Even if some use of animals for medical purposes can be justified in principle, their use for xenotransplantation raises specific issues that need further consideration. Particular concerns are raised by the use of primates, such as baboons. The high degree of evolutionary relatedness between human beings and primates both suggests that xenotransplantation of primate organs and tissue might be successful and also raises questions about whether it is ethical to use primates in ways that it is not considered acceptable to use human beings. Certainly, any harm suffered by primates should be given great weight. This position is reflected in the principles underlying current practice in the U.K. **The Working Party endorses the special protection afforded to primates used for medical and scientific purposes.**

10.10   The Working Party would accept the use of very small numbers of primates as **recipients of organs** during research to develop xenotransplantation of organs and tissue from non-primates. In this case, using a small number of primates for research, while undesirable, can be justified by the potential benefits if xenotransplantation were to become a successful procedure.

10.11   The routine use of higher primates to supply organs for xenotransplantation on a scale sufficient to meet the organ shortage would represent a new use of primates in the U.K. In addition to the special harm suffered by primates other considerations must be taken into account. The endangered status of chimpanzees rules out their use for xenotransplantation. The potential risk of extinction, even to a specis like the baboon that is not currently endangered, must be taken seriously. Xenotransplantation using primate organs or tissue may pose particular risks of disease transmission.

10.12   Given the ethical concerns raised by the use of primates for xenotransplantation attention has turned to developing the pig as an alternative source of organs and tissue. As discussed below, in the view of the Working Party, the use of pigs for xenotransplantation raises fewer ethical concerns. To develop the use of primates for xenotransplantation, when there is an ethically acceptable alternative, would not be justifiable. **The Working Party recommends that non-primate specis should be regarded as the source animals of choice for xenotransplantation.** However, possibilities for alleviating the organ shortage which do not involve the use of animals, such as increased donation of human organs, and the development of artificial organs and tissue, should be actively pursued.

10.13   The Working Party considered the possibility that, after a number of years of research, it might be found that pig organs and tissue could not be used for xenotransplantation. Would it then be ethically acceptable to use primate organs and tissue for xenotransplantation? The members of the Working Party were agreed that the use of primates would be ethically **unacceptable** if **any** of the following conditions obtained:

— improving the supply of human organs and the use of alternative methods of organ replacement such as mechanical organs and tissue replacement could meet the organ shortage;
— the use of higher primates would result in them becoming an endangered species;
— concerns about the possible transmission of disease from higher primates to human beings could not be met; or
— the welfare of animals could not be maintained to a high standard.

These conditions would rule out all use of chimpanzees on conservation grounds. When considering the hypothetical situation in which the conditions might be satisfied for a species such as a baboon, some members of the Working Party felt that the use of primates for xenotransplantation would never be acceptable. Other members of the Working Party felt that, should these circumstances come to prevail, it would be appropriate to reconsider the use of higher primates to supply organs for xenotransplantation.

The use of pigs for xenotransplantation

10.14   While the pig is an animal of sufficient intelligence and sociability to make welfare considerations paramount, there is less evidence that is shares capacities with human beings to the extent that primates do. As such, the adverse effects suffered by pigs used to supply organs for transplantation would not outweigh the potential benefits to human beings . It is also difficult to see how, in a society in which the breeding of pigs for food and clothing is accepted, their use for life-saving medical procedures such as xenotransplantation could be acceptable. **The Working Party concluded that the use of pigs for the routine supply of organs for xenotransplantation was ethically acceptable.**

10.15 If pigs are used for xenotransplantation they are likely to have been genetically modified so the human response to pig organs and tissue is reduced. The production of transgenic pigs for xenotransplantation is likely to involve the transfer of a gene or a few genes of human origin. This is a very small and specific change. It is only in combination with all the other genes that make up the human genome that a particular gene contributes to the specification of the characteristics of the human species. Thus, inserting these genes into a transgenic pig would not destroy the integrity of either species. Species boundaries in any case, are not inviolable but change through a number of other processes. **The Working Party concluded that the use of transgenic pigs that have been genetically modified to reduce the human immune response to pig organs was ethically acceptable . . .**

Animal Concerns: practice

10.18 In the U.K., animals used for scientific purposes are protected by the Animals (Scientific Procedures) Act 1986 (the 1986 Act). Before the use of animals is permitted, the likely effects on the animals must be weighed against the benefits likely to accrue from their use. The Home Office Inspectorate grants licences, in consultation where necessary with the Animals Procedures Committee. The use of animals for xenotransplantation raises questions about their breeding, especially if they are genetically modified, the welfare implications of producing animals free of infectious organisms, and their slaughter. **The Working Party recommends that the convention by which the Animal Procedures Committee advises on project licences in difficult areas should extend to applications for the use of animals for xenotransplantation.**

10.19 Xenotransplantation research may require the use of limited numbers of primates as xenograft recipients. Primates are afforded special protection by the 1986 Act. Project applications involving primates are examined by the Animals Procedures Committee and the Home Office sets standards for the care and welfare of primates involved in research. The Working Party recommended that non-primate species should be regarded as the source animals of choice for xenotransplantation. What follows, therefore, refers to the welfare implications of the use of non-primate animals, notably transgenic pigs, to supply organs and tissue for xenotransplantation.

10.20 The breeding of transgenic animals is under the control of the 1986 Act. Transgenic animals can, in principle, be released from the control of the 1986 Act if there is no significant effect on the animals' welfare after two generations. If they are released welfare concerns would be covered by the less demanding standards regulating agricultural practice and animal husbandry.

10.21 Animals used to provide organs and tissue will need to be free, as far as possible, from infectious organisms in order to reduce the risk that xenotransplantation will lead to the transmission of diseases into the human population. Repeated testing of animals and other procedures may adversely effect animal welfare. **The Working Party recommends that, when decisions are made about the acceptability of using animals for xenotransplantation, particular attention is paid to reducing the adverse effects associated with the need to produce animals free from infectious organisms.**

10.22 Removal of organs or tissue from anaesthetised animals will come under the control of the 1986 Act. It is possible, however, that killing animals and removing their organs without the use of anaesthetic would not come under the control of the 1986 Act. It would be possible, in principle, to remove non-vital organs, or tissues that regenerate, sequentially from animals. This could well result in an increase in animal suffering. The Home Office has stated that the provisions of the 1986 Act regarding re-use of animals would preclude the sequential removal of organs or tissue. **The Working Party recommends that the Animals (Scientific Procedures) Act should continue to be interpreted as prohibiting sequential removal from animals of tissue and organs for transplantation.**

10.23   Important welfare considerations are raised by the breeding of transgenic animals; producing animals free from infectious organisms; and removing organs and tissue from animals used for xenotransplantation. There is some uncertainty about whether, in practice, all these aspects would be covered by the 1986 Act. In view of the important welfare implications raised by xenotransplantation, **the Working Party recommends that the Home Office should require that all animals used for xenotransplantation are protected under the Animals (Scientific Procedure) Act 1986.** Any reputable company producing animals in order to supply organs and tissue for xenotransplantation would, in any case, wish to be licensed under the 1986 Act in order to reassure the public that their activities were meeting the highest standards of animal welfare. **The Working Party recommends that the standards set by the 1986 Act become the minimum for the industry.**

Transmission of infectious diseases

10.24   Xenotransplantation of animal organs and tissue carries with it the potential risk that diseases will be transmitted from animals to xenograft recipients and to the wider human population. It is difficult to assess this risk, since it is impossible to predict whether infectious organisms that are harmless in their animal host will cause disease in human xenograph recipients or whether the disease will spread into the wider human population. There are certain to be infectious organisms of both primates and pigs that are currently unknown, and some of these might cause disease in human beings. There is evidence that infectious organisms of both primates and pigs that are currently unknown, and some of these might cause disease in human beings. There is evidence that infectious organisms of primates, notably viruses, can pass into the human population and cause disease. This supports the recommendation that non-primate species should be regarded as the source animals of choice for xenotransplantation. The possible risk of disease transmission from pigs, however, also requires careful consideration.

10.25   It is not possible to predict or quantify the risk that xenotransplantation will result in the emergence of new human diseases. But in the worst case, the consequences could be fare reaching and difficult to control. The principle of precaution required that action is taken to avoid risks **in advance** of certainty about their nature. It suggests that the burden of proof should lie with those developing the technology to demonstrate that it will not cause serious harm. **The Working Party concluded that the risks associated with possible transmission of infectious diseases as a consequence of xenotransplantation have not been adequately dealt with. It would not be ethical therefore to begin clinical trials of xenotransplantation involving human beings. . ..**

The Report recommends that a new body an Advisory Committee on Xenotransplantation should be established. It takes the view that before initial transplantation procedures are undertaken on human subjects the approval of both this committee and the local research ethics committee should be obtained.

Early patients

10.34 Even where the results from animal experiments suggest that xenotransplantation involving human recipients is justifiable, the early clinical trials will involve unknown and unpredictable risks. The question then becomes how best to protect early patients' welfare and interests. It is of the utmost importance that potential patients give free and properly informed consent to participation in the first xenotransplantation trials. **The Working Party recommends that the consent of patients to participation in xenotransplantation trials is sought by appropriately trained professionals who are independant of the xenotransplantation team. The information given to prospective recipients should include an estimation of likely success, attendant risks and subsequent quality of life.** Patients consenting to xenotransplantation should be informed that post-operative monitoring for infectious organisms is an integral part of the procedure and that their consent to the operation includes consent to this monitoring.

10.35 Teams conducting experimental trials on patients are under a scientific and ethical obligation to research and report the subsequent quality of life of the recipients. **The Working Party recommends that no protocol to conduct a trial should be accepted unless it contains a commitment to a robust description and assessment of the patient's pre-operative and post operative quality of life** . . .

10.36 Special issues arise in the case of children. Xenotransplantation has been proposed as a method of reducing the especially acute shortage of organs for babies and children. Early clinical trials of xenotransplantation will be a form of therapeutic research. Therapeutic research must offer some prospect of genuine benefit for the patient, but it involves greater uncertainties than treatment, and therefore greater caution must be exercised. The British Paediatric Association and the Medical Research Council have advised that therapeutic research should not involve children if it could equally well be performed with adults. It would be difficult to justify the involvement of children in major and risky xenotransplantation trials before some of the uncertainties have been eliminated in trials involving adults. **The Working Party therefore recommend that the first xenotransplantation trials involve adults rather than children.**

10.37 Similar issues arise for adults who are considered incapable of consenting to participation in therapeutic research because they are mentally incapacitated. The law would appear to be that incapacitated adults may be involved in therapeutic research if this is in their best interests. It would be difficult to justify the involvement of incapacitated adults in the first xenotransplantation trials before some of the major uncertainties have been eliminated in trials involving adults who are capable of weighing the benefits and risks on their own behalf. **The Working Party recommends that the first xenotransplantation trials should not involve adults incapable of consenting to participation on their own behalf.**

[Author's Note: In January 1997 it was announced that xenotransplantation would not be undertaken at present but would be reviewed by a new body, the Xenotransplantation Interim Regulatory Authority. See further M. Fox and J. McHale, "Regulating Xenotransplantation" (1997) 147 NLJ 139.]

NOTES:

1. As with other organ technologies, the use of xenotransplantation is not cost free. The Nuffield Report notes that developments in xenographs should be addressed in the light of other transplantation resource allocation matters (paras. 8.1–8.13). It also proposes that the introduction of xenographs should be supervised by the body which is responsible for the regulation of other specialist services

within the NHS, the Supra Regional Service Advisory Body (paras. 10.43).

2. The major risks of disease transmission identified by the Working Party led it to recommend the establishment of a regulatory framework to control the safety and quality of animal organs and tissue used for transplantation, with monitoring mechanisms for xenograph recipients (paras 10.27–10.28). The need to ensure public confidence here can be seen as of particular importance in relation to the current BSE "crisis".

3. The Report recognises that the transplantation of animal organs into a human subject may involve difficult questions in relation to the identity of the recipients of organs. They recommend that counselling of potential recipients should include discussion of the effect transplantation may have on them personally.

4. The Report also considers the question of conscientious objection. Such objections may derive from religious or other ethical beliefs — for example, evidence to the Working Party from the Union of Muslim Organisations in United Kingdom and Eire indicated that its members would support the practice of xenotransplantation but not the use of pigs which are regarded as unclean. Sensitivity surrounding this area prompted the recommendation of the Working Party that if an individual refused a xenotransplant, this should not prejudice them should they apply for a human organ (paras. 7.27–7.30). As far as conscientious objection and health professionals are concerned, while ethical objections should be taken seriously by management they should not be held to be overriding (para. 7.32). The ethical issues regarding the use of animals for xenotransplantation are given fuller consideration in Chapter 4 of the Report.

QUESTION:

1. At the present time it is questionable as to whether transplantation of animal organs into human subjects is lawful. As noted above an individual cannot consent to the infliction of any harm (see Chapter 6 above at pages 322–323). Would it be lawful to accept an organ realising that there would be a high probability of rejection? (See J. K. Mason "Organ Donation and Transplantation" in C. Dyer (ed,), *Doctors, Patients and the Law,* Blackwell: Oxford, 1992).

4. ORGAN AND TISSUE OWNERSHIP

Aspects of the legality of the use of bodily products such as gametes and organs have been considered at various points in this text. We have examined what rights individuals have to control the use of bodily products, but one question, which has been to some extent sidestepped, is to what extent an individual has any rights of ownership in such bodily products. The traditional approach is that human tissue and organs are not susceptible of ownership. *Dr Handyside's case* (1749) 3 East PC 652 is cited as authority for the proposition that there is no property in an unburied corpse, as is the case of *Williams v. Williams* (1852) 20 Ch. D. 657, (see also *Dobson and Another v. North Tyneside H.A., The Times,* July 15, 1996). While the strength of these authorities has been called into question, it appears to be the case that they are generally accepted as existing law. (See P. Matthews, "Whose Body; People As Property" (1983) 36 *Current Legal Problems* 195). Uncertainty surrounds the position of human tissue/bodily fluids. Certainly, human substances such as urine and hair may be stolen (*R. v. Welsh* [1974] R.T.R. 478 and see G. Dworkin and I. Kennedy, "Human Tissue: Rights in the Body and its Parts" (1993) 1 *Medical Law Review* 291.)

The catalyst for recent interest as to whether there is property in organs and tissue in this country was a United States case, *Moore v. University of California* 793 Pd 479 (Cal 1990). Moore had part of his spleen removed as part of treatment for hairy cell leukaemia. Unknown to Moore, some of his cells were used in the development of a lucrative cell line. Whilst the Californian Supreme Court held that Moore had no or "at least only limited" property rights in the cells removed they acknowledged that he should have been informed as to the use of the cells and that failure to do so was in contravention of the requirement of informed consent. In English law there has been no comparable case. Consideration has been given to the question of tissue ownership by the Nuffield Council on Bioethics. Below is an extract from a report of the Council examining claims which a person, from whom tissue is removed, can assert in relation to that tissue.

Nuffield Council on Bioethics, Human Tissue: *Ethical and Legal Issues,* 1995

9.3   No claim by statute is available to the person from whom tissue is removed. Indeed the implication of the Human Tissue Act 1961, the Human Organ Transplants Act 1989 and the Anatomy Act 1984, though not expressly stated is that the tissue removed pursuant to these Acts is given free of all claims, *i.e.* is an unconditional gift. The Human Fertilisation and Embryology Act 1990 is less straightforward. Donors of gametes or embryos may impose conditions on use and may vary or withdraw any consent given. By adopting a scheme of consents, however the Act avoids vesting any property claim in the donor.

9.4   At common law the issue has not been tested in English law. It is instructive to enquire why the question of a claim over tissue once removed has not received legal attention. The answer seems simple. In the general run of things a person from whom tissue is removed has not the slightest interest in making any claim to it once it is removed. This is obviously the case as regards tissue removed as a consequence of treatment. It is equally true in the case of donation of tissue whether, for example, blood, bone marrow or an organ. The word donation clearly indicates that what is involved is a gift.

9.5   It is certainly true, of course, that an appendix or gallstone may be returned to a patient who may refer to it as **her** appendix or gallstone. But this says nothing about any legal claim that she may have to the appendix. In fact, in the case of the returned appendix, one view of the legal position may be as follows: the patient consents to the operation which involves the removal of her appendix: by her consent to the operation she *abandons* any claims to the appendix, on removal the appendix acquires the status of a *res* (a thing) and comes into the possession of the hospital authority prior to disposal; in response by a request of the patient that it can be returned the hospital gives the appendix to the patient as a gift; the appendix then becomes the property of the patient.

9.6   While what has been said about the lack of interest of the patient in the fate of tissue removed from him may be true, some have enquired whether a claim to tissue which has been removed can be advanced in certain circumstances. One such circumstance is the removal of foetal tissue subsequent to an abortion. Does a mother, it may be asked, have any claim to the tissue? The report of the Polkinghorne Committee did not claim to resolve the question. Instead it provided for a scheme whereby the woman has to give explicit and unconditional consent to the use of the foetal tissue before it may be used. The same scheme of consents, circumventing the need to resolve questions of property and ownership, was employed in the Human Fertilisation and Embryology Act.

9.7   But there are other circumstances in which the question posed in paragraph 9.6 may arise. In some circumstances, it could be argued, and has been by a number of commentators, that tissue once removed becomes the property of the person from whom it is removed. This is to say that consent to removal does not *entail* an intent to abandon. The tissue may well, in fact, be abandoned or donated, but these imply a prior coming into existence of a *res* and the exercise of rights over it. Indeed, such an analysis is logically essential, it is argued, even if the resulting property (*i.e.* a person's assertion of a property right over the new res) exists merely for the moment (a *scintilla temporis*). On this view the person from whom tissue is removed must have a property right in the tissue which he expressly or by implication he could waive on the removal so that the property passes to another. The consequence is, of course, that if the property right were not waived, it would be retained. To return to the example in paragraph 9.5, the appendix would have become (and remained) the patient's property had she not by implication waived any right to it.

9.8   The case of *Venner v. State of Maryland* decided by the Court of Special Appeals in Maryland USA, may be of assistance. Powers J. held that, 'By the force of social custom . . . when a person **does nothing and says nothing to indicate an intent to assert his rights of ownership, possession and control over [bodily] material,** the only rational inference is that he intends to abandon the material'. The emphasis of this approach is clear.

1. The legal presumption is in favour of abandonment
2. Abandonment may be prospective
3. Where, however, the circumstances are such that abandonment may not be presumed, it must follow that if no consent were given, or a consent expressed to be 'on terms' were given, property rights over the tissue *would not necessarily pass* but would be retained by the person from whom the property was removed.

9.9   It is fair to say that some support for this approach can be derived from various statutes already referred to. While we have seen (in paragraph 9.3) that no claim arises by reference to these statutes, the approach to tissue adopted by them may assist in understanding the current state of the common law. While the Human Tissue Act 1961 is of no assistance, both the Human Organ Transplants Act 1989 and the Human Fertilisation and Embryology Act 1990 appear to endorse a property approach. Indeed the latter, though relying upon a scheme of consents so as to avoid the need to decide the issue of property, contemplates that the control

and disposal of gametes and embryos rests with the donor(s) and allows for the transfer of the reproductive material between those with a licence to deal with them. A final statutory provision section 25 of the National Health Service Act 1977 also seems implicitly to adopt a property approach. The section provides that:
  where the Secretary of State has acquired:

  (a) supplies of human blood . . . or
  (b) any part of a human body . . .

he may arrange to make such supplies or that part available (on such terms, including terms as to charges as he thinks fit) to any person . . .

The statutory language is therefore, that of things, of property, of the reification of blood and body parts . . .
9.11 . . . we have noticed the following as possible legal approach to any claims made by the person from whom tissue is removed: either

  1. consent to removal entails abandonment: or
  2. on removal, property rights vest in the person from whom it is removed. It is presumed that these are abandoned, but they can be retained.

A further legal approach is to argue that tissue once removed becomes property, but at the time of its removal it is *res nullis*, *i.e.* that it belongs to no one until it is brought under domininion (the traditional legal example is the wild animal or plant). This would reflect the traditional view of 'no property in the body'. It would also mean that a person could not prospectively donate 'his' tissue once removed from the body. All he could do would be to consent to the removal. If this analysis were adopted, the tissue would be the property of the person who removed it or subsequently came into possession of it. The person from whom it was removed would not, however, have any property claim to it.
9.12 The current state of English law makes it unclear (at best) which of these approaches (or another) represents the law. Interest in the validity of property claims over removed tissue has, however, been rekindled because of the awareness of circumstances in which tissue has been removed and then developed in some way so as to serve as the basis for a commercial product. The *locus classicus* is the well known *Moore* case. In *Moore* the Supreme Court of California trying a preliminary point of law, decided that Moore had no property right over the tissue taken from his body. Although not expressed in such a way, if we impose the language that we have employed, the court appears to have found that Moore's consent to the operation entailed an abandonment of any claim to the removed tissue. Thus, he could not assert a claim in property as the basis either for objecting to the removal of his tissue or for having a share in whatever profit was gained through its use. The issue of the validity of the consent he gave to the operation and subsequent procedures then becomes the focus of the case.
9.13 It is not easy to predict whether an English court would adopt the Supreme Court of California's conclusion. Certainly the reasons advanced by the majority of the court for rejecting Moore's claim are somewhat unconvincing. The majority found that there were three 'reasons to doubt' Moore's claim, all of which Mosk J. sharply criticised in his dissenting judgment. The first was the absence of precedent. Mosk J.'s response was that the Supreme Court was there precisely to make law where necessary. The second was that the matter was more appropriately for the legislature, a view which Mosk J. said was out of place in a decision of the highest court, one of whose roles was to develop the law. The third was that the patent granted to the University of California preempted any claim Moore might have but, the grant of the patent did not mean, according to Mosk J. that Moore ,could not share in any profits arising from it. Notwithstanding these weaknesses,

the *conclusion* of the Supreme Court, if not the reasoning may recommend itself, not least because of the consequences of adopting the alternative. For, if the alternative approach were adopted and a potential property claim were recognised, the consequences could be far reaching. Consent to even the most minor procedures would have to refer to possible property rights in removed tissue and seek a waiver of such rights. Patients might be encouraged to bargain over tissue (if thought to be unusually valuable, for example, for research). Agencies to negotiate such bargains might appear and research may be impeded in a welter of contractual arrangements.

9.14   Of the various approaches referred to, therefore, it may be that a preferable approach for the English courts would be the following:

1. It will be entailed in any consent to **treatment** that tissue removed **in the course of treatment** will be regarded in law as having been abandoned by the person from whom it was removed.
2. tissue removed in **circumstances other than treatment** which is **voluntarily donated** will be regarded as a gift. Use for purposes other than those for which consent was given could give rise to a claim on the part of the person from whom the tissue was removed. Such a claim will depend upon the terms of the original consent;
3. where tissue is removed voluntarily but is intended to be kept for the **donor**, for example autologous blood donations, the donor will be able to claim the tissue by virtue of the agrement under which it is kept. (The donation of gametes and embryos is subject to a specific statutory framework of consent regulating *inter alia* the giving and withdrawal of consent to use):
4. where tissue is removed without **explicit** knowledge and consent, any claim the person from whom it was removed may have as regards the subsequent use of that tissue will turn on the validity of any general consent which may have been given, *i.e.* as to whether removal and subsequent use of the tissue could legitimately be said to be implied.

9.15   From this summary it will be seen that, on the reasoning proposed legal claims may be open to persons from whom tissue is removed. It is suggested that they should properly proceed on the basis of consent given to the procedure which resulted in the removal, or its absence, rather than a claim in property . . .

The Report went on to consider the question of the claims of users of tissue.

10.1   In Chapter 9 we discussed whether or not the person from whom tissue is removed may have a property right in the tissue. Whatever view is taken, it does not follow that the user (broadly defined) has no such right. The tissue once removed comes into the possession of the remover and may then be passed to others. The nineteenth-century doctrine that a body may not be property would suggest, however, that no possessory or property right vests in the user of a body or, arguably, parts of a body. In this chapter we examine the claims users may have over human tissue . . .

10.3   The early twentieth-century Austrialian case of *Doodeward v. Spence* is cited as authority for the no property rule. *"There can be no property in a human body dead or alive. I go further and say that if a limb or any portion of a body is removed that no person has a right of property in that portion of the body so removed"*, *per* Pring J. On appeal to the High Court of Australia the judgment of Griffiths C.J. in the New South Wales Court of Appeal decided that if some work was carried out on the body part, for example to preserve it, which changed the part, then it could acquire the characteristics of property and be subject to property rights.

10.4 By contrast to the view of Pring J. Stephen expressed the view that anatomical specimens could constitute personal property. More recently, as Magnusson points out, *"there are a handful of English decisions in which human tissue has been treated as property"*. He cites criminal cases where a defendant was convicted of theft as well as assault when he cut a quantity of hair from a woman's head, where a defendant poured a urine sample he had given to establish his sobriety down the sink and was convicted of theft, and where the defendant was convicted of theft when he removed the blood sample, taken for the same reason, from the police station. The last two cases, albeit that the point was not directly discussed in either case, suggest that property vested in the police. Admittedly, two of these cases involve hair and urine, neither of which are, strictly speaking, tissue, but if they are treated as property, *a fortiori,* so would what we define as tissue by virtue of its identification as an organised collection of cells and the tangible quality such identification suggests, Finally, it must be recalled that Broussard J. in his dissenting opinion in the *Moore* case wrote that ". . . *the majority's analysis cannot rest on the broad proposition that a removed part is not property, but . . . on the proposition that a patient retains no ownership interest in a body part once the body part has been removed.*" [Our emphasis]

10.6 The continued absence of clear legal authority admittedly leaves the law uncertain. It is suggested, however, that common sense as well as the common law require that the user of tissue acquires at least possessory rights and probably a right of ownership over tissue once removed. It cannot plausibly be argued that University College London does own not Bentham's skeleton. *Mutatis mutandis,* a hospital which has tissue in its possession, for example for transplant, has such property rights over the tissue as to exclude any claim of another to it, as does a coroner or pathologist who has carried out a post-mortem and retains body parts for examination. Equally, it would follow, they have the right to recover the tissue if it were taken without permission. The same must be true who operate a tissue bank or an archive of specimens used for research or teaching.

(The embalmed body of Jeremy Bentham is kept at University College London.)

NOTES:

1. The rejection of the property approach by the Nuffield Report has been criticised. Matthews argues that the earlier case law does not provide conclusive evidence of a "no-property" approach. He also sees inconsistencies in the Nuffield Report. For instance, he regards statements made later in the Report to the effect that defects in blood and bodily products may be actionable under the Consumer Protection Act 1987 as being at variance with its earlier conclusions. (See P. Matthews, "The Man of Property" (1995) 3 *Medical Law Review* 251.)

2. Many of the assumptions made in the Report rely on the fact that the individual has consented to the removal of tissue. Difficulties may arise in relation to the mentally incompetent adult, as we noted above, with regard to the transplantation of organs. The Nuffield Report proposed that the courts should regard it as lawful to remove tissue from a mentally incompetent adult in the public interest where such use is a justifiable use (para. 9.17). This of course leaves open the question of what would constitute such a use.

3. The Report emphasises the concept of abandonment. However, again Matthews, *op. cit.*, has questioned its reliance upon this approach. He notes that the doctrine has only been used in certain specific areas of law and that it is doubtful whether it could be said to be of general application. Furthermore he states that there is no authority in English law for treating property as *res nullis*. He also criticises the approach taken in the Nuffield Report to the *Moore* case. In that case abandonment was irrelevant because the court held that there were no rights to abandon.

4. It is likely that scientists will increasingly attempt to obtain intellectual property rights, such as patents, as a consequence of developments involving the use of bodily products with the aim of profiting from their invention. Some would oppose the granting of such rights on the basis that it may inhibit future research in the area. One consideration which is taken into account when patents are granted are the ethics underlying the proposed development. Such elements are to be found in both the European Patent Convention and in the Patent Acts. Article 5(3) of the Convention provides that a patent should not be granted where the publication or exploitation of an invention would be contrary to public order or morality. The Patents Act (U.K.) 1977 provides in section 1(3)(a) that a patent would not be given in relation to "an invention, the publication or exploitation of which would be generally accepted to encourage offensive, immoral or anti-social behaviour". The Nuffield Report recommended that a protocol should be drawn up giving guidance to national courts who have to interpret the European Patent Convention and consider those exclusions under this convention which relate to immoral use (Article 53(a) EPC and section 1(3)c Patent Act (U.K.) 1977). The Nuffield Report concluded that rather than these issues being dealt with by the European Patent office they should instead be left to national courts. The Report leaves open what the protocol should contain. The Report was criticised for its failure to adequately address existing tensions in this area, particularly in relation to the need to promote research as against growing public controversy regarding the use of certain technologies. (See further on this issue, L. Bentley and B. Sherman, "The Ethics of Patenting; Towards a Transgenic Patent System" (1995) 3 *Medical Law Review* 275.)

5. The development of biotechnology has meant that it is possible to remove cells/tissue from a person and then later use them to produce a lucrative new cell line. The person may claim that s/he has a claim upon the profits made from that cell line, as in *Moore v. Regents of the University of California* (1990) 13 P 2d 479 has not yet come before an English court. One possibility is that such use amounted to the tort of conversion. Conversion is the term used to describe an "intentional dealing with goods which is seriously inconsistent with the possession/right to immediate possession" (M. Brazier, (9th ed.),

Street on Torts, (9th edn.) London: Butterworth, 1992, at page 389). It is unclear as whether bodily products could be classed as "goods". Secondly, it is uncertain whether a person who has undergone an operation has any right to possession of tissue subsequently removed. Dworkin and Kennedy have suggested that an action for conversion may be possible if the individual expressly stipulate the manner in which he intends his tissue to be used after it was removed from him. Alternatively, it may be the case that the use to which the tissue was put was different than the patient had been given to understand and that the information given could be regarded as a deception, thus vitiating the patient's consent regarding removal of that tissue. Nevertheless, even if a court were to accept such a claim, the measure of damages available would be uncertain. (See G. Dworkin and I. Kennedy, "Human Tissue" [1993] 1 *Medical Law Review* 291.)

6. The Nuffield Report suggested that where work is undertaken on a body/tissue then a person acquires proprietory rights. Matthews *op. cit.* disagreed with this approach and noted that at common law unauthorised work on anothers goods gives no rights to those goods.

SELECT BIBLIOGRAPHY

M. R. Brazier, *Medicine, Patients and the Law* (2nd ed.) Harmondsworth: Penguin, 1992, Chapter 18.

R. Chadwick, "Corpses, Recycling and Therapeutic Purposes" in R. Lee and D. Morgan (eds.), *Deathrights: Law and Ethics at the End of Life*, London: Routledge (1994).

J. Dukeminier, "Supplying Organs for Transplantation" (1970) 68 *Mich. L.R.* 811.

G. Dworkin, "The Law Relating to Organ Transplantation in England" (1970) 33 *M.L.R.* 35.

G. Dworkin and I. Kennedy, Human Tissue: Rights in the Body and Its Parts (1993) 1 *Medical Law Review* 291.

D. Lamb, *Organ Transplants and Ethics,* London: Routledge, 1990.

D. Lamb, *Death, Brain Death & Ethics,* Beckenham: Croom Helm, 1988.

D. Lanham, "Transplants and the Human Tissue Act 1961" (1971) 11 *Med. Sci. and the Law* 16.

J. K. Mason, "Organ Donation and Transportation" C. Dyer (ed.) *"Doctors, Patients and the Law"* Oxford: Blackwells, 1992.

J. K. Mason, R. A. McCall Smith, *Law and Medical Ethics* (4th ed.), London: Butterworths, 1994, Chapter 14.

P. McCullagh, *Brain Dead, Brain Absent, Brain Donors,* Chichester: Wiley, 1993.

G. Northoff, "Do brain tissue transplants alter personal identity? Inadequacies of some 'standard arguments'" (1996) 22 *Journal of Medical Ethics* 174.

C. Pallis, *The ABC of Brain Stem Death,* (2nd ed.) London: BMJ, 1996.

P. Singer, *Rethinking Life and Death: The Collapse of Our Traditional Ethics*, Oxford: OUP (1995), Chapters 2 and 3.

P. D. G. Skegg, *Law Ethics and Medicine,* Oxford: OUP, 1988, Chapter 10.

P. D. G. Skegg, "Liability for the Unauthorised Removal of Cadarveric Transplant Material" (1974) *Med. Sci. and Law* 53; (1977) *Med. Sci. and Law* 123.

APPENDICES

APPENDIX A

PARENTAL REFUSAL OF TREATMENT OF INCOMPETENT MINORS

In Chapter 7 it was noted that most of the legal cases relating to the medical treatment of minors are concerned with adolescent children at the borderlines of capacity. It was further noted that most of the cases which have dealt with the medical treatment of younger children have arisen because parents refuse their consent to medical treatment on the basis of their religious beliefs, and in such cases the courts have ordered treatment in the child's best interests. However, the recent Court of Appeal decision in *Re T (A Minor), The Times,* October 25, 1996, (1996) *NLJLR* 1577, the Court of Appeal dealt with a more unusual situation and in this case the Court respected the parents' wishes.

The Court of Appeal unanimously overturned the ruling of Connell J. that it was in the best interests of an 18 month old child to undergo a liver transplantation, notwithstanding his mother's refusal to consent to the operation. The medical prognosis was that the child would not live beyond two and a half years without the liver transplant and that the operation had a good chance of success. However, the Court of Appeal took the view that the case raised issues which were broader than purely clinical considerations. Butler Sloss L.J. emphasised that the welfare of the child was dependent upon his mother who would be the primary carer. She pointed to the opinion of one doctor who foresaw grave difficulties in carrying out the operation and treatment without the wholehearted support of the mother. Hence, although the welfare principle carried a very strong presumption in favour of a course of action which would prolong life; in the particular circumstances of this case the judges agreed that the best interests of the child respecting mother's wishes that her son should not be subjected to the pain and distress of this very invasive surgery.

It is however crucial to emphasise the very unusual features of this case — something which was particularly stressed in the judgment of Waite L.J. It is particularly significant that the parents were health professionals themselves, that their son had already undergone an unsuccessful operation called "Kasai" when he was three and a half weeks old which had caused him considerable pain and distress, and that they were now living abroad and would have to bring their son back to the United Kingdom in order for the treatment to be performed. Waite L.J. distinguished this case from those where parental opposition to medical treatment was prompted by "scruple or dogma of a kind which is patently irreconcilable with principles of child health and welfare widely accepted by the generality of mankind". In view of these peculiar features it is unlikely that this case signals a shift in judicial attitudes with regard to parental rights, and it is probably better regarded as a one-off case decided on its own facts.

APPENDIX B

POSTHUMOUS INSEMINATION AND HFEA

As we saw in Chapter 11, the Human Fertilisation and Embryology Act 1990 places great emphasis on the importance of informed consent. Thus, prior to donating gametes a donor must give his or her written consent and must have been adequately counselled. Moreover, section 28 of the Act provides in subsection (6)(b) that where a woman is inseminated with frozen sperm or implanted with an embryo created from such sperm after her partner or husband's death he is not to be treated posthumously as the father. This legislative provision was a result of the Warnock Committee's disapproval of posthumous insemination. As this text was going to print these issues commanded masive media attention in the United Kingdom as a result of the Case of Diane Blood.

Mrs Blood's husband contracted meningitis and lapsed into a coma. Prior to his illness she had been trying to conceive and consequently she asked the doctors to take and store her husband's sperm while he was unconscious. She later claimed that her husband would have consented to the procedure as they had discussed the issue of posthumous insemination after reading a magazine article on the subject.

The frozen sperm was stored in a licensed clinic which brought it within the remit of the 1990 Act, and the HFEA refused its permission for her to use the sperm because there was no valid consent from her husband. Mrs Blood sought judicial review of HFEA's decision, but in October 1996 the High Court ruled that she could not use sperm taken from her deceased husband for artificial insemination in the absence of his written consent as required by section 4(1) of the 1990 Act (*R v. Human Fertilisation and Embryology Authority ex p. Blood* (1996) *N.L. Law Reports* 1542; *The Times,* October 18, 1996). She appealed to the Court of Appeal and in February 1997 it held that, although insemination in Britain would be unlawful because taking and storing the man's sperm without his written consent was unlawful, the HFEA should reconsider its ban on taking the sperm abroad in the light of European Community law. Although the High Court had held that E.C. law was of no assistance to Mrs Blood, the Court of Appeal held that her right to receive medical treatment in another Member State, granted by Articles 59 and 60 of the E.C. Treaty, was directly enforceable in English law. The Court of Appeal stressed that this was a one-off decision which set no precedent for the future, as it confirmed that the act of taking and storing the sperm without Mr Blood's consent was unlawful (*R v. Human Fertilisation and Embryology Authority ex p. Blood, The Times,* February 7, 1997). Three weeks later, in the light of the Court of Appeal ruling, the HFEA met and announced that it had reversed its decision. It issued a direction to the Jessop Hospital in

Sheffield, which had stored the sperm, to send it to the Centre for Reproductive Medicine, Brussels, which had agreed to treat Mrs Blood (*The Daily Telegraph*, February 28, 1996).

It remains to be seen whether the Court of Appeal is correct in its view that is decision sets no precedent for future cases. It is also significant that an issue raising fundamental questions about the significance of informed consent, reproductive autonomy and the status of gametes was transposed into the context of freedom to avail of services.

APPENDIX C

CAESAREAN SECTIONS

In Chapter 13 above we explored the controversy regarding judicial authorisation of caesarean section operations against the wishes of the women involved. There were further instances of judicial authorisation of caesarean sections upon women who were opposed to such a procedure during 1996. In *Rochdale NHS Trust v. Chowdury* (1996, unreported) the woman in question was found by the judge not to be competent (although the obstetrician had accepted that she was competent). The woman had previously undergone a caesarean section and suffered backache and pain around the scar. She told the consultant she "would rather died than have a caesarean section again." In the case of *Norfolk & Norwich NHS Trust v. W* (1996 2 FLR 613) a woman came into accident and emergency in a state of arrested labor. She denied that she was pregnant. She had undergone three previous caesarean sections. There was a risk that unless the fetus was delivered soon it would suffocate and its continued presence would represent a danger to the woman's health. Alternatively there was the possibility that her scar would rupture. The woman was found incompetent by the court despite the fact that the psychiatrist at the hospital had stated that she was not suffering from a mental disorder and that she was capable of instructing a solicitor. A caesarean was authorised. It has been commented that in neither of these cased did the woman have legal representation (See B. Hewson "Womens Rights and Legal Wrongs" (1996) 146 *NLJ* 1385). In a subsequent case of an enforced caesarean in February 1997 (unreported) a woman did receive legal representation. This case was referred to the Court of Appeal who upheld the decision at first instance.

Legal proceedings are, at the time of writing, being brought by a woman who underwent a caesarean section against a social worker and two NHS Trusts who were involved in her commitment to a psychiatric hospital (See D. Dyer "Birth of a Dilemma" *The Guardian*, March 11, 1997). The woman was a trained health care professional and had planned a home birth. She went to see a G.P. when eight months pregnant and she was told that she was suffering from pre-eclampsia, a condition which was potentially life threatening for woman and fetus. She was advised to immediately go into hospital. When she refused a social worker was called and she was sectioned under the Mental Health Act 1983. The judge authorised the caesarean in an expedited hearing during her lunch hour.

The cases on forced caesareans are of significance not only for their impact on the reproductive choices of women but also because they demonstrate how the concepts of capacity and consent, considered in Chapters 5 and 6, may operate in a gendered manner. Hewson has argued that the recent cases appear to assume that "pregnant women are not really autonomous individuals entitled to equal protection, but merely a subdivision of what courts once called infants and lunatics, incapable of making decisions for themselves, for whom doctors and courts should be surrogate decision makers". (See B. Hewson, "Women's rights and legal wrongs" (1996) 146 *NLJ* 1385; R. Ladd, "Women in Labor: Some Issues about Informed Consent" in H. Holmes and L. Purdy (eds) *Feminist Perspectives in Medical Ethics,* Bloomington and Indianapolis: Indiana University Press, 1992.)

APPENDIX D

WITHDRAWAL OF TREATMENT FROM PATIENTS IN PVS

Guidance to those handling cases concerning withdrawal of treatment from patients in a persistent vegetative state was provided in a Practice Note issued in 1996 (Practice Note (persistent vegetative state: withdrawal of treatment) [1996] 4 All E.R. 766). This provides that diagnosis of PVS should be in accordance with guidelines accepted by the medical profession. Recent guidance published by the Royal College of Physicians on this issue is noted in this Practice Note ("The Permanent Vegetative State: Review by a Working Group Convened by the Royal College of Physicians and Endorsed by the Conference of Medical Royal Colleges and their Faculties of the United Kingdom" (1996) 30 *Journal of the Royal College of Physicians of London* 119). This states that PVS diagnosis may not be reasonably made until the patient has been in a continuing vegetative state following head injury for more than six months or in the case of other brain damage for more than 12 months. Two independent reports should be obtained from neurologists/doctors experienced in assessing disturbances of consciousness. The practitioners should draw up their reports separately. Applications should only be made to terminate artificial nutrition/hydration where the condition is permant, which may necessitate the commission of reports over a period of time. The Practice Note states that: "If there is any uncertainty in the mind of the assessor then the diagnosis shall not be made and a reassessment undertaken after further time has elapsed." This is particularly important in view of recent research questioning the conclusive nature of some PVS diagnosis. Where an application is made the Official Solicitor should normally be involved to represent the patient. The Official Solicitor's representative will normally see the patient and interview next of kin/others close to the patient. The Practice Note states that "the patient's previously expressed views, if any, will always be an important component in the decision of the doctor and the court, particularly if they are clearly established and were intended to apply to the circumstances which have in fact arisen."

APPENDIX E

TRANSPLANTATION AND THE INCOMPETENT ADULT

The English courts were asked to rule upon the legality of the performance of a non-therapeutic transplant procedure upon a mentally incompetent adult in the case of *Re Y* [1996] 2 FLR 791: see A. Grubb "Adult Incompetent: Legality of Non-Therapeutic Procedure" [1996] 4 *Medical Law Review* 204). Y was a 25 year old mentally retarded woman whom it was proposed to use as a bone marrow donor for her 36 year old sister. It was likely that without the transplant the sister would develop acute myeloid leukaemia within three months. The court authorised the performance of test on Y to ascertain suitability and, if necessary, the undertaking of a bone marrow harvesting operation. The court held that it was necessary to consider whether the procedure was in the best interests of Y and they held that this was the case here. They noted the exceptionally close family relationship which existed, the effect that the death of Y's sister would have on Y's mother who was not in good health and had to look after a grandchild. In addition the harvesting was not unduly onerous and the bone marrow itself would regenerate. The court did indicate that in such a situation application to the court for a declaration would be appropriate. It appears that cases such as this in which use of mentally incompetent adults as transplant donors are authorised are likely to be exceptional in nature. (Comparisons can be drawn with the earlier United States decision in *Strunk v. Strunk,* see page 905, above). The impact of *Re Y* to decisions regarding the performance of non-therapeutic procedures generally on incompetent adults and children, for example, their involvement in clinical research, may be limited in view of the exceptional nature of the facts such as the close emotional "psychological" bond and the low risk levels involved in the procedure.

INDEX